P9-CEH-695

BIOLOGY

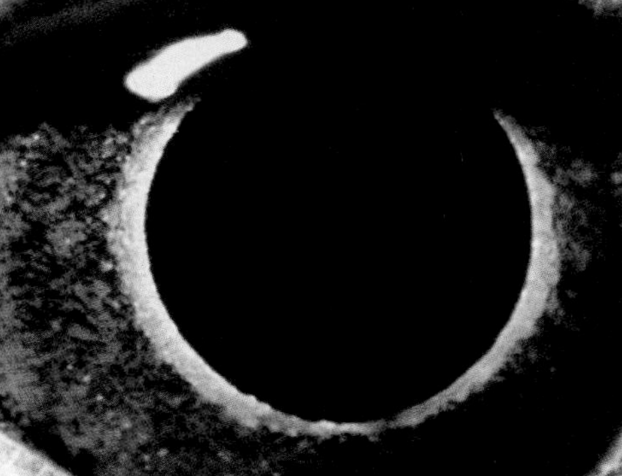

Exploring Life

Neil A. Campbell
Department of Botany and Plant Sciences
University of California, Riverside, California

Brad Williamson
Biology Instructor
Olathe School District
Olathe, Kansas

Robin J. Heyden
Education Consultant
Wellesley, Massachusetts

PEARSON
Prentice Hall
Boston, Massachusetts
Upper Saddle River, New Jersey

BIOLOGY

Exploring Life

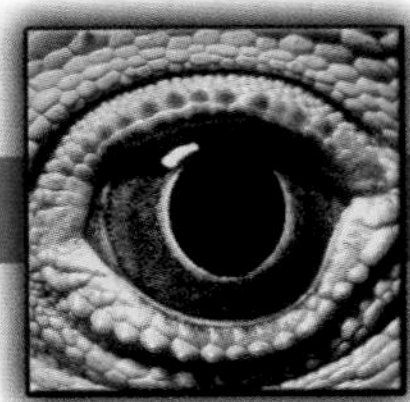

PROGRAM COMPONENTS

Student Edition
Teacher's Edition
Program Web Site: www.biology.com
Online Activities CD-ROM
Learning Log for Online Activities
Laboratory Manual, Student Edition
Laboratory Manual, Teacher's Edition
Teaching Resources
Guided Reading and Study Workbook
Guided Reading and Study Workbook Answer Key
Color Transparencies
Resource Pro® CD-ROM with Planning Express® and Presentation Pro
Computer Test Bank with ExamView® Book and CD-ROM

Acknowledgments appear on page 846, which constitutes an extension of this copyright page.

ISBN 0-13-062592-2
17 18 19 20 V063 14 13 12 11 10

Program Authors

NEIL A. CAMPBELL

Neil Campbell is the lead author of biology textbooks used each year by over 500,000 high-school and college students worldwide, including *Biology, Biology: Concepts and Connections,* and *Essential Biology.* He has 30 years of teaching experience in diverse environments including Cornell University, Pomona College, and San Bernardino Valley College. He is currently a visiting scholar in the Department of Botany and Plant Sciences at the University of California, Riverside.

BRAD WILLIAMSON

Brad Williamson, the 2002 President of the National Association of Biology Teachers (NABT), has taught high-school biology for more than 25 years in a variety of settings with a broad range of students. He specializes in integrating the active learning opportunities provided by laboratory and field investigations into the biology classroom. He currently teaches in the Olathe School District, Olathe, Kansas.

ROBIN J. HEYDEN

Robin Heyden has worked in science publishing since 1984. In addition to editorial roles on Campbell's *Biology* and *Biology: Concepts and Connections*, she has produced the *Interactive Physiology* series with A.D.A.M. Software and a number of other interactive products for the life and physical sciences. She currently lives and works in Wellesley, Massachusetts.

Student Edition Contributing Writers

Susan W. Nourse
Biology Instructor
Tabor Academy
Marion, MA

James McLaren
Science Department Chair
Newton South High School
Newton, MA

Development Team

TEACHER'S EDITION

Suzanne Black
Teacher's Edition Lead Writer
Science Department Chair
Inglemoor High School
Kenmore, WA

James McLaren
Teacher's Edition Contributing Writer
Science Department Chair
Newton South High School
Newton, MA

Mya R. Nelson
Teacher's Edition Contributing Writer
Biology Writer
Brookline, MA

Edward Schiele
Teacher's Edition Contributing Writer
Former Biology Instructor
Buskirk, NY

Diane L. Sweeney
Teacher's Edition Contributing Writer
Biology Instructor
Prince of Peace Lutheran School
Fremont, CA

LABORATORY PROGRAM

Diane L. Sweeney
Laboratory Investigation Creator and Lead Writer
Biology Instructor
Prince of Peace Lutheran School
Fremont, CA

Ruth Hathaway
Safety Reviewer
Hathaway Consulting
Cape Girardeau, MO

WEB SITE

Richard Benz
Web Content Contributor
Biology Instructor
Wickliffe High School
Wickliffe, OH

Hilair Chism
Media Activities Developer
Oakland, CA

Susan Eldert
Web Content Creator
Biology Instructor
Fessenden School
West Newton, MA

Graham R. Kent
Web Content Creator
Professor of Biological Sciences
Smith College
Northhampton, MA

Richard Leider
Web Developer
Applied Rhetoric
San Francisco, CA

Steve McEntee
Lead Web Art Developer
Healdsburg, CA

Jacqueline S. McLaughlin
Web Content Creator
Assistant Professor of Biology
The Pennsylvania State University/Berks-Lehigh Valley
Fogelsville, PA

Audre W. Newman
Media Activities Developer
Berkeley, CA

Susan W. Nourse
Web Content Contributor
Biology Instructor
Tabor Academy
Marion, MA

Red Hill Studios
Web Development
Larkspur, CA

Beryl Simon
Media Art Director
Arlington, MA

Content Reviewers

John Alcock
Department of Biology
Arizona State University
Tempe, AZ

Wayne M. Becker
Department of Botany
University of Wisconsin
Madison, WI

Jim Bray
Department of Biology
Blackburn College
Carlinville, IL

Craig Clifford
College of Math, Science, and Nursing
Northeastern State University
Tahlequah, OK

Roger del Moral
Department of Botany
University of Washington
Seattle, WA

Gregory Demas
Department of Biology
Indiana University
Bloomington, IN

Fred A. Diehl
Department of Biology
University of Virginia
Charlottesville, VA

Susan Dunford
Department of Biological Sciences
University of Cincinnati
Cincinnati, OH

Susan Fahrbach
Department of Entomology
University of Illinois
Urbana-Champaign, IL

Daphne G. Fautin
Division of Biological Sciences
University of Kansas
Lawrence, KS

Alan D. Gishlick
National Center for Science Education
Oakland, CA

Elizabeth Godrick
Biology Department
Boston University
Boston, MA

Erick Greene
Division of Biological Sciences
University of Montana
Missoula, MT

William J. Higgins
Department of Biology
University of Maryland
College Park, MD

Robert J. Huskey
Department of Biology
University of Virginia
Charlottesville, VA

Paula C. Jackson
Department of Biology
Kennesaw State University
Kennesaw, GA

Elaine A. Johnson
Bio-Link Director
City College of San Francisco
San Francisco, CA

Nickolas Kapp
Department of Biology
Skyline College
San Bruno, CA

Cathy Kemper
Department of Biology
Tomball College
Tomball, TX

Tyler Kokjohn
Arizona College of Osteopathic Medicine
Midwestern College
Glendale, AZ

Janet Lanza
Biology Department
University of Arkansas
Little Rock, AR

Rene D. Massengale
Department of Biology
Baylor University
Waco, TX

Philip M. Meneely
Department of Biology
Haverford College
Haverford, PA

Robert Miller
Department of Microbiology and Molecular Genetics
Oklahoma State University
Stillwater, OK

Susan J. Mitchell
Department of Biological Sciences
Onondaga Community College
Syracuse, NY

Martha Newsome
Department of Biology
Tomball College
Tomball, TX

Michael Palladino
Department of Biology
Monmouth University
West Long Branch, NJ

Hudson Kern Reeve
Neurobiology and Behavior
Cornell University
Ithaca, NY

David Reznick
Department of Biology
University of California
Riverside, CA

Mark Ridley
Department of Zoology
Oxford University
Oxford, England

Thomas L. Rost
Section of Plant Biology
University of California
Davis, CA

David J. Schimpf
Department of Biology
University of Minnesota
Duluth, MN

David S. Smith
Biology Department
San Antonio College
San Antonio, TX

Thomas M. Terry
Molecular and Cell Biology
University of Connecticut
Storrs, CT

Robert M. Thornton
Section of Plant Biology
University of California
Davis, CA

Lisa A. Urry
Biology Department
Mills College
Oakland, CA

Adam Welman
Department of Natural Resources
Cornell University
Ithaca, NY

Clarence Wolfe
Biology and Natural Science
Northern Virginia Community College
Annandale, VA

Edward Zalisko
Department of Biology
Blackburn College
Carlinville, IL

National Science Foundation Evaluation Team

Alec M. Bodzin
Primary Investigator
Department of Education and Human Services
Lehigh University
Bethlehem, Pennsylvania

Betsy Price
Program Evaluator

Ward Mitchell Cates
Program Evaluator

Michelle Heist Gannon
Project Manager

Dawn Bothwell
Data Management

John Bishop
Data Management

Sherrie Moore
Administrative Support

National Science Foundation Evaluation Pilot Testers

Jeffrey Anderson
Riverside University High
Milwaukee, WI

Duane Ashenfalder
Parkland High School
Allentown, PA

Melissa Azzarello
Governor Mifflin High
Shillington, PA

Sharon Bajema
Ottawa Hills High School
Grand Rapids, MI

Gena Barnhardt
Hickory High School
Hickory, NC

Laura Berry
Tinley Park High School
Tinley Park, IL

Patricia Berger
Souderton Area High School
Souderton, PA

Cheryl Blaukovitch
Moravian Academy
Bethlehem, PA

Patrick Boehemer
Carrington Public School
Carrington, ND

Deon H. Branch
Hunter-Kinard-Tyler High
Neeses, SC

Stacey Britton
Pearl River Central High
Carriere, MS

Judy M. Cassani
Great Bridge High School
Chesapeake, VA

Kelly Champney
Georgetown Visitation Prep
Washington, DC

Jim Christian
Colville High School
Colville, WA

Myrna Cole
Narragansett High School
Narragansett, RI

Karen Culberson
Nipmuc Regional School
Upton, MA

Nicole Della Santina
Aptos High School
Aptos, CA

David Devore
University School
Chagrin Falls, OH

Tami Dickerson
Caldwell High School
Caldwell, ID

Randy Dix
Olathe North High School
Olathe, KS

Kenneth Dunlap
Lenoir City High School
Lenoir City, TN

Alison Emblidge
Methuen High School
Methuen, MA

Loretta Fair
Freedom High School
Bethlehem, PA

Deborah Ferrer
Wahtonka High School
The Dalles, OR

Gary Fortenberry
Monterey High School
Lubbock, TX

R. Drew Frank
State College Area High
State College, PA

Sara Franzen
Cocoa Beach High School
Cocoa Beach, FL

Sherri Garcia
Seabury Hall
Makawao, HI

Tami Gilmour
State College Area High
State College, PA

Rachel Gladney
Elmwood Park High School
Elmwood Park, IL

Patricia Glynn
Plymouth North High
Plymouth, MA

Frances Grant
Grafton High School
Grafton, WI

Hallie Hammond
Harrodsburg High School
Harrodsburg, KY

Marilyn Havlik
Walter Payton High School
Chicago, IL

Melissa Heffner
Parkland High School
Allentown, PA

Harmon Hoff
Sherburne-Earlville High
Sherburne, NY

Michael Hotz
Wyandotte High School
Kansas City, KS

Steve Huffman
Sacred Heart Academy
Honolulu, HI

Lisa Hughes
Bayside High School
Palm Bay, FL

Sherie Jenkins
West Shore Jr./Sr. High
Melbourne, FL

Beth Jewell
West Springfield High
Springfield, VA

Jennifer Jordan
McNeil High School
Austin, TX

Shana Just
Hiram Johnson High School
Sacramento, CA

Dave Klindienst
State College Area High
State College, PA

Wendy Klintworth
Northwest High School
Jackson, MI

Dan Kunkle
Freedom High School
Bethlehem, PA

Patti Kupferer
Taylor Junior High School
Mesa, AZ

JoAnn Lane
St. Ignatius High School
Cleveland, OH

Brian Lemmings
Gardendale High School
Gardendale, AL

Linda Lentz
Wando High School
Mount Pleasant, SC

Valesca Lopez Dwyer
The Capitol School
Tuscaloosa, AL

Kay Lucas
Albuquerque High School
Albuquerque, NM

Jeff Lukens
Roosevelt High School
Sioux Falls, SD

Jack Lyke
State College Area High
State College, PA

Laura L. Maitland
W.C. Mepham High School
Bellmore, NY

Carolyn Martin
Many High School
Many, LA

Michael Marvin
Burlington High School
Burlington, VT

Michelle Mason
State College Area High
State College, PA

Wendy Matsumoto
Independence High School
San Jose, CA

Kevin McGinity
Ottumwa High School
Ottumwa, IA

Becky S. Nutt
Oneida Nation High School
Oneida, WI

Emily Parker
Novi High School
Novi, MI

Patsye Peebles
University Lab School
Baton Rouge, LA

Rosemary Ramos
John Marshall High School
Rochester, NY

Tammy Rickard
Hoover High School
Hoover, AL

Miguel Rivas
New Brunswick High School
New Brunswick, NJ

Eloise Roche
Carl Schurz High School
Chicago, IL

Kimberly Roundy
Deposit Jr./Sr. High School
Deposit, NY

Roberto Sepulveda
Menchville High School
Newport News, VA

Asha Shipman
Suffield High School
Suffield, CT

Janis Smoke
Tok School
Tok, AK

Jan Snyder
Camelback High School
Phoenix, AZ

Israel Solon
Greenhill School
Addison, TX

Peter Stetson
Coventry High School
Coventry, RI

Pamela Temons
Central Mountain High
Mill Hall, PA

Holly Thomas
Little Chute High School
Little Chute, WI

Monica Tullo
Putnam Valley High School
Putnam Valley, NY

Karla Walker
DeSoto High School
DeSoto, WI

Patricia L. Waller
Emmaus High School
Emmaus, PA

Sarah Weber
Comstock Park High School
Comstock Park, MI

Mary-Lee Wesberry
Hutchison High School
Memphis, TN

Hubert White
State College Area High
State College, PA

Ruth Babe Wiley
Fremont-Ross High School
Fremont, OH

Marilyn Yoachum
Will Rogers High School
Tulsa, OK

Additional Pilot Testers

Andrea Abraham
Lake Orion High School
Lake Orion, MI

Kayode C. Adebowale
Science Skills Center High
Brooklyn, NY

Janice L. Anderson
Chaminade-Julienne
Catholic High School
Dayton, OH

Bonnie Arons-Polan
Beverly High School
Beverly, MA

Donna Artola
Bethpage High School
Bethpage, NY

James Baglivi
Southold Jr./Sr. High
Southold, NY

Margaret Bahe
John Burroughs School
Ladue, MO

Shelley Barker
Danville High School
Danville, IL

William H. Barkley
North High School
Wichita, KS

Annie L. Barnes
East High School
Memphis, TN

Jim Barnstable
Clinton High School
Clinton, WI

Sister Christine Marie Beach
Roncalli High School
Manitowoc, WI

Steve Beckelhimer
Cabell Midland High School
Ona, WV

Andrew F. Bednarik
Fairfield High School
Fairfield, CT

Henriette Been
Mercy High School
San Francisco, CA

Jonathan Beener
Proviso East High School
Maywood, IL

Barbara R. Beitch
Hamden Hall Country Day
Hamden, CT

Christine Bennett
Naugatuck High School
Naugatuck, CT

Chuck Blaney
Coloney High School
Palmer, AR

Dennis L. Bluge
Trinity Preparatory School
Winter Park, FL

Louise D. Boyd
Neshaminy High School
Langhorne, PA

Ernest Boyett
Lufkin High School
Lufkin, TX

Wendy Jean Bowles
Apopka High School
Apopka, FL

Hortense Brice
King College Preparatory
Chicago, IL

Liz Brimhall
Palo Alto High School
Palo Alto, CA

Kathryn A. Britt
Marquette High School
Chesterfield, MO

Signe L. Brousseau
Taconic Hills High School
Craryville, NY

Marty Buehler
Hastings High School
Hastings, MI

Lornie D. Bullerwell
Dedham High School
Dedham, MA

Jimmy Cantrell
North Mesquite High School
Mesquite, TX

Erica Carnahan
Pius XI High School
Milwaukee, WI

Clarissa Caro
Kerr High School
Houston, TX

Sheila Chilton-Davis
Nazareth Academy
LaGrange, IL

Patricia Cloud
Convenant Christian High
Indianapolis, IN

Glen Cochrane
Half Hollow Hills
High School East
Dix Hills, NY

Brenda Crouch
Marianna High School
Marianna, FL

Linda C. Curley
Pittsfield High School
Pittsfield, MA

Elizabeth M. Daigle
Newton Country Day
Newton, MA

Tina Davies
The John Cooper School
The Woodlands, TX

Amanda Dawson
The King's Academy
Sunnyvale, CA

Taylor A. Delaney
Saint Edwards School
Vero Beach, FL

Kyle DeHorn
Hastings High School
Hastings, MI

Martha S. DeWeese
Berkeley Preparatory School
Tampa, FL

Barbara Divinski
St. Louis Park Senior High
Minneapolis, MN

Pam Dooling
Jones High School
Jones, OK

John Drew
Concord Academy
Concord, MA

Patricia J. Dugan
Holy Comforter Episcopal
Middle School
Tallahassee, FL

Pamela C. Edgerton
Maggie L. Walker
Governor's School
Richmond, VA

Angela M. Ermi
John P. Stevens High School
Edison, NJ

Erica Everett
Manchester-Essex
Regional High School
Manchester, MA

Nancy A. Farley
King William High School
King William, VA

Eloise Farmer
Torrington High School
Torrington, CT

Maryellen Fealy
Iona Preparatory School
New Rochelle, NY

Janice M. Ferry
Mount St. Charles Academy
Woonsocket, RI

Aulikki Flagan
Ramona Convent
Secondary School
Alhambra, CA

Roxanne Frillmann
Nazareth Academy
LaGrange, IL

Penny A. Ghinaudo
East Central High School
San Antonio, TX

Melissa Gibbons
Paschal High School
Fort Worth, TX

Darrell E. Gibson
The Prout School
Wakefield, RI

Jack G. Gilbey
Andrean High School
Merrillville, IN

William R. Giles
North Yarmouth Academy
Yarmouth, ME

Ruth Gleicher
Niles West High School
Skokie, IL

Mark Gottfried
N. Miami Beach Sr. High
N. Miami Beach, FL

Marguerite A. Graham
Gulliver Preparatory School
Miami, FL

Frances Grant
Grafton High School
Grafton, WI

Jennifer R. Grimley
Pope John Paul II
Catholic High School
Slidell, LA

Robin Groch
San Ramon Valley High
Danville, CA

Ann R. Gulley
Harper Woods High School
Harper Woods, MI

Thomas Hall
Brighton High School
Rochester, NY

Vicki Hantman
Palisades Park Jr./Sr. High
Palisades Park, NJ

Susan Helwig
N. Kansas City High School
N. Kansas City, MO

Paula J. Herbes
Bridgewater-Raritan
Regional High School
Bridgewater, NJ

Bobbie Hinson
Providence Day School
Charlotte, NC

John L. Hollingshead
Fallston High School
Fallston, MD

Theresa Holtzclaw
Clinton High School
Clinton, TN

Katrenia Hosea-Flanigan
Frank Cody High School
Detroit, MI

Annette Howk
Center Senior High School
Kansas City, MO

Bettina Hughes
Drake High School
San Anselmo, CA

Elaine G. Irons
Medina Central High School
Medina, NY

Tracie L. Jeffries
St. Stephens High School
Hickory, NC

Kelly Jolley
Rio Rancho High School
Rio Rancho, NM

June Kasminoff
Bethpage High School
Bethpage, NY

Bernadette Kegelman
St. Elizabeth High School
Wilmington, DE

Nicole Kirschten
Newfield High School
Newfield, NY

Carl F. Koch
Riverside-Brookfield High
Riverside, IL

Duane Koenen
Rushford-Peterson Public
Rushford, MN

Kimberly Kondrat
Summit High School
Summit, NJ

Susan M. Kostovny
Baldwin High School
Bethel Park, PA

Rick E. Kroll
Lufkin High School
Lufkin, TX

Deanna Lankford
Blue Springs South High
Blue Springs, MD

Joseph LaPointe
Dedham High School
Dedham, MA

Mary Launi
Pottsgrove High School
Pottstown, PA

Donna Light-Donovan
Croton-Harmon High School
Croton-on-Hudson, NY

John Magee
Fremont High School
Sunnyvale, CA

Marlene J. Mahle Bernal
David Posnack Hebrew
Day School
Plantation, FL

Elaine Mahoney
Mililani High School
Mililani, HI

Patrick Malone
Junipero Serra High School
San Mateo, CA

Zonda Martin
Putnam City High School
Oklahoma City, OK

Darryl Martino
MICDS
St Louis, MO

Cheryl Massengale
Stuttgart High School
Stuttgart, AR

Angela C. McBride
Seekonk High School
Seekonk, MA

Linda J. McIntosh
Dana Hall School
Wellesley, MA

Elizabeth McLean
Sweetser School
Saco, ME

Ed Mellado
North Mesquite High School
Mesquite, TX

Elisabeth Merrill
The Masters School
Dobbs Ferry, NY

Frank Michalski
Villa Walsh Academy
Morristown, NJ

Lisa Miller
Mission Viejo High School
Mission Viejo, CA

Douglas Mizukami
Jordan High School
Los Angeles, CA

Bob Moore
Noble and Greenough School
Dedham, MA

David K. Moser
Putnam City High School
Oklahoma City, OK

Stephen T. Nakano
Waipau High School
Waipau, HI

Shawn W. Neely
Pennsbury High School
Fairless Hills, PA

John Neuberger
Greendale High School
Greendale, WI

Jennifer Newitt
Friends Academy
Locust Valley, NY

Marsha Newton-Graham
Charlotte Country Day
Charlotte, NC

Susan Nishiura
Iolani High School
Honolulu, HI

Gary Norgan
West Valley High School
Hemet, CA

Connie O'Callagan
Cardinal Newman High
West Palm Beach, FL

Kristina M. O'Connor
King George Middle School
King George, VA

Gail O'Meara
Pope John XXIII High School
Everett, MA

Sylvester N. Onyeneho
Southwest High School
Minneapolis, MN

Susan J. Pastor
Weston High School
Weston, CT

Martin W. Perlaky
Springfield High School
Holland, OH

Alma Phifer
Plymouth High School
Plymouth, NC

Frank Pickett
Thorne Bay Schools
Thorne Bay, AK

Kimberley B. Porterfield
Boone High School
Orlando, FL

Sharon Radford
Paideia School
Atlanta, GA

Don Reid
Cypress High School
Cypress, CA

Fidela A. Robertson
Norwalk High School
Norwalk, CA

Sue S. Royster
Norfolk Christian High
Norfolk, VA

Catherine Russell
Southgate-Anderson High
Southgate, MI

Deb Schenk
Lima Central Catholic High
Lima, OH

Stuart D. Schnell
John C. Fremont High
Los Angeles, CA

Jessica Schultz
Yeshiva High School
Boca Raton, FL

Keri Schumacher
Blue Valley Northwest High
Overland Park, KS

Patricia Schwartz
Big Bay de Noc High School
Cooks, MI

Marian H. Scott
Campolindo High School
Moraga, CA

Lois V. Sinclair
Lake Braddock Secondary
Burke, VA

Brodie Sivley
Southwest Christian School
Ft. Worth, TX

Ronald E. Smith
Town of Webb School
Old Forge, NY

Linda Soja
Belleville High School
Belleville, MI

Scott Stein
Springside School
Philadelphia, PA

Mindy Steiner
Palo Alto High School
Palo Alto, CA

Martin Stickle
Summit High School
Summit, NJ

Kathy Stier
Mohawk Trail Regional High
Shelbourne Falls, MA

Sharon Sullivan-Piscopia
Sayville High School
West Sayville, NY

Candy L. Swan
Oakland High School
Murfreesboro, TN

Trudy J. Swan
McKay High School
Salem, OR

Ruth Sweeney
Belmont Hill School
Belmont, MA

Ruth A. Toseland
George Jenkins High School
Lakeland, FL

Ruth Tummey
Southern Regional High
Manahawkin, NJ

Kelley Twilley
Forest City Regional High
Forest City, PA

Clarisa Vasquez
Santa Rosa ISD
Santa Rosa, TX

Ann Vercler
University High School
Normal, IL

Mike Virlee
University High School
Normal, IL

Richard Wasserman
Sand Creek High School
Colorado Springs, CO

A. Collier Webb
Catholic High School
Virginia Beach, VA

Julie M. Weigle
Cumberland Valley High
Mechanicsburg, PA

Sally Winecke
Lakeville High School
Lakeville, MN

Bryan P. Woods
Poughkeepsie High School
Poughkeepsie, NY

Peggy Workman
Henry Clay High School
Lexington, KY

Eric Wright
Spotsylvania High School
Spotsylvania, VA

Glen T. Young
Northampton Senior High
Northampton, PA

Pamela Zeigler
Kenston High School
Chagrin Falls, OH

Contents

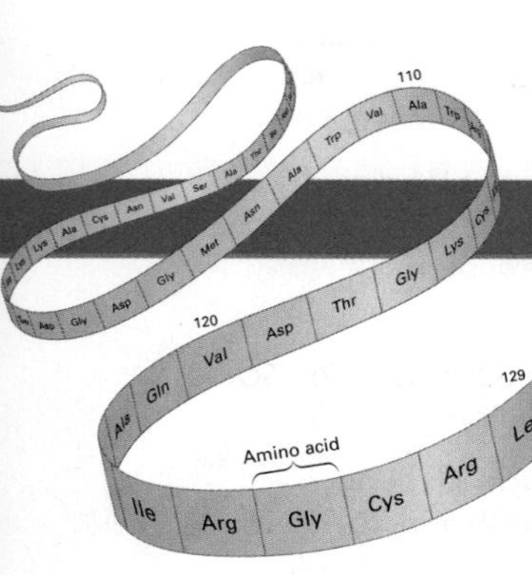

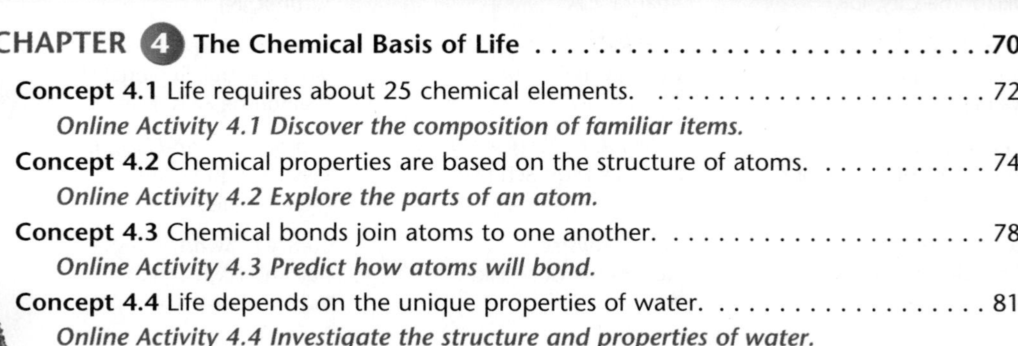

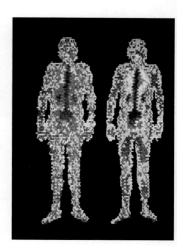

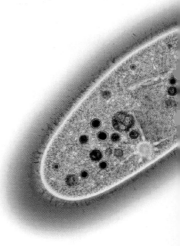

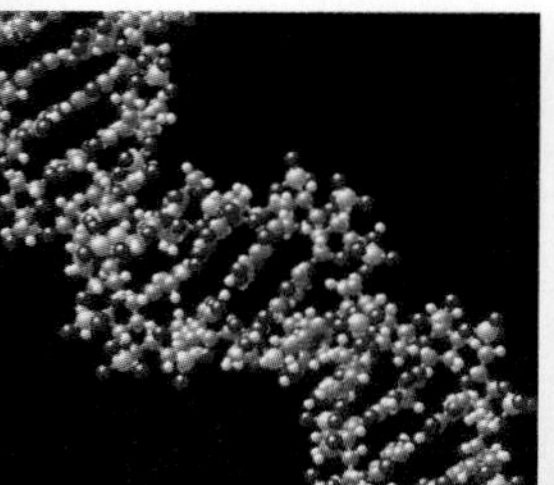
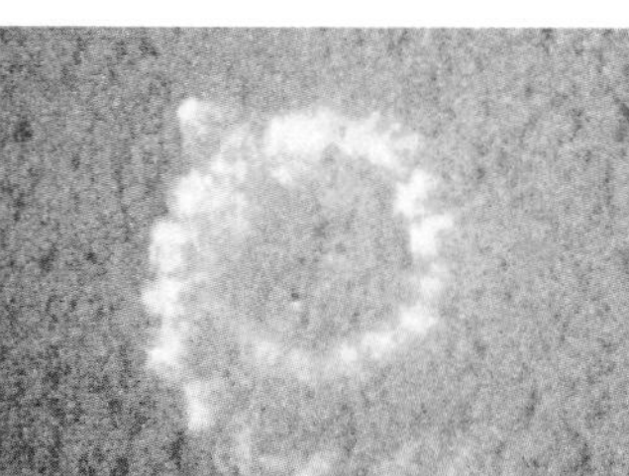

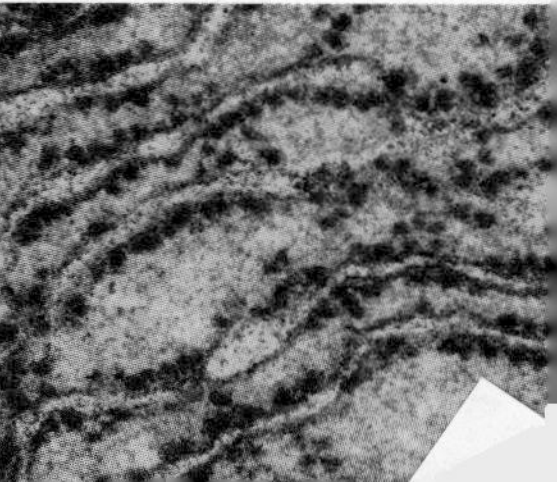

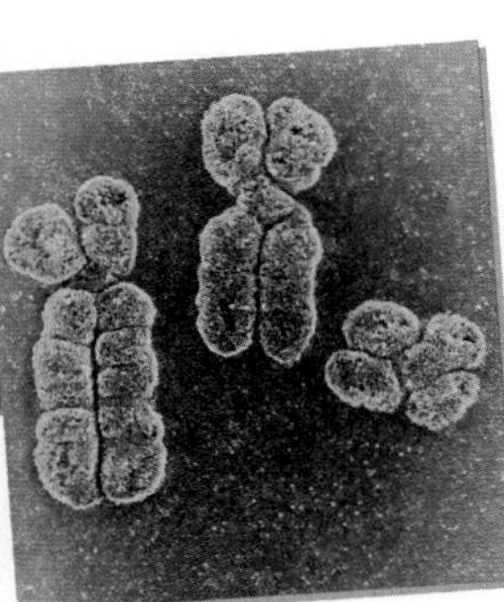

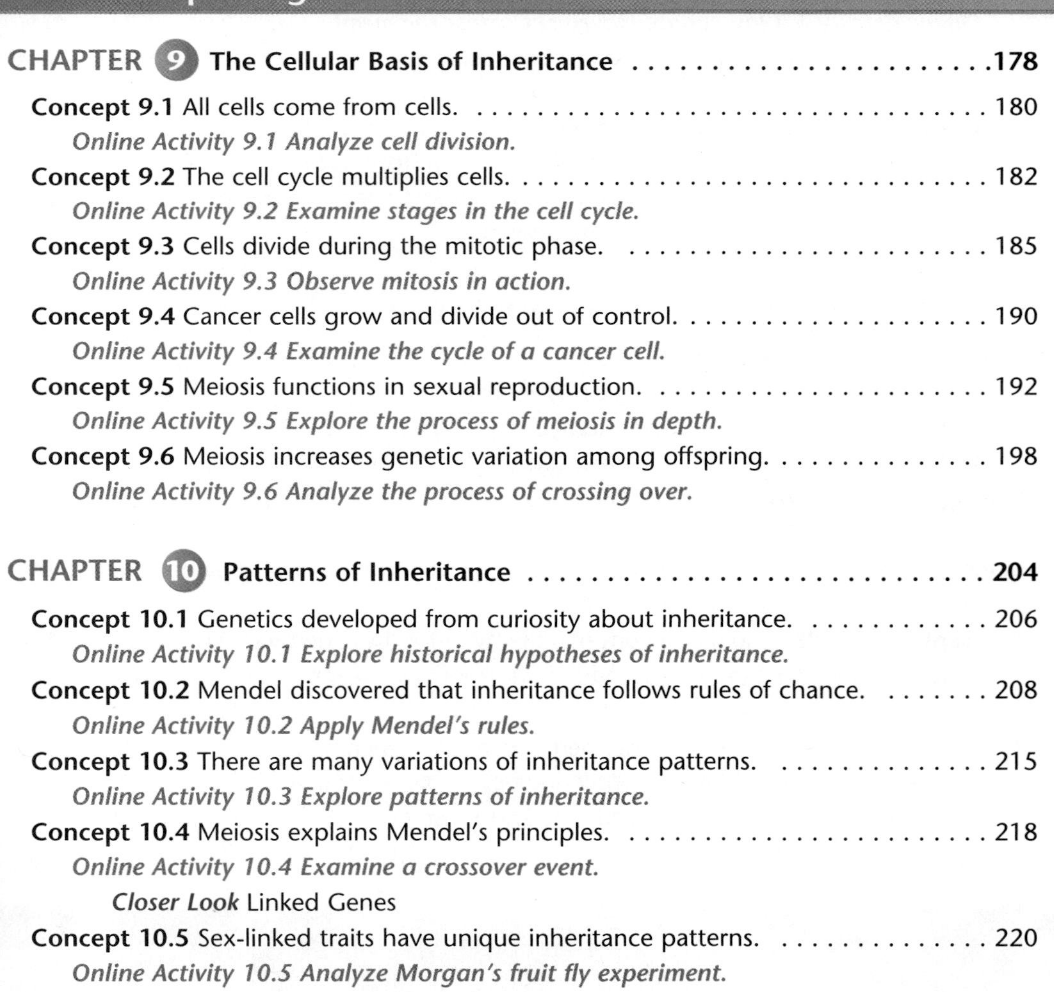

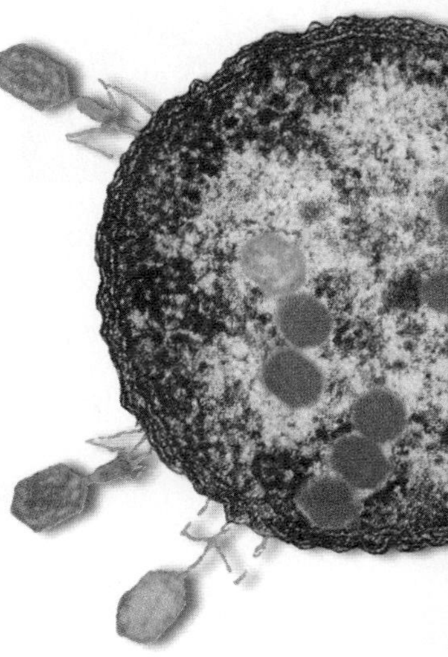

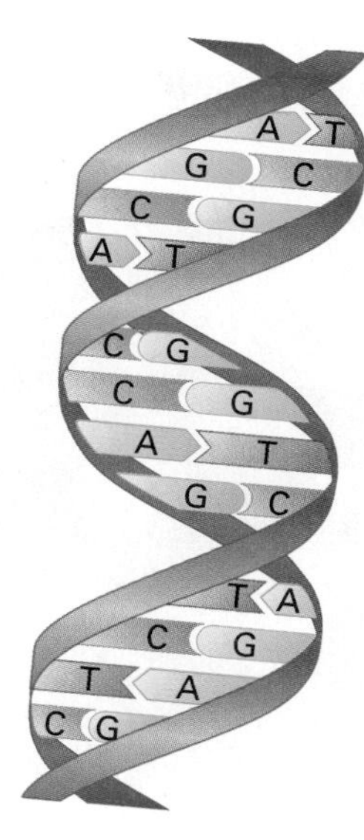

A T
G C
C G
A T
C G
C G
A T
G C
T A
C G
T A
C G

UNIT 4: Exploring the History of Life 288

UNIT 5: Exploring the Microbial World 352

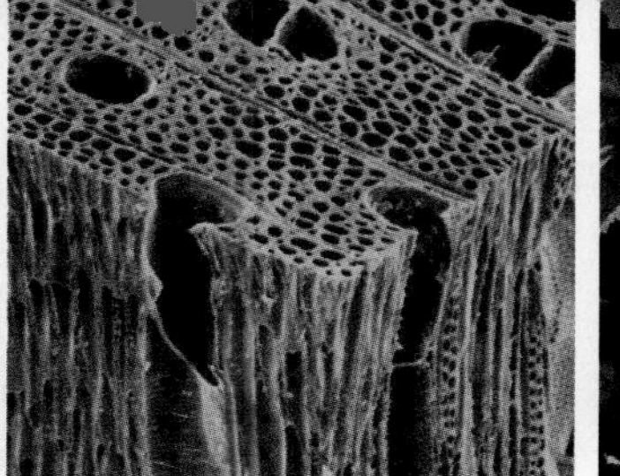

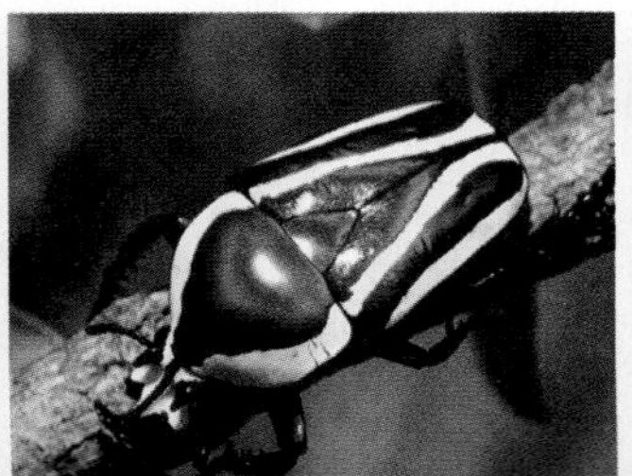

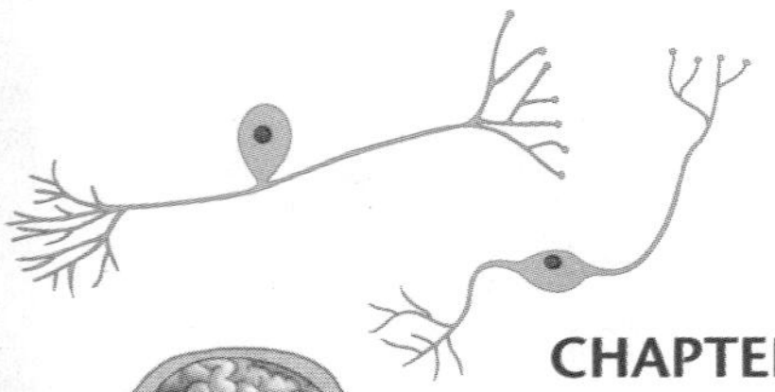

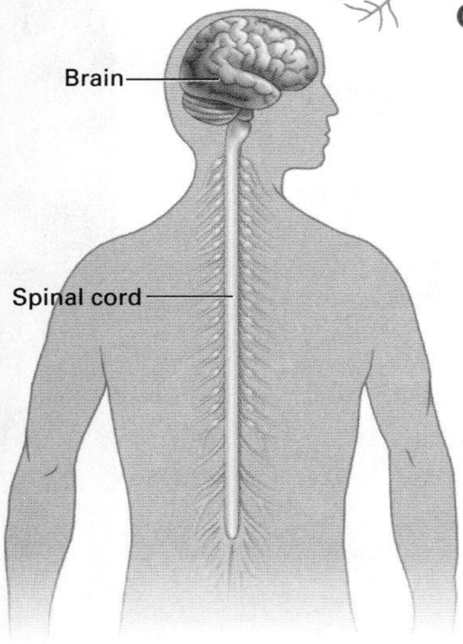

Brain
Spinal cord

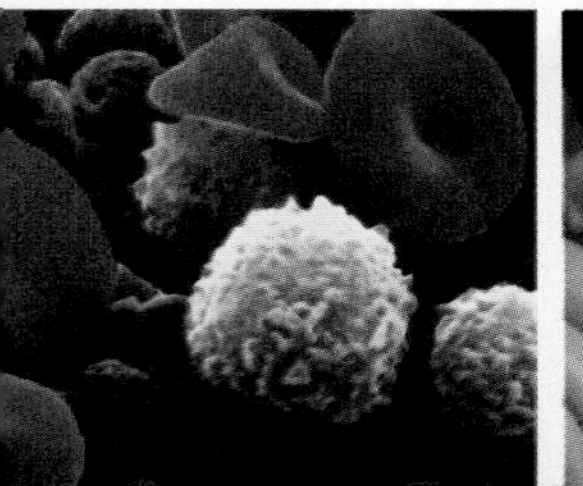

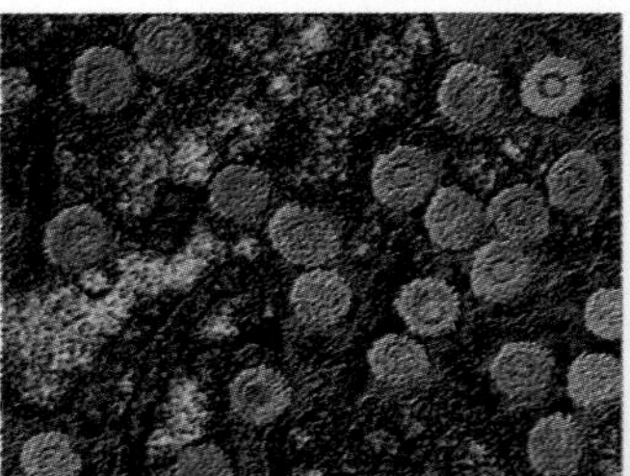

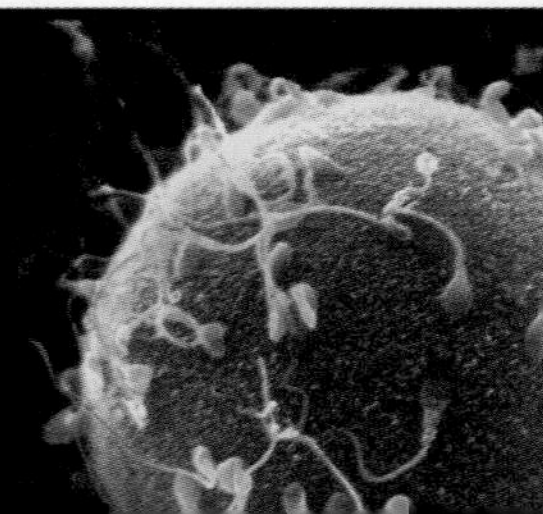

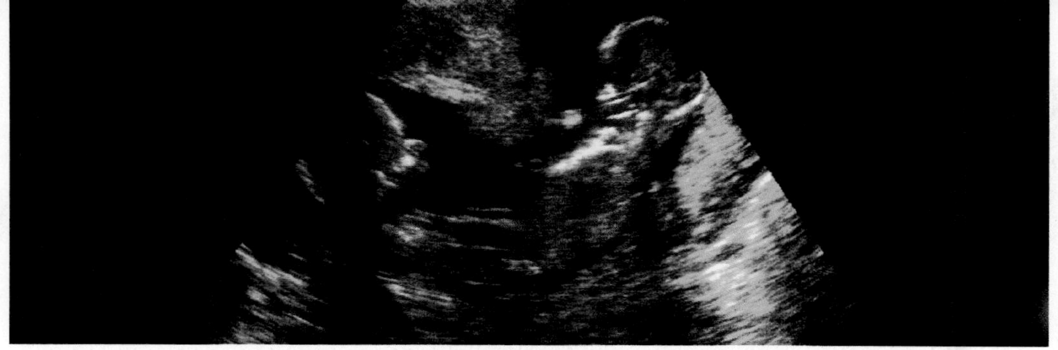

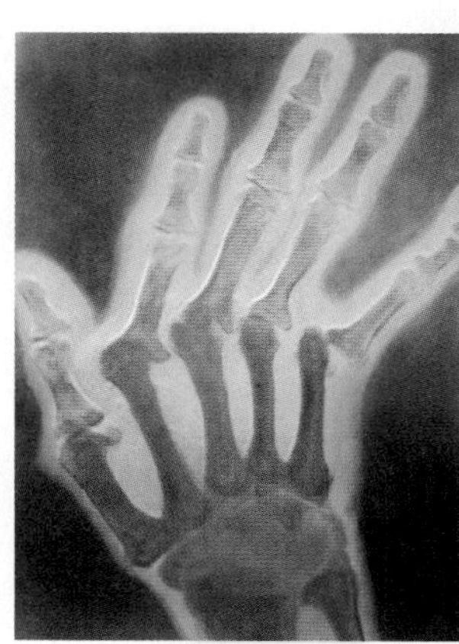

WebQuests

Labs

Investigative Labs

Online Collaborative Science

Guided Research Labs

Features

Careers

History of Science

Science, Technology, & Society

WELCOME TO *Biology: Exploring Life*

Perhaps you've never thought much about the way a textbook works. But in the case of *Biology: Exploring Life*, we thought you might like to know that the authors first talked with many students and teachers about how a book and other materials could help students learn biology better. As the program was being developed, the National Science Foundation (NSF) organized a classroom piloting program to get feedback from thousands of students and their teachers. The result is a unique three-part program that combines a shorter textbook; interactive activities; and interesting, creative labs. These three parts were all created to work together to make biology a successful and fun experience for you! Get started with *Biology: Exploring Life* by reading this overview.

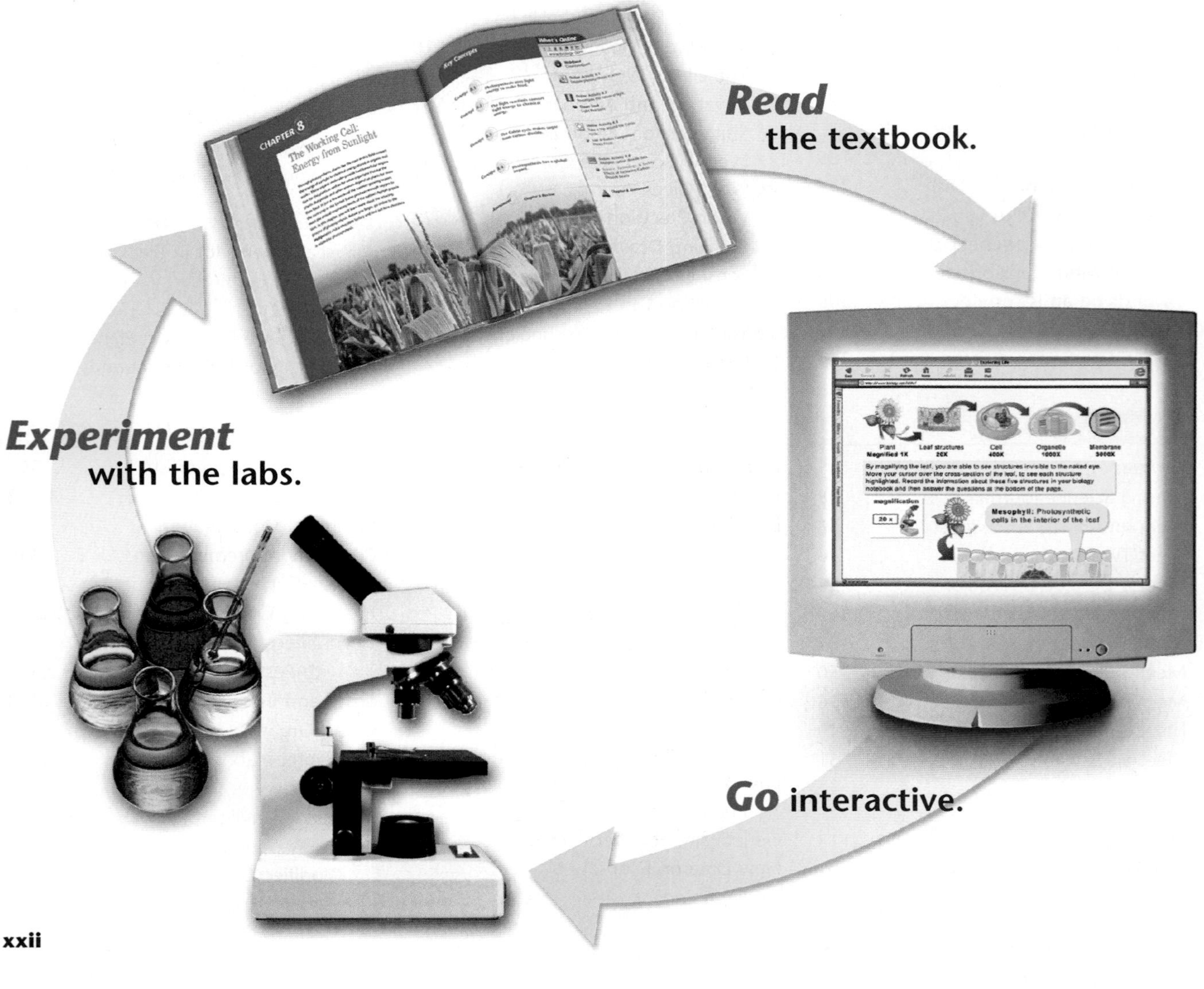

Read the textbook.

Go interactive.

Experiment with the labs.

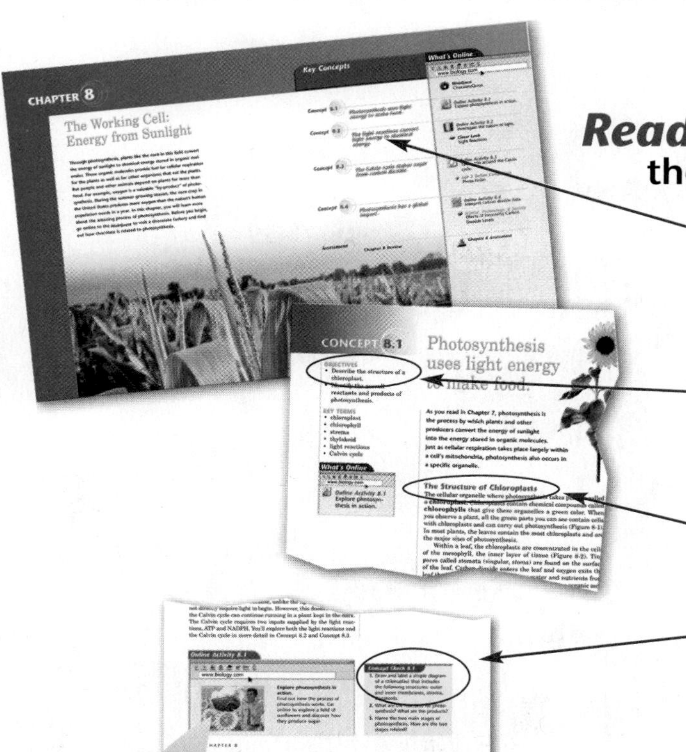

Read the textbook.

- Each chapter is built around a framework of just a few **Key Concepts**. These Key Concept statements help you focus on the "big ideas" of biology.
- Support to guide your reading is built into the book.

Before you read, check out the **Objectives** and **Key Terms** to get a sense of what you'll be learning. The Objectives and Key Terms are a good way to review when you're studying for a test, too.

As you read, note that each section within the text corresponds to one of the Objectives. Use these blue section titles to quickly find the information you need.

After you read, answer the **Concept Check** questions. If you have trouble answering a question, you know which section of the text you need to review.

Go interactive.

- Each Concept has an **Online Activity** (available on Web and CD-ROM) that lets you explore the same core content interactively.
- The optional ***Learning Log for Online Activities*** provides worksheets that guide you through the activities and give you a written record of your online work.
- More interactive activities in each chapter include **WebQuests; Skills Activities; Careers Activities; Science, Technology, & Society Activities; History of Science Activities;** and **Lab Online Companions.**

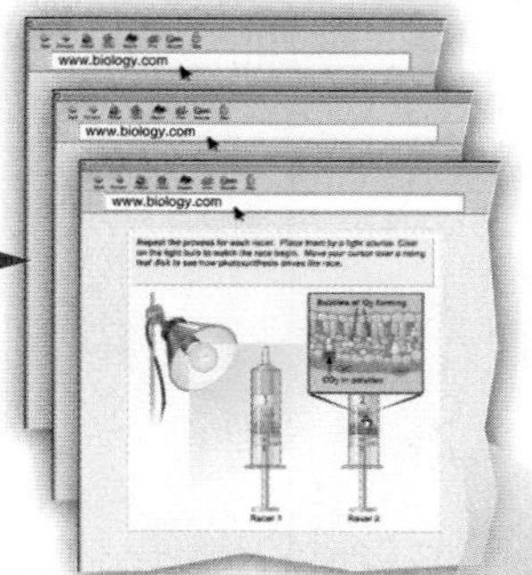

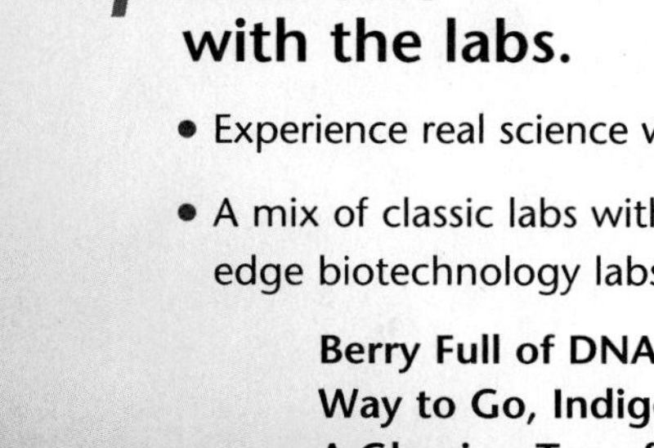

Experiment with the labs.

- Experience real science with the laboratory program.
- A mix of classic labs with new twists, plus cutting-edge biotechnology labs including:

Berry Full of DNA
Way to Go, Indigo!
A Glowing Transformation
You Are a Medical Technologist

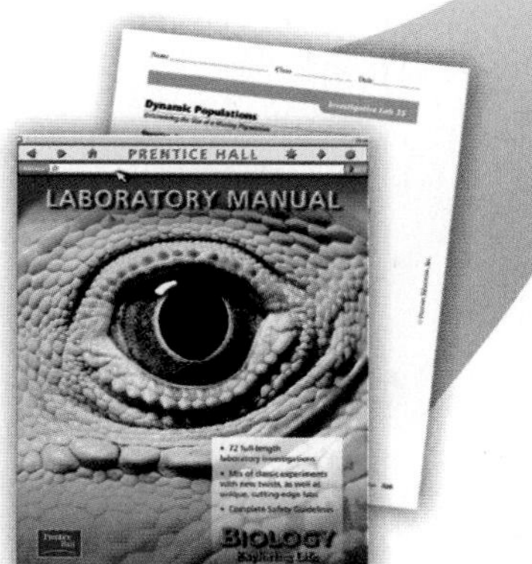

UNIT 1

Exploring Life: Introducing Biology

Chapters

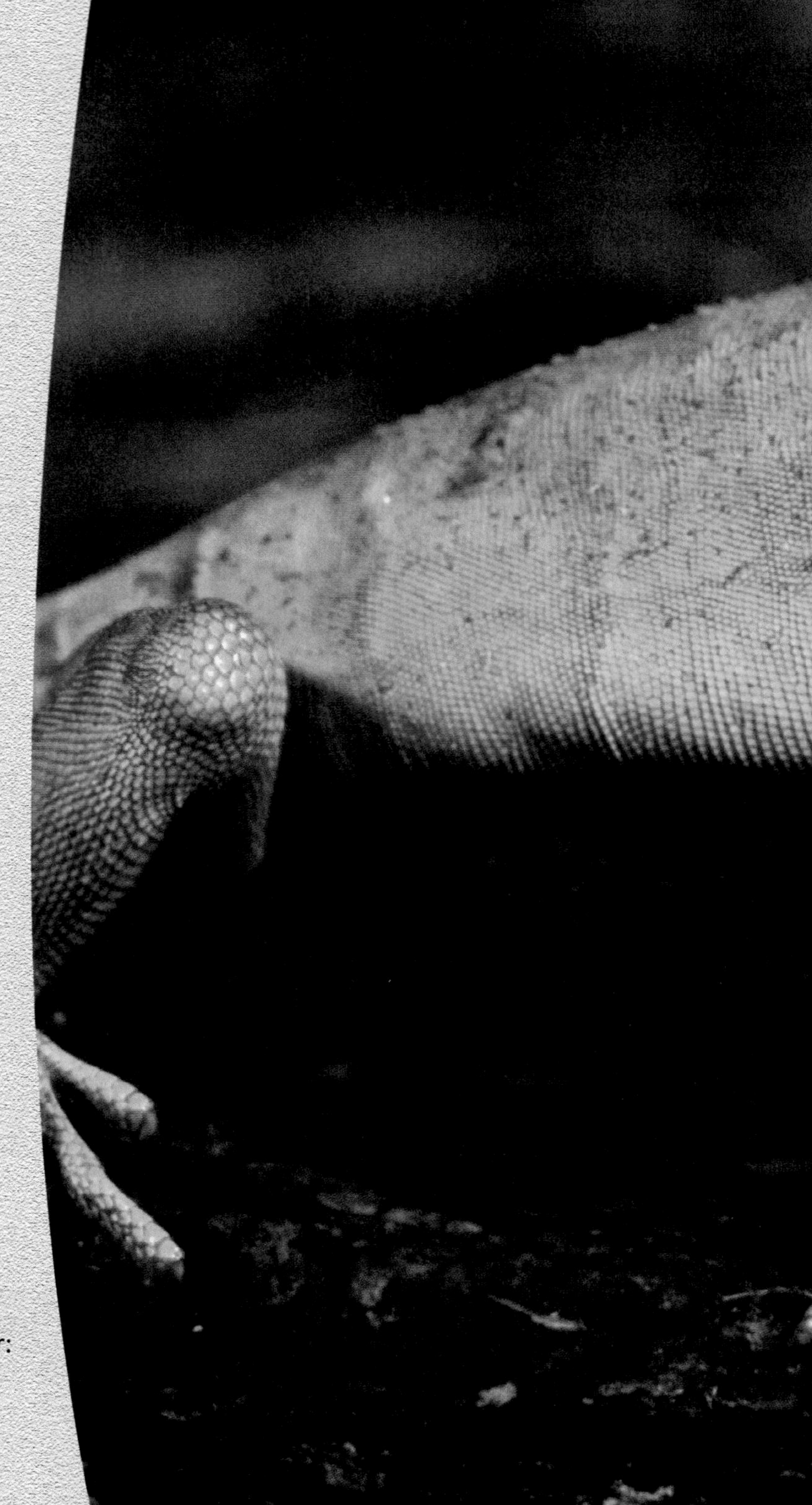

▶ The organism on this book's cover: a green iguana *(Iguana iguana)*

Science is a living thing—not a dead dogma.
Cecilia Payne-Gaposchkin

CHAPTER 1

The Scope of Biology

Welcome to biology, the study of life. All you need to get started is your curiosity. Curiosity about life drives biologists to explore nature. For example, how can animals thrive in such extreme environments as the Antarctic home of the penguins in this photo? How does a plant use sunlight to power the production of food? How do viruses cause disease? Why are there so many kinds of insects? What causes cancer? How do migrating birds and whales find their way? What caused the extinction of the dinosaurs? How does the human brain work? These are just a few of the questions you'll explore in your biology class this year.

As you set off to explore life, it helps to start with a panoramic view of the subject. This chapter provides an overview that will guide you through the very broad scope of biology. First, go online to the ***WebQuest*** to learn how curiosity fuels scientific exploration.

Key Concepts

Concept 1.1

Biology explores life from the global to the microscopic scale.

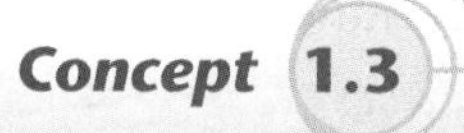

Concept 1.2

Biology explores life in its diverse forms.

Concept 1.3

Ten themes unify the study of life.

Assessment

Chapter 1 Review

What's Online

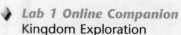

www.biology.com

WebQuest
CuriosityQuest

Online Activity 1.1
Activate a metric scale bar.

Online Activity 1.2
Visit a tropical rain forest.

Lab 1 Online Companion
Kingdom Exploration

Online Activity 1.3
Identify biology themes.

Careers
Meet a Science Journalist

Chapter 1 Assessment

CONCEPT 1.1

Biology explores life from the global to the microscopic scale.

OBJECTIVE

- Identify major organizational levels of life.

KEY TERMS

- biosphere
- ecosystem
- organism
- cell
- DNA
- gene

What's Online

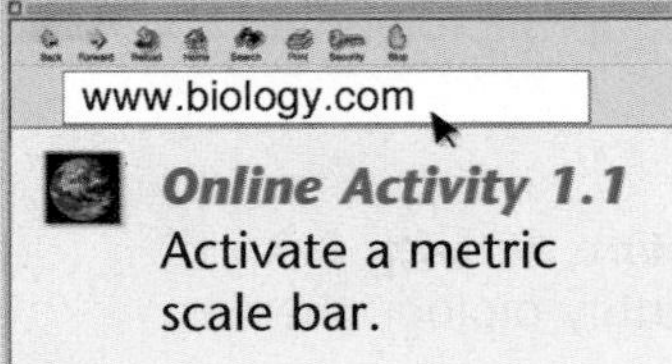

Online Activity 1.1
Activate a metric scale bar.

The science of biology reaches from the global scale of the entire planet down to the microscopic world of cells and molecules. Some biologists ask questions they can answer only with images of Earth beamed down from satellites in space. Other biologists use the world's most powerful microscopes to explore life in its tiniest dimensions. Biologists divide this enormous range of scales into different levels of organization.

The Biosphere

Suppose you could approach Earth from space, zooming in for a closer and closer look at life. The photographs on these two pages show what you might see if you explored New York City's Central Park in this way. Each photograph takes you about a thousand times closer.

In the first view you begin to see signs of life at the global scale of the **biosphere,** which consists of all the parts of the planet that are inhabited by living things (Figure 1-1). The biosphere includes most regions of land; most bodies of water, such as oceans, lakes, and rivers; and the atmosphere to an altitude of several kilometers. (See the Skills Appendix to review metric measurements.) Even from space you can see evidence of life—the dark green regions of forests on the continents. Zoom in a thousand times closer, and you can see your selected site, Central Park in the middle of Manhattan.

Figure 1-1 A view from space includes the entire biosphere (left). A satellite photograph "zooms in" on Central Park in New York City (right). The red areas in this photograph indicate dense plant growth.

Ecosystems

Zooming in another thousand times closer brings you to an area of woodland around a pond within Central Park (Figure 1-2). Such a woodland is an example of what biologists call an ecosystem. An **ecosystem** is the community of living things in an area, along with the nonliving features of the environment that support the living community. For example, this woodland ecosystem's community includes various types of trees and other plants, squirrels and other animals, and countless microscopic forms of life such as bacteria. The woodland's nonliving features include the sunlight, water, air, and soil upon which the living things depend.

Earth's ecosystems vary widely. Perhaps you live in a desert ecosystem in the southwestern United States or along a seacoast. Or perhaps you live in an area where prairies were once widespread. A tropical rain forest and even a small pond are other examples of ecosystems. Each of these ecosystems has a different community of living things and different nonliving features. All of Earth's ecosystems combined make up the biosphere.

Organisms

Another thousand times closer and you can begin to identify individual living things, or **organisms.** The squirrel in Figure 1-2 is an organism, and so is the oak tree that produced the acorn the squirrel is eating. There are many insects living on and around the tree and in the soil.

Some organisms are too small to see at the scale of this photograph. Microscopic organisms—also called microorganisms—in the soil are decomposing (breaking down) the leaf litter and other wastes on the woodland floor. Interactions among the organisms of a community make each ecosystem a dynamic (constantly changing) place.

▼ **Figure 1-2** Even a city contains ecosystems, such as this area of woodland (left). An ecosystem includes a community of living things (organisms), such as squirrels, trees, and grass (right).

Cells

A view a thousand times closer takes you into a leaf such as one from the oak tree on the previous page. Now you can see that the leaf consists of cells, which look somewhat like microscopic "rooms" in the photograph. **Cells** are life's basic units of structure and function. All organisms are made of one or more cells.

A microscope was used to take the photograph of a leaf interior in Figure 1-3a. Each of the cells you see is only about 25 µm (micrometers) across. (1 µm = one millionth of a meter.) It would take more than 700 of these cells to reach across a penny. Yet, as small as these cells are, they contain even tinier structures. One such structure visible in some of these leaf cells is the nucleus. The nucleus directs all of the activities throughout the cell. You will read more about cells and their structures and processes in Unit 2.

DNA and Genes

Coming closer once again, you can see inside the nucleus of a single cell. Figure 1-3b is a computer model of a very important chemical within a cell's nucleus. The spheres represent atoms, the basic building blocks of all materials both living and nonliving. As you'll read in Chapter 4, atoms can bond together, forming molecules such as this one—a molecule called DNA. **DNA** is the chemical responsible for inheritance—the passing on of traits from parent organisms to their offspring. A DNA molecule contains the instructions for a cell to make all the other molecules it needs to function. Along the length of each DNA molecule are units of inherited information called **genes.**

From such molecular machinery of cells on up to the workings of the whole biosphere, biology explores life at its many levels.

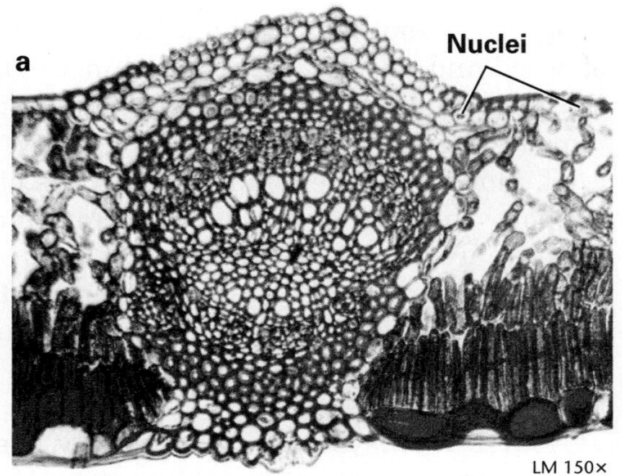

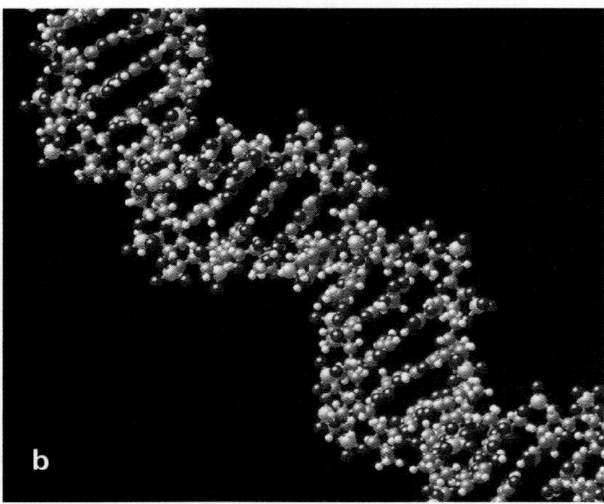

▲ **Figure 1-3** The next two views are not visible to the unaided eye. **a.** A microscope reveals an array of different cells in the cross section of a leaf. **b.** A computer model represents the molecular structure of DNA within a cell's nucleus.

Online Activity 1.1

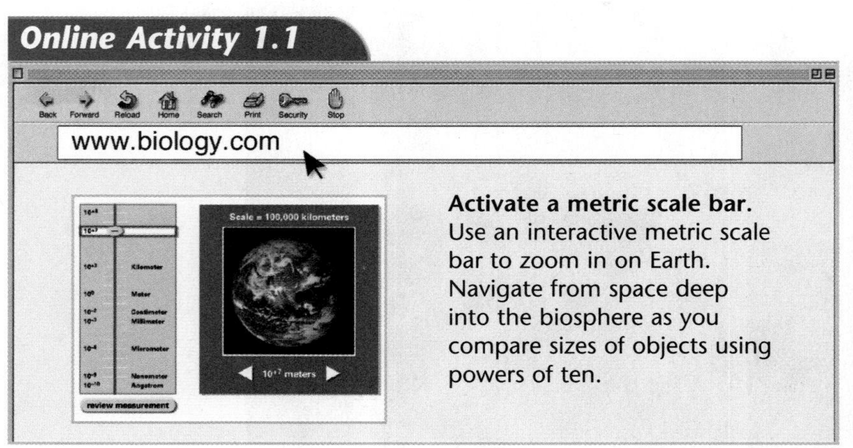

Activate a metric scale bar. Use an interactive metric scale bar to zoom in on Earth. Navigate from space deep into the biosphere as you compare sizes of objects using powers of ten.

Concept Check 1.1

1. Which level of life includes all of the other levels in this list: organisms, cells, biosphere, molecules, ecosystems? Explain your answer.
2. Identify an ecosystem in the area where you live.
3. What are genes? How are they related to DNA?

CONCEPT 1.2

Biology explores life in its diverse forms.

OBJECTIVES

- Use the term *species* in discussing life's diversity.
- Explain the basic strategy biologists use in classifying organisms.
- Identify a characteristic that separates the domains Bacteria and Archaea from the domain Eukarya.

KEY TERMS

- species
- domain
- unicellular
- prokaryotic cell
- eukaryotic cell
- multicellular

What's Online

Online Activity 1.2
Visit a tropical rain forest.

Lab 1 Online Companion
Kingdom Exploration

Biology explores a vast frontier. As you learned in Concept 1.1, biology extends from the giant scale of the biosphere down to the molecular world within a cell. But the scope of biology also includes the broad diversity of organisms that inhabit Earth.

Life's Diversity of Species

On your next walk through your neighborhood, notice how many kinds of living things you can spot. You may observe various insects, spiders, birds, and plants. Now suppose you're walking in a tropical rain forest such as the one pictured in Figure 1-4. The enormous variety of life overloads your senses with sights, sounds, and smells. Insects crawl, jump, and fly everywhere—their hum and buzz surround you. Now and then, they are drowned out by loud calls of birds or howls of monkeys. You struggle through a dense tangle of plants. Showy orchids fill the air with sweet fragrance. Colorful mushrooms poke up from the logs they are decomposing. Inspecting the forest floor with a magnifying glass, you find an astonishing assortment of organisms so tiny that they would otherwise escape notice.

Each different type of organism you observe during either walk is an example of a **species,** or a distinct form of life. Biologists have so far identified more than 1.5 million species, and new species are discovered almost daily. This growing catalog of known life forms includes approximately 5,000 species of bacteria; 8,600 species of birds; 30,000 species of fishes; 100,000 species of fungi; 280,000 species of plants; and 1,000,000 species of insects, by far the most diverse of all animals. There are also thousands of species of amphibians, reptiles, and mammals. Tropical rain forests are especially rich in species diversity, as you will read more about later in this book.

Figure 1-4 Rain forests are homes to a wide diversity of species. This spider monkey and orchid blossom are just two of the thousands of species that inhabit the forests of the Yucatán peninsula in Mexico.

Classifying Life: The Basic Idea

Humans have a tendency to place items in categories. For instance, perhaps you organize your music collection according to artist. And then maybe you group the various artists into even broader categories, such as study-time music, dance music, and exercise music. This behavior may explain why one of the oldest branches of biology is the study of classification—organizing similar species into larger groups. Grouping species probably seems natural to you. You may speak of butterflies, recognizing that there are many types (species) of butterflies (Figure 1-5). You may sort groups of animals into broader categories, such as the insect group (which includes groups such as ants and bees as well as butterflies). And you probably recognize that insects and reptiles, as different as they are, both belong to the larger animal group, which in turn is very different from the plant group.

You can compare an organism's biological classification to a postal address. A postal address describes a location by using broader and broader categories. For example, an address specifies a particular house or apartment number, but also a street (which includes many houses), a city (which includes many streets), and a state (which includes many cities).

Figure 1-6 illustrates the basic idea of grouping species into broader and broader categories using the animal found on your textbook's cover (the species *Iguana iguana*) as an example. This species is one of many large lizards called iguanas. All iguanas belong to a larger group of animals called reptiles, and so on. You'll learn more about the complete system of classifying organisms in Chapter 15.

▲ **Figure 1-5** Despite their very different appearances, these three insects share certain characteristics that identify them all as butterflies.

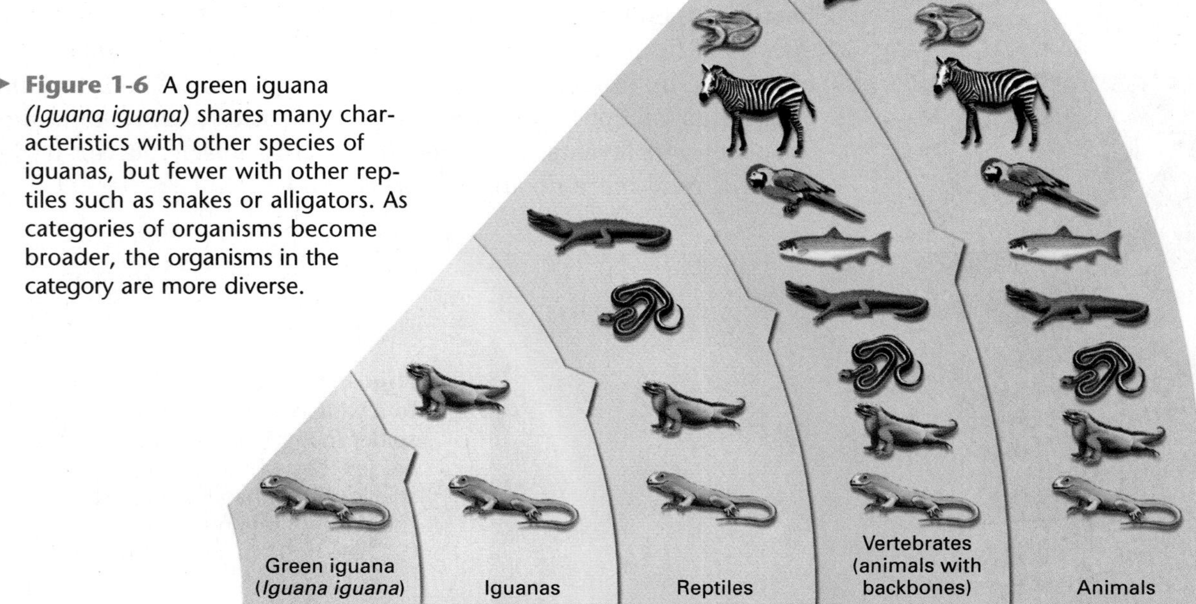

▶ **Figure 1-6** A green iguana (*Iguana iguana*) shares many characteristics with other species of iguanas, but fewer with other reptiles such as snakes or alligators. As categories of organisms become broader, the organisms in the category are more diverse.

The Three Domains of Life

In classifying life forms, many biologists call the broadest category a **domain.** According to this classification scheme, there are three domains: Archaea, Bacteria, and Eukarya (Figure 1-7). The organisms of domains Archaea and Bacteria are very tiny. Most of these organisms are **unicellular,** meaning that their entire bodies consist of just a single cell. These cells are relatively simple. For example, they lack nuclei—their DNA is not separated from the rest of the cell. These cells without nuclei are called **prokaryotic cells.** Though domains Bacteria and Archaea both consist of prokaryotic organisms, they are otherwise very different from each other, as you'll learn in Chapter 16.

Biologists divide each domain into subgroups called kingdoms. For example, domain Eukarya includes four kingdoms: protists, fungi, plants, and animals. All the organisms of these four subgroups consist of eukaryotic cells. **Eukaryotic cells** contain nuclei that separate DNA from the rest of the cell. Like the prokaryotes, many protists and certain fungi are unicellular and microscopic in size. But other protists, most fungi, and all animals and plants are multicellular. **Multicellular** organisms are made of many cells, not just one. Your own body, for example, has trillions of cells.

You will learn much more about the diversity of life in later chapters. The last section of this chapter will focus on some basic themes that apply to *all* species, from prokaryotes to animals, and to *all* levels of organization, from the biosphere to cells.

Domain Archaea

Colorized SEM 10,700×

Domain Bacteria

Colorized SEM 5,000×

Domain Eukarya

LM 120×

Kingdom Protista (protists)

Kingdom Fungi

Kingdom Plantae (plants)

Kingdom Animalia (animals)

▲ **Figure 1-7** All known organisms currently are classified into one of three domains—Archaea, Bacteria, or Eukarya. This figure also shows the four kingdoms that make up domain Eukarya.

Online Activity 1.2

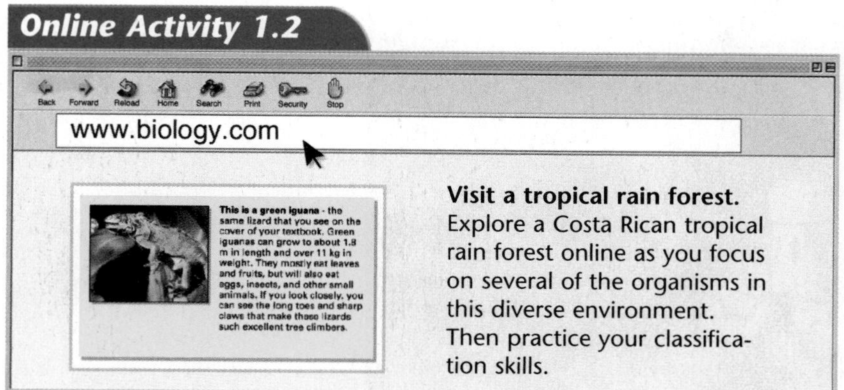

Back Forward Reload Home Search Print Security Stop
www.biology.com
This is a green iguana - the same lizard that you see on the cover of your textbook. Green iguanas can grow to about 1.8 m in length and over 11 kg in weight. They mostly eat leaves and fruits, but will also eat eggs, insects, and other small animals. If you look closely, you can see the long toes and sharp claws that make these lizards such excellent tree climbers.

Visit a tropical rain forest. Explore a Costa Rican tropical rain forest online as you focus on several of the organisms in this diverse environment. Then practice your classification skills.

Concept Check 1.2

1. Explain the relationship between the terms *species* and *organism.*
2. Explain two different ways that you could classify the following items: banana, lemon, sandwich, milk, orange, meatball, salad.
3. Explain the main difference between organisms of the domains Bacteria and Archaea and organisms of the domain Eukarya.

Kingdom Exploration

Observing Organisms With a Microscope

Question How do microscopes help biologists explore the diversity of life?

Lab Overview In this investigation you will use a microscope to observe representatives of each of the four kingdoms of organisms in domain Eukarya. You will sketch them as you see them, then make a final drawing of each based on their relative sizes.

Preparing for the Lab To help you prepare for the investigation, go to the *Lab 1 Online Companion.* ······➔ Identify the parts of a microscope and learn how to obtain a focused image. Prepare for the lab procedure by previewing the steps you will take.

Completing the Lab Use your Laboratory Manual or lab page printouts from the *Lab 1 Online Companion* to do the investigation and draw conclusions from the observations you made. **CAUTION:** *Be sure to follow your teacher's instructions and all safety guidelines in the investigation.*

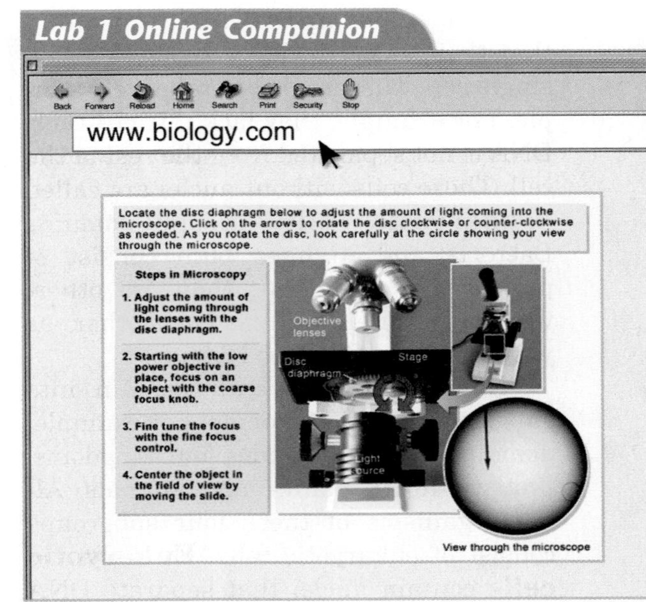

Lab 1 Online Companion
Back
Forward
Reload
Home
Search
Print
Security
Stop
www.biology.com
Locate the disc diaphragm below to adjust the amount of light coming into the microscope. Click on the arrows to rotate the disc clockwise or counter-clockwise as needed. As you rotate the disc, look carefully at the circle showing your view through the microscope.
Steps in Microscopy
1. Adjust the amount of light coming through the lenses with the disc diaphragm.
2. Starting with the low power objective in place, focus on an object with the coarse focus knob.
3. Fine tune the focus with the fine focus control.
4. Center the object in the field of view by moving the slide.
Objective lenses
Disc diaphragm
Stage
View through the microscope

CONCEPT 1.3

Ten themes unify the study of life.

OBJECTIVE

- Identify ten themes of biology.

KEY TERMS

- system
- photosynthesis
- producer
- consumer
- homeostasis
- adaptation
- population
- natural selection
- evolution

What's Online
www.biology.com
Online Activity 1.3
Identify biology themes.
Careers
Meet a Science Journalist

With life's many levels of organization and great diversity of organisms, biologists have a huge subject to study. And it gets bigger every year as researchers continually make new discoveries. How can anyone make sense of all this information? Fortunately, there are some basic ideas, or themes, that apply to biology at all levels and for all organisms. The ten themes described here will help you connect the many things you'll learn as you explore life.

Biological Systems

Have you ever heard the saying "The whole is greater than the sum of its parts"? This saying captures the importance of how a combination of parts can form a more complex organization called a **system.** A system has properties that are based on the arrangement and interactions of its parts. For example, a bicycle is a mechanical system you can use for exercise or transportation. But just try to get around on a box full of bicycle parts!

Your body, like that of any organism, is a living system. You make use of the interactions among its parts when you type on a keyboard or click a computer mouse (Figure 1-8). The joints in your fingers and wrist give your hand a wide range of movements. But your bones themselves cannot move. Movement depends on contractions of the muscles attached to the bones. Muscles are coordinated by signals from the brain, carried by nerves. Finally, blood vessels supply all of these parts with oxygen and food. Together, the parts of your body enable you to work the computer. You are certainly more than the sum of your parts, and so are all biological systems.

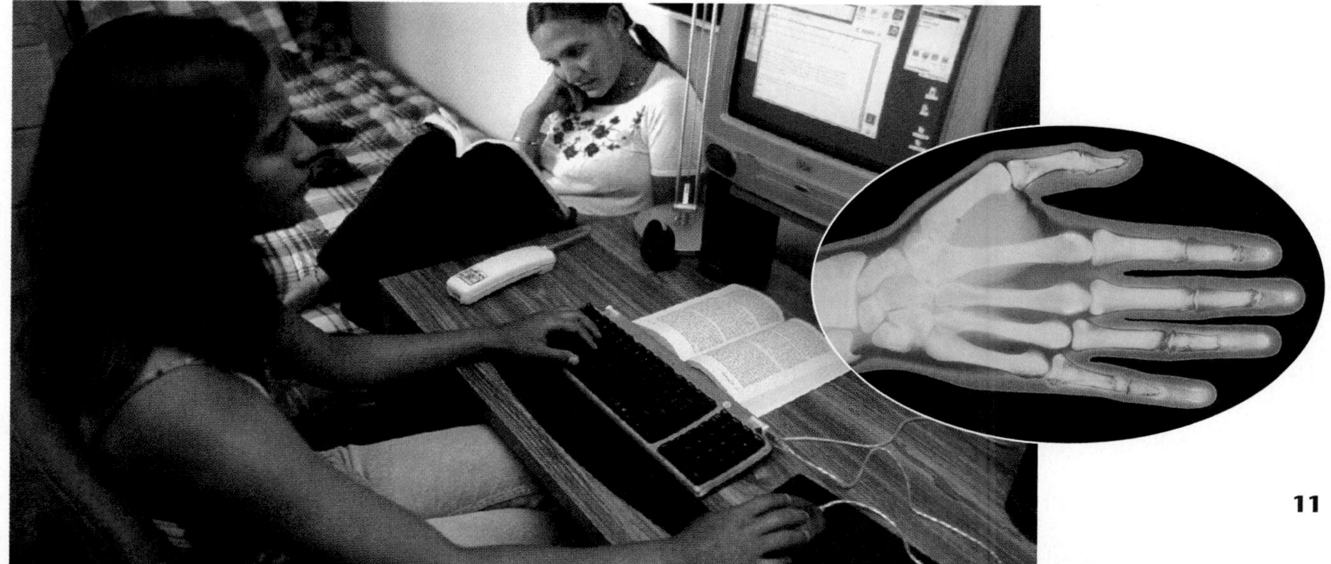

Figure 1-8 In performing tasks such as using a computer, a person's bones, muscles, nerves, and other parts of the body interact as an organized, living system.

An ecosystem such as a forest is also a biological system. Like your body, an ecosystem has properties that depend on how its parts interact. For example, the organisms in the ecosystem require a steady supply of certain chemicals to live. Plants obtain most of their necessary chemicals from the soil, water, and air. Animals acquire most of the chemicals they need by eating plants or other animals. Chemicals are returned to the soil by bacteria and fungi that decompose the wastes and remains of organisms (Figure 1-9). You could say that such interactions of organisms with each other and with the nonliving environment "put the *system* in *ecosystem*." The biological systems theme applies to all levels of life, from the biosphere all the way down to the interactions of molecules in cells.

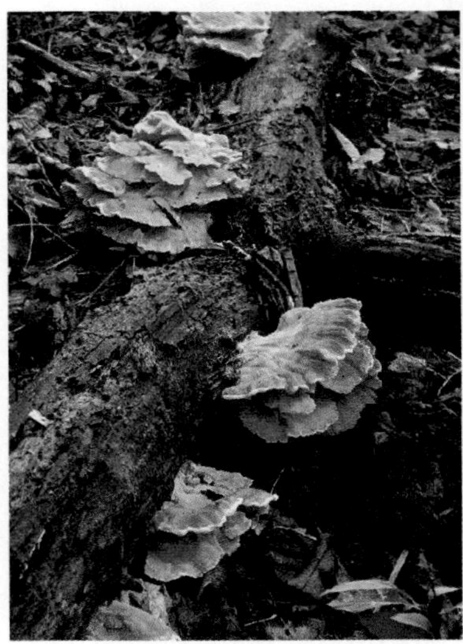

▲ **Figure 1-9** Decomposers such as these mushrooms break down wastes and remains of plants and animals, recycling the chemicals in an ecosystem.

The Cellular Basis of Life

As you read in Concept 1.1, all organisms are made of cells. Most multicellular organisms have cells that are specialized for different functions. Two examples of specialized cells in your body are your muscle cells, which contract and enable you to move, and your nerve cells, which transmit impulses that control your muscles.

In most multicellular organisms, cells are organized into higher levels of organization (Figure 1-10). Beginning with the cellular level, the next level is a tissue, which is a group of similar cells that together perform a specific function. For example, nerve tissue consists of many nerve cells organized into a complex network. Several types of tissue together may make up a structure called an organ. The brain is an organ that consists of nerve tissue and other types of tissues. Finally, several organs that together carry out a major body function make up an organ system. In this example, the brain, spinal cord, and nerves make up the organ system called the nervous system.

A multicellular organism's development and survival are based on the functions and interactions of its many cells. This cellular basis of life is a theme you will encounter often as you explore the living world.

▼ **Figure 1-10** The human body, like most multicellular organisms, consists of many levels of organization.

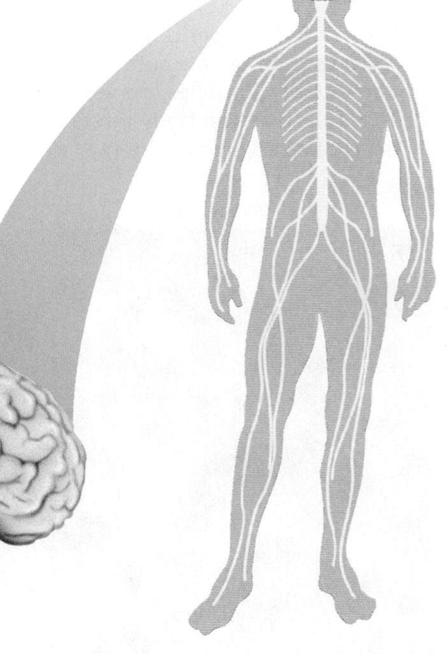

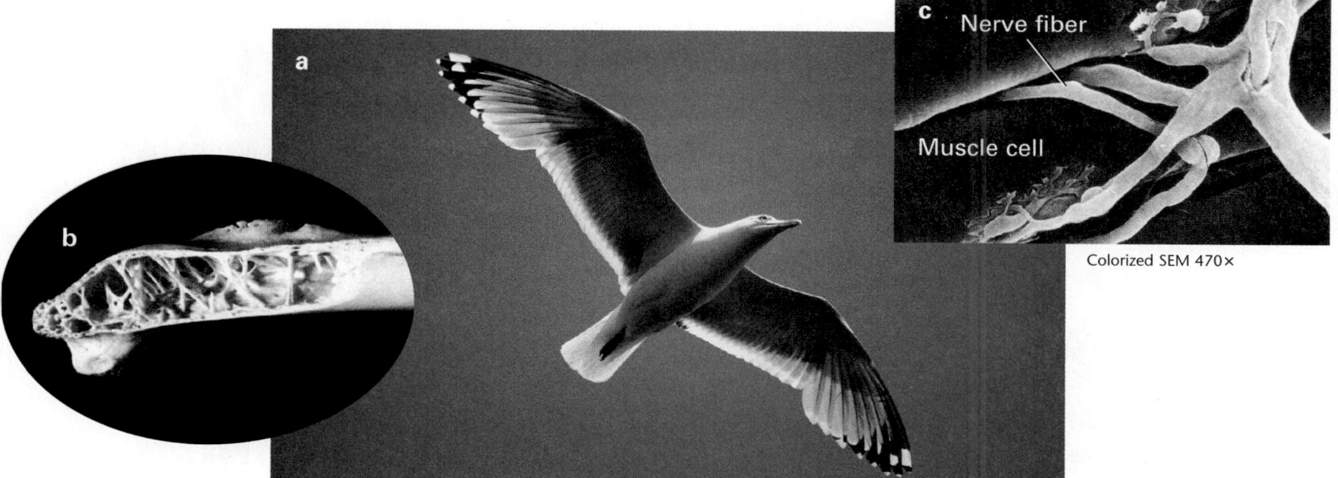

▲ **Figure 1-11** A bird's ability to fly provides several examples of form fitting function. **a.** The aerodynamic shape of a bird's wing allows it to glide through the air. **b.** The honeycomb structure of the bones makes them strong but lightweight. **c.** Nerve cells have long fibers that signal the bird's muscles, coordinating its flying movements.

Form and Function

Which is the better tool: a hammer or a screwdriver? The answer depends on what you want to do. You probably would not choose a hammer to loosen a screw or a screwdriver to pound in a nail. The heavy head of a hammer is suited to driving in nails, and the thin, flat edge of a screwdriver is suited to turning screws. How something works is related to its structure. In other words, form fits function.

The aerodynamic shape of a bird's wing is a living example of the form-fits-function theme (Figure 1-11a). The structure of the bird's bones contributes to the bird's ability to fly. Inside the bones, an open, honeycomb-like structure provides great strength with little weight (Figure 1-11b). The form-fits-function theme also extends down to the cellular level. Figure 1-11c shows the long extensions of the nerve cells that control the bird's flight muscles. These fibers make it possible for the bird's brain to coordinate flying movements. As you explore the structure of life, you'll discover the harmony of form and function everywhere.

Reproduction and Inheritance

"Like begets like" is an old saying that describes the ability of organisms to reproduce their own kind. For example, the Japanese macaque monkey and her baby in Figure 1-12 closely resemble each other. The baby macaque in turn may grow up and produce similar-looking offspring of its own.

What explains the similarity between parents and their offspring? You read earlier in the chapter that offspring inherit units of information called genes from their parents. Genes are responsible for family resemblance.

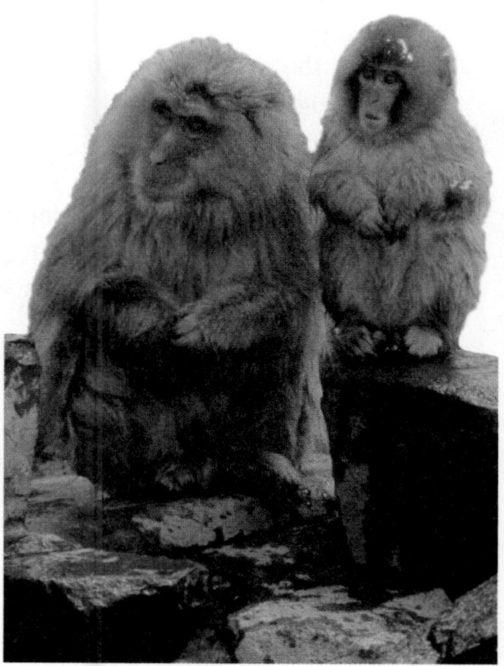

▶ **Figure 1-12** This baby Japanese macaque resembles its mother because of genes.

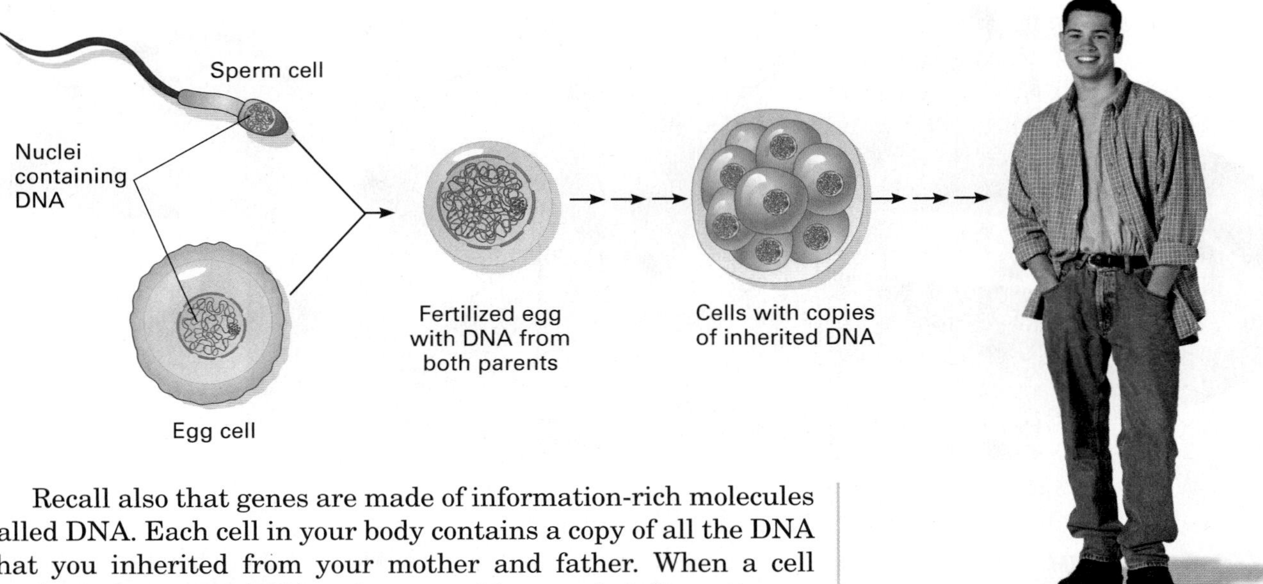

▲ **Figure 1-13** When an egg cell and sperm cell fuse, DNA from each parent is combined in the fertilized egg. The inherited DNA directs the eventual transformation of the fertilized egg into a person.

Recall also that genes are made of information-rich molecules called DNA. Each cell in your body contains a copy of all the DNA that you inherited from your mother and father. When a cell divides, it copies its DNA and passes this genetic information on to each of the two cells it produces. How is this information passed from parent organisms to offspring? In humans, an egg cell from the mother fuses with a sperm cell from the father (Figure 1-13). The result is a fertilized cell containing a combination of DNA from both parents. The inherited DNA directs the transformation of the fertilized egg into a person, with his or her own eye color, facial features, and other characteristics.

This brief introduction to DNA suggests several questions.

- How does DNA store information?
- How do cells copy and pass along this information?
- How does the inherited DNA bring about such traits as the color of eyes or the shape of a nose?

Later chapters in this book will help you answer these questions. For now, the key point is that inherited information in the form of DNA enables organisms to reproduce their own kind.

Interaction With the Environment

No organism is completely isolated from its surroundings. As part of an ecosystem, each organism interacts continuously with its environment. For example, a plant obtains water and nutrients from the soil, carbon dioxide gas from the air, and energy from sunlight. The plant uses these three "inputs" from its environment for **photosynthesis**—the process by which plants make food.

But the plant also has an impact on its surroundings. For example, as a plant grows, its roots break up rocks and release acids that change the soil. This affects the types of organisms that can live in the soil. Plants also release oxygen as a byproduct of photosynthesis. Other organisms as well as plants use this oxygen for their own survival.

The transfer of chemicals between organisms and their environments is a key process in any ecosystem. Think about your own chemical exchanges with the outside world. You breathe air, drink water, eat food, and get rid of waste products. Living requires a daily balance of such "inputs" and "outputs."

In addition to chemical exchange, there are many other ways you interact with your environment. If you go outside on a bright summer day, the sun may cause you to squint. Perhaps the bark of an approaching dog causes you to turn your head quickly. Just as you are constantly sensing and responding to changes in your environment, so are all other organisms. For example, a specialized leaf of the Venus' flytrap in Figure 1-14 sensed the light footsteps of this soon-to-be-digested green bottle fly. The plant responded to this environmental stimulus by rapidly folding the leaf together. You will discover many such examples of organism-environment interactions as you explore life.

▲ **Figure 1-14** Venus' flytraps have specialized cells that can detect touch. When an insect lands and stimulates these leaf cells, it may become the plant's next meal.

Energy and Life

Moving, growing, reproducing, and other activities of life require organisms to perform work. Work depends on a source of energy. You obtain your energy in chemical form—in the sugars, fats, and other "fuel-like" molecules in your food. Your cells use this energy for all their work. You "burn" fuel to move, to think, and even to keep your heart beating when you are asleep.

On a bigger scale, you can trace energy through an ecosystem. Energy flows into an ecosystem as sunlight and exits in the form of heat. Figure 1-15 is a simplified diagram of this energy flow through a forest ecosystem. Note how the ecosystem's organisms convert one form of energy to another. For example, in the process of photosynthesis, plants convert light energy to the chemical energy stored in sugars and other foods. Plants and other photosynthetic organisms are an ecosystem's **producers,** so named because they produce the food upon which the entire ecosystem depends. The plants use some of the food they produce for their own fuel and building material. A portion of the stored energy reaches **consumers,** which are animals and other organisms that eat (consume) the food made by the producers.

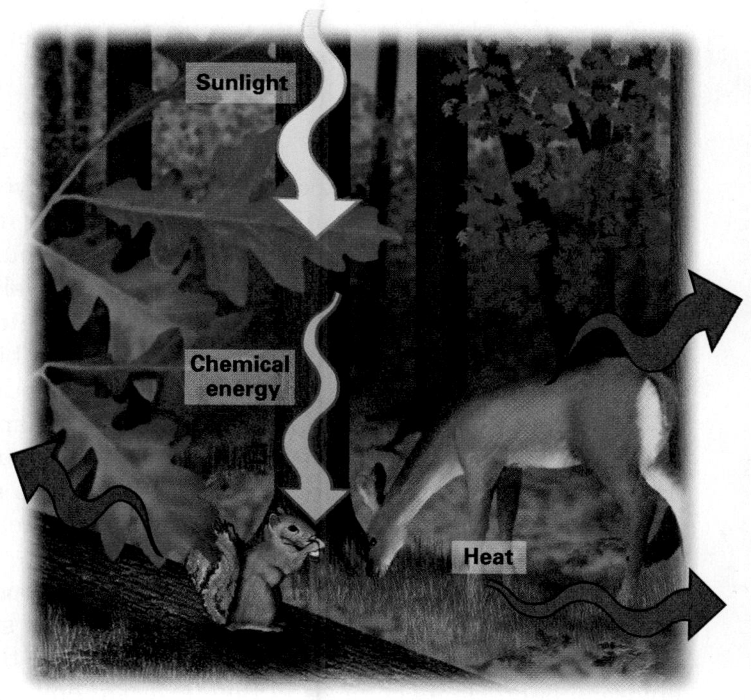

▶ **Figure 1-15** Energy enters an ecosystem as sunlight. Plants are producers that convert light energy to chemical energy stored in food. Animals and other consumers obtain their energy in chemical form by eating. Energy exits an ecosystem as heat, which all organisms generate as they perform work.

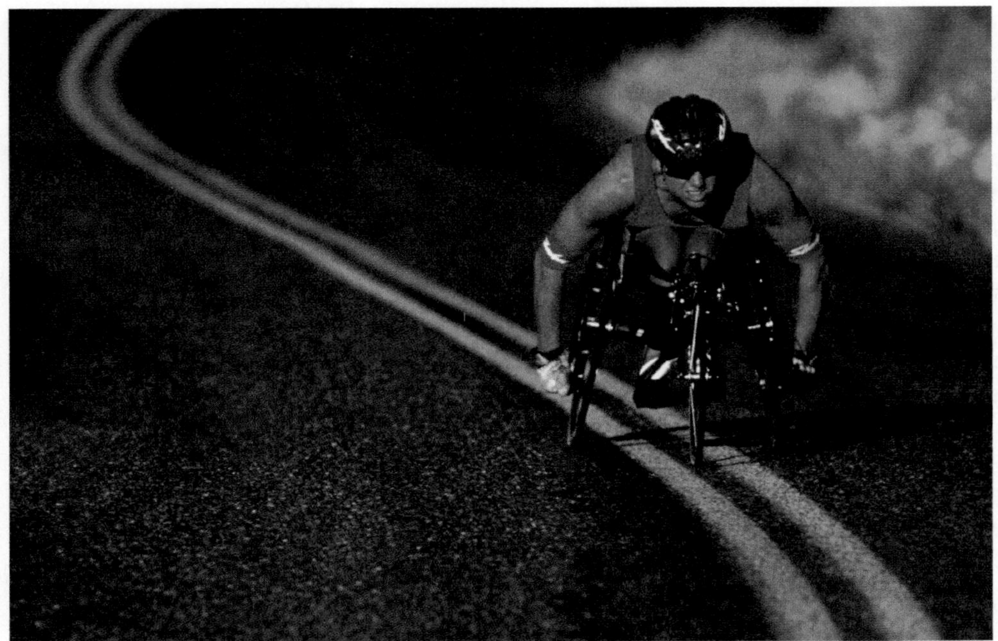

▲ **Figure 1-16** Energy is required for all the activities of life. The source of this racer's energy is the chemical energy stored in food.

What happens to the chemical energy stored in the food consumers eat? It is converted to other forms of energy as the organism carries out its life activities (Figure 1-16). Moving, thinking, breathing, seeing, and everything else you do requires your cells to convert some of the chemical energy of food into other forms of energy. You can compare this energy conversion to a car converting the chemical energy stored in gasoline to the mechanical energy of moving wheels. Whenever an organism or a car performs work, it converts some of its energy supply to heat. The heat is released to the environment. Even when you are sitting still in class, you produce about as much heat as a 100-watt light bulb. Because all organisms lose energy in the form of heat, an ecosystem cannot recycle energy. Life on Earth depends on a continuous supply of energy from the sun.

Regulation

Another theme you will encounter frequently in your study of biology is the ability of organisms to regulate their internal conditions. For example, you have a "thermostat" in your brain that reacts whenever your body temperature varies slightly from 37°C (about 98.6°F). If this internal thermostat detects a slight rise in your body temperature on a hot day, your brain signals your skin to produce sweat. Sweating helps cool your body.

Panting is another example of a cooling mechanism. You've probably seen a dog pant on a hot day, but did you know that some birds also pant (Figure 1-17)? Panting causes moisture on the large surface of the animal's lungs to evaporate, cooling the body as a result.

The ability of mammals and birds to regulate body temperature is just one example of **homeostasis,** or "steady state." Mechanisms of homeostasis enable organisms to regulate their *internal* environment, despite changes in their *external* environment.

▼ **Figure 1-17** This great blue heron in the Florida Everglades is panting, a mechanism that releases heat from the bird's body.

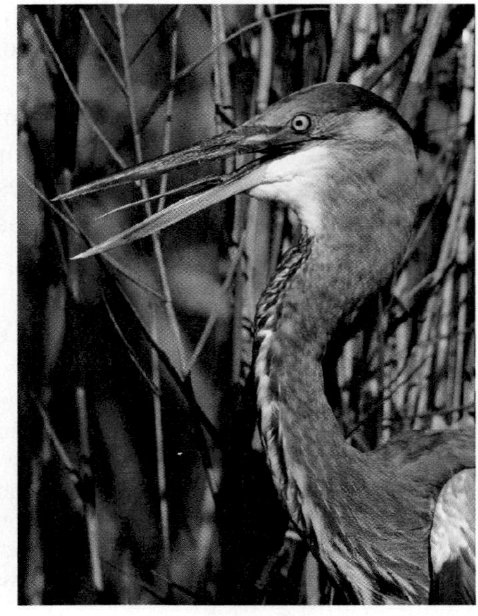

Adaptation and Evolution

Can you find the three animals in Figure 1-18? These organisms are three species of insects called mantids. Their shapes and colors enable them to blend into their backgrounds. This camouflage makes the mantids less visible to animals that feed on insects. It also makes them less visible to the insects the mantids feed on!

Adaptations The unique characteristics that camouflage each mantid species are examples of adaptations. An **adaptation** is an inherited trait that helps the organism's ability to survive and reproduce in its particular environment.

How do mantids and other organisms adapt to their environments? Part of the answer is the variation among individuals in a population. A **population** is a localized group of organisms belonging to the same species. Just as you and your classmates are not exactly alike, individuals of all populations, including mantids, also vary in some of their traits. These variations reflect each individual's particular combination of inherited genes. And this hereditary variation is the raw material that makes it possible for a population to adapt to its environment. If a particular variation is helpful, individuals with the variation may live longer and produce more offspring than those that do not have it. This process is called **natural selection** because it works by the natural environment "selecting" certain inherited traits.

Figure 1-19 illustrates a hypothetical example of natural selection in a beetle population. The individual beetles vary in their coloring, from light gray to charcoal. Each beetle's color is determined by its genes. Now suppose that the soil has recently been blackened by a fire. For birds that eat the beetles, it is easiest to spot the beetles that are lightest in color. On average, the darker beetles have a better chance of surviving and reproducing, passing their genes for dark color on to their offspring. In contrast, the lighter beetles are captured more easily, and fewer survive to produce offspring. After many generations, most of the beetles in the population are dark. This abundance of dark color is an adaptation of the beetle population to its environment.

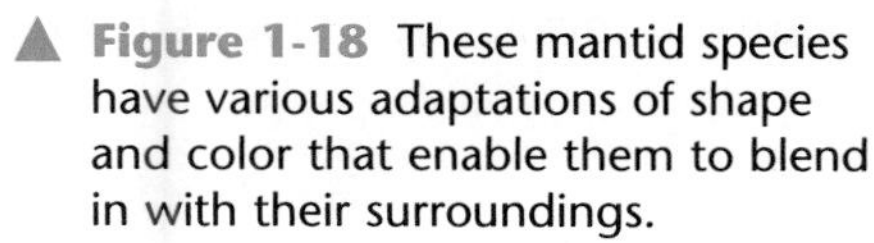

▲ **Figure 1-18** These mantid species have various adaptations of shape and color that enable them to blend in with their surroundings.

▼ **Figure 1-19** In this hypothetical example of natural selection, darker beetles are more likely to survive longer and reproduce, passing their genes on to more offspring.

a. A beetle population includes individuals of different colors.

b. Birds capture more light beetles than dark beetles.

c. Survivors (mostly dark beetles) reproduce.

d. Dark beetles become more frequent in the population over time.

Evolution Natural selection is the mechanism by which evolution occurs. The term *evolution* means "a process of change." Biologists use the word **evolution** specifically to mean a generation-to-generation change in the proportion of different inherited genes in a population. For example, in the beetle example, genes for dark color are becoming more common and genes for light color are becoming less common over the generations of beetles. The beetle population is said to be undergoing evolution, or evolving.

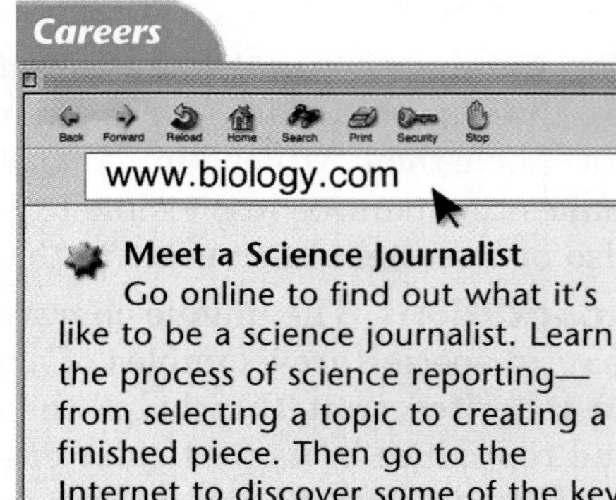

Meet a Science Journalist
Go online to find out what it's like to be a science journalist. Learn the process of science reporting—from selecting a topic to creating a finished piece. Then go to the Internet to discover some of the key science resources available there.

Biology and Society

More than ever before, modern biology is changing humans' everyday lives. New findings about DNA affect such fields as medicine and agriculture. Research on the nervous system is improving the treatment of certain mental illnesses. The study of evolution is helping health professionals understand how disease-causing bacteria become resistant to antibiotic drugs. Environmental issues such as water and air pollution are changing how people think about their relationship to the biosphere. If you watch the evening news or read a newspaper for a week, it's likely you'll hear about many issues that relate to biology, such as stem cell research, animal cloning, environmental issues, genetically modified crops, or new ways to treat diseases (Figure 1-20). The concepts you study this year will help you to have informed opinions about the impact of biology's rapid progress.

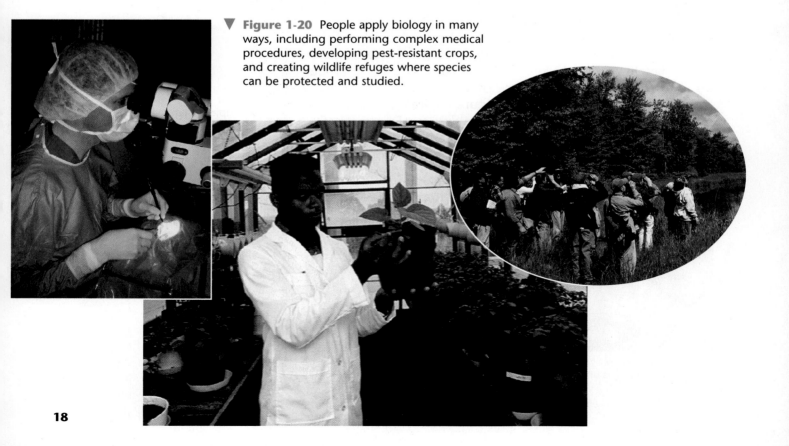

▼ **Figure 1-20** People apply biology in many ways, including performing complex medical procedures, developing pest-resistant crops, and creating wildlife refuges where species can be protected and studied.

Figure 1-21 This Atlantic loggerhead turtle is being fitted with a radio transmitter that will enable scientists to track its movements.

Scientific Inquiry

Biology is a science and, as such, relies on certain processes of inquiry. As you will read in Chapter 2, scientific inquiry involves asking questions about nature and then using observations or experiments to find possible answers to those questions. For example, the biologist in Figure 1-21 is fitting an Atlantic loggerhead turtle with a radio transmitter. Researchers will use signals from the transmitter to monitor the animal as it moves throughout its range. Such research is helping biologists determine how large a nature preserve must be to support a population of Atlantic loggerheads.

In your biology class this year, you will have many opportunities to conduct your own scientific inquiries in laboratory and field settings. The many Online Activities in the *Biology: Exploring Life* program will provide you with additional practice in the process of science. Throughout this adventure, you will find many connections to the ten themes introduced in this first chapter. Enjoy your exploration of life!

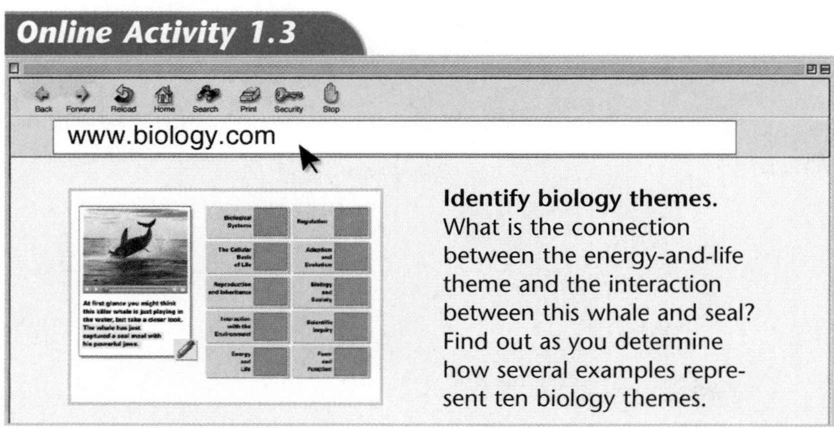

Online Activity 1.3
Back Forward Reload Home Search Print Security Stop
www.biology.com
Identify biology themes.
What is the connection between the energy-and-life theme and the interaction between this whale and seal? Find out as you determine how several examples represent ten biology themes.

Concept Check 1.3

1. Using examples, describe three biology themes.
2. Describe four ways you have interacted with your environment today.
3. In biological terms are you a producer or a consumer? Explain your answer.

Multiple Choice

Choose the letter of the best answer.

1. A biologist studying interactions between an animal species and its environment is studying biology at which level?
   a. cell b. biosphere
   c. organism d. ecosystem

2. Which of the following is *not* considered an organism?
   a. an oak leaf
   b. a spider
   c. an elephant
   d. a bacterial cell

3. To which domain of life do humans belong?
   a. Animals
   b. Eukarya
   c. Archaea
   d. none of the above

4. DNA is found in the nucleus of
   a. all cells.
   b. eukaryotic cells only.
   c. prokaryotic cells only.
   d. unicellular organisms only.

5. Which is a chemical product of photosynthesis that is used by consumers?
   a. water
   b. carbon dioxide
   c. food
   d. heat

6. Which of the following processes provides the raw material for the other three to occur?
   a. natural selection
   b. adaptation
   c. genetic variation
   d. evolution

7. Some poisonous organisms are brightly colored, which warns others not to eat them. Which theme does this *best* represent?
   a. adaptation
   b. regulation
   c. the cellular basis of life
   d. biology and society

Short Answer

8. Explain why cells are considered the most basic unit of life.

9. What is the main difference between organisms in domain Archaea and domain Eukarya?

10. Describe how a sports team could be considered a system.

11. You read that a mantid's camouflage is an example of adaptation. How does its camouflage also represent the form-fits-function theme?

12. Choose two objects that were not discussed in the text and describe how their form fits their function.

13. Describe the interaction between a plant and its environment. What does the plant obtain from the environment and how does the plant affect its environment?

14. Explain why life on Earth requires a continuous supply of energy from the sun.

15. Explain why plants are called producers.

16. Describe the process of natural selection.

Visualizing Concepts

17. Organize the terms below into a flowchart. Explain why you placed the term *population* where you did.

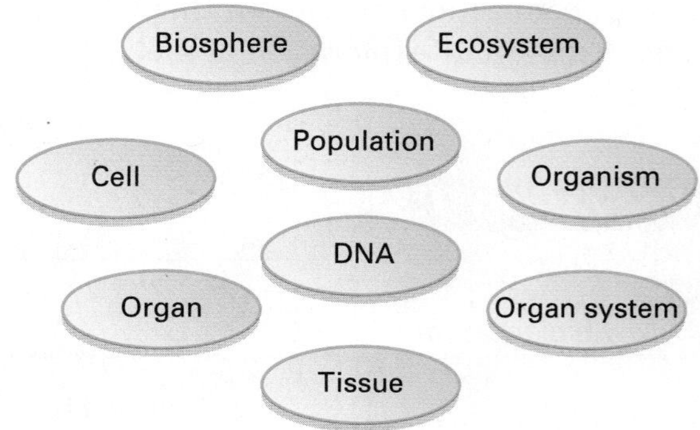

Analyzing Information

18. **Analyzing Photographs** Suggest five questions a biologist might ask about the scene below. In your questions consider the various levels (scales) of life, the diversity of life, and biology themes.

19. **Analyzing Diagrams** Study the incomplete diagram below and answer the following questions.

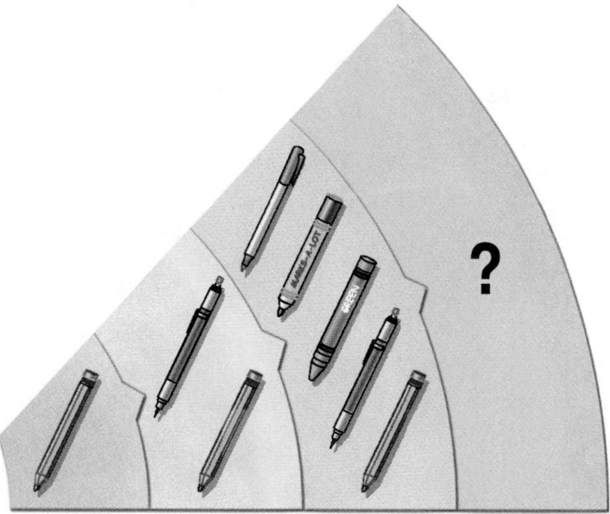

a. Describe the purpose of a diagram such as this one.
b. Create a list of items that you would place in the blank section of this diagram. Include at least eight items on your list.
c. How would you label each section? Explain your answer.

Critical Thinking

20. **Making Generalizations** You have read that an ecosystem is a system, and a system is dependent on the interaction of its parts. What do you think might happen in an ecosystem if it lost all of its plant species?

21. **Evaluating Models** Describe how your home could be considered an ecosystem.

22. **Relating Cause and Effect** In this chapter you read that DNA is responsible for the similarities between animal parents and their offspring. You also read that DNA is responsible for variations in organisms of the same population. Explain how both these statements can be true.

23. **Evaluating the Impact of Research** Discuss a few positive ways in which the study of biology has affected you.

24. **What's Wrong With These Statements?** *Briefly explain why each statement is inaccurate or misleading.*
   a. Many organs working together make up a tissue.
   b. Energy is recycled constantly in an ecosystem.
   c. DNA is made of genes.

Performance Assessment

Biology Research Project News media and magazines frequently report stories that are connected to biology. In the next 24 hours, collect two biology-related stories from different sources. Briefly describe how each story relates to one or more of the ten themes you read about in this chapter.

Online Assessment/Test Preparation

Back Forward Reload Home Search Print Security Stop

www.biology.com

- **Chapter 1 Assessment**
  Check your understanding of the chapter concepts.
- **Standardized Test Preparation**
  Practice test-taking skills you need to succeed.

The Science of Biology

Science is a quest to understand nature. As in all quests, science includes elements of challenge, surprise, and adventure. Indeed, some scientists go to great extremes to explore nature. The biologist in these photos is Nalini Nadkarni from Evergreen State College in Washington. Using ropes, she often climbs more than 50 meters above the ground to study small plants that grow on the upper limbs of the giant trees. In this Costa Rican rain forest, Dr. Nadkarni inspects plants for signs of visiting birds.

Science also has a tamer side. Careful planning, reasoning, persistence, patience, setbacks, and tiny steps of progress also mark the work of scientists who seek answers to questions about nature. In this chapter, you will learn how science works and how you can use the process of science to help answer your own questions. To get started, go online to the ***WebQuest*** to explore the pioneering work of Jane Goodall.

Key Concepts

What's Online

www.biology.com

WebQuest
GoodallQuest

Concept 2.1

Discovery science emphasizes inquiry and observation.

Online Activity 2.1
Observe and infer.

Concept 2.2

Hypothesis-based science is a search for explanations.

Online Activity 2.2
Form a hypothesis.

Lab 2 Online Companion
Making a "Rip-o-meter"

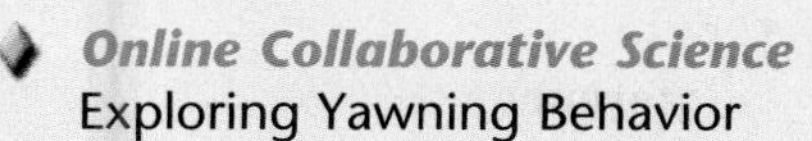
Online Collaborative Science 1
Exploring Yawning Behavior

Concept 2.3

Understanding science will help you evaluate many issues.

Online Activity 2.3
Trace a famous scientific discovery.

Science, Technology, & Society
Scientific Collaboration on the Internet

Assessment

Chapter 2 Review

Chapter 2 Assessment

CONCEPT 2.1

Discovery science emphasizes inquiry and observation.

OBJECTIVES
- Describe the nature of scientific inquiry.
- Compare quantitative and qualitative data.
- Summarize the nature of discovery science.
- Distinguish between observations and inferences.
- Explain the term *generalization.*

KEY TERMS
- observation
- data
- inference
- generalization

Any science textbook, including this one, is packed with information based on what scientists have discovered in the past. Indeed, science has built an impressive body of knowledge that continues to increase and change with new discoveries. Much of what's known is fascinating, but the real fun in science begins when you turn from what's *known* to what's *unknown.*

Biology blends two main forms of scientific exploration: discovery science and hypothesis-based science. Discovery science, as you'll read later in this section, is mostly about *describing* nature. Hypothesis-based science, as you'll read in Concept 2.2, is mostly about *explaining* nature. Most scientists practice a combination of these two approaches.

Science as Inquiry

Biology is defined as the scientific study of life. But what does *scientific* mean? What is science? The word is derived from a Latin verb meaning "to know." In other words, science is a way of knowing. It is a way to answer questions about the natural world.

At the heart of science is inquiry—people asking questions about what they observe in nature and actively seeking answers. For example, have you ever noticed that most houseplants grow toward a light source, such as a window (Figure 2-1)? Rotate the plant, and its direction of growth will shift until the leaves again face the window. Such observations inspire questions. How does the plant sense the direction of light? What enables the plant to bend toward light as it grows? In what direction would a plant grow in the dark?

Your own curiosity is the starting point for exploring life through inquiry. But inquiry means more than asking questions. Inquiry is a process of investigation, with thoughtful questions leading to a search for answers. Asking questions is a natural activity for all curious minds, but even figuring out what to ask takes practice. You can develop this and other skills that support scientific inquiry through the activities on the *Biology: Exploring Life* Web site and through your laboratory investigations. By the end of this school year, you'll have plenty of experience with science as a process of inquiry.

▼ **Figure 2-1** How do plants sense and respond to the direction of light? Such questions stimulate scientific inquiry.

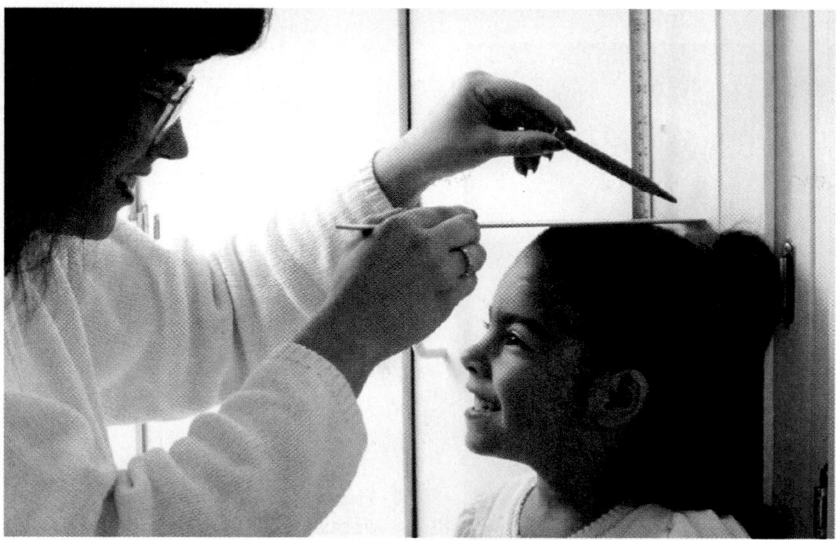

Growth Chart

Age (years)	Height (cm)
2.0	86
2.5	90
3.0	93
3.5	98
4.0	100
4.5	104
5.0	107
5.5	110
6.0	114

Figure 2-2 For several years, this mother has recorded the data of her daughter's growth by marking her height on a doorframe. Organizing data in a table makes the information easy to track.

Observations and Data

The questions that drive scientific inquiry are based on observations. In science, **observation** is the use of the senses—such as vision or hearing—to gather and record information about structures or processes. Recorded observations are called **data.** Put another way, data are items of information. For example, the penciled marks along a doorframe that track a child's height at different ages are biological data (Figure 2-2).

All observations depend on human senses. But, without help the senses are too limited to penetrate some of the most interesting realms of nature. Scientific instruments vastly increase the range of possible observations. In astronomy, telescopes reveal craters on the moon. In biology, microscopes make it possible to observe life that is invisible to the unaided eye. Other equipment enables humans to observe DNA and other molecules.

Observations are often recorded as measurements, also called *quantitative* data. Scientists worldwide use an international system of measurements based on the metric system. (See the Skills Appendix at the back of this book.)

Data also may be *qualitative*—that is, in the form of descriptions instead of measurements. For example, Jane Goodall spent decades recording her observations of chimpanzee behavior in a jungle in Gambia, an east African nation (Figure 2-3). In addition to keeping careful notes as data in her field notebooks, Goodall also documented her observations with photographs and movies. Data can best support science when they are clearly organized, consistently recorded, and reliable.

▼ **Figure 2-3** By carefully recording her observations in field notebooks, photos, and movies, Jane Goodall has provided a wealth of qualitative data on chimpanzee behavior. Her notes often contain sketches of the animals she observed.

◀ **Figure 2-4** These high school students are setting out equipment to collect data during biological field research.

What Is Discovery Science?

Jane Goodall's research on chimpanzees is an example of discovery science (also called descriptive science). Discovery science describes natural structures or processes as accurately as possible through careful observation and data collection. The students in Figure 2-4 are taking part in a research project to collect and identify organisms in a river—an example of discovery science. When a biologist uses a microscope to describe the arrangement of cells in the interior of a leaf, that's discovery science, too. In 2000, an international team of scientists announced that they had completed a detailed chemical "map" of human DNA. Their achievement is discovery science at the molecular level.

In contrast to the carefully planned mapping of human DNA, observant people sometimes discover something important about nature entirely by accident. One famous example is Alexander Fleming's 1928 discovery that certain fungi produce chemicals that kill bacteria. Fleming, a Scottish physician, was culturing (growing) bacteria for research in his laboratory. He found that a mold (a type of fungus) had contaminated some of his cultures of bacteria. As he was discarding the "spoiled" cultures, Fleming noticed that no bacteria were growing near the mold (Figure 2-5). The fungus turned out to be *Penicillium,* a common mold. It produces an antibacterial substance that was later named penicillin. Fleming's accidental discovery revolutionized medicine. Penicillin proved to be just one of many lifesaving antibiotics that are made by fungi and other organisms. These drugs help treat strep throat, bacterial pneumonia, syphilis, and many other diseases caused by bacteria. The use of antibiotics has greatly extended the average human lifespan in many countries.

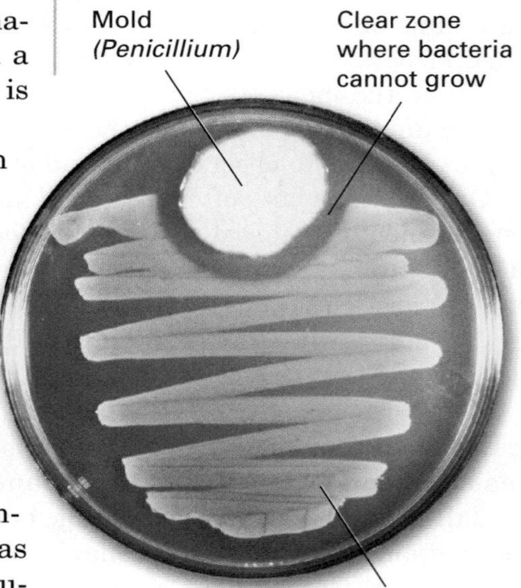

▲ **Figure 2-5** A bacterial culture like this one led Fleming to the accidental discovery that certain molds can prevent the growth of bacteria.

Inferences in Science

A logical conclusion based on observations is called an **inference.** An example of an inference is the statement that the mold in Figure 2-5 on page 26 is killing nearby bacteria. Often, a person makes an inference by relating observations to his or her prior knowledge. For instance, you infer someone is at the door when you hear the doorbell ring because you know the same thing has happened before. Examine the picnic table in Figure 2-6. What can you infer from the place settings and other objects you observe on the table? Can you infer anything from what is *absent*? Can you make reasonable inferences about the weather and time of day when this photograph was taken?

Inferences are important in science because they help refine general questions into specific questions that can be explored further. For example, a scientist might ask: "What substance produced by this particular mold kills bacteria?" However, keep in mind that scientists are skeptical of inferences that "stretch" far beyond the data. An example would be inferring, *solely* from Fleming's observation, that some molds could be used to produce antibiotics capable of curing bacterial diseases in humans. It took much more research before this conclusion was accepted among scientists. Also, it is important not to confuse inferences with the observations on which they are based. Hearing the doorbell ring is an observation. Inferring that someone is at the door, though reasonable, has less certainty. Maybe an electrical short circuit is causing the bell to ring.

Figure 2-6 Take time to look at the scene in this photograph. What observations can you make? What inferences can you suggest based on your observations?

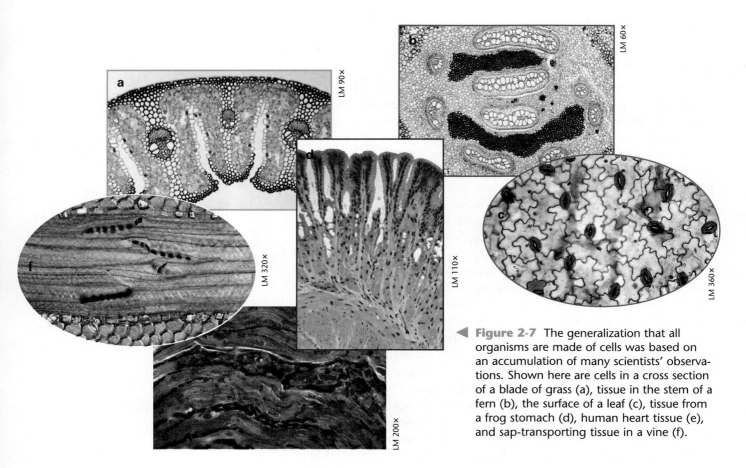

Figure 2-7 The generalization that all organisms are made of cells was based on an accumulation of many scientists' observations. Shown here are cells in a cross section of a blade of grass (a), tissue in the stem of a fern (b), the surface of a leaf (c), tissue from a frog stomach (d), human heart tissue (e), and sap-transporting tissue in a vine (f).

Generalizations in Discovery Science

Carefully recorded observations provide "raw data" for science. However, some of the biggest breakthroughs in discovery science come when scientists put together many specific observations to reach a general conclusion, or **generalization.** For instance, in the 1800s, scientists used microscopes to examine bits of tissue from a diversity of organisms. In both plants and animals, the scientists observed the tiny units called cells in all of the specimens they studied (Figure 2-7). Cells were actually discovered in the 1600s in oak bark. But it was the accumulation of observations of cells in all organisms examined that finally gave biologists confidence that they had uncovered a general feature of life. This generalization that "all living things are made of cells" became part of what is known as the cell theory, one of the most important products of discovery science in the nineteenth century.

It is also sometimes possible to generalize from quantitative data. This usually requires pooling (combining) measurements from a very large sample. To look for general patterns in measurements, it often helps to put the data in a graph. For example, the graph in Figure 2-8 compares the changes in heights of teenage boys and girls over time. Each point on the graph is an average measurement for many thousand boys or girls. The graph makes it

Figure 2-8 A graph is a visual way to uncover general patterns in data. For example, a generalization from the data graphed here is that girls stop growing, on average, before boys do.

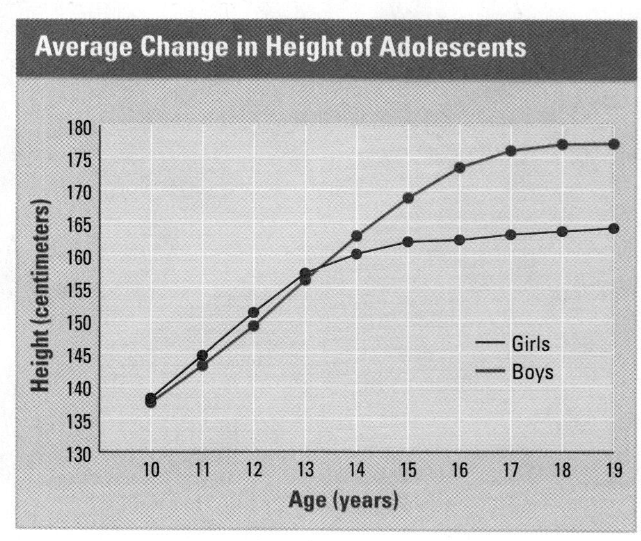

Figure 2-9 Observations of distinct "tree lines" on many mountainsides may lead to questions about environmental factors that limit the growth of trees.

easier to spot the general pattern that girls, *on average,* stop growing at a younger age than boys. Of course, there are many individual exceptions. *Some* females do continue to grow well past the average age when males stop growing. But the generalization still holds across the very large sample of teens.

Observations, data, inferences, and generalizations all advance people's understanding of life. But these processes of discovery science are often just the beginning of a scientific inquiry. For example, notice in Figure 2-9 that no trees are growing above a certain altitude in this mountain range. Observations of this "treeline" phenomenon in many mountain ranges in Western North America may lead you to a generalization: At a particular latitude, trees don't generally grow above a certain altitude. And you might go on to infer that environmental conditions at high altitude are unfavorable to tree growth. But which environmental factors influence tree growth most? Low temperatures? "Thin" atmosphere? Strong winds? Lack of soil? Or is it some combination of such factors that limit tree growth? Discovering something interesting inspires curious minds to seek an explanation. And that's when hypothesis-based science comes into play.

Online Activity 2.1

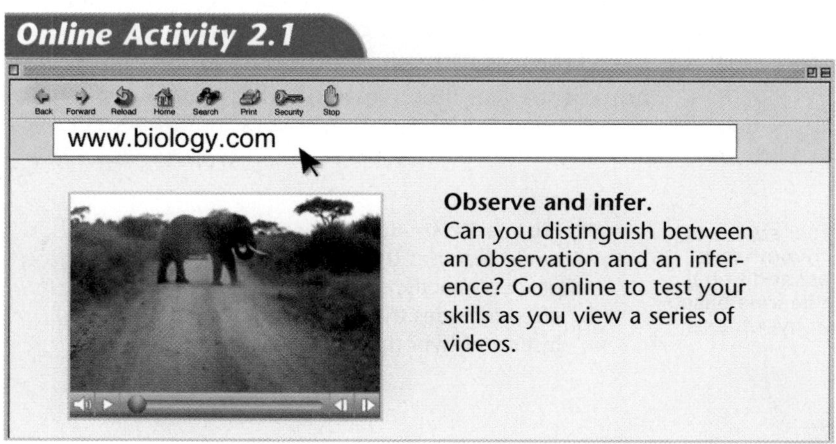

Observe and infer.
Can you distinguish between an observation and an inference? Go online to test your skills as you view a series of videos.

Concept Check 2.1

1. How does scientific inquiry differ from simply asking questions?
2. Are the data recorded in the table in Figure 2-2 quantitative or qualitative? Explain.
3. How is Jane Goodall's work an example of discovery science?
4. Describe an observation you made today and an inference you can make from that observation.
5. How are the terms *generalization* and *observation* related?

CONCEPT 2.2

Hypothesis-based science is a search for explanations.

OBJECTIVES
- Outline the generalized steps of hypothesis-based science.
- Trace the process of hypothesis-based science through a case study.

KEY TERMS
- hypothesis
- variable
- controlled experiment

What's Online

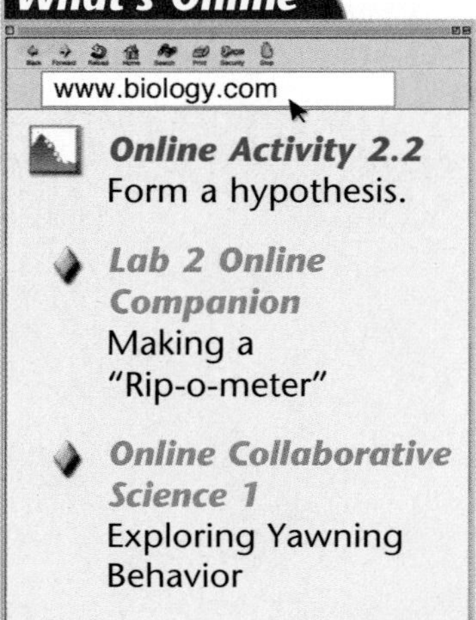
www.biology.com

Online Activity 2.2
Form a hypothesis.

Lab 2 Online Companion
Making a "Rip-o-meter"

Online Collaborative Science 1
Exploring Yawning Behavior

It is one thing to describe and measure the growth of a plant toward light (discovery science). But what *causes* this phenomenon? How can scientists *explain* the plant's ability to detect and respond to the direction of light? Such questions about causes and explanations are at the center of hypothesis-based science.

Methods of Hypothesis-Based Science

You may have heard of "the scientific method." The steps of this idealized method are diagrammed in Figure 2-10. At one time or another in their research, scientists may use all or most of these steps. Often, however, the sequence of steps does not exactly match the generalized scheme of Figure 2-10. For example, a scientist may start to plan an experiment, but then decide that more observations are needed first. In other cases, observations are too puzzling to even suggest key questions until other lines of research bring more understanding. Or, at some point in a research project, scientists may realize they have been "barking up the wrong tree." That is, they've been asking the wrong questions. Many scientific inquiries are abandoned before any questions are answered, though the data from observations and experiments may prove useful later. And accidental discoveries, such as Fleming's findings about mold and bacteria, are certainly not products of a rigid, step-by-step scientific method. Science is actually less structured than most people realize.

Despite all the variation in scientific inquiry, one key element is common to all hypothesis-based science. In fact, this form of inquiry is named for this key element: the hypothesis.

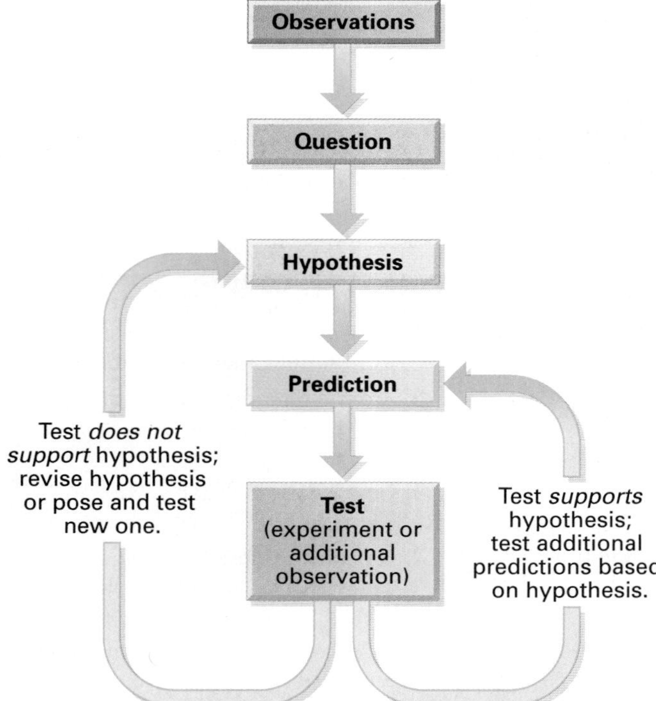
Observations
Question
Hypothesis
Prediction
Test (experiment or additional observation)
Test *does not support* hypothesis; revise hypothesis or pose and test new one.
Test *supports* hypothesis; test additional predictions based on hypothesis.

Figure 2-10 Although science rarely matches this step-by-step process exactly, scientific inquiry often includes the posing and testing of hypotheses.

Forming and Testing a Hypothesis

A **hypothesis** (plural, *hypotheses*) is a suggested answer to a well-defined scientific question—an explanation on trial. Most hypotheses are concerned with the causes of natural phenomena, such as the growth of a plant toward light. A hypothesis is often based on past experience or knowledge gained from discovery science or other sources.

People use hypotheses almost instinctively, as a natural way to solve everyday problems. For example, suppose your flashlight stops working during a camping trip. That's an observation. The question is obvious: Why doesn't the flashlight work? A reasonable hypothesis based on past experience is that the batteries in the flashlight are dead.

Scientists don't just *propose* hypotheses. They *test* these ideas by making additional observations or by designing experiments. A hypothesis allows you to make certain predictions. It is these predictions that scientists then test. Consider the case of the failed flashlight in Figure 2-11. Note that the prediction is written as an *"If . . . , then . . ."* statement. *If* a particular hypothesis is correct, and you test that hypothesis with a suitable experiment, *then* you should expect a certain result for the experiment.

What if the flashlight still doesn't work after changing the batteries? Here's where things get interesting. Keep in mind that in science, an incorrect hypothesis doesn't mean failure. It just means the hypothesis that led to the prediction was probably wrong. The inquiry continues with tests of alternative hypotheses. What would be your next step in the flashlight problem? Perhaps, you could test another hypothesis by replacing the flashlight's bulb.

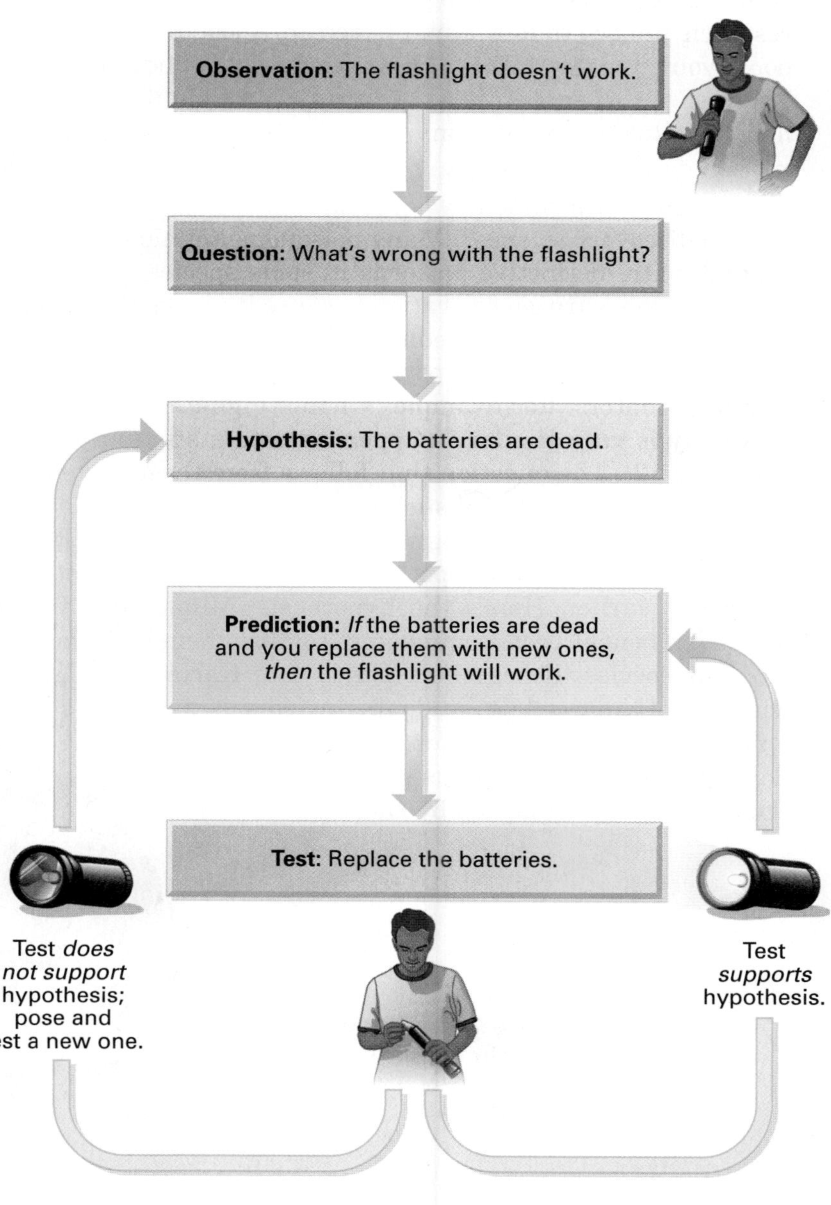
Observation: The flashlight doesn't work.
Question: What's wrong with the flashlight?
Hypothesis: The batteries are dead.
Prediction: *If* the batteries are dead and you replace them with new ones, *then* the flashlight will work.
Test: Replace the batteries.
Test *does not support* hypothesis; pose and test a new one.
Test *supports* hypothesis.

Figure 2-11 Applying hypothesis-based science to the problem of a failed flashlight leads to a test in the form of an experiment. If the results of the test do not support the hypothesis, other hypotheses can be suggested and tested.

Even when experiments support a hypothesis, curiosity can send you in new directions. (How long do batteries last in a flashlight? Do some brands of batteries last longer than others?) Opportunities for creativity and new challenges make scientific inquiry as exciting as exploring a new landscape. As you reach the top of a hill or round the corner of a trail, you may become curious to see the view from the next hill or around the next corner. Science generates new questions in a similar manner.

A Case Study of Hypothesis-Based Science

One way to learn more about how hypothesis-based science works is to examine a case study. In contrast to a made-up example, such as the flashlight problem, a case study is an in-depth examination of something that actually happened. For instance, students in law school train to become lawyers by analyzing the actual documents of past legal cases. Similarly, a case study of a research project that was published in a scientific journal will boost your understanding of how scientists go about their work. The rest of this section is a case study of an inquiry about what harmless snakes might gain by imitating poisonous ones.

From Observations to Question and Hypothesis The story begins with some key observations. (Do you recognize this step as discovery science?) Many poisonous animals are brightly colored, with distinctive patterns in some species. This appearance is called warning coloration because it marks the animal as dangerous to potential predators. But there are also mimics. These imposters look like a poisonous species but are really harmless to predators. For example, a non-stinging insect called the flower fly is very similar in appearance to a stinging honeybee (Figure 2-12). The question that follows from these observations is: What is the function of such mimicry?

In 2001, a team of biologists designed a simple but clever set of experiments to test a hypothesis that was first suggested over a century earlier. Here's the hypothesis: Mimics (such as the flower fly) benefit because predators confuse them with the actual harmful species. Researchers David and Karin Pfennig, along with one of their college students, tested this hypothesis by studying mimicry in snakes that live in North and South Carolina. A poisonous snake called the eastern coral snake is marked by rings of red, yellow,

Figure 2-12 The non-stinging flower fly (top) mimics the appearance of a stinging honeybee (bottom).

▲ Figure 2-13 The scarlet kingsnake (left) is a nonpoisonous species that mimics the dangerous eastern coral snake (right).

and black. Predators rarely attack these snakes. A nonpoisonous snake named the scarlet kingsnake mimics the ringed coloration of the coral snake (Figure 2-13).

Testing a Prediction of the Hypothesis What is the explanation for this case of look-alike snakes? According to the mimicry hypothesis, the coral-snakelike appearance of kingsnakes repels predators. The hypothesis predicts that predators will attack snakes with the bright rings of red, yellow, and black less frequently than they will attack snakes lacking such warning coloration. To test this prediction, the researchers made hundreds of artificial kingsnakes out of wire and a claylike substance called plasticine. There were two types of artificial snakes: those with the red, yellow, and black ring pattern of coral snakes; and snakes with plain brown coloration.

The researchers placed equal numbers of the two types of artificial snakes in various sites throughout North and South Carolina. After four weeks, the team retrieved the artificial snakes and counted how many had been attacked by looking for bite or claw marks. The most common predators were foxes, coyotes, and raccoons, but black bears also attacked some of the artificial snakes.

Designing a Controlled Experiment Why did the experiment include artificial snakes that were plain brown along with the ringed snakes? A quick answer is that the contrast in coloration was necessary to see if predators attack snakes based on their color. If all the snakes were the same, the number of attacks would indicate nothing at all about the effect of the colored rings. This point illustrates an important requirement for designing experiments that test hypotheses. If you want to test the effect of one condition, you need to provide a contrasting condition as well. A condition that can differ within the experiment is called a **variable.** In the artificial snakes, the variable is the presence versus the absence of the colored rings. Most often, experiments test the effect of a difference in just one variable. An experiment that tests the effect of a single variable is called a **controlled experiment.**

Online Collaborative Science 1

Back Forward Reload Home Search Print Security Stop

www.biology.com

Exploring Yawning Behavior
Why do people yawn? Have you ever noticed that yawning seems to be "contagious"? In this investigation, you will develop hypotheses about yawning behavior in humans and design experiments to test them. Then share, compare, and discuss your results with students in other classes around the country.

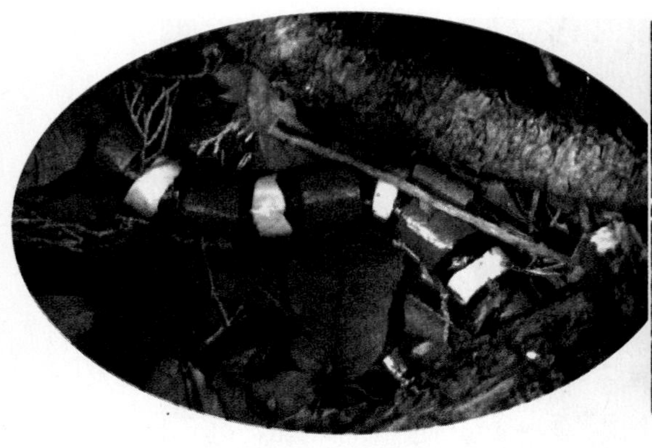

◀ **Figure 2-14** Artificial kingsnakes (left) were fashioned from plasticine and wire. Bite marks show a black bear's attack on this artificial brown snake (right).

By conducting a controlled experiment, scientists try to eliminate (control) other variables that could affect the outcome. This is not usually a simple task. For example, variables such as temperature or other weather conditions could influence the activities of predators in the snake experiment. In an ideal setting—such as a laboratory—scientists can keep temperature and other environmental conditions as constant as possible. But such control is usually impossible in a field experiment. And even in a laboratory, total regulation of *all* but one variable is often not practical.

Eliminating Unwanted Variables What is the solution to the problem of unwanted variables? Researchers divide the subjects (the artificial snakes, for example) into two groups: a control group and an experimental group. Since the snake experiment was designed to test the effect of the colored rings, the artificial snakes with the colored rings were the experimental group. The brown snakes served as a control group by showing what happens in the absence of colored rings. Everything else about the two snake groups was the same. For example, both ringed snakes and brown snakes were made of the same materials (Figure 2-14). Both kinds of snakes were placed at random in the same locations. Conditions such as light, temperature, and appetite of the predators varied, but both kinds of snakes were subject to the same variations. In this way, the brown snakes *controlled,* or cancelled out, the effects of the unwanted variables, leaving colored rings as the only consistent difference between the two groups of snakes. Then any difference in the number of attacks on the ringed snakes compared to the brown snakes could only have been due to the difference in coloration.

"If . . . , then . . ." Reasoning You should now be able to recognize in this case study the same type of reasoning you learned about in the flashlight example. Using the flowchart in Figure 2-15, you can follow the steps taken by the Pfennig team. Observations of snake coloration and attacks by predators led to a question. The Pfennigs posed

Observation: Both poisonous coral snakes and nonpoisonous kingsnakes have red, yellow, and black rings.

↓

Question: What is the function of the kingsnakes' mimicry of coral snakes?

↓

Hypothesis: Mimicry of coral snakes helps protect the kingsnakes from predators.

↓

Prediction: *If* predators confuse kingsnakes with coral snakes, *then* predators should attack fewer ringed artificial snakes than brown artificial snakes.

↓

Experiment: Compare data on attacks on ringed versus brown artificial snakes.

▲ **Figure 2-15** This flowchart summarizes the inquiry process followed during the snake mimicry research.

a hypothesis that seemed reasonable based on other scientists' past research on different animal species. The Pfennigs then designed and performed a controlled experiment to test their hypothesis. The next step was analyzing the data.

Organizing Data and Interpreting Results Scientific inquiry is far from over once the data have been collected. Often, the results of an experiment only begin to make sense after much analysis of the data. For quantitative data, note again that it is often helpful to put the data in the form of a table or graph. These efforts may reveal patterns that were not obvious when the "raw" data were first collected.

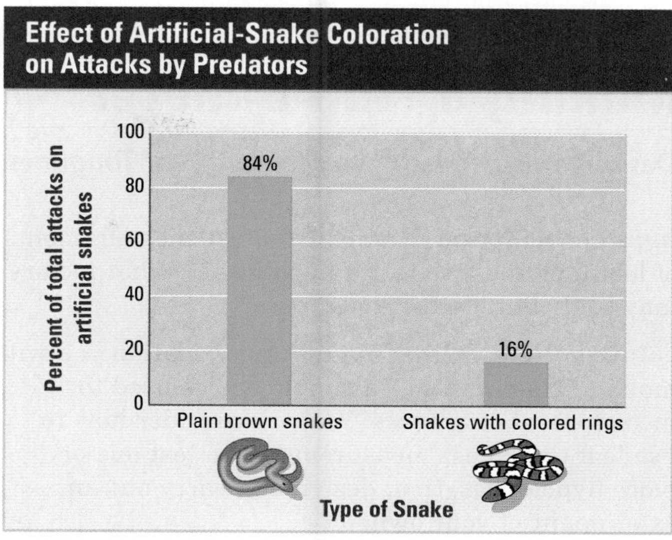

▲ **Figure 2-16** Results of mimicry experiments using artificial snakes show a dramatic difference in the frequency of attacks on plain brown snakes compared to the snakes with colored rings.

The bar graph in Figure 2-16 summarizes the results of the artificial snake experiment. The graph also reinforces the purpose of using two groups of snakes. Of all attacks on artificial snakes, about 84 percent of attacks were on the plain brown snakes compared to about 16 percent for the snakes with colored rings. These data fit the prediction based on the mimicry hypothesis. The experiment supports the hypothesis that the kingsnakes' mimicry of coral-snake coloration helps protect against predators.

The research on look-alike snakes provides an example of how scientists use hypothesis-based science to test their explanation of natural phenonena. Notice again how hypothesis-based science works along with discovery science. Questions about nature usually arise from the observations of discovery science. Hypothesis-based science is a process for testing the possible answers to such questions.

The upcoming section broadens the view of science you've seen so far, showing how scientific ideas fit in with other ways of picturing and knowing the world around you.

Online Activity 2.2

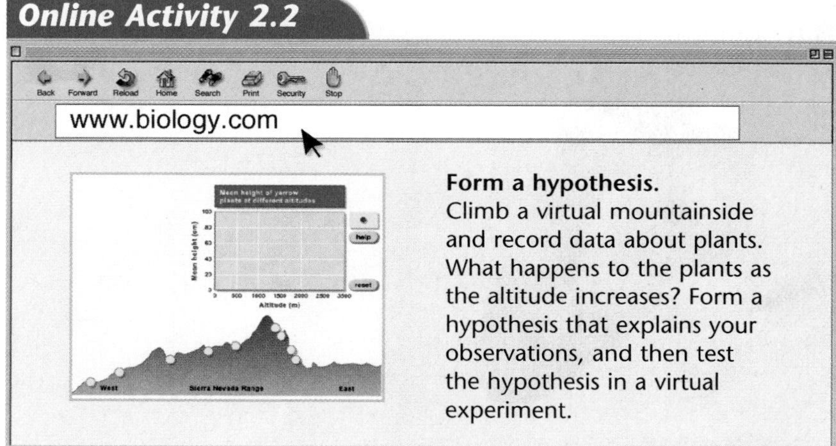

Form a hypothesis.
Climb a virtual mountainside and record data about plants. What happens to the plants as the altitude increases? Form a hypothesis that explains your observations, and then test the hypothesis in a virtual experiment.

Concept Check 2.2

1. Write a hypothesis to explain why a door hinge squeaks. Then use your hypothesis to make a prediction that could be tested.
2. Why do experiments usually test only one variable at a time?
3. In the snake experiment, what was the basis for the hypothesis that mimic species benefit from looking like unrelated harmful species?
4. What role did the brown artificial snakes have in the experiment?

Making a "Rip-o-meter"

Designing Experiments to Measure Leaf Toughness

Inquiry Challenge How can you use measurements of leaf toughness to test a hypothesis? What factors may contribute to leaf toughness?

Lab Overview In this inquiry investigation you will make a "rip-o-meter"—a simple device used to measure leaf toughness. You will consider how to use leaf toughness measurements to test one or more hypotheses, then design and carry out an experiment of your own.

Preparing for the Lab To prepare to design your own experiment go to the *Lab 2 Online Companion*. See how an experiment is designed, practice analyzing data, and use a virtual rip-o-meter to test the toughness of leaves.

Completing the Lab Use your Laboratory Manual or lab page printouts from the *Lab 2 Online Companion* to design your own experiment and analyze your results. **CAUTION:** *Be sure to follow your teacher's instructions and all safety guidelines in the investigation.*

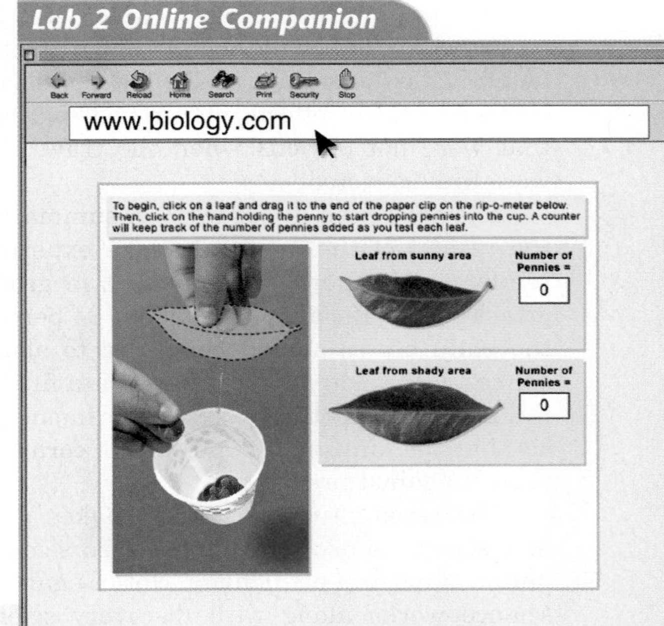
Lab 2 Online Companion
Back
Forward
Reload
Home
Search
Print
Security
Stop
www.biology.com
To begin, click on a leaf and drag it to the end of the paper clip on the rip-o-meter below. Then, click on the hand holding the penny to start dropping pennies into the cup. A counter will keep track of the number of pennies added as you test each leaf.
Leaf from sunny area
Number of Pennies =
0
Leaf from shady area
Number of Pennies =
0

CONCEPT 2.3 Understanding science will help you evaluate many issues.

OBJECTIVES

- State how the terms *evidence, hypothesis,* and *theory* are used in science.
- Explain how scientific models are useful in understanding ideas.
- Describe the importance of communication in science.
- Distinguish between the roles of science and technology in society.

KEY TERMS

- evidence
- theory
- model
- technology

What's Online

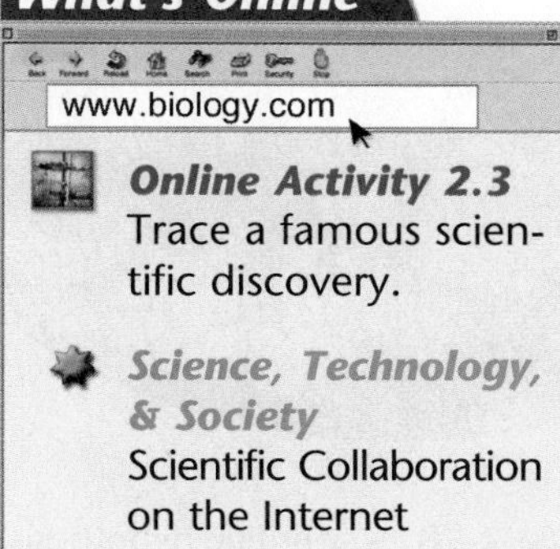

Online Activity 2.3
Trace a famous scientific discovery.

Science, Technology, & Society
Scientific Collaboration on the Internet

What you learn this year about biology and the process of science will help you evaluate many issues that affect your personal life, such as health issues. Your understanding of science will also help you make decisions that affect your community and even the entire nation. In just a few years you may be voting in local, state, and national elections. Democracy works best when voters understand the issues. And science now impacts many issues that voters face. This section explores some of the things you need to know.

Evidence in Science

Unconfirmed observations filling supermarket tabloids would have you believe that some of your classmates are aliens from space and that humans are occasionally born with the heads of dogs. Most people, especially if they understand science, do not find the eyewitness accounts and computer-rigged photos to be convincing evidence. But judgments are harder when you read, for example, a magazine ad for a food supplement. You might find testimonials from enthusiastic users, graphs, quotes from "experts," and so on. To avoid wasting money and endangering your health, you need to know how to judge the quality of the evidence.

Evidence is a word that comes up as often in science as it does in courtrooms. In general, evidence is the information upon which inferences are based. In science, **evidence** consists of a collected body of data from observations and experiments. And such evidence doesn't begin to convince scientists until the observations and experiments have been repeated multiple times with similar results. The scientists who studied snake mimicry in the Carolinas obtained similar data when they repeated their experiments with different species of coral snakes and kingsnakes in Arizona. And *you* should be able to obtain similar data if you were to repeat the snake experiment. Such attempts to repeat independently the observations and experiments of others are common in science. Repeatability is a hallmark of scientific evidence.

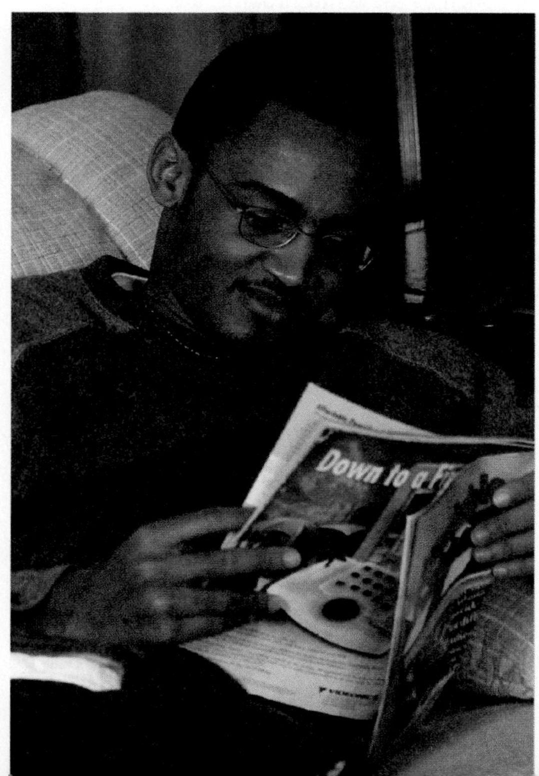

Figure 2-17 Have you ever read an ad that made claims about a product? What evidence would you use to evaluate such a claim?

What Makes a Hypothesis Scientific?

Magazines and television programs have no shortage of hypotheses that are claimed to be scientific. But how do you know which of the hypotheses make scientific sense? Look at whether the hypothesis can be tested (and if it has been). In science, the only hypotheses that count are those that meet this standard of testability. You saw this process at work in both the flashlight and snake examples. Each hypothesis led to a prediction that could be tested in an experiment. And notice that the experiments could either support or contradict the hypotheses. The flashlight experiment could show that the hypothesis of dead batteries was incorrect. And though the experiments with artificial snakes supported the mimicry hypothesis, the data could have gone the other way. Suppose both groups of snakes had been attacked equally. Such results would have cast doubt on the hypothesis that the mimic coloration helped discourage predators. In contrast, try to think of a way to test the hypothesis that invisible "space aliens" were fooling with your flashlight. How could you show that such an idea is false? A scientific hypothesis must be *falsifiable*—that is, there must be some observation or experiment that *could* reveal if such a hypothesis is false.

Scientists test a hypothesis many times and in different ways. Even hypotheses that stand up to repeated testing may later be revised or even rejected. One way such change occurs is when new research tools make new kinds of observations and experiments possible. A few decades ago, for example, most biologists accepted the hypothesis that fungi are closely related to plants (Figure 2-18). The evidence included some similarities in structure, growth pattern, and reproduction. That hypothesis has been challenged by new methods that make it possible to analyze and compare the DNA of diverse organisms.

▲ **Figure 2-18** A scientific hypothesis can be challenged by new evidence. Based on DNA comparisons, fungi, such as these mushrooms, are now thought to be more closely related to animals than to plants.

The Limitations of Science

Science is powerful, but limited in the kinds of questions it can help answer. Science requires repeatable observations and testable hypotheses. These standards restrict science to a search for *natural* causes for natural phenomena. For example, science can neither prove nor disprove that unobservable or supernatural forces cause storms, rainbows, illnesses, or cures of disease. Supernatural explanations of natural events are simply outside the bounds of science. There is no way to show that such hypotheses are false.

Although science is "a way of knowing," keep in mind that it is not the *only* way. Not everything you "know" is based on science. For example, you *know* what kind of music you like and what your favorite color is. These personal tastes are not the results of a careful testing of hypotheses. And you *know* right from wrong. This concept is an ethical value, not a scientific fact. Each human mind develops a unique database of knowledge of many different kinds. Science-based knowledge is the type built from confirmed observations and testable hypotheses.

Theories in Science

Many people think of science mainly as a collection of facts. But collecting facts is not what really defines science. A telephone book is an impressive catalog of factual information, yet it has little to do with science. It is true that factual data provide the raw material for science. But scientists are mostly interested in finding patterns in the data and explaining these patterns. What really advances science is some new theory that ties together a variety of facts that previously seemed unrelated. People like Isaac Newton, Charles Darwin, and Albert Einstein stand out in the history of science because their theories connected so many observations and experimental results.

How is a theory different from a hypothesis? In science, a **theory** is a well-tested explanation that makes sense of a great variety of scientific observations. It gives rise to many hypotheses that can be tested. This definition contrasts with the everyday use of *theory* to mean a speculation, as in "It's only a theory."

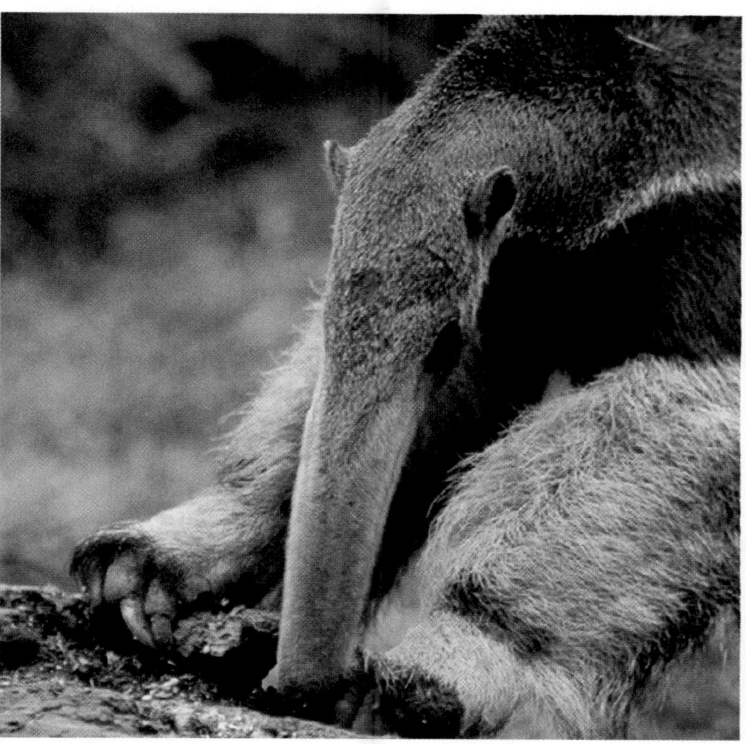

▲ **Figure 2-19** This anteater is feeding on ants in a fallen log. The animal's long snout and long tongue are adaptations for reaching insects in hard-to-reach places. The theory of natural selection can explain the evolution of the anteater's feeding adaptations as well as other adaptations of organisms to their environment.

Compared to a hypothesis, a theory is much broader in scope. *This* is a hypothesis: "Mimicking poisonous snakes is an adaptation that protects nonpoisonous snakes from predators." But *this* is a theory: "Adaptations such as mimicry evolve by natural selection." The theory of natural selection explains the evolution of the many cases of mimicry, as well as a variety of other adaptations of organisms to their environments (Figure 2-19).

Theories, such as the theory of natural selection, only become widely accepted in science when they are supported by an extensive body of evidence. That evidence also provides a framework for further research and predictions. If new evidence that contradicts a theory is uncovered, scientists first verify the evidence many times. They then modify or discard the theory accordingly.

Models

Have you ever drawn a simple map for a friend who needed directions to your home? If so, you created a model. **Models** are physical, mental, or mathematical representations of how people understand a process or an idea. Models can be very useful tools of scientific thinking. A model can take the form of

Science, Technology, & Society

Back Forward Reload Home Search Print Security Stop

www.biology.com

Scientific Collaboration on the Internet

Making observations and collecting data can be challenging—for example, think of tracking the migration of animals that travel thousands of kilometers each year. This kind of research requires the collaboration of many people. Thanks to modern technology, teams of scientists around the world can now share their observations. Go online to explore how scientists are using the Internet to collaborate on scientific investigations.

a drawing, graph, three-dimensional object, computer program, or mathematical equation. Even a description in words of how a natural process works is a model. The diagrams in Figure 2-20 are two different models that represent blood flow through the human heart. You can tell that the pictures are not images of a real heart. Models are not exact replicas of something real. Rather, they are useful because they help people explain and evaluate ideas about the natural world.

Analogies are another type of model in science. An analogy is a comparison that shows a likeness between two things. For example, you might say the brain is like a computer. Analogies are valuable aids to memory and creative thinking because they usually compare something that you are just starting to understand with something that you know from everyday life.

Scientists judge the value of a model several ways. Does it explain all the observations related to it? Can predictions be made from the model? Is it compatible with other, related models or ideas? For example, does the description of blood flow in the diagram in Figure 2-20 match the path blood actually follows in a working heart? Can this model be used as a basis for designing a plan for an artifical heart? A model that explains, predicts, or matches new observations becomes increasingly useful to scientists. And, models that fail to meet these requirements don't last.

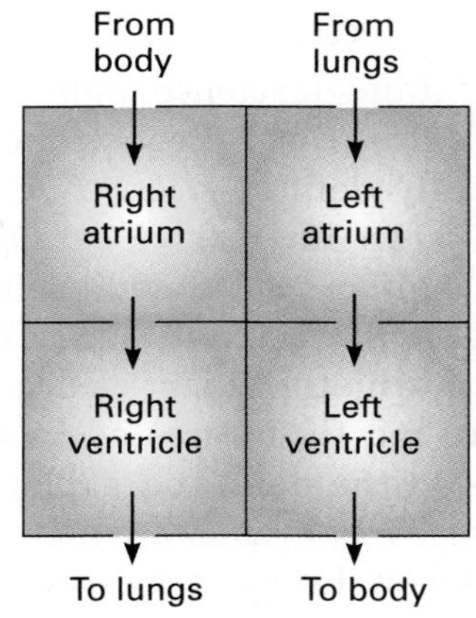

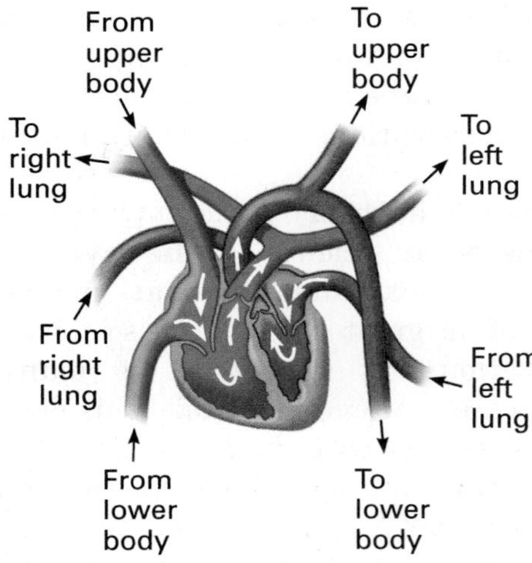

▲ **Figure 2-20** Though neither of these diagrams looks realistic, both can help you understand a key process in the body. The top model simply shows the path of blood flow into and out of the heart's four chambers. The bottom model shows more detail about the connecting blood vessels. (The models are "face-on" views, with the "right" and "left" labels referring to the person's right and left sides.) Red indicates blood that is rich in oxygen; blue represents oxygen-depleted blood.

Communication in Science

Cartoons and movies sometimes portray scientists as loners working in isolated laboratories. In reality, science is an intensely social activity. Most scientists work in teams, and most successful scientists are good communicators. Researchers share their findings by publishing articles in journals and by giving talks or presenting posters at meetings. The Internet has become an increasingly important way for scientists to exchange ideas and data with colleagues all over the world. It also allows the general public easy access to the work of many scientists. As you conduct biological research this year, you'll have a chance to share some of your ideas and data via the *Biology: Exploring Life* Web site.

Both cooperation and competition characterize the scientific culture. Scientists working in the same research field often check one another's claims by attempting to repeat experiments. Sometimes, science provides all the excitement of a race. Most scientists enjoy the challenge to "get there first" with an important discovery or key experiment.

Science, Technology, and Society

The strong link between science and society becomes even clearer when you add technology to the picture. Science and technology are related, but their goals and methods are different. The goal of science is to understand nature through careful observation and testing of hypotheses. The goal of **technology** is to *apply* scientific understanding for some specific purpose. Scientists—such as biologists—speak of "discoveries." On the other hand, technologists—such as engineers—speak of "inventions."

Fifty years ago, scientists James Watson and Francis Crick discovered the structure of DNA, the chemical material of genes. Their discovery eventually led to a variety of DNA technologies. An example is the genetic engineering that pharmaceutical companies are now using to produce a new generation of medicines (Figure 2-21). Perhaps Watson and Crick wondered if their discovery would someday have important applications, but they probably did not predict exactly what those applications would be.

The direction technology takes depends less on the curiosity that drives basic science than it does on the current needs and wants of humans and on the social environment of the times. An example of how society makes choices about technology is the issue of whether people should be tested to see if they have genes for heritable diseases. Should such tests be voluntary or required? Should insurance companies or employers have access to the information? How should people who learn that they carry genetic diseases make decisions about whether to have children? Who should decide the answers to these questions? Such hotly debated issues about technology often are not about "*can* it be done," but "*should* it be done." Such issues make front-page news. Technology and the science on which it depends cannot be separated from the society in which they occur. More than ever, good citizens must make an effort to gain a basic understanding of science and technology. Whether you are making lifestyle choices that affect your health or democratic choices that affect the future of society, your understanding of biology and the process of science should serve you well.

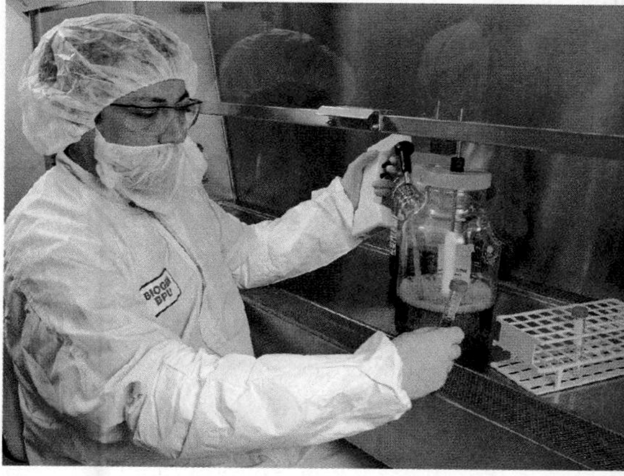

▲ **Figure 2-21** This technician checks on the production of a genetically engineered protein used to treat multiple sclerosis (a disease of the nervous system). The protein is made by specialized cells that have been manipulated through DNA technology.

Online Activity 2.3

www.biology.com

Trace a famous scientific discovery. DNA technology would not be possible without the discovery of the structure of DNA by James Watson and Francis Crick in 1953. Go online to explore how Watson and Crick collaborated, built a model, and communicated their discovery.

Concept Check 2.3

1. How is a theory different from a hypothesis?
2. What features are used to evaluate a scientific model?
3. How is communication an important part of science?
4. What is technology?
5. A magazine ad lists 10 celebrities who claim that the advertised product improved their memory. Why doesn't this example qualify as scientific evidence?

Developing and Practicing Skills

What's your favorite after-school activity? Whether it's playing a sport or a musical instrument, acting in plays, or taking photographs, you rely on certain skills that help you to succeed. Similarly, throughout your study of biology and other sciences, you are developing a set of skills to interpret information and to design and carry out scientific investigations. The Skills Activities described on these two pages will help you learn and improve your science skills. You can find all of these activities on the *Biology: Exploring Life* Web site and the Online Activities CD-ROM.

Making Measurements

A common system of units enables scientists around the world to speak the same "language" of data. Learn this language and develop good measuring skills with tutorials on laboratory equipment, practice problems, and common equivalents.

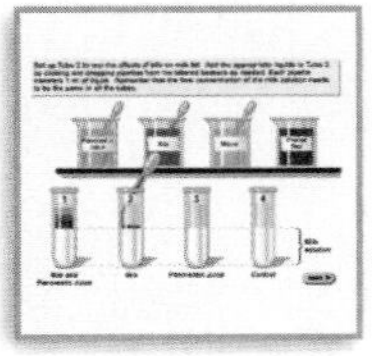

Conducting a Scientific Investigation

Through virtual experiments, practice making observations and inferences, developing hypotheses, designing experiments, collecting and interpreting data, drawing conclusions, and communicating your results.

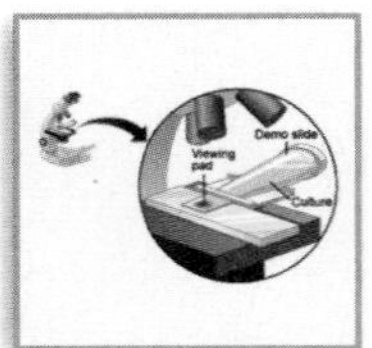

Using a Microscope

Get to know the parts of a microscope and important techniques for using one in the laboratory. Then compare images from different types of microscopes and at different magnifications.

Lab Safety Primer

Learn about the safety precautions in your *Biology: Exploring Life* Laboratory Manual, and discover reliable ways to avoid hazards in the lab. Then check your safety IQ by playing *"What's Wrong With This Lab?"*

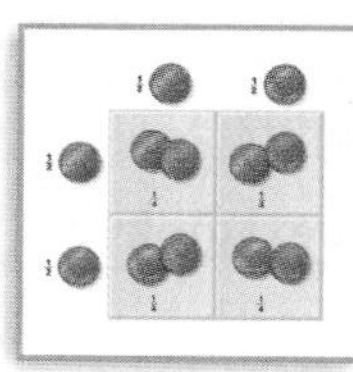

Math Review

What does math have to do with biology? You'll find out as you sharpen your skills with tutorials and practice problems on fractions, percents, decimals, exponents, probability, and significant figures.

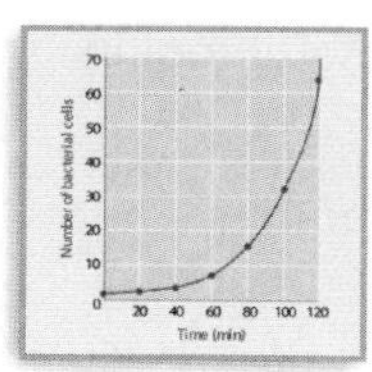

Graphing

You will encounter many graphs in your study of biology. Practice reading, interpreting, and making your own line, bar, and circle graphs.

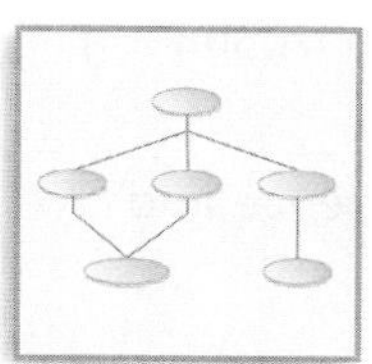

Organizing Information

Learning how to create graphic organizers such as concept maps, flowcharts, cycle diagrams, Venn diagrams, and tables can help you in all your studies. Explore examples and try your hand at building different organizers.

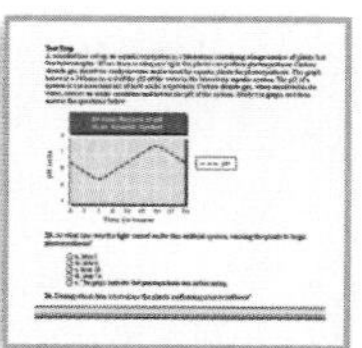

Studying for Standardized Tests

Taking standardized tests can be very stressful. Preparing well can ease your anxiety and help you succeed. Go online to review test question types and strategies for selecting correct answers and eliminating incorrect answers. Then practice your test-taking techniques on sample questions.

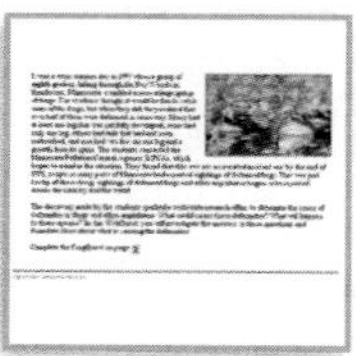

Reading a Scientific Article

Should you believe everything you read? Get some experience reading and interpreting a scientific article. Sifting through the facts, posing questions, and considering potential bias will help you understand and critically evaluate any scientific article.

Critical Thinking for Web Research

The Internet is like the biggest library in the world—except in this library, the books are scattered all over the floor! Find out how to select research topics and locate appropriate Web sites for information so that you can use the Internet wisely and efficiently. Once you know how to ask the right questions, use search engines, and assess whether Web sites are credible you will be able to fully harness the research power of the Web.

Multiple Choice

Choose the letter of the best answer.

1. Which of the following is the *best* definition of science?
   a. a body of knowledge gathered through experiments
   b. a process of accidental discovery
   c. a search for answers to questions about the natural world
   d. a method of asking testable questions based on hypotheses

2. Which of the following is an example of qualitative data?
   a. The temperature decreased from 20°C to 15°C.
   b. The fish swam in a zig-zag motion across the pond.
   c. The plant's height is 25 centimeters.
   d. The six pairs of robins hatched an average of three chicks per nest.

3. Discovery science is to __________ as hypothesis-based science is to __________.
   a. description; explanation
   b. data; observations
   c. theory; technology
   d. inquiry; inference

4. What is a hypothesis?
   a. a prediction
   b. a collection of data
   c. a possible explanation that can be tested
   d. a controlled experiment

5. A factor that can change in an experiment is called a(n)
   a. control.
   b. hypothesis.
   c. inference.
   d. variable.

6. Which of the following is an example of technology?
   a. searching for causes of cancer
   b. understanding how muscles contract
   c. studying migration routes of birds
   d. using artificial skin to treat burns

Short Answer

7. In what ways does discovery science increase understanding about the natural world?

8. What are quantitative data? Give an example of quantitative data.

9. Describe a generalization about nature that you can make based on your own observations.

10. Why is a controlled experiment a useful tool in hypothesis-based science?

11. List characteristics that make a hypothesis scientific.

12. What is the purpose of a scientific model?

13. Describe the benefits scientists gain by sharing information with one another?

14. Explain the differences between science and technology.

Visualizing Concepts

15. Copy the concept map below and complete it.

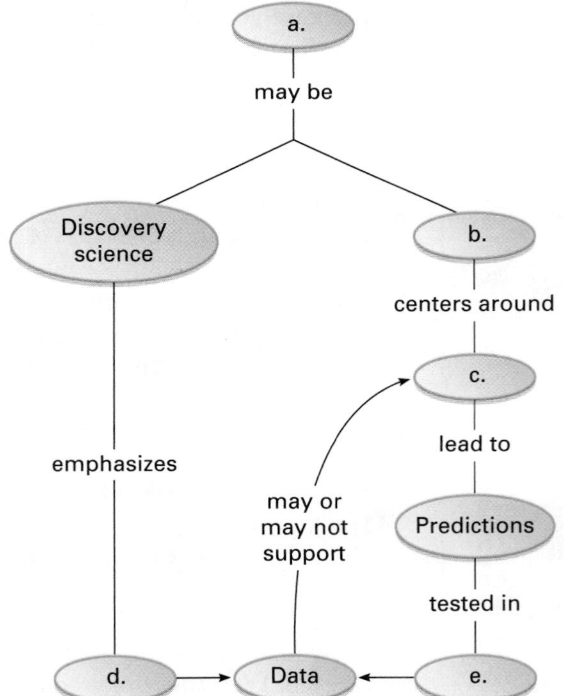

Analyzing Information

16. **Analyzing Photographs** Study the photograph below. Then answer the questions that follow.

a. Make and list at least four observations about the photo.
b. Write one possible inference.
c. Make a prediction about what will happen next.

17. **Analyzing Graphs** The graph shows the results of an experiment in which mice learned to run through mazes.

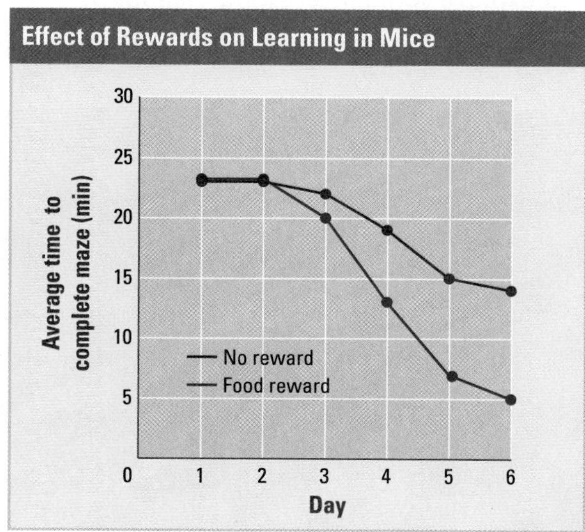

a. State the hypothesis that you think this experiment tested.
b. Identify the experimental variable. List at least two variables that must have been controlled so as not to affect the results.
c. Do the data support the hypothesis? Explain.

Critical Thinking

18. **Problem Solving** Suppose you observe your neighbor's dog barking at various times of the day and night. What other observations would help you hypothesize why the dog barks when it does?

19. **Developing Hypotheses** Based on the results of the snake mimicry case study, suggest another hypothesis researchers might investigate further.

20. **Evaluating Promotional Claims** Describe the strategies you would use to judge whether an advertisement for a diet supplement was reliable.

21. **What's Wrong With These Statements?** *Briefly explain why each statement is inaccurate or misleading.*
    a. An inference is the answer to a scientific question.
    b. An experiment that shows a hypothesis to be false is wasted effort.
    c. Discovery science is not as scientific as hypothesis-based science.
    d. New evidence that does not fit an existing, widely accepted theory can be ignored.

Performance Assessment

Design an Experiment Plan an investigation to determine the direction in which plants grow in the dark. Write a reasonable hypothesis. Use the hypothesis to make a prediction that could be tested. Describe how you would set up the experiment. Identify the variable you want to test, and tell how you would control other variables.

Online Assessment/Test Preparation

Back Forward Reload Home Search Print Security Stop

www.biology.com

- **Chapter 2 Assessment**
  Check your understanding of the chapter concepts.
- **Standardized Test Preparation**
  Practice test-taking skills you need to succeed.

The Process of Science: Studying Animal Behavior

Many kilometers from shore, you scan the surface of the ocean for a glimpse of the knobby heads or bright white flippers of several humpback whales nearby. Suddenly, an enormous humpback launches itself completely out of the water, shattering the calm. The whale twists and falls back into the sea with a resounding splash. This amazing behavior is called "breaching." What causes whales to breach? Why would these large animals go to such an effort? Biologists have a few hypotheses. One is that breaching is one way that the whale communicates with other humpbacks. Another hypothesis is that splashing hard into the water knocks off small animals called barnacles that stick to the whale's skin.

As you read in Chapter 2, asking and searching for answers to such questions are what make biology challenging and fun to do. In this chapter you will learn how biologists apply the process of science to learn about animal behaviors. Before you begin, go online to the *WebQuest* to explore some interesting examples.

Key Concepts

Concept 3.1

Biologists study behavior through observations and experiments.

Concept 3.2

Experiments show that both genes and environment affect behavior.

Concept 3.3

Learning is behavior based on experience.

Concept 3.4

Social behaviors are important adaptations in many species.

Assessment

Chapter 3 Review

What's Online

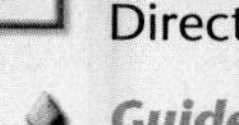

www.biology.com

WebQuest
AnimalBehaviorQuest

Online Activity 3.1
Direct a digger wasp.

Guided Research Lab 1
Escape Behavior in Blackworms

Lab 3 Online Companion
Termite Tracking

Online Activity 3.2
Cause a chick to peck.

Online Activity 3.3
Investigate how birds learn songs.

Careers
Meet an Animal Behaviorist

Online Activity 3.4
Interpret canine behavior.

Chapter 3 Assessment

CONCEPT 3.1

Biologists study behavior through observations and experiments.

OBJECTIVES
- Define *animal behavior.*
- Describe examples of studying behavior through observations and experiments.
- Distinguish between immediate and ultimate causes of behavior.

KEY TERMS
- animal behavior
- immediate cause
- ultimate cause

What's Online

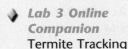

Online Activity 3.1
Direct a digger wasp.

Guided Research Lab 1
Escape Behavior in Blackworms

Lab 3 Online Companion
Termite Tracking

Have you ever observed a pet cat or dog at play and wondered what the animal's behavior meant? For thousands of years, people have been curious about the activities of other animals that share their surroundings.

Asking Questions About Animal Behavior

When you ask questions about an animal's actions, you are taking the first step in the study of **animal behavior**—what an animal does as it interacts with its environment.

For example, in observing the humpback whales you read about in this chapter's introduction, you might ask many questions about their distinctive behaviors. Consider the spectacular scene illustrated in Figure 3-1. As the humpback whale spirals to the surface, it releases a stream of bubbles. What is the function of this bubble-blowing behavior? Through many observations, biologists learned that this "bubble net" temporarily traps small fish and shrimp on which the whale feeds. This observation raises further questions. What causes the whale to blow bubbles? Is this behavior learned, or is the whale born knowing how to use bubble nets? These questions in turn can set a direction for further inquiry.

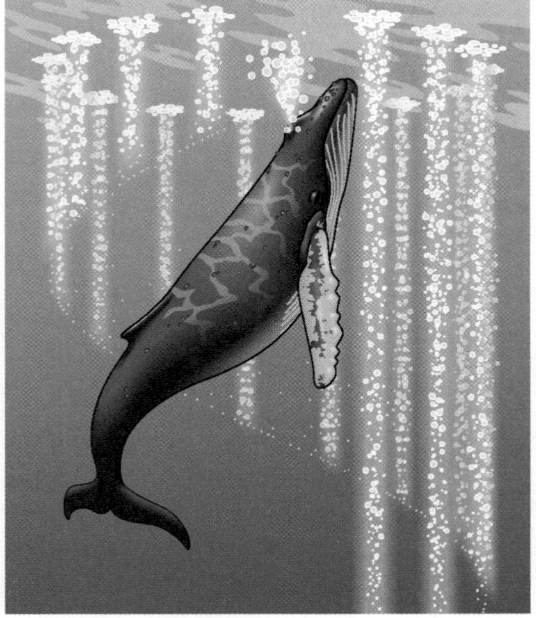

Figure 3-1 A humpback whale can surround itself with a "bubble net," illustrated at left and seen in an aerial photograph at right. The whales in the photograph below are feeding inside a bubble net.

You read in Chapter 2 that scientists rely on two approaches to explore life: discovery science (observation and careful description) and hypothesis-based science (testing explanations, usually with experiments). As in other areas of biology, most investigations of animal behavior involve some combination of these two approaches. Often, the scientist observes an animal closely and describes an interesting behavior (discovery science). This leads to asking a question about the behavior and developing a testable hypothesis to explain it (hypothesis-based science).

Figure 3-2 Based on her observations in the field, Jane Goodall has developed many hypotheses regarding the complicated social interactions of chimpanzees.

Observing Behavior in Natural Environments

When scientists study animals in the wild, using controlled experiments to test hypotheses is often impractical. Imagine trying to carry out controlled experiments to answer questions about humpback whale behaviors. The animals are too large and range too far to study in a controlled experiment. But that does not mean that the questions are unanswerable. In such situations, scientists can test their hypotheses through further observation.

One example is Jane Goodall's field study on chimpanzees (introduced in Chapter 2). Dr. Goodall's tools were minimal: a notebook, binoculars, and patience. When she began studying the chimps, she was only able to glimpse the chimps from afar. After six months the chimps allowed her to approach close enough to make detailed observations (Figure 3-2). By this time she could recognize many of the individual chimps, and she gave them names to distinguish them in her notes. By tracking individuals she noticed patterns in the animals' interactions with each other. Each animal had a social rank within the group. She hypothesized that higher-ranking chimps must have certain advantages over lower-ranking chimps. Her further observations of female chimps supported this hypothesis. The highest-ranking females had access to the best food and could thus provide their infants with the richest milk.

Guided Research Lab 1

Back Forward Reload Home Search Print Security Stop

www.biology.com

Escape Behavior in Blackworms

In this laboratory exploration, you will first study how California blackworms detect and avoid predators in their aquatic habitat. After learning about blackworm responses, you will apply this knowledge to design and carry out your own investigation.

Designing Experiments on Animal Behavior

As you learned in Chapter 2, scientists often design experiments to test their hypotheses. Sometimes it is even possible to conduct experiments on an animal's behavior in its natural environment, as the following example shows.

In the 1920s, an insect called a digger wasp sparked the curiosity of Dutch biologist Niko Tinbergen. Female digger wasps build their nests in a small burrow in sandy ground. The nest consists of four or five cells branching from a main tunnel. After laying an egg in each cell, the wasp flies off to hunt bees, which she paralyzes and carries back to the nest to feed her young. Tinbergen observed this behavior among several female wasps in a small area with many burrows. He wondered whether each wasp returned to only her own nest. By marking the wasps with different-colored drops of paint, he was able to track individuals and conclude that they did return to only their own nests.

Next he asked, "How does each wasp keep track of her nests?" Tinbergen hypothesized that the wasps use landmarks to locate their burrows. To test his hypothesis, he placed a circle of pine cones around a nest opening (Figure 3-3). He observed that when a female wasp emerged from her nest, she sometimes flew about as if she were getting her bearings. When the wasp flew away, he moved the pine cones to one side of the nest. The next time the wasp returned, she flew to the center of the pine-cone circle instead of the actual nest. Tinbergen concluded that the wasp did use landmarks to find her nests, and that she could learn new ones.

Tinbergen's results raised a new question: Did the wasp respond to the pine cones themselves or to their circular arrangement? To answer this, Tinbergen arranged the pine cones in a triangle around the nest and made a circle of small stones off to one side of the nest opening. This time, the wasp flew to the stones, indicating that she was responding to the arrangement of the landmarks rather than the landmarks themselves.

▼ **Figure 3-3** Tinbergen used simple materials in his experiment—pine cones and stones—and a simple procedure. The results led him to conclude that digger wasps use a pattern of landmarks to find their nests.

1 A digger wasp carries food (a paralyzed bee) back to her nest.

2 When the landmarks are moved, the wasp follows the landmarks rather than returning to the nest site.

3 Changing the landmarks reveals that the wasp responds to the arrangement of the landmarks, rather than the type of landmark.

Immediate and Ultimate Causes of Behavior

Tinbergen's studies looked for the **immediate cause** of the wasp's behavior—that is, an explanation in terms of the organism's immediate interactions with the environment. Such explanations usually answer "how" questions. For example, the immediate cause of nest-locating behavior is the wasp's ability to recognize an arrangement of landmarks. This observation answers "how" the wasp locates her nest.

But behavioral biologists also ask "why" questions—why do organisms behave as they do? Answering "why" questions involves finding the **ultimate cause** of a behavior—an explanation based on the organism's evolutionary adaptations. How did the behavior first arise? What is the function of the behavior—in other words, how does it help the organism to survive and reproduce (Figure 3-4)?

To illustrate the difference between immediate and ultimate causes of behavior, consider this example. When you accidentally touch a hot plate, your arm quickly pulls away. The immediate cause of this behavior—the how—is the reaction of your nervous system, which sends signals to the muscles in your arm. A reasonable hypothesis for the ultimate cause—the why—is that natural selection has favored this response, which minimizes damage to the body in a dangerous situation.

▲ **Figure 3-4** At times, adult musk oxen arrange themselves in a ring facing out, with their young offspring in the center. What could be the ultimate cause of this striking behavior? Researchers hypothesize the ring formation is a behavioral adaptation that protects the young oxen.

Online Activity 3.1

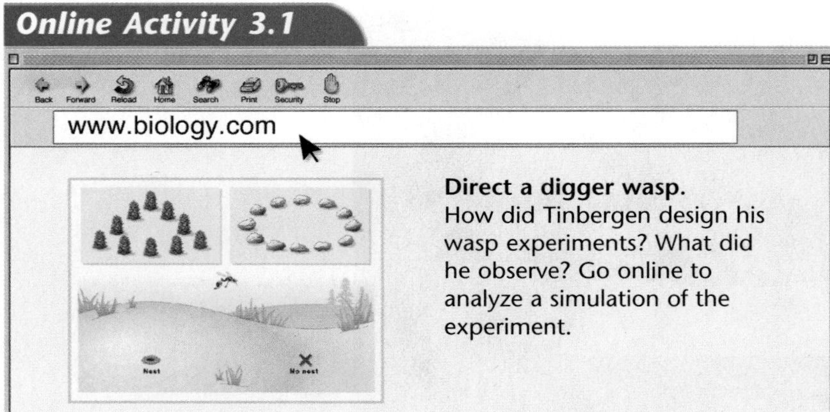

Direct a digger wasp.
How did Tinbergen design his wasp experiments? What did he observe? Go online to analyze a simulation of the experiment.

Concept Check 3.1

1. Pose another question about the behavior of one of the animals described in this section.
2. Explain how Tinbergen's wasp research involved both observations and experiments.
3. Contrast immediate and ultimate causes of behavior.

Termite Tracking

Learning About Termite Behavior

Inquiry Challenge How do termites navigate in their environment?

Lab Overview In this inquiry investigation you will discover how worker termites locate wood and how they signal other worker termites to follow.

Preparing for the Lab To prepare to design your own experiment, go to the *Lab 3 Online Companion.* Examine the tunnels and chambers in a termite mound, and find out more about how termites live.

Completing the Lab Use your Laboratory Manual or lab page printouts from the *Lab 3 Online Companion* to design and perform your own experiment and draw conclusions from your observations. **CAUTION:** *Be sure to follow your teacher's instructions and all safety guidelines in the investigation.*

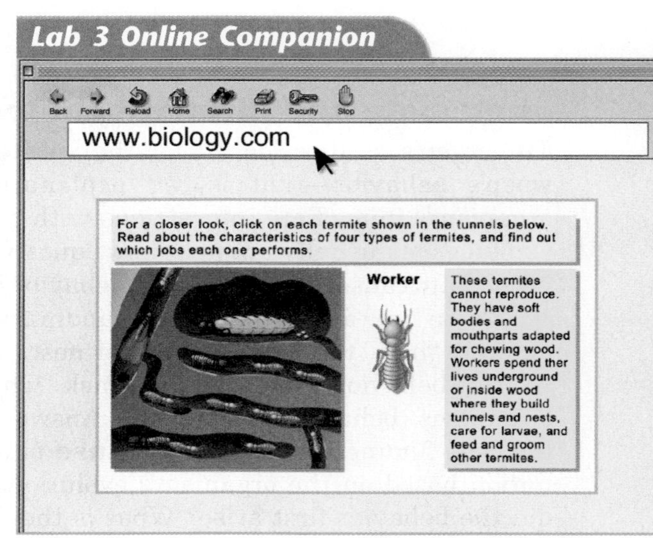

Lab 3 Online Companion
Back Forward Reload Home Search Print Security Stop
www.biology.com
For a closer look, click on each termite shown in the tunnels below. Read about the characteristics of four types of termites, and find out which jobs each one performs.
Worker
These termites cannot reproduce. They have soft bodies and mouthparts adapted for chewing wood. Workers spend ther lives underground or inside wood where they build tunnels and nests, care for larvae, and feed and groom other termites.

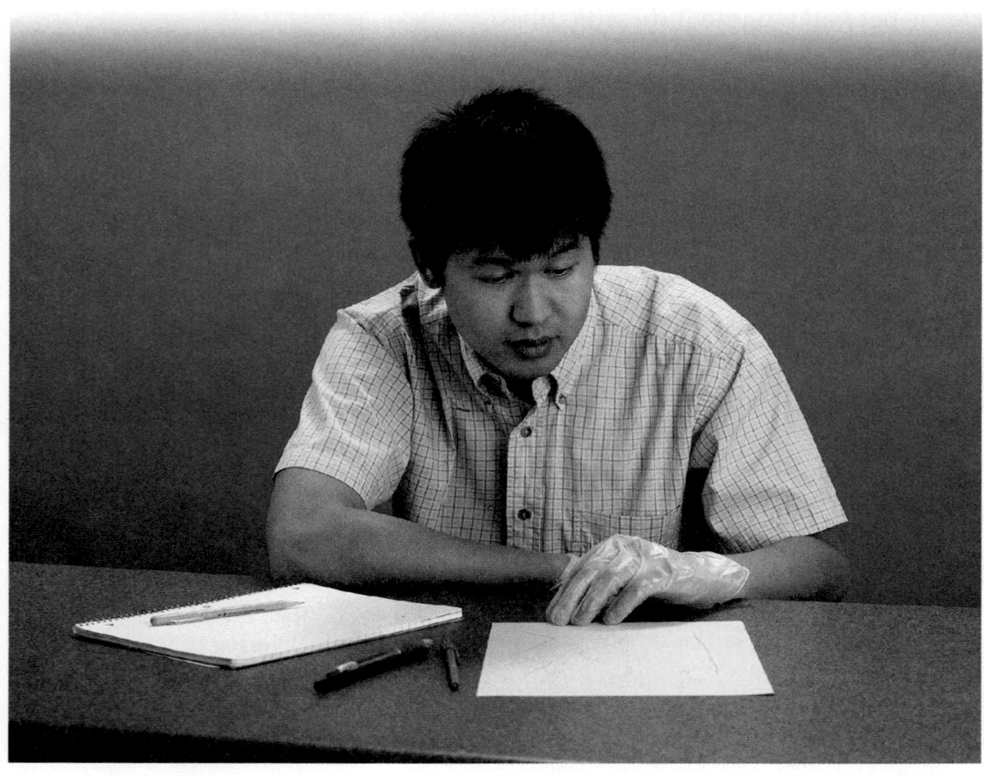

CONCEPT 3.2

Experiments show that both genes and environment affect behavior.

OBJECTIVES

- Explain the term *innate behavior*.
- Describe the influence of environmental cues on rhythmic behaviors.
- Describe how both genes and experience can influence behavior.

KEY TERMS

- innate behavior
- fixed action pattern
- circadian rhythm

What's Online

Online Activity 3.2
Cause a chick to peck.

Have you ever heard the phrase "nature versus nurture"? This expression refers to the idea that behavior is due either to genes (nature) or to environmental influences (nurture). For example, is the digger wasp born "knowing" how to use landmarks to find its nests? Or, does each wasp learn this skill during its lifetime? The answer is more complex than either/or. All of an animal's behaviors depend on some combination of genes and environment.

Innate Behaviors

Researchers have observed that digger wasps raised in isolation build nests in the same way as wasps raised among other wasps. The conclusion is that a digger wasp is born "knowing" how to build a nest—it does not have to learn this behavior from another wasp. A behavior that is performed correctly by all individuals of a species, even if they have no previous experience with the behavior, is called an **innate behavior.** Figure 3-5 illustrates another example of an innate behavior.

Note that this concept of innate behavior does not mean that such behaviors are *only* determined by genes. Even the most programmed behavior is influenced by the environment. For example, perhaps the appropriate type of sandy nesting site must be available to trigger the wasp's behavior. Furthermore, the wasp has to have the physical skills to carry out the behavior. Both genetic and environmental factors (such as nutrition) contributed to the development of the insect's nervous and muscular systems that together enable it to perform the behavior.

◀ **Figure 3-5** The large hatchling in this warbler nest is a cowbird, deposited there as an egg by the cowbird's mother. Opening its mouth to receive food is an innate behavior. The adult warbler is also exhibiting innate behavior by feeding the loudest openmouthed chick in the nest, even though it is the foreign cowbird. Meanwhile, she ignores her own smaller, quieter offspring.

Niko Tinbergen and Austrian biologist Konrad Lorenz observed innate behaviors in many organisms. One famous study involved an interesting behavior in the graylag goose. If the goose bumps one of her eggs out of her nest area, she always uses her beak to retrieve it in the same way (Figure 3-6). When Lorenz and Tinbergen pulled the egg away from the goose during this process, she continued as though the egg were still there. Only after the goose sat down on her nest did she seem to notice that the egg was still outside the nest, and she started the process all over again. The scientists even substituted other objects, such as small toys or balls, for the egg, yet the goose did not alter her behavior.

The goose's egg-retrieving response is an example of a **fixed action pattern** (abbreviated FAP)—an innate behavior that occurs as an unchangeable sequence of actions. An animal can only perform a FAP as a whole "script," from beginning to end. Once an animal starts a particular FAP, it usually completes the sequence no matter what happens along the way.

A FAP is usually triggered by a specific stimulus. In the goose example, the stimulus is the sight of an egg (or other similar object) outside the nest. What is the ultimate cause of such behavior? Why might a FAP evolve, even if it could cause the goose to roll a strange object into her nest? A FAP allows an animal to perform a task correctly the first time, without learning the behavior. You might hypothesize that it would increase an organism's likelihood of success if it could perform important tasks without practicing first. Observations that FAPs often involve activities that are critical to survival and reproductive success, such as feeding or defending offspring, support this hypothesis.

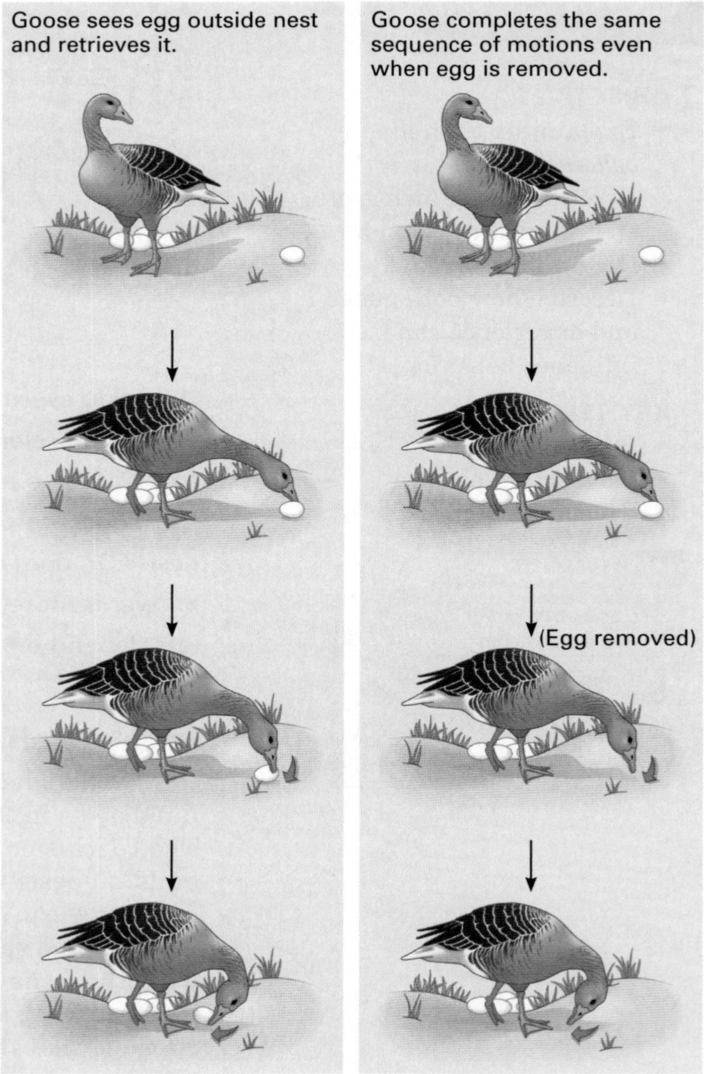

Goose sees egg outside nest and retrieves it.

Goose completes the same sequence of motions even when egg is removed.

(Egg removed)

▲ **Figure 3-6** The graylag goose responds to an egg outside her nest with a set of specific actions. Even when the egg is removed, the goose will continue to push at the air with her beak until she completes the FAP (fixed action pattern).

Rhythms of Behavior

Another example of the interplay of programmed behavior with environmental influences is the ability of many animals to synchronize their activities with their environment. For example, if you have traveled to another time zone, you may have experienced "jet lag"—a period when you were "out of sync" with your surroundings. However, within a few days, you were adjusted to the night and day cues in the environment of the new time zone.

CONCEPT 3.3

Learning is behavior based on experience.

OBJECTIVES
- Distinguish habituation, imprinting, and conditioning as forms of learning.
- Explain the term *insight*.
- Summarize two hypotheses about the purpose of play behavior.

KEY TERMS
- learning
- habituation
- imprinting
- conditioning
- insight

What's Online

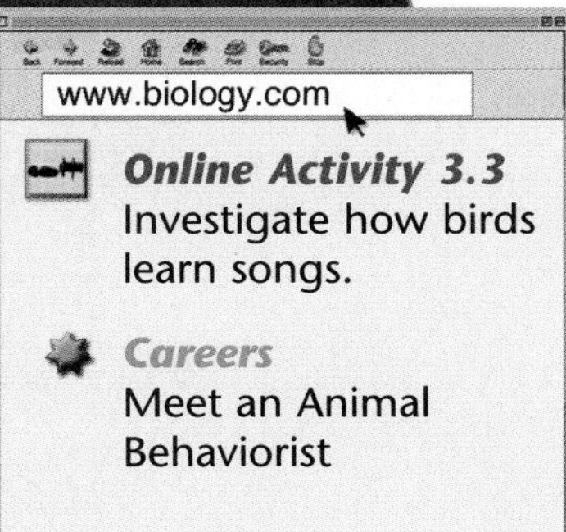

You never had to learn to jerk your hand away from a hot stovetop. That reflex is an innate behavior. But such a painful experience does help you learn to avoid touching hot surfaces in the future. Of course, you are also capable of learning far more complex lessons. A human's ability to learn is unmatched in the animal kingdom. Perhaps that is why many people find investigations into the biology of learning particularly engaging. Humans have much to learn about learning!

Habituation

A change in an animal's behavior resulting from experience is called **learning.** A simple form of learning is **habituation,** in which an animal learns *not* to respond to a repeated stimulus that conveys little or no important information. Think of something you hear that carries no meaning, like the ticking of a clock. Eventually, you stop paying attention to it. Once habituated to a stimulus, an animal still senses the stimulus—its sensory organs detect it—but the animal has learned not to respond. In other words, your ears detect the clock's constant sounds, but after awhile your brain does not initiate a response.

Many animals undergo habituation. For example, a microscopic freshwater organism, the hydra, contracts when disturbed by a slight touch. However, if it is disturbed repeatedly by such a stimulus, the hydra stops responding. Likewise, scarecrows can keep birds away from a garden for a time. But the birds soon become habituated to the scarecrow and may even land on it on their way to the garden (Figure 3-10).

How does habituation benefit an animal? One hypothesis is that habituation allows an animal's nervous system to focus on stimuli that signal food, mates, or real danger, and not waste time or energy on other, less important stimuli.

Figure 3-10 At first, crows may be frightened away by a scarecrow. Over time, however, they become habituated to the scarecrow and will even rest on it.

Imprinting

Many behaviors have both learned and unlearned components. Some of the most interesting cases involve imprinting. **Imprinting** is learning that is limited to a specific time period in an animal's life and that is usually irreversible. One result of imprinting is the formation of a strong bond between two animals, often a newborn and its parent.

In a famous study, Konrad Lorenz used the graylag goose to study imprinting. He divided a batch of eggs from a nest, leaving some with the mother and putting the rest in an incubator. The young reared by the mother served as the control group. They showed normal behavior, following their mother as goslings and eventually growing up, mating, and interacting with other geese. The geese from the artificially incubated eggs formed the experimental group. These geese spent their first two days after hatching with Lorenz rather than with their mother. From then on, they followed Lorenz and showed no recognition of their mother or other adults of their own species (Figure 3-11). This early imprinting lingered into adulthood. The birds continued to prefer the company of Lorenz and even other humans to that of their own species.

In contrast to other kinds of learning, imprinting takes place during a particular time period in an animal's development called a *critical learning period*. For example, Lorenz found that the critical period for graylag geese is the first two days after hatching. If geese were isolated from any moving objects during those first two days, they failed to imprint on anything afterward.

Careers

Back Forward Reload Home Search Print Security Stop

www.biology.com

Meet an Animal Behaviorist
What does an animal behaviorist do? Go online to explore an animal behaviorist's experiences and daily work caring for animals in a zoo. Link to Web sites to learn more about this profession.

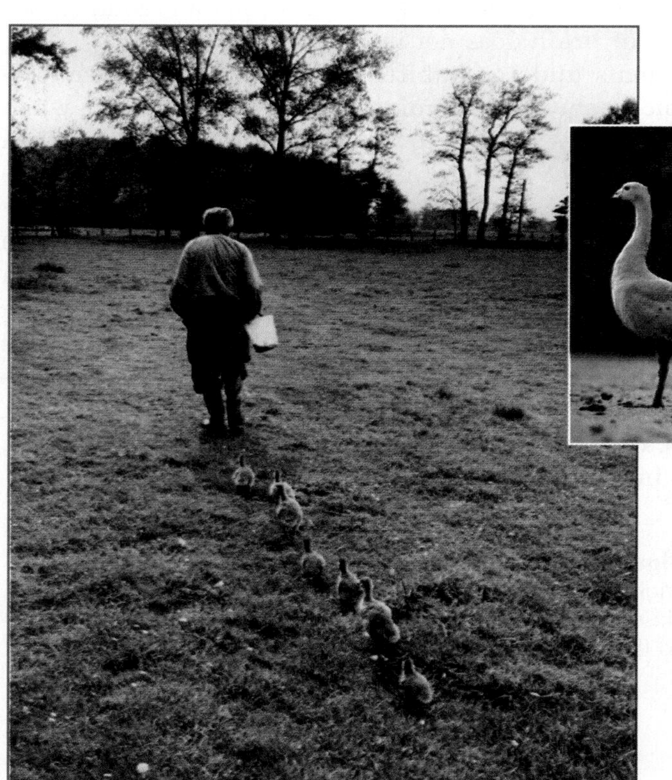

Figure 3-11 The goslings in the photograph on the left spent their first days of life with Lorenz. From then on they preferred the company of Lorenz to their own species. They followed Lorenz as other goslings would follow their mother (above).

1 A dog salivates when it sees or smells food.

2 A dog does not salivate when it hears a sound it does not associate with food, such as a bell.

3 In an experiment, Pavlov rang a bell every time he fed a dog.

4 Eventually, the dog associated the bell with food. It salivated every time it heard the bell, even if no food was present.

▲ **Figure 3-12** In a classical conditioning experiment, Pavlov trained a dog to associate a ringing bell with food. Afterward, when the dog heard the bell, it would begin to salivate even when no food was present.

Conditioning

Learning that a particular stimulus or a particular response is linked to a reward or punishment is called **conditioning.** If you have a pet, you probably have observed many examples of conditioning. For example, a cat may associate the sound of a can opener with mealtime. A dog may associate a hand signal or command with a particular behavior—heeling or staying still. This type of learning, in which an otherwise meaningless stimulus is associated with a reward or a punishment, is called *classical conditioning.* Eventually, the animal learns to respond to the stimulus even in the absence of a reward or punishment. The scientist Ivan Pavlov conducted a famous experiment on classical conditioning in which he trained a dog to salivate at the sound of a bell (Figure 3-12).

In nature, a much more common form of conditioning is *operant conditioning,* also called trial-and-error learning. An animal learns to associate one of its own behavioral acts with a positive or negative effect. The animal then tends to repeat the response if it is rewarded. But the animal avoids the response if it is harmed. For example, predators quickly learn to associate certain kinds of prey with painful experiences. The coyote in Figure 3-13 learned the hard way not to attack a porcupine nose-first. Learning by trial and error often reinforces behaviors that are important to survival.

▶ **Figure 3-13** Through operant conditioning, an animal associates a behavior with positive or negative results. This coyote most likely has learned not to attack porcupines nose-first.

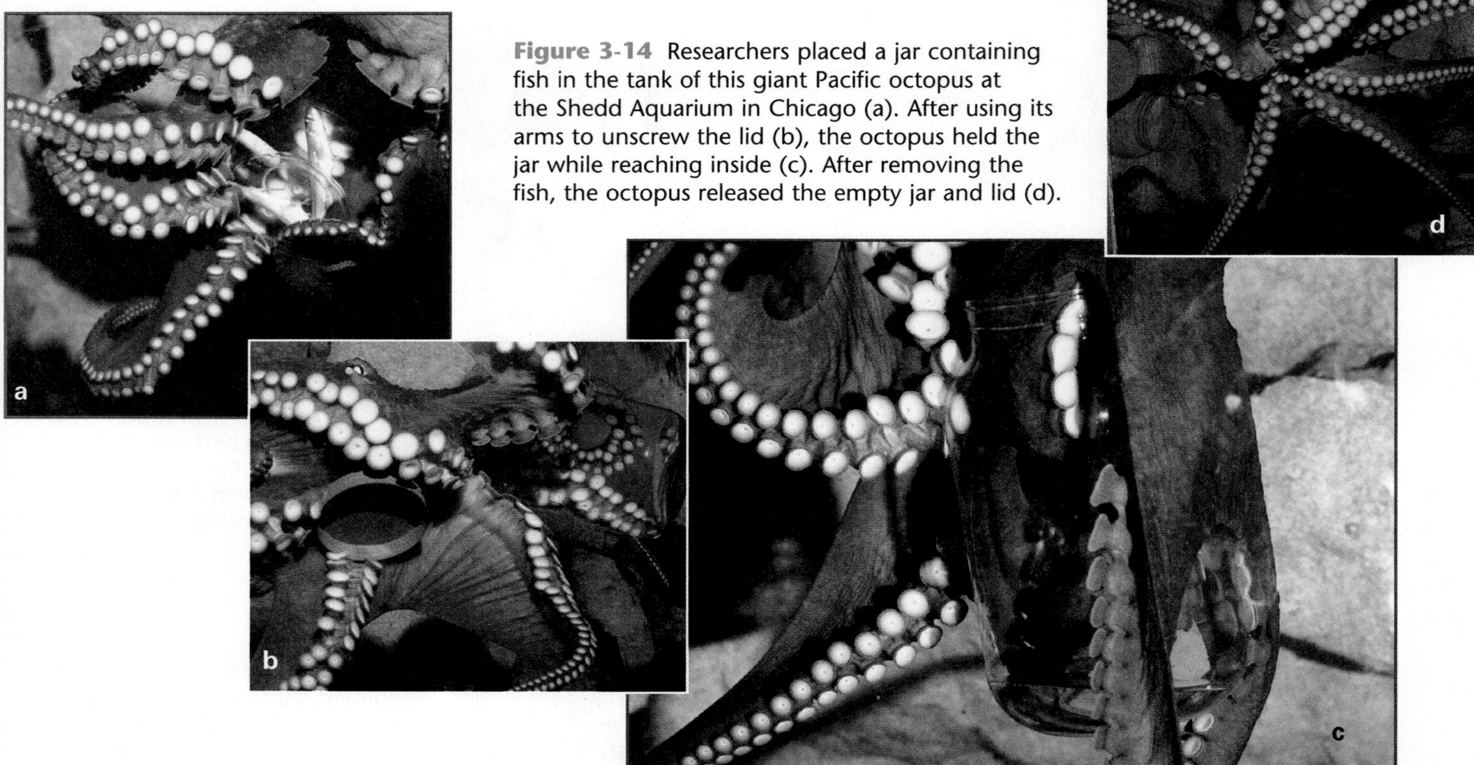

Figure 3-14 Researchers placed a jar containing fish in the tank of this giant Pacific octopus at the Shedd Aquarium in Chicago (a). After using its arms to unscrew the lid (b), the octopus held the jar while reaching inside (c). After removing the fish, the octopus released the empty jar and lid (d).

Insight

At a level above operant conditioning is the ability to respond appropriately to a new situation without previous experience, called **insight** or innovation. Insight involves the ability to analyze problems and to test possible solutions. For example, the octopus in Figure 3-14 figured out how to unscrew the lid of a jar and obtain the food inside. Since in nature an octopus never obtains food exactly in this manner, researchers infer that the octopus' behavior represents insight. In another example, a chimpanzee was placed in a room with several boxes on the floor and a banana hung high above its head. The chimp eventually "sized up" the situation and then stacked the boxes in order to reach the food.

Since it takes place without previous experience, insight is not technically a form of learning. However, successful insight contributes to learning. (The same chimp solves the same problem faster the next time.) Furthermore, insight may itself be based on trial-and-error experience with related problems. In this example, the chimp may have once stood on a rock or tree stump to reach food. Here, the chimp demonstrates insight by applying a past experience to a new, slightly different situation.

Play Behavior

Many mammals and some birds engage in behavior that can best be described as play. For example, young foxes playfully stalk and "attack" their parents or siblings (Figure 3-15). Although the bites are not usually painful, the animals grab one another using movements similar to those used to capture and kill prey.

Play obviously consumes energy, and can even risk damaging the animals' bodies. What could be the ultimate cause for such seemingly pointless behavior? One hypothesis suggests that play is a type of learning that allows animals to practice behaviors required for survival. This "practice hypothesis" is supported by the observation that play is most common in young animals. However, researchers observe that young animals don't seem to improve their movements much even after a few practices.

Another ultimate explanation for play is the "exercise hypothesis." This hypothesis suggests that play is an adaptation that keeps the animal's muscular and cardiovascular systems in top condition. The exercise hypothesis also predicts that play should be especially common in young animals, because they typically do not have to exert themselves in useful activities while under the protection and care of their parents.

Note that both these hypotheses make the same prediction about what to expect from further observation—that young animals should play more than older animals. The data uphold this prediction, but they don't help distinguish which hypothetical explanation is best. Neither the "practice" nor the "exercise" hypothesis can be rejected. For the researcher, the next step is to make further predictions that would help distinguish between the hypotheses.

▶ **Figure 3-15** Play is a common behavior among many young mammals, such as these young foxes, as well as some birds. Researchers have different hypotheses about the ultimate adaptive causes of such play.

Online Activity 3.3

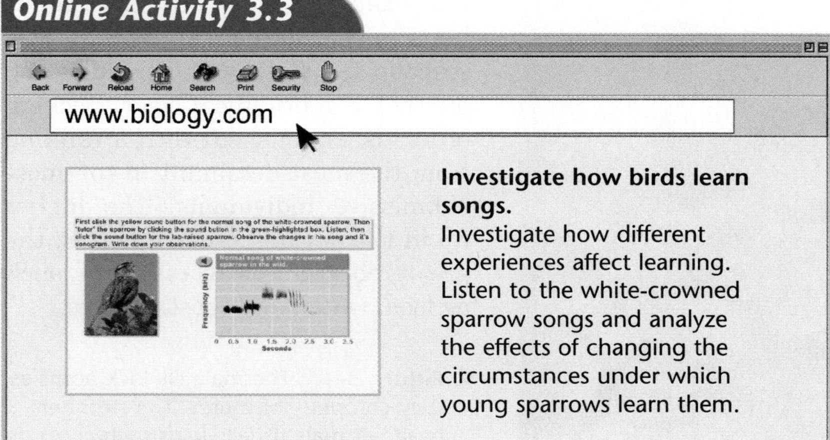

Back
Forward
Reload
Home
Search
Print
Security
Stop
www.biology.com
Investigate how birds learn songs.
Investigate how different experiences affect learning. Listen to the white-crowned sparrow songs and analyze the effects of changing the circumstances under which young sparrows learn them.

Concept Check 3.3

1. Create a table that includes definitions and examples of habituation, imprinting, and conditioning.
2. Explain how insight is different from operant conditioning.
3. Identify two possible explanations for the ultimate cause of playing in young animals.

CONCEPT 3.4

Social behaviors are important adaptations in many species.

OBJECTIVES

- Identify examples of competitive behaviors.
- Explain the significance of courtship rituals.
- Relate communication to other social behaviors.
- Give an example of cooperation in an animal species.

KEY TERMS

- aggressive behavior
- dominance hierarchy
- territory
- courtship ritual
- communication
- cooperation

What's Online

www.biology.com

Online Activity 3.4 Interpret canine behavior.

Many animals live in groups (such as colonies of ants, packs of wolves, herds of antelope, pods of whales, and households and communities of people). As part of a group, such social animals may migrate, hunt, feed, or raise young in a way that offers some benefit compared to living alone. Interactions between two or more individuals of the same species are called *social behaviors.* Careful observations and experiments have resulted in much of the current understanding of social behaviors.

Competitive Behaviors

Animals that live in social groups must sometimes compete for resources such as food, space, or mates. Sometimes these competitions result in conflicts between individuals (Figure 3-16).

Aggressive Behaviors Actual physical struggles or threatening behaviors between animals are classified as **aggressive behaviors.** They include tests of strength or, more commonly, symbolic displays that reveal which individuals are larger, stronger, or more determined. In most cases one individual eventually stops threatening and "surrenders" to the winner.

Dominance Hierarchies Aggressive behaviors within a group of animals often result in a ranking of individuals, called a **dominance hierarchy.** Once the hierarchy is set, the animals do not need to spend energy fighting with each other. Instead, they can concentrate on finding food, raising young, or other necessary behaviors. For example, if several unfamiliar hens are placed together, they respond by chasing and pecking one another. Eventually, a clear "pecking order" is established, with a ranking from the most dominant to the most submissive individuals. The higher up in the pecking order a hen is, the greater her access to resources such as food, water, and roosting sites.

Figure 3-16 The male elk lock horns as they compete for mates. The stronger, healthier male usually wins such contests.

Territorial Behavior Many animals exhibit territorial behavior. A **territory** is an area that individuals defend and from which other members of the same species are usually excluded. The size of the territory varies with the species, the territory's function (for example, feeding or raising young), and the resources available. The gannets in Figure 3-17 maintain territories just large enough for their nests. Even so, they constantly defend their tiny spaces by calling out and pecking at other birds.

Individuals that have established a territory usually proclaim their territorial rights continually. This is the function of most bird songs, as well as the noisy bellowing of sea lions and the chattering of squirrels. Scent markers are frequently used by mammals to signal territories. For example, male cheetahs mark their territories by spraying urine on trees. The odor serves as a chemical "No Trespassing" sign. Other males that approach the area sniff the marked tree and recognize that the urine is not their own. Usually, the intruder avoids the marked territory, steering clear of a risky confrontation with its owner. Defending a territory takes energy, but the result can mean exclusive access to food supplies, breeding areas, and places to raise young.

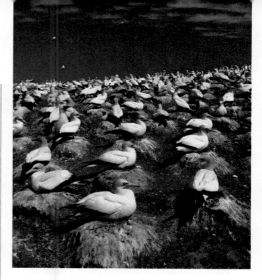

▲ **Figure 3-17** Space is very limited for these gannets nesting on a crowded coastline in Australia. The birds call and peck at each other to maintain their tiny territories—literally "one peck apart" from each other.

Courtship Behavior

In some species, animals perform elaborate behaviors before mating, called a **courtship ritual.** Courtship rituals may confirm that individuals are of the same species but of the opposite sex, that they are ready to mate, and perhaps that they are not threats to each other. Certain rituals may also be an opportunity for an animal to advertise positive qualities to a potential mate. For example, an impressive fanning of tail feathers by a peacock may indicate good health to peahens who are choosing mates. Dull, skimpy tail feathers could be caused by infections or other health problems. By choosing a healthy mate, a female is more likely to have healthy offspring. Note that such a behavior is not an example of

◀ **Figure 3-18** A peacock's radiant tail feathers are a dramatic example of a courtship display.

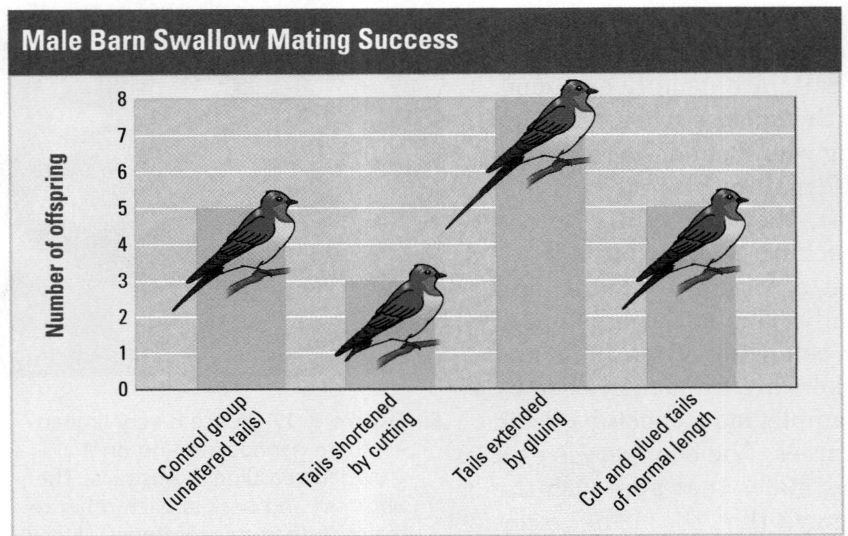

Figure 3-19 A controlled experiment demonstrated that female barn swallows tend to prefer mates with the longest tails. One hypothesis to explain this result is that a male must be healthy for long tail feathers to develop. Natural selection would favor female birds choosing these longer-tailed males.

high-level thinking by the peahens. Rather, it is an example of natural selection refining courtship rituals that improve reproductive success.

The following case study illustrates how biologists used an experimental approach to investigate courtship rituals in barn swallows. Researchers observed that when males first arrive at their breeding grounds each season, they establish territories and display their long tails. Females choose their mates, and the pair then raise the young together.

The researchers hypothesized that the length of a male's tail influenced its mating success—the longer a male's tail, the more attractive he is to females. To test this hypothesis they used a control group of male swallows with natural-length tails and three experimental groups: a group with tails cut short, a group with tails extended by gluing on additional feathers, and a group with cut and glued tails of natural length. (The purpose of this last group was to test whether the gluing process itself had any effect on the females' choices.) Figure 3-19 shows the results of the experiment.

Why would females prefer to mate with males with unusually long tails? As in the peacocks, one hypothesis is that good health is required to produce long feathers. The researchers designed new experiments to test this hypothesis, studying birds with naturally varying tail lengths. They found that long-tailed swallows and their offspring had fewer parasites than short-tailed swallows.

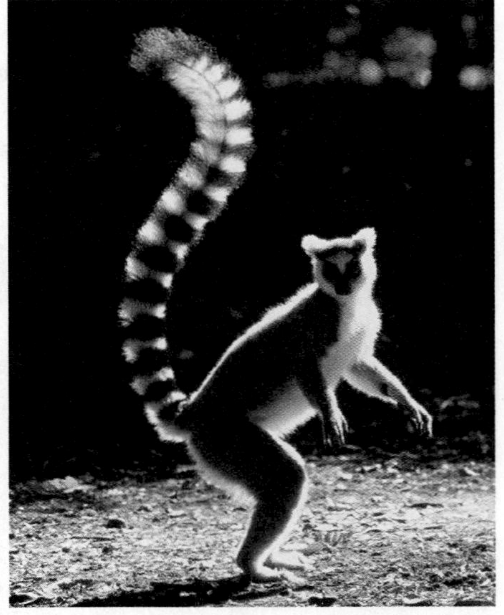

▲ **Figure 3-20** This ring-tailed lemur is communicating aggression through both visual and chemical signals. Before this display, it smeared its tail with strong-smelling secretions from glands on its forelegs.

Communication

The social behaviors you have just read about all depend on some form of signaling, or **communication,** among the participating animals (Figure 3-20). Animals use a variety of signals, including sounds, odors, visual displays, and touches.

Species with complex social structures tend to have complex communication systems. One of the most complex social systems is found in honeybees. In the 1940s, biologist Karl von Frisch carried out several experiments to study bee communication. He put out dishes of sugar water at various distances and directions from a study hive. He also modified the hive so that he could observe the bees inside. Von Frisch observed that worker bees returning to the hive from different dishes performed variations of a "waggle dance." He hypothesized that these dance variations communicated information about the location of the food to other bees in the hive (Figure 3-21).

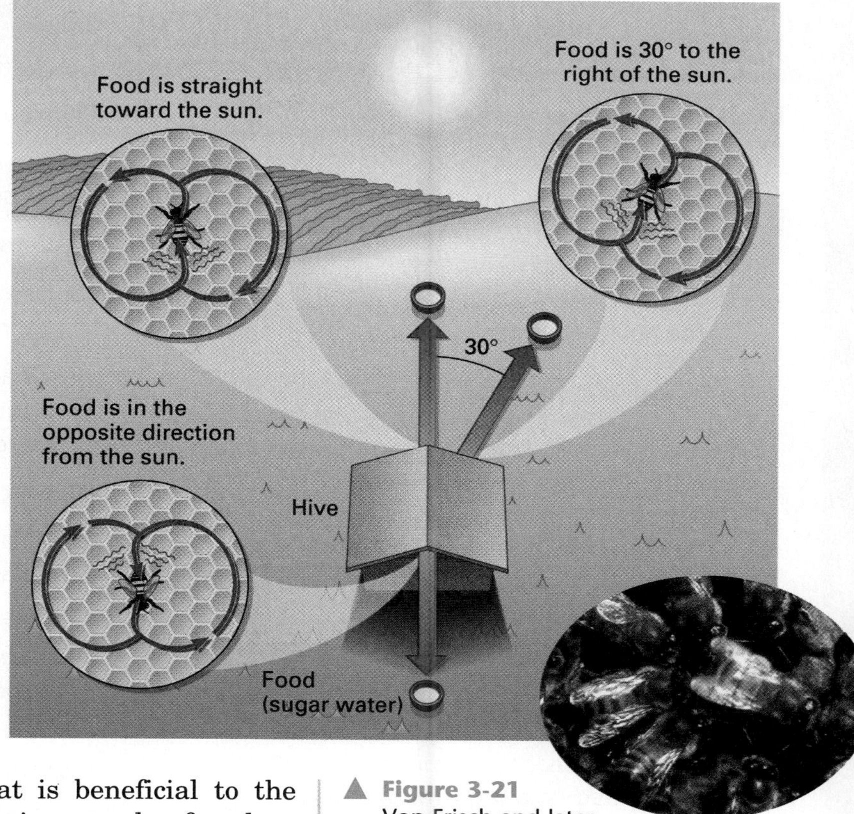

▲ **Figure 3-21**
Von Frisch and later researchers determined that the angle of a returning honeybee's "waggle dance" signals the direction of the food source from the hive compared to the position of the sun.

Cooperation

The social system of the honeybees is one example of a group of behaviors described as **cooperation,** in which individuals work together in a way that is beneficial to the group. Another example of cooperation is a pack of wolves together capturing a much larger prey animal such as a moose. The musk oxen in Figure 3-4 on page 51 are also cooperating, forming a defensive ring around the young oxen. The complete ring of many adults is more effective in protecting all the young than any one ox defending its own young.

In this chapter, you have seen many examples of how biologists use a combination of discovery and hypothesis-based science to understand animal behavior. Analyzing these examples will help you use the process of science in your own inquiries in biology.

Back Forward Reload Home Search Print Security Stop
www.biology.com
Interpret canine behavior.
Have you seen a dog with its ears drawn back and lowered? What does it mean? Find out online when you compare aggressive and submissive behaviors in two canine species: dogs and coyotes.

Concept Check 3.4

1. Explain how aggressive behaviors relate to dominance hierarchies.
2. Summarize one hypothesis about the ultimate cause of tail displays in male barn swallows.
3. Give an example showing the importance of communication in a social behavior.
4. Explain *cooperation* and give an example.

Multiple Choice

Choose the letter of the best answer.

1. What is the immediate cause of a fixed action pattern?
   a. a stimulus and a response
   b. the task
   c. the ability to perform important tasks without practice
   d. imprinting

2. Researchers who studied flying squirrels found that the squirrels that were kept in complete darkness
   a. lost their ability to keep rhythms.
   b. maintained identical rhythms to the control squirrels.
   c. had rhythms that varied slightly from 24 hours.
   d. never returned to normal daily rhythms even after the study was complete.

3. Ants remove dead ants from the anthill. If a live ant is painted with a chemical of a dead ant, other ants carry it out of the anthill even as it kicks and struggles. When the ant returns to the anthill, they carry it out again. Which of the following best describes this behavior?
   a. The chemical triggers a fixed action pattern.
   b. The ants have become imprinted on the chemical.
   c. The ants continue the behavior until they become habituated.
   d. The ants can learn only by trial and error.

4. Your brain ignores the constant sensations of touch from your clothing because of
   a. imprinting.
   b. habituation.
   c. operant conditioning.
   d. fixed action pattern.

5. Swimming in a large school protects certain fish from predators, who may see the school as a single large organism. The schooling behavior is most likely an example of
   a. aggressive behavior.
   b. insight.
   c. territoriality.
   d. cooperation.

Short Answer

6. Compare and contrast immediate and ultimate causes of behavior. Give an example of each.

7. Compare and contrast innate and learned behavior.

8. Describe one hypothesis that explains how habituation benefits animals.

9. What is a fixed action pattern? Describe an example of a fixed action pattern exhibited by the graylag goose.

10. Describe two hypotheses about play behavior.

11. What are courtship rituals? Discuss how these rituals may benefit animals.

12. What is one hypothesis that could explain how a dominance hierarchy benefits the animals in a social group?

Visualizing Concepts

13. Copy the concept map about behavior onto a separate sheet of paper and complete it.

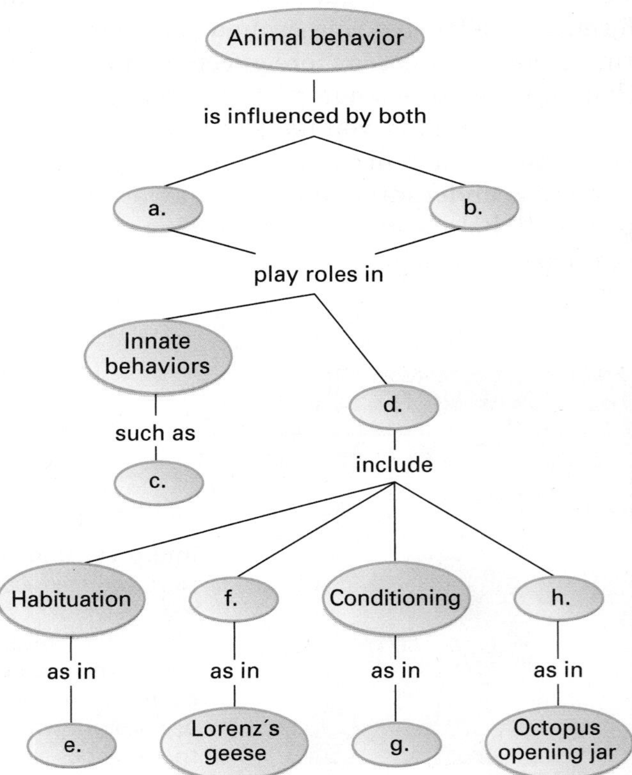

Analyzing Information

14. **Analyzing Data** Crows break the shells of certain mollusks before eating them. Hypothesizing that crows drop the mollusks from a height that gives the most food for the least effort, a researcher dropped shells from different heights and counted the drops it took to break them.

Height of drop (m)	Average number of drops required to break shell	Total flight height (number of drops × height per drop)
2	55	110
3	13	39
5	6	30
7	5	35
15	4	60

   a. Which height provides the most food for the least energy for the crows? Explain.
   b. If crows do fly to the most energy-efficient height, describe an experiment to determine if this is learned or innate behavior.

15. **Analyzing Diagrams** Researchers captured birds at a point on their normal migration route and moved them to a new location to the south.

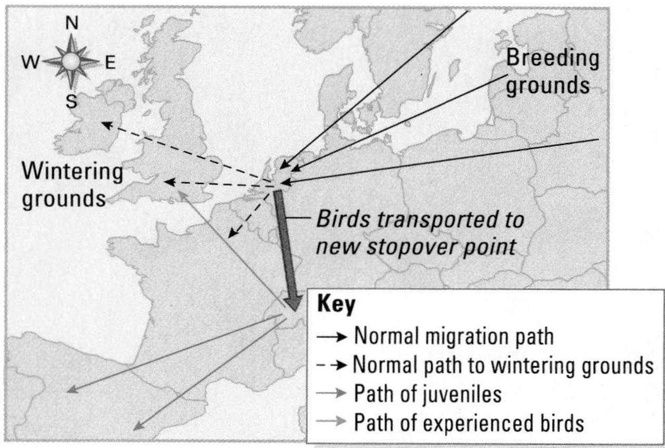

   a. Describe the path the experienced birds flew from the new location. Describe the path of the inexperienced juvenile birds.
   b. Does this graph support the hypothesis that these birds' migration is a combination of innate and learned behaviors? Explain.

Critical Thinking

16. **Making Generalizations** A fish in an aquarium often swims to the top when it sees a person approach. What type of learning could this reflect? Explain your answer.

17. **Giving an Example** Give one example of how you have solved a problem through insight.

18. **Comparing and Contrasting** Compare and contrast insight and operant conditioning.

19. **Making Generalizations** Which social behavior discussed in the chapter would you say is the foundation of all of the others? Explain your choice.

20. **What's Wrong With These Statements?** *Briefly explain why each statement is inaccurate or misleading.*
   a. Innate behaviors are influenced only by genes.
   b. Once habituation has occurred an animal no longer senses a stimulus.
   c. Circadian rhythms cannot exist without environmental cues.

Performance Assessment

Design an Experiment Male stickleback fish attack other male sticklebacks that enter their territory. A biologist notices that the male fish also behave aggressively whenever a red-colored object passes their tank. Since male sticklebacks have red undersides, the biologist hypothesizes that they do not respond to other sticklebacks, but rather to the color red. Design a controlled experiment to test this hypothesis.

Online Assessment/Test Preparation

www.biology.com

- **Chapter 3 Assessment**
  Check your understanding of the chapter concepts.
- **Standardized Test Preparation**
  Practice test-taking skills you need to succeed.

UNIT 2 Exploring Cells

Chapters

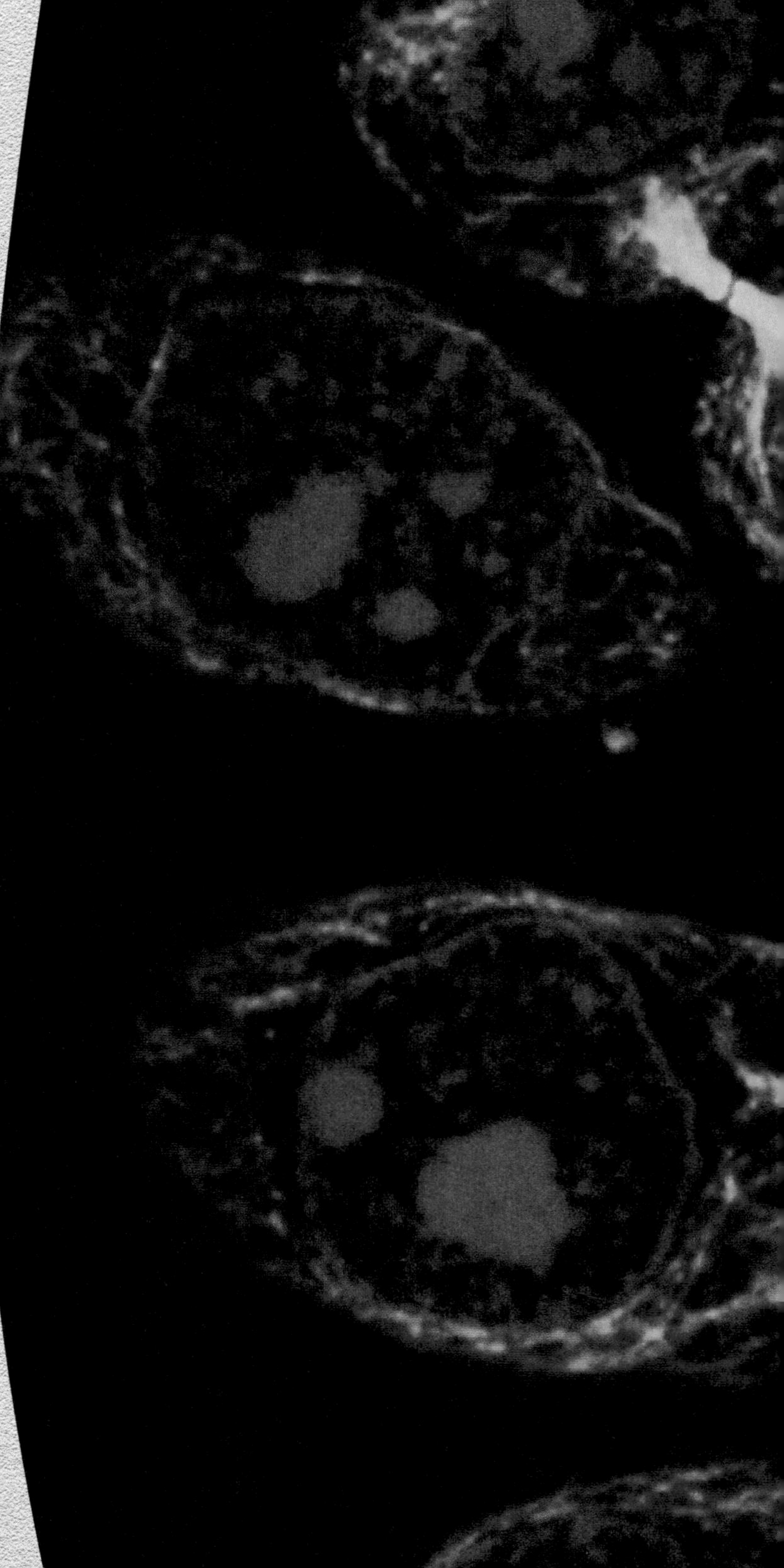

▶ Dividing cancer cells

It is not a simple life to be a single cell, although I have no right to say so, having been a single cell so long ago myself that I have no memory of [it].

Lewis Thomas

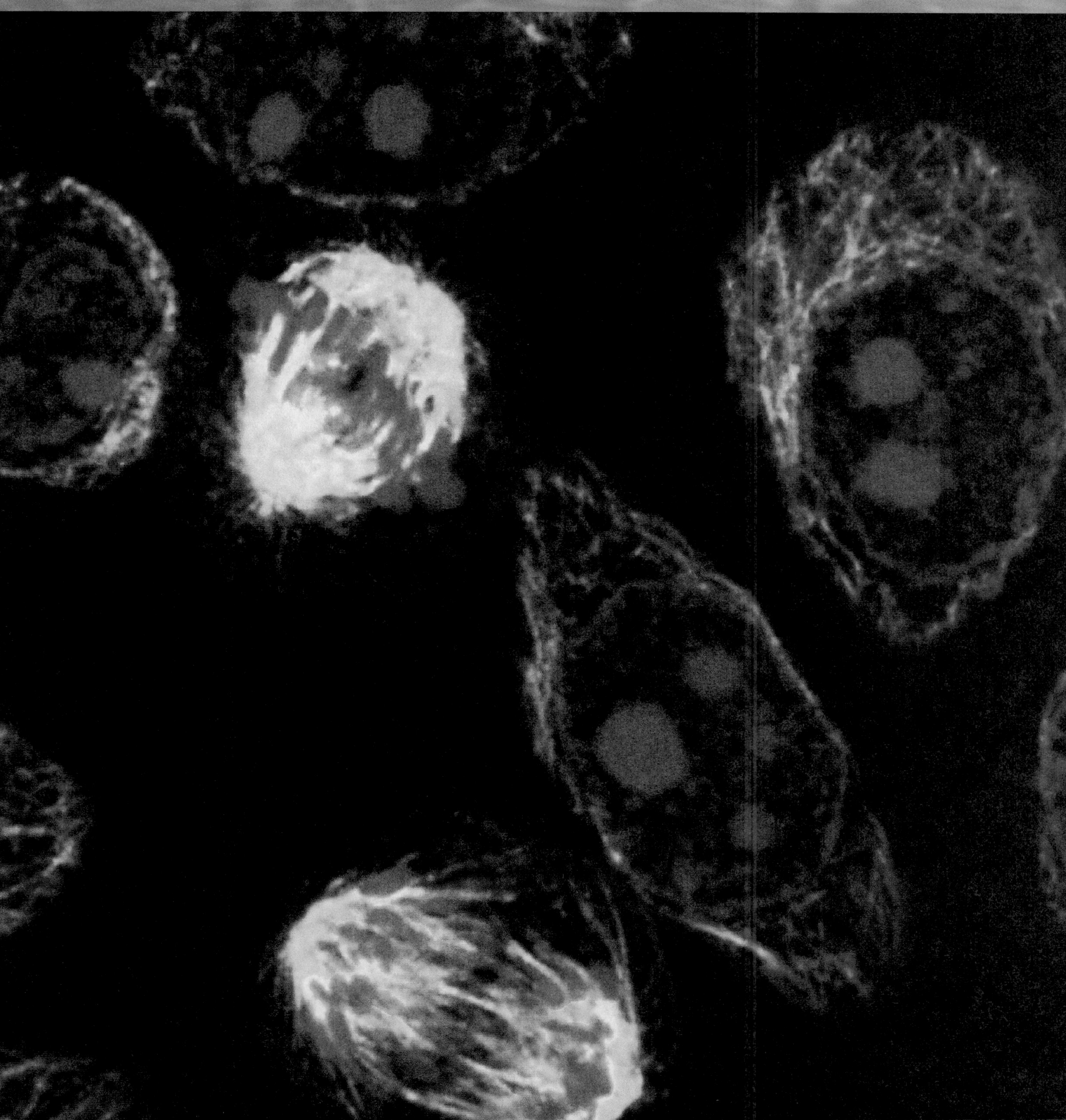

The Chemical Basis of Life

Your body is an elaborate chemical system. Chemical reactions power the muscles that move your eyes as you watch a soccer game. Your ability to see the players results from light interacting with chemicals in your eyes. Chemical signals between brain cells enable your mind to understand what you see. You nourish those brain cells and all the other cells of your body with chemicals obtained from food. In fact, at its most basic level, life is all about chemicals and how they interact. In this chapter you will learn some chemistry that will be helpful throughout your study of biology. Before you begin, go online to the ***WebQuest*** to explore what happens when rainwater mixes with an acid.

Key Concepts

Concept 4.1
Life requires about 25 chemical elements.

Concept 4.2
Chemical properties are based on the structure of atoms.

Concept 4.3
Chemical bonds join atoms to one another.

Concept 4.4
Life depends on the unique properties of water.

Assessment
Chapter 4 Review

What's Online

www.biology.com

WebQuest
AcidRainQuest

Online Activity 4.1
Discover the composition of familiar items.

Science, Technology, & Society
Fluoridation

Online Activity 4.2
Explore the parts of an atom.

Online Activity 4.3
Predict how atoms will bond.

Online Activity 4.4
Investigate the structure and properties of water.

Lab 4 Online Companion
Soil Solutions

Chapter 4 Assessment

CONCEPT 4.1

Life requires about 25 chemical elements.

OBJECTIVES
- List the most common elements in living things.
- Compare and contrast elements and compounds.

KEY TERMS
- matter
- element
- trace element
- compound

Are you wondering why you're reading about chemistry in a biology textbook? The answer is that all of biology involves chemistry. All living things share the same chemical building blocks and depend on chemical processes for survival.

Elements

Humans and other organisms and everything around them are examples of matter. **Matter** is anything that occupies space and has mass—the physical "stuff" of the universe. Rock, wood, air, metal, water, and animals are all matter.

The various forms of matter are composed of one or more chemical elements. An **element** is a pure substance that cannot be broken down into other substances by chemical means. Examples of naturally occurring elements include some you have probably heard of, such as gold, helium, mercury, and oxygen. Elements are often described as the "basic ingredients" of matter because the more complex forms of matter (including you) are made from elements.

About 25 elements are essential to life (Figure 4-1). Four of these elements—oxygen (O), carbon (C), hydrogen (H), and nitrogen (N)—make up about 96 percent of the living matter in your body. Calcium (Ca), phosphorus (P), potassium (K), sulfur (S), and a few other elements account for most of the remaining 4 percent. **Trace elements,** elements that make up less than 0.01 percent of your body mass, are nevertheless critical to your health. For example, you need about 0.15 milligram (mg) of the trace element iodine each day. If you don't get enough iodine, your thyroid gland (a gland in your throat that regulates certain chemical processes in your body) does not function properly. Another trace element, iron, makes up only about 0.004 percent of your body mass, but it is essential for carrying oxygen in your blood. Examples of other trace elements include copper, fluorine, manganese, and selenium. A balanced diet will usually provide you with the trace elements you need.

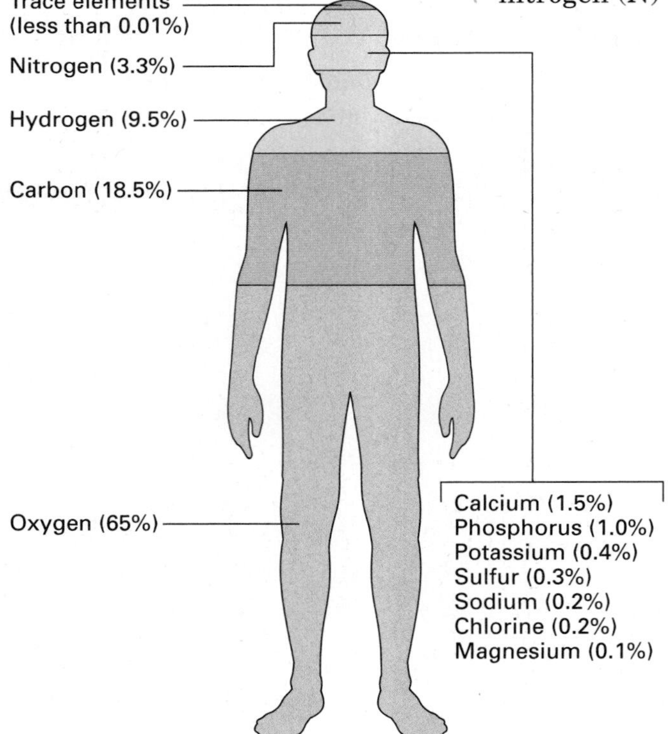

Figure 4-1 This chart compares percentages of various elements in your body. All of the elements represented are essential to life.

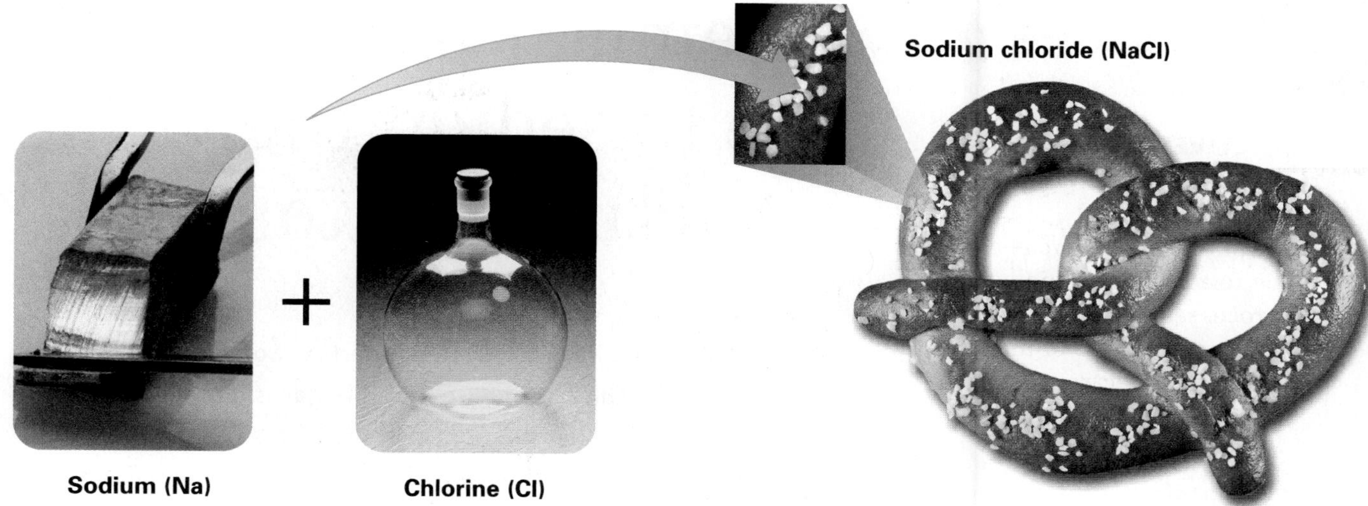

Compounds

Most elements can interact with other elements, forming more complex types of matter called compounds. A **compound** is a substance containing two or more elements that are chemically combined in a fixed ratio. For example, water (H_2O) is a compound that always contains the same ratio of hydrogen combined with oxygen.

A compound's properties may differ greatly from those of its component elements. As you can see in Figure 4-2, the white crystals of table salt, or sodium chloride (NaCl), on a pretzel look very different from the silvery gray sodium metal and yellowish-green chlorine gas. Similarly, while water is a liquid at room temperature, both oxygen and hydrogen in their elemental form are gases.

Though simple compounds like sodium chloride and water play important roles in living things, most compounds found in organisms are more complex, containing at least three or four elements. For example, the sugars in flower nectar and in maple tree sap are composed of carbon, hydrogen, and oxygen. The compounds in the muscles that wag a dog's tail or blink your eyes consist mostly of carbon, hydrogen, oxygen, and nitrogen.

▲ **Figure 4-2** At room temperature, sodium metal is soft enough to cut with a knife, but too dangerous to touch with bare skin. Chlorine is a poisonous gas. When chemically combined, these elements form sodium chloride, a compound essential to life (and often used to flavor food).

Science, Technology, & Society

www.biology.com

Fluoridation

Adding fluoride to drinking water has been shown to decrease tooth decay. But some people question the safety of this practice. Go online to find out about the issues and participate in a debate.

Online Activity 4.1

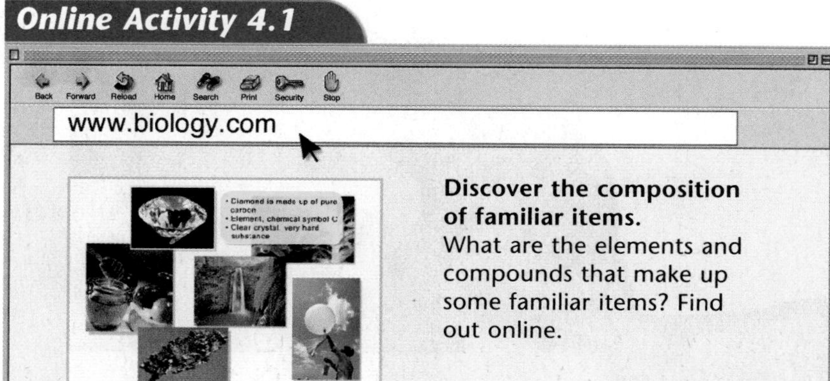

Back
Forward
Reload
Home
Search
Print
Security
Stop
www.biology.com
Discover the composition of familiar items.
What are the elements and compounds that make up some familiar items? Find out online.

Concept Check 4.1

1. List the four most abundant elements in your body, in order of decreasing percent of body mass.
2. How are elements and compounds different?
3. Give an example showing the importance of trace elements to the human body.

CONCEPT 4.2

Chemical properties are based on the structure of atoms.

OBJECTIVES

- Describe the structure of an atom.
- Explain how isotopes can be used to study biological processes.
- Explain the role of an element's electrons in determining its chemical reactivity.

KEY TERMS

- atom
- proton
- electron
- neutron
- nucleus
- atomic number
- isotope
- radioactive isotope

What's Online

www.biology.com
Online Activity 4.2
Explore the parts of an atom.

Different elements have different properties. Some are solid metals at room temperature. Some are invisible gases. Some elements readily react with other elements, while others hardly react at all. These properties affect the roles that different elements play in biological processes. This section describes how an element's properties are related to its structure.

Atoms

Each element consists of a single kind of atom that is different from the atoms of all other elements. An **atom,** which gets its name from the Greek word *atomos* meaning "indivisible," is the smallest possible particle of an element. In other words, a carbon atom is the smallest possible "piece" of the element carbon. And that's a very small piece—it would take more than three million carbon atoms to stretch across the period printed at the end of this sentence.

Atoms of all elements are made up of even smaller components called subatomic particles. A **proton** is a subatomic particle with a single unit of positive electrical charge (+). An **electron** is a subatomic particle with a single unit of negative electrical charge (−). A third type of subatomic particle, the **neutron,** is electrically neutral, meaning it has no electrical charge. An element's physical and chemical properties depend on the number and arrangement of its subatomic particles. For example, the shiny luster of copper metal and the boxy crystals of sulfur are based on the structure and interactions of the atoms that make up those elements (Figure 4-3).

Figure 4-3 Copper (left) and sulfur (right) each display unique properties that are determined by the structure of their atoms.

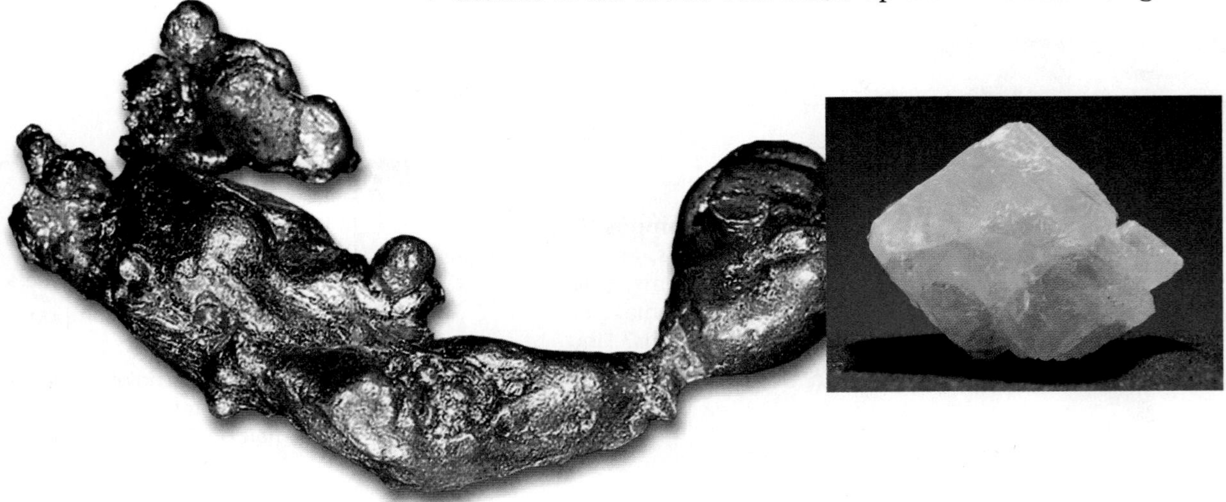

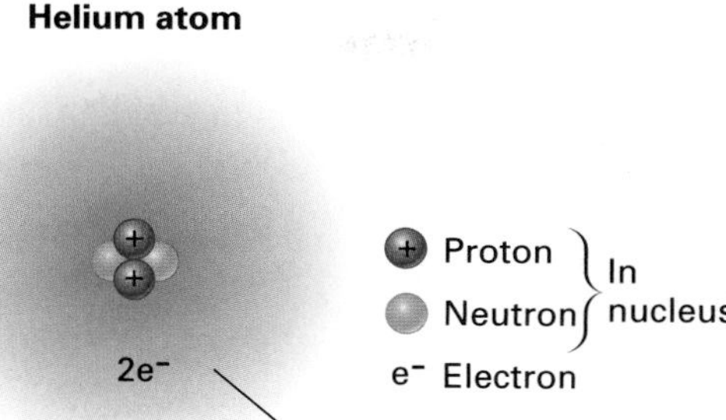

Figure 4-4 This parade balloon floats because it is filled with helium gas, which is less dense than air. The model of a helium atom to the left indicates the number of each kind of subatomic particle it contains. Though no visual model can accurately show an atom's structure, models can help you in understanding certain aspects of an element's chemical behavior.

An atom's protons and neutrons are tightly packed together, forming a central core called the **nucleus.** Electrons, which have much less mass than neutrons and protons, continually move about the outside of the nucleus at great speed. The attraction between the negatively charged electrons and the positively charged protons keeps the electrons close to the nucleus.

Notice that the model of the helium atom in Figure 4-4 has 2 protons and 2 neutrons in its nucleus. This model, which is not drawn to scale, represents the moving electrons as a spherical "cloud" of negative charge surrounding the nucleus. Because the exact path of any electron cannot be determined, the cloud model is helpful. An electron may visit every point around a nucleus over time. Thus you can think of the electron's negative charge as spread out, like a cloud, in all the places the electron might be. In a real atom, the electron cloud is much larger than the nucleus. To give you an idea of the difference, consider that if the electron cloud of an atom were big enough to fill a baseball stadium, the nucleus would be only the size of a housefly on the field!

An important difference among elements is the number of protons in their atoms. All atoms of a particular element have the same number of protons, known as the element's **atomic number.** Thus, a helium atom, with 2 protons, has an atomic number of 2. Left alone, an atom tends to hold as many electrons as protons. In that state, the atom is electrically neutral—the positive charges on the protons exactly balance the negative charges on the electrons. However, the number of electrons is not constant like the number of protons. Certain atoms can lose one or more electrons, while some atoms can gain one or two electrons. As you'll see later, the number of electrons determines how the atom interacts with other atoms. Indirectly then—by setting the usual number of electrons—the number of protons determines the atom's properties. No two elements have the same atomic number (proton number), so no two elements have the exact same chemical behavior.

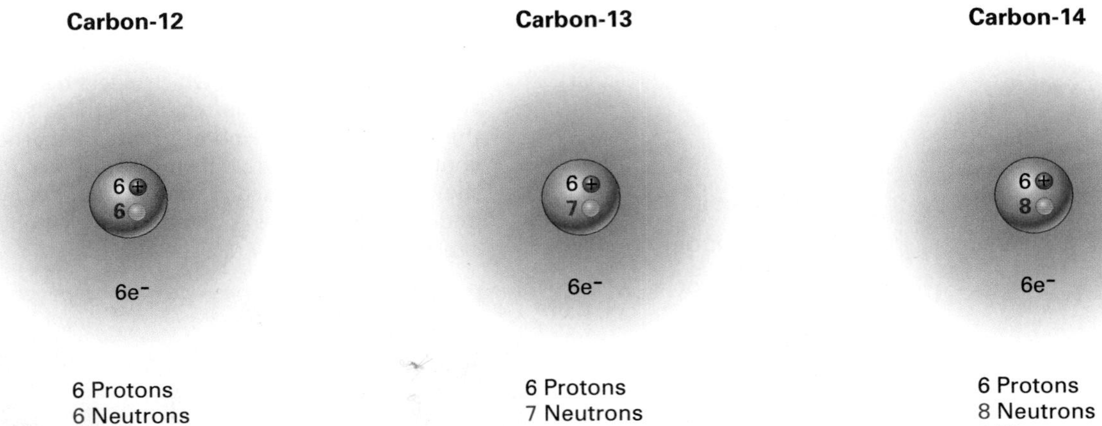

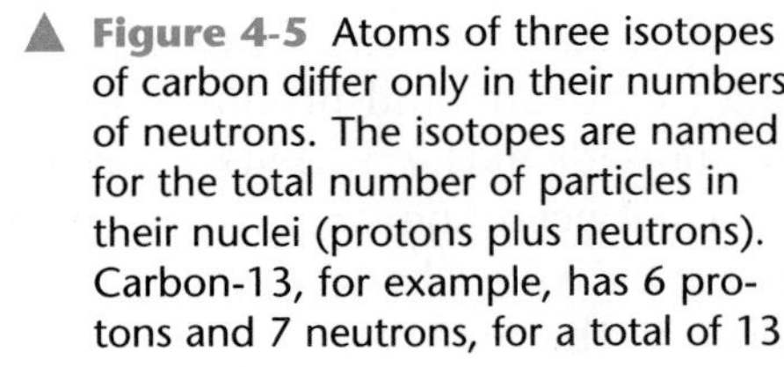

▲ **Figure 4-5** Atoms of three isotopes of carbon differ only in their numbers of neutrons. The isotopes are named for the total number of particles in their nuclei (protons plus neutrons). Carbon-13, for example, has 6 protons and 7 neutrons, for a total of 13.

Isotopes

Some elements have alternate forms called isotopes. **Isotopes** of an element have the same number of protons in their atoms but different numbers of neutrons. Figure 4-5 shows the numbers of subatomic particles in atoms of the three isotopes of carbon. Carbon-12 (usually written ^{12}C), which has atoms containing 6 neutrons, makes up about 99 percent of all naturally occurring carbon. Most of the other 1 percent is carbon-13 (^{13}C), which has atoms with 7 neutrons. A third isotope, carbon-14 (^{14}C), has atoms with 8 neutrons and is very rare. Notice that atoms of all three carbon isotopes still have 6 protons—otherwise, they would not be carbon. Both ^{12}C and ^{13}C are stable isotopes, meaning their nuclei do not change with time. The isotope ^{14}C, on the other hand, is unstable, or radioactive. A **radioactive isotope** is one in which the nucleus decays (breaks down) over time, giving off radiation in the form of matter and energy.

Radioactive isotopes have many uses in research and medicine. Living cells use radioactive isotopes just as they would use the nonradioactive forms. Thus, radioactive isotopes are useful as "biological spies" for observing what happens to different atoms within organisms. Scientists can track the presence of radioactive isotopes with instruments that detect radioactive decay. Though radioactive isotopes have many beneficial uses, the particles and energy they give off can also damage cells. However, the doses of most isotopes used in medical diagnosis, such as the body scan in Figure 4-6, are relatively safe.

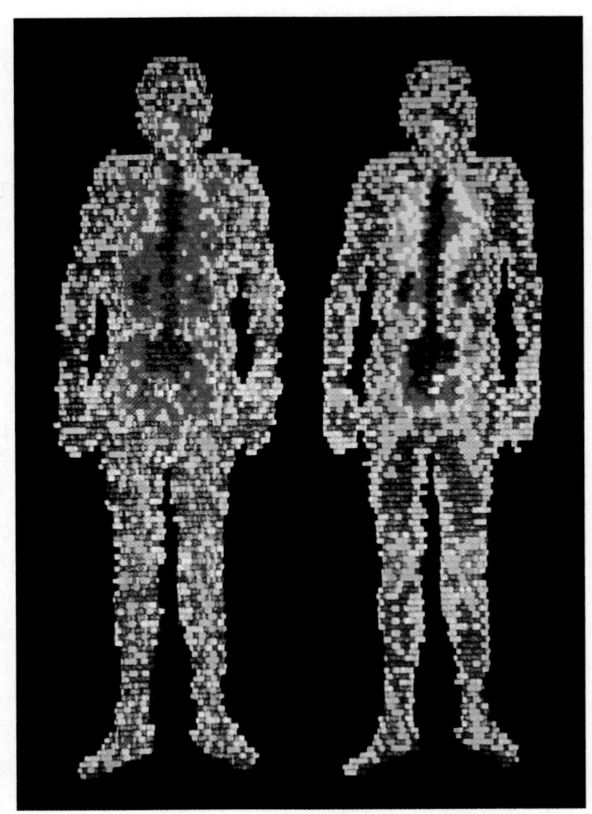

▶ **Figure 4-6** The radioactive isotope used in this body scan concentrates in bone, notably the spine, ribs, and pelvis. Color-coding indicates the intensity of radiation, which ranges from blue (lowest) to brown (highest). The left-hand image is the person's front, while the right-hand image is the back.

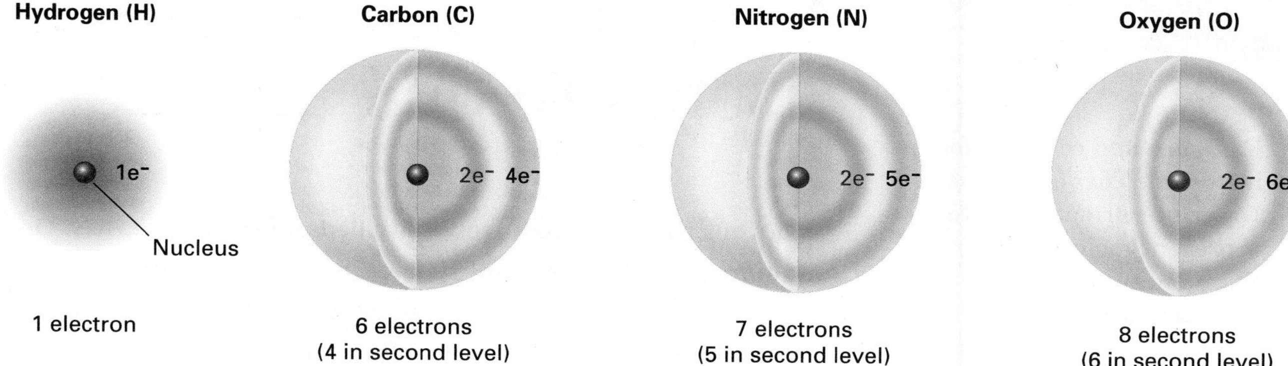

▲ **Figure 4-7** An atom's lowest (first) energy level can hold up to 2 electrons. The second level can hold up to 8. Notice that the second energy levels of carbon, nitrogen, and oxygen atoms are unfilled with 4, 5, and 6 electrons, respectively. (Remember that atomic models are limited in what they can represent. Energy levels are not actual physical locations.)

Electrons and Reactivity

How does an atom's structure determine how it reacts with other atoms? The key is the atom's electrons. Electrons differ in the amount of energy they have and how tightly they are held by the protons in the nucleus. Based on these properties, chemists describe an atom's electrons as belonging to certain energy levels. Usually it is the electrons in the highest energy level of an atom that determine how that atom reacts.

The first, or lowest, energy level (nearest the nucleus) can hold 2 electrons, while the second energy level can hold 8 electrons. For example, a hydrogen atom has 1 electron. Since electrons fill the lowest energy level first, hydrogen's electron occupies its first energy level (Figure 4-7). Helium (modeled in Figure 4-4) has 2 electrons, filling its lowest energy level. Carbon has 2 electrons in its lowest energy level, and 4 more electrons in its second level. Note that both hydrogen and carbon have a partly-filled energy level, as do nitrogen and oxygen. That condition makes these atoms chemically reactive—they tend to react with other atoms, filling their highest occupied energy levels. In contrast, a helium atom, which has no partly-filled energy levels, is inert—it does not tend to react. In the next section, you'll read more about the ways electrons are involved in the reactions among atoms.

Online Activity 4.2

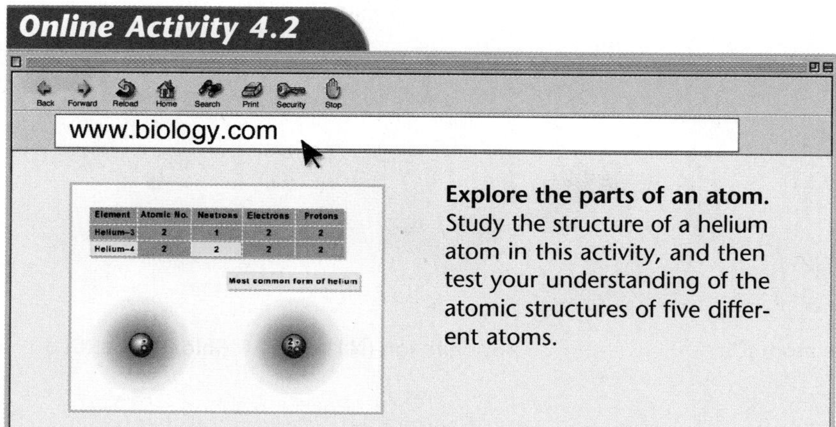

Explore the parts of an atom. Study the structure of a helium atom in this activity, and then test your understanding of the atomic structures of five different atoms.

Concept Check 4.2

1. Describe three kinds of subatomic particles and tell how they are arranged in an atom.
2. What is an isotope? Explain how radioactive isotopes are useful to researchers.
3. Describe the significance of the number of electrons in an atom's highest energy level.
4. Explain the significance of an element's atomic number.

CONCEPT 4.3 Chemical bonds join atoms to one another.

OBJECTIVES

- Compare and contrast ionic bonds and covalent bonds.
- Describe various ways to represent molecules.
- Summarize what happens in a chemical reaction.

KEY TERMS

- ionic bond
- ion
- covalent bond
- molecule
- chemical reaction
- reactant
- product

What's Online

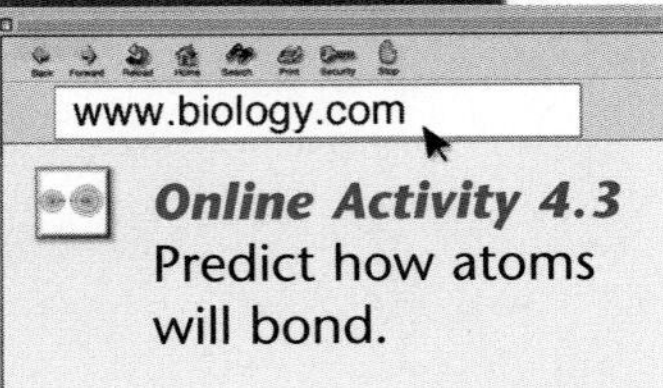

Online Activity 4.3
Predict how atoms will bond.

Reactions between atoms result in filled outer energy levels. One atom may transfer electrons to another, or two atoms may share electrons. This process of transferring or sharing electrons creates an attraction—a chemical bond—that holds the atoms together.

Ionic Bonds

One type of chemical bond, an **ionic bond,** occurs when an atom transfers an electron to another atom. Table salt, or sodium chloride (NaCl), is a compound formed as a result of electron transfer between sodium (Na) atoms and chlorine (Cl) atoms. You can follow the reaction between these atoms in Figure 4-8. Notice that at the beginning, sodium has only 1 electron in its highest energy level, whereas chlorine has 7. At this point, each atom has an equal number of protons and electrons and therefore is electrically neutral.

When the two atoms collide, the chlorine atom strips away sodium's outer electron. In the process, chlorine's highest energy level, now with 8 electrons, becomes filled. In losing an electron, the sodium atom's second energy level, which already has 8 electrons, becomes the highest. It, too, is filled.

Look at how the balance of electric charges has changed. One unit of negative charge (1 electron) moved from sodium to chlorine. The two atoms are now referred to as **ions**—atoms (or groups of atoms) that have become electrically charged as a result of gaining or losing electrons. Losing an electron leaves the sodium ion with a charge of 1+, while gaining an electron gives chlorine (now called chloride) a charge of 1−. The attraction holding the oppositely charged Na^+ and Cl^- ions together is the ionic bond.

▼ **Figure 4-8** The transfer of an electron from a sodium atom to a chlorine atom results in oppositely charged ions. The attraction between these ions is an ionic bond.

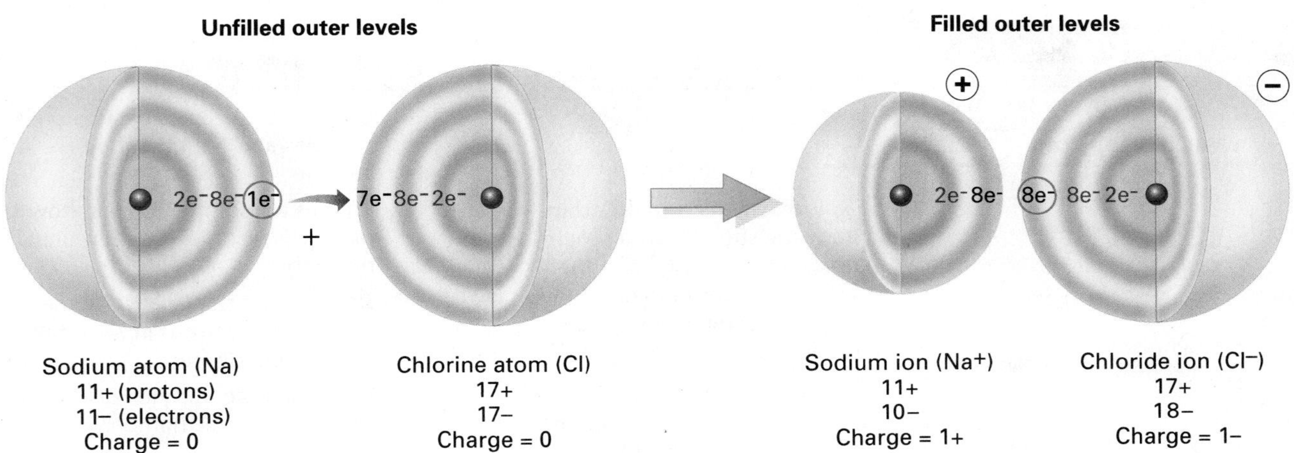

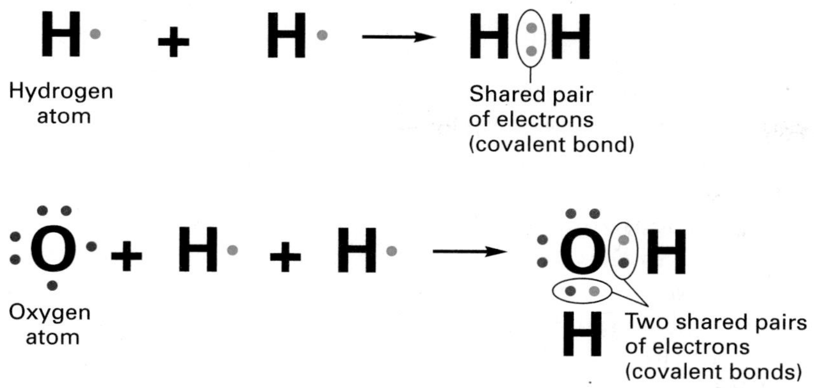

$H\cdot + H\cdot \rightarrow H{:}H$

Hydrogen atom

Shared pair of electrons (covalent bond)

$:\ddot{O}\cdot + H\cdot + H\cdot \rightarrow :\ddot{O}{:}H$ (with second H bonded below O)

Oxygen atom

Two shared pairs of electrons (covalent bonds)

Figure 4-9 A pair of electrons (dots) between atoms represents a covalent bond. The electron pair counts in the total of outermost electrons for both atoms. You can count 8 electrons around the oxygen atom on the bottom right. Its highest energy level is filled as a result of sharing electrons with the hydrogen atoms.

Covalent Bonds

In contrast to the transfer of electrons that results in an ionic bond, a **covalent bond** forms when two atoms *share* electrons. Electron sharing can be modeled using element symbols, with dots representing the atoms' outermost electrons (Figure 4-9). In the first example, each hydrogen atom (H) shares its electron with another hydrogen atom. This shared pair of electrons is one covalent bond. In the second example, an oxygen atom (O) shares a pair of electrons with each of two hydrogen atoms, forming two covalent bonds.

Numbers of Bonds The number of bonds an atom can form usually equals the number of additional electrons that will fill its highest energy level. A hydrogen atom can accept one additional electron, so it can form one bond. In contrast, an oxygen atom can accept two electrons in its highest energy level, so it can form two bonds.

Molecules Two or more atoms held together by covalent bonds form a **molecule.** Molecules can be modeled in different ways (Figure 4-10). A *chemical formula* tells you the number and types of atoms in a molecule. For example, the chemical formula H_2O indicates that a water molecule contains two atoms of hydrogen and one atom of oxygen. (The absence of a subscript after the oxygen symbol is understood to mean "1.") A *structural formula* indicates how atoms in a molecule are linked by bonds. Each line between symbols represents a single covalent bond—a shared pair of electrons. Double or even triple bonds form when two atoms share two or three pairs of electrons between them. The two lines in the structural formula for oxygen (O_2) indicate that an oxygen molecule contains a double bond. A *space-filling model,* in which color-coded spheres symbolize atoms, is a drawing that depicts a three-dimensional model of a molecule. You will see all three of these representations used in this book.

Figure 4-10 Some molecules consist of atoms of only one element, as in molecules of hydrogen (H_2) and oxygen (O_2). However, most molecules are made of two or more different types of atoms, as in water (H_2O).

Modeling Molecules

Chemical formula	Structural formula	Space-filling model
H_2	H—H	
O_2	O=O	
H_2O	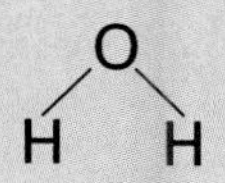 H—O—H (bent)	

Chemical Reactions

Within your cells certain molecules constantly become rearranged into other molecules as existing chemical bonds break (absorbing energy from the surroundings) and new ones form (releasing energy to the surroundings). Such changes, which result in the formation of one or more new substances, are called **chemical reactions.** Some chemical reactions absorb more energy than they release, while others release more energy than they absorb. An example of a reaction that has a net release of energy is the one that occurs between hydrogen and oxygen, forming water (Figure 4-11). In fact, this reaction can be so explosive that it is harnessed to help power the space shuttle.

Figure 4-11 Space-filling models for molecules of hydrogen, oxygen, and water illustrate the chemical reaction that is described by the equation. A water molecule always consists of hydrogen atoms and oxygen atoms in a ratio of 2 to 1.

The expression above, called a chemical equation, is a convenient way to describe a chemical reaction. Just like a math equation, such as 1 + 1 = 2, you read this equation from left to right. It states that two molecules of hydrogen ($2 \times H_2$) react with one molecule of oxygen (O_2), forming two molecules of water ($2 \times H_2O$). The starting materials for the reaction (hydrogen and oxygen) are called **reactants.** The ending materials (in this case, only water) are called **products.**

Notice that the same number of hydrogen atoms (4) is present on both sides of the equation, although the atoms are combined in different molecules. The same is true of the oxygen atoms (2 on each side). Chemical reactions do not create or destroy atoms, but only rearrange them. These rearrangements usually involve breaking chemical bonds in reactants and forming new bonds in products.

Online Activity 4.3

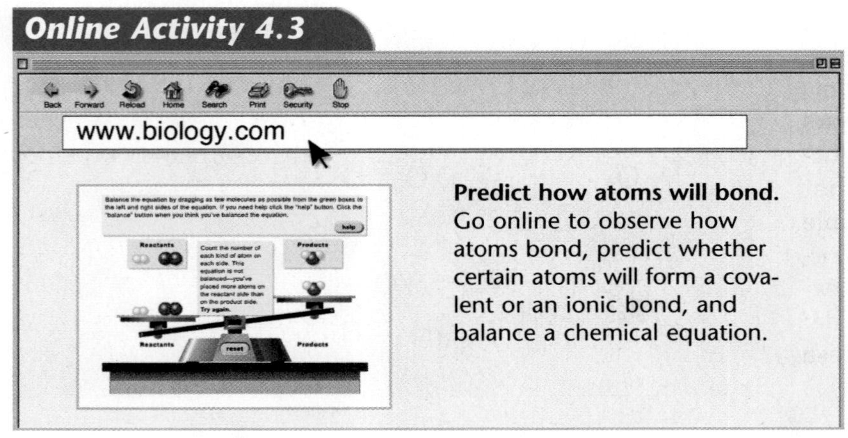

www.biology.com
Predict how atoms will bond.
Go online to observe how atoms bond, predict whether certain atoms will form a covalent or an ionic bond, and balance a chemical equation.

Concept Check 4.3

1. Describe how an ionic bond forms. How is this process different from the formation of a covalent bond?
2. In a molecule represented by the chemical formula $C_6H_{12}O_6$, how many atoms of each element are present?
3. What information does a chemical equation provide about a chemical reaction?
4. A carbon atom has 4 electrons in its highest energy level. How many hydrogen atoms could become bonded to a single carbon atom?

CONCEPT 4.4

Life depends on the unique properties of water.

OBJECTIVES

- Describe the structure of a water molecule.
- List and describe water's unique properties.
- Distinguish between an acid and a base.
- Explain how Earth's conditions are fit for life.

KEY TERMS

- polar molecule
- hydrogen bond
- cohesion
- adhesion
- thermal energy
- temperature
- solution
- solvent
- solute
- aqueous solution
- acid
- base
- pH scale
- buffer

What's Online
www.biology.com
Online Activity 4.4
Investigate the structure and properties of water.
Lab 4 Online Companion
Soil Solutions

All living things are dependent on water. Inside your body, your cells are surrounded by a fluid that is mostly water, and your cells themselves are 70 to 95 percent water. The abundance of water is a major reason Earth can support life. Water is so common that it is easy to overlook its extraordinary properties, which are linked to the structure and interactions of its molecules.

The Structure of Water

A water molecule at first may seem pretty simple. Its two hydrogen atoms are each joined to an oxygen atom by a single covalent bond (Figure 4-12). However, the key to water's unusual properties is that the electrons of each covalent bond are not shared equally between oxygen and hydrogen atoms. Oxygen pulls electrons much more strongly than does hydrogen. Part of the reason is that the oxygen nucleus has eight protons, and therefore has a stronger positive charge than the hydrogen nucleus, which has one proton. This unequal pull results in the shared electrons spending more of their time in the "neighborhood" of the oxygen atom. Note the "V" shape of the water molecule, with the oxygen atom at the base of the "V" opposite the two hydrogen atoms. The unequal sharing of electrons causes the oxygen end of the molecule to have a slight negative charge, while the end with the two hydrogen atoms is slightly positive. A molecule in which opposite ends have opposite electric charges is called a **polar molecule.** Water is a compound consisting of polar molecules.

Water molecules are attracted to one another in a specific way. The slightly negative oxygen end of one molecule attracts the slightly positive hydrogen ends of adjacent water molecules, causing the molecules to become arranged as you see in Figure 4-12. This type of weak attraction between the hydrogen atom of one molecule and a slightly negative atom within another molecule is a type of chemical bond called a **hydrogen bond.** Because the atoms within the water molecules have not transferred an electron (and thus a full unit of charge) to another atom, the attraction in a hydrogen bond is not as strong as that in an ionic bond.

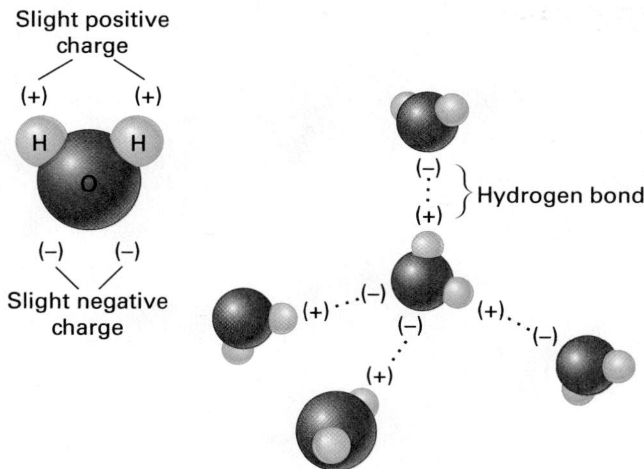

▲ **Figure 4-12** Hydrogen bonds form readily among polar water molecules.

Water's Life-Supporting Properties

The polar nature of water and the effects of hydrogen bonding explain most of water's unique properties. These properties include cohesion and adhesion, temperature moderation, the lower density of ice compared to liquid water, and water's ability to dissolve other substances.

Cohesion and Adhesion Each hydrogen bond between molecules of liquid water lasts for only a few trillionths of a second. Yet, at any instant most of the molecules are involved in hydrogen bonding with other molecules because new hydrogen bonds form as fast as old ones break. This tendency of molecules of the same kind to stick to one another is called **cohesion.** Cohesion is much stronger for water than for most other liquids. Water molecules are also attracted to certain other molecules. The type of attraction that occurs between unlike molecules is called **adhesion.**

Both cohesion and adhesion are important in the living world. One of the most important effects of these forces is keeping large molecules organized and arranged in a way that enables them to function properly in cells. You will read more about this role of water in Chapters 5 and 6.

As another example, trees depend on cohesion and adhesion to help transport water from their roots to their leaves (Figure 4-13). The evaporation of water from leaves pulls water upward from the roots through narrow tubes in the trunk of the tree. Adhesion between water molecules and the walls of the tubes helps resist the downward pull of gravity on the water. And because of cohesion between water molecules, the pulling force caused by evaporation from the leaves is relayed through the tubes all the way down to the roots. As a result, water moves against the force of gravity even to the top of a very tall tree. You've witnessed another example of cohesion if you've ever seen an insect "skating" across the surface of a pond. Cohesion pulls the molecules at the surface tightly together, forming a filmlike boundary that can support the insect. This effect is known as surface tension.

▼ **Figure 4-13** Cohesion and adhesion contribute to the rise of water molecules within a tree's water transport system. The dotted lines in the diagram indicate hydrogen bonds.

Cohesion

Adhesion

▲ **Figure 4-14** The body temperature of this swimmer is higher than that of the surrounding water. She loses thermal energy to the water when heat flows from her body (indicated by the red arrows). In colder water, a greater loss of thermal energy could quickly cause a swimmer to feel chilled.

Temperature Moderation If you have ever burned your finger on a metal pot while waiting for the water in it to boil, you know that water heats up much more slowly than metal. In fact, because of hydrogen bonding, water has a better ability to resist temperature change than most other substances. To understand why, it is first helpful to know a little about energy and temperature. **Thermal energy** is the total amount of energy associated with the random movement of atoms and molecules in a sample of matter. **Temperature** is a measure of the average energy of random motion of the particles in a substance. When two substances differ in temperature, thermal energy in the form of heat is transferred from the warmer substance to the cooler one (Figure 4-14).

When you heat a substance—such as a metal pan or water—its temperature rises because its molecules move faster. But in water, some of the thermal energy that is absorbed goes to break hydrogen bonds. That doesn't happen in the metal pan, which has no hydrogen bonds. As a result, the water absorbs the same amount of thermal energy but undergoes less temperature change than the metal. Conversely, when you cool a substance, the molecules slow and the temperature drops. But as water cools, it forms hydrogen bonds. This releases thermal energy in the form of heat, so there is less of a drop in temperature than in metal.

One result of this property is that it causes oceans and large lakes to moderate the temperatures of nearby land areas. In other words, coastal areas generally have less extreme temperatures than inland areas. For example, a large lake can store a huge amount of thermal energy from the sun during the day. Then at night, heat given off by the gradually cooling water moderates the otherwise more rapid cooling of the air and land.

Water also moderates temperature through evaporation, such as when you sweat. Evaporation occurs when molecules at the surface of a liquid escape to the air. As water molecules evaporate, the remaining liquid becomes cooler. The process of evaporation requires thermal energy to break hydrogen bonds and release water molecules into the air. In sweating, this energy is absorbed from the skin, cooling the body.

Low Density of Ice Density is the amount of matter in a given volume. A high-density substance is more tightly "packed" than a low-density substance. In most substances, the solid state is more dense than the liquid state. Water is just the opposite—its solid form (ice) is less dense than the cold liquid form. Once again, hydrogen bonds are the reason. Every water molecule in ice forms four long-lasting hydrogen bonds with neighboring water molecules, which keep the molecules spaced in a regular pattern (Figure 4-15). Because the molecules in liquid water are moving faster than those in ice, there are fewer and more short-lived hydrogen bonds between molecules. The liquid water molecules can fit more closely together than the molecules in ice. Since substances of lesser density float in substances of greater density, ice floats in liquid water.

How is the fact that ice floats important to living things? If ice sank, it would form on the bottom of a body of water as the water was cooling. Ponds and lakes would freeze from the bottom up, trapping the fish and other organisms in a shrinking layer of water without access to the nutrients from the muddy bottom. Instead, when a deep body of water cools, the floating ice insulates the liquid water below, allowing life to persist under the frozen surface.

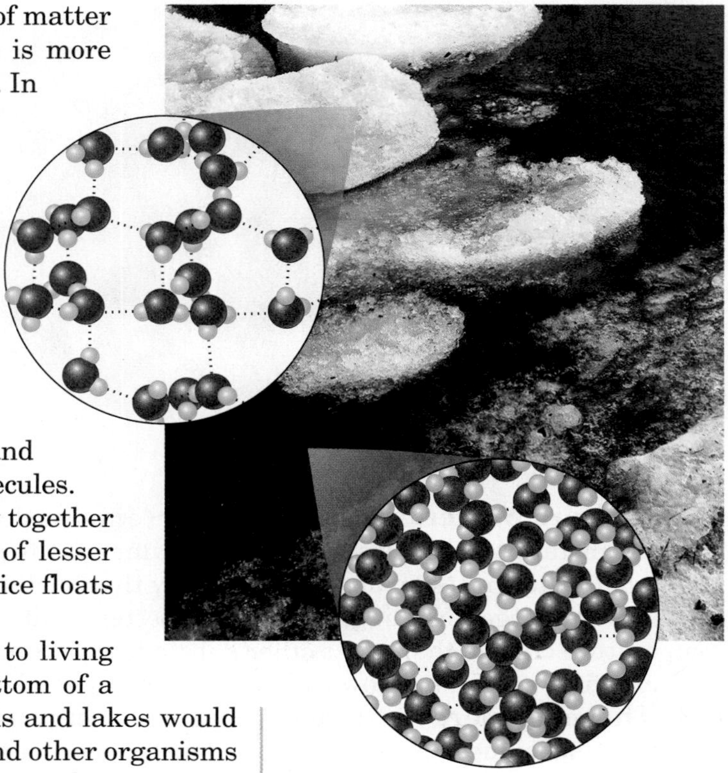

▲ **Figure 4-15** Ice floats because its molecules are less densely packed than those in liquid water.

Water's Ability to Dissolve Other Substances When you stir table salt into a glass of water, you are forming a **solution,** a uniform mixture of two or more substances. The substance that dissolves the other substance and is present in the greater amount is the **solvent** (in this case, water). The substance that is dissolved and is present in a lesser amount is the **solute** (in this case, salt). When water is the solvent, the result is called an **aqueous solution** (from the Latin word *aqua*, "water").

Water is the main solvent inside all cells, in blood, and in plant sap. Water dissolves an enormous variety of solutes necessary for life. Figure 4-16 illustrates how water dissolves ionic compounds such as table salt (sodium chloride). The positive sodium ions at the surface of a sodium chloride crystal attract the oxygen ends of the water molecules. The negative chloride ions attract the hydrogen ends of the water molecules. As a result, water molecules surround each ion, breaking the salt crystal apart in the process.

Water can also dissolve many nonionic compounds, such as sugars. The structures of sugar molecules include polar areas where electrons are shared unevenly between atoms. These areas of slight electric charge attract the polar ends of water molecules. Water molecules cling to these charged regions and separate the sugar molecules from one another.

▲ **Figure 4-16** Sodium chloride dissolves as Na^+ and Cl^- ions become attracted to water molecules and break away from the surface of the solid.

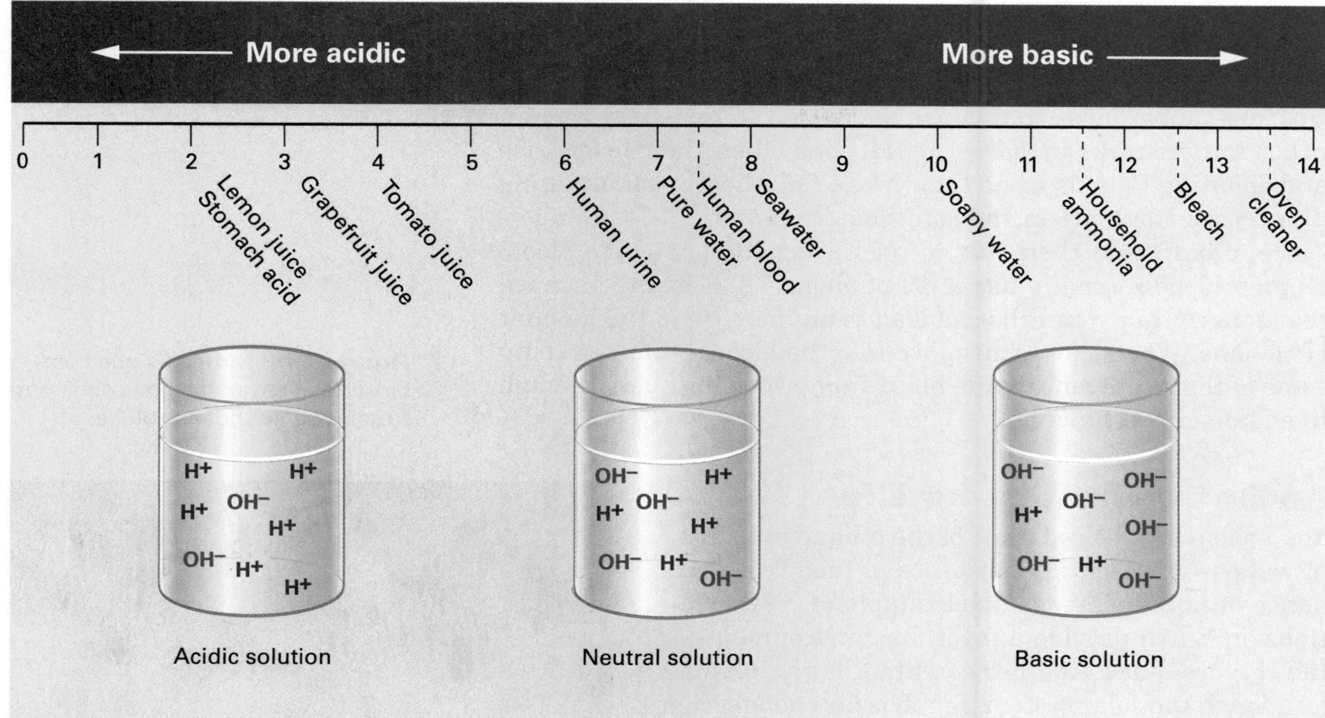

▲ **Figure 4-17** A solution having a pH of 7 is neutral. Many fruits have pH values less than 7, making them acidic. Various household cleaners have pH values greater than 7, making them basic.

Acids, Bases, and pH

In aqueous solutions, a very small percentage of the water molecules themselves break apart into ions. The ions formed are positively charged hydrogen ions (H^+) and negatively charged hydroxide ions (OH^-). (A hydroxide ion is a combination of an oxygen atom and a hydrogen atom that carries a 1– charge.) For the chemical processes of life to work correctly, the right balance of H^+ ions and OH^- ions is critical.

Some chemical compounds contribute additional H^+ ions to an aqueous solution while others remove H^+ ions from it. A compound that donates H^+ ions to a solution is called an **acid.** An example is hydrochloric acid (HCl), the acid in your stomach. In an aqueous solution, hydrochloric acid breaks apart completely into H^+ and Cl^- ions. A compound that removes H^+ ions from an aqueous solution is called a **base.** Some bases, such as sodium hydroxide (NaOH), do this by adding OH^- ions, which then combine with H^+ ions and form water molecules.

The pH Scale The **pH scale** describes how acidic or basic a solution is. The scale ranges from 0 (most acidic) to 14 (most basic) (Figure 4-17). Each pH unit represents a tenfold change in the concentration of H^+ ions. For example, lemon juice at pH 2 has 10 times more H^+ ions than an equal amount of grapefruit juice at pH 3. Pure water and aqueous solutions that have equal amounts of H^+ and OH^- ions are said to be neutral. They have a pH of 7 and are neither acidic nor basic. The pH of the solution inside most living cells is close to 7.

Buffers Because the molecules in cells are very sensitive to concentrations of H^+ and OH^- ions, even a slight change in pH can be harmful to organisms. Many biological fluids contain **buffers,** substances that cause a solution to resist changes in pH. A buffer works by accepting H^+ ions when their levels rise and donating H^+ ions when their levels fall, thereby maintaining a fairly constant pH in the solution. An example of the importance of buffers is their role in regulating the pH of the blood. Human blood normally has a pH of about 7.4. Certain chemical reactions within your cells can lead to an increase in the amount of H^+ ions. When these ions move into the blood, buffers take up some of them, preventing the blood from becoming acidic enough to endanger cell function.

An Environment Fit for Life

You have just explored some of the unique properties of water—an essential substance of life. The abundance of liquid water is one example of how conditions on Earth provide a favorable environment for life (Figure 4-18). Another condition is the planet's location in the solar system. Earth is far enough from the sun that the planet receives a moderate quantity of the energy radiating from the sun, but not so far away that temperatures are too cold to sustain life. At the same time, ozone (a gas made of oxygen atoms) in Earth's upper atmosphere shields the planet's surface from some of the sun's harmful radiation. Yet another factor is the availability in the soil, rock, and atmosphere of elements essential to life. As you will read in Chapter 36, carbon, hydrogen, oxygen, and nitrogen are recycled through living and nonliving parts of the environment and so are constantly available to living organisms. In the next chapter, you will explore how these essential elements are arranged into the molecules of life.

▼ **Figure 4-18** Earth's unique combination of environmental conditions sustains an abundance of life.

Online Activity 4.4

Investigate the structure and properties of water. Go online to examine how the polarity of water contributes to processes in nature. Then conduct virtual experiments to learn about acids, bases, and buffers.

Concept Check 4.4

1. Explain how the structure of water molecules results in attractions among them.
2. Give an example of how cohesion among water molecules is important to living things.
3. Describe the information the pH scale provides.
4. Name three conditions on Earth that make the planet suitable for life.
5. Explain one way in which water can moderate temperature.

Soil Solutions

Exploring Ions Found in Soil

Questions Which ions will be dissolved when soil is mixed with water? How do the amounts of these ions vary in soils from different locations?

Lab Overview In this investigation you will collect and test soil from two locations. One sample will be soil you predict to be high in ions important to plants, and the other will be soil you predict to be low in these ions. You will use a soil testing kit to find out if your predictions were correct.

Preparing for the Lab To help you prepare for the investigation, go to the *Lab 4 Online Companion.* ······➔ Explore how ions in soil provide a source of nutrients for plant growth. The activity will also provide clues that will help you choose where to collect your soil samples. Prepare for the lab procedure by previewing the steps you will take.

Completing the Lab Use your Laboratory Manual or lab page printouts from the *Lab 4 Online Companion* to do the investigation and analyze your results. **CAUTION:** *Be sure to follow your teacher's instructions and all safety guidelines given in the investigation.*

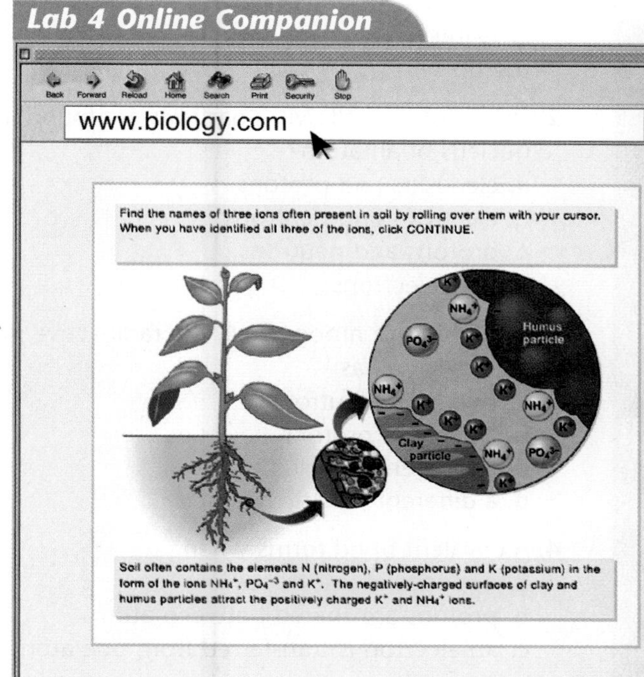

Lab 4 Online Companion
Back
Forward
Reload
Home
Search
Print
Security
Stop
www.biology.com
Find the names of three ions often present in soil by rolling over them with your cursor. When you have identified all three of the ions, click CONTINUE.
K^+
NH_4^+
PO_4^{3-}
Humus particle
Clay particle
Soil often contains the elements N (nitrogen), P (phosphorus) and K (potassium) in the form of the ions NH_4^+, PO_4^{-3} and K^+. The negatively-charged surfaces of clay and humus particles attract the positively charged K^+ and NH_4^+ ions.

Multiple Choice

Choose the letter of the best answer.

1. Which of the following is not an element?
 a. hydrogen
 b. carbon
 c. water
 d. iron

2. Which of the following particles are found in the nucleus of an atom?
 a. electrons and protons
 b. electrons and neutrons
 c. protons and neutrons
 d. only electrons

3. Compared to nitrogen-14, the radioactive isotope nitrogen-16 has
 a. two more neutrons.
 b. two more protons.
 c. a different atomic number.
 d. a different electric charge.

4. A covalent bond forms when
 a. opposite ions attract.
 b. protons are shared between atoms.
 c. an electron is transferred from one atom to another.
 d. two atoms share a pair of electrons.

5. Substances formed by a chemical reaction are called
 a. reactants.
 b. products.
 c. chemical formulas.
 d. chemical equations.

6. Which of the following properties of water is *not* a result of hydrogen bonding?
 a. cohesion
 b. ability to dissolve many substances
 c. lower density of ice compared to liquid water
 d. ratio of hydrogen to oxygen in water molecules

7. A solution with a pH of 9 is
 a. acidic.
 b. basic.
 c. neutral.
 d. higher in H^+ ions than in OH^- ions.

Short Answer

8. What four essential elements make up most of living matter?

9. List three subatomic particles. For each particle, state where it is located in the atom and what electric charge it has (if any).

10. How are the number of electrons in an atom's highest energy level related to the reactivity of that atom?

11. How is a potassium atom (K) different from a potassium ion (K^+)?

12. Summarize the information represented in a chemical equation.

13. Explain what makes a water molecule polar.

14. Explain how water can absorb large amounts of thermal energy without having a similarly large increase in temperature.

15. Describe how the properties of water molecules contribute to the upward movement of water through a tall tree.

16. What is an aqueous solution?

17. How does a buffer keep a solution from becoming too acidic?

18. Describe two conditions on Earth that make the planet favorable for life.

Visualizing Concepts

19. The diagrams below represent atoms of carbon and hydrogen. These two elements can combine to form the compound methane, which has a ratio of one carbon atom to four hydrogen atoms in its molecules. Using these diagrams and colored pencils or pens, draw a model of a molecule of methane. Then write the chemical formula for the compound.

Carbon atom

H·

Hydrogen atom

Analyzing Information

20. Analyzing Diagrams Use the diagrams of atoms below to answer the following questions:

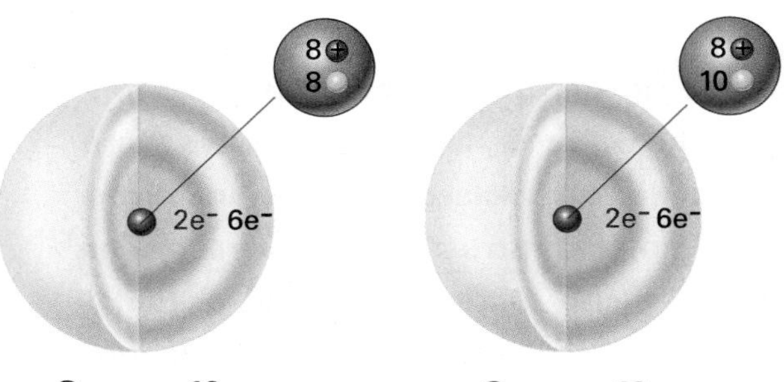

a. What is the relationship between these two atoms of oxygen? Explain.

b. What is the atomic number of oxygen? How do you know?

c. How many covalent bonds can either one of these oxygen atoms form? Explain.

21. Analyzing Data Use the data table below to answer the following questions.

pH Values of Familiar Solutions

Solution	pH
Lime juice	1.8
Vinegar	3.0
Tomato juice	4.2
Normal rainfall	5.5
Milk	6.3
Baking soda solution	8.3
Drain cleaner	14.0

a. Which sample in the table is most acidic?

b. Which sample listed has a pH that is closest to neutral?

c. In equal volumes of normal rainfall and baking soda solution, which sample would have a greater amount of hydrogen ions (H^+) present? Explain.

Critical Thinking

22. Relating Cause and Effect Element X has 8 electrons in the highest energy level of its atoms. Is element X likely to be very reactive? Explain.

23. Comparing and Contrasting How is an aqueous solution of table salt different from an aqueous solution of table sugar? Describe how each solution forms.

24. Evaluating Promotional Claims Suppose a cosmetics manufacturer advertises a shampoo as "having a pH as gentle as rainwater." Describe how you might determine whether the promotional claim is valid.

25. Making Generalizations How is energy involved in the chemical reaction that produces water from hydrogen and oxygen?

26. What's Wrong With These Statements? *Briefly explain why each statement is inaccurate or misleading.*

a. An ion is electrically neutral.

b. A chemical reaction occurs whenever matter is created.

c. Ice floats because it is lighter than liquid water.

Performance Assessment

Design an Experiment You have learned that attractions between water molecules help move water through a plant. Design an experiment that would demonstrate that the direction of this movement is from the roots to the leaves and not the opposite.

Online Assessment/Test Preparation

Back Forward Reload Home Search Print Security Stop

www.biology.com

- **Chapter 4 Assessment**
  Check your understanding of the chapter concepts.
- **Standardized Test Preparation**
  Practice test-taking skills you need to succeed.

The Molecules of Life

From the giant lily pads in this pond to the slender tree trunks on its banks to the delicate wings of insects humming in the warm air, all life's structures share a common element: carbon. The carbon-containing molecules of life range from simple structures of just a few atoms to complex constructions of several million atoms. Some of these molecules function as sources of energy, others as tools and machinery, and still others as storage for massive amounts of information. In this chapter, you will read about how these carbon-based molecules are made and how they function. Before you begin, go online to the ***WebQuest*** to explore biological molecules in some familiar foods.

Key Concepts

Concept 5.1

Carbon is the main ingredient of organic molecules.

Concept 5.2

Carbohydrates provide fuel and building material.

Concept 5.3

Lipids include fats and steroids.

Concept 5.4

Proteins perform most functions in cells.

Concept 5.5

Enzymes are proteins that speed up specific reactions in cells.

Assessment

Chapter 5 Review

What's Online

www.biology.com

WebQuest
PizzaQuest

Online Activity 5.1
Examine carbon-based molecules.

Online Activity 5.2
Analyze the role of glucose in life processes.

Careers
Meet Two Biochemists

Online Activity 5.3
Explore the properties of lipids.

Online Activity 5.4
Build amino acid chains.

Closer Look
Protein Structure

Online Activity 5.5
Investigate the role of enzymes in nature.

Lab 5 Online Companion
Way to Go, Indigo!

Chapter 5 Assessment

CONCEPT 5.1

Carbon is the main ingredient of organic molecules.

OBJECTIVES

- Identify carbon skeletons and functional groups in organic molecules.
- Relate monomers and polymers.
- Describe the processes of building and breaking polymers.

KEY TERMS

- organic molecule
- inorganic molecule
- hydrocarbon
- functional group
- hydrophilic
- monomer
- polymer

What's Online

www.biology.com

Online Activity 5.1
Examine carbon-based molecules.

Life without carbon would be as unlikely as life without water. Other than water, most molecules of a cell are carbon-based. These "biomolecules" are composed of a backbone of carbon atoms bonded to one another. Atoms of other elements may branch off this carbon backbone. This basic structure is the foundation of the wide range of life's molecules.

Carbon Skeletons and Functional Groups

Why are carbon atoms so common in living things? Remember from Chapter 4 that an atom's bonding ability is related to the number of electrons in its highest occupied energy level. Carbon has only 4 electrons in its highest occupied energy level. Because this energy level can hold 8 electrons, carbon can form up to 4 bonds with other atoms. Each carbon atom is a connecting point from which other atoms can branch off in up to four directions.

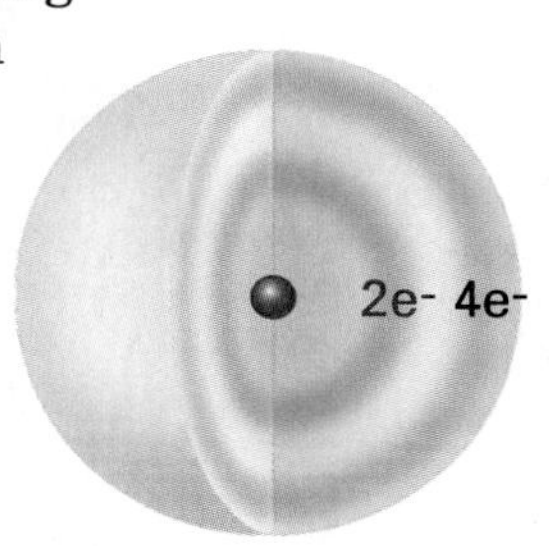

Carbon (C)

Carbon can form bonds with one or more other carbon atoms, producing an endless variety of carbon skeletons (Figure 5-1). Most carbon-based molecules are classified as **organic molecules.** In contrast, non-carbon-based molecules such as water (H_2O), oxygen (O_2), and ammonia (NH_3) are classified as **inorganic molecules.**

Besides bonding with other carbon atoms, carbon may also bond with atoms of other elements. For example, organic molecules that are composed of only carbon and hydrogen are known as **hydrocarbons.** Many hydrocarbons are important fuels. Methane (CH_4) is one of the most abundant hydrocarbons

Figure 5-1 The carbon backbones of organic molecules can take many shapes. These molecules may include single, double, and rarely, triple bonds. The only rule is that each carbon forms a total of four bonds.

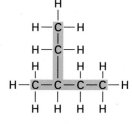

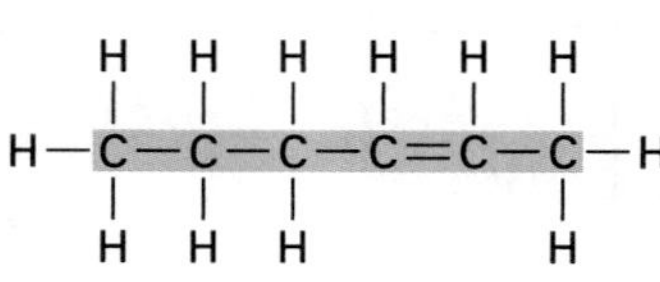
Straight chain

Branched chain

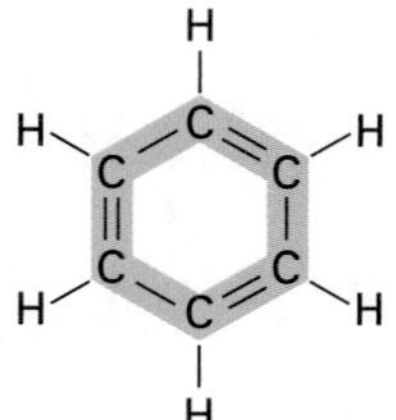
Ring

Hydroxyl group

Carbonyl group

Carboxyl group

Amino group

▲ **Figure 5-2** These four common functional groups give specific properties to the organic molecules that contain them.

in natural gas, a fuel used to heat homes. In your body, energy-storing fat molecules contain long hydrocarbon chains. In addition to hydrogen, two other atoms frequently found in organic molecules are oxygen and nitrogen.

A group of atoms within a molecule that interacts in predictable ways with other molecules is called a **functional group.** Figure 5-2 shows some of the functional groups important in the chemistry of life. Together, the carbon skeleton and the attached functional groups determine the properties of an organic molecule. For example, hydroxyl groups are **hydrophilic,** meaning they attract water molecules. Thus, most organic molecules that contain hydroxyl groups are hydrophilic, which literally means "water-loving." These molecules tend to become surrounded by water molecules in an aqueous environment.

Monomers and Polymers

Some biomolecules may be composed of hundreds or even millions of atoms. These large molecules are built from many similar, smaller molecular units called **monomers.** Your cells link monomers together into long chains called **polymers.** A polymer may be a straight chain of monomers, much as a train is a string of many individual cars. Other polymers have branching chains or chains that fold back on themselves.

The diversity of life's polymers is vast. Every living cell has thousands of different kinds of polymers. The specific molecules vary from cell to cell within an organism. The variety of polymers differs among individuals of the same species, and even more among organisms of different species (Figure 5-3). And yet, all of these polymers are built from a collection of fewer than 50 kinds of monomers.

Life's large molecules are classified into four main categories: carbohydrates, lipids, proteins, and nucleic acids. In the next sections of this chapter, you'll explore the properties of carbohydrates, lipids, and proteins. The structure and role of nucleic acids, such as DNA, will be explored in depth in Chapter 11. But first, turn the page to find out how polymers are constructed and broken down.

▲ **Figure 5-3** The protein that makes up a spider's web is one example of a polymer.

Building a Polymer Chain

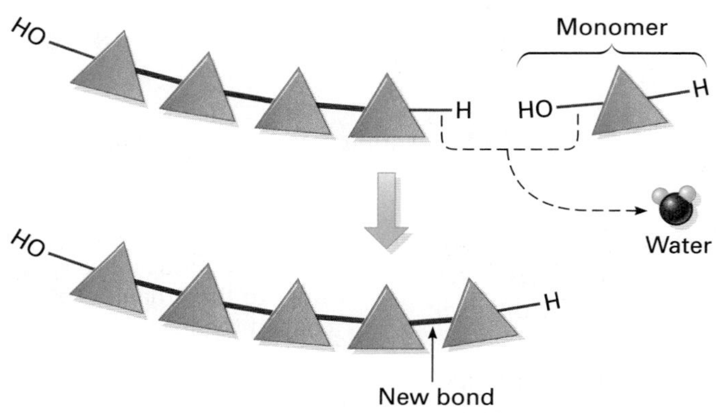

▲ **Figure 5-4** In the dehydration reaction, two monomers bond to each other, making a polymer chain longer. The hydroxyl group of one monomer reacts with a hydrogen atom from the other monomer. The reactions involved ultimately release a water molecule.

Building and Breaking Polymers

Each time a monomer is added to a chain, a water molecule is released (Figure 5-4). This is called a *dehydration reaction* because it involves removing (*de-*) water (*hydro-*). This same type of reaction occurs regardless of the specific monomers and the type of polymer being produced.

Organisms not only build polymers; they also have to break them down. For example, many of the molecules in your food are polymers. You must break down these giant molecules to make their monomers available to your cells. Your cells can either further break down the monomers to obtain energy, or, alternatively, use them to build new polymers. Cells break bonds between monomers by adding water to them, the reverse of dehydration (Figure 5-5). This process is called a *hydrolysis reaction* because water (*hydro-*) is used to break down (*-lysis*) the polymer. To summarize, water is removed to build a polymer, and water is added to break it down.

Breaking a Polymer Chain

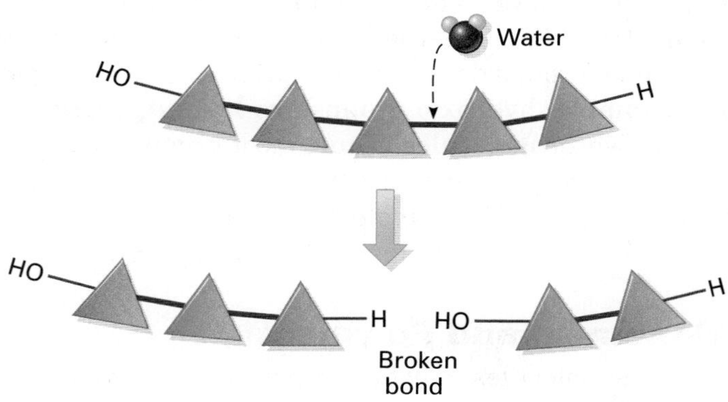

▲ **Figure 5-5** In the hydrolysis reaction, the addition of a water molecule breaks the polymer chain.

Online Activity 5.1

www.biology.com

Examine carbon-based molecules.
Go online to classify inorganic and organic molecules. Then examine how a polymer chain is built and broken down.

Concept Check 5.1

1. Draw a molecule that has a three-carbon skeleton and a hydroxyl group on the middle carbon. (*Hint:* The molecule's formula is C_3H_8O.)
2. Explain the connection between monomers and polymers.
3. What molecule is released during construction of a polymer? What is this reaction called?
4. Draw at least three ways in which five carbon atoms could be joined to make different carbon skeletons.

CONCEPT 5.2

Carbohydrates provide fuel and building material.

OBJECTIVES

- Describe the basic structure and function of sugars.
- Name three polysaccharides and describe their functions.

KEY TERMS

- carbohydrate
- monosaccharide
- disaccharide
- polysaccharide
- starch
- glycogen
- cellulose

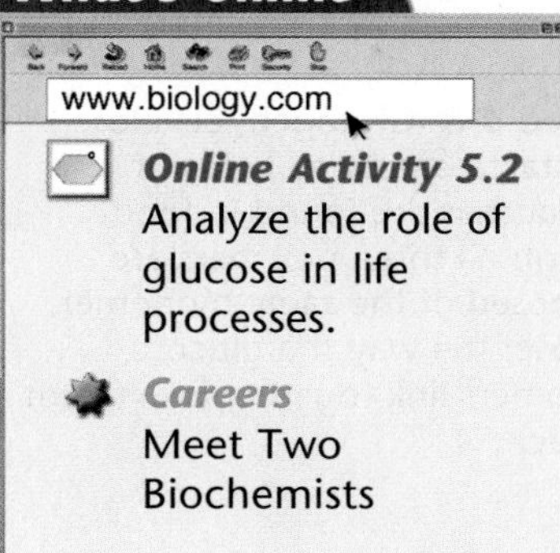

What's Online
www.biology.com
Online Activity 5.2
Analyze the role of glucose in life processes.
Careers
Meet Two Biochemists

Have you ever heard athletes talk about "carbs"? What are they referring to? "Carbs," which is short for *carbohydrates,* include the small sugar molecules dissolved in sport drinks as well as the long starch molecules in pasta and potatoes. Carbohydrates can be called upon as an energy source just minutes after a meal, or can be stored away for later use. They are an important source of energy for athletes (and everyone else). In this section you will learn how carbohydrates are used by living things.

Sugars

A **carbohydrate** is an organic compound made up of sugar molecules. Sugars contain the elements carbon, hydrogen, and oxygen in the ratio of 1 carbon: 2 hydrogen: 1 oxygen. The molecular formula of any carbohydrate is a multiple of the basic formula CH_2O. At the core of most sugar molecules found in nature are carbon skeletons that have a ring shape.

Monosaccharides Simple sugars contain just one sugar unit and are called **monosaccharides** (mahn oh SAK uh rydz). Glucose, fructose, and galactose are examples of monosaccharides. (Notice that the names of sugars end in the suffix *-ose*.) One or more of these simple sugars are found in many sweet things you eat. Honey, for example, contains both glucose and fructose.

Glucose exists in both straight-chain and ring-shaped forms. Figure 5-6 shows the complete molecular structure of glucose in its ring form, as well as a simplified diagram that shows only its core ring. This book will use the simplified representation of sugars in most diagrams.

Figure 5-6 The complete structural diagram of the monosaccharide glucose (left) shows all its atoms. The simplified representation (right) shows just the core ring formed by some of the carbon and oxygen atoms. Ring shapes are common in sugar molecules found in nature.

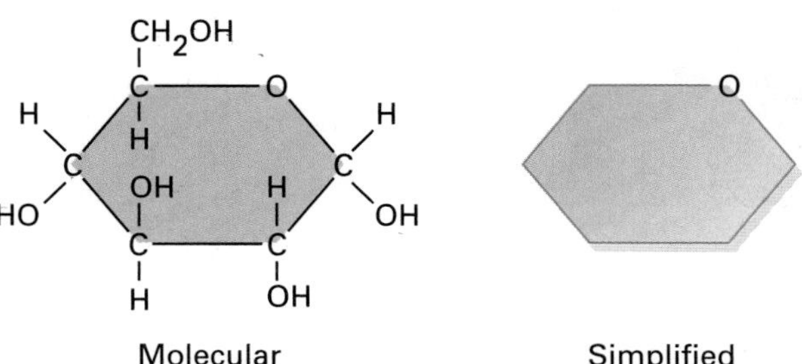

Sugar molecules, particularly glucose, are the main fuel supply for cellular work. Similar to an automobile engine burning gasoline, cells break down glucose molecules and extract their stored energy. This process is described in detail in Chapter 7. Cells also use the carbon skeletons of monosaccharides as raw material for manufacturing other kinds of organic molecules. Glucose molecules that are not used immediately by cells are usually incorporated into larger carbohydrates, or they may be used to make fat molecules.

Disaccharides Using the dehydration reaction, cells construct a **disaccharide** (dy SAK uh ryd) or "double sugar," from two monosaccharides. The most common disaccharide is sucrose (Figure 5-7). Sucrose consists of a glucose molecule linked to a fructose molecule. Sucrose is a major carbohydrate in plant sap, and it nourishes all the parts of the plant. For example, the sap of maple trees (maple syrup) contains sucrose. Table sugar is sucrose processed from the stems of sugarcane or the roots of sugar beets. Once consumed, sucrose can be broken down into glucose and fructose and used right away. The body can also store glucose in larger molecules for later use.

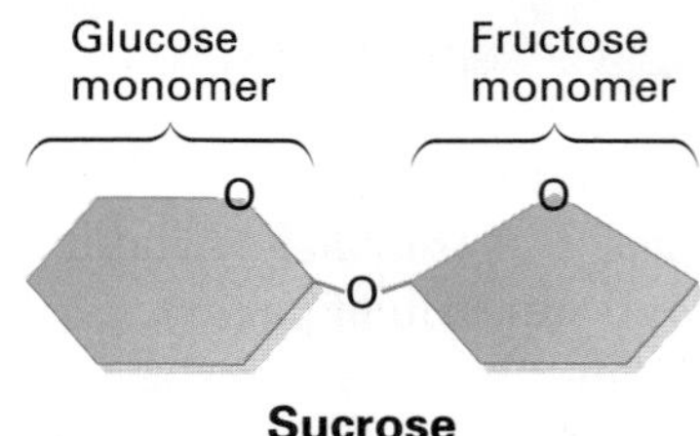
Glucose monomer
Fructose monomer
O
O
O
Sucrose

▲ **Figure 5-7** Sucrose is a disaccharide (double sugar) consisting of two monosaccharides linked together.

Polysaccharides

Long polymer chains made up of simple sugar monomers are called **polysaccharides** (pah lih SAK uh rydz), or complex carbohydrates (Figure 5-8). For example, **starch** is a polysaccharide found in plant cells that consists entirely of glucose monomers. Inside a plant cell, such as a potato cell, starch chains branch and coil up like the loops of a telephone cord. The starch chains serve as sugar stockpiles. Plant cells, like animal cells, need sugar for energy to perform work, and as raw material for building other molecules. When plants break down starch molecules, the stored glucose becomes available. Humans and most other animals are also able to use plant starch as food by breaking it down within their digestive systems. Potatoes, rice, and corn are examples of foods rich in starch.

▼ **Figure 5-8** Glycogen, cellulose, and starch are three types of polysaccharides found in food. Though all three polymers are composed of the same monomer, glucose, the way the glucose monomers link together is different for each.

Glycogen stores energy in turkey muscle cells.
Cellulose makes broccoli stem fibers rigid.
Glucose monomer
Starch stores energy in potato cells.

Animal cells do not contain starch. Instead, animals such as turkeys (and humans) store excess sugar in the form of a polysaccharide called **glycogen** (GLY kuh jun). Glycogen, like starch, is a chain of many glucose monomers. However, a glycogen polymer is more highly branched than a starch polymer. In humans, most glycogen is stored as granules in liver and muscle cells. When the body needs energy, it breaks down these glycogen granules, releasing glucose.

Some polysaccharides in plants, such as **cellulose,** serve as building materials. They protect cells and stiffen the plant, preventing it from flopping over. Like starch and glycogen, cellulose is also made of glucose monomers. Multiple cellulose chains are linked together with hydrogen bonds, forming cable-like fibers in the tough walls that enclose plant cells, such as the cells of broccoli stems.

Most animals, including people, cannot digest cellulose because they lack the molecule necessary to break the bonds between the glucose monomers in cellulose. Therefore, cellulose from plant foods, commonly referred to as "fiber," passes unchanged through your digestive system. Cellulose helps keep your digestive system healthy, but it does not serve as a nutrient. In contrast, some organisms, such as cows and termites, can derive nutrition from cellulose. Microorganisms that inhabit their digestive tracts break down the cellulose, making glucose available to the cow or termite.

Almost all carbohydrates are hydrophilic. This is due to the many hydroxyl groups in their sugar units. (Recall that the hydroxyl functional group attracts water.) Therefore, monosaccharides and disaccharides dissolve readily in water, forming sugary solutions. Cellulose and some forms of starch, however, are such large molecules that they do not dissolve in water. If they did, then your cotton T-shirt or jeans, which are mostly cellulose, would dissolve the first time you were caught in a rainstorm! But though they are not soluble in water, note that these large carbohydrates are still hydrophilic. That is one reason why cotton bath towels can absorb so much water.

Careers

Back Forward Reload Home Search Print Security Stop

www.biology.com

Meet Two Biochemists

Kay Gray and her son, Chris Nelson, are biochemists working at different companies. They have a common mission: to find a drug that will destroy cancer cells without harming the human body. Go online to explore their career choices and why they find their work rewarding.

Online Activity 5.2

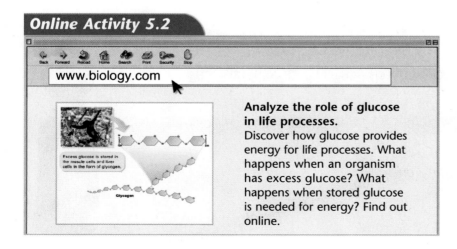

Back Forward Reload Home Search Print Security Stop

www.biology.com

Excess glucose is stored in the muscle cells and liver cells in the form of glycogen.

Glycogen

Analyze the role of glucose in life processes.

Discover how glucose provides energy for life processes. What happens when an organism has excess glucose? What happens when stored glucose is needed for energy? Find out online.

Concept Check 5.2

1. Explain the difference between a monosaccharide and a disaccharide. Give an example of each.
2. Compare and contrast starch, glycogen, and cellulose.
3. How do animals store excess glucose molecules?

CONCEPT 5.3 Lipids include fats and steroids.

OBJECTIVES

- Identify a general characteristic of lipids.
- Describe the structure and function of fats.
- Describe the structure and function of steroids.

KEY TERMS

- lipid
- hydrophobic
- fat
- saturated fat
- unsaturated fat
- steroid
- cholesterol

What's Online

Online Activity 5.3
Explore the properties of lipids.

Have you ever noticed the instruction "Shake well before using" on a bottle of salad dressing? The oil in most dressings doesn't mix well with the vinegar, which is mostly water. When you shake the bottle you force a temporary mixture long enough to douse your salad with dressing. However, the dressing will quickly separate again once you stop shaking the bottle.

Characteristics of Lipids

Oil's inability to mix with water is typical of the class of water-avoiding compounds called **lipids.** Water-avoiding molecules are said to be **hydrophobic,** meaning "water-fearing." This property of lipids is important to their function. For example, lipids act as a boundary that surrounds and contains the aqueous (watery) contents of your cells. Other types of lipid molecules circulate in your body as chemical signals to cells. Still other lipids known as fats store energy in your body.

Fats

A **fat** consists of a three-carbon backbone called glycerol attached to three fatty acids, which contain long hydrocarbon chains (Figure 5-9). Some fats are solid at room temperature. Other fats called oils are liquids at room temperature. In addition to storing energy for later use, fatty tissues cushion your organs and provide your body with insulation.

You have probably seen the terms *saturated fat* and *unsaturated fat* on food labels. A **saturated fat** is a fat in which all three fatty acid chains contain the maximum possible number of hydrogen atoms. In other words, all the carbon atoms in the fatty acid chains

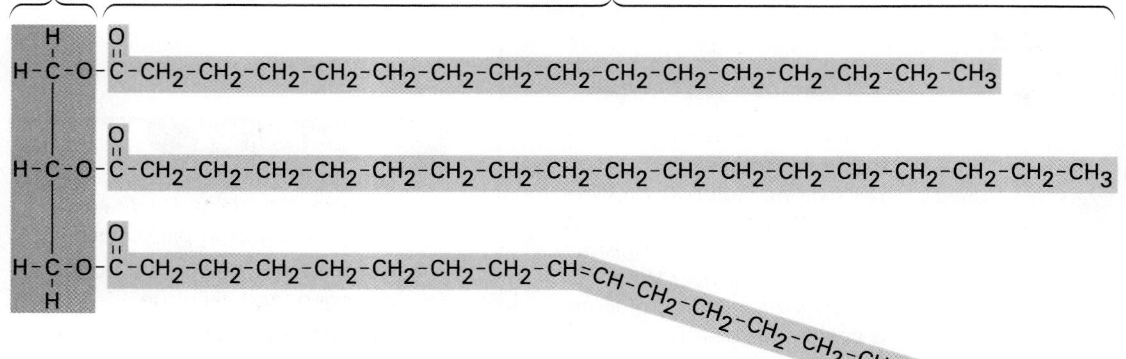

Figure 5-9 Certain vegetable oils contain unsaturated fat molecules, which have at least one double bond in at least one of the fatty acid chains. In this case, the double bond is located about halfway along the bottom chain.

form single bonds with each other, and the rest of their bonds are with hydrogen atoms. Most animal fats, such as lard and butter, are saturated. They are solid at room temperature. An **unsaturated fat,** such as the one in Figure 5-9, contains less than the maximum number of hydrogen atoms in one or more of its fatty acid chains because some of its carbon atoms are double-bonded to each other. The fats in fruits, vegetables, and fish are generally unsaturated, as are corn oil, olive oil, and other vegetable oils.

Diets rich in saturated fats may be unhealthy. Such diets may promote the buildup of lipid-containing deposits, called plaques, within the walls of blood vessels. These plaques can reduce blood flow and contribute to heart disease.

Steroids

A lipid molecule in which the carbon skeleton forms four fused rings is called a **steroid.** While all steroids have a core set of four rings, they differ in the kinds and locations of functional groups attached to the rings.

Steroids are classified as lipids because they are hydrophobic, but they are very different from fats in structure and function. Some steroids circulate in your body as chemical signals. The steroids estrogen, a female sex hormone, and testosterone, a male sex hormone, function in this way (Figure 5-10). Notice the small differences in their functional groups. These variations cause some major differences in appearance between male and female mammals, including men and women.

▲ **Figure 5-10** The only difference in these two steroid hormones is the location of their functional groups. Yet, these two molecules contribute to major differences in the appearance and behavior of male and female mammals.

Perhaps the best-known steroid is cholesterol. **Cholesterol** is an essential molecule found in the membranes that surround your cells. It is also the starting point from which your body produces other steroids. Despite its necessity, cholesterol has a bad reputation because high levels of particular cholesterol-containing substances in the blood are linked to increased risk for cardiovascular (heart and blood vessel) disease.

Online Activity 5.3

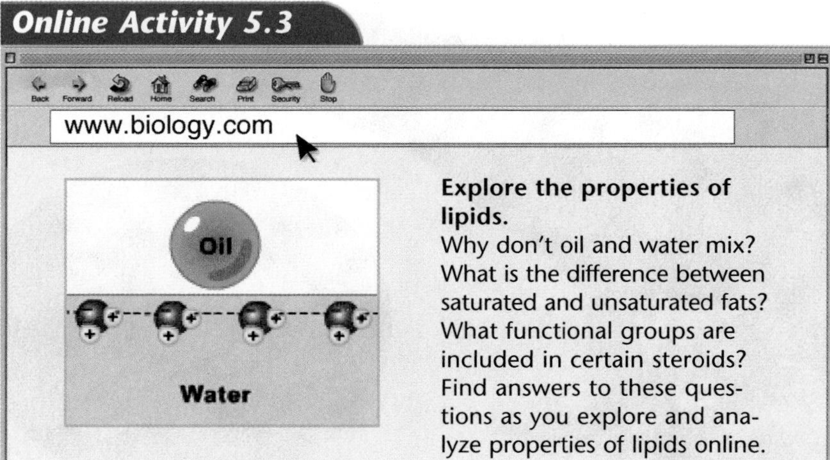

Explore the properties of lipids.
Why don't oil and water mix? What is the difference between saturated and unsaturated fats? What functional groups are included in certain steroids? Find answers to these questions as you explore and analyze properties of lipids online.

Concept Check 5.3

1. What property do lipids share?
2. What are the parts of a fat molecule?
3. Describe two ways that steroids differ from fats.
4. What does the term *unsaturated fat* on a food label mean?

CONCEPT 5.4

Proteins perform most functions in cells.

OBJECTIVES

- List functions of proteins.
- Describe the structure of amino acids and proteins.
- Describe factors that influence protein shape.

KEY TERMS

- protein
- amino acid
- polypeptide
- denaturation

What's Online

Online Activity 5.4 Build amino acid chains.

Closer Look Protein Structure

The word *protein* comes from the Greek word meaning "first place." This term suggests the importance of this class of polymers. There are tens of thousands of different kinds of proteins. Each one has a unique, three-dimensional structure that corresponds to a specific function. This diversity enables proteins to provide the molecular tool kit for almost everything cells do.

The Functions of Proteins

A **protein** is a polymer constructed from a set of just 20 kinds of monomers called amino acids. Proteins are responsible for almost all of the day-to-day functioning of organisms. For example, proteins form structures such as hair and fur, make up muscles, and provide long-term nutrient storage (Figure 5-11). Proteins with less-visible functions include proteins that circulate in the blood and defend the body from harmful microorganisms, and others that act as signals, conveying messages from one cell to another. Another group of proteins controls the chemical reactions in a cell. As you might expect, the structure of proteins is the key to understanding their elaborate and diverse functions.

▼ **Figure 5-11** Proteins have many functions in organisms. Along with other roles, they provide the texture of an animal's coat (left), the powerful muscles of a crouching panther (middle), and much of the food value of nuts in a chipmunk's cache (right).

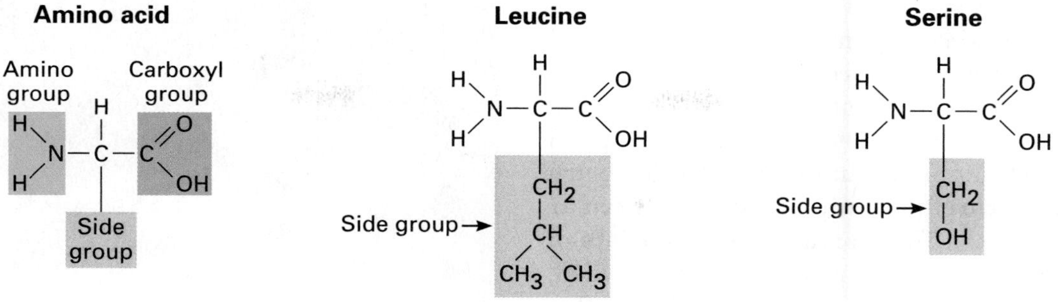

Amino acid — Amino group; Carboxyl group; Side group

Leucine — Side group

Serine — Side group

Amino Acids

Each **amino acid** monomer consists of a central carbon atom bonded to four partners (a carbon atom, remember, forms four covalent bonds). Three of the central carbon's partners are the same in all amino acids. One partner is a hydrogen atom. Two others are a carboxyl group and an amino group, functional groups that you read about in Concept 5.1.

What is different about each type of amino acid is the "side group" that attaches to the fourth bond of the central carbon (Figure 5-12). The side group, sometimes called the "R-group," is responsible for the particular chemical properties of each amino acid. For example, the side group of the amino acid called leucine is a hydrocarbon. That region of leucine is hydrophobic. In contrast, the side group of the amino acid serine contains a hydroxyl group that attracts water.

▲ **Figure 5-12** All amino acids consist of a central carbon bonded to an amino group, a carboxyl group, and a hydrogen atom. The fourth bond is with a unique side group. The differences in side groups convey different properties to each amino acid.

Building a Protein

Cells create proteins by linking amino acids together into a chain called a **polypeptide.** Each link is created by a dehydration reaction between the amino group of one amino acid and the carboxyl group of the next amino acid in the chain. Proteins are composed of one or more polypeptide chains.

Your body can make an enormous variety of proteins by arranging different amino acids in different orders. Think of how you can make thousands of different English words by using different combinations of 26 letters. Though the protein alphabet is slightly smaller, with just 20 "letters" (amino acids), the "words" are much longer. Most polypeptide chains are at least 100 amino acids in length. Because there are 20 choices for each amino acid in the chain, there is a very large number of possible amino acid sequences and therefore, a very large number of possible polypeptides. Just as each word in the English language is constructed from a unique sequence of letters, each protein has a unique sequence of amino acids (Figure 5-13).

▼ **Figure 5-13** The order of amino acids makes each polypeptide unique. There are 129 amino acids in this protein, called lysozyme. The three-letter symbols are abbreviations for the amino acid names.

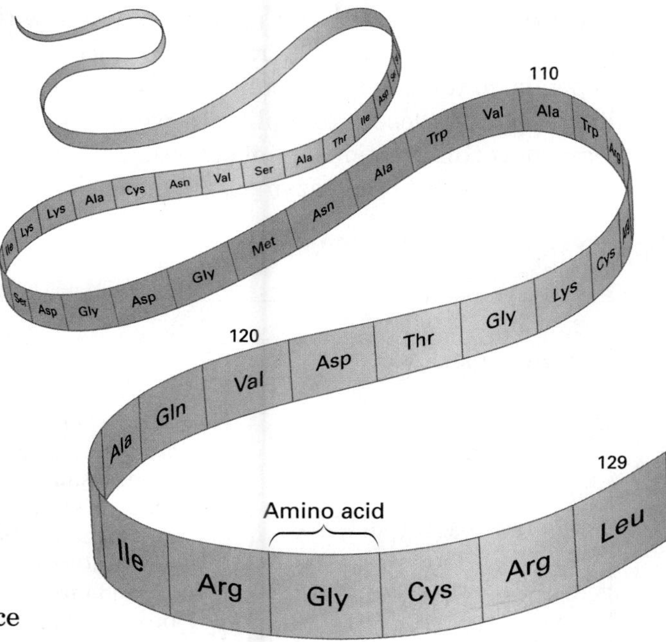

Protein Shape

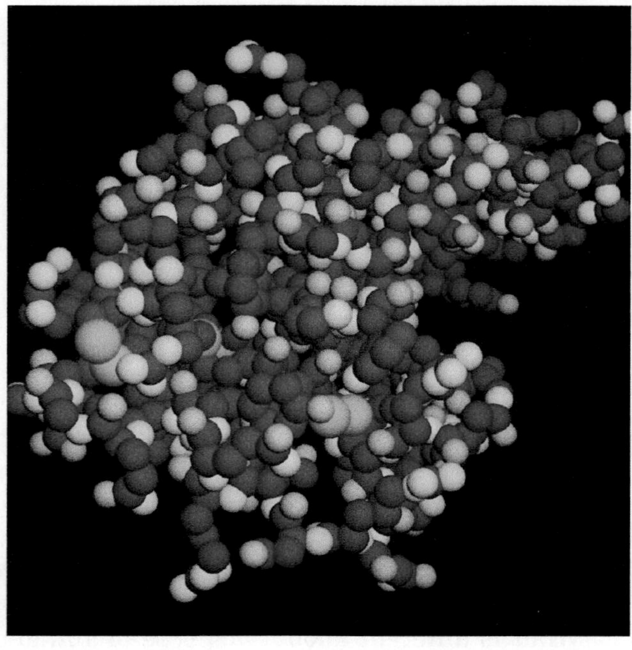

▲ **Figure 5-14** The three-dimensional shape of a protein molecule is determined by the interactions of its amino acids. This computer model shows the shape of the same protein (lysozyme) whose amino acid sequence you saw in Figure 5-13.

A protein in the simple form of amino acids linked together cannot function properly. You might compare this with the relationship between a long strand of yarn and a finished sweater. A functional sweater is not simply a bundle of yarn, but yarn that has been carefully knitted into a particular shape. Likewise, a functional protein consists of one or more polypeptides precisely twisted, folded, and coiled into a unique shape (Figure 5-14). But how does the protein fold in exactly the right way? The answer is not fully understood, but the sequence of amino acids is certainly important. For example, some side groups form bonds with each other. These forces help to fold a polypeptide and to keep it folded.

A protein's shape is also influenced by the surrounding environment, which is usually aqueous. Water attracts hydrophilic side groups and rejects hydrophobic ones. Therefore, hydrophilic amino acids tend to orient towards the outside edges of the protein, and hydrophobic amino acids cluster in the center of the protein.

An unfavorable change in temperature, pH, or some other quality of the environment can cause a protein to unravel and lose its normal shape. This process is called **denaturation** of the protein. You may have witnessed denaturation in action while frying an egg. The egg white changes from a clear liquid to a white solid during cooking because heat denatures the egg's proteins. The polypeptide chains become tangled up with one another. Heating unfolds proteins because most of the forces that maintain folding are weak attractions between pairs of side groups, and between side groups and water. Hot molecules collide with enough force to overcome these weak attractions. Since a protein's function depends on its shape, a protein that becomes denatured and loses its shape also loses its ability to work properly. Next, you will learn how this relationship of structure to function applies to proteins that perform as enzymes.

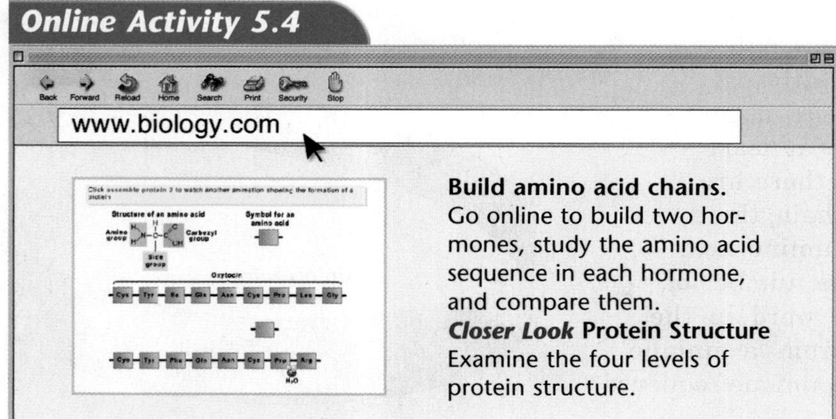

Online Activity 5.4
www.biology.com
Build amino acid chains.
Go online to build two hormones, study the amino acid sequence in each hormone, and compare them.
Closer Look Protein Structure
Examine the four levels of protein structure.

Concept Check 5.4

1. Give at least two examples of proteins you can "see" in the world around you. What are their functions?
2. Relate amino acids, polypeptides, and proteins.
3. Explain how heat can destroy a protein.
4. Which parts of an amino acid's structure are the same in all amino acids? Which part is unique?

CONCEPT 5.5

Enzymes are proteins that speed up specific reactions in cells.

OBJECTIVES

- Explain how enzymes affect activation energy.
- Describe how an enzyme's shape is important to its function.

KEY TERMS

- activation energy
- catalyst
- enzyme
- substrate
- active site

What's Online

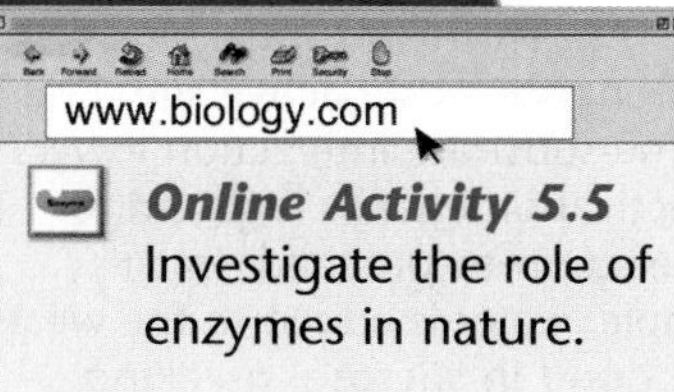

Online Activity 5.5
Investigate the role of enzymes in nature.

Each of your cells is like a miniature chemical factory capable of performing thousands of different reactions. As a cell's needs change, some of these reactions speed up, while others slow down. In this section you'll read about a group of specialized proteins that coordinate the cell's chemistry.

Enzymes and Activation Energy

To start a chemical reaction, it is first necessary to weaken chemical bonds in the reactant molecules. This activation process requires that the molecules absorb energy. For example, to burn a candle you need to provide the initial energy with a match. This "start-up" energy is called **activation energy** because it activates the reactants and triggers a chemical reaction.

One way to provide activation energy is to heat up the mixture of molecules. Hotter molecules may collide with enough energy to weaken bonds, whereas cooler molecules collide with less energy. However, heating up a cell would cause many unnecessary reactions to occur at once, including reactions that destroy the cell's delicate structures. Instead, cellular reactions depend on the assistance of **catalysts,** compounds that speed up chemical reactions. The main catalysts of chemical reactions in organisms are specialized proteins called **enzymes.**

Enzymes provide a way for reactions to occur at the cell's normal temperature. An enzyme doesn't supply activation energy to the reacting molecules, but instead lowers the energy requirement barrier so that the reaction can proceed at normal cell temperatures. Figure 5-15 shows an analogy to help explain why reactions run faster if they require less activation energy. The rock wall represents the activation energy barrier. The frogs represent reactants and products of the reaction.

Each enzyme catalyzes a specific kind of chemical reaction. At any moment in the cell's life, the specific enzymes that are present and active determine which reactions occur.

▼ **Figure 5-15** The activation energy barrier is like a wall between two parts of a pond. If an enzyme lowers the wall, more frogs have enough energy to reach the other side.

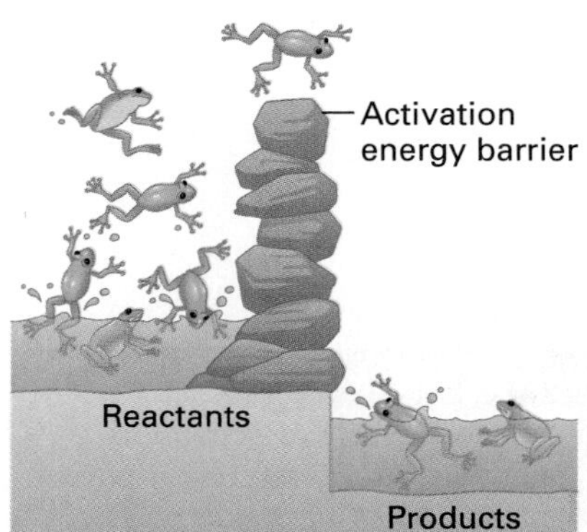

Without enzyme

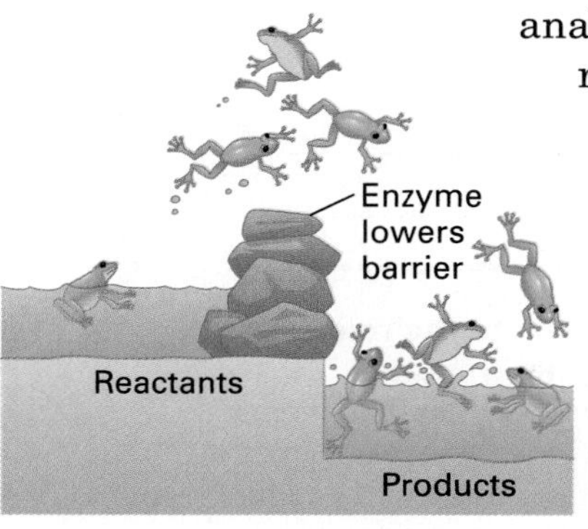

With enzyme

How Enzymes Work

Just how does an enzyme catalyze only one type of reaction? The reason is that the shape of each enzyme fits the shape of only particular reactant molecules. A specific reactant acted upon by an enzyme is called the enzyme's **substrate.** The substrate fits into a particular region of the enzyme, called the **active site.**

The fit between substrate and enzyme is not rigid. As the substrate enters, the active site changes shape slightly, fitting the substrate more snugly. This places certain functional groups of the active site in position to catalyze the reaction. The tighter grip may also bend the substrate, weakening its bonds.

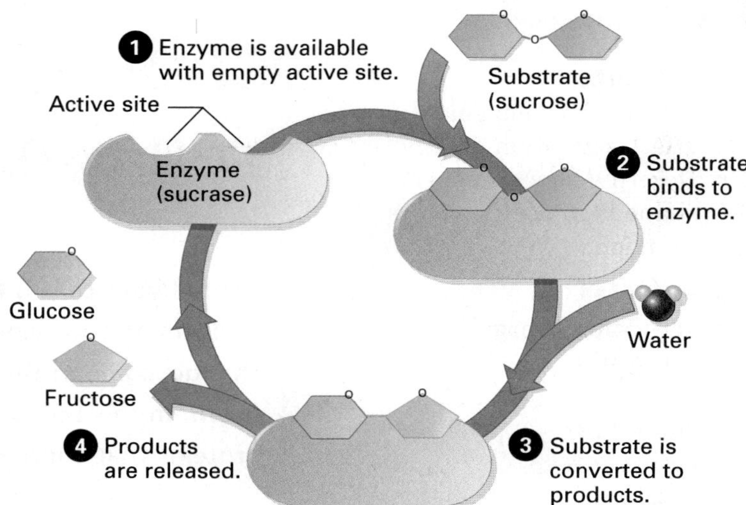

1 Enzyme is available with empty active site.
Active site
Enzyme (sucrase)
Substrate (sucrose)
2 Substrate binds to enzyme.
Water
3 Substrate is converted to products.
4 Products are released.
Glucose
Fructose

▲ **Figure 5-16** A substrate binds to an enzyme at an active site. The enzyme-substrate interaction lowers the activation energy required for the reaction to proceed. In this example, water is added to the weakened bond in sucrose, breaking sucrose into glucose and fructose.

Figure 5-16 follows the action of the enzyme sucrase, which catalyzes the hydrolysis of sucrose (the substrate). (Most enzymes have names that end in *-ase.*) Sucrose is slightly distorted as it enters the active site. The weakened bond reacts with water. The result is two products: a glucose molecule and a fructose molecule. Once these products are released, the enzyme's active site is ready to accept another molecule of sucrose. In fact, this recycling ability is a key characteristic of enzymes.

Another way that an enzyme can lower activation energy is by accepting two reactant molecules (substrates) into adjacent sites. Holding the reactants together enables them to react more easily. In this way, enzymes can catalyze the formation of larger molecules from smaller molecules.

As with any other protein, an enzyme's structure and shape are essential to its function. And like other proteins, an enzyme's shape is sensitive to changes in its surrounding environment. Therefore, factors such as pH and temperature can greatly affect how well an enzyme works or if it can work at all. This is one reason why cells (and hence organisms) can only survive and function within certain ranges of conditions.

Online Activity 5.5

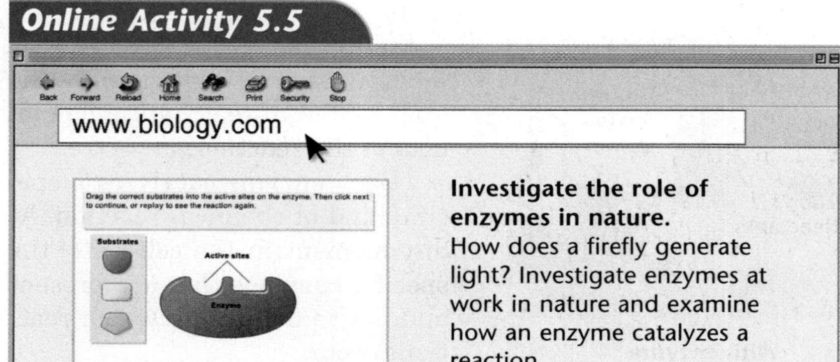

Back Forward Reload Home Search Print Security Stop
www.biology.com
Drag the correct substrates into the active sites on the enzyme. Then click next to continue, or replay to see the reaction again.
Substrates
Active sites
Enzyme

Investigate the role of enzymes in nature.
How does a firefly generate light? Investigate enzymes at work in nature and examine how an enzyme catalyzes a reaction.

Concept Check 5.5

1. Explain the role of activation energy in a reaction. How does an enzyme affect activation energy?
2. Describe how a substrate interacts with an enzyme.

Way to Go, Indigo!

Biological Molecules and Denim Processing

Question How does the enzyme cellulase affect denim fabric?

Lab Overview In this investigation you will take on the role of an industrial scientist as you examine a process used by jeans manufacturers to soften and lighten denim fabric. You will identify problems with one industrial process and investigate a possible solution by using your understanding of biological molecules.

Preparing for the Lab To help you prepare for the investigation, go to the *Lab 5 Online Companion.* ·····➔ Find out more about an industrial process used by denim manufacturers, take a closer look at the structure of denim cloth, and propose another method that manufacturers could use to soften and lighten denim. Prepare for the lab procedure by previewing the steps you will take.

Completing the Lab Use your Laboratory Manual or lab page printouts from the *Lab 5 Online Companion* to do the investigation and analyze your results. **CAUTION:** *Be sure to follow your teacher's instructions and all safety guidelines given in the investigation.*

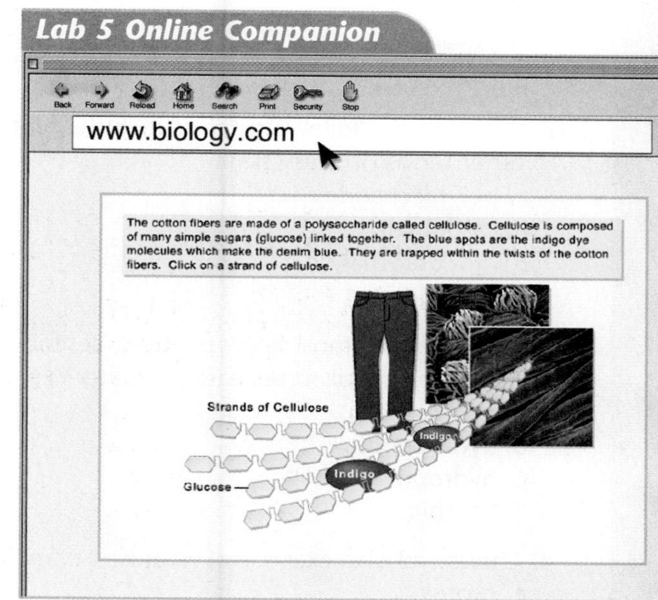
Lab 5 Online Companion
Back
Forward
Reload
Home
Search
Print
Security
Stop
www.biology.com
The cotton fibers are made of a polysaccharide called cellulose. Cellulose is composed of many simple sugars (glucose) linked together. The blue spots are the indigo dye molecules which make the denim blue. They are trapped within the twists of the cotton fibers. Click on a strand of cellulose.
Strands of Cellulose
Indigo
Indigo
Glucose

Multiple Choice

Choose the letter of the best answer.

1. Which of the following is *not* an organic molecule?
   a. cellulose
   b. sucrose
   c. water
   d. testosterone

2. Which of the following terms includes all the other terms on this list?
   a. polysaccharide
   b. carbohydrate
   c. monosaccharide
   d. glycogen

3. Which term is most appropriate to describe a molecule that dissolves easily in water?
   a. hydrocarbon
   b. hydrophobic
   c. hydrophilic
   d. organic

4. Cholesterol is an example of what kind of molecule?
   a. protein
   b. lipid
   c. amino acid
   d. carbohydrate

5. The 20 amino acids vary only in their
   a. carboxyl goups.
   b. side groups.
   c. amino groups.
   d. lipid groups.

6. A specific reactant an enzyme acts upon is called the
   a. catalyst.
   b. sucrase.
   c. active site.
   d. substrate.

7. An enzyme does which of the following?
   a. adds heat to a reaction, speeding it up
   b. lowers the activation energy of a reaction
   c. cools a reaction, slowing it down
   d. raises the activation energy of a reaction

Short Answer

8. Besides satisfying your hunger, why else might you consume a big bowl of pasta the night before a race?

9. How are glucose, sucrose, and starch related?

10. What are steroids? Describe two functions they have in cells.

11. How are polypeptides related to proteins?

12. How does denaturation affect the ability of a protein to function?

Visualizing Concepts

13. Copy the concept map below onto a separate sheet of paper, and complete it.

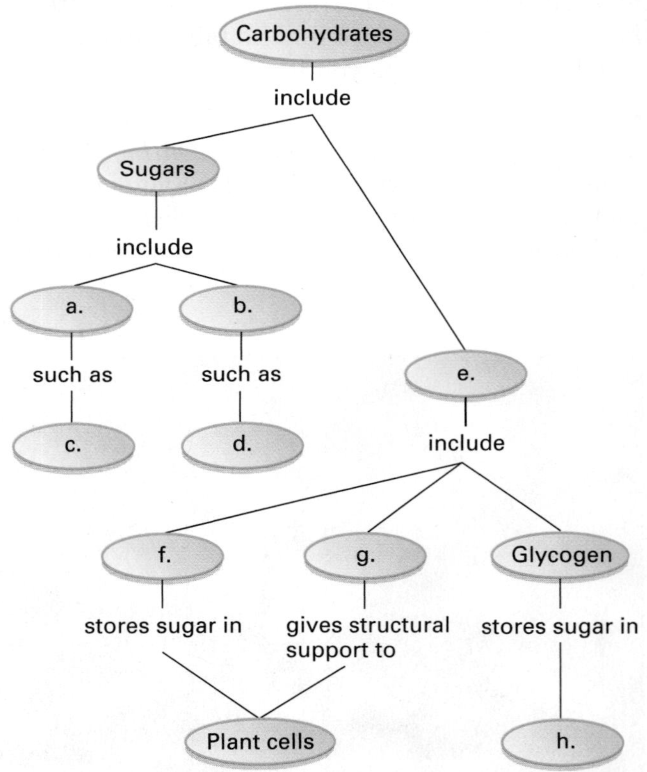

Analyzing Information

14. Analyzing Diagrams The reaction below shows two amino acids joining together.

Leucine **Serine**

a. One product of this reaction is represented by a question mark. Which molecule is it?
b. What is this kind of reaction called? Explain.
c. If an amino acid were added to this chain, at what two places could it attach?

15. Analyzing Graphs Use the graph to answer the questions below.

Effect of Temperature on Enzyme Activity

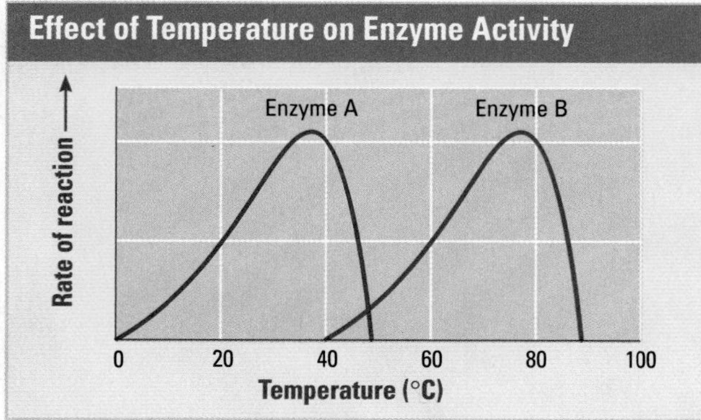

a. At which temperature does enzyme A perform best? Enzyme B?
b. Knowing that one of these enzymes is found in humans and the other in thermophilic (heat-loving) bacteria, hypothesize which enzyme came from which organism.
c. Propose a hypothesis that explains why the rate of the reaction catalyzed by enzyme A slows down at temperatures above 40°C.

Critical Thinking

16. Making Judgments Some food labels list the ingredient "partially hydrogenated vegetable oil." This means that hydrogens have been added to some of the double bonds in the oil's fatty acid chains. Does this make the food more or less healthful? Explain your answer.

17. Evaluating Promotional Claims You hear a television commercial claiming that a snack food is low-fat because it is made with vegetable oil. What may be misleading about this claim?

18. Developing Hypotheses Which of the three polysaccharides you learned about in this chapter is most likely found in paper? Explain.

19. Developing Hypotheses Many humans are lactose-intolerant, meaning they cannot digest milk products containing the disaccharide lactose. Hypothesize the reason behind lactose intolerance.

20. What's Wrong With These Statements?
Briefly explain why each statement is inaccurate or misleading.

a. The structure of a protein is like a long strand of yarn.
b. Enzymes provide activation energy for reactions.

Performance Assessment

Biology Research Project Research lactose intolerance and dietary solutions for lactose-intolerant individuals. Do any of the solutions relate to your hypothesis from Question 19? Write a report that summarizes your findings.

Online Assessment/Test Preparation

www.biology.com

- **Chapter 5 Assessment**
  Check your understanding of the chapter concepts.
- **Standardized Test Preparation**
  Practice test-taking skills you need to succeed.

A Tour of the Cell

What may look like a telescope's view of a supernova in the picture below is actually a microscope's view of the "world" of a single cell. Each of your cells is a miniature marvel. Consider taking a complex machine with millions of parts—say a jumbo jet—and shrinking it to microscopic size while keeping everything in working order. It would still seem simple compared to a living cell. Everything you do, every action and every thought, reflects processes occurring at the cellular level. In this chapter, you will tour cells to explore cell structures and how they function. Before you begin, go online to the ***WebQuest*** to compare sizes, shapes, and characteristics of different cells.

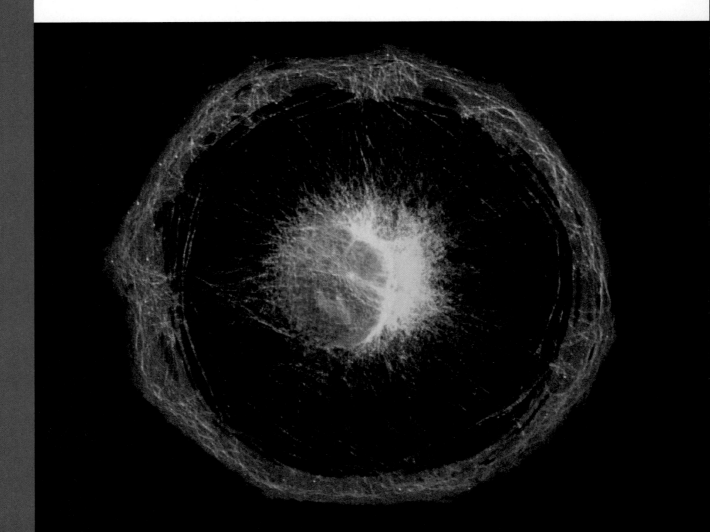

Key Concepts

Concept 6.1 All organisms are made of cells.

Concept 6.2 Membranes organize a cell's activities.

Concept 6.3 Membranes regulate the traffic of molecules.

Concept 6.4 The cell builds a diversity of products.

Concept 6.5 Chloroplasts and mitochondria energize cells.

Concept 6.6 An internal skeleton supports the cell and enables movement.

Assessment Chapter 6 Review

What's Online

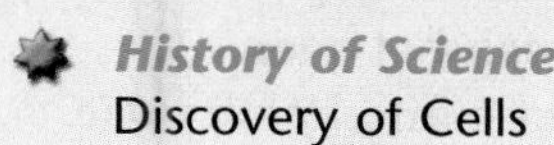

WebQuest
CellQuest

Online Activity 6.1
Compare how cells measure up.

History of Science
Discovery of Cells

Online Activity 6.2
Dissect a plasma membrane.

Online Activity 6.3
Investigate movement across the membrane.

Lab 6 Online Companion
Design a Cell

Online Activity 6.4
Transport insulin to the bloodstream.

Online Activity 6.5
Magnify a choloroplast and a mitochondrion.

Online Activity 6.6
Predict how protists move.

Chapter 6 Assessment

CONCEPT 6.1

All organisms are made of cells.

OBJECTIVES

- Explain the main ideas of the cell theory.
- Describe how microscopes aid the study of cells.
- Compare and contrast animal cells and plant cells.
- Distinguish between prokaryotic and eukaryotic cells.

KEY TERMS

- cell theory
- micrograph
- organelle
- plasma membrane
- nucleus
- cytoplasm
- cell wall
- prokaryotic cell
- eukaryotic cell

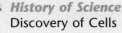

What's Online

Online Activity 6.1 Compare how cells measure up.

History of Science Discovery of Cells

Cells are as basic to biology as atoms are to chemistry. All organisms are made of cells. Organisms are either unicellular (single-celled), such as most bacteria and protists, or multicellular (many-celled), such as plants, animals, and most fungi. Because most cells cannot be seen without magnification, people's understanding of cells and their importance is relatively recent.

The Cell Theory

Human understanding of nature often follows the invention and improvement of instruments that extend human senses. The development of microscopes provided increasingly clear windows to the world of cells.

Light microscopes, the kind used in your classroom, were first developed and used by scientists around 1600. In a light microscope, visible light passes through an object, such as a thin slice of muscle tissue, and glass lenses then enlarge the image and project it into the human eye or a camera.

In 1665, an English scientist named Robert Hooke observed "compartments" in a thin slice of cork (oak bark) using a light microscope (Figure 6-1). He named the compartments *cells.* Actually, Hooke was observing the walls of dead plant cells. Many more observations by many other scientists were needed to understand the importance of Hooke's discovery. By 1700, Dutch scientist Anton van Leeuwenhoek (LAY vun hook) had developed simple light microscopes with high-quality lenses to observe tiny living organisms, such as those in pond water. He described what he called "animalcules" in letters to Hooke and his colleagues.

For the next two centuries, scientists, using microscopes, found cells in every organism they examined. By the mid-1800s, this evidence led to the **cell theory**—the generalization that all living things are composed of cells, and that cells are the basic unit of structure and function in living things. Later, the cell theory was extended to include the concept that all cells come from pre-existing cells.

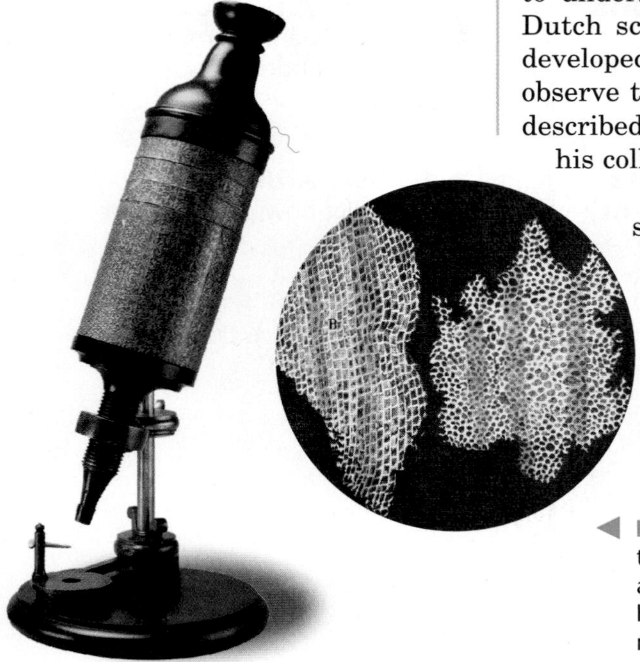

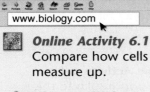

Figure 6-1 This microscope is a replica of the one used by Robert Hooke. Shown here are Hooke's drawings of cork (oak bark) that he saw under the microscope. The image reminded him of a honeycomb.

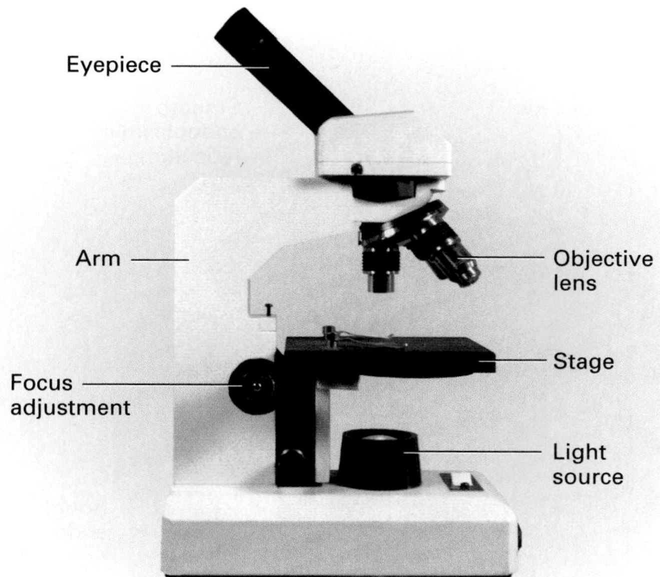

◀ **Figure 6-2** A light microscope like the one shown here can magnify objects up to about 1000 times.

Microscopes as Windows to Cells

Light microscopes (abbreviated LM) are useful for magnifying objects up to about 1000 times their actual size. This type of microscope works for viewing objects about the size of a bacterium or larger. But much of a cell's structure is so small that even magnifying it 1000 times is not enough to see it. Knowledge of cell structure took a giant leap forward as biologists began using electron microscopes in the 1950s. Instead of light, the electron microscope uses a beam of electrons. Certain electron microscopes can magnify objects as much as a million (1,000,000) times, enough to reveal details of the structures inside a cell.

Biologists use the scanning electron microscope (SEM) to study the surface structures of cells. The transmission electron microscope (TEM) is used to explore their internal structure. Specimens for both types of electron microscopes must be killed and preserved before they can be examined. For this reason, light microscopes are still useful for observing living cells.

A photograph of the view through a microscope is called a **micrograph.** In Figure 6-3, you can compare the differences among micrographs of a cell taken with each of the various microscopes. Throughout this book, most micrographs have a notation alongside the image that indicates the kind of microscope used to view the object and its final magnification. For example, "LM 200×" next to photo (a) in Figure 6-3 indicates that the micrograph is an image made with a light microscope and shown here at a magnification of 200×, or 200 times its actual size. (You may notice that some light micrographs in this book have magnifications listed of more than 1000×. That is because the photographs have been further enlarged from the originals.)

As you tour the parts of a cell in this chapter, you will encounter comparisons to a scale model of a cell enlarged to the size of your classroom. At this magnification, the "classroom cell" is over 300,000 times larger than a normal cell.

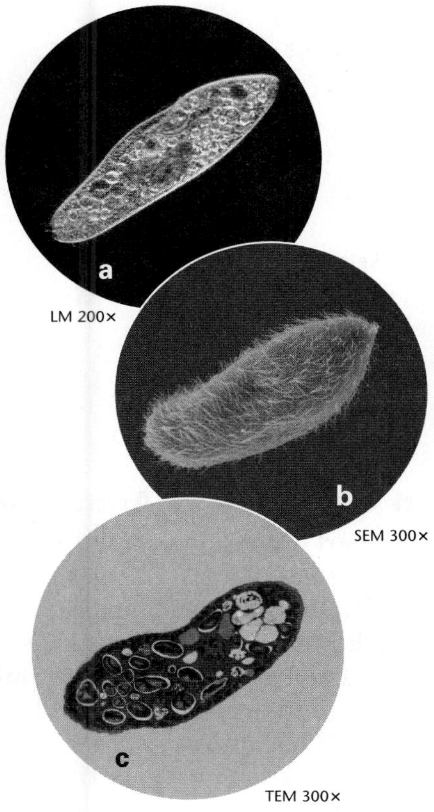

▲ **Figure 6-3** Different microscopes reveal different views of a paramecium. **a.** A light microscope shows the interior of a live cell. **b.** A scanning electron microscope shows the cell's surface structure. **c.** A transmission electron microscope shows internal details of a preserved cell.

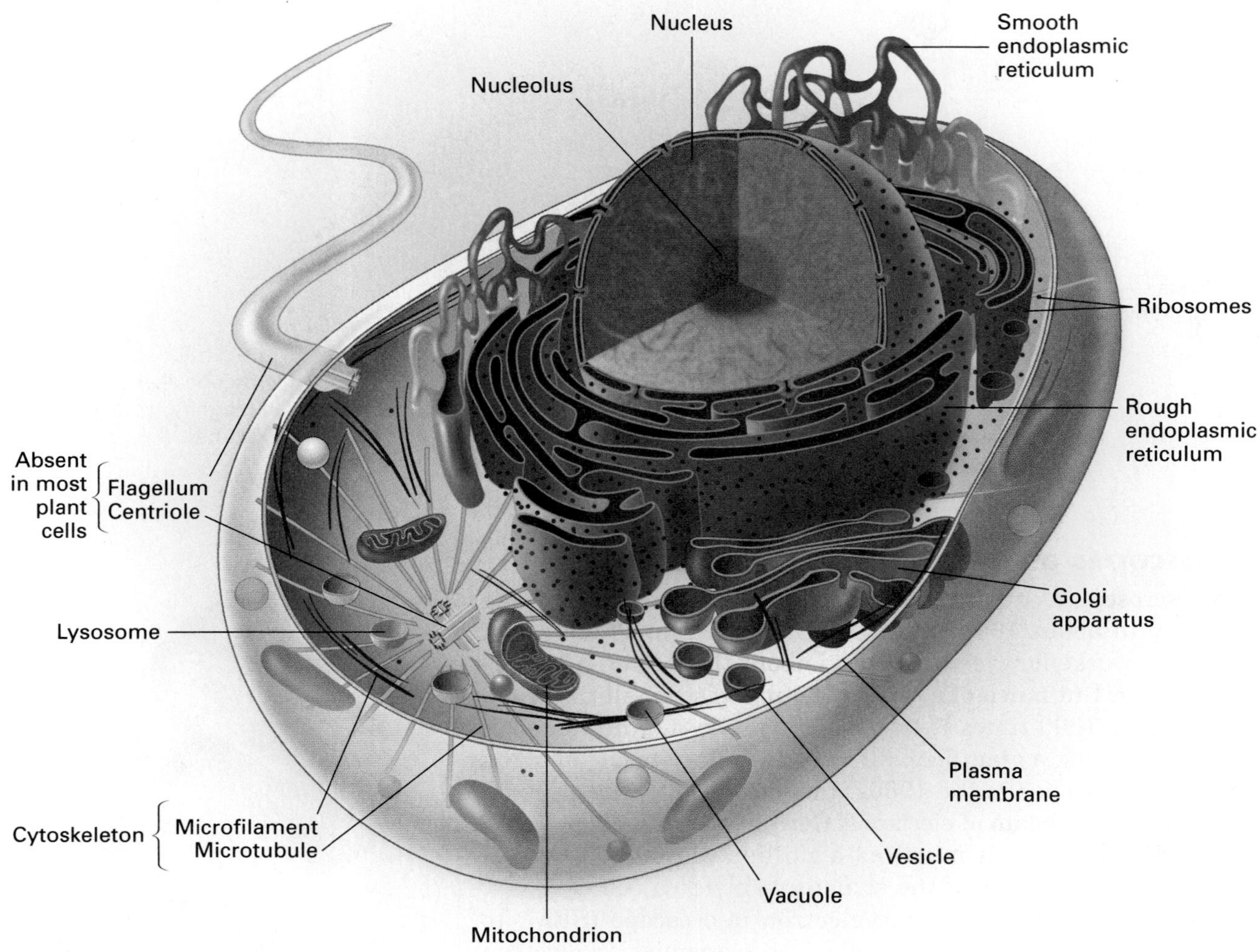

▲ **Figure 6-4** This diagram provides an overview of a generalized animal cell. Later in the chapter, watch for miniature versions of the diagram with "you-are-here" highlights. They will serve as road maps on your tour of cells.

An Overview of Animal and Plant Cells

Each part of a cell with a specific job to do is called an **organelle,** meaning "mini-organ." Cutaway diagrams of a generalized animal cell (Figure 6-4) and plant cell (Figure 6-5) show the organelles in each kind of cell. For now, the cell parts labeled in the figures are just words and structures, but these organelles will come to life as you take a closer look at how each of them works, here and later in the chapter.

There are more similarities between animal and plant cells than there are differences. Both kinds of cells have a thin outer covering, called the **plasma membrane,** which defines the boundary of the cell and regulates the traffic of chemicals between the cell and its surroundings. Each cell also has a prominent **nucleus** (plural, *nuclei*), which houses the cell's genetic material in the form of DNA. In the classroom-cell scale model, the nucleus would be the size of a small car in the middle of your classroom.

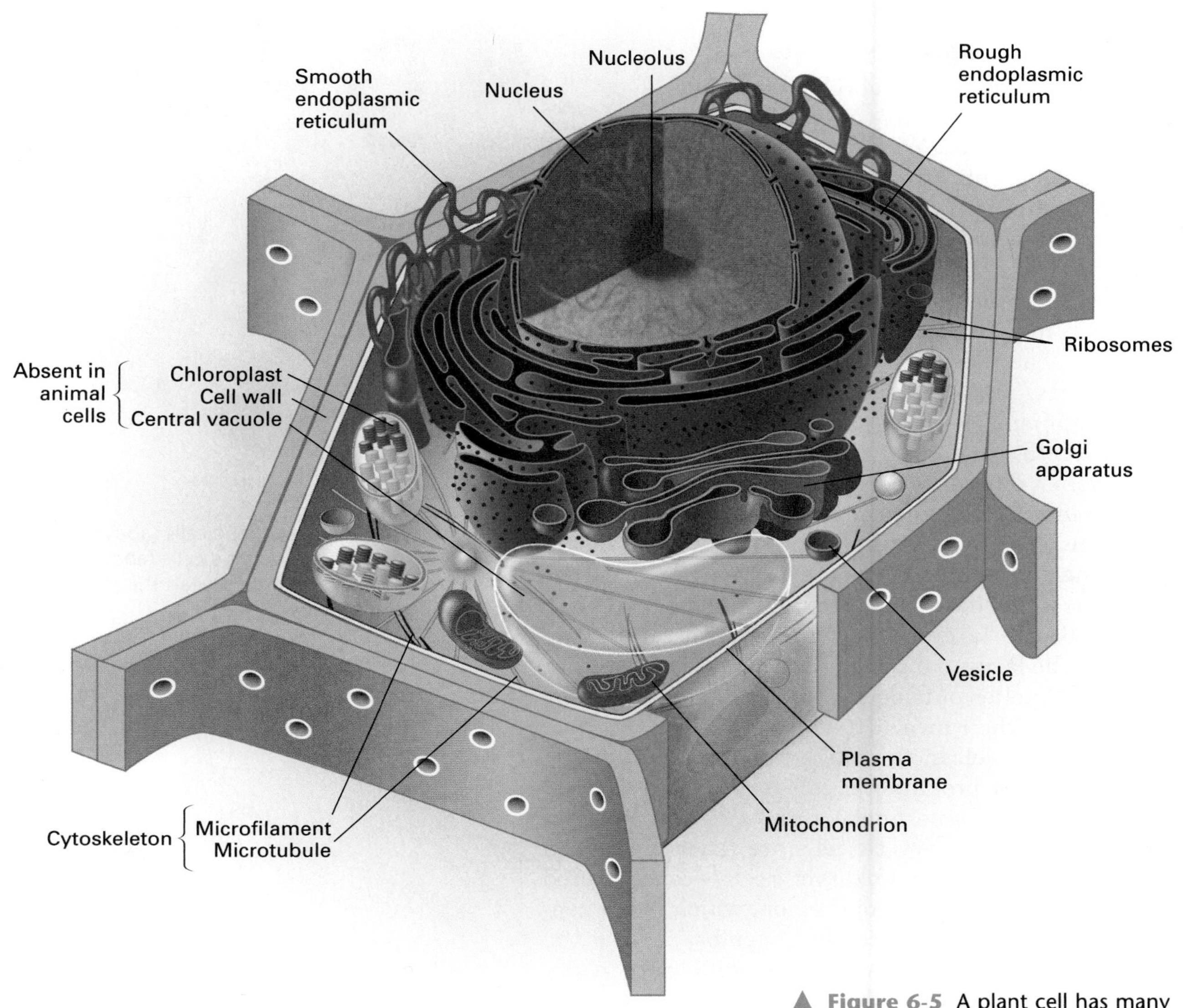

▲ **Figure 6-5** A plant cell has many of the same structures as an animal cell. Miniature versions of this generalized plant cell diagram will appear in parts of the chapter where its unique organelles are discussed.

The entire region of the cell between the nucleus and the plasma membrane is called the **cytoplasm** (SYT oh plaz um), which consists of various organelles suspended in a fluid. Many of these organelles are enclosed by their own membranes. These membranes help to maintain chemical environments inside the organelles that are different from the environment of the rest of the cell.

If you compare Figures 6-4 and 6-5, you will see that there are a few key differences in cell structure between plants and animals. One difference is the presence of chloroplasts in some plant cells, but not in animal cells. A chloroplast is the organelle in which photosynthesis occurs. Photosynthesis converts light energy to the chemical energy stored in molecules of sugars and other organic compounds. Also, a plant cell is encased by a strong cell wall outside its plasma membrane. The **cell wall** protects the plant cell and maintains its shape. Animal cells do not have cell walls.

History of Science

Back Forward Reload Home Search Print Security Stop

www.biology.com

Discovery of Cells

Before microscopes, nobody even knew that cells existed. Go online to learn more about the people and instruments that have been critical in building today's understanding of cell structures and functions.

Two Major Classes of Cells

There are two basic kinds of cells. One kind—a **prokaryotic cell** (pro KAR ee oh tik)—lacks a nucleus and most other organelles. Bacteria and another group of organisms called the archaea are prokaryotic cells. Prokaryotic organisms appear earliest in Earth's fossil record. In contrast, a **eukaryotic cell** (yoo KAR ee oh tik) has a nucleus surrounded by its own membrane, and has other internal organelles bounded by membranes. Protists, fungi, plants, and animals consist of eukaryotic cells. Organisms with eukaryotic cells appeared later in Earth's history.

The major difference between these two main classes of cells is indicated by their names. The word *eukaryotic* is from the Greek *eu* meaning "true," and *karyon* meaning "kernel." The kernel refers to the nucleus that eukaryotic cells have and prokaryotic cells lack. In Figure 6-6, the larger cell is a eukaryotic cell. The nucleus is the largest organelle. You can see many other types of organelles outside the nucleus, surrounded by membranes of their own.

The smaller cell in the micrograph is a bacterium, an example of a prokaryotic cell (*pro* means "earlier than"). Without a true nucleus and the organelles of eukaryotic cells, prokaryotic cells are much simpler in structure. The DNA in a prokaryotic cell is concentrated in an area called the nucleoid region, which is not separated from the rest of the cell by a membrane, as is the case in a eukaryotic cell. Also, note the difference in size between these two cells. Most bacteria are 1 to 10 micrometers in diameter, whereas eukaryotic cells are typically 10 to 100 micrometers in diameter. You'll examine prokaryotic cells in more detail in Chapter 16. Eukaryotic cells are the main focus of this chapter.

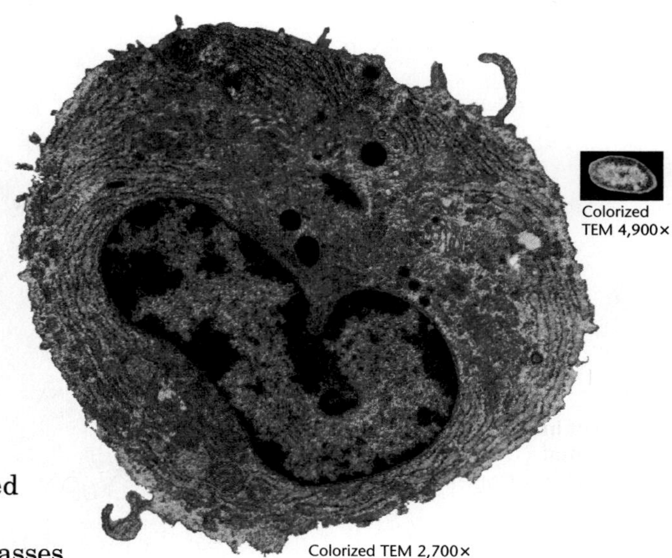

Figure 6-6 Most eukaryotic cells (above left) are much larger than prokaryotic cells (above right). Below, a cutaway diagram reveals the structure of a generalized prokaryotic cell.

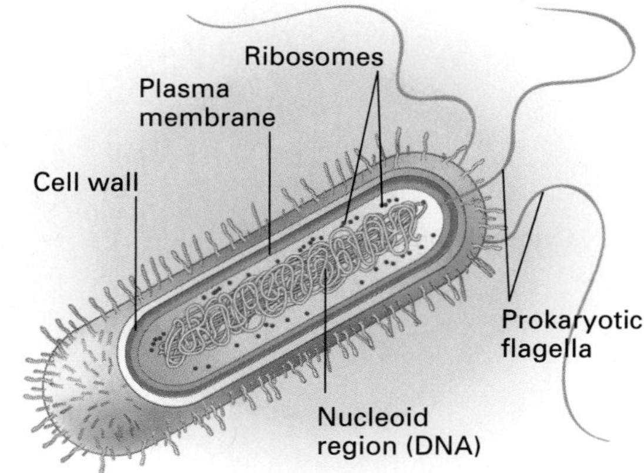

Online Activity 6.1

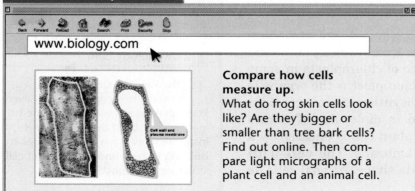

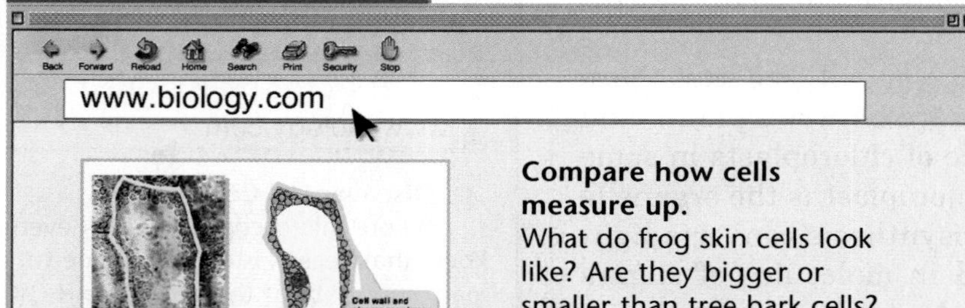

Compare how cells measure up.
What do frog skin cells look like? Are they bigger or smaller than tree bark cells? Find out online. Then compare light micrographs of a plant cell and an animal cell.

Concept Check 6.1

1. What evidence led to the development of the cell theory?
2. How do the various kinds of microscopes differ as tools in the study of cells?
3. Identify two similarities and two differences between plant and animal cells.
4. How is a eukaryotic cell different from a prokaryotic cell?

CONCEPT 6.2 Membranes organize a cell's activities.

OBJECTIVES
- Describe the structure of cellular membranes.
- Identify functions of proteins in cellular membranes.

KEY TERM
- phospholipid bilayer

The plasma membrane can be thought of as the edge of life—it is the boundary that separates the interior of a living cell from its surroundings. The membrane is a remarkable film so thin that you would have to stack 8,000 of them to equal the thickness of the page you are reading. Yet the plasma membrane can regulate the traffic of chemicals into and out of the cell. The key to how a membrane works is its structure.

Membrane Structure

Membranes help keep the functions of a eukaryotic cell organized. As partitions, the membranes isolate teams of enzymes within a cell's compartments. But membranes are more than cellular room dividers. Membranes, unlike walls, regulate the transport of substances across the boundary, allowing only certain substances to pass. In this way, a membrane maintains a specific chemical environment within each compartment it encloses.

The plasma membrane and other membranes of a cell are composed mostly of proteins and a type of lipid called phospholipids. A phospholipid molecule (Figure 6-7) is structured much like the fat molecules you learned about in Chapter 5 but has only two fatty acids instead of three. The two fatty acids at one end (the tail) of the phospholipid are hydrophobic (not attracted to water). The other end (the head) of the molecule includes a phosphate group (PO_4^{3-}), which is negatively charged and hydrophilic (attracted to water). Thus, the tail end of a phospholipid is pushed away by water, while the head is attracted to water.

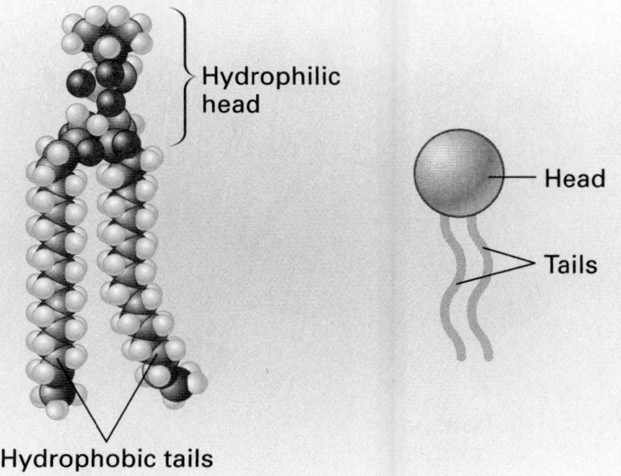

Figure 6-7 A space-filling model of a phospholipid depicts the hydrophilic head region and the hydrophobic fatty acid tails. The simplified representation of phospholipids used in this book looks something like a lollipop (the head) with two sticks (the tails).

The structure of phospholipids enables them to form boundaries, or membranes, between two watery environments. For example, the plasma membrane separates a cell's aqueous cytoplasm from the aqueous environment surrounding the cell (Figure 6-8). At such boundaries, the phospholipids form a two-layer "sandwich" of molecules, called a **phospholipid bilayer,** that surrounds the organelle or cell. In the bilayer membrane, the phosphate ends face the watery inside and watery outside of the cell. The hydrophobic fatty acid tails are tucked inside the membrane, shielded from the water. These hydrophobic tails play a key role in the membrane's function as a selective barrier. Nonpolar molecules (such as oxygen and carbon dioxide) cross with ease, while polar molecules (such as sugars) and many ions do not.

Together, the phospholipids, proteins, and other membrane components form a dynamic structure. Membranes are fluid-like, rather than sheets of molecules locked rigidly in place. Most of the proteins drift about freely in the plane of the membrane, much like "icebergs" floating in a "sea" of phospholipids.

Figure 6-8 A cell's plasma membrane contains a diversity of proteins that drift about in the phospholipid bilayer. Even the phospholipid molecules themselves can move along the plane of the fluid-like membrane. Some membrane proteins and lipids have carbohydrate chains attached to their outer surfaces.

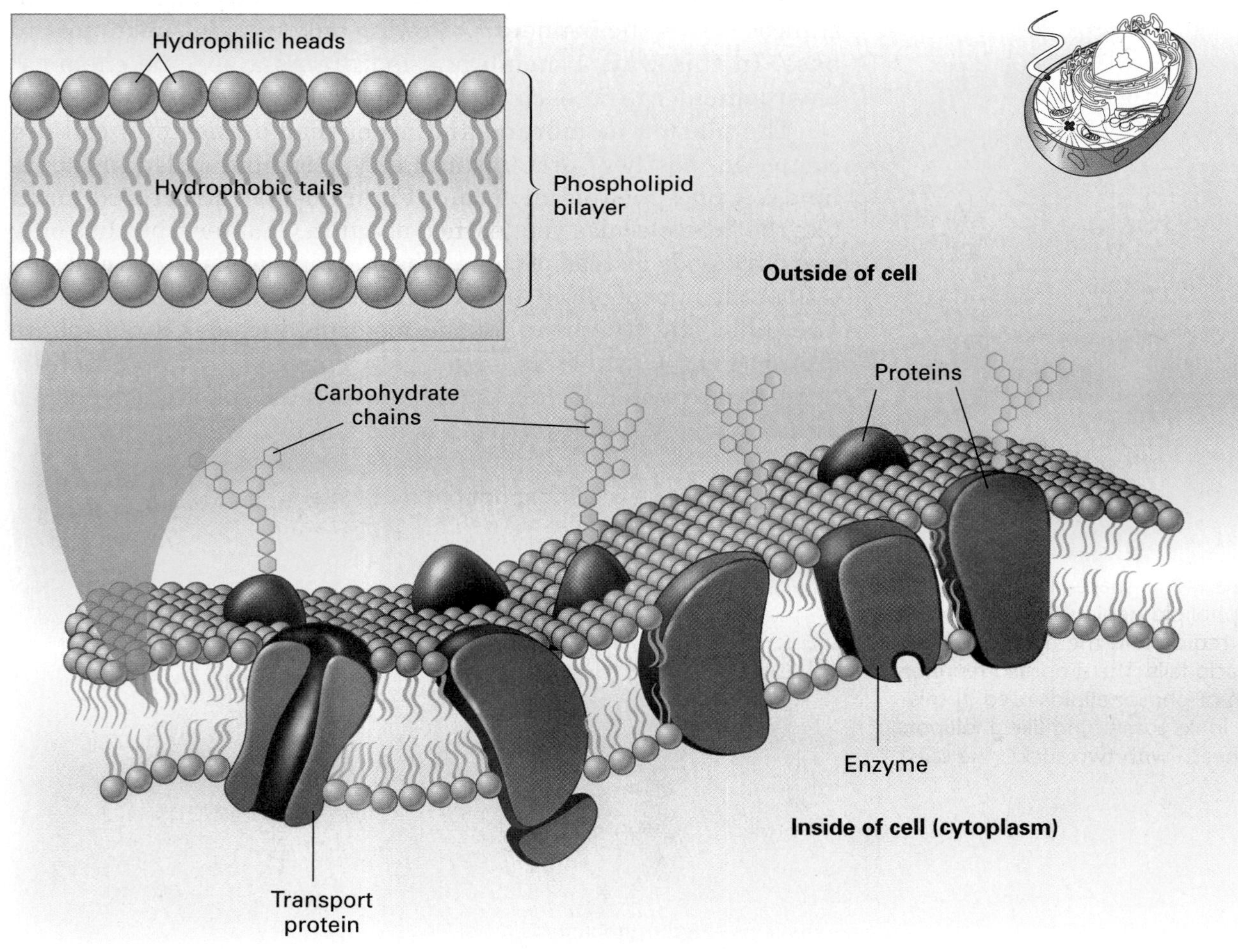

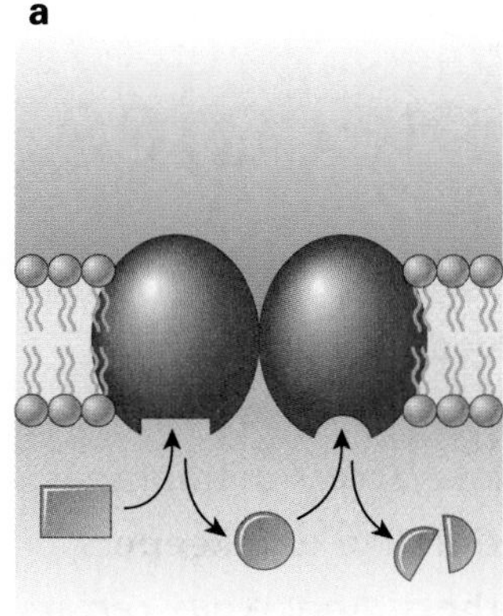

Enzyme activity

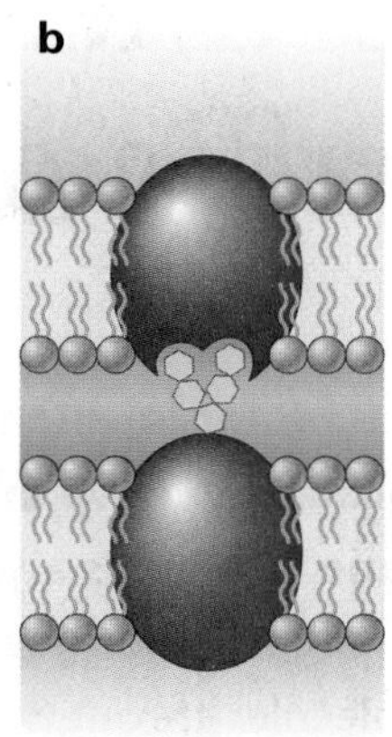

Cell-to-cell recognition

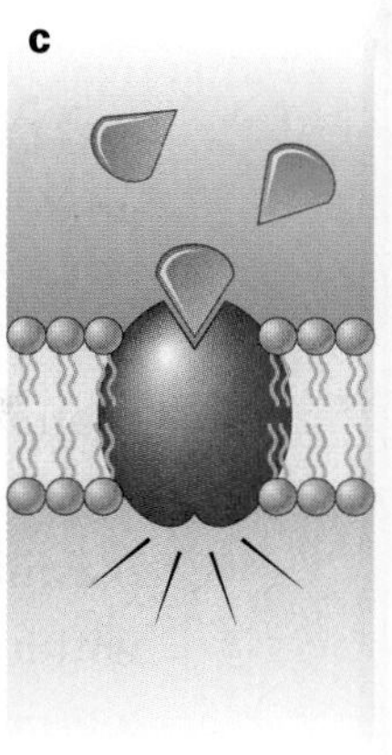

Cell signaling

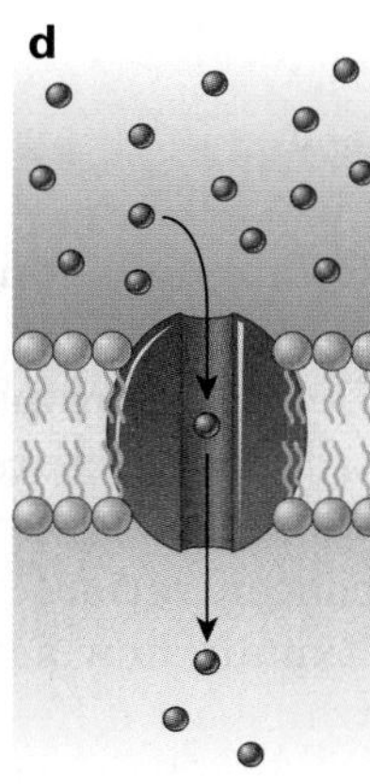

Transport of materials

▲ **Figure 6-9** Many functions of the plasma membrane involve its embedded proteins. **a.** Enzymes catalyze reactions of nearby substrates. **b.** Molecules on the surfaces of other cells are "recognized" by membrane proteins. **c.** A chemical messenger binds to a membrane protein, causing it to change shape and relay the message inside the cell. **d.** Transport proteins provide channels for certain solutes.

The Many Functions of Membrane Proteins

Many types of proteins are embedded in the membrane's phospholipid bilayer. Other molecules, such as carbohydrates, may be attached to the membrane as well, but the proteins perform most of the membrane's specific functions. For example, sets of closely placed enzymes built into the membrane carry out some of a cell's important chemical reactions (Figure 6-9a). In Chapters 7 and 8, you will learn more about how such membrane-bound enzymes contribute to cellular processes.

Another function of membrane proteins is to help cells—especially cells that are part of a multicellular organism—communicate and recognize each other (Figure 6-9b and c). For example, chemical signals released by one cell may be "picked up" by the proteins embedded in the membrane of another cell.

Still other membrane proteins, called transport proteins, help move certain substances such as water and sugars across the membrane (Figure 6-9d). Although small nonpolar molecules such as carbon dioxide and oxygen pass freely through the membrane, many essential molecules need assistance from proteins to enter or leave the cell. You will read more about how molecules move across a membrane in Concept 6.3.

Online Activity 6.2

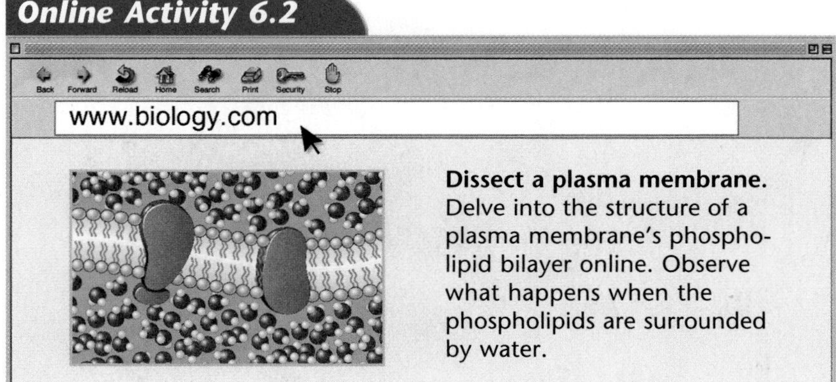

Dissect a plasma membrane. Delve into the structure of a plasma membrane's phospholipid bilayer online. Observe what happens when the phospholipids are surrounded by water.

Concept Check 6.2

1. Describe how phospholipid molecules are oriented in the plasma membrane of a cell.
2. What is the function of a transport protein?

CONCEPT 6.3

Membranes regulate the traffic of molecules.

OBJECTIVES

- Relate diffusion and equilibrium.
- Describe how passive transport occurs.
- Relate osmosis to solute concentration.
- Explain how active transport differs from passive transport.
- Describe how large molecules move across a membrane.

KEY TERMS

- diffusion
- equilibrium
- selectively permeable membrane
- passive transport
- facilitated diffusion
- osmosis
- hypertonic
- hypotonic
- isotonic
- active transport
- vesicle
- exocytosis
- endocytosis

What's Online

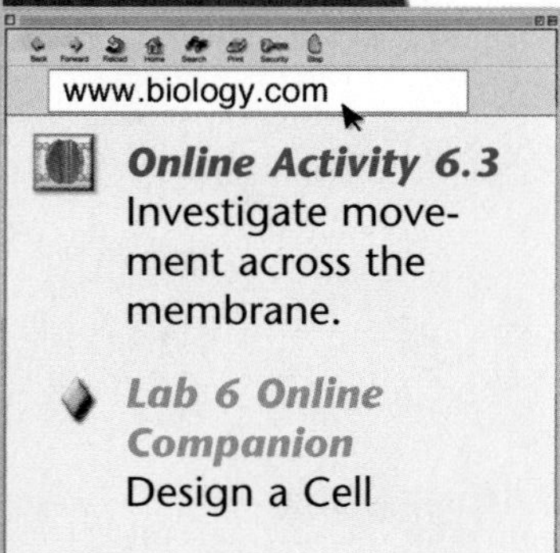

Online Activity 6.3 Investigate movement across the membrane.

Lab 6 Online Companion Design a Cell

Materials such as water, nutrients, dissolved gases, ions, and wastes must constantly move in two-way traffic across a cell's plasma membrane. Materials also must move across membranes within the cell. Cellular membranes function like gatekeepers, letting some molecules through but not others. And, while certain molecules pass freely through the "gates," others move only when the cell expends energy.

Diffusion

Molecules in a fluid are constantly in motion, colliding and bouncing as they spread out into the available space. One result of this motion is **diffusion,** the net movement of the particles of a substance from where they are more concentrated to where they are less concentrated (Figure 6-10).

Suppose there is a container of water in which a membrane separates pure water from a solution of dye and water. This membrane happens to be *permeable* to both the dye and water molecules—that is, the molecules can pass through the membrane freely (Figure 6-11). As the molecules of water and dye move randomly, the dye eventually diffuses across the membrane until the concentration of dye—the ratio of dye to water—on each side is the same. At this point, the number of dye molecules moving in one direction is equal to the number moving in the other direction, and the system is said to be in **equilibrium,** or balance.

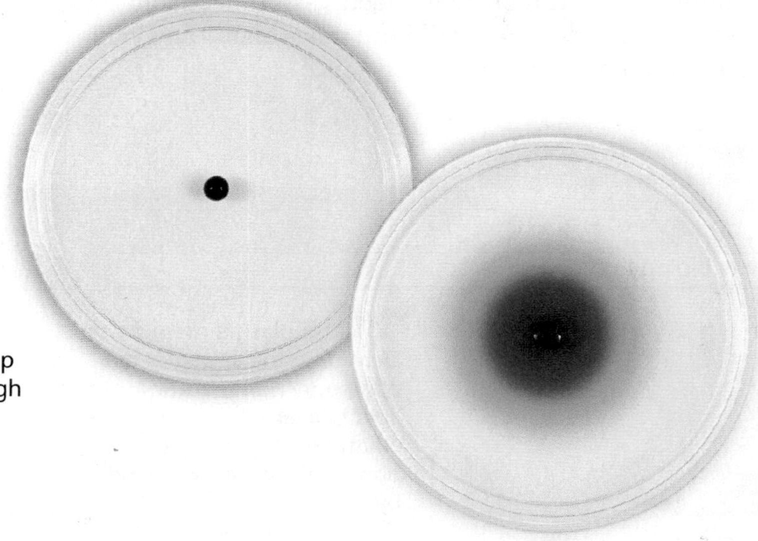

Figure 6-10 Over time, a drop of food coloring diffuses through gelatin in a petri dish.

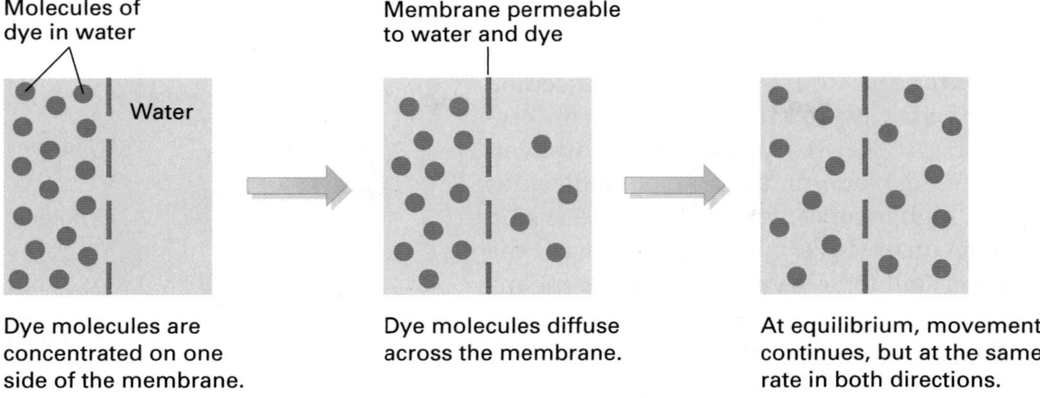

Molecules of dye in water
Water
Membrane permeable to water and dye
Dye molecules are concentrated on one side of the membrane.
Dye molecules diffuse across the membrane.
At equilibrium, movement continues, but at the same rate in both directions.

Figure 6-11 Dye molecules diffuse across a membrane. At equilibrium, the concentration of dye is the same throughout the container.

Passive Transport

Cellular membranes are barriers to the diffusion of some substances. A **selectively permeable membrane** allows some substances to cross the membrane more easily than others and blocks the passage of some substances altogether. (Think of a window screen that lets a breeze through but blocks the entry of mosquitoes.) In a typical cell, a few molecules (primarily oxygen and carbon dioxide) diffuse freely through the plasma membrane (Figure 6-12, left). Water also diffuses through the membrane, but mostly through protein channels. Other molecules pass less easily or only under specific conditions. Diffusion across a membrane is called **passive transport** because no energy is expended by the cell in the process. Only the random motion of the molecules is required to move them across the membrane.

Though small molecules generally pass more readily by passive transport than large molecules, most small molecules have restricted access. For example, sugars do not pass easily through the hydrophobic region of the plasma membrane. The traffic of such substances can only occur by way of transport proteins (Figure 6-12, right). In this process, known as **facilitated diffusion,** transport proteins provide a pathway for certain molecules to pass. (The word *facilitate* means "to help.") Specific proteins allow the passive transport of different substances. In this way, substances including some ions and small polar molecules, such as water and sugars, diffuse into or out of the cell.

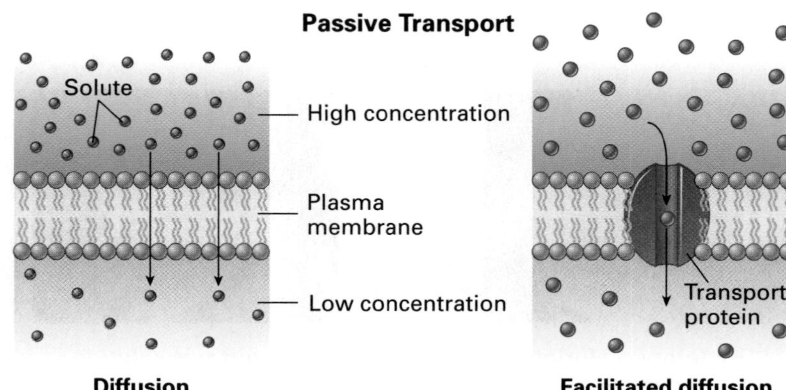

Figure 6-12 Both diffusion and facilitated diffusion are forms of passive transport, as neither process requires the cell to expend energy. In facilitated diffusion, solute particles pass through a channel in a transport protein.

Osmosis

The passive transport of water across a selectively permeable membrane is called **osmosis** (ahs MOH sis). Consider a sealed bag of concentrated sugar water placed in a container of less-concentrated sugar water (Figure 6-13). Suppose that water can pass through the bag (the membrane) but the sugar molecules cannot. The solution with a higher concentration of solute is said to be **hypertonic** (*hyper* means "above"). The solution with the lower solute concentration is said to be **hypotonic** (*hypo* means "below"). Think now, which solution has the higher concentration of water? By having less solute, the hypotonic solution has the higher water concentration. What will happen?

As a result of osmosis, water from the container (hypotonic solution) will diffuse across the membrane to the inside of the bag (hypertonic solution). The sugar molecules, however, cannot cross the membrane. In time, the volume of water increases inside the bag. If the volume of the bag is large enough, the concentration of sugar will become the same in the water on either side of the membrane (Figure 6-13). Solutions in which the concentrations of solute are equal are said to be **isotonic** (*isos* means "equal").

Water Balance in Animal Cells Although the solution in Figure 6-13 became isotonic, the bag got bigger as it took on water. What happens to an animal cell in a hypotonic solution? The cell gains water, swells, and may even pop like an overfilled balloon. A hypertonic environment is also harsh on an animal cell. The cell loses water, shrivels, and may die. Figure 6-14 shows how these various conditions affect red blood cells. A normal red blood cell has a shape that looks something like a rounded pillow pressed inward at its middle. Notice how the shape changes when the environment is not isotonic.

Animals living in aquatic environments may encounter conditions that are not isotonic with their body tissues. These animals depend on mechanisms that make up for the gain or loss of water that results from osmosis. For example, the body of a freshwater fish constantly gains water from its hypotonic environment. One function of the fish's gills and kidneys is to prevent an excessive buildup of water in the body.

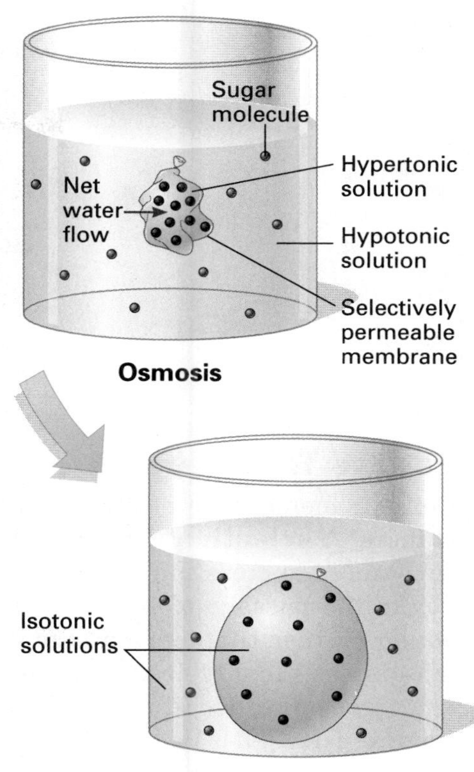

▲ **Figure 6-13** A selectively permeable membrane (the bag) separates two solutions of different sugar concentrations. Sugar molecules cannot pass through the membrane.

▼ **Figure 6-14** In an isotonic solution, the flow of water (shown by arrows) into and out of a cell is equal. In a hypotonic solution, the net flow inward causes the cell to swell. The opposite effect occurs in a hypertonic solution, causing the cell to shrivel.

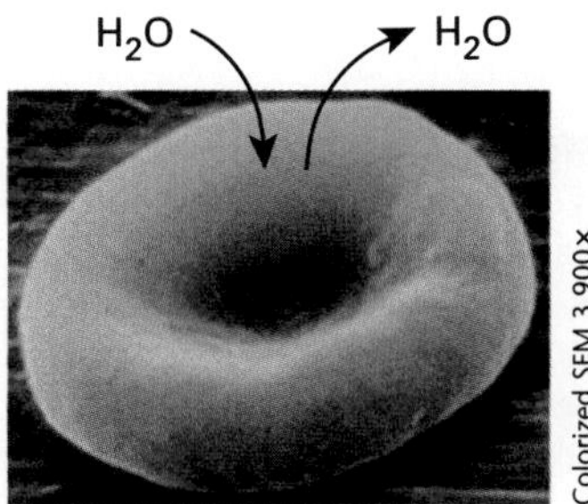

Isotonic solution
Water flow is equal in both directions.

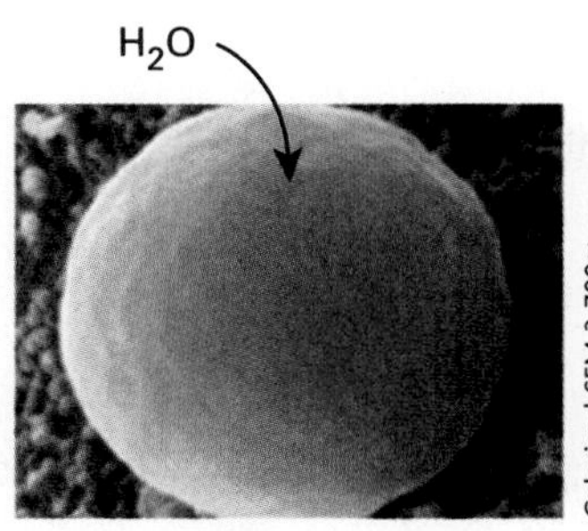

Hypotonic solution
Net water flow is into cell.

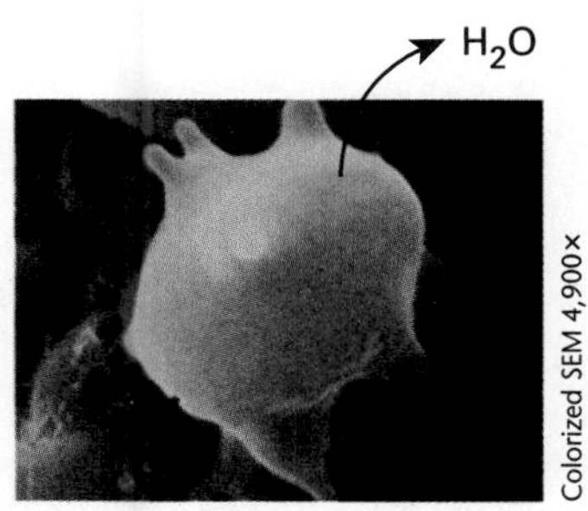

Hypertonic solution
Net water flow is out of cell.

Water Balance in Plant Cells Water balance problems are somewhat different for plant cells because of their strong cell walls (Figure 6-15). A plant cell is firm and healthiest in a hypotonic environment—when bathed by rainwater, for example. The cell becomes firm as a result of the net flow of water inward. Although the cell wall expands a bit, it applies pressure that prevents the cell from taking in too much water and bursting, as an animal cell would. In contrast, a plant cell in an isotonic environment has no net inward flow of water. It becomes limp. Non-woody plants, such as most houseplants, wilt in this situation. In a hypertonic environment, a plant cell is no better off than an animal cell. As a plant cell loses water, it shrivels, and its plasma membrane pulls away from the cell wall. This situation usually kills the cell.

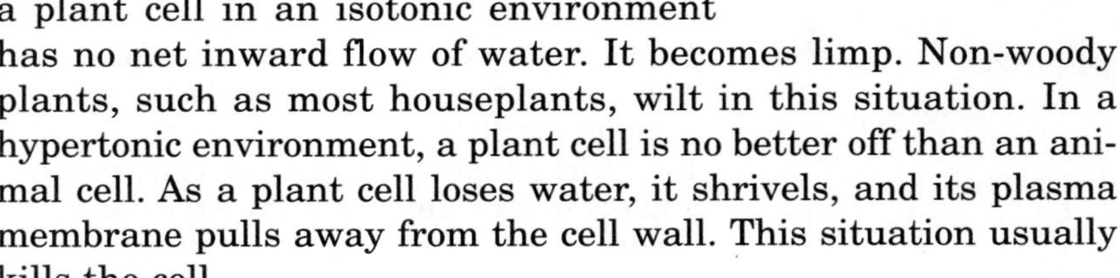

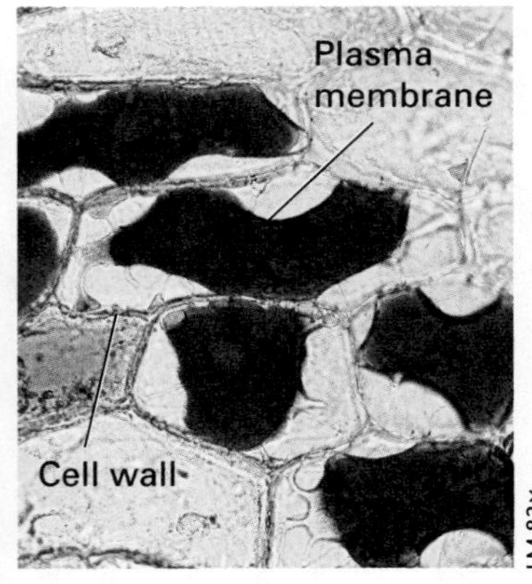

▲ **Figure 6-15** Skin from a red onion is placed in an isotonic solution (left) and a hypertonic solution (right). Compare the same cell in both photographs. You can see how the plasma membrane has pulled away from the cell wall in the image on the right.

Active Transport

When a cell expends energy to move molecules or ions across a membrane, the process is known as **active transport.** During active transport, a specific transport protein pumps a solute across a membrane, usually in the opposite direction to the way it travels in diffusion (Figure 6-16). This action requires chemical energy supplied primarily by the mitochondria, which you will read more about in Concept 6.5.

Active transport plays a part in maintaining the cell's chemical environment. For example, an animal cell has a much higher concentration of potassium ions (K^+) and a much lower concentration of sodium ions (Na^+) than its fluid surroundings. The plasma membrane helps maintain these differences by pumping K^+ ions into the cell and Na^+ ions out of the cell. This particular case of active transport is central to how your nerve cells work, as you'll learn in Chapter 28.

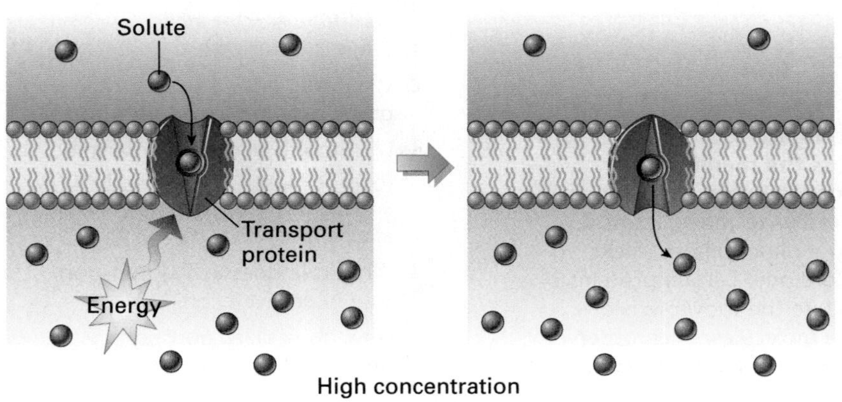

◀ **Figure 6-16** Like an enzyme, a transport protein recognizes a specific solute (a molecule or ion). During active transport, the protein uses energy, usually moving the solute in a direction from lesser concentration to greater concentration.

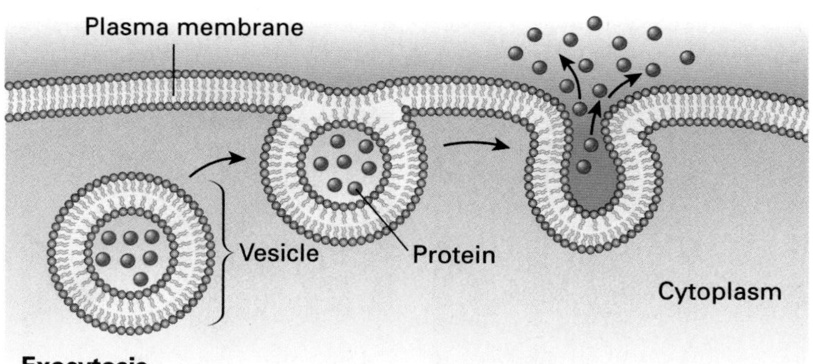

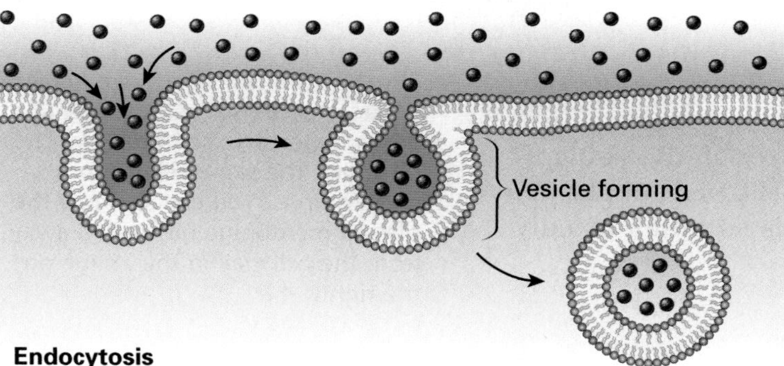

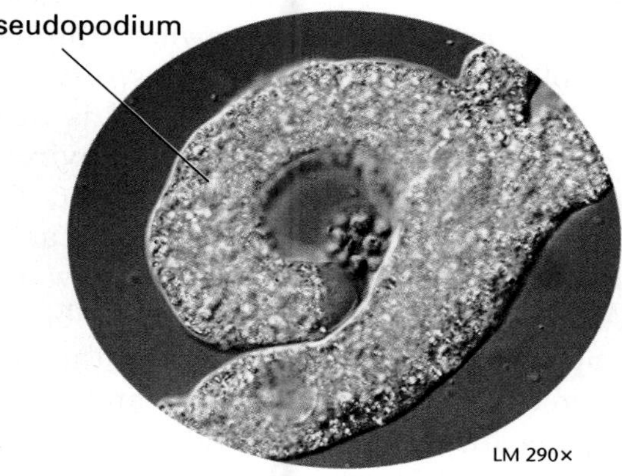

Figure 6-17 Exocytosis (above left) expels molecules from the cell that are too large to pass through the plasma membrane. Endocytosis (below left) brings large molecules into the cell and packages them in vesicles. An amoeba (above) uses a cellular extension called a pseudopodium to engulf food within a large membrane-bound sac.

Transport of Large Molecules

So far you've seen how water and small particles of solutes enter and leave a cell by moving through the plasma membrane. The process is different for large particles. Their movement depends on being packaged in **vesicles** (VES i kuhlz), which are small membrane sacs that specialize in moving products into, out of, and within a cell (Figure 6-17). For example, in exporting protein products from a cell, a vesicle containing the proteins fuses with the plasma membrane and spills its contents outside the cell—a process called **exocytosis.** The reverse process, **endocytosis,** takes material into the cell within vesicles that bud inward from the plasma membrane. Larger membrane sacs are also formed by endocytosis when food particles are ingested.

Online Activity 6.3

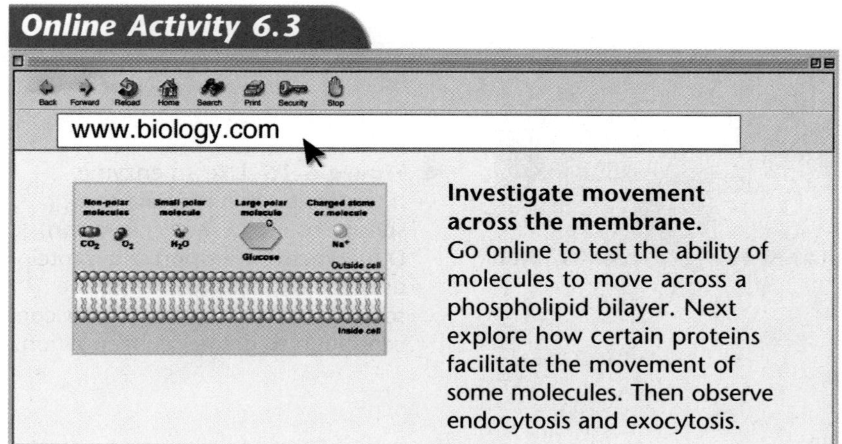

Investigate movement across the membrane.
Go online to test the ability of molecules to move across a phospholipid bilayer. Next explore how certain proteins facilitate the movement of some molecules. Then observe endocytosis and exocytosis.

Concept Check 6.3

1. What is diffusion?
2. What role does a cellular membrane play in passive transport?
3. Distinguish between hypertonic, hypotonic, and isotonic solutions, and give an example of how each affects an animal cell.
4. What role does active transport play in cell function?
5. How do vesicles transport large molecules out of a cell?

Design a Cell

Comparing the Effects of Cell Shape on Diffusion Rate

Question Which cell shapes are the most efficient at bringing in substances by diffusion?

Lab Overview In this investigation, you will design your own cell shapes, carve model cells from gel cubes, and test how rapidly a substance can diffuse throughout each model cell. Your team will then design and make a model cell for a class "diffusion race," in which the cell with the largest ratio of mass to diffusion time wins.

Preparing for the Lab To help you prepare for the investigation, go to the *Lab 6 Online Companion.* ·····➔ Find out how the ratio of surface area to volume affects the rate of diffusion in gel cubes of different sizes. Prepare for the lab procedure by previewing the steps you will take.

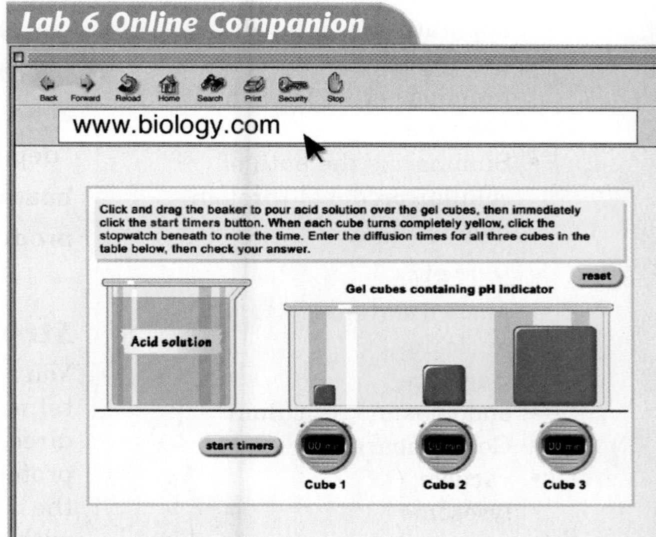
Lab 6 Online Companion
Back Forward Reload Home Search Print Security Stop
www.biology.com
Click and drag the beaker to pour acid solution over the gel cubes, then immediately click the start timers button. When each cube turns completely yellow, click the stopwatch beneath to note the time. Enter the diffusion times for all three cubes in the table below, then check your answer.
reset
Gel cubes containing pH indicator
Acid solution
start timers
Cube 1
Cube 2
Cube 3

Completing the Lab Use your Laboratory Manual or lab page printouts from the *Lab 6 Online Companion* to do the investigation and analyze your results. **CAUTION:** *Be sure to follow your teacher's instructions and all safety guidelines in the investigation.*

CONCEPT 6.4

The cell builds a diversity of products.

OBJECTIVES

- Identify the role of the nucleus in a cell.
- Describe how the functions of ribosomes, the endoplasmic reticulum, and the Golgi apparatus are related.
- Distinguish between the functions of vacuoles and lysosomes.
- Summarize the path of cellular products through membranes.

KEY TERMS

- nuclear envelope
- nucleolus
- ribosome
- endoplasmic reticulum
- Golgi apparatus
- vacuole
- lysosome

What's Online

Just as a factory has a number of different departments and equipment specialized for specific jobs, a cell is similarly specialized. If you think of a cell as a factory, then the nucleus is its executive boardroom. The top managers are the DNA molecules that direct almost all the business of the cell. The other organelles are the "departments" that carry out the instructions of the executive board. They build, package, transport, export, and even recycle products of the cell.

Structure and Function of the Nucleus

You read in Concept 6.1 that the nucleus of a eukaryotic cell contains most of the cell's DNA. The information stored in the DNA directs the activities of the cell. This DNA is attached to certain proteins, forming long fibers called chromatin. Most of the time, the chromatin looks like a tangled mess to anybody examining it with a microscope. But you will read in Chapter 9 that chromatin becomes much more organized when cells reproduce. A pair of membranes called the **nuclear envelope** surrounds the nucleus (Figure 6-18). Substances made in the nucleus move into the cell's cytoplasm through tiny holes, or pores, in the nuclear envelope. These substances include molecules that carry out the instructions from the DNA of the nucleus. In addition to the chromatin, the nucleus contains a ball-like mass of fibers and granules called the **nucleolus** (plural, *nucleoli*). The nucleolus contains the parts that make up organelles called ribosomes.

Figure 6-18 A cell's nucleus contains DNA—information-rich molecules that direct cell activities.

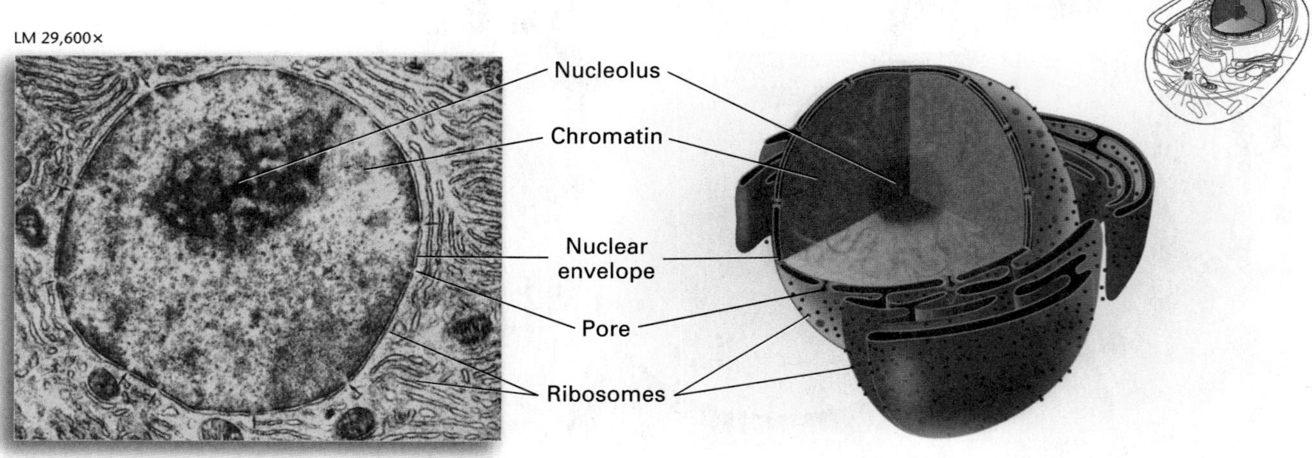

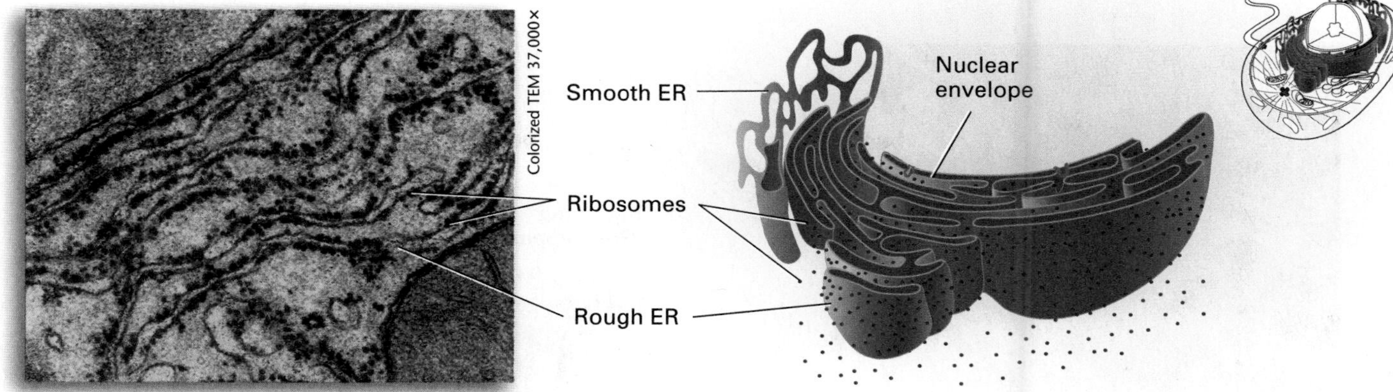
Colorized TEM 37,000×
Smooth ER
Nuclear envelope
Ribosomes
Rough ER

Ribosomes

The DNA in the nucleus contains instructions for making proteins. Proteins are constructed in a cell by the **ribosomes.** These organelles work as protein "assembly lines" in the cellular factory. Ribosomes themselves are clusters of proteins and nucleic acids assembled from components made in the nucleolus. In the classroom-cell scale model, a ribosome would be about the size of a marble. Some ribosomes are bound to the outer surface of a membrane network within the cytoplasm (Figure 6-19). These ribosomes make the proteins found in membranes, as well as other proteins that are exported by the cell. Other ribosomes are suspended in the cytoplasm. The suspended ribosomes make enzymes and other proteins that remain in the cytoplasm.

▲ **Figure 6-19** A ribosome is either suspended in the cytoplasm or temporarily attached to the rough endoplasmic reticulum (ER). Though different in structure and function, the two types of ER form a continuous maze of membranes throughout a cell. The ER is also connected to the nuclear envelope.

The Endoplasmic Reticulum

Within the cytoplasm of a cell is an extensive network of membranes called the **endoplasmic reticulum** (ER). You could think of the ER as one of the main manufacturing and transportation facilities in the cell factory. The ER produces an enormous variety of molecules. It is a maze of membranes, arranged as tubes and sacs that separate the inside of the ER from the surrounding cytoplasm (Figure 6-19). There are two distinct regions: rough ER and smooth ER. These two regions are physically connected, but they differ in structure and function.

Rough ER The rough ER gets its name from the bound ribosomes that dot the outside of the ER membrane. These ribosomes produce proteins that are inserted right into (or through) the ER membrane. Ribosomes bound to the ER also produce proteins that are packaged in vesicles by the ER and later exported, or secreted, by the cell (Figure 6-20). Cells that secrete a lot of protein—such as the cells of your salivary glands that secrete enzymes into your mouth—are especially rich in rough ER.

Smooth ER This part of the ER lacks the ribosomes that cover the rough ER. A number of different enzymes built into the smooth ER membrane enable the organelle to perform many functions. One function is to build lipid molecules. For example, cells in the ovaries and testes that produce sex hormones contain an especially large amount of smooth ER.

▼ **Figure 6-20** Some proteins are made by ribosomes (the red structure) on the rough ER and packaged in vesicles. After further processing in other parts of the cell, these proteins will eventually move to other organelles or to the plasma membrane.

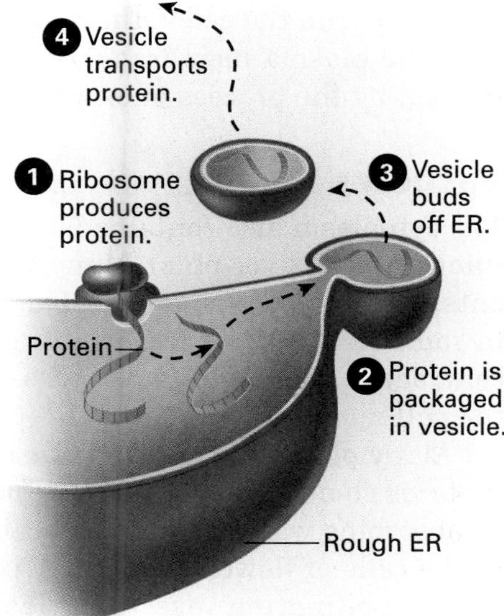
4 Vesicle transports protein.
1 Ribosome produces protein.
3 Vesicle buds off ER.
Protein
2 Protein is packaged in vesicle.
Rough ER

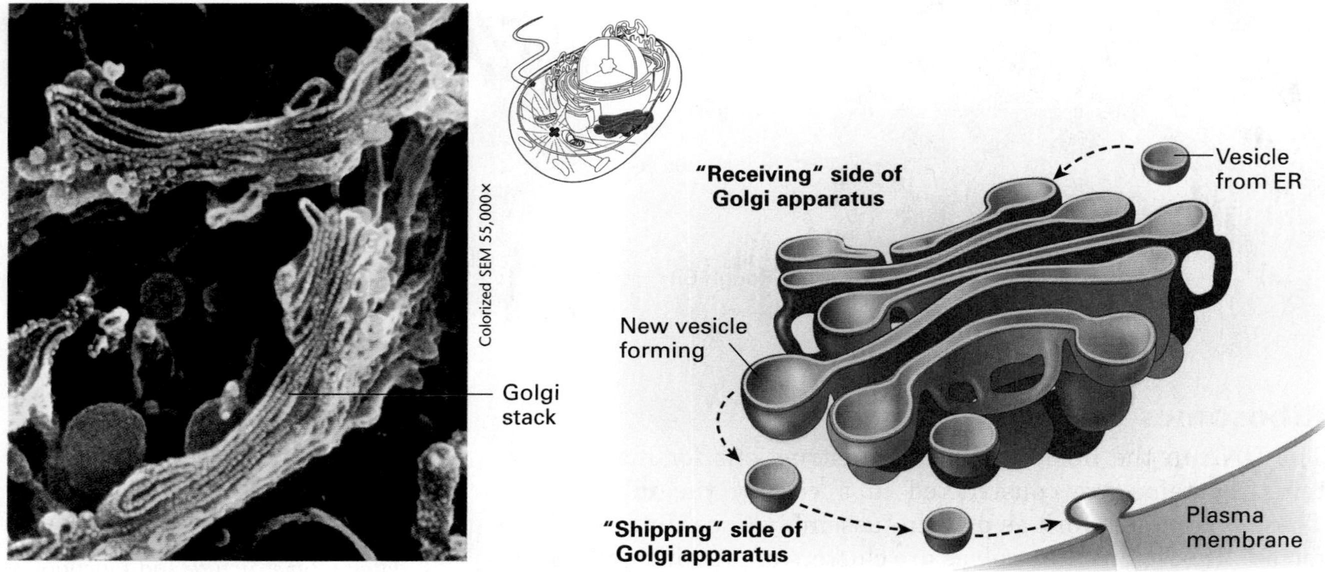

▲ **Figure 6-21** Two Golgi stacks (light green) are visible in the micrograph at left. The stacks receive, modify, and dispatch finished products.

The Golgi Apparatus

Some products that are made in the ER travel in vesicles to the **Golgi apparatus,** an organelle that modifies, stores, and routes proteins and other chemical products to their next destinations. The membranes of the Golgi apparatus are arranged as a series of flattened sacs that might remind you of a stack of pita bread. A cell may contain anywhere from just a few of these stacks to hundreds. In the classroom-cell scale model, a Golgi stack is about the size of a bass drum. This organelle is like the factory's processing and shipping center all in one. One side of a stack serves as a "receiving dock" for vesicles transported from the ER (Figure 6-21). Enzymes in the Golgi apparatus refine and modify the ER products by altering their chemical structure. From the "shipping" side of a stack, the finished products can be moved in vesicles to other locations. Some of these vesicles travel to specific targets within the cell. Others export cellular products by fusing with the plasma membrane and releasing the products outside the cell by the process of exocytosis.

Vacuoles

The cytoplasm also contains large, membrane-bound sacs called **vacuoles** (VAK yoo ohlz). Many vacuoles store undigested nutrients. One type of vacuole, called a contractile vacuole, is found in some single-celled freshwater organisms (Figure 6-22a). The contractile vacuole pumps out excess water that diffuses into the cell.

Many plant cells have a large central vacuole (Figure 6-22b). It stores chemicals such as salts and contributes to plant growth by absorbing water and causing cells to expand. Central vacuoles in the cells of flower petals may contain colorful pigments that attract pollinating insects. In leaf cells, central vacuoles may contain poisons that protect against plant-eating animals.

▼ **Figure 6-22** A large membrane-bound sac is called a vacuole. **a.** This paramecium has two contractile vacuoles. **b.** The central vacuole in a mature plant cell is often the cell's largest organelle.

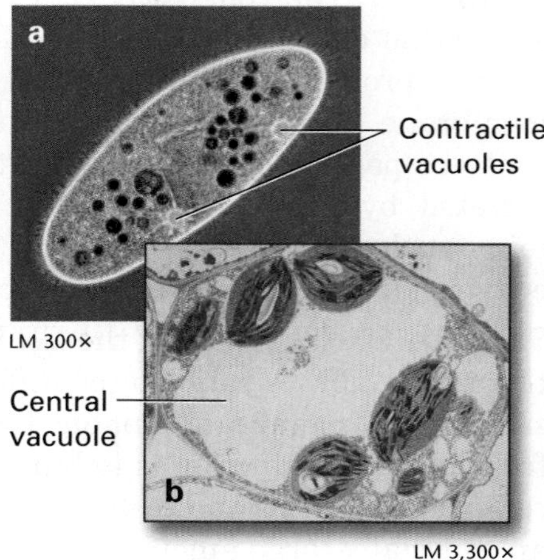

Lysosomes

Membrane-bound sacs called **lysosomes** contain digestive enzymes that can break down such macromolecules as proteins, nucleic acids, and polysaccharides (Figure 6-23). Lysosomes have several functions. They fuse with incoming food vacuoles and expose the nutrients to enzymes that digest them, thereby nourishing the cell. Lysosomes also function like safety officers when they help destroy harmful bacteria. In certain cells—for example, your white blood cells—lysosomes release enzymes into vacuoles that contain trapped bacteria and break down the bacterial cell walls. Similarly, lysosomes serve as recycling centers for damaged organelles. Without harming the cell, a lysosome can engulf and digest another organelle. This makes molecules available for the construction of new organelles.

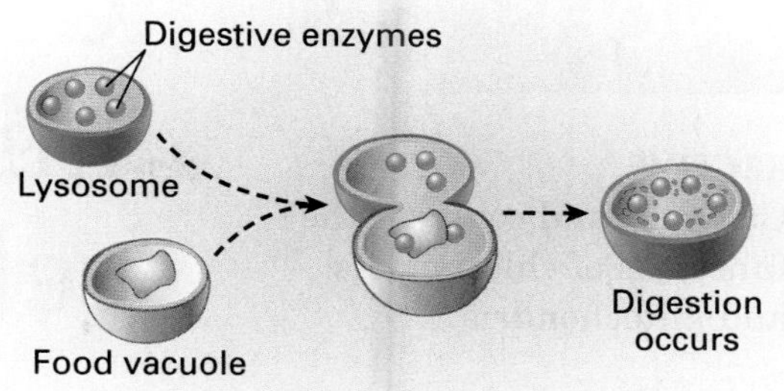

▲ **Figure 6-23** Lysosomes contain digestive enzymes that break down food for cell use.

Membrane Pathways in a Cell

Follow the pathway of activity in Figure 6-24 to see how some of a cell's organelles function together. Vesicles bud from one organelle (1) and fuse with another (2), transferring membranes as well as products. The arrows show some of the pathways cell products follow on their journey through the cell (3 and 4). You may notice that the internal side of a vesicle membrane can eventually turn up as part of the outward face of the plasma membrane at the cell's surface (5). Exocytosis has turned the vesicle inside out! Membranes are constantly being transferred throughout the cell. An ER product can eventually exit the cell without ever crossing a membrane.

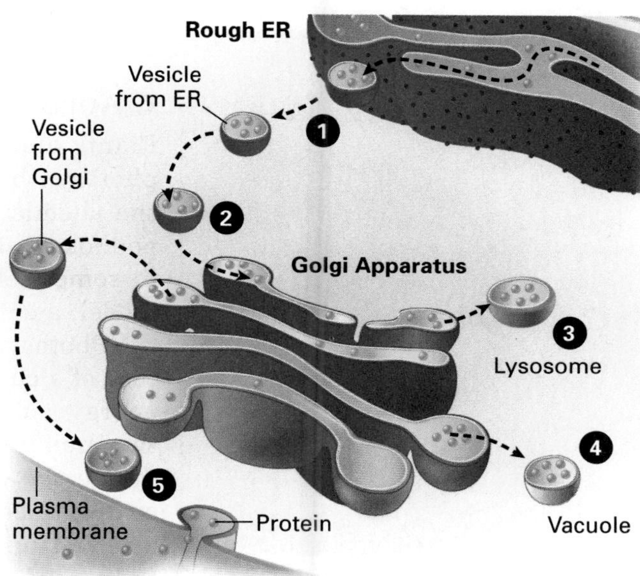

▲ **Figure 6-24** Products made in the ER move through membrane pathways in a cell.

Online Activity 6.4

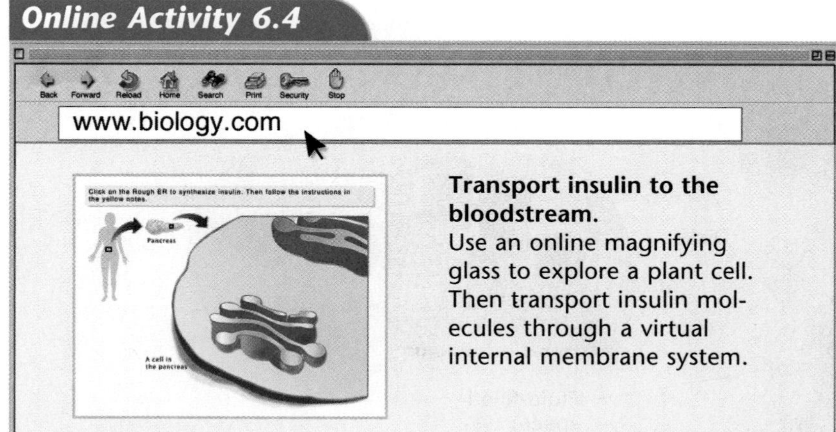

Back
Forward
Reload
Home
Search
Print
Security
Stop
www.biology.com
Transport insulin to the bloodstream.
Use an online magnifying glass to explore a plant cell. Then transport insulin molecules through a virtual internal membrane system.

Concept Check 6.4

1. In what way does the nucleus direct the activities of a cell?
2. Trace the path of a protein from the time it is produced by a ribosome on the ER until it reaches its destination.
3. How are undigested nutrients in a vacuole made available to a cell?

CONCEPT 6.5

Chloroplasts and mitochondria energize cells.

OBJECTIVE
- Compare and contrast the functions of chloroplasts and mitochondria.

KEY TERMS
- chloroplast
- mitochondria
- ATP

What's Online

Online Activity 6.5
Magnify a chloroplast and a mitochondrion.

The cellular machinery requires a continuous energy supply to do all the work of life. The two types of cellular power stations are organelles called chloroplasts and mitochondria. One harnesses light energy from the sun, and the other "unpacks" this captured energy into smaller packets that are useful for powering cellular work.

Chloroplasts

Plants and algae harness light energy through the process of photosynthesis—the conversion of light energy from the sun to the chemical energy stored in sugars and other organic compounds. **Chloroplasts** are the photosynthetic organelles found in some cells of plants and algae. In the classroom-cell scale model, a chloroplast would be the size of a table.

Photosynthesis is a complex, multi-step process. The structure of a chloroplast provides the organization necessary for the energy conversion process to take place. An envelope made of two membranes encloses the chloroplast. Internal membranes divide the chloroplast into compartments (Figure 6-25). One compartment is a fluid-filled space inside the chloroplast's envelope. Suspended in that thick fluid is a network of membrane-bounded disks and tubules that form another compartment. The disks are a chloroplast's solar "power packs"—the structures that actually trap light energy and convert it to chemical energy. In Chapter 8, you'll learn more about a chloroplast's structure and how it works.

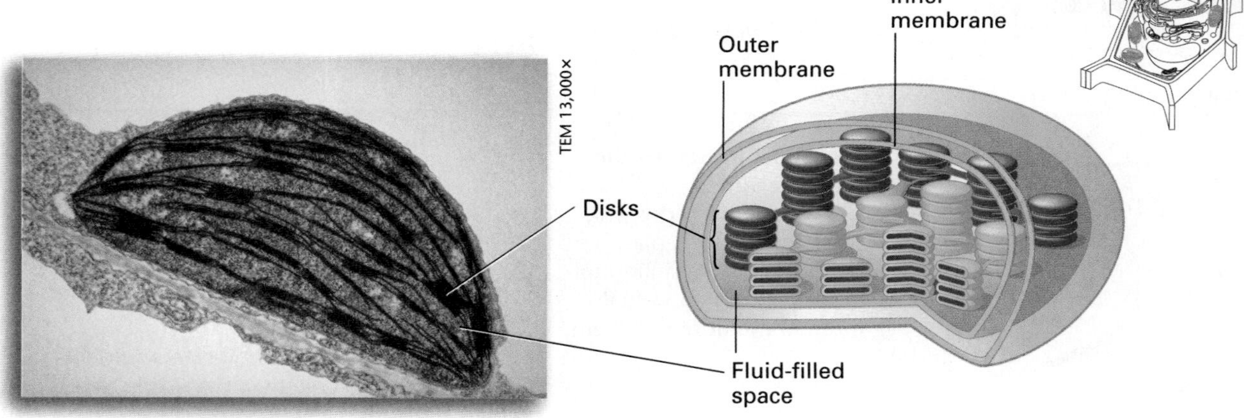

▼ **Figure 6-25** A chloroplast is a miniature "solar collector," transforming light energy into chemical energy through photosynthesis. The green color of the disks is due to the presence of a pigment called chlorophyll that reacts with light.

Mitochondria

Most organisms access the energy needed for the activities of life through a process known as cellular respiration. In eukaryotic cells, **mitochondria** (singular, *mitochondrion*) are the sites where cellular respiration occurs. This process releases energy from sugars and certain other organic molecules and then uses it in the formation of another organic molecule called ATP. **ATP** (adenosine triphosphate) is the main energy source that cells use for most of their work. You can think of ATP as a kind of energy currency, recognized and used in "transactions" throughout the cell.

Unlike chloroplasts, which are found only in cells that carry out photosynthesis, mitochondria are found in almost all eukaryotic cells (including plants and algae). A mitochondrion would be a little bigger than a football in the classroom-cell scale model.

A mitochondrion's structure is related to its function. As in a chloroplast, an envelope of two membranes surrounds a mitochondrion (Figure 6-26). The inner membrane of the envelope has numerous infoldings. Many of the enzymes and other molecules that function in cellular respiration are built into the inner membrane. The folds increase the surface area of this membrane, increasing the number of sites where cellular respiration can occur. Thus the folds maximize the organelle's production of ATP. In Chapter 7, you will read more about how mitochondria convert the chemical energy stored in molecules of sugars and other organic compounds to the chemical energy stored in ATP.

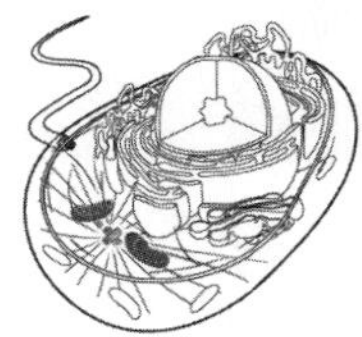

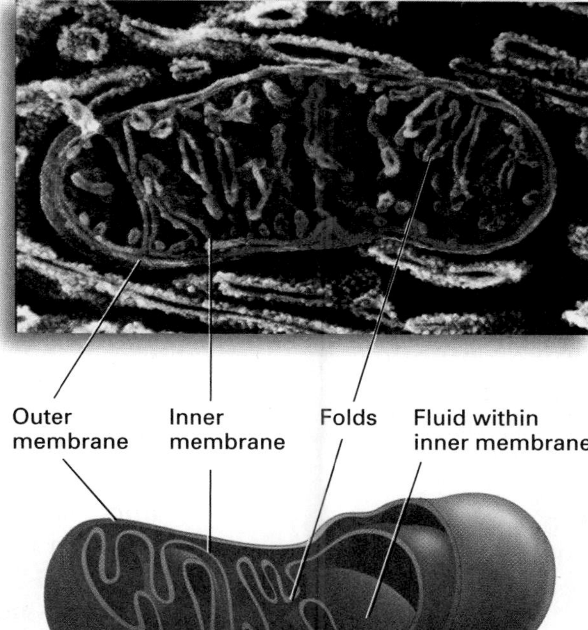

▲ **Figure 6-26** Cellular respiration in the mitochondria releases the energy that drives a cell. The many folds of each mitochondrion's inner membrane are the sites of ATP production.

Online Activity 6.5

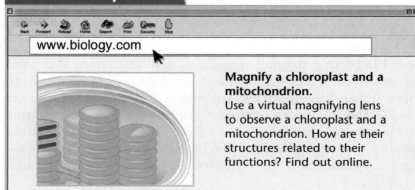

Magnify a chloroplast and a mitochondrion.
Use a virtual magnifying lens to observe a chloroplast and a mitochondrion. How are their structures related to their functions? Find out online.

Concept Check 6.5

1. How are the functions of chloroplasts and mitochondria similar?
2. How does a cell use the energy produced by mitochondria?
3. In what way is energy changed by reactions in a chloroplast?
4. How is membrane structure important to the functions of mitochondria and chloroplasts?

CONCEPT 6.6

An internal skeleton supports the cell and enables movement.

OBJECTIVES
- Describe the role of the cytoskeleton in cell movement.
- Compare and contrast the functions of flagella and cilia.
- Explain why a cell can be described as a coordinated unit.

KEY TERMS
- microtubule
- microfilament
- flagella
- cilia

What's Online

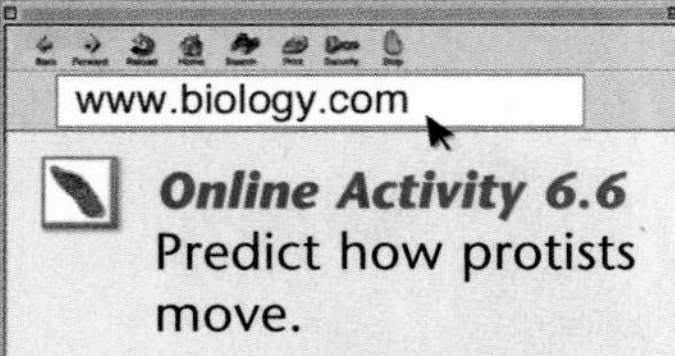

Online Activity 6.6
Predict how protists move.

Some cells are capable of moving by extending parts of themselves and "oozing" from one place to another. Just as you have an internal skeleton that serves several functions in your body, a cell has its own kind of internal support system that enables it to move, support organelles, and maintain shape.

The Cytoskeleton

Biologists once thought that the organelles of a cell drifted about freely in the cytoplasm. However, improvements in microscopes and research techniques revealed a cytoskeleton (*cyto* means "cell"), a network of fibers extending throughout the cytoplasm (Figure 6-27). Unlike your body's skeleton, the skeleton of most cells does not keep the same structural pattern all the time. It is always changing, with new extensions building at the same time that others are breaking apart.

Different kinds of fibers make up the cytoskeleton. Straight, hollow tubes of proteins that give rigidity, shape, and organization to a cell are called **microtubules.** As protein subunits are added or subtracted from the microtubules, these structures lengthen or shorten. One function of microtubules is to provide "tracks" along which other organelles can move. For example, a lysosome might reach a food vacuole by moving along a microtubule. Thinner, solid rods of protein called **microfilaments** enable the cell to move or change shape when protein subunits slide past one another. This process contributes to the oozing movements of an amoeba and some white blood cells.

▼ **Figure 6-27** Microfilaments and microtubules are two fibers that form the cytoskeleton, which appears in the inset as orange and green fibers around a cell's nucleus (blue).

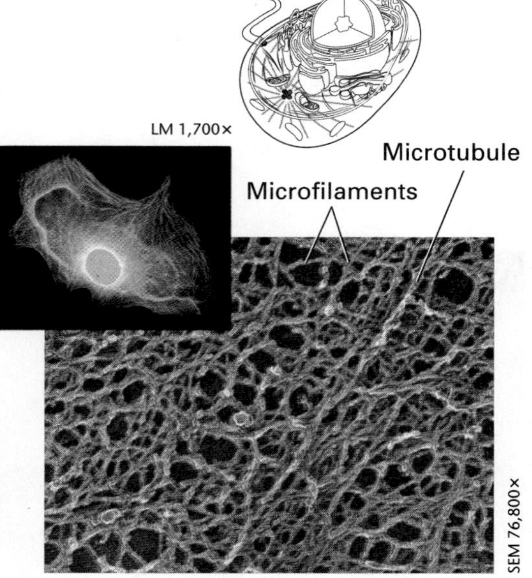

Flagella and Cilia

Unlike an amoeba that moves as changes occur to microfilaments in its cytoplasm, many other kinds of cells move as a result of the action of specialized structures that project from the cell. **Flagella** (singular, *flagellum*) are long, thin, whip-like structures, with a core of microtubules, that enable some cells to move. A flagellum usually waves with an "S"-shaped motion that propels the cell. **Cilia** (singular, *cilium*) are generally shorter and more numerous than flagella. Like flagella, cilia also contain bundles of microtubules, but cilia have a back-and-forth motion—something like the oars of a rowboat—that moves a cell through its surroundings.

Cilia or flagella can also extend out from stationary cells that are held in place as part of a layer of tissue in a multicellular organism. Here, their motion moves fluid over the surface of the tissue. For example, the cells lining your windpipe have cilia that sweep mucus with trapped debris out of your lungs. This sweeping action helps keep your respiratory system clean and allows air to flow through it smoothly (Figure 6-28).

Figure 6-28 The cilia lining your respiratory tract sweep mucus and trapped debris out of your lungs.

The Cell as a Coordinated Unit

From the overview of a cell's organization to a close-up inspection of each organelle's architecture, this tour of the cell has provided many opportunities to connect structure with function. As you study the parts of a cell, remember that none of its organelles works alone.

Consider the scene in Figure 6-29. The large cell in the micrograph is a type of white blood cell that helps defend the body against infections by ingesting bacteria (the small cells). The cell moves toward the bacteria using thin cytoplasmic extensions created by the interaction of parts of the cytoskeleton. After the cell engulfs the bacteria, they are destroyed by lysosomes that were produced by the ER and Golgi apparatus. Ribosomes made the proteins of the cytoskeleton and the enzymes within the lysosomes. And the production of these proteins was programmed by messages dispatched from the DNA in the nucleus. All these processes require energy, which mitochondria supply in the form of ATP. The cooperation of cellular organelles makes a cell a living unit that is greater than the sum of its parts.

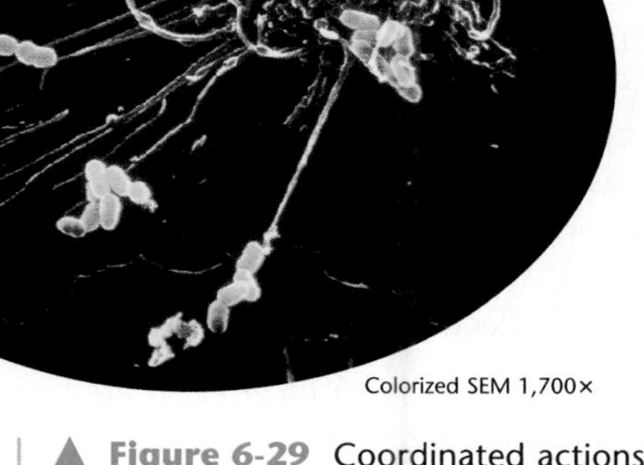

Figure 6-29 Coordinated actions of its cell structures enable a white blood cell (orange) to move toward and destroy bacteria (yellow).

Online Activity 6.6

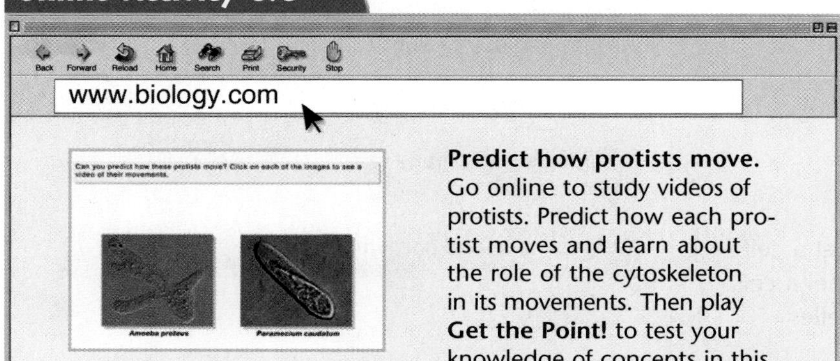

Predict how protists move. Go online to study videos of protists. Predict how each protist moves and learn about the role of the cytoskeleton in its movements. Then play **Get the Point!** to test your knowledge of concepts in this chapter.

Concept Check 6.6

1. How do microfilaments function in the cytoskeleton of a cell?
2. How do flagella differ in structure and function from cilia?
3. Give an example of coordination within a cell.

Multiple Choice

Choose the letter of the best answer.

1. A structure found in plant cells but not in animal cells is the
   a. nucleus.
   b. plasma membrane.
   c. endoplasmic reticulum.
   d. cell wall.

2. Which best describes the structure of a cell's plasma membrane?
   a. proteins sandwiched between two layers of phospholipid
   b. proteins embedded in two layers of phospholipid
   c. phospholipids sandwiched between two layers of proteins
   d. a layer of protein coating two layers of phospholipids

3. During diffusion, molecules move
   a. from areas of lesser concentration to areas of greater concentration.
   b. from areas of greater concentration to areas of lesser concentration.
   c. by active transport.
   d. only through selectively permeable membranes.

4. Which of the following is an *incorrect* match of organelle and function?
   a. ribosome—protein synthesis
   b. lysosome—digestion
   c. Golgi apparatus—photosynthesis
   d. plasma membrane—active transport

5. In mitochondria, chemical energy becomes available to cells through a process called
   a. photosynthesis.
   b. cellular respiration.
   c. osmosis.
   d. exocytosis.

6. Which best describes flagella?
   a. thin, solid rods that aid cell motion
   b. short, hair-like structures that propel a cell
   c. long, whip-like structures that propel a cell
   d. long, solid rods that anchor organelles

Short Answer

7. What are the three key ideas of the cell theory?

8. Identify the type of microscope most useful for viewing each of the following: a group of cells in a thin layer of onion skin; the details of the surface of a human hair; the detailed structure of a mitochondrion in a muscle cell.

9. What characteristics do eukaryotic cells share?

10. How does the structure of a phospholipid molecule contribute to the way such molecules are organized in a cellular membrane?

11. How is diffusion related to passive transport?

12. Describe how the structure of a plasma membrane is involved in facilitated diffusion.

13. What happens to an animal cell placed in a hypotonic environment? Explain.

14. What is the function of the Golgi apparatus?

15. How might a cell be affected if one of its lysosomes were to rupture?

16. What does photosynthesis accomplish?

17. Describe two different ways in which the motion of cilia can function in organisms.

Visualizing Concepts

18. Copy and complete the following table that lists cell structures and their functions.

Action or Process	Cell Structure(s) Involved
Cell movement such as an amoeba oozing	a.
Endocytosis	b.
Movement of organelles within a cell	c.
Digesting a food particle	d.

Analyzing Information

19. Analyzing Diagrams Examine the diagram of a cell below and answer the following questions.

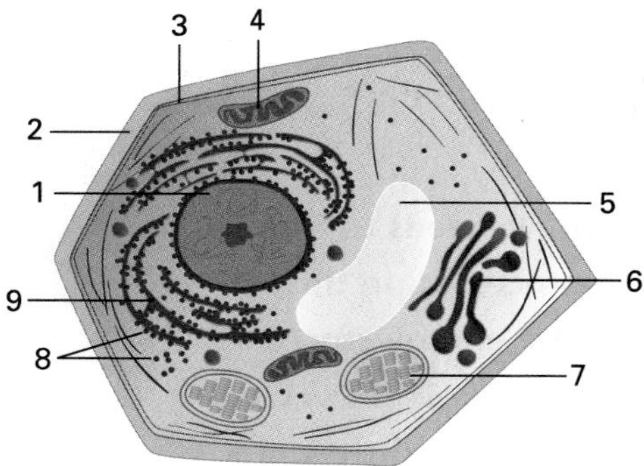

a. Is this a diagram of a eukaryotic cell or a prokaryotic cell? Explain.
b. Which structure in the diagram carries out photosynthesis?
c. Name three processes that involve Structure 3.
d. Which structure manufactures proteins?
e. In which structure would you expect to find many newly produced molecules of ATP?
f. How are the functions of structures 9 and 6 related?

20. Analyzing Diagrams In the diagram below, a U-shaped glass tube contains two different sugar-water solutions. The solutions are separated by a selectively permeable membrane that sugar molecules cannot penetrate. Use the diagram to answer the questions that follow.

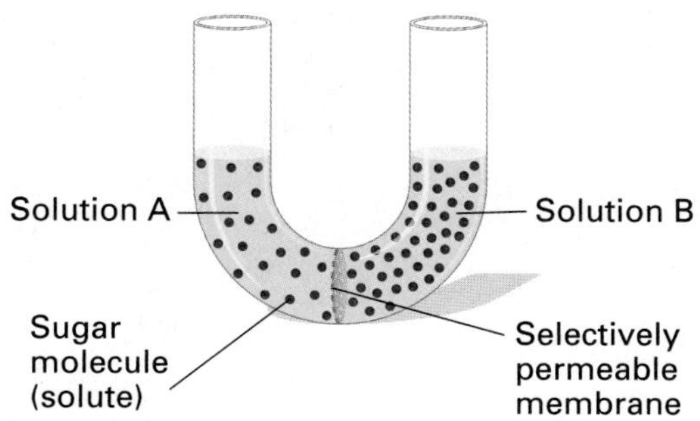

a. Which solution (A or B) contains a greater concentration of solute?
b. Predict the direction in which osmosis will occur. Explain your reasoning.
c. Draw a diagram of how the water levels in the tube will look at equilibrium.

Critical Thinking

21. Comparing and Contrasting How are active transport and facilitated diffusion different? How are they similar?

22. Relating Cause and Effect Explain how a protein inside the ER can be exported from the cell without ever crossing a membrane.

23. Making Generalizations Give examples of how structure and function are interdependent in a cell.

24. Evaluating the Impact of Research How have electron microscopes changed cell biology?

25. Evaluating Models How is the classroom-size scale model of cells that was described in this chapter helpful in understanding cell structure? What drawbacks does the model have?

26. What's Wrong With These Statements? *Briefly explain why each statement is inaccurate or misleading.*

a. Cells are the same in all living things.
b. Molecules of a solution stop moving when concentration equilibrium is reached.
c. Ribosomes direct the activities of a cell because they produce proteins.

Performance Assessment

Design an Experiment Suppose you wanted to explore the effects of osmosis on plant cells. You peel a raw potato and cut it into rectangular blocks each about 3 cm × 1 cm × 1 cm. You place three pieces in a 15 percent salt solution, and three in distilled water. Predict how you think the potato pieces will change. What measurements would you include?

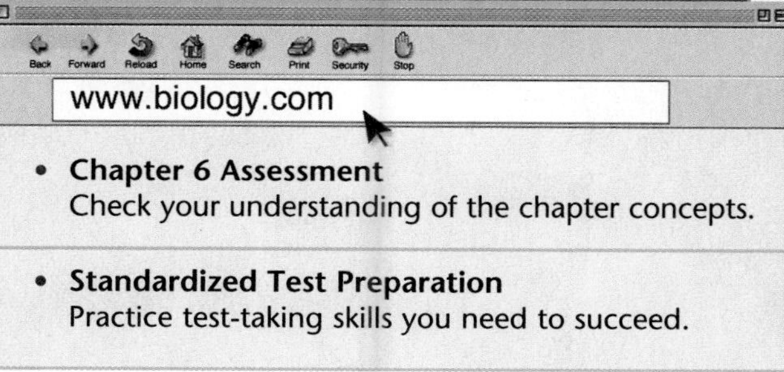

- **Chapter 6 Assessment**
  Check your understanding of the chapter concepts.
- **Standardized Test Preparation**
  Practice test-taking skills you need to succeed.

The Working Cell: Energy from Food

Nectar provides a hummingbird with the energy it needs to fly, breathe, build a nest, and carry out other life processes. In this chapter, you will learn how organisms release the energy stored in food. Before you start the chapter, go online to the *WebQuest* to explore the connection between the food you eat and the energy you burn.

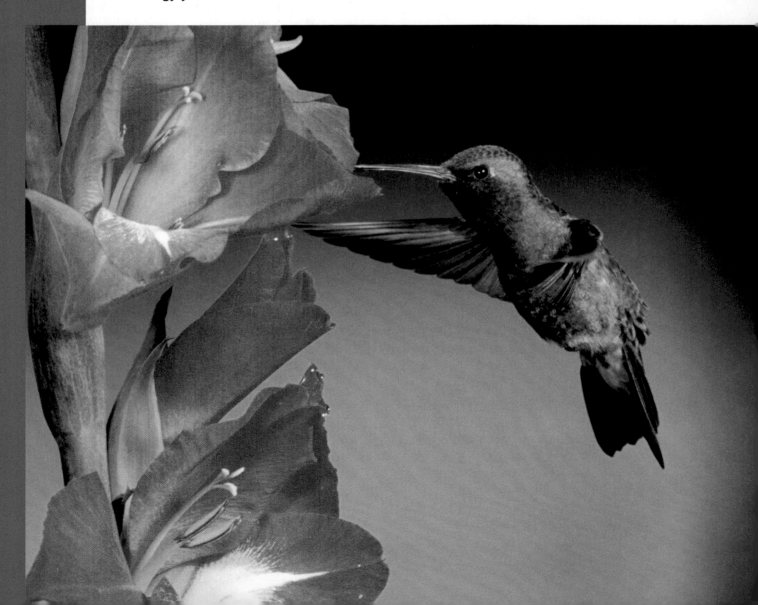

Key Concepts

Concept 7.1 **Sunlight powers life.**

Concept 7.2 **Food stores chemical energy.**

Concept 7.3 **ATP provides energy for cellular work.**

Concept 7.4 **Electrons "fall" from food to oxygen during cellular respiration.**

Concept 7.5 **Cellular respiration converts energy in food to energy in ATP.**

Concept 7.6 **Some cells can harvest energy without oxygen.**

Assessment **Chapter 7 Review**

What's Online

www.biology.com

WebQuest
CalorieQuest

Online Activity 7.1
Explore light energy in action.

Online Activity 7.2
Burn a marshmallow.

Lab 7 Online Companion
Food as Fuel

Online Activity 7.3
Examine how ATP stores energy.

Online Activity 7.4
Make electrons fall.

Guided Research Lab 2
Cellular Respiration in Fast Plants™

Online Activity 7.5
Explore a pinball analogy for cellular respiration.

Closer Look
Respiration Stages

Science, Technology, & Society
Aerobic Performance

Online Activity 7.6
Explore a pinball analogy for fermentation.

Closer Look
Fermentation in Muscle and Yeast

Chapter 7 Assessment

CONCEPT 7.1 Sunlight powers life.

OBJECTIVES
- Compare and contrast how autotrophs and heterotrophs obtain food.
- Explain how cellular respiration harvests the energy in food.

KEY TERMS
- autotroph
- photosynthesis
- producer
- heterotroph
- consumer
- cellular respiration

What's Online

Online Activity 7.1
Explore light energy in action.

Look up on a clear day, and you will see the sun burning brightly almost 150 million kilometers away. A tiny fraction of the light energy radiated from the sun reaches Earth's surface. And a tiny fraction of that sunlight powers most of the planet's life. This is true because certain organisms can convert the energy of sunlight to the chemical energy in food—sugars and other organic molecules.

Obtaining Food

All organisms need food for energy and building materials. Biologists classify organisms according to how they obtain food.

Autotrophs An organism such as a plant that makes its own food is called an **autotroph,** which means "self-feeder" in Greek. Starting with inorganic molecules, autotrophs make organic molecules. For example, plants use the sun's energy to convert water and carbon dioxide into sugars. This process is called **photosynthesis** (from the Greek *photo-* meaning "light," and *synthesis* meaning "making something"). You will read more about photosynthesis in Chapter 8.

Autotrophs are also called **producers** because they produce the organic molecules that serve as food for the organisms in their ecosystem. On land, plants are the major producers. In oceans, lakes, and streams, producers include algae and certain photosynthetic bacteria (Figure 7-1).

Heterotrophs Organisms that cannot make their own food, such as humans, are called **heterotrophs,** meaning "other eaters." Heterotrophs, also called **consumers,** must obtain food by eating producers or other consumers. Heterotrophs depend on producers to supply energy and materials for life and growth. Since most producers depend on sunlight as their energy source, you could say that life on Earth is solar-powered.

▼ **Figure 7-1** Seaweed (left), a cherry tree (middle), and microscopic *Euglena* (right) are just a few of the diverse organisms that are classified as producers.

Harvesting the Energy in Food

As you have read, plants and certain other producers use light energy to make organic molecules. These organic molecules are a source of energy and building materials for organisms.

Many organisms, including both producers and consumers such as the woodchucks in Figure 7-2, harvest the energy stored in foods through cellular respiration. **Cellular respiration** is a chemical process that uses oxygen to convert the chemical energy stored in organic molecules into another form of chemical energy—a molecule called adenosine triphosphate (ATP). Cells in plants and animals then use ATP as their main energy supply. You will read about cellular respiration and ATP in more detail later in this chapter.

▲ **Figure 7-2** These two woodchucks are consumers (heterotrophs). They rely on organic molecules from producers, such as grass, for energy and building materials.

The processes of photosynthesis and cellular respiration recycle a common set of chemicals: water, carbon dioxide, oxygen, and organic compounds such as glucose. The diagram in Figure 7-3 visually summarizes this chemical recycling. Water and carbon dioxide are the raw ingredients for photosynthesis. Plants use energy from sunlight to rearrange the atoms of water and carbon dioxide, producing glucose and oxygen. Oxygen is used by both plant and animal cells during cellular respiration to release the energy stored in glucose. The released energy enables cells to produce ATP. Cellular respiration also produces carbon dioxide and water. The result is a continual cycling of these chemical ingredients.

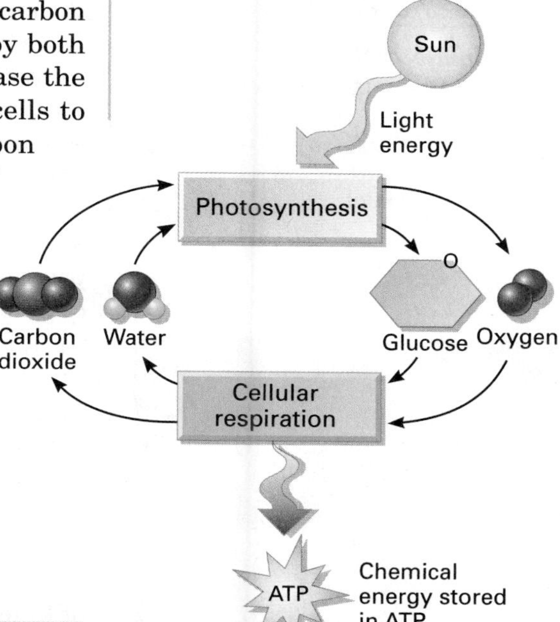

▶ **Figure 7-3** The products of photosynthesis are the chemical ingredients for cellular respiration, while the products of cellular respiration are the chemical ingredients for photosynthesis.

Online Activity 7.1

Back
Forward
Reload
Home
Search
Print
Security
Stop
www.biology.com
Sun
Explore light energy in action.
How are photosynthesis and cellular respiration related? Explore an animated apple tree to learn how sunlight powers life.

Concept Check 7.1

1. Define *autotroph* and *heterotroph*, and give an example of each.
2. Explain the role of food (glucose) in both photosynthesis and cellular respiration.
3. Explain how life on Earth depends on the sun.

CONCEPT 7.2

Food stores chemical energy.

OBJECTIVES

- Distinguish between kinetic and potential energy.
- Explain what chemical energy is and how cells release it from food.
- Define calories and kilocalories as units of energy.

KEY TERMS

- kinetic energy
- potential energy
- thermal energy
- chemical energy
- calorie

What's Online

www.biology.com

Online Activity 7.2
Burn a marshmallow.

Lab 7 Online Companion
Food as Fuel

If you've ever felt tired or groggy from being hungry, you probably know that you need food for energy. But how does your body use the energy stored in food? To understand this, you first need to know some basic facts about energy.

Introduction to Energy

Energy is the ability to perform work. In the physical science sense of the word, work is performed whenever an object is moved against an opposing force. For example, your leg muscles do work when you climb the steps to the top of a water slide—your legs move your body against the opposing force of gravity.

The two basic forms of energy are kinetic energy and potential energy. While you climb the stairs, you have **kinetic energy,** the energy of motion. Anything that is moving has kinetic energy. In fact, the word *kinetic* comes from a Greek word meaning "motion." Once you reach the top of the stairs and are standing still, you have low kinetic energy. Where has the energy gone? Although it is not possible to destroy or create energy, energy can be converted from one form to another. By climbing the stairs, your body converted kinetic energy to potential energy. **Potential energy** is energy that is stored due to an object's position or arrangement. As you climb higher against the force of gravity, your body gains potential energy due to its position—its higher location. The potential energy is converted back to kinetic energy as you move down the slide (Figure 7-4).

What becomes of the energy once you have splashed into the pool and come to a stop? As you go down the slide, your body collides with air and water molecules, increasing their motion. And when you splash into the pool, the rest of your motion is transferred to the water. The air and water molecules transfer their motion in random directions as they collide again and again. This type of kinetic energy—random molecular motion—is called **thermal energy.** (Thermal energy that is transferred from a warmer object to a cooler one is referred to as *heat*.) Overall, your trip down the slide converted potential energy into the directed kinetic energy of your sliding body, and then into the random kinetic energy of molecular motion (thermal energy). You cannot retrieve this thermal energy and put it to work again. So, to climb the stairs again, you need a fresh supply of energy. That energy is provided by food.

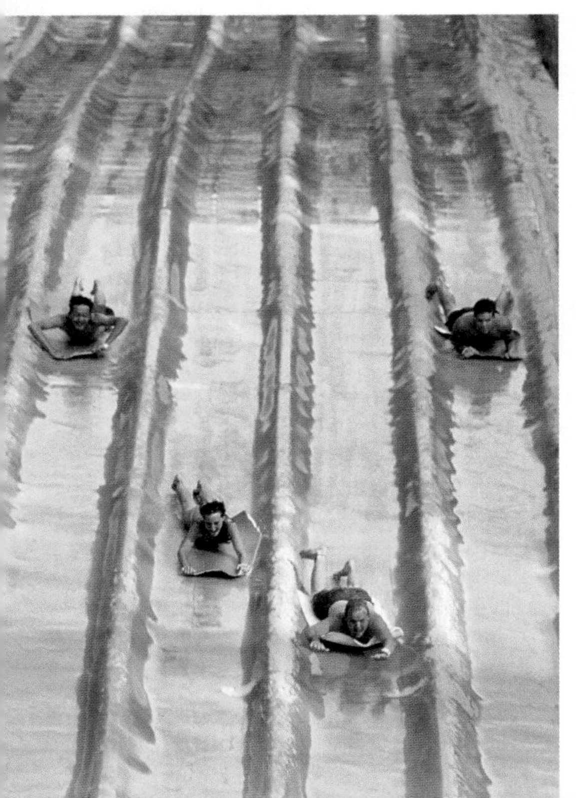

Figure 7-4 The sliders' potential energy at the top of the slide is converted to kinetic energy on the way down.

Chemical Energy

How do the organic compounds in food provide energy for a climb up a water slide? Just like the molecules in gasoline and other fuels, these organic compounds have a form of potential energy called **chemical energy.** In the case of chemical energy, the potential to perform work is due to the arrangement of the atoms within the molecules. Put another way, chemical energy depends on the structure of molecules. Organic molecules such as the carbohydrates, fats, and proteins you learned about in Chapter 5 have structures that make them especially rich in chemical energy (Figure 7-5).

Figure 7-6 compares potential energy due to position and chemical structure (chemical energy). In the case of potential energy due to position, the potential energy is converted to kinetic energy in the forms of motion and thermal energy (which is released to the surroundings as heat). In the case of chemical energy, the rearrangement of atoms during chemical reactions releases the potential energy. This energy is then available for work such as contracting a muscle.

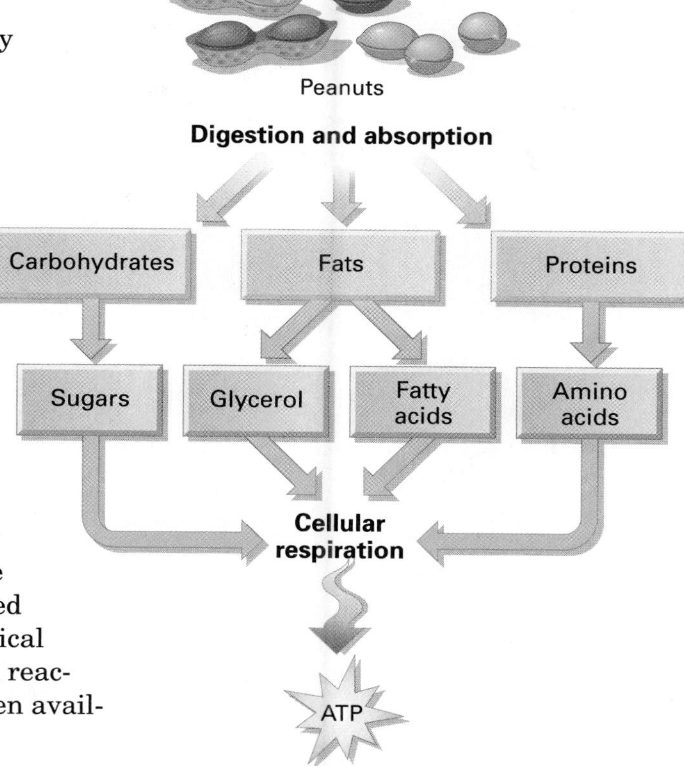

▲ **Figure 7-5** The stored chemical energy of foods such as peanuts can be released through cellular respiration.

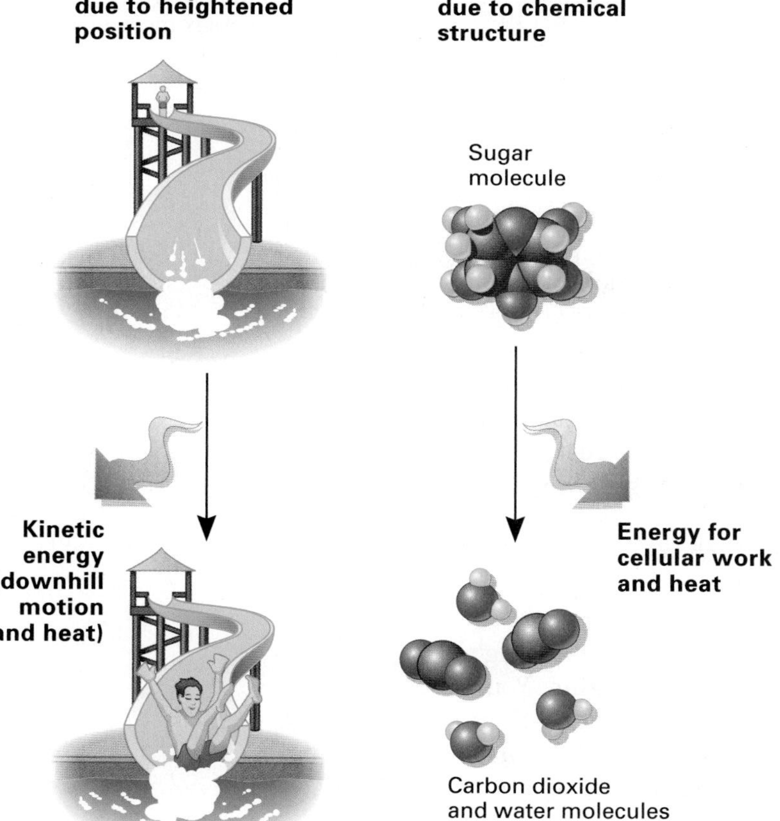

◀ **Figure 7-6** Potential energy can be converted to other types of energy.

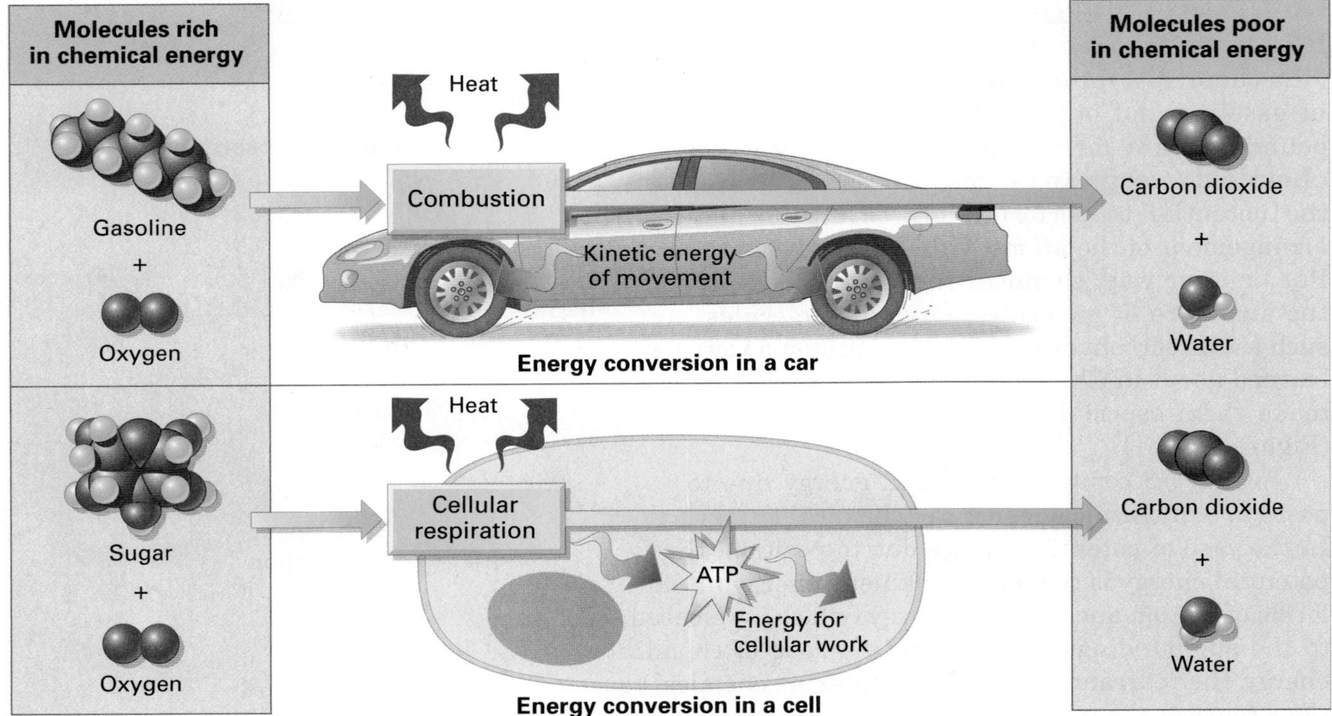

▲ **Figure 7-7** Both engines and cells use oxygen to convert the potential energy in complex molecules to energy that can be used for work.

Putting Chemical Energy to Work

The organic molecules in food are high in chemical energy, just as the organic molecules in gasoline are. Cells and automobile engines make chemical energy available for work through similar processes. In both cases, a complex molecule is broken into smaller molecules that have less chemical energy than the original substance (Figure 7-7).

An automobile engine is called an internal combustion (burning) engine. This type of engine mixes oxygen with gasoline in a very fast chemical reaction that results in the molecules of gasoline breaking down. The reaction releases thermal energy as heat, which is then used to power the car. The main waste products emitted from the automobile's exhaust pipe are carbon dioxide and water. Only about 25 percent of the energy from the gasoline is converted into the car's kinetic energy (motion). The rest is lost to the surroundings as heat, which explains why it gets very hot under the hood of a running car.

Within your cells, organic molecules such as glucose also react with oxygen in the process of cellular respiration. And similar to an automobile engine, working cells produce carbon dioxide and water as their "exhaust." Fortunately, the "burning" is much slower in your cells than in an automobile engine. Your cells are also more efficient than automobile engines—they convert about 40 percent of the energy from food into useful work. The other 60 percent of the energy is converted to thermal energy, which is lost from your body in the form of heat.

The heat generated by cellular respiration is not completely wasted. Retaining some of this heat enables your body to maintain a constant temperature, even when the surrounding air is cold. When you are sitting still in class, you radiate about as much heat as a 100-watt lightbulb. You've probably experienced the discomfort of this heat while sitting in a closed room crowded with other "human lightbulbs." When you exercise, your cells increase the rate of cellular respiration. This is why you feel warm after exercise such as running or inline skating. Excess heat is lost through sweating and other cooling methods, much as a car's radiator keeps the engine from overheating.

Calories: Units of Energy

You have probably heard the term *calorie* used to refer to food or exercise. A **calorie** is the amount of energy required to raise the temperature of 1 gram (g) of water by 1 degree Celsius (°C). However, a calorie is such a tiny unit of energy that it is not very practical for measuring the energy content of food. Instead, people usually express the energy in food in kilocalories. One kilocalorie (kcal) equals 1,000 calories. The "calories" shown on a food label are actually kilocalories.

You can actually measure the energy content of a food such as a peanut in the laboratory. First you dry the peanut and burn it under an insulated container of water. Burning the peanut converts its stored chemical energy to thermal energy, releasing heat. By measuring the increase in water temperature and using the definition of a calorie, you can calculate the number of calories in the peanut. One peanut has about 5,000 calories, or 5 kcal. That is enough chemical energy to raise the temperature of 1 kilogram (1,000 g) of water by 5°C. Of course, your cells don't burn molecules from peanuts or other foods with a flame. Cells use enzymes to break down organic molecules through the more controlled process of cellular respiration. As a result, the released energy is easier to manage for work. As shown in Figure 7-8, just a handful of peanuts provides enough fuel to power an hour-long walk.

Energy Consumed by Various Activities

Activity	kcal per hour*
Bicycling (slowly)	170
Bicycling (racing)	514
Dancing (slow)	202
Dancing (fast)	599
Running	865
Sitting (writing)	28
Swimming	535
Walking	158

*Energy consumed by a 67.5-kg person, not including energy necessary for body maintenance

▲ **Figure 7-8** Different daily activities require different amounts of energy. Organic molecules in food are the source of this energy.

Online Activity 7.2

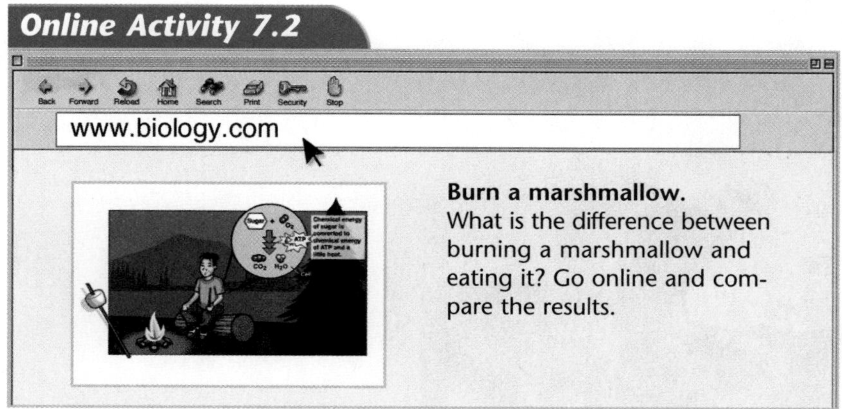

Burn a marshmallow.
What is the difference between burning a marshmallow and eating it? Go online and compare the results.

Concept Check 7.2

1. Identify the types of energy you have at the top of a staircase and as you go down the stairs.
2. Explain how your body uses chemical energy during exercise.
3. If a food has 10 kcal of energy, how much could it increase the temperature of 100 g of water?

Food as Fuel

Measuring the Chemical Energy Stored in Food

Question How can you measure the calorie content of a peanut?

Lab Overview In this investigation, you will construct and use a simple calorimeter to measure the approximate number of calories in a peanut. You will compare the number of calories in a peanut with the calorie content of other foods.

Preparing for the Lab To help you prepare for the investigation, go to the *Lab 7 Online Companion.* Find out more about how a calorimeter works. Prepare for the lab procedure by previewing the steps you will take.

Completing the Lab Use your Laboratory Manual or lab page printouts from the *Lab 7 Online Companion* to do the investigation and analyze your results. **CAUTION:** *Be sure to follow your teacher's instructions and all safety guidelines in the investigation.*

Lab 7 Online Companion

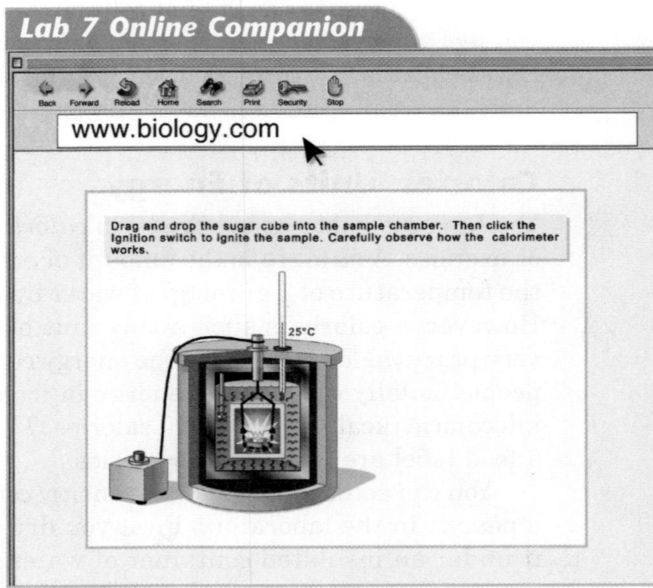
Back
Forward
Reload
Home
Search
Print
Security
Stop
www.biology.com
Drag and drop the sugar cube into the sample chamber. Then click the Ignition switch to ignite the sample. Carefully observe how the calorimeter works.
25°C

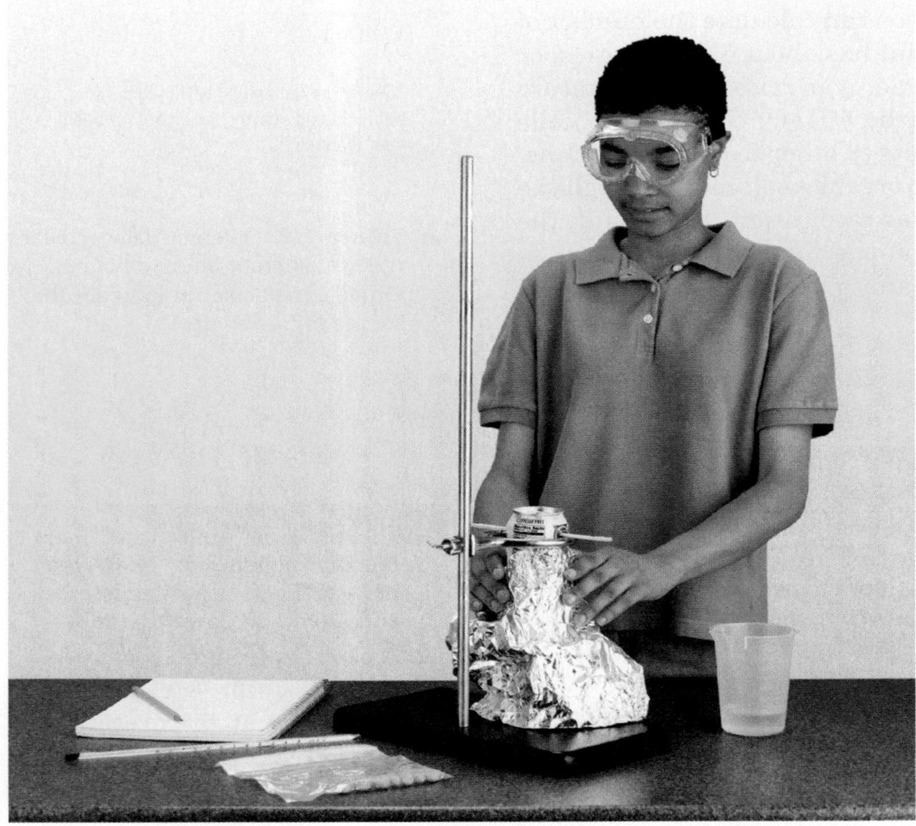

CONCEPT 7.3

ATP provides energy for cellular work.

OBJECTIVES
- Describe the structure of ATP and how it stores energy.
- Give examples of work that cells perform.
- Summarize the ATP cycle.

KEY TERM
- ATP

What's Online

www.biology.com

Online Activity 7.3
Examine how ATP stores energy.

It's a good thing that food doesn't fuel your cells by burning like the torched peanut described in Concept 7.2. In fact, the carbohydrates, fats, and proteins obtained from food do not drive work in your cells in any direct way. The chemical energy stored in these compounds must first be converted to energy stored in another molecule.

How ATP Packs Energy

As you read in Chapter 6, **ATP** stands for adenosine triphosphate. The "adenosine" part consists of a nitrogen-containing compound called adenine and a five-carbon sugar called ribose (Figure 7-9). The triphosphate "tail" consists of three phosphate groups. The tail is the "business" end of ATP—it is the source of energy used for most cellular work.

Each phosphate group is negatively charged. Because like charges repel, the crowding of negative charge in the ATP tail contributes to the potential energy stored in ATP. You can compare this to storing energy by compressing a spring. The tightly coiled spring has potential energy. When the compressed spring relaxes, its potential energy is released. The spring's kinetic energy can be used to perform work such as pushing a block attached to one end of the spring.

The phosphate bonds are symbolized by springs in Figure 7-9. When ATP is involved in a chemical reaction that breaks one or both of these phosphate bonds, potential energy is released. In most cases of cellular work, only one phosphate group is lost from ATP. Then the tail of the molecule has only two phosphate groups left. The resulting molecule is called adenosine diphosphate, or ADP.

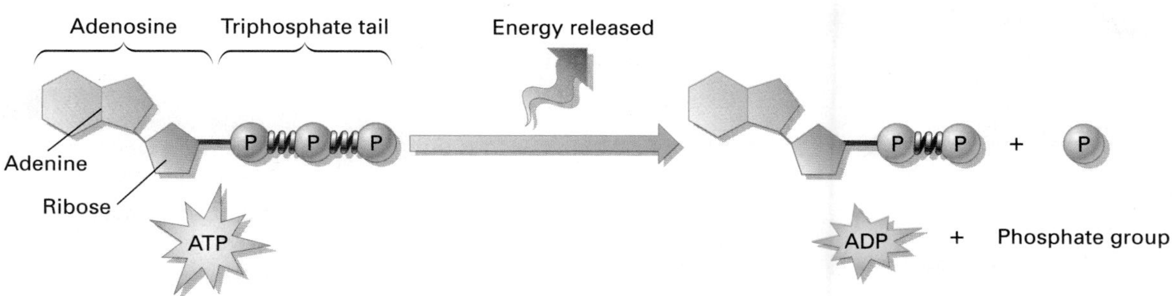

Figure 7-9 An ATP molecule contains potential energy, much like a compressed spring. When a phosphate group is pulled away during a chemical reaction, energy is released.

ATP and Cellular Work

During a chemical reaction that breaks one of ATP's bonds, the phosphate group is transferred from ATP to another molecule. Specific enzymes enable this transfer to occur. The molecule that accepts the phosphate undergoes a change, driving the work.

Your cells perform three main types of work: chemical work, mechanical work, and transport work (Figure 7-10). An example of chemical work is building large molecules such as proteins. ATP provides the energy for the dehydration synthesis reaction that links amino acids together. An example of mechanical work is the contraction of a muscle. In your muscle cells, ATP transfers phosphate groups to certain proteins. These proteins change shape, starting a chain of events which cause muscle cells to contract. An example of transport work is pumping solutes such as ions across a cellular membrane. Again, the transfer of a phosphate group from ATP causes the receiving membrane protein to change shape, enabling ions to pass through.

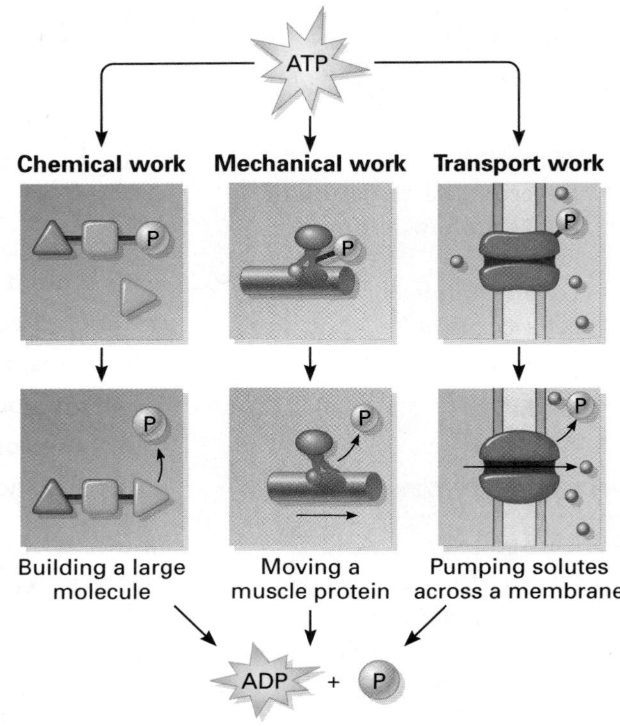

▲ **Figure 7-10** The energy in ATP drives three main types of cellular work.

The ATP Cycle

ATP is continuously converted to ADP as your cells do work. Fortunately, ATP is "recyclable." For example, ATP can be restored from ADP by adding a third phosphate group (Figure 7-11). Like compressing a spring, adding the phosphate group requires energy. The source of this energy is the organic molecules from food. Thus, ATP operates in a cycle within your cells. Work consumes ATP, which is then regenerated from ADP and phosphate.

The ATP cycle churns at an astonishing pace. A working muscle cell recycles all of its ATP molecules about once each minute. That's 10 million ATP molecules spent and regenerated per second! The next concept focuses on how your cells keep pace with this incredible demand for ATP.

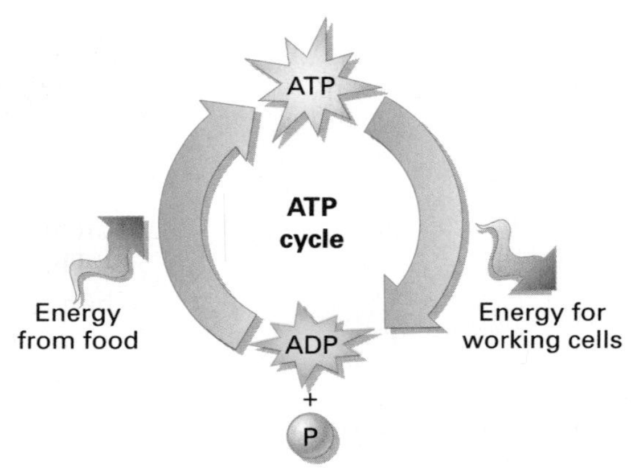

▲ **Figure 7-11** ATP is constantly recycled in your cells.

Online Activity 7.3

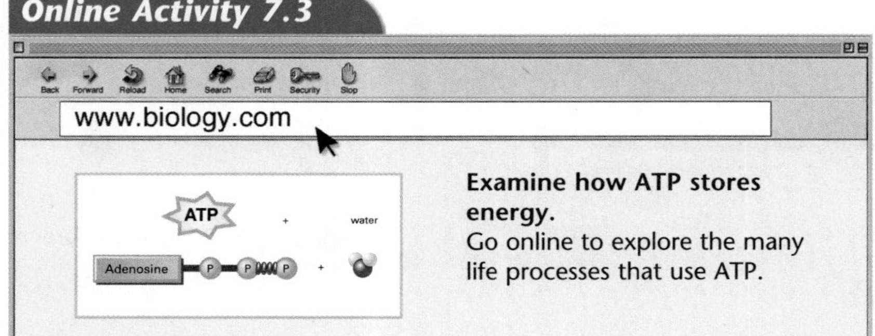

Examine how ATP stores energy.
Go online to explore the many life processes that use ATP.

Concept Check 7.3

1. In what way is ATP like a compressed spring?
2. List three main types of cellular work.
3. What is the source of energy for regenerating ATP from ADP?

CONCEPT 7.4

Electrons "fall" from food to oxygen during cellular respiration.

OBJECTIVES
- Relate breathing and cellular respiration.
- Summarize the cellular respiration equation.
- Tell how "falling" electrons are a source of energy.
- Explain the role of electron transport chains.

KEY TERMS
- aerobic
- electron transport chain

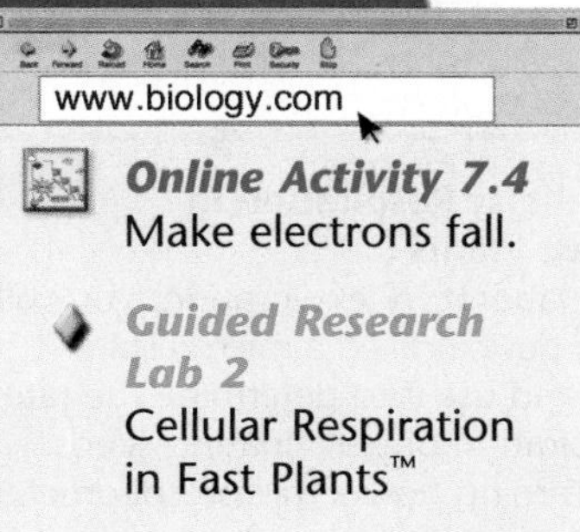

You have read that cells, like automobile engines, use oxygen in the process of breaking down fuel. The cell's living version of internal combustion is cellular respiration. Cellular respiration converts the energy stored in food to energy stored in ATP. But how is oxygen involved?

Relationship of Cellular Respiration to Breathing

Cellular respiration is an **aerobic** process, meaning that it requires oxygen. You have probably heard the word *respiration* used to describe breathing. Although breathing for a whole organism is not the same as cellular respiration, the two processes are related (Figure 7-12).

During cellular respiration, a cell exchanges two gases with its surroundings. The cell takes in oxygen and releases carbon dioxide. Your bloodstream delivers oxygen to cells and carries away carbon dioxide. The process of breathing results in the exchange of these gases between your blood and the outside air. This exchange takes place in tiny air sacs in your lungs. Oxygen in the air you inhale diffuses from your lungs across the lining of the air sacs and into your bloodstream. The carbon dioxide diffuses from your blood across the air sacs' lining and into your lungs. From there it is exhaled.

▼ **Figure 7-12** Breathing supports cellular respiration by providing the body with oxygen and removing carbon dioxide.

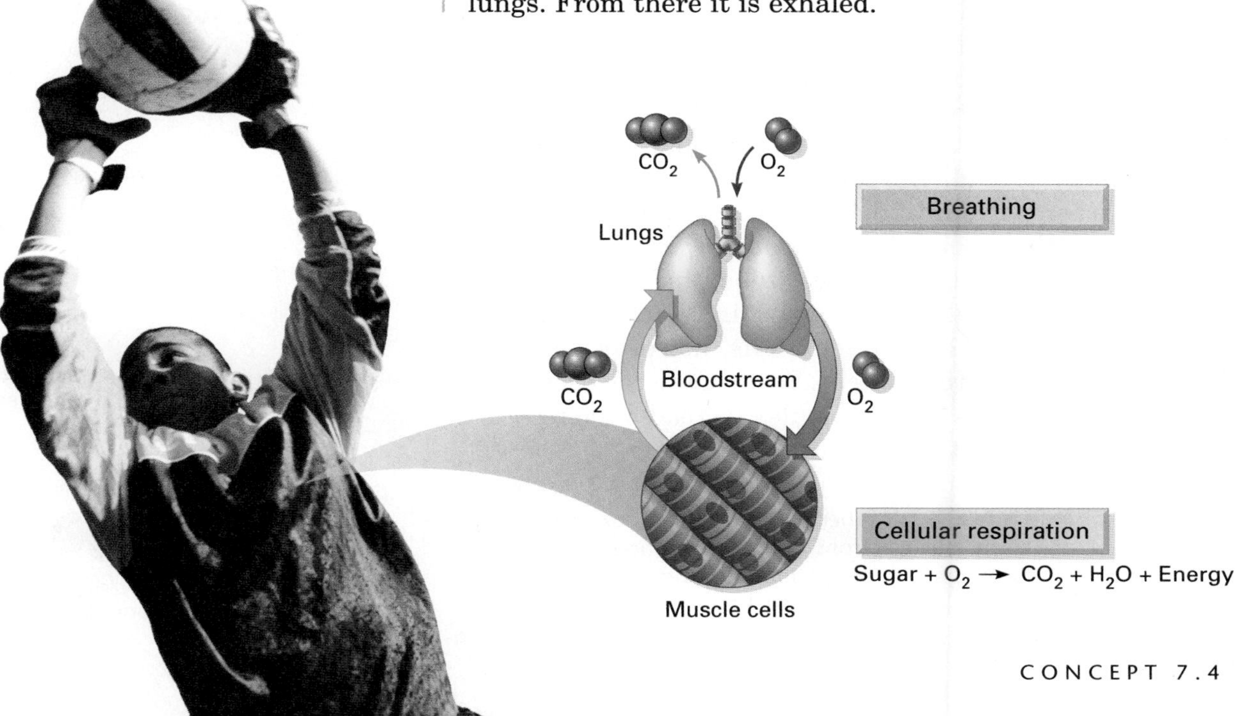

Overall Equation for Cellular Respiration

Glucose is a common fuel for cellular respiration. Figure 7-13 shows the overall equation of what happens to glucose during cellular respiration. The series of arrows indicates that cellular respiration consists of many chemical steps, not just a single chemical reaction.

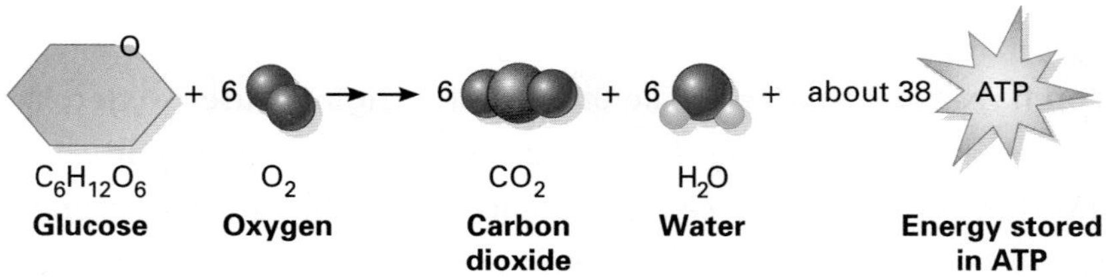

$C_6H_{12}O_6$ + 6 O_2 →→ 6 CO_2 + 6 H_2O + about 38 ATP

Glucose + **Oxygen** →→ **Carbon dioxide** + **Water** + **Energy stored in ATP**

◀ **Figure 7-13** In cellular respiration, the atoms in glucose and oxygen are rearranged, forming carbon dioxide and water. The cell uses the energy released to produce ATP.

Cellular respiration's main function is to generate ATP for cellular work. In fact, the process can produce up to 38 ATP molecules for each glucose molecule consumed. Notice that cellular respiration also transfers hydrogen and carbon atoms from glucose to oxygen atoms, thus forming water and carbon dioxide. Now, take a closer look at how these events release energy.

Guided Research Lab 2

Back Forward Reload Home Search Print Security Stop

www.biology.com

Cellular Respiration in Fast Plants™

In this laboratory exploration, you will build a device called a microrespirometer and use it to determine the rate of respiration of germinating seeds. After learning how a microrespirometer works, you will apply what you have learned to design and carry out your own investigation.

"Falling" Electrons as an Energy Source

Why does the process of cellular respiration release energy? For an analogy, recall the water slide. At the top, your potential energy is high. As you are pulled down the slide by the force of gravity, the potential energy is converted to kinetic energy. Similarly, an atom's positively charged nucleus exerts an electrical "pull" on negatively charged electrons. When an electron "falls" toward the nucleus, potential energy is released.

Here is how "falling" electrons relate to cellular respiration. Oxygen attracts electrons very strongly, similar to how gravity pulls objects downhill. In fact, oxygen is sometimes called an "electron grabber." In contrast to oxygen, carbon and hydrogen atoms exert much less pull on electrons. A sugar molecule has several carbon-hydrogen bonds. During cellular respiration, the carbon and hydrogen atoms change partners and bond with oxygen atoms instead. The carbon-hydrogen bonds are replaced by carbon-oxygen and hydrogen-oxygen bonds. As the electrons of these bonds "fall" toward oxygen, energy is released. If you burn sugar in a test tube, this reaction happens very quickly, releasing energy in the form of heat and light (Figure 7-14). In your cells, however, the "burning" happens in controlled steps. Some of the released energy is used to generate ATP molecules instead of being converted to heat and light.

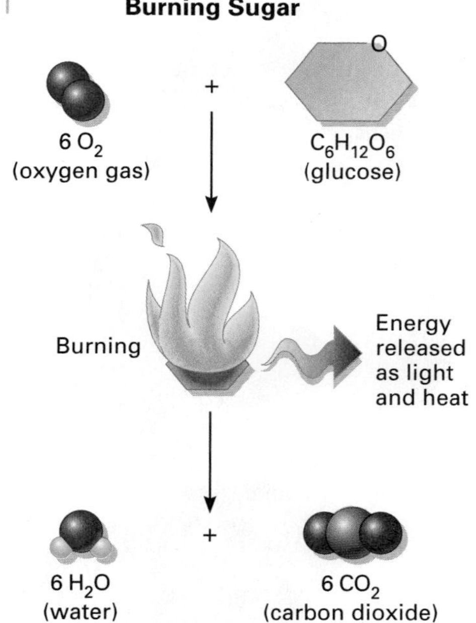

▶ **Figure 7-14** When sugar is burned, oxygen atoms pull electrons from carbon and hydrogen, forming new chemical bonds. Burning releases energy in the form of heat and light.

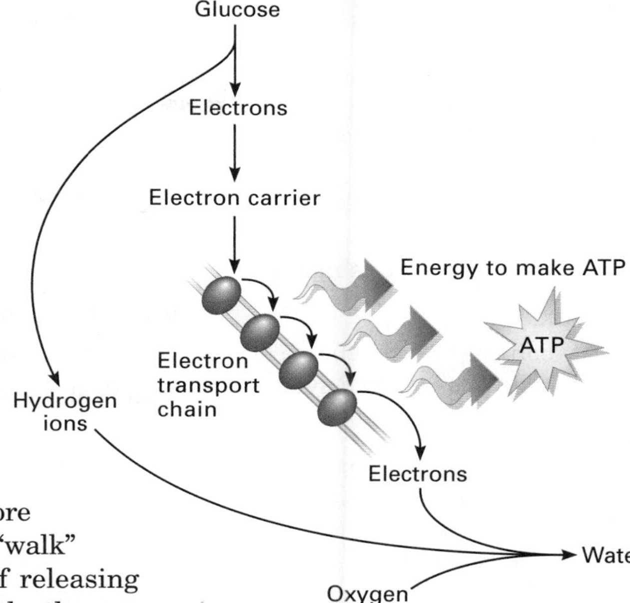

▲ **Figure 7-15** An electron transport chain is like a staircase—as electrons move down each step in the chain, a small amount of energy is released.

Electron Transport Chains

Compared with burning, cellular respiration is a more controlled fall of electrons—more like a step-by-step "walk" of electrons down an energy staircase. Instead of releasing energy in a burst of flame, cellular respiration unlocks the energy in glucose in small amounts that cells can put to productive use—the formation of ATP molecules.

In contrast to burning, where oxygen reacts directly with glucose, cellular respiration involves breaking down glucose in several steps. Oxygen only enters as an electron acceptor in the final electron transfer. During the breakdown, molecules called electron carriers accept many of the high-energy electrons from the glucose molecule. The electron carriers pass the electrons on to other carriers in a series of transfers called an **electron transport chain** (Figure 7-15). Each carrier holds the electrons more strongly than the carrier before it. At the end of the chain, oxygen—the electron grabber—pulls electrons from the final carrier molecule and joins them with hydrogen ions, forming water.

As electrons undergo each transfer in the chain, they release a little energy. The cell has a mechanism that traps this released energy and uses it to make ATP. You will read about these events in more detail in Concept 7.5.

Online Activity 7.4

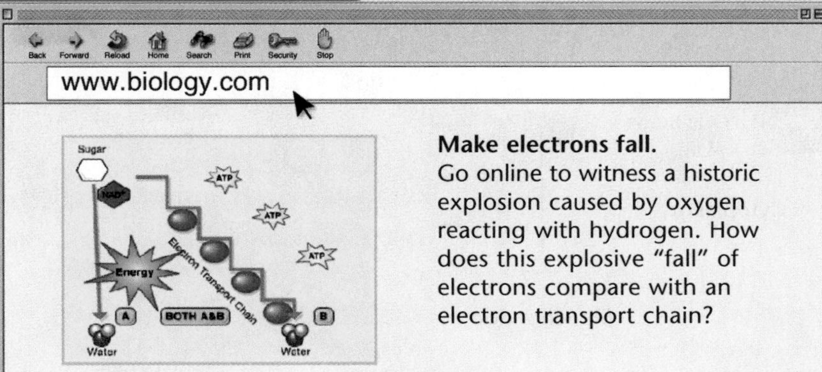

Make electrons fall.
Go online to witness a historic explosion caused by oxygen reacting with hydrogen. How does this explosive "fall" of electrons compare with an electron transport chain?

Concept Check 7.4

1. Compare and contrast breathing and cellular respiration.
2. List the reactants and products in cellular respiration.
3. What is meant by the "falling" of electrons to oxygen? How does this process release energy?
4. How does an electron transport chain result in the gradual release of energy stored in glucose?

CONCEPT 7.5

Cellular respiration converts energy in food to energy in ATP.

OBJECTIVES

- Describe the structure of a mitochondrion.
- Summarize the three stages of cellular respiration and identify where ATP is made.

KEY TERMS

- metabolism
- glycolysis
- Krebs cycle
- ATP synthase

What's Online

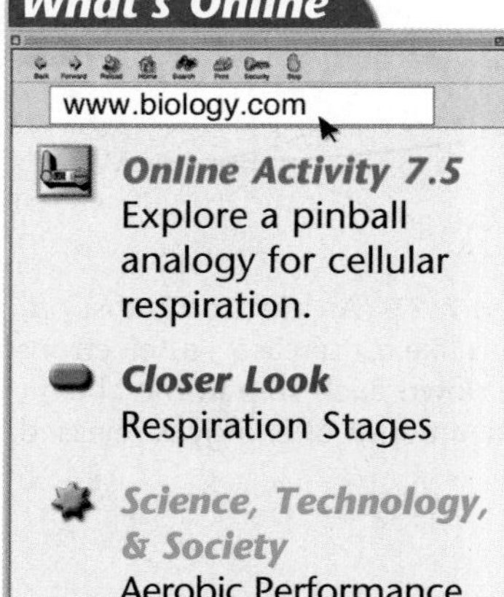

www.biology.com
Online Activity 7.5
Explore a pinball analogy for cellular respiration.
Closer Look
Respiration Stages
Science, Technology, & Society
Aerobic Performance

While the above sentence summarizes the outcome of cellular respiration, the process actually consists of more than two dozen chemical reactions. Many of the reactions take place in specialized organelles—mitochondria.

Structure of Mitochondria

Mitochondria (singular, *mitochondrion*) are found in almost all eukaryotic cells. A mitochondrion's structure is key to its role in cellular respiration. An envelope of two membranes encloses the mitochondrion (Figure 7-16). There is a space between the outer and inner membranes. The highly folded inner membrane encloses a thick fluid called the matrix. Many enzymes and other molecules involved in cellular respiration are built into the inner membrane. The complex folding pattern of this membrane allows for many sites where these reactions can occur. This maximizes the mitochondrion's ATP production.

A Road Map for Cellular Respiration

Cellular respiration is one type of chemical process that takes place in cells. All together, a cell's chemical processes make up the cell's **metabolism.** Because cellular respiration consists of a series of reactions, it is referred to as a metabolic pathway. A specific enzyme catalyzes (speeds up) each reaction in a metabolic pathway.

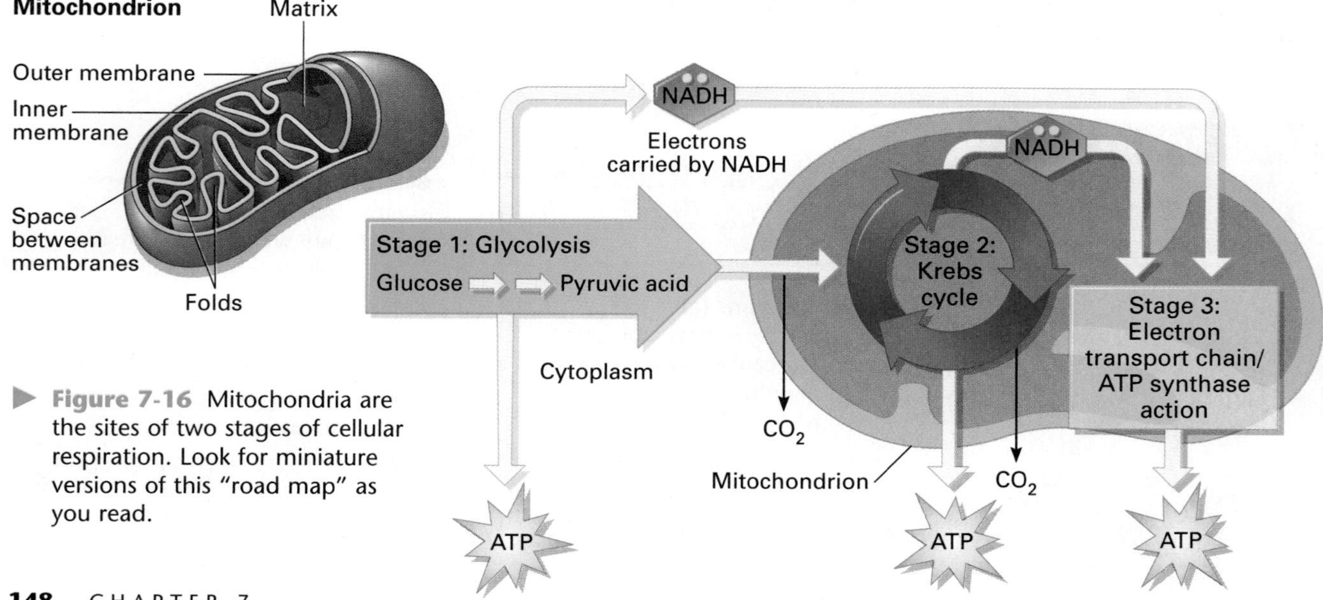

Figure 7-16 Mitochondria are the sites of two stages of cellular respiration. Look for miniature versions of this "road map" as you read.

Figure 7-16 on the facing page is a simplified "road map" of cellular respiration. You can use the diagram to follow glucose through the metabolic pathway of cellular respiration. The three main stages are color-coded: glycolysis (green), the Krebs cycle (purple), and electron transport and ATP synthase (gold). The road map also shows where in your cells each stage occurs.

Stage I: Glycolysis

The first stage in breaking down a glucose molecule, called **glycolysis,** takes place outside the mitochondria in the cytoplasm of the cell. The word *glycolysis* means "splitting of sugar." Figure 7-17 illustrates this process. In the figure, note that glucose is shown as a chain of six carbon atoms (represented by gray balls) rather than as a ring. This allows you to focus on the number of carbon atoms in each molecule.

Using two ATP molecules as an initial "investment," the cell splits a six-carbon glucose molecule in half. The result is two three-carbon molecules, each with one phosphate group. Each three-carbon molecule then transfers electrons and hydrogen ions to a carrier molecule called NAD^+. Accepting two electrons and one hydrogen ion converts the NAD^+ to a compound called NADH. (The yellow dots in the NADH symbols represent electrons.) The next step is the "payback" on the ATP investment—four new ATP molecules are produced, a net gain of two ATP molecules.

In summary, the original glucose molecule has been converted to two molecules of a substance called pyruvic acid. Two ATP molecules have been spent, and four ATP molecules have been produced. The pyruvic acid molecules still hold most of the energy of the original glucose molecule.

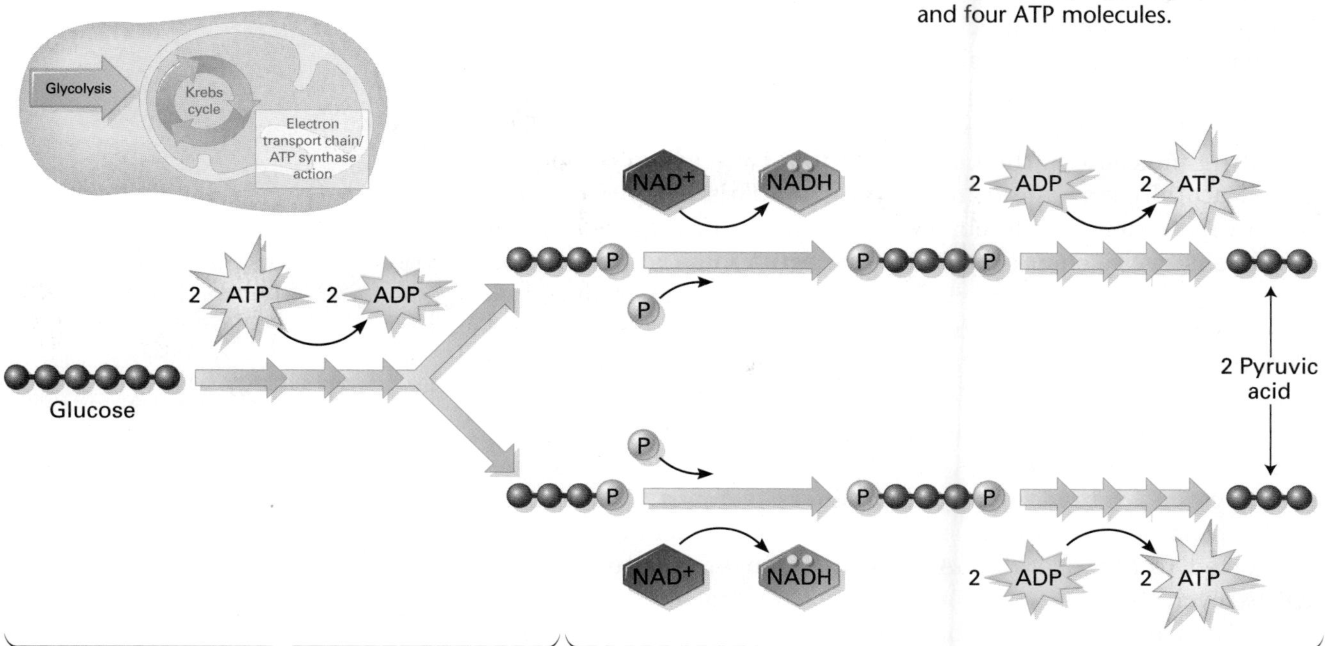

Figure 7-17 A cell invests two ATP molecules to break down glucose. The products of glycolysis are two pyruvic acid molecules, two NADH molecules and four ATP molecules.

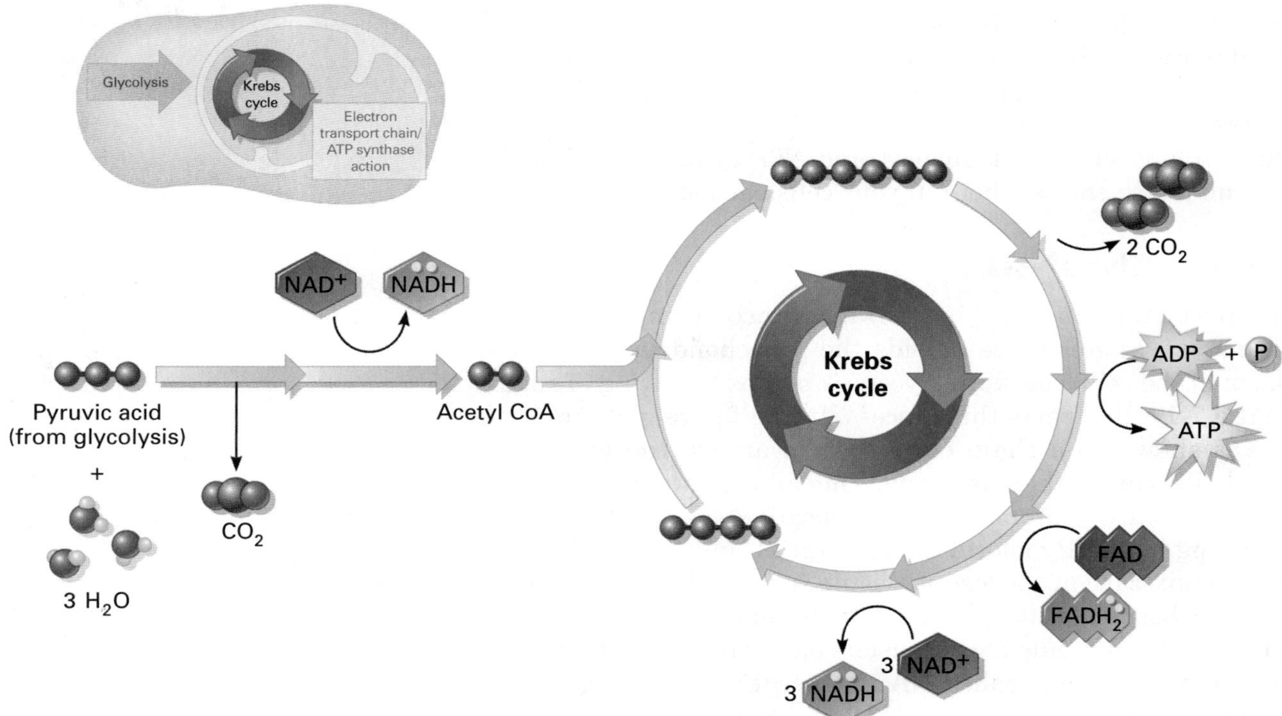

Stage 2: The Krebs Cycle

This stage is named for the biochemist Hans Krebs, who figured out the steps of the process in the 1930s. The **Krebs cycle** finishes the breakdown of pyruvic acid molecules to carbon dioxide, releasing more energy in the process. The enzymes for the Krebs cycle are dissolved in the fluid matrix within a mitochondrion's inner membrane.

Recall that glycolysis takes place outside the mitochondrion and produces two pyruvic acid molecules. These pyruvic acid molecules do not themselves take part in the Krebs cycle. Instead, after diffusing into the mitochondrion, each three-carbon pyruvic acid molecule loses a molecule of carbon dioxide. The resulting molecule is then converted to a two-carbon compound called acetyl coenzyme A, or acetyl CoA. This acetyl CoA molecule then enters the Krebs cycle, as shown in Figure 7-18. In the Krebs cycle, each acetyl CoA molecule joins a four-carbon acceptor molecule. The reactions in the Krebs cycle produce two more carbon dioxide molecules and one ATP molecule per acetyl CoA molecule. However, NADH and another electron carrier called $FADH_2$ trap most of the energy. At the end of the Krebs cycle, the four-carbon acceptor molecule has been regenerated and the cycle can continue.

As you have read, glycolysis produces two pyruvic acid molecules from one glucose molecule. Each pyruvic acid molecule is converted to one acetyl CoA molecule. Since each turn of the Krebs cycle breaks down one acetyl CoA molecule, the cycle actually turns twice for each glucose molecule, producing a total of four carbon dioxide molecules and two ATP molecules.

▲ **Figure 7-18** Since glycolysis splits glucose into two pyruvic acid molecules, the Krebs cycle turns twice for each glucose molecule.

Science, Technology, & Society

www.biology.com

Aerobic Performance

Advances in training are helping many athletes improve their performance. New methods allow aerobic athletes to be faster and stronger for longer periods of time. Find out more about these methods when you go online.

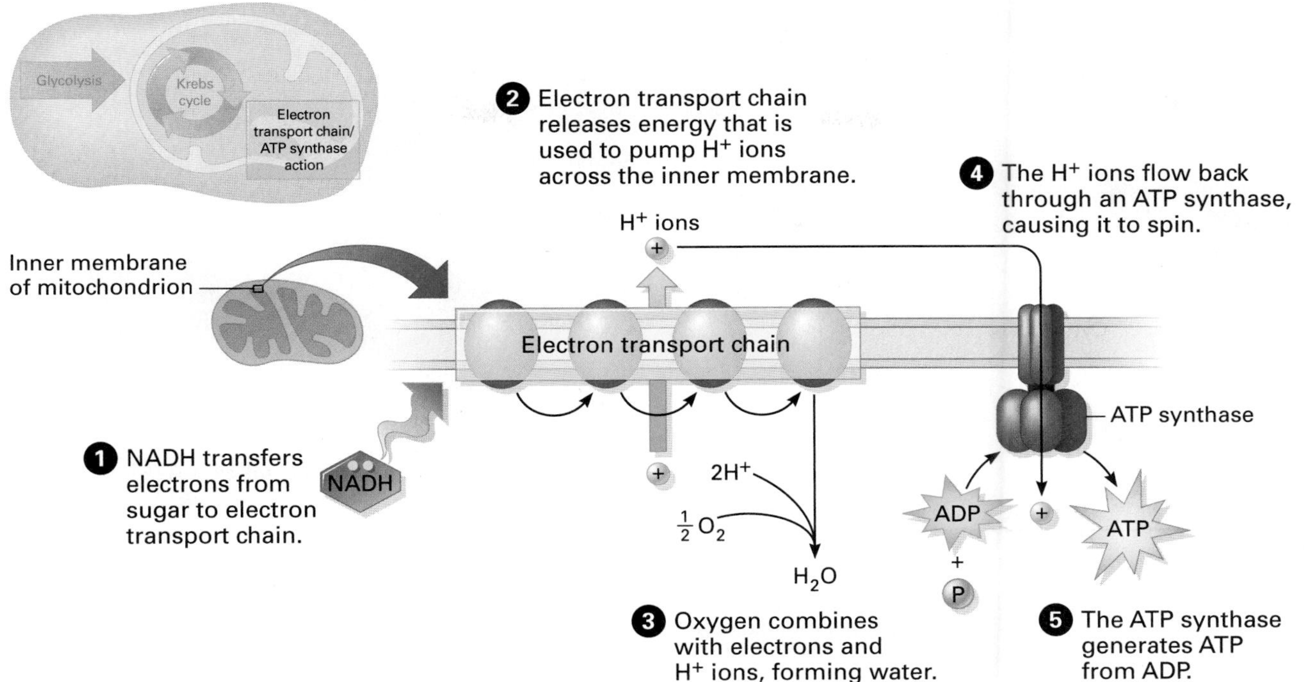
Glycolysis
Krebs cycle
Electron transport chain/ ATP synthase action
2 Electron transport chain releases energy that is used to pump H+ ions across the inner membrane.
4 The H+ ions flow back through an ATP synthase, causing it to spin.
H+ ions
Inner membrane of mitochondrion
Electron transport chain
ATP synthase
1 NADH transfers electrons from sugar to electron transport chain.
NADH
2H+
1/2 O2
ADP
+
P
ATP
H2O
3 Oxygen combines with electrons and H+ ions, forming water.
5 The ATP synthase generates ATP from ADP.

Stage 3: Electron Transport Chain and ATP Synthase Action

The final stage of cellular respiration occurs in the inner membranes of mitochondria. This stage has two parts: an electron transport chain and ATP production by ATP synthase.

First, the carrier molecule NADH transfers electrons from the original glucose molecule to an electron transport chain (Figure 7-19). As you read in Concept 7.4, electrons move to carriers that attract them more strongly. In this way the electrons move from carrier to carrier within the inner membrane of the mitochondria, eventually being "pulled" to oxygen at the end of the chain. There the oxygen and electrons combine with hydrogen ions, forming water.

Each transfer in the chain releases a small amount of energy. This energy is used to pump hydrogen ions across the membrane from where they are less concentrated to where they are more concentrated. This pumping action stores potential energy in much the same way as a dam stores potential energy by holding back water.

The energy stored by a dam can be harnessed to do work (such as generating electricity) when the water is allowed to rush downhill, turning giant wheels called turbines. Similarly, your mitochondria have protein structures called **ATP synthases** that act like miniature turbines. Hydrogen ions pumped by electron transport rush back "downhill" through the ATP synthase. The ATP synthase uses the energy from the flow of H^+ ions to convert ADP to ATP. This process can generate up to 34 ATP molecules per original glucose molecule.

Figure 7-19 Hydrogen ions pumped by electron transport rush back across the membrane. In doing so, they cause ATP synthase "turbines" to spin, like the rushing water at this hydroelectric dam spins turbines that generate electricity.

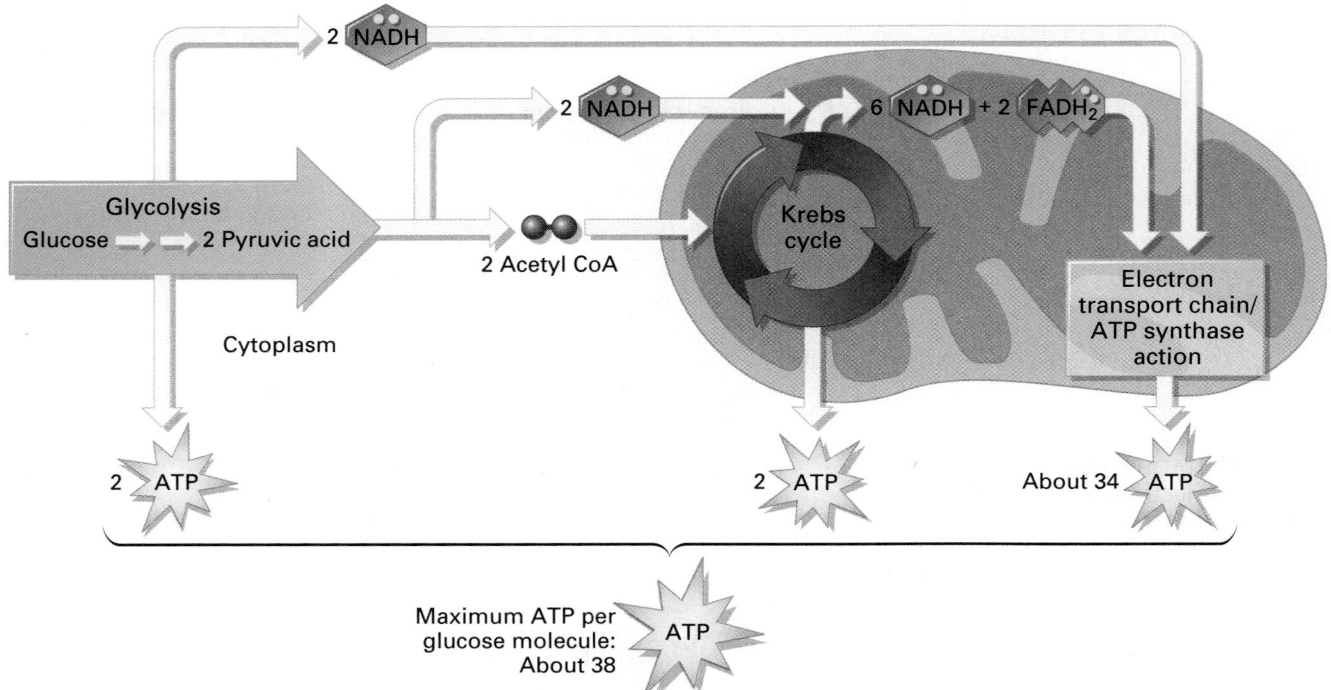

▲ **Figure 7-20** The three stages of cellular respiration together produce as many as 38 ATPs for each molecule of glucose that enters the pathway.

Adding Up the ATP Molecules

When taking cellular respiration apart to see how all its metabolic machinery works, it's easy to forget the overall function. The result of cellular respiration is to generate ATP for cellular work. A cell can convert the energy of one glucose molecule to as many as 38 molecules of ATP (Figure 7-20).

Glycolysis produces four ATP molecules, but recall that it requires two ATP molecules as an initial energy investment. So the result is a net gain of two ATP molecules. The Krebs cycle produces two more ATP molecules (one for each three-carbon pyruvic acid molecule). And finally, the ATP synthase turbines produce about 34 more molecules of ATP.

Notice that most ATP production occurs after glycolysis and requires oxygen. Without oxygen, most of your cells would be unable to produce much ATP. As a result, you cannot survive for long without a fresh supply of oxygen.

Online Activity 7.5

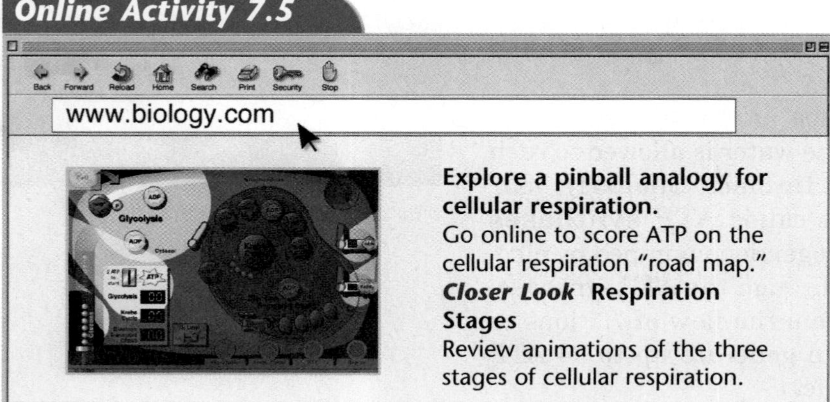

Explore a pinball analogy for cellular respiration.
Go online to score ATP on the cellular respiration "road map."

Closer Look **Respiration Stages**
Review animations of the three stages of cellular respiration.

Concept Check 7.5

1. How is the mitochondrion's structure suited to its function?
2. Identify the three stages of cellular respiration, where in the cell each takes place, and how many ATP molecules it produces.
3. Summarize the use and production of ATP in one cycle of cellular respiration.

CONCEPT 7.6 Some cells can harvest energy without oxygen.

OBJECTIVES
- Explain how fermentation in muscle cells is different from cellular respiration.
- Give examples of products that depend on fermentation in microorganisms.

KEY TERMS
- fermentation
- anaerobic

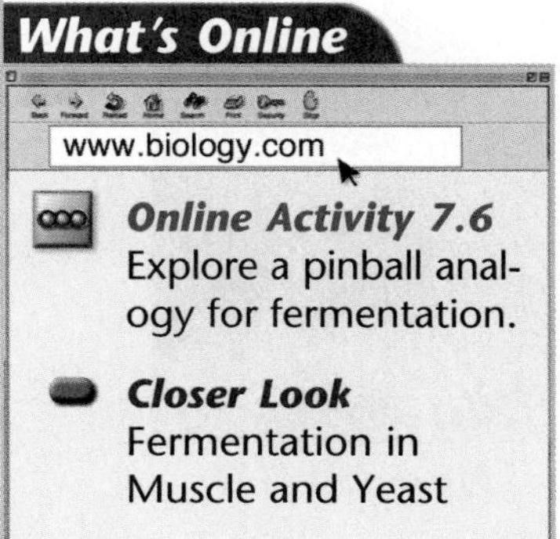

What's Online
www.biology.com
Online Activity 7.6
Explore a pinball analogy for fermentation.
Closer Look
Fermentation in Muscle and Yeast

When you walk down the street, your lungs supply your cells with oxygen at a rate that keeps pace with ATP demand. But what happens when you sprint to catch a bus? Your leg muscles are forced to work without enough oxygen because you are spending ATP more quickly than your lungs and bloodstream can deliver oxygen to your muscles for cellular respiration. Fortunately, some of your cells can produce ATP and continue working for short periods without oxygen.

Fermentation in Human Muscle Cells

If you exercise for a certain amount of time, your muscles must regenerate ATP. Normally, the cells can produce ATP through cellular respiration. But when you sprint, your lungs and bloodstream can't supply oxygen fast enough to meet your muscles' need for ATP. In such situations, your muscle cells use another process, called **fermentation,** that makes ATP without using oxygen. Cellular respiration still continues, but it is not the main source of ATP while fermentation is occurring.

Fermentation makes ATP entirely from glycolysis, the same process that is the first stage of cellular respiration. Note in Figure 7-21 that glycolysis does not use oxygen. As you read in Concept 7.5, glycolysis directly produces a net of two molecules of ATP from each molecule of glucose it consumes. Remember that glycolysis produces 4 ATP but that 2 ATP molecules are required to power this stage, yielding a net of 2 ATP. This may not seem very efficient compared to the 38 molecules of ATP generated during all of cellular respiration. However, by burning enough glucose, fermentation can regenerate enough ATP molecules for short bursts of activity such as a sprint to catch the bus.

Figure 7-21 When little oxygen is available in muscle cells, fermentation allows glycolysis to continue.

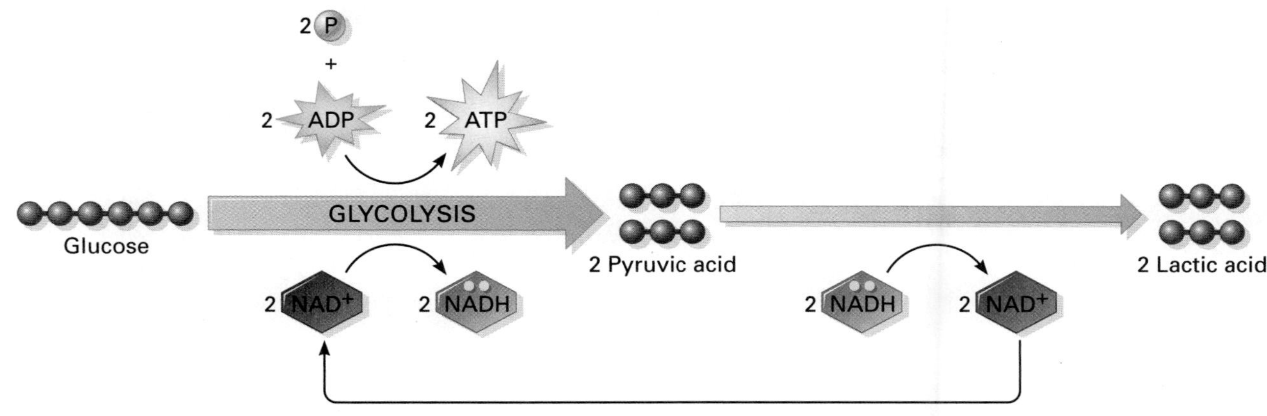

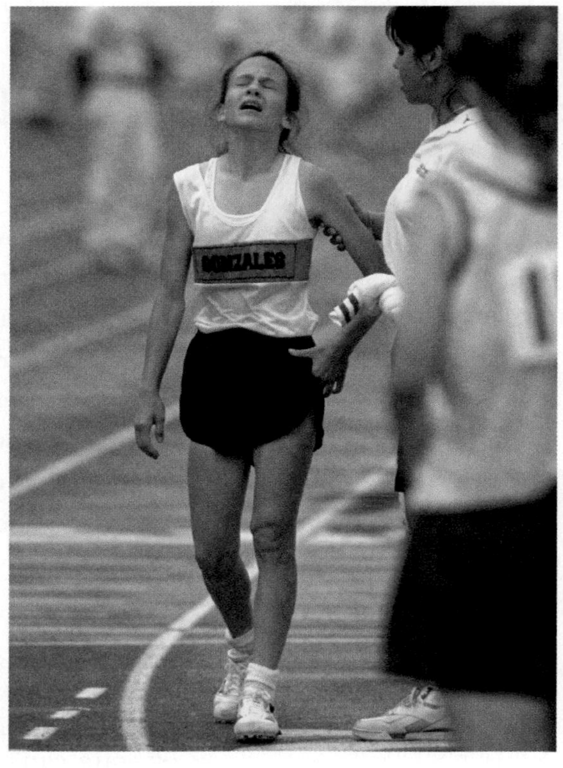

▶ **Figure 7-22** The fatigue and soreness a person feels after intense exercise partly result from a buildup of lactic acid.

Fermentation in muscle cells produces a waste product called lactic acid. The temporary buildup of lactic acid in muscle cells contributes to the fatigue you feel during and after a long run or a set of push-ups. Your body consumes oxygen as it converts the lactic acid back to pyruvic acid. You restore your oxygen supply by breathing heavily for several minutes after you stop exercising.

Fermentation in Microorganisms

Like your muscle cells, yeast (a microscopic fungus) is capable of both cellular respiration and fermentation. When yeast cells are kept in an **anaerobic** environment—an environment without oxygen—they are forced to ferment sugar and other foods. In contrast to fermentation in your muscle cells, fermentation in yeast produces alcohol, instead of lactic acid, as a waste product (Figure 7-23). This fermentation reaction, called alcoholic fermentation, also releases carbon dioxide. For thousands of years, humans have put yeast to work producing alcoholic beverages such as beer and wine. The carbon dioxide is what makes champagne and beer bubbly. In another example of "taming" microbes, the carbon dioxide bubbles from baker's yeast make bread rise.

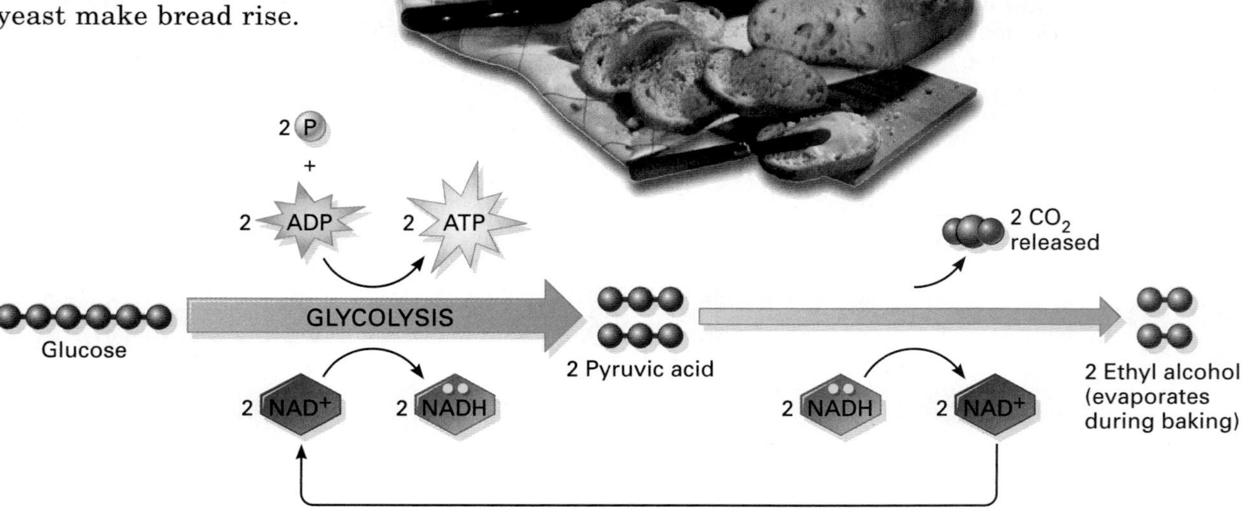

▼ **Figure 7-23** Fermentation in yeast produces ethyl alcohol. The carbon dioxide that is released during fermentation creates bubbles and pockets that make bread rise. The alcohol evaporates during baking.

There are also fungi and bacteria that produce lactic acid during fermentation, just as your muscle cells do. Humans use these microbes to transform milk into cheese and yogurt. The sharpness or sour flavor of yogurt and some cheeses is mainly due to lactic acid (Figure 7-24). Similar kinds of microbial fermentation turn soybeans into soy sauce and cabbage into sauerkraut.

Yeast cells and muscle cells are versatile in their ability to harvest energy by either respiration or fermentation. In contrast, some bacteria found in still ponds or deep in the soil are actually poisoned if they come into contact with oxygen. These bacteria generate all of their ATP by fermentation. If you had to do that—though you don't and you can't—you would have to consume almost 20 times more food than normal. Oxygen enables you to get the most energy from your food. In the next chapter, you'll learn about the original source of this energy—photosynthesis.

▲ **Figure 7-24** Bacterial fermentation gives this cheese its characteristic flavor.

Online Activity 7.6

www.biology.com

Explore a pinball analogy for fermentation.
Go online to play fermentation pinball. What is the ultimate ATP score without oxygen? How are the results different from respiration pinball?
Closer Look **Fermentation in Muscle and Yeast**
Compare products in two types of cells.

Concept Check 7.6

1. How is fermentation different from cellular respiration?
2. Describe one example of how fermentation in microorganisms produces human foods.
3. What is the waste product of fermentation in your muscle cells?

Multiple Choice

Choose the letter of the best answer.

1. Heterotrophs are also called
  a. producers.
  b. autotrophs.
  c. consumers.
  d. "self-feeders."

2. What are the waste products of cellular respiration?
  a. carbon dioxide and water
  b. ATP and ADP
  c. carbon dioxide and oxygen
  d. energy and glucose

3. What metabolic stage is part of both cellular respiration and fermentation?
  a. electron transport
  b. glycolysis
  c. Krebs cycle
  d. ATP synthase action

4. What is the *net gain* of ATP molecules produced directly by glycolysis?
  a. 2
  b. 4
  c. 34
  d. 38

5. Electron transport occurs in the
  a. cytoplasm.
  b. matrix of the mitochondria.
  c. outer membrane of the mitochondria.
  d. inner membrane of the mitochondria.

6. Which molecule accepts electrons from the final carrier in the electron transport chain?
  a. NAD
  b. pyruvic acid
  c. oxygen
  d. carbon

7. Which of the following molecules is *not* involved in fermentation?
  a. glucose
  b. pyruvic acid
  c. NADH
  d. oxygen

Short Answer

8. Explain why it can be said that most of life on Earth is solar-powered.

9. Describe what happens to the chemical energy in food that is not converted to useful cellular work.

10. How could you measure the calorie content of a peanut in the laboratory?

11. Describe how energy is stored in an ATP molecule.

12. What are the three main types of cellular work? Give an example of each.

13. Summarize the steps of glycolysis.

14. Which stage of cellular respiration uses oxygen directly to extract chemical energy from organic compounds? Explain the steps in this stage.

15. Compare and contrast fermentation that occurs in human muscle cells and in yeast cells.

Visualizing Concepts

16. Fill in the missing spaces in this fermentation concept map.

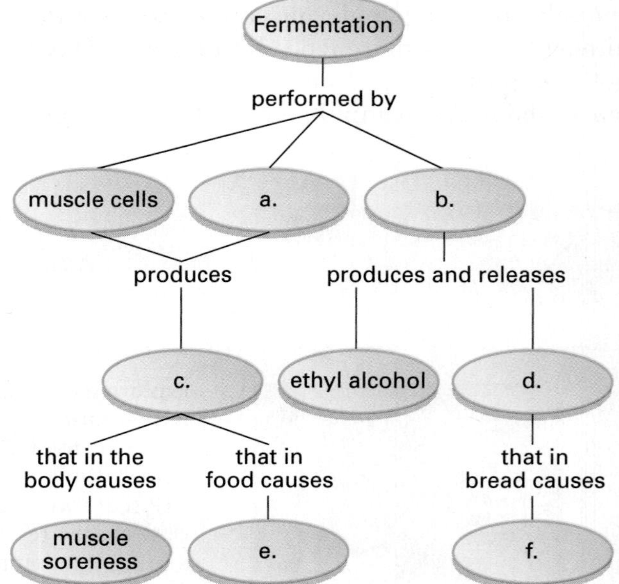

Analyzing Information

17. Analyzing Diagrams Use the diagram below to answer the questions.

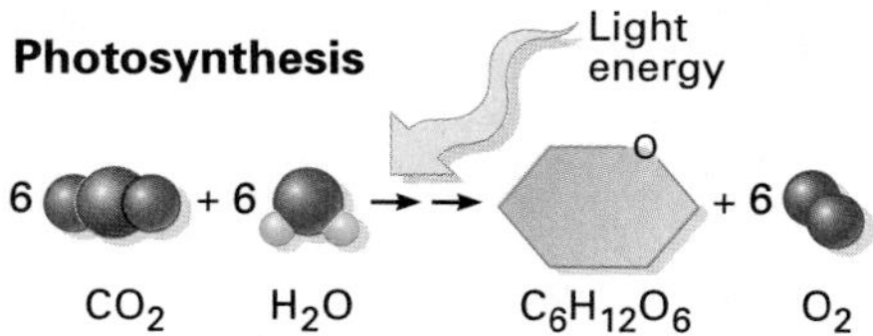

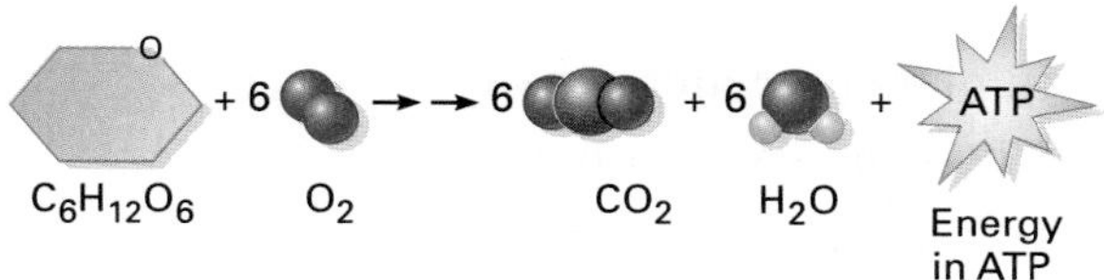

a. What are the chemical reactants in photosynthesis? What are the chemical products?
b. What do the double arrows in each reaction indicate?
c. How are photosynthesis and cellular respiration related? How are they different?

18. Analyzing Data The data table below lists the kilocalories (kcal) needed for various activities. Refer to the table to answer the questions that follow.

kcal Consumed per Hour by a 67.5-kg Person

Activity	kcal	Activity	kcal
Bicycling (slowly)	170	Running	865
Bicycling (racing)	514	Swimming	535
Dancing (fast)	599	Walking	158

a. How many hours would a 67.5-kg person have to walk to use up the energy contained in a cheeseburger containing 430 kcal?
b. How far would this person have walked if he were walking 3 km per hour?
c. What form of exercise would use up the cheeseburger's calories in the shortest amount of time? Explain your answer.

Critical Thinking

19. Relating Cause and Effect Red blood cells do not contain mitochondria. Which stage or stages of sugar breakdown can take place in these cells? Explain your answer.

20. Comparing and Contrasting How is the process by which your body extracts energy from food similar to how a car's engine extracts energy from fuel? How is it different?

21. Making Generalizations Explain the following statement: Heterotrophs depend on autotrophs for energy.

22. What Is Wrong With These Statements? *Briefly explain why each statement is inaccurate or misleading.*
a. Plants carry out photosynthesis and animals carry out cellular respiration.
b. ATP traps most of the energy released from food during the Krebs cycle.
c. While sprinting, your muscle cells stop cellular respiration and switch to fermentation to produce ATP.

Performance Assessment

Design an Experiment Choose a variable that might affect fermentation in yeast or bacteria. For example, you might choose to study the effect of the concentration of sugar available to the fermenting cells. Develop a hypothesis about the effect of this variable. Then design a controlled experiment to test your hypothesis. Be sure to check with your teacher before conducting any experiments.

Online Assessment/Test Preparation

Back Forward Reload Home Search Print Security Stop

www.biology.com

- **Chapter 7 Assessment**
  Check your understanding of the chapter concepts.
- **Standardized Test Preparation**
  Practice test-taking skills you need to succeed.

The Working Cell: Energy from Sunlight

Through photosynthesis, plants like the corn in this field convert the energy of sunlight to chemical energy stored in organic molecules. Those organic molecules provide fuel for cellular respiration for the plants as well as for other organisms that eat the plants. But people and other animals depend on plants for more than food. For example, oxygen is a valuable "by-product" of photosynthesis. During the summer growing season, the corn crop in the United States produces more oxygen than the nation's human population needs in a year. In this chapter, you will learn more about the amazing process of photosynthesis. Before you begin, go online to the *WebQuest* to visit a chocolate factory and find out how chocolate is related to photosynthesis.

Key Concepts

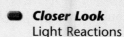

Concept 8.1 **Photosynthesis uses light energy to make food.**

Concept 8.2 **The light reactions convert light energy to chemical energy.**

Concept 8.3 **The Calvin cycle makes sugar from carbon dioxide.**

Concept 8.4 **Photosynthesis has a global impact.**

Assessment **Chapter 8 Review**

What's Online

www.biology.com

WebQuest
ChocolateQuest

Online Activity 8.1
Explore photosynthesis in action.

Online Activity 8.2
Investigate the nature of light.

Closer Look
Light Reactions

Online Activity 8.3
Take a trip around the Calvin cycle.

Lab 8 Online Companion
Photo Finish

Online Activity 8.4
Interpret carbon dioxide data.

Science, Technology, & Society
Effects of Increasing Carbon Dioxide Levels

Chapter 8 Assessment

CONCEPT 8.1

Photosynthesis uses light energy to make food.

OBJECTIVES
- Describe the structure of a chloroplast.
- Identify the overall reactants and products of photosynthesis.

KEY TERMS
- chloroplast
- chlorophyll
- stroma
- thylakoid
- light reactions
- Calvin cycle

What's Online

Online Activity 8.1
Explore photosynthesis in action.

As you read in Chapter 7, photosynthesis is the process by which plants and other producers convert the energy of sunlight into the energy stored in organic molecules. Just as cellular respiration takes place largely within a cell's mitochondria, photosynthesis also occurs in a specific organelle.

The Structure of Chloroplasts

The cellular organelle where photosynthesis takes place is called a **chloroplast.** Chloroplasts contain chemical compounds called **chlorophylls** that give these organelles a green color. When you observe a plant, all the green parts you can see contain cells with chloroplasts and can carry out photosynthesis (Figure 8-1). In most plants, the leaves contain the most chloroplasts and are the major sites of photosynthesis.

Within a leaf, the chloroplasts are concentrated in the cells of the mesophyll, the inner layer of tissue (Figure 8-2). Tiny pores called stomata (singular, *stoma*) are found on the surface of the leaf. Carbon dioxide enters the leaf and oxygen exits the leaf through the stomata. Veins carry water and nutrients from the plant's roots to the leaves. The veins also deliver organic molecules produced in the leaves to other parts of the plant.

The chloroplast's structure is key to its function. Like a mitochondrion, a chloroplast has an inner and an outer membrane. The inner membrane encloses a thick fluid called **stroma.**

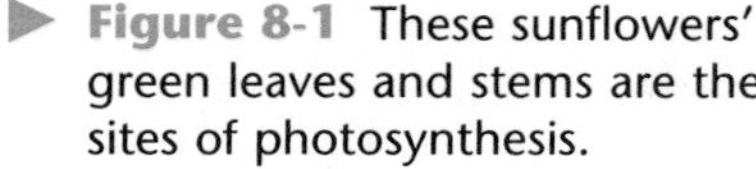

Figure 8-1 These sunflowers' green leaves and stems are the sites of photosynthesis.

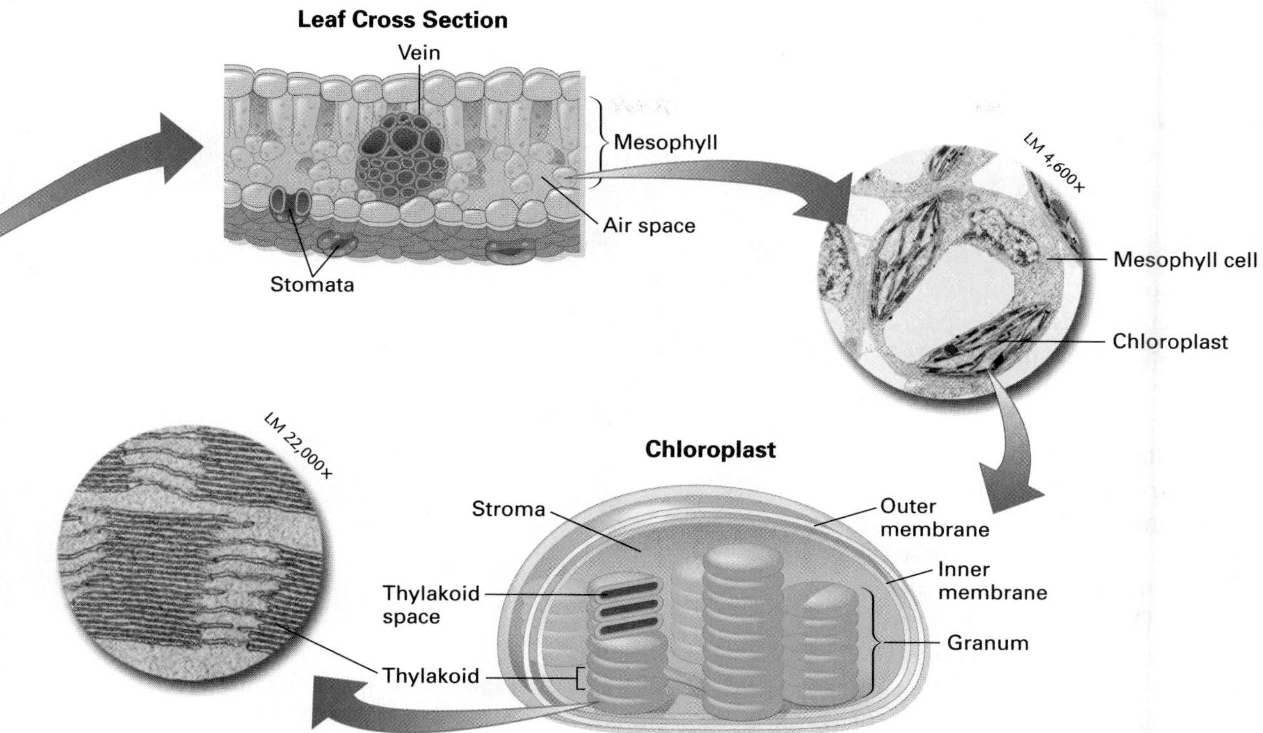

▲ **Figure 8-2** Photosynthesis takes place in cellular organelles called chloroplasts. In this sunflower, the greatest numbers of chloroplasts are located in the leaves. Chlorophylls give the chloroplasts—and in turn the leaves—their green color.

Suspended in the stroma are many disk-shaped sacs called **thylakoids.** Each thylakoid has a membrane surrounding an interior space. The thylakoids are arranged in stacks called grana (singular, *granum*). These various structures within the chloroplast organize the complex series of chemical reactions that make up the overall process of photosynthesis. Some of the steps take place in the thylakoid membranes, while others take place in the stroma.

Overview of Photosynthesis

You have read that cellular respiration involves the process of electron transfer. The "fall" of electrons from glucose to oxygen releases energy, which is then used to make ATP. The opposite occurs in photosynthesis. Electrons from water are boosted "uphill" by the energy from sunlight. The chloroplast uses these "excited" electrons, along with carbon dioxide and hydrogen ions, to produce sugar molecules. The reaction steps add up to the following overall chemical equation for photosynthesis:

$$6\,CO_2 + 6\,H_2O \rightarrow\rightarrow\rightarrow C_6H_{12}O_6 + 6\,O_2$$

Carbon dioxide + **Water** → **Glucose** + **Oxygen**

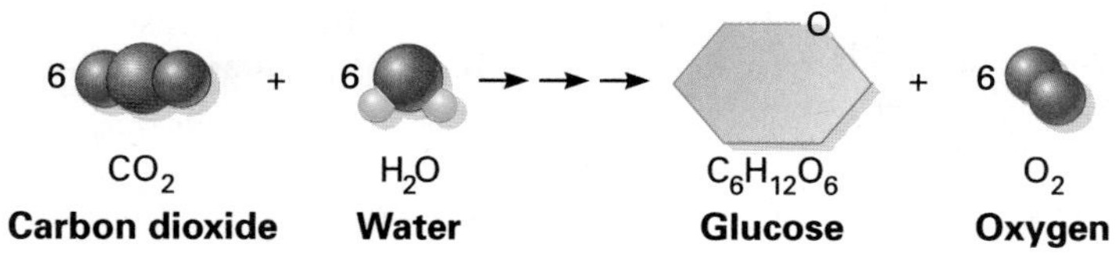

◀ **Figure 8-3** As in cellular respiration, the chemical equation for photosynthesis summarizes many reaction steps.

Photosynthesis occurs in two main stages, each with many steps: the light reactions and the Calvin cycle (Figure 8-4).

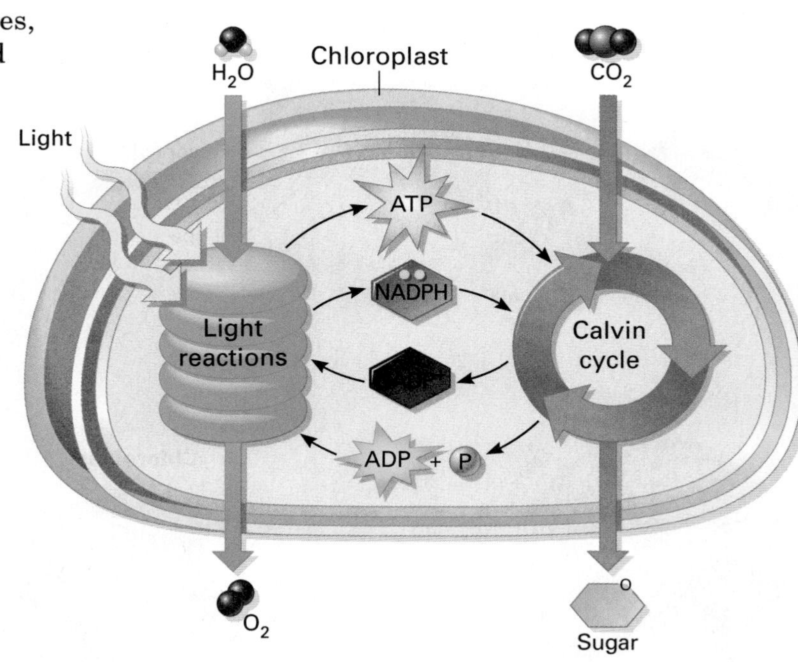

▲ **Figure 8-4** This "road map" shows the two main stages of photosynthesis: the light reactions, which occur in the thylakoids, and the Calvin cycle, which occurs in the stroma. Later in this chapter, miniature versions of this diagram will help keep you oriented as you study each stage.

The Light Reactions The **light reactions** convert the energy in sunlight to chemical energy. These reactions depend on molecules built into the membranes of the thylakoids. First, chlorophyll molecules in the membranes capture light energy. Then the chloroplasts use the captured energy to remove electrons from water. This splits the water into oxygen and hydrogen ions. The oxygen is a "waste product" of photosynthesis. It escapes to the atmosphere through the stomata of leaves. What becomes of the water's electrons and hydrogen ions? Chloroplasts use them to make an energy-rich molecule called NADPH. (NADPH is an electron carrier very similar to the NADH you read about in Chapter 7.) The chloroplasts also use the captured light energy to generate ATP. The overall result of the light reactions is the conversion of light energy to chemical energy stored in two compounds: NADPH and ATP.

The Calvin Cycle The **Calvin cycle** makes sugar from the atoms in carbon dioxide plus the hydrogen ions and high-energy electrons carried by NADPH. The enzymes for the Calvin cycle are located outside the thylakoids and dissolved in the stroma. The ATP made by the light reactions provides the energy to make sugar.

The Calvin cycle is sometimes referred to as the "light-independent reactions" because, unlike the light reactions, it does not directly require light to begin. However, this doesn't mean that the Calvin cycle can continue running in a plant kept in the dark. The Calvin cycle requires two inputs supplied by the light reactions, ATP and NADPH. You'll explore both the light reactions and the Calvin cycle in more detail in Concept 8.2 and Concept 8.3.

www.biology.com
Explore photosynthesis in action.
Find out how the process of photosynthesis works. Go online to explore a field of sunflowers and discover how they produce sugar.

Concept Check 8.1

1. Draw and label a simple diagram of a chloroplast that includes the following structures: outer and inner membranes, stroma, thylakoids.
2. What are the reactants for photosynthesis? What are the products?
3. Name the two main stages of photosynthesis. How are the two stages related?

CONCEPT 8.2

The light reactions convert light energy to chemical energy.

OBJECTIVES
- Explain how light interacts with pigments.
- Describe how photosystems help harvest light energy.
- Identify the chemical products of the light reactions.

KEY TERMS
- wavelength
- electromagnetic spectrum
- pigment
- paper chromatography
- photosystem

What's Online

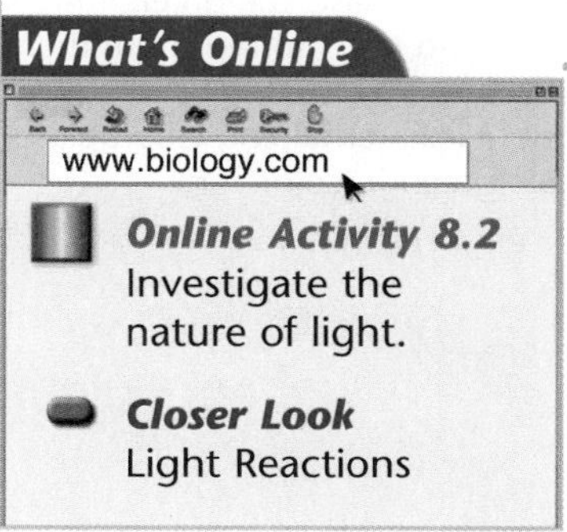

Chloroplasts are like chemical factories inside plant cells. The energy to run these factories comes from the sun, an energy source more than 150 million kilometers from Earth. In this section, you'll follow the chain of events that occurs when sunlight enters a chloroplast.

Light Energy and Pigments

Sunlight is a form of electromagnetic energy. Electromagnetic energy travels in waves that can be compared to ocean waves rolling onto a beach. The distance between two adjacent waves is called a **wavelength.** The different forms of electromagnetic energy have characteristic wavelengths, as shown in Figure 8-5. The range of types of electromagnetic energy, from the very short wavelengths of gamma rays to the very long wavelengths of radio waves, is called the **electromagnetic spectrum.**

Visible light—those wavelengths that your eyes see as different colors—makes up only a small fraction of the electromagnetic spectrum. Visible light consists of wavelengths from about 400 nanometers (nm), violet, to about 700 nm, red. Shorter wavelengths have more energy than longer wavelengths. In fact, wavelengths that are shorter than those of visible light have enough energy to damage organic molecules such as proteins and nucleic acids. This is why being exposed to the ultraviolet (UV) radiation in sunlight can cause sunburns and lead to skin cancer.

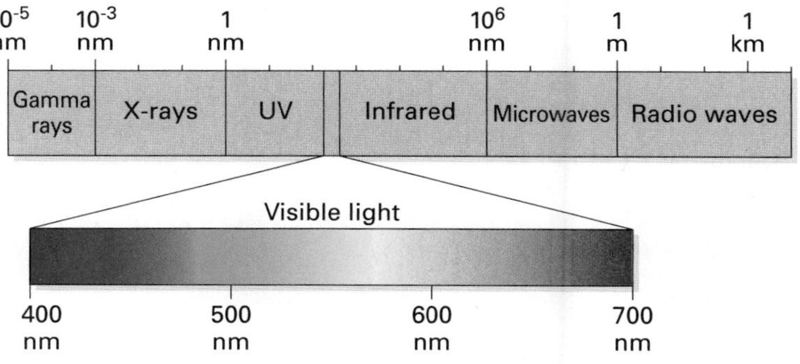

Figure 8-5 Different forms of electromagnetic energy have different wavelengths. Shorter wavelengths have more energy than longer wavelengths.

Pigments and Color A substance's color is due to chemical compounds called **pigments.** When light shines on a material that contains pigments, three things can happen to the different wavelengths: they can be absorbed, transmitted, or reflected. The pigments in the leaf's chloroplasts absorb blue-violet and red-orange light very well. The chloroplasts convert some of this absorbed light energy into chemical energy. But the chloroplast pigments do not absorb green light well. As shown in Figure 8-6, most of the green light passes through the leaf (is transmitted) or bounces back (is reflected). Leaves look green because the green light is not absorbed.

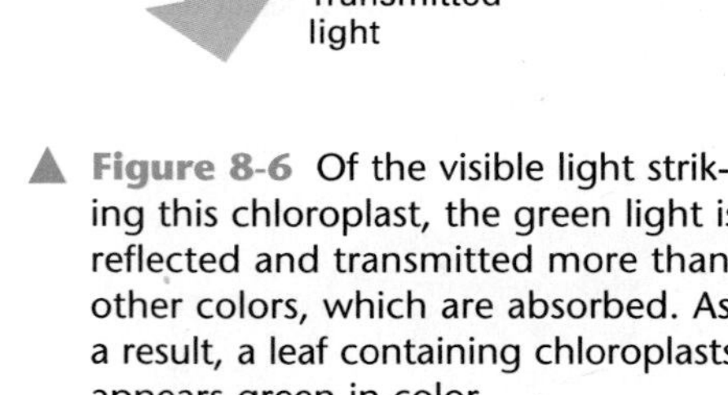

▲ **Figure 8-6** Of the visible light striking this chloroplast, the green light is reflected and transmitted more than other colors, which are absorbed. As a result, a leaf containing chloroplasts appears green in color.

Identifying Chloroplast Pigments Using a laboratory technique called **paper chromatography,** you could observe the different pigments in a green leaf. First you would press the leaf onto a strip of filter paper to deposit a "stain." Next you would seal the paper in a cylinder containing solvents, working under a vented laboratory hood. (In Online Activity 8.2, you can carry out a virtual paper chromatography experiment.)

As the solvents move up the paper strip, the pigments dissolve in the solvents and are carried up the strip. Different pigments travel at different rates, depending on how easily they dissolve and how strongly they are attracted to the paper. Figure 8-7 shows some chromatography results. Notice that several different pigments have separated out on the paper. Chlorophyll *a*, which absorbs mainly blue-violet and red light and reflects mainly green light, plays a major role in the light reactions of photosynthesis. Chloroplasts also contain other "helper" pigments. These include chlorophyll *b*, which absorbs mainly blue and orange light and reflects yellow-green; and several types of carotenoids, which absorb mainly blue-green light and reflect yellow-orange.

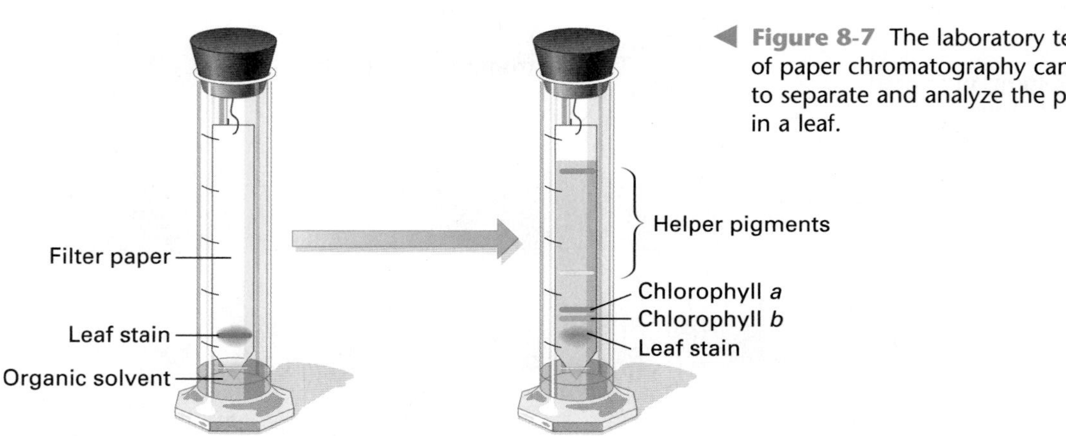

◀ **Figure 8-7** The laboratory technique of paper chromatography can be used to separate and analyze the pigments in a leaf.

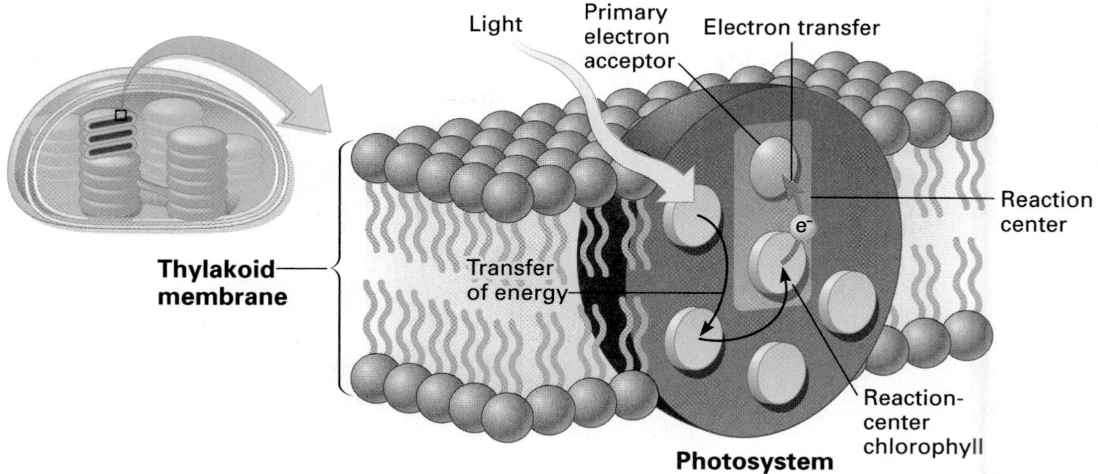

▲ **Figure 8-8** When light strikes the chloroplast, pigment molecules absorb the energy. This energy jumps from molecule to molecule until it arrives at the reaction center.

Harvesting Light Energy

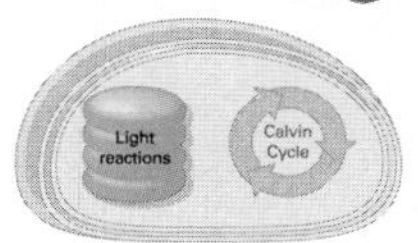

Suppose that you could observe what happens inside a chloroplast as sunlight strikes a leaf. Within the thylakoid membrane, chlorophyll and other molecules are arranged in clusters called **photosystems** (Figure 8-8). Each photosystem contains a few hundred pigment molecules, including chlorophyll *a*, chlorophyll *b*, and carotenoids. This cluster of pigment molecules acts like a light-gathering panel, somewhat like a miniature version of the solar collector shown in Figure 8-9.

Each time a pigment molecule absorbs light energy, one of the pigment's electrons gains energy—the electron is raised from a low-energy "ground state" to a high-energy "excited state." This excited state is very unstable. Almost immediately, the excited electron falls back to the ground state and transfers the energy to a neighboring molecule. The energy transfer excites an electron in the receiving molecule. When this electron drops back to the ground state, it excites an electron in the next pigment molecule, and so on. In this way, the energy "jumps" from molecule to molecule until it arrives at what is called the reaction center of the photosystem.

The reaction center consists of a chlorophyll *a* molecule located next to another molecule called a primary electron acceptor. The primary electron acceptor is a molecule that traps the excited electron from the chlorophyll *a* molecule. Other teams of molecules built into the thylakoid membrane can now use that trapped energy to make ATP and NADPH.

▶ **Figure 8-9** This solar collector captures sunlight and converts the energy to another form. Photosystems in chloroplasts can be compared to miniature solar collectors.

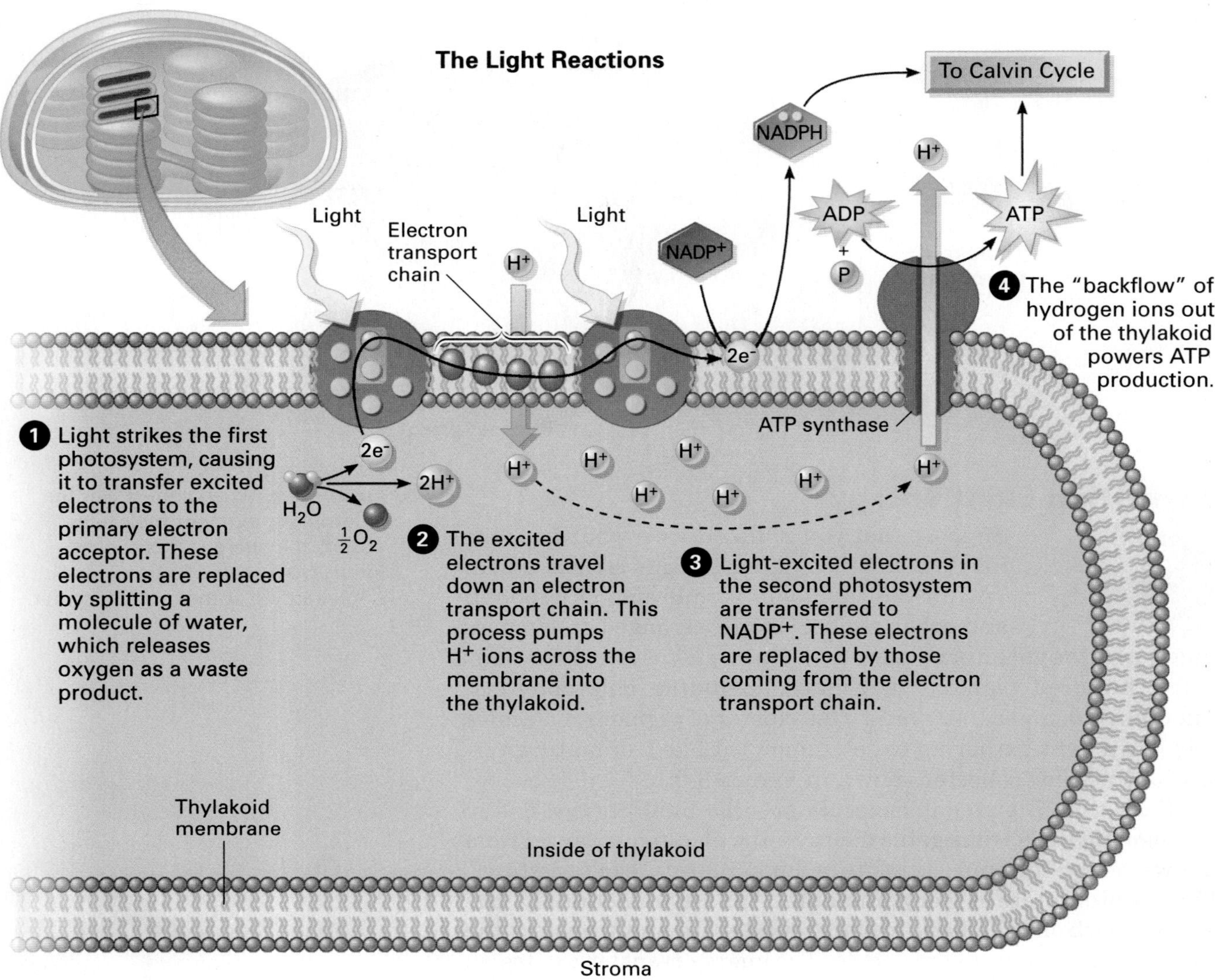
The Light Reactions
To Calvin Cycle
NADPH
H+
ADP
ATP
P
Light
Electron transport chain
Light
NADP+
H+
2e-
4 The "backflow" of hydrogen ions out of the thylakoid powers ATP production.
ATP synthase
1 Light strikes the first photosystem, causing it to transfer excited electrons to the primary electron acceptor. These electrons are replaced by splitting a molecule of water, which releases oxygen as a waste product.
2e-
2H+
H2O
1/2 O2
2 The excited electrons travel down an electron transport chain. This process pumps H+ ions across the membrane into the thylakoid.
3 Light-excited electrons in the second photosystem are transferred to NADP+. These electrons are replaced by those coming from the electron transport chain.
Thylakoid membrane
Inside of thylakoid
Stroma

▲ **Figure 8-10** The light reactions involve two photosystems connected by an electron transport chain.

Chemical Products of the Light Reactions

Two photosystems are involved in the light reactions, as shown in Figure 8-10. The first photosystem traps light energy and transfers the light-excited electrons to an electron transport chain. This photosystem can be thought of as the "water-splitting photosystem" because the electrons are replaced by splitting a molecule of water. This process releases oxygen as a waste product, and also releases hydrogen ions.

The electron transport chain connecting the two photosystems releases energy, which the chloroplast uses to make ATP. This mechanism of ATP production is very similar to ATP production in cellular respiration. In both cases, an electron transport chain pumps hydrogen ions across a membrane—the inner mitochondrial membrane in respiration and the thylakoid membrane in photosynthesis. The main difference is that in respiration food

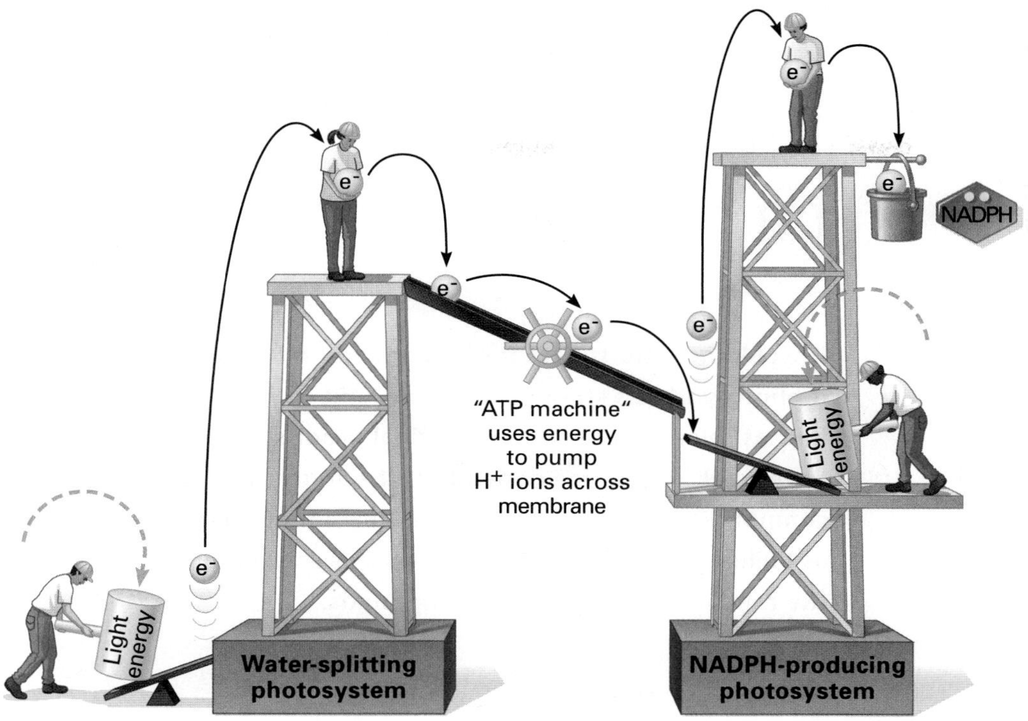

provides the electrons for the electron transport chain, while in photosynthesis light-excited electrons from chlorophyll travel down the chain.

The second photosystem can be thought of as the "NADPH-producing photosystem." This photosystem produces NADPH by transferring excited electrons and hydrogen ions to $NADP^+$. Figure 8-11 shows a mechanical analogy for the light reactions. Note how the light energy "bumps up" the electrons to their excited state in each photosystem.

The light reactions convert light energy to the chemical energy of ATP and NADPH. But recall that photosynthesis also produces sugar. So far no sugar has been produced. That is the job of the Calvin cycle, which uses the ATP and NADPH produced by the light reactions.

▲ **Figure 8-11** In this "construction analogy" for the light reactions, the input of light energy is represented by the large yellow mallets. The light energy boosts the electrons up to their excited states atop the platform in each photosystem. The energy released as the electrons move down the electron transport chain between the photosystems is used to pump hydrogen ions across a membrane and produce ATP.

Online Activity 8.2

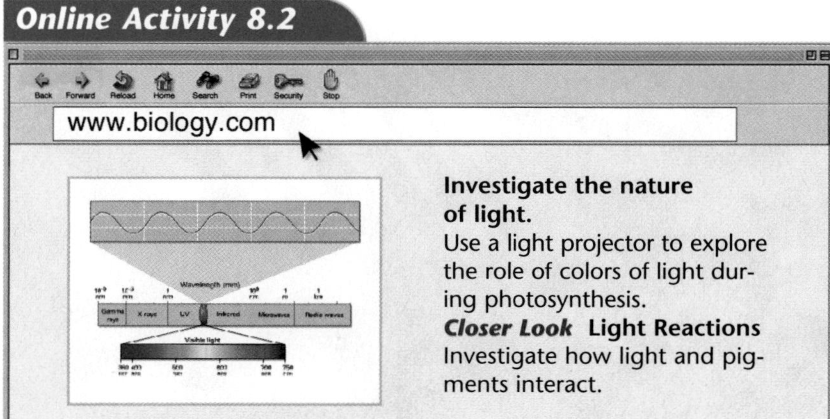

Investigate the nature of light.
Use a light projector to explore the role of colors of light during photosynthesis.
Closer Look **Light Reactions**
Investigate how light and pigments interact.

Concept Check 8.2

1. Explain why a leaf appears green.
2. Describe what happens when a molecule of chlorophyll *a* absorbs light.
3. Besides oxygen, what two molecules are produced by the light reactions?
4. Where in the chloroplast do the light reactions take place?

CONCEPT 8.3 The Calvin cycle makes sugar from carbon dioxide.

OBJECTIVES
- Explain how the Calvin cycle makes sugar.
- Summarize the overall process of photosynthesis.

What's Online

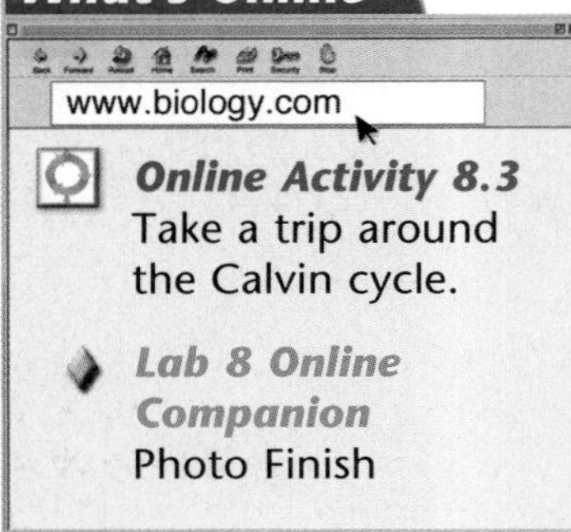

It would be unfortunate for humans and most other living things if photosynthesis stopped after the light reactions. The process so far has released one important final product, oxygen. But as you have read, organisms depend on the sugars and other organic compounds produced by plants as fuel for cellular respiration and as building materials. The Calvin cycle is responsible for producing the raw materials for these compounds.

A Trip Around the Calvin Cycle

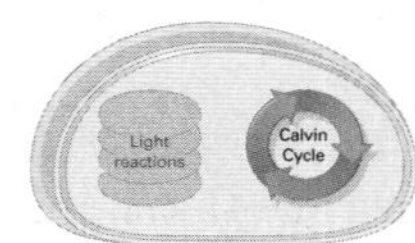

You can think of the Calvin cycle as being somewhat like a sugar factory within a chloroplast. It is called a cycle because, like the Krebs cycle in cellular respiration, the starting material is regenerated each time the process occurs. In this case, the starting material that gets regenerated is a compound called RuBP, a sugar with five carbons.

With each turn of the Calvin cycle, there are chemical inputs and outputs. The inputs are carbon dioxide from the air and the ATP and NADPH produced by the light reactions. The Calvin cycle uses carbon from the carbon dioxide, energy from the ATP, and high-energy electrons and hydrogen ions from the NADPH. The cycle's output is an energy-rich sugar molecule. That sugar is not yet glucose, but a smaller sugar named G3P. The plant cell uses G3P as the raw material to make glucose and other organic molecules it needs (Figure 8-12). You can follow the process of the Calvin cycle in Figure 8-13 on the facing page.

▼ **Figure 8-12** The Calvin cycle uses atmospheric carbon dioxide to build organic matter, such as all the plant life you see in this tropical forest.

▼ **Figure 8-13** Follow the fate of three carbon dioxide molecules through the Calvin cycle. This diagram shows simplified representations of some of the molecules formed during the reactions. Each gray ball represents a carbon atom.

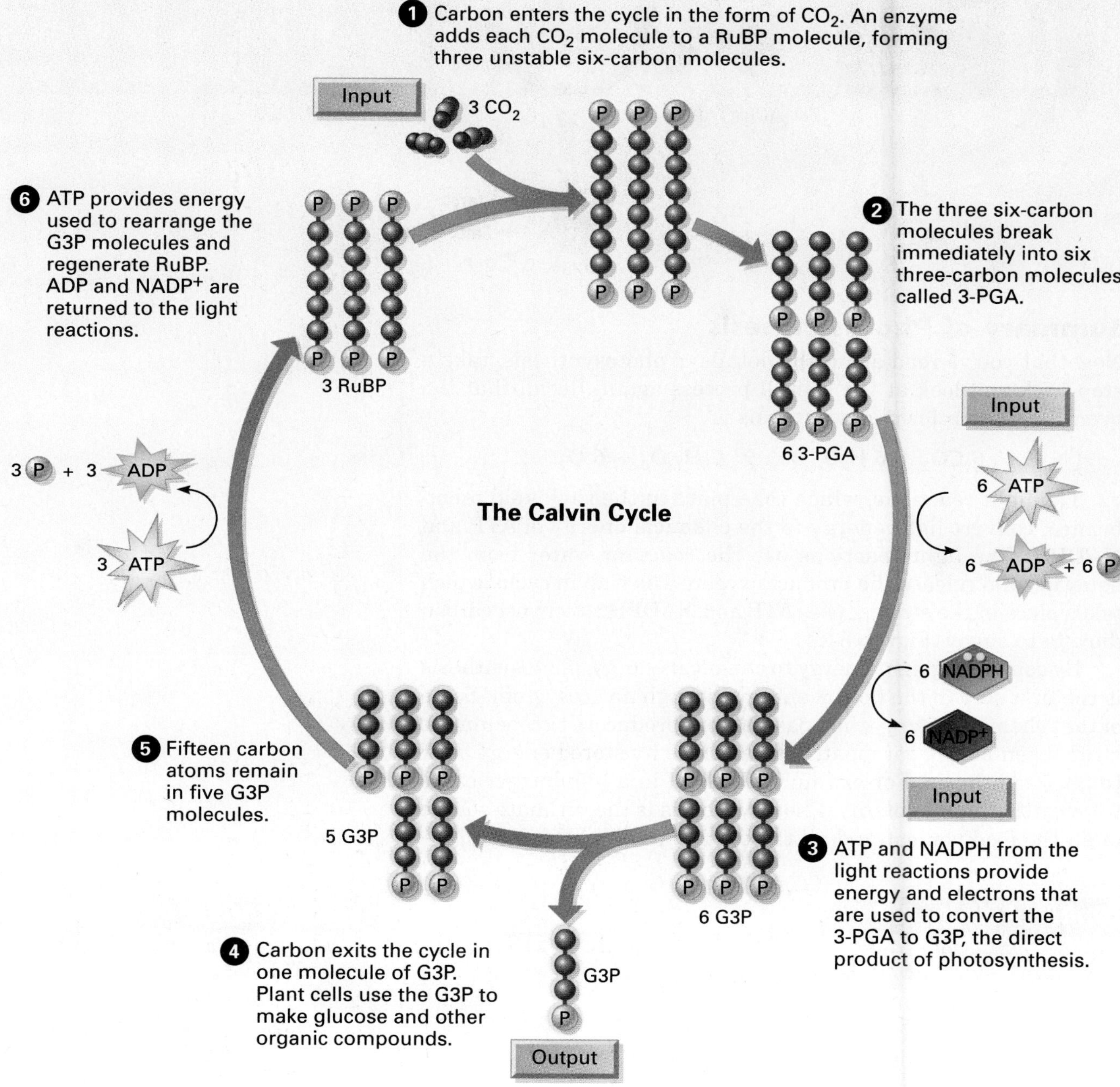

1 Carbon enters the cycle in the form of CO_2. An enzyme adds each CO_2 molecule to a RuBP molecule, forming three unstable six-carbon molecules.
Input
3 CO_2
2 The three six-carbon molecules break immediately into six three-carbon molecules called 3-PGA.
6 3-PGA
Input
6 ATP
6 ADP + 6 P
6 NADPH
6 $NADP^+$
Input
3 ATP and NADPH from the light reactions provide energy and electrons that are used to convert the 3-PGA to G3P, the direct product of photosynthesis.
6 G3P
The Calvin Cycle
G3P
Output
4 Carbon exits the cycle in one molecule of G3P. Plant cells use the G3P to make glucose and other organic compounds.
5 G3P
5 Fifteen carbon atoms remain in five G3P molecules.
3 P + 3 ADP
3 ATP
3 RuBP
6 ATP provides energy used to rearrange the G3P molecules and regenerate RuBP. ADP and $NADP^+$ are returned to the light reactions.

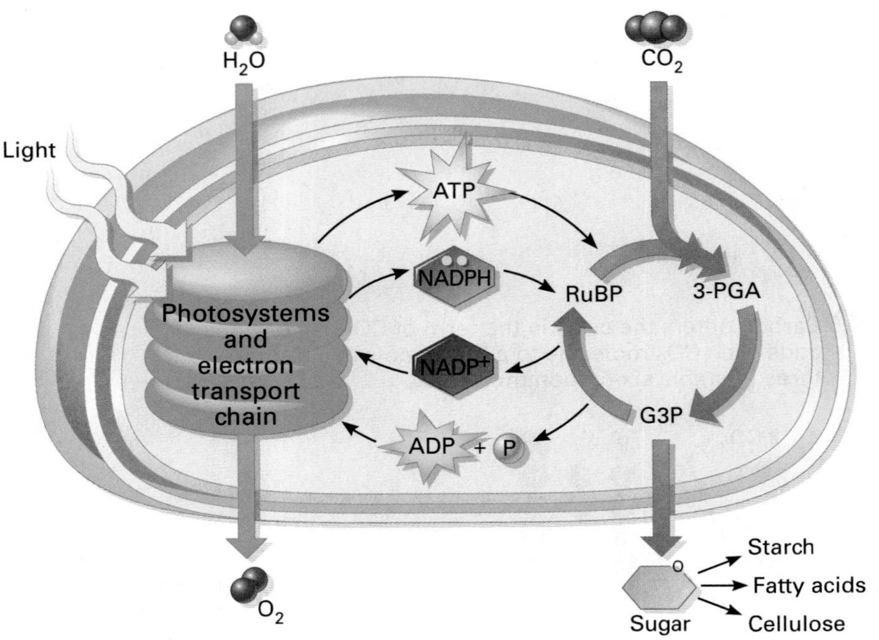

Figure 8-14 The light reactions and the Calvin cycle together convert light energy to the stored chemical energy of sugar. The plant can use the sugar to build other organic molecules.

Summary of Photosynthesis

Now that you've read about the details of photosynthesis, take a step back and look at the overall process again. Recall that the overall equation for photosynthesis is

$$6\ CO_2 + 6\ H_2O \rightarrow\rightarrow\rightarrow C_6H_{12}O_6 + 6\ O_2$$

The light reactions, which take place in the thylakoid membranes, convert light energy to the chemical energy of ATP and NADPH. The light reactions use the reactant water from the equation and release the product oxygen. The Calvin cycle, which takes place in the stroma, uses ATP and NADPH to convert carbon dioxide to sugar (Figure 8-14).

By converting light energy to chemical energy, photosynthesis is the first step in the flow of energy through an ecosystem. Some of that chemical energy then passes from producers to consumers. Even when people eat meat, you can trace its stored energy back to photosynthesis. For example, the beef in a hamburger came from cattle that ate plants. Photosynthesis is the ultimate source of all the food you eat and all the oxygen you breathe.

Online Activity 8.3

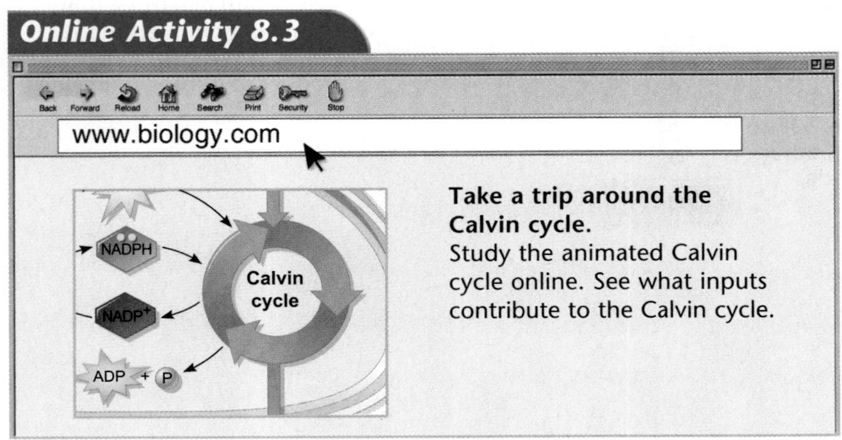

Take a trip around the Calvin cycle.
Study the animated Calvin cycle online. See what inputs contribute to the Calvin cycle.

Concept Check 8.3

1. What are the inputs and outputs of the Calvin cycle?
2. Which stage of photosynthesis uses each reactant from the overall photosynthesis equation? Which stage generates each product from the overall photosynthesis equation?
3. Why is the Calvin cycle called a cycle?
4. What molecule is the direct product of photosynthesis? How is that molecule then used by plant cells?

Photo Finish

Comparing Rates of Photosynthesis

Question Which will photosynthesize at a faster rate, a young ivy leaf or an older ivy leaf?

Lab Overview In this investigation you will compare rates of photosynthesis in old and young ivy leaves by measuring the length of time it takes pieces of each leaf type to generate enough oxygen gas to float upward in a solution-filled syringe.

Preparing for the Lab To help you prepare for the investigation, go to the *Lab 8 Online Companion.* Learn about the characteristics of leaf structure that make it possible to use oxygen production as an indirect measure of the rate of photosynthesis. Prepare for the lab procedure by previewing the steps you will take.

Completing the Lab Use your Laboratory Manual or lab page printouts from the *Lab 8 Online Companion* to do the investigation and analyze your results. **CAUTION:** *Be sure to follow your teacher's instructions and all safety guidelines in the investigation.*

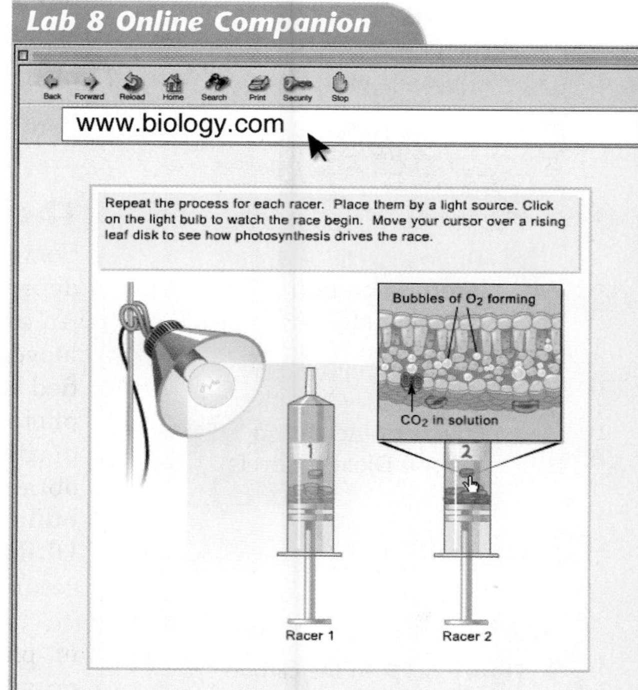
Lab 8 Online Companion
Back
Forward
Reload
Home
Search
Print
Security
Stop
www.biology.com
Repeat the process for each racer. Place them by a light source. Click on the light bulb to watch the race begin. Move your cursor over a rising leaf disk to see how photosynthesis drives the race.
Bubbles of O_2 forming
CO_2 in solution
1
2
Racer 1
Racer 2

CONCEPT 8.4

Photosynthesis has a global impact.

OBJECTIVES
- Describe the path of carbon in the carbon cycle.
- Explain how photosynthesis is related to climate.

KEY TERMS
- carbon cycle
- greenhouse effect

What's Online

www.biology.com

Online Activity 8.4 Interpret carbon dioxide data.

Science, Technology, & Society Effects of Increasing Carbon Dioxide Levels

For the past several chapters, you have been navigating the microscopic world of cells as though you were a miniature explorer. Now imagine you could zoom out into space and look at planet Earth as a whole. Keep reading to see how these cellular processes fit into your new perspective of life on Earth.

The Carbon Cycle

Some of the processes that occur on a global scale on Earth depend on the metabolism of tiny chloroplasts and mitochondria. An example is the **carbon cycle,** the process by which carbon moves from inorganic to organic compounds and back. A simplified version of the carbon cycle is shown in Figure 8-15. Through photosynthesis, producers such as grass convert inorganic carbon dioxide to organic compounds. Consumers such as a Cape buffalo obtain the organic compounds by eating the producers. Cape buffalo may in turn be eaten by a lioness or another consumer. Ultimately, cellular respiration by both producers and consumers returns carbon dioxide to the atmosphere.

No other chemical process on the planet matches the output of photosynthesis. Earth's plants and other photosynthetic organisms make about 160 billion metric tons of organic material per year. That's about equal to 80 trillion copies of this book—25 stacks of books reaching from Earth to the sun!

▼ **Figure 8-15** In the carbon cycle, carbon continuously moves from inorganic carbon dioxide to organic molecules and back.

CO_2 in atmosphere
Cellular respiration by producers and consumers releases CO_2.
Photosynthesis by producers builds organic compounds.

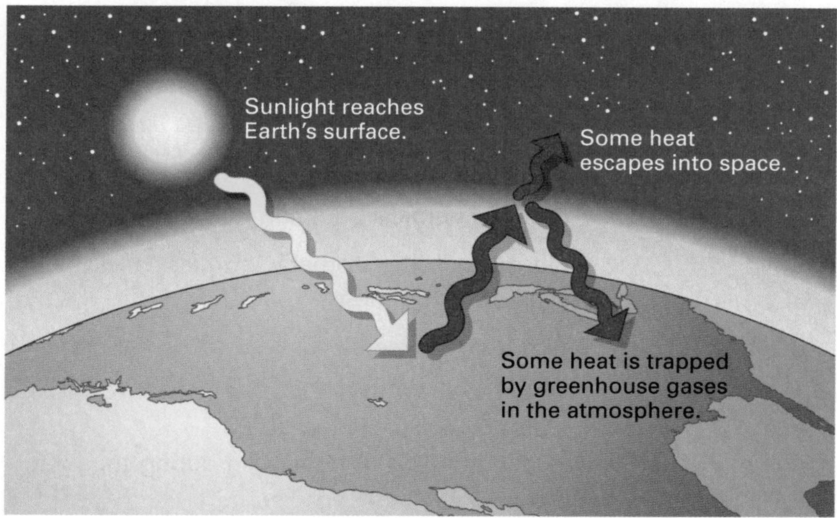

Figure 8-16 Some heat radiating from Earth's surface back out toward space is trapped by carbon dioxide (along with some other types of gases) in the atmosphere. This greenhouse effect keeps Earth warm enough for living things.

Photosynthesis and Global Climate

As you have just read, a key element of the carbon cycle is carbon dioxide. Plants use carbon dioxide to make sugars in photosynthesis, and most organisms give off carbon dioxide as waste from cellular respiration. Though any one organism may use or produce relatively small amounts of carbon dioxide, the total effect of all the organisms on Earth has a very large effect on the amount of carbon dioxide in the atmosphere.

Before this century, carbon dioxide made up about 0.03 percent (300 parts per million) of Earth's atmosphere. This amount of carbon dioxide is enough to provide plants with plenty of carbon for photosynthesis. Carbon dioxide in the atmosphere also traps heat from the sun that would otherwise escape from Earth back into space (Figure 8-16). This important property, known as the **greenhouse effect,** keeps the world climate warm enough for living things. The greenhouse effect keeps the average temperature on Earth some 10°C warmer than it would be otherwise.

In the past century, the amount of atmospheric carbon dioxide has been rising, reaching more than 360 parts per million. In Chapter 36, you'll read more about this change and about its possible effects.

Science, Technology, & Society

Back Forward Reload Home Search Print Security Stop

www.biology.com

Effects of Increasing Carbon Dioxide Levels

Carbon dioxide levels have been steadily increasing since the 1750s. Go online to find out how this increase is affecting plants and some organisms that depend on plants for food.

Online Activity 8.4

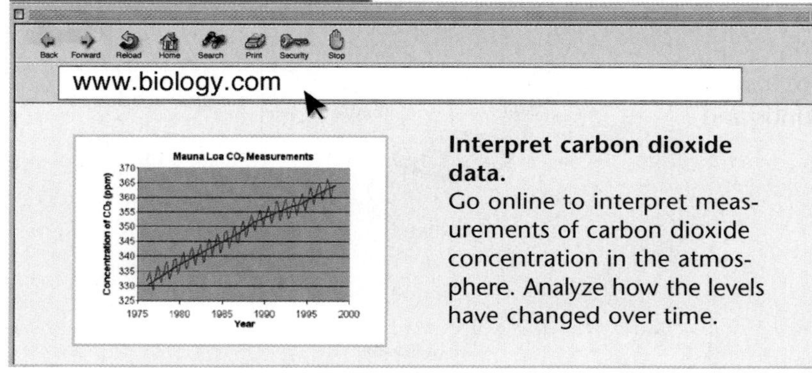

Interpret carbon dioxide data.

Go online to interpret measurements of carbon dioxide concentration in the atmosphere. Analyze how the levels have changed over time.

Concept Check 8.4

1. Give an example of carbon moving from an inorganic compound to an organic compound in the carbon cycle. Give an example of carbon moving from an organic to an inorganic compound.
2. How is carbon dioxide important to Earth's climate?

Multiple Choice

Choose the letter of the best answer.

1. In the diagram below, the part of the leaf where most photosynthesis occurs is the
   a. vein. b. mesophyll.
   c. stomata. d. air space.

Leaf Cross Section

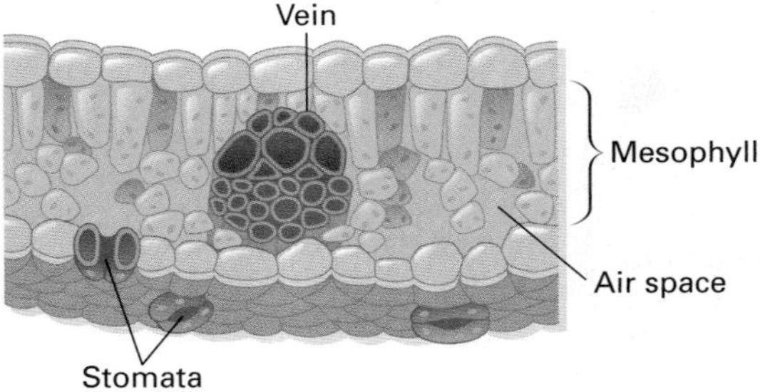

2. In a plant cell, where do the light reactions of photosynthesis occur?
   a. the stomata b. the stroma
   c. the thylakoids d. the mitochondria

3. The chemical products of the light reactions are oxygen,
   a. $NADP^+$, and ADP.
   b. sugar, and water.
   c. carbon dioxide, and ATP.
   d. ATP, and NADPH.

4. The stage of photosynthesis that uses the most ATP molecules is
   a. the light reactions.
   b. the Calvin cycle.
   c. the electron transport chain.
   d. glycolysis.

5. The Calvin cycle converts carbon dioxide to
   a. ADP and NADPH. b. water.
   c. a sugar called G3P. d. chlorophyll.

6. The process by which carbon moves from inorganic carbon dioxide to organic compounds and back is called
   a. the electron transport chain.
   b. the carbon cycle.
   c. the electromagnetic spectrum.
   d. chromatography.

Short Answer

7. Write the chemical equation for photosynthesis.

8. What roles do the stomata in a plant's leaves play in photosynthesis?

9. Describe the three things that could happen to light of a particular wavelength after it strikes a leaf.

10. Describe how ATP is generated during the light reactions.

11. Why is the term "light-independent reactions" a misleading description of the Calvin cycle?

12. What is the function of NADPH in the Calvin cycle?

13. What is the significance of the sugar G3P?

14. Describe how the processes of photosynthesis and cellular respiration each contribute to the carbon cycle.

Visualizing Concepts

15. Copy the concept map below and fill in the blank spaces to describe the process of photosynthesis.

Photosynthesis

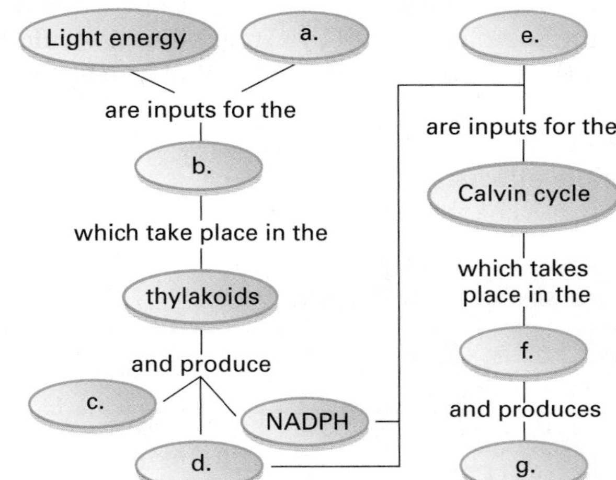

Applying Concepts

Analyzing Information

16. Analyzing Diagrams Use the diagram below to answer the questions.

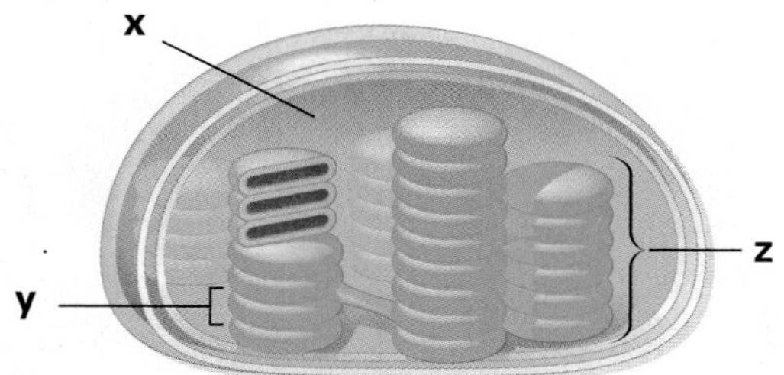

a. What organelle is depicted above?
b. Name the parts of the organelle labeled x, y, and z.
c. Describe where in this organelle each of the two stages of photosynthesis occurs.

17. Analyzing Data Three students are investigating the effect of light intensity on photosynthesis by the aquatic plant *Elodea.* They varied the light intensity by placing a lamp at five different distances from the aquarium. The students left the room lights on and the window shades up. Then they measured how much oxygen gas the plant produced per hour at the different lamp distances. Here is their data table.

Rate of Photosynthesis in *Elodea*

Lamp distance (cm)	15	30	45	60	75
Oxygen gas produced (mL/hr)	7.25	6.25	5.0	4.5	4.5

a. Use the data to make a graph.
b. At which lamp distance(s) is photosynthesis occurring at the fastest rate? At which lamp distance(s) is photosynthesis occurring at the slowest rate?
c. The students designed the experiment to test this hypothesis: the closer the lamp, the faster photosynthesis will occur. Do their results support their hypothesis? Why or why not?
d. Can you suggest a possible reason for the results being the same at 60 and 75 cm? Does this suggest any new questions to investigate? Explain.

Critical Thinking

18. Making Generalizations How is the structure of a chloroplast suited to its function?

19. Relating Cause and Effect Explain why a leaf containing chloroplasts looks green in color.

20. Comparing and Contrasting Describe at least two similarities and two differences between photosynthesis and cellular respiration.

21. Making Generalizations In terms of energy flow, what is the key result of the light reactions?

22. Problem Solving A friend challenges you to grow a houseplant using mainly one color of light—either red or green. Which would you choose? Explain your answer.

23. Making Generalizations Explain how producers and consumers play a role in cycling carbon within the biosphere.

24. What's Wrong With These Statements? *Briefly explain why each statement is inaccurate or misleading.*
a. Plants can convert sunlight into sugar.
b. Plants don't need sunlight to make sugar as long as they have a source of carbon dioxide and water.
c. The Calvin cycle produces glucose directly.

Performance Assessment

Biology Research Project In many parts of the United States, leaves change colors in the fall. Young children are often very curious about this process. With a partner, research, write, and illustrate a children's story that explains why leaves change color.

Online Assessment/Test Preparation

Back Forward Reload Home Search Print Security Stop

www.biology.com

- **Chapter 8 Assessment**
  Check your understanding of the chapter concepts.
- **Standardized Test Preparation**
  Practice test-taking skills you need to succeed.

UNIT 3 Exploring Inheritance

Chapters

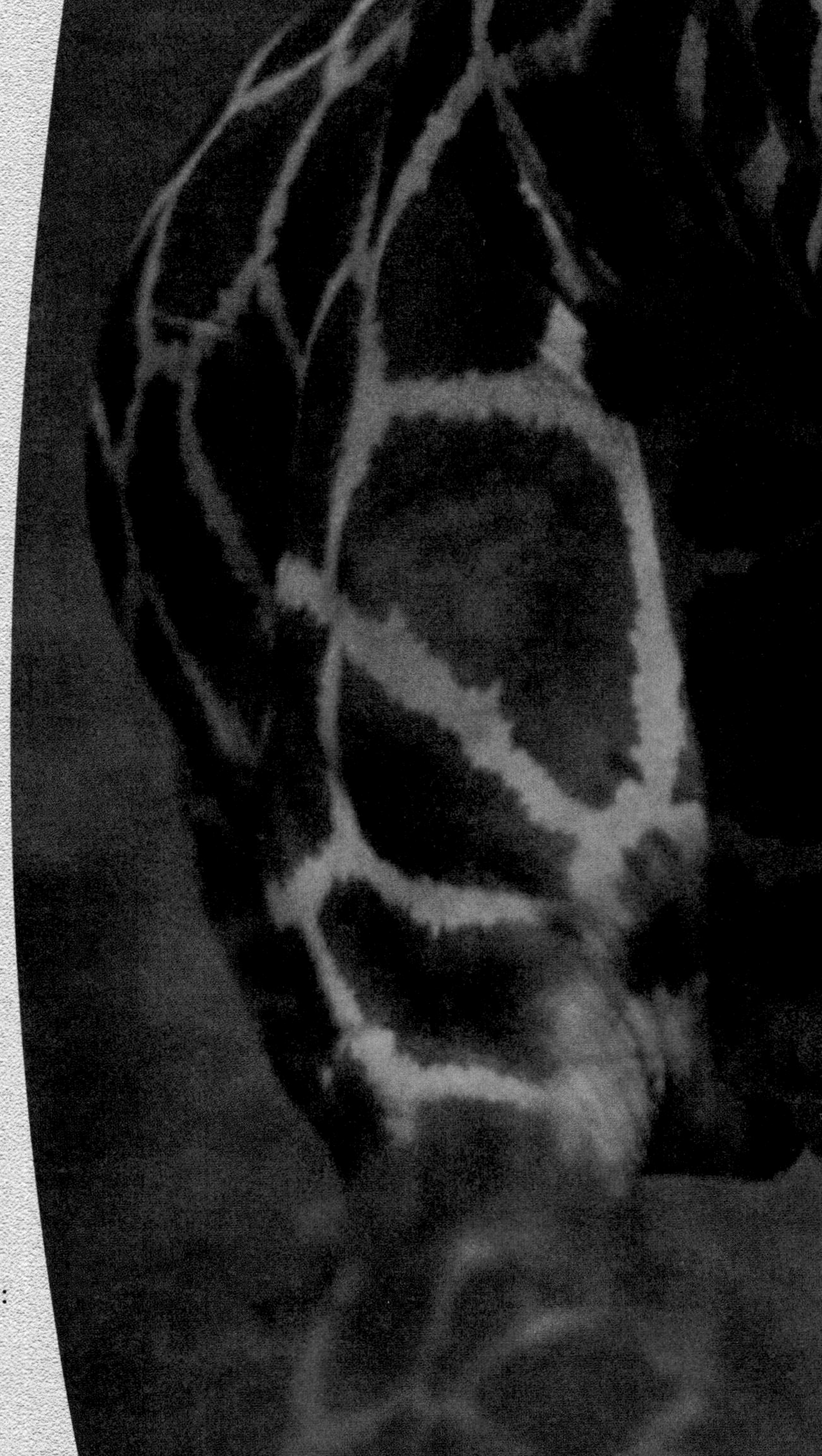

Resemblance of parents and offspring: a mother giraffe and her young

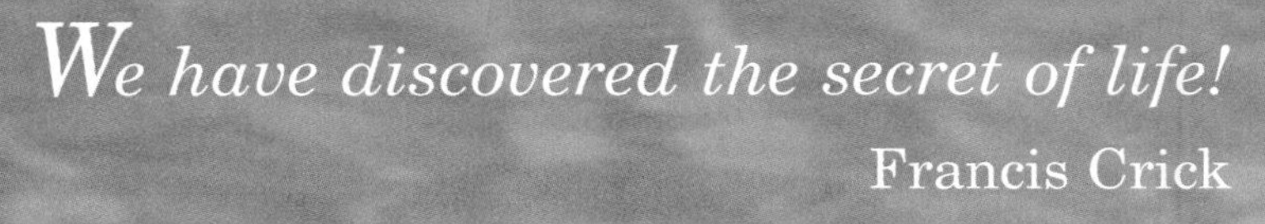

We have discovered the secret of life!

Francis Crick

The Cellular Basis of Inheritance

Your body developed from a single cell formed from the union of a unique sperm cell and a unique egg cell. How did that single cell give rise to the trillions of cells that make up your body—more cells than the Milky Way galaxy has stars? And how are these cells related to the cells of your parents? The answers to these questions involve the process occurring in the photograph below—cell reproduction. Before you begin reading this chapter about how cells reproduce, go online to the *WebQuest* to explore the cellular connection between a young animal and its adult form.

LM 2,600×

Key Concepts

Concept 9.1

All cells come from cells.

Concept 9.2

The cell cycle multiplies cells.

Concept 9.3

Cells divide during the mitotic phase.

Concept 9.4

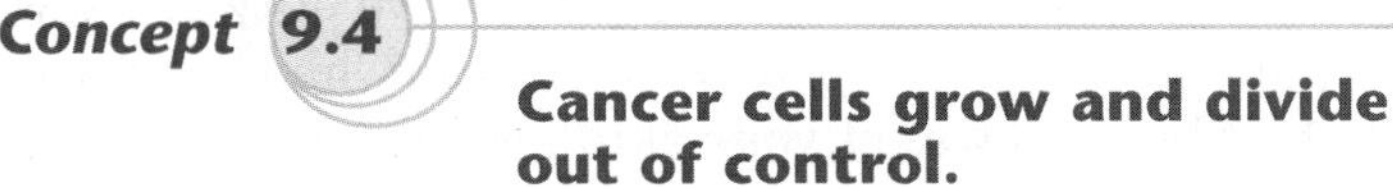

Cancer cells grow and divide out of control.

Concept 9.5

Meiosis functions in sexual reproduction.

Concept 9.6

Meiosis increases genetic variation among offspring.

Assessment

Chapter 9 Review

What's Online

www.biology.com

WebQuest
GrowthQuest

Online Activity 9.1
Analyze cell division.

Online Activity 9.2
Examine stages in the cell cycle.

Online Activity 9.3
Observe mitosis in action.

Lab 9 Online Companion
You Are a 19th-Century Cell Biologist

Online Activity 9.4
Examine the cycle of a cancer cell.

Online Activity 9.5
Explore the process of meiosis in depth.

Online Activity 9.6
Analyze the process of crossing over.

History of Science
Discovery of Chromosomes

Chapter 9 Assessment

CONCEPT 9.1

All cells come from cells.

OBJECTIVES

- Describe how cell reproduction contributes to repair and to growth.
- Contrast the two main ways that organisms reproduce.

KEY TERMS

- asexual reproduction
- sexual reproduction

What's Online

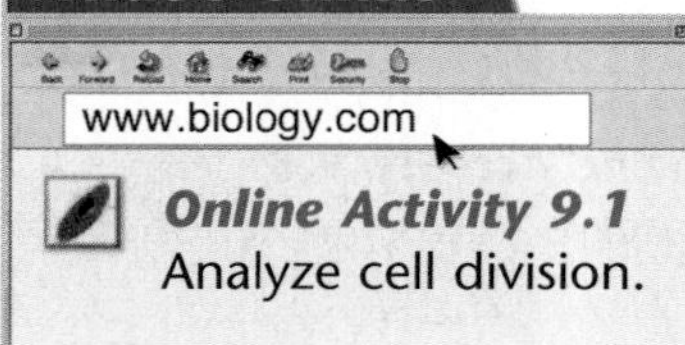
www.biology.com

Online Activity 9.1
Analyze cell division.

All organisms reproduce their own kind. The ability to reproduce is an important characteristic of living things. Like all life processes, reproduction has a cellular basis. Rudolf Virchow, a German physician, put it this way in 1855: "Where a cell exists, there must have been a preexisting cell . . ." The division of cells into more cells enables living things to repair damage, to grow, and to produce offspring.

Repair and Growth

Take a moment to look at the skin on your arm. You might be surprised to learn that the outermost layer of skin is actually a layer of dead cells. Underneath the surface layer are living cells busily carrying out the chemical reactions you studied in Unit 2. The living cells are also engaged in another vital activity: They are reproducing. The new cells gradually move outward toward the skin's surface, replacing dead cells that have rubbed off (Figure 9-1). This renewal of your skin goes on throughout your life. And when your skin is injured, additional cell reproduction helps heal the wound.

The replacement of lost or damaged cells is just one of the important roles cell reproduction plays in your life. Another is growth—simply increasing in size from a baby to a child to an adult. All of the trillions of cells in your body result from cell reproduction, a series of cell divisions that began with a single fertilized egg cell.

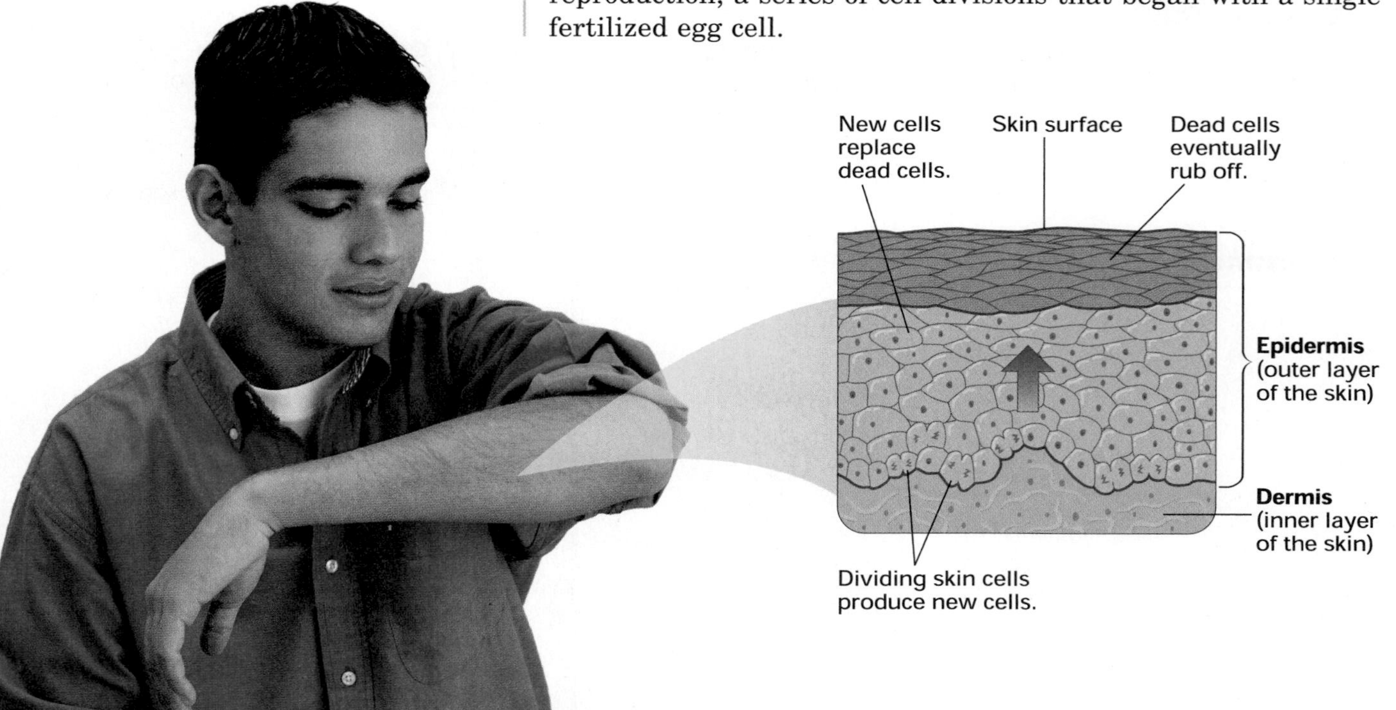
New cells replace dead cells.
Skin surface
Dead cells eventually rub off.
Epidermis (outer layer of the skin)
Dermis (inner layer of the skin)
Dividing skin cells produce new cells.

▼ **Figure 9-1** Cell reproduction enables your body to produce new skin cells that replace dead cells at your skin's surface.

Reproduction

While the production of new cells can result in growth and repair *within* organisms, cell division also has an essential role in the reproduction of *entire* organisms. Some organisms reproduce by simple cell division, in which a single cell or group of cells each duplicates its genetic material and then splits into two new genetically identical cells. This process, which is known as **asexual reproduction,** produces offspring that inherit all their genetic material from just one parent. As a result, the offspring are genetically identical to one another and to their parent. Single-celled organisms such as *Paramecium* usually reproduce this way (Figure 9-2). Many multicellular organisms can also reproduce asexually at certain times. For example, some sea stars, when divided into two pieces, can regrow into two whole new individuals through simple cell division. And if you've ever grown a geranium from a leaf cutting, you've taken advantage of the plant's ability to reproduce asexually.

In contrast, when two parents are involved in the production of offspring, the process is called **sexual reproduction.** In sexual reproduction genetic material from each of two parents combines, producing offspring that differ genetically from either parent. Sexual reproduction involves the union of sex cells, such as an egg and a sperm. These cells are produced by a specialized kind of cell division that you'll read about later in the chapter.

In unicellular organisms, simple cell division results in the asexual reproduction of new organisms. Some unicellular organisms are also capable of sexual reproduction. Most multicellular organisms reproduce sexually, but some may also reproduce asexually. And whether reproduction is sexual or asexual, all multicellular organisms depend on cell division for growth. In this chapter, you'll learn what happens inside cells during both kinds of cell division—the cell division responsible for growth and repair and the cell division that produces sex cells.

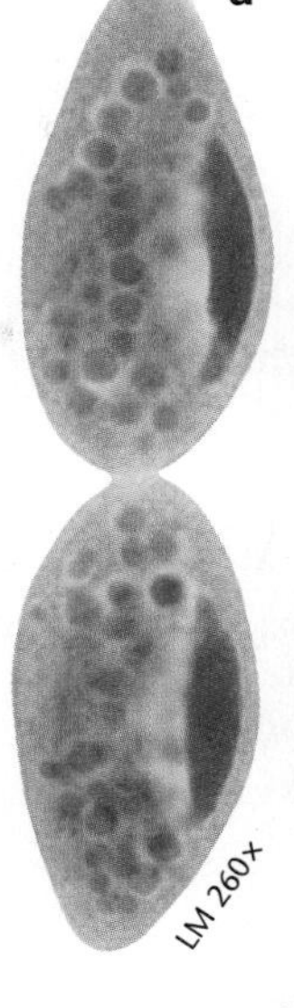
a
LM 260×

b

c

▲ **Figure 9-2** Both asexual and sexual reproduction occur as a result of cell division. **a.** A single-celled paramecium reproduces asexually by simple cell division. **b.** Some multicellular organisms, such as this kalanchoe plant, can reproduce both sexually and asexually. **c.** These birds called tanagers reproduce sexually through the union of an egg cell and a sperm.

Online Activity 9.1

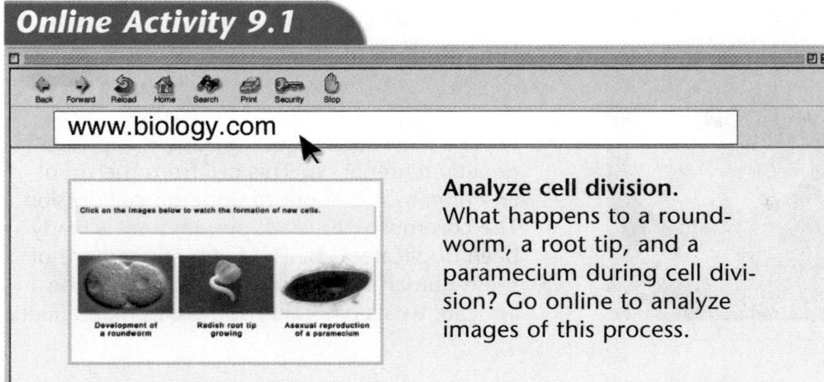
Back
Forward
Reload
Home
Search
Print
Security
Stop
www.biology.com
Click on the images below to watch the formation of new cells.
Development of a roundworm
Radish root tip growing
Asexual reproduction of a paramecium
Analyze cell division.
What happens to a roundworm, a root tip, and a paramecium during cell division? Go online to analyze images of this process.

Concept Check 9.1

1. Relate cell reproduction to the replacement of skin cells.
2. Describe two ways in which asexual and sexual reproduction differ.
3. How is cell division involved in growth?

CONCEPT 9.2

The cell cycle multiplies cells.

OBJECTIVES

- Describe the structure of a chromosome.
- Name the stages of the cell cycle and explain what happens during each stage.

KEY TERMS

- chromatin
- chromosome
- sister chromatid
- centromere
- cell cycle
- interphase
- mitotic phase
- mitosis
- cytokinesis

What's Online

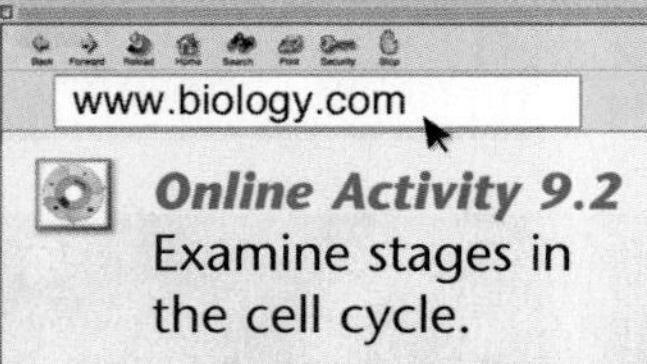

Online Activity 9.2
Examine stages in the cell cycle.

At this moment, millions of cells in your body are dividing, each forming two new cells. However, the vast majority of your cells (about 200 trillion) aren't dividing but are going about other cell activities—building proteins, breaking down food, consuming energy, and so on. How does cell division fit into the life of a cell?

Chromosomes and Cell Division

Almost all the genes of a eukaryotic cell are located in the cell nucleus. Most of the time, this genetic material exists as a mass of very long fibers that are too thin to be seen under a light microscope. These fibers consist of **chromatin,** a combination of DNA and protein molecules. As a cell prepares to divide, its chromatin fibers condense, becoming visible as the compact structures called **chromosomes.** In the stained cell in Figure 9-3a, each dark purple thread is an individual chromosome. The number of chromosomes in a eukaryotic cell depends on the species. For example, human body cells generally each have 46 chromosomes. Each chromosome may contain many hundreds of genes.

Before cell division begins, a cell duplicates all of its chromosomes. Each chromosome now consists of two identical joined copies called **sister chromatids** (Figure 9-3b). (Biologists use the term "sister" to identify joined chromatids, but it does not imply female gender.) The region where the two chromatids are joined tightly together is called the **centromere.**

A dividing human skin cell starts with 46 pairs of duplicated chromosomes (each made up of two sister chromatids). When the cell divides, the sister chromatids separate from each other (Figure 9-4). Once separated from its sister, each chromatid is considered a full-fledged chromosome. The result of the division is two offspring nuclei, each containing 46 chromosomes.

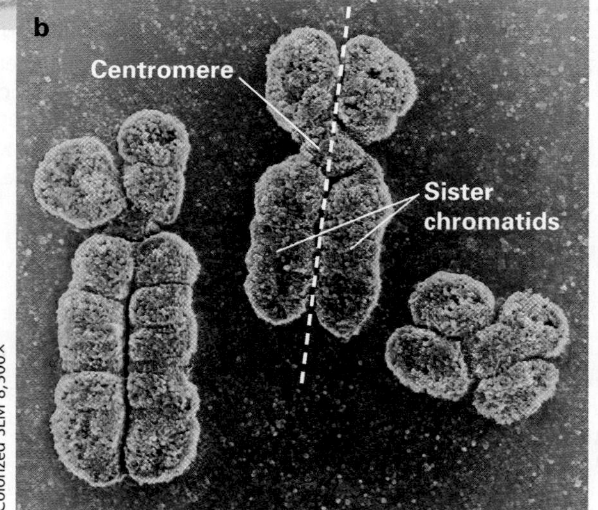

Figure 9-3 Before a cell divides, it copies its genetic material. **a.** This cell from the tip of an onion root is about to undergo cell division. The chromosomes (dark purple) have already been duplicated. **b.** The fuzzy appearance of these human chromosomes comes from the intricate twists and folds of the chromatin fibers.

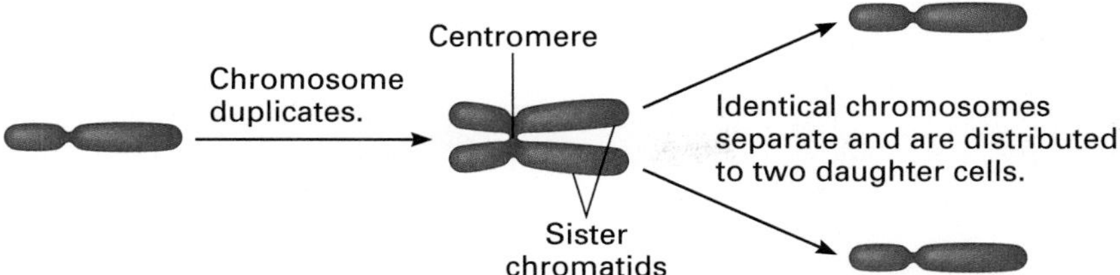

Figure 9-4 Each chromosome in a reproducing cell undergoes the duplication and separation process shown here. Duplication occurs during interphase, in preparation for cell division.

The Cell Cycle

How often a cell divides depends on the type of cell. Some cells divide once a day. Some divide more often; others, less often. Some highly specialized cells, such as mature muscle cells, do not divide at all. Eukaryotic cells that do divide undergo an orderly sequence of events known as the **cell cycle.** The cell cycle extends from the "birth" of a cell as a result of cell reproduction to the time the cell itself reproduces (Figure 9-5). Understanding the cell cycle will help you understand how cells function and how irregularities in the cell cycle can lead to disease.

Interphase The cell may spend as much as 90 percent of the cell cycle in interphase. **Interphase** is the stage during which a cell carries out its metabolic processes and performs its functions. For example, a cell in your stomach lining might be making and releasing enzyme molecules that help digest your food. During interphase, a cell increases its supply of proteins, increases the number of many of its organelles (such as mitochondria and ribosomes), and grows in size.

Interphase also includes cellular functions leading up to cell division. One key event is the duplication of the DNA in the cell's chromosomes. This period is called the S phase (*S* stands for DNA *synthesis*). The interphase periods before and after the S phase are called the G_1 and G_2 phases (*G* stands for *gap*). During the G_2 phase, each duplicated chromosome remains loosely packed as chromatin fibers. The cell is now ready to begin mitosis.

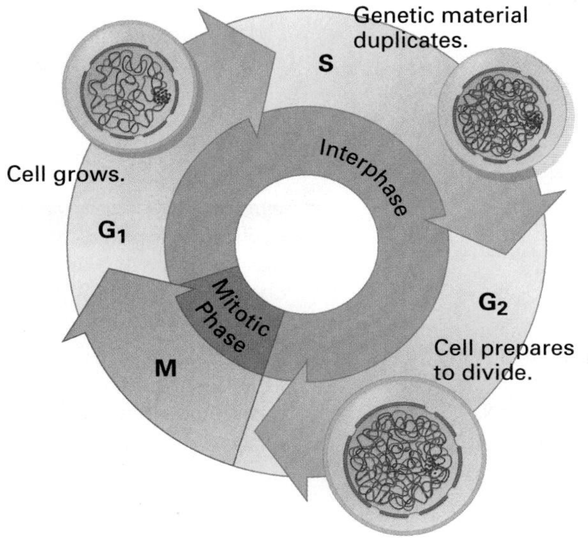

Figure 9-5 In humans and other mammals, cells that reproduce daily have a cell cycle that usually lasts 10 to 20 hours. The S phase takes about 3 to 6 hours, while the G_2 phase is slightly shorter.

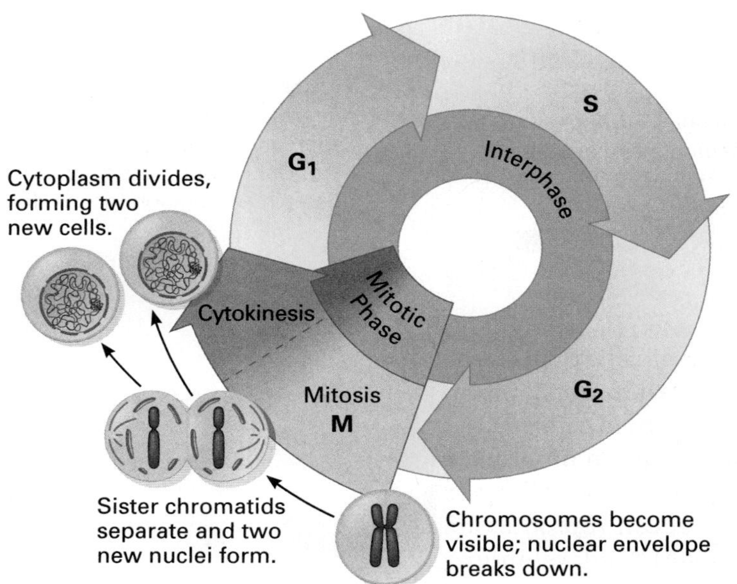

Figure 9-6 This diagram of the cell cycle, showing only one chromosome, highlights the mitotic phase (M). The duplicated chromosomes are separated during mitosis and distributed into daughter cells that form through cytokinesis. (The term "daughter" refers to offspring cells and does not imply female gender.)

Mitotic Phase The stage of the cell cycle when the cell is actually dividing is called the **mitotic phase** (M phase). The mitotic phase includes two processes, mitosis and cytokinesis (Figure 9-6). During **mitosis,** the nucleus and the duplicated chromosomes divide and are evenly distributed, forming two "daughter" nuclei. You will read about mitosis in more detail in Concept 9.3. **Cytokinesis** is the process by which the cytoplasm is divided in two. Cytokinesis usually begins before mitosis is completed. The combination of mitosis and cytokinesis produces two genetically identical daughter cells since the chromosomes were duplicated precisely in the S phase. Each daughter cell has a single nucleus, some surrounding cytoplasm, and a plasma membrane.

Mitosis is a very accurate way of distributing identical copies of a large amount of genetic material to two daughter cells. Experiments with yeast cells, for example, indicate that an error in chromosome distribution occurs only once in about 100,000 cell divisions. Mitosis is unique to eukaryotes. Prokaryotes use a simpler mechanism for distributing DNA to daughter cells, as you will read later in Chapter 16.

Online Activity 9.2

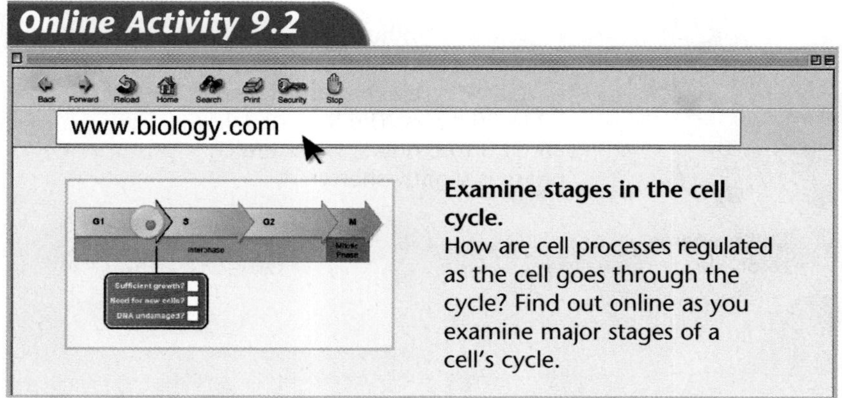

Examine stages in the cell cycle.
How are cell processes regulated as the cell goes through the cycle? Find out online as you examine major stages of a cell's cycle.

Concept Check 9.2

1. Describe how the appearance of chromosomes changes as a cell is about to divide.
2. Interphase used to be described as a "resting phase." Why is this description inaccurate?
3. Summarize the events that occur during mitosis and cytokinesis.

CONCEPT 9.3

Cells divide during the mitotic phase.

OBJECTIVES
- Summarize the major events that occur during each phase of mitosis.
- Explain how cytokinesis differs in plant and animal cells.

KEY TERMS
- spindle
- centrosome
- prophase
- metaphase
- anaphase
- telophase
- cell plate

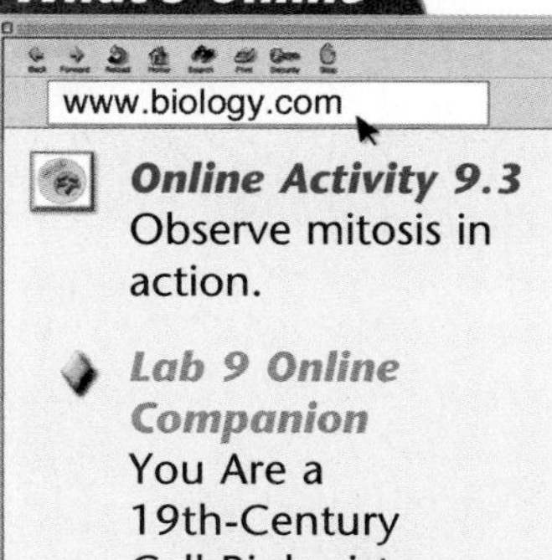

You can think of mitosis as a lively "dance" of the chromosomes. Before the action begins, the chromatin of each chromosome doubles during interphase. Then the elaborately "choreographed" stages of the mitotic phase take place rapidly, distributing the duplicate sets of chromosomes to two daughter nuclei. Finally, cytokinesis divides the cytoplasm, producing two daughter cells. In this section you will read in more detail about the processes that occur during mitosis.

The Mitosis Dance

During mitosis, the chromosomes' movements are guided by a football-shaped framework of microtubules called the **spindle.** The spindle microtubules grow from two **centrosomes,** regions of cytoplasmic material that in animal cells contain structures called centrioles. The role of centrioles in cell division remains a mystery in spite of much research into this question. Destroying them does not interfere with normal spindle formation, and most plant cells lack them entirely.

Figure 9-8, on the next two pages, reveals the events taking place within an animal cell during each phase of the cell cycle. Although mitosis is a continual process, biologists divide the mitotic phase into four main stages in order to study it: prophase, metaphase, anaphase, and telophase. Try using different-colored toothpicks or pieces of yarn to represent chromosomes as you follow the steps of the mitosis dance.

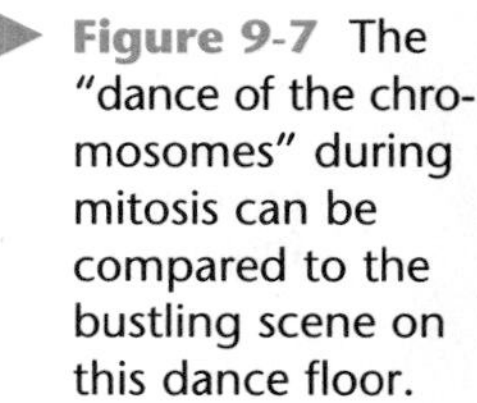

Figure 9-7 The "dance of the chromosomes" during mitosis can be compared to the bustling scene on this dance floor.

Interphase As you read in Concept 9.2, during interphase the cell is busy making new molecules and organelles. The cell shown here is in late interphase (G_2). By this time the cell has duplicated its DNA. However, you can't see the individual chromosomes yet because they are still loosely packed chromatin fibers. The presence of the nucleolus indicates that the cell is still producing ribosomes.

Prophase In **prophase,** the first stage of mitosis, the chromosome "dancers" make their appearance on the dance floor. In the nucleus, the chromatin fibers have condensed and are thick enough to be seen with a light microscope. With high magnification, each chromosome can be clearly seen now to consist of a pair of sister chromatids joined at the centromere. The nucleolus disappears, and the cell stops making ribosomes. Late in prophase, the nuclear envelope breaks down. Meanwhile, in the cytoplasm, a football-shaped structure called the mitotic spindle forms. The chromatids now attach to microtubules that make up the spindle. The spindle starts tugging the chromosomes toward the center of the cell for the next step in the dance.

Metaphase During **metaphase,** the second stage, the chromosomes all gather in a plane across the middle of the cell. The mitotic spindle is now fully formed. All the chromosomes are attached to the spindle microtubules, with their centromeres lined up about halfway between the two ends, or poles, of the spindle.

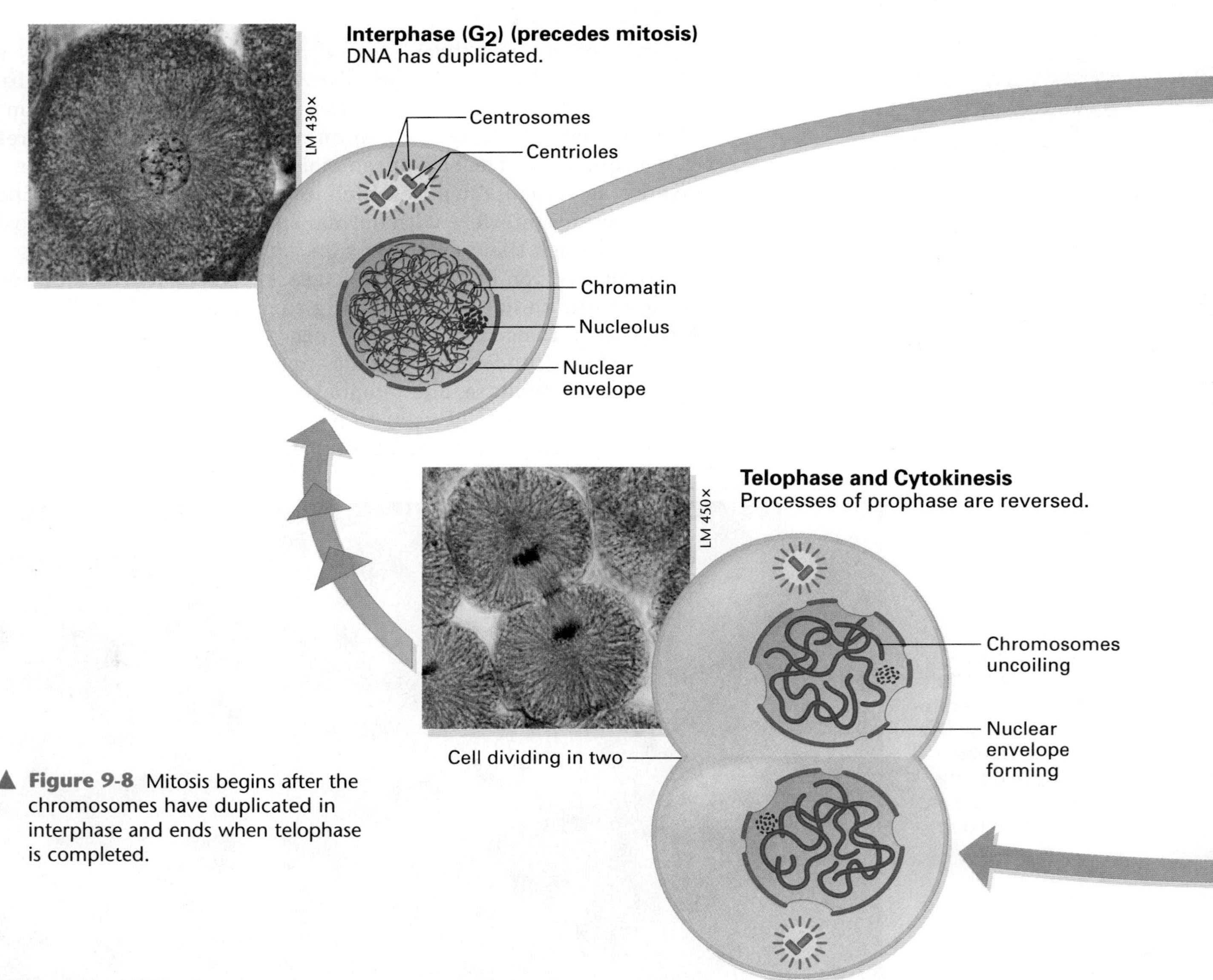

▲ **Figure 9-8** Mitosis begins after the chromosomes have duplicated in interphase and ends when telophase is completed.

Anaphase **Anaphase** is the third stage of the mitosis dance. The sister chromatids suddenly separate from their partners. Each chromatid is now considered a daughter chromosome. Proteins at the centromeres help move the daughter chromosomes along the spindle microtubules toward the poles. At the same time, these microtubules shorten, bringing the chromosomes closer to the poles. However, spindle microtubules that are not attached to centromeres do just the opposite—they grow longer, pushing the poles farther apart.

Telophase and Cytokinesis The final stage of mitosis, **telophase,** begins when the chromosomes reach the poles of the spindle. During this stage, the processes that occurred in prophase are reversed. The spindle disappears, two nuclear envelopes reform (one around each set of daughter chromosomes), the chromosomes uncoil and lengthen, and the nucleoli reappear. Mitosis, the division of one nucleus into two genetically identical daughter nuclei, is now finished.

Cytokinesis completes the cell division process by dividing the cytoplasm into two daughter cells, each with a nucleus. Usually this process occurs along with telophase.

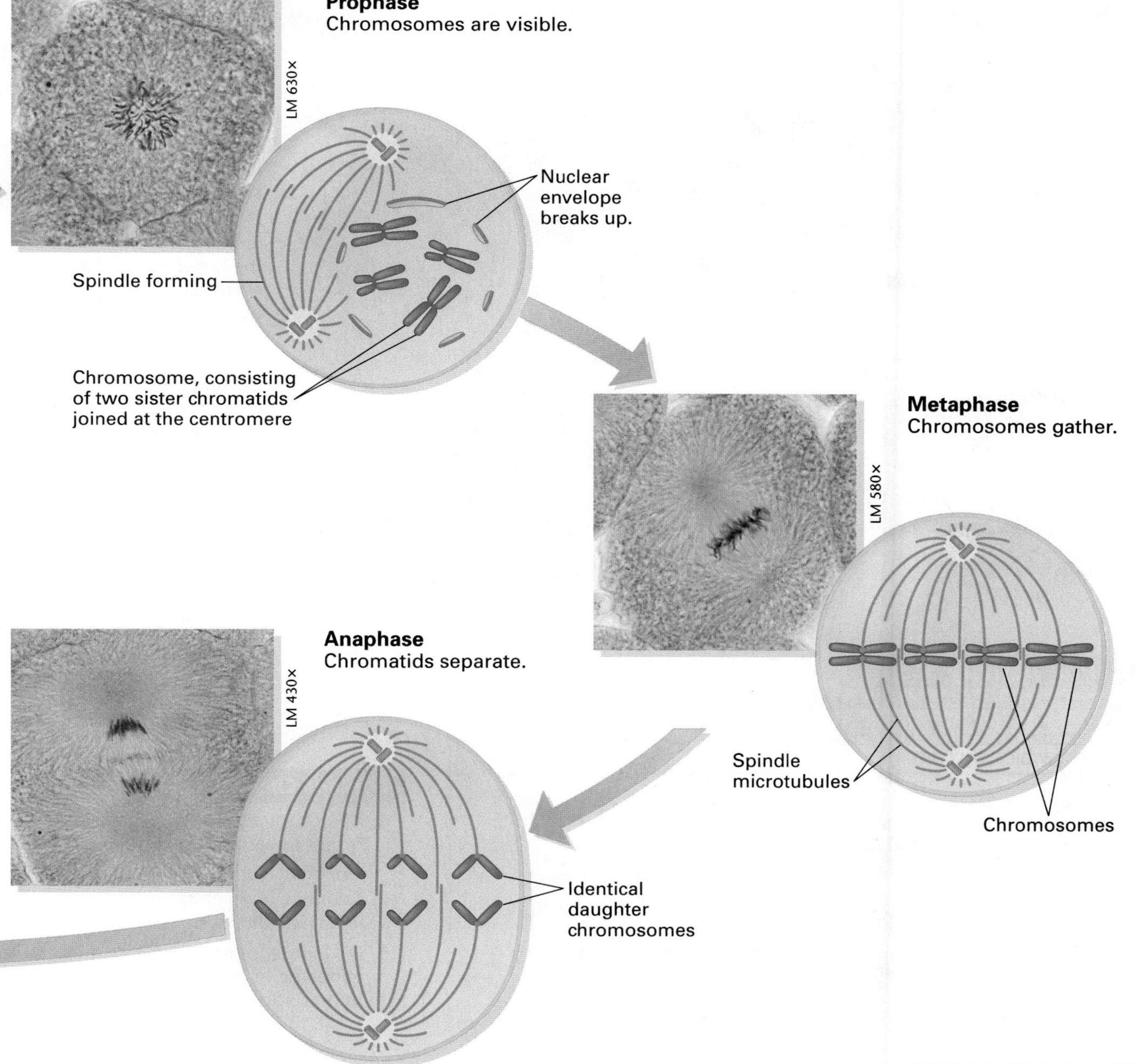

Cytokinesis in Animals and Plants

Cytokinesis, the actual division of the cytoplasm into two cells, typically occurs during telophase. In animal cells, the first sign of cytokinesis is the appearance of an indentation around the middle of the cell, as shown in Figure 9-8 on page 186. This indentation is caused by a ring of microfilaments in the cytoplasm just under the plasma membrane. The ring contracts like the pulling of a drawstring, deepening the indentation and pinching the parent cell in two. Because the two new nuclei are forming at the ends of the cell, cytokinesis results in two new cells.

Cytokinesis in a plant cell occurs differently (Figure 9-9). A disk containing cell wall material called a **cell plate** forms inside the cell and grows outward. Eventually this new piece of cell wall divides the cell in two. The result is two daughter cells, each bounded by its own continuous membrane and its own cell wall.

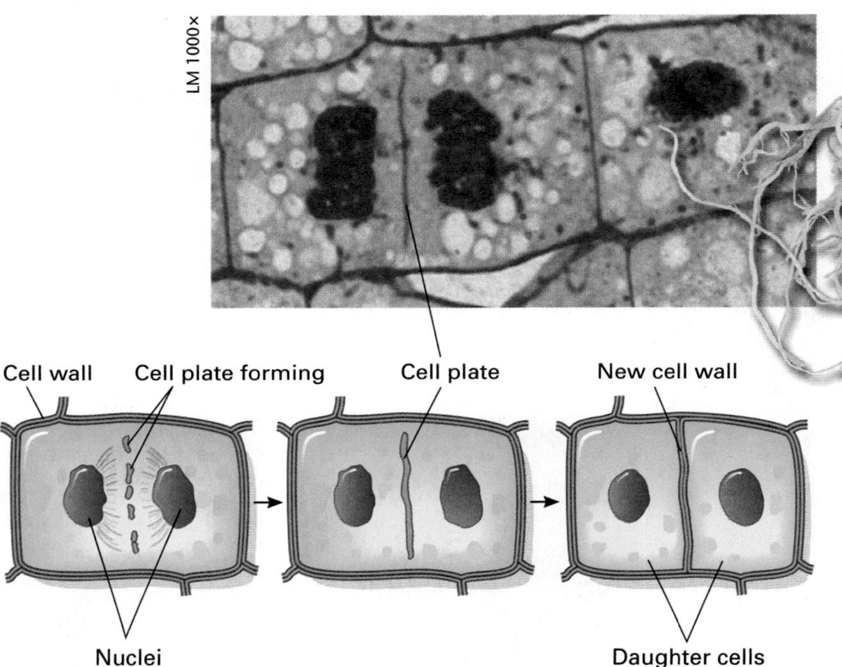

Figure 9-9 In a dividing plant cell, such as in the root tips of a green onion, the growing cell plate eventually fuses with the plasma membrane of the parent cell, and the cell wall material joins the existing cell wall. Two daughter cells result, each with its own plasma membrane and cell wall.

Online Activity 9.3

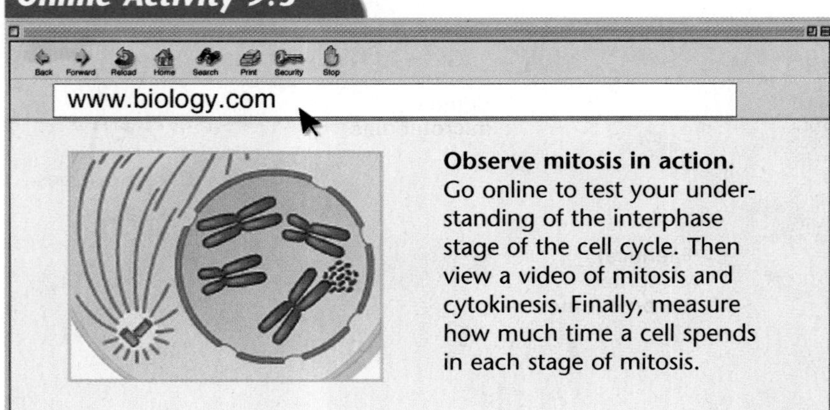

Observe mitosis in action. Go online to test your understanding of the interphase stage of the cell cycle. Then view a video of mitosis and cytokinesis. Finally, measure how much time a cell spends in each stage of mitosis.

Concept Check 9.3

1. Describe a significant event that occurs in each of the four stages of mitosis.
2. Compare and contrast cytokinesis in animal and plant cells.
3. In what sense may prophase and telophase in mitosis be characterized as opposites?

You Are a 19th-Century Cell Biologist

Observing Cell Division

Question What is the sequence of events that occurs during cell division?

Lab Overview In this investigation, you will prepare slides of onion root tips, observe cells in the process of dividing, and discover for yourself the important events of cell division.

Preparing for the Lab To help you prepare for the lab, proceed to the *Lab 9 Online Companion* to learn about the tools 19th century biologists used to study cell division. Prepare for the lab procedure by previewing the steps you will take.

Completing the Lab Use your Laboratory Manual or lab page printouts from the *Lab 9 Online Companion* to do the investigation and analyze your results. **CAUTION:** *Be sure to follow your teacher's instructions and all safety guidelines in the investigation.*

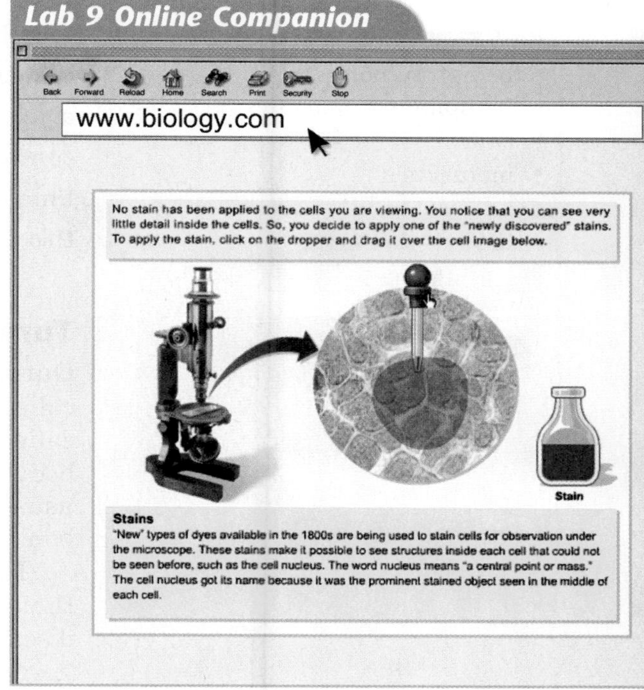

Lab 9 Online Companion
Back
Forward
Reload
Home
Search
Print
Security
Stop
www.biology.com
No stain has been applied to the cells you are viewing. You notice that you can see very little detail inside the cells. So, you decide to apply one of the "newly discovered" stains. To apply the stain, click on the dropper and drag it over the cell image below.
Stain
Stains
"New" types of dyes available in the 1800s are being used to stain cells for observation under the microscope. These stains make it possible to see structures inside each cell that could not be seen before, such as the cell nucleus. The word nucleus means "a central point or mass." The cell nucleus got its name because it was the prominent stained object seen in the middle of each cell.

CONCEPT 9.4

Cancer cells grow and divide out of control.

OBJECTIVES
- Compare benign and malignant tumors.
- Explain how cancer treatments can work at the cellular level.

KEY TERMS
- benign tumor
- malignant tumor
- cancer
- metastasis

What's Online

www.biology.com
Online Activity 9.4
Examine the cycle of a cancer cell.

The timing of cell division is critical to normal growth and development. A "control system" consisting of certain proteins within a cell directs the sequence of events in the cell cycle. When this control system malfunctions, cells may reproduce at the wrong time or in the wrong place. In this section, you'll discover how this abnormal cycle affects the body.

Tumors and Cancer

Out-of-control cell reproduction can produce a mass of cells called a tumor. An abnormal mass of essentially normal cells is called a **benign tumor.** Depending on their location in the body, benign tumors can sometimes cause health problems, but usually they can be completely removed by surgery. The cells of benign tumors always remain at their original site in the body.

More problematic are **malignant tumors,** masses of cells that result from the reproduction of cancer cells. **Cancer** is a disease caused by the severe disruption of the mechanisms that normally control the cell cycle. This disruption leads to uncontrolled cell division, which if unchecked can result in death.

The most dangerous characteristic of cancer cells is their ability to spread. A malignant tumor displaces normal tissue as it grows, as shown in Figure 9-11 on the facing page. If a malignant tumor is not killed or removed, it can spread into surrounding tissues. More alarming still, cells may split off from the tumor and travel to other parts of the body, where they can form new tumors. The spread of cancer cells beyond their original site is called **metastasis** (muh TAS tuh sis).

Many different biochemical changes can affect the cell cycle and result in cancer. For this reason, there is no single "cure," but rather multiple approaches to controlling or halting the progress of the disease.

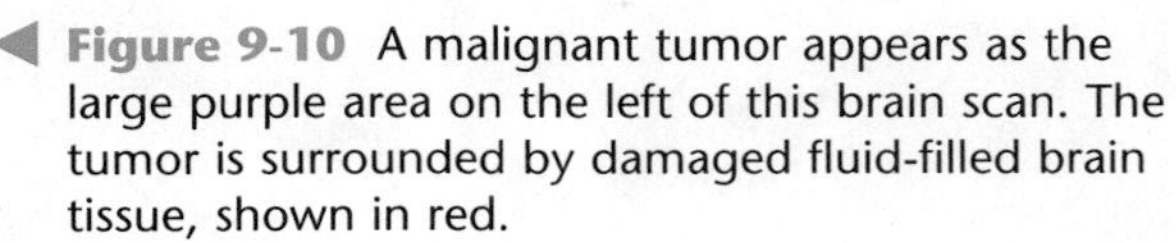

Figure 9-10 A malignant tumor appears as the large purple area on the left of this brain scan. The tumor is surrounded by damaged fluid-filled brain tissue, shown in red.

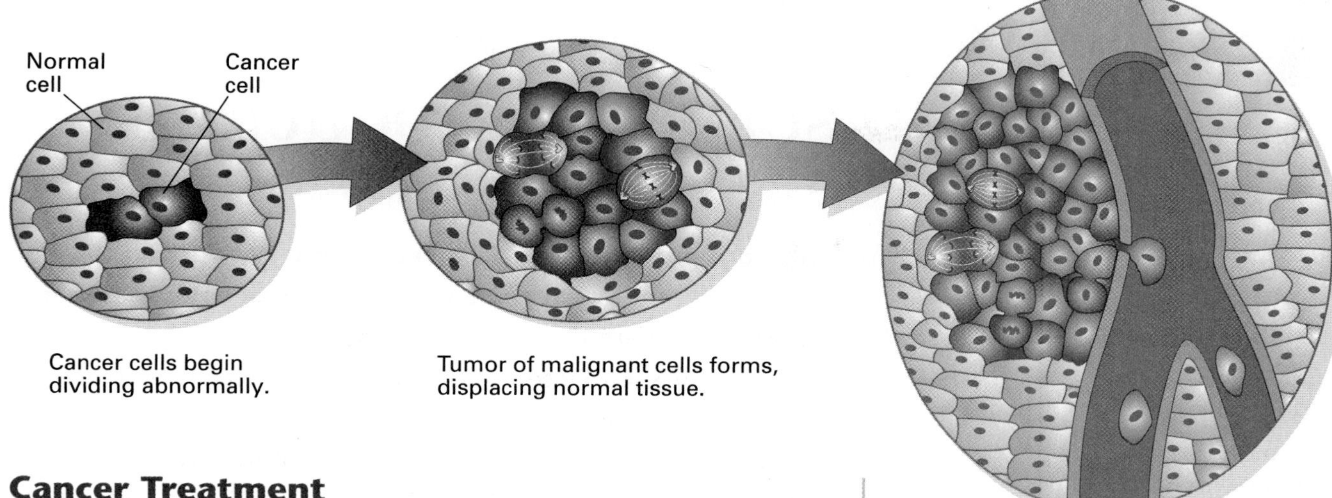

Cancer cells begin dividing abnormally.

Tumor of malignant cells forms, displacing normal tissue.

Cancer cells invade blood or lymph vessels and spread to other parts of the body.

▲ **Figure 9-11** Cells in a cancerous tumor reproduce at an abnormally fast rate and become irregular in appearance. When individual cells metastasize (travel from the original tumor), the cancer can spread.

Cancer Treatment

When possible, malignant tumors are removed by surgery. However, it's difficult to successfully remove all traces of cancer cells with surgery. To treat cancer at the cellular level, physicians sometimes use radiation therapy or chemotherapy. Both of these treatments attempt to stop cancer cells from dividing.

In radiation therapy, the parts of the body with cancerous tumors are exposed to high-energy radiation, which disrupts cell division. Because cancer cells divide more often than most normal cells, they are more likely to be dividing at any given time. So radiation can often destroy cancer cells with minimal damage to normal cells.

Chemotherapy involves treating the patient with drugs that disrupt cell division. These drugs work in a variety of ways. Some, called antimitotic drugs, prevent cell division by interfering with the mitotic spindle. One antimitotic drug prevents the spindle from forming in the first place. Another drug "freezes" the spindle after it forms, keeping it from functioning.

Both radiation and chemotherapy can cause undesirable side effects in normal body cells that divide fairly often. Radiation, for example, can damage cells of the ovaries or testes, causing sterility. Intestinal cells or hair follicle cells can be affected by chemotherapy, leading to nausea or hair loss.

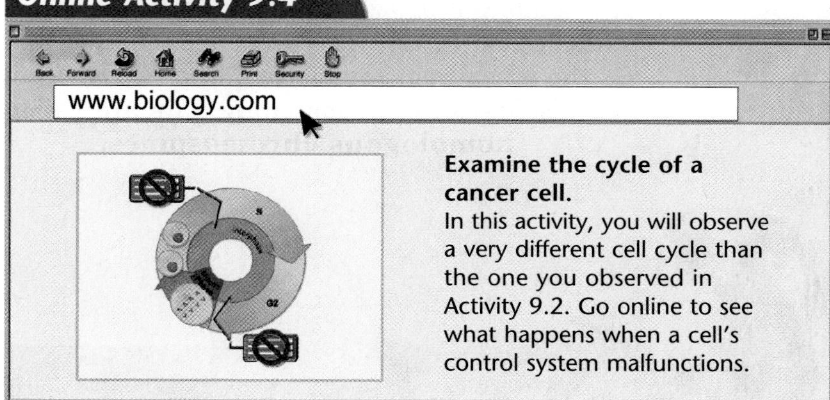

www.biology.com
Examine the cycle of a cancer cell.
In this activity, you will observe a very different cell cycle than the one you observed in Activity 9.2. Go online to see what happens when a cell's control system malfunctions.

Concept Check 9.4

1. List two differences between benign tumors and malignant tumors.
2. How might drugs that interfere with mitosis be effective in treating cancer?
3. How is cancer related to cell reproduction?

CONCEPT 9.5

Meiosis functions in sexual reproduction.

OBJECTIVES

- Describe how homologous chromosomes are alike and how they differ.
- Contrast haploid and diploid cells.
- Summarize the process of meiosis.

KEY TERMS

- meiosis
- karyotype
- homologous chromosome
- sex chromosome
- diploid
- gamete
- haploid
- fertilization
- zygote
- tetrad

What's Online

Online Activity 9.5
Explore the process of meiosis in depth.

▼ **Figure 9-12** These terrier puppies resemble their parents and one another. Yet, each dog has a unique combination of genes that makes it an individual unlike any of the others.

Only dogs produce more dogs, only maple trees produce more maple trees, and only people produce more people. These simple facts of life are the basis of the saying, "Like begets like." However, for sexually reproducing species, it might be more accurate to say, "Like begets similar to, but not exactly like." Most people resemble the other members of their families more closely than they resemble a stranger, but they do not look exactly like their parents or siblings. Each offspring in a sexually reproducing species inherits a unique combination of genes from its two parents. This combined set of genes contributes to a unique combination of traits in each individual.

Homologous Chromosomes

Sexual reproduction depends in part on **meiosis** (my OH sis)—a type of cell division that produces four cells, each with half the number of chromosomes as the parent cell. In animals, meiosis occurs in the sex organs—the testes in males and the ovaries in females. To understand the process of meiosis, you first need to learn a little more about chromosomes and their role in the life cycles of sexually reproducing organisms.

If you examined a number of cells from any individual organism, you would see that almost all the cells have the same number and types of chromosomes. Likewise, cells from different male or female individuals of a single species have the same number and types of chromosomes. For example, a typical human body cell has 46 chromosomes. A display of the 46 chromosomes of an individual, such as the one in Figure 9-13 on the facing page, is called a **karyotype** (KAR ee uh type). Notice that each of these chromosomes has a twin that resembles it in size and shape. You inherit one chromosome of each pair from your mother and the other from your father. The two chromosomes of each matching pair are called **homologous chromosomes.**

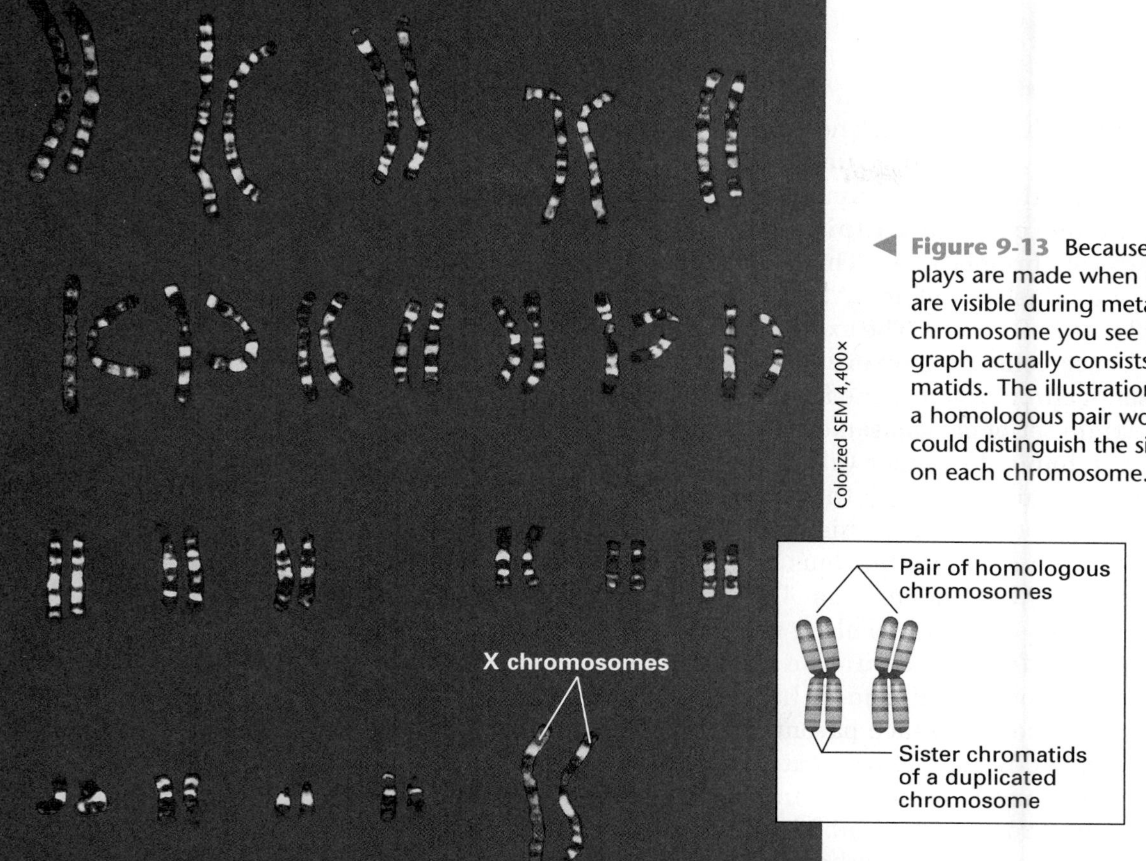

◀ **Figure 9-13** Because karyotype displays are made when chromosomes are visible during metaphase, each chromosome you see in the photograph actually consists of two chromatids. The illustration shows how a homologous pair would look if you could distinguish the sister chromatids on each chromosome.

Each homologous chromosome in a pair carries the same sequence of genes controlling the same inherited characteristics. For example, if a gene influencing eye color is located at a particular place on one chromosome, then the homologous chromosome also has a gene for eye color in the same place. However, the two genes may be slightly different versions. One chromosome might have the form of the gene for brown eye color, while the homologous chromosome might have another form for blue eye color. Note how this comparison is different from that of the sister chromatids you read about earlier in this chapter. Sister chromatids are duplicated copies of a single chromosome that are attached to each other and are identical—both chromatids contain exactly the same forms of each gene.

Altogether, humans have 23 homologous pairs of chromosomes. For the karyotype of a human female, such as Figure 9-13, the 46 chromosomes fall neatly into 23 homologous pairs. But in males, the two chromosomes of one pair do *not* look alike (Figure 9-14). This 23rd pair of chromosomes, called the **sex chromosomes,** determines the person's sex. The sex chromosomes occur in two forms, called X and Y. Like all mammals, human males have one X chromosome and one Y chromosome, while females have two X chromosomes. Only small parts of the X and Y chromosomes are homologous. Most of the genes carried on the X chromosome do not have counterparts on the tiny Y, and the Y has genes that are lacking on the X.

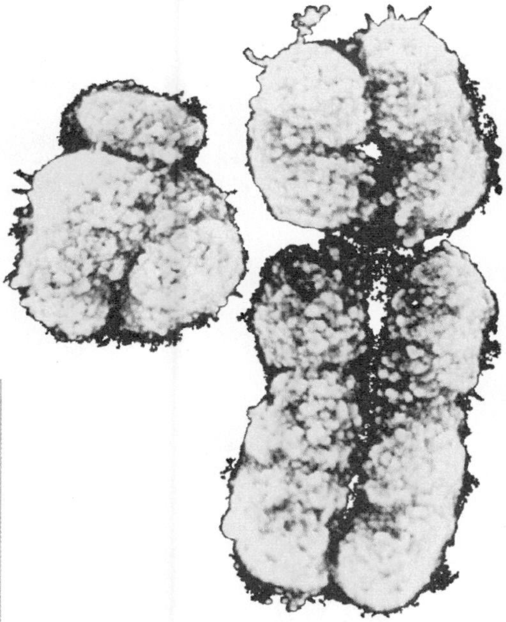

Colorized SEM 18,000×

▲ **Figure 9-14** In human males, the Y chromosome (left) and the X chromosome (right) differ greatly in size. In contrast, the two X chromosomes of a female (at lower magnification in Figure 9-13) match in size.

Diploid and Haploid Cells

Having two sets of chromosomes, one inherited from each parent, is key to the life cycles of all sexually reproducing organisms. Follow chromosomes through the human life cycle in Figure 9-15.

Almost all human cells are **diploid;** that is, they contain two homologous sets of chromosomes. The total number of chromosomes, 46 in humans, is referred to as the diploid number (abbreviated $2n$, as in $2n = 46$). The exceptions are egg and sperm cells, known as sex cells, or **gametes** (GAM eets). Each gamete has a single set of chromosomes, one from each homologous pair. A cell with a single set of chromosomes is called a **haploid** cell. For humans, the haploid number (abbreviated n) is 23. These haploid cells are produced through the process of meiosis, which you will read more about later in this section.

In the human life cycle, the nucleus of a haploid sperm cell from the father fuses with the nucleus of a haploid egg cell from the mother. The fusion of the nuclei along with the cytoplasm from the gametes is called **fertilization.** The resulting fertilized egg, called a **zygote** (ZY goht), is diploid. It has two homologous sets of chromosomes, one set from each parent. During the rest of the life cycle, the zygote develops into a sexually mature adult with trillions of cells produced by mitosis. In this way, fertilization restores the diploid chromosome number, and the zygote's 46 chromosomes are passed on to all the other diploid body cells.

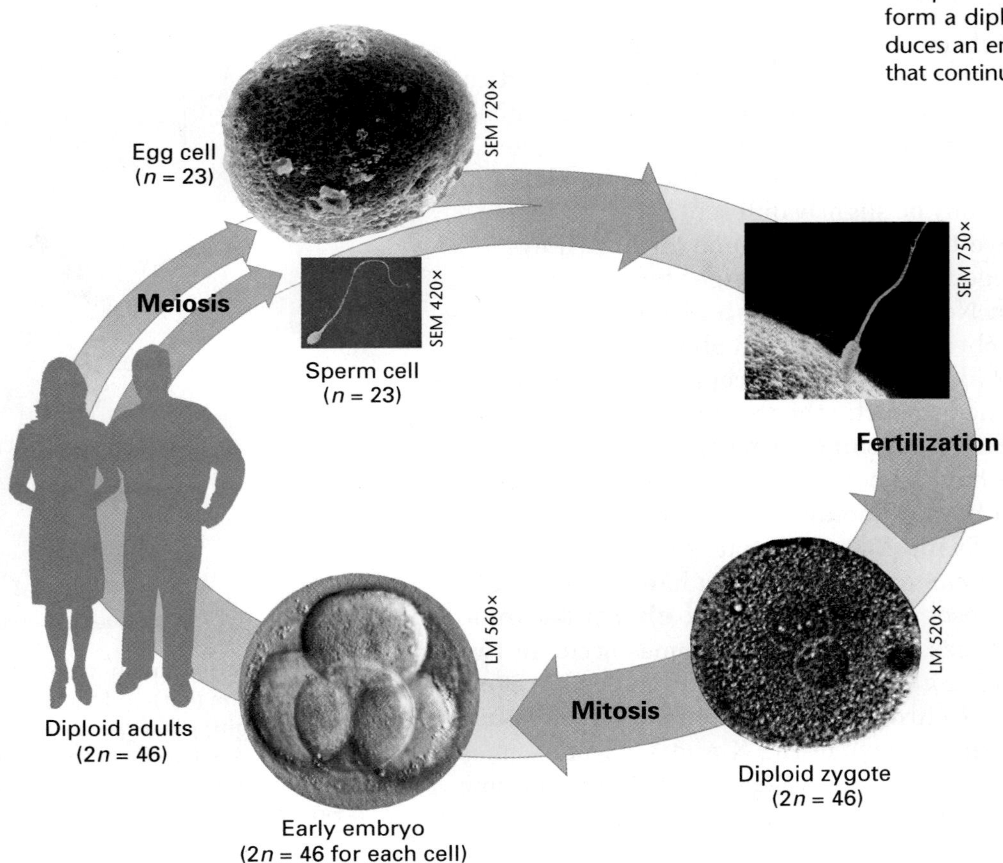

▼ **Figure 9-15** In the human life cycle a haploid egg and sperm fuse and form a diploid zygote. Mitosis produces an embryo with numerous cells that continue to multiply and develop.

The Process of Meiosis

As a result of the alternation of fertilization and meiosis, life cycles of all sexually reproducing organisms involve alternating diploid and haploid stages. Producing haploid gametes by meiosis keeps the chromosome number from doubling in every generation. If meiosis did not occur, cells involved in fertilization would produce new organisms having twice the number of chromosomes as those in the previous generation. Within only a few generations, there would be no more room in a cell for all the chromosomes! The alternation of meiosis and fertilization keeps the number of chromosomes in a species the same from generation to generation.

Meiosis Versus Mitosis Meiosis produces haploid daughter cells from specialized cells in diploid organisms. Despite the similarity in their names, meiosis is different from mitosis in two major ways. The first major difference is that meiosis produces four new offspring cells, each with one set of chromosomes—thus half the number of chromosomes as the parent cell (Figure 9-16). In contrast, mitosis produces two offspring cells, each with the same number of chromosomes as the parent cell. The second major difference is that meiosis involves the exchange of genetic material between homologous chromosomes. You'll read more about this swapping process, called crossing over, in Concept 9.6.

As you follow the stages of meiosis in Figure 9-17 on the next two pages, keep in mind the difference between homologous chromosomes and sister chromatids. The two chromosomes of a homologous pair are individual chromosomes that were inherited from different parents. The homologous chromosomes in Figure 9-17 (and later figures) are colored red and blue to remind you that each comes from a different parent. These homologous chromosomes may contain different versions of some of their genes. For example, one chromosome may contain a form of the gene for freckles, while the homologous chromosome, at the same location, contains a form of the gene for the absence of freckles. In contrast, when sister chromatids are formed, they are identical—they carry the same versions of all their genes because one was produced as an exact copy of the other. As with mitosis, meiosis begins after the chromosomes have been duplicated during interphase.

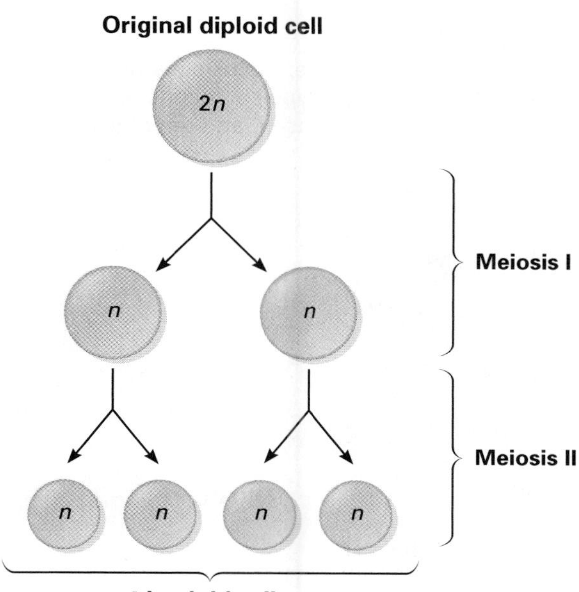

▲ **Figure 9-16** This simplified diagram highlights the major points that distinguish meiosis from mitosis. Meiosis produces four haploid cells, rather than two diploid cells. Also, meiosis involves two divisions, whereas mitosis involves only one.

The Two Meiotic Divisions Meiosis consists of two distinct parts—meiosis I and meiosis II. In meiosis I, homologous chromosomes, each composed of two sister chromatids, are separated from one another. In meiosis II, sister chromatids are separated much as they are in mitosis. However, the resulting cells are haploid rather than diploid.

▼ **Figure 9-17** The stages of meiosis begin after interphase. (This example starts with a cell that has two homologous pairs of chromosomes, $2n = 4$.)

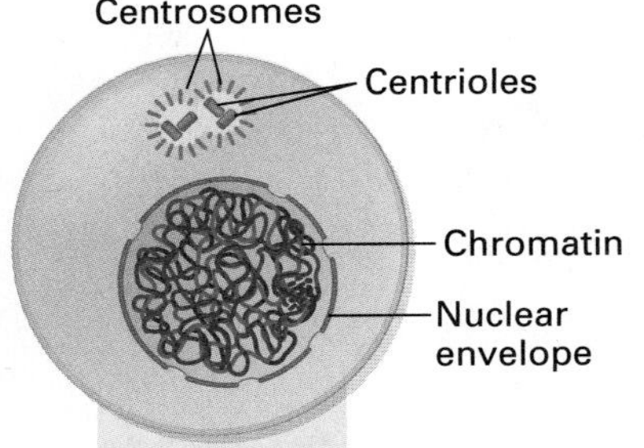

Interphase
Just as in mitosis, the cell duplicates its DNA. Each chromosome then consists of two identical sister chromatids that can be seen more clearly in prophase.

Meiosis I:

In contrast to mitosis, meiosis involves two divisions. The first division is called meiosis I. It consists of four stages: prophase I, metaphase I, anaphase I, and telophase I.

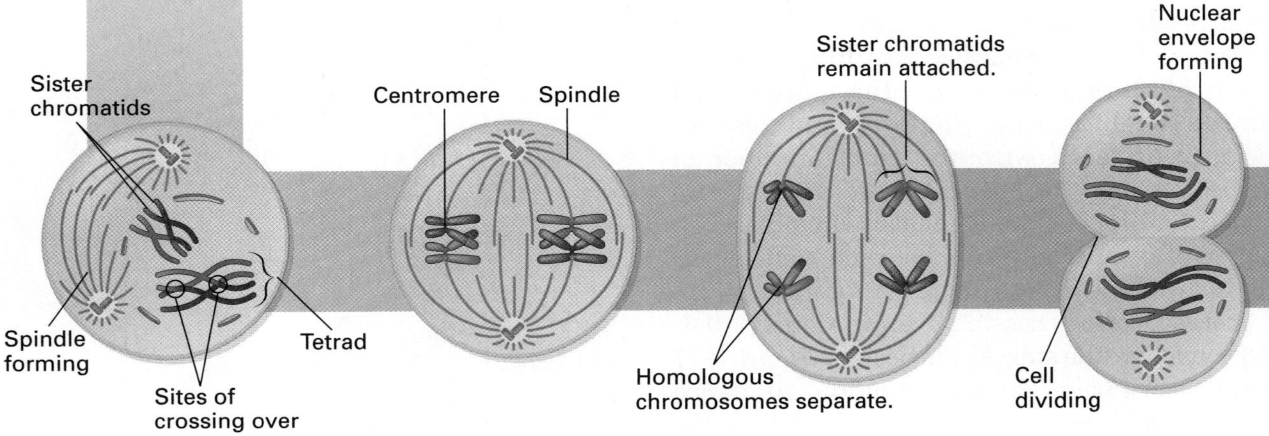

Prophase I **Metaphase I** **Anaphase I** **Telophase I and Cytokinesis**

Prophase I: In prophase I, meiosis adds two new steps to the mitosis dance routine. One new step is that proteins cause the homologous chromosomes to actually stick together along their length. The paired chromosomes, now consisting of four chromatids, are referred to as **tetrads.** The tetrads attach to the spindle. The second new step is that the sister chromatids in the tetrads exchange some genetic material in the process known as crossing over. The different colors in this illustration indicate that one chromosome in the tetrad was originally inherited from the male parent and the other from the female parent.

Metaphase I: During metaphase I, the tetrads move to the middle of the cell and line up across the spindle.

Anaphase I: In this stage, homologous chromosomes separate as they migrate to opposite poles of the spindle. Notice that the sister chromatids migrate together—each chromosome is made up of two copies. Although this cell started with four chromosomes, there are only two chromosomes (each with two copies) moving to each pole.

Telophase I and Cytokinesis: In telophase I, the chromosomes arrive at the poles. Each pole now has a *haploid* daughter nucleus because it has only one set of chromosomes, even though each chromosome consists of two sister chromatids. Cytokinesis usually occurs along with telophase I, forming two haploid daughter cells. The chromosomes in each daughter cell are still duplicated.

Prophase II: In each haploid daughter cell, a spindle forms, attaches to the centromeres, and moves the individual chromosomes to the middle of the cell.

Metaphase II: The chromosomes line up in the middle of the cell with spindle microtubules attached to each sister chromatid.

Anaphase II: The sister chromatids separate and move to opposite poles.

Telophase II and Cytokinesis: The chromatids, now considered individual chromosomes, arrive at the poles. Cytokinesis splits the cells one more time. The process of meiosis is completed, producing four haploid daughter cells as a final result.

Meiosis II:

The steps of meiosis II are very similar to the steps of mitosis. The difference is that instead of starting with a diploid cell, meiosis II starts with a haploid cell.

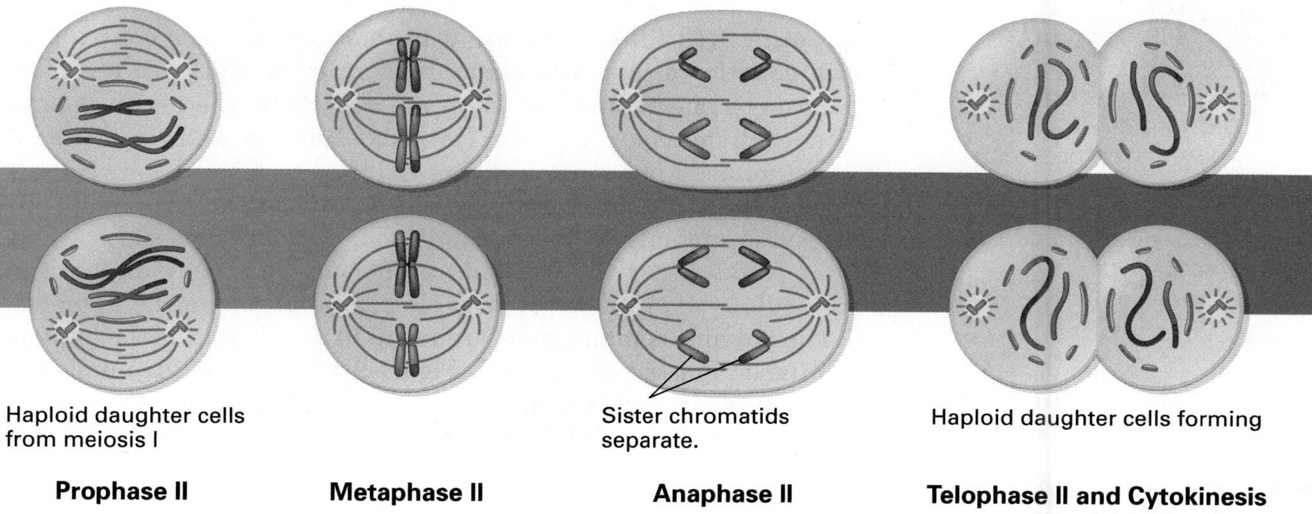

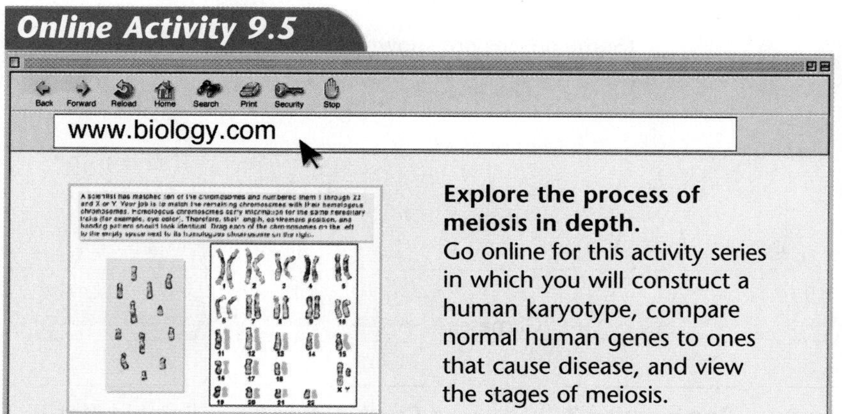

Online Activity 9.5
Back
Forward
Reload
Home
Search
Print
Security
Stop
www.biology.com
Explore the process of meiosis in depth.
Go online for this activity series in which you will construct a human karyotype, compare normal human genes to ones that cause disease, and view the stages of meiosis.

Concept Check 9.5

1. Describe how homologous chromosomes are different from sister chromatids.
2. Compare the number of sets of chromosomes in human gametes with the number of sets in other cells in the body.
3. How does meiosis I reduce the number of chromosomes in the daughter cells?
4. What is the final result of meiosis?

CONCEPT 9.6

Meiosis increases genetic variation among offspring.

OBJECTIVES

- Describe how chromosome assortment during meiosis contributes to genetic variation.
- Explain how crossing over contributes to genetic variation.
- Compare and contrast mitosis and meiosis.

KEY TERMS

- crossing over
- genetic recombination

As you have read, offspring that result from sexual reproduction are genetically different from their parents and from one another. This genetic variety in offspring is the raw material for natural selection, which will be discussed in Unit 4. This section explores how genetic variety arises through meiosis and fertilization.

Assortments of Chromosomes

Figure 9-18 illustrates one way in which meiosis contributes to genetic variety. The example is an organism with a diploid chromosome number of four ($2n = 4$). How the chromosomes in each homologous pair (tetrads) line up and separate at metaphase I is a matter of chance, like the flip of a coin. So, the assortment of chromosomes that end up in the resulting cells occurs randomly. In this example, four combinations are possible.

If you know the haploid number for an organism, you can calculate the number of possible combinations in the gametes. The possible combinations are equal to 2^n, where n is the haploid number. For the organism in Figure 9-18, $n = 2$, so the number of chromosome combinations is 2^2, or 4. For a human, $n = 23$, so there are 2^{23}, or about 8 million, possible chromosome combinations!

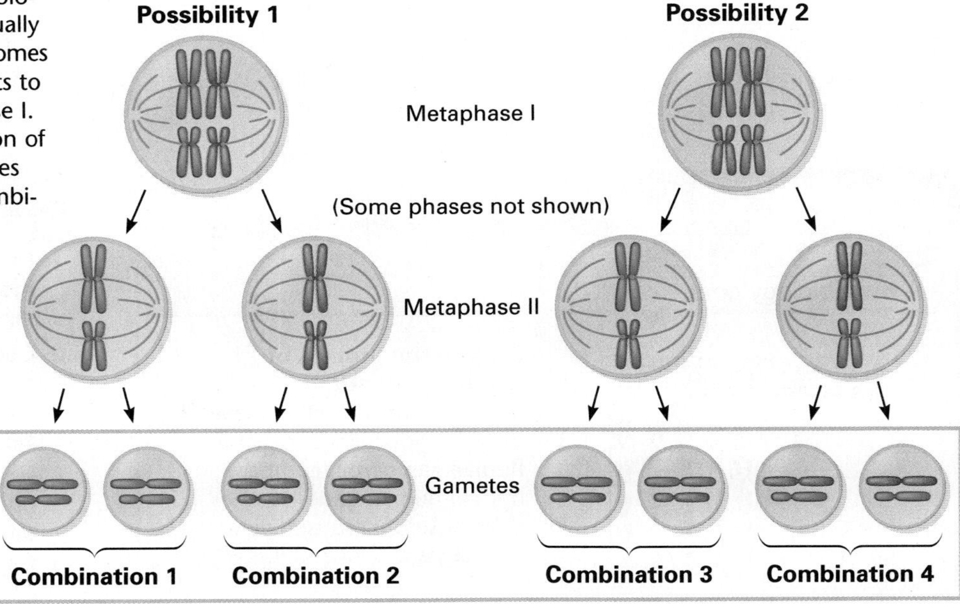

Figure 9-18 In a diploid cell with four chromosomes (two homologous pairs), there are two equally possible ways for the chromosomes inherited from the two parents to be arranged during metaphase I. This variation in the orientation of chromosomes leads to gametes with four equally possible combinations of chromosomes.

Crossing Over

The number of different chromosome combinations in gametes is one factor that contributes to genetic variation. A second factor is **crossing over**—the exchange of genetic material between homologous chromosomes. This exchange occurs during prophase I of meiosis. Figure 9-19 shows the results of crossing over in one tetrad. When crossing over begins, homologous chromosomes are closely paired all along their lengths. There is a precise gene-by-gene alignment between adjacent chromatids of the two chromosomes. Segments of the two chromatids can be exchanged at one or more sites.

So, on top of all the possible chromosome combinations, crossing over adds another source of variation. Crossing over can produce a single chromosome that contains a new combination of genetic information from different parents, a result called **genetic recombination.**

Because chromosomes may contain many hundreds of genes, a single crossover event can affect many genes. Since more than one crossover can occur in each tetrad, it is no wonder that gametes and the offspring that result from them can be so varied.

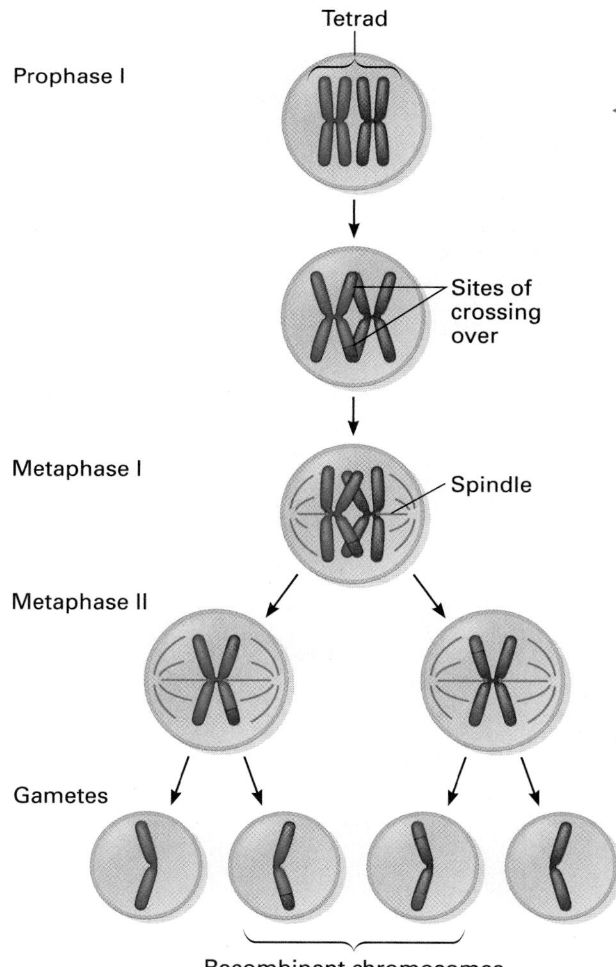

Figure 9-19 This diagram illustrates an example of crossing over in one pair of homologous chromosomes, shown here side-by-side for ease of viewing. (The process can occur in all pairs.) Early in prophase I, a chromatid from one chromosome exchanges a segment with the corresponding segment from the other chromosome. These altered chromosomes give rise to what are known as "recombinant chromosomes" in the gametes.

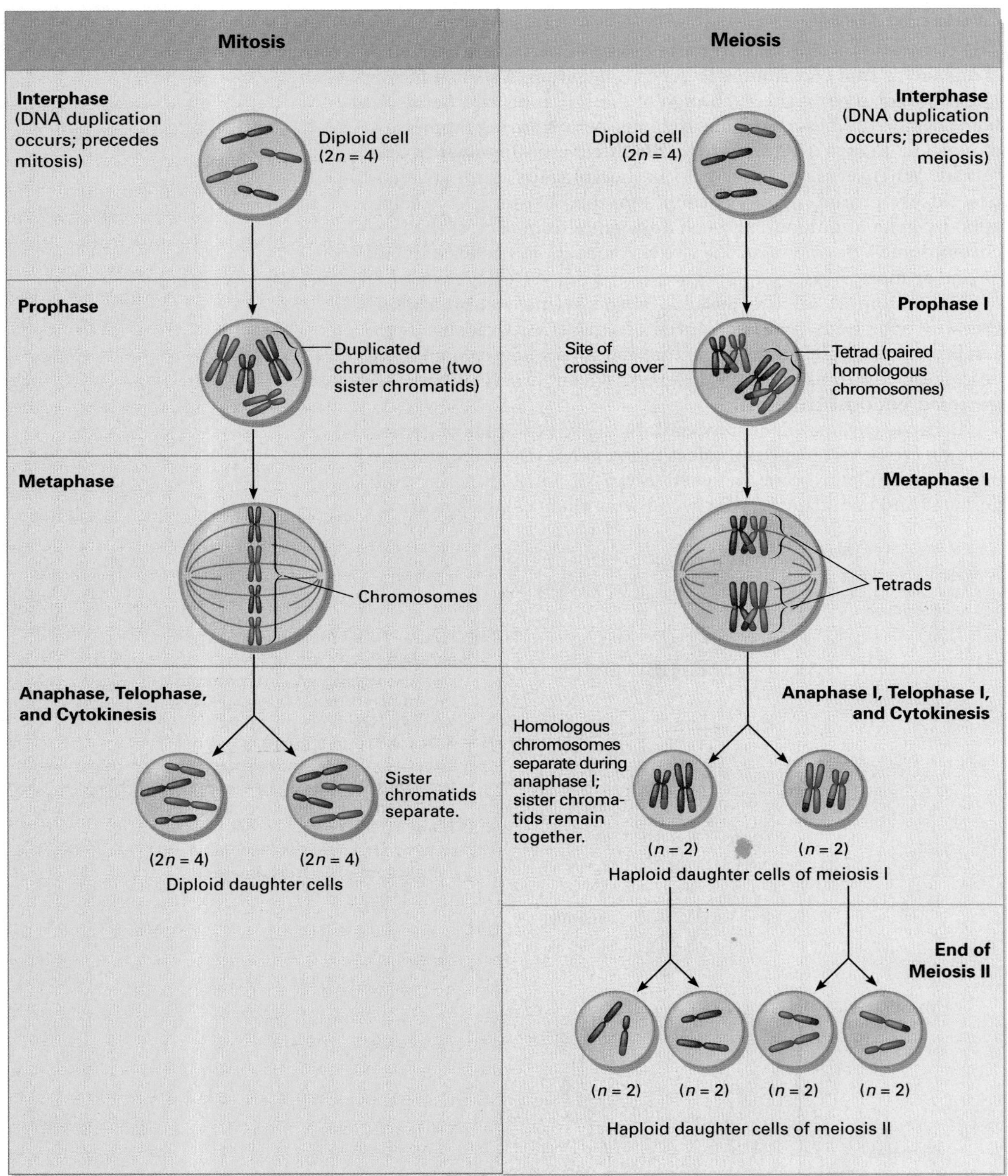

▲ **Figure 9-20** Both mitosis and meiosis begin after the chromosomes have been duplicated during interphase. Though similar, the results of the two processes differ in the number of cells produced and in the number of chromosomes the cells contain.

Review: Comparison of Mitosis and Meiosis

You have now learned about two versions of cell reproduction in eukaryotic organisms. Figure 9-20 compares these processes. Mitosis, which provides for growth, repair, and asexual reproduction, produces daughter cells that are genetically identical to the parent cell. Meiosis, which takes place in a subset of specialized cells in sexually reproducing organisms, yields haploid daughter cells with only one set of homologous chromosomes. This set consists of one member of each homologous pair.

In both mitosis and meiosis, the chromosomes duplicate only once, in the preceding interphase. Mitosis involves one division of the genetic material in the nucleus, and it is usually accompanied by cytokinesis, producing two diploid cells. Meiosis involves two nuclear divisions, yielding four haploid cells.

The key events that distinguish meiosis from mitosis occur during the stages of meiosis I. In prophase I, the duplicated homologous chromosomes form tetrads, and crossing over occurs. Then, during metaphase I, the tetrads (rather than individual doubled chromosomes) are aligned at the center of the cell. In anaphase I, sister chromatids stay together and go to the same pole when the homologous chromosomes separate. At the end of meiosis I, the chromosome number in each of the two daughter cells is haploid, but each chromosome still consists of two sister chromatids. Meiosis II is basically identical to mitosis. The sister chromatids separate, and each cell divides in two. Because these cells are already haploid, the cells they produce are haploid, too.

Mitosis and meiosis both make it possible for cells to inherit genetic information in the form of chromosome copies. In the next chapter, you will have the opportunity to connect this property of chromosomes to the inheritance of genes for specific traits, such as your blood type. Keep in mind the process of meiosis and the production of gametes as you study the patterns of inheritance. You'll find that an understanding of how meiosis distributes chromosomes will make it easier for you to follow how specific traits are inherited.

History of Science

www.biology.com

Discovery of Chromosomes
When and how were chromosomes identified in the nucleus of a cell? How was the role of chromosomes in heredity determined? Find out online when you explore and research scientists who opened the door to current knowledge of chromosomes.

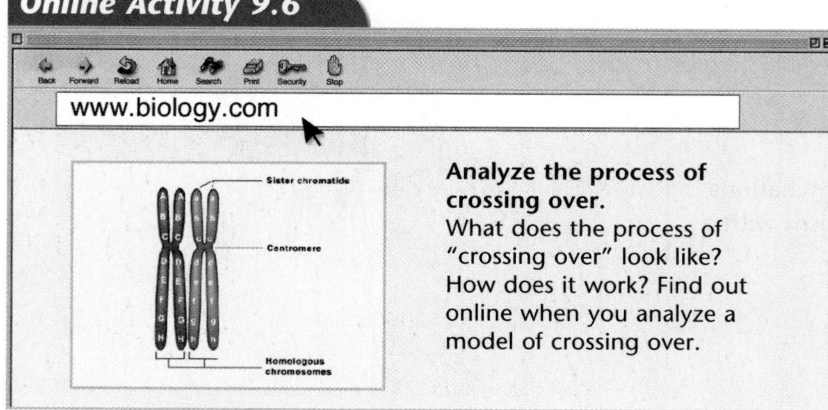
Online Activity 9.6
www.biology.com
Sister chromatids
Centromere
Homologous chromosomes
Analyze the process of crossing over.
What does the process of "crossing over" look like? How does it work? Find out online when you analyze a model of crossing over.

Concept Check 9.6

1. Draw a diagram that shows the chromosome combinations that are possible in the haploid gametes of an organism with a diploid number of 6.
2. Describe how crossing over during meiosis in an individual organism recombines the genetic material of the organism's two parents.
3. Describe two differences between meiosis and mitosis.

Multiple Choice

Choose the letter of the best answer.

1. Which of the following processes occurs in eukaryotic organisms that only reproduce asexually?
   a. mitosis
   b. meiosis
   c. both mitosis and meiosis
   d. fertilization

2. Which of the following is a key event during the S phase of the cell cycle?
   a. The genetic material is duplicated.
   b. A cell grows in size.
   c. The number of organelles increases.
   d. The cytoplasm is divided in two.

3. The cytoplasm is divided into two daughter cells during
   a. metaphase.
   b. prophase.
   c. cytokinesis.
   d. anaphase.

4. Which of the following steps occurs during prophase in mitosis?
   a. Sister chromatids separate.
   b. Nuclear envelope disappears.
   c. Nuclear envelope reappears.
   d. Chromosomes undergo duplication.

5. The spread of cancer cells beyond their original tumor site is called
   a. mitosis.
   b. fertilization.
   c. cytokinesis.
   d. metastasis.

6. The products of meiosis from one parent cell are
   a. two diploid cells.
   b. four chromosome pairs.
   c. four haploid cells.
   d. two haploid cells.

7. How many possible chromosome combinations are there for the gametes of an organism with a haploid number equal to 4?
   a. $2^2 = 4$ b. $2^8 = 256$
   c. $2^1 = 2$ d. $2^4 = 16$

Short Answer

8. Give three examples of organisms that reproduce asexually.

9. Describe four events that happen in a typical cell during interphase.

10. Identify the two major events that occur during the mitotic phase of the cell cycle.

11. What is the function of the spindle during mitosis?

12. Explain how cancer tumors spread.

13. Describe the most obvious way the karyotypes of a sister and brother look different.

14. Explain how having a haploid number of chromosomes contributes to the function of gametes in a life cycle.

15. Describe the structure of a tetrad. When do tetrads form?

16. Describe one similarity between mitosis and meiosis II. Describe one difference.

17. Name two factors that introduce genetic variation during the process of meiosis. Explain how they introduce variation.

Visualizing Concepts

18. The diagram below represents metaphase I of meiosis in a cell that has two pairs of homologous chromosomes. Using colored pencils or pens, draw a similar diagram to show how the chromosomes would look if the cell were in metaphase of mitosis.

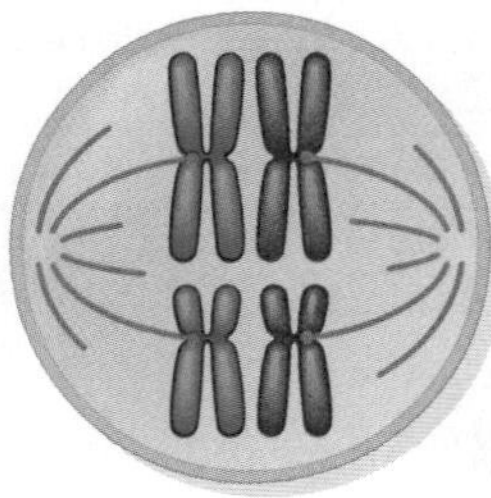

Analyzing Information

19. Analyzing Diagrams Use the diagram below of a cell undergoing cytokinesis to answer the following questions.

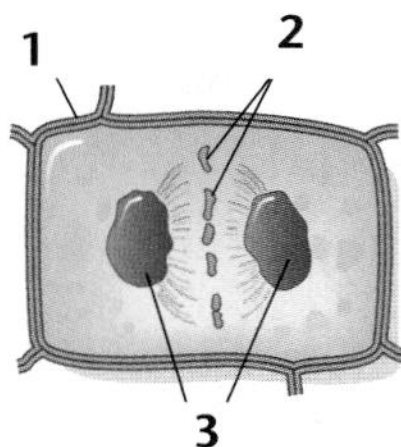

a. Does the diagram show a plant cell or an animal cell? Explain.
b. Identify each of the numbered structures in the diagram.
c. Draw and label a diagram of the final step in this process.

20. Analyzing Photographs Strawberry plants, such as those shown in the photograph below, can reproduce by a process in which an existing plant sends out tiny new plants on long, trailing stems. These new plants grow roots when they come in contact with soil. If the trailing stems are severed, the separated plants become completely independent of the parent plant.

a. Is the process in strawberry plants an example of asexual or sexual reproduction? Explain your answer.
b. Which process, mitosis or meiosis, is involved in producing the trailing stems, leaves, and new roots?
c. How do the new strawberry plants compare genetically to the original plant?

Critical Thinking

21. Developing Hypotheses The cells of organisms called plasmodial slime molds have multiple nuclei. Suggest how a variation on the cell cycle could give rise to such a situation.

22. Comparing and Contrasting How are the growth of a malignant tumor and the repair of a cut on your finger similar? How are they different?

23. Making Judgments Suppose you read about a study that relates exposure to a certain chemical to an increased risk of cancer in rats. What types of effects at the cellular level do you think the researchers observed? Would you expect to observe similar effects in humans exposed to the chemical? Why or why not?

24. What's Wrong With These Statements? *Briefly explain why each statement is inaccurate or misleading.*
a. The first stage of mitosis is the duplication of the chromosomes.
b. Every cell of a sexually reproducing organism has the same number of chromosomes.
c. Cells spend most of their time in the mitotic (M) phase of the cell cycle.

Performance Assessment

Writing Like animals, plants can get malignant tumors. (Such tumors cannot metastasize, however, because plant cells do not move about.) Apply what you learned about cytokinesis in plants to hypothesize a way to stop the growth of a plant tumor. What would the side effects be? Would your method work on certain kinds of plants better than others?

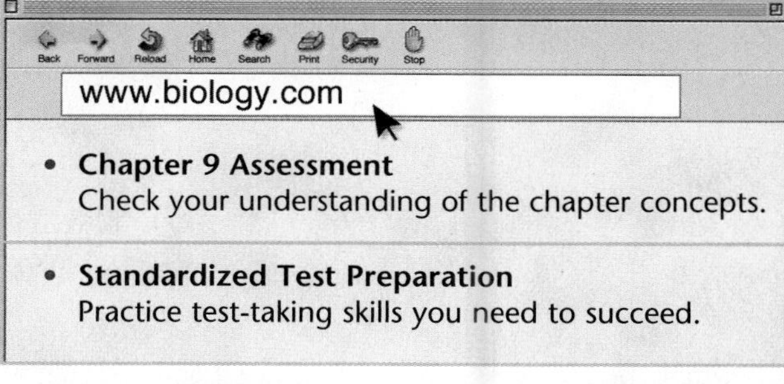

Online Assessment/Test Preparation
Back Forward Reload Home Search Print Security Stop
www.biology.com
• **Chapter 9 Assessment**
Check your understanding of the chapter concepts.
• **Standardized Test Preparation**
Practice test-taking skills you need to succeed.

CHAPTER 10

Patterns of Inheritance

Fish of red, black, orange, yellow, and white—koi come in various patterns of all these colors and more. Koi are bred all over the world for their beautiful color patterns. When two fish are bred, what patterns will appear in the offspring? While age and diet affect color, the basic patterns are inherited. In the mid-1800s, the rules underlying patterns of inheritance were uncovered in a series of experiments performed by an Austrian monk named Gregor Mendel. Later research revealed some interesting variations on his basic principles.

In this chapter, you will read about Mendel's experiments. You will also learn some rules of probability and other tools that will help you to predict how certain traits are inherited. In addition, you'll find out how meiosis, the process you learned about in Chapter 9, explains Mendel's principles of inheritance. But first, go online to the ***WebQuest*** to explore probability.

Key Concepts

Concept 10.1 Genetics developed from curiosity about inheritance.

Concept 10.2 Mendel discovered that inheritance follows rules of chance.

Concept 10.3 There are many variations of inheritance patterns.

Concept 10.4 Meiosis explains Mendel's principles.

Concept 10.5 Sex-linked traits have unique inheritance patterns.

Assessment Chapter 10 Review

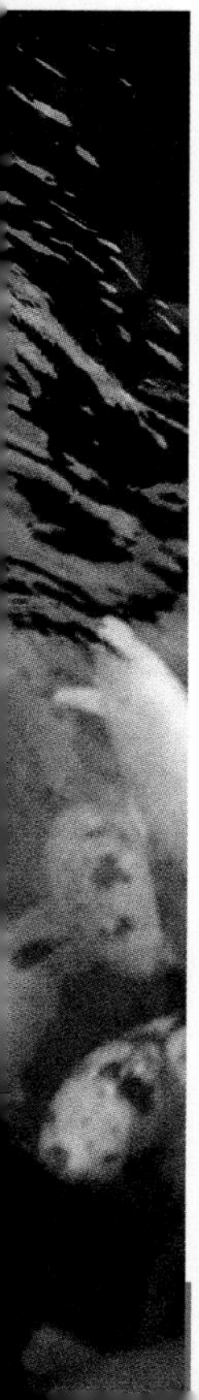

What's Online

www.biology.com

WebQuest
ProbabilityQuest

Online Activity 10.1
Explore historical hypotheses of inheritance.

Guided Research Lab 3
Inheritance Patterns in Plants

Online Activity 10.2
Apply Mendel's rules.

Science, Technology, & Society
Environmental Effects on Phenotypes

Lab 10 Online Companion
Family Reunion in a Dish

Online Activity 10.3
Explore patterns of inheritance.

Online Activity 10.4
Examine a crossover event.

Closer Look
Linked Genes

Online Activity 10.5
Analyze Morgan's fruit fly experiment.

Chapter 10 Assessment

CONCEPT 10.1

Genetics developed from curiosity about inheritance.

OBJECTIVES

- Compare and contrast the blending hypothesis and the particulate hypothesis of inheritance.
- Describe the methods Mendel used in his plant-breeding experiments.

KEY TERMS

- trait
- genetics
- cross-fertilization

What's Online

www.biology.com

Online Activity 10.1 Explore historical hypotheses of inheritance.

Guided Research Lab 3 Inheritance Patterns in Plants

▲ Figure 10-1 Gregor Mendel carried out a series of well-designed experiments that led him to draw conclusions about inheritance patterns in pea plants.

For centuries, plant and animal breeders had many questions about the inheritance of flower colors, fur length, and other characters of organisms. Observations alone could not answer all these questions. Then an Austrian monk named Gregor Mendel devised a series of experiments that revealed the basic rules underlying patterns of inheritance.

The Blending Hypothesis of Inheritance

A **trait** is a variation of a particular character. For example, one plant might have the trait of red flowers, while another might have the trait of yellow flowers. In the early 1800s, biologists proposed the *blending hypothesis* to explain how offspring inherit traits from both parents. For example, suppose a red-flowered plant were crossed with a yellow-flowered plant of the same species. According to the blending hypothesis, the red and yellow hereditary material in the offspring would blend, producing orange-flowered plants—like blending red and yellow paint to make orange paint. Based on this hypothesis, all offspring of orange-flowered plants would also have orange flowers.

But people observed many exceptions to blending. For example, red-flowered parents sometimes produced yellow-flowered offspring. The blending hypothesis was eventually discarded because it could not explain how traits that disappear in one generation can reappear in later ones.

Mendel's Plant Breeding Experiments

In the nineteenth century, most biologists worked by observing and describing nature. Gregor Mendel was one of the first to apply an experimental approach to the question of inheritance (Figure 10-1). His work eventually gave rise to **genetics,** the study of heredity.

For seven years, Mendel bred pea plants and recorded inheritance patterns in the offspring. Based on his results, he developed a *particulate hypothesis* of inheritance. This hypothesis states that parents pass on to their offspring separate and distinct factors (today called genes) that are responsible for inherited traits. Mendel stressed that these heritable factors retain their identity generation after generation. In other words, genes are more like marbles of different colors than paints. Just as marbles retain their individual colors, genes retain their own identities.

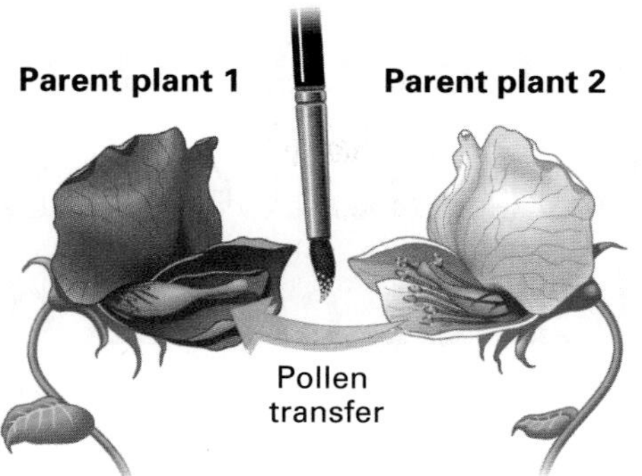

1. To prevent self-fertilization, Mendel cut off the immature stamens (structures that produce pollen).
2. He then dusted the carpel (egg-producing structure) with pollen from another plant's mature stamens.
3. The carpel matured into a pod containing seeds (peas). Once planted, these seeds grew into offspring plants.

▲ **Figure 10-2** Mendel cross-fertilized his plants by hand. This enabled him to control which plants would serve as the "parents."

Mendel's first step was to identify pea plants that were true-breeding. When self-fertilized, a true-breeding plant produces offspring identical in appearance to itself generation after generation. For instance, Mendel identified a purple-flowered pea plant that, when self-fertilized, always produced offpring plants that had purple flowers. To ensure self-fertilization, Mendel tied a little cloth bag around the flowers so that pollen from other plants could not enter.

To test the particulate hypothesis, Mendel crossed true-breeding plants that had two distinct and contrasting traits—for example, purple or white flowers. These contrasting pea varieties served as parents for the next generation. In a method called **cross-fertilization,** or cross, sperm from the pollen of one flower fertilizes the eggs in the flower of a different plant (Figure 10-2). The fertilized eggs developed into embryos within seeds (peas) that Mendel planted. The seeds grew into offspring that eventually produced their own flowers. Mendel apparently wondered, if a purple-flowered pea plant were fertilized with pollen from a white-flowered plant, what color flowers would the offspring have? You'll read about his results in Concept 10.2.

Guided Research Lab 3

www.biology.com

Inheritance Patterns in Plants
In this laboratory exploration, you will learn how to grow and to cross different strains of plants as a way to determine the inheritance patterns of certain traits. After learning these skills you will design and carry out your own investigation about inheritance patterns in plants.

Online Activity 10.1

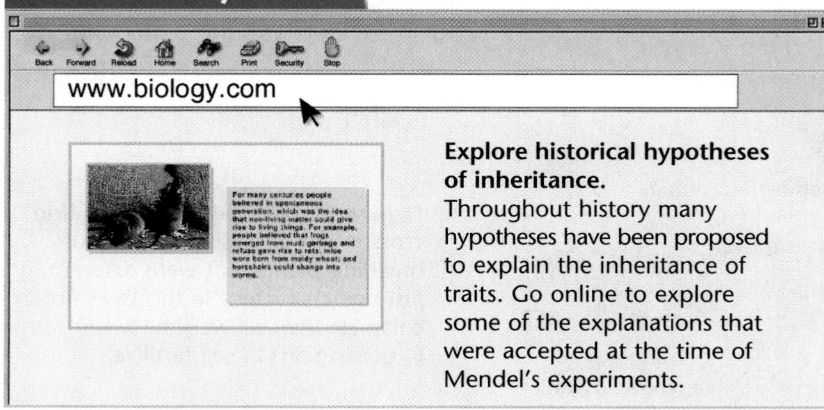

Explore historical hypotheses of inheritance.
Throughout history many hypotheses have been proposed to explain the inheritance of traits. Go online to explore some of the explanations that were accepted at the time of Mendel's experiments.

Concept Check 10.1

1. Explain how Mendel's particulate hypothesis is different from the blending hypothesis of inheritance.
2. What is the difference between self-fertilization and cross-fertilization?
3. Describe a pattern of inheritance that the blending hypothesis fails to explain.

CONCEPT 10.2 Mendel discovered that inheritance follows rules of chance.

OBJECTIVES
- Explain Mendel's principle of segregation.
- Describe how probability applies to genetics.
- Contrast genotype and phenotype.
- Explain Mendel's principle of independent assortment.

KEY TERMS
- hybrid
- monohybrid cross
- allele
- homozygous
- heterozygous
- dominant
- recessive
- Punnett square
- phenotype
- genotype
- testcross
- dihybrid cross

What's Online

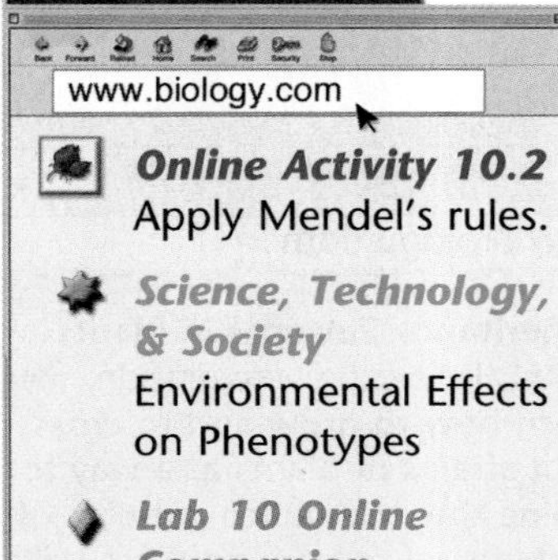

Mendel performed many experiments in which he tracked the inheritance of characters in pea plants, such as flower color and seed shape (pea shape). The results led him to formulate several hypotheses about inheritance. Take a look at some of his experiments and follow the reasoning that led to his hypotheses.

Mendel's Principle of Segregation

In the language of genetics, the offspring of two different true-breeding varieties are called **hybrids.** The parental plants are called the P generation (*P* for *parental*), and the hybrid offspring are the F_1 generation (*F* for *filial,* from the Latin word for "son"). When the F_1 plants self-fertilize or fertilize each other, their offspring are the F_2 generation.

In one experiment, Mendel crossed purple-flowered pea plants with white-flowered pea plants (Figure 10-3). This is an example of a **monohybrid cross,** a pairing in which the parent plants differ in only one (*mono*) character. Mendel saw that the F_1 hybrid plants were not a blend of purple and white. The F_1 hybrids all had purple flowers, the same color as the purple-flowered parent. Was the factor for white flowers now lost as a result of the crossing? By allowing the F_1 plants to self-fertilize, Mendel found the answer to be no. About one fourth of the F_2 plants had white flowers. Mendel concluded that the factor for white flowers did not disappear in the F_1 plants. Instead, only the purple flower factor was affecting F_1 flower color. He reasoned that the F_1 plants must have carried two factors for the flower color character, one for purple and one for white. Today, Mendel's "factors" are called genes.

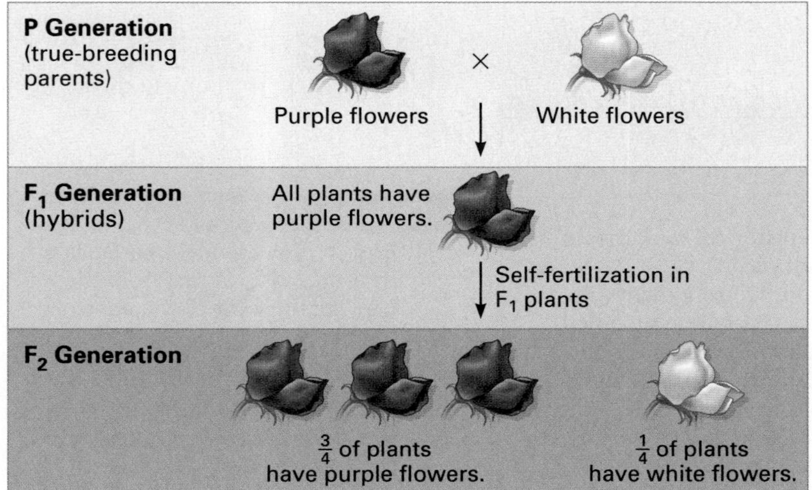

Figure 10-3 For each monohybrid cross, Mendel cross-fertilized true-breeding plants that were different in just one character—in this case, flower color. He then allowed the hybrids (the F_1 generation) to self-fertilize.

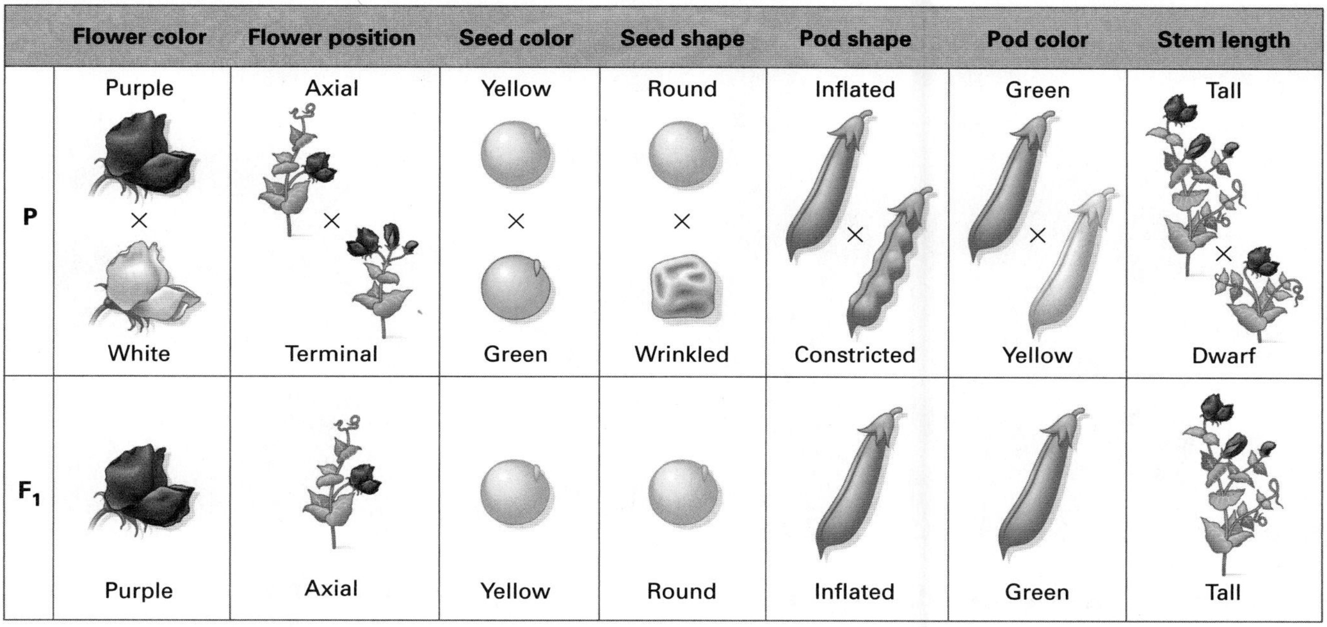

	Flower color	Flower position	Seed color	Seed shape	Pod shape	Pod color	Stem length
P	Purple × White	Axial × Terminal	Yellow × Green	Round × Wrinkled	Inflated × Constricted	Green × Yellow	Tall × Dwarf
F_1	Purple	Axial	Yellow	Round	Inflated	Green	Tall

▲ **Figure 10-4** Mendel examined the inheritance patterns of seven different pea-plant characters. For each character, one of the two parent traits disappeared in the F_1 hybrids, but reappeared in approximately one quarter of the F_2 generation (not shown here).

In addition to studying the inheritance patterns of flower color, Mendel used monohybrid crosses to investigate six other pea plant characters (Figure 10-4). Each cross produced the same pattern. One of the two parent traits disappeared in the F_1 generation, but then reappeared in about one fourth of the F_2 offspring. From these results, Mendel developed four hypotheses. Using modern terms (such as *gene* instead of *factor*), these hypotheses are as follows:

1. There are alternative forms of genes. For example, the gene for flower color in pea plants exists in one form for purple and in another form for white. These alternative forms of genes are called **alleles** (uh LEELZ).
2. For each inherited character, an organism has two alleles for the gene controlling that character, one from each parent. If the two alleles are the same, the individual is **homozygous** (hoh moh ZY gus) for that character. If the two alleles are different, the individual is **heterozygous** (het ur oh ZY gus).
3. When only one of the two different alleles in a heterozygous individual appears to affect the trait, that allele is called the **dominant** allele. And in such cases, the other allele that does not appear to affect the trait is called the **recessive** allele. In this book, a capital letter is used to represent the name of a dominant allele (in the flower color example, P). The lowercase version of the same letter is used to represent the recessive allele (p).
4. The two alleles for a character segregate (separate) during the formation of gametes (sex cells), so that each gamete carries only one allele for each character. This is known as Mendel's *principle of segregation*. The union of gametes during fertilization reforms allele pairs in the offspring.

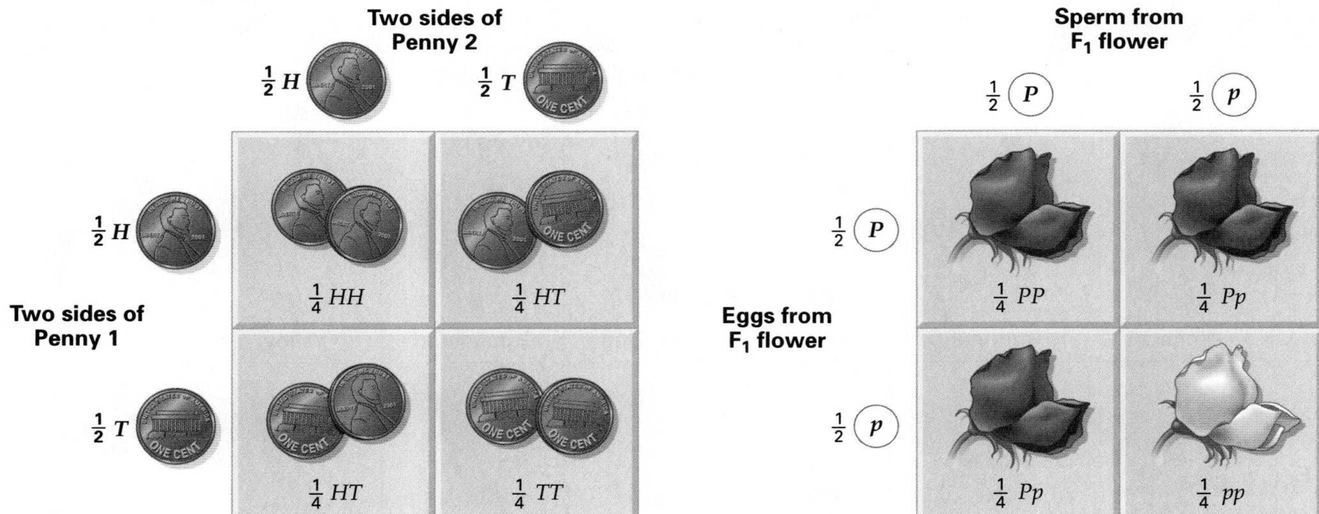

▲ **Figure 10-5** Punnett squares are used to calculate the probabilities of outcomes resulting from a genetic cross. The grid on the left predicts the probabilities of certain combinations of the two sides (alleles) of two pennies. The Punnett square on the right predicts that the two alleles for flower color will randomly pair in the same proportions as the two sides of the pennies.

Probability and Punnett Squares

In a monohybrid cross of true-breeding (homozygous) purple-flowered and white-flowered plants, Mendel's hypotheses predict that each F_1 plant will get the dominant purple-flower allele (*P*) from one parent and the recessive white-flower allele (*p*) from the other parent. Each F_1 plant will be heterozygous: *Pp.* Then the F_1 plants grow up and make gametes of their own. Each gamete receives only one allele for flower color, *P* or *p,* with equal likelihood.

As the F_1 plants fertilize each other, gametes combine randomly and form zygotes with pairs of alleles. The likelihood of each specific pair forming is key to the inheritance pattern seen in the F_2 generation. Consider the analogy of being handed two pennies (Figure 10-5, left). As you look at the two pennies, you will see *2 heads* or *1 head and 1 tail* or *2 tails.* (Note that there are *two* different ways to get the outcome of 1 head and 1 tail.) The side shown by one coin is unaffected by the side shown by the other coin. But what is the probability of a particular combination occurring? For example, what is the probability that you will see 2 heads? You can build a table that shows the probability of each combination. List the probabilities for the first coin along the top of a piece of paper, and the probabilities for the second coin along the edge of the paper. Create a grid as shown in Figure 10-5. The probability of a particular combination is the product of the separate probabilities for each coin. For example, the probability of 2 heads showing is $1/2 \times 1/2 = 1/4$.

In the same way, you can calculate the probabilities for different combinations of alleles resulting from a genetic cross. The gametes of the purple F_1 flowers pair randomly, making the allele combinations in the F_2 generation *PP* or *Pp* or *pp* (Figure 10-5, right). (Again, note that there are two ways to get the heterozygous—*Pp*—outcome.) This type of diagram that shows all possible outcomes of a genetic cross is called a **Punnett square.** You can use a Punnett square to predict probabilities of particular outcomes if you know the genetic makeup of both parents.

Genotype and Phenotype

Now that you know how to predict the genetic makeup of the F_2 plants, what can you say about their appearance? In the prediction based on the Punnett square, one fourth of the F_2 plants are homozygous for the purple allele—they have two alleles specifying purple flowers (*PP*). Clearly, these plants will have purple flowers. One half (1/4 + 1/4) of the F_2 offspring are heterozygous—they have both types of allele (*Pp*). Like the F_1 plants, these plants will also have purple flowers, the dominant trait. Finally, one fourth of the F_2 plants are homozygous for the white-flower allele (*pp*). They will display the recessive trait, white flowers. Thus, Mendel's hypotheses account for the 3/4 : 1/4 or 3 : 1 ratio of flower color that he observed in the F_2 generation.

An observable trait (such as purple flowers) is called the **phenotype** (FEE noh type). The genetic makeup, or combination of alleles (such as *PP*), is called the **genotype** (JEE noh type). For the F_2 plants, the ratio of plants with purple flowers to those with white flowers (3 purple : 1 white) is called the phenotypic ratio. The genotypic ratio is 1 *PP* : 2 *Pp* : 1 *pp*.

The Testcross

What is the genotype of an organism that displays the dominant phenotype? Suppose, for example, that you have a purple-flowered pea plant. Its genotype could be either of two possibilities: *PP* or *Pp*. To determine whether the purple-flowered plant is homozygous (*PP*) or heterozygous (*Pp*), you need to perform what geneticists call a testcross. A **testcross** breeds an individual of unknown genotype, but dominant phenotype (your purple-flowered mystery plant) with a homozygous recessive individual—in this case, a white-flowered plant (*pp*).

The appearance of the offspring resulting from the testcross will reveal the genotype of the mystery plant. Because the homozygous recessive parent can only contribute a recessive allele to the offspring, the phenotype will indicate the allele contributed by the mystery plant. If the purple-flowered parent is homozygous, you would expect all of the offspring to be purple-flowered since the mystery plant can only contribute a *P* allele. Thus, all offspring would be *Pp* (Figure 10-6, left). However, if the purple-flowered parent is heterozygous, you would expect both purple-flowered (*Pp*) and white-flowered (*pp*) offspring (Figure 10-6, right). Figure 10-6 also shows that the white-flowered and purple-flowered offspring of a *Pp* × *pp* testcross are predicted to have a 1 : 1 (1 purple to 1 white) ratio of phenotypes.

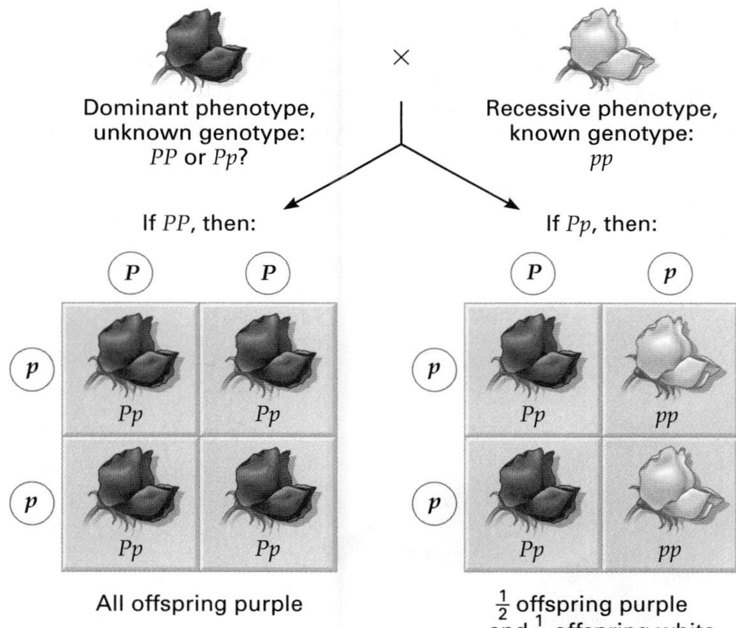

▲ **Figure 10-6** A testcross can reveal whether an organism that displays the dominant phenotype is homozygous or heterozygous.

Mendel's Principle of Independent Assortment

Two of the seven characters Mendel studied were qualities of the peas themselves: shape and color (see Figure 10-4 on page 209). From his monohybrid crosses, Mendel knew that round pea shape was dominant to wrinkled shape, and yellow color was dominant to green. What would be the result of a **dihybrid cross**—crossing organisms differing in *two* characters? Figure 10-7 outlines Mendel's results. Mendel crossed a true-breeding plant grown from a round yellow seed (genotype *RRYY*) with a true-breeding plant grown from a wrinkled green seed (genotype *rryy*). The first parent could only produce *RY* gametes. The other could only produce *ry* gametes. The union of these *RY* and *ry* gametes yielded hybrid peas heterozygous for both characters (*RrYy*). All peas had the dominant phenotype: They were round and yellow.

The hybrid peas grew into F_1 plants, which Mendel allowed to self-fertilize. This produced four phenotypes of peas. Assuming there are four equally likely combinations of alleles in the gametes produced by the F_1 generation—*RY, rY, Ry,* and *ry*—a Punnett square predicts a phenotypic ratio of 9 : 3 : 3 : 1 (Figure 10-8). And in fact, Mendel counted 315 round yellow, 108 round green, 101 wrinkled yellow, and 32 wrinkled green peas, a ratio that is approximately 9 : 3 : 3 : 1.

The Punnett square in Figure 10-8 also reveals that a dihybrid cross has the same outcome as two monohybrid crosses occurring at the same time. If you just look at seed shape, there are 12 plants with round seeds to every 4 with wrinkled seeds. If you look at just seed color, there are 12 yellow-seeded plants to every 4 green-seeded ones. A 12 : 4 ratio is the same as a 3 : 1 ratio, the phenotypic ratio for the F_2 generation of a monohybrid cross.

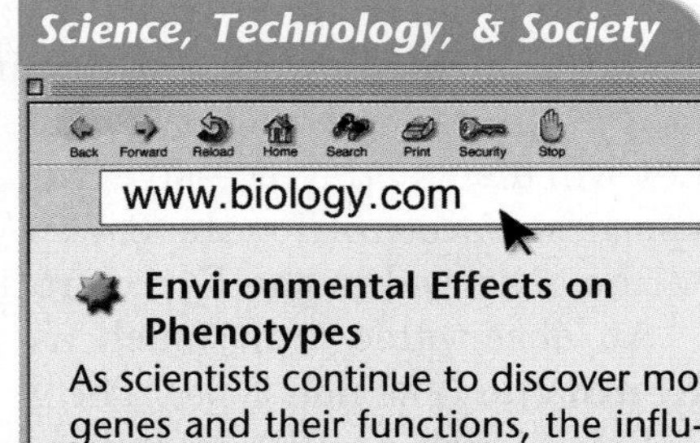

Environmental Effects on Phenotypes

As scientists continue to discover more genes and their functions, the influence of environmental factors on the expression of traits is a growing field of investigation. Find out more about this topic when you go online.

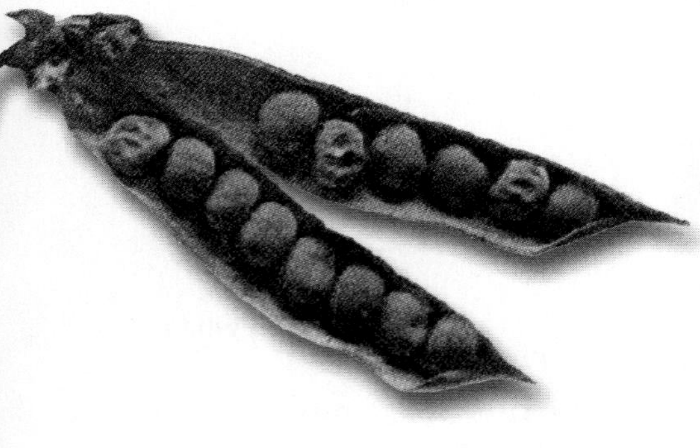

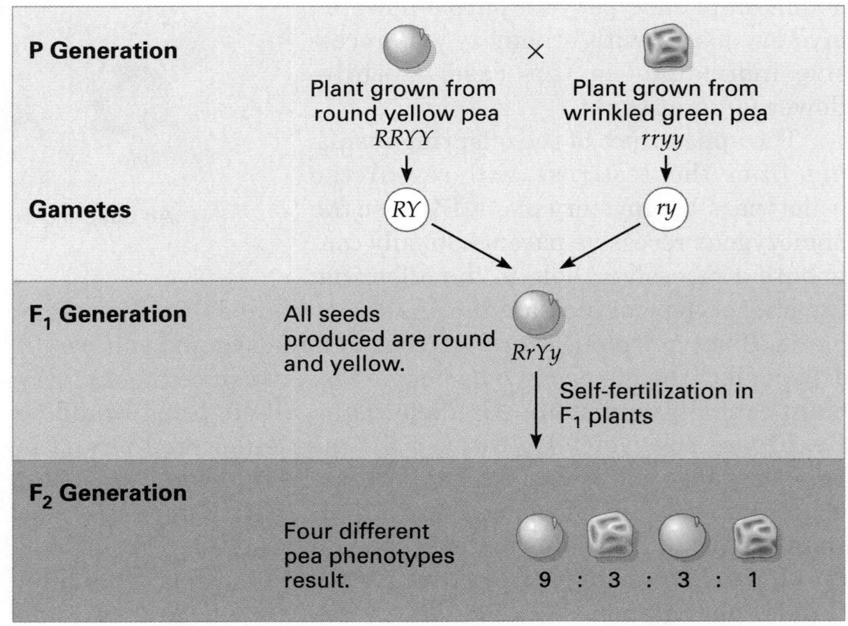

Figure 10-7 For each dihybrid cross, Mendel cross-fertilized true-breeding plants that were different in two characters. Then he allowed the F_1 hybrids to self-fertilize. In this case, the two characters, seed color and shape, are displayed by the first stage of each new generation, the seed (pea).

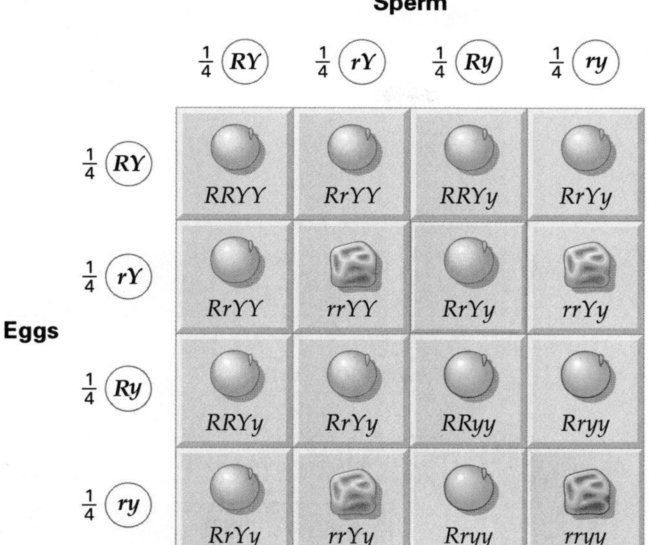

Figure 10-8 A Punnett square predicts a 9 : 3 : 3 : 1 phenotypic ratio for the F_2 offspring resulting from the dihybrid cross for seed shape and color.

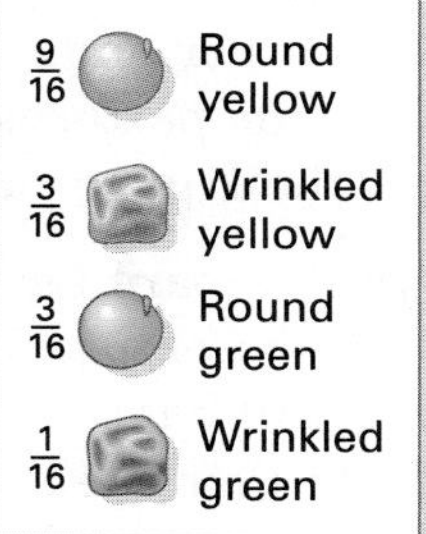

Mendel tested his seven pea characters in various dihybrid combinations. The ratio of phenotypes in the F_2 generation was always very close to the predicted ratio of 9 : 3 : 3 : 1. Based on these results Mendel proposed his *principle of independent assortment.* This principle states that during gamete formation in an F_2 cross, a particular allele for one character can be paired with either allele of another character. For instance, in the above example, *R* can end up with either *Y* or *y,* and *r* can end up with either *Y* or *y.* The alleles for different genes are sorted into the gametes independently of one another.

Mendel's principle of independent assortment accurately described the seven pea plant characters he studied. But you will learn later in this chapter that there are certain exceptions to this principle.

Online Activity 10.2

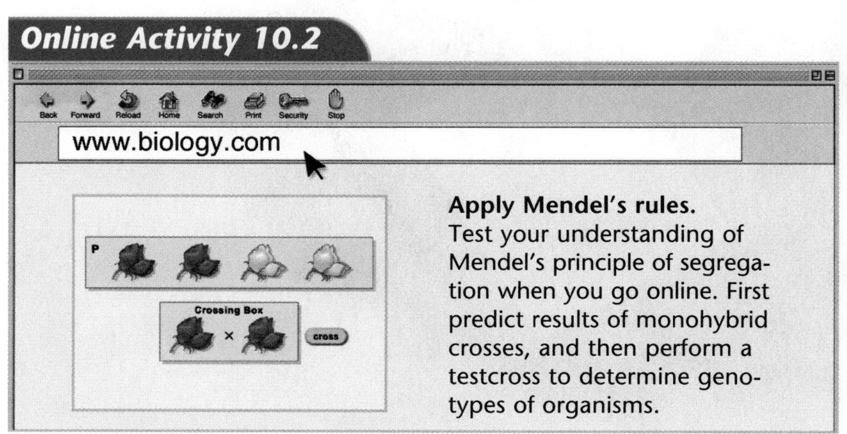

Back
Forward
Reload
Home
Search
Print
Security
Stop
www.biology.com
P
Crossing Box
cross
Apply Mendel's rules.
Test your understanding of Mendel's principle of segregation when you go online. First predict results of monohybrid crosses, and then perform a testcross to determine genotypes of organisms.

Concept Check 10.2

1. What are the two possible gametes produced by a plant that has the genotype *Aa*? Give the probability of each type of gamete.
2. Use a Punnett square to predict the genotypes produced if the plant in Question 1 is self-fertilized. Calculate the probability of each outcome.
3. List all the possible genotypes of a pea plant with purple flowers and round seeds.
4. List the four possible allele combinations in the gametes of a plant with genotype *PpWw.*

Family Reunion in a Dish

Determining P Phenotypes From F_1 and F_2 Phenotypes

Question How can you determine the traits of plants from the P generation by observing the traits of the F_1 and F_2 generations?

Lab Overview In this investigation you will germinate seeds from two consecutive crosses of Fast Plants™. By observing the stem color and height of the seedlings, you will determine the patterns of inheritance and the phenotypes of the P generation.

Preparing for the Lab To help you prepare for the investigation, go to the *Lab 10 Online Companion.* ·····➔ Find out more about the seeds you will be using by doing a virtual genetic cross. Prepare for the lab procedure by previewing the steps you will take.

Completing the Lab Use your Laboratory Manual or lab page printouts from the *Lab 10 Online Companion* to do the investigation and analyze your results. **CAUTION:** *Be sure to follow your teacher's instructions and all safety guidelines in the investigation.*

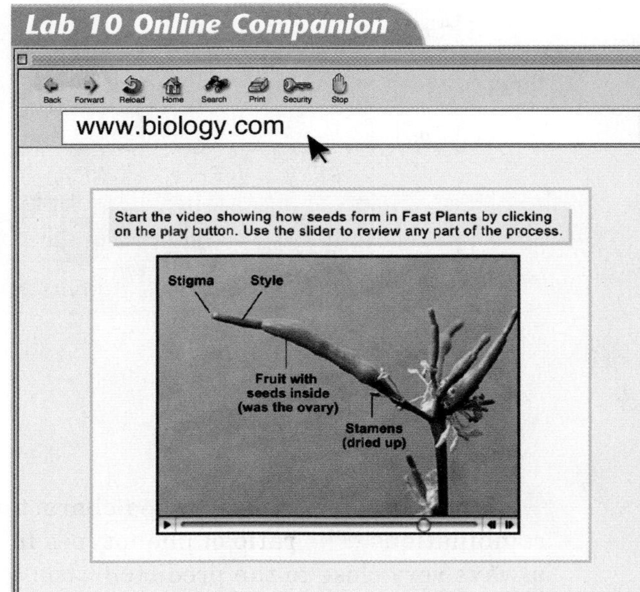

CONCEPT 10.3

There are many variations of inheritance patterns.

OBJECTIVES

- Describe how alleles interact in intermediate inheritance.
- Describe inheritance patterns involving multiple alleles.
- Explain how polygenic inheritance can result in a wide range of phenotypes.
- Describe how environmental conditions can affect phenotype expression.

KEY TERMS

- intermediate inheritance
- codominance
- polygenic inheritance

What's Online

Online Activity 10.3
Explore patterns of inheritance.

For his experiments Mendel carefully selected simple pea plant characters to study. His choice increased the chance that he might be able to determine the basic rules behind inheritance patterns. However, many characters of organisms have more complicated inheritance patterns than those studied by Mendel. In this section, you will explore the reasons for these patterns.

Intermediate Inheritance

The F_1 offspring of Mendel's pea crosses always looked like the dominant homozygous parent. This is because *one* dominant allele was enough to produce the dominant phenotype, but the recessive phenotype required inheriting *two* recessive alleles. But for some characters of organisms, neither allele is dominant. The heterozygotes have a phenotype that is intermediate between the phenotypes of the two homozygotes. This pattern of inheritance is called **intermediate inheritance.** For example, in a particular breed of chicken called Andalusians, black and white parents produce F_1 hybrid offspring, called "blues," with grayish-blue feathers (Figure 10-9). Because neither the black nor white allele is dominant, capital and lowercase letters are not used to represent them. Instead, a *C* for "color" is paired with a superscript *B* for "black" or *W* for "white" to represent the two alleles. A heterozygote chicken has one of each allele, C^BC^W, and is blue in color.

Although the F_1 phenotypes are intermediate, this inheritance pattern does not support the blending hypothesis. This is because the parent phenotypes can reappear in the F_2 generation. In the chicken example, the predicted phenotypes in the F_2 are 1 black : 2 blue : 1 white. Note that 1 : 2 : 1 is also the ratio of genotypes.

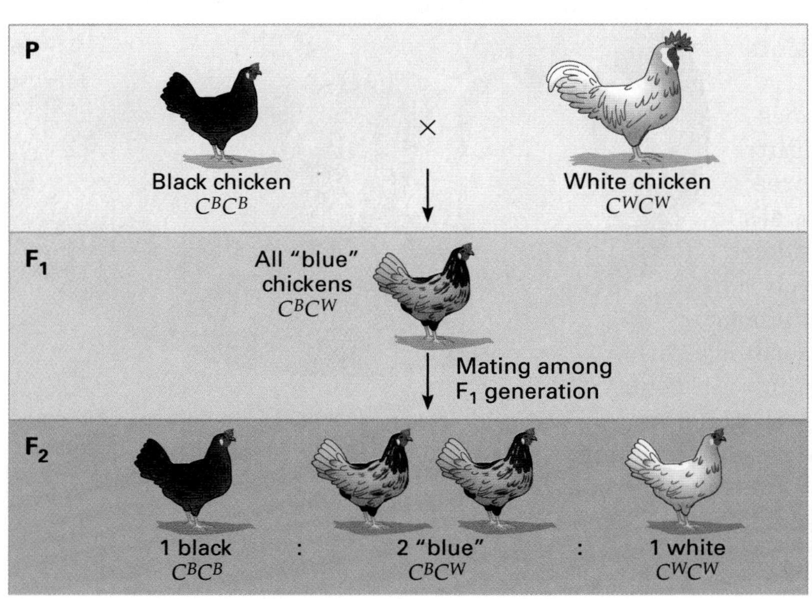

Figure 10-9 In a monohybrid cross where neither parent trait is dominant, the hybrids have an intermediate phenotype. But the parent phenotypes can appear again in the F_2 generation.

Multiple Alleles

The inheritance patterns you have explored so far have involved only two contrasting alleles for each inherited character. But for many genes *several* alleles exist in the population. This expands the number of possible genotypes and phenotypes.

For example, multiple alleles control the character of blood type in humans. A person's blood type may be A, B, AB, or O. The letters refer to two carbohydrates, designated A and B, which are found on the surface of red blood cells. A person's red blood cells may be coated with one carbohydrate (type A) or the other (type B), with both (type AB), or with neither (type O).

Figure 10-10 shows how these four blood types result from various combinations of three alleles, symbolized as I^A (for carbohydrate A), I^B (for carbohydrate B), and i (for neither A nor B). Each person inherits one of these alleles from each parent. There are six possible ways to pair the alleles—in other words, there are six possible genotypes. The alleles I^A and I^B exhibit **codominance,** meaning that a heterozygote expresses *both* traits. Note that this is different from intermediate inheritance. The individual's phenotype is not intermediate, but rather shows the separate traits of both alleles.

Genetic Determination of Blood Type

Phenotype (Blood type)	Genotypes
O	ii
A	I^AI^A or I^Ai
B	I^BI^B or I^Bi
AB	I^AI^B

▲ **Figure 10-10** There are three alleles for blood type in the human population. (But note that any one person has only two alleles for blood type.) The combinations of these alleles result in six genotypes and four phenotypes. Alleles I^A and I^B are codominant. Allele i is recessive.

Polygenic Inheritance

Each of the seven characters Mendel studied occurred in two distinct phenotypes. For example, flower color was either white or purple. For some characters, intermediate inheritance, codominance of alleles, or multiple types of alleles can lead to more than two phenotypes in a population. When multiple *genes* affect a character, the variation in phenotypes can become even greater. When two or more genes affect a single character, it is called **polygenic inheritance** (pahl uh JEN ik). In humans, height and skin color have polygenic inheritance (Figure 10-11). For example, the height of students in a large high school might range from about 125 cm to 200 cm, with students of every possible height in between.

Consider how three hypothetical genes could produce the variation of height observed in humans. Assume that the three genes are inherited separately, like Mendel's pea genes. Suppose there are three "tall" alleles for each gene (*A, B,* and *C*), each of which contributes one "unit" of tallness to the phenotype. These tall alleles exhibit intermediate inheritance with three "short" alleles (*X, Y,* and *Z*). A person with genotype *AABBCC* would be very tall, a person with genotype *AXBBCC* would be slightly less tall, and so on. The potential combinations of alleles (and thus range of phenotypes) for a character increases with the number of genes that affect that character. Some characters are affected by dozens of genes.

▲ **Figure 10-11** In humans, skin color and height have polygenic inheritance. Both characters show a large range of phenotypes.

The Importance of Environment

An individual's phenotype depends on environment as well as on genes. For example, although a tree's genotype does not change throughout its lifetime, the tree's leaves vary in size, shape, and greenness from year to year depending on exposure to wind and sunlight.

Temperature has a very interesting effect on the phenotype of certain organisms. For example, a Siamese cat such as the one in Figure 10-12 is covered with creamy white fur, except on its ears, face, feet, and tail. The enzyme responsible for black fur color is only active at the cooler temperatures found at the cat's extremities, giving the cat a unique appearance.

In humans, nutrition influences height, exercise affects build, and exposure to sunlight darkens the skin. Even identical twins, who have the same genotype for every character, accumulate some differences in phenotype as a result of their exposure to environmental differences. For example, each twin may have a different diet, activity level, history of illnesses, and exposure to sunlight.

Whether genes or the environment have more of an influence on human characters is a very old and hotly contested topic of debate. There *are* cases where genes determine phenotype with little or no influence from the environment. Human blood type is an example. More common, however, are characters such as a person's blood count (numbers of red and white blood cells), which is very sensitive to environment as well as genotype. Blood count depends on such factors as the altitude of one's home, a person's customary level of physical activity, and the presence of infection.

In summary, the product of a genotype is generally not a single, rigidly defined phenotype, but a range of possibilities influenced by the environment.

Figure 10-12 Some hereditary characters are influenced by environmental conditions. In Siamese cats, fur color is affected by temperature. The cat's face, ears, paws, and tail are cooler than the rest of its body, and have a darker color.

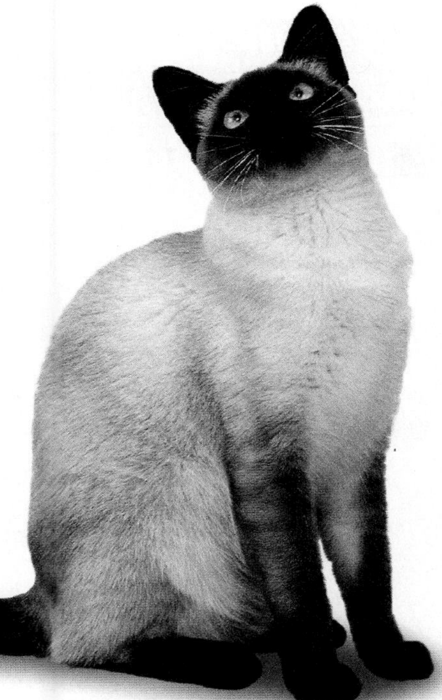

Online Activity 10.3

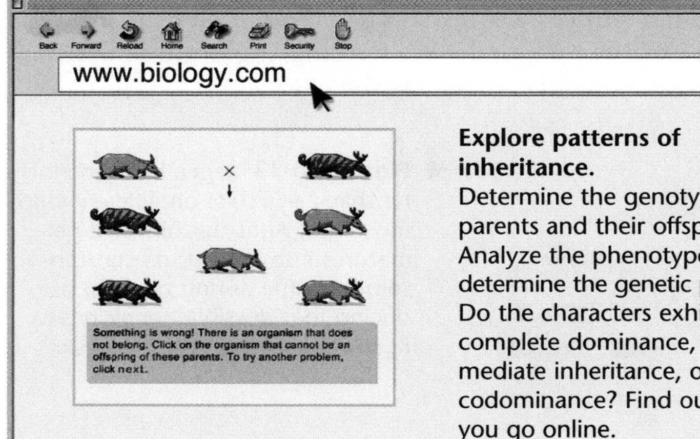

Back
Forward
Reload
Home
Search
Print
Security
Stop
www.biology.com
Something is wrong! There is an organism that does not belong. Click on the organism that cannot be an offspring of these parents. To try another problem, click next.

Explore patterns of inheritance.
Determine the genotypes of parents and their offspring. Analyze the phenotypes to determine the genetic patterns. Do the characters exhibit complete dominance, intermediate inheritance, or codominance? Find out when you go online.

Concept Check 10.3

1. For a trait with intermediate inheritance, what is the phenotypic ratio for F_2 offspring of a monohybrid cross? How is that different from a simple dominant-recessive cross?
2. Two parents have type O blood. What blood type would you expect for their first child?
3. What is the likely mechanism of inheritance for a character with a large range of phenotypes? Explain.
4. Give three examples of human physical characters affected by environment.

CONCEPT 10.4

Meiosis explains Mendel's principles.

OBJECTIVES

- Summarize the chromosome theory of inheritance.
- Explain how genetic linkage provides exceptions to Mendel's principle of independent assortment.

KEY TERMS

- chromosome theory of inheritance
- gene locus
- genetic linkage

What's Online

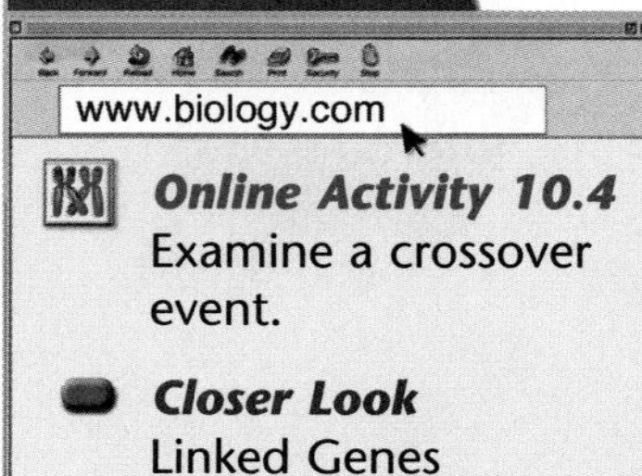

Mendel's discoveries were not widely known or accepted in his lifetime. During the years from 1866 when Mendel published his work on pea plants to 1900 when Mendel's work was "rediscovered," biologists began to study chromosomes. New evidence about the role of chromosomes in cell reproduction helped biologists to understand Mendel's principles.

Chromosome Theory of Inheritance

Cell biologists worked out the processes of mitosis and meiosis in the late 1800s. (See Chapter 9 to review these processes.) Then, around 1900, researchers noticed parallels between the behavior of chromosomes and the behavior of Mendel's heritable factors ("genes"). One of biology's most important theories—the chromosome theory of inheritance—emerged.

The **chromosome theory of inheritance** states that genes are located on chromosomes, and the behavior of chromosomes during meiosis and fertilization accounts for inheritance patterns. Indeed, it is chromosomes that undergo segregation and independent assortment during meiosis and thus account for Mendel's two principles of the same name.

Recall that every diploid individual, such as a pea plant or a human, has two sets of homologous chromosomes. One set comes from the organism's female parent, and the other set comes from the male parent. In Figures 10-13 and 10-14, chromosomes from one parent are shown in blue, and from the other parent in red. The alleles of a gene reside at the same location, called a **gene locus** (plural, *loci*), on homologous chromosomes (Figure 10-13). Notice that the homologous chromosomes may bear either the same alleles or different ones at a particular locus, making the organism either homozygous or heterozygous for each gene.

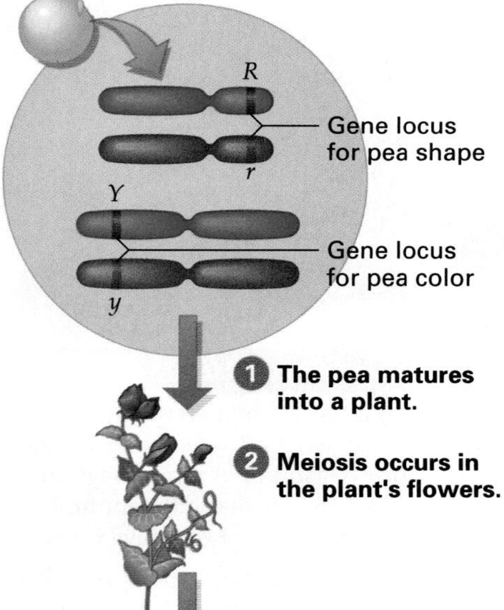

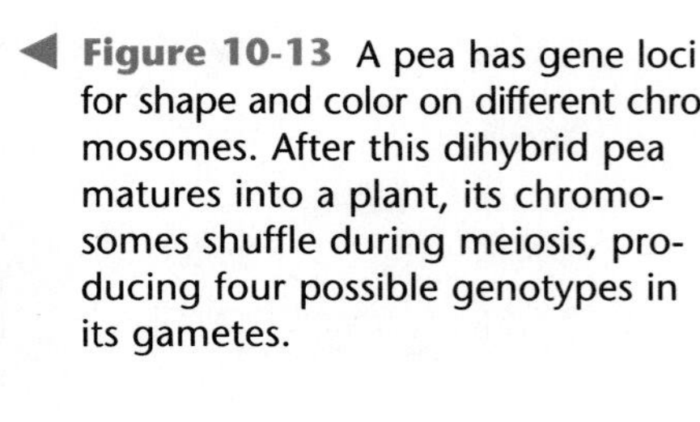

Figure 10-13 A pea has gene loci for shape and color on different chromosomes. After this dihybrid pea matures into a plant, its chromosomes shuffle during meiosis, producing four possible genotypes in its gametes.

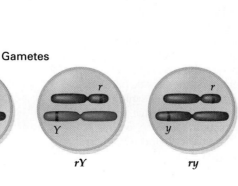

Scenario 1: Gene loci close together

Q M / *q m*

1 Homologous chromosomes pair up at prophase I of meiosis.

2 . . .then cross over.

Q M / *Q M* / *q m* / *q m*

3 The alleles tend to stay together.

Scenario 2: Gene loci far apart

B L / *b l*

1 Homologous chromosomes pair up at prophase I of meiosis.

2 . . .then cross over.

B L / *b L* / *B l* / *b l*

3 New combinations of the alleles are created.

Figure 10-14 Crossing over can recombine gene loci on homologous chromosomes. This is unlikely when the genes are very close together (Scenario 1). A crossover is more likely to recombine the alleles when the genes are far apart (Scenario 2).

Genetic Linkage and Crossing Over

When genes are located on separate chromosomes, they sort independently of each other during meiosis. But what happens when genes are located on the *same* chromosome? The alleles for these genes would not tend to be sorted into gametes independently since they would stay together during meiosis. The only way such alleles can sort independently is if crossing over during meiosis separates them.

The tendency for the alleles on one chromosome to be inherited together is called **genetic linkage.** The closer two genes are on a chromosome, the greater the genetic linkage (Figure 10-14). The farther apart the genes are, the more likely it is that a crossover event will separate them. For example in Scenario 2 of Figure 10-14, allele B can be found with either allele L or l. Looking at the proportion of gametes with recombined alleles allows scientists to map the distance between genes on a chromosome.

Online Activity 10.4

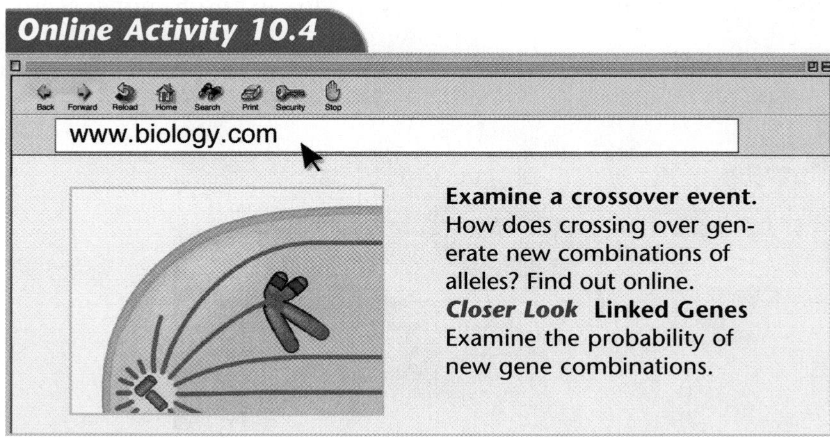

Back
Forward
Reload
Home
Search
Print
Security
Stop
www.biology.com
Examine a crossover event.
How does crossing over generate new combinations of alleles? Find out online.
Closer Look **Linked Genes**
Examine the probability of new gene combinations.

Concept Check 10.4

1. Draw a picture of the possible arrangements of chromosomes in the gametes produced by a pea plant with genotype *RRYy*. Label the gene loci. (Remember that these genes are located on separate chromosomes.)
2. Explain how the distance between two gene loci on the same chromosome affects genetic linkage.

CONCEPT 10.5

Sex-linked traits have unique inheritance patterns.

OBJECTIVES

- Explain how sex-linked genes produce different inheritance patterns in males and females.
- Explain why most sex-linked disorders are more common in males.

KEY TERM

- sex-linked gene

What's Online

www.biology.com

Online Activity 10.5
Analyze Morgan's fruit fly experiment.

The work of biologists that established the chromosome basis of Mendel's principles also led to an understanding of the role that sex chromosomes play in a unique pattern of inheritance.

Sex-Linked Genes

As you learned in Chapter 9, many species including humans have sex chromosomes, designated X and Y, that are associated with determining an individual's sex. The eggs contain a single X chromosome. Of the sperm cells, half contain an X chromosome and half contain a Y chromosome. An offspring's sex depends on whether the sperm cell that fertilizes the egg carries an X or a Y.

Any gene that is located on a sex chromosome is called a **sex-linked gene.** In humans, most sex-linked genes are found on the X chromosome, which is considerably larger than the Y chromosome. Sex-linked genes were discovered by Thomas Hunt Morgan while he was studying the inheritance of white eye color in fruit flies. White eyes are very rare in natural fruit fly populations. Normally, fruit flies have red eyes (Figure 10-15).

Figure 10-16 on the facing page shows the eye color inheritance patterns that Morgan observed, along with the genotypes that he eventually figured out. When he mated a white-eyed male fly with a red-eyed female fly, all the F_1 offspring had red eyes. This result suggested that the allele for red eyes was dominant. When Morgan bred those F_1 offspring with each other, he got the classical 3 : 1 phenotypic ratio of red-eyed to white-eyed flies in the F_2 generation.

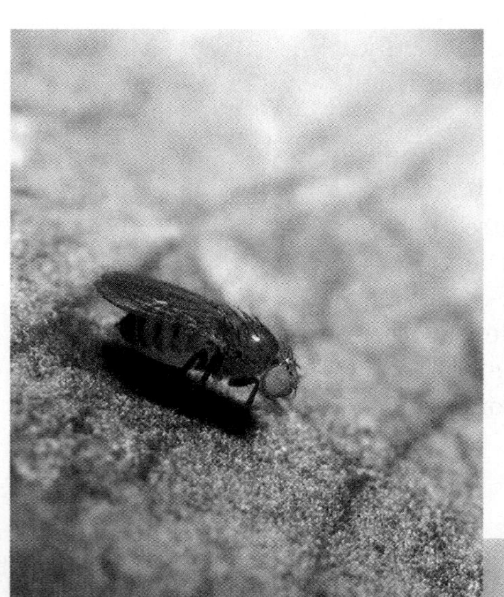

Figure 10-15 The inheritance patterns of the white-eyed trait in fruit flies led to the discovery of sex-linked genes. The red eyes of the fly on the right are more common. White eye color, as in the fly above, is rare.

However, there was a surprising twist: none of the flies with white eyes was female. Morgan realized that in these flies, eye color must somehow be tied to sex.

From this and other evidence, Morgan deduced that the gene involved in this inheritance pattern is located only on the X chromosome. There is no corresponding eye color locus on the Y. Thus, females (XX) carry two copies of the gene for this character, while males (XY) carry only one. Because the white-eye allele is recessive, a female will have white eyes only if she has the white-eye allele on *both* her X chromosomes. However, in males, a *single* copy of the white-eye allele on the lone X chromosome will lead to white eyes because no other allele is present. In Figure 10-16, X^R represents the dominant, red-eye allele located on the X chromosome. X^r represents the recessive, white-eye allele located on the X chromosome.

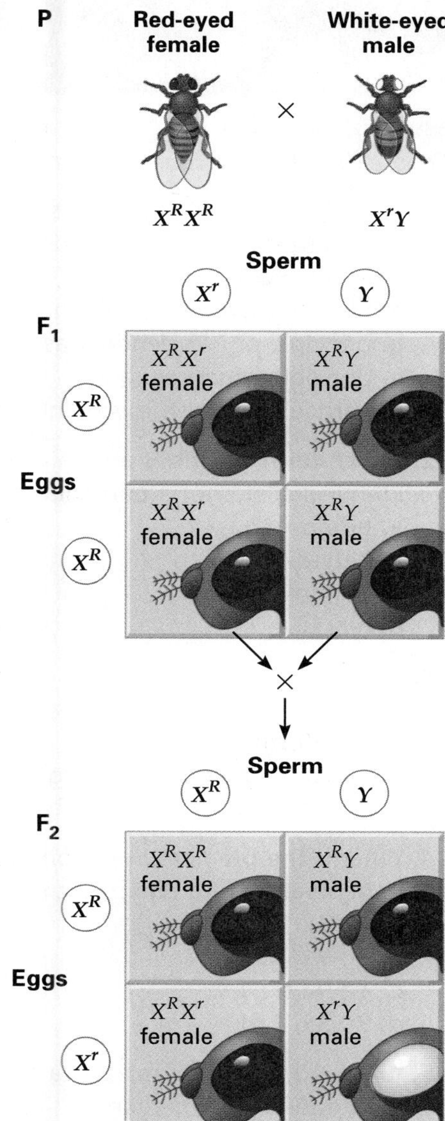

Sex-linked Disorders

Fruit fly genetics helps explain certain patterns in human inheritance. For example, a number of human conditions, including red-green color blindness and hemophilia (a disease in which blood fails to clot normally), are inherited as sex-linked (X-linked) recessive traits. These human conditions are inherited in the same way as the white-eye trait in fruit flies. The fruit fly model also shows why recessive sex-linked traits are much more common in men than in women. Like a male fruit fly, if a human male inherits the sex-linked recessive allele from his mother, the allele will be expressed. In contrast, a female must inherit two such alleles—one from each parent—to exhibit the trait. You will read more about sex-linked disorders in humans in Chapter 12.

▶ **Figure 10-16** Morgan's monohybrid cross for fly eye color produced a 3 : 1 phenotypic ratio of red to white eyes in the F_2 generation. However, none of the flies with white eyes was female.

Online Activity 10.5

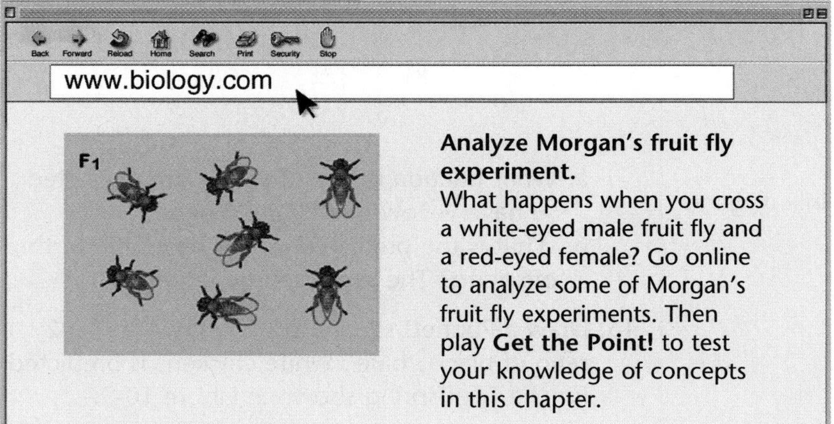

Analyze Morgan's fruit fly experiment.
What happens when you cross a white-eyed male fruit fly and a red-eyed female? Go online to analyze some of Morgan's fruit fly experiments. Then play **Get the Point!** to test your knowledge of concepts in this chapter.

Concept Check 10.5

1. Describe why one would expect to find more white-eyed male fruit flies than white-eyed females in natural populations.
2. A man with hemophilia and a homozygous non-hemophiliac woman have a son. Is it possible that the son will inherit hemophilia? Why or why not?

Multiple Choice

Choose the letter of the best answer.

1. Which of the following states that heritable factors (genes) retain their identity generation after generation?
   a. blending hypothesis of inheritance
   b. principle of independent assortment
   c. principle of segregation
   d. particulate hypothesis of inheritance

2. Which term describes an individual with two identical alleles for a particular character?
   a. homozygous
   b. heterozygous
   c. dominant
   d. recessive

3. If you want to know the genotype of a pea plant that has purple flowers, which would you perform?
   a. dihybrid cross **b.** genetic linkage
   c. Punnett square **d.** testcross

4. What is the predicted phenotypic ratio of the F_2 generation of a dihybrid cross?
   a. 1 : 3 : 1
   b. 3 : 9 : 1 : 1
   c. 1 : 9 : 9 : 1
   d. 9 : 3 : 3 : 1

5. AB blood type in humans is a result of
   a. intermediate inheritance.
   b. codominance.
   c. sex-linked inheritance.
   d. environmental effects.

6. The farther apart the alleles for two genes are on the same chromosome, the more likely they are to
   a. separate during meiosis.
   b. stay together during meiosis.
   c. be inherited only by male offspring.
   d. both be recessive.

7. How many alleles for a sex-linked (X-linked) gene does a male carry?
   a. four
   b. one
   c. none
   d. two

Short Answer

8. Describe the *blending hypothesis.* Explain why it was discarded as a valid hypothesis.

9. Suppose you have two fully grown pea plants, one tall and one dwarf. Dwarf height is a recessive trait. Using *T* and *t* as the alleles, what is the the dwarf plant's genotype? How could you learn the tall plant's genotype?

10. List the possible combinations of alleles in the gametes of an individual with genotype *AaBb.*

11. Explain Mendel's *principle of independent assortment.* When might this principle *not* apply?

12. If a father's blood type is B and a mother's blood type is A, is it possible that their child could have blood type O? Explain your response.

13. Define polygenic inheritance and give an example of a character that is polygenic.

14. Explain how a white-eyed male fruit fly can have a red-eyed father.

Visualizing Concepts

15. The Punnett square below represents the self-fertilization of a pea plant that is heterozygous for yellow peas. Copy the diagram and fill in the missing alleles to predict the resulting offspring.

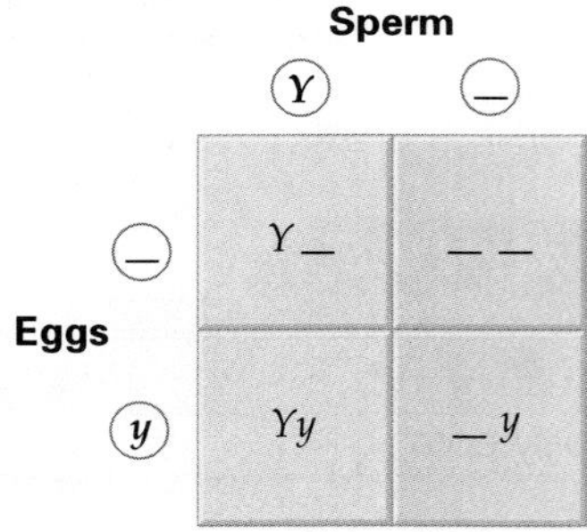

   a. What fraction of the offspring are predicted to have yellow peas? Green peas?
   b. What is the predicted phenotypic ratio of the offspring? The predicted genotypic ratio?

16. Draw a Punnett square to show how the 1 : 2 : 1 ratio of black : blue : white chickens is predicted for the F_2 offspring shown in Figure 10-9.

Analyzing Information

17. Analyzing Data The table below shows the results of a cross of two red-eyed fruit flies. Some of the offspring have "ruby"-colored (deep pink) eyes instead of the usual red-colored eyes.

Numbers of Offspring

	Males	Females
Red eyes	77	151
"Ruby" eyes	75	0

a. Are ruby-colored eyes dominant or recessive?
b. How do the results of the cross indicate that ruby eye color is sex-linked?
c. Using X^R for the dominant allele and X^r for the recessive allele, write the genotypes of the two parents.
d. Do the female offspring all have the same genotype? List the likely genotype(s) of the female offspring.
e. List the genotype of the red-eyed males and the genotype of the ruby-eyed males.

18. Analyzing Diagrams The diagram shows three gene loci on a pair of homologous chromosomes.

Homologous chromosomes

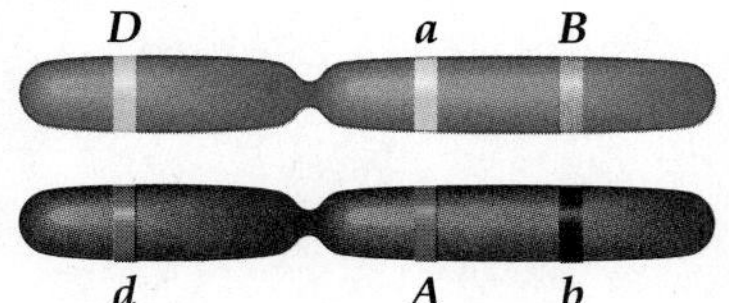

a. Of the three genes found on this pair of homologous chromosomes, which two are most likely to be separated from each other by a crossover event? Explain.
b. If no crossovers occurred between any of the genes, list the possible combinations of alleles in this individual's gametes.

Critical Thinking

19. Evaluating Models Explain how the table of outcomes for the pennies presented in Concept 10.2 helps explain the outcome of a cross of two F_1 offspring. What do the two sides represent?

20. Problem Solving Tim and Christine have freckles (a dominant trait that is not sex-linked), but their son Michael does not. Show with a Punnett square how this is possible. Tim and Christine are expecting a baby. What is the probability of freckles in that child?

21. Analyzing Scientific Explanations Suppose a friend in biology class says: "There are just two alleles for every gene." Another of your friends says: "There are many alleles for some genes." In what way are they both correct? Explain.

22. What's Wrong With These Statements? *Briefly explain why each statement is inaccurate or misleading.*
a. If the first time you flip a penny you see a tail, the next flip is more likely to show a head.
b. If you buy two plants of the same species that have different-colored flowers, they must have different genotypes.

Performance Assessment

Design an Experiment When a horse breeder mates two true-breeding horses, one of which is dark brown and the other white, she produces a horse called a palomino that is creamy gold in color. Formulate a hypothesis to explain what kind of inheritance pattern this is. Design an experiment the horse breeder could perform to test this hypothesis.

Online Assessment/Test Preparation

Back Forward Reload Home Search Print Security Stop

www.biology.com

- **Chapter 10 Assessment**
  Check your understanding of the chapter concepts.
- **Standardized Test Preparation**
  Practice test-taking skills you need to succeed.

DNA and the Language of Life

Many people find beauty in nature's elaborate patterns: the radiating petals of a flower, the alternating branches of a tree, the spiral of a snail shell. Underlying this beauty is an important pattern on the molecular level, the double helix of life's "instruction molecule"—DNA. The work leading to the understanding of DNA's structure and function might be the most significant biological discovery of the twentieth century. DNA's function is to store genetic information and provide a way for that information to be copied. DNA's structure provides a way to achieve these functions, as you will learn in this chapter. But first, go online to the *WebQuest* to explore how deciphering codes can unlock a wide range of mysteries.

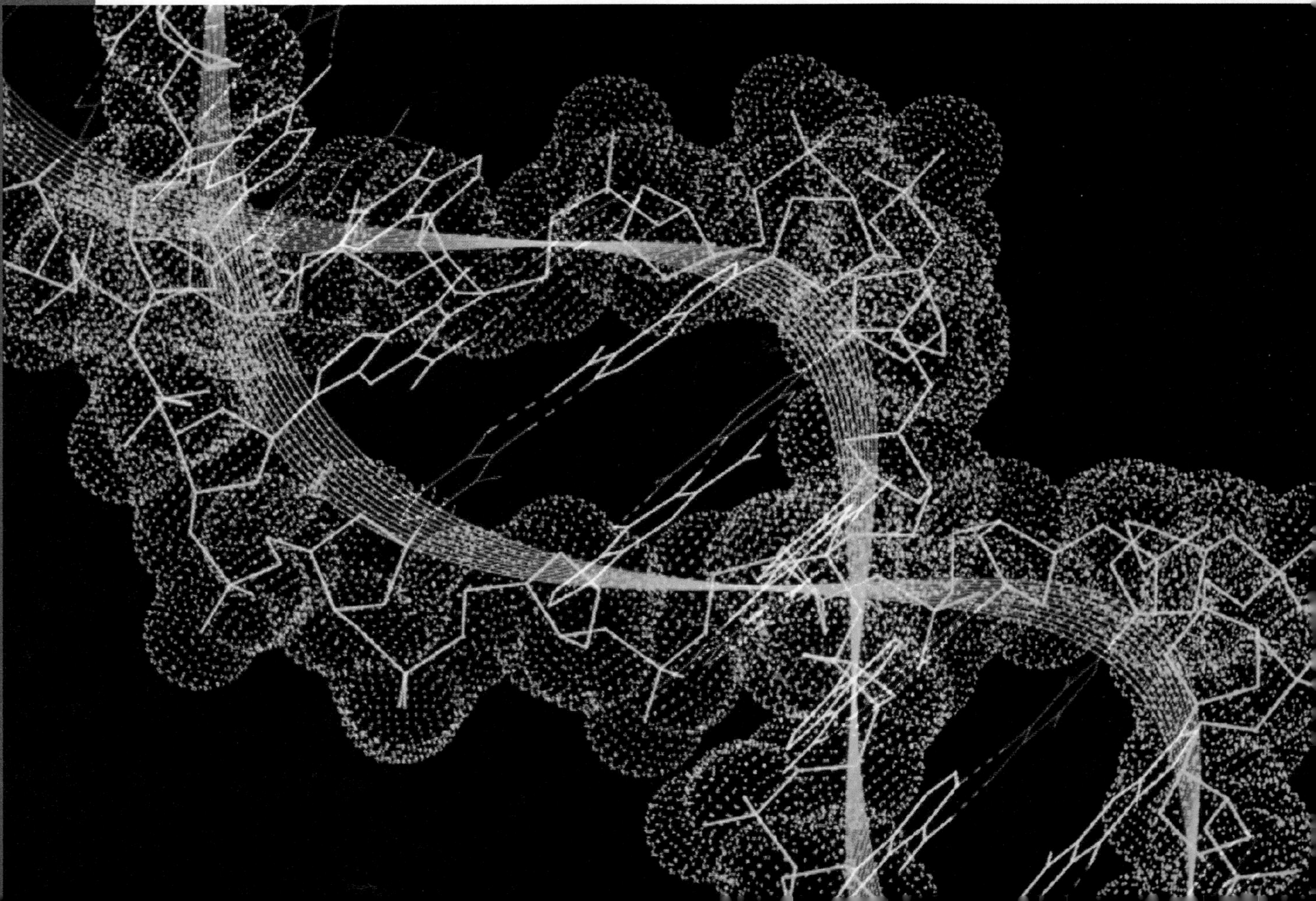

Key Concepts

Concept 11.1 Genes are made of DNA.

Concept 11.2 Nucleic acids store information in their sequences of chemical units.

Concept 11.3 DNA replication is the molecular mechanism of inheritance.

Concept 11.4 A gene provides the information for making a specific protein.

Concept 11.5 There are two main steps from gene to protein.

Concept 11.6 Mutations can change the meaning of genes.

Assessment Chapter 11 Review

What's Online

www.biology.com

WebQuest
CodeQuest

Online Activity 11.1
Experiment with bacteriophages.

Online Activity 11.2
Pair up nucleotide bases.

Lab 11 Online Companion
Berry Full of DNA

Online Activity 11.3
Replicate DNA strands.

Online Activity 11.4
Follow the path from gene to protein.

History of Science
Discovery of DNA

Online Activity 11.5
Translate RNA to a protein.

Online Activity 11.6
Mutate a DNA molecule.

Chapter 11 Assessment

CONCEPT 11.1 Genes are made of DNA.

OBJECTIVES

- Describe Griffith's experiments and conclusion.
- Describe Avery's experiments and conclusion.
- Explain how experiments with viral DNA further supported Avery's conclusion.

KEY TERMS

- virus
- bacteriophage

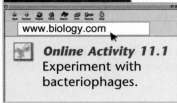

What's Online

www.biology.com

Online Activity 11.1 Experiment with bacteriophages.

Scientists identified DNA as a chemical in the nucleus of cells more than 100 years ago. Even so, Mendel, Morgan, and other early geneticists did all their work without any knowledge of how DNA played a role in heredity. How biologists learned that DNA is the genetic material is one of the great stories of science.

Griffith's "Transforming Factor" Is the Genetic Material

The story opens in 1928. British biologist Frederick Griffith was studying two forms, or strains, of a bacterial species: one strain caused a kind of pneumonia fatal to mice, while the other strain was harmless. Figure 11-1 shows each step in Griffith's experiments. When he injected heat-treated bacteria into mice, the mice remained healthy. Heat kills the deadly strain of the bacterium, making it harmless.

Griffith's important discovery came when he injected mice with a mixture of the harmless strain and the heat-treated deadly strain. Since neither of these treatments on its own could kill the mice, he expected the mice to survive. However, the mixture killed the mice. Some of the harmless bacteria had been "transformed," becoming deadly. Furthermore, Griffith discovered that all of the descendants of the transformed bacteria inherited the killer trait. Clearly, some substance in the deadly strain remained active despite the heat treatment. This substance caused a heritable change in the other strain.

▼ **Figure 11-1** Griffith showed that although a deadly strain of bacteria could be made harmless by heating it, some factor in that strain is still able to change other harmless bacteria into deadly ones. He called this the "transforming factor."

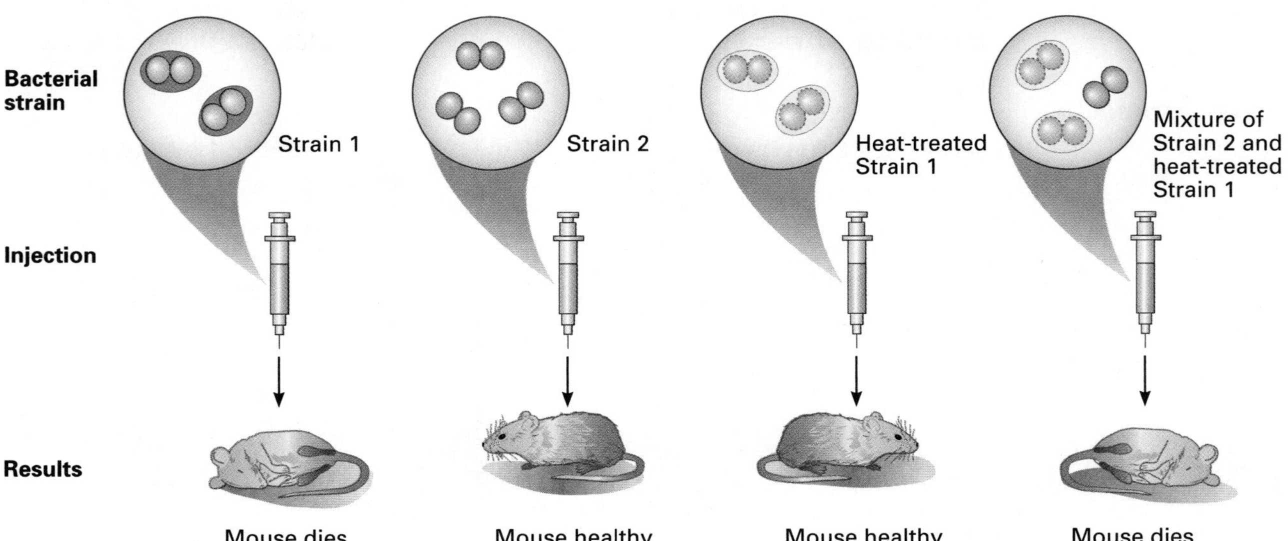

Avery Shows DNA Is the Transforming Factor

Other scientists began to search for this "transforming factor." Attention focused on two types of chemicals: protein and DNA. These chemicals were the most likely candidates because scientists already knew that chromosomes, which function in inheritance, consist of protein and DNA. In 1944, American biologist Oswald Avery and his colleagues took Griffith's experiments one step further. To test whether protein was the transforming factor, they treated Griffith's mixture of heat-treated deadly strain and live harmless strain with protein-destroying enzymes. The bacterial colonies grown from the mixture were still transformed. Avery and his colleagues concluded that protein could not be the transforming factor. Next, they treated the mixture with DNA-destroying enzymes. This time the colonies failed to transform. Avery concluded that DNA is the genetic material of the cell (Figure 11-2). As the experiments of Griffith and Avery illustrate, science is a process in which discoveries often build upon the results of previous experiments.

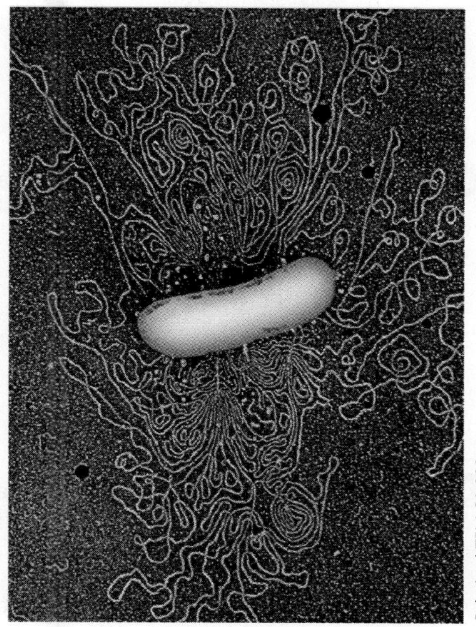

▲ **Figure 11-2** This colorized micrograph shows a bacterium surrounded by its DNA, which was expelled as a result of a modern chemical treatment. Though Avery could not "see" a bacterium's DNA in this manner, he provided evidence that DNA is the "transforming factor."

Virus Experiments Provide More Evidence

Despite Avery's findings, many scientists remained skeptical that genes were made of DNA rather than protein. Proteins are made of 20 different amino acid building blocks. DNA, on the other hand, has only four nucleotide building blocks. Many people thought DNA seemed too simple to account for the large variety of traits inherited by organisms. Which one, DNA or protein, was truly the hereditary material? In 1952, biologists Alfred Hershey and Martha Chase provided more evidence to distinguish between these two possibilities. They conducted a series of experiments using viruses.

A **virus** is a package of nucleic acid wrapped in a protein coat. Unlike living things, viruses are not made of cells. Also, a virus can only reproduce by infecting a living cell with its genetic material. The viral genetic material then directs the cell's machinery to make more viruses. A virus that infects bacteria is called a **bacteriophage** (bak TEER ee oh fayj), or phage for short (Figure 11-3). You'll read more about viruses in Chapter 16.

Hershey and Chase knew that the particular phage they worked with has two basic components: DNA on the inside, coated with protein on the outside. One of these components must be the hereditary material, but which one? They devised an experiment to determine which part of the phage, the DNA or the protein,

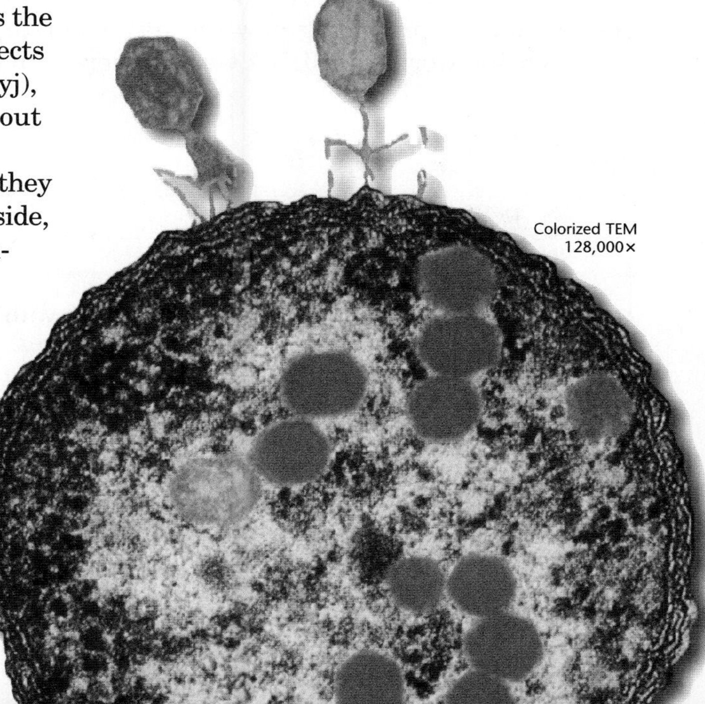

▶ **Figure 11-3** This colorized micrograph shows phages (orange) injecting a bacterial cell with their genetic material. Notice the new phages forming inside the bacterial cell.

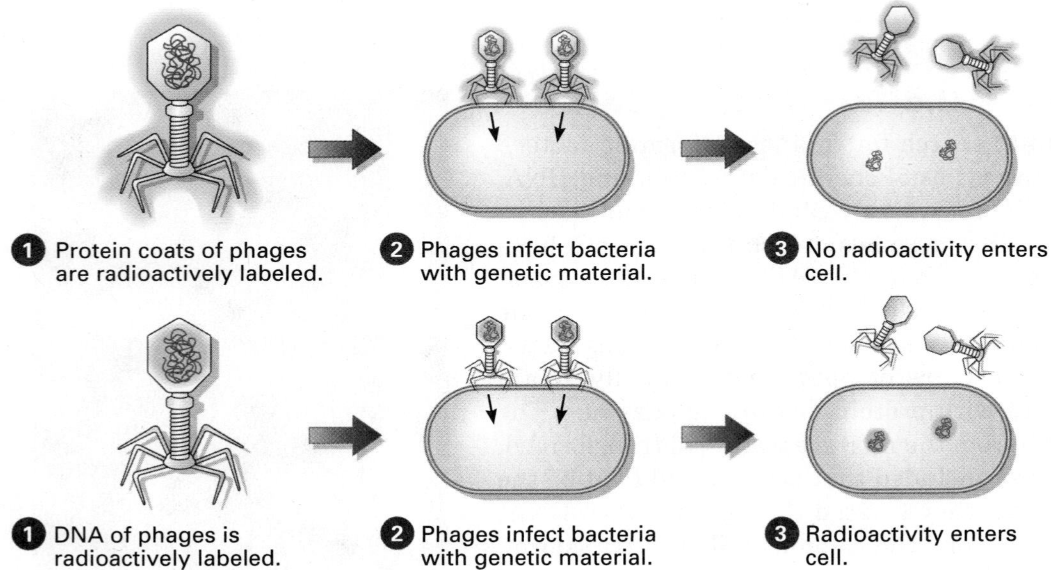
1 Protein coats of phages are radioactively labeled.
2 Phages infect bacteria with genetic material.
3 No radioactivity enters cell.
1 DNA of phages is radioactively labeled.
2 Phages infect bacteria with genetic material.
3 Radioactivity enters cell.

▲ **Figure 11-4** Hershey and Chase offered further evidence that DNA, not proteins, is the genetic material. Only the DNA of the old generation of viruses is incorporated into the new generation.

enters a bacterium and directs it to make more phages. For one batch of infecting phages, they used a radioactive isotope of sulfur to label only the phages' protein coats. (Sulfur is an element found in proteins but not in DNA.) In another batch of phages, they used a radioactive isotope of phosphorus to label only DNA. (Phosphorus is an element found in DNA but not in proteins.)

Next, they allowed each batch of phages to infect separate cultures of nonradioactive bacterial cells. They then whirled each culture in a blender to shake loose any parts of the phages that remained outside the bacterial cells. They measured radioactivity in the loose phage parts and in the bacterial cells.

When only phage protein coats were labeled, most of the radioactivity was detected outside the cells (Figure 11-4). But when phage DNA was labeled, most of the radioactivity was detected inside the cells.

Hershey and Chase concluded that the phage's DNA entered the bacterial cell during infection, but the proteins did not. They further concluded that DNA must carry the genetic information responsible for producing new phages. Their results convinced the scientific world that DNA was the hereditary material.

Online Activity 11.1

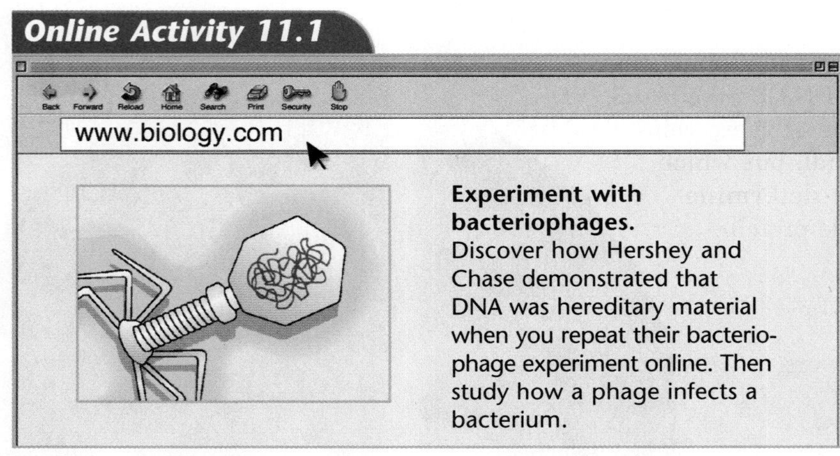
Back Forward Reload Home Search Print Security Stop
www.biology.com

Experiment with bacteriophages.
Discover how Hershey and Chase demonstrated that DNA was hereditary material when you repeat their bacteriophage experiment online. Then study how a phage infects a bacterium.

Concept Check 11.1

1. How did Griffith's experiments indicate the presence of a "transforming factor" in bacteria?
2. What did Avery's experiments add to the knowledge gained from Griffith's experiments?
3. Describe the experimental design that allowed Hershey and Chase to distinguish between the two options for genetic material.

CONCEPT 11.2 Nucleic acids store information in their sequences of chemical units.

OBJECTIVES
- Identify the building blocks of DNA.
- Describe DNA's structure and the rules for base pairing in DNA.

KEY TERMS
- deoxyribonucleic acid (DNA)
- nucleotide
- nitrogenous base
- pyrimidine
- purine
- double helix

What's Online

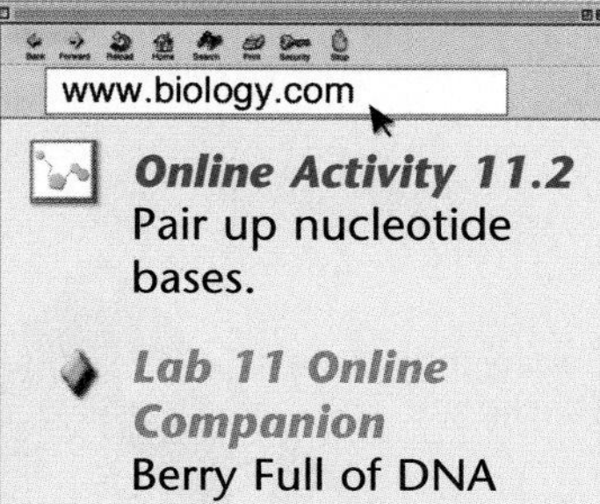

Online Activity 11.2
Pair up nucleotide bases.

Lab 11 Online Companion
Berry Full of DNA

Once most biologists were convinced that DNA is the genetic material, new questions arose. What is it about the specific arrangement of atoms that gives DNA its unique properties? How is DNA able to store genetic information, copy it, and pass it from generation to generation? The challenge became one of determining how the structure of this molecule could account for its role in heredity.

The Building Blocks of DNA

The heritable genetic information of an organism is stored in the molecule called **deoxyribonucleic acid (DNA).** DNA is a kind of nucleic acid, a polymer built from monomers called nucleotides. Another group of nucleic acids, called ribonucleic acids (RNAs), also plays a key role in cells. You will learn about the function of RNAs later in this chapter.

Nucleotides are the building blocks (the monomers) of nucleic acid polymers. Only four types of nucleotides make up DNA. Examine the chemical structure of a single nucleotide in Figure 11-5. Notice that each nucleotide has three parts:

1. A ring-shaped sugar called deoxyribose
2. A phosphate group (a phosphorus atom surrounded by four oxygen atoms)
3. A **nitrogenous base** (ny TRAW juhn us): a single or double ring of carbon and nitrogen atoms with functional groups (*nitrogenous* means "nitrogen-containing")

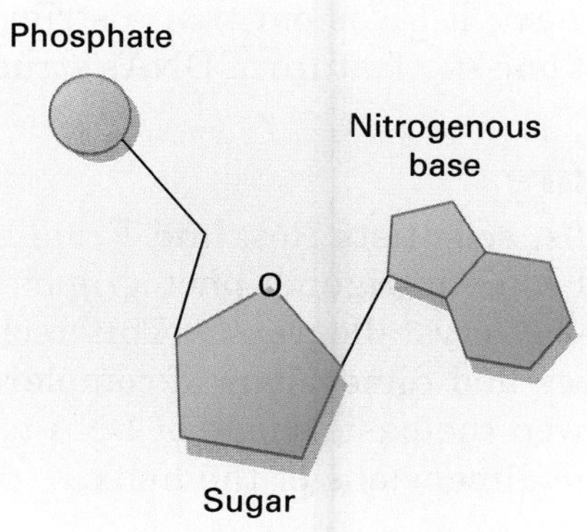

Figure 11-5 A nucleotide has three components: a sugar, a phosphate group, and a nitrogenous base.

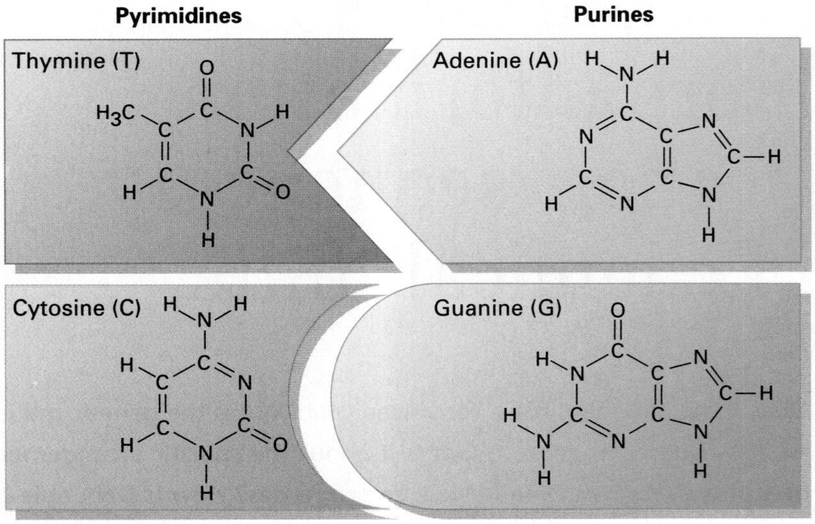

Pyrimidines

Thymine (T)

Cytosine (C)

Purines

Adenine (A)

Guanine (G)

◀ **Figure 11-6** DNA contains four different nitrogenous bases. Thymine and cytosine have single-ring structures. Adenine and guanine have double-ring structures.

Nitrogenous Bases The four nucleotides found in DNA differ only in their nitrogenous bases, called bases for short (Figure 11-6). The bases thymine (T) and cytosine (C) are single-ring structures called **pyrimidines** (py RIM uh deenz). Adenine (A) and guanine (G) are larger, double-ring structures called **purines** (PYOOR eenz). The one-letter abbreviations stand for both the bases alone and for the nucleotides containing them.

DNA Strands Nucleotides are joined to one another by covalent bonds that connect the sugar of one nucleotide to the phosphate group of the next. This repeating pattern of sugar-phosphate-sugar-phosphate is called a sugar-phosphate "backbone." The nitrogenous bases are lined up along this backbone (Figure 11-7).

Just as amino acid monomers combine and form a polypeptide, the nucleotides of a nucleic acid polymer can combine in many different sequences. For example, the part of a nucleic acid shown in Figure 11-7 has nine nucleotides arranged in the order CTGCTATCG. This arrangement is only one of many possible. Since nucleotide chains also vary in length, from only a few hundred nucleotides to millions of nucleotides, the number of possible nucleotide sequences is essentially unlimited.

For years, people wondered how strings of nucleotides could serve as the hereditary material. As you will read next, it turns out that a string of nucleotides is just one key feature of DNA's structure.

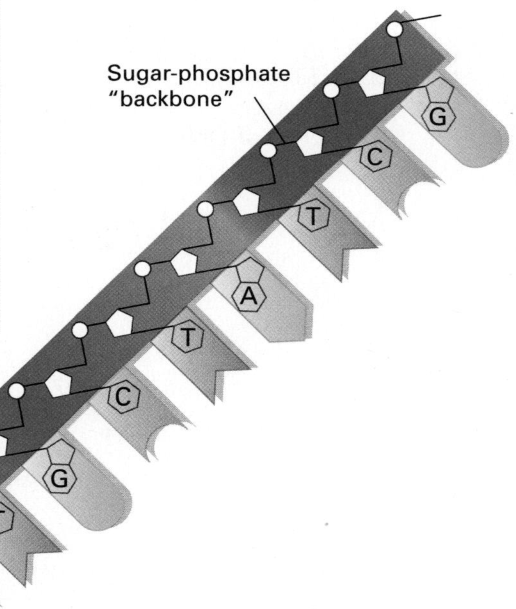

▲ **Figure 11-7** Nucleotide monomers join together by covalent bonds between the sugar of one nucleotide and the phosphate of the next, forming a sugar-phosphate backbone.

DNA's Structure

In the early 1950s, scientists Rosalind Franklin and Maurice Wilkins produced some intriguing photographs of DNA using a method called X-ray crystallography. This technique provides clues to the shapes and dimensions of complex molecules. The photographs showed the basic shape of DNA to be a helix, and revealed the basic dimensions of the helix.

The Double Helix Meanwhile, scientists James Watson and Francis Crick modeled DNA's structure with tin and wire. Their early models failed to explain DNA's chemical properties. Then one day, Watson saw one of Franklin's X-ray crystallography photos of DNA. Using the clues provided by Franklin's work, Watson and Crick created a new model in which two strands of nucleotides wound about each other. This formed a twisting shape called a **double helix** (Figure 11-8). Their model placed the sugar-phosphate backbones on the outside of the double helix and the nitrogenous bases on the inside. They hypothesized that the nitrogenous bases that aligned across the two strands formed hydrogen bonds. This new model successfully represented DNA's structure.

▲ **Figure 11-8** Watson (left) and Crick are shown with their model of DNA's structure—the double helix. The bases pair up between the two intertwined sugar-phosphate backbones. A pairs with T, and G pairs with C.

Complementary Base Pairs Watson and Crick realized that the individual structures of the nitrogenous bases determine very specific pairings between the nucleotides of the two strands of the double helix. These pairings are due to the sizes of the bases and their abilities to form hydrogen bonds with each other. The purine adenine pairs with the pyrimidine thymine, and the purine guanine pairs with the pyrimidine cytosine. In the biologist's shorthand, A pairs with T, and G pairs with C. A is also said to be "complementary" to T, and G is complementary to C. So, while the *sequence* of nucleotides along the length of one of the two DNA strands can vary in countless ways, the bases on the second strand of the double helix are determined by the sequence of the bases on the first strand. Each base must pair up with its complementary base. Base-pairing rules set the stage for understanding how the information in DNA is passed through generations, as you will learn in Concept 11.3.

In 1953, Watson and Crick described their model in a two-page article in the science journal *Nature*. Few milestones in the history of biology have been as important as the discovery of the double helix and the pairing of complementary bases.

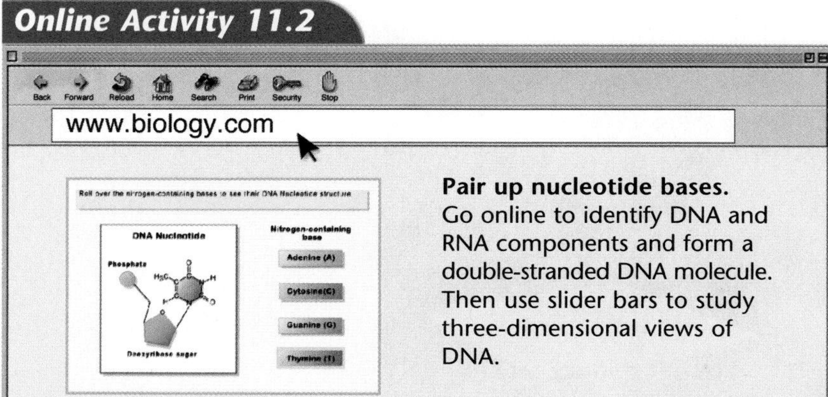

Online Activity 11.2
Back Forward Reload Home Search Print Security Stop
www.biology.com
DNA Nucleotide
Phosphate
Deoxyribose sugar
Nitrogen-containing base
Adenine (A)
Cytosine (C)
Guanine (G)
Thymine (T)
Pair up nucleotide bases.
Go online to identify DNA and RNA components and form a double-stranded DNA molecule. Then use slider bars to study three-dimensional views of DNA.

Concept Check 11.2

1. What are the three parts of a nucleotide? Which parts make up the backbone of a DNA strand?
2. List the two base pairs found in DNA.
3. If six bases on one strand of a DNA double helix are AGTCGG, what are the six bases on the complementary section of the other strand of DNA?

Berry Full of DNA

Exploring Properties of Strawberry DNA

Question What properties of DNA can be observed in a test tube?

Lab Overview In this investigation you will break open strawberry cells, prepare a filtered extract containing strawberry DNA, and separate out molecules of DNA in a test tube.

Preparing for the Lab To help you prepare for the lab, go to the *Lab 11 Online Companion.* Explore the parts of a plant cell in which DNA molecules are located. Prepare for the lab procedure by previewing the steps you will take.

Completing the Lab Use your Laboratory Manual or lab page printouts from the *Lab 11 Online Companion* to do the investigation and draw conclusions from the observations you made. **CAUTION:** *Be sure to follow your teacher's instructions and all safety guidelines in the investigation.*

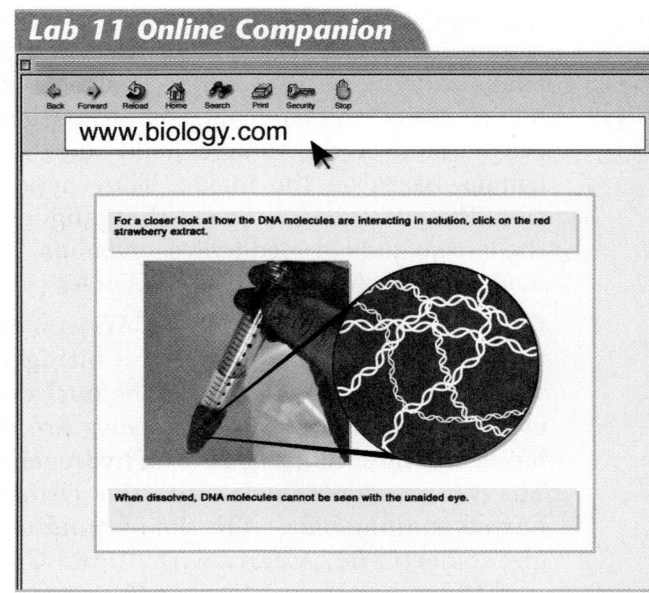
Lab 11 Online Companion
Back
Forward
Reload
Home
Search
Print
Security
Stop
www.biology.com
For a closer look at how the DNA molecules are interacting in solution, click on the red strawberry extract.
When dissolved, DNA molecules cannot be seen with the unaided eye.

CONCEPT 11.3 DNA replication is the molecular mechanism of inheritance.

OBJECTIVES
- Explain how the template mechanism is important in DNA replication.
- Describe the process of DNA replication.

KEY TERMS
- DNA replication
- DNA polymerase

What's Online

Have you ever had additional copies of a favorite photo made from a photo negative? Even if you've lost your negative, a new negative can be made from your print, from which more prints can be made. In this section, you'll read how this same principle enables a cell to make a copy of its genetic material.

The Template Mechanism

When a cell divides, forming new cells, a complete set of genetic instructions is generated for each new cell. And when an organism reproduces, genetic instructions pass from one generation to the next. For this to occur, there must be a means of copying the instructions. Long before DNA was identified as the genetic material, some people proposed that gene-copying must be based on a template mechanism. A template mechanism works like the negative and photograph example described in the introduction. The cell somehow uses a "negative" of the DNA to make more DNA.

Watson and Crick's model for DNA structure immediately suggested to them that DNA-copying involved a template mechanism. Their hypothesis was based on the specific pairing rules of complementary bases: A pairs with T, and G pairs with C. If you know the sequence of bases on one strand of DNA, you can determine the sequence on the other by applying these rules.

Watson and Crick's hypothesis was confirmed by experiments performed in the 1950s. During DNA copying, the two strands of the double helix separate. Each single strand acts as a "negative" for producing a new, complementary strand (Figure 11-9). Nucleotides line up one at a time across from the existing strand as predicted by the base-pairing rules. Enzymes link the nucleotides together to form the two new DNA strands, called daughter strands. This process of copying the DNA molecule is called **DNA replication.**

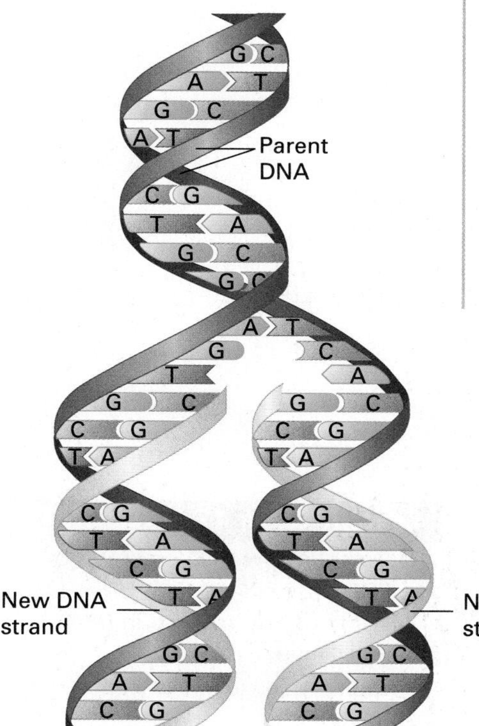

Figure 11-9 During DNA replication, the two strands of the original (parent) DNA molecule, shown in blue, each serve as a template for making a new strand, shown in yellow. Replication results in two daughter DNA molecules, each consisting of one original strand and one new strand.

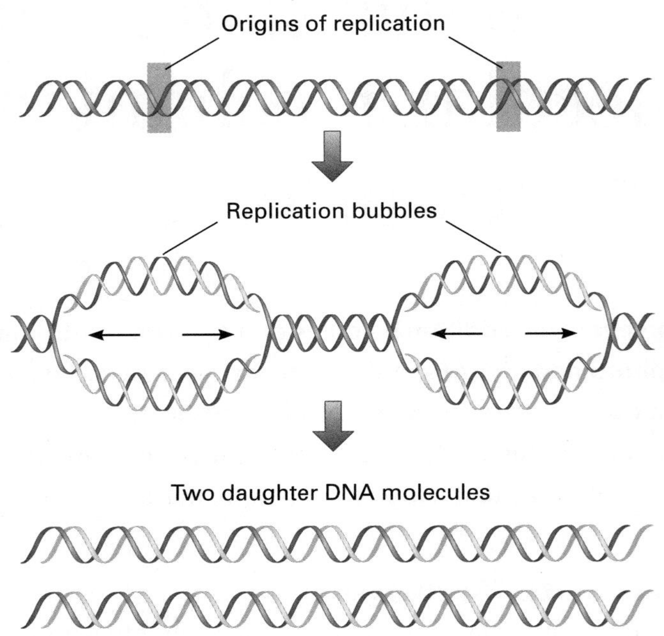

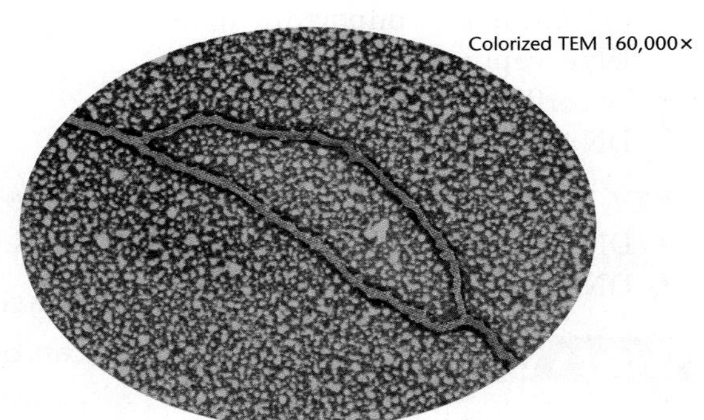

▲ **Figure 11-10** DNA replication begins at origins of replication and proceeds in both directions, producing "bubbles," like the one shown above. Eventually, all the bubbles merge, resulting in two separate daughter DNA molecules.

Replication of the Double Helix

More than a dozen enzymes are involved in DNA replication. Each "incoming" nucleotide pairs with its complementary nucleotide on the parent strand. Enzymes called **DNA polymerases** (PAHL ih mur ayz ez) make the covalent bonds between the nucleotides of the new DNA strand. The process is fast and amazingly accurate—an error occurs in only about one of a billion nucleotides.

DNA replication begins at specific sites called origins of replication. The copying proceeds outward in both directions, creating replication "bubbles" (Figure 11-10). The parent DNA strands open up as daughter strands grow on both sides of each bubble. A eukaryotic DNA molecule has many origins where replication can start at the same time. This shortens the total time to copy all the DNA. Eventually, all the bubbles merge, yielding two double-stranded DNA molecules, each with one new and one old strand.

DNA replication occurs before a cell divides, ensuring that the cells in a multicellular organism all carry the same genetic information. It is also the mechanism for producing the DNA copies that offspring inherit from parents during reproduction.

Online Activity 11.3

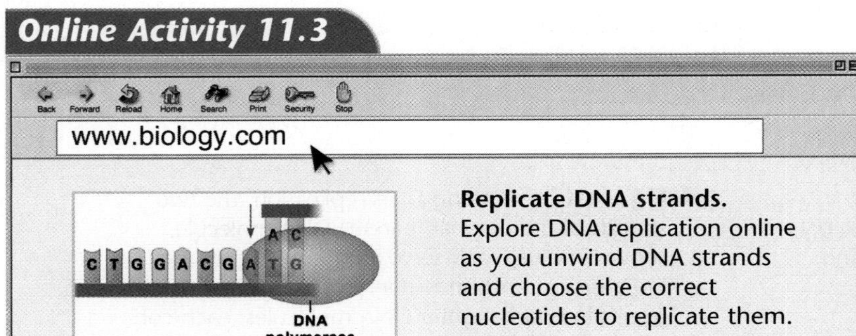

Replicate DNA strands.
Explore DNA replication online as you unwind DNA strands and choose the correct nucleotides to replicate them.

Concept Check 11.3

1. Describe how DNA replicates by using a template.
2. List the steps involved in DNA replication.
3. Under what circumstances is DNA replicated?

CONCEPT 11.4 A gene provides the information for making a specific protein.

OBJECTIVES

- Explain the "one gene–one polypeptide" hypothesis.
- Trace the information flow from DNA to protein.
- Describe how amino acids are coded.

KEY TERMS

- RNA (ribonucleic acid)
- transcription
- translation
- codon

What's Online

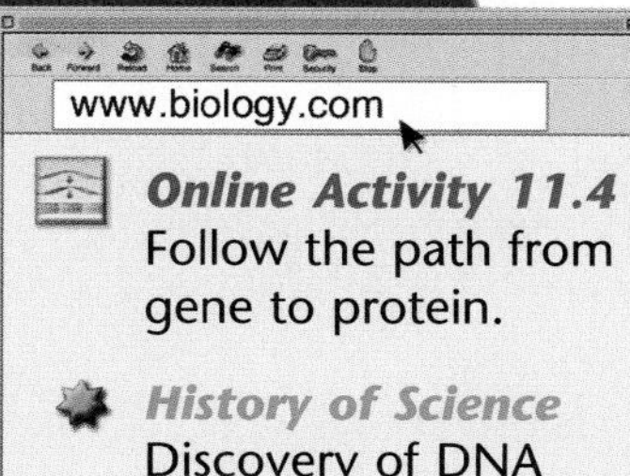

When you were younger, did you ever use codes to send secret messages to your friends? Your first codes might have had simple rules such as using the alphabet backwards or using numbers to represent letters. Perhaps you developed codes with even more complex rules. Code-breaking can be an interesting challenge. Just think of the challenges scientists faced in breaking the genetic code.

One Gene, One Polypeptide

With the structure of DNA in mind, you can now put into molecular terms the concepts of genotype and phenotype you learned about in Chapter 10. An organism's *genotype,* its genetic makeup, is the sequence of nucleotide bases in its DNA. The molecular basis of the *phenotype,* the organism's specific traits, lies in proteins and their wide variety of functions. What is the connection between the DNA that defines the genotype and the proteins that, along with environmental influences, determine the phenotype?

The major breakthrough in demonstrating the relationship between genes and proteins came in the 1940s. American geneticists George Beadle and Edward Tatum worked with the orange bread mold *Neurospora crassa* (Figure 11-11). Beadle and Tatum studied mutant strains of the mold that were unable to grow on the usual nutrient medium. Each of these mutant strains turned out to lack a single enzyme needed to produce some molecule the mold needed, such as a vitamin or an amino acid. Beadle and Tatum also showed that each mutant was defective in a single gene. Their research led them to propose the "one gene–one enzyme" hypothesis. This hypothesis states that the function of an individual gene is to dictate the production of a specific enzyme.

Since then, scientists have learned that most genes actually dictate the production of a single *polypeptide,* which may make up part of an enzyme or another kind of protein. Beadle and Tatum's hypothesis is now generally stated as one gene–one *polypeptide.*

▼ **Figure 11-11** Experiments with mutant strains of the orange bread mold shown here led Beadle and Tatum to propose the "one gene–one enzyme" hypothesis. It is now known that each gene directs the manufacture of a particular polypeptide (which is part of an enzyme or other protein).

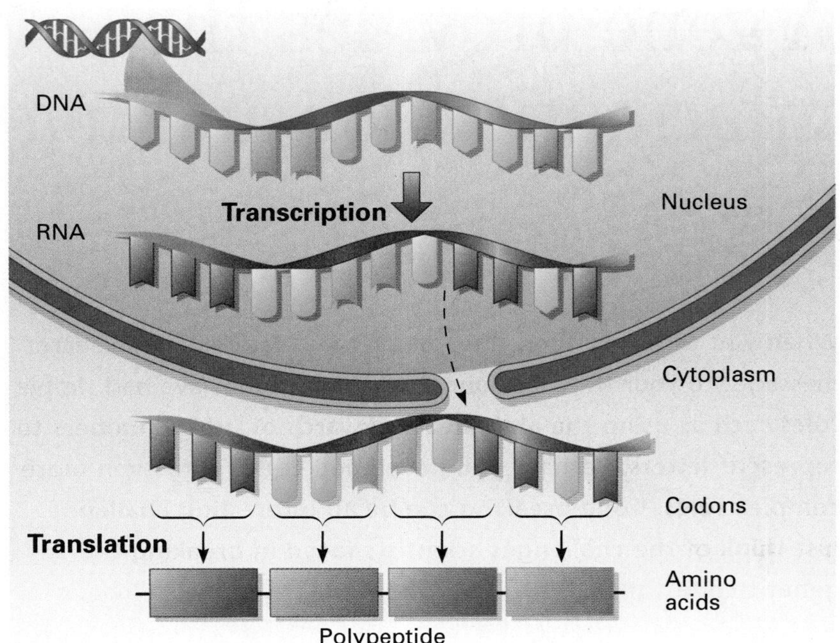

Figure 11-12 Information flows from gene to polypeptide. First, a sequence of nucleotides in DNA (a gene) is transcribed into RNA in the cell's nucleus. Then the RNA travels to the cytoplasm where it is translated into the specific amino acid sequence of a polypeptide.

Information Flow: DNA to RNA to Protein

The language of genes is written as a sequence of bases along the length of a DNA chain. If the bases are the language's letters, each gene is like a sentence. Specific strings of bases make up each gene "sentence" on one DNA strand.

What is the connection between these genes and the polypeptides in a cell? The answer involves RNA, another kind of nucleic acid with a structure similar to that of DNA. **RNA (ribonucleic acid)** is any nucleic acid whose sugar is ribose rather than the deoxyribose of DNA. Another difference between RNA and DNA is that RNA contains a nitrogenous base called uracil (U) instead of the thymine of DNA. Uracil is very similar to thymine, and pairs with adenine. The other components of RNA are the same as those for DNA. RNA typically forms a single, sometimes twisted strand, not a double helix like DNA.

Several RNA molecules play a part in the intermediate steps from gene to protein. In the first step, DNA's nucleotide sequence is converted to the form of a single-stranded RNA molecule in a process called **transcription** (Figure 11-12). This "transcribed" message leaves the nucleus and directs the making of proteins in the cytoplasm, while the DNA remains in the nucleus.

When a reporter transcribes a speech, the language remains the same. However, the form of the message changes from spoken language to written language. Similarly, when DNA is transcribed, the result is RNA—a different form of the same message. The next step, however, does require changing languages. Much as English can be translated into Russian, genetic **translation** converts nucleic acid language into amino acid language. The flow of information from gene to protein is based on codons. A **codon** is a three-base "word" that codes for one amino acid. Several codons form a "sentence" that translates into a polypeptide.

History of Science

Back Forward Reload Home Search Print Security Stop

www.biology.com

Discovery of DNA

Stories about the latest advances in DNA science are reported nearly every day in the news. Although DNA is nearly as old as life itself, what people know about it has been discovered in only the last hundred years. Go online to learn about the people and the experiments behind the current understanding of DNA.

The Triplet Code

What are the rules for translating the nucleotide sequence of RNA into an amino acid sequence? In other words, which codons are translated into which amino acids? American biochemist Marshall Nirenberg began cracking this code in the early 1960s. He built an RNA molecule that only had uracil nucleotides, called "poly U." (Recall that RNA has U instead of T.) Because it contained only uracil nucleotides, it contained only one type of codon: UUU, repeated over and over. Nirenberg added poly U to a test-tube mixture containing all 20 amino acids, plus the enzymes and other chemicals required for building polypeptides. The result was translation of the poly U into a polypeptide consisting entirely of a single kind of amino acid: phenylalanine. Nirenberg concluded that the RNA codon UUU codes for the amino acid phenylalanine (Phe).

Using similar methods, Nirenberg and others determined the amino acids represented by each codon. As Figure 11-13 shows, 61 of the 64 triplets code for amino acids. Notice that some amino acids are coded for by more than one codon, but no codon represents more than one amino acid. For example, codons UUU and UUC both specify phenylalanine, and neither of them ever codes for any other amino acid. The three codons that do not code for amino acids are "stop codons" that come at the end of each gene sequence.

This same genetic coding system is shared by almost all organisms. In experiments, genes can be transcribed and translated after being transferred from one species to another, even when the species are as different as a human and a bacterium! The universal nature of the genetic code suggests that it arose very early in the history of life and has been passed on over time to all the organisms living on Earth today.

▼ **Figure 11-13** Each codon stands for a particular amino acid. (The table uses abbreviations for the amino acids, such as Ser for serine.) The codon AUG not only stands for methionine (Met), but also functions as a signal to "start" translating an RNA transcript. There are also three "stop" codons that do not code for amino acids, but signal the end of each genetic message.

Second base in codon

First base in codon	U	C	A	G	Third base in codon
U	UUU Phe	UCU Ser	UAU Tyr	UGU Cys	U
U	UUC Phe	UCC Ser	UAC Tyr	UGC Cys	C
U	UUA Leu	UCA Ser	UAA Stop	UGA Stop	A
U	UUG Leu	UCG Ser	UAG Stop	UGG Trp	G
C	CUU Leu	CCU Pro	CAU His	CGU Arg	U
C	CUC Leu	CCC Pro	CAC His	CGC Arg	C
C	CUA Leu	CCA Pro	CAA Gln	CGA Arg	A
C	CUG Leu	CCG Pro	CAG Gln	CGG Arg	G
A	AUU Ile	ACU Thr	AAU Asn	AGU Ser	U
A	AUC Ile	ACC Thr	AAC Asn	AGC Ser	C
A	AUA Ile	ACA Thr	AAA Lys	AGA Arg	A
A	AUG Met or start	ACG Thr	AAG Lys	AGG Arg	G
G	GUU Val	GCU Ala	GAU Asp	GGU Gly	U
G	GUC Val	GCC Ala	GAC Asp	GGC Gly	C
G	GUA Val	GCA Ala	GAA Glu	GGA Gly	A
G	GUG Val	GCG Ala	GAG Glu	GGG Gly	G

Online Activity 11.4

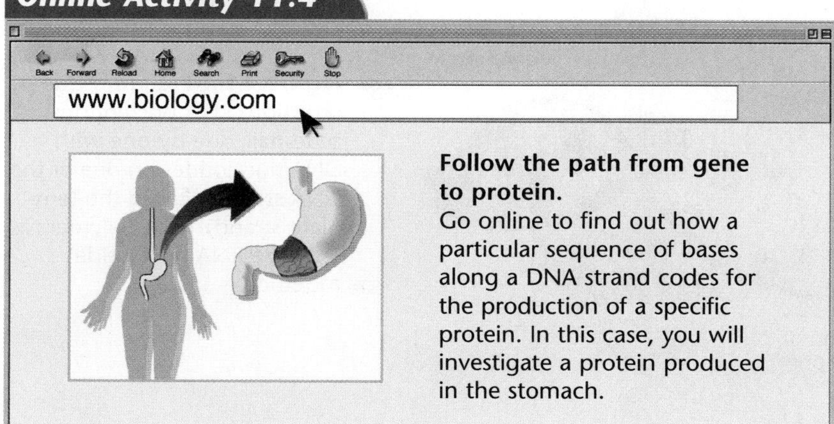

Back
Forward
Reload
Home
Search
Print
Security
Stop
www.biology.com
Follow the path from gene to protein.
Go online to find out how a particular sequence of bases along a DNA strand codes for the production of a specific protein. In this case, you will investigate a protein produced in the stomach.

Concept Check 11.4

1. How did Beadle and Tatum's research result in the "one gene–one polypeptide" hypothesis?
2. Which molecule completes the flow of information from DNA to protein?
3. Which amino acid is coded for by the RNA sequence CUA?
4. List two ways RNA is different from DNA.

CONCEPT 11.5

There are two main steps from gene to protein.

OBJECTIVES

- Describe the process of DNA transcription.
- Explain how an RNA message is edited.
- Describe how RNA is translated to a protein.
- Summarize protein synthesis.

KEY TERMS

- messenger RNA (mRNA)
- RNA polymerase
- intron
- exon
- RNA splicing
- transfer RNA (tRNA)
- anticodon
- ribosomal RNA (rRNA)

What's Online

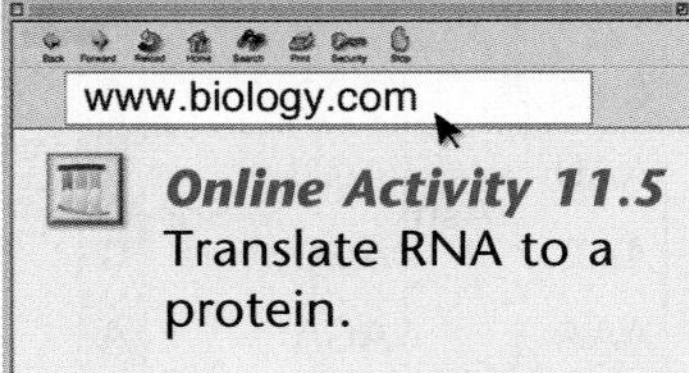

Online Activity 11.5
Translate RNA to a protein.

You have just learned how genetic information flows from DNA to RNA to protein. A sequence of DNA base triplets is transcribed into RNA codons, which are translated into a sequence of amino acids that form a polypeptide. In this section, you will learn the details of the mechanisms of transcription and translation.

Transcription: DNA to RNA

There are three types of ribonucleic acids (RNAs) involved in making proteins from the instructions carried in genes. Starting with transcription, the RNA molecule called **messenger RNA (mRNA)** is transcribed from a DNA template. The transcription process resembles replication of a DNA strand. However, in transcription, only one of the DNA strands serves as a template for the newly forming mRNA molecule. The two DNA strands first separate at the place where transcription will start. Then RNA bases pair with complementary DNA bases (Figure 11-14).

The base-pairing during transcription is the same as when DNA replicates, except that RNA has uracil instead of thymine: the base U in RNA pairs with A in DNA. A transcription enzyme called **RNA polymerase** links the RNA nucleotides together. In the transcription of a gene, specific sequences of DNA nucleotides tell the RNA polymerase where to begin and end the transcribing process.

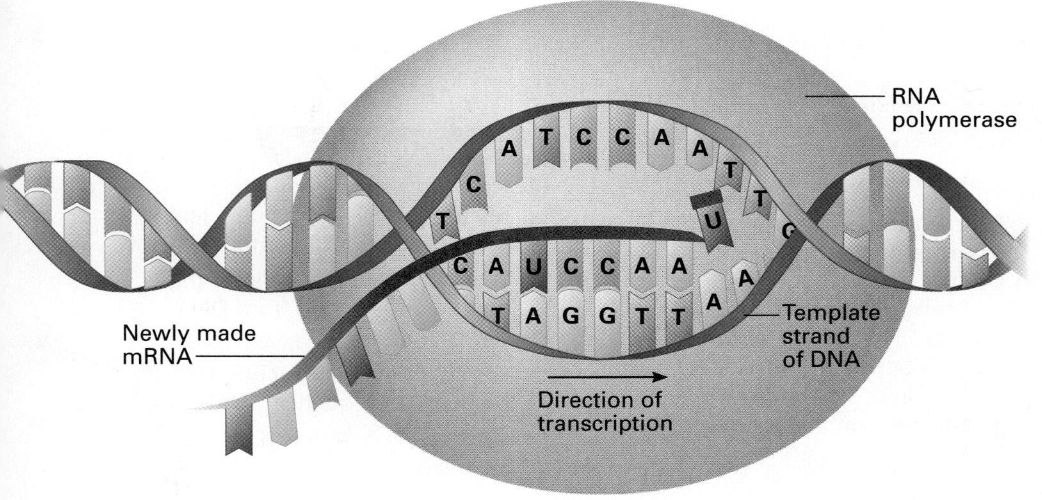

Figure 11-14 During transcription, RNA nucleotides base-pair one by one with DNA nucleotides on one of the DNA strands (called the template strand). RNA polymerase links the RNA nucleotides together.

Editing the RNA Message

In prokaryotic cells, the mRNA transcribed from a gene directly serves as the messenger molecule that is translated into a protein. But this is not the case in eukaryotic cells. In a eukaryotic cell, the RNA transcribed in the nucleus is modified or processed before it leaves the nucleus as mRNA to be translated.

The initial RNA transcripts have stretches of noncoding nucleotides that interrupt nucleotide sequences that actually code for amino acids. It is as if nonsense groups of letters were randomly scattered in an otherwise normal document. Such internal noncoding regions are called **introns,** and are found in most plant and animal genes. (Many researchers are now trying to determine the functions of introns and how they evolved.) The coding regions of the RNA transcript—the parts of a gene that remain in the mRNA and will be translated, or "expressed"—are called **exons.** Before the RNA leaves the nucleus, the introns are removed and the exons are joined together, producing an mRNA molecule with a continuous coding sequence (Figure 11-15). This process is called **RNA splicing.** With splicing completed, the "final draft" of eukaryotic mRNA is ready for translation.

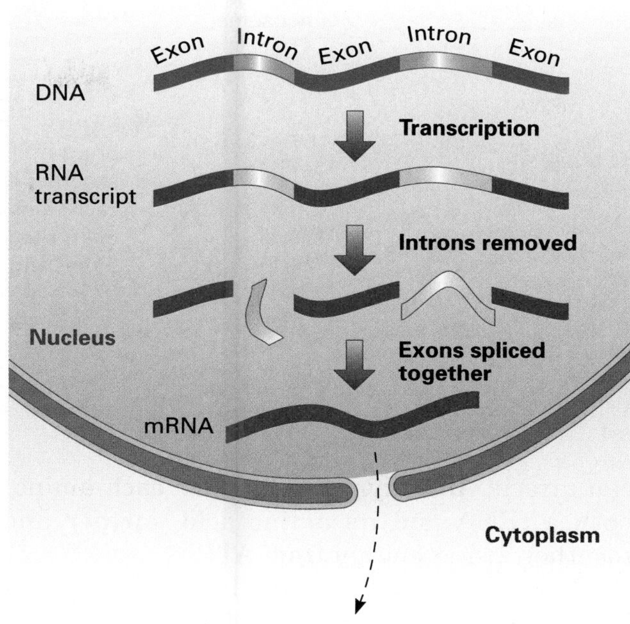

▲ **Figure 11-15** In eukaryotes, the RNA transcript is edited before it leaves the nucleus. Introns are removed, and the exons are spliced together before the "final draft" transcript moves into the cytoplasm where it gets translated.

Translation: RNA to Protein

Translating the nucleic acid language to the protein language is an elaborate process. Like other cellular processes, the translation of mRNA requires enzymes and sources of chemical energy such as ATP. The main players in the mRNA translation process are ribosomes and another kind of RNA called transfer RNA.

The Players Translating one language into another language requires an interpreter. Some person or device must recognize the words of one language and convert them into the other. For the cell, that interpreter is transfer RNA. **Transfer RNA (tRNA)** translates the three-letter codons of mRNA to the amino acids that make up proteins (Figure 11-16).

To perform this task, a tRNA molecule must (1) become bound to the appropriate amino acid and (2) recognize the appropriate codon in the mRNA. The unique structure of tRNA molecules enables them to perform both functions. There is a different version of tRNA molecule that matches each codon.

At one end of the folded tRNA molecule is a specific triplet of bases called an anticodon. The three bases of the **anticodon** are complementary to a specific codon in the mRNA. During translation, the anticodon on tRNA recognizes a particular codon on mRNA by using base-pairing rules. At the other end of the tRNA molecule is a site where a particular amino acid

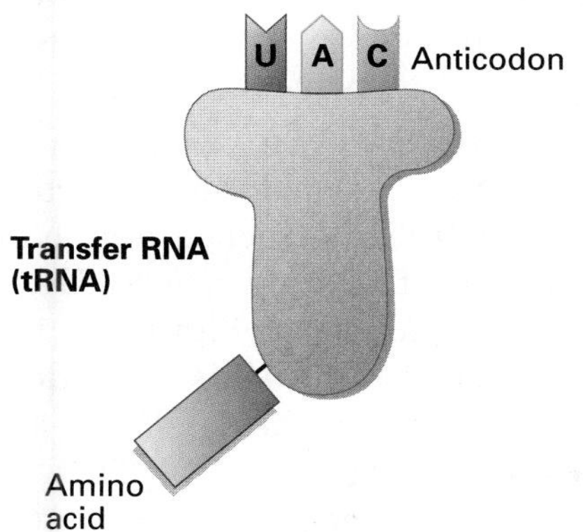

▲ **Figure 11-16** During translation, tRNAs transport and match amino acids to their appropriate codons on the mRNA transcript. One end of the tRNA attaches to an amino acid. At the other end, a triplet of bases called the anticodon matches to the complementary mRNA codon.

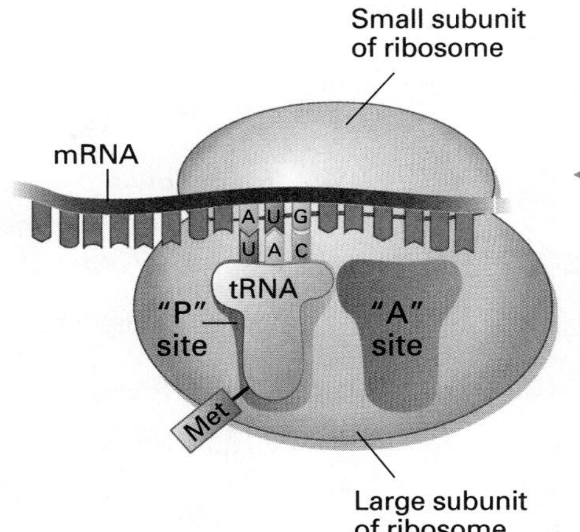

◀ **Figure 11-17** Ribosomes bring mRNA and tRNAs together during translation. Each ribosome has an attachment site for an mRNA transcript, and two sites for tRNAs.

can attach. An enzyme specific for each amino acid recognizes both a tRNA and its amino acid partner and links the two together, using energy from ATP.

The ribosome, an organelle to which you were introduced in Chapter 6, coordinates the functioning of mRNA and tRNA. The ribosome consists of two parts or subunits, each of which is made up of proteins and a considerable amount of yet another kind of RNA, **ribosomal RNA (rRNA).** A complete ribosome has a binding site for mRNA on its small subunit and two binding sites for tRNA on its large subunit (Figure 11-17). The subunits of the ribosome act like a vise, holding the mRNA and tRNA molecules close together.

One of the tRNA-binding sites, the "P" site, holds the tRNA carrying the growing polypeptide chain. The other site, the "A" site, holds a tRNA carrying the next amino acid to be added to the chain. (An easy way to remember which site is which is that "P" stands for "polypeptide" while "A" stands for "amino acid.") The ribosome connects the newly arrived amino acid to the growing polypeptide chain.

The Process The first step in translation brings together all the pieces needed during translation: the mRNA, the first tRNA with its attached amino acid, and the two subunits of a ribosome. The start codon AUG dictates where translation will begin, as shown in Figure 11-17.

Next, amino acids are added one by one to the growing chain of amino acids. Each addition occurs in a three-step process (Figure 11-18). This lengthening process continues until the ribosome reaches a stop codon—UAA, UAG, or UGA. Remember that the three stop codons do not code for amino acids. When a new amino acid fails to arrive at the "A" site, the translation stops. The completed polypeptide, which is typically several hundred amino acids long, is set free by hydrolysis from the tRNA. A single ribosome can make an average-sized polypeptide in less than a minute. The whole process of translation is summarized in Figure 11-19 on the facing page.

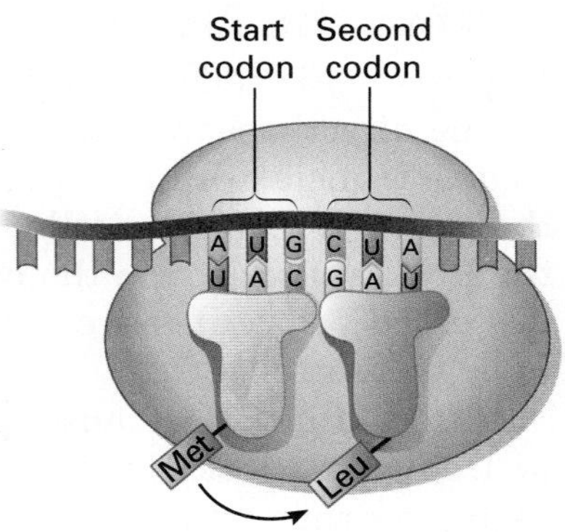

1 Methionine binds to the next amino acid that arrives at the ribosome.

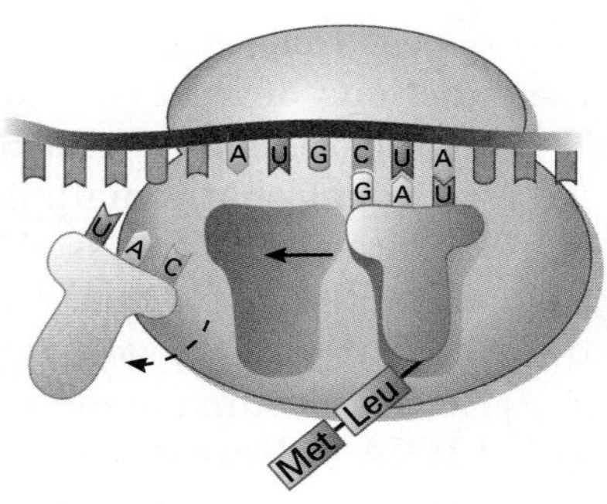

2 The tRNA for methionine leaves the ribosome, and the tRNA holding the polypeptide chain moves to the empty site.

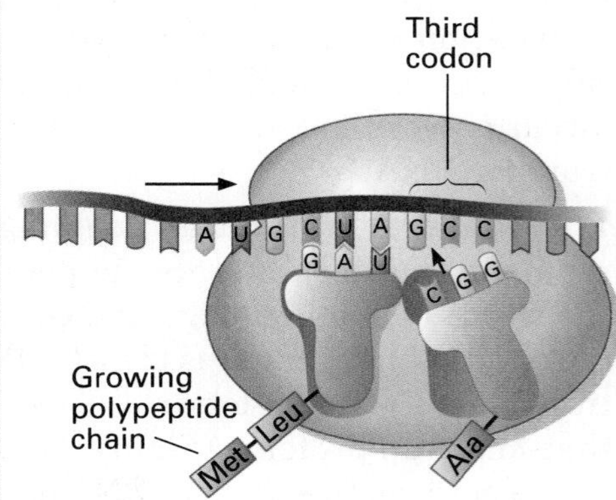

3 The ribosome moves down the mRNA to the next codon.

▲ **Figure 11-18** During translation, the ribosome adds amino acids to the polypeptide chain. The ribosome moves down the transcript, codon by codon, until translation is completed.

Figure 11-19 Translation begins with the attachment of a ribosome and the first tRNA to a "start" (AUG) codon. The ribosome then moves along the mRNA transcript. The polypeptide elongates as an amino acid is added for each codon. When the ribosome arrives at a "stop" codon, the completed polypeptide is released.

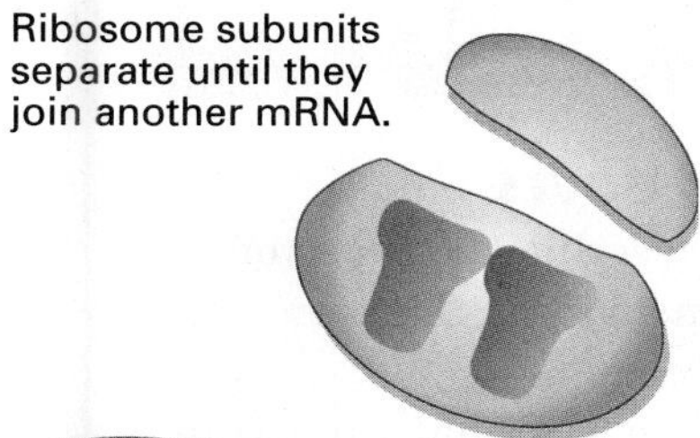

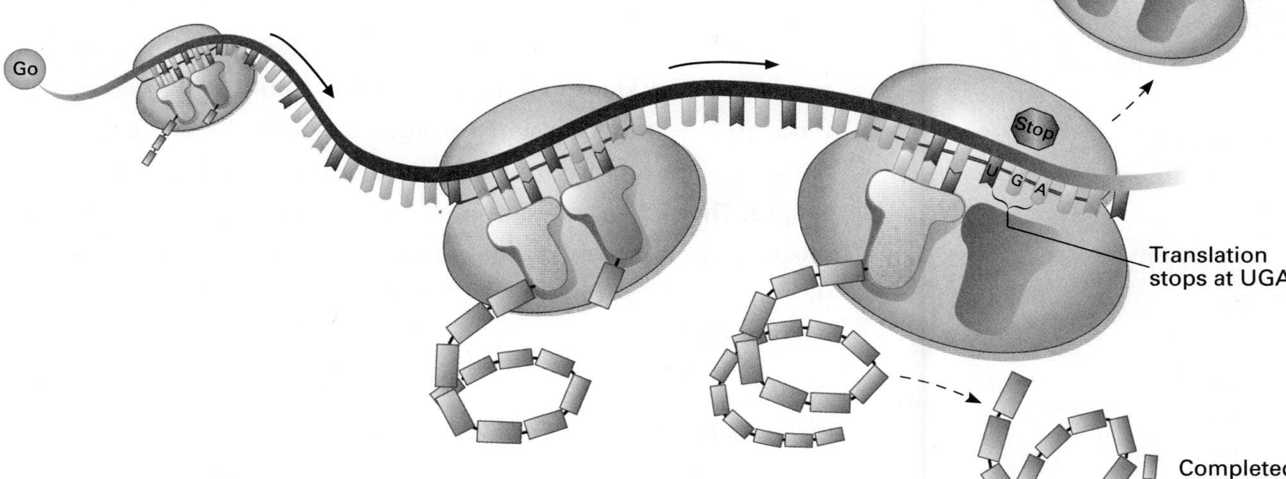

Review of Protein Synthesis

What is the overall significance of transcription and translation? In learning these processes, you now understand how genes are responsible for the polypeptides and proteins that make up the structures and perform the activities of cells. Put more broadly, this is the way that genotype relates to phenotype. The chain of command originates with the information in the DNA of a gene. The DNA serves as a template, dictating transcription of a complementary strand of mRNA. In turn, mRNA specifies the sequence of amino acids in a polypeptide built with the assistance of tRNA and the rRNA of a ribosome. Finally, the proteins that form from the polypeptides determine the appearance and functioning of the cell and of the whole organism.

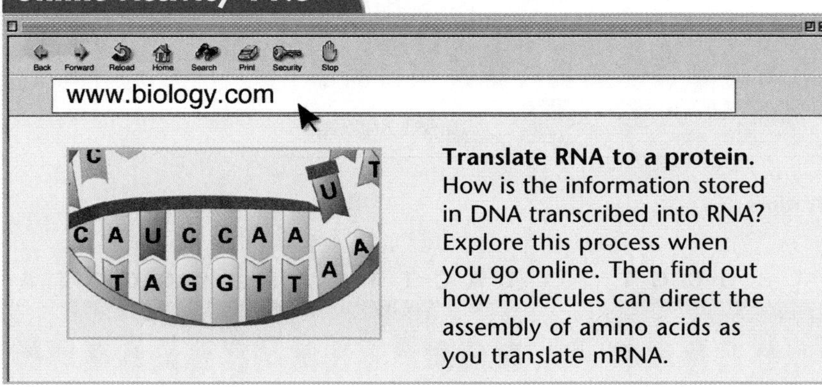

Translate RNA to a protein. How is the information stored in DNA transcribed into RNA? Explore this process when you go online. Then find out how molecules can direct the assembly of amino acids as you translate mRNA.

Concept Check 11.5

1. What kind of nucleic acid is made during transcription?
2. How do introns and exons relate to RNA splicing?
3. List the three RNA types involved in transcription and translation, and describe the role of each.
4. Briefly describe the steps of protein synthesis.

CONCEPT 11.6

Mutations can change the meaning of genes.

OBJECTIVES
- Describe the types of mutations that can affect genes.
- Explain what can cause a mutation.

KEY TERMS
- mutation
- mutagen

What's Online

Online Activity 11.6 Mutate a DNA molecule.

Sickle cell disease is an example of a disorder caused by a genetic mutation. In sickle cell disease, the hemoglobin in red blood cells tends to bind together when oxygen levels are low. The hemoglobin crystals deform the red blood cells into sickle, or crescent, shapes. The sickle-shaped cells clog tiny blood vessels, dangerously blocking the normal flow of blood. The molecular basis for the disease lies in the difference of only one DNA nucleotide out of a 438-base sequence.

How Mutations Affect Genes

A **mutation** is any change in the nucleotide sequence of DNA. Mutations can involve large regions of a chromosome or just a single nucleotide pair, as in the sickle cell allele described above. How can small changes such as altering a single nucleotide in the DNA sequence cause such big changes in the phenotype?

Mutations within a gene can be divided into two general categories: base substitutions and base insertions or deletions. A base substitution is the replacement of one base or nucleotide with another (Figure 11-20a). Occasionally, a base substitution causes no change to a protein, but sometimes it results in a change that affects the function of a protein, sometimes drastically (as in the base substitution leading to sickle cell disease).

How can some base substitutions show no effect on the protein that is made? Remember that in the genetic code, several amino acids have more than one codon. For example, both GAA and GAG code for the same amino acid (Glu). If a mutation to

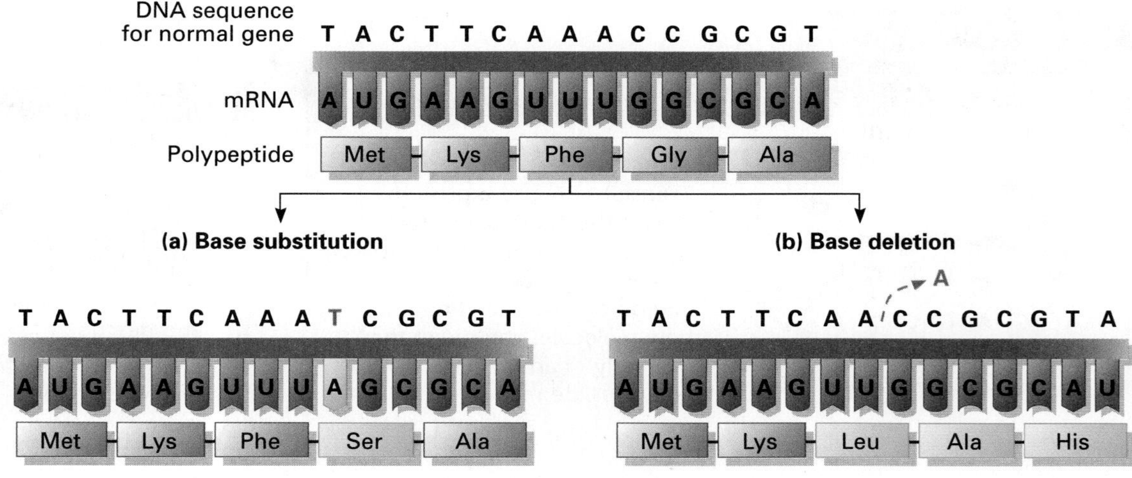

Figure 11-20 There are two general categories of gene mutation: base substitution and base insertion (or deletion). The effect on the resulting polypeptide is shown here, following substitution (a) and deletion (b).

DNA causes the mRNA codon to change from GAA to GAG, no change in the protein product would result. This kind of mutation is called a "silent mutation." Other changes of a single nucleotide may result in an mRNA that codes for an amino acid whose chemical properties are similar enough to the original amino acid that there is little effect on the overall function of the protein.

Insertion or deletion of one or more nucleotides in a gene is usually more disastrous than the effects of a base substitution. Because mRNA is read as a series of triplets, adding or subtracting nucleotides may alter the triplet groupings of the genetic message. Therefore, all the nucleotides that are "downstream" of the mutation will be regrouped into different codons (Figure 11-20b). These new codons code for new amino acids. The result will be a different, and probably nonworking, protein.

What Causes Mutations?

Mutations may occur when errors are made during DNA replication, or when errors are made during chromosome crossovers in meiosis. Physical or chemical agents that cause mutations are called **mutagens** (MYOOT uh junz). One type of physical mutagen is high-energy radiation, such as X-rays and ultraviolet light. One type of chemical mutagen consists of chemicals that are similar to normal DNA bases but cause incorrect base-pairing when incorporated into DNA.

Although mutations are often harmful, they can alter a protein in a way that may be beneficial in certain environments. For example, a genetic mutation is responsible for the dark color seen in some females of the tiger swallowtail butterfly species, *Papilio glaucus* (Figure 11-21). The mutation may be advantageous when the environment includes a related species, the poisonous black swallowtail *Battus philenor.* Predators that avoid eating the black swallowtail may also avoid eating its mimic, the dark form of *P. glaucus.*

If a mutation is present in an organism's gametes, it can be passed on to its offspring. Mutations are the ultimate source of genetic diversity in the living world—a topic you will explore in the next several chapters.

▲ **Figure 11-21** Inheritance of a genetic mutation causes dark-winged butterflies in some populations of tiger swallowtails.

Online Activity 11.6

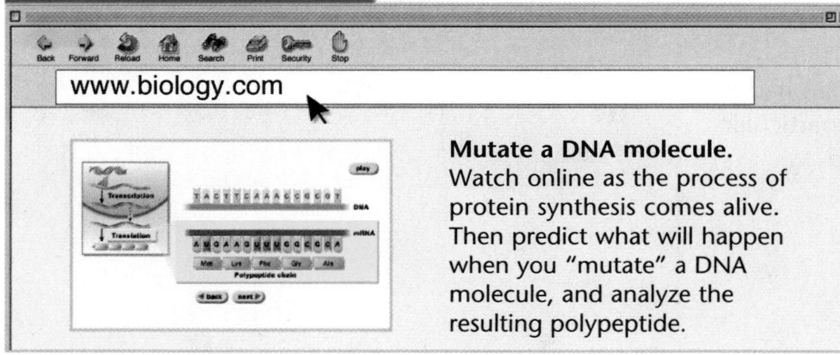

www.biology.com
Mutate a DNA molecule.
Watch online as the process of protein synthesis comes alive. Then predict what will happen when you "mutate" a DNA molecule, and analyze the resulting polypeptide.

Concept Check 11.6

1. Explain why a base substitution is often less harmful than a base deletion or insertion.
2. Describe how a mutation could be helpful rather than harmful.
3. Give an example of a mutagen.

Multiple Choice

Choose the letter of the best answer.

1. The work of several scientists helped to show that the hereditary material is
   a. DNA. b. proteins.
   c. ribosomes. d. codons.

2. The backbone of nucleic acid polymers is composed of
   a. nitrogenous bases and phosphates.
   b. polypeptides.
   c. sugars and phosphates.
   d. nucleotides.

3. Excluding the stop sequence, how many nucleotides are necessary to code for a polypeptide that is 100 amino acids long?
   a. 33 b. 66
   c. 100 d. 300

4. Which of the following occurs first during the process of transcription?
   a. Introns are removed and exons are joined together.
   b. Two DNA strands start to separate.
   c. DNA polymerases join together complementary base pairs.
   d. tRNA translates codons.

5. Stretches of noncoding nucleotides found in RNA transcripts that interrupt coding sequences are called
   a. exons.
   b. codons.
   c. anticodons.
   d. introns.

6. Which of the following does not directly participate in translation?
   a. ribosomes b. tRNA
   c. mRNA d. DNA

7. A geneticist found that a certain mutagen had no effect on the polypeptide coded by a particular gene. This mutagen most likely caused
   a. a silent mutation.
   b. loss of one nucleotide.
   c. addition of one nucleotide.
   d. deletion of a gene.

Short Answer

8. What did Hershey and Chase conclude from their experiments with viruses and bacteria?

9. Explain why DNA's structure is called "the double helix."

10. Describe the rule of complementary base-pairing.

11. What is the function of DNA polymerases in DNA replication?

12. Explain the "one gene–one polypeptide" hypothesis.

13. Identify three differences between the structures of DNA and RNA.

14. Explain why the triplet code is so named.

15. Explain why the RNA transcripts in eukaryotic cells must be edited.

16. Describe the roles of mRNA, tRNA, and the ribosomes during translation.

17. List and describe two types of mutations that can occur within a gene.

Visualizing Concepts

18. Copy the table below that compares the structure and function of DNA and mRNA, and fill in the missing information.

Comparison of DNA and mRNA

	DNA	mRNA
Nitrogenous bases	A, T, G, C	a.
Sugar	b.	c.
Structure	d.	single-stranded polymer
Function	e.	f.

Applying Information

19. Analyzing Diagrams Examine the diagram to answer the questions below.

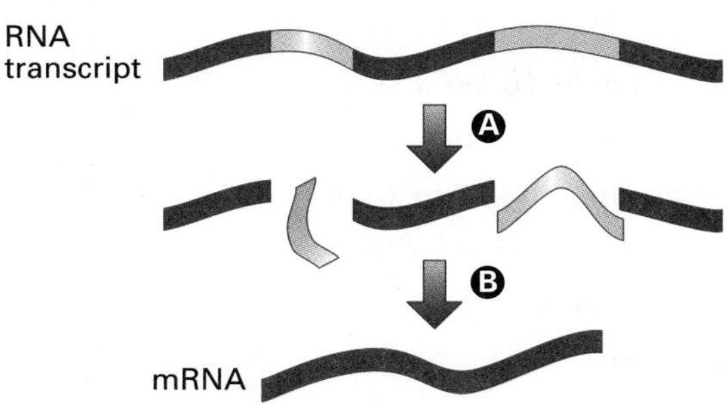

a. Describe what is happening in Step A of the diagram.
b. Describe what is happening in Step B of the diagram.
c. Where in the cell does this process take place?
d. What happens to the mRNA next? Where?

20. Analyzing Diagrams Fill in the missing information in the diagram by answering the questions below.

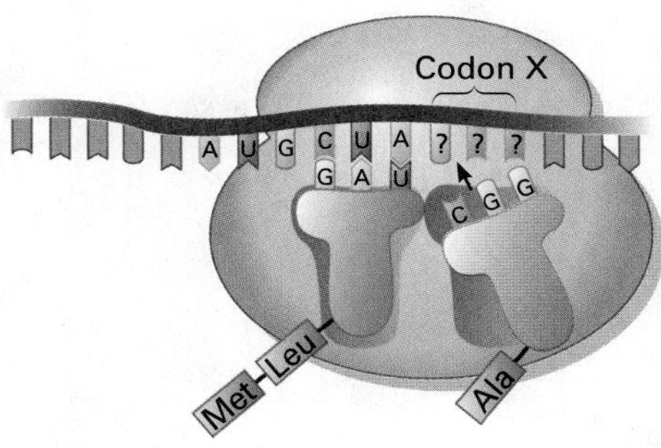

a. What is the name of the process shown?
b. What is the first amino acid in the polypeptide chain?
c. What are the nitrogenous bases in the codon indicated (Codon X)?
d. What type of codon must be reached for the polypeptide to be released?

Critical Thinking

21. Evaluating the Impact of Research Explain why scientists communicate the results of their experiments. Use an example from this chapter.

22. Comparing and Contrasting How are DNA transcription and replication similar and different?

23. Making Generalizations In a variation on Nirenberg's experiment, suppose you made a "poly-C" RNA molecule. What is the composition of the polypeptide it codes for? Note that you will need to refer to Figure 11-13.

24. Problem Solving For the DNA sequence TACCAAGTGAAAATT, write the sequence of its RNA transcript and the sequence of the polypeptide it codes. (Assume the entire RNA transcript is an exon region.) Refer to Figure 11-13.

25. Making Generalizations Summarize how the insertion of a nucleotide in a DNA sequence can change the effectiveness of a protein.

26. What's Wrong With These Statements? *Briefly explain why each statement is inaccurate or misleading.*
a. Viruses inject bacteria with proteins.
b. Some codons can code for more than one amino acid.
c. All mutations have harmful effects on organisms.

Performance Assessment

Writing Write a short biography about one of the scientists mentioned in this chapter. Include a description of this person's contribution to the understanding of DNA's role in genetics.

Online Assessment/Test Preparation

Back Forward Reload Home Search Print Security Stop

www.biology.com

- **Chapter 11 Assessment**
  Check your understanding of the chapter concepts.
- **Standardized Test Preparation**
  Practice test-taking skills you need to succeed.

Human Genetics

At first glance, this graduation scene might appear to be a sea of faces that all look the same. But look closer and you will notice differences among individuals—in the coloring and shape of their features, in their height, and in other characteristics. These differences are partly determined by inheritance. The genetic information lies in the giant library of DNA called the genome.

In this chapter, you'll learn about the challenges biologists face in interpreting the human genome, explore what happens when meiosis doesn't work quite right, and see how Mendel's principles explain many inheritance patterns in humans. Finally, you'll explore the chain of genetic events that can lead to the development of cancer. But first, go online to the *WebQuest* to explore some observable human characteristics that are genetically controlled.

Key Concepts

Concept 12.1 The nucleus contains an information-rich genome.

Concept 12.2 Accidents affecting chromosomes can cause disorders.

Concept 12.3 Mendel's principles apply to humans.

Concept 12.4 Genetic changes contribute to cancer.

Assessment Chapter 12 Review

What's Online

www.biology.com

WebQuest
TraitQuest

Online Activity 12.1
Explore DNA's storage system.

Online Activity 12.2
Discover effects of chromosome changes.

Lab 12 Online Companion
You Are a Cytogeneticist

Online Activity 12.3
Interpret a pedigree.

Careers
Meet a Genetic Counselor

Online Activity 12.4
Explore the DNA–cancer connection.

Chapter 12 Assessment

CONCEPT 12.1

The nucleus contains an information-rich genome.

OBJECTIVES

- Describe how DNA is packed within the nucleus.
- Explain the significance of the Human Genome Project.

KEY TERMS

- genome
- histone

What's Online

Online Activity 12.1
Explore DNA's storage system.

DNA can store a vast amount of information in a tiny space. The DNA in just one set of your chromosomes contains 3 billion base pairs. Therefore, in each of your diploid body cells, the nucleus contains 6 billion base pairs. This information provides the instructions for all the parts and processes that have become you.

DNA Packing in a Single Cell

Each of your chromosomes consists of a single DNA molecule. That DNA molecule is thousands of times longer than the diameter of the nucleus that contains it. If you could straighten out all the DNA molecules in a cell's 46 chromosomes and place them end to end, the DNA would stretch for 2 meters!

The complete set of genetic material in an organism, as defined by the order of bases in the DNA, is called its **genome** (JEE nohm). The genome can fit into the nucleus of a single cell because of DNA's elaborate packing system (Figure 12-1). First, DNA wraps around small proteins called **histones,** much as you might tightly wrap a length of thread around a spool. Next the DNA is wrapped into a tight helical fiber, and then coils further into a thick "supercoil." Looping and folding further compacts the DNA in each chromosome.

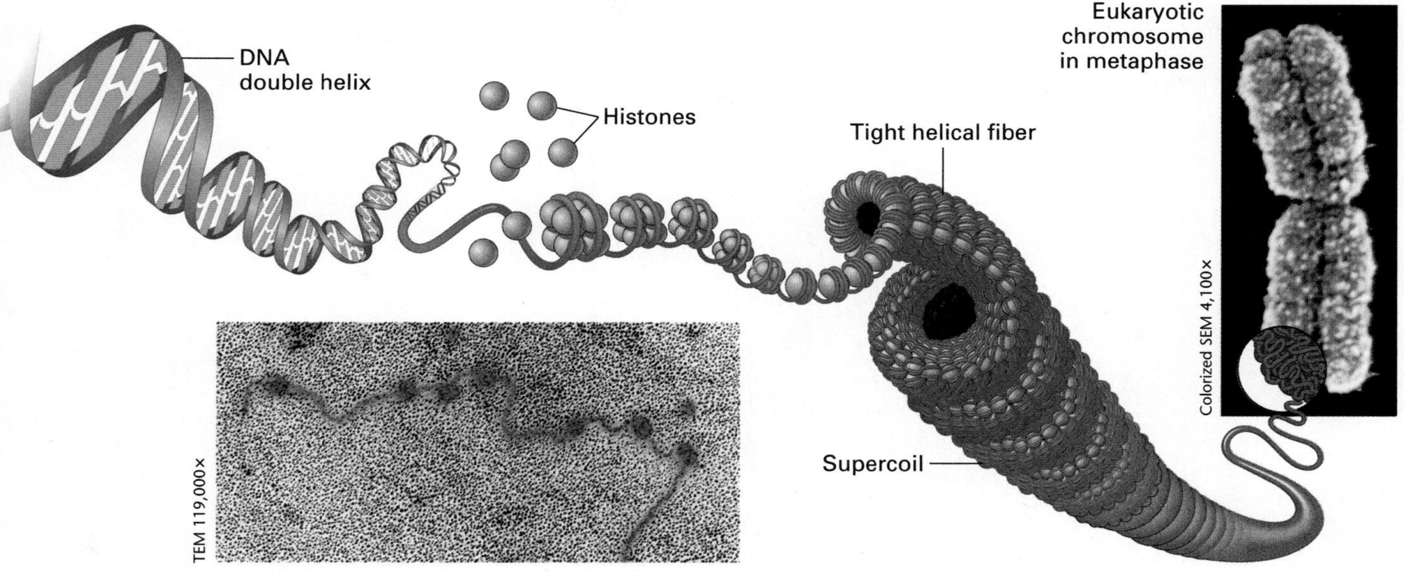

Figure 12-1 An intricate packing system compacts the DNA of each chromosome. In an electron micrograph, the combination of histones and DNA looks like a series of beads on a string.

The Human Genome Project

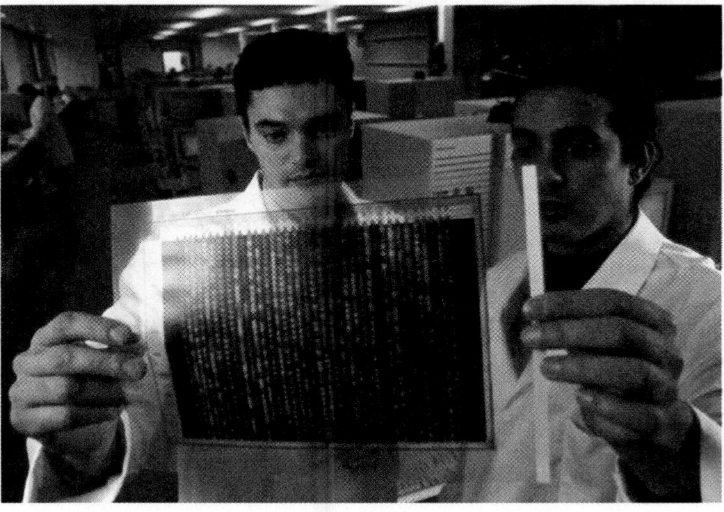

▲ **Figure 12-2** These biologists are analyzing genome data. Such data are providing insight into human development and health.

Now that you have a sense of the amount of DNA in the human genome, consider the difficulty of trying to determine the sequence of all the nucleotides. Recall from Chapter 11 that each polymer in DNA's double helix is a long chain of nucleotides. Each nucleotide contains one of four nitrogenous bases: A, T, G, or C. The order of bases (the sequence) is unique for different species. Even among individuals of the same species, there are small differences in certain regions of the sequence.

By 1990, advances in DNA technology enabled scientists to tackle the challenge of completely sequencing the human genome (Figure 12-2). The government-funded Human Genome Project began. A rough draft of the entire sequence was completed in 2000. Scientists at private companies have contributed data for this huge project as well.

Knowing the sequence of nucleotides is just one step toward understanding the human genome. Regions of DNA that code for polypeptides (the genes) must be distinguished from non-coding regions. Then, the *functions* of the resulting polypeptides must be determined.

The DNA sequences determined by the Human Genome Project are entered into a database that is available to researchers all over the world through the Internet. The potential benefits of having a complete map of the human genome are great. Comparing human sequences with those from other species is already providing insight into human embryonic development and evolutionary relationships. For human health, identifying genes will aid in diagnosing, treating, and possibly preventing many common ailments. These include allergies, diabetes, and cancer. Researchers have already identified hundreds of disease-associated genes.

Online Activity 12.1

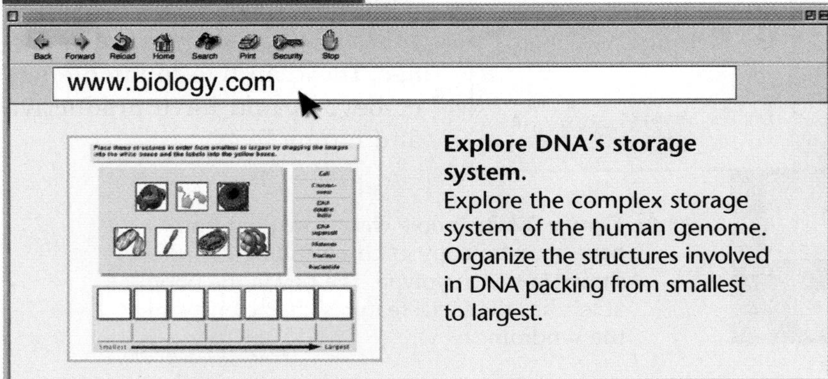

Explore DNA's storage system.
Explore the complex storage system of the human genome. Organize the structures involved in DNA packing from smallest to largest.

Concept Check 12.1

1. Draw a simple diagram showing the different levels of DNA-packing within a nucleus.
2. How might a complete map of the human genome be useful?

CONCEPT 12.2 Accidents affecting chromosomes can cause disorders.

OBJECTIVES

- Relate Down syndrome and nonseparation of chromosomes.
- Describe how chromosomes can be damaged.
- Explain how a "jumping gene" can affect other genes.

KEY TERMS

- trisomy 21
- Down syndrome
- nondisjunction
- duplication
- deletion
- inversion
- translocation
- transposon

What's Online

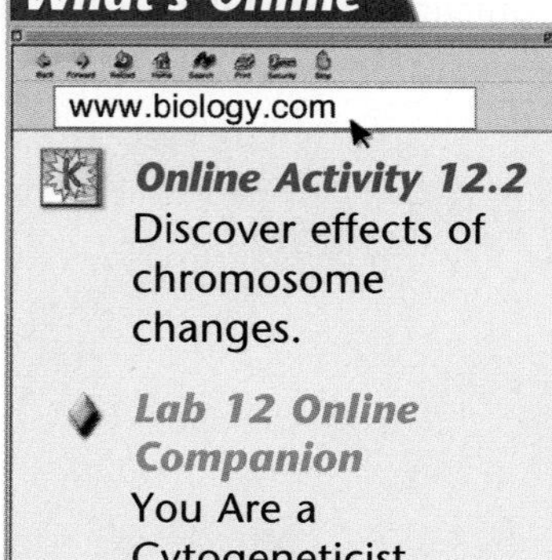

Meiosis occurs repeatedly in a person's lifetime as the testes produce sperm or the ovaries complete production of eggs. Almost always, the meiotic spindle distributes chromosomes to the daughter cells without error. But occasionally an accident occurs that can have serious consequences.

Down Syndrome

In Chapter 9 you read that a normal human karyotype has 46 total chromosomes, or 23 pairs. The karyotype in Figure 12-3 is different. Notice that there are not two, but *three* number 21 chromosomes. This condition is called **trisomy 21** (TRY soh mee). Trisomy 21 results from an error during either stage of meiosis, but most commonly during meiosis I.

In most cases, a human embryo with an abnormal number of chromosomes results in a miscarriage (meaning the embryo does not survive). But many embryos with trisomy chromosome 21 do survive. Trisomy 21 affects about one out of every 700 children born in the United States.

People with trisomy 21 have a general set of symptoms called **Down syndrome,** named after John Langdon Down, who described the syndrome in 1866. These symptoms include certain characteristic facial features and below-average height. Other symptoms typically include heart defects, an impaired immune system, and varying degrees of mental disability. Though people with Down syndrome have lifetimes that are shorter than average, they can live to middle age or beyond and have productive and happy lives.

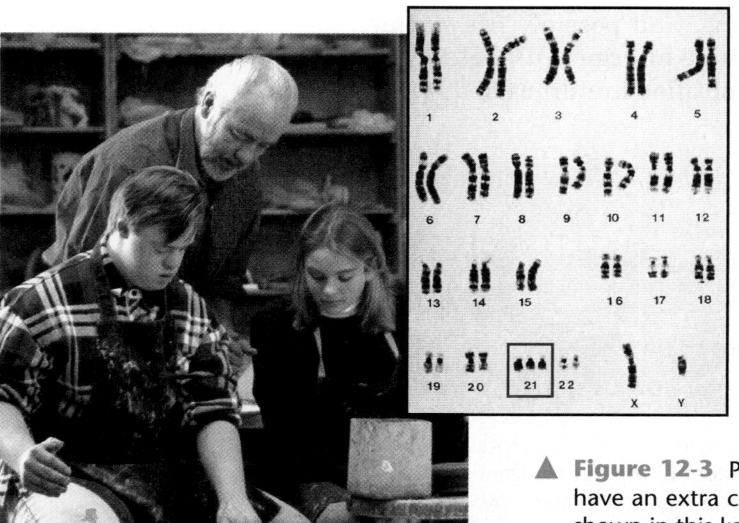

▲ **Figure 12-3** People with Down syndrome have an extra copy of chromosome 21, as shown in this karyotype. The boy in the photo at left has the facial features characteristic of the syndrome.

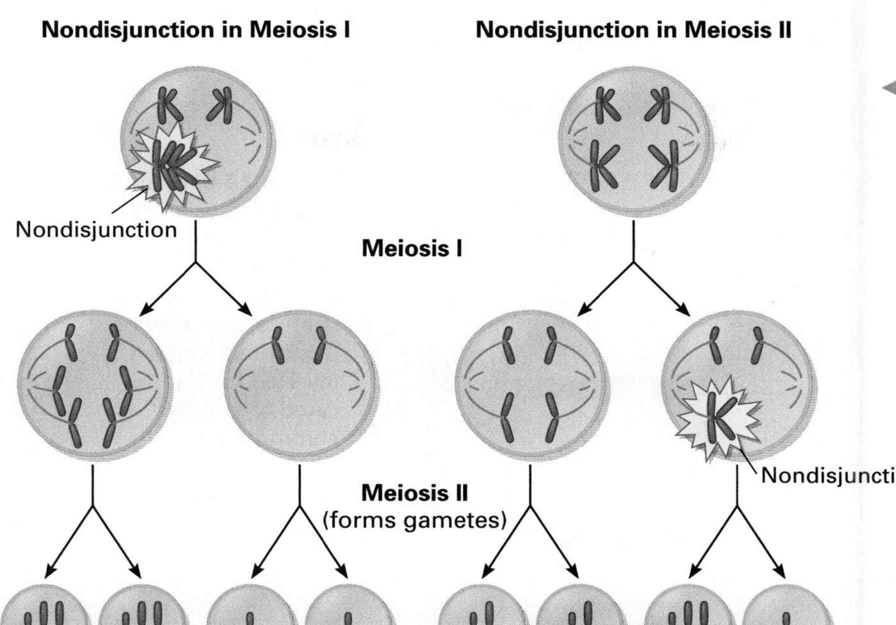

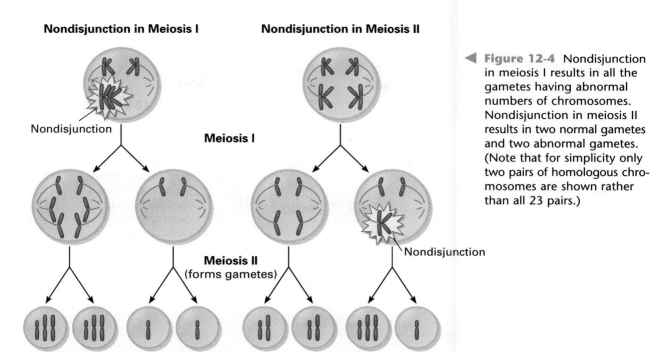

Figure 12-4 Nondisjunction in meiosis I results in all the gametes having abnormal numbers of chromosomes. Nondisjunction in meiosis II results in two normal gametes and two abnormal gametes. (Note that for simplicity only two pairs of homologous chromosomes are shown rather than all 23 pairs.)

Nonseparation of Chromosomes

Trisomy 21 and other errors in chromosome number are usually caused by homologous chromosomes or sister chromatids failing to separate during meiosis, an event called **nondisjunction** (nahn dis JUNK shun). Nondisjunction can occur in anaphase of meiosis I or II, resulting in gametes with abnormal numbers of chromosomes (Figure 12-4). Trisomy 21 can occur when a normal sperm fertilizes an egg cell with an extra chromosome 21, resulting in a zygote with 3 copies of chromosome 21 and a total of 47 chromosomes, instead of the usual 46. As a result of mitosis, all the new cells in the developing embryo will also have 47 chromosomes.

What causes nondisjunction to occur? The answer is not fully understood, but it is known that as a woman gets older, she is more likely to have offspring with trisomy 21 (Figure 12-5). This finding suggests a connection to the time line of egg cell development. Meiosis begins in the pre-egg cells in a girl's ovaries before she is born but then pauses until years later. At puberty, meiosis resumes. Usually only one egg resumes meiosis and is released from the ovaries each month until menopause, at about age 50. This means that a cell might remain stopped in the middle of meiosis for decades. It seems that the longer the time lag, the greater the chance that there will be errors such as nondisjunction when meiosis is finally completed. Some researchers hypothesize that damage to the cell during this lag time contributes to errors in meiosis.

Figure 12-5 As a woman ages, the likelihood of her having a baby with Down syndrome increases.

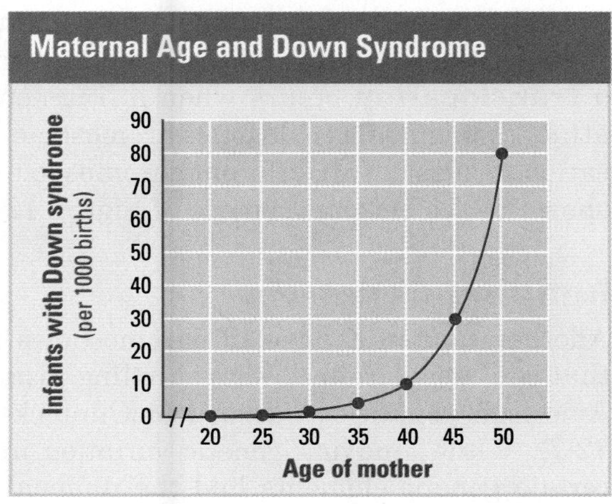

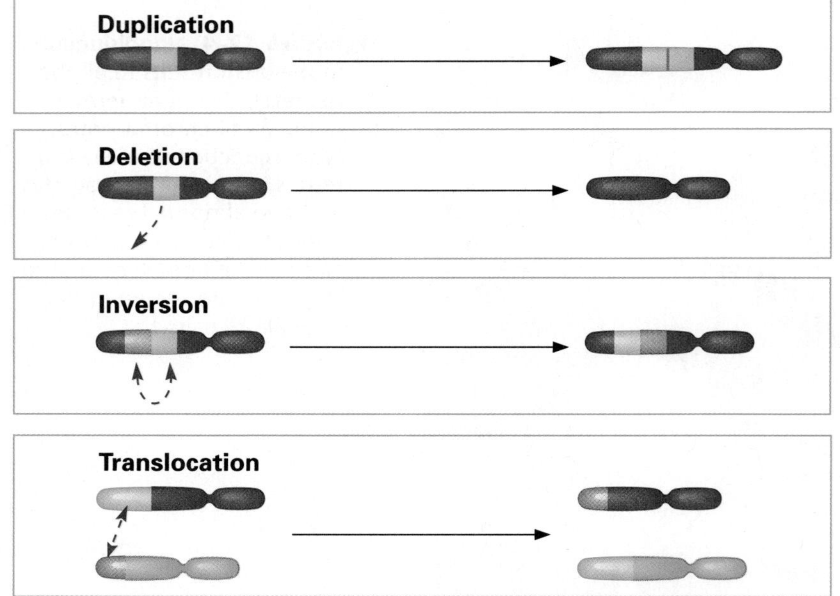

Figure 12-6 Changes to a chromosome's structure may lead to various human disorders. Part of the chromosome may be duplicated, deleted, inverted, or translocated to another chromosome.

Damaged Chromosomes

Even if all chromosomes are present in normal numbers in a cell, changes in chromosome structure may also cause disorders. For example, a chromosome may break, leading to a variety of new arrangements that affect its genes (Figure 12-6).

The first type of change, a **duplication,** occurs when part of a chromosome is repeated. Duplications within certain chromosomes are not always fatal but often result in developmental abnormalities. A second type of change, a **deletion,** occurs when a fragment of a chromosome is lost. Remember that losing a fragment of a chromosome means losing part or all of the genes that code for certain proteins. Those proteins have specific functions in the body. Therefore, as you might expect, large deletions tend to have very serious effects on the body.

Another type of change, an **inversion,** involves reversing a fragment of the original chromosome. Because most of the genes are still present in their normal number, inversions are less likely than deletions or duplications to produce harmful effects. Finally, a **translocation** occurs when a fragment of one chromosome attaches to a nonhomologous chromosome. Sometimes a translocation results in two different chromosomes exchanging parts, as shown in the bottom scenario of Figure 12-6 above.

Jumping Genes

Another type of change in chromosomes involves single genes that can move around. This startling discovery was the work of American geneticist Barbara McClintock in the 1940s (Figure 12-7). While studying genetic variation in corn, she found that certain genetic elements had the unusual ability to move from one location to another in a chromosome. They could even move to an entirely different chromosome. (Note that this is different from a translocation, where a whole piece of the chromosome moves, not just a gene.)

McClintock discovered that these "jumping genes" could land in the middle of other genes and disrupt them. For instance, jumping genes could disrupt pigment genes in corn cells, leading to spotted kernels. McClintock's jumping genes are now called **transposons.** Current evidence suggests that all organisms, including humans, have transposons. In 1983, McClintock received a Nobel Prize for her pioneering work.

Figure 12-8 shows the simplest kind of transposon and how its movement can interfere with another gene. The transposon includes a gene (shown in green) that codes for an enzyme. The enzyme catalyzes movement of the gene by attaching to the ends of the transposon and another site on the DNA. The enzyme then cuts the DNA and catalyzes insertion of the transposon at the new site, sometimes disrupting another gene (shown in red).

▲ **Figure 12-7** Barbara McClintock found that "jumping genes" could cause spotty corn kernels by disrupting the genes controlling pigments in the kernels.

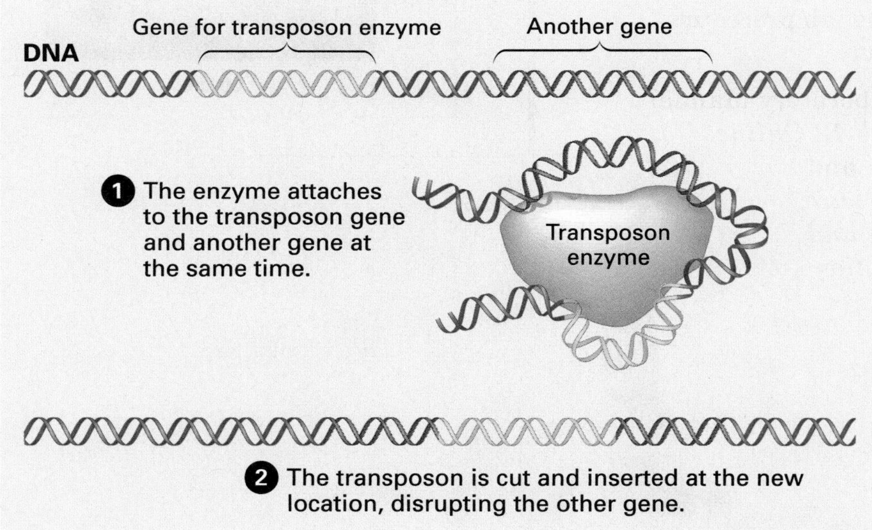

DNA
Gene for transposon enzyme
Another gene
1 The enzyme attaches to the transposon gene and another gene at the same time.
Transposon enzyme
2 The transposon is cut and inserted at the new location, disrupting the other gene.

◀ **Figure 12-8** When a transposon moves to a new site within the genome, it can disrupt another gene.

Online Activity 12.2

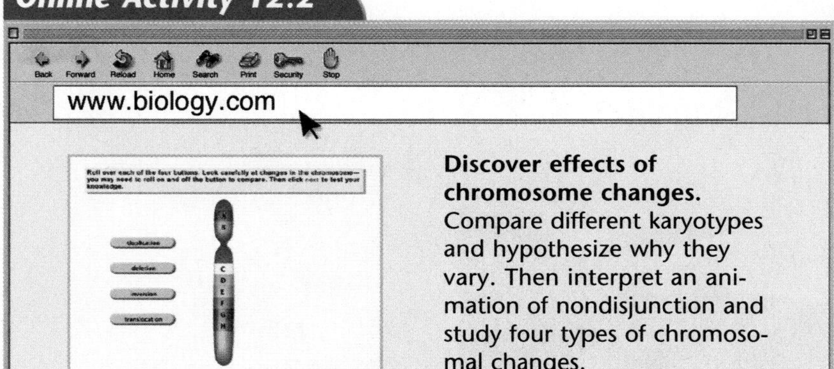

Discover effects of chromosome changes. Compare different karyotypes and hypothesize why they vary. Then interpret an animation of nondisjunction and study four types of chromosomal changes.

Concept Check 12.2

1. What is the relationship between trisomy 21 and Down syndrome? Describe how nondisjunction can result in trisomy 21.
2. List and define four types of damage to chromosome structure that can cause disorders.
3. What is a "jumping gene," or transposon?
4. How is a mother's age related to the probability of nonseparation of chromosomes in her gametes?

You Are a Cytogeneticist

Observing Human Chromosomes

Question What can you learn about chromosome structure and number from observing cultured human cells using cytogenetic (syt oh juh NET ik) techniques?

Lab Overview You will take on the role of a cytogeneticist as you prepare and analyze a chromosome spread from cultured human cells. You will observe human chromosomes and study their different shapes. It is possible that you will observe chromosomal mutations as well.

Preparing for the Lab To help you prepare for the investigation, go to the *Lab 12 Online Companion.* Find out more about the human cells with which you will be working. Prepare for the lab procedure by previewing the steps you will take.

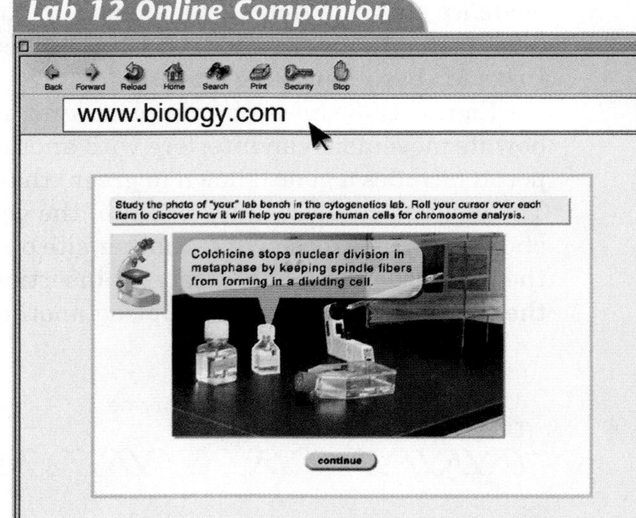
Lab 12 Online Companion
Back Forward Reload Home Search Print Security Stop
www.biology.com
Study the photo of "your" lab bench in the cytogenetics lab. Roll your cursor over each item to discover how it will help you prepare human cells for chromosome analysis.
Colchicine stops nuclear division in metaphase by keeping spindle fibers from forming in a dividing cell.
continue

Completing the Lab Use your Laboratory Manual or lab page printouts from the *Lab 12 Online Companion* to do the investigation and analyze your results. **CAUTION:** *Be sure to follow your teacher's instructions and all safety guidelines in the investigation.*

CONCEPT 12.3 Mendel's principles apply to humans.

OBJECTIVES
- Summarize the information provided in a pedigree.
- Explain how recessive, dominant, and sex-linked disorders are inherited.
- Describe how it is possible to predict certain genetic disorders.

KEY TERMS
- pedigree
- carrier
- genetic counselor

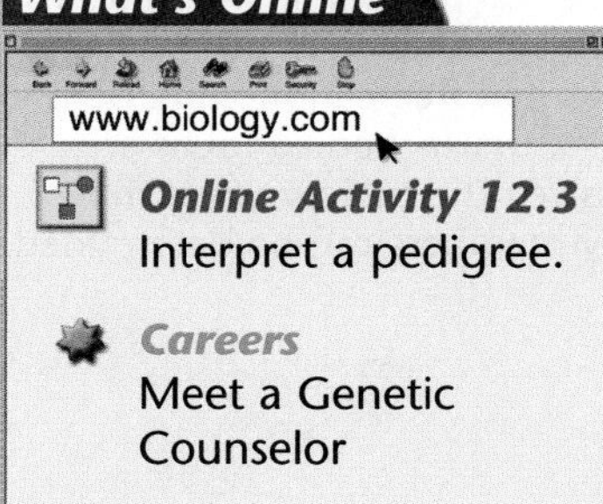

In Chapter 10 you read about Mendel's principles, which explain the inheritance patterns of certain characteristics in organisms. In humans, these principles explain the inheritance of certain alleles that help define individual appearance, as well as those responsible for some diseases.

Working With Human Pedigrees

Unlike researchers working with pea plants or fruit flies, geneticists who study humans cannot control matings to study the resulting offspring! Instead, they must analyze the patterns in existing families. For example, attached earlobes are an inherited trait (Figure 12-9). To study their inheritance, you would first need to collect information about a family's history for the trait. Next you would organize the information in a family tree. Then you could analyze this information by applying Mendel's concepts of dominant and recessive alleles and his principle of segregation.

A **pedigree** is a family tree that records and traces the occurrence of a trait in a family. For example, the pedigree below records the occurrence of attached earlobes in three generations. A typical pedigree uses squares to represent males and circles to represent females. The colored shapes represent individuals that show the trait. Parents are connected by horizontal lines, with their children beneath them. For example, the couple at the top left of the pedigree below had four children: one girl and three boys.

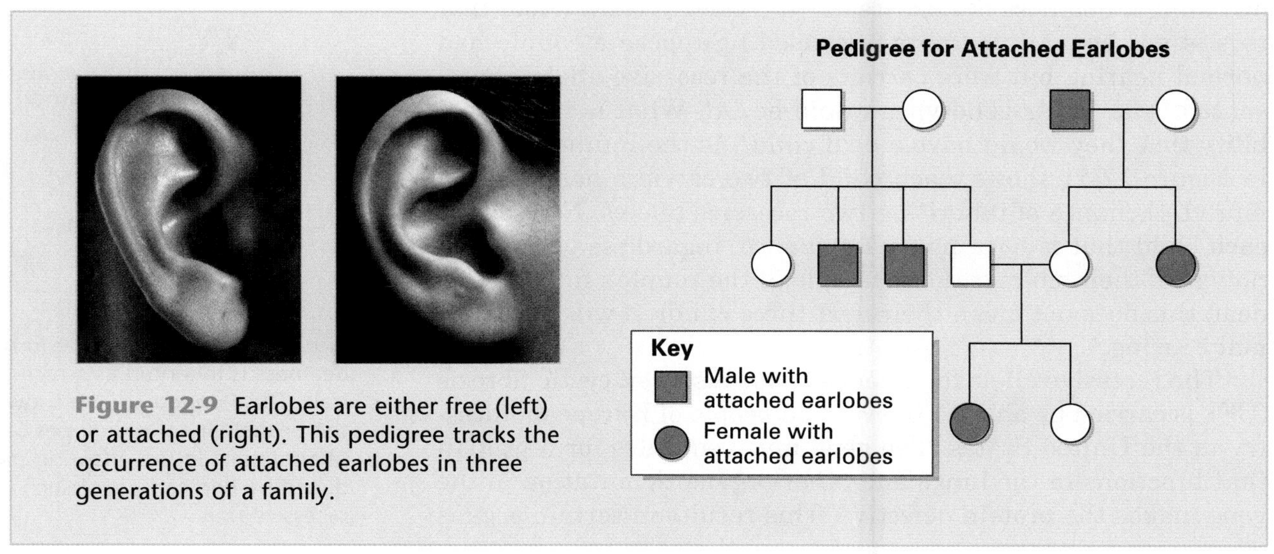

Figure 12-9 Earlobes are either free (left) or attached (right). This pedigree tracks the occurrence of attached earlobes in three generations of a family.

The genotypes of most of the individuals in this pedigree can be determined by examining the pattern in which the trait occurs (Figure 12-10). Notice that the first-born daughter in the third generation has attached lobes, although both of her parents have free earlobes. By applying Mendel's principles, you can figure out that the attached-earlobe trait must therefore be recessive. If the trait for attached earlobes were dominant, then at least one of her parents would have attached earlobes. It is possible to figure out the genotypes for most of the other people in the pedigree in this way. For some individuals, such as the second daughter in the third generation, there is not enough information to determine the genotype.

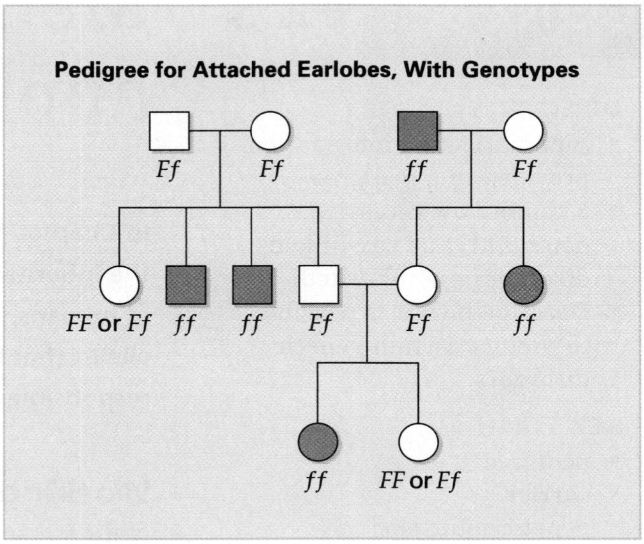

Pedigree for Attached Earlobes, With Genotypes

Ff *Ff* *ff* *Ff*

FF or *Ff* *ff* *ff* *Ff* *Ff* *ff*

ff *FF* or *Ff*

▲ **Figure 12-10** Examining patterns of trait appearance in this pedigree reveals that free earlobes are dominant, and attached earlobes are recessive. The genotypes of most family members can be determined.

Disorders Inherited as Recessive Traits

Pedigree analysis is a more serious matter when the alleles in question cause disabling or lethal (deadly) disorders. Over a thousand human genetic disorders are known to have Mendelian inheritance patterns. Each of these disorders is inherited as a dominant or recessive trait controlled by a single gene. Most human genetic disorders are recessive.

Recessive disorders range in severity. Some such as albinism (lack of skin and hair pigmentation) are not life-threatening. Others such as Tay-Sachs disease, which leads to major nerve damage, are fatal. The vast majority of people with recessive disorders are born to parents who are heterozygous and do not have the recessive disorder. An individual who has one copy of the allele for a recessive disorder and does not exhibit symptoms is a **carrier** of the disorder.

Using Mendel's principles, you can predict the probability that a child of two carriers will have the disorder. For example, one kind of deafness is inherited as a recessive trait. (Note that this is not how all deafness is caused.) Suppose a couple had normal hearing but were carriers of the recessive allele, represented by *d*. Their genotypes would be *Dd*. What is the probability that they would have a deaf child? As the Punnett square in Figure 12-11 shows, each child of two carriers has a one in four (1/4) chance of inheriting two recessive alleles. Notice that each child that is born has a 1/4 chance, regardless of the phenotype of their siblings. For example, if the couple's first child is deaf, this does not mean their next three children will have normal hearing.

The recessive allele for a very serious disorder, cystic fibrosis (CF), is carried by about 1 in every 25 people of European ancestry in the United States. The gene involved codes for a protein that functions in the lungs and other organs. A mutation in the gene makes the protein defective. This results in certain organs

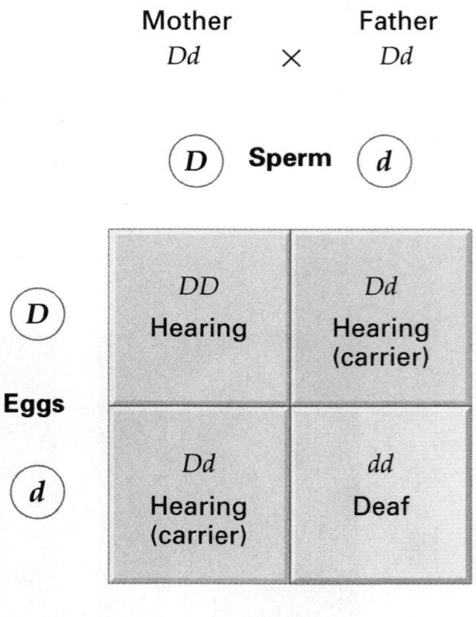

Mother *Dd* × Father *Dd*

Eggs \ Sperm	*D*	*d*
D	*DD* Hearing	*Dd* Hearing (carrier)
d	*Dd* Hearing (carrier)	*dd* Deaf

▲ **Figure 12-11** A particular form of deafness is inherited as a recessive trait. This Punnett square shows the probability of genotypes (and phenotypes) in the offspring produced by two carriers of such a recessive trait.

secreting excessive amounts of very thick mucus. This mucus can interfere with breathing, digestion, and liver function. A person with CF is also particularly vulnerable to pneumonia and other infections. Treatments such as a restricted diet, antibiotics to prevent infection, and exercises to clear the lungs can improve and prolong the lives of people with CF (Figure 12-12).

▲ **Figure 12-12** The girl on the right has cystic fibrosis. In order to raise awareness of the disease, and money for research to find a cure, she toured the major league baseball parks around the United States.

Disorders Inherited as Dominant Traits

A smaller number of human disorders are inherited as dominant traits. One example is being born with extra fingers and toes. A serious dominant disorder is a form of dwarfism called achondroplasia (ay kahn droh PLAY zhuh). The person's torso may develop normally, but the arms and legs are short. About 1 out of 25,000 people has achondroplasia. All individuals with this disorder are heterozygous—they have a single copy of the dominant allele. Inheriting two copies of the allele is fatal. More than 99.99% of the population is homozygous for the normal, recessive allele. This example makes it clear that dominant alleles are not necessarily more plentiful than recessive alleles in a population.

Dominant alleles that are lethal are, in fact, much less common than lethal recessives. This is because for most dominant disorders, the affected person dies before producing any offspring that could inherit the allele. (However, the disorder may return to a population if a natural mutation creates a new copy of the dominant allele in a sperm or egg cell.) In contrast, lethal recessive alleles usually do not have a large effect on heterozygous carriers. As a result, alleles for recessive disorders may pass undetected from generation to generation, until two carriers happen to produce a homozygous offspring with the disorder.

Lethal dominant disorders that don't cause death until adulthood can affect multiple generations of a family. By the time the symptoms show, the person may have already transmitted the lethal gene to his or her children. One example is Huntington's disease (Figure 12-13). Huntington's causes a degeneration of

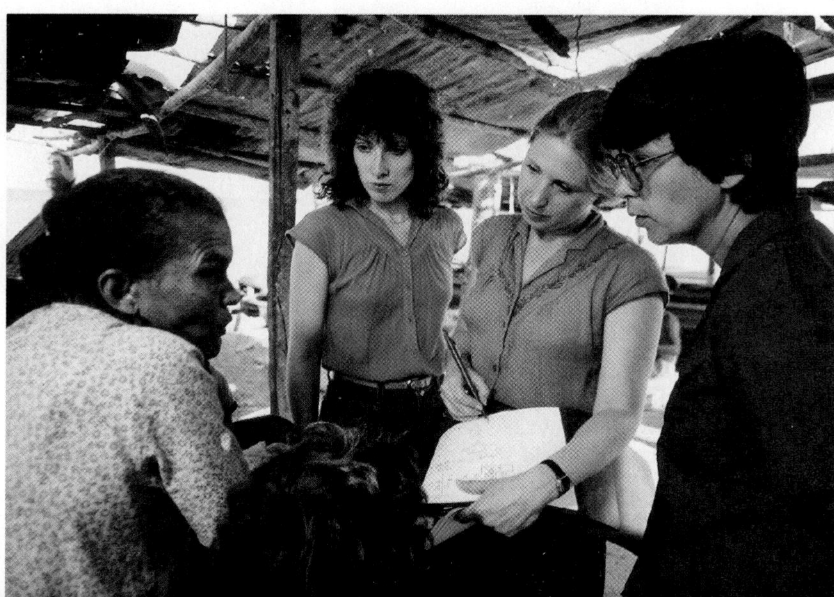

◀ **Figure 12-13** Analyzing numerous pedigrees is an important first step in establishing the inheritance patterns of a particular disease. In this photograph taken in 1983, scientist Nancy Wexler (taking notes) collects pedigree information on Huntington's disease from villagers in Venezuela.

the nervous system that usually does not begin until middle age. As the disease progresses, it causes loss of mental ability and muscle control, and eventually death.

Until recently, it was impossible to tell if a person with a family history of Huntington's disease had actually inherited the allele until the person developed symptoms. But then geneticists tracked the disease allele to chromosome 4 and developed a test to detect it. Researchers now hope to find a treatment that prevents people who carry the allele from ever developing the disease.

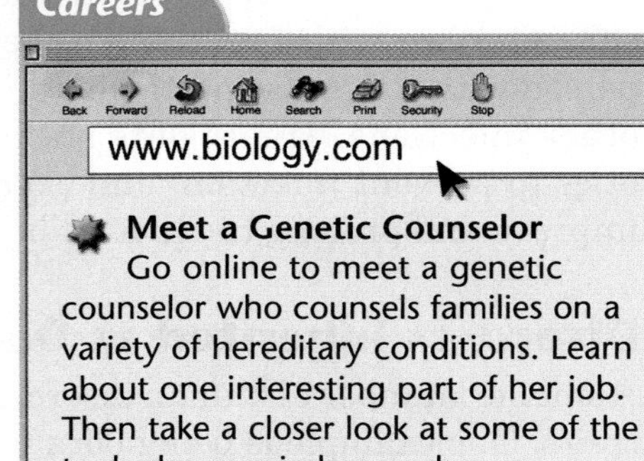

Meet a Genetic Counselor
Go online to meet a genetic counselor who counsels families on a variety of hereditary conditions. Learn about one interesting part of her job. Then take a closer look at some of the tools she uses in her work.

Sex-linked Disorders

Another Mendelian inheritance pattern that occurs in humans involves recessive alleles that are sex-linked. As you learned in Chapter 10, sex-linked alleles are those located on one sex chromosome but not on the other. In humans, most sex-linked alleles are located on the X chromosome. A male only receives such sex-linked alleles from his mother. (The homologous Y chromosome is always inherited from the father.) A male therefore needs only one copy of a sex-linked recessive allele to exhibit the recessive trait. In contrast, a female must inherit two such recessive alleles—one from each parent—to exhibit the trait.

Red-green colorblindness is a common sex-linked disorder that involves a malfunction of light-sensitive cells in the eyes. Some affected people have difficulty distinguishing reds from greens. The pedigree in Figure 12-14 shows the occurrence of colorblindness in four generations of a family. The half-filled circles represent carriers. Circles representing females whose genotypes are unknown are marked with a question mark.

It is rare—but not impossible—for females to exhibit sex-linked (X-linked) traits. Suppose a woman who is a carrier married a man with a sex-linked trait. There would be a 50 percent chance that any of their children (male *or* female) would have the trait.

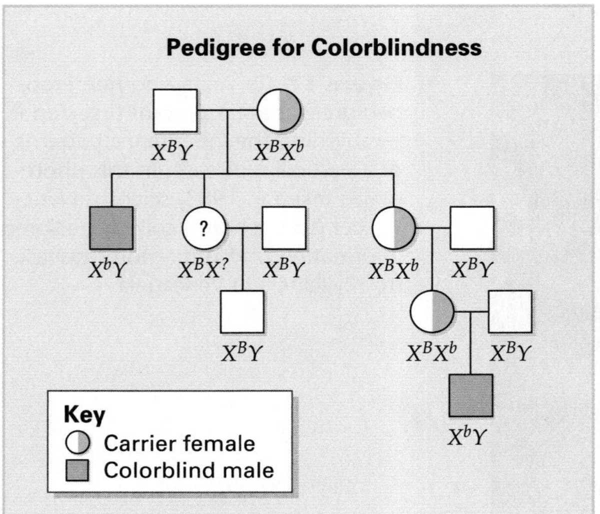

Figure 12-14 This pedigree at left shows the appearance of colorblindness in four generations of a family. The photograph above right approximates how a "red-weak" colorblind person might see the house and field shown in full color at left.

Predicting and Treating Genetic Disorders

▲ **Figure 12-15** A genetic counselor helps this couple determine the risk of passing on a disease trait to their offspring.

When two people are considering having children, and one or both has a family history of a genetic disease, it may be helpful for the couple to visit a genetic counselor. A **genetic counselor** is trained to collect and analyze data about inheritance patterns and to explain the results and their significance (Figure 12-15). The genetic counselor examines the couple's family histories for any disorders that have Mendelian inheritance patterns. He or she can also interpret genetic tests performed on the parents to detect disorder alleles (recessive alleles with effects that would be hidden in a carrier, for example). The counselor can then help the couple determine the risk of passing on a disease trait to their child. The knowledge provided by genetic counseling can help couples make informed decisions about whether to have a child or how they might be able to treat the child if a disorder is in fact inherited.

Before a baby is born, doctors can perform certain tests to detect chromosomal and other genetic disorders in the fetus. For example, karyotyping is a test for chromosome abnormalities, such as the trisomy 21 that leads to Down syndrome (see Figure 12-3 on page 250). Other tests analyze the fluid surrounding the fetus to detect chemical imbalances that point to specific disorders.

Furthermore, standard tests are performed on every baby born at a hospital in the United States, whether or not the baby has any family history for a particular disease. One such test is for phenylketonuria (fen ul kee toh NOOR ee ah), a recessive disorder in which a person cannot process the amino acid phenylalanine. If the baby tests positive for phenylketonuria, the parents can put the baby on a phenylalanine-controlled diet. Such a diet is effective in preventing the mental disability that is characteristic of the untreated disorder.

Online Activity 12.3

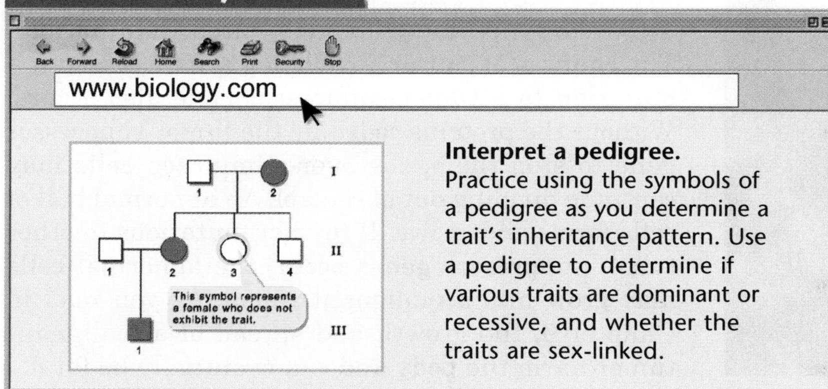

Interpret a pedigree.
Practice using the symbols of a pedigree as you determine a trait's inheritance pattern. Use a pedigree to determine if various traits are dominant or recessive, and whether the traits are sex-linked.

Concept Check 12.3

1. What information is collected to create a pedigree for a particular trait?
2. Give examples of a recessive disorder, a dominant disorder, and a sex-linked recessive disorder, and describe how each is inherited.
3. What does a genetic counselor do?

CONCEPT 12.4

Genetic changes contribute to cancer.

OBJECTIVES

- Explain how mutations to genes that play a role in regulating the cell cycle can lead to cancer.
- Describe how inheriting certain mutations can increase a person's risk for cancer.

KEY TERMS

- growth factor
- tumor-suppressor gene
- oncogene

What's Online

www.biology.com

Online Activity 12.4
Explore the DNA–cancer connection.

Cancer was once a mystery. But now scientists know that the usual cause of cancer is an accumulation of mutations in DNA. As you read in Chapter 11, mutations can be caused by exposure to mutagens such as UV light and certain chemicals. Mutations can also be inherited. Here you will read how several such mutations can add up, sometimes leading to cancer.

Cancer Genes

Chapter 9 described what happens when the cell-cycle control system does not work properly. Cells grow and divide too quickly (Figure 12-16). Eventually, out-of-control cell division can result in a mass of abnormal cells called a tumor. All of the cells of a tumor are descendants of a single cell that malfunctioned.

What is required for the cell cycle to function properly? Normally, two classes of genes direct the production of proteins that regulate cell growth and division. One class of genes produces proteins called **growth factors** that initiate cell division. The other class of genes, known as **tumor-suppressor genes,** produces proteins that stop cell division in particular situations—for example, when cells contain damaged DNA or when cells start to exceed a specific amount of space. Tumor-suppressor genes can even cause such cells to self-destruct.

A single mutation to a single gene involved in regulating the cell cycle does not usually lead to cancer. Rather, cancer develops when several mutations to such genes accumulate (Figure 12-17). For example, the path to cancer often starts with a mutation to a gene that produces growth factors. If the mutation results in producing too much growth factor or increasing growth-factor activity, the gene may have become an **oncogene** (AHNG kuh jeen)—a cancer-causing gene. Cells with an oncogene become over-stimulated to divide more often than normal. The chances of cancer developing are increased if a mutation to a tumor-suppressor gene also occurs. Without the proteins coded by the tumor-suppressor gene to stop them, the over-stimulated cells may continue dividing out of control. An abnormal ball of cells forms and grows. If further mutations to other tumor-suppressor genes occur, the abnormal cells may grow into a malignant tumor. As you read in Chapter 9, the growth and spread of a malignant tumor harm the body and can eventually be fatal.

▼ **Figure 12-16** This micrograph of human skin shows both normal skin cells (green) and cancer cells (orange). Accumulations of mutations can lead to out-of-control cell division and tumor formation.

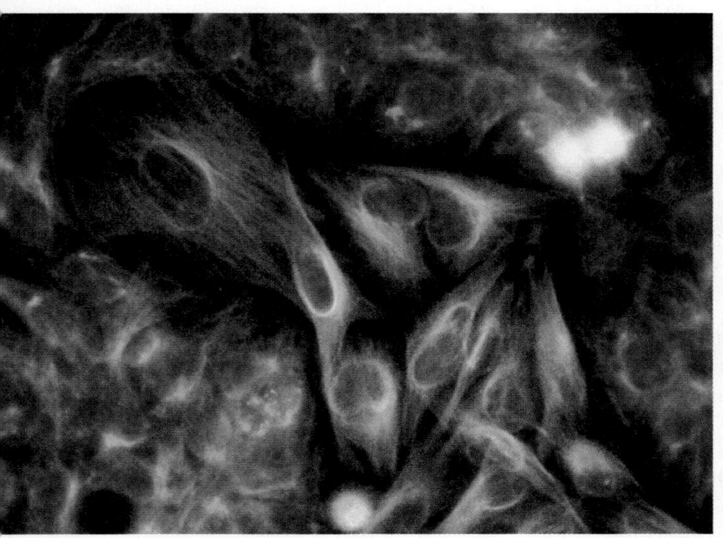

LM 1,200×

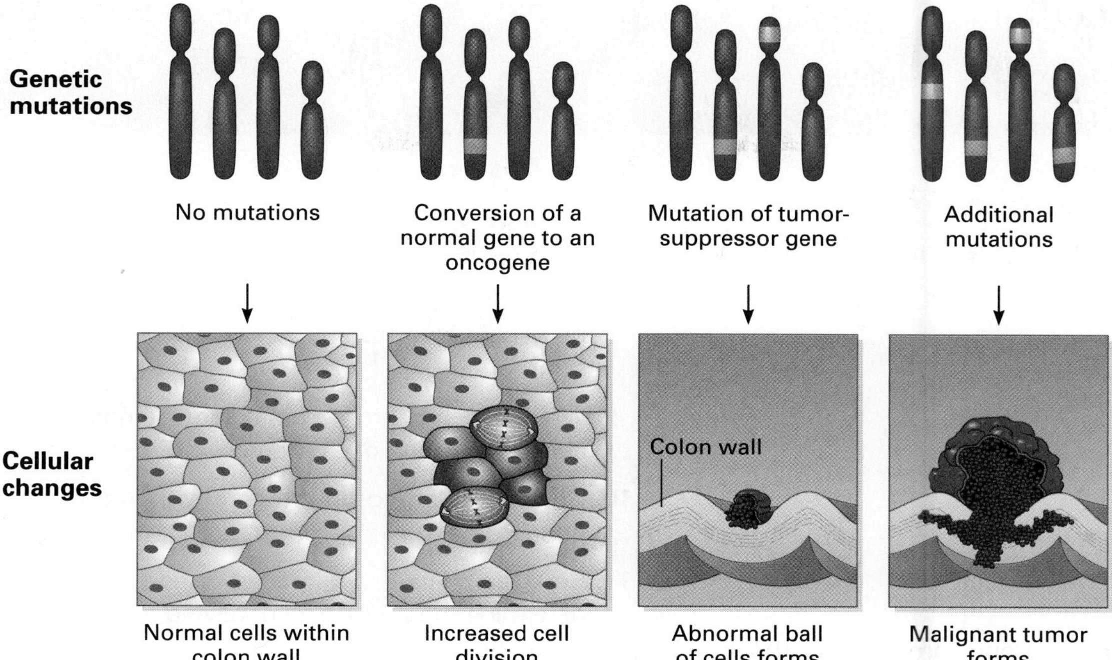

▲ **Figure 12-17** A series of mutations within a cell in the colon (large intestine) can eventually cause a malignant tumor to form on the colon wall.

"Inherited" Cancer

Cancer is always a genetic disease in the sense that it always results from changes in DNA. Most mutations that lead to cancer occur in the organ where the cancer starts. Because these mutations do not affect the cells that give rise to eggs or sperm, they are not passed from parent to child. In some cases, however, a mutation to one or more of these same genes does occur in a cell that gives rise to gametes. Such mutations are passed on and increase the risk of cancer in offspring over the following generations. An example of an inherited cancer gene is a mutated version of a tumor-suppressor gene called *BRCA1.* Women with this gene are at higher risk for breast cancer. Although women who inherit this mutation will not necessarily develop cancer, their risk is higher because they have an unfortunate "head-start" on accumulating the mutations that lead to cancer.

Online Activity 12.4

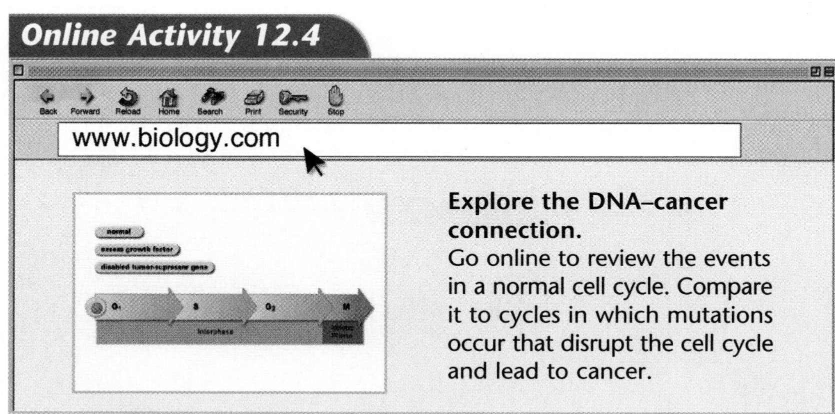

Explore the DNA–cancer connection.
Go online to review the events in a normal cell cycle. Compare it to cycles in which mutations occur that disrupt the cell cycle and lead to cancer.

Concept Check 12.4

1. Compare and contrast the two classes of genes involved in regulating the cell cycle.
2. Describe how a woman inheriting a mutated *BRCA1* gene is at a higher risk for breast cancer.
3. What is an oncogene? What effect does an oncogene have on a cell?

Multiple Choice

Choose the letter of the best answer.

1. The complete set of genetic material in an organism is called its
   a. chromosome.
   b. histone.
   c. transposon.
   d. genome.

2. Trisomy 21 is a condition usually caused by
   a. nondisjunction.
   b. chromosome deletion.
   c. chromosome inversion.
   d. Down syndrome.

3. When a fragment of one chromosome attaches to a nonhomologous chromosome, this process is called a
   a. duplication.
   b. translocation.
   c. deletion.
   d. nondisjunction.

4. What is the probability that each child born to two carriers of a recessive-disorder allele will have the disorder?
   a. 1/3
   b. 1/8
   c. 1/4
   d. 0

5. A person who is a carrier for a sex-linked recessive disorder
   a. is male.
   b. is heterozygous for the disorder.
   c. is homozygous for the disorder.
   d. cannot pass the allele for the disorder to offspring.

6. The chances of cancer developing in an individual increases if a cell that has an oncogene also
   a. has a mutation in a tumor-suppressor gene.
   b. does not make growth factors.
   c. self-destructs.
   d. all of the above.

Short Answer

7. Describe how 2 meters of DNA can fit inside a cell's nucleus.

8. What is the name for the set of symptoms shown by people with trisomy 21? List some of the symptoms.

9. Which type of chromosomal damage might affect more than one chromosome? Explain.

10. How can a tranposon interfere with another gene?

11. How can a family pedigree be used to help determine the probability of having a child with a genetic disorder?

12. Which are more common, lethal dominant alleles or lethal recessive alleles? Explain your answer.

13. Why are there more men than women with colorblindness?

14. Describe the job of a genetic counselor.

15. Is it certain that someone who inherits a cancer gene will get cancer? Explain.

Visualizing Concepts

16. Draw three sketches depicting what the chromosomes below would look like after the described damage affects the indicated area.

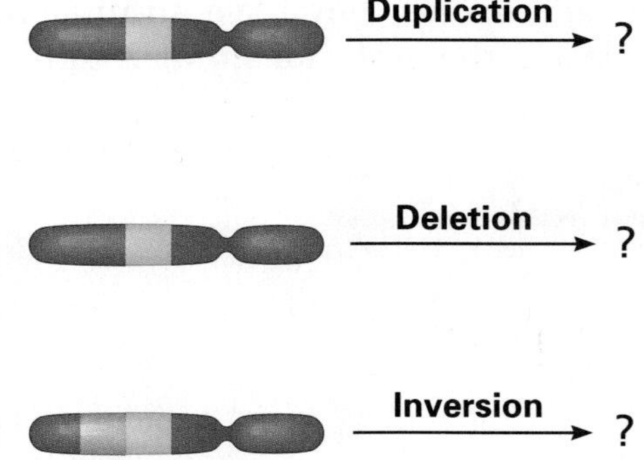

Analyzing Information

17. Analyzing Diagrams Use the pedigree below to answer the questions.

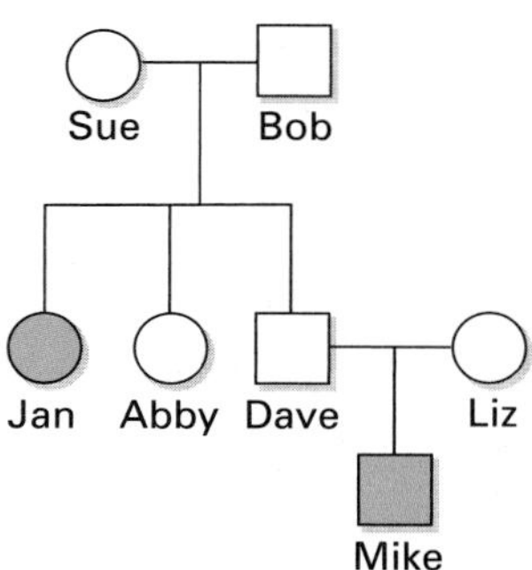

a. List the names of people with the trait.
b. Is this a recessive or dominant trait? Is it a sex-linked trait? Explain.
c. List the names of any carriers of the trait.
d. If Jan married a man who was heterozygous for this trait, what is the probability that any one of their children would have the trait?

18. Analyzing Diagrams Use the diagram below to answer the questions.

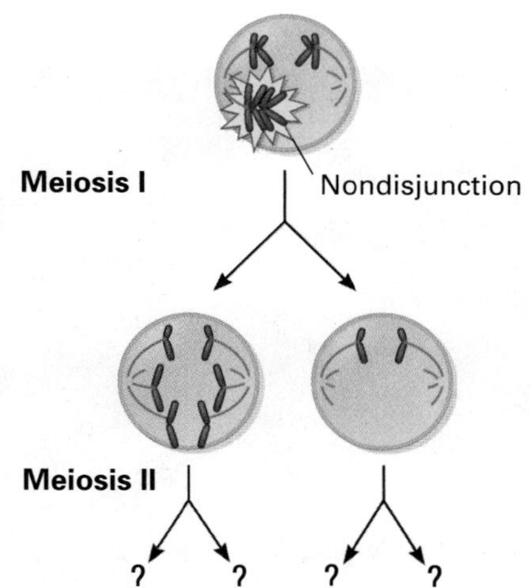

a. On a separate piece of paper, draw the four gametes produced, including the number of chromosomes in each. Explain how each gamete is abnormal.
b. Note that the process shown is simplified, showing only two pairs of chromosomes at meiosis I. In a human, how many pairs of chromosomes would there actually be at meiosis I?

Critical Thinking

19. Evaluating the Impact of Research Describe some benefits of having a complete map of the human genome.

20. Making Generalizations Which kinds of chromosomal abnormalities would be hard to detect in a karyotype? Explain.

21. Problem Solving Note again that the woman whose genotype is unknown in the pedigree for colorblindness (Figure 12-14) has one son with normal vision. Suppose she has a second son who is colorblind. Now can you determine her genotype? Explain. Alternatively, suppose her second son had normal vision. Can you determine her genotype then? Explain.

22. What's Wrong With These Statements? *Briefly explain why each statement is inaccurate or misleading.*

a. Jumping genes jump from one organism into another.
b. Sex-linked traits don't occur in females.
c. Cancer is a genetic disease and therefore is always inherited.

Performance Assessment

Biology Research Project Go to the library or the Internet to research non-disorder traits that have simple Mendelian inheritance (like earlobe attachment). Choose one such trait and write a brief report. Include in your report a made-up pedigree that illustrates how the trait is inherited. Be sure that it follows the inheritance rules for the trait.

Online Assessment/Test Preparation

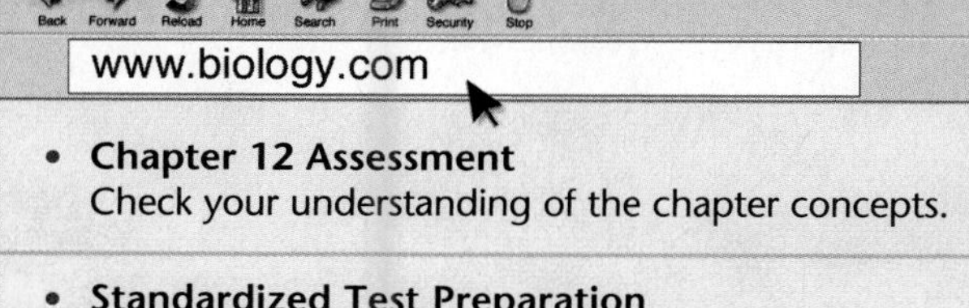

- **Chapter 12 Assessment**
  Check your understanding of the chapter concepts.
- **Standardized Test Preparation**
  Practice test-taking skills you need to succeed.

Frontiers of Genetics

The essence of what makes a particular person genetically unique could be revealed in a simple pattern of glowing bands much like the ones below. This technique compares the genomes of different individuals by separating fragments of their DNA. Variations on this technique provide many useful types of information about genes and genomes.

More and more topics relating to genetic technologies are making news headlines. Many recent advances in agriculture, medicine, and forensics are based on techniques that isolate and manipulate DNA. This chapter will help you build a framework of concepts that you can use to interpret these news stories and be an informed citizen. But first, go online to the ***WebQuest*** to explore how DNA sequencing helps solve mysteries and identify criminals.

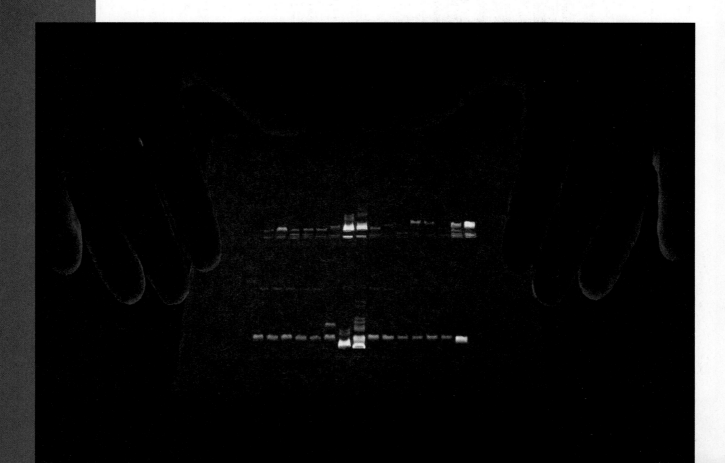

Key Concepts

Concept 13.1 **Biologists have learned to manipulate DNA.**

Concept 13.2 **Biologists can engineer bacteria to make useful products.**

Concept 13.3 **Biologists can genetically engineer plants and animals.**

Concept 13.4 **DNA technologies have many applications.**

Concept 13.5 **Control mechanisms switch genes on and off.**

Assessment **Chapter 13 Review**

What's Online

www.biology.com

WebQuest
ForensicQuest

Online Activity 13.1
Discover DNA applications.

Online Activity 13.2
Cut and paste DNA.

Lab 13 Online Companion
A Glowing Transformation

Online Activity 13.3
Model a cloning procedure.

Science, Technology, & Society
Genetically Modified Foods

Online Activity 13.4
Apply the PCR technique.

Online Activity 13.5
Activate a *lac* operon.

Chapter 13 Assessment

CONCEPT 13.1

Biologists have learned to manipulate DNA.

OBJECTIVES

- Explain how the use of bacteria has contributed to the development of DNA technology.
- List some recent research trends in recombinant DNA technology.

KEY TERMS

- biotechnology
- recombinant DNA technology

What's Online

Online Activity 13.1 Discover DNA applications.

For thousands of years humans have relied on other organisms to do certain jobs. People used yeast to make bread long before they understood the chemistry of fermentation. And farmers bred animals and plants to produce offspring with desired traits without knowing about the activities of DNA and chromosomes. Now, as researchers learn more about biology at the molecular level, they are developing astonishing new ways to modify organisms in the laboratory.

The Beginnings of DNA Technology

The use of organisms to perform practical tasks for humans is called **biotechnology.** On the forefront of biotechnology today are applications that analyze and manipulate the genomes of organisms at the molecular level. This branch of biotechnology is called DNA technology.

During the last 35 years, many of the developments in DNA technology came from research with the common bacterium *Escherichia coli. E. coli* and other bacterial species have been very useful models for gene manipulations. In Chapter 9, you read how sexual reproduction can lead to new combinations of genetic information in offspring. Unlike plants and animals, bacteria do not undergo meiosis, produce gametes, or reproduce by fertilization. Yet, they have their own means of genetic recombination, which you will read about in more detail in Chapter 16. Scientists have been able to apply these natural processes to transfer DNA into bacteria.

Through their experiments in the 1940s, American scientists Joshua Lederberg and Edward Tatum demonstrated that two bacteria can form a tunnel-like connection. One bacterium can pass genes to the other through the connection (Figure 13-1). Since Lederberg and Tatum's discovery, researchers have identified two other ways that bacteria acquire new combinations of genes. Viruses can carry bacterial genes from one bacterial cell to another, and bacteria also can take up loose pieces of DNA from their surrounding environment. In fact, this last method was the cause of the "transformation" of the harmless strain of bacteria in Griffith's experiment, discussed in Chapter 11. In all three processes, a bacterial cell can incorporate new DNA into its genome.

▼ **Figure 13.1** Although bacteria do not undergo meiosis or produce gametes, they can form new combinations of DNA. Here one bacterium passes some of its DNA to another through a tunnel-like connection.

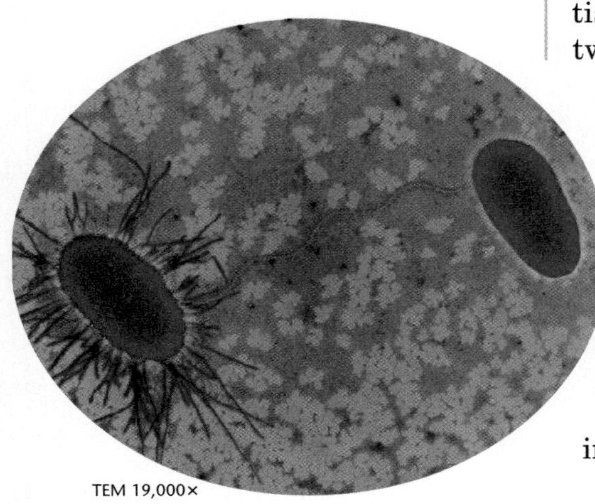

TEM 19,000×

Using this knowledge about the different ways that DNA can be transferred and recombined, scientists have developed a set of laboratory techniques called recombinant DNA technology. **Recombinant DNA technology** combines genes from different sources—even different species—into a single DNA molecule. You will learn about the basic techniques of recombinant DNA technology in Concept 13.2.

▲ **Figure 13-2** Techniques for DNA technology often involve working with bacteria. This scientist is examining a culture of bacteria in a petri dish.

DNA Technology and Frontiers of Research in Biology

In Chapter 12 you read about the ongoing work of the Human Genome Project. In addition, biologists are also sequencing the genomes of many other important research organisms. Some organisms whose genomes have already been sequenced include the fruit fly, baker's yeast, the bacterium *E. coli,* and the rice plant.

Knowledge about genomes can lead to useful applications. For example, sequencing the genome of rice could lead to ways of making it a more nutritious food source. The many similarities among the genomes of different kinds of organisms also means that research on simpler organisms can sometimes be applied to human biology. For example, researchers can sometimes learn how a human gene works by studying its counterpart in another organism, such as yeast.

In addition to the many applications in fields such as medicine and agriculture, analyzing and manipulating genomes can help answer one of biology's most important questions: "How does a complex multicellular organism develop from a single cell?" Concept 13.5 will explore this topic further. Throughout this chapter, in addition to learning about the techniques of DNA technology, you will explore some of the benefits and risks of this growing field of study.

Online Activity 13.1

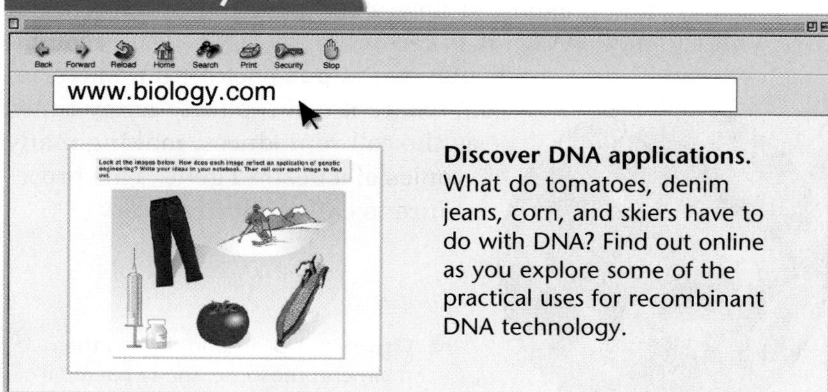

Discover DNA applications. What do tomatoes, denim jeans, corn, and skiers have to do with DNA? Find out online as you explore some of the practical uses for recombinant DNA technology.

Concept Check 13.1

1. How has the bacterium *E. coli* played a role in the development of biotechnology?
2. Describe one use of DNA technology.
3. List three ways genetic recombination occurs in bacteria.

CONCEPT 13.2 Biologists can engineer bacteria to make useful products.

OBJECTIVES

- Explain the role of plasmids in engineering bacteria.
- Explain how biologists "cut and paste" DNA.
- Describe the procedure used in cloning a specific gene.
- Identify the usefulness of recombinant microorganisms.

KEY TERMS

- plasmid
- restriction enzyme
- genomic library
- nucleic acid probe

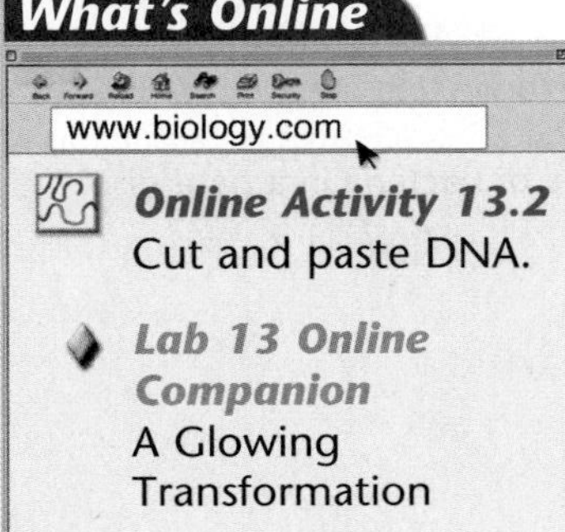

Bacteria are the "workhorses" of modern biotechnology. Biologists can use bacteria to mass-produce useful genes and proteins. These products can then be introduced into other organisms. To understand how this is possible, you first need to know more about how bacteria naturally transfer genes among themselves.

Engineering Bacteria: An Introduction

Many bacteria contain plasmids. A **plasmid** is a small, circular DNA molecule separate from the much larger bacterial chromosome (Figure 13-3). Like a chromosome, a plasmid may carry a number of genes, and can make copies of itself. When a plasmid replicates, one copy can pass from one bacterial cell to another, resulting in gene "sharing" among bacteria. In some instances, gene transfer by plasmids can spread traits that help the bacterial cells survive. For example, some bacteria carry plasmids containing genes that make them resistant to antibiotics. The plasmids carrying these genes can be copied and spread throughout a bacterial population and can even be shared between bacterial species. As a result, an increasing variety of bacteria that cause human disease are becoming resistant to current antibiotics.

While plasmids can spread antibiotic resistance, they can also be used for human benefit. Biologists use plasmids to move pieces of DNA, such as genes for useful products, into bacteria (Figure 13-4). To do this, a plasmid is removed from a bacterial cell, and the desired gene (from any kind of cell) is inserted into the plasmid. The plasmid is now a combination of its original DNA and the new DNA—it is recombinant DNA. The recombinant plasmid is put back into a bacterial cell, where it can replicate many times as the cell reproduces, making many copies of a desired gene. This procedure is called *gene cloning.*

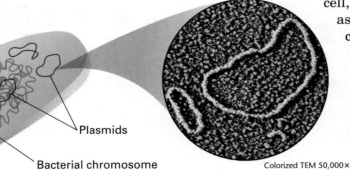

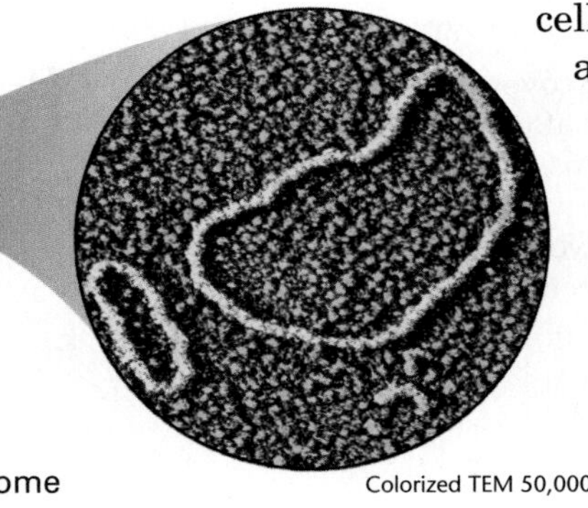

Figure 13-3 In addition to their main chromosome, many bacterial cells contain small, circular DNA molecules called plasmids.

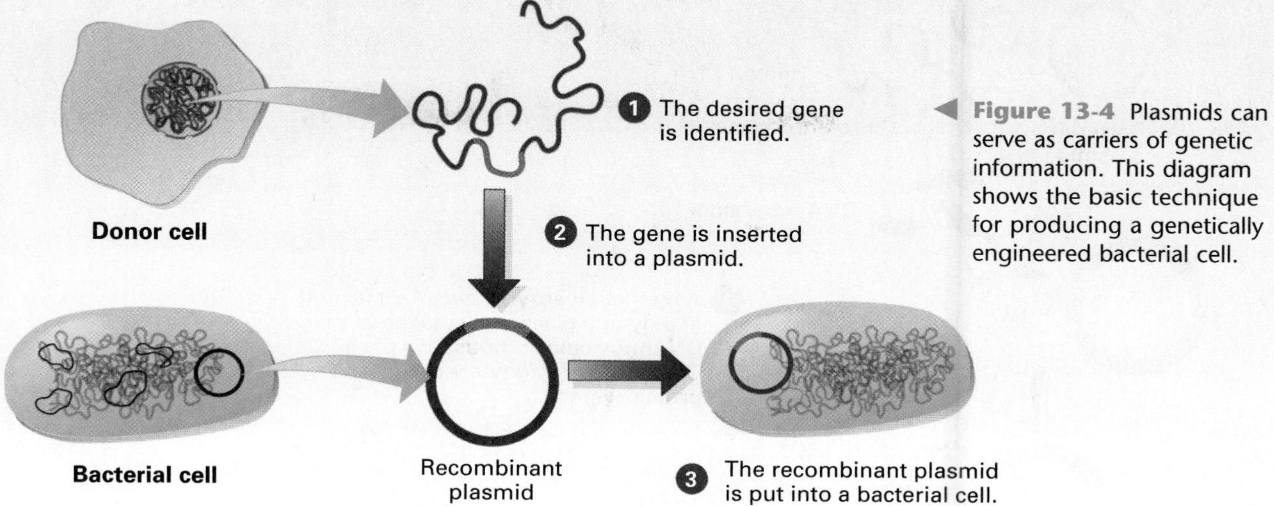

1 The desired gene is identified.
Donor cell
2 The gene is inserted into a plasmid.
Bacterial cell
Recombinant plasmid
3 The recombinant plasmid is put into a bacterial cell.

Figure 13-4 Plasmids can serve as carriers of genetic information. This diagram shows the basic technique for producing a genetically engineered bacterial cell.

"Cutting and Pasting" DNA

You've just read that biologists can engineer a bacterium by inserting a specific gene into its plasmid. But how does a biologist remove a gene from one DNA molecule and put it into another? First, a piece of DNA containing the desired gene must be "cut" out of a much longer DNA molecule. The "tools" used to cut DNA are called **restriction enzymes.** In nature, these enzymes are found in bacteria and protect the bacteria against intruding DNA from other organisms and phages. The restriction enzymes work by chopping up the foreign DNA into small pieces. (The bacterium's DNA is chemically protected from being chopped up by its own restriction enzymes.) In the laboratory, restriction enzymes become a useful tool for moving DNA from one place to another. Each restriction enzyme recognizes particular short nucleotide sequences in DNA molecules, and cuts sugar-phosphate bonds in the DNA backbone at specific points within these sequences (Figure 13-5).

Most restriction enzymes make staggered cuts (meaning not straight across the double-stranded DNA). These staggered cuts leave single-stranded DNA hanging off the ends of the fragments. The single-stranded portion of DNA is called a "sticky end" because it is available to bind to any sequence that is complementary to it. Sticky ends are useful for recombining DNA. The complementary sticky ends of two DNA fragments can join together by base-pairing with each other. Another enzyme, called DNA ligase, "pastes" the sticky ends together, thus repairing the DNA backbone.

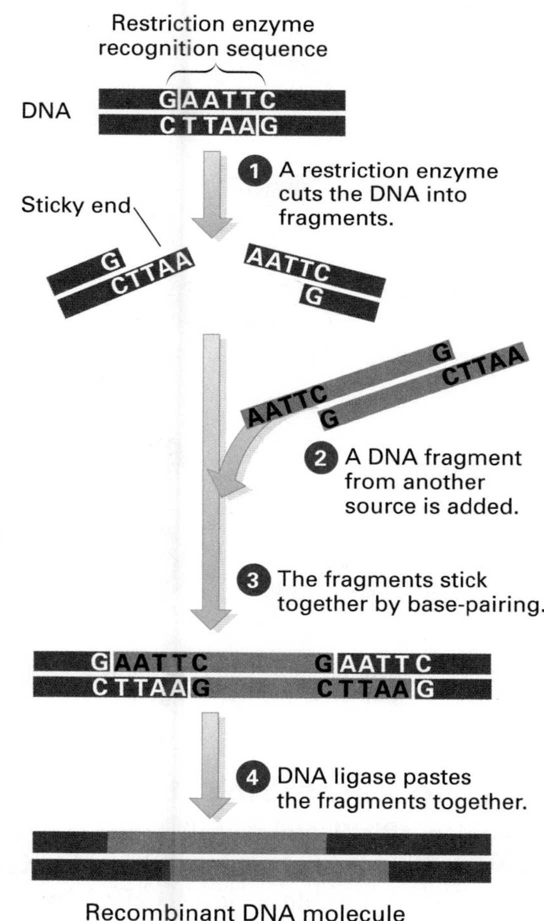

2 A DNA fragment from another source is added.

Figure 13-5 Restriction enzymes cut DNA molecules at specific locations. Splicing together fragments of DNA from two different sources produces a recombinant DNA molecule.

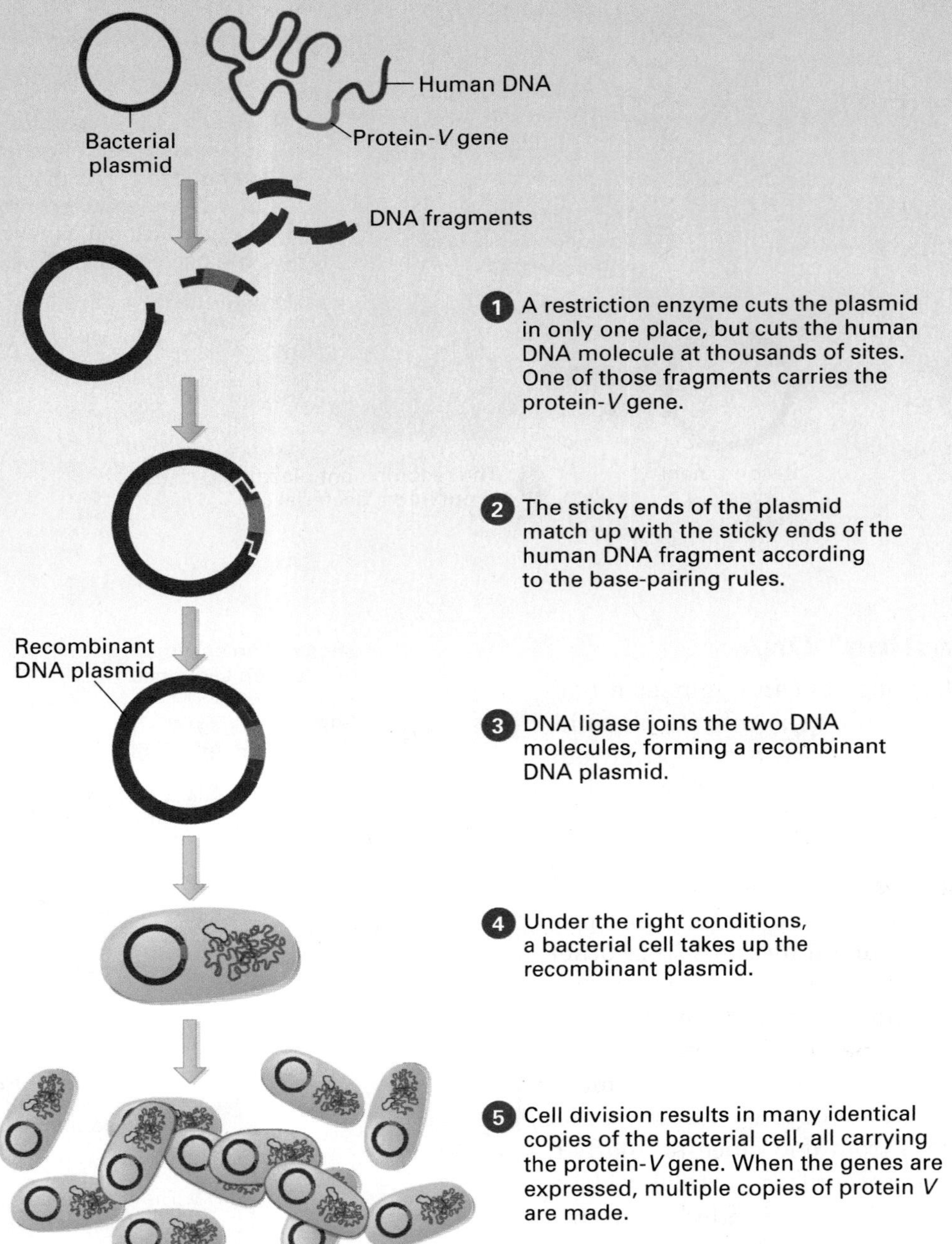

Human DNA
Bacterial plasmid
Protein-V gene
DNA fragments
1 A restriction enzyme cuts the plasmid in only one place, but cuts the human DNA molecule at thousands of sites. One of those fragments carries the protein-V gene.
2 The sticky ends of the plasmid match up with the sticky ends of the human DNA fragment according to the base-pairing rules.
Recombinant DNA plasmid
3 DNA ligase joins the two DNA molecules, forming a recombinant DNA plasmid.
4 Under the right conditions, a bacterial cell takes up the recombinant plasmid.
5 Cell division results in many identical copies of the bacterial cell, all carrying the protein-V gene. When the genes are expressed, multiple copies of protein V are made.
Bacterial clone carrying many copies of the human gene

▲ **Figure 13-6** This diagram traces the cloning of the human gene for a hypothetical protein *V*.

Cloning Recombinant DNA

Consider this example of a genetic engineering challenge. Suppose a molecular biologist has identified a human gene that codes for a valuable product called "protein *V*." By putting the gene in bacterial cells that can express the gene as protein, the biologist sets up a system for making large amounts of the protein. Making recombinant DNA in large enough amounts to be useful requires several steps. You can follow the process in Figure 13-6.

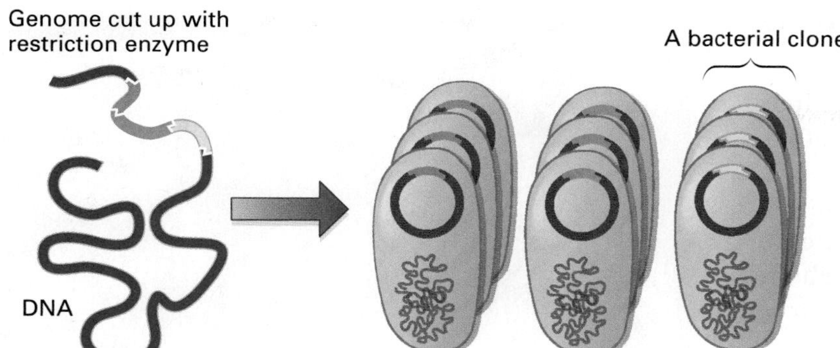

Figure 13-7 A genomic library contains the complete collection of cloned DNA fragments from one organism.

Libraries of Cloned Genes Step 5 of Figure 13-6 only depicts the production of the bacterial clone containing the desired gene. In reality, the procedure produces many different clones, each containing a different portion of the source DNA (human DNA, in this example) because the restriction enzyme makes cuts all over the source DNA. The result is that many genes are cloned in addition to the target gene.

The complete collection of cloned DNA fragments from an organism is called a **genomic library** (Figure 13-7). A typical plasmid contains a DNA fragment big enough to carry only one or a few genes. Together, the different recombinant plasmids in a genomic library contain the entire genome of the organism from which the DNA was derived—in this case, a human.

Identifying Specific Genes With Probes Once a genomic library is created for an organism, how does a biologist find a specific gene in that library? Just as you rely on a card catalog or computer system to help you find a particular book in a large library, biologists need tools to locate a specific gene among the possible thousands in a genomic library.

One method requires knowing at least part of the gene's nucleotide sequence. For example, suppose that the gene for protein *V* contains the base sequence TAGGCT. Knowing this, a biologist can use nucleotides labeled with a radioactive isotope to build a complementary single strand of DNA with the sequence ATCCGA (Figure 13-8). This complementary, radioactively labeled nucleic acid molecule is called a **nucleic acid probe.**

Next the biologist treats the DNA being searched with chemicals or heat to separate the two DNA strands. The nucleic acid probe is mixed in with these single strands. The probe tags the correct DNA portion by pairing with the complementary sequence in the protein-*V* gene. Once the biologist uses this radioactive marker to identify the bacterial cells with the desired gene, those cells are allowed to multiply further, producing the desired gene in large amounts.

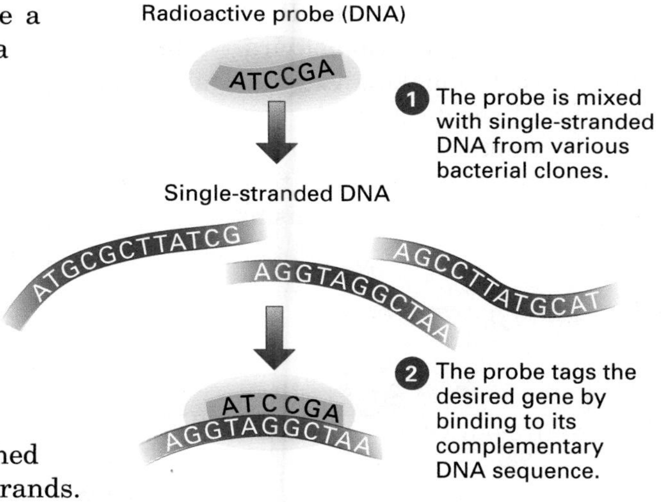

Radioactive probe (DNA)
ATCCGA
1 The probe is mixed with single-stranded DNA from various bacterial clones.
Single-stranded DNA
ATGCGCTTATCG
AGGTAGGCTAA
AGCCTTATGCAT
2 The probe tags the desired gene by binding to its complementary DNA sequence.
ATCCGA
AGGTAGGCTAA

Figure 13-8 Scientists use nucleic acid probes to locate specific genes. Besides labeling probes with radioactive isotopes, biologists can also use fluorescent (glow-in-the-dark) dyes to "tag" the probes.

Useful Products From Genetically Engineered Microorganisms

The news is full of examples of recombinant DNA technology in action. Some kinds of bacteria engineered with recombinant DNA can break down certain chemicals and help to clean up toxic waste sites. Other engineered bacteria are mass-producing useful chemicals, from pesticides to therapeutic drugs (Figure 13-9).

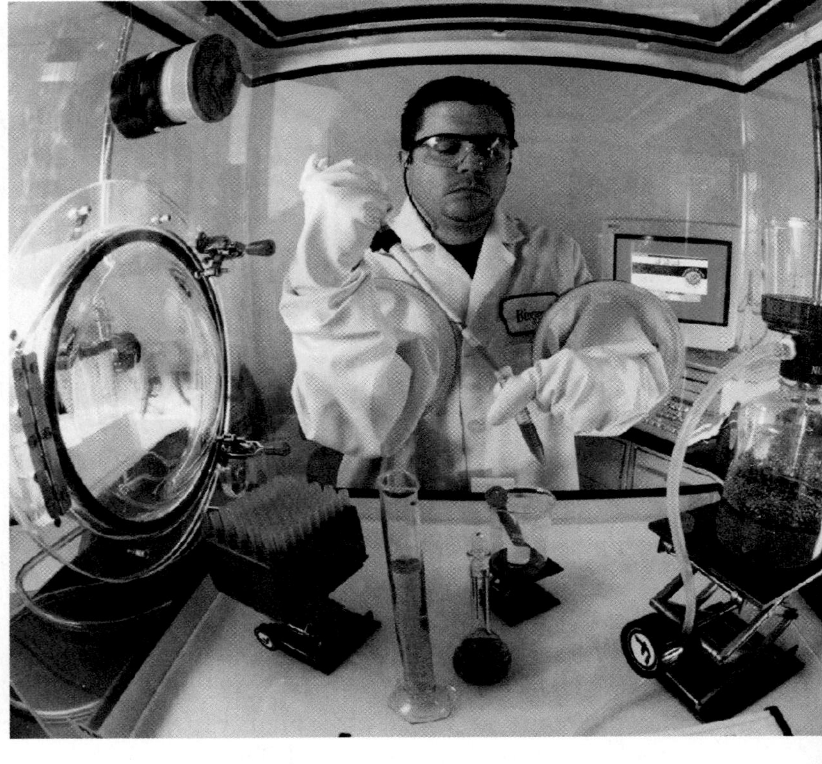

▲ **Figure 13-9** This scientist is isolating proteins produced by genetically engineered bacteria. These proteins will be used to make a medicine for humans.

The genetic engineering of bacteria has many useful applications in medicine. Consider insulin, a hormone that helps regulate blood sugar levels in people with diabetes. Before 1982, the main sources of insulin were pig and cattle tissues. Insulin obtained from these animals is chemically similar, but not identical, to human insulin. As a result, some people using those sources of insulin experienced negative side effects. Now some types of diabetes can be treated without the side effects by using pure human insulin produced by recombinant DNA technology.

Recombinant DNA technology is also helping to develop effective vaccines against disease-causing microbes. A vaccine exposes a person's immune system to disabled microbes (or parts of microbes). This enables the immune system to recognize and quickly defend the body against any later exposures to actual disease-causing agents. For example, genes for proteins of the virus that causes hepatitis B have been cloned in yeast cells, allowing mass-production of viral proteins. These viral proteins are then used to make a vaccine against this serious and sometimes fatal liver disease.

In Concept 13.3, you will learn about ways in which scientists use recombinant DNA technology to produce genetically modified multicellular organisms.

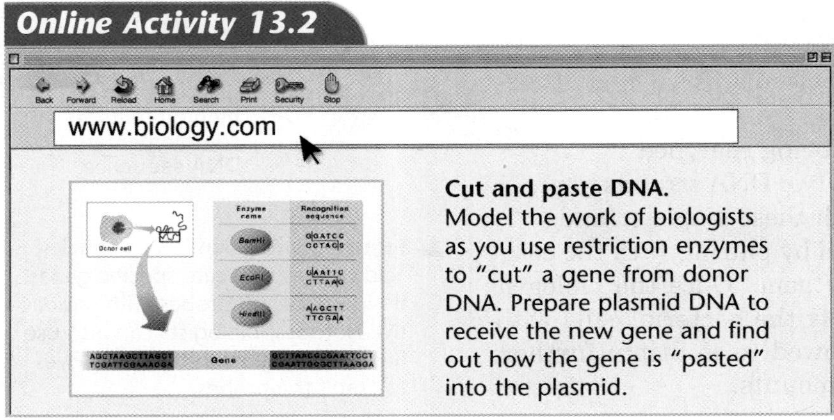

Online Activity 13.2
Back Forward Reload Home Search Print Security Stop
www.biology.com
Donor cell
Enzyme name
Recognition sequence
BamHI
EcoRI
HindIII
Gene
Cut and paste DNA.
Model the work of biologists as you use restriction enzymes to "cut" a gene from donor DNA. Prepare plasmid DNA to receive the new gene and find out how the gene is "pasted" into the plasmid.

Concept Check 13.2

1. How can a biologist use plasmids to produce bacteria that carry a specific gene?
2. Explain how the "sticky ends" that result from the action of restriction enzymes can be useful.
3. Explain how a nucleic acid probe enables researchers to identify a specific gene.
4. Give an example of a use of recombinant DNA technology in medicine.

A Glowing Transformation

Inserting Useful Genes Into Bacteria

Question How can bacterial cells be genetically transformed with plasmid DNA containing a jellyfish gene?

Lab Overview In this investigation you will mix plasmid DNA containing the gene for green fluorescent protein (GFP) with *E. coli* bacteria. You will culture the bacteria, and then check for "glowing" bacteria that have the GFP gene and produce the GFP protein.

Preparing for the Lab To prepare for the investigation, go to the *Lab 13 Online Companion*. See how a bacterial cell takes in plasmid DNA during transformation and find out how scientists select for bacterial cells that contain and express new genetic information. Prepare for the lab procedure by previewing the steps you will take.

Completing the Lab Use your Laboratory Manual or lab page printouts from the *Lab 13 Online Companion* to do the investigation and analyze your results. **CAUTION:** *Be sure to follow your teacher's instructions and all safety guidelines in the investigation.*

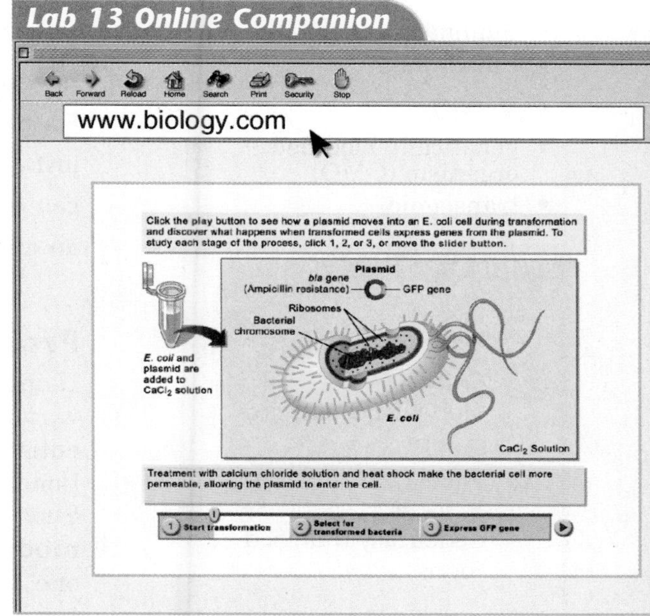
Lab 13 Online Companion
Back
Forward
Reload
Home
Search
Print
Security
Stop
www.biology.com
Click the play button to see how a plasmid moves into an E. coli cell during transformation and discover what happens when transformed cells express genes from the plasmid. To study each stage of the process, click 1, 2, or 3, or move the slider button.
Plasmid
bla gene (Ampicillin resistance)
GFP gene
Ribosomes
Bacterial chromosome
E. coli and plasmid are added to $CaCl_2$ solution
E. coli
$CaCl_2$ Solution
Treatment with calcium chloride solution and heat shock make the bacterial cell more permeable, allowing the plasmid to enter the cell.
1 Start transformation
2 Select for transformed bacteria
3 Express GFP gene

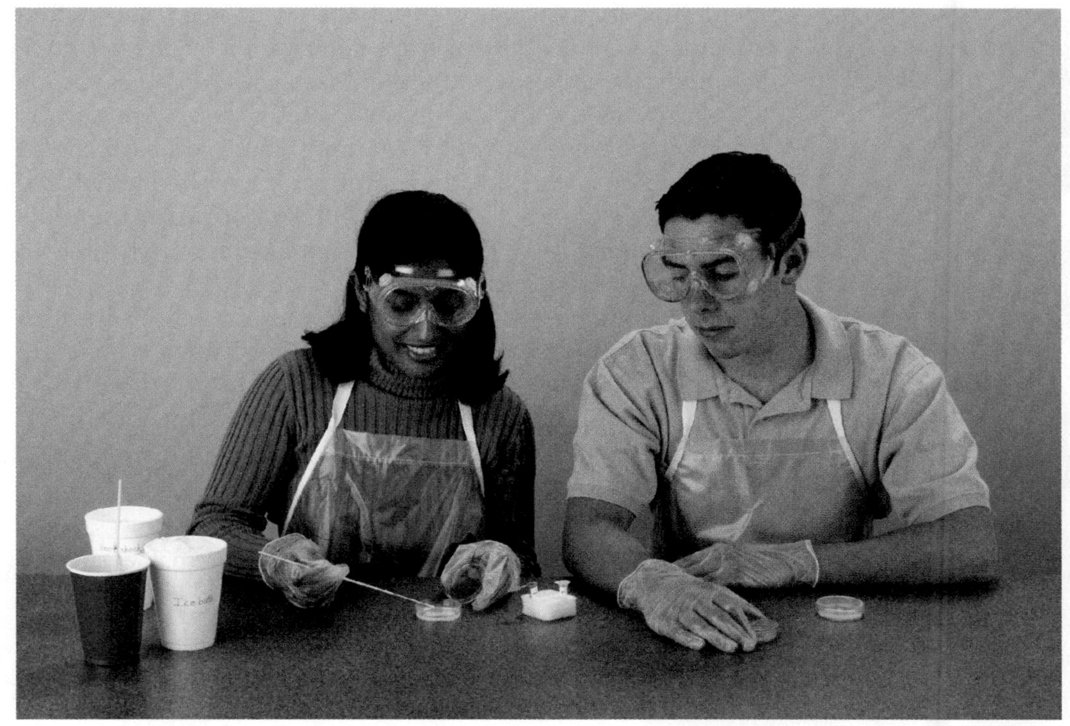

CONCEPT 13.3

Biologists can genetically engineer plants and animals.

OBJECTIVES

- Describe how biologists genetically modify plants and animals.
- Explain a technique used to clone animals.
- Summarize the GMO controversy.

KEY TERMS

- genetically modified organism (GMO)
- transgenic

What's Online

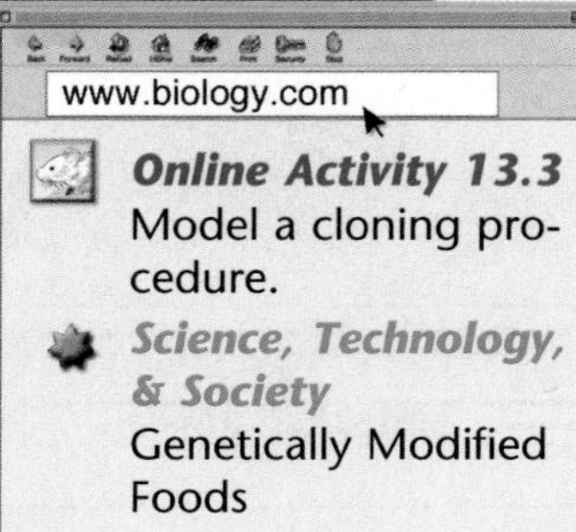

Online Activity 13.3 Model a cloning procedure.

Science, Technology, & Society Genetically Modified Foods

If you've ever grown a plant from a cutting, you know that some new plants can be easy to grow without actually planting seeds. For many species, a new plant can be grown in the laboratory from just one adult plant cell. Taking advantage of this fact, biologists can produce a genetically engineered plant cell that grows into an entire plant with new traits.

Producing Genetically Modified Plants

Using recombinant DNA technology, scientists are able to improve various characteristics of certain crop plants. For example, scientists have inserted genes for delayed ripening, improved nutritional content, and resistance to spoilage or disease (Figure 13-10). Such crops are said to be genetically modified. A **genetically modified organism (GMO)** is any organism that has acquired one or more genes by artificial means. A GMO is said to be **transgenic** if the source of the new genetic material is a different species.

Genetic engineering is replacing traditional methods of plant breeding in many situations. It is used most often when a plant's useful traits are determined by one or only a few genes. In the year 2000, about half the crops of soybeans and corn grown in the United States were genetically modified in some way. For example, many crops received genes for herbicide resistance. Herbicides applied to fields of these plants destroy the weeds but do not harm the crop. Other genetically modified plants are being engineered to resist pest insects and fungi.

Biologists often use a plasmid from the soil bacterium *Agrobacterium tumefaciens* to introduce new genes into plant cells. Figure 13-11 on the facing page outlines the procedure for producing a genetically modified (GM) plant.

Figure 13-10 This scientist is measuring a melon's output of ethylene gas, a natural ripening chemical. These GM melons contain altered genes hypothesized to affect ethylene production. The inset shows the ethylene-measuring device strapped to a melon.

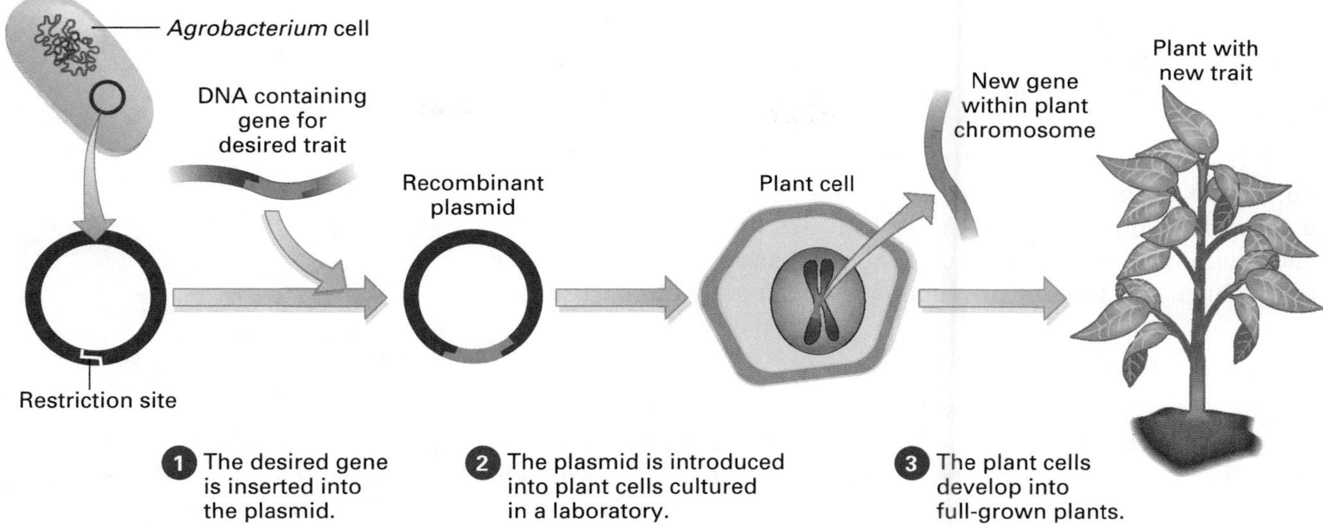
Agrobacterium cell
DNA containing gene for desired trait
Recombinant plasmid
Plant cell
New gene within plant chromosome
Plant with new trait
Restriction site
1 The desired gene is inserted into the plasmid.
2 The plasmid is introduced into plant cells cultured in a laboratory.
3 The plant cells develop into full-grown plants.

▲ **Figure 13-11** To genetically modify a plant, researchers insert a plasmid containing the desired gene into a plant cell. There, the gene is incorporated into the plant cell's DNA. The engineered plant cell then grows into a genetically modified plant.

Producing Genetically Modified Animals

Biologists routinely use DNA technology to make vaccines and growth hormones for treating farm animals. However, only recently have researchers tested ways to genetically modify the animals. Genetically modifying animals is more difficult than producing GM plants. In mammals, the procedure requires extracting an egg cell from a female. Sperm from the same species is used to fertilize the egg in a "test-tube" environment. Then the desired gene is injected into the fertilized egg, and the egg is returned to a uterus (womb) where it can develop into an embryo. It usually takes many attempts before an egg actually incorporates the DNA. If the embryo develops successfully, the result is a GM animal. The offspring contains a gene or genes from a third "parent" that may even be of another species.

The goals of genetically modifying an animal are often the same as the goals of traditional breeding. For instance, researchers try to make a sheep with better-quality wool, a pig with leaner meat, or a fish that will mature in a shorter time (Figure 13-12). In other cases the goal is to make a transgenic

◄ **Figure 13-12** Getting products to market faster is one goal of recombinant DNA technologies. These two salmon are the same age, but the genetically modified salmon (top) is larger because it grew at about twice the rate of the control salmon (bottom).

animal that produces a large amount of an otherwise rare biological substance for medical use. Most cases involve adding a gene for a desired human protein, such as a hormone, to the genome of a farm mammal. The gene is added in such a way that the desired human protein is secreted in the animal's milk. The human protein can then be purified. This is a good method for cloning certain genes that are not expressed well in bacterial clones (meaning that when the same genes are placed in bacteria, the protein products are not made well, or at all).

Animal Cloning

You have so far learned how individual genes can be cloned in bacteria, plants, or animals. Entire genomes can be cloned, too. For centuries plants have been cloned from cuttings, as you will learn in Chapter 20. In recent years, scientists have figured out how to clone animals—first the famous sheep named "Dolly," and more recently, cats and pigs.

In cloning an entire animal, the nucleus from a single cell of that adult animal replaces the nucleus of an unfertilized egg cell from another animal of the same species (Figure 13-13). The procedure is much the same as that described above for producing a GM animal, except that instead of inserting a gene into the egg cell, an entire foreign nucleus (and all its genes) replaces the egg's own nucleus. The egg then develops into an animal that has the same genome as the nuclear donor. The new animal is a clone of the animal that supplied the nucleus.

Cloning offers the potential to mass-produce an animal with a desirable set of traits. This is much faster than using traditional animal breeding to select for a certain set of traits over several generations of animals. One particularly useful application is cloning a GM animal. This could prove easier than starting from scratch to produce each new animal.

Science, Technology, & Society

Back Forward Reload Home Search Print Security Stop

www.biology.com

Genetically Modified Foods
Genetic engineering is enabling scientists to alter the genetic makeup of some crops so that they are more resistant to extreme environmental conditions and insects. However, this technology could also have some negative consequences for organisms and ecosystems. Explore both sides of this topic when you go online.

Figure 13-13 These five piglets are clones of an adult pig. Researchers cloned the adult by using nuclei from its cells to replace the nuclei in the eggs from which these piglets developed. The inset shows an egg cell receiving a new nucleus.

The GMO Controversy

You may have heard news stories questioning the safety of crops carrying artificially inserted genes. Could they be harmful to human health or to the environment? For example, could GM crops pass their new genes to closely related plants in nearby wild areas? Pollen from plants carrying genes for resistance to herbicides might fertilize the flowers of wild plants. The offspring might then become "superweeds" that would be very difficult to control. The National Academy of Sciences released a study in 2000 finding no evidence that crops genetically modified to resist pests pose significant health or environmental risks. However, the authors of the study recommended stricter regulations on how GM crops are used and suggested further research.

▲ **Figure 13-14** This consumer examines some genetically modified tomatoes. Look for genetically modified products next time you go shopping.

Another concern is that GM plants or animals could have unknown risks to human consumers. Some consumers think labeling that clearly identifies GM products should be required (Figure 13-14). Transgenic farm animals used to make medicines may also pose certain risks. For example, human proteins produced in the milk of an engineered animal might differ slightly from natural human proteins. For this reason the proteins have to be tested very carefully. It is important to make sure that the proteins in medicines or foods produced by GMOs will not cause allergic reactions or other negative effects in individuals receiving them.

Governments and regulatory agencies throughout the world are dealing with issues of how to ensure that new biotechnology products and procedures are safe. In the United States, several government agencies evaluate all genetic engineering projects for risks.

Online Activity 13.3

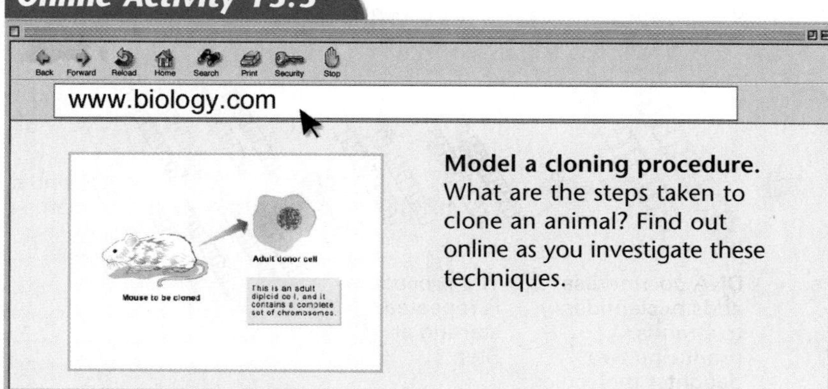

Model a cloning procedure. What are the steps taken to clone an animal? Find out online as you investigate these techniques.

Concept Check 13.3

1. How is producing a GM plant different from producing a GM animal?
2. Compare and contrast the techniques for producing a GM animal and a cloned animal.
3. Give an example of one potential risk posed by GMOs.

CONCEPT 13.4 DNA technologies have many applications.

OBJECTIVES
- Describe the technique that enables scientists to mass-produce specific segments of DNA in a test tube.
- Describe a technique used to compare DNA samples.

KEY TERMS
- polymerase chain reaction (PCR)
- gel electrophoresis
- genetic marker
- DNA fingerprint

What's Online
www.biology.com
Online Activity 13.4
Apply the PCR technique.

Almost every week the news media announce a new advance in medicine, agriculture, law, or genetics. DNA technology is behind many of these advances—it is rapidly changing the way society solves certain problems. You have already learned about some types of DNA technology. This section explores some additional techniques and their applications.

Mass-Producing DNA in a Test Tube

The **polymerase chain reaction (PCR)** is a technique that makes many copies of a certain segment of DNA without using living cells. Starting with a single DNA molecule, PCR can generate 100 billion identical molecules in just a few hours (Figure 13-15). A great advantage of PCR is that it can copy one *specific segment* from within a tremendous length of DNA. The technique is so precise and powerful that its starting material does not even have to be purified DNA. Only a tiny amount (less than 1 μg, one millionth of a gram) of DNA needs to be present in the starting material. Using living cells instead would require a much longer time and a larger amount of the desired DNA.

Using PCR to produce multiple copies of a DNA sample can make further analysis of the sample much easier. It also enables scientists to make copies of very rare DNA. For example, scientists have used the technique to clone DNA pieces recovered from 5,000-year-old human remains, from a 40,000-year-old woolly mammoth frozen in a glacier, and from a 30-million-year-old plant fossil. PCR also has applications in medicine. For example, PCR makes it possible to detect viral genes in cells infected with the virus that causes AIDS.

▼ **Figure 13-15** PCR produces multiple copies of a segment of DNA.

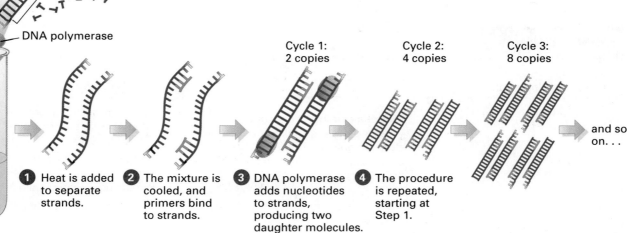

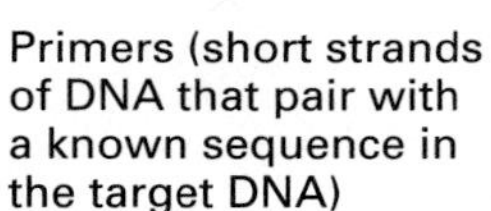

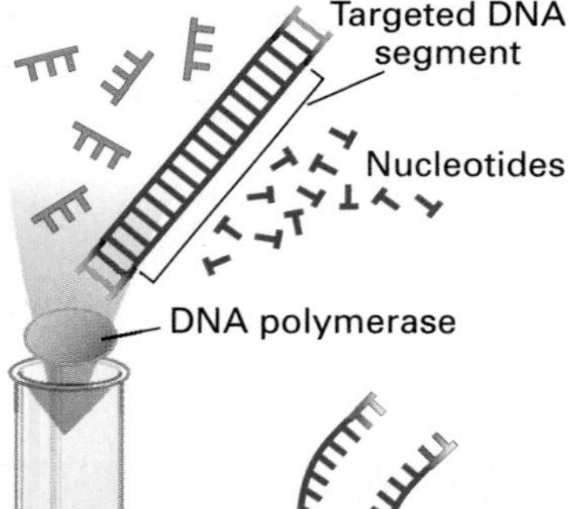

Primers (short strands of DNA that pair with a known sequence in the target DNA)
Targeted DNA segment
Nucleotides
DNA polymerase
Cycle 1: 2 copies
Cycle 2: 4 copies
Cycle 3: 8 copies
and so on. . .
1 Heat is added to separate strands.
2 The mixture is cooled, and primers bind to strands.
3 DNA polymerase adds nucleotides to strands, producing two daughter molecules.
4 The procedure is repeated, starting at Step 1.

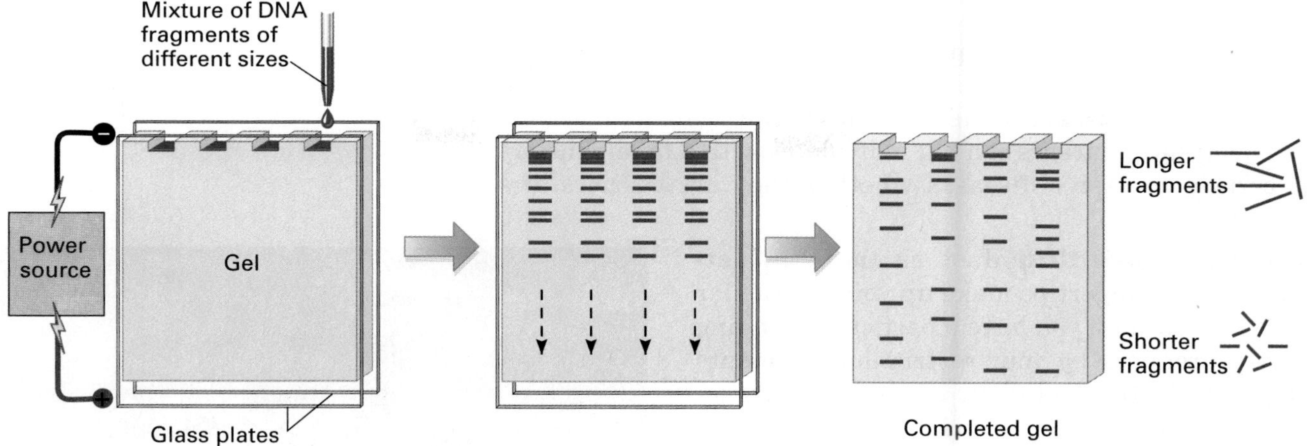

Comparing DNA

Often scientists want to compare DNA samples from different sources. One useful technique for sorting molecules or fragments of molecules by length is called **gel electrophoresis.** Figure 13-16 shows this technique applied to DNA samples from four different individuals. First, each DNA sample is cut up into fragments by a group of restriction enzymes. Remember that restriction enzymes recognize and cut within specific DNA sequences. These specific sequences are located at different places along the DNA, depending on the source. Therefore, the assortment of fragments for each sample is unique. A few drops of each sample are placed in a small pocket, or well, at one end of a thin slab of gelatin-like material called a gel. The other end of the gel has a positive charge. All DNA molecules are negatively charged, so they move through pores in the gel toward the positive pole.

The shorter DNA fragments slip more easily through the pores of the gel. Therefore, after a set period of time, the shorter DNA fragments will travel farther through the gel and be closer to the positive end of the gel than the longer fragments. In the last step, the gel is treated with a stain that makes the DNA visible under ultraviolet light (as in the photograph on page 264). The DNA fragments show up as a series of bands in each "lane" of the gel. Each band consists of many DNA fragments of one particular size. The pattern of bands will be different for each of the four samples because each sample has a unique set of DNA fragment lengths.

Genetic Markers Cutting up an organism's entire genome with even just one kind of restriction enzyme produces thousands of differently sized DNA fragments. This in turn produces thousands of individual bands on a gel. With so many bands to look at, how does a biologist find any differences in the banding patterns between individual samples? The solution is to examine the banding pattern produced by specific portions of the genome called genetic markers. As illustrated in Figure 13-8 on page 271, radioactively labeled DNA probes can "tag" the bands containing particular genetic markers.

Figure 13-16 The gel electrophoresis technique shown above can be used to compare DNA of individuals or species. In the photo below, a biologist uses a pipette to load DNA into the wells at the end of the gel.

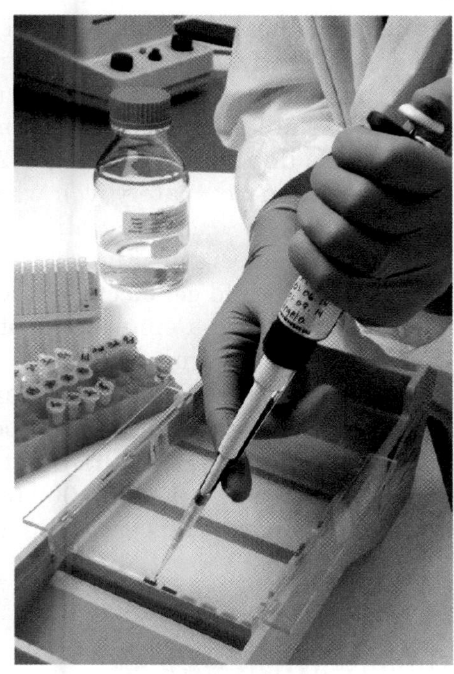

Genetic markers are particular stretches of DNA that are variable among individuals. For example, DNA fragments that include certain disease alleles contain distinct genetic markers. Analyzing such markers can tell individuals with a family history for certain recessive diseases whether they are carriers of a disease allele.

DNA Fingerprinting Just as the skin patterns on your fingertips make up your particular set of fingerprints, you have a particular banding pattern produced by your restriction fragments called a **DNA fingerprint.** Unless you have an identical twin, no one else is likely to have the exact same DNA fingerprint as you. As you have just read, genetic markers can help to pick out the differences between two DNA fingerprints. Genetic markers can occur in alleles for diseases or other traits. Markers can also be located in one of the many noncoding stretches of the human genome (such as the introns you learned about in Chapter 11). These noncoding regions make up about 97 percent of the human genome. When DNA fingerprints are used in court as evidence, genetic markers from these highly variable noncoding regions are used. Why is this important? To use DNA to identify a specific person accurately, you want to compare genetic markers that are unlikely to be shared with any other person (Figure 13-17).

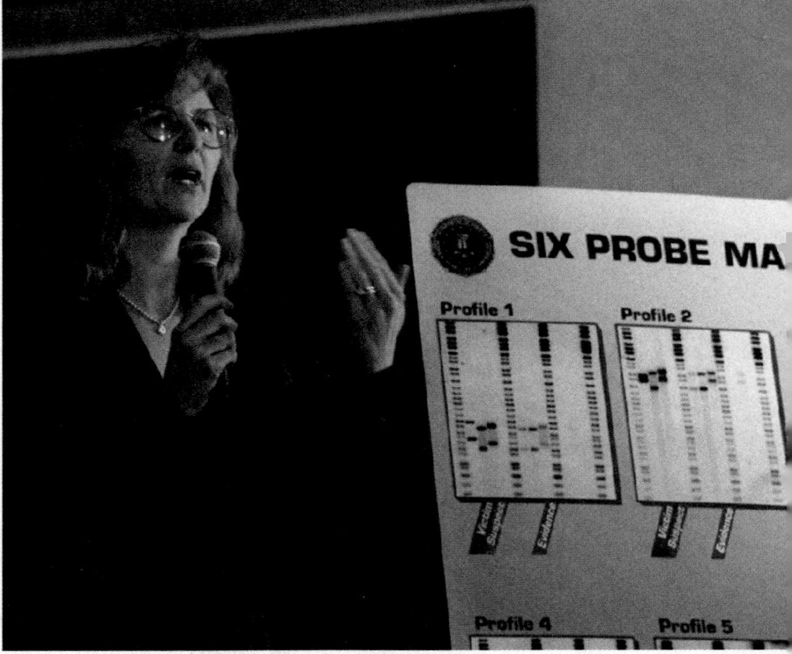

▲ **Figure 13-17** DNA fingerprinting can provide evidence in legal cases. For example, DNA collected from a crime scene (from blood or hair, for example) can be compared to DNA from a suspect's blood sample.

Using PCR and gel electrophoresis, a DNA fingerprint can be made from cells in a single drop of blood or from a hair follicle. DNA is extracted from the small sample, and multiple copies are made using PCR. Genetic markers are then compared. In most cases, the probability of two people having identical genetic markers is small—somewhere between one chance in 100,000 and one chance in 1,000,000,000 (one billion), depending on the number of genetic markers compared.

Online Activity 13.4

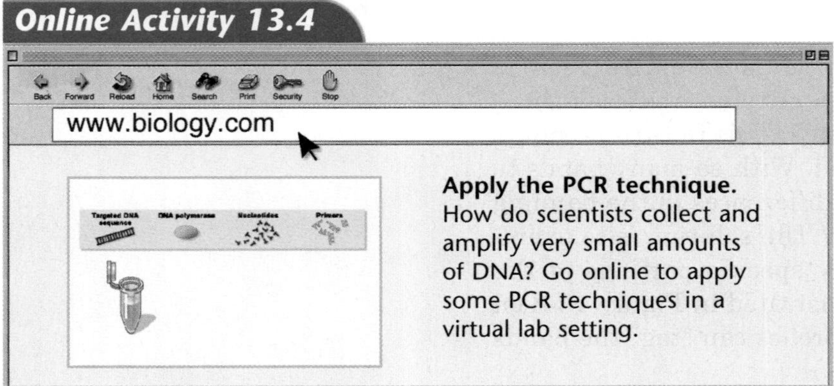

Apply the PCR technique. How do scientists collect and amplify very small amounts of DNA? Go online to apply some PCR techniques in a virtual lab setting.

Concept Check 13.4

1. Name one application of the mass-production of DNA using PCR.
2. Explain how gel electrophoresis compares DNA samples.
3. Why are genetic markers from noncoding regions useful in distinguishing DNA fingerprints?

CONCEPT 13.5 Control mechanisms switch genes on and off.

OBJECTIVES

- Explain how operons enable a prokaryote to respond to changes in its environment.
- Describe how transcription factors regulate genes in eukaryotes.
- Summarize the importance of cellular differentiation in the development of an egg into an organism.
- Identify the unique features of stem cells.
- Describe a homeotic gene.

KEY TERMS

- operon
- promoter
- operator
- repressor
- transcription factor
- gene expression
- cellular differentiation
- stem cell
- homeotic gene

What's Online

Online Activity 13.5
Activate a *lac* operon.

Though each of your cells has the same set of genes, there are clearly many differences in how your cells look and function. This is because a different subset of genes is active in different cells. As with many other topics in genetics, biologists first began to understand gene regulation from their studies of bacteria.

Regulation of Genes in Prokaryotes

Most bacteria are unicellular and do not have the ability to turn genes on or off to produce different kinds of cells as more complex organisms do. However, a bacterium can change its functions in response to changes in its environment. For example, consider the *E. coli* living in the constantly changing chemical environment of your intestine. Suppose you've just had a glass of milk. One of the main nutrients in milk is the sugar lactose. When lactose is plentiful in the intestine, *E. coli* makes the three enzymes necessary to absorb and use this disaccharide. When lactose is not plentiful, *E. coli* does not waste energy producing those enzymes.

The three genes coding for the enzymes that process lactose are next to each other in the *E. coli* chromosome (Figure 13-18). Before the genes, there are two short stretches of DNA called control sequences. Such a cluster of genes, along with its control sequences, is called an **operon.** The operon discussed here is the *lac* operon, for "lactose." The first control sequence, the **promoter,** is the site where RNA polymerase attaches to the DNA. (Recall that RNA polymerase transcribes genes by making mRNA.) Between the promoter and the enzyme genes is a second control sequence called the operator. The **operator** acts like a switch, determining whether or not RNA polymerase can attach to the promoter.

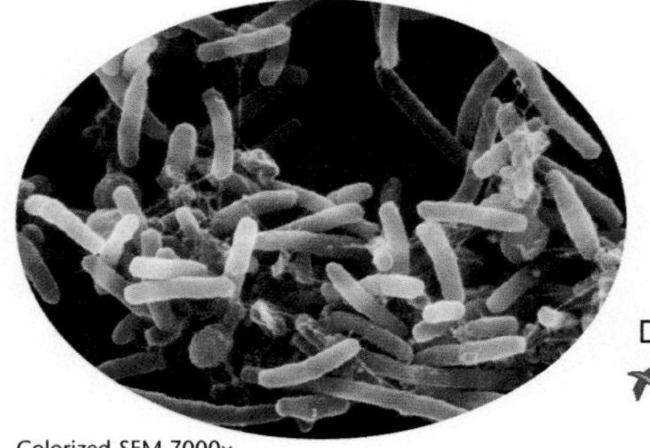

Colorized SEM 7000×

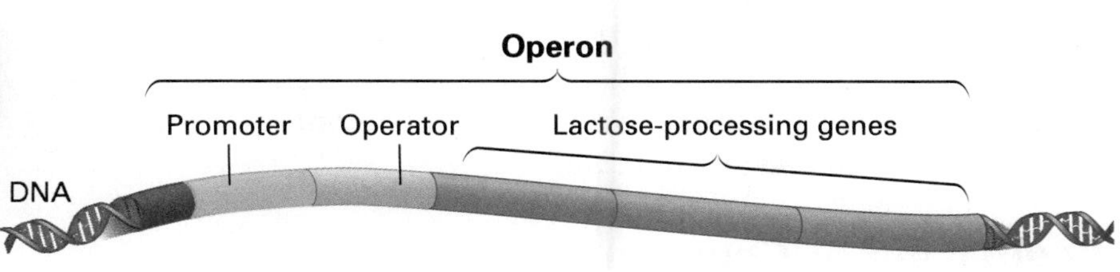

Figure 13-18 *E. coli* bacteria, natural inhabitants of your intestine, break down the sugar lactose. The genes that code for lactose-processing enzymes are located next to control sequences. Altogether, this stretch of DNA is called the *lac* operon.

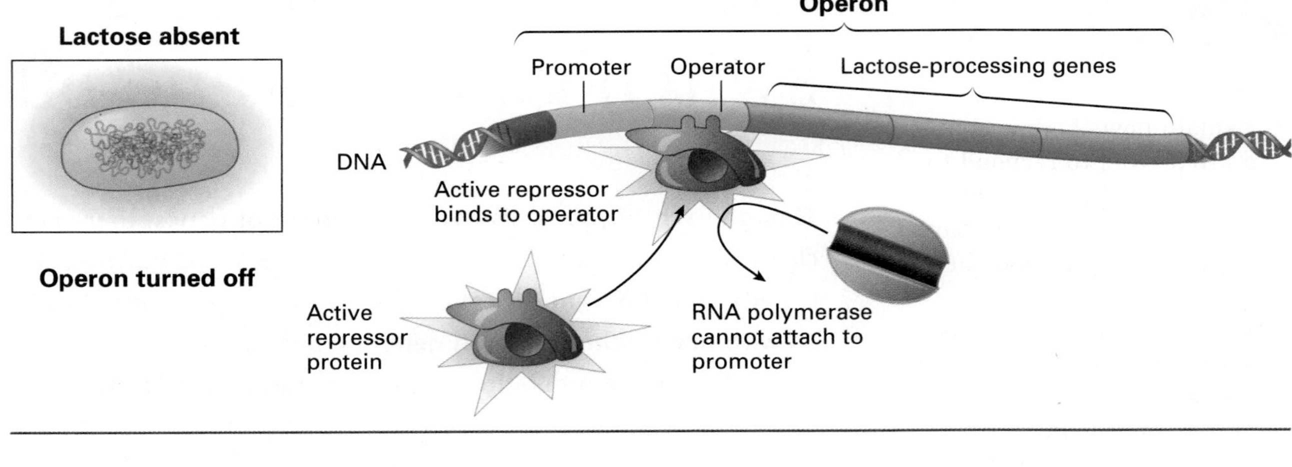

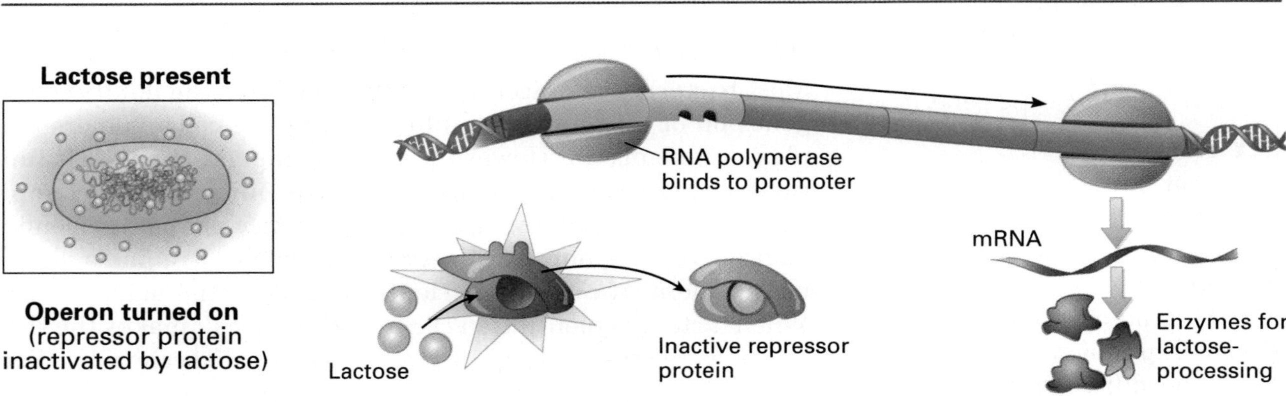

▲ **Figure 13-19** The *lac* operon is inactive in the absence of lactose (top) because a repressor blocks attachment of RNA polymerase to the promoter. With lactose present (bottom), the repressor is inactivated, and transcription of lactose-processing genes proceeds.

But what determines whether the operator switch is on or off? Transcription is turned off by a molecule called a **repressor,** a protein that functions by binding to the operator and blocking the attachment of RNA polymerase to the promoter. In the absence of lactose, the repressor is active, and the lactose-processing genes are "turned off" (Figure 13-19, top). In contrast, when lactose molecules are present, they bind to the repressor protein and change its shape. In this new shape, the repressor cannot bind to the operator. RNA polymerase can now attach to the promoter and transcribe the DNA. The lactose-processing genes are "turned on" (Figure 13-19, bottom). When the bacterial cell uses up the available lactose, the repressor turns the genes off again by reattaching to the operator.

Scientists have discovered many operons in prokaryotes. Similar to the *lac* operon, these other operons enable the prokaryotes to tailor their cell chemistry to the changing environment. As a result, prokaryotes waste little energy providing enzymes for unnecessary reactions.

Regulation of Genes in Eukaryotes

Eukaryotic cells have more elaborate mechanisms than bacteria for regulating genes, but some of the general principles are the same. Eukaryotic DNA includes promoter sequences located before the point where transcription of certain genes begins.

Many types of proteins called **transcription factors** regulate transcription by binding to those promoters or to RNA polymerases. These transcription factors are in turn activated and deactivated by certain chemical signals in the cell. For example, by attaching to transcription factors, some hormones signal cells in the body to express certain genes. **Gene expression** is the transcription and translation of genes into proteins.

▲ Figure 13-20 All the cells in an early frog embryo (inset) are very similar. But as the embryo develops, the cells differentiate into the distinct cells making up muscles, nerves, and other parts of the tadpole.

From Egg to Organism

Gene expression is regulated in the cells of a eukaryotic organism starting when an egg is fertilized and begins to divide into a multicellular embryo. The position of each new cell in the embryo promotes expression of particular groups of genes. For example, genes associated with the head are expressed only in a particular region of "pre-head" cells in the embryo. Throughout development, a cell's position relative to its neighbors affects which genes it expresses. As the embryo continues to develop, individual cells undergo **cellular differentiation**—they become increasingly specialized in structure and function (Figure 13-20).

A particular cell only expresses genes that code for proteins with functions in that cell. For example, genes coding for enzymes required during glycolysis are active in all human cell types shown in the diagram in Figure 13-21. The gene for making insulin, though present in each type of cell, is only active (expressed—transcribed and translated) in certain cells of the pancreas. Similarly, the gene coding for a transparent protein that coats the eye lens is only active in the developing eye of the embryo. The hemoglobin gene is inactive in all three cell types—none of these cells produce hemoglobin.

Biologists can track the expression of thousands of genes at once using a "DNA chip," shown in Figure 13-21. DNA chips can be used to track changes in gene activity in any cell during the course of development, or to diagnose genetic disorders by revealing abnormal expression of certain genes in different cell types.

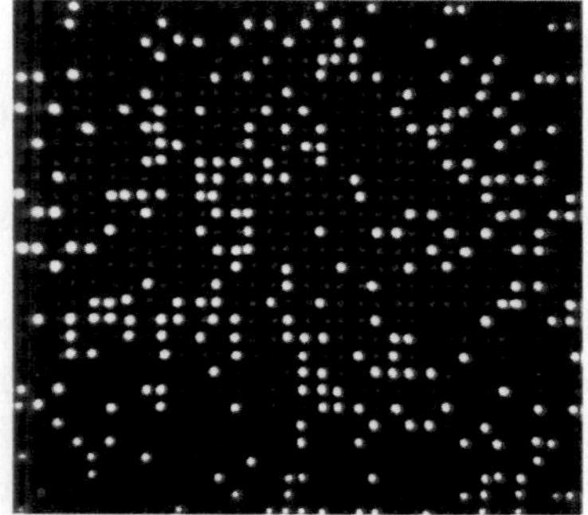

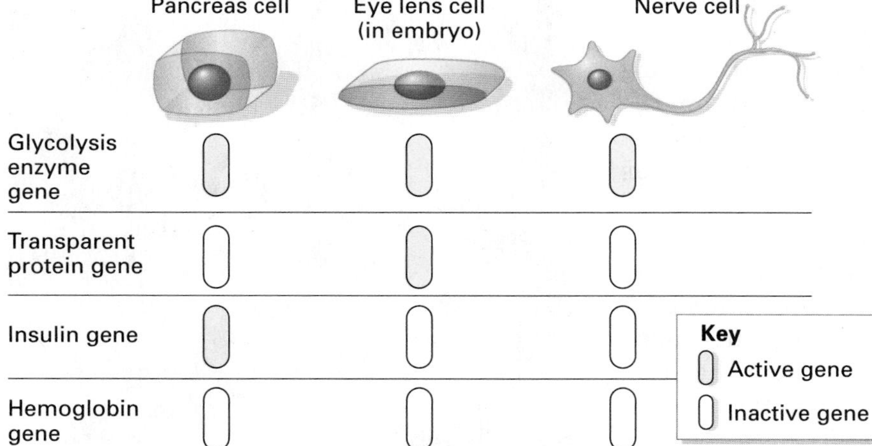

Figure 13-21 Though all the genes of the genome are present in every type of cell, only a small, specific fraction of these genes are actually expressed in each type of cell. The image above shows an actual DNA chip, which indicates the expression of hundreds of genes in a cell at a time. The yellow dots indicate a gene that is "turned on" (expressed).

Stem Cells

During most organisms' development, certain groups of cells, called **stem cells,** remain undifferentiated. Stem cells have the potential to differentiate into various types of cells.

A human embryo seven days after fertilization is a mostly hollow ball of about 100 cells, with embryonic stem cells in the center (Figure 13-22). After birth, clusters of stem cells remain in several organs. For example, your bone marrow contains stem cells that can develop into more than a dozen different types of blood cells throughout your life. In a bone marrow transplant, bone marrow from a healthy person is transplanted into a person with a bone marrow or blood disease such as leukemia. This enables the sick person to start making healthy blood cells again.

However, stem cell clusters present after birth cannot make the full range of new tissues with the ease that embryonic stem cells can. And there are some types of tissues, such as nervous tissue and heart muscle, for which stem cells may not exist in the adult individual. Embryonic stem cells may be able to help people with disabling diseases that affect such tissues, but some people question the ethics of this technology.

While the ethics of research on embryonic stem cells continues to be debated, new breakthroughs are being made with bone marrow stem cells. Recent laboratory experiments have shown that under the right conditions, bone marrow stem cells can sometimes develop into nerve cells. The procedure does not have a good success rate yet, but perhaps in the future, doctors will be able to "grow new parts" using a patient's very own stem cells.

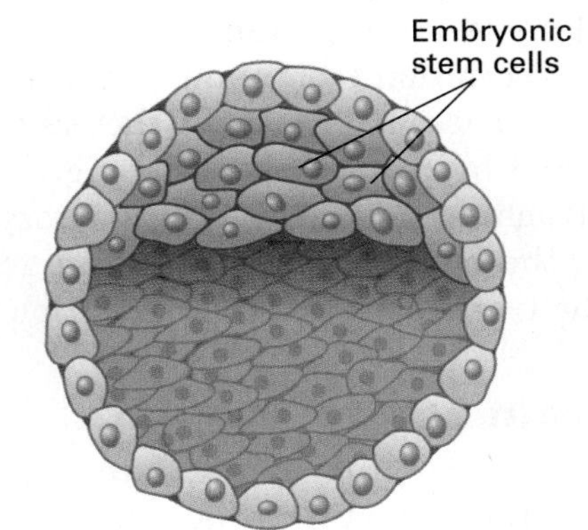

▲ **Figure 13-22** Present at a very early stage of human development, stem cells have the potential to develop into any type of human cell.

▼ **Figure 13-23** This *Drosophila* is a homeotic mutant. In place of antennae, it has developed an extra pair of eyes.

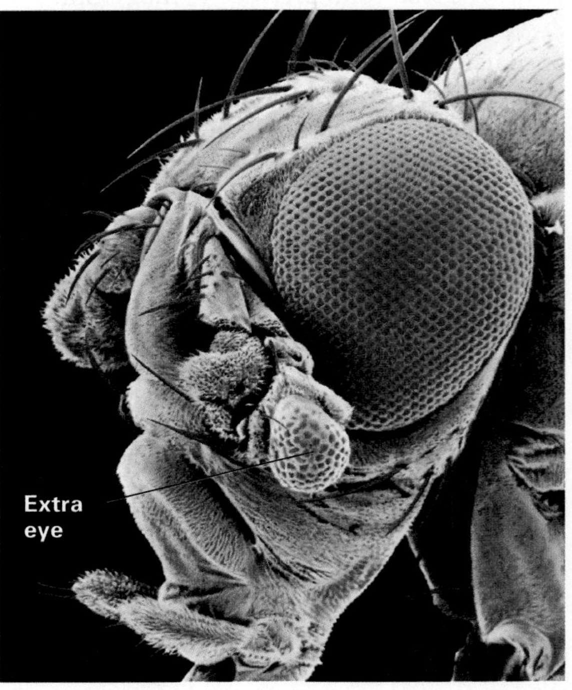

Colorized SEM 50×

Homeotic Genes

Studying the effects of genetic mutations is another way to understand more about gene expression during development. For example, researchers have demonstrated that a particular gene functions as a master switch that triggers the development of eyes in *Drosophila* (Figure 13-23). A mutation that leads to expression of this gene in the wrong cells of the embryonic fly is like flipping on a switch in the wrong location. In the mutant flies, eyes develop on the antennae, legs, and wings, in addition to their normal location on the head. Some of the mutants grow as many as 14 eyes!

This gene is one of a class of **homeotic genes,** master control genes that direct development of body parts in specific locations in many organisms. In *Drosophila* each homeotic gene contains a 180-nucleotide sequence called a homeobox. A homeobox codes for a protein that promotes the transcription of genes involved in the development of specific body parts. This basic process of one

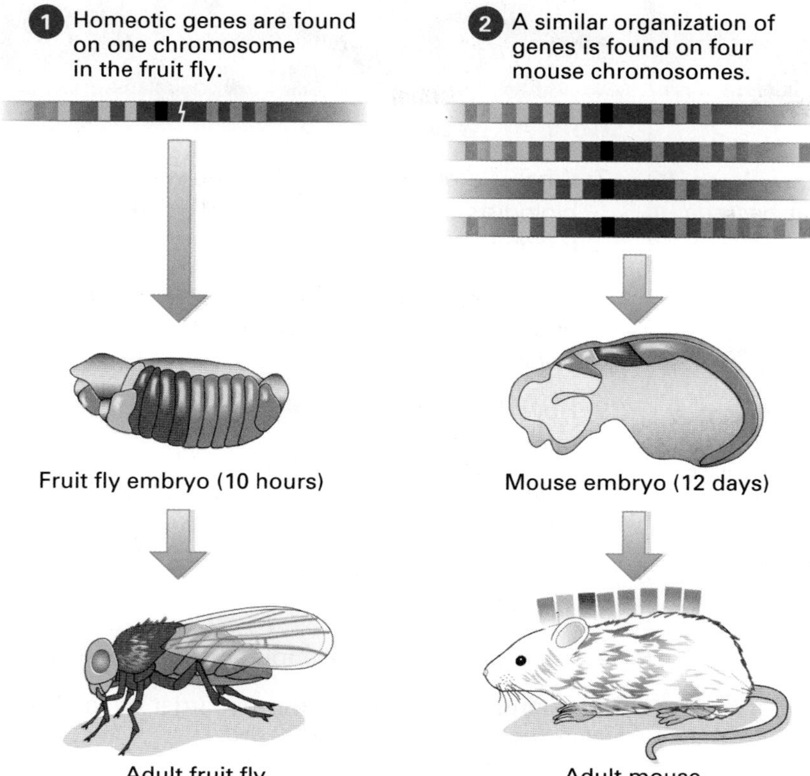
1 Homeotic genes are found on one chromosome in the fruit fly.
2 A similar organization of genes is found on four mouse chromosomes.
Fruit fly embryo (10 hours)
Mouse embryo (12 days)
Adult fruit fly
Adult mouse

Figure 13-24 The highlighted portions of the fruit fly and mouse chromosomes carry very similar homeotic genes. The color coding identifies the parts of the embryo and adult animals that are affected by these genes.

gene product regulating the expression of other genes is common in the development of all multicellular organisms. In fact, the same or very similar homeobox sequence found in *Drosophila* also occurs in the homeotic genes of many other animals, including humans and other mammals (Figure 13-24).

The more scientists learn about the mechanisms of development in different organisms, the more underlying similarities they find. The similarities support the hypothesis that certain genes in diverse species were inherited from ancestors common to those species. In the next unit, you will explore how diverse organisms can evolve from a common ancestor.

Online Activity 13.5

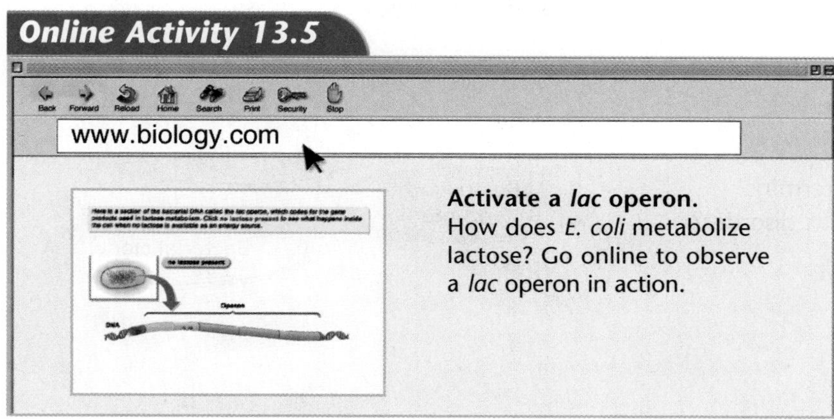
Back
Forward
Reload
Home
Search
Print
Security
Stop
www.biology.com

Activate a *lac* operon.
How does *E. coli* metabolize lactose? Go online to observe a *lac* operon in action.

Concept Check 13.5

1. Describe how the presence of lactose turns on the *lac* operon in bacteria.
2. Give an example of a molecule in your body that can affect transcription factors.
3. Define cellular differentiation.
4. Give examples of two types of cells that probably cannot be regenerated by stem cells in an adult human.
5. Give an example of a homeotic gene.

Multiple Choice

Choose the letter of the best answer.

1. Which of the following is *not* a way that bacteria obtain new combinations of genes?
   a. Two bacteria join together and one passes genes to the other.
   b. Bacteria produce haploid gametes that undergo fertilization.
   c. Viruses carry bacterial genes from one cell to another.
   d. Bacteria take up free pieces of DNA from their environment.
2. Which tool do biologists use to cut a section of DNA from a chromosome?
   a. plasmids
   b. restriction enzymes
   c. nucleic acid probes
   d. genetic markers
3. Why would a scientist use a nucleic acid probe?
   a. to test for the presence of a certain gene
   b. to build a genomic library
   c. to cut DNA
   d. to introduce new genes into other cells
4. Which of the following would be considered a transgenic organism?
   a. a plant grown in culture from a single plant cell
   b. a human treated with insulin produced by *E. coli* bacteria
   c. a sheep developed from an egg cell fertilized in the laboratory
   d. a sheep that produces a cow protein
5. Why do scientists use gel electrophoresis?
   a. to build a genomic library
   b. to inject a gene into a fertilized egg
   c. to mass-produce a specific segment of DNA
   d. to compare DNA samples from different sources
6. What might a scientist examine to determine whether a person is a carrier for a genetic disorder?
   a. cellular differentiation
   b. recombinant plasmids
   c. operons
   d. genetic markers

Short Answer

7. What is a plasmid? Describe one way in which biologists use plasmids as a tool in genetic engineering.
8. In making recombinant DNA, what is the benefit of using a restriction enzyme that cuts DNA in a staggered fashion?
9. How do scientists locate a specific gene in a genomic library?
10. Give examples of at least two useful products from genetically engineered microorganisms.
11. Contrast a genetically modified animal with a cloned animal.
12. What is PCR? Give examples of its uses.
13. During gel electrophoresis do larger or smaller molecules move faster? Explain.
14. Why is it helpful to use genetic markers from noncoding regions when comparing DNA fingerprints as evidence in court?
15. Explain how the *lac* operon is regulated.
16. What is a homeotic gene?

Visualizing Concepts

17. Using the terms in the ovals below, create a flowchart to show the sequence of steps involved in cloning a gene using recombinant bacterial plasmids.

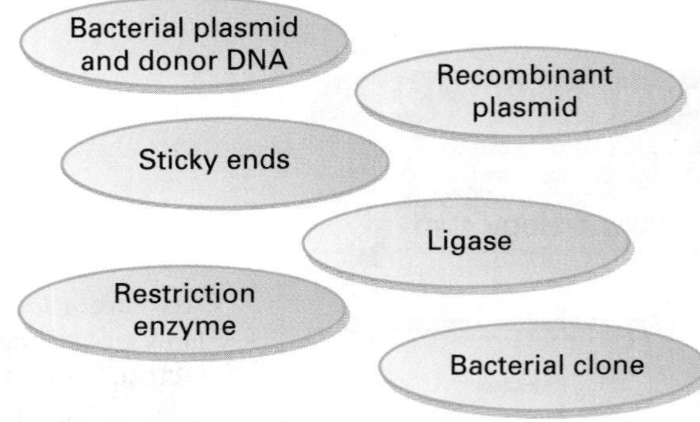

Analyzing Information

18. Analyzing Diagrams Use the diagram to answer the questions below.

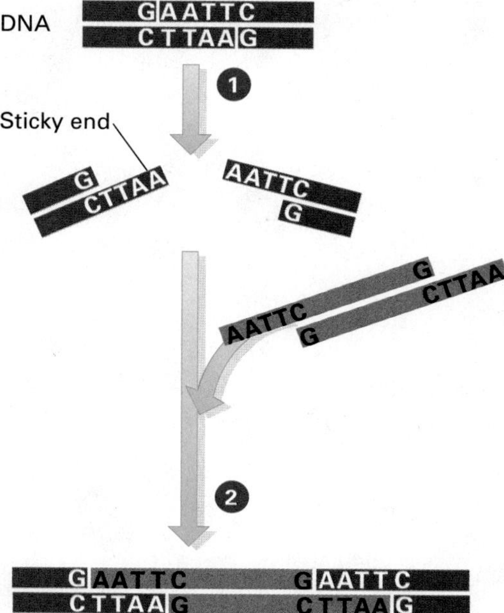

a. Describe what is happening in Step 1.
b. Describe what is happening in Step 2.

19. Analyzing Data This gel shows results of DNA fingerprinting in a criminal case.

Victim | Hair from victim's shirt | Suspect 1 | Suspect 2

a. Give a reason why the restriction enzyme treatment produced different lengths of fragments for the victim and each suspect.
b. Does the DNA evidence indicate that either suspect was present at the scene of the crime? Explain.

Critical Thinking

20. Comparing and Contrasting Distinguish between two different "cloning" techniques discussed in this chapter.

21. Problem Solving A scientist has collected a genomic library using just one restriction enzyme. She fails to locate the desired gene using a nucleic acid probe. She tries a different restriction enzyme. Suggest why her first attempt might have failed and why her second might succeed.

22. Comparing and Contrasting Compare and contrast the procedures for producing genetically modified plants and animals.

23. Making Generalizations Your nerve cells and skin cells contain the same genes. Explain why these cells are different.

24. What's Wrong With These Statements? *Briefly explain why each statement is inaccurate or misleading.*

a. PCR is a technique by which living cells make many copies of a segment of DNA.
b. Each of your cells expresses your genome.
c. The *lac* operon is the gene that makes lactose in *E. coli.*

Performance Assessment

Design an Experiment A scientist is attempting to clone a cow. The female cow into which the altered embryo is implanted eventually gives birth to two calves, indicating that the cow was already carrying an embryo when the altered one was implanted. Explain how you could detect which calf is the clone.

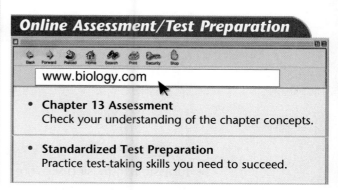

Online Assessment/Test Preparation

Back Forward Reload Home Search Print Security Stop

www.biology.com

- **Chapter 13 Assessment**
  Check your understanding of the chapter concepts.
- **Standardized Test Preparation**
  Practice test-taking skills you need to succeed.

UNIT 4 Exploring the History of Life

Chapters

Jurassic fish fossil discovered in a quarry in Germany

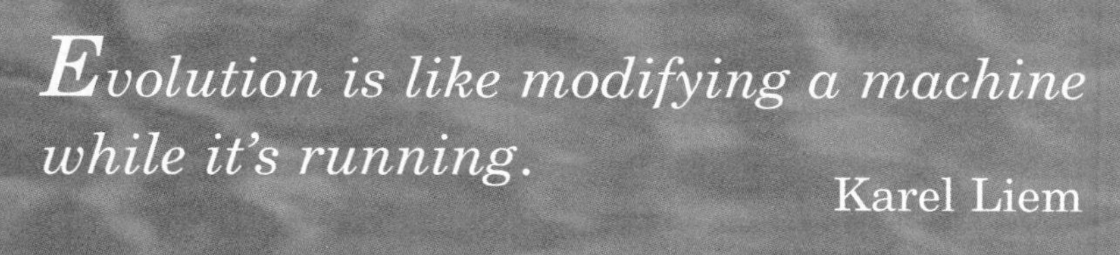

Evolution is like modifying a machine while it's running.

Karel Liem

Evolution: A History and a Process

There's an expression that the only constant in the universe is change. According to evolutionary theory, this expression certainly applies to life. The kinds of organisms on Earth—the species—have changed over time. The imprints in the rock in this photograph are remnants of marine organisms called ammonites that lived more than a hundred million years ago. Many other species have come and gone, and new species have emerged. But even as change is part of life, so is continuity. Scientific evidence suggests that all of life is united by descent from the first microbes that appeared on early Earth. In this chapter, you will learn how life evolves through the process of natural selection. Before you begin, go online to the ***WebQuest*** to explore connections between birds and reptiles based on the fossil record.

Key Concepts

Concept 14.1 Darwin developed a theory of evolution.

Concept 14.2 Evolution has left much evidence.

Concept 14.3 Darwin proposed natural selection as the mechanism of evolution.

Concept 14.4 Microevolution is a change in a population's gene pool.

Concept 14.5 Evolutionary biology is important in health science.

Assessment Chapter 14 Review

What's Online

www.biology.com

WebQuest
ArchaeopteryxQuest

Online Activity 14.1
Travel with Darwin.

History of Science
History of Evolutionary Theory

Online Activity 14.2
Locate homologous structures.

Online Activity 14.3
Model the spread of pesticide resistance.

Lab 14 Online Companion
Birds on an Island

Online Activity 14.4
Alter a gene pool.

Closer Look
Hardy-Weinberg Equilibrium

Online Activity 14.5
Analyze sickle cell genotypes.

Chapter 14 Assessment

CONCEPT 14.1 Darwin developed a theory of evolution.

OBJECTIVES

- Summarize ideas from Darwin's time that influenced his work.
- Identify some key observations from Darwin's voyage that led to his theory.
- Describe the two main points of Darwin's theory.

KEY TERMS

- evolution
- adaptation
- descent with modification
- natural selection

What's Online

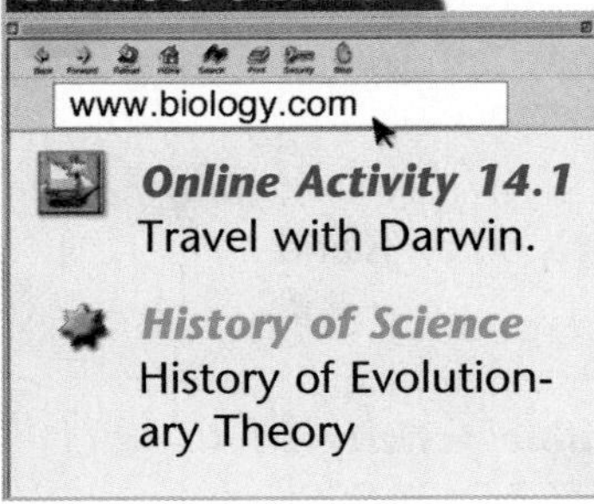

Online Activity 14.1 Travel with Darwin.

History of Science History of Evolutionary Theory

A new view of life came into focus in 1859, when Charles Darwin published his book *The Origin of Species.* Darwin's ideas provided a framework for understanding Earth's diversity of organisms and their relationships to one another and with their environments.

Ideas From Darwin's Time

On its grandest scale, **evolution** is all of the changes that have transformed life over an immense time. In a sense, evolution is the biological history of life on Earth. Before Darwin, two ideas about life on Earth prevailed. One was that species are fixed, or permanent. In other words, they do not change. The other idea was that Earth itself is less than 10,000 years old and also relatively unchanging. These ideas were challenged as people became aware of the incredible diversity of organisms, past and present, and the nature of Earth's geologic processes.

In the mid-1700s, the study of fossils led French naturalist Georges Buffon to suggest that Earth might be much older than a few thousand years. He also observed that specific fossils and certain living animals were similar but not exactly alike. In the early 1800s, another French naturalist, Jean Baptiste Lamarck suggested an explanation of Buffon's observations. Lamarck proposed that life evolves, or changes. He recognized that species are not permanent. Lamarck explained evolution as a process of adaptation. Today, biologists consider an **adaptation** to be an inherited characteristic that improves an organism's ability to survive and reproduce in a particular environment. An example of evolutionary adaptation is the massive hind legs of a kangaroo that moves about by hopping and leaping (Figure 14-1).

Figure 14-1 Powerful muscles in the large hind legs of a kangaroo are an adaptation that help the animal move about quickly and efficiently. The large tail provides balance when the kangaroo is leaping or sitting on the ground.

Today, Lamarck is unfairly remembered in large part for his mistaken explanation of how adaptations evolve. He proposed that by using or not using certain body parts, an organism develops certain characteristics. Lamarck thought that these enhanced characteristics would be passed on to the offspring. Lamarck called this idea *inheritance of acquired characteristics.* For example, Lamarck might explain that a kangaroo's powerful hind legs were the result of ancestors strengthening their legs by jumping and then passing that acquired leg strength on to offspring. However, an acquired characteristic would have to somehow modify the DNA of specific genes in order to be inherited. There is no evidence that this happens (Figure 14-2). Still, it is important to note that Lamarck proposed that evolution occurs when organisms adapt to their environments. This idea helped set the stage for Darwin.

▲ **Figure 14-2** A bonsai tree is "trained" to grow as a dwarf by pruning and shaping. But seeds from this tree would produce offspring that could grow to normal size.

The Voyage of the *Beagle*

On a cold December day in 1831, the HMS *Beagle* set sail on a voyage around the world. Figure 14-3 shows the route the ship followed. The main mission of the voyage was to chart poorly known stretches of the South American coastline for the British navy. Accompanying the captain was a 22-year-old college graduate, Charles Darwin. Darwin's main interest was to study the geology, plants, and animals encountered on the voyage. It was a tour that would greatly affect Darwin's thinking and eventually the thinking of many others.

▼ **Figure 14-3** The route of the *Beagle* (top inset) took Darwin around the world during a five-year voyage.

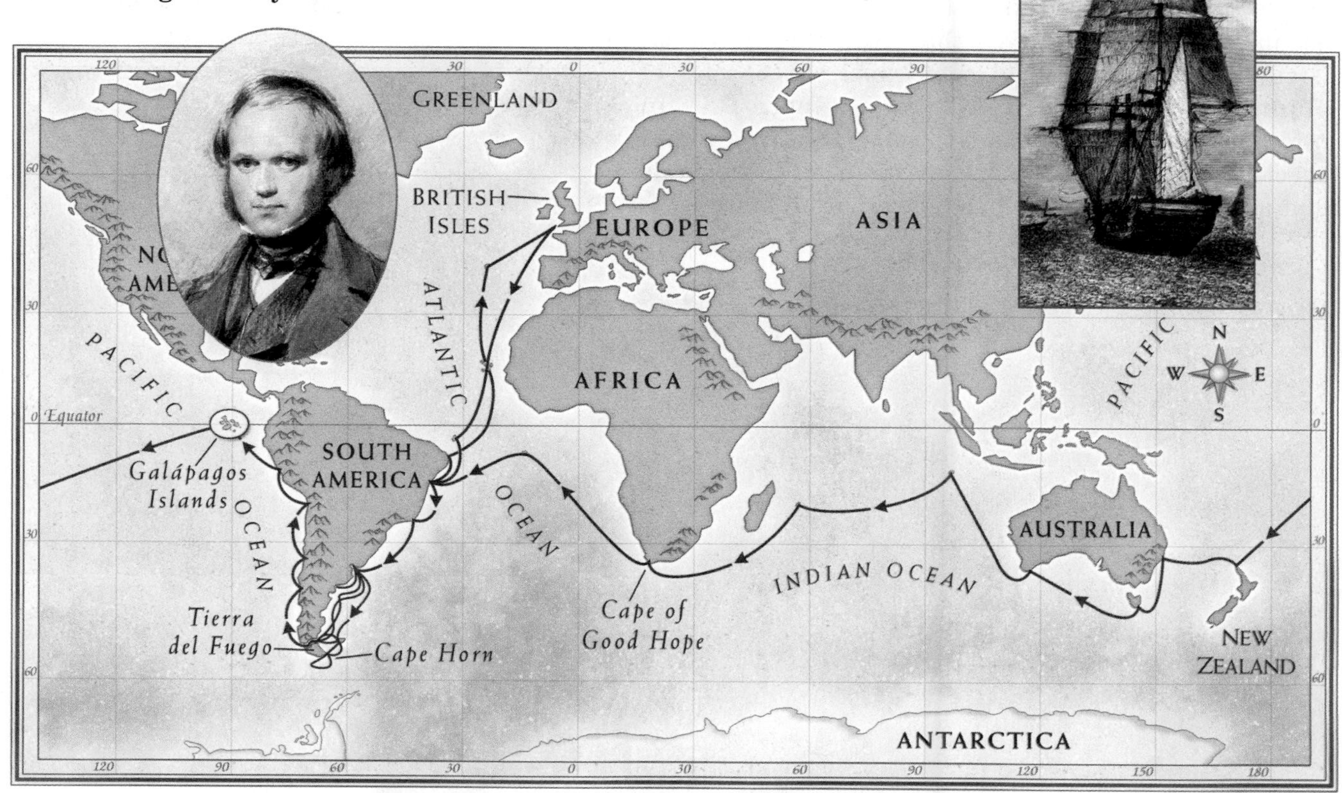

Darwin's Observations Darwin spent most of his time on shore while the ship's crew was busy surveying. There, he observed and collected thousands of specimens of South American plants and animals from diverse environments. He studied organisms and their adaptations from places as different as the Brazilian jungle, the grasslands of the pampas, and the frigid lands near Antarctica.

Throughout the voyage and the rest of his life, Darwin maintained extensive journals of his observations, studies, and thoughts. These journals provide a window into Darwin's thinking. His writings indicate that before the voyage he felt that the concept of fixed or unchanging species best described nature. During the voyage, he began to question this concept. Sometime after he returned to England, Darwin became convinced that species change as they adapt to their changing environments.

Darwin noticed that the plants and animals throughout the continent all had a definite South American character. They were quite distinct from the species of Europe. Even the fossils that Darwin found were uniquely South American. Some of the fossils were gigantic versions of the modern animals. His observations supported the idea that species living in South America today were descended from ancestral species on that continent.

Darwin was intrigued by life on islands such as the Galápagos. The Galápagos are a chain of relatively young volcanic islands about 900 kilometers off the western coast of South America. Darwin observed that the islands had many unique organisms (Figure 14-4). Most of the species on the islands were similar to, but different from the plants and animals of the nearest mainland. He observed that even the individual islands in the chain had some different species of plants and animals from one another. Darwin inferred from these observations that mainland species had changed after they colonized the islands and adapted to their various new environments.

▼ **Figure 14-4** Marine iguanas of the Galápagos dive into the ocean to feed on algae. Very large, slightly webbed feet are one of the adaptations that make these animals such good swimmers. Their charcoal skin color provides camouflage on the islands' lava rocks. The dark skin also absorbs sunlight and helps to warm the iguanas as they bask on rocks.

Ideas From Geology During the *Beagle's* long sails between ports, Darwin managed to do a lot of reading in spite of his seasickness. The writings of the geologist Charles Lyell had a particularly strong influence on Darwin. Lyell proposed that gradual and observable geologic processes such as erosion could explain the physical features of today's Earth. For example, the gradual erosion of a riverbed over thousands or millions of years can result in a deep, river-carved canyon (Figure 14-5). A mighty mountain range can be thrust up centimeter by centimeter by earthquakes occurring over millions of years. All that was required for an understanding of these changes was an Earth far older than previously thought.

▲ **Figure 14-5** Gradual erosion by the Colorado River produced this dramatic rock formation named Horseshoe Bend in what is now Arizona.

Darwin personally experienced an earthquake while doing field studies in the Andes Mountains of Chile. In a harbor, he observed a block of land that had been underwater move upward above the water level as a result of the quake. He also collected fossils of ocean organisms high in the Andes (Figure 14-6). Applying Lyell's ideas, Darwin reasoned that earthquakes gradually lifted the rock bearing those marine fossils from the sea floor.

The geologic evidence presented by Lyell and others pointed to two conclusions. First, the slow processes of mountain building and erosion suggested an Earth that must be very old. Second, these slow and gradual processes occurring over vast spans of time could cause enormous change on Earth. Darwin would eventually apply this idea of gradual change to the evolution of Earth's life forms.

▼ **Figure 14-6** Darwin found fossils of marine organisms like this one high above sea level in the Andes Mountains. These findings were evidence of major geologic changes in Earth's history.

Darwin Publishes His Theory

Darwin and the *Beagle* returned to England after five years at sea. Letters and specimens he had sent back to England established Darwin's reputation with other scientists. He left as a young graduate and returned as a famous naturalist. After his return, he analyzed his collection and became convinced that Earth was ancient and that species can change through time. As Darwin contemplated a mechanism for evolutionary change, he began to construct a scientific theory built on observations, inferences, and ideas from his own work and the work of others. Figure 14-7 summarizes some of Darwin's experiences.

▼ **Figure 14-7** The ideas of others and observations during his voyage changed Darwin's thinking about Earth and its life. At home, observations of selective breeding (discussed in Concept 14.3) and the ideas of Malthus also influenced Darwin.

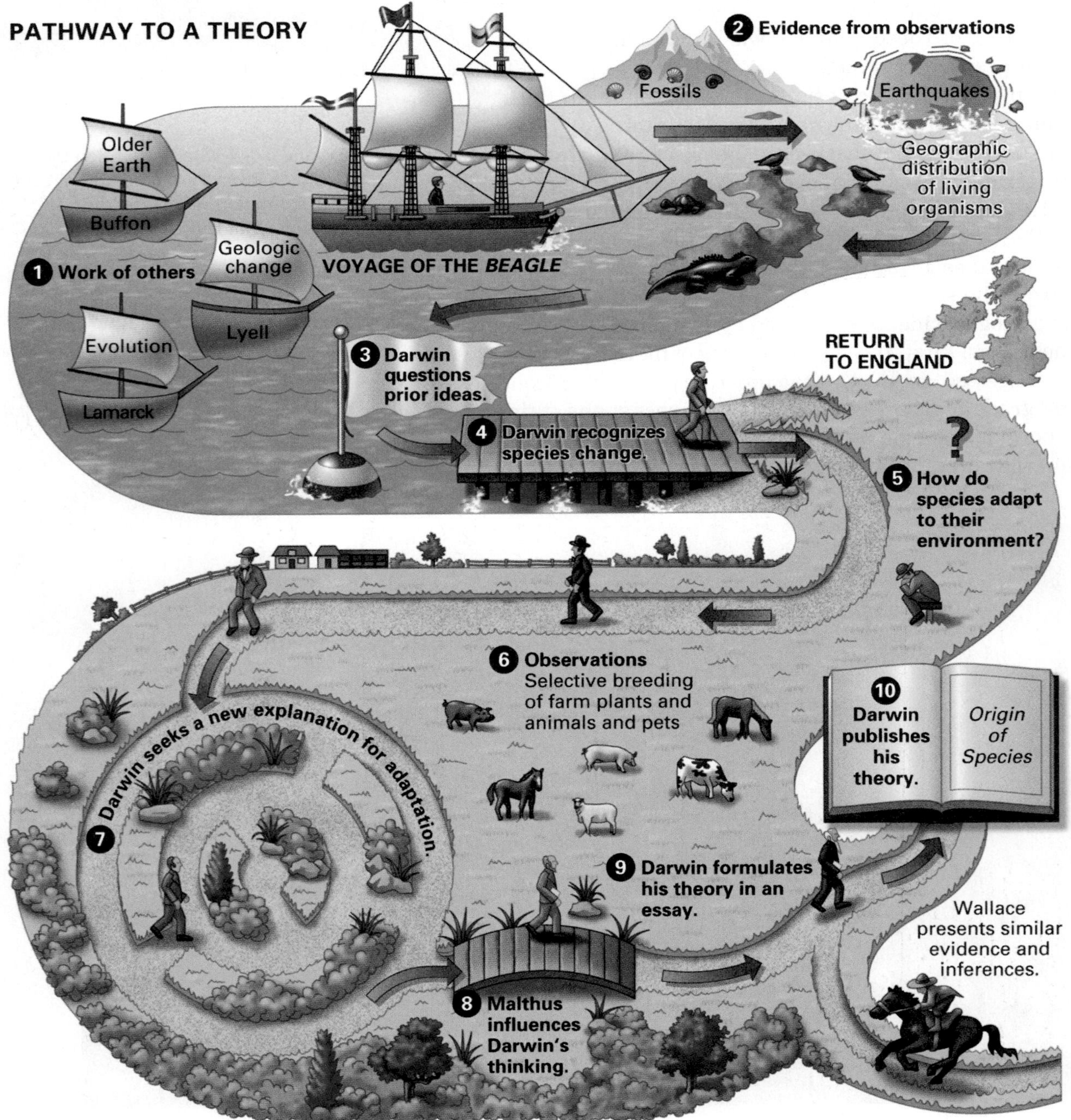
PATHWAY TO A THEORY
1 Work of others
Older Earth
Buffon
Geologic change
Lyell
Evolution
Lamarck
VOYAGE OF THE BEAGLE
2 Evidence from observations
Fossils
Earthquakes
Geographic distribution of living organisms
3 Darwin questions prior ideas.
4 Darwin recognizes species change.
RETURN TO ENGLAND
5 How do species adapt to their environment?
6 Observations
Selective breeding of farm plants and animals and pets
7 Darwin seeks a new explanation for adaptation.
8 Malthus influences Darwin's thinking.
9 Darwin formulates his theory in an essay.
10 Darwin publishes his theory.
Origin of Species
Wallace presents similar evidence and inferences.

In 1838, as Darwin continued to think about the question of how species change, he read an essay on human populations written a few decades earlier by Thomas Malthus. Malthus contended that much of human suffering, such as disease, famine, and homelessness, was due to the human population's potential to grow. That is, populations can grow much faster than the rate at which supplies of food and other resources can be produced. Darwin recognized that Malthus's ideas applied to all species. The production of more individuals than the environment can support leads to a struggle for existence. This concept helped Darwin to propose a mechanism of evolutionary change.

In 1844, Darwin wrote a 200-page essay that outlined his idea, but he didn't release it to the public. Instead, for the next several years he continued to accumulate more evidence to support his idea. He told only a few of his closest colleagues, who encouraged him to publish his work before someone else came to the same conclusions. In 1858, another British naturalist, Alfred Wallace, *did* come to the same conclusion. Darwin was shocked to receive a letter from Wallace that described the same basic mechanism for evolutionary change that Darwin had proposed. Within a month, some of Wallace's and Darwin's writings were jointly presented in public. Darwin published his book *The Origin of Species* about a year later.

History of Science

Back Forward Reload Home Search Print Security Stop

www.biology.com

History of Evolutionary Theory

Earth is home to more than a million species of organisms. Where did they all come from? How do scientists study the history of life? Go online to learn about some individuals who have interpreted physical evidence to explain how life on Earth came to be the way it is today.

Darwin's Two Main Points

Darwin made two main points in his book. First, he argued from evidence that the species of organisms living on Earth today descended from ancestral species. In other words, life has a history of change. Darwin proposed that the descendants of the earliest organisms spread into various habitats over millions of years. In these habitats, they accumulated different modifications, or adaptations, to diverse ways of life. Darwin called this process **descent with modification.** He saw descent with modification as a way to account for the diversity of life. Figure 14-8 shows two species of hares that are adapted to living in different environments. The jackrabbit benefits from fur that blends well in the desert and ears that help cool its body. White fur provides protective camouflage in the snowy northern regions of the snowshoe hare's range.

Figure 14-8 The large ears of the jackrabbit (left) are an adaptation to the animal's hot environment. Rich with blood vessels, the ears radiate heat, which helps cool the jackrabbit's body. The white fur of the snowshoe hare (right) camouflages the animal in its environment.

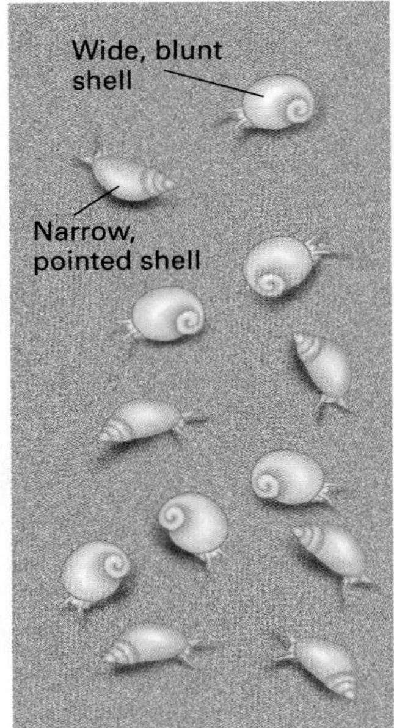

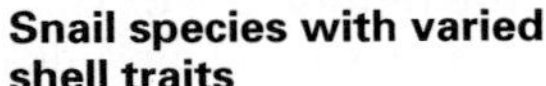
Snail species with varied shell traits

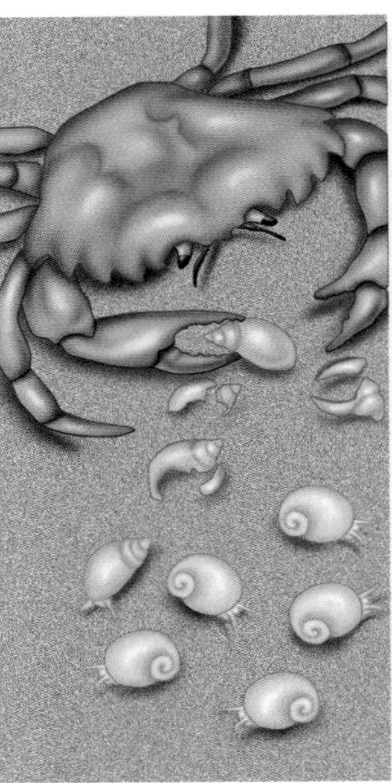
Capture of snails with narrow, pointed shells

Reproduction of survivors

Over many generations, there is an increase in snails with wide, blunt shells.

▲ **Figure 14-9** In this hypothetical population of snails, inherited shell variations make some snails less likely than others to be attacked by predators. Wide, blunt shells increase the chances for snails to survive and pass their traits to the next generation by reproducing.

Darwin's second main point was his argument for natural selection as the mechanism for evolution. **Natural selection** is the process by which individuals with inherited characteristics well-suited to the environment leave more offspring on average than do other individuals. Figure 14-9 models how certain inherited traits can give individuals some advantage over other individuals of the same species in the same environment. This process, which you will read more about later in this chapter, can cause a population to change over time. When biologists speak of "Darwin's theory of evolution," they are referring to natural selection as a cause of evolution. The result of natural selection is adaptation. This process of natural selection is another way of defining evolution. But the term *evolution* can also be used on a much broader scale to mean the history of life, from the earliest microbes to the enormous diversity of modern organisms.

Online Activity 14.1

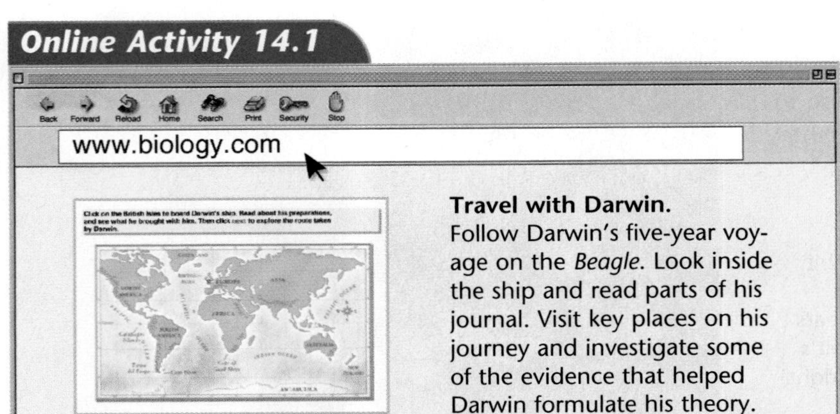

Travel with Darwin.
Follow Darwin's five-year voyage on the *Beagle*. Look inside the ship and read parts of his journal. Visit key places on his journey and investigate some of the evidence that helped Darwin formulate his theory.

Concept Check 14.1

1. How did the work of Lyell and Malthus influence Darwin as he developed his theory of evolution?
2. What characteristics of the Galápagos Islands were particularly important for Darwin?
3. What is natural selection?
4. Which of the following is an adaptation: the sharp teeth of a house cat, or a scar on the cat's ear? Explain.

CONCEPT 14.2

Evolution has left much evidence.

OBJECTIVES
- Describe information the fossil record contains about life on Earth.
- Tell how the geographic distribution of organisms relates to evolution.
- Explain how similarities in structure and development among different species are evidence for evolution.
- Describe molecular evidence for evolution.

KEY TERMS
- fossil
- fossil record
- extinct
- homologous structure
- vestigial structure

What's Online

Online Activity 14.2 Locate homologous structures.

Evolution leaves observable signs. Such clues to the past are essential to any historical science. Biological evolution has left marks on all aspects of life—in the fossil record and in the diverse assortment of modern species.

The Fossil Record

Preserved remains or markings left by organisms that lived in the past are called **fossils.** Most fossils are found in sedimentary rocks. Sand and silt eroded from the land are carried by rivers to seas and swamps, where the particles settle to the bottom. Over millions of years, deposits pile up and compress the older sediments below into rock. Rock strata, or layers, form when the rates of sedimentation or the types of particles forming the sediments vary over time. Aquatic organisms can become fossils when they die and are buried in sediments in a way that preserves some of their structure. Land organisms can become fossils in a similar way, if they are swept into rivers, lakes, swamps, and seas. Other remains of land dwellers may become fossils after being covered by windblown dust, sand, or volcanic ash.

Younger rock strata usually are layered on top of older ones, as illustrated in Figure 14-10. Thus, the positions of fossils in the rock strata can reveal their relative age. The **fossil record** is this chronological collection of life's remains in the rock layers, recorded during the passage of time.

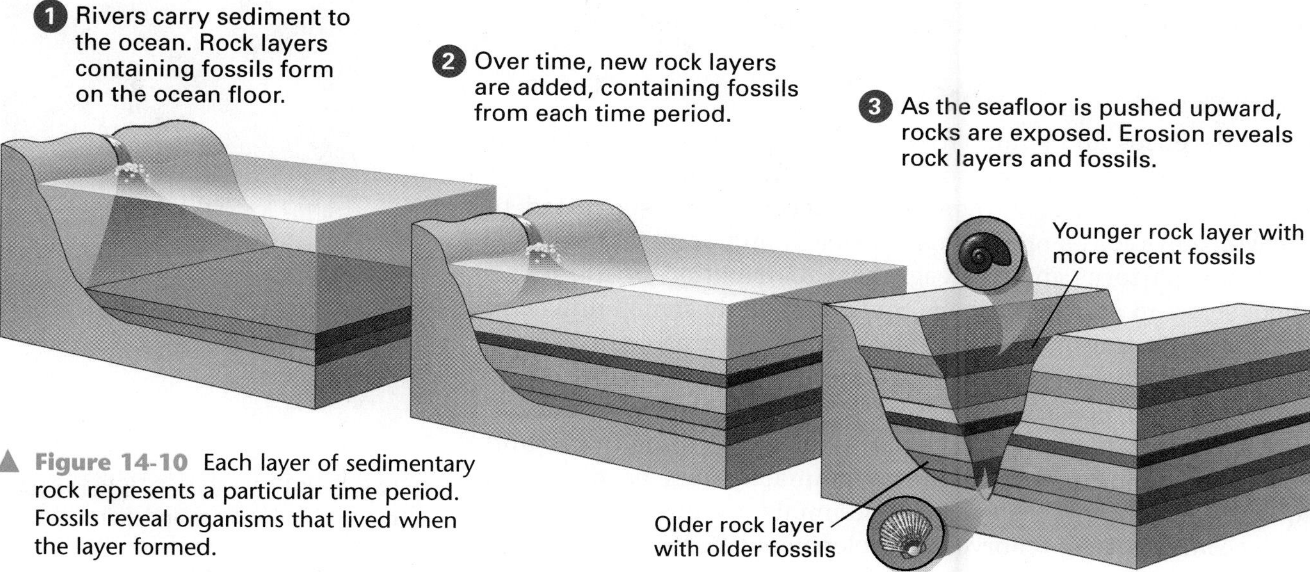

1 Rivers carry sediment to the ocean. Rock layers containing fossils form on the ocean floor.
2 Over time, new rock layers are added, containing fossils from each time period.
3 As the seafloor is pushed upward, rocks are exposed. Erosion reveals rock layers and fossils.
Younger rock layer with more recent fossils
Older rock layer with older fossils

▲ **Figure 14-10** Each layer of sedimentary rock represents a particular time period. Fossils reveal organisms that lived when the layer formed.

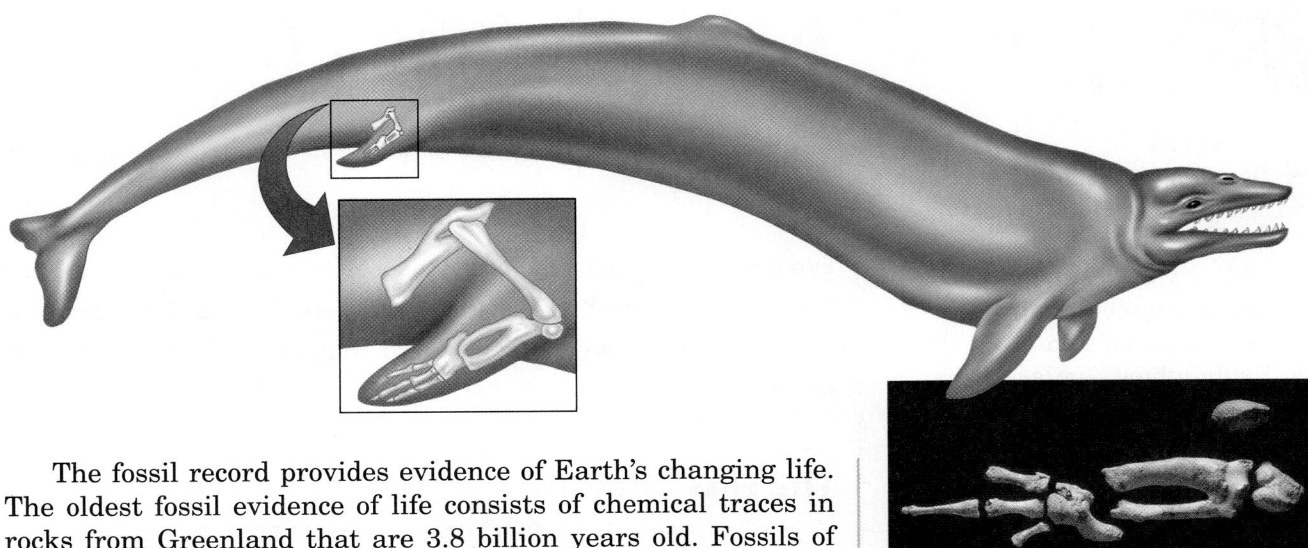

▲ **Figure 14-11** Fossil evidence suggests that ancient whales evolved from ancestors with hind limbs. The photograph shows the fossilized hind flipper of an early whale species, *Basilosaurus*.

The fossil record provides evidence of Earth's changing life. The oldest fossil evidence of life consists of chemical traces in rocks from Greenland that are 3.8 billion years old. Fossils of prokaryotes (bacteria and archaea) have been found in rocks of about 3.5 billion years in age. These data fit with the molecular and cellular evidence that prokaryotes are the oldest form of life. Fossils in younger layers of rock record the evolution of various groups of eukaryotic organisms. Fossils of species that became **extinct**—species that no longer exist—help scientists reconstruct the past.

Paleontologists (scientists who study fossils) have discovered fossils of many ancestral life forms that link past and present. For example, fossil evidence supports the hypothesis that whales, which have no hind limbs, evolved from land-dwelling ancestors that had four limbs. Paleontologists digging in Egypt and Pakistan have identified ancient whales that had hind limb bones. Figure 14-11 shows the fossilized hind leg bones of *Basilosaurus,* one of those early whales. These whales, which lived about 40 million years ago, were aquatic animals that no longer used their legs to support their weight. Even larger leg bones are found in fossils of older whale species that may have split their time between living on land and in water.

Geographic Distribution

The differences and similarities between organisms in different parts of the world were some of the first observations that Darwin made on his voyage. These observations suggested to Darwin that today's organisms evolved from ancestral forms.

Many patterns in the geographic distribution of life forms make sense in an evolutionary context. Why do some animals of the South American tropics share more features with certain species in the South American deserts than they do with species in the African tropics? Why is Australia home to so many kinds of pouched mammals (marsupials)—such as kangaroos and koalas—while very few placental animals—such as deer and squirrels—live there? (Placental mammals are mammals whose young complete their embryonic development before birth.) It is *not* because placental mammals are unable to survive in Australia.

▲ **Figure 14-12** Australia is home to many unique plants and animals, such as the koala, that evolved in relative isolation from other continents.

Humans have introduced rabbits, foxes, dogs, cats, and many other placental mammals to Australia. Several of these species have thrived to the point of becoming ecological and economic nuisances. The most widely accepted hypothesis suggests that Australia's diverse marsupial species evolved from marsupial ancestors on an island continent that was isolated from placental mammals.

Just as the fossil record documents the history of species of the past, the geographic distribution of organisms serves as a clue to how modern species may have evolved. As an example, consider two islands with similar environments in different parts of the world. The species on each island have more similarities to species on the nearest mainland than they do to species on the other island. If species evolved from ancestors that lived in one geographic region, the presence of related species in that region today makes sense. As you'll read in Chapter 15, the origin of new species is closely linked to Earth's changing geography and environmental conditions.

Similarities in Structure

Certain similarities in structure among species provide clues to evolutionary history. For example, the forelimbs of all mammals consist of the same skeletal parts. Human arms, cat forelegs, whale flippers, and bat wings all have the same basic combination of bones (Figure 14-13). The functions of these forelimbs differ, however. You know that a whale's flipper does not do the same job as a bat's wing. Since the functions of these limbs are completely different, you might expect that their structures would also be entirely different. Yet, that is not the case. Arms, forelegs, flippers, and wings of different mammals are variations on a common structural theme—one that has become adapted to different functions. Such similar structures in species sharing a common ancestor are called **homologous structures.**

▼ **Figure 14-13** The forelimbs of all mammals consist of the same skeletal parts. The hypothesis that all mammals descended from a common ancestor predicts that their forelimbs would be variations of the structural form in that ancestor.

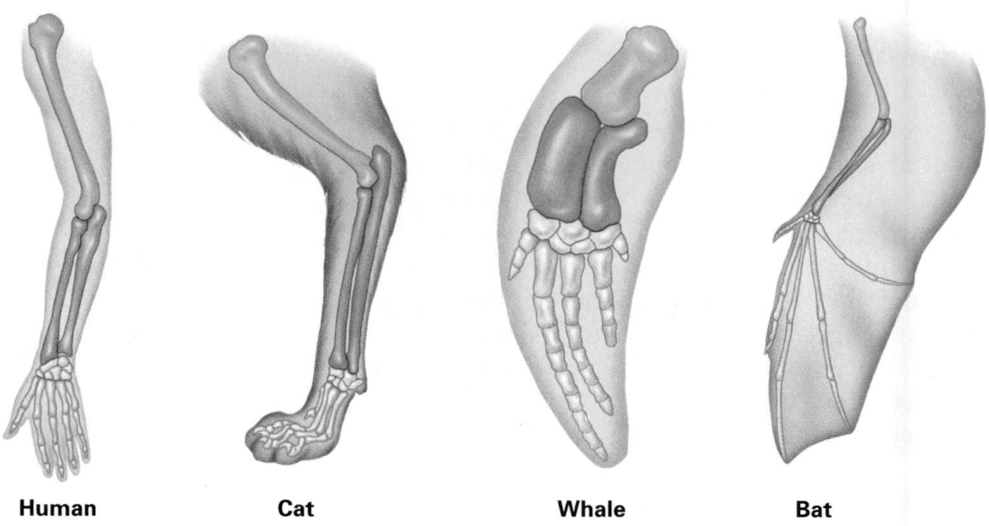

Homologous structures support other evidence that evolution is a remodeling process. Structures that originally functioned one way in ancestral species become modified as they take on new functions. This idea is what Darwin meant by "descent with modification." The limitations of this retrofitting are evident in structures that are less than perfect. For example, almost no person reaches old age without some form of knee or back problem. The human spine and knee joint were derived from ancestral structures that supported four-legged mammals—not two-legged mammals that walked upright.

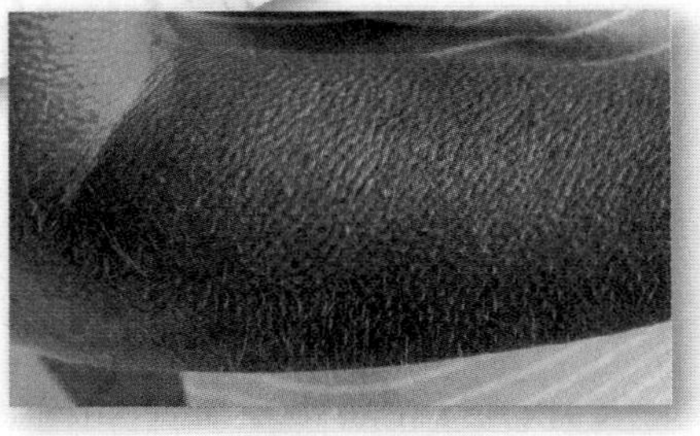

Some of the most interesting homologous structures are those that have a major function in one species but are less important in a related species. **Vestigial structures** (ves TIJ ee uhl) are remnants of structures that may have had important functions in an ancestral species, but have no clear function in some of the modern descendants (Figure 14-14). Often, vestigial organs are reduced in size. For example, the whales of today lack hind limbs, but some have small vestigial hipbones probably derived from their four-footed ancestors described earlier. Lamarck's idea of *inheritance of acquired characteristics* (see Concept 14.1) could account for the reduced size of vestigial structures. However, genetic evidence does not support such a process of inheritance. Natural selection provides a different explanation for vestigial structures that is consistent with known processes of inheritance. Natural selection would favor the survival and reproduction of individuals with genes for reduced versions of those structures. Consider also that if species arose independently, remnants of structures similar to working organs in other species would be unlikely. But the presence of these structures makes sense if certain species descended from a common ancestor.

▲ **Figure 14-14** Homologous structures in a lynx and a human cause a similar reaction to cold temperatures—making hairs stand on end. In the lynx, this puffiness functions as insulation by trapping air and keeping the animal warm. "Goosebumps" are homologous to the tiny muscles that raise the fur of hairier mammals. Since goosebumps have no known significant function, they can be considered vestigial.

Similarities in Development

Other clues to evolutionary history come from comparing the development of different organisms. Embryos of closely related organisms often have similar stages in development. All vertebrates, for example, have an embryonic stage in which pouches appear on the sides of the throat. At this stage, the embryos of fishes, frogs, snakes, birds, and primates look relatively alike (Figure 14-15). These different vertebrates take on more distinctive features as development progresses. In fishes, for example, most of the throat pouches develop into gills. In land vertebrates, however, these embryonic features are involved in the development of other structures, such as bones of the skull. Yet, the similarities of these structures during development support other evidence that all vertebrates evolved from a common ancestor.

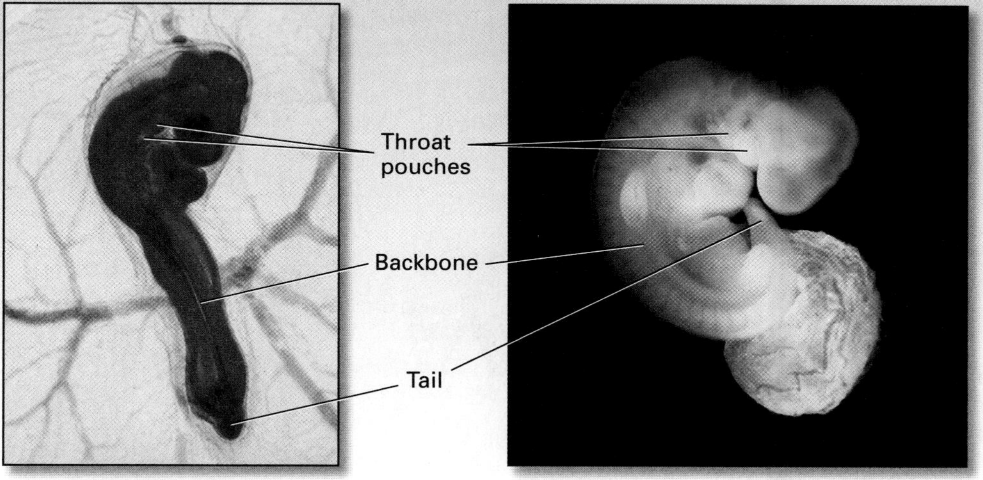

▲ **Figure 14-15** Even at this early stage of development, the kinship of vertebrates is evident. Notice, for example, the throat pouches and tails of both the bird embryo (left) and the human embryo (right).

Comparing the development of organisms supports other evidence of homologous structures. The forelimbs of the mammals described earlier are an example. As the skeletons of the forelimbs take form in the embryos of different mammals, there is a common pattern in the development of many bones. Structural differences become clear later in development. The specific type of limb is shaped by differences in the rates at which different bones of the skeleton grow. This evidence further supports the hypothesis that all mammals are related and descended, with modification, from a common ancestor.

Molecular Biology

In recent decades, biologists have been reading a molecular history of evolution in the DNA sequences of organisms. The sequences of bases in DNA molecules are passed from parents to offspring. As you learned in Chapter 11, these DNA sequences determine the amino acid sequences of proteins. These information-rich molecules are the records of an organism's ancestry (hereditary background). Among siblings, the DNA and protein sequences are very similar. However, the sequences of unrelated individuals of the same species show more differences.

This idea of molecular comparison extends to studying relationships between species. If two species have genes and proteins with sequences that match closely, biologists conclude that the sequences must have been inherited from a relatively recent common ancestor. In contrast, the greater the number of differences in DNA and protein sequences between species, the less likely they share as close a common ancestry.

Testable hypotheses are at the heart of science. DNA and protein analyses are new tools for testing hypotheses about evolution. For example, fossil evidence and studies of anatomy support the hypothesis that humans, chimpanzees, and gorillas are closely related. This hypothesis is testable. It can be used to make predictions about what to expect if the hypothesis is correct. For example, *if* humans and other primates are closely related, *then* they

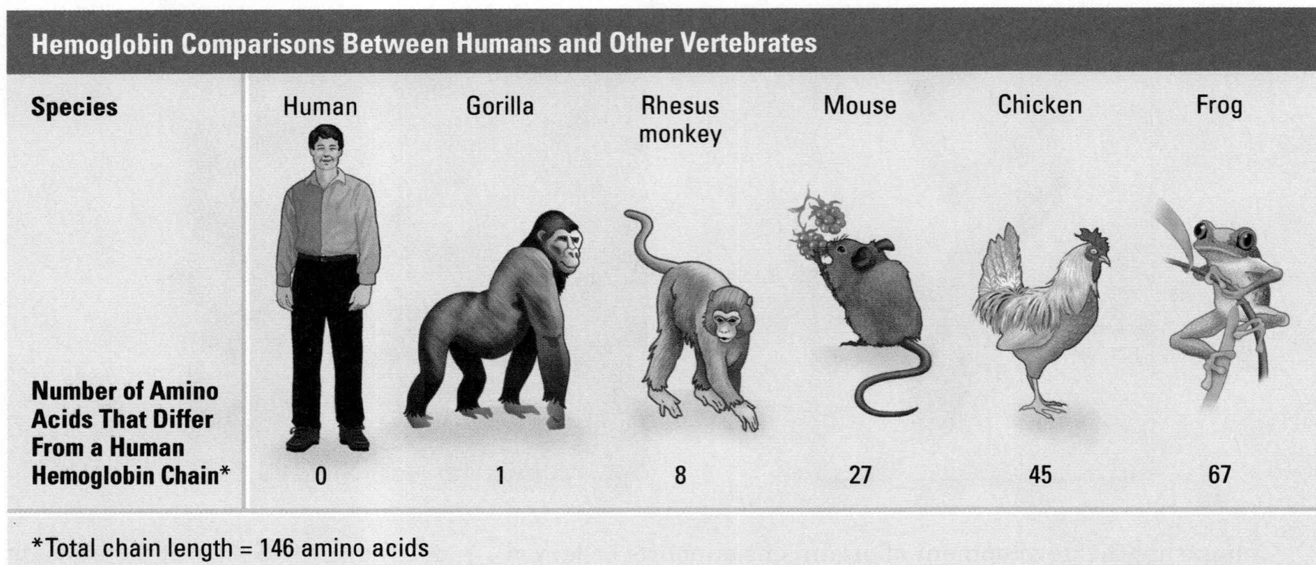

Hemoglobin Comparisons Between Humans and Other Vertebrates

Species	Human	Gorilla	Rhesus monkey	Mouse	Chicken	Frog
Number of Amino Acids That Differ From a Human Hemoglobin Chain*	0	1	8	27	45	67

*Total chain length = 146 amino acids

▲ **Figure 14-16** This table shows the results of a comparison of the amino acid sequences of hemoglobin in humans and other vertebrates. The data reveal the same pattern of evolutionary relationships that researchers find when they compare species using nonmolecular methods.

should share much of their inherited DNA and protein sequences. The sequences of distantly related species should have more differences. If molecular analysis did not confirm this prediction, that would cast doubt on the hypothesis that apes and humans are closely related.

Figure 14-16 compares the amino acid sequence of human hemoglobin (the protein that carries oxygen in blood) with the hemoglobin of other vertebrates. The data support the hypothesis that humans are more closely related to primates than to other vertebrates. Other evidence comes from DNA sequences in humans and chimpanzees. There is approximately 5 percent difference in the total DNA between these two species.

Darwin's boldest hypothesis was that *all* life forms are related. The molecular evidence includes the common genetic code shared by all species (Chapter 11). This genetic language has been passed along through all the branches of evolution. And, it has added to the evidence that supports evolution as an explanation for the unity and diversity of life.

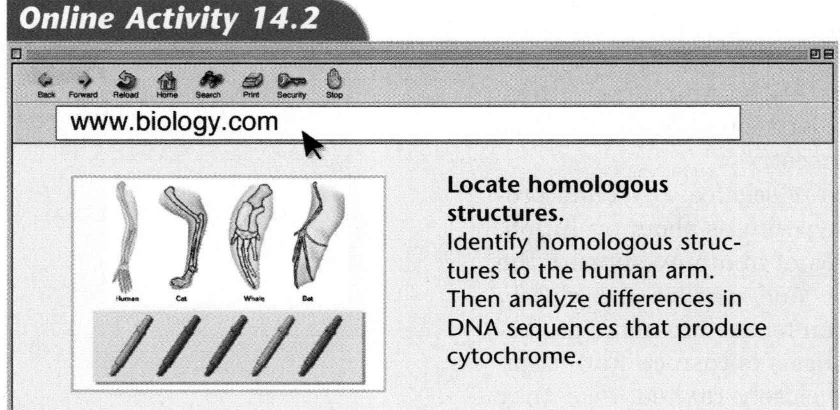

Online Activity 14.2
www.biology.com
Locate homologous structures.
Identify homologous structures to the human arm. Then analyze differences in DNA sequences that produce cytochrome.

Concept Check 14.2

1. Why are older fossils generally in deeper rock layers than younger fossils?
2. How can evolutionary theory explain why Australia is home to relatively few native placental mammals?
3. What are homologous structures?
4. What can you infer about species that differ significantly in their DNA sequences?

CONCEPT 14.3

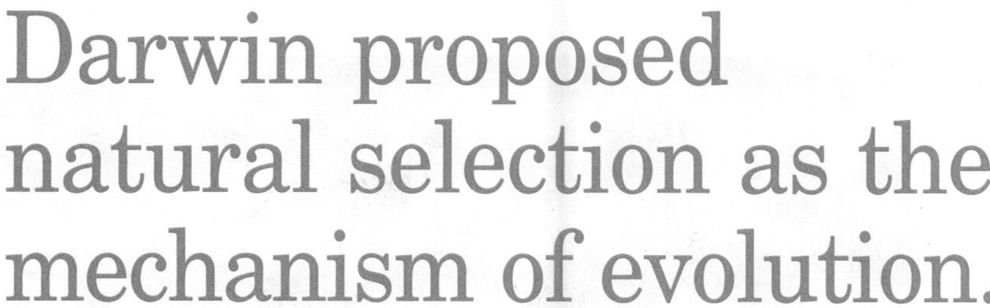

Darwin proposed natural selection as the mechanism of evolution.

OBJECTIVES

- Summarize Darwin's theory of natural selection.
- Compare and contrast artificial selection with natural selection.
- Relate pesticide resistance in insects to natural selection.

KEY TERMS

- population
- variation
- artificial selection

What's Online

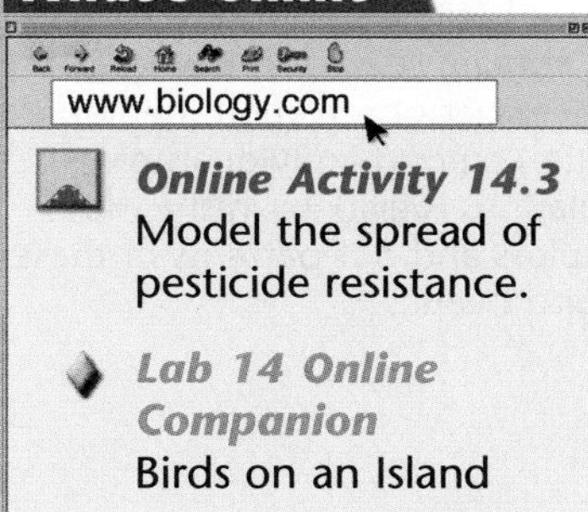

Online Activity 14.3 Model the spread of pesticide resistance.

Lab 14 Online Companion Birds on an Island

Darwin saw a link between adaptation to the environment and the origin of new species. He realized that the key to understanding the mechanism of evolution was in explaining how adaptations arise. His theory of natural selection remains biology's best explanation for adaptive evolution.

Darwin's Theory of Natural Selection

In biology, a **population** is a group of individuals of the same species living in the same area at the same time. Suppose an animal species from a mainland colonizes a chain of distant and isolated islands. The individuals of that species on each island make up a separate population. Populations on the different islands would adapt to their local environments. Over time, the isolated populations would become more and more different. And over many generations, the populations could become different enough to be separate species. The evolution of finches on the Galápagos Islands is an example. Darwin did not realize the significance of these finches until later, after he returned to England. Still, these finches are known as "Darwin's finches" for their contribution to the theory of natural selection.

Observations Lead to a Question There are 13 species of finches unique to the Galápagos islands. However, they most closely resemble one finch species living on the South American mainland. A reasonable hypothesis is that the islands were colonized by a single finch species that strayed from the mainland. This single species adapted to the varied habitats on the islands and eventually diversified into the 13 species seen today. A key characteristic of the finches is their beaks, which are adapted to specific foods available on the different islands (Figure 14-17). A question that follows is, "How did these different beaks arise?" Darwin's theory proposes that these differences arose through natural selection.

◀ **Figure 14-17** The beaks of the cactus finch (top) and the medium ground finch (middle) are specialized for eating different kinds of seeds. The woodpecker finch (bottom) has a long, narrow beak specialized for capturing insects, sometimes with the help of a twig or cactus spine.

▲ **Figure 14-18** Two key observations led to Darwin's theory of natural selection. **a.** One observation was overproduction of offspring, such as the numerous "whirlybirds" on this variety of maple tree. The whirlybirds contain seeds for new trees. **b.** The other observation, heritable variation among individuals of a population, is evident in the different colors and dot patterns of these ladybird beetles.

More Observations Lead to an Idea Darwin based his theory of natural selection on two key sets of observations. First, drawing from Malthus's ideas about humans, Darwin recognized that all species tend to produce excessive numbers of offspring (Figure 14-18a). But in nature, resources are limited. The production of more individuals than the environment can support leads to a struggle for existence among the individuals of a population. In most cases, only a small percentage of offspring will survive in each generation. Many eggs are laid, many young are born, and many seeds are spread, but only a tiny fraction complete their development and leave offspring of their own. The rest are starved, eaten, frozen, diseased, unmated, or unable to reproduce for other reasons.

Darwin's second set of observations was his awareness of variation among the individuals of a population. **Variation** refers to differences among members of the same species. You need only look around your classroom to see how hair color, skin tone, and facial features, for example, vary among just a small group of people. Just as no two people in a human population are alike, individual variation is widespread in all species (Figure 14-18b). Much of this variation is heritable and passes from generation to generation. This explains why siblings usually share more traits with one another and with their parents than they do with unrelated members of the same population.

From these two sets of observations Darwin developed his theory of natural selection, summarized in Figure 14-19. Individuals with inherited traits that are best suited to the local environment are more likely to survive and reproduce than less fit individuals. In other words, the individuals that function best tend to leave the most offspring. When this process repeats over many generations, each new generation has a higher proportion of individuals with the advantageous traits.

Darwin also reasoned that natural selection could eventually cause two isolated populations of the same species to become separate species as they adapted to their different environments. This would explain patterns such as those observed in the Galápagos finches.

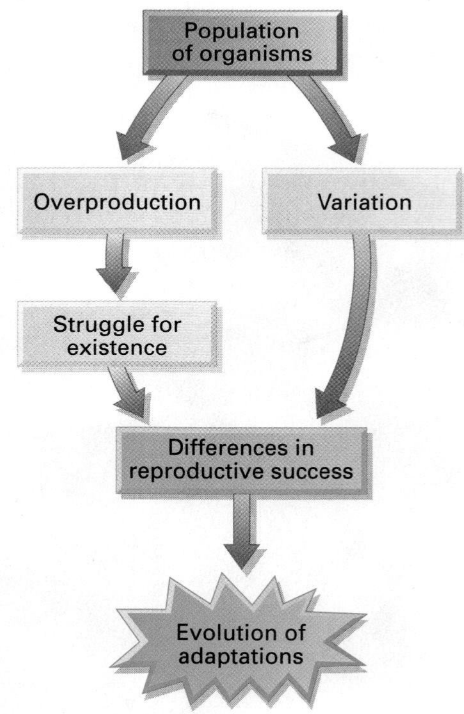

▲ **Figure 14-19** This flowchart summarizes Darwin's theory of natural selection.

▲ **Figure 14-20** As a result of artificial selection over just a few centuries, dog breeders have produced dogs that range widely in size, coat, body shape, head shape, and ear shape.

Artificial Selection

Darwin found convincing evidence for his ideas in the results of artificial selection. **Artificial selection** is the selective breeding of domesticated plants and animals to produce offspring with genetic traits that humans value. For instance, a plant breeder might seek to improve traits such as grain production, disease resistance, or protein content. An animal breeder might select for growth rate or temperament. Darwin observed that breeders selected individuals with the desired traits as breeding stock. Breeders play the role of the environment, allowing only those plants or animals with desired traits to reproduce.

In fact, humans have been modifying species for thousands of years. You can see evidence of Darwin's point in the enormous diversity that dog breeders have produced within this single species in just the last 500 years (Figure 14-20).

Darwin observed that artificial selection could produce a great deal of change in a species in a short time. He reasoned that over thousands of generations, natural selection could also cause major change. Of course, there are important differences between artificial and natural selection. The traits that become more common in a population through artificial selection are those that humans choose. In contrast, natural selection favors traits that benefit the organisms in their particular environment—environmental conditions do the "selective breeding." The result is the evolutionary adaptation to the environment.

Pesticides—Natural Selection in Action

Natural selection and the evolution it causes can be observable events. An example is the evolution of pesticide resistance in hundreds of insect species. Pesticides are poisons used to kill insects that are pests in crops and in homes.

Whenever a new type of pesticide is used to control agricultural pests, the story is usually the same. Early results are encouraging. A relatively small amount of poison dusted onto a crop may kill 99 percent of the insects. But later sprayings are less and less effective. For example, the flour beetle *(Tribolium castaneum)* is a pest species that damages stored grain. In the

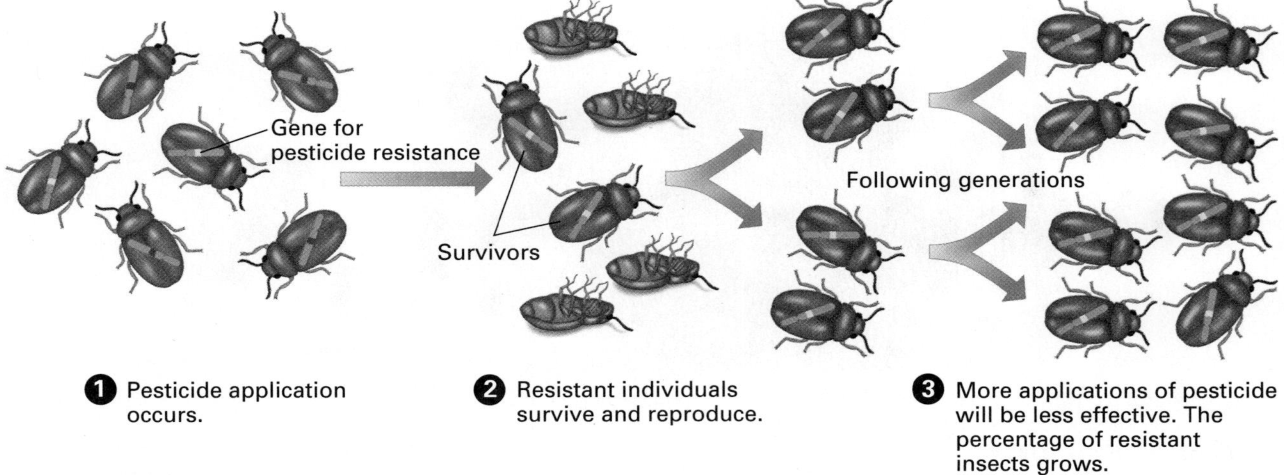

1 Pesticide application occurs.

2 Resistant individuals survive and reproduce.

3 More applications of pesticide will be less effective. The percentage of resistant insects grows.

early 1950s, the pesticide malathion was introduced to control these insects. At first only a small concentration of malathion was necessary to control them. Today, wild flour beetles are resistant to very high concentrations of malathion.

Figure 14-21 traces how pesticide resistance evolves. Most survivors of the first pesticide treatments were insects with genes that somehow enabled them to resist the chemical attack. Their offspring inherited the genes for pesticide resistance. In each generation, the percentage of pesticide-resistant individuals in the beetle population increased. The population underwent evolutionary change that resulted in adaptation to a change in the chemical environment—the presence of the pesticide.

This example highlights two key points about natural selection. First, natural selection is a process of "screening" traits that are available. A pesticide does not create resistant individuals, but selects for resistant insects that are already present in the population. Second, natural selection favors those characteristics in a varying population that fit the specific current, local environment. Pesticide resistance offered no advantage until pesticide application changed the local environment.

▲ **Figure 14-21** By spraying crops with poisons to kill insect pests, humans have favored the reproduction of insects with inherited resistance to the poisons over those with no resistance.

Online Activity 14.3

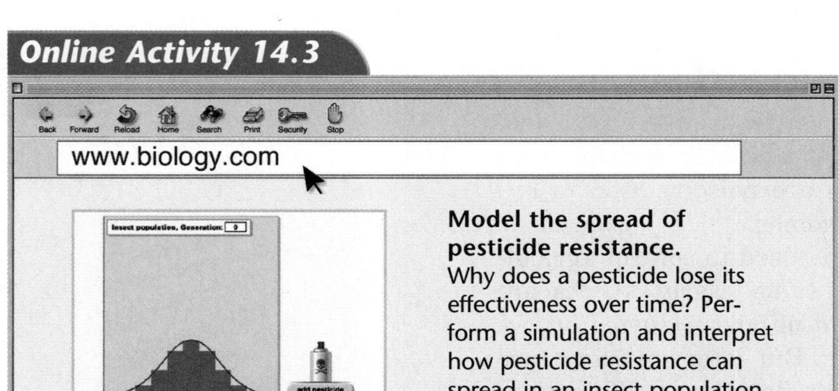

Model the spread of pesticide resistance.
Why does a pesticide lose its effectiveness over time? Perform a simulation and interpret how pesticide resistance can spread in an insect population over many generations.

Concept Check 14.3

1. In Darwin's view, what conditions lead to a struggle for existence among individuals in a population?
2. What is the goal of artificial selection?
3. Why does a specific pesticide become less effective over time?

Birds on an Island

A Simulation of Natural Selection

Question Can natural selection change the frequency of traits in a population in only a few generations?

Lab Overview In this investigation you and your classmates will use a simulation exercise to explore how the frequencies of three beak phenotypes change over several generations in a population of birds on an island.

Preparing for the Lab To help you prepare for the investigation go to the *Lab 14 Online Companion.* ·····→ Find out how researchers measure bird beaks. Compare beak measurements from one bird population between two different years. Prepare for the lab procedure by previewing the steps you will take.

Completing the Lab Use your Laboratory Manual or lab page printouts from the *Lab 14 Online Companion* to do the investigation and analyze your results. CAUTION: *Be sure to follow your teacher's instructions and all safety guidelines in the investigation.*

Lab 14 Online Companion

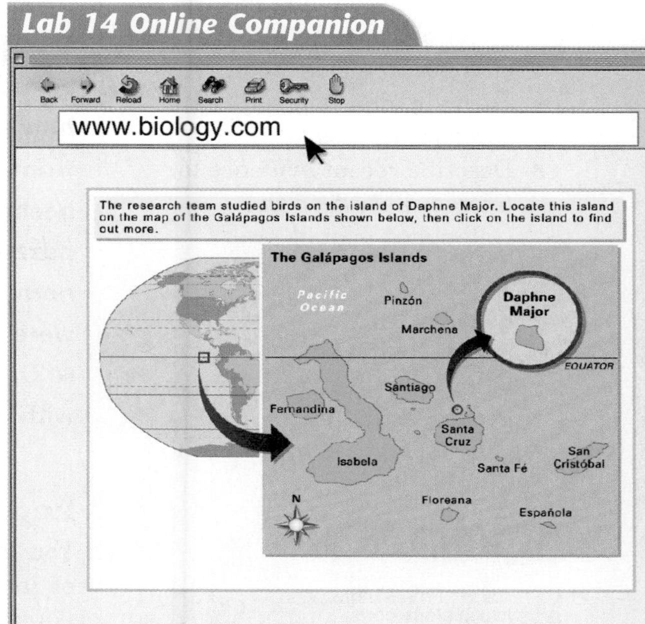

CONCEPT 14.4

Microevolution is a change in a population's gene pool.

OBJECTIVES

- Explain the significance of gene pools in understanding evolution.
- Tell how genetic drift, gene flow, mutation, and natural selection contribute to changes in a gene pool.
- Explain what is meant by the term *fitness*.
- Describe recent evidence for microevolution on the Galápagos Islands.

KEY TERMS

- gene pool
- microevolution
- Hardy-Weinberg equilibrium
- genetic drift
- gene flow
- fitness

What's Online

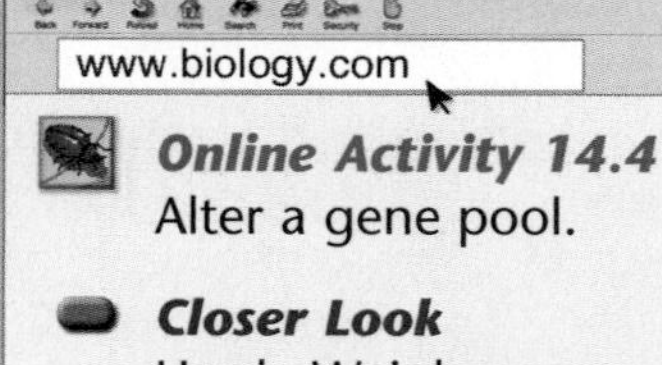

Online Activity 14.4 Alter a gene pool.

Closer Look Hardy-Weinberg Equilibrium

Darwin understood the connection between natural selection and adaptation to the environment. However, he could not explain how the variations that are the basis for natural selection pass from one generation to the next. Gregor Mendel might have been some help. Mendel figured out the inheritance piece of the puzzle. But though they lived in the same era, Darwin knew nothing of Mendel's work. It wasn't until decades after both men were dead that biologists were able to apply Mendel's genetics to Darwin's ideas about natural selection. This union of genetics with evolutionary biology focuses on change within populations.

Populations and Their Gene Pools

You learned earlier that a biological population is a local group of individuals belonging to the same species (Figure 14-22). A population is the smallest level at which evolution can occur. A common but mistaken belief is that individual organisms evolve. It is true that natural selection does act on individuals, and inherited characteristics do affect their reproductive success. However, this natural selection only becomes clear when an entire population is tracked over time.

A key concept in understanding the evolution of populations is the gene pool. The **gene pool** consists of all the alleles (alternative forms of genes) in all the individuals that make up a population. You can think of the gene pool as the reservoir from which the next generation draws its genes. As such, the population's gene pool is where genetic variation—the raw material of evolution—is stored.

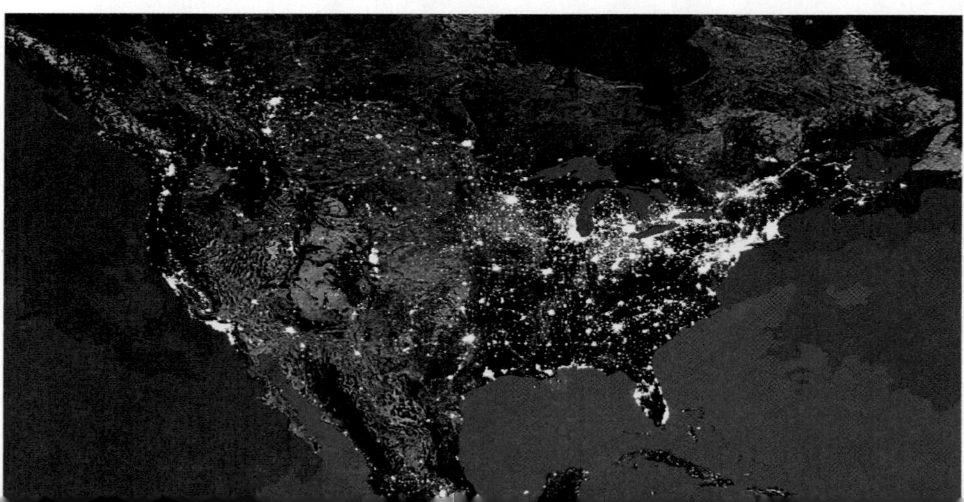

Figure 14-22 This nighttime satellite view shows the lights of human population centers in most of the United States.

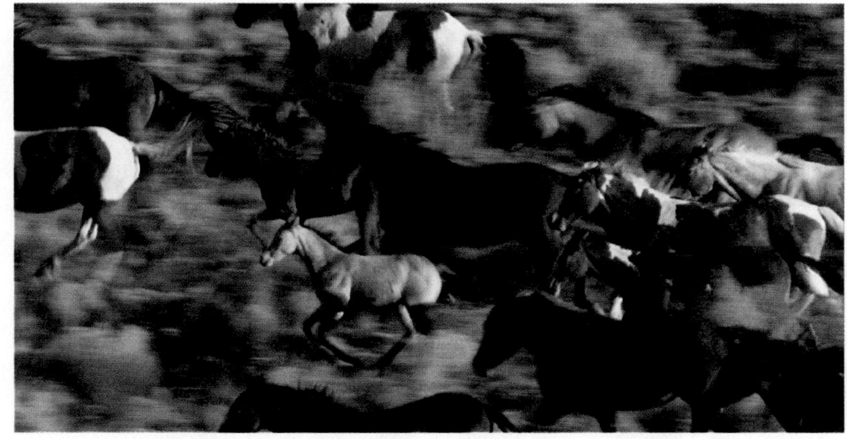

Figure 14-23 The many different colors of the wild mustangs in this population are one reflection of the genetic variation in its gene pool.

You can observe evidence of a gene pool's reservoir of variations in the population of wild mustangs in Figure 14-23. Each mustang has a unique combination of genes. This uniqueness is reflected in individual variations such as the horses' coloring. The variety expressed among individuals is largely the result of sexual recombination, and it is typical in populations that reproduce sexually. The processes of meiosis and fertilization (see Chapter 9) shuffle alleles within the gene pool and deal them out to offspring in fresh combinations.

Changes in Gene Pools

The processes that lead to genetic variation—mutations and sexual recombination—are random. That is, the precise outcome of these processes for any individual can't be predicted. However, natural selection (and thus evolution) is *not* random. The environment favors genetic combinations that contribute to survival and reproductive success. Thus, some alleles may become more common than others in the gene pool. In other words, there is a change in the *frequency of alleles*—how often certain alleles occur in the gene pool. This frequency is usually expressed as a decimal or a percentage, as shown by the example in Figure 14-24.

Merging Mendel's and Darwin's theories led to a way of looking at evolution based on genetic changes. **Microevolution** is evolution on the smallest scale—a generation-to-generation change in the frequencies of alleles within a population.

In contrast to microevolution, populations that do not undergo change to their gene pools are not presently evolving. This condition is known as the **Hardy-Weinberg equilibrium** (named for the two scientists who first described it). Such equilibrium of a gene pool means that the frequency of alleles in that gene pool are constant over time. In fact, populations rarely remain in Hardy-Weinberg equilibrium for long in nature. But the concept is useful because it provides a "no change" baseline that makes it possible to recognize when a gene pool *is* changing.

What mechanisms can change a gene pool? The two main factors are genetic drift and natural selection, as you'll read in the following pages.

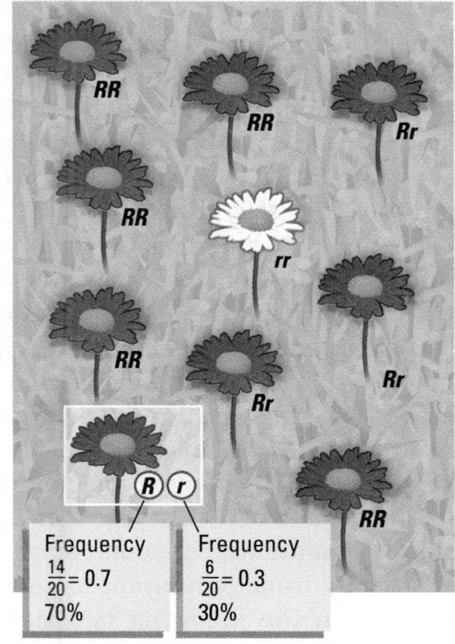

Figure 14-24 Each plant in this hypothetical population of wildflowers has 2 alleles for flower color. In all, there are 14 red-flower alleles (*R*) and 6 white-flower alleles (*r*). The frequency of each allele is calculated as a ratio based on the total of 20.

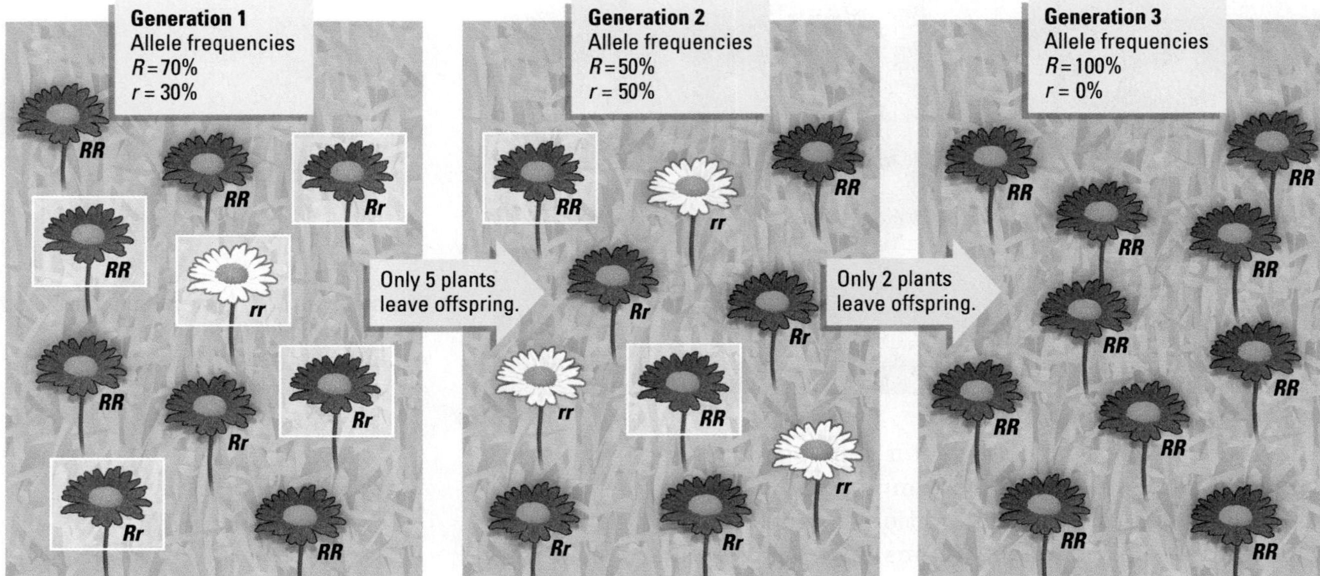

▲ **Figure 14-25** Only the alleles of organisms that successfully reproduce in one generation appear in the gene pool of the next generation. In this population of ten plants, the frequency of white-flower alleles was reduced to zero due to genetic drift.

Genetic Drift

A change in the gene pool of a population due to chance is called **genetic drift.** For example, the first generation of the small wildflower population illustrated in Figure 14-25 consists of nine plants with red flowers (*RR* and *Rr*) and one plant with white flowers (*rr*). It is partly chance that affects which plants reproduce. By the third generation, no plants carry the allele for white flowers. The result is a change in allele frequencies in this population.

All populations are subject to some genetic drift. However the smaller the population is, the more impact genetic drift has on that population. It is like the erratic outcome from a small sample of coin tosses. Flip a coin 1,000 times, and a result of 700 heads and 300 tails would make you very suspicious about that coin. But flip a coin ten times, and an outcome of seven heads and three tails would seem within reason. The smaller the sample is, the greater the chance that the results will differ from an expected result—in this case, a roughly equal number of heads and tails. As in coin tosses, the frequencies of alleles in a gene pool will be more stable from one generation to the next when a population is large. But in small populations, the allele frequencies can vary erratically from generation to generation. As you will see in the following two situations, genetic drift can have major effects on a population.

The Bottleneck Effect Disasters such as earthquakes, floods, droughts, and fires may drastically reduce the size of a population. Reducing the size of the population also reduces the size of its gene pool (Figure 14-26). By chance, certain

▼ **Figure 14-26** Marbles falling through the narrow neck of a bottle serve as an analogy for the bottleneck effect. Compared to the original population (in the bottle) the new population has less variation.

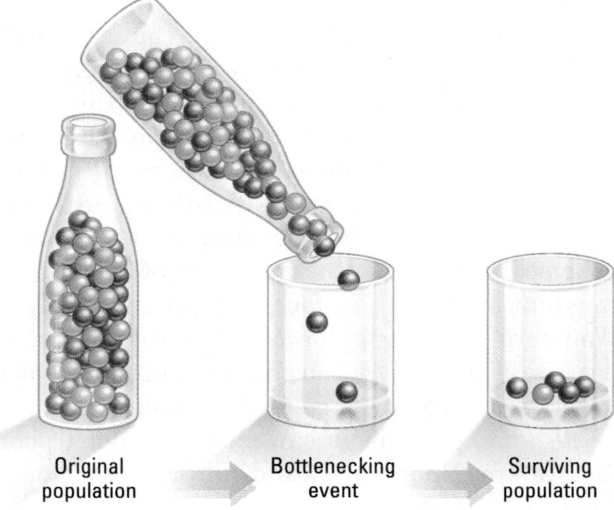

alleles may then be represented more frequently than others among the survivors. Some alleles may be eliminated altogether. Such genetic drift, called the bottleneck effect, decreases genetic variation in a population.

▲ **Figure 14-27** Some endangered species, such as the cheetah, may have relatively little genetic variation.

The loss of variation due to a bottleneck effect could reduce the ability of a population to adapt to environmental change. For example, the cheetah—the fastest running of all animals—may have suffered one or more bottleneck events (Figure 14-27). Like many African mammals, a sharp decrease in the cheetah population occurred during the last ice age about 10,000 years ago. In the nineteenth century, farmers hunted the animals to near extinction. Today only a few small populations of cheetahs exist in the wild. There is some evidence from genetic studies that variation is relatively low among cheetahs compared to other mammals. Some biologists who study cheetahs are concerned that with relatively little variation in their gene pools, the cheetah populations may not be able to resist disease or adapt to other environmental challenges to their survival.

Founder Effect Genetic drift is also likely when a few individuals colonize an isolated island, lake, or some other new habitat. The smaller the colony, the less its genetic makeup will represent the gene pool of the larger population from which the colonists came. Again, chance reduces genetic variation. Genetic drift in a new colony is known as the founder effect because the change relates to the genetic makeup of the founders of the colony. The founder effect likely contributed to changes in the gene pools of the finches and other South American organisms that arrived as strays on the Galápagos Islands.

Gene Flow and Mutation

Although genetic drift and natural selection are the main causes of changes in gene pools from one generation to the next, other mechanisms also have a role. These mechanisms include gene flow and mutation.

Gene Flow The exchange of genes with another population is referred to as **gene flow**. Gene flow occurs when fertile individuals or their gametes (sex cells) migrate between populations. For example, suppose a population that neighbors the wildflowers pictured in Figure 14-25 consists entirely of white-flowered individuals. A windstorm may blow pollen from these neighbors to the mostly red-flowered population. Interbreeding would increase the frequency of the white-flower allele in the original population. Gene flow tends to reduce genetic differences between populations. If it is extensive enough, gene flow can eventually mix neighboring populations into a single population with a common gene pool.

Figure 14-28 These two albino deer are homozygous for a genetic mutation that causes their lack of coloring. Their chances of surviving (and passing on their genes) are probably less than that of brown deer. However, the albino allele can persist in the population through the reproduction of brown deer that are heterozygous (carry one copy of the recessive albino allele).

Mutation From Chapter 11, you may remember that a mutation is a change in an organism's DNA. If this mutation is carried by a gamete, the mutation enters the population's gene pool.

Natural selection or genetic drift (or both) can influence whether the frequency of a new mutation increases in a population. For example, consider the albino deer in Figure 14-28. They carry a type of mutation, found in many vertebrate species, that results in a lack of coloration. Natural selection can affect the frequency of the mutant allele in the population. White fur may lend an advantage to animals that live in snowy climates most of the year and must escape predators to survive. In such a population, this allele might increase in frequency. But deer live in wintry conditions only one season out of four. White fur could prove harmful most of the time, so the frequency of such an allele in deer populations would most likely not increase.

Over the long term, mutation plays a key role in evolution as the original source of the genetic variation that is the raw material for natural selection. Mutations are especially important as a source of variation in asexually reproducing organisms that clone themselves rapidly, such as bacteria. For example, a new mutation that is favorable can rapidly increase in frequency in a bacteria population due to natural selection. In sexually reproducing organisms with relatively long generation spans, most of the variation is not due to new mutations but to the scrambling of existing alleles, including those that originated as mutations in earlier generations.

Natural Selection and Fitness

Genetic drift, gene flow, and mutation can cause microevolution, or changes in allele frequencies. But they do not necessarily lead to adaptation. Only blind luck would improve a population's fitness in its environment through these processes. Of all causes of microevolution, only natural selection usually leads to adaptation. Natural selection is a blend of chance and sorting. Chance stems from mutations and the sexual recombination of alleles. These random events produce genetic variation in a population. Sorting, which is *not* random, is accomplished by differences in reproductive success among members of the varying population.

The phrases "struggle for existence" and "survival of the fittest" are sometimes used to describe natural selection. But these phrases are misleading since they suggest that natural selection usually involves direct contests between individuals. There *are* animal species in which individuals, usually the males, lock horns or otherwise do combat for mates. But competition is generally less dramatic. In a varying population of moths, certain individuals may average more offspring than others because their wing colors hide them better from predators. Plants in a wildflower population may differ in reproductive success because slight variations in flower color, shape, or fragrance make the plants better able to attract pollinators (Figure 14-29).

▲ **Figure 14-29** The fragrance of wild roses is an adaptation that lures insects. As this beetle travels from flower to flower, it transfers pollen, ensuring another generation of wild roses.

These examples point to a biological definition of **fitness**—the contribution that an individual makes to the gene pool of the next generation compared to the contributions of other individuals. Survival to reproductive maturity, of course, is necessary for reproductive success. But even the biggest, fastest, toughest frog in the pond has a fitness of zero if it is sterile. Production of healthy, fertile offspring is all that counts in natural selection.

A Return to the Galápagos

Earlier you learned how Darwin's observations of island species influenced his thinking. The geology, plants, and animals of the Galápagos Islands were a particularly rich source of information for him. Even today, the unique conditions of the Galápagos continue to serve as a living laboratory for studying natural selection. One of the best studied examples of natural selection involves the birds called "Darwin's finches."

For 30 years, Peter and Rosemary Grant and their students have been studying the finches of Daphne Major in the Galápagos. Daphne Major is an isolated, uninhabited island about the size of a football stadium. Two species of finch inhabit the island, the medium ground finch and the cactus finch. The island's small size and limited population of finches make it an excellent setting for studying natural selection. Each year the Grants and their students have captured, marked, measured, and studied every finch on the island. With these data, they have been able to provide clear evidence for natural selection.

▼ **Figure 14-30** These photographs show Rosemary and Peter Grant setting out equipment to catch and study finches on Daphne Major.

One of the Grants' research projects focuses on beak size in the medium ground finch. This finch uses its strong beak to crush seeds. Given a choice of small or large seeds, the birds eat mostly small ones, which are easier to crush. Large seeds from one plant species are common on the island. But these large seeds are particularly difficult to crack. During wet years, small seeds are so abundant that ground finches eat relatively few large seeds. However, in dry years all seeds are in short supply, and the large seeds make up a greater part of the birds' diet. Those birds with larger beaks are more successful at cracking the large seeds. Dry years are difficult, and there are usually more deaths. The surviving finches tend to be those with larger beaks that can crack the toughest seeds. This trend of larger beaks continues into the next generation of finches in the following year. The most likely explanation is that those birds with stronger beaks have a feeding advantage. Thus, they have more reproductive success during droughts and pass the genes for thicker beaks on to their offspring.

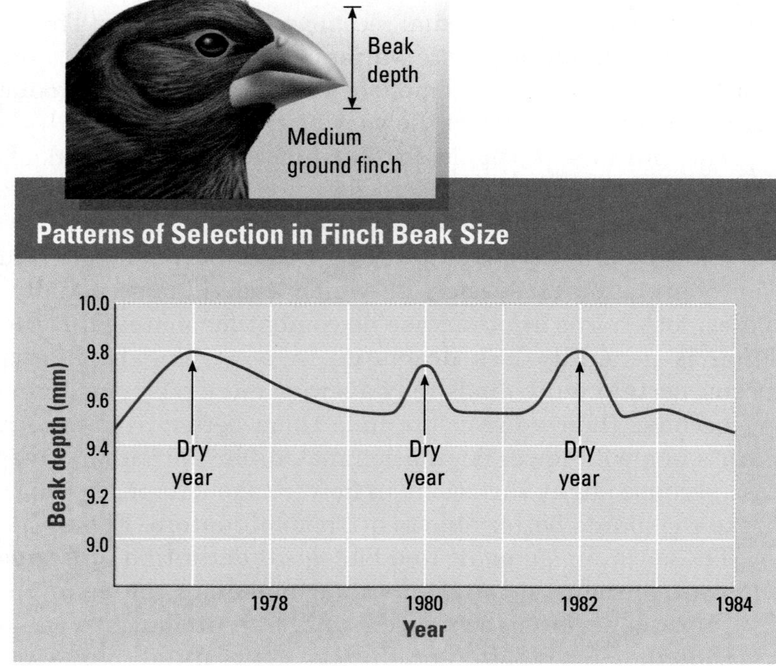

▲ **Figure 14-31** The Grants documented changes in beak size among medium ground finches over many years.

When wet years return to Daphne Major, the plants that produce small seeds recover. Small seeds are a more efficient food source for finches than large seeds. During wet years, birds with smaller beaks appear to forage for seeds more efficiently than the large-beaked birds. The average beak size in the population of birds changes again. The Grants have documented several such cycles of natural selection over their 30-year study. Figure 14-31 presents a simplified graph of some of their results.

Darwin thought that natural selection always works too slowly to actually be measured during a human lifetime. But the research of the Grants and many others has changed that view and provided many examples of natural selection in action.

Online Activity 14.4

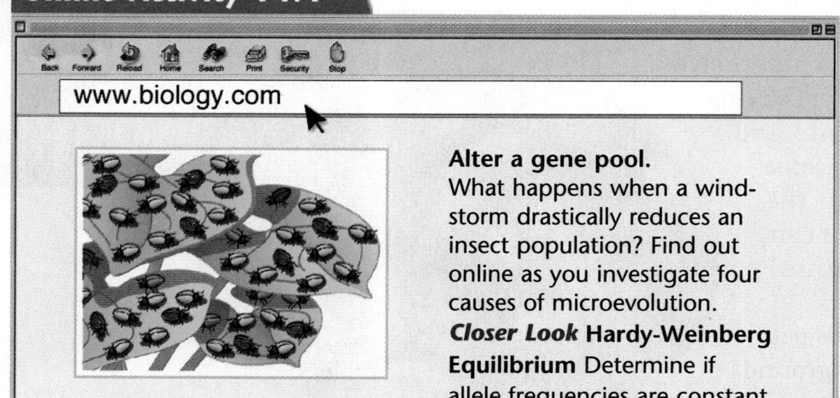

Alter a gene pool.
What happens when a windstorm drastically reduces an insect population? Find out online as you investigate four causes of microevolution.
Closer Look **Hardy-Weinberg Equilibrium** Determine if allele frequencies are constant over time.

Concept Check 14.4

1. What is a gene pool?
2. How has genetic drift affected the world's populations of cheetahs?
3. Describe what is meant by a "biologically fit" organism.
4. Describe the Grants' hypothesis about how environmental conditions led to microevolution among the finches of Daphne Major.
5. What are the two main forces of evolutionary change in gene pools?

CONCEPT 14.5

Evolutionary biology is important in health science.

OBJECTIVES

- Explain how natural selection causes the sickle cell allele to persist in some gene pools.
- Explain how antibiotic resistance may evolve in bacteria.

KEY TERM

- antibiotic

What's Online

www.biology.com

Online Activity 14.5
Analyze sickle cell genotypes.

How does evolutionary biology fit into everyday life? One clear connection is in the efforts of scientists to understand some health problems in an evolutionary context. What can evolution reveal about inherited disease? How can infectious diseases that were once seemingly defeated or controlled by drugs now be on the rise? Biologists are now seeking answers to these questions in an evolutionary framework. Two examples are described here.

Natural Selection and Sickle Cell Disease

In some African populations, sickle cell disease affects about 1 out of every 25 individuals. The disease is named for the abnormal shape of red blood cells in individuals who inherit the disorder (Figure 14-32). People with the disease suffer a range of symptoms that include general weakening of the body, pain, damage to organs, and sometimes death. Sickle cell disease is caused by a recessive allele. Only homozygous individuals—those who inherit the recessive allele from both parents—have the disorder. Heterozygous individuals—those with a single copy of the sickle cell allele—do not have the disease. But they can pass the allele on to their children. (You can review the inheritance of sickle cell disease in Chapters 10 and 11.)

Why do many African populations have such high frequencies of an allele with the potential to shorten life (and thus reproductive success)? Evolutionary biology holds a possible answer. Although the sickle cell allele has harmful effects, in the African tropics it is also beneficial. Individuals with just one copy of the sickle cell allele are resistant to the disease malaria. This resistance is an important advantage in environments where malaria is a major cause of death in infants.

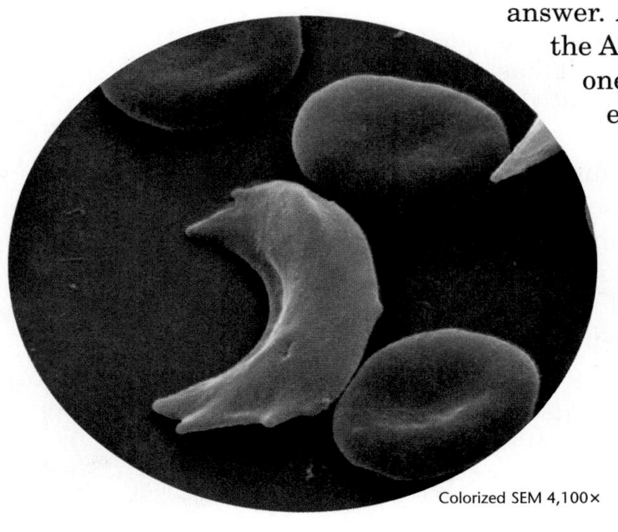

Figure 14-32 Sickle cell disease gets its name from the characteristic shape of affected red blood cells, which resemble the crescent-shaped cutting tool called a sickle. (Normal red blood cells, also visible in this micrograph, have a rounded shape.)

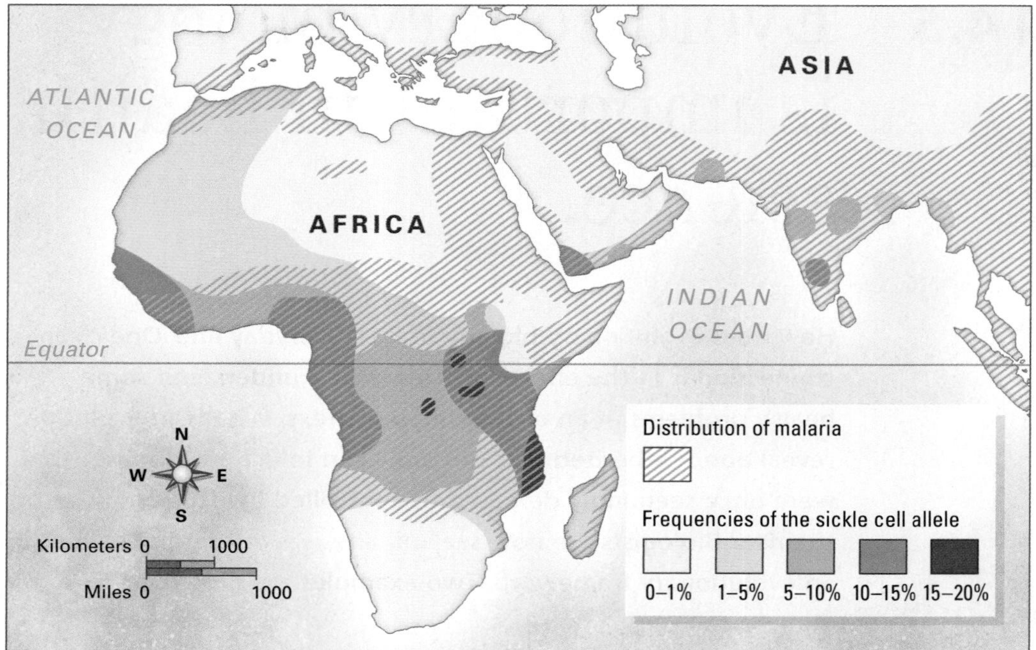

▲ **Figure 14-33** Malaria is transmitted by the bite of certain mosquitoes that transfer the disease-causing protist from one person to another.

The map in Figure 14-33 indicates that the frequency of the sickle cell allele in Africa is generally highest in areas where the malaria parasite is most common. For some populations, as many as one out of three people carry a single copy of the sickle cell allele and are resistant to malaria. In populations with a high frequency of the sickle cell allele, 4 percent of the population is homozygous and suffers from the disease. However, 32 percent of the population is heterozygous and gains protection from malaria. With malaria common in the environment, natural selection maintains a higher frequency of the sickle cell allele than would be expected from the negative effects of the allele alone.

Evolution of Antibiotic Resistance in Bacteria

Medicines that kill or slow the growth of bacteria are called **antibiotics.** These drugs help to cure many infections caused by bacteria. Antibiotics have saved the lives of millions of people. But the widespread use of antibiotics also brings risk. It has caused the evolution of antibiotic-resistant populations of the very bacteria the drugs are meant to kill.

Antibiotic resistance evolves by natural selection, much as pesticide resistance evolves in insects. An antibiotic causes selection among the varying bacteria of a population, leaving those individuals that can survive the drug. While the drug kills most of the bacteria, the resistant bacteria multiply and quickly become the norm in the population rather than the exceptions.

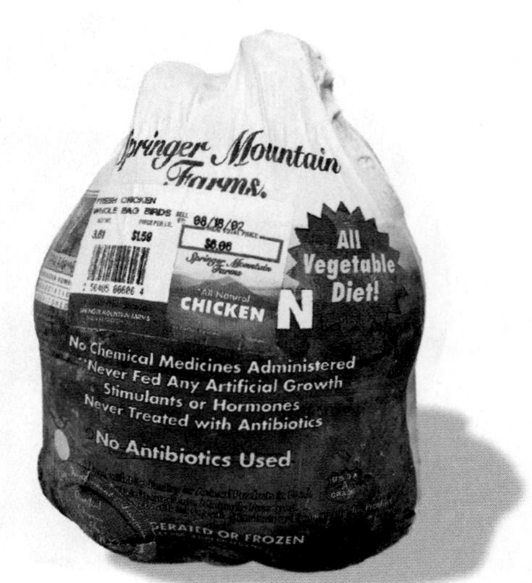

▶ **Figure 14-34** This chicken's packaging indicates that it was fed an antibiotic-free diet. Reducing the widespread use of antibiotics may help slow the evolution of antibiotic-resistant bacteria.

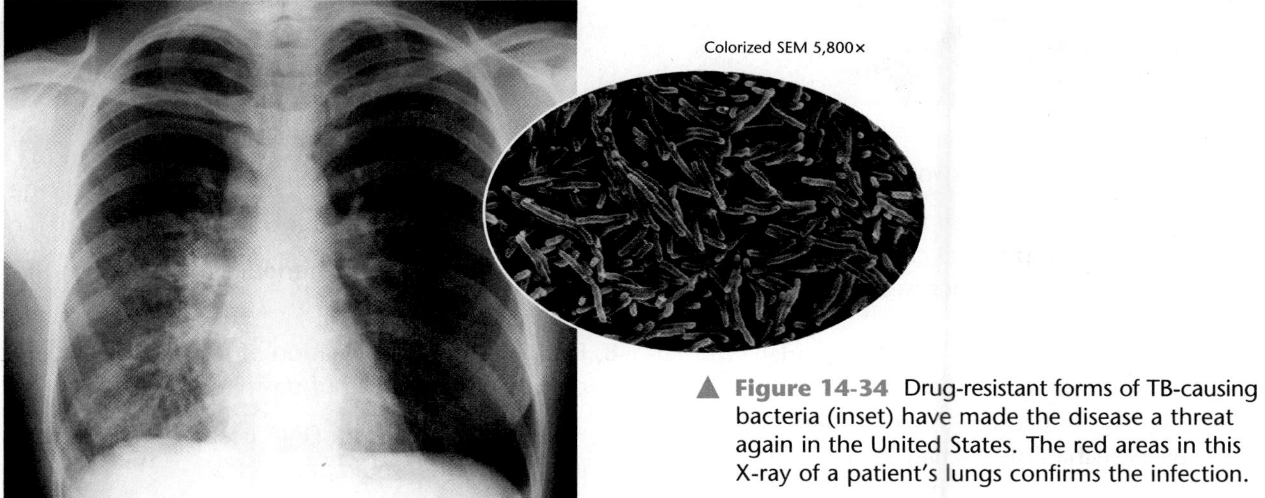

▲ **Figure 14-34** Drug-resistant forms of TB-causing bacteria (inset) have made the disease a threat again in the United States. The red areas in this X-ray of a patient's lungs confirms the infection.

The evolution of antibiotic-resistant bacteria is a huge problem in public health. For example, in New York City, there are now some strains of the tuberculosis-causing bacteria that are resistant to all three antibiotics used to treat the disease. Unfortunate people infected with one of these resistant strains have no better chance of surviving than tuberculosis patients did a century ago.

Understanding how populations of bacteria adapt to antibiotics is beginning to influence how doctors prescribe antibiotics. Realizing that the overruse of these drugs is speeding the evolution of resistant bacteria, many doctors are less likely to prescribe antibiotics unless absolutely necessary.

It will take an organized effort by scientists, health care professionals, and patients to effectively meet this challenge to public health. Underlying the effort is the need to see that evolution is not *just* a powerful theory for understanding life. On both a short-term and a long-term basis, grasping the principles of evolution helps people understand human interactions with the rest of the living world.

Online Activity 14.5

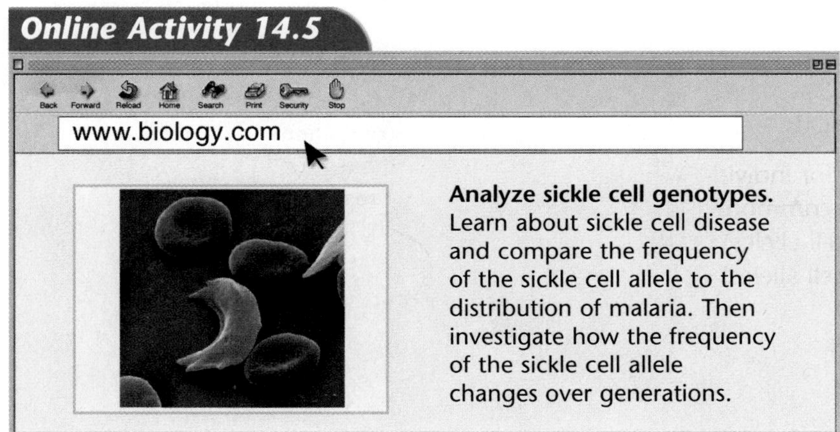

Analyze sickle cell genotypes. Learn about sickle cell disease and compare the frequency of the sickle cell allele to the distribution of malaria. Then investigate how the frequency of the sickle cell allele changes over generations.

Concept Check 14.5

1. Under what conditions is the sickle cell allele beneficial to a heterozygous individual?
2. Identify a possible risk of overuse of antibiotics.

Multiple Choice

Choose the letter of the best answer.

1. Which of the following is an *incorrect* match?
   a. Lyell—suggested physical changes to Earth result from geologic processes occurring over long periods of time.
   b. Lamarck—proposed that organisms adapt to their environment.
   c. Darwin—developed the theory of natural selection as a mechanism of change in species.
   d. Malthus—thought that characteristics acquired during an organism's lifetime can be passed on to the next generation.

2. Which of the following provides clues about the size and structure of once-living organisms?
   a. fossils
   b. DNA and proteins from the organisms
   c. vestigial structures
   d. development of embryos

3. What statement is *not* an observation or inference on which Darwin's theory of natural selection is based?
   a. Variations among individuals exist in a population.
   b. Poorly adapted individuals never produce offspring.
   c. Individuals whose inherited characteristics give them advantages in their environment will generally produce more offspring.
   d. Species living today descended with modification from earlier species.

4. Artificial selection is similar to natural selection in that both processes
   a. were suggested by Darwin.
   b. adapt species to their environments.
   c. occur over many millions of years.
   d. depend on variation among individuals.

5. What genotype is the most beneficial for individuals living in regions where malaria is common?
   a. homozygous dominant (no sickle cell alleles)
   b. homozygous recessive (two sickle cell alleles)
   c. heterozygous (one sickle cell allele)
   d. no difference among the genotypes

Short Answer

6. How did Darwin's experiences during his voyage later affect his views about species?

7. How does descent with modification explain the diversity of life?

8. Explain how the formation of fossils provides a chronological record of past life forms.

9. How is evidence from DNA useful in understanding the evolution of species?

10. How are pesticide-resistant insects an example of natural selection?

11. Describe what can happen to a gene pool as a result of the bottleneck effect.

12. What is microevolution?

13. How does natural selection lead to adaptation?

Visualizing Concepts

14. Copy the concept map below and complete it.

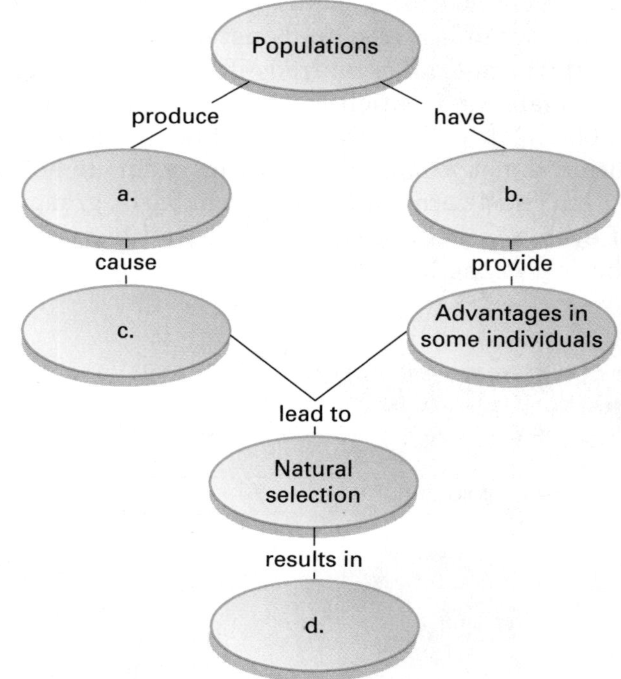

Analyzing Information

15. **Analyzing Graphs** The following graph shows drug resistance that develops over time in the virus that causes AIDS. Use the graph to answer the questions below.

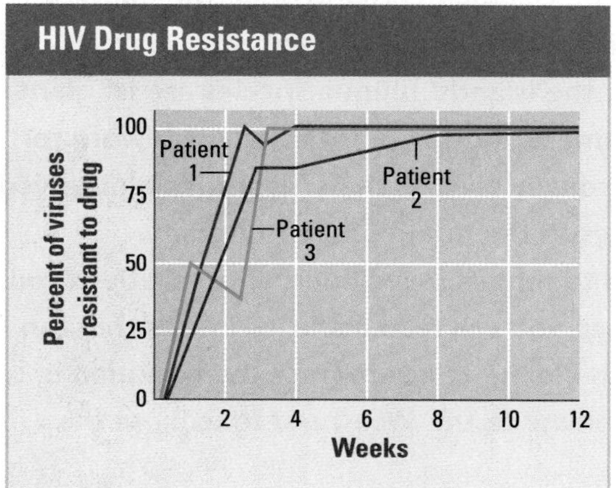

a. What trend appears in all the patients by the end of the third week?
b. Explain what happened to the virus population over the ten weeks of exposure to the drug.
c. How do these data reflect a problem in treating patients with the virus?

16. **Analyzing Data** A population containing striped and unstriped snails has recently moved into a new region. Birds break the snails open by dropping them onto rocks. The birds eat the bodies of the snails and leave the shells. In one area, researchers counted both live snails and broken shells. The data are summarized below.

	Striped shells	Unstriped shells
Living snails	264	296
Broken shells	486	377

a. Based on the data, tell which form of snail (striped or unstriped) is more likely to be caught by the birds for food. Explain.
b. Suggest a hypothesis to explain what is happening to the snails.
c. Predict how the frequencies of striped and unstriped individuals in the population might change over the generations.

Critical Thinking

17. **Comparing and Contrasting** Describe how the ideas of Lamarck and Darwin are similar and how they differ.

18. **Analyzing Scientific Explanations** How do Lyell's ideas about geology and evidence from the fossil record reinforce each other as ideas about the age of Earth?

19. **Analyzing Scientific Explanations** Tell how the forelimbs of a bat, a whale, a cat, and a human contribute evidence to support the hypothesis that these mammals evolved from a common ancestor.

20. **Relating Cause and Effect** Explain how the effectiveness of an antibiotic decreases with time.

21. **Evaluating the Impact of Research** Explain the significance of the Grants' research.

22. **What's Wrong With These Statements?** *Briefly explain why each statement is inaccurate or misleading.*
   a. Individuals adapt to their environment and pass the adaptations on to their offspring.
   b. Homologous structures have the same function in unrelated species.
   c. Pesticides have created pesticide-resistant insects.

Performance Assessment

Writing Some people say that living in a technological society makes humans unlikely to be affected by natural selection. Decide whether you agree with this statement, and write a short essay defending your position. Give examples to support your argument.

Online Assessment/Test Preparation

Back Forward Reload Home Search Print Security Stop

www.biology.com

- **Chapter 14 Assessment**
  Check your understanding of the chapter concepts.
- **Standardized Test Preparation**
  Practice test-taking skills you need to succeed.

Origins of Biological Diversity

Darwin realized, following his travels to the Galápagos Islands, that he had visited a birthplace of new species. The islands are home to many plants and animals found nowhere else in the world. Among the islands' unique species are its giant tortoises, for which the Galápagos are named. (*Galápago* is the Spanish word for "tortoise.") After his voyage, Darwin was convinced that the organisms he observed on the Galápagos and elsewhere were clues to the origin of life's diversity.

How is the origin of new species related to the microevolution of populations you learned about in Chapter 14? In this chapter, you will read about processes that can lead to new species and about the methods biologists use to trace the evolution of biological diversity. Before you begin, go online to the *WebQuest* to explore the movement of Earth's continents.

Key Concepts

Concept 15.1 The diversity of life is based on the origin of new species.

Concept 15.2 Evolution is usually a remodeling process.

Concept 15.3 The fossil record provides evidence of life's history.

Concept 15.4 Modern taxonomy reflects evolutionary history.

Assessment Chapter 15 Review

What's Online

www.biology.com

WebQuest
ContinentalDriftQuest

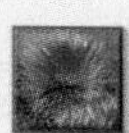

Online Activity 15.1
Explore speciation.

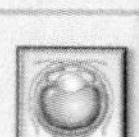

Online Activity 15.2
Build a complex eye.

Online Activity 15.3
Solve a fossil mystery.

Science, Technology, & Society
New Data on Dinosaur Evolution

Online Activity 15.4
Build a cladogram.

Lab 15 Online Companion
Eat Your Greens

Chapter 15 Assessment

CONCEPT 15.1

The diversity of life is based on the origin of new species.

OBJECTIVES

- Describe the biological species concept.
- Distinguish between microevolution and macroevolution.
- List types of reproductive barriers between species.
- Explain how geographic isolation and adaptive radiation contribute to species diversity.
- Summarize models for the tempo of speciation.

KEY TERMS

- biological species concept
- macroevolution
- speciation
- reproductive isolation
- geographic isolation
- adaptive radiation
- punctuated equilibrium

What's Online
www.biology.com
Online Activity 15.1
Explore speciation.

In 1928, a young biologist named Ernst Mayr led an expedition into the remote mountains of New Guinea to study the wildlife. He found a great variety of birds, eventually identifying 138 species based on their different appearances. Mayr was surprised to learn that his list of bird species agreed almost exactly with the species of birds recognized by the local natives. To Mayr, the experience was evidence that species represent recognizably distinct forms of life. How do today's biologists identify species? How do species arise? These questions are essential to understanding the diversity of life on Earth.

What Is a Species?

In Chapter 1, you learned that a species can be described as a distinct form of life. Now it's time to clarify that description. Many biologists use the **biological species concept,** which defines a species as a population or group of populations whose members have the ability to breed with one another in nature and produce fertile offspring. (Fertile offspring are capable of mating and producing offspring.) Members of one species also cannot successfully interbreed with members of other species. This definition has limitations, however. For example, organisms that only reproduce asexually (produce offspring from a single parent) are not included. Fossils, of course, are no longer reproducing, so they cannot be evaluated by this definition either. Even with these exceptions, the biological species concept is useful. This species concept helps biologists understand the origin of new species.

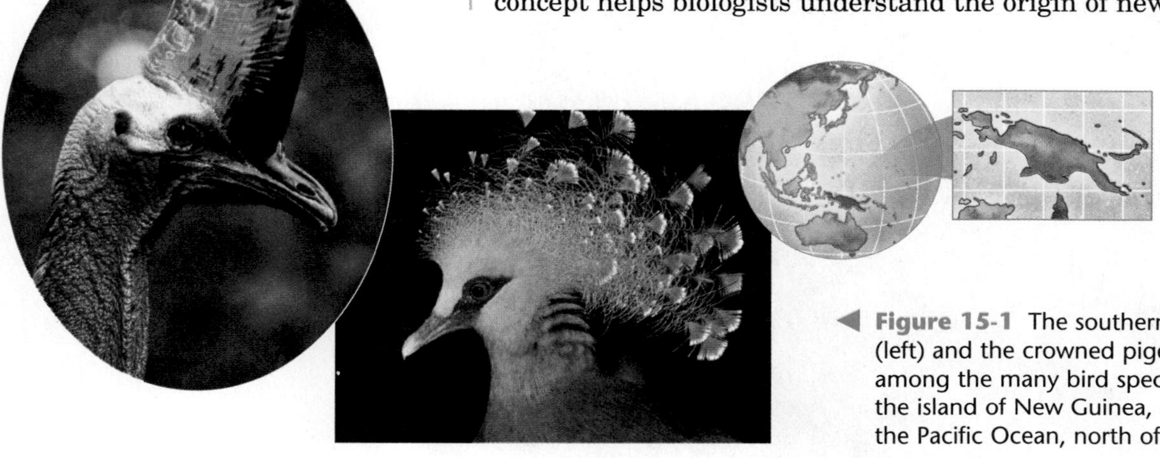

Figure 15-1 The southern cassowary (left) and the crowned pigeon (right) are among the many bird species found on the island of New Guinea, a country in the Pacific Ocean, north of Australia.

From Microevolution to Macroevolution

Microevolution and adaptation explain how populations evolve, as you read in Chapter 14. But if that were *all* that happened, Earth would be inhabited only by a highly adapted version of the first form of life.

Recall from Chapter 14 that microevolution refers to change in the allele frequencies within a population. In contrast, the term **macroevolution** encompasses more dramatic biological changes, many of which are evident in the fossil record. These changes include the origin of different species, the extinction of species, and the evolution of major new features of living things, such as wings or flowers. The origin of new species is known as **speciation** (spee shee AY shun). It is the main focus of the study of macroevolution, for with speciation comes biological diversity. Figure 15-2 shows a simple example of how speciation can lead to an increase in the number of species. In this case, the ancestral (original) species branches into two separate species, increasing the diversity of life.

▲ **Figure 15-2** If one species evolves into two or more surviving species, diversity increases.

Reproductive Barriers Between Species

Clearly, a fly will not mate with a frog or a fern. But what about species that are not so different? The inability to interbreed marks species as separate. If so, what keeps existing species that are similar and closely related from interbreeding? For example, the western spotted skunk and the eastern spotted skunk shown in Figure 15-3 are so similar that only other spotted skunks and expert biologists can tell them apart. Where the skunks' ranges overlap in the Great Plains region, individuals from these two species do not mate. Why not? Some kind of reproductive barrier keeps the two species from interbreeding—a condition known as **reproductive isolation.** Some of the barriers that contribute to reproductive isolation include the following circumstances.

Timing Two similar species may have different breeding seasons. The skunks below fit this category. Western spotted skunks breed in the fall, but the eastern species breeds in late winter. The timing of their breeding seasons keeps these species separate even where they coexist in the Great Plains.

▼ **Figure 15-3** Despite their similarities, the eastern spotted skunk (left) and the western spotted skunk (right) are two species kept separate by different breeding seasons.

Behavior Two similar species may have different courtship or mating behaviors. For example, eastern and western meadowlarks are almost identical in shape, coloring, and habitat. Like the skunks, the ranges of these birds in the central United States overlap. Yet they remain separate species because their courtship rituals differ, including the songs that attract mates.

Habitat Some species remain reproductively isolated because they are adapted to different habitats in the same general location. For example, certain lakes in British Columbia, Canada, contain two different species of three-spined stickleback fish. One species is adapted to living along the lake bottom, feeding on small snails. Fish of the other species spend most of their lives in the open water, filtering plankton (small floating organisms). The two species' preferences for different habitats help maintain their isolation.

Other Reproductive Barriers In addition to timing, behavior, and habitat, other barriers can keep species reproductively isolated. For instance, two seemingly similar species may be unable to mate because their reproductive structures are physically incompatible. Or, as in the case of some plants, the insects or other animals that transfer flower pollen may do so only among plants of a single species.

Some reproductive barriers come into play *after* fertilization takes place. A hybrid zygote may fail to develop. Or, some hybrid offspring may mature into adults, but they are infertile (Figure 15-4). (Remember that the definition of a species requires that its members be able to produce fertile offspring.)

In most cases, reproductive isolation results from a combination of two or more barriers. Such barriers often come about as "side effects" of other adaptations. For example, the different breeding seasons of the eastern and western spotted skunks probably were individual adaptations of each skunk species. These adaptations likely arose when the ancestral populations of the two species were isolated in different locations. If reproductive isolation keeps species separate after the species arise, then the origin of these barriers is the key to the origin of new species.

▼ **Figure 15-4** Horses and donkeys remain separate species because their hybrid offspring—mules—are infertile.

▲ **Figure 15-5** The Grand Canyon forms a geologic barrier between Harris's antelope squirrel (left) and the white-tailed antelope squirrel (right).

Geographic Isolation and Speciation

Geologic processes constantly change and rearrange Earth's features. Such change can separate different populations of one species. A mountain range may gradually emerge, slowly splitting a population of organisms that cannot cross it. A creeping glacier may slowly divide a population. In other cases, populations become separated when a small group disperses from the main population and colonizes an isolated location, such as an island. Separation of populations as a result of geographic change or dispersal to geographically isolated places is called **geographic isolation.**

How well a geographic barrier keeps populations apart depends on the ability of organisms to move about. For example, biologists hypothesize that the two species of antelope squirrels in Figure 15-5 evolved from geographically separate populations. These species live on opposite rims of the Grand Canyon. Harris's antelope squirrel (*Ammospermophilus harrisii*) lives on the south rim. Just a few miles away on the north rim is the closely related white-tailed antelope squirrel (*Ammospermophilus leucurus*). Such small rodents may find a deep canyon or wide river too daunting to cross. In contrast, birds, mountain lions, and coyotes can navigate mountain ranges, rivers, and canyons. The windblown pollen of pine trees or the seeds of plants carried on animals also move back and forth.

The separation of a small "splinter" population from its main population is a crucial event in the origin of species. Once separate, the splinter population may follow its own evolutionary course. Recall from Chapter 14 that genetic drift—change in a gene pool due to chance—plays a key role in microevolution. Changes in allele frequencies caused by genetic drift and natural selection can accumulate in the splinter population, making it less and less like the main population.

For each small, isolated population that becomes a new species, many more simply perish. Life in some environments is harsh, and most colonizing populations probably fail to survive in their new location. Even if such populations survive and adapt to their local environments, they do not necessarily evolve into new species. Speciation has occurred only if one population can no longer breed with the other population, even if the two populations should come back into contact. Figure 15-6 shows two possible outcomes for populations that meet again after having been geographically separate. In one case, the changes do not prevent interbreeding, and the populations are still one species. In the other case, the two populations have evolved in ways that prevent them from interbreeding. They have become two species.

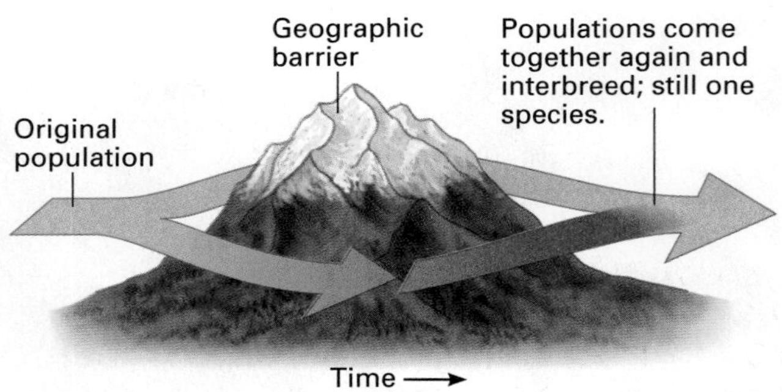

Speciation does not occur.

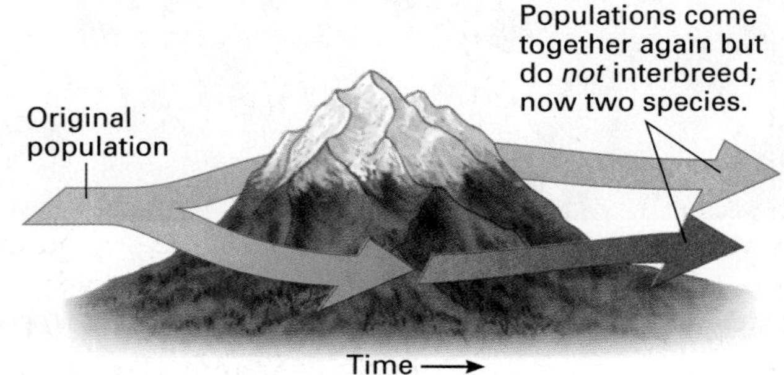

▲ **Figure 15-6** In this model, arrows symbolize populations that become geographically separated, then come together again at a later time.

Adaptive Radiation

Since Darwin's time, islands have served as living laboratories for studying speciation. Islands often have species found nowhere else. The isolation and diverse habitats of some islands create conditions that seem to favor speciation. Only a few organisms manage to be the first to colonize new islands. Those that do, enter a diverse, "empty" environment. The small populations of colonizing species may undergo evolutionary change. Some of these organisms may move on to other islands in the chain, where the process repeats itself. New and varying species may evolve through genetic drift and adaptation to the different habitats. Such evolution from a common ancestor that results in diverse species adapted to different environments is called **adaptive radiation.**

Figure 15-7 illustrates a simplified model for adaptive radiation of birds. In this example, one species is the common ancestor of several new species that arise on the islands. After migrating

▼ **Figure 15-7** Adaptive radiation on an island chain may lead to several new bird species evolving from one founding population.

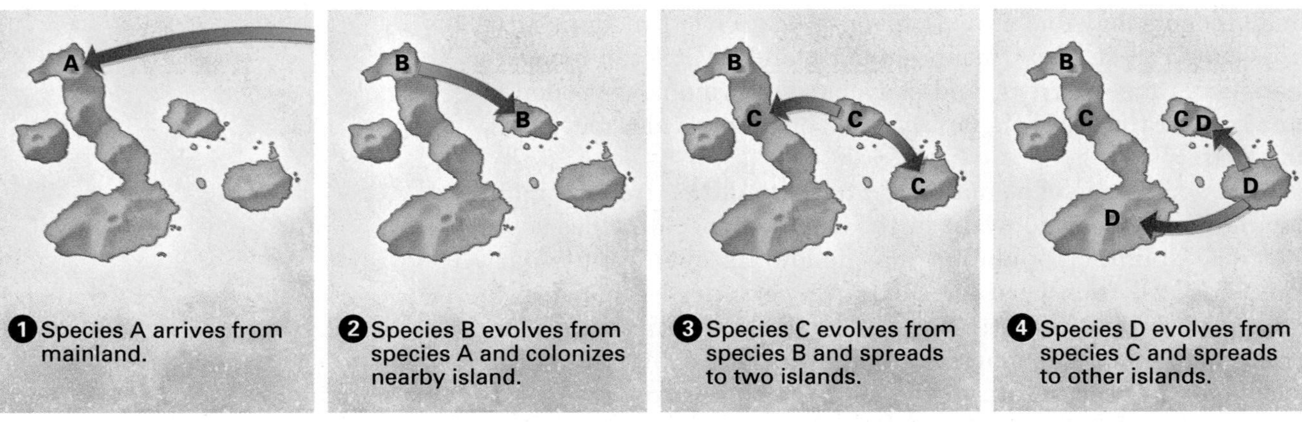

A
B
B
B
C
C
C
B
C
C D
D
D
1 Species A arrives from mainland.
2 Species B evolves from species A and colonizes nearby island.
3 Species C evolves from species B and spreads to two islands.
4 Species D evolves from species C and spreads to other islands.

from the mainland, species A may have undergone significant change in its gene pool and become species B. Later, a few birds of species B may have migrated to a neighboring island. This population could have evolved into species C. Some of these birds could later move back to the first island. They might coexist with species B if reproductive barriers keep the two species separate. Species C could also move among other islands where the same evolutionary processes might continue. Geographic isolation is a key factor in this example because it prevents the splinter populations from breeding with the "parent" population on the mainland.

The Hawaiian Islands are one of the world's great showcases of evolution. The islands are about 4,000 kilometers from the nearest continent, and each island is itself physically diverse. A range of altitudes and differences in rainfall on each island create multiple environments. Originally, the islands were uninhabited. New lava flows continually increased the amount of vacant land (and still do). These conditions supported repeated instances of adaptive radiation. Most of the thousands of native species on the islands are found nowhere else in the world (Figure 15-8).

▲ **Figure 15-8** The silversword is a unique plant species found in the Haleakala crater on the island of Maui, Hawaii.

The Tempo of Speciation

On the time scale of the fossil record, species often seem to arise abruptly. A new fossil species may appear rather suddenly (in geological terms) in a layer of rock, and persist for thousands or millions of years without noticeable change. Then, it may disappear from the fossil record as suddenly as it appeared.

Over the past 30 years, some evolutionary biologists have developed a model to address these observations. Now known as **punctuated equilibrium,** the model suggests that species often diverge in spurts of relatively rapid change. Then many newly formed species may remain mostly unchanged, at least in ways that are evident in the fossil record. The term *punctuated equilibrium* comes from the idea that long periods of little change (equilibrium) in a species are broken, or punctuated, by shorter times of speciation.

Given a model of gradual adaptation through natural selection, how could species have sudden bursts of change? Speciation can sometimes be quite rapid. In just a few hundred to a few thousand generations, genetic drift and natural selection can cause significant change in a small population that is occupying a challenging new environment.

You may also wonder how speciation in a few thousand generations can be called abrupt. The fossil record indicates that successful species last, on average, about one to five million years. A particular species may have accumulated most of its unique changes in its first 50,000 years. Though this time span may seem long on a human scale, it only represents a hundredth of

Gradual Adaptation Model

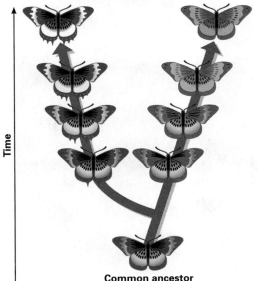

Time

Common ancestor

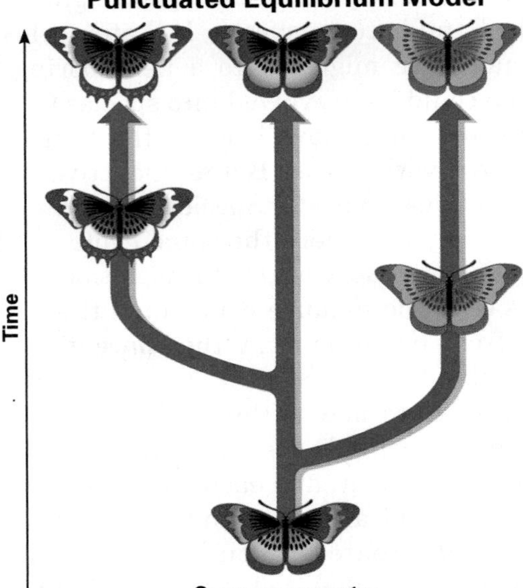

the lifetime of a typical species and a short interval of time on the scale of the fossil record. This explanation would account for the punctuated equilibrium that scientists often observe in the fossil record. Remember, too, that the best candidates for speciation are small populations. Fossils from such populations are rare. By the time a new species grew in number and became widespread enough that it might leave a fossil record, its distinctive features would have already evolved.

Keep in mind that punctuated equilibrium does not contradict or weaken Darwin's theory. The theory of natural selection can account for observations of punctuated equilibrium in the fossil record. Natural selection and adaptation still happen, but mostly during that time when a species is "young." The addition of punctuated equilibrium to evolutionary biology demonstrates a principle you learned about in Chapter 2—refining a scientific theory to reflect new evidence.

▲ **Figure 15-9** In contrast to a more gradual model of evolution, punctuated equilibrium suggests that a new species changes most as it buds from a parent species. There is little change for the rest of the time the species exists.

Online Activity 15.1
Back Forward Reload Home Search Print Security Stop
www.biology.com
Explore speciation.
Go online to visit the Hawaiian Islands and investigate adaptive radiation in silversword plants. Then examine the evolutionary history of elephants.

Concept Check 15.1

1. Why are donkeys and horses considered different species?
2. What is macroevolution?
3. Give an example of a reproductive barrier that may separate two similar species.
4. Describe conditions that could make a new island a likely place for adaptive radiation.
5. How does punctuated equilibrium relate to Darwin's theory of natural selection?

CONCEPT 15.2

Evolution is usually a remodeling process.

OBJECTIVES
- Describe how evolution can refine existing adaptations.
- Explain how existing structures can take on new functions through evolution.
- Explain the role of developmental biology in understanding evolutionary change.

KEY TERM
- embryology

What's Online
www.biology.com
Online Activity 15.2
Build a complex eye.

So far, you've been reading about examples in which one species gives rise to another similar species. Yet most people think of evolution as involving more dramatic transformations, such as new body forms or the intricate structure of an eye. Can Darwin's theory of gradual change account for such "breakthroughs" in form and function?

Refinement of Existing Adaptations

Any living organism has a number of adaptations. Examples might include the fins and flippers of swimming animals, bodies adapted for flight, or the structure of an eye or a flower. How does natural selection account for these adaptations? In some cases, a complex structure may have evolved from a simpler structure having the same basic function—a process of refinement. For example, the camera-like eye of a mammal is an amazing structure with many interacting parts (Figure 15-10). Some people cannot consider that such complex organs could evolve by gradual refinement of simpler structures. If the eye needs all of its parts to work, the argument goes, how could a partial eye be of any use as an evolutionary stage? What's the use of a retina (layers of cells on which light is focused), for instance, without a lens that focuses light? Yet, evidence shows that eyes don't have to be complicated to be useful adaptations.

Figure 15-10 The camera-like eye of a mammal such as this bighorn sheep has many interacting parts. This complex structure could have evolved through refinements of simpler types of eyes.

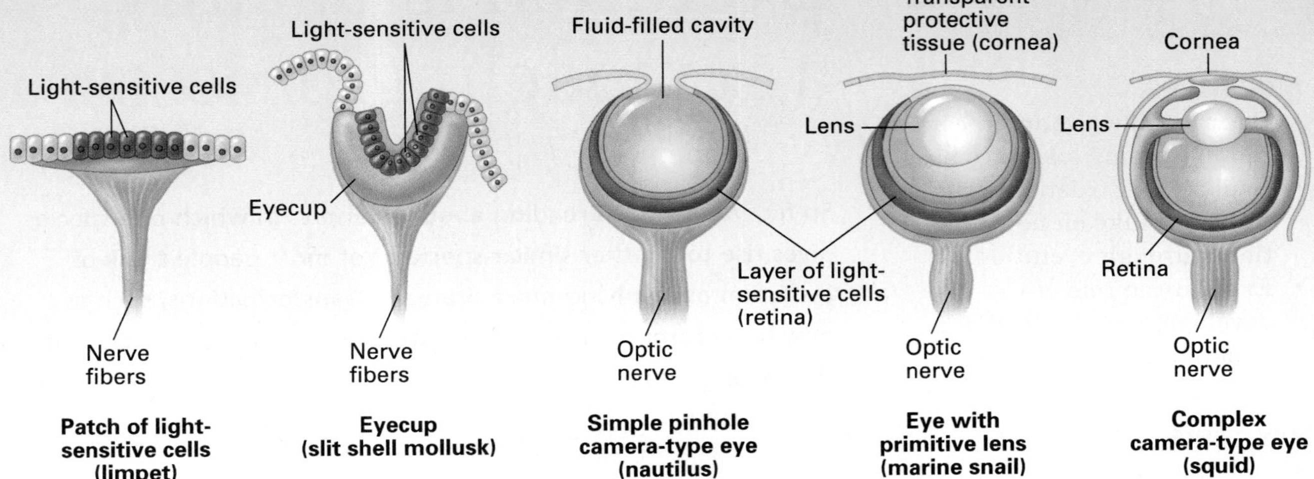

▲ **Figure 15-11** These diagrams show the range of complexity in the structure of eyes among various species of mollusks living today.

Among living mollusks (animals that include squids, octopuses, snails, and clams), you can find eyes ranging in complexity from clusters of light-sensitive cells to camera-like eyes with lenses (Figure 15-11). Some mollusks have very simple eyes. Other mollusks have structures called eyecups that have no lenses or other means of focusing images. However, all these animals can at least distinguish light from dark. Considering the long survival of many species with simple eyes, simple eyes are obviously enough to meet these animals' needs. In those animals that do have complex eyes, the organs did not have to evolve from simpler ones in one giant evolutionary jump. Instead, complex eyes probably evolved by small steps of adaptation, refining organs that worked and benefited their owners at each stage. Evidence of these small steps can be seen in other mollusk eyes.

Adaptation of Existing Structures to New Functions

When World War I ended in 1918, an American paper products company was stuck with a surplus of 375 tons of material for bandage dressings. The company found new functions for the material. For example, they used the paper sheets to make the first facial tissues—the "ancestor" of the products you rely on when you have a cold.

In the history of life there are also instances of existing materials or structures that evolved as adaptations for certain functions and later fulfilled different functions. An example is the material called chitin (KY tun). Chitin forms the exoskeleton (shell) of arthropods, which are animals such as insects, spiders, scorpions, and lobsters. In the ocean, where arthropods originated, the exoskeleton helped to protect the animals from predators (Figure 15-12). More than a hundred million years later, when the arthropod ancestors of insects, spiders, and scorpions began to colonize land, the exoskeleton became adapted to an additional function. Land-dwelling organisms face the severe environmental

▼ **Figure 15-12** In marine arthropods such as this reef lobster (top), the exoskeleton protects the animal from predators. In land arthropods such as this scorpion (bottom), the exoskeleton fulfills the additional function of resisting water loss.

challenge of dehydration—the loss of body water by evaporation. The chitin of the arthropod exoskeleton resists water loss. Chemical changes to this material made it even more watertight as the animals became adapted to living on land.

The flippers of penguins are another example of how natural selection can modify existing structures for different functions. Penguins are birds. The flippers they use to swim are actually modified wings (Figure 15-13). Penguins inhabit small, barren islands and other remote locations in the Southern Hemisphere where flight would offer little advantage for either escape or hunting. Large predators are rare on these rocky or icy islands. Also, food is far more abundant in the surrounding sea than on the land or ice. Though penguins cannot fly through the air, they are strong, fast underwater swimmers. They can dive into the sea to hunt small fish and other prey. Natural selection has remodeled the wings into powerful flippers for swimming.

▲ **Figure 15-13** A penguin's modified wings do not function in true flight and are of limited use on land. But the "flipper-wings" enable the penguin to "fly" through the water.

Evolution and Development

What is the genetic basis for the evolutionary remodeling of body form? Some answers to this question are coming from the field of developmental biology, including embryology. **Embryology** is the study of the processes of multicellular organisms as they develop from fertilized eggs to fully formed organisms. One important focus of embryology are genes that control the development of an organism as it begins to take shape. For example, the homeotic genes you learned about in Chapter 13 program the placement of body parts, such as the locations of wings, legs, and antennae in insects. A mutation in such a master control gene can produce bizarre effects, such as a fly with legs developing where antennae would normally be located (Figure 15-14). Less dramatic, but more important in evolution, are more subtle changes in the developmental programs of organisms.

▼ **Figure 15-14** A mutation in a homeotic gene caused this fly to grow extra legs in place of antennae.

Figure 15-15 Compared to ground-dwelling salamanders (right), the feet of tree-dwelling salamanders (left) have shorter toes and more webbing—an adaptation to the tree salamander's climbing lifestyle.

In some cases, the remodeling process of evolution involves changes in the rate or timing of some event in the development of an organism. An example is the evolutionary adaptation of feet in various salamander species. (Salamanders are vertebrates closely related to frogs.) Most salamanders live on the ground or in the water, but some species live in trees. The feet of these tree-dwelling salamanders are adapted for climbing. They have shorter toes and more webbing than the feet of salamanders that live on the ground (Figure 15-15). The difference occurs because growth of the feet of the tree-dwellers ends sooner in development, even as the rest of the body continues to grow. As scientists investigate genetic programs that control development, they hope to learn more about the remodeling mechanisms of evolution.

Online Activity 15.2

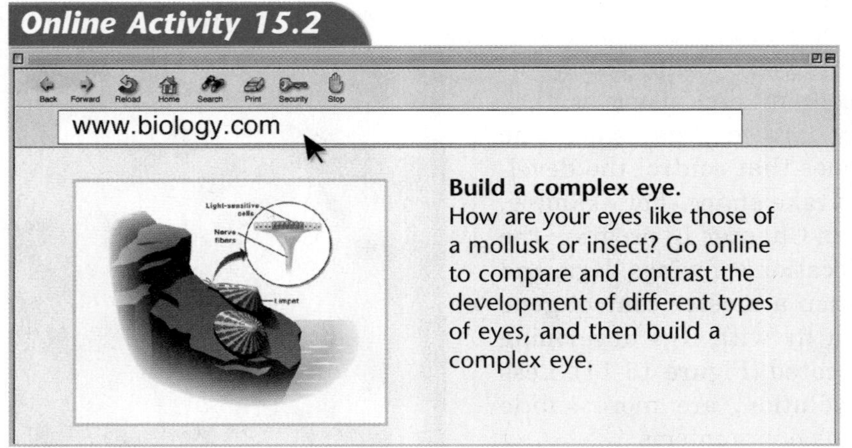

www.biology.com
Build a complex eye.
How are your eyes like those of a mollusk or insect? Go online to compare and contrast the development of different types of eyes, and then build a complex eye.

Concept Check 15.2

1. How can evolution explain the range of complexity of eyes in modern organisms?
2. Give an example of evolutionary remodeling of an exisiting structure to a new function.
3. Identify one possible event during an organism's embryonic development that can result in a change in body form.

CONCEPT 15.3

The fossil record provides evidence of life's history.

OBJECTIVES

- Explain how fossils can form.
- Describe the geologic time scale.
- Summarize methods used to determine the ages of fossils.
- Describe how continental drift and mass extinctions relate to macroevolution.

KEY TERMS

- geologic time scale
- radiometric dating
- half-life
- continental drift
- mass extinction

What's Online

Online Activity 15.3
Solve a fossil mystery.

Science, Technology, & Society
New Data on Dinosaur Evolution

Have you ever seen exposed layers of rock alongside a highway? If the rock contains fossils, such layers are like pages in the history of life. Each layer records a snapshot of organisms from a particular time. Here, you'll explore how the story of life as told by fossils can be read.

How Fossils Form

In Chapter 14, you learned that fossils can form from the remains of organisms buried by sediments, dust, or volcanic ash. The soft body parts of dead organisms usually decay rapidly in these conditions. However, hard parts such as shells, bones, or teeth, are long-lasting and may become preserved as fossils (Figure 15-16). Many of these relics are hardened even more and preserved by chemical changes. Under the right conditions, minerals dissolved in groundwater seep into the tissues of a dead organism and replace its organic material. The plant or animal remains become petrified—they turn to stone.

Some rare fossils actually retain organic material. Usually, these are found as thin films pressed between layers of sandstone or shale. For example, in Idaho, paleontologists have discovered plant leaves millions of years old that are still green with chlorophyll. DNA from such cells can sometimes be extracted and studied.

Other fossils consist of footprints, animal burrows, or other impressions left in sediments. Dinosaur tracks, for example, provide clues about whether the animal walked or ran and about its size and speed. Even animal dung can form fossils that give biologists clues to an animal's diet and digestive processes.

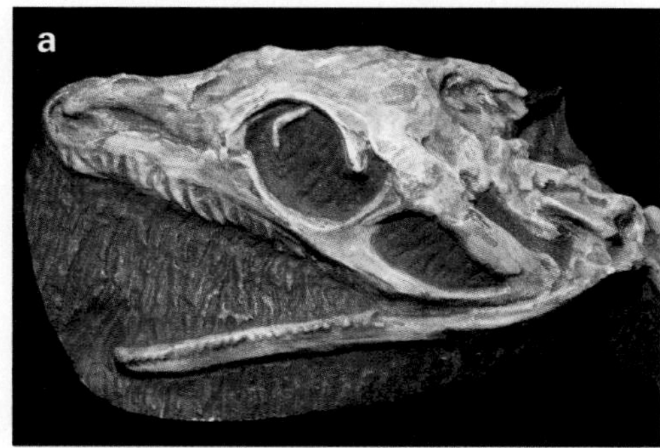

Figure 15-16 The fossil remains of organisms exist in various forms. **a.** This skull of an ancient animal is preserved bone. **b.** Leaves from a fern left these impressions in sedimentary rock.

Sometimes an organism happens to die in a place where bacteria and fungi cannot decompose the corpse. In such rare cases, the entire body, including soft parts, may be preserved as a fossil (Figure 15-17). For example, mammoths, bison, and even prehistoric humans have been found frozen in ice, where conditions slow decomposition. Such rare discoveries make the news, but biologists rely mainly on fossils that are found in sedimentary rocks to reconstruct the history of life.

▲ **Figure 15-17** These insects were trapped in plant sap when they died. The sap hardened into amber, preserving the entire organisms inside.

The Fossil Record and Geologic Time Scale

The fossil record is a rich storehouse of information about macroevolution. In each layer of rock, the fossils are samples of the organisms that existed in that place at the time the sediment was deposited. Geologists have studied and compared sediments from sites around the world. The data collected provide a consistent and extensive record of Earth's history.

The **geologic time scale** (Figure 15-18 on the facing page) organizes Earth's history into four distinct ages known as the Precambrian, Paleozoic, Mesozoic, and Cenozoic eras. These eras are divided into shorter time spans called periods. Periods are divided into epochs. The boundaries between eras are marked in the fossil record by a major change (or turnover) in the forms of life. For example, the beginning of the Paleozoic Era (the start of the Cambrian period) is marked by the appearance of a diversity of multicellular animals with hard parts. Fossils of these animals are absent in rocks of the Precambrian Era. The boundaries between eras and between some periods are also marked by widespread extinctions. For example, many of the animals that lived during the late Paleozoic Era became extinct at the end of that era.

Some of the organisms included in the geologic time scale may not be familiar to you now. But as you study Units 5, 6, and 7, you will learn more about these groups of organisms. When you read these later chapters, you may want to refer occasionally to Figure 15-18 to help you keep track of the "big picture" of the history of life.

Dating Fossils

Fossils aren't much help in learning about the past unless you know their age. Because younger sediments are usually layered over older ones, you can tell which layers formed before others. The *relative ages* of fossils reflect the order in which groups of species existed compared to one another. However, position in the rocks won't tell you the actual ages in years, or *absolute ages,* of the fossils. The situation is like peeling layers of wallpaper from the walls of an old house. You could determine the sequence in which the wallpapers had been applied, but not the year that each layer was added.

Relative Time Span
Era
Period
Epoch
Millions of Years Ago
Some Important Events in the History of Life
Cenozoic
Mesozoic
Paleozoic
Precambrian
Quaternary
Tertiary
Cretaceous
Jurassic
Triassic
Permian
Carboniferous
Devonian
Silurian
Ordovician
Cambrian
Recent
Pleistocene
Pliocene
Miocene
Oligocene
Eocene
Paleocene
0.01
1.8
5
23
35
57
65
144
206
245
290
363
409
439
510
543
600
2,200
2,700
3,500
3,800
4,600
Historical time
Ice ages; humans appear
Ancestors of humans appear
Mammals and flowering plants continue to diversify
Many primate groups, including apes, appear
Flowering plants increase in abundance; most modern mammals appear
Mammals, birds, and pollinating insects increase greatly in diversity
Flowering plants appear; many groups of organisms, including dinosaurs, become extinct at end of period (Cretaceous extinctions)
Cone-bearing plants dominate landscape; dinosaurs diversify
Cone-bearing plants continue to dominate kingdom; dinosaurs abundant and diverse
Many marine and terrestrial organisms go extinct; reptiles diversify; mammal-like reptiles and most modern insects appear
Forests of vascular plants; first seed plants; reptiles appear; amphibians dominant
Bony fishes diversify; first amphibians and insects
Diversity of jawless fishes; first jawed fishes; early vascular plants diversify
Marine algae abundant; plants and arthropods colonize land
Most modern animal groups appear (Cambrian explosion)
Diverse soft-bodied invertebrate animals; diverse algae
Oldest fossils of eukaryotic cells
Atmospheric oxygen begins to increase
Oldest fossils of cells (prokaryotes)
Earliest traces of life
Approximate time of origin of Earth

Figure 15-18 This diagram of geologic time indicates some key events in the history of life on Earth. Note the relative time spans of the eras, depicted in the lower left corner.

▲ **Figure 15-19** If the ages of two volcanic rock layers are measured using radioactive isotopes, the data can be used to estimate the age of fossils found in the sedimentary rock between the volcanic layers.

Radiometric dating is based on the measurement of certain radioactive isotopes in objects. It is the method most often used to determine the absolute ages of rocks and fossils. Every radioactive isotope has a fixed rate of decay. An isotope's **half-life** is the number of years it takes for 50 percent of the original sample to decay. The half-life is unaffected by temperature, pressure, and other environmental conditions.

Geologists use radioactive isotopes with long half-lives to date rocks. For example, uranium-238, which has a half-life of 4.5 billion years, has been used to date rocks of the Precambrian era and the Cambrian period. Uranium-238 is not present in living organisms. It occurs in molten lava and volcanic rock that forms as lava cools. After volcanic rock forms, no more uranium-238 is incorporated. The rock's original stock of the isotope decays, eventually becoming lead-206. By measuring the ratio of uranium-238 to lead-206, researchers can date (find the absolute age of) volcanic rocks. Paleontologists can use these measurements to date fossils found in rock layers above or below the volcanic rocks (Figure 15-19).

Sometimes the ages of fossils themselves can be determined directly. Fossils contain isotopes of elements that accumulated in the organisms when they were alive—for example, carbon-12 and radioactive carbon-14. Plants take in both isotopes in the carbon dioxide used for photosynthesis. Animals consume the isotopes in food. When an organism dies, this intake stops, but radioactive decay continues. Changes in the ratio of carbon-14 to carbon-12 can be measured, allowing researchers to calculate how long the organism has been dead.

"Carbon dating" can only be used to find the age of recent fossils because carbon-14 has a half-life of just 5,730 years. You can see from Figure 15-20 that if fossils are much older than about 50,000 years, the fraction of carbon-14 remaining is too small to measure accurately. To estimate the ages of older fossils, scientists can use surrounding rocks that contain uranium-238 and other radioactive isotopes having longer half-lives.

▼ **Figure 15-20** From the time an organism dies, decay of half the carbon-14 present in its body takes 5,730 years. Half of that remainder decays in another 5,730 years, and so on.

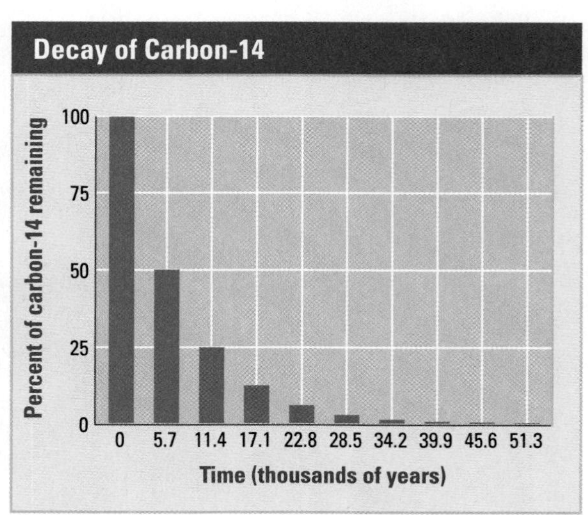

Continental Drift and Macroevolution

Earth's continents are not locked in place. They move about the planet's surface like passengers on great plates of crust, floating on the hot mantle. Landmasses on different plates change position relative to each other as a result of movement known as **continental drift.** North America and Europe, for example, are presently drifting apart at a rate of about 2 centimeters per year.

Continental drift is the solution to many biological puzzles. For example, paleontologists have discovered matching Mesozoic fossils in West Africa and Brazil. How could these two parts of the world, now separated by 3,000 kilometers of ocean, be home to the same organisms? The evidence makes sense if these two regions were part of one landmass in the early Mesozoic Era. Similarly, continental drift explains why the plants and animals of Australia are so different from those in the rest of the world. After Australia became an isolated landmass, the organisms living there would have evolved independently of those living on other continents.

Two major events in the history of continental drift had an especially strong influence on life on Earth. The first occurred about 250 million years ago, near the end of the Paleozoic Era (Figure 15-21). Plate movements brought all the landmasses together into one supercontinent, named Pangaea (meaning "all land"). A variety of environmental changes followed. The amount of shoreline was reduced. Also, evidence suggests that sea levels dropped and shallow coastal seas were drained. Such changes would have destroyed the shallow water environments inhabited by many marine species. On land, continental interiors—which are drier and have more extreme climates than coastal areas—would have been affected as well. Additionally, species that had been evolving in isolation would have come together and competed. All these changes likely caused the extinction of huge numbers of species.

The second major event in the history of continental drift was written about 180 million years ago as Pangaea began to break up. As the continents drifted apart, each became an isolated and separate evolutionary arena. The species living on the different continents would have diverged in their evolution as they continued to adapt and diversify on the now-separate continents.

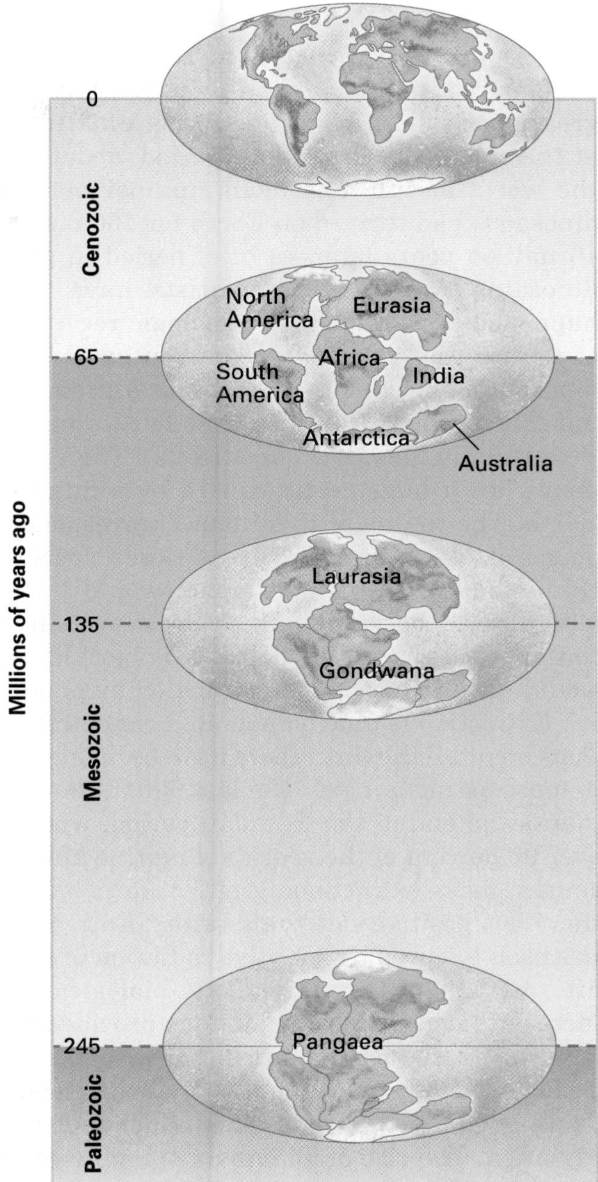

▲ **Figure 15-21** About 180 million years ago, Pangaea split into northern and southern landmasses that later separated into the modern continents. India collided with Eurasia just 40 to 50 million years ago, forming the Himalaya mountain range. The continents continue to drift today.

Mass Extinctions

The fossil record reveals that Earth's history has long periods of relative stability broken by comparatively brief episodes of great species loss known as **mass extinctions.** For example, at the end of the Cretaceous period, about 65 million years ago, the world lost an enormous number of species. Before then, dinosaurs had thrived on Earth for 150 million years. Less than 10 million years later—a brief period in geologic time—all the dinosaurs were gone. Scientists have been debating what happened for decades. The geologic record indicates a number of events that may have contributed to the extinction of the dinosaurs. The climate was cooling, and shallow seas were receding. But perhaps the final blow left its mark near the Yucatán Peninsula in Mexico (Figure 15-22). There, buried beneath sediment, lies a huge crater caused by a large meteor that struck Earth. The timing of this impact corresponds with the last evidence of dinosaurs and many other species. Many scientists think that such a huge impact would have polluted the sky with dusty debris for months. (Rock layers from that time period contain evidence of this debris.) By blocking sunlight, this event would have reduced food production by photosynthesis.

Extinction is unavoidable in a changing world. While extinctions occur all the time, there have been five or six distinct periods of mass extinction over the last 600 million years. One example marks the end of the Permian period, when extinction claimed over 90 percent of the species of marine animals. Whatever their causes, mass extinctions greatly affect biological diversity. Yet, there is a positive side to this story. Each massive loss of species has been followed by adaptive radiation of some survivors. In the aftermath of mass extinctions, biological diversity gradually increased again. Mass extinctions provided the surviving organisms with new opportunities. For example, just after the mass extinction marking the end of the Cretaceous period, fossil evidence suggests that mammals underwent widespread adaptive radiation. The rise of mammals probably resulted, in part, from the void left by the extinction of dinosaurs.

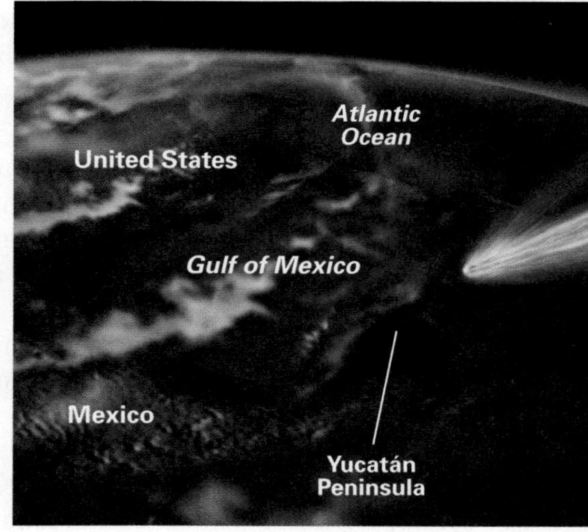

▲ **Figure 15-22** The impact of a meteor 65 million years ago near the Yucatán Peninsula in Mexico may be one cause of the extinction of many land plants and animals in North America.

Science, Technology, & Society

New Data on Dinosaur Evolution
Roving deserts in search of new finds . . . digging in scorching heat to unearth ancient bones . . . The job description of a paleontologist reads a bit like a movie script! But while fossil hunting may be a great adventure, it's also serious work. Go online to find out how "dinosaur hunters" use the fossil record to learn more about evolution.

Online Activity 15.3

Solve a fossil mystery.
How do scientists date fossils? Find out online as you use a carbon-14 dating calculator to solve a fossil mystery. Then scroll through an interactive geologic time scale to observe how life changed through the eras.

Concept Check 15.3

1. Which parts of organisms are most commonly found as fossils?
2. What main characteristic distinguishes the fossil record of the Paleozoic Era from that of the Precambrian Era?
3. How are the relative ages of fossils in sedimentary rock determined?
4. How does a mass extinction change conditions for species that survive?

CONCEPT 15.4

Modern taxonomy reflects evolutionary history.

OBJECTIVES

- State the goals of taxonomy.
- Describe how evolutionary biology and molecular biology influence classification.
- Summarize the meaning of a cladogram.
- Compare the use of domains and kingdoms in various classification schemes.

KEY TERMS

- taxonomy
- binomial
- phylogenetic tree
- convergent evolution
- analogous structures
- derived character
- cladogram

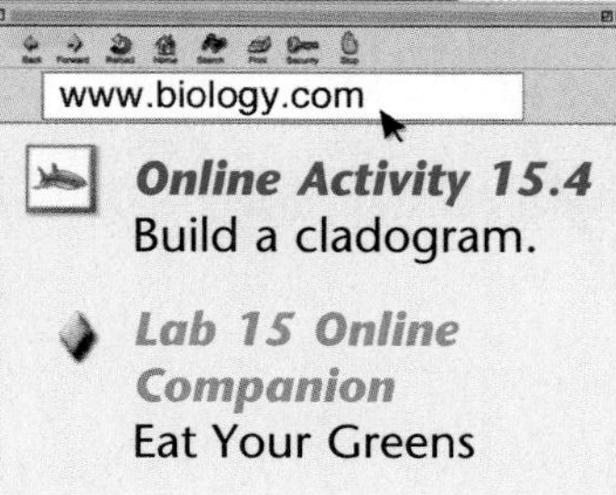
What's Online
www.biology.com
Online Activity 15.4
Build a cladogram.
Lab 15 Online Companion
Eat Your Greens

As the science of biology developed in the eighteenth and nineteenth centuries, a major goal was to name and classify Earth's diverse species. You might think this task would be fairly complete by now—but in fact that is not the case. New discoveries, methods, technology, and molecular evidence have revitalized the field, making it one of today's most exciting areas of biological research.

What Is Taxonomy?

A branch of biology called **taxonomy** involves the identification, naming, and classification of species. Assigning scientific names to species is an important part of studying the history of life. Although common names such as monkey, fruit fly, and pine generally work well in everyday language, common names can also cause confusion. Each of the names above actually refers to many different species. And sometimes the same common name can even refer to *very* different organisms. For example, a tortoise might be called a gopher in Florida, but in Kansas, "gopher" might refer to either a ground squirrel or a pocket gopher. Often, a common name doesn't accurately reflect the organism (Figure 15-23). Consider the names catfish, crayfish, and silverfish—the first is a fish, the second is a small freshwater lobster, and the third is an insect. Then there's the fact that organisms have different common names in different languages. Yet biologists must be able to communicate with one another about the species they study, no matter what language they speak.

To reduce this confusion in discussing organisms, one goal of taxonomy is to assign a universal scientific name to each known species. But taxonomists also attempt to organize the diversity of life by classifying species into larger groups of related species. This section describes some of their methods.

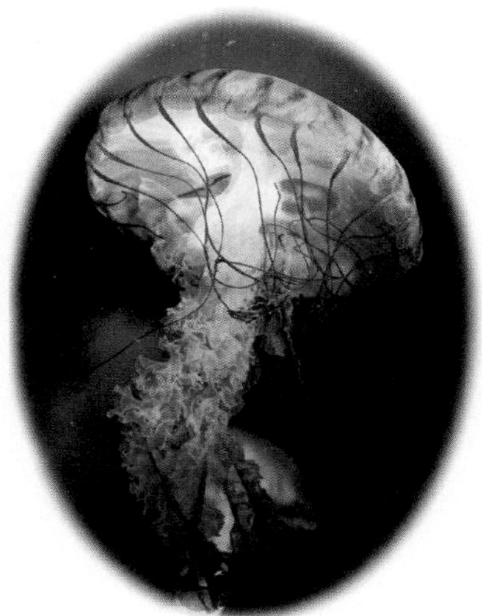

▲ **Figure 15-23** Most people would call this sea nettle a jellyfish, but it's another example of a "-fish" that isn't a fish!

The Linnaean System of Classification

The system of classification most widely used in biology dates back to Swedish botanist Carolus Linnaeus (1707–1778). The system has two main characteristics—a two-part Latin name for each species and a hierarchy, or ordering, of species into broader and broader groups.

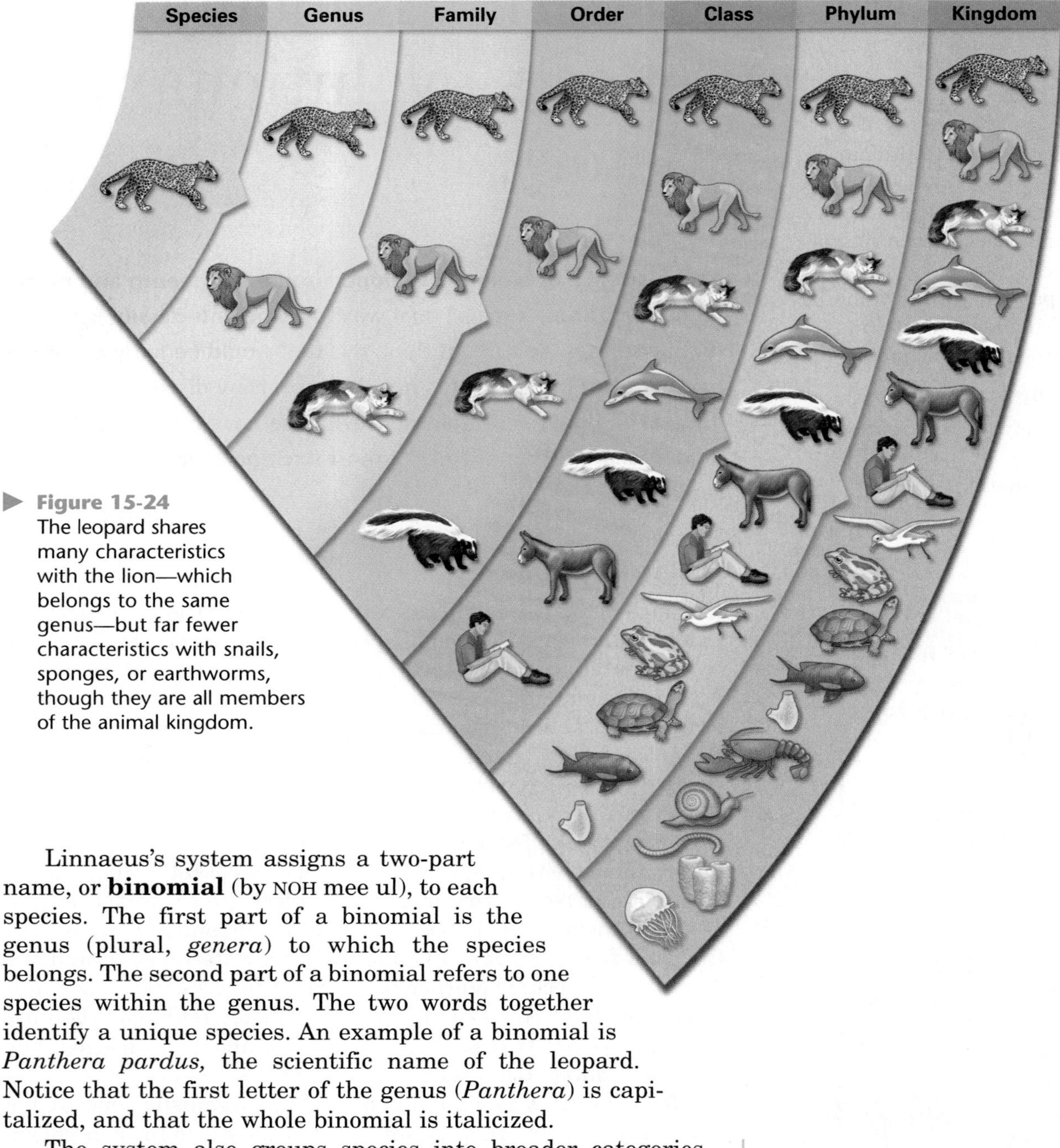

Figure 15-24
The leopard shares many characteristics with the lion—which belongs to the same genus—but far fewer characteristics with snails, sponges, or earthworms, though they are all members of the animal kingdom.

Linnaeus's system assigns a two-part name, or **binomial** (by NOH mee ul), to each species. The first part of a binomial is the genus (plural, *genera*) to which the species belongs. The second part of a binomial refers to one species within the genus. The two words together identify a unique species. An example of a binomial is *Panthera pardus,* the scientific name of the leopard. Notice that the first letter of the genus (*Panthera*) is capitalized, and that the whole binomial is italicized.

The system also groups species into broader categories, starting with the genus in the binomial (Figure 15-24). Closely related species are grouped into the same genus. For example the leopard, and the African lion (*Panthera leo*) both belong to the genus *Panthera.* Taxonomists group similar genera in the same family. Next, similar families are placed into orders, orders into classes, and classes into phyla (singular, *phylum*). Phyla are grouped into kingdoms. Classifying a species by kingdom, phylum, and so on, is like placing students in a large school system. First a student might be identified by school, then by specific grade, and finally as a unique individual by name.

Classification and Evolution

Darwin viewed Linnaeus's system of classification in the context of evolution. Ever since, biologists have strived to have classification represent the evolutionary relationships among species. Species are classified into groups within groups. A diagram that reflects such hypotheses of evolutionary relationships has a branching pattern called a **phylogenetic tree** (Figure 15-25). (The diagram's name comes from the word *phylogeny,* meaning "evolutionary history.")

Homologous structures are one of the best clues to assess how closely organisms are related. Recall from Chapter 14 that homologous structures—like a whale's flipper and a bat's wing—may look different and function very differently in different species. However, they will have basic underlying similarities if they both evolved from a single structure in a common ancestor. The greater the number of homologous structures two species have, the more closely the species are thought to be related.

There are, however, pitfalls in the search for homologous characteristics. Not all similar structures are inherited from a common ancestor. **Convergent evolution** is a process in which unrelated species from similar environments have adaptations that seem very similar (Figure 15-26). Similar adaptations that result from convergent evolution are called **analogous structures.** For example, the wings of insects and those of birds are analogous, not homologous, flight equipment—they evolved independently. And, they are built from entirely different structures. There is no evidence that insects and birds shared a common winged ancestor.

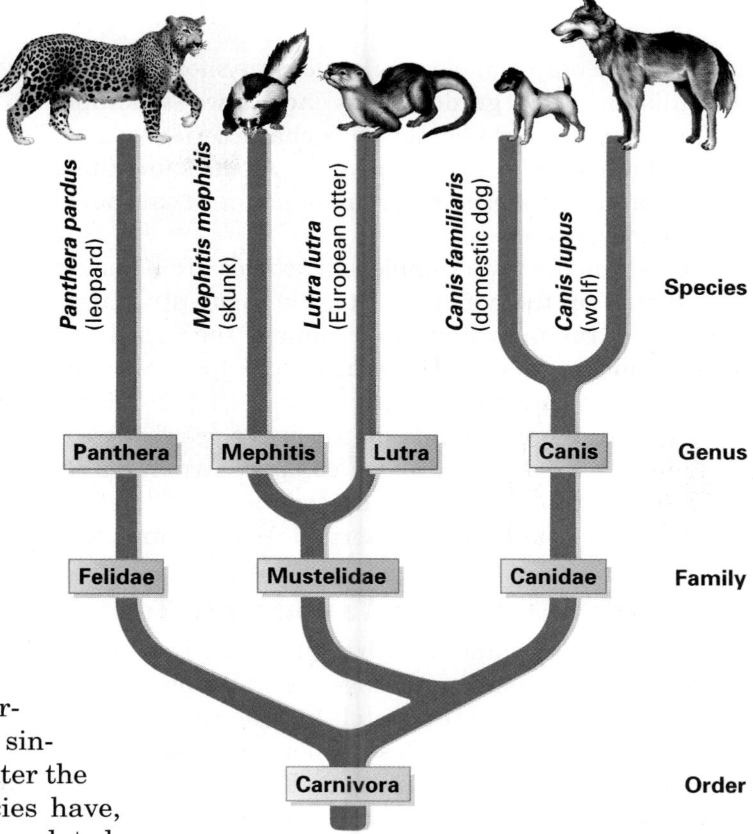

▲ **Figure 15-25** In a phylogenetic tree, each branch point represents a common ancestor of the species above that point. In this diagram, the branches are labeled to reinforce how taxonomy reflects the branching pattern of evolution.

◀ **Figure 15-26** The ocotillo of southwestern North America (left) and the allauidia of Madagascar (right) are not closely related. They owe their resemblance to analogous adaptations that evolved independently in similar environments.

Though only homologous structures should be used to classify organisms, this guideline is not always simple to apply. Adaptation can hide homologous characteristics, as it does in the wing of a bat and flipper of a whale. At the same time, convergent evolution can produce analogous structures that could be mistaken for homologous ones.

One clue that two complex structures are homologous is if you can match up their many parts. The more structural details two complex structures have in common, the less likely it is they evolved independently. The skulls of chimpanzees and humans, for example, are not single bones. Rather, they are a fusion of many bones. And, the two skulls match almost perfectly, bone for bone. It is highly unlikely that such complex structures that match in such detail could have separate origins. Most likely the bone patterns of these skulls were inherited from a common ancestor.

Molecular Data as a Taxonomic Tool

You know from Chapter 14 that the relatedness of species can be measured by comparing their genes and gene products (proteins). The more the sequences match up, the more closely the species are probably related. Researchers are now sequencing the genomes of species at a rapid rate. The data—readily available on the Internet—have sparked a boom in the study of evolutionary history. Such molecular data are independent of the structural data that have traditionally been used for classification.

Such molecular comparisons provide a new way to test hypotheses about evolutionary history. The strongest support for any such hypothesis is when molecular data agree with evidence from other sources, such as anatomy (body structure). For instance, fossil data have indicated that whales are closely related to the group of mammals that includes hippos, cows, deer, and pigs. Molecular data have backed up this hypothesis.

▼ **Figure 15-27** When independent types of evidence support the same hypothesis, the hypothesis is strengthened. Fossil evidence and molecular evidence both suggest that whales (left) and the group of mammals that include hippos (middle) are closely related. The painting at right is an artist's depiction of an early ancestor of whales, based on fossils discovered in the early 2000s.

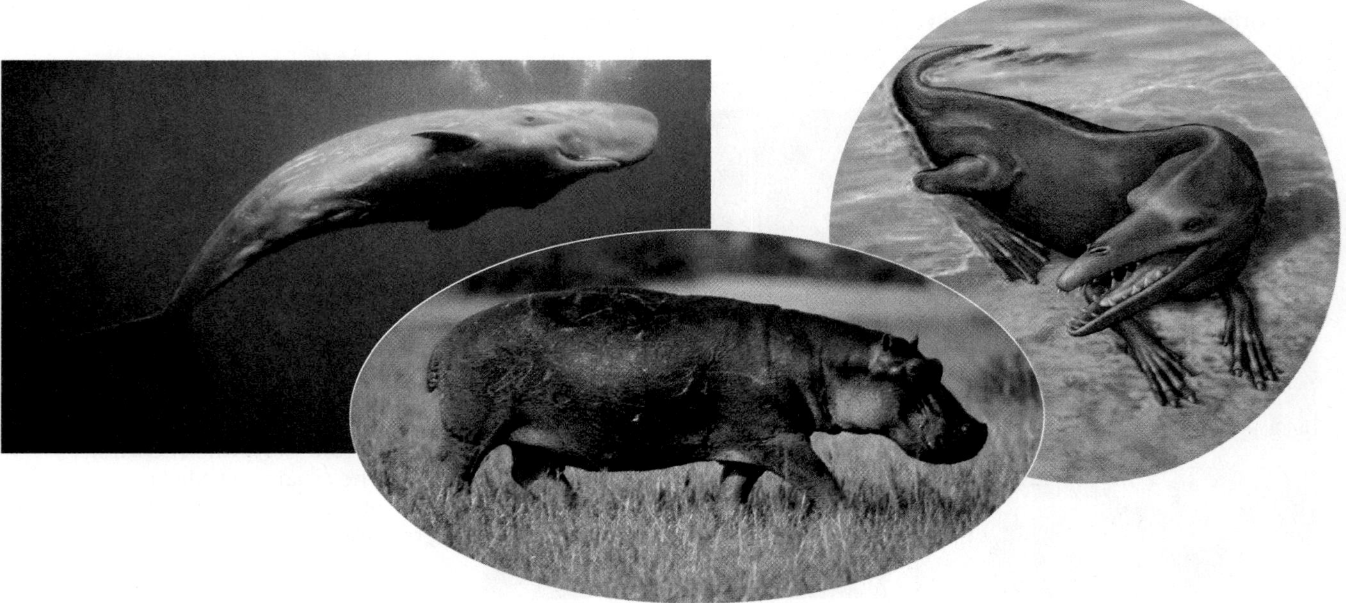

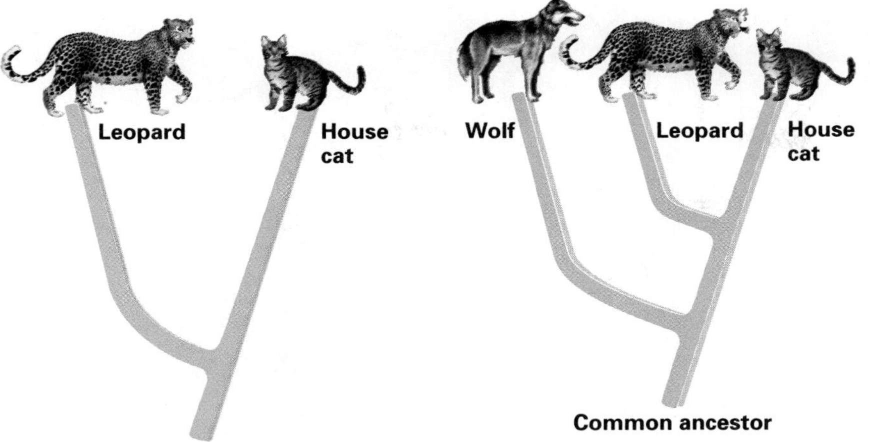

Figure 15-28 Leopards and house cats compose a branch of two species that share a common ancestor (far left). A larger branch that also includes wolves (near left) has a common ancestor that would have lived longer ago than the ancestor of leopards and house cats.

A Closer Look at Phylogenetic Trees

Taxonomy began a new era in the 1960s. One advance that led the way occurred when the molecular methods just described became available for comparing species' DNA. At the same time, computer technology provided greater power to analyze information. These innovations coincided with new ways of building phylogenetic trees as hypotheses about evolutionary relationships.

A key feature of phylogenetic trees is the pattern of branches. Figure 15-28 shows two simple trees constructed from a series of two-way branch points. A particular branching in the cat family could be represented as the diagram on the left. The tree can be expanded to include additional species, as in the diagram on the right. The "deeper" branch point represents the evolutionary split from a common ancestor of the wolf and cat groups. This phylogenetic tree represents the hypothesis that the wolf and cat groups diverged earlier in their evolution than did leopards and house cats.

Identifying Clades Each evolutionary branch in a phylogenetic tree is called a clade. Clades, like taxonomic levels in classification, can nest within larger clades. Continuing with the above example, the cat group represents a clade within a larger clade that also includes the dog group. Each item in a clade may be an individual species, a genus, a family, or some other taxonomic group. However, every clade consists of an ancestral species and *all* of its descendants. Look at the phylogenetic tree in Figure 15-29. Species B through H are members of a clade (yellow). So are species I through K (orange). But these two groups only become part of a larger clade (blue) when you include species A. Species A is an ancestral species to all of the others in this larger clade. (See if you can identify all five clades in the figure.)

Figure 15-29 Each shaded area in the phylogenetic tree highlights one clade, such as the yellow area including species B through H.

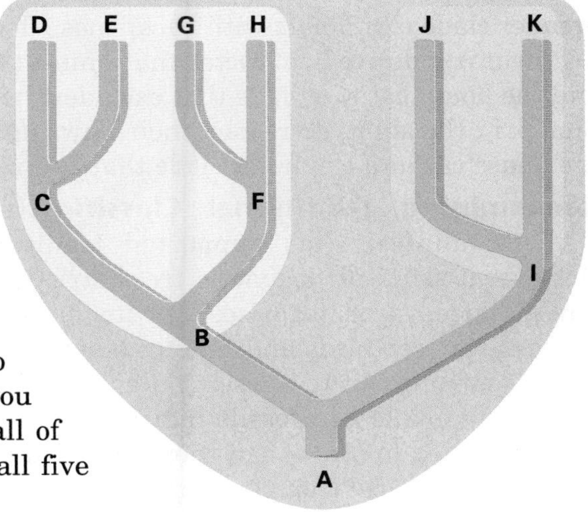

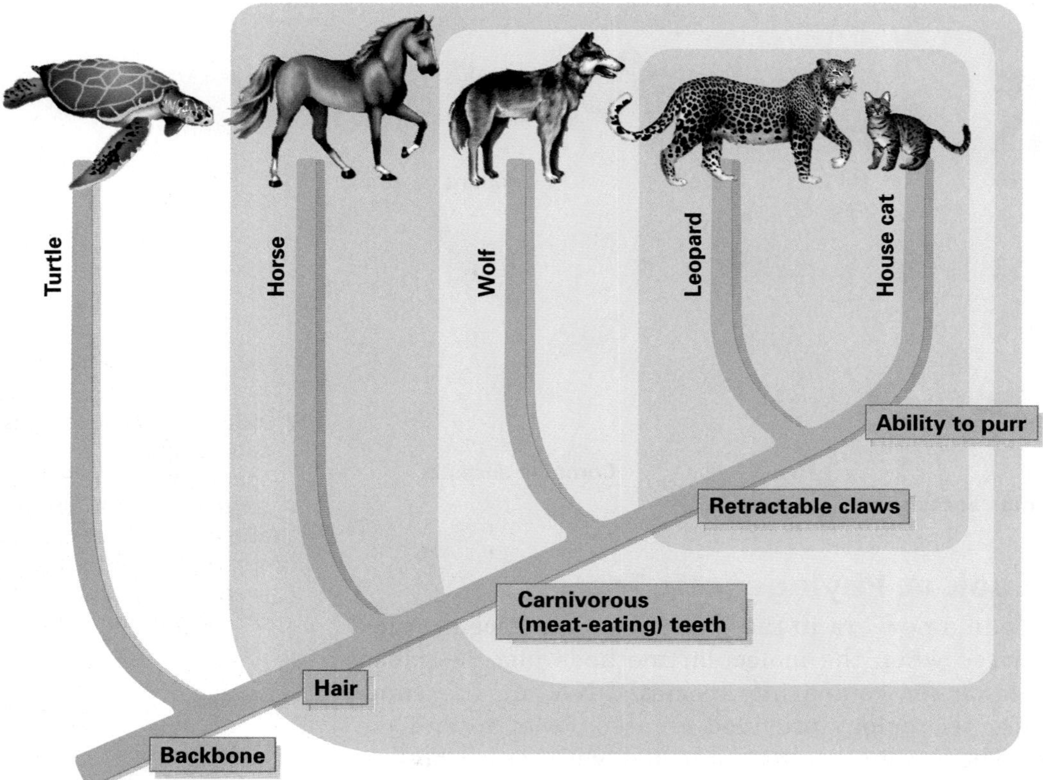

▲ **Figure 15-30** This cladogram shows how derived characters can be used to identify clades among certain vertebrates (animals with backbones). All the species shown here share a common ancestor that had a backbone. (Each clade is actually defined by several derived characters, not just one.)

Cladistics How can a biologist determine the sequence of branching in a phylogenetic tree? The most common method today is called cladistics (from the word *clade,* meaning branch). The key rule in cladistics is that all of the organisms of a particular clade must share homologous structures that do not occur outside the clade. These unique features that unite the organisms as a clade are called **derived characters.**

A phylogenetic diagram that specifies the derived characters of clades is called a **cladogram.** For example, compare the animals in the cladogram in Figure 15-30. The horse, wolf, leopard, and house cat all have hair. This derived character unites a clade that doesn't include the turtle. (The turtle would be included in a broader clade of animals with backbones.) Teeth adapted for eating meat is a derived character that unites the wolf, the leopard, and the house cat in a clade that excludes the plant-eating horse. Similarly, the ability to retract their claws unites the leopard and the house cat into a smaller clade that doesn't include the wolf.

Reexamining Traditional Classification In most cases, cladistic analysis has supported traditional classification. However, basing phylogenetic trees strictly on derived characters produces some surprises. For instance, biologists have traditionally placed birds and reptiles (such as lizards, snakes, and crocodiles) in separate classes. Yet analysis of derived characters in living animals and fossils indicates that crocodiles are more closely related to birds than they are to lizards and snakes. The tree in Figure 15-31 on the facing page shows birds and crocodiles in one clade, and lizards and snakes in another. Now look at the larger clade that includes the ancestor that crocodiles

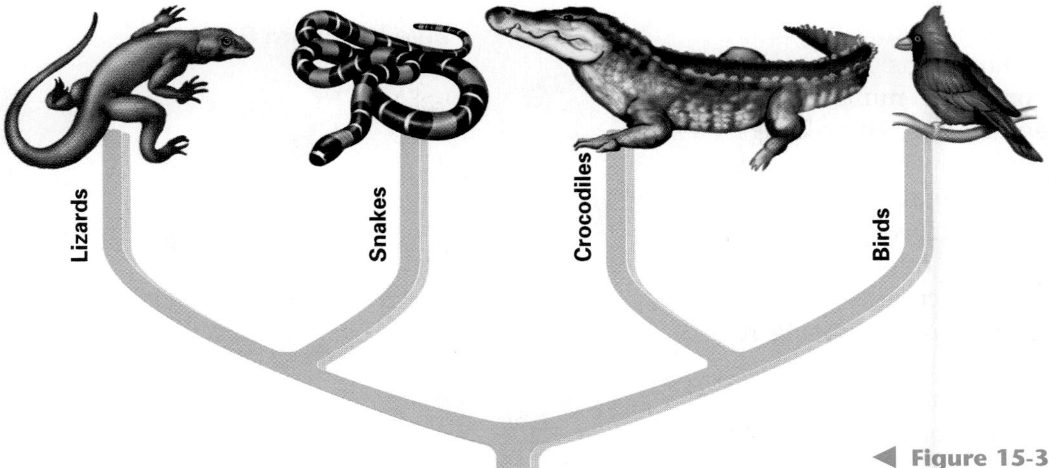

Figure 15-31 Biologists have traditionally placed reptiles and birds in separate classes of vertebrates. However, the tree shown here is more consistent with both the fossil record and analysis of derived characters among living species.

share with lizards and snakes. In this scheme, the reptile group must also include birds. This classification seems to go against common sense and tradition. For some, the unique flight adaptations of birds justify separating them from the crocodiles and other reptiles. However, keeping birds in a separate group from reptiles probably does not accurately reflect evolutionary relationships.

Comparing Classification Schemes

Phylogenetic trees and classifications represent hypotheses about evolutionary history. Like all hypotheses, they are revised to correspond with the discovery of new evidence. In some cases they are even rejected. Cladistic analysis of molecular data is changing scientists' understanding of certain evolutionary relationships. The changes even affect classification at the kingdom level.

Two- and Three-Kingdom Schemes Biologists have traditionally considered the kingdom to be the broadest taxonomic category. Each of the authors of this book first learned a different scheme for kingdom classification. In high school, the oldest author learned that there are only two kingdoms of life—plants and animals. The two-kingdom system had a long tradition in taxonomy. Linnaeus divided all known forms of life between the plant and animal kingdoms. (None of the authors is as old as Linnaeus!) The two-kingdom system prevailed for over 200 years, but it had its problems. Where do prokaryotes fit in such a system? Can they be considered members of the plant kingdom? And what about fungi? Another author of this book learned a three-kingdom model in high school biology. This model placed protists such as protozoans into their own kingdom. But this model also failed to fit new evidence about the biology and evolutionary history of certain forms of life.

A Five-Kingdom Scheme In 1969, American ecologist Robert H. Whittaker proposed a five-kingdom system. This is the system that the youngest author first learned. It places prokaryotes such as bacteria in the kingdom Monera. Organisms of the other four kingdoms all consist of eukaryotic cells (see Chapter 6). The kingdoms for plants, fungi, and animals consist of multicellular eukaryotes. Among eukaryotes, these kingdoms differ in structure, development, and modes of nutrition. Plants make their own food by photosynthesis. Fungi live by decomposing the remains of other organisms and absorbing small organic molecules. Most animals live by ingesting food and digesting it within their bodies.

In the five-kingdom system, the kingdom Protista contains all eukaryotes that do not fit the definitions of plant, fungus, or animal. Most protists are unicellular. Amoebas and other so-called protozoa are examples. But protists also include certain large, multicellular organisms that are thought to be close relatives of unicellular protists.

Three Domains In the last decade, molecular data and cladistics have led to a reevaluation of the five-kingdom system. Figure 15-32 shows a three-domain system as one alternative to the five-kingdom system. A domain is a taxonomic category above the kingdom level. This newer scheme recognizes three basic groups: two domains of prokaryotes—the Bacteria and the Archaea—and one domain of eukaryotes, the Eukarya. The Bacteria and the Archaea differ in a number of ways, as you'll read in Chapter 16. What is most important to understand here is that classifying Earth's diverse species of life is a work in progress. As more is learned about organisms and their evolution, classification schemes will continue to be revised. It is quite possible that if you continue your study of biology in the coming years, you may learn about new and different taxonomic systems.

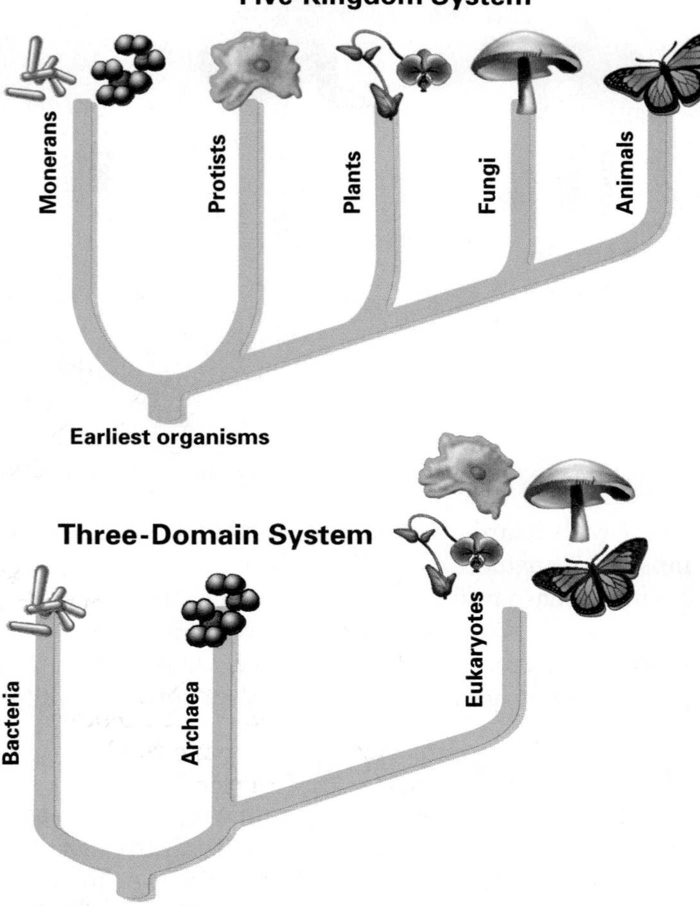

▲ **Figure 15-32** For many years, most biologists classified organisms according to a five-kingdom system. Based on molecular data, however, many biologists now prefer a three-domain classification. Within each domain there are multiple kingdoms (only listed here for Eukarya).

Online Activity 15.4

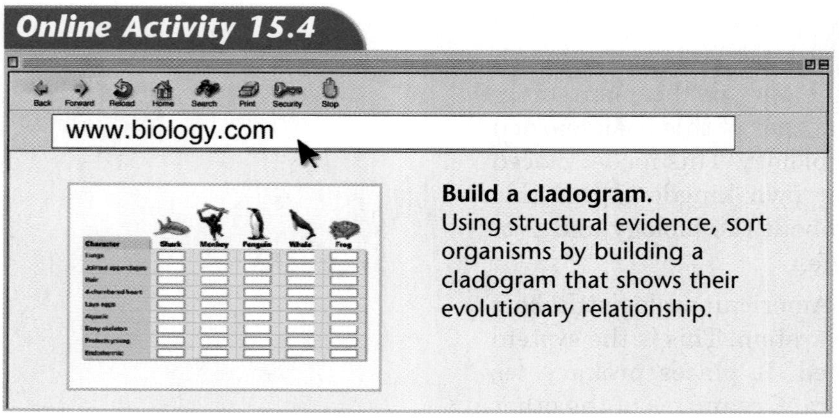

Build a cladogram.
Using structural evidence, sort organisms by building a cladogram that shows their evolutionary relationship.

Concept Check 15.4

1. Give two reasons why common names of organisms can lead to confusion.
2. Why are analogous structures not useful for classifying species in an evolutionary context?
3. What does a branch point in a cladogram represent?
4. How does the three-domain model of classification differ from the five-kingdom model?

Eat Your Greens

Exploring Classification

Questions What adaptations have evolved in white cabbage butterflies and plants in the crucifer family in response to one another? How do these adaptations relate to the classification of crucifers?

Lab Overview In this investigation, you will classify plants in the crucifer family, examine the relationship between crucifers and the white cabbage butterfly, and look for adaptations in the plants and butterflies that have occurred through natural selection. To begin, you will distinguish crucifers from unrelated plants. Then, you will do an experiment to find out if white cabbage butterfly larvae can distinguish the leaves of crucifers from the leaves of other plants.

Preparing for the Lab To help you prepare for the investigation, go to the *Lab 15 Online Companion.* Find out more about crucifers and learn to identify them with a dichotomous key. Prepare for the lab procedure by previewing the steps you will take.

Completing the Lab Use your Laboratory Manual or lab page printouts from the *Lab 15 Online Companion* to do the investigation and analyze your results. **CAUTION:** *Be sure to follow your teacher's instructions and all safety guidelines in the investigation.*

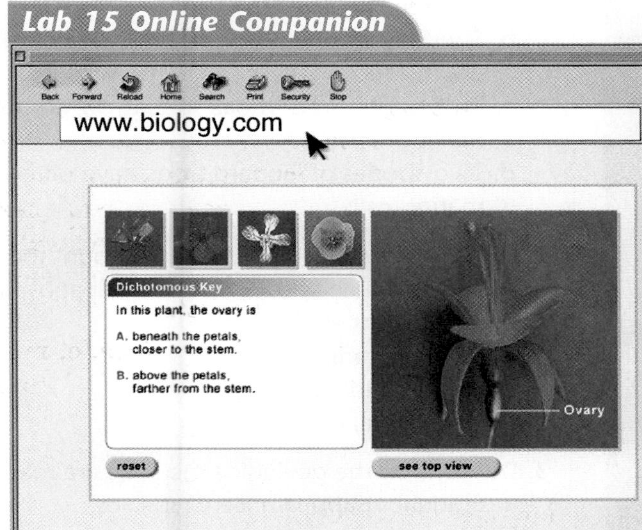

Multiple Choice

Choose the letter of the best answer.

1. Which of the following is *not* an example of a reproductive barrier?
   a. Mallard ducks and pintail ducks mate at different times of the year.
   b. Two species of flowers are pollinated by different insects.
   c. Two populations of oak trees grow on opposite banks of a river.
   d. Two species of leopard frogs have different mating calls.
2. What process most likely could account for the diversity of finch species on the Galápagos Islands?
   a. convergent evolution
   b. adaptive radiation
   c. punctuated equilibrium
   d. continental drift
3. Divisions on the geologic time scale are marked by
   a. gradual disappearance of species.
   b. regular intervals of time.
   c. distinct changes in the types of fossilized life.
   d. radioactive dating.
4. Mass extinctions that occurred in the past
   a. were followed by diversification of some of the survivors.
   b. occurred roughly every million years.
   c. cut the number of species to the few left today.
   d. wiped out land animals but had little effect on marine life.
5. Two worms in the same class must also be grouped in the same
   a. order.
   b. genus.
   c. family.
   d. phylum.
6. Organisms in the same clade must
   a. belong to the same genus.
   b. belong to the same species.
   c. share a common ancestor that belongs to the same clade.
   d. not share a common ancestor.

Short Answer

7. How does the biological species concept define a *species*?
8. Give an example in which differences in behavior prevent similar species from interbreeding.
9. Describe conditions that make it possible for a species to undergo adaptive radiation.
10. How does punctuated equilibrium account for the relatively rare number of fossils that link newer species to older ones?
11. In what ways can evolution be termed a "remodeling process"? Give an example.
12. How is developmental biology helpful to biologists who study evolution?
13. Use the geologic time scale (Figure 15-18) to estimate how long prokaryotes inhabited Earth before eukaryotes evolved.
14. How does continental drift contribute to macroevolution?
15. How much of the classification in Figure 15-24 do humans share with the leopard?
16. What are derived characters, and how are they used in taxonomy?

Visualizing Concepts

17. Copy and complete the table below.

Term	Definition	Example
Reproductive isolation	a.	b.
Adaptive radiation	c.	d.
e.	f.	Breakup of Pangaea
g.	Episode of great species loss	h.
i.	j.	Bird wings and insect wings

Analyzing Information

18. Analyzing Diagrams Use the diagram of sedimentary rock layers below to answer the questions.

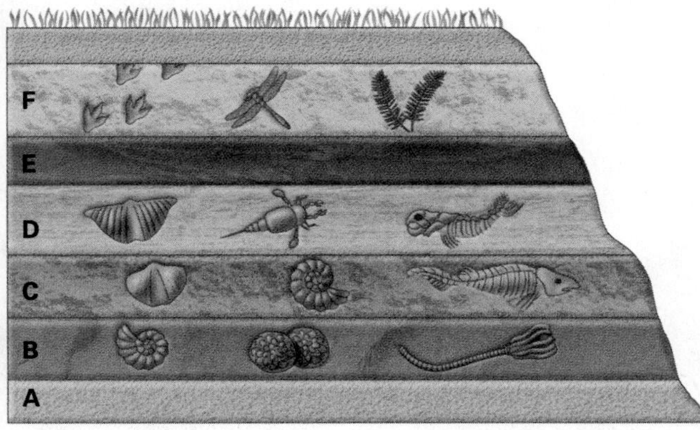

a. What major change in the environment occurred after layers D and E? Explain.
b. What inferences can you make about life forms at the time layer A was formed?
c. If radiometric dating identifies the rock in layer C as 425 million years old, what can you infer about the age of the fossils in layer C? In layers B and D? Explain.

19. Analyzing Diagrams Use the diagram below to answer the questions that follow.

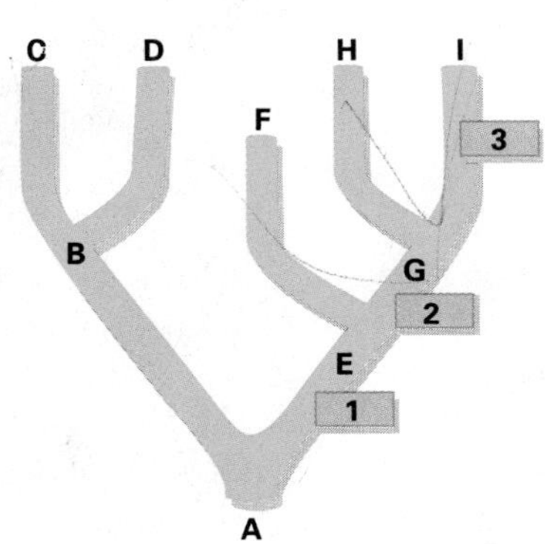

a. Which species is the common ancestor of all those shown?
b. What do 1, 2, and 3 represent?
c. To which living species is species H most closely related?
d. How many clades are contained in the diagram? List the species in each clade.

Critical Thinking

20. Comparing and Contrasting How do analogous structures and homologous structures differ?

21. Developing Hypotheses Suggest an explanation for observations that animals and plants of India are almost completely different from the species found in nearby Southeast Asia.

22. Problem Solving A geologist estimates that a certain rock contained 12 mg of radioactive potassium-40 when it formed. The rock now contains 3 mg of the isotope. The half-life of potassium-40 is 1.3 billion years. About how old is the rock?

23. Relating Cause and Effect How does geographic isolation contribute to speciation?

24. Evaluating Models Discuss reasons why classification systems have changed over time.

25. What's Wrong With These Statements? *Briefly explain why each statement is inaccurate or misleading.*
a. Two populations of mice living on opposite sides of a river are separate species.
b. Lightweight bones evolved in birds so the birds could fly.

Performance Assessment

Biology Research Project Choose an organism other than the examples in the chapter and use library references or the Internet to identify its classification from species to domain. Then identify at least one other organism with which it shares a derived character, enabling you to define a clade.

Online Assessment/Test Preparation

Back Forward Reload Home Search Print Security Stop

www.biology.com

- **Chapter 15 Assessment**
Check your understanding of the chapter concepts.
- **Standardized Test Preparation**
Practice test-taking skills you need to succeed.

UNIT 5 Exploring the Microbial World

Chapters

Colonies of the microscopic protist *Volvox*

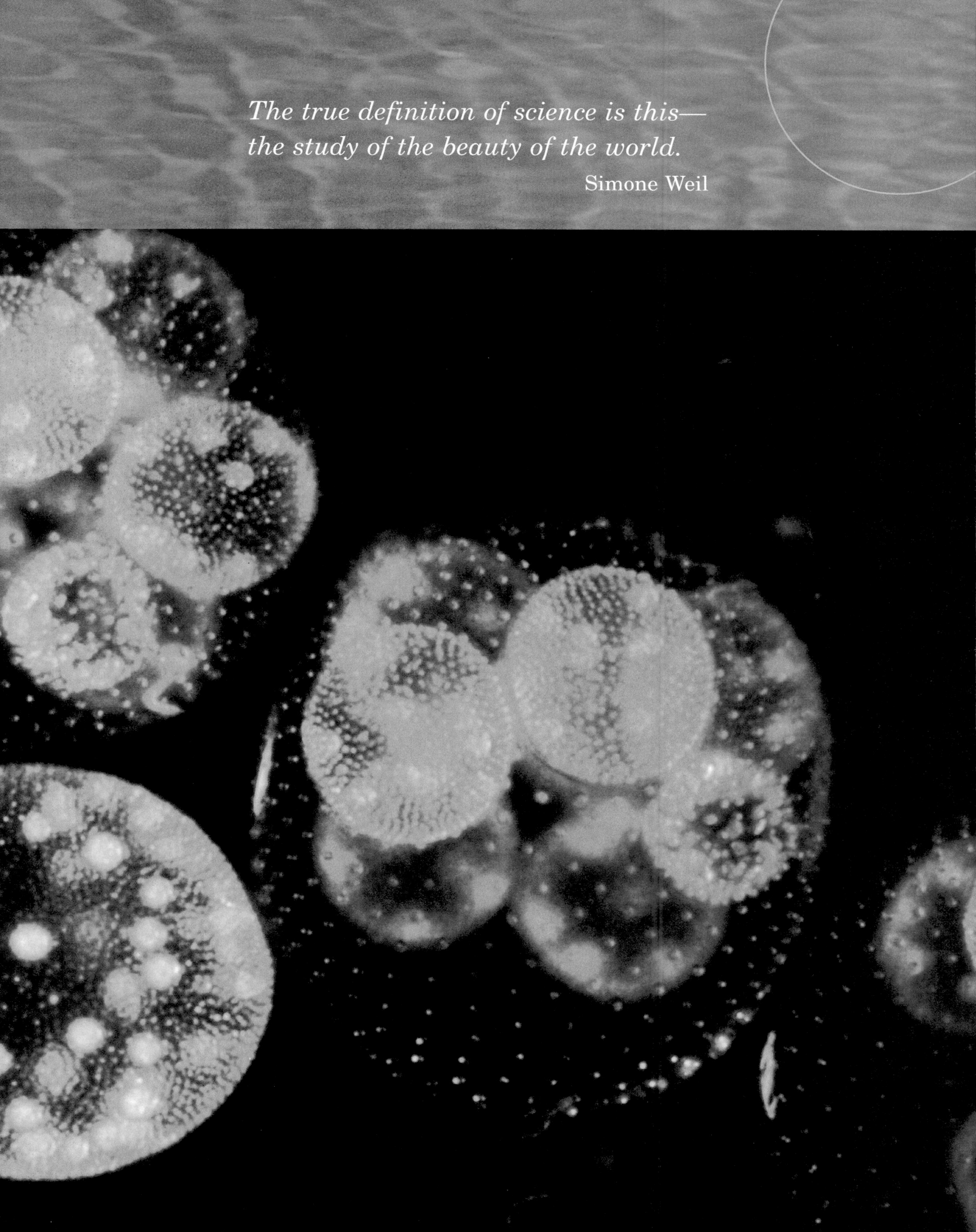
The true definition of science is this—
the study of the beauty of the world.
Simone Weil

Prokaryotes and Viruses

The water in this hot spring in Nevada is literally boiling—heated to over 100°C by thermal energy from Earth's interior. The vivid reds, oranges, and yellows that paint the rocks are microorganisms that thrive in these extreme conditions. In heat that would kill any eukaryotic cell, these prokaryotes flourish. In fact, they would die at "normal" temperatures.

Some species of prokaryotes thrive in places that are too hot, too cold, too salty, or too acidic for any eukaryote. However, the vast majority of prokaryotes live in more moderate environments. You can find them everywhere: on doorknobs, in food, on your skin, and even in your intestines. In this chapter you will read about prokaryotes that are beneficial as well as those that are harmful. Before you begin, go online to the ***WebQuest*** to explore some interesting prokaryotes.

Key Concepts

Concept 16.1

Prokaryotic life began on a young Earth.

Concept 16.2

Diverse prokaryotes populate the biosphere.

Concept 16.3

Prokaryotes perform essential functions in the biosphere.

Concept 16.4

Some prokaryotes cause disease.

Concept 16.5

Viruses infect cells by inserting genes.

Assessment

Chapter 16 Review

What's Online

www.biology.com

WebQuest
BacteriaQuest

Online Activity 16.1
Visit early Earth.

Online Activity 16.2
Determine modes of nutrition.

Careers
Meet a Medical Technologist

Online Activity 16.3
Tour a water treatment plant.

Online Activity 16.4
Stop bacteria from dividing.

Closer Look
Bacterial Pathogens

Lab 16 Online Companion
Sari Solution

Online Activity 16.5
Investigate how viruses infect cells.

Chapter 16 Assessment

CONCEPT 16.1

Prokaryotic life began on a young Earth.

OBJECTIVES

- Explain what Earth's oldest fossils indicate about the history of life.
- Summarize a hypothetical four-stage sequence for how life could have begun.
- Identify two hypotheses about where life began.

KEY TERM

- stromatolite

What's Online

www.biology.com

Online Activity 16.1
Visit early Earth.

As you learned in Chapter 15, scientific evidence indicates that Earth is about 4.6 billion years old. Think of a time scale that compresses Earth's entire history into one year—365 days. On this scale Earth formed at midnight on January 1. The time you are living in right now is 11:59:59—one second before midnight on December 31. When did life begin in this "year"?

The Oldest Fossils

On this one-year time scale, Earth's crust began to cool and solidify in early February—about 400 million years after the planet formed. Fossil evidence indicates that life existed by late March (about 3.5 billion years ago). These ancient fossils are found in dome-shaped rocks called stromatolites. **Stromatolites** are composed of thin layers of sediment pressed tightly together, resembling the layers of an onion (Figure 16-1). The structure of stromatolites is very similar to the layered mats formed by colonies of photosynthetic prokaryotes living today in salty marshes. Fossils resembling photosynthetic prokaryotes have been found in stromatolites that scientists have measured to be about 3.5 billion years old. Recall from Chapter 6 that prokaryotes are simple organisms that lack true nuclei and many of the organelles found in eukaryotes.

Today, photosynthetic prokaryotes are among the simplest organisms that can produce their own food. However, photosynthesis is a complex process, and it is not likely that photosynthetic bacteria were the first forms of life on Earth. The evidence that photosynthetic prokaryotes existed 3.5 billion years ago suggests that life in simpler forms began even earlier, perhaps around mid-February (3.9 billion years ago), when Earth had cooled enough for liquid water to exist.

Figure 16-1 Stromatolite fossils (top) provide evidence that early prokaryotes lived in colonies similar to the layered mats of photosynthetic prokaryotes that live today (middle). The inset (bottom) shows a cross section through a modern layered mat.

How Did Life Begin?

How do scientists study how early forms of life arose on Earth? After all, no people were there to see it happen. But researchers can still apply the scientific process to investigate this mystery—forming hypotheses and designing experiments to test them.

Origin of Small Organic Molecules One important question is how organic compounds first formed before there was life on early Earth. Geologic evidence suggests that the young Earth was a very different place from the planet today. The atmosphere contained carbon monoxide, carbon dioxide, nitrogen, and water vapor, but little or no oxygen. Also, energy sources such as active volcanoes, lightning, and ultraviolet radiation from the sun were all more intense than they are today.

In 1953, Stanley Miller, a graduate student at the University of Chicago, designed an experiment that simulated conditions on early Earth (Figure 16-2). Miller placed gases in a flask to represent Earth's ancient atmosphere. He used electric sparks to represent lightning as an energy source. The experiment produced a variety of small organic molecules that are essential to life, including amino acids—the building blocks of proteins. Many scientists have since repeated and extended this research. They have tested a variety of assumptions about available atmospheric gases and energy sources. Under many different conditions, these experiments have produced all 20 amino acids, several sugars, lipids, the nitrogenous bases found in DNA and RNA, and even ATP.

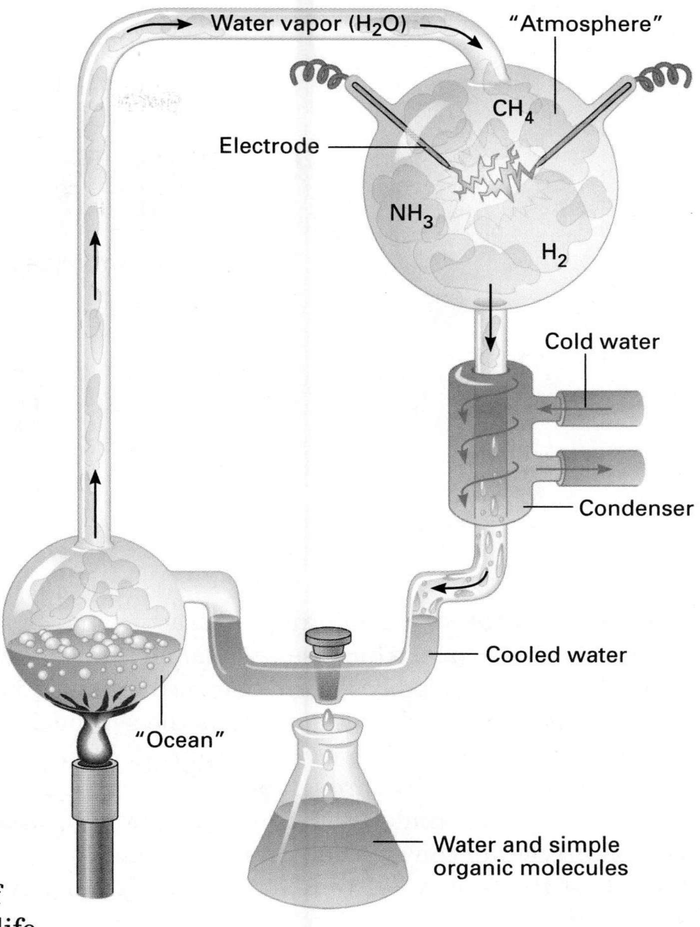

▲ **Figure 16-2** Simulating Earth's ancient atmosphere, oceans, and sources of energy, Stanley Miller's experiment produced some of the organic compounds that are essential for life.

Formation of Organic Polymers Miller's experiment provided evidence that small organic molecules could have formed from chemical and physical processes on early Earth. The next question is how the large molecules characteristic of life—polymers such as polypeptides and polysaccharides—formed without living cells or enzymes being present. In other experiments, scientists have taken solutions of amino acids and dripped them onto the surface of hot sand, clay, or rocks. Heat vaporizes the water in the solutions, leaving behind high concentrations of amino acids. Some of the concentrated amino acids then bond together and form polypeptides. Clay, in particular, concentrates amino acids and other organic monomers and could have held monomers close together. These experiments suggest that organic polymers such as polypeptides could have formed under the conditions found on early Earth.

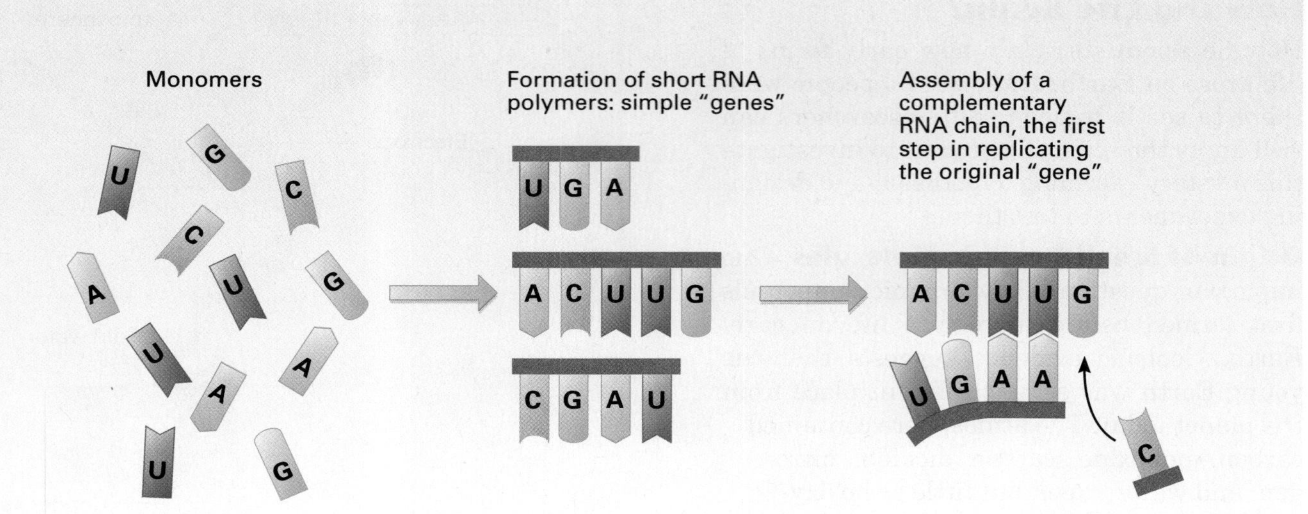

▲ **Figure 16-3** Some scientists hypothesize that self-copying RNA molecules might have arisen in the conditions of early Earth.

"The RNA World" A defining characteristic of life is the process of inheritance, which is based on molecules that can copy themselves. Cells in today's world transcribe genetic information from DNA into RNA, which then directs the synthesis of enzymes and other proteins. This mechanism of information flow could have emerged gradually through a series of changes.

Following this thinking, the next question is, what was the original process of copying hereditary information? One hypothesis is that the first genes were short strands of RNA that could replicate without the help of enzymes. In laboratory experiments, scientists have observed short RNA molecules copy themselves in solutions containing nucleotides (Figure 16-3). This copying took place without enzymes or cells being present. The early history of life may have included an "RNA world," a period when RNA served as both the molecule that stored genetic information and the molecule that directed protein synthesis.

Formation of Pre-Cells Solutions of organic compounds such as RNA and polypeptides were still far simpler than a living cell. Life today depends on complex organic molecules interacting in an organized and coordinated manner. How did this greater organization and coordination develop? Some biologists hypothesize that early organic molecules became organized into increased levels of order by becoming encased in a membrane.

This hypothesis, too, is testable. Experiments have shown that polypeptides can come together and form microscopic, fluid-filled spheres. If certain kinds of lipids are included in the solution, they form selectively permeable membranes similar to those of cells. Such molecular packages are called pre-cells (Figure 16-4). They are not living but do have some of the properties of living cells. It is important to keep in mind that even the simplest living organism is far more complex than any pre-cell produced in a laboratory so far.

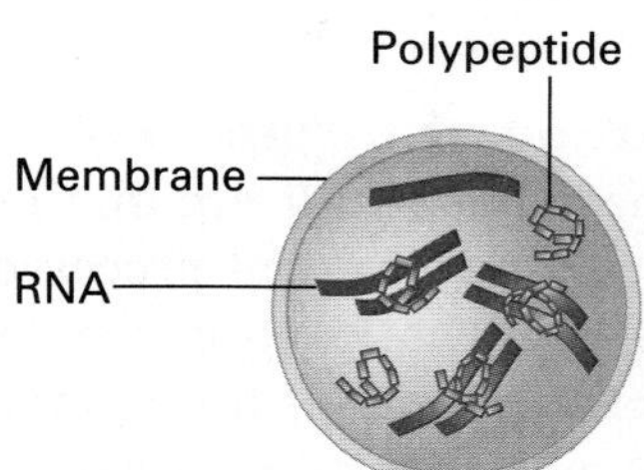

▲ **Figure 16-4** Experiments show that membranes can form around organic polymers in a solution.

All of these experiments together support a hypothetical four-stage sequence for how life could have first developed on Earth. First, small organic molecules, such as amino acids and nucleotides, formed from simpler molecules present in the environment. Second, these small molecules joined together into larger ones such as proteins and nucleic acids. Third, molecules that could copy themselves provided a basis for the inheritance of molecular information. In the last stage, these various organic molecules became packaged within membranes and separated from their surroundings. In other words, they formed pre-cells.

Laboratory simulations cannot prove that the chemical evolution described above actually led to life on primitive Earth. They only show that such events *could* have taken place. Debate abounds about the nature of each step and about missing steps that have not yet been tested by experiments. But such debates represent what science is all about: seeking possible explanations, developing hypotheses, and testing those hypotheses through experiments.

Where Did Life Begin?

One of the questions that scientists also continue to debate is *where* life might have originated. Until recently, most researchers thought that the most likely sites for the origin of life were shallow water or moist sediments such as clay. But during Earth's early history, the land surface may have been too hot and too extreme for complex organic molecules or pre-cells to "survive" for long. The discovery of deep-sea hydrothermal vents raised the possibility that similar environments might have supplied the energy and chemical raw materials for the origin of life (Figure 16-5). Today's deep-sea vents are populated with prokaryotic organisms that may resemble some of the earliest living cells.

▲ **Figure 16-5** Many researchers think that the environments where life first formed might have been similar to deep-sea hydrothermal vents like this one.

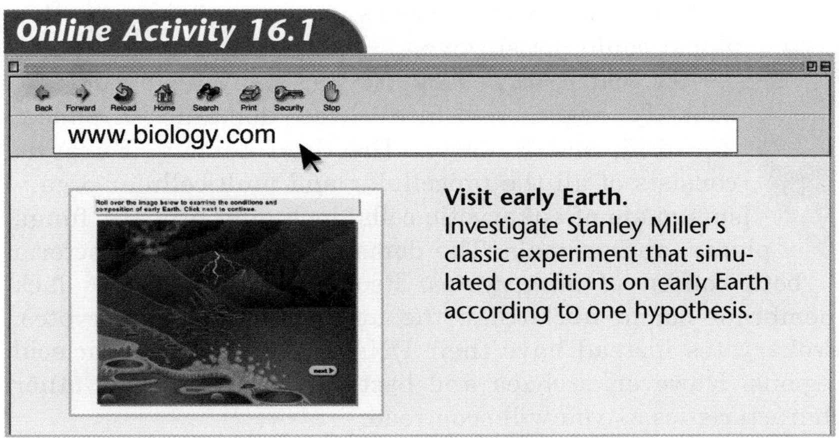

Online Activity 16.1
Back Forward Reload Home Search Print Security Stop
www.biology.com
Visit early Earth.
Investigate Stanley Miller's classic experiment that simulated conditions on early Earth according to one hypothesis.

Concept Check 16.1

1. What do fossils found in stromatolites indicate about early life on Earth (3.5 billion years ago)?
2. What did Stanley Miller's experiment contribute to hypotheses of how life began?
3. Describe two environments where life might have first appeared.

CONCEPT 16.2

Diverse prokaryotes populate the biosphere.

OBJECTIVES

- Identify two domains of prokaryotes.
- Describe three physical features that are used to classify prokaryotes.
- Explain how prokaryotes reproduce.
- Describe the four modes of nutrition and identify which one cyanobacteria use.

KEY TERMS

- archaea
- bacteria
- coccus
- bacillus
- spirochete
- binary fission
- endospore
- cyanobacteria

What's Online

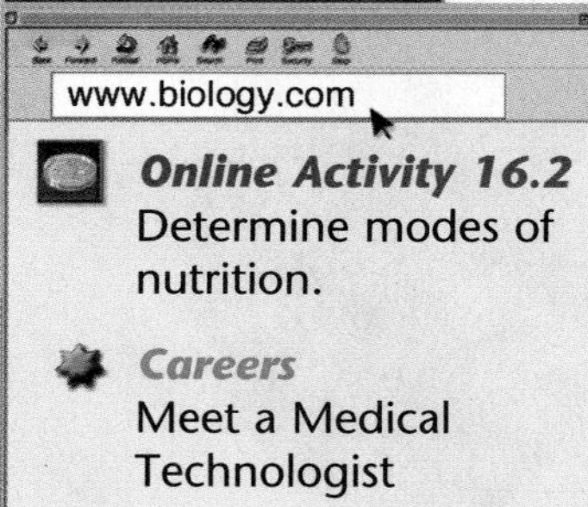

Online Activity 16.2
Determine modes of nutrition.

Careers
Meet a Medical Technologist

There are more prokaryotes living in a handful of fertile soil than the total number of people who have ever lived. In fact, prokaryotic organisms outnumber all eukaryotic organisms combined. Prokaryotes inhabit some of the most extreme environments imaginable. But they also inhabit "normal" environments in huge numbers. Though individual prokaryotes are small organisms, their combined impact on Earth and life is enormous.

Diversity of Prokaryotic Life

Some prokaryotes are well-known because they cause diseases in humans—a fact first recognized only in the 1860s. For example, the disease tuberculosis (TB) is caused by a bacterium called *Mycobacterium tuberculosis.* This tiny microbe causes more deaths worldwide than any other infection. Other bacteria cause strep throat *(Streptococcus pyogenes)*, diphtheria *(Corynebacterium diphtheriae)*, many sexually transmitted diseases, and certain kinds of food poisoning. These diseases may give the impression that all microorganisms are harmful. Far more common, however, are prokaryotes that are either not harmful or are actually helpful to humans and other organisms. For example, the bacterium *Escherichia coli* (*E. coli*) that lives in your intestines releases certain vitamins that are important to your health. Other bacteria in your mouth prevent harmful fungi from growing there (Figure 16-6). On a global scale, prokaryotes cycle vital chemicals between organic matter and the soil and atmosphere. For example, some species of soil bacteria convert nitrogen gas (N_2) from the atmosphere to nitrogen-containing compounds that plants can absorb from the soil. Plants use these nitrogen-containing compounds to build proteins. Without prokaryotes, larger organisms on this planet could not survive.

As you read in Chapter 15, many biologists now classify organisms into three domains—Archaea, Bacteria, and Eukarya. The third domain, Eukarya, consists of all the unicellular and multicellular organisms made of eukaryotic cells, including protists, fungi, plants, and animals. The domains Archaea and Bacteria both consist of prokaryotes. Recall that prokaryotes lack membrane-bound nuclei like the nuclei found in eukaryotes. Prokaryotes instead have their DNA concentrated in nucleoid regions. However, archaea and bacteria differ in many other characteristics as you will soon read.

Colorized SEM 4,300×

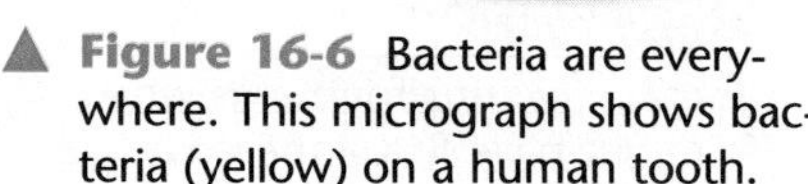

▲ **Figure 16-6** Bacteria are everywhere. This micrograph shows bacteria (yellow) on a human tooth.

Figure 16-7 Many archaea are adapted to thrive in environments too harsh for other organisms. The red and yellow areas near these evaporation ponds are vast colonies of halophilic (salt-loving) prokaryotes.

Archaea The word *archaea* comes from a Greek word meaning "ancient." **Archaea** (ahr KEE a) are prokaryotes, many of which live in some of the most extreme environments on Earth. These habitats, while harsh compared with other Earth environments today, may resemble the conditions that existed on early Earth. Biologists refer to such archaea as *extremophiles,* meaning "lovers of the extreme." For example, thermophiles (heat lovers) live in hot water such as the hot springs of Yellowstone National Park or deep-sea vents where super-heated water exceeds 100°C. Halophiles (salt lovers) thrive in such environments as Utah's Great Salt Lake, or in seawater evaporating ponds (Figure 16-7). Still other species of archaea live in oxygen-free environments such as the mud at the bottom of lakes and swamps where they produce bubbles of "swamp gas" (methane). Some archaea also live in less extreme environments, such as cool seawater.

Biologists hypothesize that archaea and bacteria diverged very early in their evolution from ancient prokaryotic ancestors. Genetic analysis of organisms from all three domains indicates that archaea may be at least as closely related to eukaryotes as they are to bacteria.

Bacteria Prokaryotic organisms classified as **bacteria** differ from archaea in several features of cell structure and chemical makeup (Figure 16-8). Scientists place the two groups of prokaryotes in separate domains partly because of key differences in the information contained in their nucleic acids (DNA and RNA). There are also differences in RNA polymerases, the enzymes that catalyze the synthesis of RNA. Bacteria polymerases are relatively small and simple, while archaea polymerases are complex and similar to those of eukaryotes. Introns, the noncoding portions of genes, are absent in bacteria but are present in some genes of archaea. Certain antibiotics that kill bacteria have no effect on archaea. And finally, bacterial cell walls contain a polymer called peptidoglycan, which consists of sugars and short polypeptides and is not found in archaea or eukaryotes.

Figure 16-8 Bacteria have a basic cell structure that includes a cell wall, plasma membrane, ribosomes, DNA that is not enclosed in a membrane, pili, and flagella for movement.

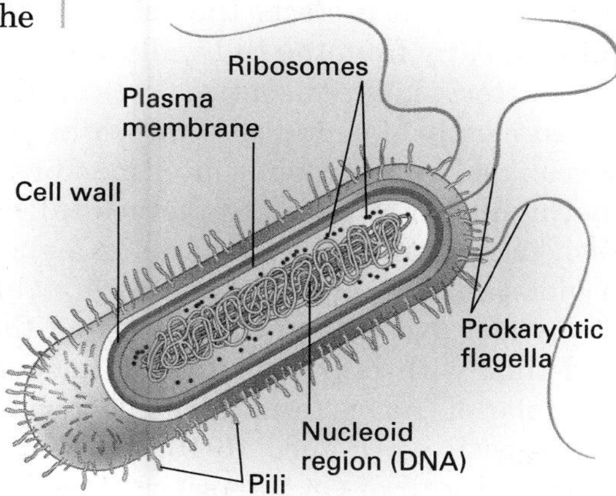

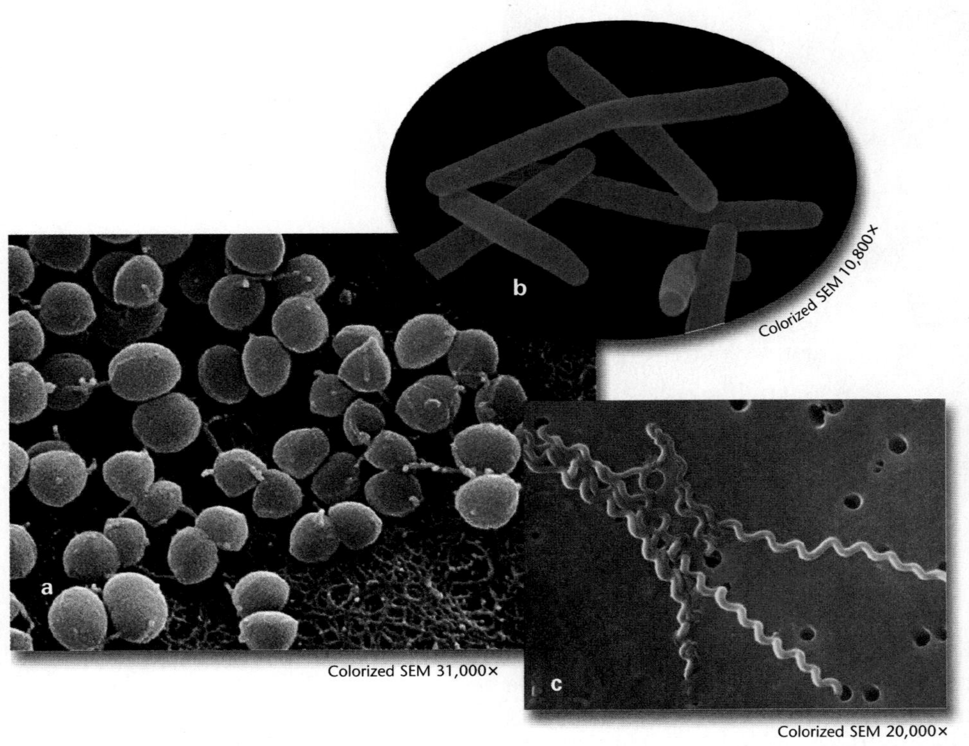

Figure 16-9 Bacteria have three basic shapes. **a.** *Staphylococcus aureus* are cocci that can cause food poisoning. **b.** *Capnocytophaga sputigena* are bacilli. **c.** *Leptospira* are spirochetes that can cause liver and kidney disease.

Structure and Function of Bacteria

Biologists identify and distinguish bacteria based partly on three important characteristics: cell shape, cell wall structure, and motility (method of movement).

Cell Shape Bacteria come in three basic shapes: spherical, rod-shaped, and spiral-shaped (Figure 16-9). Spherical bacteria, such as the bacteria that cause pneumonia, are called **cocci** (singular, *coccus*), from the Greek word for "berries." Some species form clusters of spherical cells, while others, such as *Streptococcus*, form chains. Rod-shaped bacteria are called **bacilli** (singular, *bacillus*). The *E. coli* bacteria in your intestine are bacilli. A third group of bacteria is curved or spiral-shaped. The largest spiral-shaped bacteria are called **spirochetes.** The bacterium that causes syphilis and another that causes Lyme disease are spirochetes.

Cell Wall Structure Nearly all bacteria have a cell wall outside their plasma membrane. As in plants, the wall maintains cell shape and protects the cell. But the cell walls of bacteria differ greatly from the cell walls of plants, fungi, and protists.

Bacteria have one of two types of cell walls. One type is composed mostly of peptidoglycan, while the other has less peptidoglycan and an additional outer membrane. The two types can be distinguished by a testing method called Gram staining. In this test, technicians place bacteria on a glass slide. Next they wash a violet-colored dye over the slide, which stains the bacteria. The violet dye is then rinsed off and the slide is washed a second time with pink dye. Then a microscope is used to observe the color of the bacteria. If the bacteria appear purple, they are Gram-positive (Figure 16-10, left). This is because the extra-thick cell wall of Gram-positive bacteria retains the violet dye.

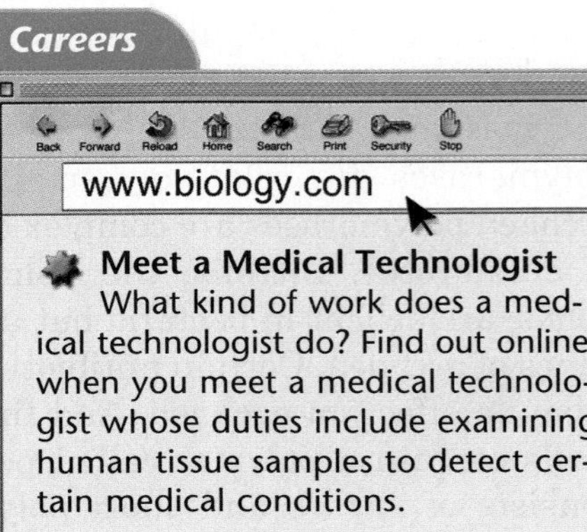

Meet a Medical Technologist
What kind of work does a medical technologist do? Find out online when you meet a medical technologist whose duties include examining human tissue samples to detect certain medical conditions.

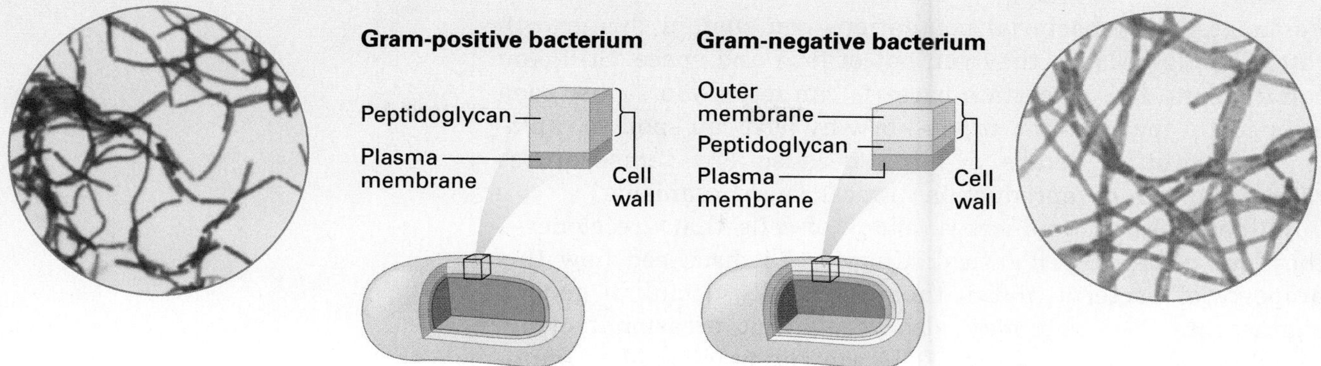

▲ **Figure 16-10** Gram-positive bacteria (left) have cell walls made mostly of peptidoglycan and retain the violet dye. Gram-negative bacteria (right) have an outer membrane in their cell walls and lose the violet dye but retain the pink dye.

In contrast, Gram-negative bacteria do not retain the violet dye, but take on the pink dye. As a result, they appear pink (Figure 16-10, right). How is this classification useful? Some antibiotics only work against Gram-positive bacteria. Doctors use Gram staining to identify bacteria in order to prescribe the correct antibiotics.

Motility About half of all prokaryotes are motile, meaning that they can move. Motile prokaryotes can move toward or away from chemical and physical signals in their environment. They might, for example, move toward food, light, or oxygen and away from toxic substances.

Most motile bacteria have a bacterial flagellum (plural, *flagella*), which is different in structure from the flagella of eukaryotic cells. The filament of the bacterial flagellum is anchored in the plasma membrane and cell wall. Flagella may be scattered over the entire cell surface or concentrated at one or both ends of the cell. In addition, many bacteria possess structures called pili that are shorter and thinner than flagella (see Figure 16-8). Pili help bacteria stick to each other and to surfaces such as rocks in flowing streams or the lining of animal intestines.

Flagella are not the only mechanism of prokaryotic motility. Some bacteria form chains of cells that secrete slimy threads that anchor to surfaces. The bacteria glide along by extending their slime threads as they go.

Reproduction

Most prokaryotes can reproduce at a phenomenal rate under the right conditions. Prokaryotic cells copy their DNA almost continuously and divide repeatedly. With each division, called **binary fission,** the DNA copies move to opposite ends of the cell as the cell splits in the middle (Figure 16-11). Binary fission is much simpler than the process of mitosis that occurs in eukaryotes. This is another important difference between prokaryotes and eukaryotes.

Rapid Reproduction Many bacteria are capable of copying themselves every 20 minutes. In just 12 hours, a single cell could give rise to a bacterial colony containing more than 68 billion cells!

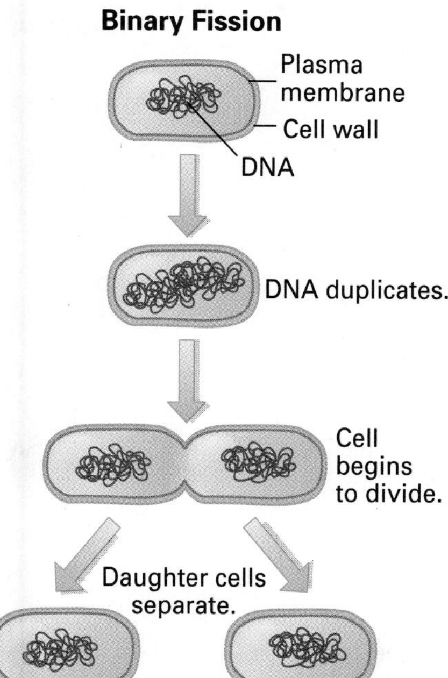

▲ **Figure 16-11** Binary fission enables prokaryotes to reproduce very quickly in the right conditions.

Fortunately, few bacterial populations can sustain this growth rate for long because they run out of food and space. Still, you can understand why certain bacteria can make you sick so soon after just a few cells infect you—or why food can spoil so rapidly. Refrigeration delays spoiling because low temperatures reduce the rate of reproduction in most microorganisms.

Binary fission produces a colony of cells that are clones—they are genetically identical. Chapter 13 discussed how this property of bacteria makes them especially useful in genetic engineering. But you may also recall that occasional errors called mutations occur in the DNA copying process. Most mutations are harmful, but occasionally a mutation aids survival in a particular environment. For example, as you read in Chapter 14, a mutation for resistance to a particular antibiotic favors the reproduction of the mutant cells over the non-resistant ones when the antibiotic is present. Soon, most of the bacteria in the population carry the mutated gene.

Genetic Variation Although prokaryotic cells do not undergo meiosis, they can undergo certain processes that result in genetic mixing, or recombination (Figure 16-12). In *transformation,* some bacteria take up pieces of DNA from the environment. Such pieces of DNA might come from nearby bacteria that have died. In *conjugation,* two bacterial cells temporarily join and directly transfer genetic material between them. Conjugation usually involves plasmids, separate rings of DNA apart from the cell's main chromosome. There is also a third method by

▼ **Figure 16-12** Bacteria are capable of receiving or exchanging genetic material. The result of these processes is greater variety within a population of bacteria.

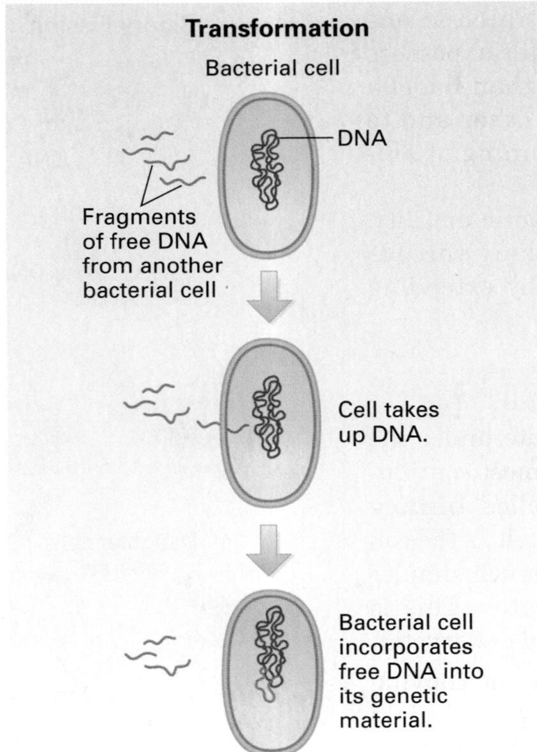
Transformation
Bacterial cell
DNA
Fragments of free DNA from another bacterial cell
Cell takes up DNA.
Bacterial cell incorporates free DNA into its genetic material.

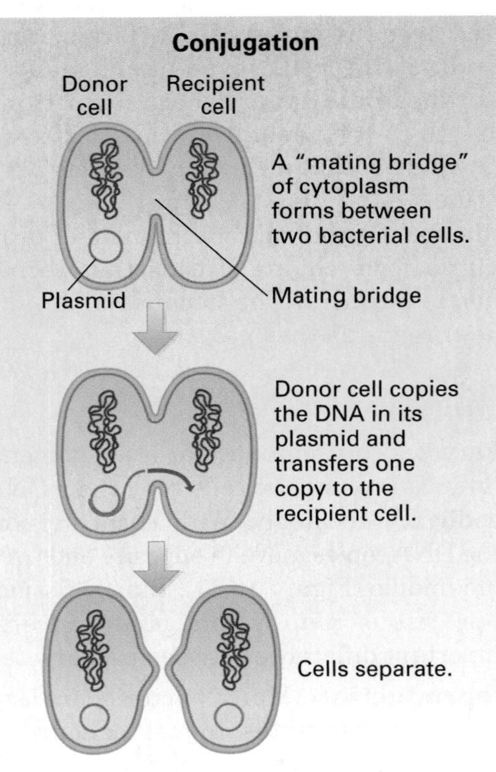
Conjugation
Donor cell
Recipient cell
A "mating bridge" of cytoplasm forms between two bacterial cells.
Plasmid
Mating bridge
Donor cell copies the DNA in its plasmid and transfers one copy to the recipient cell.
Cells separate.

which bacteria can receive new genetic material. This method, called *transduction,* involves viruses that infect bacteria (bacteriophages). These viruses carry genes from one cell and inject them into another.

Endospore Formation Some bacteria can survive extended periods of very harsh conditions by forming specialized "resting" cells, or **endospores,** within themselves (Figure 16-13). One example is *Bacillus anthracis,* the bacterium that causes the disease anthrax in cattle, sheep, and humans. The original cell copies its chromosome, and one copy becomes surrounded by a thick protective coat. The outer cell disintegrates, leaving the highly resistant endospore. Some endospores can survive lack of water and nutrients, heat, cold, and most poisons for many years. When the environment becomes more favorable, endospores can absorb water and grow again.

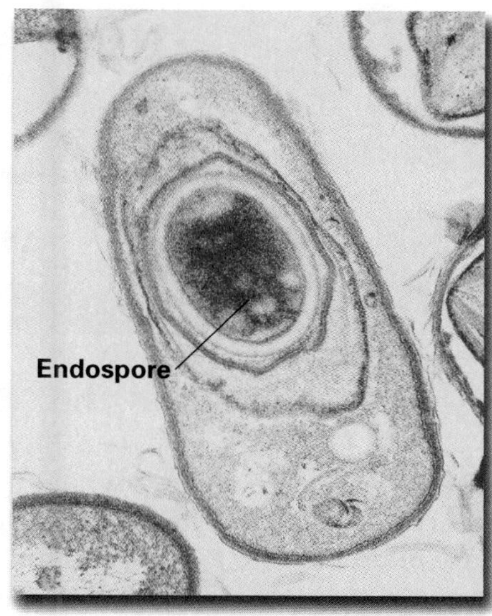

▲ **Figure 16-13** This bacterium contains an endospore that can survive harsh conditions even if the outer cell is destroyed.

Modes of Nutrition

The phrase "mode of nutrition" describes how organisms obtain energy and carbon atoms. Some organisms obtain energy by photosynthesis (identified by the prefix *photo-*). Others obtain energy from chemical sources (*chemo-*). *Autotrophs* obtain carbon atoms from carbon dioxide. *Heterotrophs* obtain carbon from existing organic molecules (such as those in food).

Adding a prefix, *photo-* or *chemo-*, to either *autotroph* or *heterotroph* fully describes the mode of nutrition (Figure 16-14). For example, photoautotrophs harness light energy and make organic compounds from carbon dioxide. Plants and many prokaryotes are photoautotrophs. Chemoautotrophs use carbon dioxide as a carbon source, but they extract energy from inorganic substances such as hydrogen sulfide or ammonia. All chemoautotrophs are prokaryotes. Photoheterotrophs use light energy to make ATP but obtain their carbon in organic form. This mode of nutrition is only found in certain prokaryotes. Chemoheterotrophs consume organic molecules for both energy and carbon. This nutritional mode exists in many prokaryotes and protists, as well as in all fungi and animals.

Nutritional Classification of Organisms

Nutritional Type	Energy Source	Carbon Source
Photoautotroph (photosynthesizers)	Sunlight	CO_2
Chemoautotroph	Inorganic chemicals	CO_2
Photoheterotroph	Sunlight	Organic compounds
Chemoheterotroph	Organic compounds	Organic compounds

▶ **Figure 16-14** This table summarizes the four nutritional lifestyles of organisms.

LM 370×

Figure 16-15 These filaments are examples of cyanobacteria, one group of photosynthetic prokaryotes.

Cyanobacteria and the "Oxygen Revolution"

Fossil evidence indicates that the photoautotrophic mode of nutrition is very ancient. As you read in Concept 16.1, scientists have inferred the early existence of photoautotrophs from the structure of prokaryote fossils in stromatolites. One photoautotrophic group of bacteria, called **cyanobacteria,** generates oxygen as a waste product of their photosynthesis (Figure 16-15).

Earth's early atmosphere was anaerobic, meaning it had very little or no free oxygen (O_2). However, as cyanobacteria evolved, they began generating oxygen as a byproduct of photosynthesis. The oxygen would have bubbled to the surface of lakes and oceans and entered the atmosphere.

The oxygen produced by early cyanobacteria resulted in a crisis for early life forms. Oxygen attacks the bonds of organic molecules, making it toxic to most organisms living at that time. The oxygen probably caused the extinction of many species. Some species survived in habitats that the oxygen did not reach, such as deep in the mud. Their descendants, called anaerobic organisms, survive in such oxygen-free environments today. Other organisms adapted and began using oxygen in extracting energy from food, the key process of cellular respiration. These are called aerobic organisms. The atmospheric oxygen required for cellular respiration is recycled by photosynthesis in cyanobacteria, algae, and plants. Today many prokaryotes and nearly all eukaryotes are aerobic. The "oxygen revolution" was a major episode in the history of life.

Online Activity 16.2

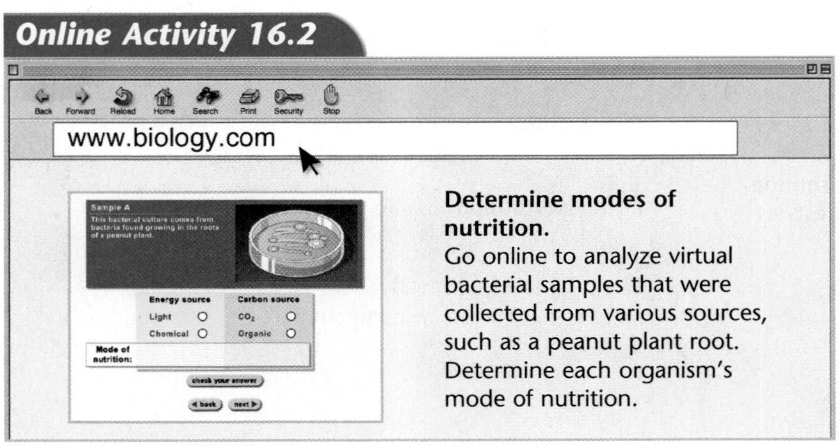

Determine modes of nutrition.
Go online to analyze virtual bacterial samples that were collected from various sources, such as a peanut plant root. Determine each organism's mode of nutrition.

Concept Check 16.2

1. In what major ways are archaea different from bacteria?
2. What are the three major cell shapes of bacteria?
3. Describe three ways bacteria can recombine their genetic material.
4. Name the four major modes of prokaryotic nutrition. For each, identify the energy source and carbon source.
5. How did cyanobacteria change Earth's early atmosphere?

CONCEPT 16.3

Prokaryotes perform essential functions in the biosphere.

OBJECTIVES

- Explain how prokaryotes recycle chemicals between organic matter and the nonliving environment.
- Describe ways that prokaryotes are helpful to humans.

KEY TERM

- bioremediation

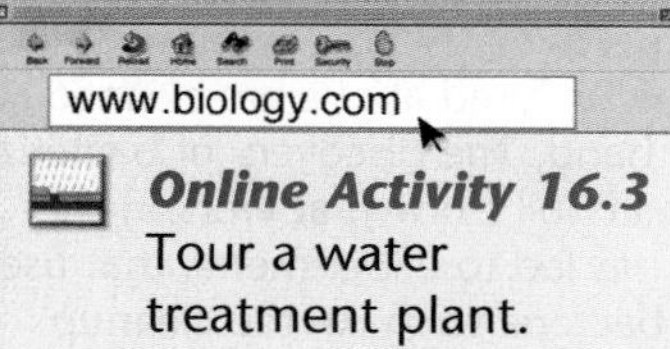

What's Online
www.biology.com
Online Activity 16.3
Tour a water treatment plant.

Not long ago, in geologic terms, the atoms of the organic molecules in your body were parts of the inorganic compounds of soil, air, and water. Life depends on the cycling of chemical elements between the biological and nonliving parts of ecosystems. Prokaryotes play a vital role in chemical recycling.

Chemical Recycling

Many prokaryotes perform an essential function by breaking down, or decomposing, organic waste products and dead organisms in the environment. For example, heterotrophic prokaryotes consume complex organic molecules and return carbon to the atmosphere in the form of carbon dioxide. If it were not for decomposers, organic wastes and dead organisms would literally pile up on Earth. The atoms composing them would not become available for reuse by later generations of organisms.

You have read how cyanobacteria restore oxygen to the atmosphere through photosynthesis. Some species of bacteria convert nitrogen gas in the air to nitrogen compounds in soil and water (Figure 16-16). This converted nitrogen can be used by plants. In fact, all the nitrogen that plants use to make proteins and nucleic acids is first processed by prokaryotes. That nitrogen is then passed on to animals when they eat the plants. Chapter 36 describes the chemical cycles of carbon, oxygen, and nitrogen in more detail.

Figure 16-16 The roots of clover plants have nodules (shown in the inset) that contain nitrogen-fixing bacteria. These bacteria convert nitrogen gas from the atmosphere to nitrogen compounds the plants can use.

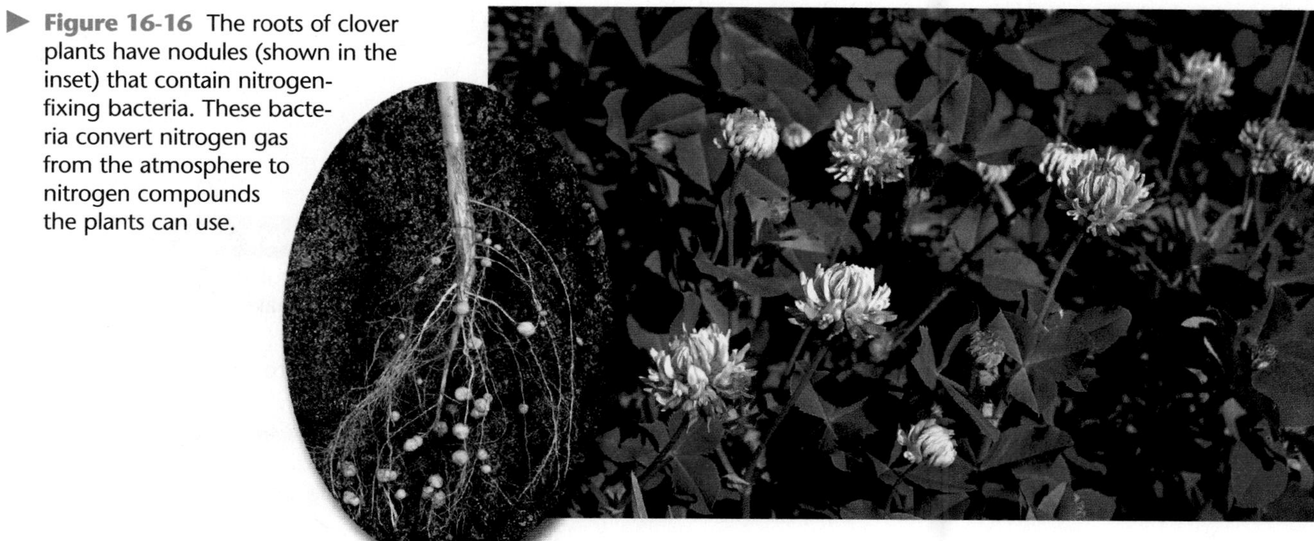

Human Uses of Prokaryotes

Humans have discovered many ways of using prokaryotes. For example, the use of organisms to remove pollutants from water, air, and soil is called **bioremediation.** One example of bioremediation is the treatment of sewage. In treatment plants, raw sewage first passes through a series of screens and shredders. Solid matter settles out from the liquid waste. This solid matter, called sludge, is then gradually added to a mixture of anaerobic prokaryotes. The prokaryotes decompose the organic matter in the sludge. The resulting material can be used as landfill or fertilizer after it is sterilized.

▲ **Figure 16-17** Normally, oil spills like the one pictured above are cleaned up by hand. The discovery of bacteria that "eat" oil (shown at work in the inset) has led to experiments that use these bacteria to make the cleanup process more efficient.

Biologists have also had some success using the bacterium *Pseudomonas* to clean up oil spills on beaches (Figure 16-17). More common still is the use of certain prokaryotes to clean up old mining sites. The water that drains from mines is highly acidic and laced with chemicals such as arsenic, copper, zinc, lead, and mercury. These toxic substances can contaminate nearby soil and groundwater. Cleaning these sites has traditionally been very expensive. But using prokaryotes may cut those costs. For example, some companies are using bacteria called *Thiobacillus*, which thrive in the acidic waters of mines, to extract lead and mercury from mine runoff. Unfortunately, the use of these bacteria is limited because their metabolic processes also add sulfuric acid to the water. If this problem is solved, perhaps through genetic engineering, *Thiobacillus* and other prokaryotes may help overcome some serious environmental problems.

In another example of the usefulness of prokaryotes, pharmaceutical companies raise bacteria that make vitamins and antibiotics. And as described in Chapter 13, genetic engineering involves using prokaryotes to make copies of eukaryotic genes and proteins for uses that are just beginning to be explored.

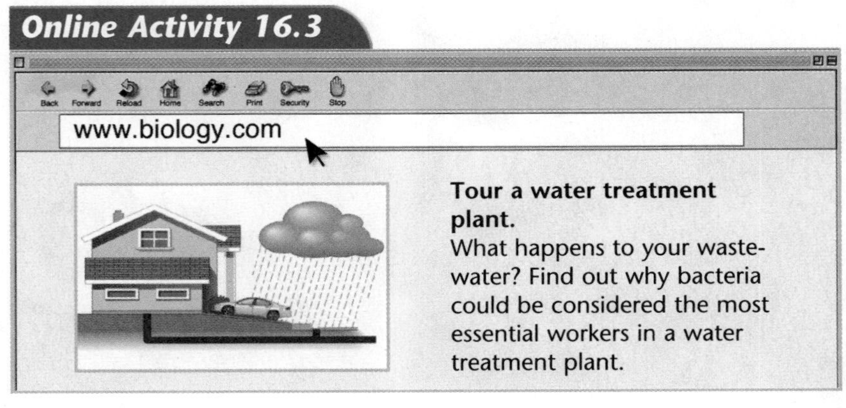

Online Activity 16.3
www.biology.com
Tour a water treatment plant.
What happens to your wastewater? Find out why bacteria could be considered the most essential workers in a water treatment plant.

Concept Check 16.3

1. How do prokaryotes recycle carbon and make nitrogen available to plants?
2. How are prokaryotes used to treat sewage?
3. Give an example, other than sewage treatment, of how prokaryotes can be used by humans.

CONCEPT 16.4 Some prokaryotes cause disease.

OBJECTIVES
- Describe two ways in which bacteria cause illness.
- Identify ways that humans defend against bacterial diseases.

KEY TERM
- pathogen

What's Online

Online Activity 16.4
Stop bacteria from dividing.

Closer Look
Bacterial Pathogens

Lab 16 Online Companion
Sari Solution

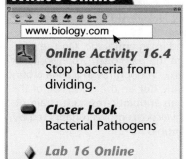

You are constantly exposed to bacteria. They are in the air you breathe, in the water and food you ingest, and on the surfaces you touch. Though most bacteria are either harmless or helpful to you, some bacteria can make you ill.

How Bacteria Cause Illness

Bacteria and other microorganisms that cause disease are called **pathogens.** Most people are usually healthy only because the body's defenses prevent the growth of pathogens. But occasionally, the balance shifts in favor of the pathogen and a person becomes ill. Even some of the bacteria that are normal residents of the body can make you sick when you are weakened by lack of sleep, poor nutrition, or another disease.

In Chapter 31 you will read about discoveries that helped scientists understand how pathogens are transmitted. For example, bacteria that cause anthrax and tuberculosis can be inhaled or transmitted by touching. Syphilis and gonorrhea are transmitted through sexual contact. Lyme disease is caused when the bite of a tick transfers the spirochete bacterium to the person bitten. Several organisms found on improperly stored or prepared foods cause food poisoning.

Some bacteria cause disease by invading tissues and destroying cells. The pathogen that causes tuberculosis is an example. This bacterium destroys the white blood cells that engulf them. Most pathogenic bacteria, however, cause disease by producing one of two types of bacterial poisons. One type consists of the poisonous proteins secreted by bacterial cells. *Clostridium botulinum* produces a highly toxic protein that causes botulism, a kind of food poisoning (Figure 16-18). *Staphylococcus aureus* is a common, usually harmless, resident of the skin surface. However, if the bacterium enters the body through a cut or is swallowed in food, the proteins it produces can cause serious illness.

The other type of poison is not a cell secretion but a component of the bacterial cell wall. These components can lead to fever, aches, and sometimes a dangerous drop in blood pressure (shock). The severity of symptoms varies with the host's health and with the species of bacterium. Different species of *Salmonella,* for example, produce cell wall components that cause food poisoning and typhoid fever.

▼ **Figure 16-18** This can has been deformed by gases from bacteria growing inside. It is possible that the bacterium is *Clostridium botulinum,* shown in the inset.

Colorized SEM 34,000×

Defense Against Bacterial Diseases

Since the discovery that bacteria cause many diseases, cases of such diseases have declined dramatically. You might think that doctors and medicines are mainly responsible for this decline. However, the major reasons for this decline are better hygiene and public health measures. Behaviors such as washing hands, careful preparation of food, and attention to water quality help minimize the risk of pathogen infection. Because of the link between hygiene and disease prevention, many think that installing water treatment systems is a public health priority throughout the world.

Even when in contact with disease-causing bacteria, the human body protects itself against infection. Your skin and the mucous lining of your mouth, nose, and digestive system provide a physical barrier to bacteria. Those bacteria that do manage to enter (through a cut, for example) meet chemical and cellular defenses that make up the immune system. You will learn in more detail how this system functions in Chapter 31.

Of course, doctors and medicines do play a role in fighting bacterial diseases. One way is to use antibiotics, chemicals that slow or prevent the growth of microorganisms. Many antibiotics act by damaging or preventing the formation of the bacterial cell wall. These antibiotics can cripple many species of infectious bacteria without affecting human cells, which do not have cell walls. (Vaccines, which you will read about in Concept 16.5, are also effective in preventing some bacterial diseases.)

While antibiotics are important medicines, public health officials are concerned about their overuse. As you will soon read, these substances are ineffective against viral diseases, yet some people expect to be given antibiotics whenever they are ill. As described earlier, any mutation that enables a bacterium to resist an antibiotic is likely to spread rapidly in a bacterial population exposed to that antibiotic. Many bacteria strains exist now that can resist most current antibiotics (Figure 16-19).

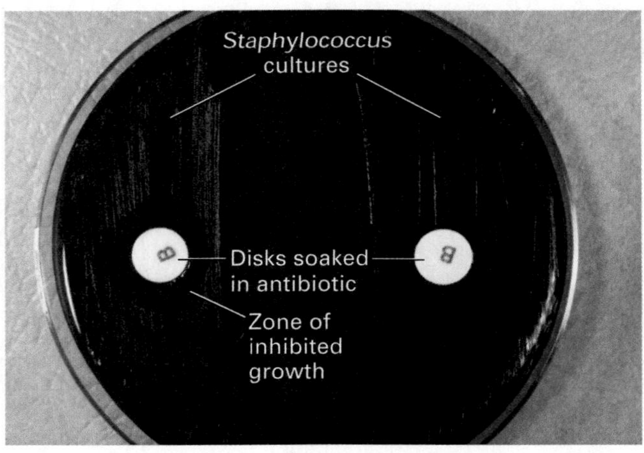

▲ **Figure 16-19** The white disks are soaked in an antibiotic. On the left side of the petri dish, *Staphylococcus* bacteria do not grow in a zone around the disk. But on the right side of the dish, an antibiotic-resistant strain of *Staphylococcus* grows, unaffected by the antibiotic.

Online Activity 16.4

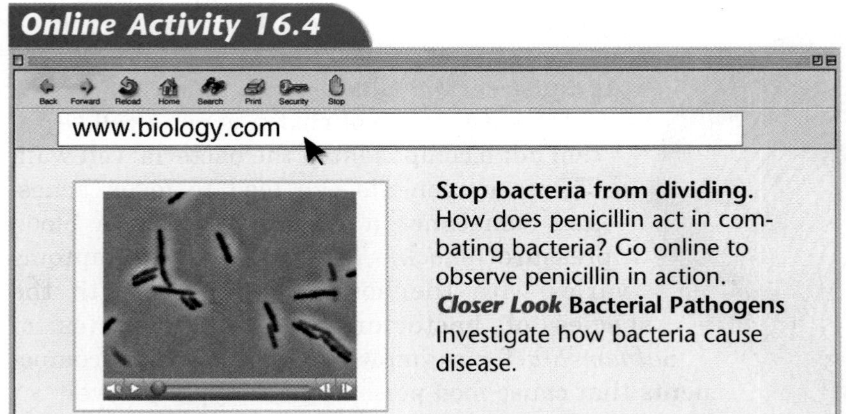

Stop bacteria from dividing. How does penicillin act in combating bacteria? Go online to observe penicillin in action.

Closer Look **Bacterial Pathogens** Investigate how bacteria cause disease.

Concept Check 16.4

1. Describe two kinds of bacterial poisons.
2. List and describe three ways in which humans can fight bacterial disease.
3. Describe one concern about the overuse of antibiotics.

Sari Solution

Discovering Methods to Prevent Cholera Epidemics

Inquiry Challenge How can the bacteria that cause cholera (*Vibrio cholerae*) be removed from river water without the use of chemicals or expensive equipment?

Lab Overview In this inquiry investigation you will learn how *Vibrio cholerae* can live in and on the bodies of copepods, tiny animals that live in river water. Using simulated river water, you will develop an inexpensive filtering method to remove copepods.

Preparing for the Lab To prepare to design your own experiment, go to the *Lab 16 Online Companion.* ···➔ Find out more about *Vibrio cholerae* in river water and learn about the simple filtering method developed by scientists working in Bangladesh.

Completing the Lab Use your Laboratory Manual or lab page printouts from the *Lab 16 Online Companion* to design and perform your own experiment and analyze your results. **CAUTION:** *Be sure to follow your teacher's instructions and all safety guidelines in the investigation.*

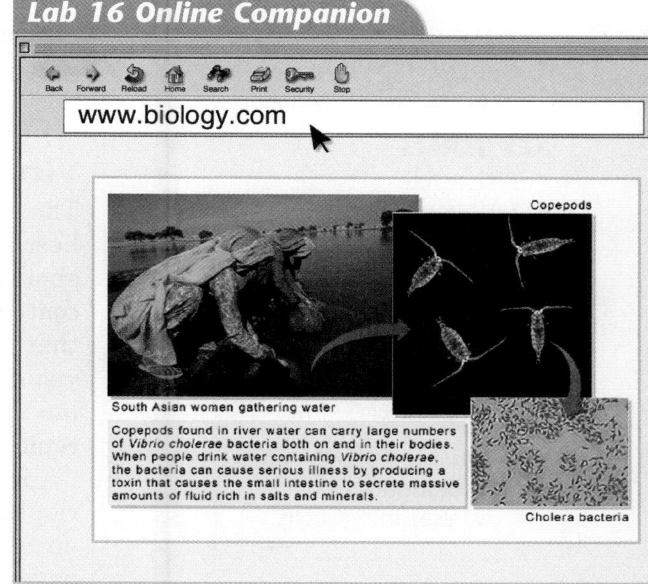

Lab 16 Online Companion
Back
Forward
Reload
Home
Search
Print
Security
Stop
www.biology.com
Copepods
South Asian women gathering water
Copepods found in river water can carry large numbers of *Vibrio cholerae* bacteria both on and in their bodies. When people drink water containing *Vibrio cholerae*, the bacteria can cause serious illness by producing a toxin that causes the small intestine to secrete massive amounts of fluid rich in salts and minerals.
Cholera bacteria

CONCEPT 16.5 Viruses infect cells by inserting genes.

OBJECTIVES
- Describe the structure and reproduction of viruses.
- Explain how viruses cause disease.
- Describe the life cycle of a retrovirus.
- Explain how humans defend against viral diseases.

KEY TERMS
- lytic cycle
- lysogenic cycle
- retrovirus
- vaccine

What's Online

As you've read, prokaryotes are very small. However, viruses are even smaller. In fact, a virus isn't even a cell. Since a virus cannot reproduce on its own, it must infect and use living cells to reproduce. Nearly all cells are vulnerable to infection by specific viruses.

Virus Structure and Reproduction

The structure of a virus is well-suited to its function: entering a host cell and reproducing. A virus is composed of a relatively short piece of nucleic acid, DNA or RNA, surrounded by a protein coat (Figure 16-20). Some viruses also have outer membranes that merge with a host cell's membrane, making it easier for the virus to infect the cell. Since a virus doesn't have its own cellular machinery, it must use the host cell's machinery to make copies of itself.

Early research on viruses that infect bacteria (called bacteriophages, or phages for short) uncovered two basic ways that viruses reproduce. As an example, Figure 16-21 on the facing page shows these two reproductive cycles for a type of phage that infects *E. coli.*

In the **lytic cycle,** the phage attaches to the host cell and injects its DNA. The host cell's enzymes and synthesis machinery make copies of the viral DNA and viral proteins. The viral proteins and nucleic acids then assemble themselves inside the host cell, making many copies of the original infecting virus. The host cell then bursts open, releasing hundreds of new viruses. These offspring infect new host cells and repeat the cycle.

In the **lysogenic cycle,** a virus injects its genes into the host. The viral DNA then adds itself directly to the host cell's DNA. Each time the host cell reproduces, the viral DNA is copied along with the host's DNA. Occasionally, the viral DNA separates from the host DNA and starts a lytic cycle. New phages are then made and released.

Some viruses that infect animals have even more complex life cycles. For example, the herpes viruses that cause chicken pox and cold sores reproduce in the host cell's nucleus. The outer coat of these viruses comes from the host cell's nuclear membrane.

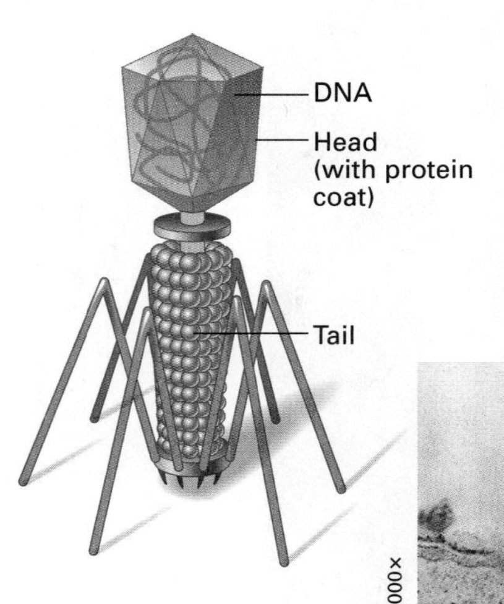

Colorized TEM 107,000×

Figure 16-20 A phage's tail fibers enable it to attach to and inject its genetic material into a bacterial host cell, as shown in the micrograph.

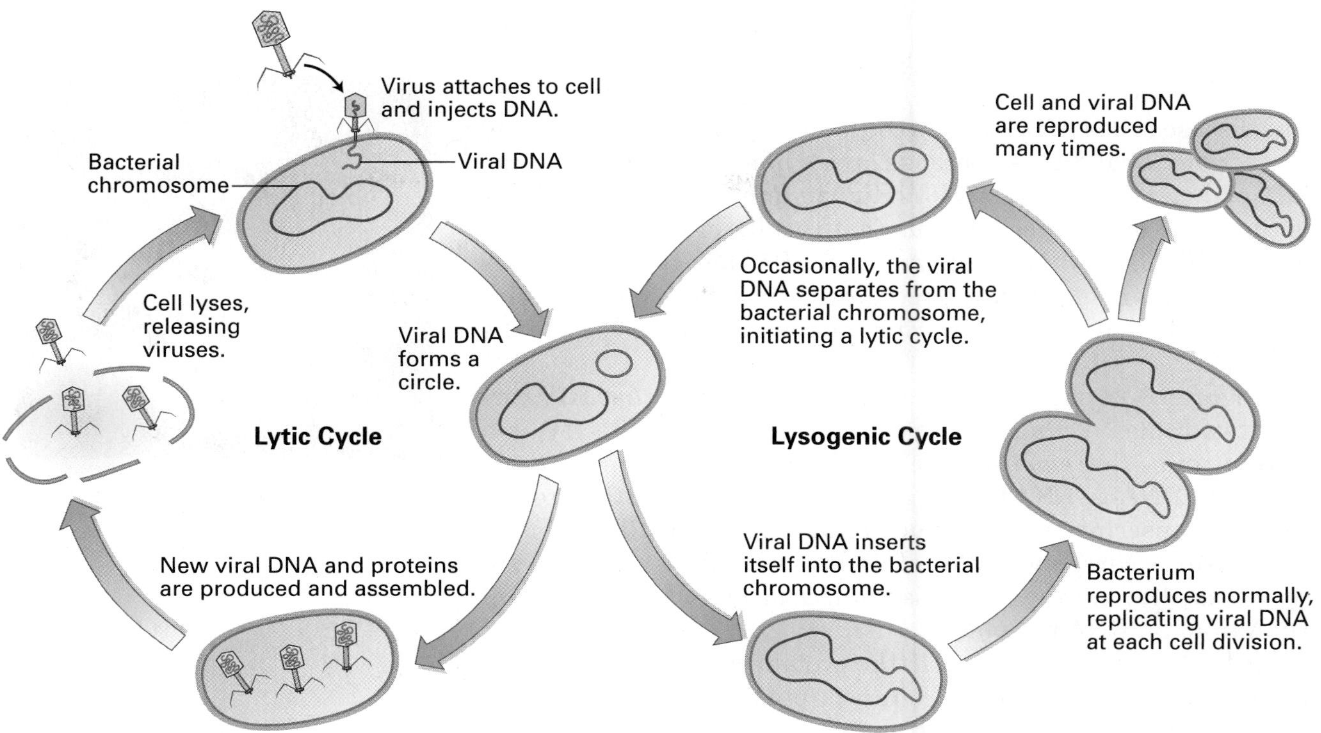
Virus attaches to cell
and injects DNA.
Bacterial
chromosome
Viral DNA
Cell lyses,
releasing
viruses.
Viral DNA
forms a
circle.
Lytic Cycle
New viral DNA and proteins
are produced and assembled.
Cell and viral DNA
are reproduced
many times.
Occasionally, the viral
DNA separates from the
bacterial chromosome,
initiating a lytic cycle.
Lysogenic Cycle
Viral DNA inserts
itself into the bacterial
chromosome.
Bacterium
reproduces normally,
replicating viral DNA
at each cell division.

▲ **Figure 16-21** Viruses such as a bacteriophage are capable of reproducing in two general ways, the lytic and lysogenic cycles.

While inside the nucleus, the herpes DNA may insert itself into the cell's DNA and remain dormant within the body. From time to time, physical stress such as sunburn or emotional stress may cause the herpes DNA to begin production of the virus, resulting in unpleasant symptoms such as cold sores. Once acquired, herpes infections may flare up repeatedly throughout a person's life.

Viruses and Disease

In your life you have probably suffered from the flu, caused by a variety of influenza (flu) virus (Figure 16-22). Like many animal viruses, this one has an outer envelope made of a phospholipid membrane with projecting spikes of protein. The envelope helps the virus enter and leave a cell. Also, like many other animal viruses, flu viruses use RNA rather than DNA as their genetic material. Other RNA viruses include those that cause the common cold, measles, and mumps, as well as ones that cause more serious human diseases, such as AIDS and polio. Diseases caused by DNA viruses include hepatitis and herpes infections.

The way viruses cause disease is radically different from the way bacteria cause disease. A disease-causing virus uses the equipment of the host cell to reproduce. Therefore, the approaches to control and cure viral infections are different from bacterial infection controls. You may recall from your own experience with the common cold that you must wait for your body's defense system to destroy the virus. Antibiotics have no effect on viruses. This is because antibiotics target specific parts of bacterial cells that are not found in either a virus or the cells in your body that host the virus.

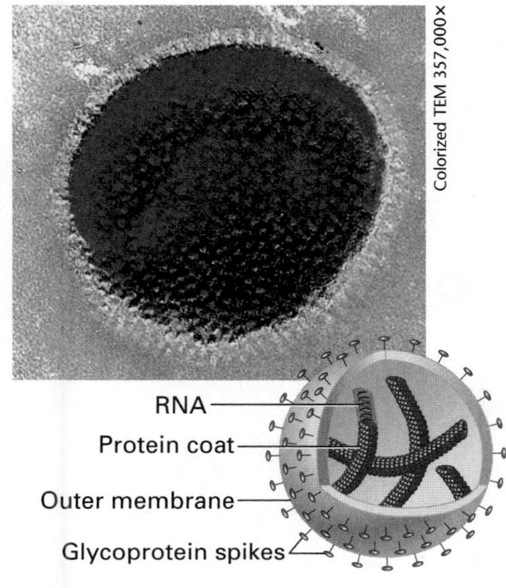
Colorized TEM 357,000×
RNA
Protein coat
Outer membrane
Glycoprotein spikes

▲ **Figure 16-22** The virus that causes the flu is an RNA virus. Its structure is different than that of the bacteriophage shown on the facing page.

HIV: A Retrovirus

The disease called AIDS (Acquired Immune Deficiency Syndrome) is a serious viral disease because, as its name implies, it attacks cells of the immune system. HIV (Human Immunodeficiency Virus) is the name of the specific virus that results in AIDS. Shown in Figure 16-23, HIV is an RNA virus. HIV has a membranous envelope that helps the virus recognize host cells and merge with the host cell membrane, delivering the contents of the virus to the host cell.

Figure 16-24 shows the life cycle of HIV. Notice that HIV carries two copies of its RNA genome rather than one. HIV is a **retrovirus.** Retroviruses are so named because they reverse the usual DNA-to-RNA flow of genetic information in the process called transcription that you read about in Chapter 11. Retroviruses carry molecules of an enzyme called reverse transcriptase that catalyze *reverse transcription,* the synthesis of DNA from an RNA template.

After HIV enters a host cell, the protein coat surrounding the RNA is removed. The reverse transcriptase uses the RNA as a template to make a double-stranded viral DNA molecule. The double-stranded DNA then enters the nucleus and integrates itself into the host cell DNA, like the lysogenic viruses described earlier. The viral DNA can remain in the host cell for years, but occasionally it is transcribed into RNA. The cell then makes new virus particles that leave (or bud off) the host cell and infect new cells. When the virus remains inactive in the host cell DNA, the disease symptoms are not evident. Only when the virus reproduces and destroys host cells does the immune system become damaged, and the individual becomes ill with AIDS.

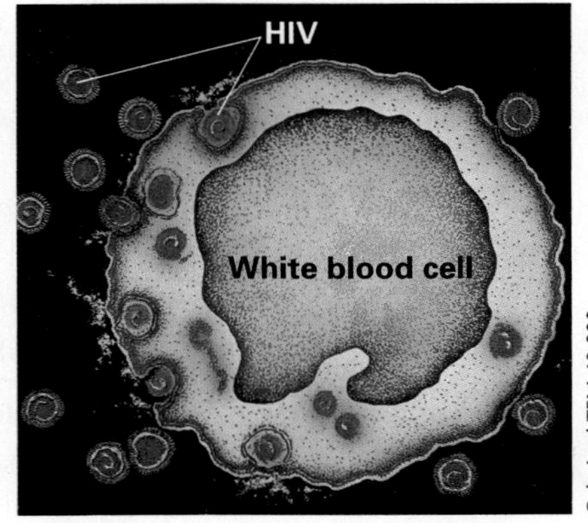
HIV
White blood cell
Colorized TEM 40,000×

▲ **Figure 16-23** HIV infects a white blood cell.

▼ **Figure 16-24** HIV, a retrovirus, uses immune system cells to reproduce itself. These host cells are eventually destroyed, weakening the patient's immune system.

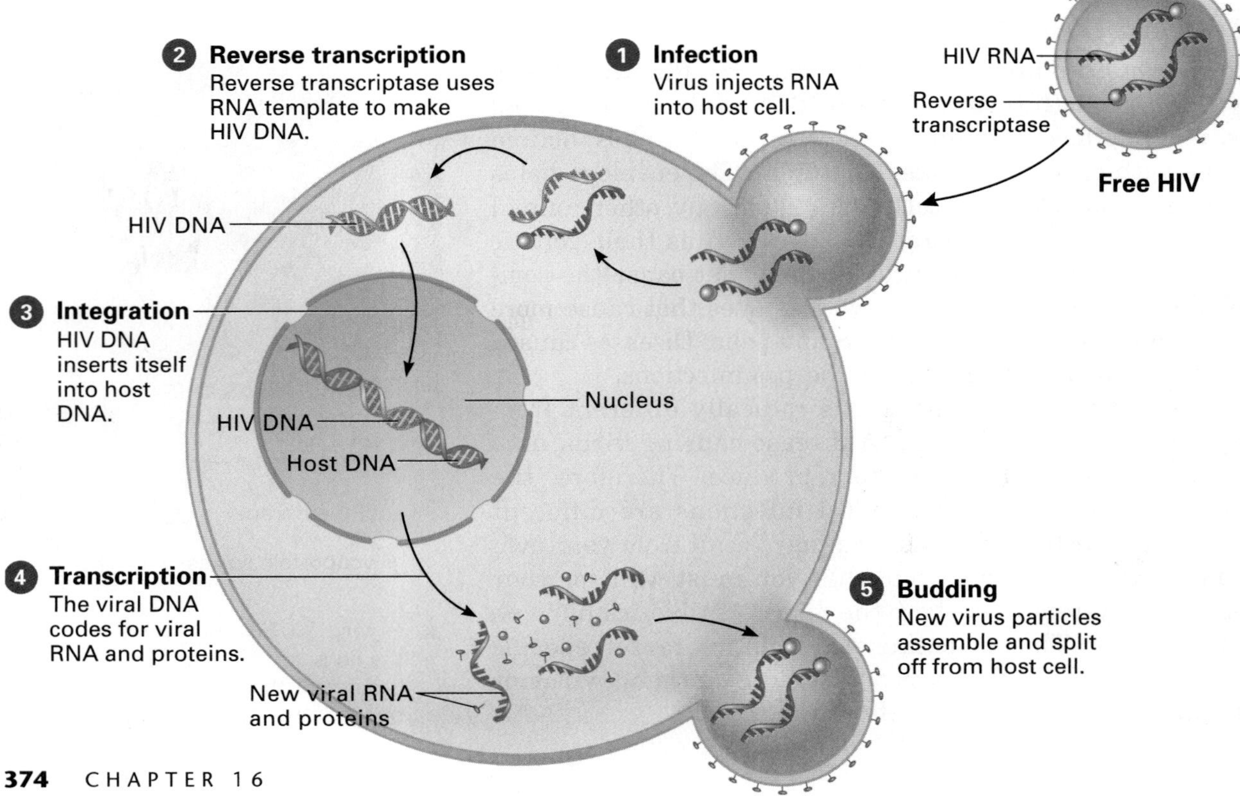
1 Infection
Virus injects RNA into host cell.
2 Reverse transcription
Reverse transcriptase uses RNA template to make HIV DNA.
3 Integration
HIV DNA inserts itself into host DNA.
4 Transcription
The viral DNA codes for viral RNA and proteins.
5 Budding
New virus particles assemble and split off from host cell.
HIV RNA
Reverse transcriptase
Free HIV
HIV DNA
Nucleus
HIV DNA
Host DNA
New viral RNA and proteins

Defense Against Viral Diseases

For the same reason that good hygiene helps control bacterial diseases, it also limits the spread of viral diseases. The immune system is also critical to fighting infections and provides the basis for the major medical weapon for preventing certain viral and bacterial infections from occurring at all—vaccines. **Vaccines** are deactivated varieties or small pieces of pathogens that stimulate the immune system to defend against the actual pathogen.

The first vaccine was made against the virus that causes smallpox, an often fatal disease. In the late 1700s, Edward Jenner, an English physician, learned that milkmaids who had contracted cowpox (a milder disease that usually infects cows) were resistant to later infections of smallpox. In a famous experiment, Jenner scratched a farmboy with a needle containing fluid from the sore of a milkmaid who had cowpox. When the boy was later exposed to smallpox, he resisted the disease (Figure 16-25). The cowpox and smallpox viruses are so similar that the immune system cannot distinguish them. Vaccination with the cowpox virus "fools" the immune system, which reacts and defends the body if it is ever exposed to the actual smallpox virus. Vaccines have since been developed against several other viral diseases, including polio, measles, and mumps, and against certain bacterial diseases such as whooping cough.

Although vaccines can prevent certain viral illnesses, they are not effective in preventing others. Some viruses, including the common cold virus and HIV, mutate rapidly. The resulting new strains are not recognized by a previously vaccinated immune system. This means that vaccines could not protect you from every existing strain and could quickly become outdated.

Medical technology can do little, at present, to cure most viral infections. The antibiotics that help you recover from bacterial infections are powerless against viruses. However, a few drugs have been developed that do combat viruses, primarily by interfering with their nucleic acid synthesis or with the action of reverse transcriptase. In Chapter 31, you will learn more about the immune system and why HIV makes the body so vulnerable to other diseases.

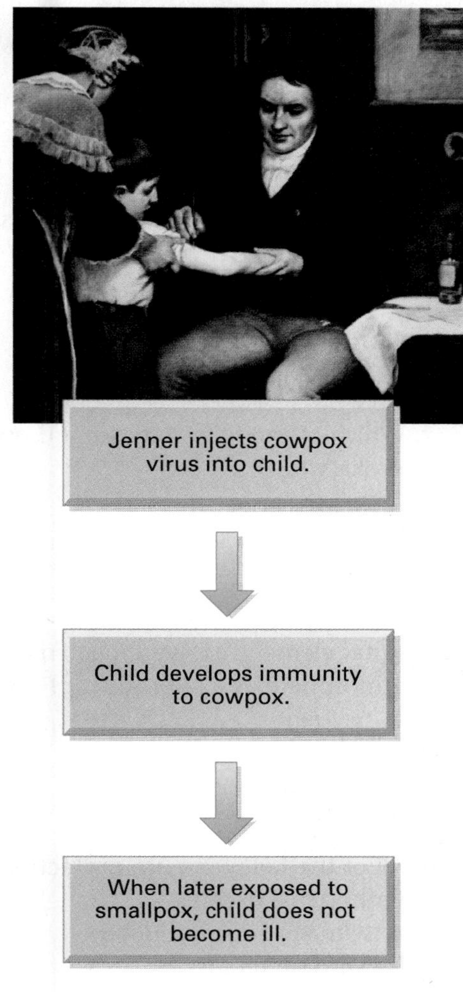
Jenner injects cowpox virus into child.
Child develops immunity to cowpox.
When later exposed to smallpox, child does not become ill.

Figure 16-25 Edward Jenner was an early pioneer in the development of vaccines.

Online Activity 16.5

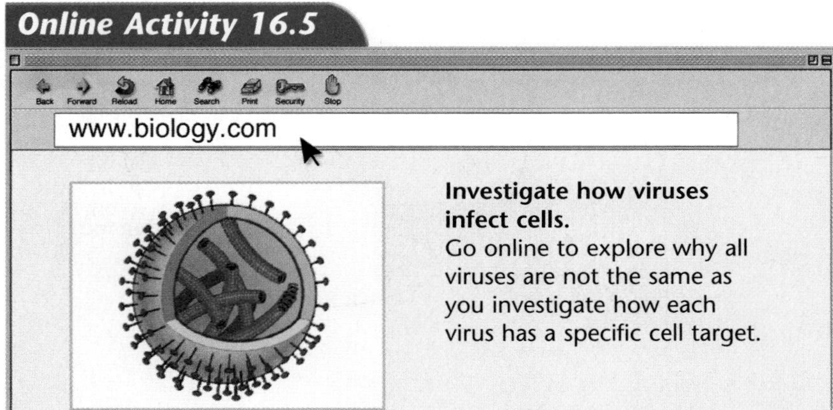
Back
Forward
Reload
Home
Search
Print
Security
Stop
www.biology.com

Investigate how viruses infect cells.
Go online to explore why all viruses are not the same as you investigate how each virus has a specific cell target.

Concept Check 16.5

1. Describe the lytic and lysogenic life cycles of viruses.
2. How is a viral infection different from a bacterial infection?
3. During what point of the HIV life cycle does an infected person develop AIDS?
4. Describe techniques used to fight viruses in humans.

Multiple Choice

Choose the letter of the best answer.

1. How many years old are the oldest fossils estimated to be?
   a. 4.0 billion
   b. 3.5 billion
   c. 600 million
   d. 4.0 million

2. Which of the following is *not* used to classify prokaryotes?
   a. cell shape
   b. cell wall structure
   c. type of nucleus
   d. motility

3. What element do cyanobacteria release to the atmosphere as a byproduct of photosynthesis?
   a. oxygen
   b. carbon
   c. nitrogen
   d. phosphorus

4. All of the following are protections against pathogens, except
   a. skin and mucous lining.
   b. washing hands.
   c. immune system.
   d. avoiding sunlight.

5. Which of the following is part of the structure of a virus?
   a. nucleus
   b. protein coat
   c. mitochondrion
   d. cell wall

6. Viruses can reproduce through which of the following processes?
   a. binary fission
   b. lysogenic cycle
   c. conjugation
   d. endospore formation

Short Answer

7. Why do scientists think that photosynthetic prokaryotes were probably not the first life forms on Earth?

8. Identify three differences between archaea and bacteria.

9. Summarize three mechanisms of genetic recombination in prokaryotes.

10. Explain how early Earth's atmosphere shifted from anaerobic to aerobic.

11. Explain the role prokaryotes play in nitrogen recycling.

12. Describe two examples of bioremediation.

13. Compare two ways that bacteria cause illness.

14. Explain how a virus reproduces itself.

15. What is the single most effective method of reducing bacterial and viral infections?

16. What is the purpose of a vaccine?

Visualizing Concepts

17. Copy this simplified diagram of the life cycle of a retrovirus and fill in the blank boxes. Write a sentence explaining each statement you entered into the boxes.

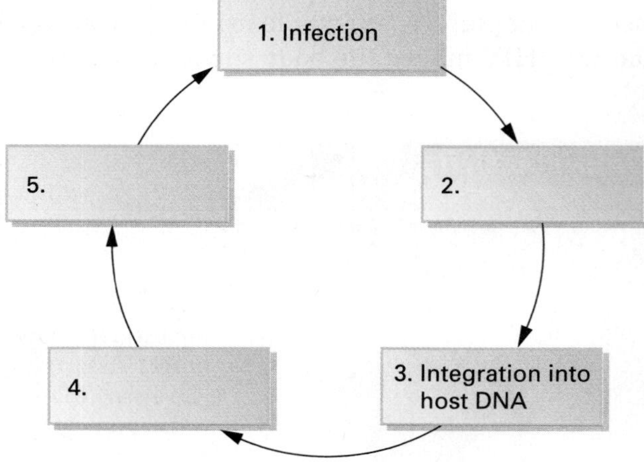

Analyzing Information

18. Analyzing Graphs Examine the graph below to answer the questions.

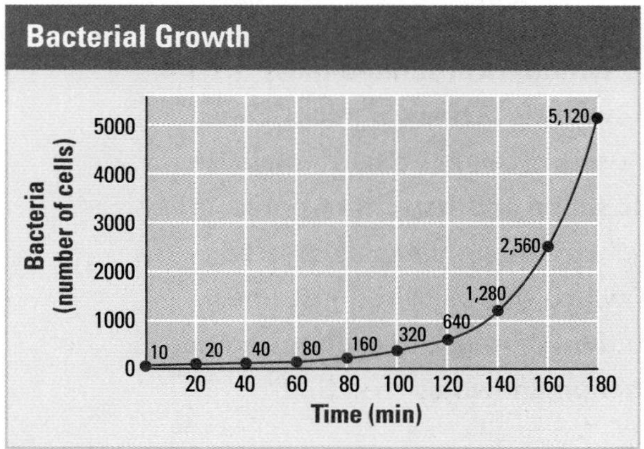

a. How many bacteria were produced during the second hour?
b. At this rate, how many bacteria would be present at the end of 4 hours?
c. What type of a bacterial reproduction that you read about in this chapter would account for this type of rapid growth?
d. If one cell became resistant to an antibiotic due to a mutation at the 80-minute mark, how many cells would be resistant at the end of the 180-minute mark? (Assume the same growth rate.)

19. Analyzing Photographs Look at the photograph of the bacteria below and answer the following questions.

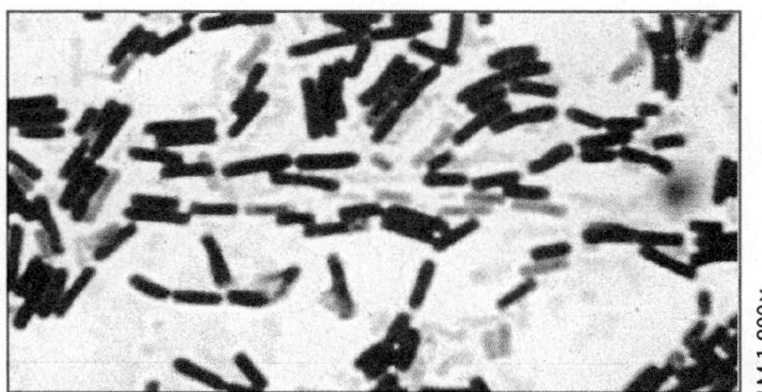
LM 1,900×

a. Based on the colors of these bacteria, what testing method was used on this slide?
b. What inferences can you make about the cell walls of these bacteria?

Critical Thinking

20. Evaluating Models Describe the model Stanley Miller built to simulate the different conditions thought to have existed on early Earth. Explain what inference he reached based on this model.

21. Developing Hypotheses Reread the description in Concept 16.5 about Edward Jenner's experiment with cowpox and smallpox viruses. Write a hypothesis that states the idea Jenner was testing when he performed his experiment.

22. Comparing and Contrasting Discuss the similarities and differences between the ways that bacteria and viruses cause disease, and the ways that those diseases are treated.

23. What's Wrong With These Statements? *Briefly explain why each statement is inaccurate or misleading.*
a. All bacteria cause disease.
b. Viruses are living cells.
c. Antibiotics will cure a cold.
d. Bacteria are closely related to eukaryotes.

Performance Assessment

Writing The average diameters of a human cell, a bacterial cell, and a virus are about 50µm, 5µm, and 0.5µm, respectively. Use this information to select household or classroom objects with which you can model these size differences on a larger scale. Write a paragraph to accompany your model, explaining how you chose your objects and how your model is useful in making comparisons between cells and viruses.

Online Assessment/Test Preparation

Back Forward Reload Home Search Print Security Stop

www.biology.com

- **Chapter 16 Assessment**
  Check your understanding of the chapter concepts.
- **Standardized Test Preparation**
  Practice test-taking skills you need to succeed.

CHAPTER 17

Protists

Despite its resemblance to an intricate, symmetrical stained-glass window, the object in the photograph below is actually a microscopic organism called a diatom. The diatom's single cell has a hard, glasslike cell wall with a characteristic geometric shape and pattern of pores. In this chapter you will become acquainted with the remarkably diverse group of organisms called protists—of which this diatom is just one example. Before you begin, go online to the *WebQuest* to explore another type of protist that causes the phenomenon known as "red tide."

LM 1,800×

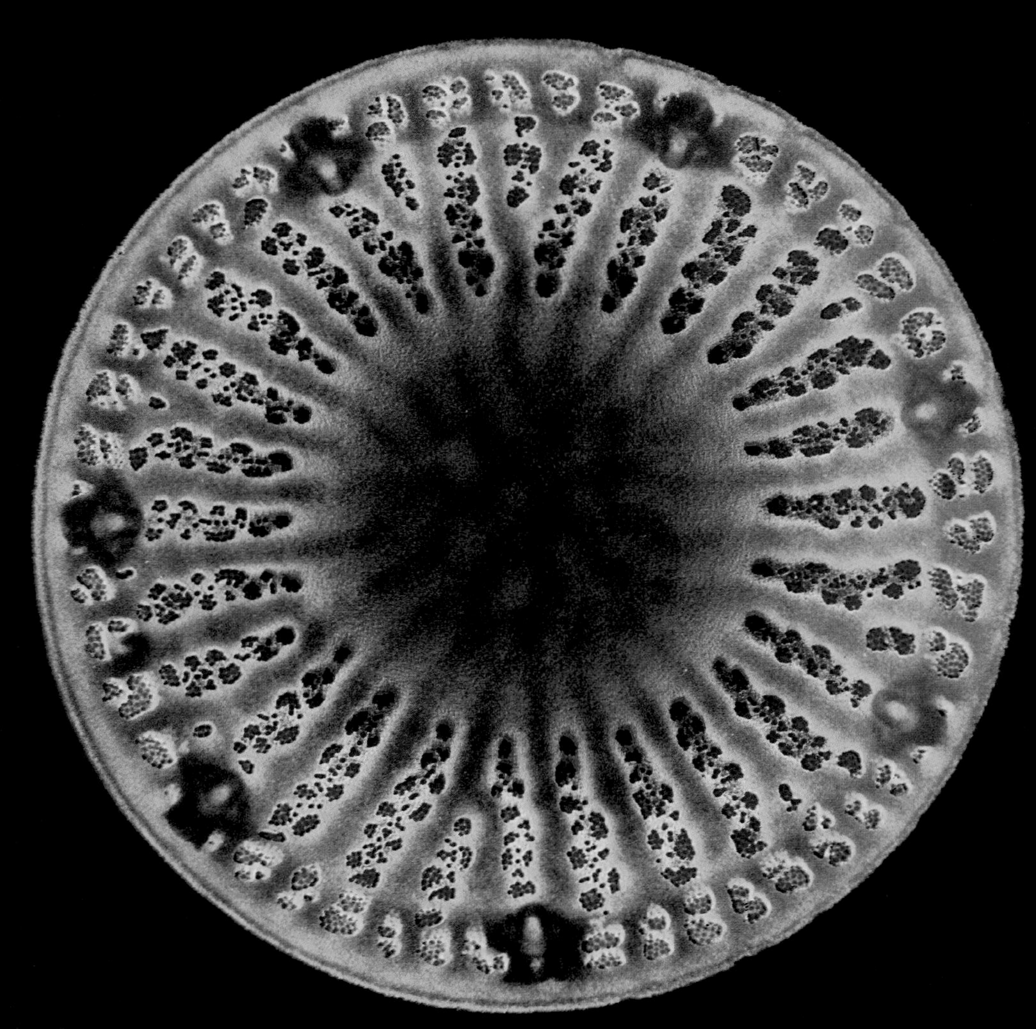

Key Concepts

Concept 17.1 Protists are the most diverse of all eukaryotes.

Concept 17.2 Protozoans ingest their food.

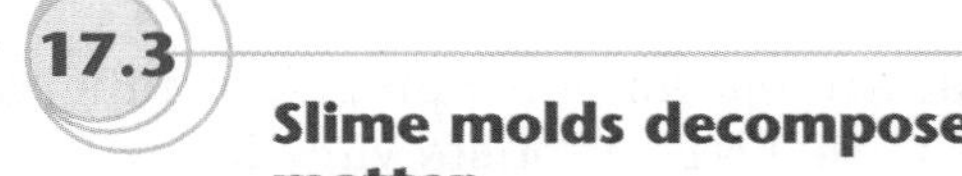

Concept 17.3 Slime molds decompose organic matter.

Concept 17.4 Algae are photosynthetic protists.

Concept 17.5 Plants, fungi, and animals evolved from protists.

Assessment Chapter 17 Review

What's Online

www.biology.com

WebQuest
RedTideQuest

Online Activity 17.1
Explore protist diversity.

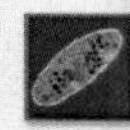

Online Activity 17.2
Explore protozoans.

Lab 17 Online Companion
Protists Feast on Yeast

Online Activity 17.3
Explore fungus-like protists.

Online Activity 17.4
Explore photosynthetic protists.

Science, Technology, & Society
Depletion of Kelp Forests

Online Activity 17.5
Initiate endosymbiosis.

Chapter 17 Assessment

CONCEPT 17.1

Protists are the most diverse of all eukaryotes.

OBJECTIVES

- Describe characteristics that all protists have in common.
- Explain why certain unicellular protists can be considered the most complex of cells.
- Identify the three types of nutrition among protists.

KEY TERMS

- protist
- protozoan
- alga

What's Online

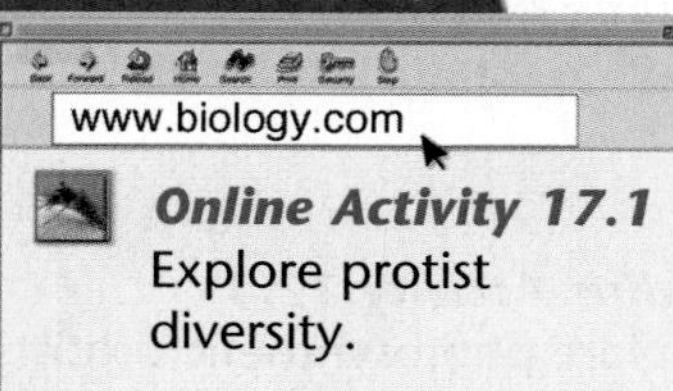

Online Activity 17.1
Explore protist diversity.

Does your family have a drawer at home where you keep "stuff"? That drawer might include a flashlight, tape measure, spare keys, rubber bands, or extra stamps. These objects have little in common except that they are kept in the same drawer for convenience. Biologists have a sort of taxonomic "stuff" drawer: the kingdom Protista. Protista is a very diverse kingdom of organisms that do not fit neatly into any of the other kingdoms.

General Characteristics of Protists

Eukaryotes that are not animals, plants, or fungi are classified as **protists** (Figure 17-1). Protists vary in structure and function more than any other group of organisms. Most protists are unicellular and free-living (not parasitic). However, some protist species are colonial—organisms consisting of many similar or identical cells. There are even some protists, such as seaweeds, that are multicellular. These multicellular protists have relatively complex bodies consisting of specialized cells.

Protists have the typical eukaryotic cell structure, including internal membranes, a nucleus surrounded by a nuclear envelope, and organelles such as mitochondria and chloroplasts (in some species). However, eukaryotic cell structure is a characteristic of *all* organisms other than bacteria and archaea. So cell structure alone does not define protists.

Most biologists think that with sufficient data the traditional protist kingdom will eventually be divided into several kingdoms within domain Eukarya. Comparing nucleic acid sequences helps researchers identify these main clades (evolutionary branches) of protists. However, evidence of these evolutionary relationships remains incomplete. Until there is a widely accepted division of these diverse organisms into multiple kingdoms, the term *protist* remains useful when studying the group.

Figure 17-1 A drop of pond water can contain a wide diversity of protists. This sample includes several types of photosynthetic protists, or algae.

LM 310×

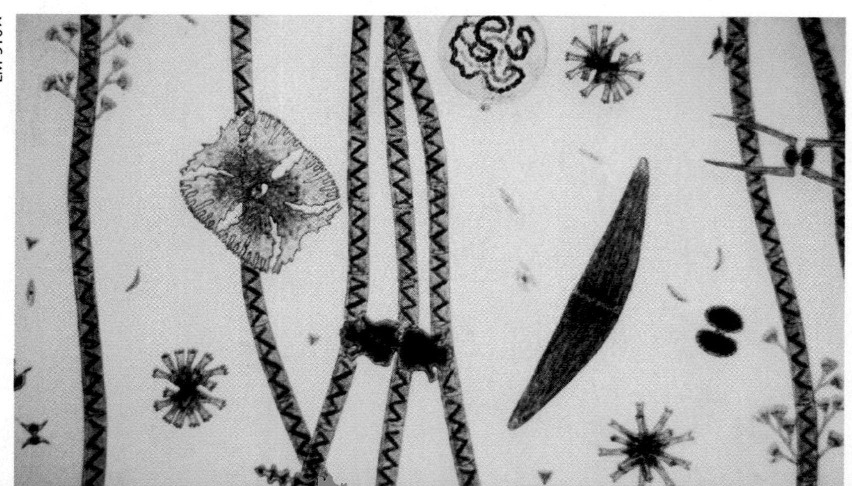

Protists as the Most Complex Cells

Being mostly unicellular, protists are considered the simplest form of eukaryotic organism. Clearly, humans are far more complex organisms than protists. However, in a way, individual human cells can be considered *less* complex than protists. Most human cells are highly specialized, carrying out only certain tasks. For example, some human cells manufacture enzymes that digest food. Other cells transmit nerve impulses in response to stimuli. By comparison, the protist's one cell must consume and process food, respond to stimuli, excrete wastes, and reproduce. At the cellular level, protists can justifiably be considered the most complex of eukaryotic cells, since each cell must carry out all of an organism's life functions. The unicellular protist in the photograph in Figure 17-2, is an example of the complexity required for single-celled organisms to perform all of the functions required for life.

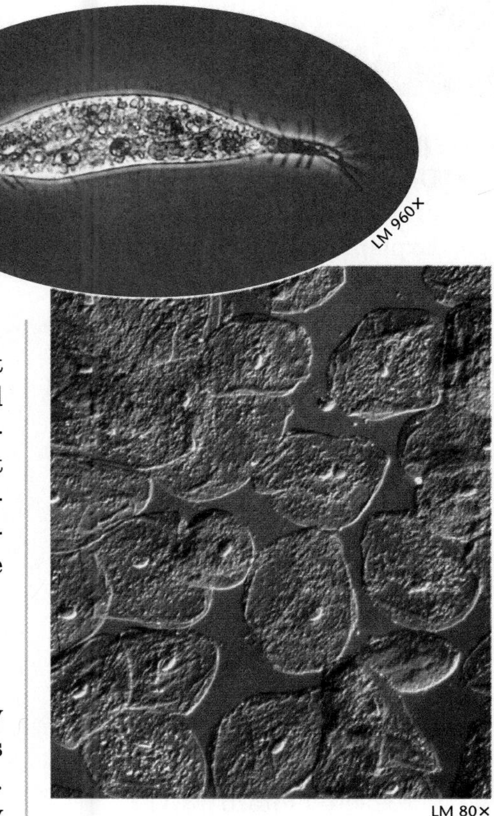

▲ **Figure 17-2** A unicellular protist such as *Urosoma cienkowski* (top) must carry out many more functions than an individual cell within a multicellular organism, such as each of these human cheek cells (bottom).

Grouping Protists by Types of Nutrition

In taxonomy, classification is based ideally on evolutionary relationships. However, in a group as diverse as protists, it is convenient to have informal groupings based on other criteria. Thus, biologists often informally group organisms by how they obtain organic molecules. For example, heterotrophs obtain food from other organisms. In contrast, autotrophs construct all of their own organic molecules. You can think of these methods of obtaining food as different "lifestyles" for organisms. Lifestyle is useful to help understand protist adaptations and the roles they play in ecosystems.

The next sections of this chapter group protists by lifestyle: animal-like, fungus-like, and plant-like protists. Animal-like protists, called **protozoans,** are heterotrophs that ingest (eat) food. Fungus-like protists are also heterotrophs, but they mostly feed on decaying organic matter. Plant-like protists, called **algae** (singular, *alga*), are autotrophs, and make their own food by photosynthesis as plants do.

Online Activity 17.1

Explore protist diversity. Go online to explore the amazing diversity of protists. Use an online microscope to zoom in on protist habitats. Then activate the diversity grid describing the major groups of protists.

Concept Check 17.1

1. Summarize why protists have traditionally been placed in their own taxonomic kingdom.
2. Explain why unicellular protists can be considered more complex than individual cells of multicellular organisms.
3. Name three types of nutrition among protists and describe each.

CONCEPT 17.2 Protozoans ingest their food.

OBJECTIVES
- Describe characteristics of protozoans with flagella.
- Explain how amoebas use pseudopodia.
- Describe the structure and function of cilia in protozoans.
- Describe the life cycle of a protist lacking motility.

KEY TERMS
- zooflagellate
- pseudopodium
- foram
- ciliate

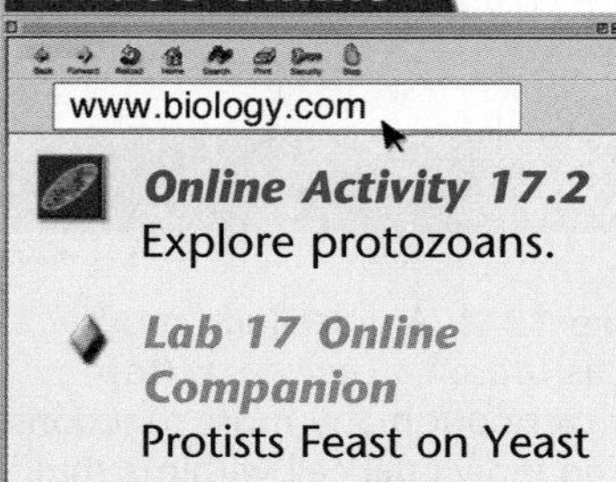

Protozoans, the animal-like protists, are heterotrophs. They eat bacteria, other protists, or nonliving organic matter. Protozoans lack a cell wall. They inhabit most aquatic environments, including tiny drops of water on plants and in soil. Some protozoans live in the body fluids of living hosts.

One convenient way to categorize protozoans is by how they move. Some move rapidly, while others creep slowly. Still others are not capable of active movement at all, but instead rely on a host organism to supply their food.

Protozoans With Flagella

Zooflagellates (zoh oh FLAJ uh lits) move by means of one or more flagella. (Recall from Chapter 6 that flagella are long, thin, whip-like cellular projections.) Zooflagellates generally reproduce asexually by binary fission. Recall that asexual reproduction results in genetically identical offspring.

Though most species of zooflagellates are free-living, some are parasites. An example of a parasitic flagellate is *Giardia,* shown in Figure 17-3. *Giardia* infects the human intestine and can cause abdominal cramps and severe diarrhea. People can become infected with *Giardia* by drinking water contaminated with feces from infected animals. Drinking such water from what may look like a clean stream or river can ruin a camping trip.

A single *Giardia* cell has two separate nuclei, a simple cytoskeleton, and other eukaryotic organelles. However, *Giardia* lacks mitochondria. These protists do not carry out cellular respiration, but instead they harvest energy from food by fermentation (see Chapter 7). *Giardia* and related flagellates have been the

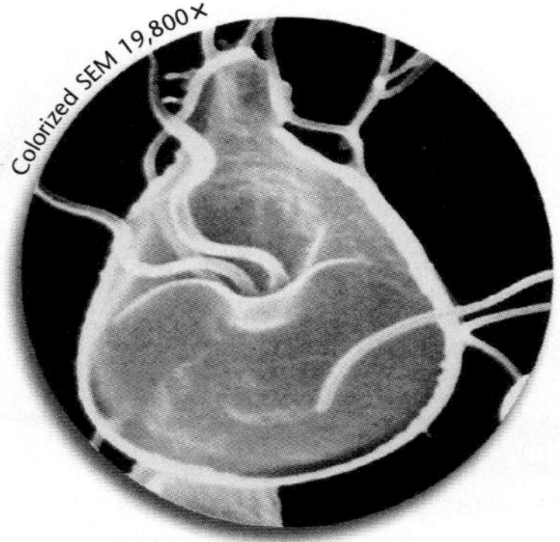

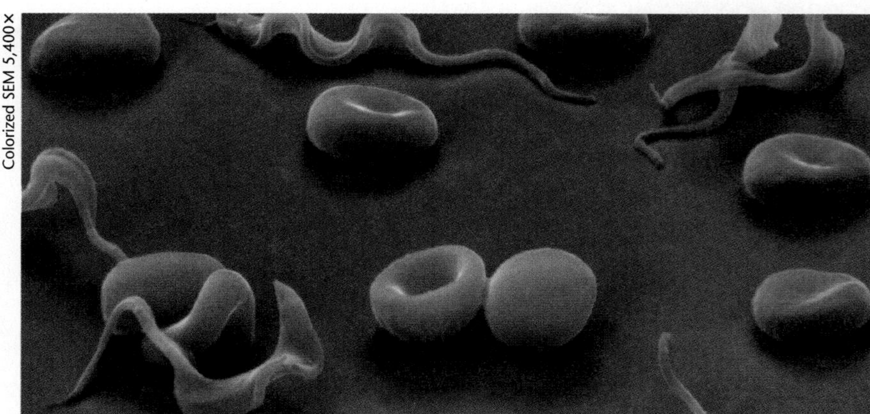

Figure 17-3 Both *Giardia lamblia* (above) and *Trypanosoma brucei* (right) are flagellated protozoans that can cause disease in humans. The *Trypanosoma* (purple) are shown amidst red blood cells.

object of much attention from evolutionary biologists. Details of cell structure and RNA sequences support the hypothesis that these organisms are the eukaryotes most closely related to prokaryotes. This would support the hypothesis that *Giardia* never had mitochondria. However, other recent evidence supports a different hypothesis—that *Giardia* and related protists once had mitochondria but lost them during their evolution.

Another parasitic zooflagellate, *Trypanosoma,* has a single large mitochondrion (Figure 17-3). This organism causes African sleeping sickness, a disease spread by the bite of the tsetse ((t)SET see) fly. Another flagellated protist, *Trichonympha,* lives in a symbiotic relationship in the gut of termites. The protist has enzymes that digest the cellulose in wood, contributing to the nutrition of the termite.

Protozoans With Pseudopodia

Another group of protozoans, the amoebas, have a distinctive way of moving about. An amoeba moves and feeds by means of temporary extensions of its cytoplasm and plasma membrane called **pseudopodia** (singular, *pseudopodium*). Cytoplasm flows from one area of the cell into a pseudopodium extending outward from the cell. This enables the cell to move in the direction of the growing pseudopodium. Amoebas can take almost any shape as they creep over moist surfaces of rocks and plants, or over the mud at the bottom of a pond or the ocean. The amoeba also uses pseudopodia to surround prey, engulfing them into a food vacuole (Figure 17-4).

Another protozoan group with pseudopodia, the forams, inhabit marine environments. **Forams** have porous shells made of organic material and hard calcium carbonate. The foram extends long, thin pseudopodia through the pores in its shell (Figure 17-5). The shells of dead forams and other protists with calcium shells build up in ocean sediments, over time forming a type of rock called limestone.

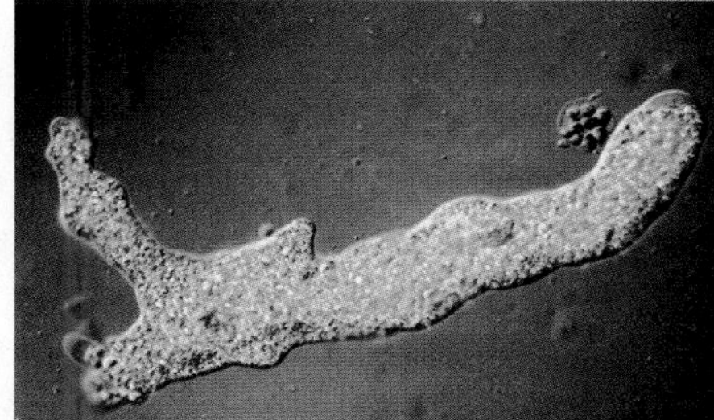

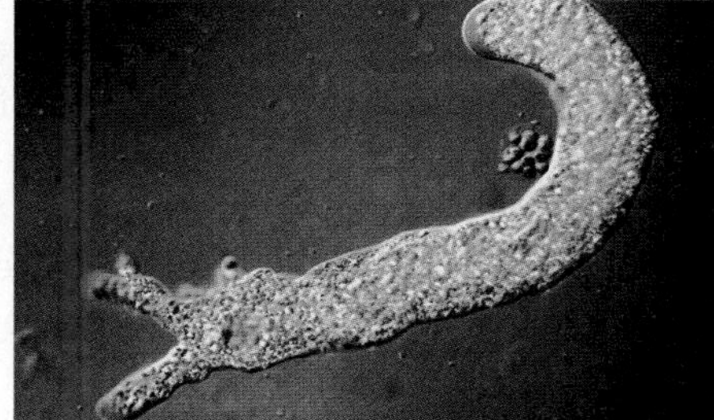

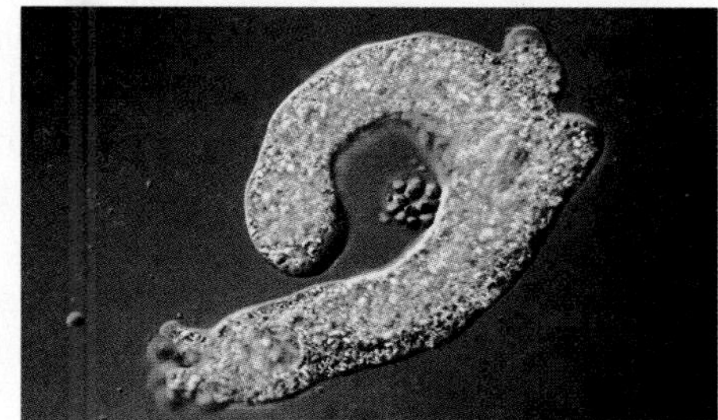

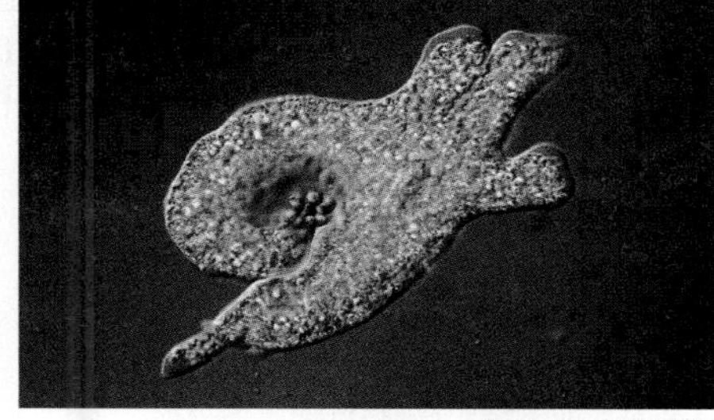

Sequence: LM 160×

▲ **Figure 17-4** This sequence of photos shows how an amoeba uses pseudopodia to surround prey and produce a food vacuole.

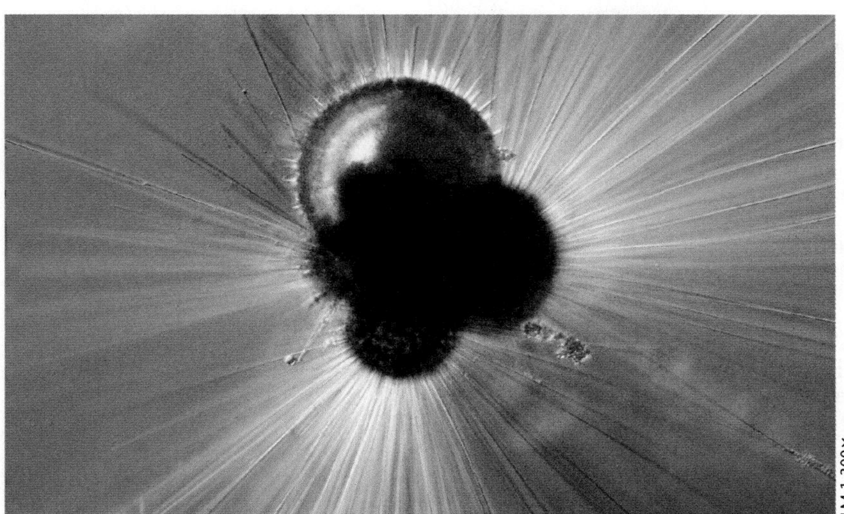

LM 1,300×

◀ **Figure 17-5** Long, thin pseudopodia extend through the porous shell and along spines of the foram *Globigerina*. These strands of cytoplasm function in locomotion and feeding. (The pseudopodia along spines are not visible in this micrograph.)

Protozoans With Cilia

Paramecium, a common pondwater organism, is an example of a ciliate. **Ciliates** are a diverse group of protozoans named for their use of hair-like projections called cilia to move and feed. Like *Paramecium,* most ciliates are free-living cells found in freshwater environments.

In contrast to flagella, cilia are shorter and usually present in much larger numbers. Researchers hypothesize that microtubules just beneath the cell's plasma membrane coordinate the movement of cilia. Some ciliates have many rows of cilia like *Paramecium,* whereas others have clusters of cilia in fewer rows or in tufts. The specific arrangements are adapted for different functions in various ciliates. *Stylonychia,* for example, scurries about on leglike structures consisting of many cilia joined together (Figure 17-6a). In contrast, *Stentor* often attaches to a surface and uses cilia ringing its "mouth" to capture food (Figure 17-6b). The cilia generate whirlpool-like currents that draw food organisms into the cell.

A unique feature of ciliates is the presence of two kinds of nuclei (Figure 17-7). Each cell has a large macronucleus and from 1 to as many as 80 micronuclei. The macronucleus coordinates various cellular activities, while the micronuclei are involved in sexual reproduction. Ciliates can reproduce asexually by fission, but they can also come together and exchange genetic material in a sexual process called conjugation.

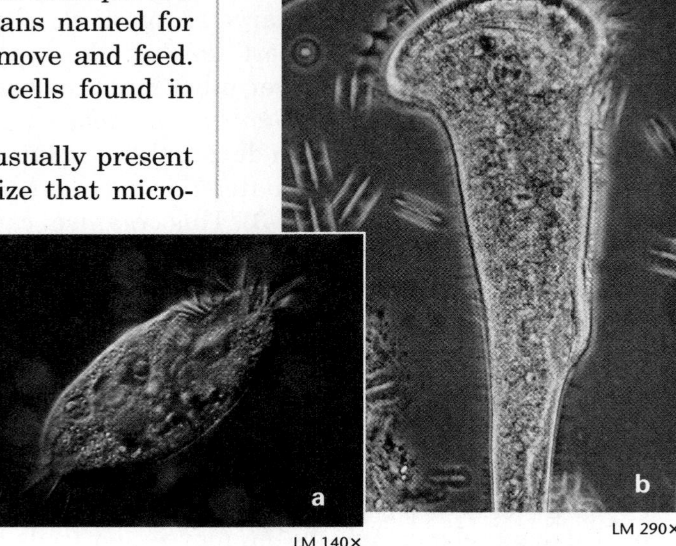
a
b
LM 140×
LM 290×

▲ **Figure 17-6** The cilia of ciliates can have different functions. **a.** The cilia of *Stylonychia* are clumped together in leg-like structures that are used for locomotion. **b.** The cilia of *Stentor* are used for locomotion and to create a whirlpool-like current that moves food into the cell's "mouth."

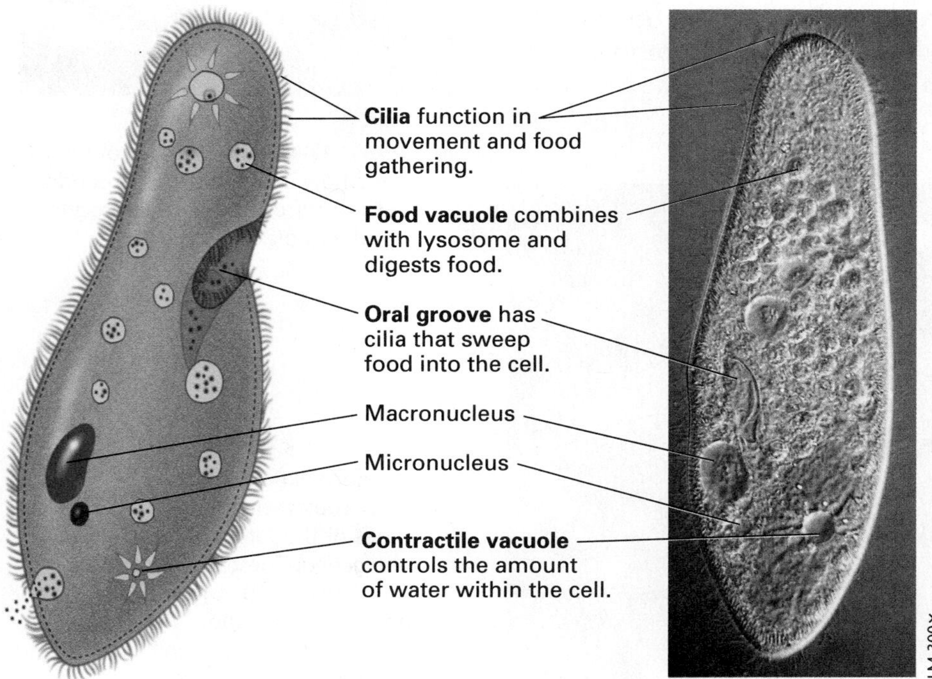
Cilia function in movement and food gathering.
Food vacuole combines with lysosome and digests food.
Oral groove has cilia that sweep food into the cell.
Macronucleus
Micronucleus
Contractile vacuole controls the amount of water within the cell.
LM 300×

◀ **Figure 17-7** *Paramecium* is a freshwater ciliate that feeds mainly on bacteria. The organism is covered by thousands of cilia that function in locomotion and feeding.

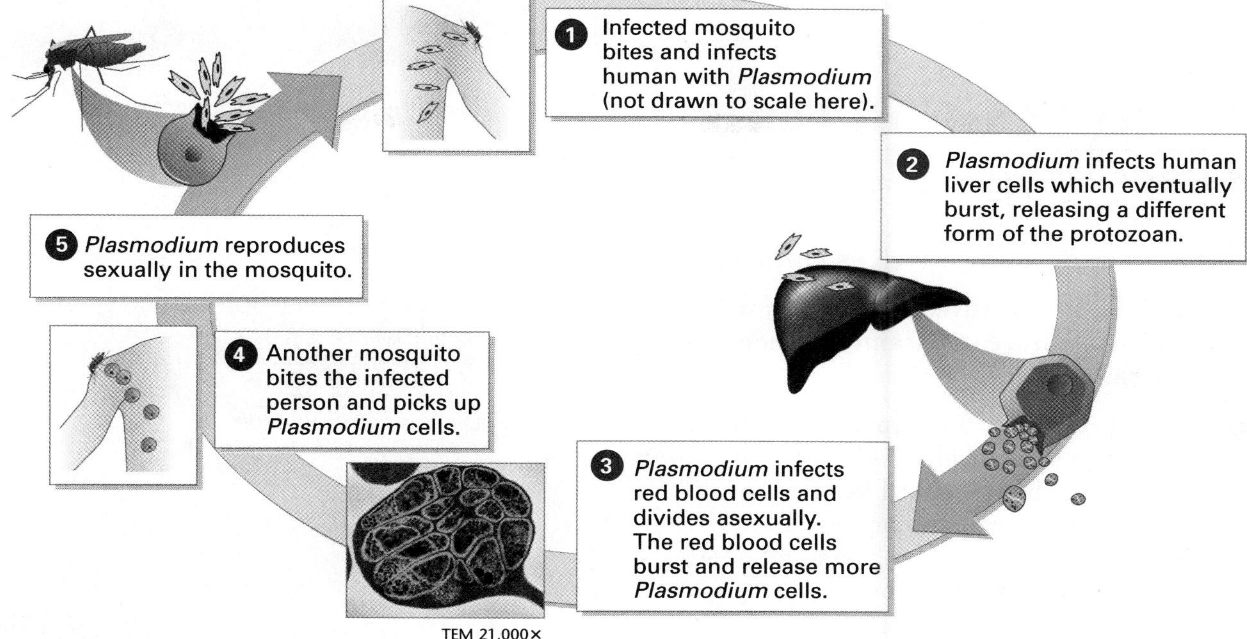

1 Infected mosquito bites and infects human with Plasmodium (not drawn to scale here).
2 Plasmodium infects human liver cells which eventually burst, releasing a different form of the protozoan.
3 Plasmodium infects red blood cells and divides asexually. The red blood cells burst and release more Plasmodium cells.
4 Another mosquito bites the infected person and picks up Plasmodium cells.
5 Plasmodium reproduces sexually in the mosquito.
TEM 21,000×

▲ **Figure 17-8** *Plasmodium,* the protozoan that causes malaria, has a complex life cycle that includes multiple hosts.

Protozoans Lacking Motility

A fourth group of protozoans called *apicomplexans* are parasites with no means of active motility. This group gets its name from a structure called the "apical complex" at the tip of the cell that contains organelles specialized for penetrating host cells. A well-known apicomplexan is *Plasmodium,* the organism that causes malaria in humans (Figure 17-8). Spread by infected mosquitoes, malaria is a harmful and widespread human disease.

Most apicomplexans have intricate life cycles that involve two or more different host species. For example, part of the life cycle of *Plasmodium* occurs in the mosquito and part occurs in the human.

In the 1960s, the rate of malaria decreased as insecticides were used to kill mosquitoes and new drugs were taken that killed *Plasmodium* in infected humans. However, the spread of resistant varieties of both the mosquitoes and the *Plasmodium* species has enabled the disease to resurge.

Online Activity 17.2

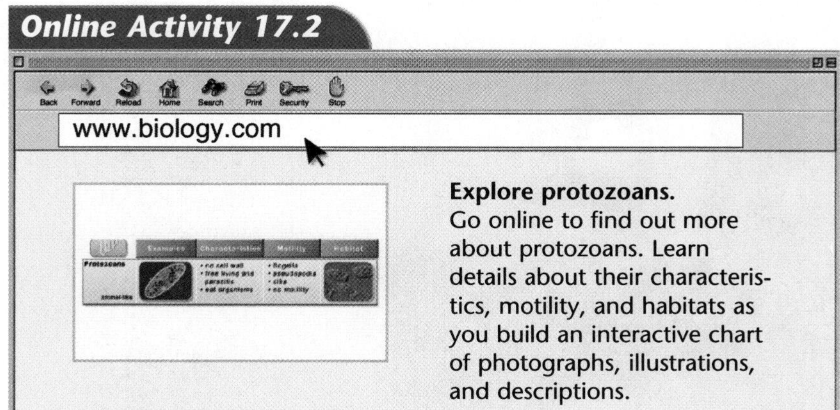

Explore protozoans.
Go online to find out more about protozoans. Learn details about their characteristics, motility, and habitats as you build an interactive chart of photographs, illustrations, and descriptions.

Concept Check 17.2

1. How are zooflagellates different from other protozoans?
2. How do amoebas use pseudopodia?
3. Distinguish between cilia and flagella.
4. Describe the life cycle of *Plasmodium.*

Investigative Lab 17

Protists Feast on Yeast

Observing Feeding in Paramecia

Question How do protists such as *Paramecium* eat?

Lab Overview In this investigation you will add dyed yeast to a culture of paramecia, then observe how the paramecia eat the yeast.

Preparing for the Lab To help you prepare for the investigation, go to the *Lab 17 Online Companion.* ······➔ Learn more about the structural features of *Paramecium* and discover the processes that occur when this unicellular protist ingests and digests a yeast cell. Prepare for the lab procedure by previewing the steps you will take.

Completing the Lab Use your Laboratory Manual or lab page printouts from the *Lab 17 Online Companion* to do the investigation and draw conclusions from the observations you made. **CAUTION:** *Be sure to follow your teacher's instructions and all safety guidelines in the investigation.*

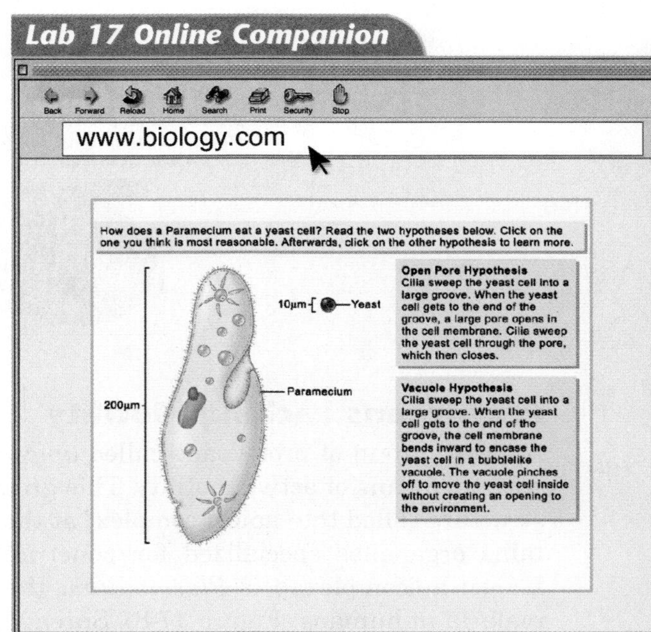

Lab 17 Online Companion
Back
Forward
Reload
Home
Search
Print
Security
Stop
www.biology.com
How does a Paramecium eat a yeast cell? Read the two hypotheses below. Click on the one you think is most reasonable. Afterwards, click on the other hypothesis to learn more.
10µm
Yeast
Paramecium
200µm
Open Pore Hypothesis
Cilia sweep the yeast cell into a large groove. When the yeast cell gets to the end of the groove, a large pore opens in the cell membrane. Cilia sweep the yeast cell through the pore, which then closes.
Vacuole Hypothesis
Cilia sweep the yeast cell into a large groove. When the yeast cell gets to the end of the groove, the cell membrane bends inward to encase the yeast cell in a bubblelike vacuole. The vacuole pinches off to move the yeast cell inside without creating an opening to the environment.

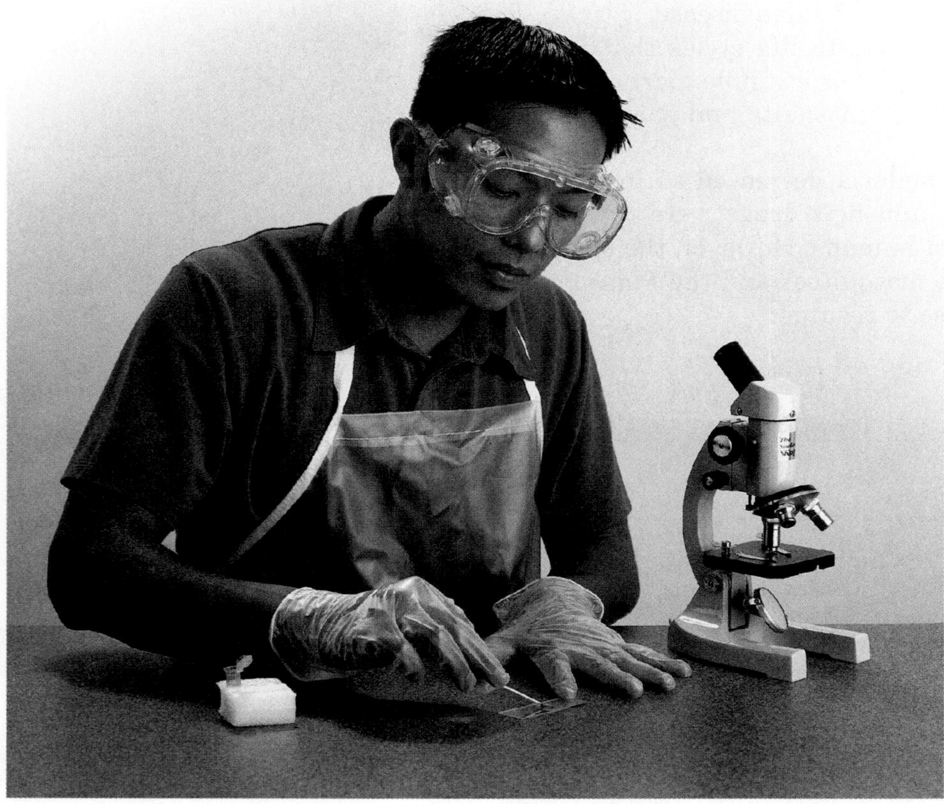

CONCEPT 17.3 Slime molds decompose organic matter.

OBJECTIVES
- Describe the general characteristics of plasmodial slime molds.
- Summarize the life cycle of cellular slime molds.
- Describe the characteristics of water molds and downy mildews.

KEY TERMS
- plasmodial slime mold
- plasmodium
- sporangia
- cellular slime mold

What's Online

Online Activity 17.3
Explore fungus-like protists.

Despite their common name, the organisms you will read about in this section are not really molds. As you will read in the next chapter, true molds are a type of fungus. What slime "molds" and fungi have in common is that both decompose dead organic material, such as the "mulch" on a forest floor.

Plasmodial Slime Molds

The brightly colored, branching growth you might observe on a decaying log is likely a protist called a **plasmodial slime mold** (Figure 17-9). These organisms are common almost anywhere there is moist, decaying organic matter. Large and branching as it is, a plasmodial slime mold is not multicellular. Rather, it is a **plasmodium,** a single mass of cytoplasm undivided by membranes or cell walls and containing many nuclei. (Do not confuse this word with the organism *Plasmodium*, the apicomplexan that causes malaria.) This giant "supercell" behaves somewhat like a large amoeba, extending pseudopodia that engulf bacteria and other bits of organic matter. Its web-like form is an adaptation that enlarges the organism's surface area, increasing its contact with food, water, and oxygen. Through a microscope, you can observe a plasmodium's cytoplasm stream in pulsing flows, first one way and then the other. Biologists hypothesize that this streaming distributes nutrients and oxygen throughout the organism.

As long as a plasmodial slime mold has ample food and water, it usually stays in the plasmodial stage. When food and water are in short supply, however, the organism stops growing and develops reproductive structures called fruiting bodies, or **sporangia** (spoh RAN jee uh) (Figure 17-9). Within the tips of the sporangia, meiosis produces haploid spores that can be dispersed by the wind. When conditions again become favorable, each spore releases an active haploid cell. Pairs of haploid cells fuse, forming diploid zygotes. Each zygote then develops into a new plasmodium, completing the life cycle.

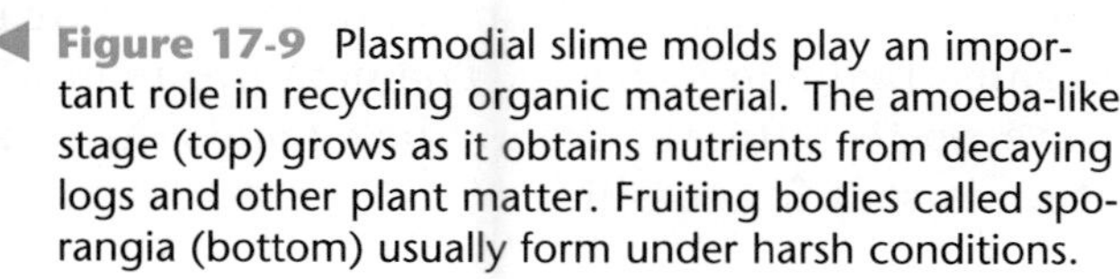
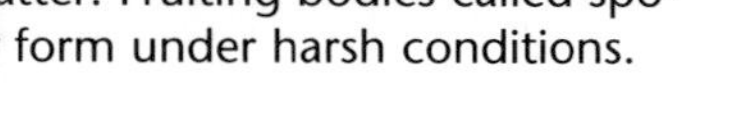

Figure 17-9 Plasmodial slime molds play an important role in recycling organic material. The amoeba-like stage (top) grows as it obtains nutrients from decaying logs and other plant matter. Fruiting bodies called sporangia (bottom) usually form under harsh conditions.

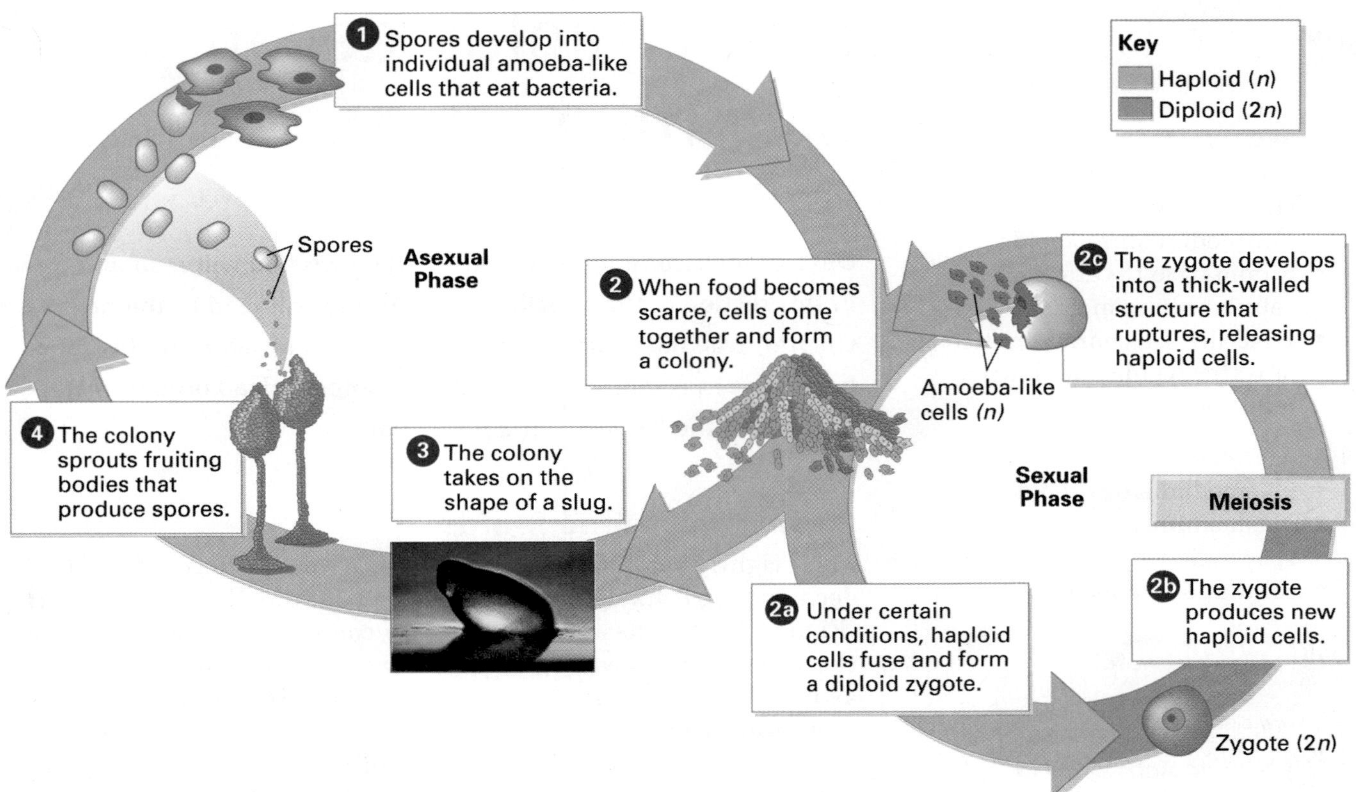

1 Spores develop into individual amoeba-like cells that eat bacteria.
Key
Haploid (n)
Diploid (2n)
Spores
Asexual Phase
2 When food becomes scarce, cells come together and form a colony.
2c The zygote develops into a thick-walled structure that ruptures, releasing haploid cells.
Amoeba-like cells (n)
4 The colony sprouts fruiting bodies that produce spores.
3 The colony takes on the shape of a slug.
Sexual Phase
Meiosis
2b The zygote produces new haploid cells.
2a Under certain conditions, haploid cells fuse and form a diploid zygote.
Zygote (2n)

▲ **Figure 17-10** The cellular slime mold *Dictyostelium* has both unicellular and multicellular stages in its life cycle.

Cellular Slime Molds

Like plasmodial slime molds, **cellular slime molds** are decomposers that live mainly on decaying organic matter. Cellular slime molds challenge biologists' understanding of what it means to be a multicellular organism. These protists have both unicellular and multicellular stages in their life cycles.

Dictyostelium, a common cellular slime mold, goes through three life cycle stages: individual, colony, and spore (Figure 17-10). Most of the time, this organism exists as solitary amoeba-like cells. These cells are haploid. They use pseudopodia to creep about and engulf bacteria and other food. When food is plentiful, the cells remain separate and reproduce asexually. But when food is scarce, the cells secrete chemicals that attract other *Dictyostelium* cells. When many *Dictyostelium* cells gather together, eventually a slug-like colony is formed. This colony of cells then migrates a few centimeters, leaving a trail of slime. At this point, the colony begins to show characteristics of multicellular organisms. Some of the cells in the colony differentiate and form a stalk, while other cells form haploid spores. Under suitable conditions, haploid amoeba-like cells emerge from the spores and begin the next generation. This form of reproduction is asexual. As Figure 17-10 shows, cellular slime molds can also reproduce sexually.

Most biologists place plasmodial and cellular slime molds in the same taxonomic group. The next group of protists, however, are quite different from slime molds. Yet their mode of nutrition is still fungus-like.

Water Molds and Downy Mildews

Another group of heterotrophic, fungus-like protists are water molds and downy mildews. Water molds generally decompose dead plants and animals in freshwater habitats (Figure 17-11a). There are also parasitic water molds that sometimes grow on the skin or gills of fishes.

Water molds exist either as unicellular organisms or as thin, branching filaments that contain many nuclei. Water molds reproduce sexually when an egg cell is fertilized by a sperm nucleus, forming a diploid zygote. When conditions are favorable, the zygote releases motile spores with two flagella.

Like water molds, downy mildews also produce an egg cell. The spores of downy mildews are spread by the wind, but these organisms can also form flagellated spores during their life cycle. Some downy mildews are plant parasites. For example, *Phytophthora infestans* infected potato plants in Ireland in the mid-1800s, causing the great Irish famine (Figure 17-11b). This fungus-like protist destroyed Irish potato crops for several years. Since each plant was grown asexually from buds of parent plants, the potato crops consisted of clones. Lacking the genetic variation generated by sexual reproduction, there were no plants resistant to the downy mildew. During the Irish famine, nearly 1,000,000 people died from starvation or famine-related illnesses. And approximately 1,500,000 more people emigrated to England and North America to escape the famine.

Despite the similarity of fungus-like lifestyles, molecular analysis indicates that water molds and downy mildews are not closely related to slime molds. Instead, it seems that water molds and downy mildews are closely related to some of the algae that you will read about in Concept 17.4.

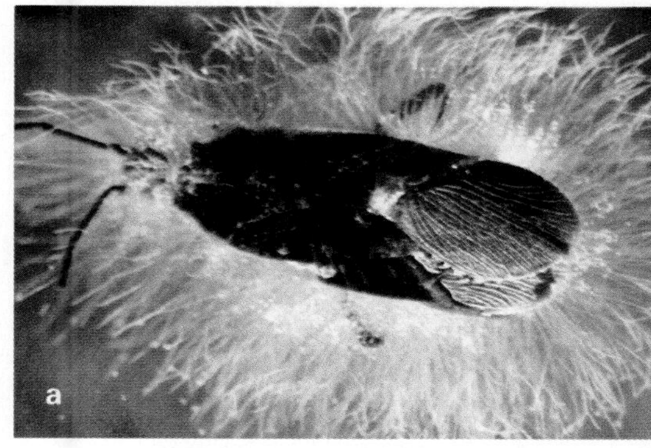

Figure 17-11 Some fungus-like protists are beneficial recyclers of organic matter, while others are harmful plant parasites. **a.** A water mold breaks down a dead insect. **b.** *Phytophthora infestans* is a plant parasite that kills potato plants and damages the potatoes.

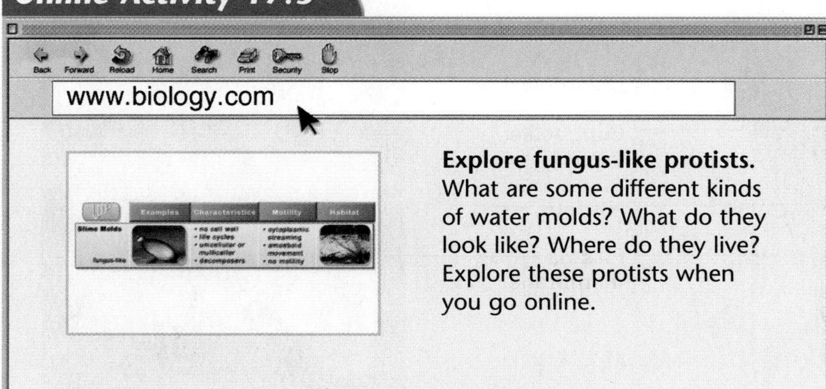

Explore fungus-like protists. What are some different kinds of water molds? What do they look like? Where do they live? Explore these protists when you go online.

Concept Check 17.3

1. What features distinguish the plasmodial slime molds from other protists?
2. How does food supply affect a cellular slime mold?
3. Compare and contrast water molds and downy mildews.

CONCEPT 17.4

Algae are photosynthetic protists.

OBJECTIVES

- Describe the characteristics of euglenoids and dinoflagellates.
- Distinguish diatoms from other photosynthetic protists.
- Compare and contrast three types of seaweeds.

KEY TERMS

- euglenoid
- dinoflagellate
- plankton
- phytoplankton
- zooplankton
- diatom
- seaweed

What's Online

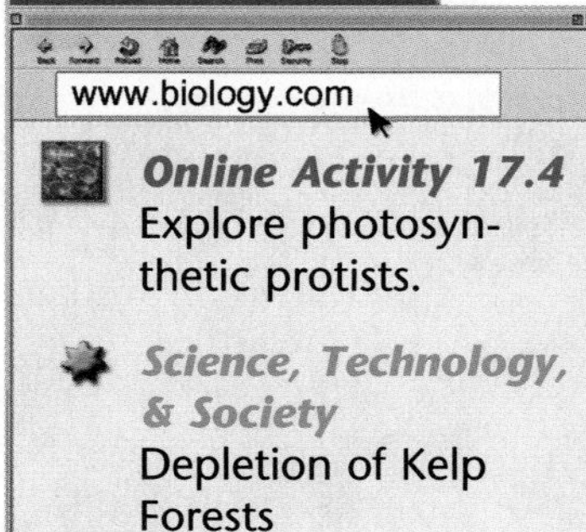

Unlike protozoans and fungus-like protists, "algae" are plant-like protists that contain chloroplasts and can make their own food. Many algae are unicellular, some live in colonies, and still others are multicellular. Most algae have both asexual and sexual mechanisms of reproduction. Biologists classify these protists by their differences in cell wall, types of photosynthetic pigments, structure, types of storage carbohydrates, and now by nucleic acid sequences.

Euglenoids

The **euglenoids** are a group of single-celled, photosynthetic protists that possess one or two flagella and lack cell walls. *Euglena,* shown in Figure 17-12, belongs to this group. Notice the presence of chloroplasts that enable the organism to carry out photosynthesis. Euglenoids live in fresh water, and though they do not have cell walls, their plasma membranes are rigid and tough but flexible. Emerging from a pocket at one end of the *Euglena* cell is a long flagellum that functions in cell movement. Near the base of the flagellum is a structure called an eyespot that functions with a light detector in sensing the direction from which light is coming. *Euglena* swims toward light, which powers photosynthesis.

Euglena is not always autotrophic. If placed in the dark, it can live as a heterotroph by absorbing organic nutrients from the environment. In fact, certain euglenoid-related species lack chloroplasts and ingest food into food vacuoles. Even though they lack a cell wall, most biologists include euglenoids with algae because they are mostly photosynthetic.

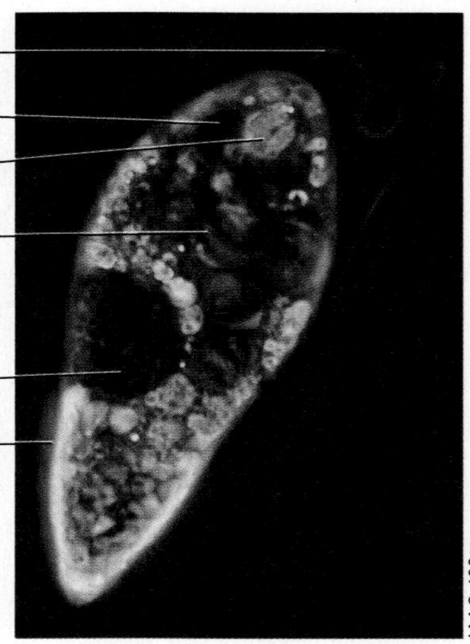

Figure 17-12 *Euglena* is one of the most common inhabitants of pond water. This single-celled protist can carry on photosynthesis in the light, and in the dark it can become heterotrophic and absorb nutrients.

Figure 17-13 Dinoflagellates are abundant members of phytoplankton. Dinoflagellate cells have protective external plates of cellulose and two flagella. The red color along this coastline is characteristic of "red tide," a condition caused by a dinoflagellate population explosion.

Dinoflagellates

The **dinoflagellates** are unicellular, mostly photosynthetic protists with a cell wall made of cellulose and two flagella (Figure 17-13). The two flagella beat in perpendicular grooves of the cell wall. This action produces the spinning movement for which these organisms are named. (*Dinos* is a Greek word that means "whirling.")

Found in both freshwater and saltwater environments, dinoflagellates are among the many unicellular algae that are components of plankton. **Plankton** are the communities of mostly microscopic organisms that drift or swim near the surface of ponds, lakes, and oceans. Photosynthetic organisms in plankton, such as dinoflagellates, are called **phytoplankton.** Those plankton that are protozoans or tiny animals are called **zooplankton.** For example, forams, which you read about in Concept 17.2, are among the zooplankton. Phytoplankton form the base of the food chain for most other aquatic organisms.

Although dinoflagellates are very small, they can have a visible impact on the environment. Dinoflagellates reproduce mainly by binary fission, and some species occasionally undergo population explosions. A large number of these organisms can cause coastal marine waters to turn pinkish-orange—a phenomenon called red tide (Figure 17-13). Toxins produced by some red tide algae kill enormous numbers of fish. These toxins can also be harmful, even deadly, to humans who eat shellfish that have ingested the toxins.

Some dinoflagellate species have an ability to produce light, a property called bioluminescence. This light can create an eerie ocean glow at night when waves, boats, or swimmers stir up water containing dense populations of the bioluminescent dinoflagellates.

Diatoms

A glass-like cell wall is a unique characteristic of **diatoms,** another group of unicellular algae. A diatom's cell wall contains silica, the same mineral that makes up glass. These rigid cell walls give diatoms a variety of geometric shapes (Figure 17-14). The cell wall consists of two halves that fit together like the bottom and lid of a shoebox. Diatoms contain chlorophyll, but appear yellow or brown because they also contain other pigments that mask the green color. Both freshwater and marine environments are rich in diatoms, which are key members of plankton. They are as important a food source for many marine animals as grasses are for many land animals.

Diatoms store their food reserves in the form of an oil, which enables them to float near the surface where they are exposed to sunlight. When diatoms die, they no longer produce this oil, and they sink to the ocean floor. The glassy cell walls do not decompose and, over time, they accumulate and can become fossilized. Enormous numbers of fossilized diatoms make up thick sediments known as diatomaceous (dy uh tuh MAY shus) earth. This soil is mined for use as a filter material, as a grinding and polishing agent, and as an ingredient in some toothpastes.

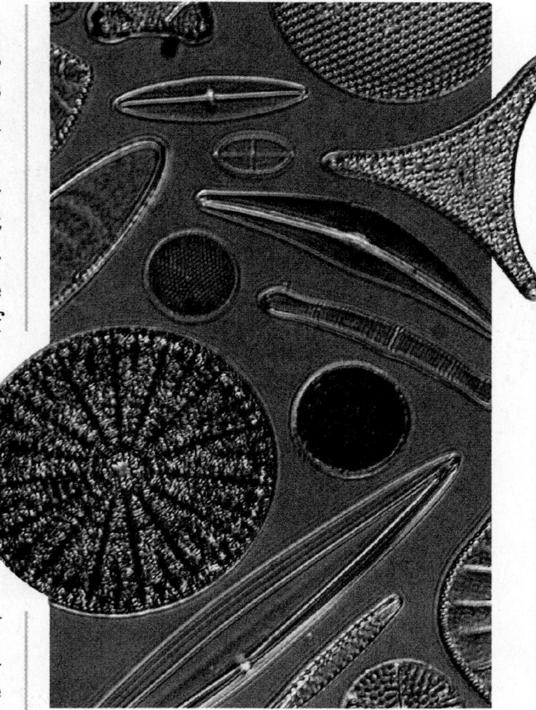

▲ **Figure 17-14** Though they may resemble tiny glass boxes, these diatoms are actually single-celled photosynthetic organisms. Tiny pores in a diatom's shell allow gases and other substances to be exchanged between the cell and its environment.

Seaweeds

Most of the protists described so far are unicellular and microscopic. In contrast, **seaweeds** are large, multicellular marine algae (Figure 17-15). Some of these organisms can be as large as many plants and have specialized structures that resemble those of plants. However, seaweeds lack the true roots, stems, and leaves of plants. Because seaweeds seem to be more closely related to certain unicellular algae than they are to true plants, most biologists include seaweeds with protists. Seaweeds are classified into three different groups depending, in part, on what pigments they contain: brown algae, red algae, and green algae.

◀ **Figure 17-15** These large seaweeds are commonly called kelp. Kelp "forests" such as this provide food and shelter for many species of fishes.

People harvest algae from all three seaweed groups for food. For example, in Japan and Korea, some seaweed species are common ingredients in soups and salads. Other seaweeds are used to wrap sushi. Marine algae are rich in iodine and other essential minerals. However, much of their organic material consists of unusual polysaccharides that humans cannot digest. Thus seaweeds are not used as a source of staple food. They are eaten mostly for their rich tastes and unusual textures.

In addition to cellulose, the cell walls of many seaweeds contain other polysaccharides that give them a slimy and rubbery feel. In their natural habitat, these substances help to cushion the organisms from wave damage in tidal areas. These polysaccharides are extracted for commercial use. For example, the extract carrageenan is widely used to thicken foods such as puddings and salad dressings. Algin, an extract of brown seaweed, is used to thicken foods and is also a common ingredient in cosmetics and paints. One extract of red algae called agar is used as the gelatin-like material on which microbiologists culture microorganisms.

Brown Algae The biggest and most complex seaweeds are the brown algae, named for their typical brown or olive color. The distinctive color is due to "accessory" pigments that are present in the chloroplasts along with chlorophyll. Many brown algae grow on rocky shores. These organisms must be able to tolerate wave action and the ebb and flow of daily tides.

Some species of brown algae called kelp may grow to heights of 60 meters (Figure 17-15). Kelp are anchored to the sea floor by root-like structures called holdfasts. However, seaweed holdfasts and plant roots have different structural details that provide evidence of separate evolutionary origins. Fishes, sea lions, sea otters, and gray whales regularly use the kelp "forest" ecosystems, feeding on the many organisms that live on and around the kelp.

Red Algae The warm, coastal waters of the tropics are home to most types of red algae, another form of seaweed (Figure 17-16). These algae are named for a reddish pigment found in addition to chlorophyll in their chloroplasts. Of all seaweeds, red algae can live in the deepest water, because the red pigment can absorb blue and green light—the light that penetrates most deeply in water.

Most red algae are multicellular, but none are as big as the giant brown kelps. Though red algae are generally soft-bodied, some, called coralline algae, have cell walls hardened by mineral deposits. Coralline algae commonly live in coral reefs (thus the name "coralline") where their hard parts contribute to the reef structure.

Life cycles in red algae are especially diverse. However, there is no stage of these life cycles that includes flagellated cells. These algae depend on water currents to bring gametes together.

Science, Technology, & Society

www.biology.com

Depletion of Kelp Forests

Off the coast of the Pacific Northwest lie huge underwater forests, home to an amazing variety of marine life. The "trees" in these forests are actually protists—a type of brown algae called kelp. Find out more about this unique marine environment when you go online.

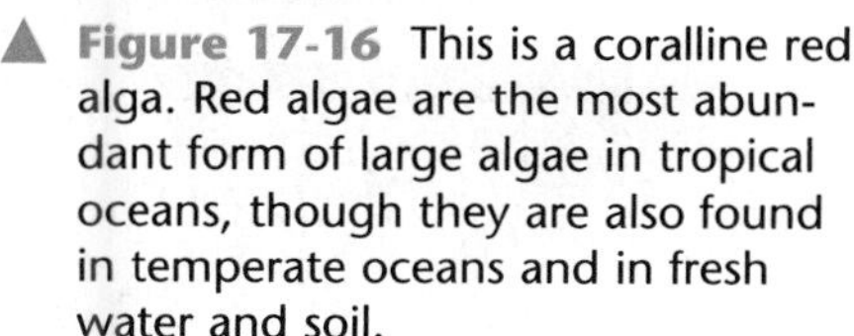

▲ **Figure 17-16** This is a coralline red alga. Red algae are the most abundant form of large algae in tropical oceans, though they are also found in temperate oceans and in fresh water and soil.

Green Algae Green algae, a group of photosynthetic protists that includes unicellular, colonial, and multicellular species, are named for their green chloroplasts. The largest green algae are seaweeds. Though there are many marine species, most green algae live in fresh water. Various species of unicellular green algae live as phytoplankton, and some even inhabit damp soil or snow.

Chlamydomonas is a single-celled green alga (Figure 17-17a). This common freshwater organism has two flagella and can sense and swim toward light. Although somewhat similar to organisms from the euglenoid group, *Chlamydomonas* has a cell wall, whereas euglenoids do not have a cell wall.

Volvox is a colonial green alga shaped like a hollow ball (Figure 17-17b). The colony consists of hundreds or thousands of cells that each look similar to *Chlamydomonas.* These cells are connected by bridges of cytoplasm.

Some multicellular green algae form filaments, long strings of cells attached end to end. Other multicellular species such as *Ulva* are large and complex enough to qualify as seaweeds along with the large brown and red algae (Figure 17-17c).

Most green algae have complex life cycles, including both asexual and sexual reproductive stages. Nearly all reproduce sexually with flagellated gametes that swim toward one another and fuse. Many plant-like features of green algae, such as cellulose cell walls, the use of starch for food storage, and similar chloroplast structure and pigmentation, suggest that the ancestor of plants was a green alga. In fact, many biologists think that at least some green algae should be classified in the plant kingdom.

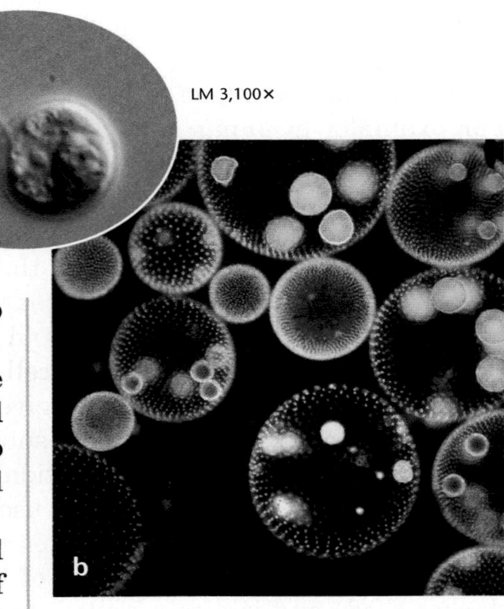

▲ **Figure 17-17** Green algae exist in a variety of forms. **a.** *Chlamydomonas* is a single-celled organism widely used in genetic research. **b.** *Volvox* is a colonial alga consisting of flagellated cells. **c.** *Ulva* (sometimes called "sea lettuce") is a multicellular seaweed used as a food source by many people.

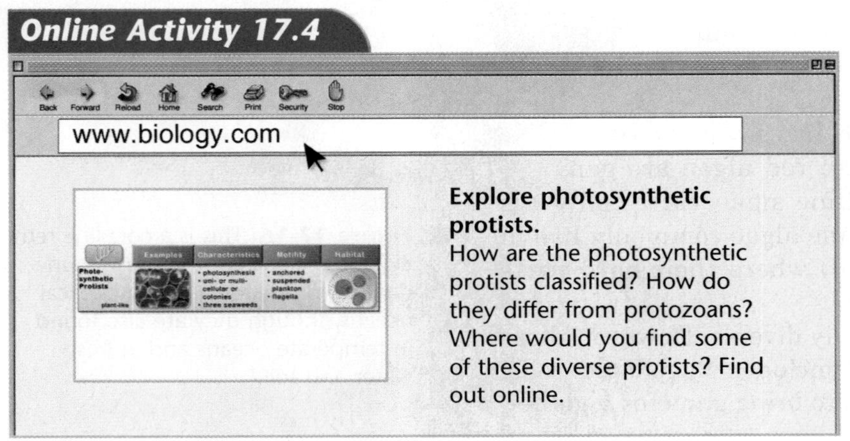

Online Activity 17.4

Explore photosynthetic protists.
How are the photosynthetic protists classified? How do they differ from protozoans? Where would you find some of these diverse protists? Find out online.

Concept Check 17.4

1. Compare and contrast euglenoids with dinoflagellates.
2. In what way are diatoms "glass-like"?
3. What are distinguishing characteristics of brown, red, and green algae?

CONCEPT 17.5 Plants, fungi, and animals evolved from protists.

OBJECTIVES
- Describe how symbiosis may have contributed to the origin of eukaryotic cells.
- Explain why the taxonomy of protists is still changing.

KEY TERM
- endosymbiosis

What's Online

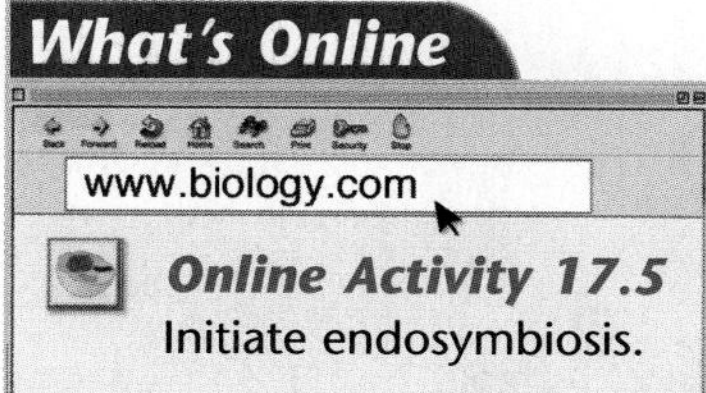

Online Activity 17.5
Initiate endosymbiosis.

The eukaryotic organisms with which you are most familiar are probably large plants and animals. How are these organisms related to protists? And how are protists related to even less complex prokaryotic organisms such as bacteria? Biologists hypothesize that protists evolved from ancient prokaryotes over a billion years ago. In turn, plants, animals, and fungi evolved from protists hundreds of millions of years ago. Can the process of science provide evidence to support these hypotheses?

The Origin of Eukaryotes

Among the most fundamental questions in biology is how the complex eukaryotic cell evolved from much simpler prokaryotic cells. A widely accepted theory is that eukaryotic cells evolved through a combination of two processes (Figure 17-18). In one process, internal membranes such as the endoplasmic reticulum, Golgi apparatus, and nuclear envelope evolved from inward folds of the plasma membrane of ancestral prokaryotic cells. Such internal membranes would allow the cell to carry out more complex chemical reactions in separate compartments.

▼ **Figure 17-18** Eukaryotic cell organelles may have evolved through a combination of two processes. Infolding of the plasma membrane could have produced internal membranes. Certain prokaryotes could have become residents within larger host cells, eventually evolving into mitochondria and chloroplasts.

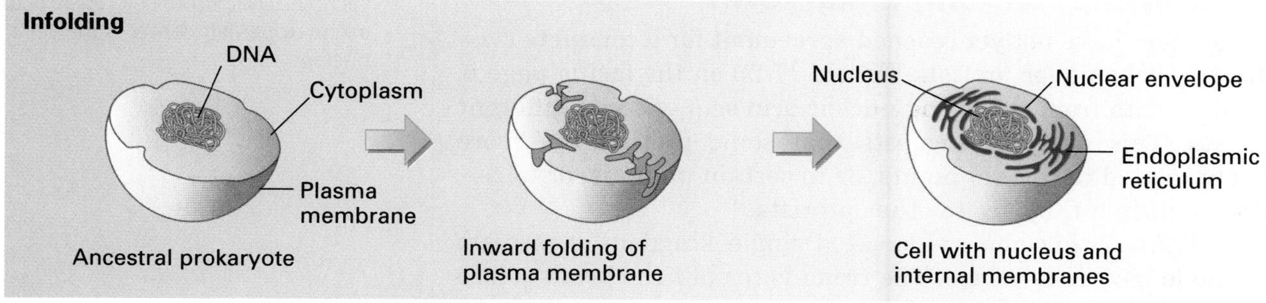

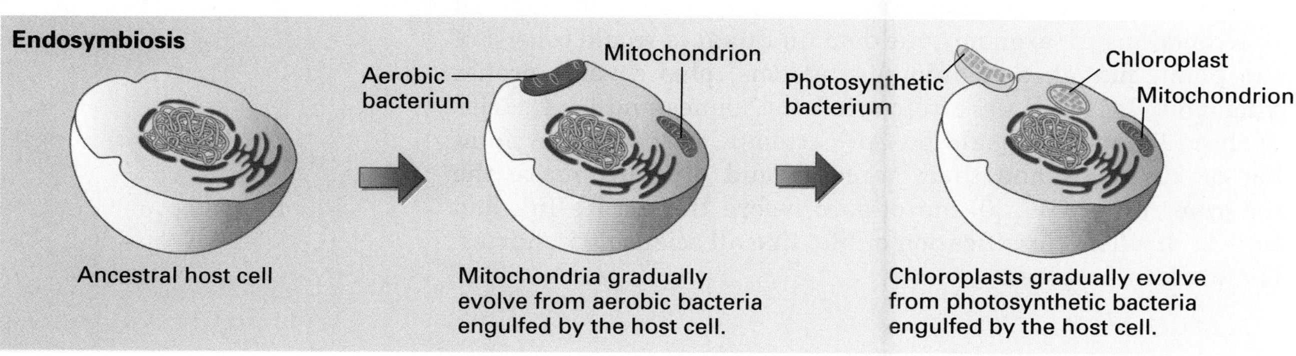

Evidence suggests that a second, very different process led to the existence of the cellular organelles mitochondria and chloroplasts. Scientists hypothesize that in this process, called **endosymbiosis,** chloroplasts and mitochondria evolved from small symbiotic prokaryotes that lived within other, larger host cells. (Symbiosis is a relationship between two organisms of different species that live in close contact with one another.)

The symbiotic ancestors of mitochondria may have been aerobic bacteria that were able to use oxygen in cellular respiration (Figure 17-19). An ancestral host cell may have ingested some of these aerobic cells for food. Instead of being digested, some of these bacterial cells might have remained alive and continued to perform respiration within the host cell. In a similar way, the ancestors of chloroplasts could have been photosynthetic bacteria that lived inside a larger host cell. Since almost all eukaryotes have mitochondria but only some have chloroplasts, it is likely that mitochondria evolved first.

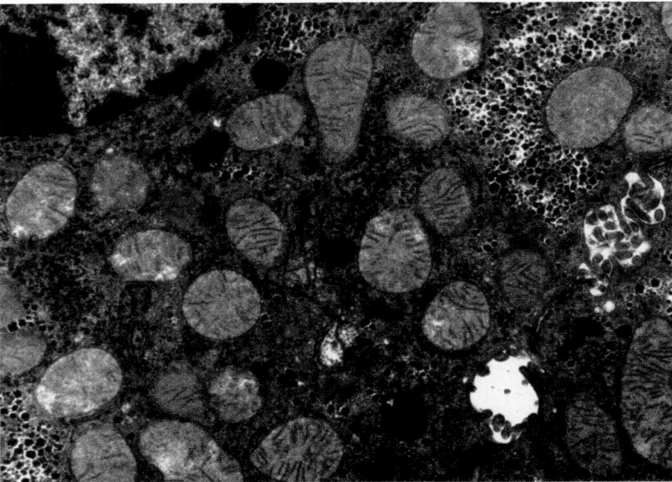

Colorized TEM 18,600×

▲ **Figure 17-19** Endosymbiosis can explain the double membranes of the mitochondria (yellow-orange) visible in this TEM. Molecular evidence suggests that the inner membrane was derived from the plasma membrane of the engulfed cell. A mitochondrion's outer membrane could have evolved from the host cell membrane that engulfed the bacterial cell into a vacuole. The purple-colored structure in the upper left corner is the cell's nucleus.

The endosymbiosis theory is supported by a variety of evidence. For instance, present-day mitochondria and chloroplasts are similar to prokaryotic cells in a number of ways. Both types of organelles contain DNA, RNA, and ribosomes, all of which resemble their counterparts in prokaryotes more than those in eukaryotes. In addition, mitochondria and chloroplasts copy their own DNA and reproduce within the host cell by a process resembling the binary fission of prokaryotes.

Relationships Among Eukaryotes

Researchers have not yet reached agreement for a complete classification scheme for protists. Figure 17-20 on the facing page is based on data from analyzing nucleic acid sequences of different protists. This analysis suggests that some protists are more closely related to certain plants, or to certain animals, or to certain fungi than they are to other protists.

In light of this new evidence, a single kingdom of protists may no longer make sense. The trend is to split the protists into several kingdoms, each a major evolutionary branch, or clade. In this remaking of taxonomy, the domain Eukarya would consist of the plant, fungal, and animal kingdoms, plus several protist kingdoms. It is still uncertain what the names and boundaries of these kingdoms should be. Any attempt to specify the number of kingdoms and their names would probably make the diagram (Figure 17-20) out-of-date before this book's ink had time to dry. The classification of life, like all scientific inquiries, is a work in progress.

Giardia and relatives
Euglenoids
Zooflagellate relatives of euglenoids
Dinoflagellates
Apicomplexans
Ciliates
Water molds
Diatoms
Brown algae
Red algae
Other green algae
Closest algal relatives of plants
Plants
Plasmodial slime molds
Cellular slime molds
Fungi
Animals

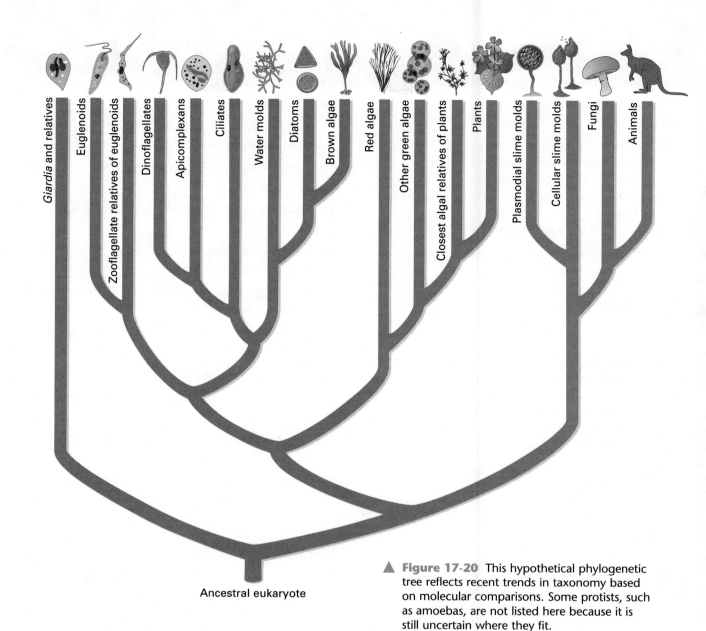

Ancestral eukaryote

▲ **Figure 17-20** This hypothetical phylogenetic tree reflects recent trends in taxonomy based on molecular comparisons. Some protists, such as amoebas, are not listed here because it is still uncertain where they fit.

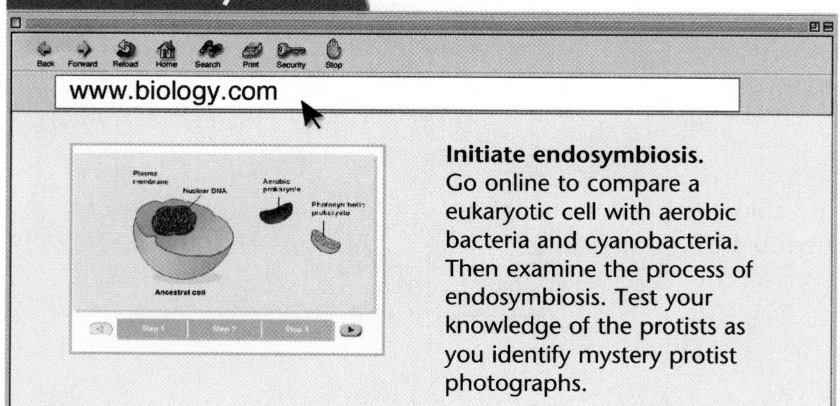

Initiate endosymbiosis.
Go online to compare a eukaryotic cell with aerobic bacteria and cyanobacteria. Then examine the process of endosymbiosis. Test your knowledge of the protists as you identify mystery protist photographs.

Concept Check 17.5

1. Describe how endosymbiosis explains the origin of mitochondria and chloroplasts in eukaryotic cells.
2. Why does it no longer seem correct to group all protists in a single kingdom?

Multiple Choice

Choose the letter of the best answer.

1. Which of the following best defines a protist?
   a. any single-celled organism
   b. another name for prokaryotes
   c. a eukaryote that is not a plant, animal, or fungus
   d. a cell lacking mitochondria and a nucleus

2. Which choice correctly pairs a protozoan with its method of locomotion?
   a. *Giardia*—pseudopodia
   b. *Plasmodium*—flagella
   c. *Amoeba*—can't move on its own
   d. *Paramecium*—cilia

3. Which of the following most completely describes the function of cilia in protozoans?
   a. reproduction and feeding
   b. locomotion and reproduction
   c. locomotion only
   d. locomotion and feeding

4. Based on nutrition, slime molds belong to the group of protists that are
   a. animal-like.
   b. plant-like.
   c. fungus-like.
   d. bacteria-like.

5. How do dinoflagellates obtain nutrients?
   a. by eating protozoans
   b. through photosynthesis
   c. by absorbing decaying organisms
   d. by eating phytoplankton

6. Large multicellular marine algae are called
   a. seaweeds.
   b. protozoans.
   c. zooplankton.
   d. diatoms.

7. Which organisms may have evolved into chloroplasts, according to the theory of endosymbiosis?
   a. heterotrophic ciliates
   b. photosynthetic bacteria
   c. photosynthetic seaweeds
   d. parasitic apicomplexans

Short Answer

8. In what sense can protists be considered the most complex type of cells?

9. Explain why protozoans are considered "animal-like" protists.

10. Contrast three modes of movement among protozoans.

11. Identify the organism that causes malaria and describe its life cycle.

12. Explain the function of the web-like structure of a plasmodium.

13. Under what circumstances do cellular slime molds form colonies?

14. Identify a harmful effect of a downy mildew.

15. Explain the role plankton play in most aquatic habitats.

16. Describe a characteristic of diatoms that distinguishes them from other algae.

17. What does the theory of endosymbiosis propose about how eukaryotes may have evolved from prokaryotes?

Visualizing Concepts

18. Copy the table below on a separate piece of paper and complete it.

Group	Example	Nutrition	Locomotion
Zooflagellates	*Trypanosoma*	Heterotrophic	a.
b.	*Stentor*	c.	Cilia
d.	e.	f.	none
Slime molds	*Dictyostelium*	g.	h.
Euglenoids	i.	j.	k.

Analyzing Information

19. **Analyzing Photographs** Use the photograph to help you answer the questions below.

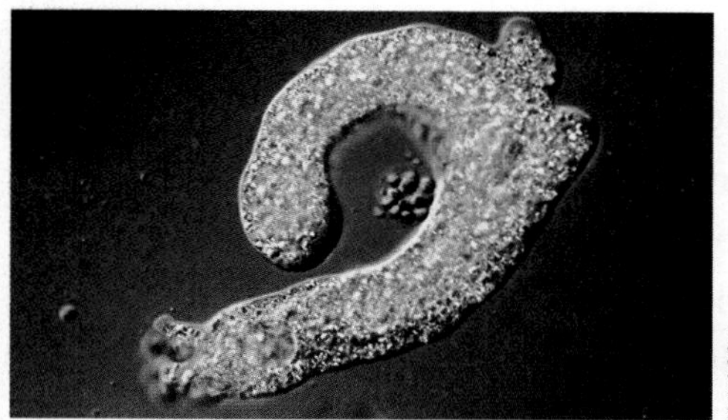

a. Explain how the organism in the photograph above obtains food.
b. Based on nutrition, to what group of protists does this organism belong?

20. **Analyzing Graphs** This graph indicates the depth that certain wavelengths (colors) of light penetrate water.

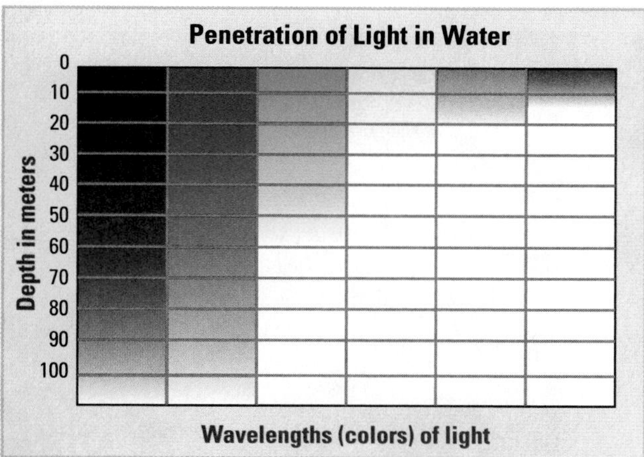

a. Which colors of light are available for photosynthesis by algae that live at a depth of 10 meters? 70 meters?
b. Green algae grow best when both blue-violet and red light are available for photosynthesis. At what depth range would you expect to find the most green algae? Explain.
c. Red algae can grow at depths of 100 meters or more. What can you infer about the type of light red algae can use for photosynthesis? Explain.

Critical Thinking

21. **Comparing and Contrasting** How are plasmodial and cellular slime molds different from one another? How are they similar to each other?

22. **Relating Cause and Effect** What advice about eating would you give to people living near the site of a red tide outbreak? Explain.

23. **Evaluating the Impact of Scientific Research** Describe the impact of molecular analysis on the classification of protists.

24. **Problem Solving** You are a healthcare worker in a clinic in the tropics. More people than usual have recently come into the clinic suffering from malaria.
a. What are some questions you could ask your patients to try to track the source of this outbreak of malaria?
b. What suggestions can you make to help reduce the occurrence of malaria in this area?

25. **What's Wrong With These Statements?** *Briefly explain why each statement is inaccurate or misleading.*
a. Slime molds are multicellular.
b. Dinoflagellates are heterotrophs.
c. Endosymbiosis is a form of sexual reproduction in protists.
d. Seaweeds are marine plants.

Performance Assessment

Biology Research Project Research, design, and create a poster to educate people about a protist-related human disease, including information about the life cycle of the protist that causes it, methods of transmission, and some methods of prevention.

Online Assessment/Test Preparation

Back Forward Reload Home Search Print Security Stop

www.biology.com

- **Chapter 17 Assessment**
  Check your understanding of the chapter concepts.
- **Standardized Test Preparation**
  Practice test-taking skills you need to succeed.

CHAPTER 18

Fungi

What do you picture when you think of a fungus? Chances are your mental image of a fungus does not resemble the graceful, curving, umbrella-like organisms in this photograph. Though some fungi have bad reputations—like poisonous mushrooms or crop-destroying parasites—fungi serve an important role in ecosystems by decomposing the wastes and the remains of other living things.

As with other kingdoms you've studied in this unit, fungi are diverse in their appearance and habitat. Before you begin the chapter, go online to the ***WebQuest*** to go on a virtual mushroom hunt and learn about some interesting fungi.

Key Concepts

Concept 18.1

Fungi are adapted for nutrition by absorption.

Concept 18.2

Kingdom Fungi consists of diverse forms.

Concept 18.3

Fungi have a major impact on other life.

Assessment

Chapter 18 Review

What's Online

www.biology.com

WebQuest
FungiQuest

Online Activity 18.1
Calculate fungal growth rate.

Science, Technology, & Society
Discovery of Giant Fungi

Online Activity 18.2
Explore the major groups of fungi.

Lab 18 Online Companion
A Twist on Fermentation

Online Activity 18.3
Investigate other fungal forms.

Chapter 18 Assessment

CONCEPT 18.1 Fungi are adapted for nutrition by absorption.

OBJECTIVES
- Describe the basic structure of fungi.
- Explain the function of spores in fungal reproduction.

KEY TERMS
- hypha
- mycelium
- absorptive nutrition
- spore

Seeing fungi growing on wet leaves or on a fallen log, you might assume they are some type of plant. But based on cell structure, molecular comparisons, reproduction, and modes of nutrition, fungi are not closely related to plants. They are assigned their own kingdom. In fact, DNA comparisons show that fungi are more closely related to you than they are to plants!

Structure and Function of Fungi

Fungi have body structures and modes of reproduction unlike those of any other eukaryotic organisms. The bodies of most fungi are made of structures called hyphae (singular, *hypha*). **Hyphae** are tiny threads of cytoplasm surrounded by a plasma membrane and covered by a cell wall (Figure 18-1). The cell walls of fungi differ from the cellulose cell walls of plants. Most fungi build their cell walls out of chitin, a strong, flexible polysaccharide that is also found in the external skeletons of insects.

The hyphae of most fungi have additional cell walls, called cross-walls, that divide the long filaments into many separate end-to-end cells. This makes most fungi multicellular. The cross-walls of many fungi have pores large enough to allow ribosomes, mitochondria, and even nuclei to flow from cell to cell. The movement of cytoplasm from one cell to another helps a fungus distribute nutrients from one part of its body to another.

The hyphae of a single fungus typically branch as they grow, forming an interwoven mat called a **mycelium** (plural, *mycelia*). The mycelium functions as the feeding structure of a fungus. Its fibrous structure maximizes contact with the food source. Fungi cannot run, swim, or fly in search of food. But the mycelium makes up for the fungus's lack of mobility by its ability to grow rapidly throughout a food source. A fungal mycelium can grow as much as a kilometer of hyphae each day as it branches within its food.

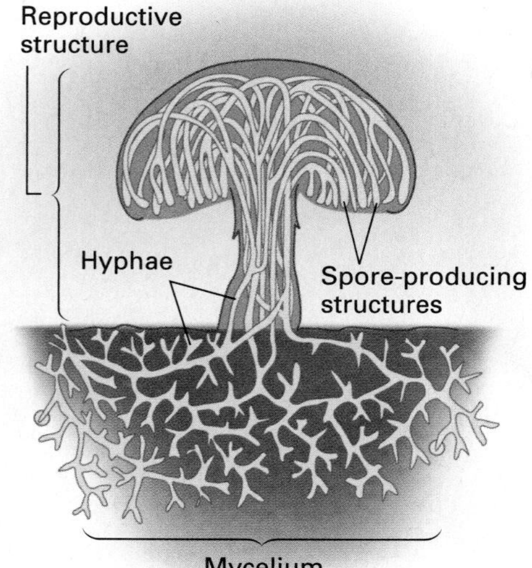

Figure 18-1 The "mushroom" that you see above ground is the reproductive structure of the fungus. This structure consists of numerous hyphae that also extend below ground, where they form the mycelium.

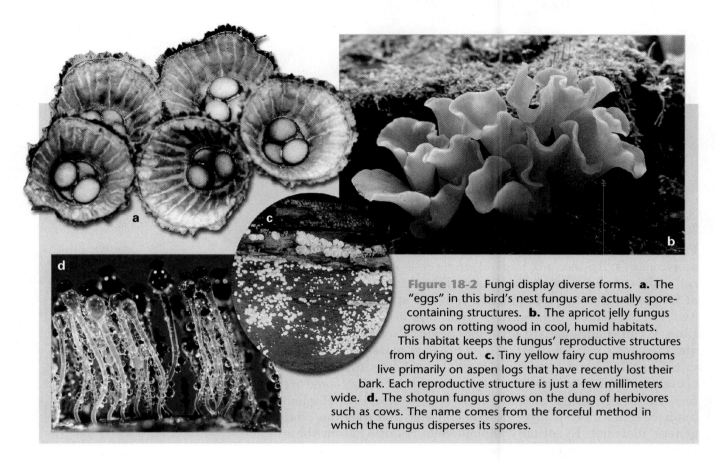

Figure 18-2 Fungi display diverse forms. **a.** The "eggs" in this bird's nest fungus are actually spore-containing structures. **b.** The apricot jelly fungus grows on rotting wood in cool, humid habitats. This habitat keeps the fungus' reproductive structures from drying out. **c.** Tiny yellow fairy cup mushrooms live primarily on aspen logs that have recently lost their bark. Each reproductive structure is just a few millimeters wide. **d.** The shotgun fungus grows on the dung of herbivores such as cows. The name comes from the forceful method in which the fungus disperses its spores.

Mycelia can be huge. Scientists have discovered one enormous mycelium in Oregon that measures 5.5 kilometers across and spreads through almost 9 square kilometers of forest (larger than 1,600 football fields). Scientists also estimate that this fungus is at least 2,400 years old, qualifying it as one of Earth's oldest and largest living organisms.

A mycelium is an efficient structure for the heterotrophic lifestyle of fungi. The branching mycelium enables the fungus to obtain food by **absorptive nutrition,** a method by which the fungus absorbs small organic molecules from its surroundings. First, the fungus digests food outside its mycelium by secreting powerful enzymes into its surroundings. These enzymes break down complex molecules into smaller molecules the mycelium can absorb.

The more than 100,000 known species of fungi have a great diversity of size, shape, and color (Figure 18-2). Many fungi play an important role as decomposers. Like some of the bacteria you read about in Chapter 16, fungi recycle nutrients such as nitrogen and carbon by breaking down organic material. Common food sources for fungi are fallen logs, bodies of dead animals, or the wastes of living organisms. In contrast, some species of fungi are parasites. These parasitic fungi absorb nutrients from the cells or body fluids of living hosts. Parasitic fungi cause about 80 percent of all plant diseases.

Science, Technology, & Society

www.biology.com

Discovery of Giant Fungi

What is the largest fungus you have ever seen? For many people, the answer to this question is most likely a hamburger-sized mushroom, called a portabella, at the grocery store. But scientists have recently discovered some truly giant fungi. Find out more about fungi and how they grow when you go online.

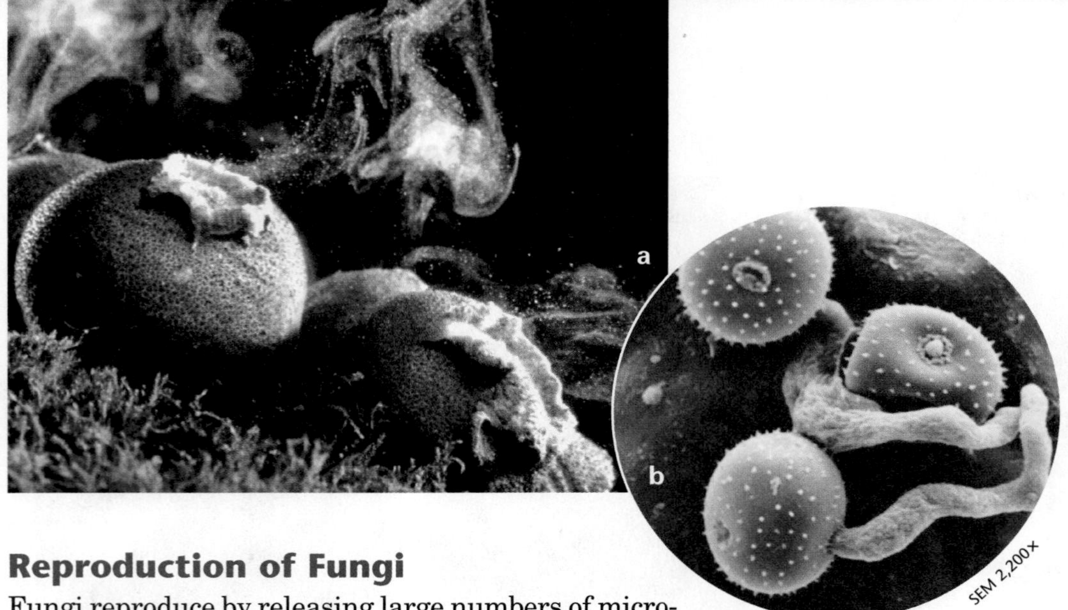

Figure 18-3 Spore dispersal is critical to the success of a fungus. **a.** A single raindrop or a nearby footstep is enough agitation to release spores in some species of mushrooms, such as these "puffballs." **b.** This micrograph shows round mold spores germinating on a plant leaf. Note the extension of hyphae that will form new mycelia.

Reproduction of Fungi

Fungi reproduce by releasing large numbers of microscopic spores. **Spores** are haploid single cells with thick cell walls that function as the dispersal stage in the reproduction of fungi. These tough reproductive cells are spread by the wind and can withstand unfavorable conditions for long periods of time. When conditions are favorable again, they can germinate and grow into new fungi. Most fungi produce spores asexually by mitosis at the tips of specialized hyphae. In these situations, the spores are haploid because the hyphae from which they come are haploid. Many fungi also produce spores sexually. Haploid hyphae from different mycelia fuse together and combine their genetic material. Eventually, diploid cells resulting from these pairings undergo meiosis. These meiotic divisions produce haploid spores.

One fungus can produce a mind-boggling output of spores. For example, puffballs, which are the reproductive structures of certain fungi, can puff out clouds containing trillions of spores (Figure 18-3). Spores can be transported easily over great distances by wind or water, which accounts for the wide geographic distribution of many species of fungi. The airborne spores of fungi have been found more than 200 kilometers above Earth's surface. Spores that land in environments where there is moisture and food can absorb water and nutrients and produce a new mycelium.

Online Activity 18.1

Calculate fungal growth rate. How fast do fungi grow? Go online to watch a time-lapse video and calculate the rate of fungal growth. Then observe a fungus releasing spores.

Concept Check 18.1

1. What features of a mycelium make it an efficient structure to obtain food by absorption?
2. Describe the function of fungal spores.

CONCEPT 18.2 Kingdom Fungi consists of diverse forms.

OBJECTIVES

- Compare and contrast the zygote fungi, sac fungi, and club fungi.
- Distinguish the yeasts from other groups of fungi.
- Explain how molds differ in lifestyle from other fungi.

KEY TERMS

- sporangia
- zygosporangium
- dikaryotic
- fruiting body
- yeast
- imperfect fungi
- mold

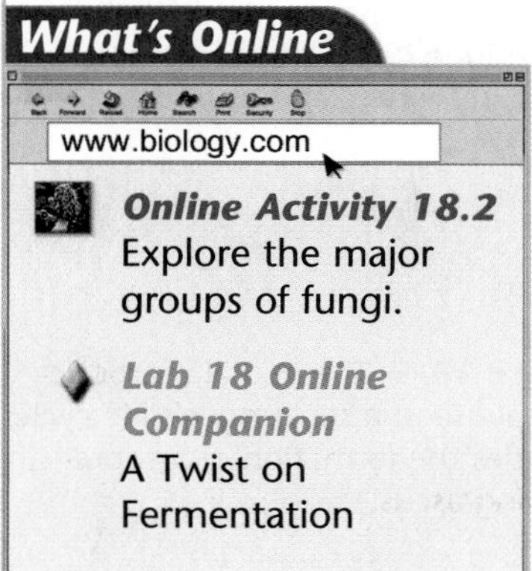

How diverse is the fungus kingdom? In size alone, fungi range from microscopic organisms to single organisms that are larger than a golf course. The major groups of fungi are distinguished primarily by their life cycles and by structures related to reproduction.

The Zygote Fungi

The fuzzy black growth often found on "moldy" bread is actually one of several species of fungi that readily grow on bread. One example is *Rhizopus stolonifer,* which belongs to a group called the zygote fungi. Zygote fungi are mostly terrestrial and live in soil or on decaying plant and animal material. When food is available, the fungus's hyphae spread out over the food and absorb nutrients. Under these conditions the fungus reproduces asexually via **sporangia** (singular, *sporangium*), spore-forming structures at the tips of the hyphae. When the food supply of a zygote fungus becomes depleted, it reproduces sexually. The "parents" in a sexual union are mycelia that are identical in appearance, but contain different genetic material. When the mycelia of the two parents come together, they form a thick-walled reproductive structure called a **zygosporangium** (Figure 18-4). Within the zygosporangium, nuclei from the two parents fuse and form diploid nuclei. The zygosporangium is able to tolerate long periods of drying or freezing. When conditions become favorable, the diploid nuclei undergo meiosis and produce haploid spores. The spores are then released and can grow into new hyphae.

Figure 18-4 The sexual reproduction of zygote fungi includes the fusion of mycelia from two different fungi. The product is a hardy zygosporangium.

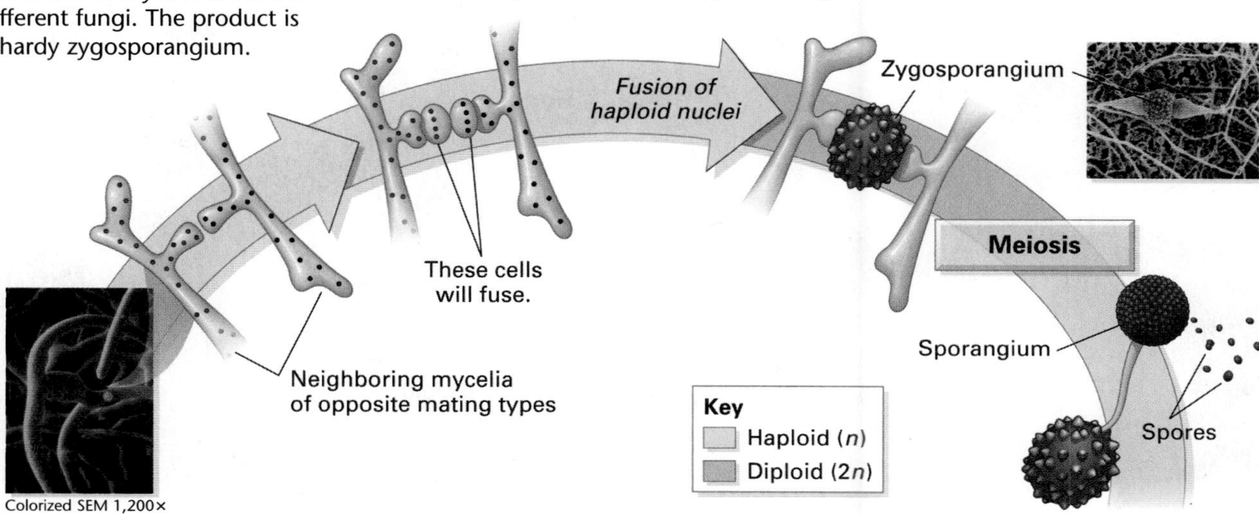

The Sac Fungi

Sac fungi live in marine, freshwater, and terrestrial habitats. They range in size from single-celled species to large morels such as those shown in Figure 18-5. Sac fungi get their name from a specialized reproductive structure or "sac," called an ascus, which contains spore cells. Like the zygote fungi, sac fungi usually reproduce asexually when conditions are suitable, and sexually when conditions become harsh. Asexual reproduction in sac fungi produces an enormous number of spores. These asexual spores are formed externally in long chains or clusters at the tips of specialized hyphae.

Also like zygote fungi, sexual reproduction in sac fungi involves the joining of two genetically different mycelia. This produces **dikaryotic** hyphae in which each cell has two separate nuclei, one from each parent fungus. The dikaryotic hyphae grow into a large aboveground reproductive structure called a **fruiting body** (Figure 18-6). An ascus develops at the tip of each specialized hypha in the fruiting body. Within the ascus the dikaryotic nuclei fuse, forming a single diploid nucleus. The diploid nucleus then undergoes meiosis and forms haploid spores.

Notice that the zygote undergoes meiosis before spores develop. Although these spores are haploid, they are the result of sexual reproduction (the fusion of genetically different mycelia). Therefore these haploid spores contain varied genetic information. This contrasts with the genetically identical spores found in asexual reproduction.

Some species of sac fungi are the most devastating of plant parasites. For example, the American chestnut tree has virtually disappeared from the landscape due to a sac fungus called *Endothia parasitica* that causes chestnut blight.

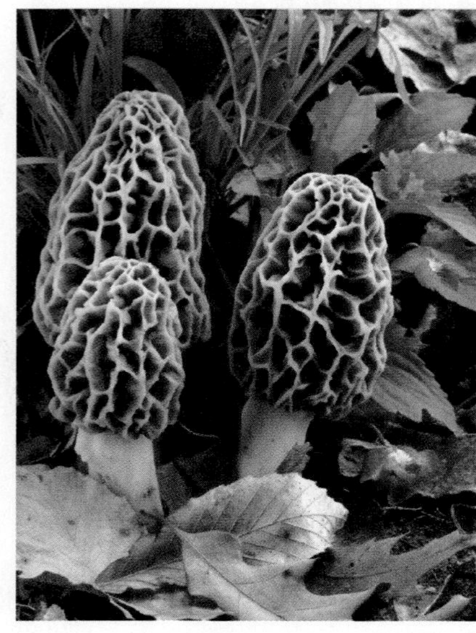

▲ **Figure 18-5** *Morchella* is the name for a group of relatively large sac fungi commonly called "morels." Within the honeycombed "flesh" of the fruiting body are sac-shaped structures where spores form.

▼ **Figure 18-6** The sexual reproduction phase of a sac fungus's life cycle includes the formation of a spore-forming ascus.

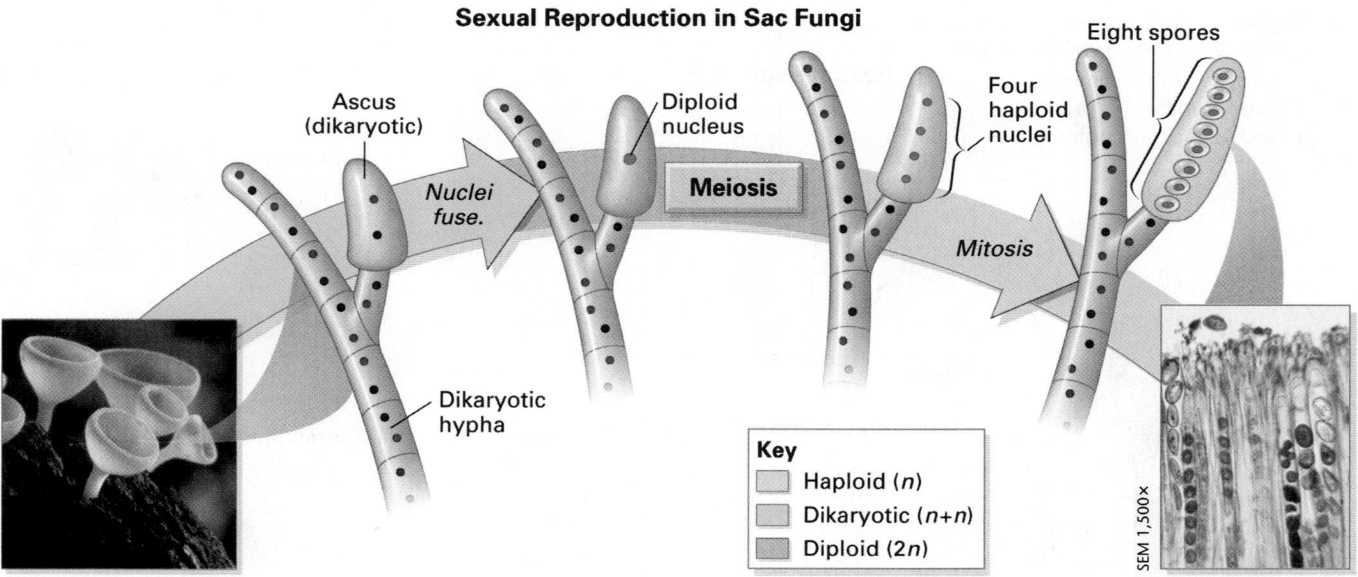

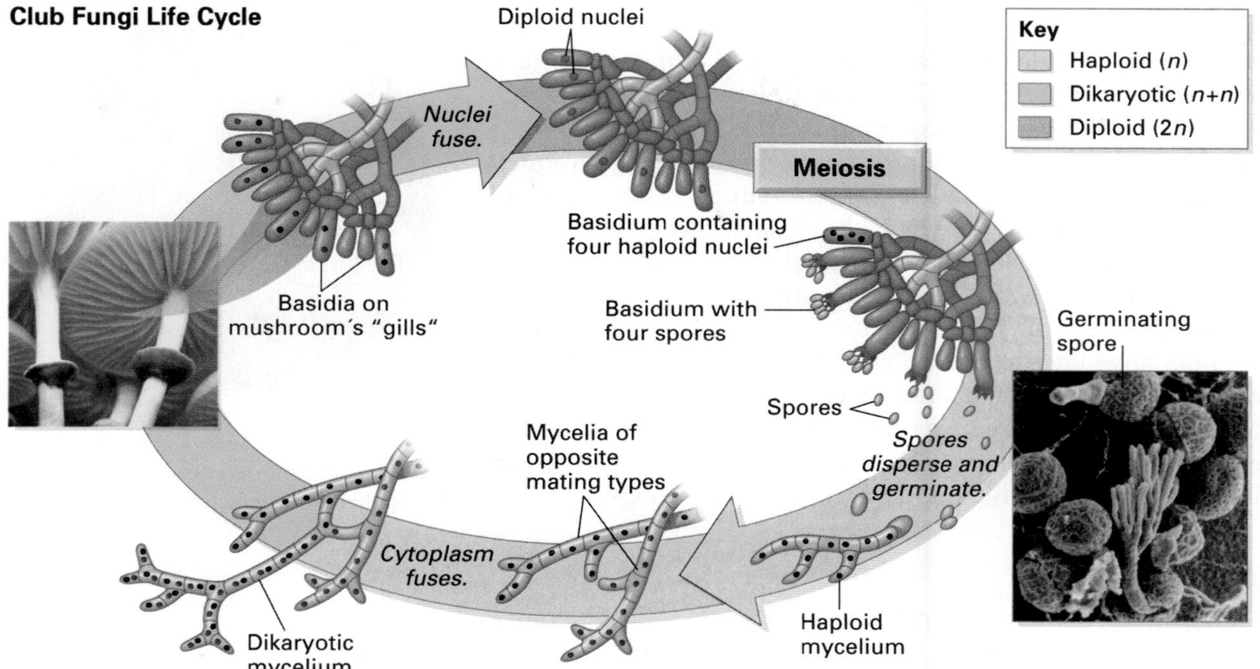

▲ **Figure 18-7** Club fungi primarily reproduce by sexual reproduction. Genetically different mycelia fuse and form dikaryotic mycelia. These grow into the umbrella-shaped structures commonly called mushrooms.

The Club Fungi

The fungi that are probably most familiar to you, mushrooms, puffballs, and rusts, are classified as club fungi. For example, *Agaricus bisporus* is a club fungus that is the commercial mushroom most often sold in grocery stores. Club fungi are named for their club-shaped, spore-producing structure called a basidium. Many club fungi are important decomposers of wood and other plant material. In many ecosystems they play a key role by breaking down the wood of weak, damaged, or dead trees. Other species of club fungi are plant parasites.

You can follow the life cycle of a club fungus in Figure 18-7. Spores are most often formed by sexual reproduction in club fungi. (Asexual reproduction is less common in club fungi than in sac fungi.) The spores drop from the "gills" on the underside of the mushroom and are carried by wind or by contact with animals. If the spores land in a favorable environment, they germinate and form a haploid mycelium. This mycelium may mate with another, starting the cycle over again.

Mycelia can sometimes grow so rapidly that a full-sized mushroom can appear in just a few hours. Once a mycelium begins to grow in an open field, it may grow outward equally in all directions. Mushrooms develop at the outer edge of the mycelium and, therefore, often appear in a circular ring, sometimes called a fairy ring (Figure 18-8). All the mushrooms in the ring are connected to the same mycelium beneath the ground. The fairy ring slowly increases in diameter as the mycelium advances and grows new mushrooms.

▼ **Figure 18-8** The mushrooms shown here grow at the outer edge of an underground fungal mycelium. Such an arrangement is often called a fairy ring.

Yeasts

Single-celled fungi, called **yeasts,** inhabit liquid or moist habitats including plant sap and animal tissues. Yeasts reproduce asexually, by simple cell division or by the pinching of small "buds" off a parent cell (Figure 18-9). Some yeast species also reproduce sexually by forming an ascus or a basidium and are classified as sac fungi or club fungi. Other yeasts have never been observed to reproduce sexually. These and other fungi with no known sexual stage of reproduction are placed in an informal category called the **imperfect fungi.**

Humans have used yeasts to raise bread dough and ferment alcoholic beverages for thousands of years. For example, baker's yeast (*Saccharomyces cerevisiae*) is a sac fungus that carries out fermentation, as you read in Chapter 7. The yeast cells release small bubbles of carbon dioxide that cause bread dough to rise.

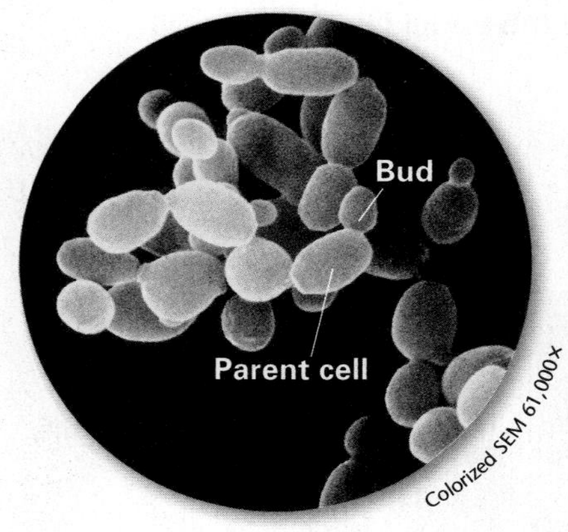

▲ **Figure 18-9** Some yeasts reproduce by budding. Each "bud" cell is genetically identical to the parent.

Molds

Any fungus that grows very rapidly on a surface is generally referred to as a **mold** (Figure 18-10). Such rapid growth usually involves asexual reproduction. Some molds are included with the imperfect fungi because they have no known sexual stage. However, many molds do have sexual stages that place them as zygote, sac, or club fungi. For example, the zygote fungus *Rhizopus,* which you read about earlier, is a common bread "mold." *Penicillium,* a sac fungus, is another common mold that often grows on fruit. One species of *Penicillium* is the source of the antibiotic penicillin. For the fungus, the antibiotic keeps bacteria from growing near it and competing for food.

Mold spores are airborne and are found almost everywhere. Warm, moist environments are ideal for spore germination and mold growth. Even the cellulose in paper and book covers provide ample nutrition for certain molds. Molds can also damage clothing, leather, paint, and even many plastics.

▼ **Figure 18-10** This holiday pumpkin has become host to a mold.

Online Activity 18.2

Explore the major groups of fungi.
Go online to find out more about zygote, sac, and club fungi, and yeast. Examine different specimens and learn details of their common characteristics and habitats. Then identify mystery fungi.

Concept Check 18.2

1. Create a table comparing and contrasting the reproductive structures and processes of the zygote fungi, sac fungi, and club fungi.
2. How are yeasts different from other fungi?
3. What characteristic defines a fungus as a mold?

A Twist on Fermentation

Studying the Rate of Yeast Growth in Dough

Question How does sugar concentration affect the rate of yeast fermentation?

Lab Overview In this investigation you will make small batches of yeast dough containing varying amounts of sugar. Then you will measure and compare the rates at which the batches of dough rise in small cylinders.

Preparing for the Lab To help you prepare for the investigation, go to the *Lab 18 Online Companion.* ···➔ Find out more about the structure of yeast cells, and discover how they make dough rise. Prepare for the lab procedure by previewing the steps you will take.

Completing the Lab Use your Laboratory Manual or lab page printouts from the *Lab 18 Online Companion* to do the investigation and analyze your results. **CAUTION:** *Be sure to follow your teacher's instructions and all safety guidelines in the investigation.*

Lab 18 Online Companion

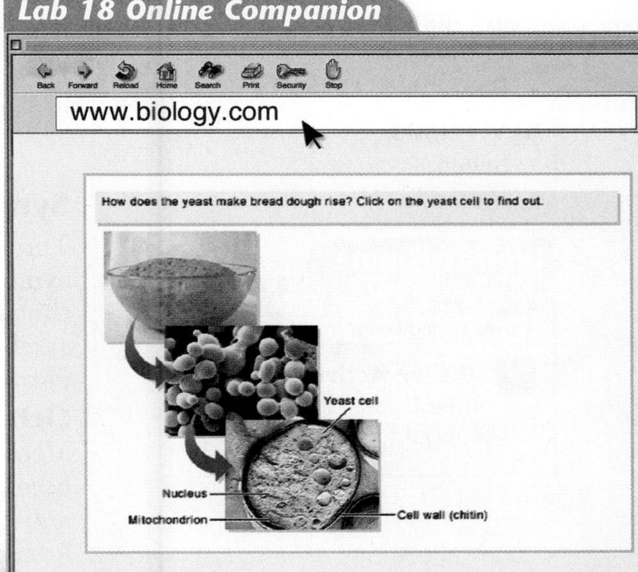

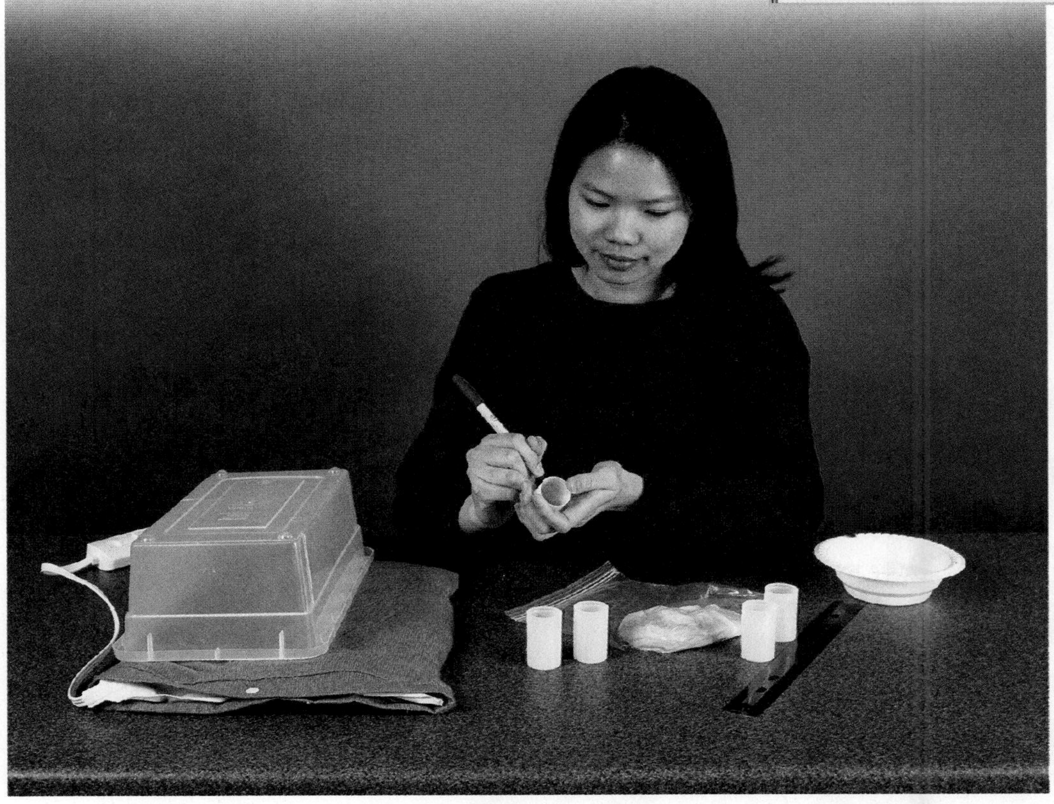

CONCEPT 18.3 Fungi have a major impact on other life.

OBJECTIVES
- Describe two examples of symbiotic fungi.
- Identify some fungal diseases of plants and of humans.
- Describe some human uses of fungi.
- Explain the role of fungi in recycling organic matter.

KEY TERMS
- lichen
- mycorrhizae

What's Online

Online Activity 18.3
Investigate other fungal forms.

As you have read, some fungi are used to make certain foods or can be eaten in their natural forms. Other fungi have less positive effects on humans. For example, if you have ever suffered from athlete's foot, you are familiar with an annoying fungus. In fact, fungi cause many diseases in animals and plants. But whether their effect is delicious or damaging, fungi play important roles in ecosystems.

Symbiotic Fungi

Throughout this unit you have read about many examples of symbiosis, a close relationship between two different species that benefits at least one of them. Recall that mutualism is a symbiotic relationship in which both organisms benefit. Fungi participate in a number of important mutualistic relationships.

Lichens A **lichen** is a mutualistic pairing of a fungus and an alga. Lichens are striking examples of how two species can become so merged that the result is essentially a new life form. At a distance, it is easy to mistake lichens growing on rocks, rotting logs, trees, or roofs for mosses (Figure 18-11). But a lichen actually consists of millions of tiny algal cells within a mesh of fungal hyphae (Figure 18-12 on the facing page). The photosynthetic algae feed the fungus. The fungal mycelium, in turn, provides a suitable habitat for the algae, helping to absorb and retain water and minerals. The fungal component of lichens is usually a sac fungus, though there are several club fungus lichens. The photosynthetic partners are usually green algae or cyanobacteria. The partnership is so complete that biologists have actually described and named more than 25,000 "species" of lichens, as though they are individual organisms.

One benefit of symbiosis is that lichens are able to live in environments where neither fungi nor algae could live alone. Lichens are important pioneer organisms on newly cleared rock and soil surfaces, such as burned forests and volcanic flows. Additionally, in the arctic tundra, caribou graze on lichens at times of the year when other foods are unavailable.

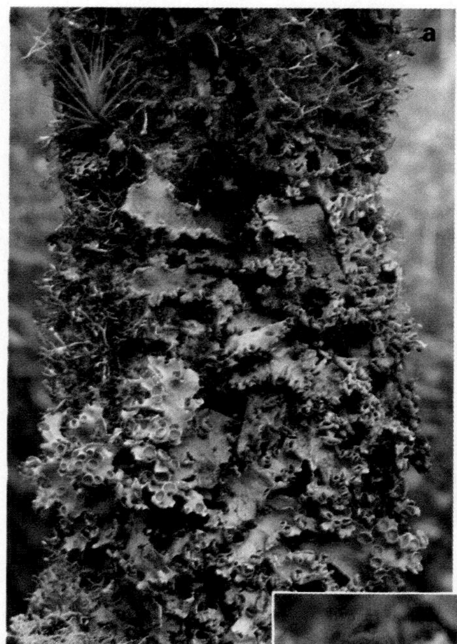

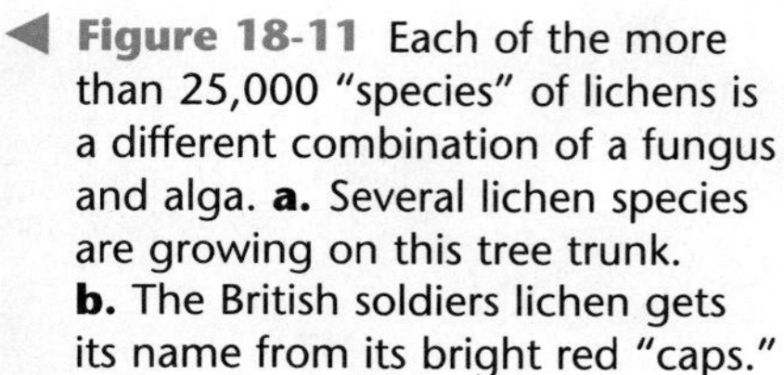

Figure 18-11 Each of the more than 25,000 "species" of lichens is a different combination of a fungus and alga. **a.** Several lichen species are growing on this tree trunk. **b.** The British soldiers lichen gets its name from its bright red "caps."

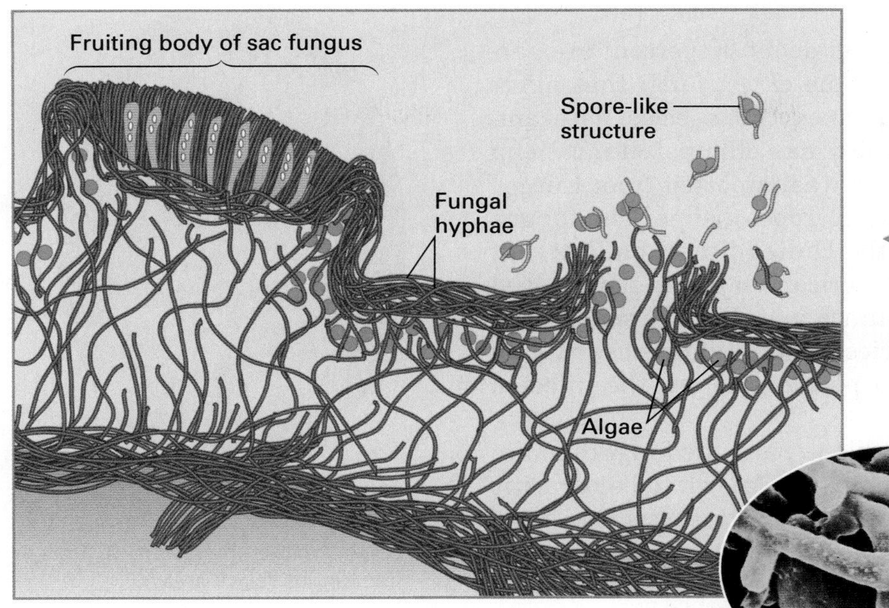

Figure 18-12 All lichens have a similar structure. Algal cells live within the interwoven mycelium of a fungus. The particular species of alga and fungus give each lichen its unique properties.

As tough as lichens are, however, many do not tolerate air pollution. Their absorption of minerals from rain and moist air makes them particularly sensitive to chemicals such as sulfur dioxide. The death of sensitive lichens in an area can be an early warning of poor air quality.

Mycorrhizae The evolution of fungi also led to important symbiotic relationships with most land plants. **Mycorrhizae** are symbiotic relationships between fungal hyphae and plant roots. The fungi absorb water and essential minerals from the soil and provide these materials to the plant. You can see in Figure 18-13 that the fungal mycelium greatly increases the surface area of the root in contact with the soil. This increases the plant's absorption of water and minerals. The sugars produced by the plant, in turn, nourish the fungi.

The importance of mycorrhizae is evident in the number of plants that have them and from the fact that they are found on some of the oldest plant fossils. Almost all plants have mycorrhizae. Nearly half of all mushroom-forming club fungi live as mycorrhizae with oak, birch, and pine trees. The mushrooms you see around the bases of these trees are the surface evidence of the underground symbiotic relationship between plants and fungi.

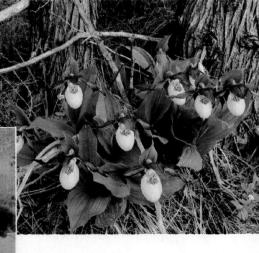

Figure 18-13 Some plants, such as *Cypripedium calceolus* (yellow lady's slipper), can only grow if mycorrhizae are present. The close-up shows the close relationship between the plant roots (thicker tubes) and the mycelium (thin threads).

Disease-causing Fungi

Of the 100,000 known species of fungi about 30 percent are parasites, mostly on or in plants. In some cases, fungi that infect plants have literally changed landscapes. One species, for example, causes Dutch elm disease, which has eliminated most elm trees in North America. The fungus was imported from Europe where it caused a minor disease in European elms. The fungus was accidentally introduced into the United States on logs sent from Europe after World War I. American elms had not evolved with this fungus and had no resistance to it. Fungi are also serious agricultural pests. Some species infect grain crops, ruining the harvest or causing disease in people who eat the infected grain (Figure 18-14).

▲ **Figure 18-14** This wheat plant has been damaged by rye ergot, a parasitic fungus (black areas).

Animals are much less susceptible to parasitic fungi than are plants. Only about 50 species of fungus are known to be parasitic in humans and other animals. Among these are yeast infections of the lungs, some of which can be fatal. Other fungal parasites produce a skin disease called ringworm, so named because it appears as circular red areas on the skin. Most commonly, these fungi attack the feet and cause intense itching and sometimes blisters. This condition, known as athlete's foot, is highly contagious, but it can be treated with various fungicides. Fungicides are substances that kill fungi without seriously harming the host organism.

Commercial Uses of Fungi

Focusing only on disease-causing fungi would give an unfair picture of the kingdom. There are many practical uses for fungi. In addition to edible mushrooms, other edible fungi include truffles (Figure 18-15). These fungi grow underground as the reproductive structures of sac fungus mycorrhizae. In nature, truffles release strong odors that attract mammals and insects that dig up the fungi and disperse their spores. Truffle hunters take advantage of those odors and use pigs or dogs to locate their prizes.

◀ **Figure 18-15** Truffles are edible sac fungi that grow underground. This truffle-sniffing dog has located a source of truffles by their strong aroma. The cross section of a truffle (inset) reveals its tightly packed hyphae.

However, since truffles cost hundreds of dollars per kilogram, you probably won't get a chance to do a taste test in the school cafeteria.

The distinctive flavors of certain kinds of cheeses come from the fungi used to "ripen" them (Figure 18-16). As mentioned earlier, yeasts are particularly important in baking, brewing, and winemaking. And a number of antibiotics also come from fungi.

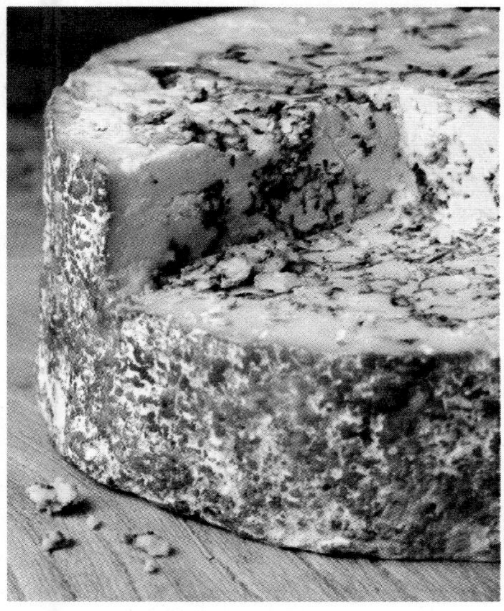

▲ **Figure 18-16** Cheese makers inject a certain strain of *Penicillium* into the young cheese, which "ripens" into blue cheese. The fungus grows as the cheese ripens, producing its characteristic taste.

The Role of Fungi in Chemical Cycling

Fungi and bacteria are the principal decomposers that supply ecosystems with the nutrients essential for plant growth. Without decomposers, elements such as carbon and nitrogen would accumulate in organic matter. Plants and the animals they feed would starve because elements taken from the soil would not be returned.

From the human perspective, there is also a destructive side to fungi. Fungi destroy 10–50 percent of the world's fruit harvest each year. Similarly, a wood-digesting fungus does not distinguish between a fallen oak limb and the oak planks of a boat. During the Revolutionary War, the British lost more ships to fungal rot than to enemy attack. Soldiers in the tropics during World War II watched as their tents, clothing, boots, and even the glue that holds binocular lenses in place were destroyed by molds. Some fungi can even decompose plastic.

Fungi are well adapted as decomposers (Figure 18-17). Their hyphae invade the tissues and cells of nonliving organic matter and break down complex molecules such as cellulose. Fungi, in concert with bacteria and some animals, are responsible for the complete breakdown of organic material. The air is so loaded with fungal spores that as soon as a leaf falls or an insect dies, it is covered with spores that quickly grow into fungal hyphae.

▶ **Figure 18-17** Club fungi such as *Pholiota aurivella* produce specialized enzymes that break down the cellulose in wood. This is an important step in recycling the chemical elements in organic matter.

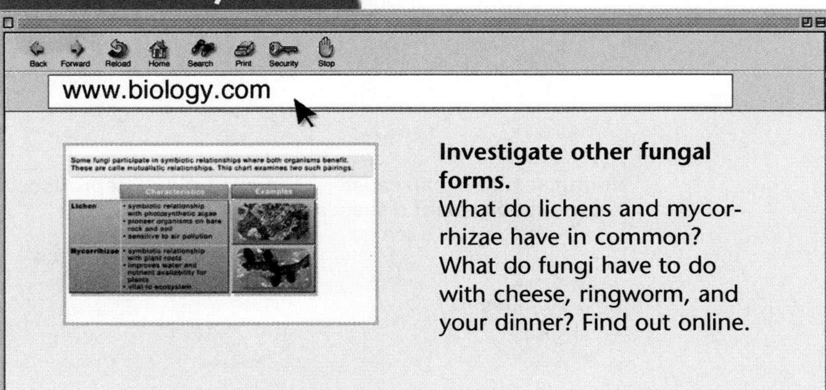

Back Forward Reload Home Search Print Security Stop
www.biology.com
Investigate other fungal forms.
What do lichens and mycorrhizae have in common? What do fungi have to do with cheese, ringworm, and your dinner? Find out online.

Concept Check 18.3

1. Identify the species that make up lichens and mycorrhizae.
2. Name and describe one fungal disease of plants and one of humans.
3. Describe two ways that fungi are economically beneficial.
4. In what way do ecosystems depend on fungi?

Multiple Choice

Choose the letter of the best answer.

1. The fine threads that make up the bodies of most fungi are called
   a. spores.
   b. hyphae.
   c. cell walls.
   d. sporangia.

2. The main function of a mycelium is to
   a. maximize contact with a food source.
   b. produce spores.
   c. flavor cheese.
   d. make bread rise.

3. The portion of a fungus that you see above the ground is usually the
   a. mycelium.
   b. reproductive structure.
   c. mycorrhizae.
   d. hyphae.

4. A dikaryotic fungal cell has two
   a. spores.
   b. nuclei.
   c. hyphae.
   d. fruiting bodies.

5. A fungus that has an asexual life cycle and no known sexual phase is called
   a. a zygote fungus.
   b. a sac fungus.
   c. an imperfect fungus.
   d. a club fungus.

6. The two symbiotic organisms found in a lichen are
   a. a fungus and an animal.
   b. a fungus and a mold.
   c. a fungus and a plant.
   d. a fungus and an alga.

7. Which of the following is *not* caused by a parasitic fungus?
   a. ringworm
   b. rye ergot
   c. Dutch elm disease
   d. formation of mychorrizae

Short Answer

8. What is a mycelium? Describe its function.

9. Describe how fungi digest food and absorb nutrients.

10. State the function of fungal spores.

11. Compare and contrast the sexual reproductive structures of sac and club fungi.

12. Explain what a dikaryotic hypha is and how it is formed.

13. Explain how one type of fungus is used to make bread.

14. Explain the symbiotic relationship that exists between the organisms that make up lichens.

15. What are mycorrhizae? Describe their function.

16. Explain the role fungi play in chemical cycling.

Visualizing Concepts

17. On a separate sheet of paper copy the concept map below and fill in the blank spaces.

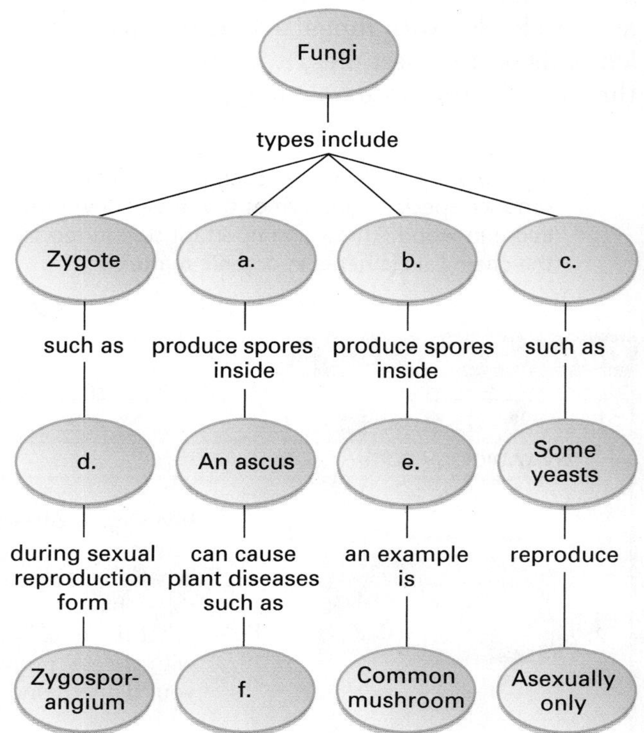

Analyzing Information

18. Analyzing Diagrams The drawing below represents one stage in the life cycle of a club fungus.

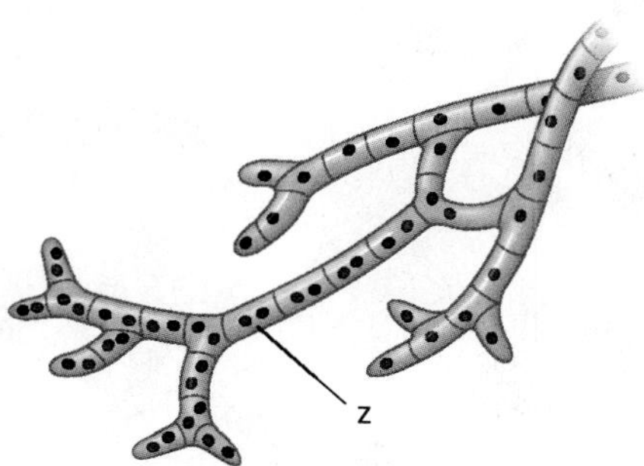

a. What type of mycelium is illustrated by structure *z*?
b. Describe what must happen in order for this structure to form.
c. Are the nuclei in the cells haploid or diploid?
d. Explain how this stage of the club fungus's life cycle introduces genetic variation.

19. Analyzing Diagrams The diagram shows a cross section of a fungus.

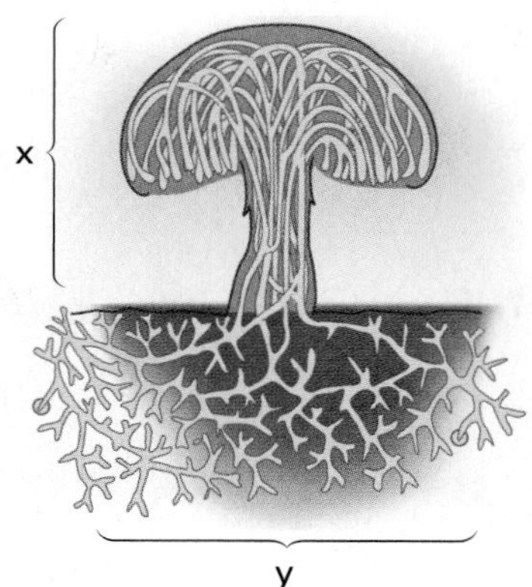

a. What is the name of structure *x*? Describe its function.
b. What is the name of structure *y*? Describe its function.
c. What information would you need to classify this fungus into its correct group?

Critical Thinking

20. Developing Hypotheses Many people are allergic to molds and mold spores. Often, these allergies flair up even if the person is outdoors in fresh air, where no mold growth can be seen. Explain why the allergic reaction can still take place.

21. Relating Cause and Effect You observe mold and bacteria growing together in the same petri dish. After a few days the bacteria growth covers the entire surface and the mold seems no longer to be growing. What conclusions can you draw about the mold and its secretion of antibiotic?

22. Comparing and Contrasting Describe one example of a mutually beneficial symbiotic relationship between a fungus and another organism. Give an example of a parasitic fungal relationship. Describe the differences in the two relationships.

23. Relating Cause and Effect In which rooms of a house would you predict that the growth of mold is most likely to occur? Explain.

24. What's Wrong With These Statements? *Briefly explain why each statement is inaccurate or misleading.*
a. A hypha consists of mycelia.
b. Fungi reproduce through diploid spores.
c. Imperfect fungi reproduce sexually.
d. Ringworm is a symbiotic fungus.

Performance Assessment

Design an Experiment Design an experiment that would test the hypothesis that the fungus called bread mold (*Rhizopus stolonifer*) is spread by airborne spores.

Online Assessment/Test Preparation

Back Forward Reload Home Search Print Security Stop

www.biology.com

- **Chapter 18 Assessment**
  Check your understanding of the chapter concepts.
- **Standardized Test Preparation**
  Practice test-taking skills you need to succeed.

UNIT 6 Exploring Plants

Chapters

Lush plant growth in Monte Verde Rainforest Park, Costa Rica

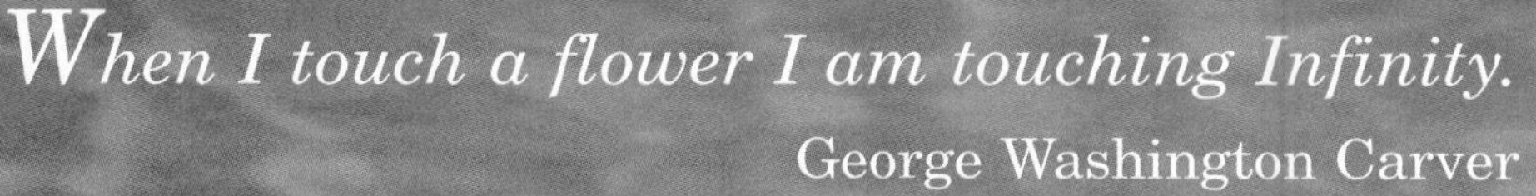

When I touch a flower I am touching Infinity.

George Washington Carver

Plant Diversity

The towering trees and densely tangled undergrowth of this wooded scene may look like they've been growing forever. Yet, land plants have only been around for a small fraction of Earth's history. If you think of Earth's history being condensed into one calendar year, life existed only in aquatic environments from March through September. By then, photosynthetic bacteria were beginning to colonize the moist soil surrounding bodies of water. But not until mid-November did plants begin to colonize land. This greening of the land transformed the biosphere. In this chapter, you will learn how plants colonized land and examine the diversity of modern plants. But first, go online to the *WebQuest* to explore how certain rain-forest plants have provided lifesaving medicines.

Key Concepts

Concept 19.1

Land plants evolved from green algae.

Concept 19.2

Mosses and other bryophytes were the first land plants.

Concept 19.3

Ferns and other pteridophytes are seedless vascular plants.

Concept 19.4

Pollen and seeds evolved in gymnosperms.

Concept 19.5

Flowers and fruits evolved in angiosperms.

Assessment

Chapter 19 Review

What's Online

www.biology.com

WebQuest
RainforestQuest

Online Activity 19.1
Drain a pond.

Online Activity 19.2
Explore mosses.

Online Activity 19.3
Explore ferns.

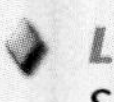

Lab 19 Online Companion
Seeds, Spores, and Sperm

Online Activity 19.4
Explore gymnosperms.

Online Activity 19.5
Explore angiosperms.

Science, Technology, & Society
Rainforest Conservation

Chapter 19 Assessment

CONCEPT 19.1 Land plants evolved from green algae.

OBJECTIVES

- Describe the hypothesis that proposes how plants evolved from algae.
- Describe four challenges to plants living on land.
- Identify the four major groups of plants.
- Explain the phrase "alternation of generations."

KEY TERMS

- plant
- vascular tissue
- lignin
- cuticle
- stomata
- ovary
- gametophyte
- sporophyte
- alternation of generations

What's Online

Figure 19-1 Charophytes such as this branching green alga are probably the closest relatives of modern plant species.

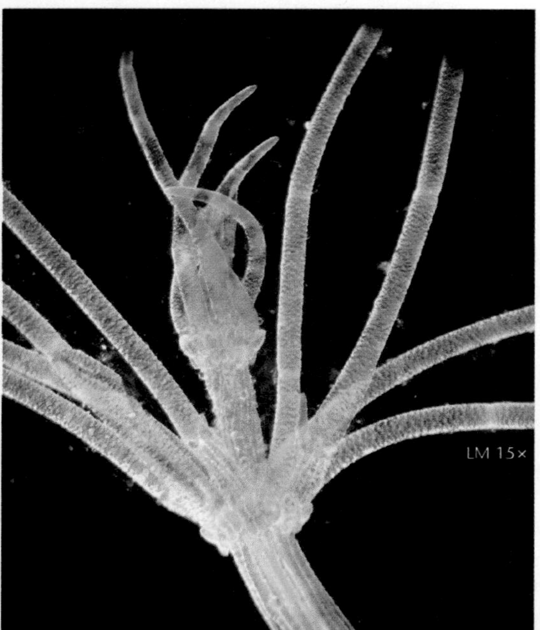

What is a plant? You might say that you know one when you see one. But plants include an enormous range of very diverse organisms, from mosses to ferns to wildflowers to pine trees. Plants are multicellular, usually photosynthetic, mostly land-dwelling organisms that are very different from their green algae ancestors.

The Origin of Plants from Algae

Based on molecular, cellular, and anatomical comparisons, the closest modern relatives of the ancestors of plants are the multicellular green algae called charophytes (Figure 19-1). Many species of modern charophytes (KAYR oh fyts) are found in shallow fresh water around the edges of ponds and lakes. Biologists hypothesize that some ancient charophytes may have lived in similar shallow-water habitats that occasionally dried out. Natural selection would have favored individual algae that could survive these dry periods.

Adaptations enabling permanent life on dry land apparently accumulated by about 475 million years ago, the age of the oldest plant fossils. Modern plants diversified from those early descendants of green algae. A **plant** is a multicellular autotroph in which the embryo develops within the female parent.

Challenges of Life on Land

Most of the differences between plants and charophytes are related to the plants' adaptations to life on land. There are four major challenges to plants living on land: obtaining resources, staying upright, maintaining moisture, and reproducing.

Obtaining Resources From Two Places at Once Algae and other aquatic organisms acquire the resources they need from the surrounding water. In contrast, the resources required by a photosynthetic organism growing on land are found in two very different environments: air and soil. Light and carbon dioxide are mainly available above ground, while water and mineral nutrients are found mainly in the soil. The bodies of most plants have specialized organ systems—shoots and roots—that provide access to these two environments (Figure 19-2 on the facing page).

Below ground, a plant's roots absorb water and essential minerals from the soil. Above ground, shoots bear leaves. Leaves use sunlight as an energy source to make food from carbon dioxide, as you learned in Chapter 8. Most plants transport materials between their roots and shoots within **vascular tissue,** a system of tube-shaped cells that branches throughout the plant.

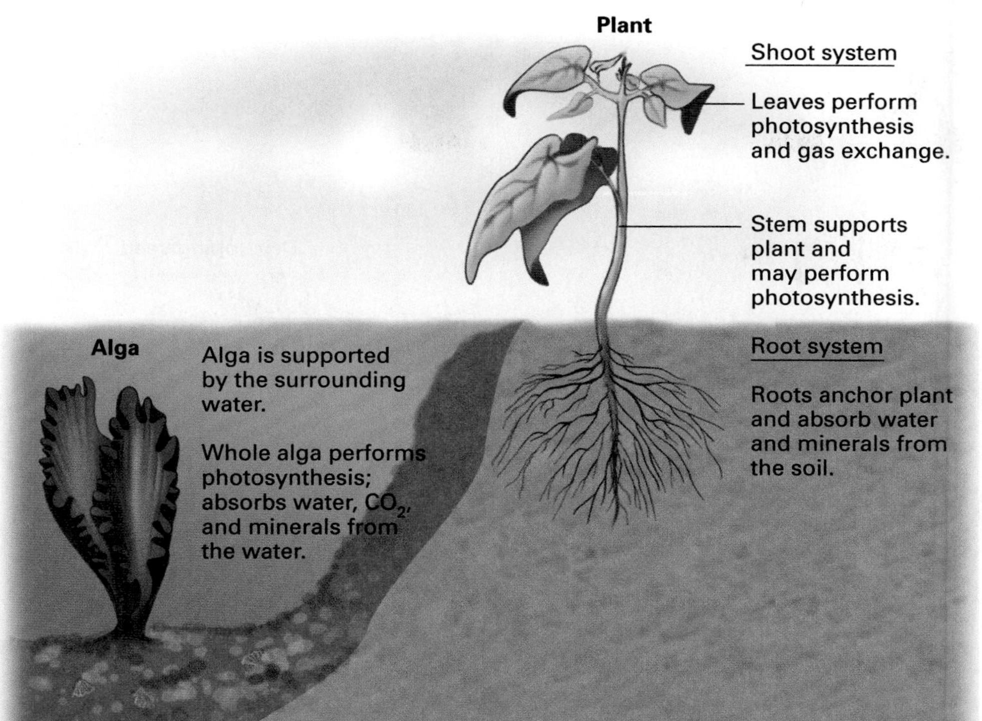

Plant
Shoot system
Leaves perform photosynthesis and gas exchange.
Stem supports plant and may perform photosynthesis.
Root system
Roots anchor plant and absorb water and minerals from the soil.
Alga
Alga is supported by the surrounding water.
Whole alga performs photosynthesis; absorbs water, CO_2, and minerals from the water.

Figure 19-2 While algae live entirely in water, a plant lives in two environments: air and soil. A plant's organ systems are adapted to these two environments.

Staying "Afloat" in Air If you have seen kelp or other seaweeds washed up on the beach, you know that these large algae are limp and flexible, yet they stay upright in water. In an aquatic environment, the buoyancy of water provides physical support for large algae.

Air does not provide the same level of support as water. Plants can only stand upright because they contain strong and rigid support tissues. An important terrestrial adaptation of plants is the production of **lignin,** a chemical that hardens the plants' cell walls. A tree would collapse if it were not for its framework of lignin-rich cell walls.

Maintaining Moisture Though most plants are exposed to dry air, their cellular processes must still take place in an aqueous environment. Plants (and other terrestrial organisms) have adaptations that maintain a watery internal environment. The waxy surfaces of a cactus or an apple are examples of such an adaptation. This waxy **cuticle** coats the leaves and other above-ground parts of most plants, helping the plant body retain water. However, the cuticle also slows down the exchange of carbon dioxide and oxygen between the surrounding air and the inside of photosynthesizing leaves. Gases are exchanged through stomata (singular, *stoma*). **Stomata** (STOH ma ta) are microscopic pores in the leaf's surface. Two surrounding cells regulate each stoma's opening and closing (Figure 19-3). Stomata are open at certain times of day, allowing gas exchange, and are closed the rest of the time, preventing water loss by evaporation.

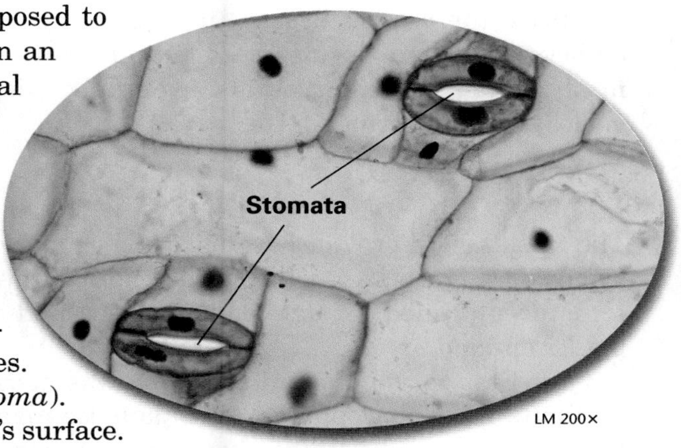

Figure 19-3 Stomata are microscopic pores in a leaf's surface that allow gas exchange while controlling water loss.

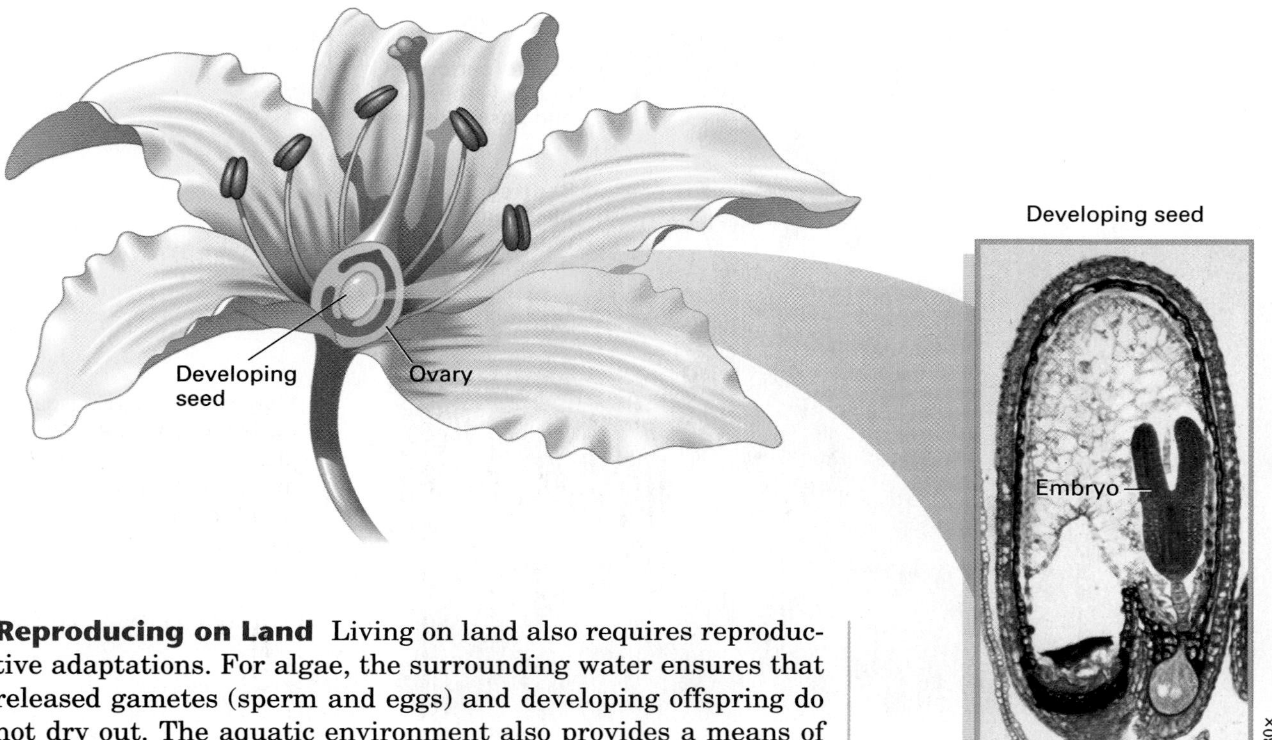

▲ **Figure 19-4** The plant zygote develops into an embryo while still contained within the female parent. This adaptation protects the embryo from drying out.

Reproducing on Land Living on land also requires reproductive adaptations. For algae, the surrounding water ensures that released gametes (sperm and eggs) and developing offspring do not dry out. The aquatic environment also provides a means of dispersing the gametes and offspring to new locations. Plants, however, must keep their gametes and developing offspring from drying out in the air. Plants must also have some means for dispersal other than water currents.

Several adaptations of plants meet these challenges. All plants produce their gametes in a "jacket" of protective cells. The protective jacket surrounds a moist chamber where gametes can develop without dehydrating. In most plants, sperm reach the eggs by traveling within pollen grains, which are carried by wind or animals. Eggs remain within the tissues of the female parent and are fertilized there. The zygote (fertilized egg) develops into an embryo while still inside the female parent (Figure 19-4). For most plants, the embryos are eventually dispersed as seeds, enclosed in protective coats.

Pollen grains

An Overview of Plant Diversity

The fossil record provides evidence of four major periods of plant evolution (Figure 19-5). During each period, the evolution of new structures opened up new opportunities and new habitats for plants on land.

The first period of plant evolution was marked by the origin of plants from charophytes, their aquatic algal ancestors. The first group to diversify from the charophytes were the bryophytes. This group includes the mosses and their relatives. Bryophytes (BRY oh fyts) do not have seeds, and most species lack lignin-hardened vascular tissue.

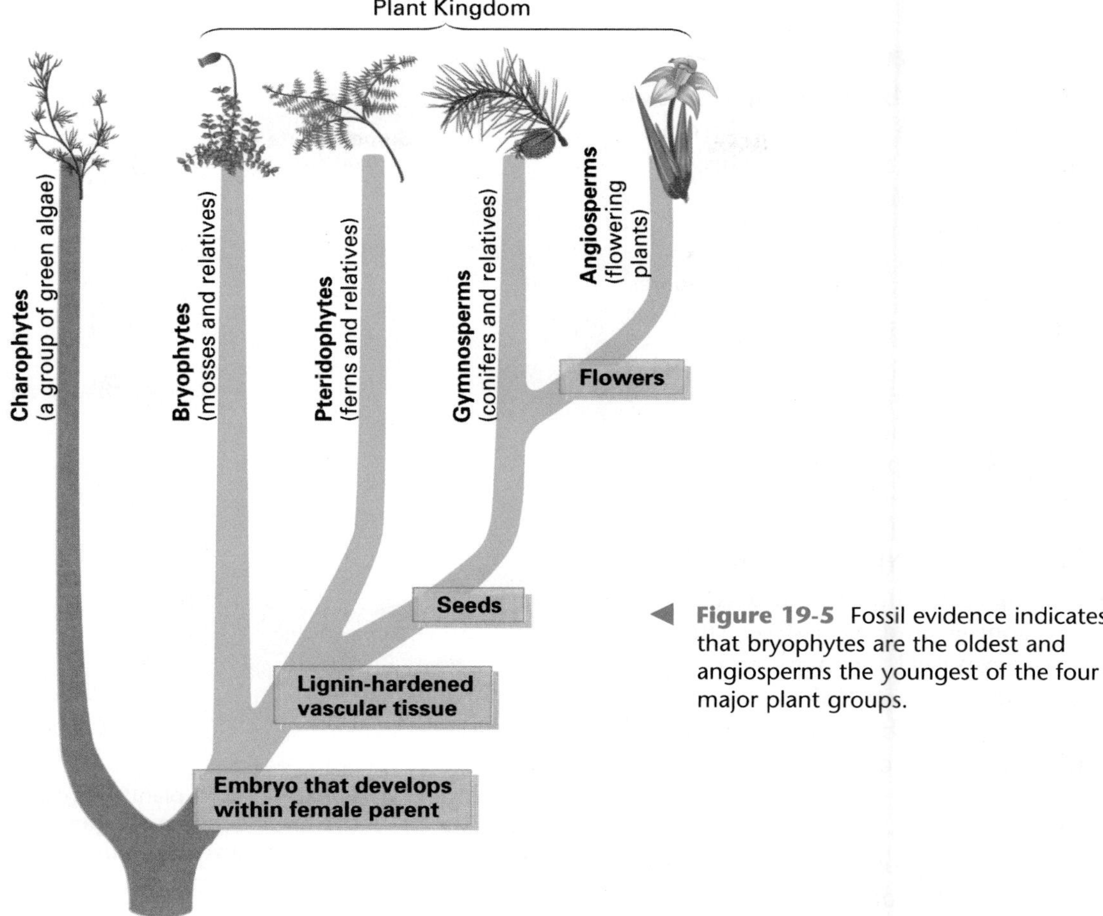

Figure 19-5 Fossil evidence indicates that bryophytes are the oldest and angiosperms the youngest of the four major plant groups.

The second period of plant evolution was marked by the development of vascular plants with lignin-hardened vascular tissues that transport water and nutrients. Early vascular plants lacked seeds. Today, one group of vascular plants called pteridophytes (teh RID oh fyts), including ferns, still have no seeds.

The third major period of plant evolution began with the origin of the seed. A seed consists of an embryo packaged along with a store of food within a protective coat. Seeds contributed to the spread of plants to diverse habitats on land by allowing plant embryos to be dispersed without drying out. Early seed plants gave rise to many types of gymnosperms (JIM noh spurmz). Gymnosperms (Greek for "naked seed") have seeds that develop "naked" (without being enclosed within a chamber) on specialized leaves of the parent plant. Today, the most widespread and diverse gymnosperms are the conifers—cone-bearing trees such as pines.

The fourth major period of plant evolution began with the appearance of flowering plants, or angiosperms (AN jee oh spurmz). The flower is a complex reproductive structure that bears seeds within protective organs called **ovaries** (see Figure 19-4 on the facing page). This contrasts with the gymnosperms' naked seeds. Most modern-day plants are angiosperms, including roses, lilies, and daffodils, as well as many species with less obvious flowers, such as grasses and oak trees.

Alternation of Generations

Plant generations alternate between diploid ($2n$) and haploid (n) forms (Figure 19-6). Recall from Chapter 9 that diploids have two sets of chromosomes, one from each parent. Haploids have just one set as a result of meiosis. In the life cycles of plants, the haploid and the diploid forms are distinct, multicellular generations. In some plants, the haploid individual is actually larger than the diploid one. In contrast, animals such as humans have a unicellular haploid stage, which is a single sperm or egg cell, as you learned in Chapter 9.

The haploid generation of plants produces gametes and is called the **gametophyte** (guh MEET uh fyt). The diploid generation produces spores and is called the **sporophyte** (SPOH ruh fyt). In a plant's life cycle, each of these generations "takes turns" giving rise to the other. The alternation between the haploid and diploid forms is called the **alternation of generations.**

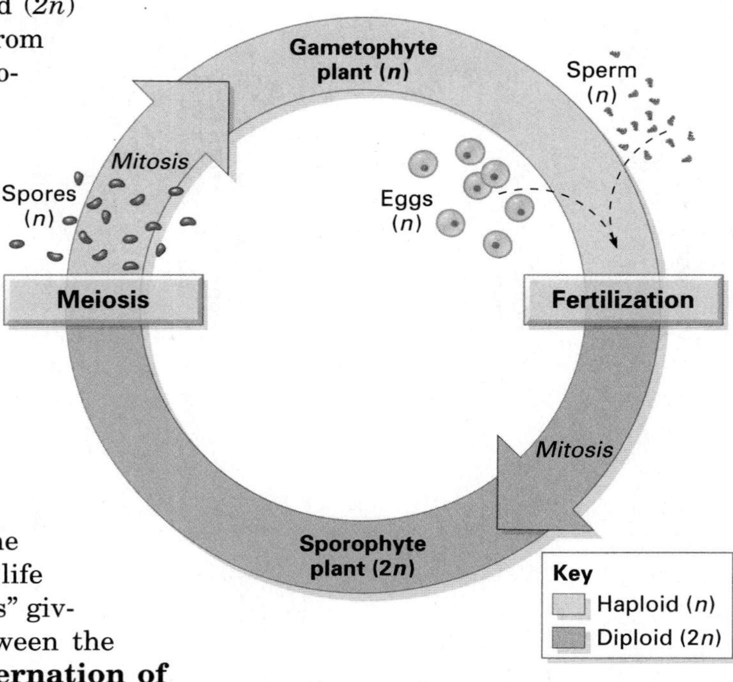

▲ **Figure 19-6** A plant's life cycle alternates between the gametophyte and sporophyte generations.

As reproductive cells, spores differ from gametes in two ways. First, a spore can develop into a new organism without fusing with another cell. In contrast, two gametes must fuse to form a zygote. Second, spores of some plants have tough coats that enable them to resist harsh environments. Gametes are not adapted to resist harsh conditions.

An alternation of generations occurs only in the life cycles of plants and certain algae. Throughout this chapter, you will read about the specific pattern of alternation of generations found in each of the four major groups of modern plants: bryophytes, pteridophytes, gymnosperms, and angiosperms.

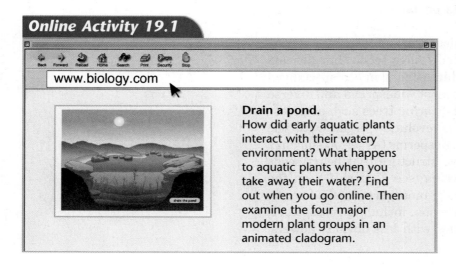

Online Activity 19.1

www.biology.com

Drain a pond.
How did early aquatic plants interact with their watery environment? What happens to aquatic plants when you take away their water? Find out when you go online. Then examine the four major modern plant groups in an animated cladogram.

Concept Check 19.1

1. Name the group of algae most closely related to plants. What is a major difference between plants and algae?
2. Make a table listing the four major challenges to plants living on land. In the second column, list at least one plant adaptation for each challenge.
3. List the four main groups of plants and describe two characteristics of each.
4. List the differences between the sporophyte and gametophyte plant generations.

CONCEPT 19.2

Mosses and other bryophytes were the first land plants.

OBJECTIVES
- Contrast the two generations of a bryophyte.
- Describe three groups of bryophytes.

KEY TERM
- bryophyte

What's Online

www.biology.com

Online Activity 19.2
Explore mosses.

Next time you are outside, look for damp habitats where mosses and other bryophytes might thrive. Bryophytes lack rigid support tissues, and therefore grow very close to the ground.

Bryophyte Adaptations

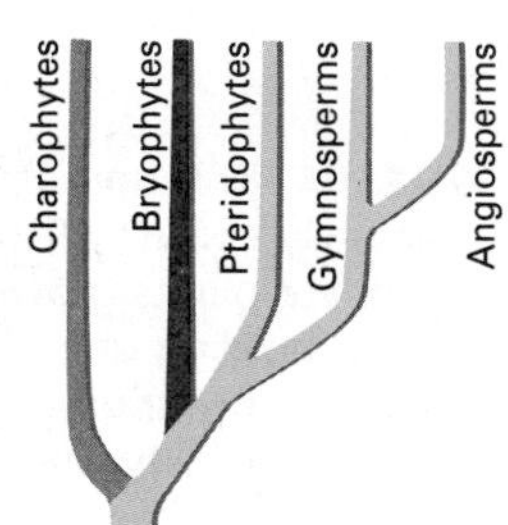

Bryophytes, which include mosses and their relatives, are sometimes described as nonvascular plants because they lack the lignin-hardened vascular tissue found in vascular plants. However, some bryophytes do have tubular cells that transport water. Male and female gametes are usually produced in reproductive structures in separate locations on the tips of the gametophytes (Figure 19-7). Sperm are flagellated and swim through a moist film to the eggs. After fertilization, the zygote grows from the tip of the female gametophyte into a sporophyte, a stalklike structure with a capsule at the top. This capsule produces and releases spores that grow into new gametophytes. The gametophyte is the dominant generation.

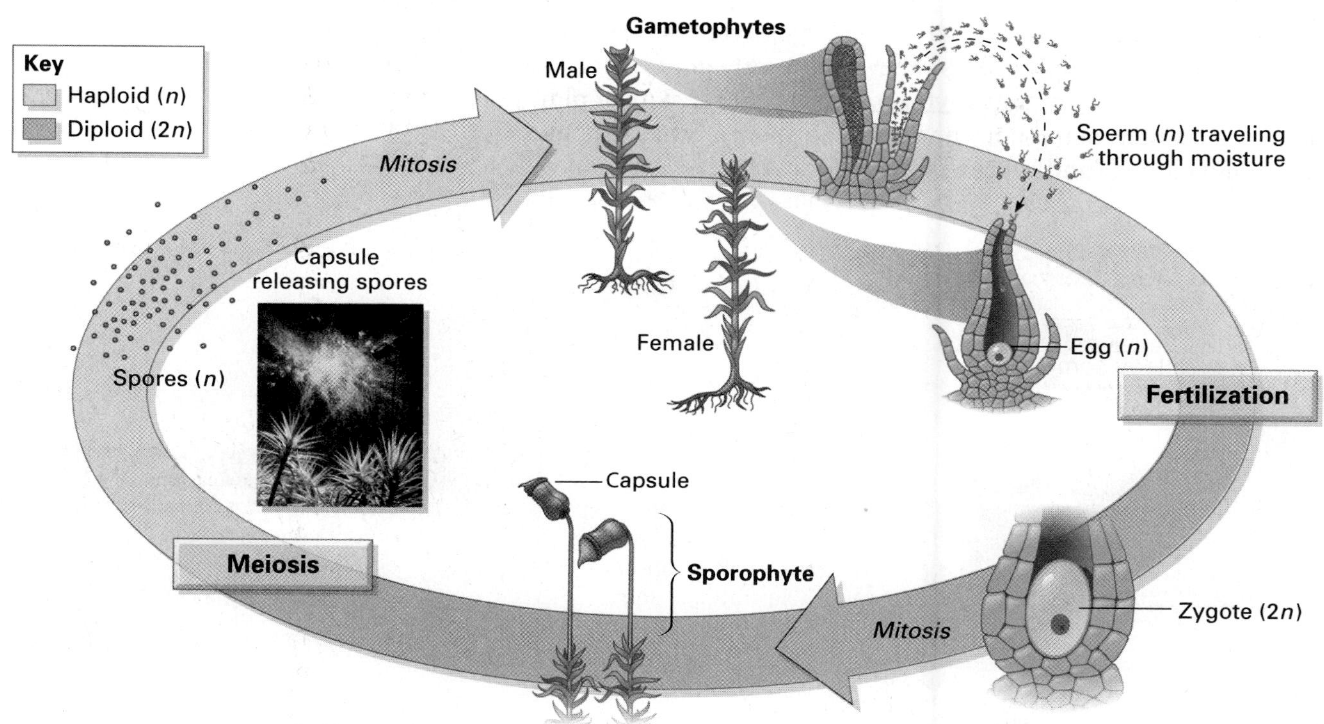

Figure 19-7 In the life cycle of a moss or other bryophyte, the sporophyte remains attached to the gametophyte. The gametophyte provides water and nutrients to the sporophyte.

◀ **Hornworts** Hornworts are bryophytes named for their hornlike sporophytes, which you can see here growing from their parental gametophytes.

▶ **Mosses** This mat of moss actually consists of many gametophyte plants growing in a tight pack, holding one another up. The stalks are the sporophytes. The mat has a spongy quality that enables it to absorb and retain water. The flagellated moss sperm swim to the eggs through a film of water on the surface of the mat.

▲ **Liverworts** Liverworts are bryophytes named for the liver-shaped appearance of the gametophyte. This liverwort (*Marchantia*) has umbrella-shaped stalks that produce the tiny sporophytes.

Figure 19-8 This photo gallery shows examples of bryophytes from three major groups.

The Diversity of Bryophytes

Mosses may be the only bryophytes you are familiar with by name. In Figure 19-8, you can examine some of the characteristics of mosses and two of their bryophyte relatives: the liverworts and hornworts.

Among plants, mosses and other bryophytes are unique in having the gametophyte as the dominant generation—the larger, more obvious form. As you continue your survey of plants, you'll see an increasing dominance of the sporophyte as the more highly developed (and more visible) generation.

Online Activity 19.2

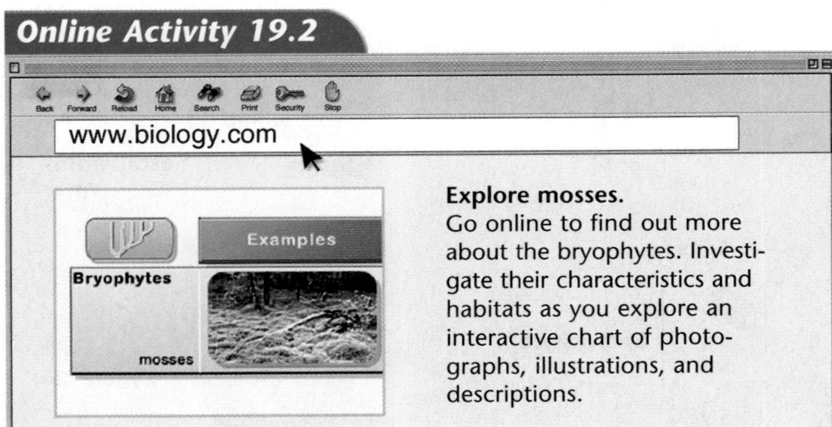

Explore mosses.
Go online to find out more about the bryophytes. Investigate their characteristics and habitats as you explore an interactive chart of photographs, illustrations, and descriptions.

Concept Check 19.2

1. Describe each generation of a bryophyte. Which generation is dominant?
2. Name three groups of bryophytes.
3. How do bryophyte sperm travel?

CONCEPT 19.3 Ferns and other pteridophytes are seedless vascular plants.

OBJECTIVES
- Describe the characteristics of a pteridophyte.
- Name three groups of pteridophytes.

KEY TERM
- pteridophyte

What's Online

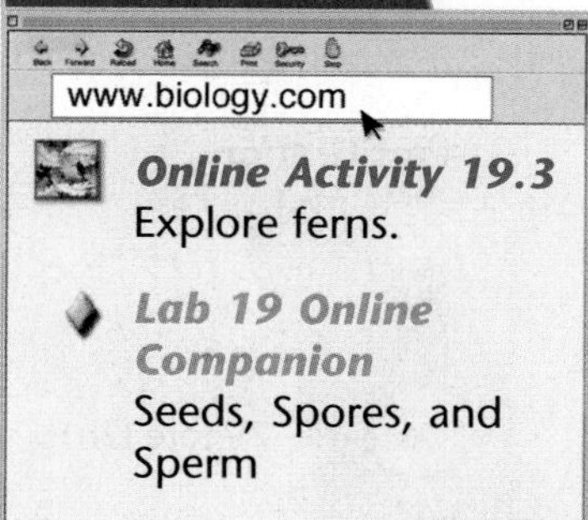

Online Activity 19.3
Explore ferns.

Lab 19 Online Companion
Seeds, Spores, and Sperm

During the Carboniferous period, from 363 to 290 million years ago, vast swampy forests covered much of what is now Eurasia and North America. These forests were dominated by large, seedless vascular plants. Today the descendants of these giants are still an important part of many plant communities.

Pteridophyte Adaptations

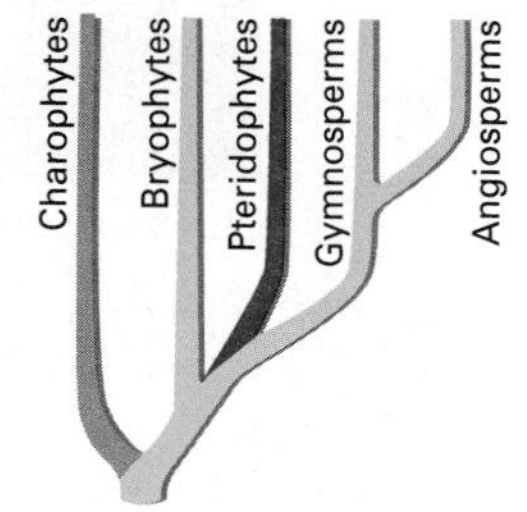

In contrast to the bryophytes, ferns and other **pteridophytes** have lignin-hardened support tissues, which include the water-conducting cells of vascular tissue. The pteridophytes and other vascular plants also have vascular tissue specialized for transporting sugar. These adaptations probably enabled pteridophytes to dominate the forests of the Carboniferous period (Figure 19-9).

The remains of these ancient forests have great significance. Under certain conditions of heat and pressure, the organic compounds in their remains formed oil, coal, and natural gas, together referred to as "fossil fuels." Fossil fuels are a major source of energy used to power vehicles and generate electricity.

▼ **Figure 19-9** An artist used fossil evidence to create this painting of what a Carboniferous forest might have looked like. The dominant plants are pteridophytes, many much larger than today's species.

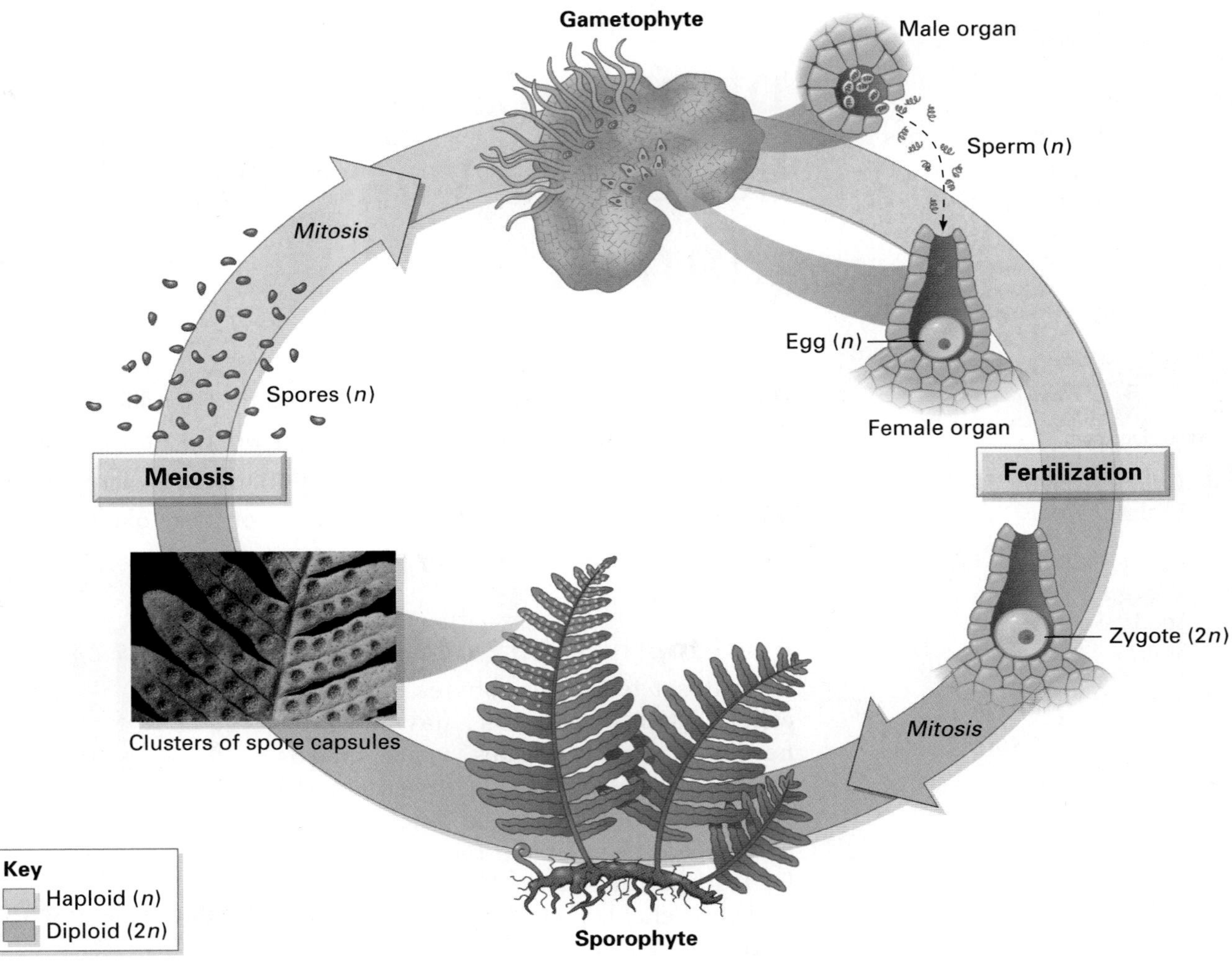

▲ **Figure 19-10** The sporophyte is the dominant generation in a fern's life cycle.

In contrast to mosses, the sporophyte is the dominant fern generation (Figure 19-10). Perhaps you have observed what look like brown dots on the undersides of mature fern fronds (leaves). In fact, each "dot" is made up of many spore capsules—small spore-filled containers. Each capsule releases a large number of tiny haploid spores that drift down to the ground and grow into tiny gametophytes on or just below the soil surface.

On the underside of the gametophyte are sperm and egg-producing structures. Pteridophyte sperm, like those of byrophytes, are flagellated. They must swim through a film of water to fertilize eggs. The zygote grows into the new sporophyte.

The Diversity of Pteridophytes

Perhaps you have seen ferns in the woods. But not all pteridophytes have the graceful leafy fronds of the familiar fern. Some pteridophytes look like little pine trees, and others like green sticks. Figure 19-11 on the facing page examines characteristics of ferns and some of their lesser-known relatives.

◄ Ferns The most diverse and widespread of the pteridophytes are the ferns, with more than 12,000 species. Most ferns have large leaves called fronds and thrive in shady forests. However, certain ferns are adapted to dry environments, such as deserts.

▼ Club "Mosses" Although this plant's common name is the "club moss," and it looks like a little pine tree, it is neither a moss nor a pine. Like other pteridophytes, it has vascular tissue but no seeds. Club mosses are common on the forest floors of the northeastern United States. Giant species of club mosses, now extinct, grew up to 40 meters tall during the Carboniferous period.

► Horsetails
Horsetails generally grow in marshy, sandy areas. During the Carboniferous period some grew as tall as 15 meters. Their outer layer of cells is embedded with silica, which gives the plant a gritty texture. Before the modern scouring pad was invented, people used the abrasive stems of horsetails to scrub pots and pans. For this reason these plants are also known as "scouring rushes."

Figure 19-11 Pteridophytes display a variety of forms, as the above examples illustrate.

Online Activity 19.3

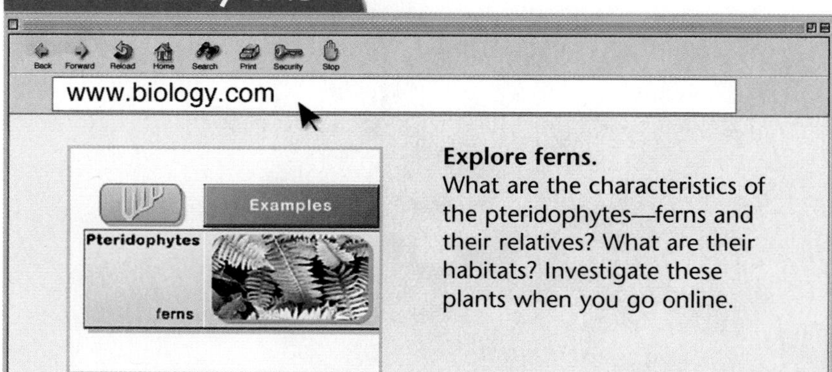

Explore ferns.
What are the characteristics of the pteridophytes—ferns and their relatives? What are their habitats? Investigate these plants when you go online.

Concept Check 19.3

1. Which generation of a pteridophyte is dominant?
2. Name three groups of pteridophytes.
3. What significance do the remains of Carboniferous pteridophytes have today?

Seeds, Spores, and Sperm

Comparing Fern and Angiosperm Life Cycles

Questions How do seeds, spores, and sperm differ in structure and function? Which types of plants have these structures and what are they used for?

Lab Overview In this investigation you will compare spores and seeds, sow them, and observe the results. You will sketch your observations over several weeks to compare fern and angiosperm life cycles. After three weeks, you will observe swimming sperm produced by the fern gametophyte.

Preparing for the Lab To help you prepare for the investigation, go to the *Lab 19 Online Companion.* ······➔ Discover how seeds, spores, and pollen differ, and learn how they are produced at different stages of plant life cycles. Prepare for the lab procedure by previewing the steps you will take.

Completing the Lab Use your Laboratory Manual or lab page printouts from the *Lab 19 Online Companion* to do the investigation and draw conclusions from the observations you made. **CAUTION:** *Be sure to follow your teacher's instructions and all safety guidelines in the investigation.*

Lab 19 Online Companion

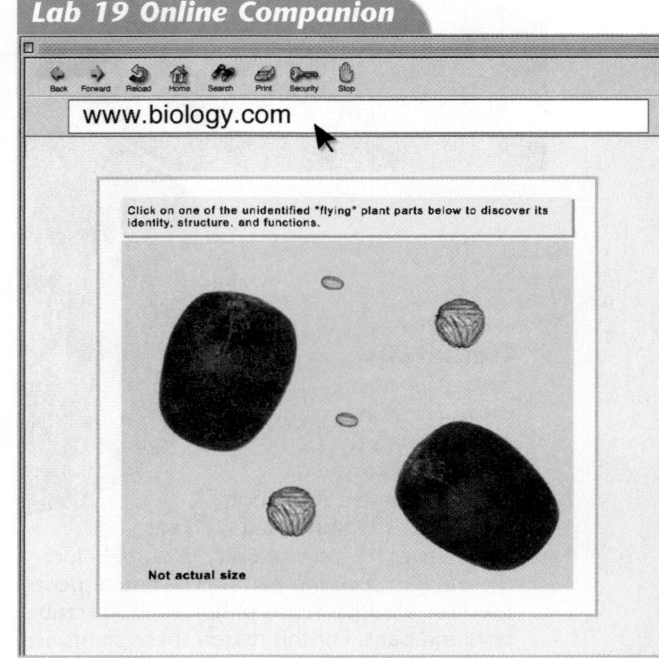
Back
Forward
Reload
Home
Search
Print
Security
Stop
www.biology.com
Click on one of the unidentified "flying" plant parts below to discover its identity, structure, and functions.
Not actual size

CONCEPT 19.4

Pollen and seeds evolved in gymnosperms.

OBJECTIVES
- Describe three plant adaptations that evolved in gymnosperms.
- List the four main groups of gymnosperms.

KEY TERMS
- gymnosperm
- pollen
- seed
- ovule

What's Online

Although you may never have thought about it, you benefit every day from the products of conifers, such as timber for buildings and furniture, and paper. Conifers, the most common gymnosperms, are among the tallest, largest, and longest-living organisms on Earth.

Gymnosperm Adaptations

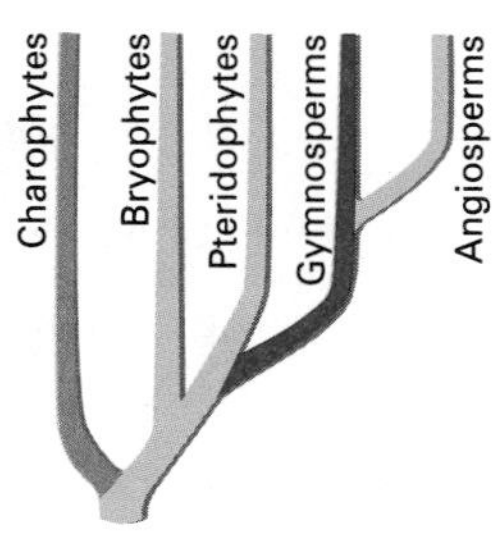

Compared to ferns, gymnosperms have three additional adaptations that make survival in diverse land habitats possible. These adaptations include an even smaller gametophyte, pollen, and the seed. **Gymnosperms** are plants that bear seeds that are "naked," meaning not enclosed in an ovary.

In gymnosperms, the diploid sporophyte generation is much more highly developed and obvious than the haploid gametophyte generation. A pine tree, for example, is actually a sporophyte on which the tiny gametophytes live in cones (Figure 19-12). This contrasts with ferns, where the small gametophytes live on their own, without the protection of the larger sporophyte.

A second adaptation of seed plants to dry land was the evolution of pollen. **Pollen** grains are the much-reduced male gametophytes that contain cells that develop into sperm. In the case of conifers, wind carries pollen from male to female cones, where eggs develop within the female gametophyte. The evolution of pollen allowed sperm to reach eggs by traveling through a dry environment rather than swimming through water.

The third important adaptation of seed plants to life on land is the seed itself. As you have read, a **seed** consists of a plant embryo packaged along with a food supply within a protective coat.

◀ **Figure 19-12** A pine tree's cones contain its gametophytes. The top inset shows male pollen cones of this Eastern white pine. The bottom inset shows its larger female seed cones.

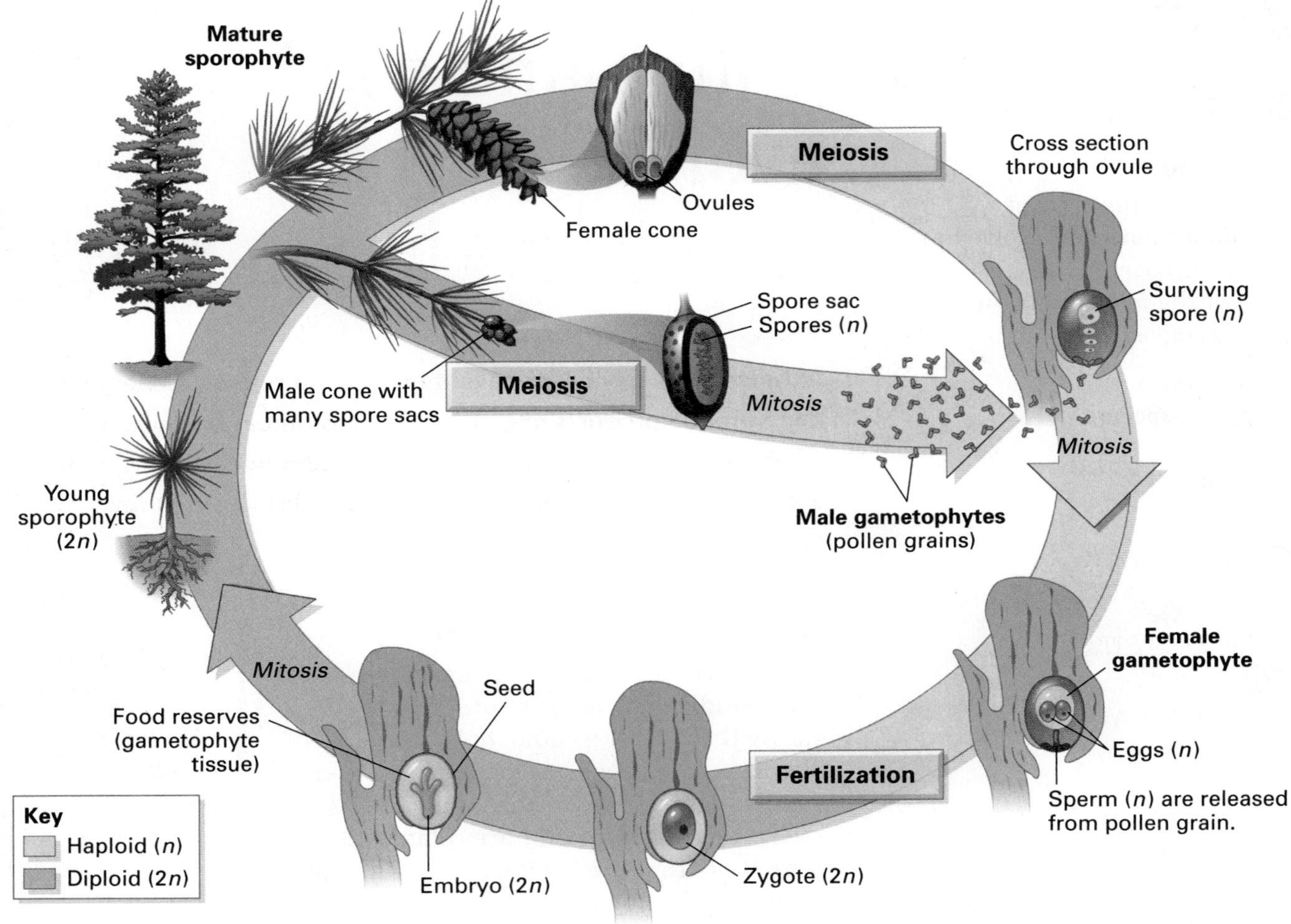

▲ **Figure 19-13** In pines and other gymnosperms, the gametophytes develop inside cones. Airborne pollen grains (the male gametophytes) carry sperm to the female gametophytes.

Figure 19-13 highlights key stages in the life cycle of a pine tree. Within a pollen cone's many spore sacs, thousands of haploid spores develop into pollen grains (male gametophytes). Meanwhile, the female gametophytes develop within structures called **ovules.** Within each of two ovules on each scale of the female cones, a large spore cell undergoes meiosis and produces four haploid cells. One of these cells survives and grows into the female gametophyte.

Wind blows pollen from one tree to another. If a pollen grain reaches a female cone, sperm cells mature and fertilize egg cells within the female gametophyte. Often two eggs in an ovule are fertilized, but just one of the zygotes develops into an embryo. This embryo is the new sporophyte plant.

The Diversity of Gymnosperms

At the end of the Carboniferous period, the global climate turned drier and colder. The vast forests of pteridophytes began to disappear. Along with this climate change came the success of seed plants, which can complete their entire life cycles on dry land. Of the earliest seed plants, the most successful were the gymnosperms. Several kinds of gymnosperms grew along with the seedless plants in the Carboniferous swamps. Four phyla of gymnosperms exist today (Figure 19-14 on the facing page).

Figure 19-14 This photo gallery includes examples of the four gymnosperm phyla.

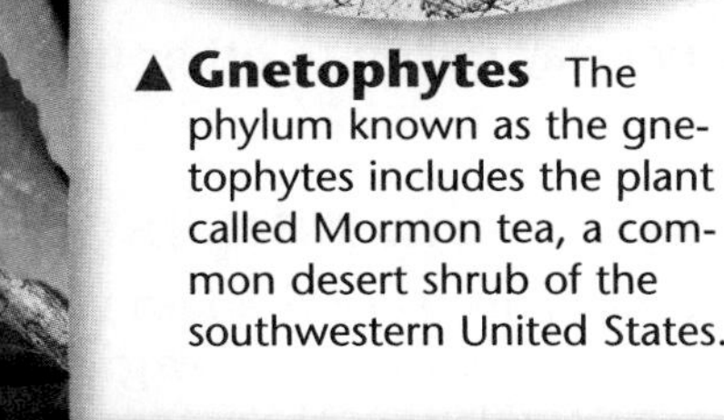

▲ **Gnetophytes** The phylum known as the gnetophytes includes the plant called Mormon tea, a common desert shrub of the southwestern United States.

▲ **Cycads** Species belonging to this phylum have large, palm-like leaves. (Don't confuse cycads with true palms, which are flowering plants, not gymnosperms.) Cycad seeds develop on the surface of specialized leaves that are packed closely together, forming a cone.

▲ **Ginkgos** *Ginkgo biloba* (the maidenhair tree) is the sole living species of the phylum known as the ginkgophytes. Many species of this phylum were common when dinosaurs were alive. The ginkgo has fanlike leaves that turn yellow and are shed in autumn. What looks like fruits are actually fleshy seeds. The gingko is a popular tree in cities, partly because it tolerates air pollution well.

▲ **Conifers** The spruces and pines in this forest are conifers, as are firs, junipers, cedars, and redwoods. Nearly all conifers are evergreens, meaning they retain leaves throughout the year. But this does not mean their leaves last forever. Leaves such as pine needles are replaced as old ones die, but they are not replaced all at once.

Online Activity 19.4

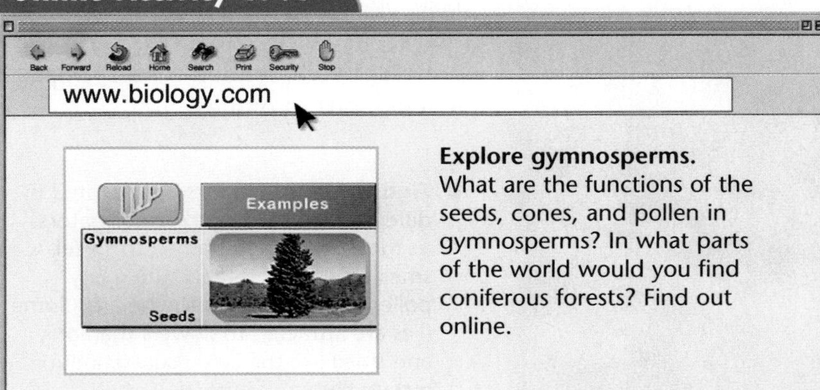

Explore gymnosperms. What are the functions of the seeds, cones, and pollen in gymnosperms? In what parts of the world would you find coniferous forests? Find out online.

Concept Check 19.4

1. Name three adaptations of gymnosperms and the advantages they provide.
2. Make a table listing the four different gymnosperm groups and a beneficial use or fact about each one.

CONCEPT 19.5 Flowers and fruits evolved in angiosperms.

OBJECTIVES

- Describe two unique features of angiosperms.
- Characterize the two largest evolutionary branches of angiosperms.
- Describe ways that humans depend on angiosperms.

KEY TERMS

- angiosperm
- flower
- stamen
- carpel
- endosperm
- fruit

What's Online

While you may think of flowers as gently perfumed, not all flowers are so sweet. The so-called carrion flowers emit the stench of rotting flesh! They attract insects that normally feed on carcasses. The odor of flowers is just one adaptation that helps attract particular animal pollinators to visit, pick up, and carry away pollen to other flowers.

Angiosperm Adaptations

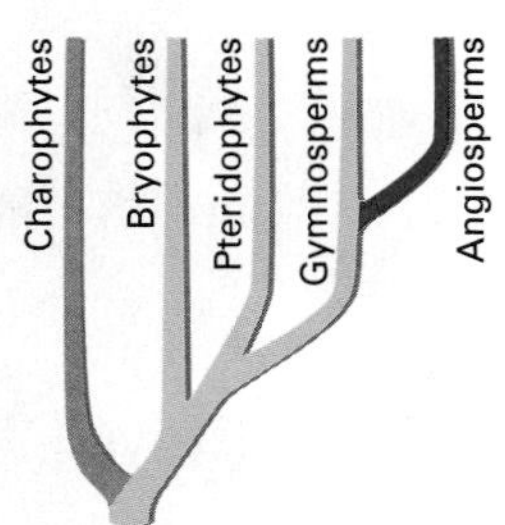

Angiosperms were the last major group of plants to evolve. In **angiosperms,** or flowering plants, the reproductive structures are flowers, in contrast to the cones of gymnosperms. The gametophytes of angiosperms develop within the flowers of the sporophyte. The **flower** is a specialized type of plant shoot that functions in reproduction and is unique to angiosperms. Flowers come in many different variations.

The flowers of many angiosperms are adapted in ways that attract insects or other animals that transfer pollen directly from one flower to another flower. The great variety of flower size, shape, odor, texture, and color reflects the diversity of interactions that angiosperms have with animal pollinators (Figure 19-15). Angiosperms such as grasses that are wind-pollinated also have flowers, but their flowers are typically smaller and less flashy than those pollinated by animals.

The male reproductive organs of a flower are called **stamens** (STAY munz). At the tip of a stamen is the anther, which produces pollen grains containing the male gametophytes. The female reproductive organs of flowers are called **carpels** (KAHR pulz). At the base of a carpel is a chamber—the ovary. Within the ovary, female gametophytes, called embryo sacs, develop within ovules.

Figure 19-15 Flowers are adapted in different ways that attract pollinators. **a.** Most bees are attracted to sweet-smelling flowers. Notice the many pollen grains stuck to the bee. **b.** Some flies are attracted to flowers that look and smell like the flies' usual dinner of rotting flesh.

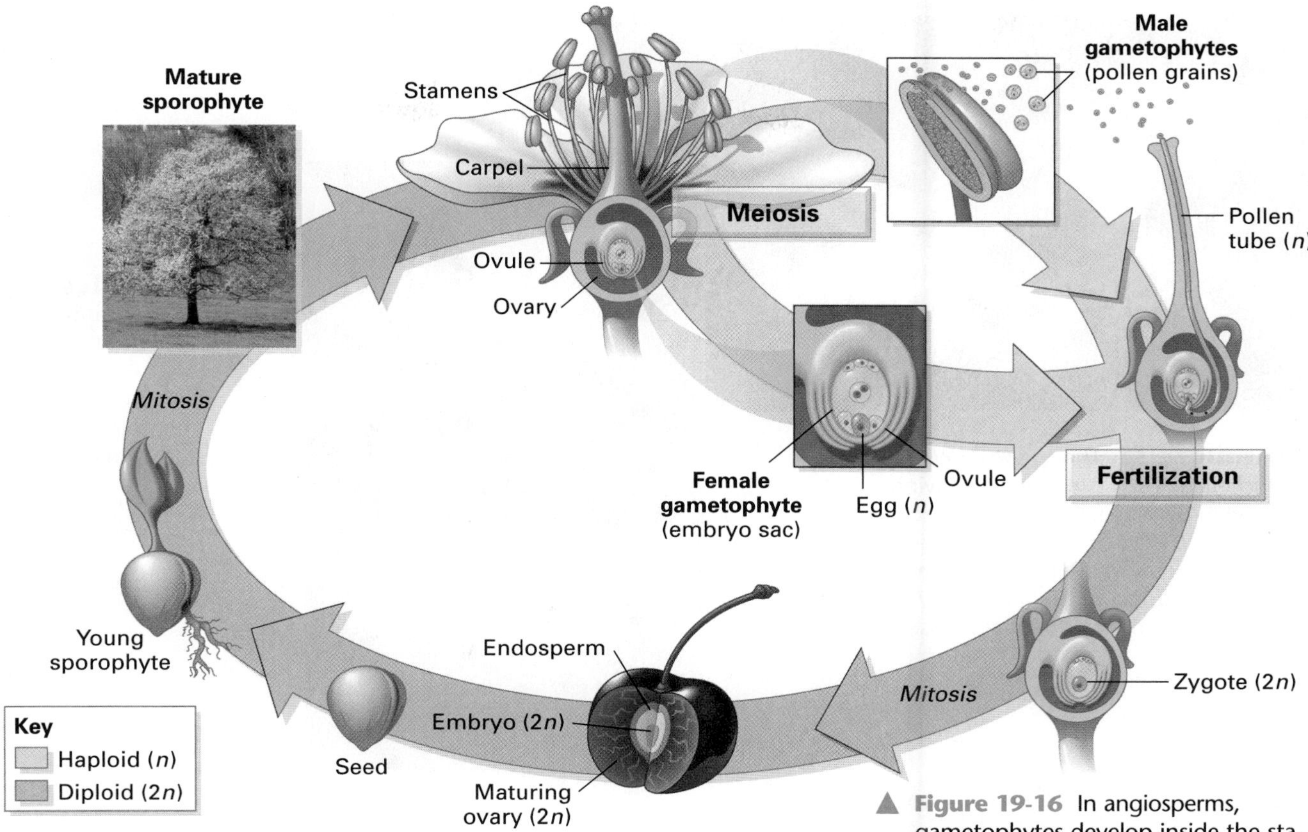

▲ **Figure 19-16** In angiosperms, gametophytes develop inside the stamens and carpels of flowers. Once a pollen grain (male gametophyte) reaches the embryo sac (female gametophyte), a double fertilization produces a zygote (start of sporophyte) and a nourishing endosperm tissue.

Figure 19-16 highlights key stages in the angiosperm life cycle. (You will read about more details of this process in Chapter 20.) During reproduction, pollen lands on sticky tips of carpels, and a tube grows from each pollen grain down the carpel toward an ovule in the ovary. Two sperm cells produced within the pollen grain are then released into the female gametophyte. One sperm cell fertilizes an egg cell. This produces a zygote, which develops into an embryo. The second sperm cell fuses with nuclei in the large center cell of the female gametophyte, which then develops into a nutrient-storing tissue called **endosperm.** The endosperm nourishes the embryo as it develops.

This "double fertilization" that simultaneously produces a zygote and an endosperm is a characteristic of angiosperms. The whole ovule (now containing the zygote and endosperm) develops into a seed. The flowers of some species contain many ovules, and thus can produce many seeds. An angiosperm's development of seeds within ovaries contrasts with the "naked" seed development of gymnosperms.

As seeds are developing from ovules, the ovary wall thickens, forming a fruit that encloses the seeds. A **fruit** is the ripened ovary of a flower (Figure 19-17). (In some angiosperms, other flower parts are incorporated along with the ovary into the fruit.) Fruits protect and help disperse seeds. For example, colorful fruits often attract animals that digest the fruits and deposit the seeds in their wastes, usually at some distance from the parent plant.

▲ **Figure 19-17** Some angiosperms, such as the apple, have one fruit-forming ovary per flower. Other angiosperms have multiple ovaries per flower, giving rise to fruit clusters, such as the raspberry and blackberry.

▲ **Amborella** The species *Amborella trichopoda* is an example of a "living fossil." It is the only surviving species of the oldest branch of the angiosperm lineage. *Amborella* lives on the island of New Caledonia in the South Pacific, and has been found nowhere else.

◀ **Water Lilies** Water lilies form another clade (evolutionary branch) of flowering plants that evolved before monocots and dicots.

Figure 19-18 While most angiosperms are either dicots or monocots, biologists have recently classified certain angiosperms into other groups. Earlier classification included these other groups in the dicot class.

The Diversity of Angiosperms

Angiosperms are the most diverse and widespread of all plants. At one time, biologists divided the angiosperms into two classes: *monocots* and *dicots.* Monocots and dicots differ in the structures of their leaves, flowers, seeds, roots, and vascular tissues. For example, monocots generally have leaves with veins that run parallel to each other. Most dicots have branched veins. In addition, monocots usually have floral parts in multiples of three. Most dicots have floral parts in multiples of four or five.

Recent research has added more branches to the evolutionary tree. Some flowering plants descended from ancestors that evolved earlier than the oldest monocot or dicot ancestor. Thus, these plants cannot be classified as either monocots or dicots. Species representing these evolutionary branches are shown in Figure 19-18.

Human Dependence on Angiosperms

Flowering plants provide nearly all the food that supports human life. All fruit and almost all vegetable crops are angiosperms. Corn, rice, wheat, and the other grains are fruits of grass species. In addition to feeding humans, grains are the main food source for domesticated animals such as cows and chickens. Angiosperms are also harvested for furniture, medicines, perfumes, decorations, and fibers for clothes (such as cotton).

Early humans probably collected wild seeds and fruits for food. Agriculture developed as humans began sowing seeds and cultivating plants to have a more dependable food source. Later, humans began to breed plants to improve food quantity and quality.

Science, Technology, & Society

Back Forward Reload Home Search Print Security Stop

www.biology.com

Rainforest Conservation

Preserving the world's rain forests helps protect nature's richest ecosystems and may lead to discoveries of important medicines. But local farmers need rainforest land to plant crops and raise cattle. Land is also needed to drill for oil and to supply lumber. How can these needs be balanced? Go online to examine some of these complicated issues.

▼ Star Anise and Others In addition to *Amborella* and water lilies, there are other early angiosperm clades that evolved before the monocots and true dicots. The star anise is a representative species.

◀ Monocots Some familiar monocots are the day lilies (such as this one), orchids, irises, palms, and grasses. Note the day lily's 6 flower petals, a multiple of 3. The monocot clade includes about 65,000 species.

▲ Dicots The true dicots include poppies (such as this California poppy), roses, peas, sunflowers, oaks, and maples. Note the California poppy's 4 flower petals. The dicot clade includes about 165,000 species.

So far, only a tiny fraction of more than 280,000 known plant species (including non-angiosperms) have been explored for potential uses. For example, almost all of the human food supply is based on the cultivation of only about two dozen species. And, while more than 120 prescription drugs are currently extracted from plants, researchers have so far investigated fewer than 5000 plant species as potential sources of new medicines. Certain human activities are threatening plant species, sometimes before their potential uses are even known. The tropical rain forest, which is losing plant species at the fastest rate of all Earth's ecosystems, may be a medicine chest of healing plants that could become extinct before they are even discovered. Chapter 36 will explore some of the issues involved in biological conservation.

Online Activity 19.5

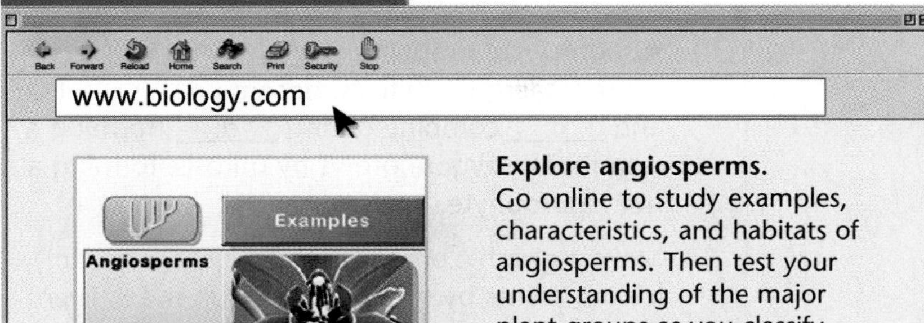

Explore angiosperms. Go online to study examples, characteristics, and habitats of angiosperms. Then test your understanding of the major plant groups as you classify mystery plant photographs.

Concept Check 19.5

1. Define and give examples of a fruit and a flower.
2. Name three examples of monocots and three examples of dicots.
3. Make a list of benefits angiosperms offer humans.
4. Explain what is meant by the term *double fertilization.*

Multiple Choice

Choose the letter of the best answer.

1. Which adaptation best helps a plant retain water?
   a. lignin
   b. cuticle
   c. vascular tissue
   d. flowers

2. A sporophyte produces
   a. gametes.
   b. eggs.
   c. spores.
   d. all of the above.

3. Which of the following structures are found in mosses?
   a. flowers
   b. seeds
   c. pollen
   d. sperm

4. Which is true of pteridophytes?
   a. They grew in Carboniferous forests.
   b. The gametophyte is dominant.
   c. Wind carries their sperm to eggs.
   d. They include the liverworts.

5. Which of the following is *not* a gymnosperm?
   a. conifer
   b. ginkgo
   c. oak
   d. cycad

6. Which structures are unique to angiosperms?
   a. seeds and pollen
   b. eggs and spores
   c. ovules and pollen grains
   d. flowers and fruits

7. In an angiosperm, double fertilization produces
   a. a diploid gametophyte.
   b. a haploid zygote and an endosperm.
   c. a diploid zygote and an endosperm.
   d. a flower.

Short Answer

8. Compare and contrast the life cycles of a moss and a fern.

9. List three key adaptations that distinguish gymnosperms from earlier plants.

10. Give examples of at least two angiosperm adaptations that help attract pollinators.

11. Compare and contrast the result of fertilization in gymnosperms and angiosperms.

12. Explain what happens to the angiosperm ovary during development of the seed.

13. Describe at least two ways angiosperms have benefited you in the last 24 hours.

Visualizing Concepts

14. Refer to the diagram to fill in the blanks in the sentences that follow.

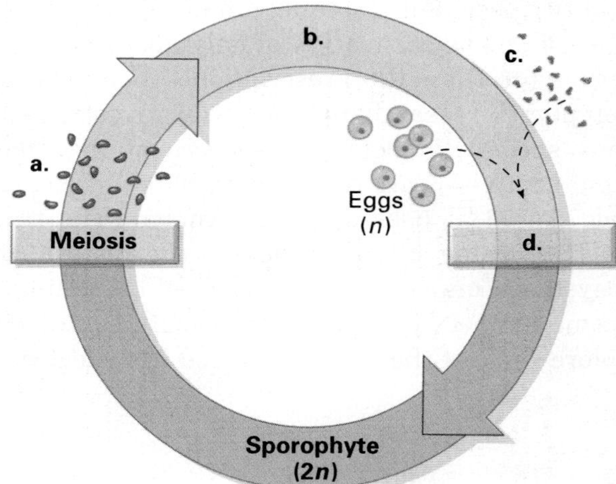

A sporophyte produces __a.__ by meiosis. A spore undergoes mitosis, becoming __b.__ Eggs and __c.__ combine during __d.__, forming a zygote. The zygote grows by mitosis, forming a new sporophyte.

15. Make a graphic organizer that classifies the following plants by group: moss, club moss, liverwort, cycad, water lily, fern, pine, maple, sunflower, horsetail, ginkgo.

Analyzing Information

16. Analyzing Photographs Examine the photograph to answer the questions that follow.

a. Describe what is happening in the photograph.
b. Identify the plant generation(s) shown in the photograph. Explain your answer.

17. Analyzing Diagrams Use the diagram to answer the questions below.

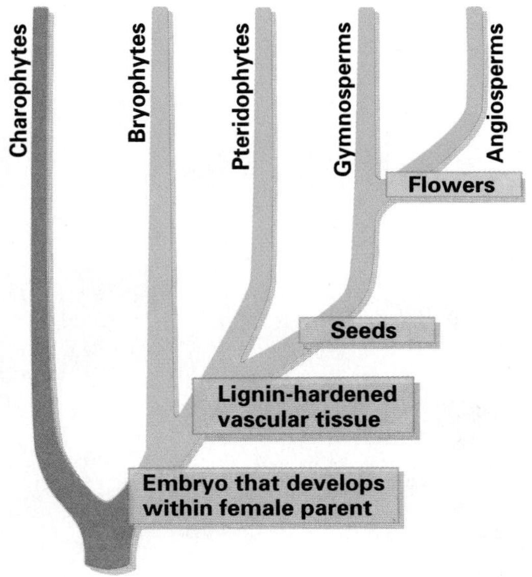

a. Which group of algae has been hypothesized to be the ancestor of plants?
b. Which group of plants evolved most recently?
c. What main adaptation separated the pteridophytes from the bryophytes?
d. In which group of plants did seeds first appear?

Critical Thinking

18. Comparing and Contrasting Contrast the habitat of bryophytes with that of charophytes. What adaptations do bryophytes have that allow them to live in a different habitat from charophytes?

19. Problem Solving Researchers have found a new species of plant growing on a damp forest floor. The plant produces flagellated sperm, and its dominant generation has diploid cells. To which major group of plants does this new species probably belong? Explain your answer.

20. Evaluating the Impact of Research Discuss how society could benefit from biologists continuing to classify and study new plant species.

21. Developing Hypotheses Researchers have used mosses to study biological damage caused by radiation leaks, such as might result from an accident at a nuclear power plant. (Recall that radiation damages organisms by causing mutations.) Suggest why it might be faster to observe the genetic effects of radiation on mosses than on other plants.

22. What's Wrong With These Statements? *Briefly explain why each statement is inaccurate or misleading.*
a. Zygotes grow into gametophytes.
b. Meiosis produces gametes in plants.
c. Ferns release seeds from their leaves.

Performance Assessment

Writing Write a storyboard (sequence of actions) for a computer animation of one of the four plant life cycles you learned about in this chapter.

Online Assessment/Test Preparation

- **Chapter 19 Assessment**
  Check your understanding of the chapter concepts.
- **Standardized Test Preparation**
  Practice test-taking skills you need to succeed.

The Life of a Flowering Plant

The delicate pink flowers and green stems of this beach vine don't seem to be going anywhere. But a plant has its ways of getting around. A plant keeps growing its entire life, becoming ever larger and branching out into new territory. This particular plant grows just above the high tide line along coastal beaches, over time forming large mats that assist in stabilizing sand and preventing beach erosion. Its seeds are dispersed by windblown sand and on ocean currents, allowing its offspring to colonize far-away beaches. This chapter and the rest of this unit focus especially on the structures and functions of flowering plants, or angiosperms, though some of the mechanisms apply to gymnosperms as well. Before you begin, go online to the *WebQuest* to explore pollen and pollinators.

Key Concepts

Concept 20.1 Reproductive adaptations contribute to angiosperm success.

Concept 20.2 Structure fits function in the plant body.

Concept 20.3 Primary growth lengthens roots and shoots.

Concept 20.4 Secondary growth increases the thickness of woody plants.

Assessment Chapter 20 Review

What's Online

www.biology.com

WebQuest
PollenQuest

Online Activity 20.1
Highlight flower structures.

Lab 20 Online Companion
Bees, Birds, and Botanists

Online Activity 20.2
Identify plant tissues.

Science, Technology, & Society
Plants and Bioremediation

Online Activity 20.3
Dissect a root.

Online Activity 20.4
Examine secondary growth.

Chapter 20 Assessment

CONCEPT 20.1

Reproductive adaptations contribute to angiosperm success.

OBJECTIVES

- Relate the structures of a flower to their reproductive functions.
- Describe various means of seed dispersal.
- Contrast mechanisms of seed germination.
- Describe different ways that plants reproduce asexually.
- List three types of life expectancies for plants.

KEY TERMS

- sepal
- petal
- anther
- embryo sac
- style
- stigma
- pollination
- pollen tube
- cotyledon
- germination
- vegetative reproduction

What's Online

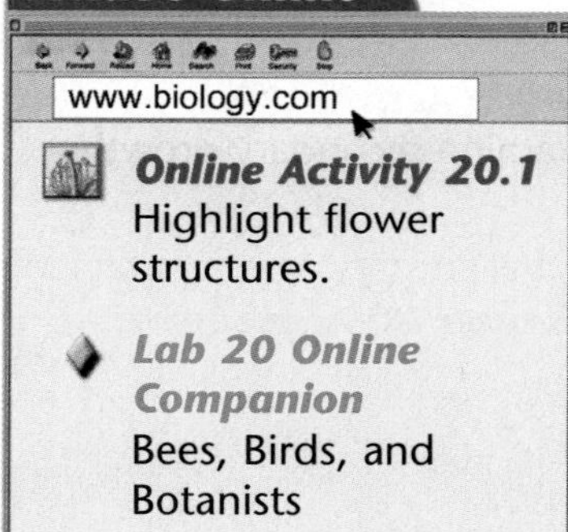

Online Activity 20.1 Highlight flower structures.

Lab 20 Online Companion Bees, Birds, and Botanists

Next time you are around flowers, look carefully inside. Many of the flowers you are familiar with are known for their pretty petals, but there's much more to a flower than petals. In fact, center stage for the plant's reproductive action is tucked inside. Read on to find out how the drama unfolds.

Flowers and Reproduction

While flowers come in all different shapes, colors, and sizes, most share the same basic pattern. A flower is a specialized shoot unique to angiosperms that usually consists of four different rings of modified leaves: sepals, petals, stamens, and carpels (Figure 20-1). The outermost ring, the **sepals,** covers and protects the flower bud before the blossom opens. (An example is a rosebud.) The next ring into the flower is composed of **petals.** Petals are often strikingly colorful—they are probably the structures you think of when you picture a flower. Some flower petals have "runway" markings that help guide insect pollinators toward the flower's reproductive parts. Finally, closest to the center of the flower are the stamens and carpels, the actual reproductive structures. Most flowers have multiple stamens surrounding one or more carpels. Some species, however, have stamens and carpels on separate flowers or even separate plants.

The male gametophytes are produced within the stamens. Each stamen consists of a long stalk topped by a sac called an **anther.** Within the anthers, meiosis produces spores that develop into pollen grains—the male haploid gametophytes (Figure 20-2). Each pollen grain consists of two cells surrounded by a thick protective wall. When smelling a flower, you may have dusted your nose with some of these tiny pollen grains.

The female gametophytes are produced in the carpels. At the base of each carpel is an ovary. Inside the ovary are structures called ovules. In each ovule, a diploid cell undergoes meiosis and forms four haploid spores. Three of the four haploid cells die.

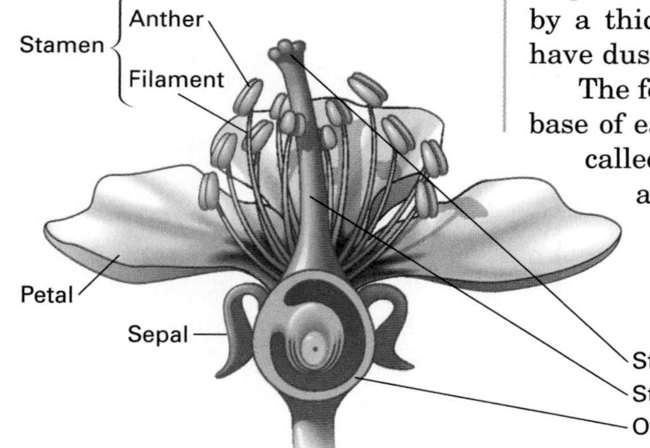

Figure 20-1 This drawing illustrates the anatomy of a typical flower. Note the male and female reproductive structures.

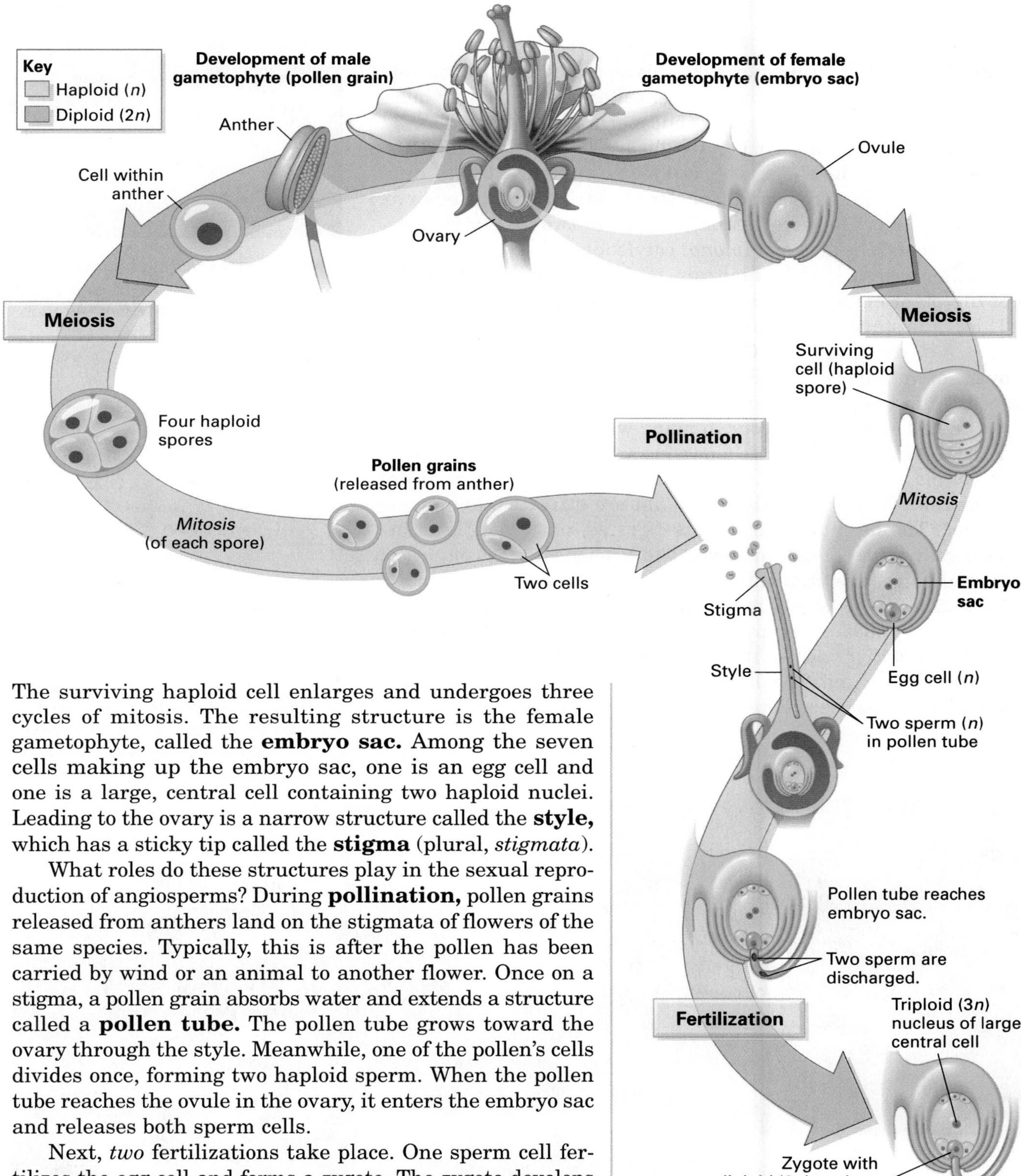

▲ **Figure 20-2** An angiosperm's life cycle includes development of male and female gametophytes, pollination, and fertilization.

The surviving haploid cell enlarges and undergoes three cycles of mitosis. The resulting structure is the female gametophyte, called the **embryo sac.** Among the seven cells making up the embryo sac, one is an egg cell and one is a large, central cell containing two haploid nuclei. Leading to the ovary is a narrow structure called the **style,** which has a sticky tip called the **stigma** (plural, *stigmata*).

What roles do these structures play in the sexual reproduction of angiosperms? During **pollination,** pollen grains released from anthers land on the stigmata of flowers of the same species. Typically, this is after the pollen has been carried by wind or an animal to another flower. Once on a stigma, a pollen grain absorbs water and extends a structure called a **pollen tube.** The pollen tube grows toward the ovary through the style. Meanwhile, one of the pollen's cells divides once, forming two haploid sperm. When the pollen tube reaches the ovule in the ovary, it enters the embryo sac and releases both sperm cells.

Next, *two* fertilizations take place. One sperm cell fertilizes the egg cell and forms a zygote. The zygote develops into the sporophyte embryo. The other sperm cell fertilizes the large central cell with the two haploid nuclei, resulting in a *triploid* cell ($3n$). This triploid cell develops into a nutrient-rich tissue called endosperm that nourishes the growing embryo.

Seed Development and Dispersal

After the double fertilization takes place, the ovule develops into a seed. Seeds have a tough outer layer called a seed coat that helps to protect the tiny embryo and endosperm inside (Figure 20-3). A miniature root and shoot take form. A structure called the cotyledon also develops. The **cotyledon** (kaht uh LEE dun) functions in the storage and transfer of nutrients to the embryo. In dicots (short for *dicotyledon*), there are two (*di*) cotyledons. In monocots, there is one (*mono*) cotyledon.

After several cycles of mitosis, the growth and development of the plant embryo within the seed is temporarily suspended. This is the stage when the seed can be dispersed from the parent plant. As you learned in Chapter 19, a fruit develops from the ovary of an angiosperm. Fruits protect seeds and help disperse seeds from the parent plant.

Seed dispersal can occur in many ways (Figure 20-4). Some seeds travel by sticking onto a passing animal's fur, as with burrs. (A burr is actually a fruit, just not a tasty one!) Other seeds are tucked inside fleshy, edible fruits that are attractive to animals as food. The flesh of the fruit gets digested, but the indigestible seed coat protects the embryo. The seed passes through the animal's digestive tract and is eventually deposited as part of the animal's feces, sometimes many kilometers from the original plant. Some seeds, such as coconuts, travel on water (again, encased in the fruit). Others are so tiny and lightweight that they can be carried by the wind. The dandelion in Figure 20-4 is one example of a plant whose seeds are dispersed by the wind.

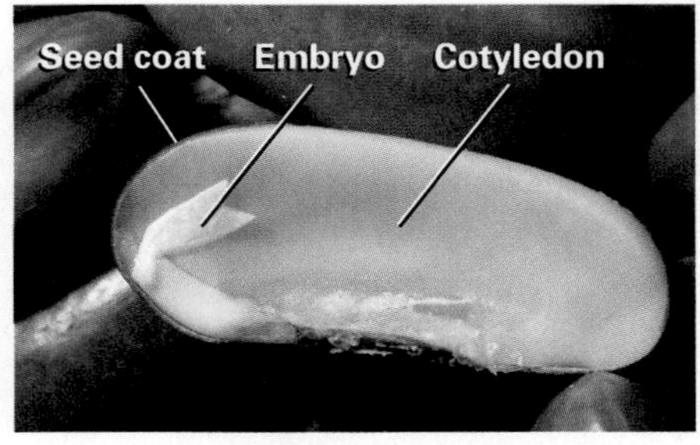

▲ **Figure 20-3** Slicing a string bean (a seed) in half reveals the embryo and one of the two cotyledons. A tough seed coat surrounds the seed.

▼ **Figure 20-4** Seeds are dispersed in different ways. Some seeds are packaged inside spiny fruits that hitch rides on animals (left). Other seeds are packaged inside tasty fruit, and are dispersed after passing through an animal's body (center). And some seeds travel on the wind (right).

Seed Germination

When conditions are favorable, the plant embryo begins to grow again. This process is called **germination.** Most seeds must soak up water in order to germinate. By taking up water, the seed expands and splits its seed coat. The water also triggers metabolic changes in the embryo that enable it to grow.

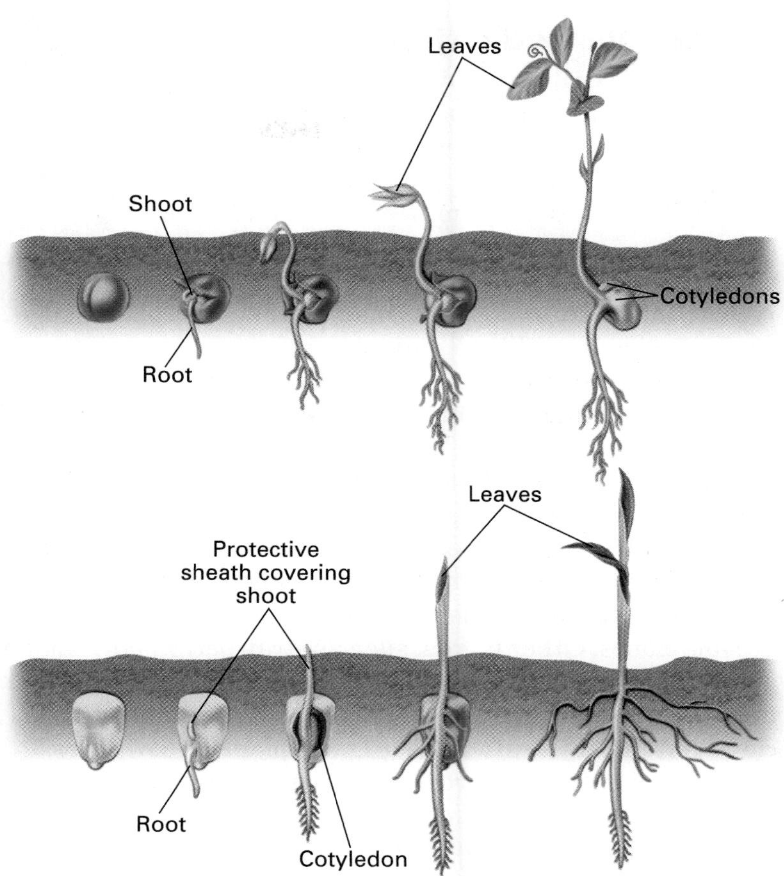

▲ **Figure 20-5** A range of adaptations protect plants during germination. In some dicots, such as peas, the shoot tip avoids traveling "face-first" by being hooked downwards as it moves through the soil (top). In some monocots, such as corn, a protective sheath penetrates the soil ahead of the shoot (bottom).

Adaptations After breaking out of the seed coat, the journey of a plant shoot through the soil to the surface is a difficult one. Have you ever scraped your knee or elbow on gravel? In a similar way, but on a smaller scale, sand and other hard particles in soil are abrasive to new plant tissues sliding past them. But plants have adaptations that protect the developing shoot as it grows toward the surface (Figure 20-5). For example, some dicots have a hooked shoot tip. This protects the delicate shoot tip by holding it downward as the shoot moves through the soil. As the shoot breaks through the soil surface, its tip is lifted gently out of the soil and straightens out. In most monocots, a sheath surrounding the shoot pushes straight upward, breaking through the soil. The delicate shoot then grows upward through this protective tunnel. After emerging into the light, the first leaves expand from the shoot and begin making food by photosynthesis. At this stage the young plant is called a *seedling*.

Environmental Conditions What environmental conditions are required for germination? If you've ever tried to grow garden vegetables, you probably noticed that simply exposing the seeds to a warm, moist environment was enough in most cases. But the conditions for germination vary among plant species. Some plants have more particular requirements. For example, some desert plants germinate only after a heavy rainfall. This allows the seedling to push more easily through the moistened soil, and ensures at least a temporary water supply that can be used by its growing tissues. In climates with harsh winters, some seeds will germinate only after being exposed to a long period of cold. This prevents them from germinating in the middle of winter. Some seeds require exposure to the intense heat of a brush fire before germinating. The fire clears dense shrubs and other growth that would otherwise totally shade the seedling.

Asexual Reproduction in Plants

There are several obstacles to successful sexual reproduction in plants. Pollen may not reach the stigma of the correct species of flower. Seeds may get damaged during the dispersal process, or they may end up somewhere they cannot germinate. Furthermore, only a small fraction of seedlings in the wild actually survive to mature into plants capable of making their own seeds. Delicate seedlings may perish from lack of water or be eaten. But, in addition to sexual reproduction, many plants are also capable of asexual reproduction.

Asexual reproduction in plants is called **vegetative reproduction.** The offspring, or clones, are genetically identical to the original plant. Vegetative reproduction can occur naturally or with human help (Figure 20-6). Some plants, such as many cacti, drop stems or other shoots that establish new roots and become clones. Other plants, such as strawberry plants and many grasses, send out runners. Some trees and shrubs send out shoots from the base of their trunks or from underground stems. These clones often persist after the original plant dies.

Using vegetative reproduction in agriculture and horticulture provides a way to propagate useful crop specimens or decorative plants without needing to wait for seeds produced by the desired plant to develop. Vegetative reproduction also offers the advantage of duplicating desired traits exactly, without sexual recombination of traits.

▲ **Figure 20-6** The cholla cactus (top) drops sections of its stems. The stem pieces take root, becoming clones of the parent. Multiple clones of the houseplant *Streptocarpus* (bottom) can be produced by cutting up a single leaf and planting each piece.

How Long Does a Plant Live?

For plants that mainly reproduce sexually, life expectancies vary. Plants called *annuals* complete their life cycle (germinate, grow, produce flowers and seeds, and die) in a single year's growing season (for example, from spring to fall). *Biennials* complete their life cycle in two years and usually only flower the second year. *Perennials* live and reproduce for multiple years.

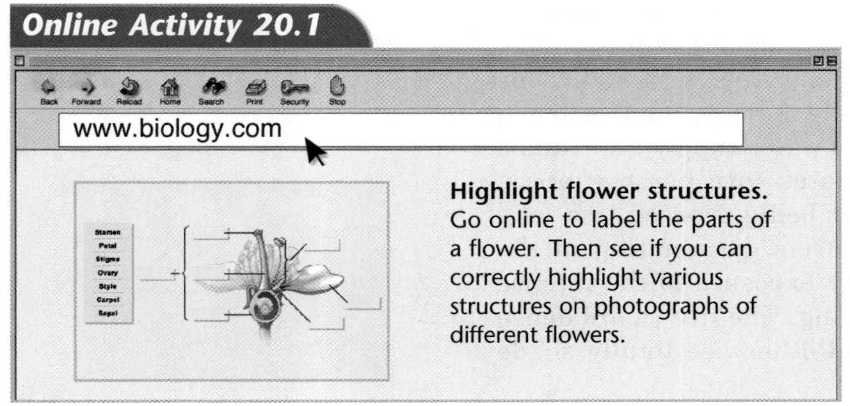

Online Activity 20.1
www.biology.com
Highlight flower structures.
Go online to label the parts of a flower. Then see if you can correctly highlight various structures on photographs of different flowers.

Concept Check 20.1

1. Diagram the reproductive structures of a flower. For each structure, include a label stating a brief description of its function.
2. Describe three different methods of seed dispersal.
3. Explain how two different adaptations of seed germination in dicots and monocots protect the developing shoot.
4. Give two examples of vegetative reproduction in plants.
5. Compare and contrast annuals, biennials, and perennials.

Bees, Birds, and Botanists

Exploring Flower Structure and Adaptations

Question How do the parts of a flower work to attract pollinators and produce seeds?

Lab Overview In this investigation you will discover how flowers attract different types of animal pollinators. Then you will dissect a flower to observe reproductive structures and learn how they work together to produce a seed.

Preparing for the Lab To help you prepare for the investigation, go to the *Lab 20 Online Companion.* → Find out more about flower structure and function. Prepare for the lab procedure by previewing the steps you will take.

Completing the Lab Use your Laboratory Manual or lab page printouts from the *Lab 20 Online Companion* to do the investigation and draw conclusions from the observations you made. **CAUTION:** *Be sure to follow your teacher's instructions and all safety guidelines in the investigation.*

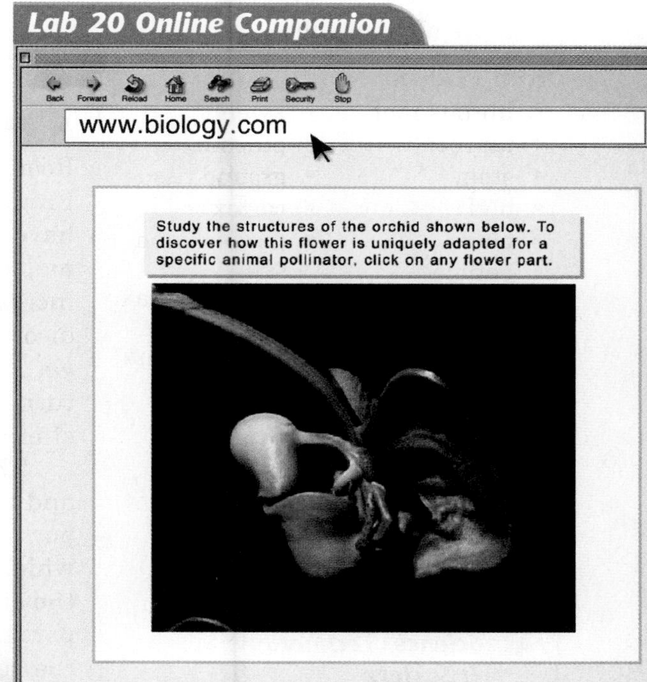
Lab 20 Online Companion
Back
Forward
Reload
Home
Search
Print
Security
Stop
www.biology.com
Study the structures of the orchid shown below. To discover how this flower is uniquely adapted for a specific animal pollinator, click on any flower part.

CONCEPT 20.2 Structure fits function in the plant body.

OBJECTIVES

- Describe root and shoot structures and functions.
- Describe three main plant tissue systems.
- Contrast three different types of plant cells.

KEY TERMS

- fibrous root
- taproot
- stem
- bud
- blade
- petiole
- dermal tissue
- vascular tissue
- xylem
- phloem
- ground tissue
- cortex
- parenchyma cell
- collenchyma cell
- sclerenchyma cell

What's Online

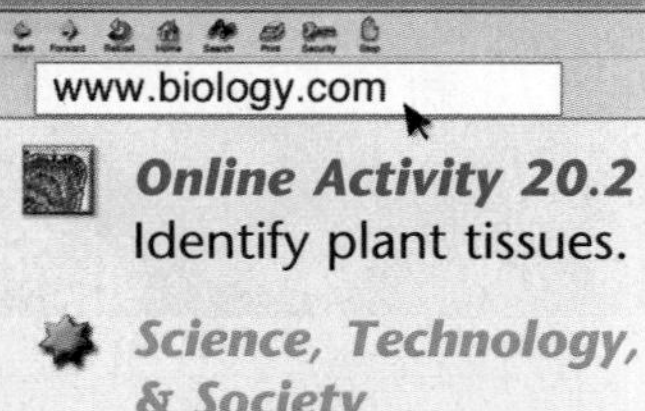

Online Activity 20.2
Identify plant tissues.

Science, Technology, & Society
Plants and Bioremediation

Like animals, plants have specialized organs, tissues, and cells. These structural adaptations enhance the survival and reproductive success of plants in the environments in which they grow.

A Plant's Root System and Shoot System

Roots anchor a plant in the soil and provide structural support. From the soil, roots absorb minerals and water. Most monocots have fibrous root systems. A **fibrous root** system consists of a mat of thin roots spread out below the soil surface, providing increased exposure to soil nutrients and water. In contrast, most dicots have a **taproot** system that is characterized by one large vertical root with many smaller branches (Figure 20-7). Carrots, turnips, and beets are examples of dicots that have very large, starch-storing taproots.

The shoot system of an angiosperm consists of stems, leaves, and flowers (Figure 20-8). **Stems** are parts of a plant that support leaves and flowers. Nodes are the points on the stem at which leaves are attached, and internodes are the portions of the stem between nodes. Stems play an important role in transporting materials in a plant. Vascular tissue runs vertically in the stem, transporting water and minerals from the roots up to the leaves, and food from the leaves down through the stem to the roots. Stems may also conduct some photosynthesis and store nutrients.

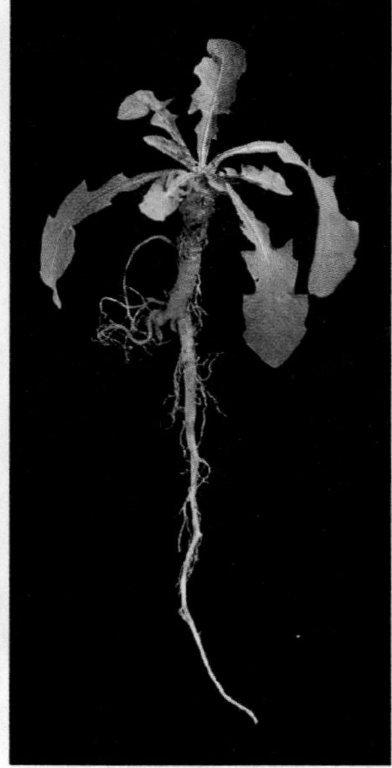

Figure 20-7 A fibrous root system, typical of grasses and other monocots, consists of a mat of thin roots (left). In contrast, most dicots have a taproot system consisting of one thick central root with thin branches (right).

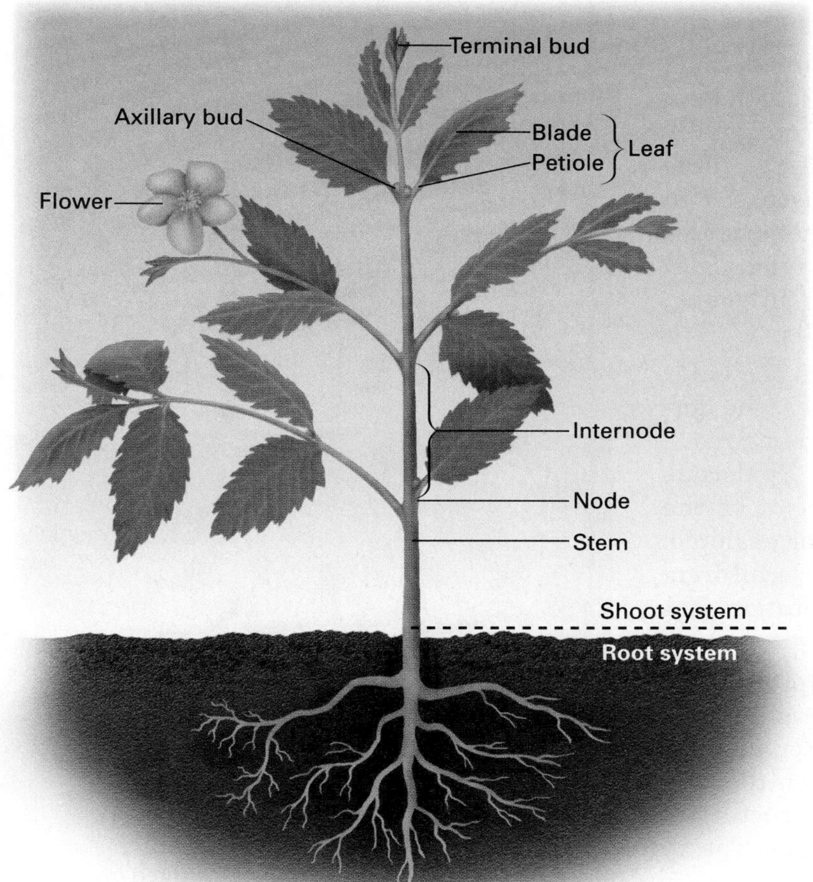

Figure 20-8 A plant has a root system below the ground and a shoot system above. A shoot consists of stems, leaves, and flowers. New shoots grow from buds throughout the plant's life.

Science, Technology, & Society

Back Forward Reload Home Search Print Security Stop

www.biology.com

Plants and Bioremediation

All plants store starches, nutrients, and water in their cells. But did you know that some plants also store metals that aren't nutrients? Go online to learn how scientists are exploring their possible use in cleaning contaminated soil.

Undeveloped shoots are called **buds.** A terminal bud is found at the tip of a stem. Axillary buds are found in the angles (the axils) formed by a leaf and the main stem. Growth from axillary buds forms the plant's branches.

Leaves are the primary food-manufacturing sites of a plant. As you read in Chapter 8, leaves capture sunlight and convert light energy to chemical energy during photosynthesis. Most leaves are flattened and thin. The main part of the leaf is the **blade.** A stalk called a **petiole** (PET ee ohl) connects the leaf to the stem. Running through the petiole and into the blade are leaf veins. The veins carry water and nutrients and consist of vascular tissue and support tissue.

Some plants have highly modified leaves (Figure 20-9). For example, the long leaves of grasses lack petioles altogether. Celery, on the other hand, has enormous petioles—the "stalks" that you eat. Some leaves, such as the spines on a cactus, are modified so much they hardly resemble a typical leaf. The tendrils on a pea plant or a grapevine are modified leaves that allow a plant to attach to and climb along a surface.

Figure 20-9 The red "petals" of a poinsettia are actually leaves (bottom). An onion bulb is a modified underground shoot (top). The layers of the onion are modified leaves.

A Plant's Main Tissue Systems

A plant has three main tissue systems: the dermal, vascular, and ground tissue systems. (A fourth kind of tissue called meristematic tissue continually produces the cells that will differentiate into these other three tissue types. It will be discussed in Concept 20.3.) The three main tissue systems change as a plant ages. Here you will read about the three tissue systems as they occur in young, nonwoody parts of a plant (Figure 20-10).

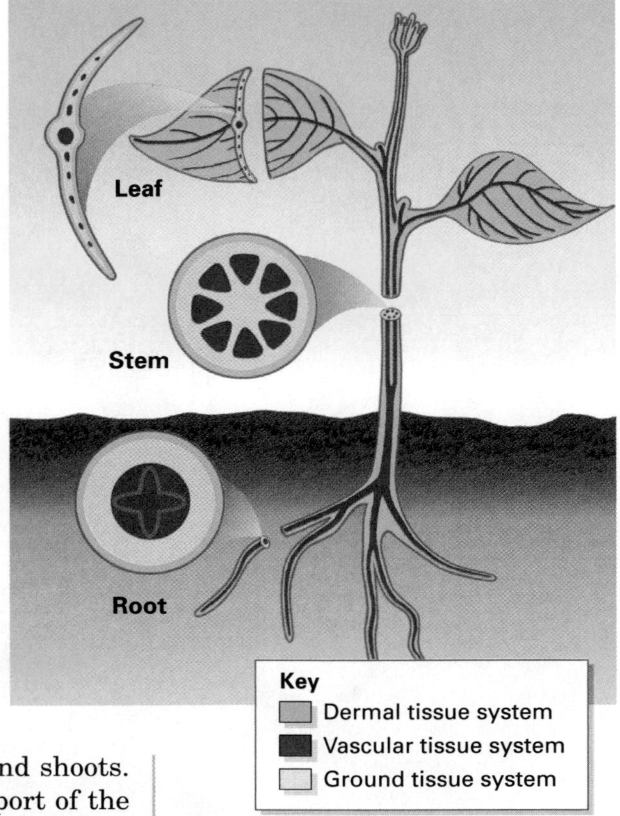

▲ **Figure 20-10** The three main tissue systems are present throughout a plant.

Dermal Tissue The **dermal tissue** is the outer covering or "skin" of the plant. Epidermis, the dermal tissue of nonwoody organs such as young roots, consists of one or more layers of cells. Epidermis covers and protects all the young parts of the plant. Some epidermis is specialized. For example, leaf epidermis secretes a waxy cuticle. Recall from Concept 19.1 that the cuticle is an adaptation that helps plants retain water.

Vascular Tissue One of the key adaptations of plants that you read about in Chapter 19 is vascular tissue. **Vascular tissue** transports water, mineral nutrients, and organic molecules between the roots and shoots. Vascular tissue also contributes to the structural support of the plant. There are two types of vascular tissue. The **xylem** (ZY lum) transports water and dissolved minerals upward from roots into shoots. The **phloem** (FLOH um) transports food made in mature leaves to the roots and parts of the shoot system that don't photosynthesize, such as developing leaves and fruits.

Vascular tissue is located in the centers of roots, but in the stems it is arranged in many separate strands called vascular bundles. The monocot stem has vascular bundles scattered throughout its ground tissue, whereas the vascular bundles of the dicot stem are arranged in a ring (Figure 20-11). You'll read more about the structure and function of vascular tissue in Chapter 21.

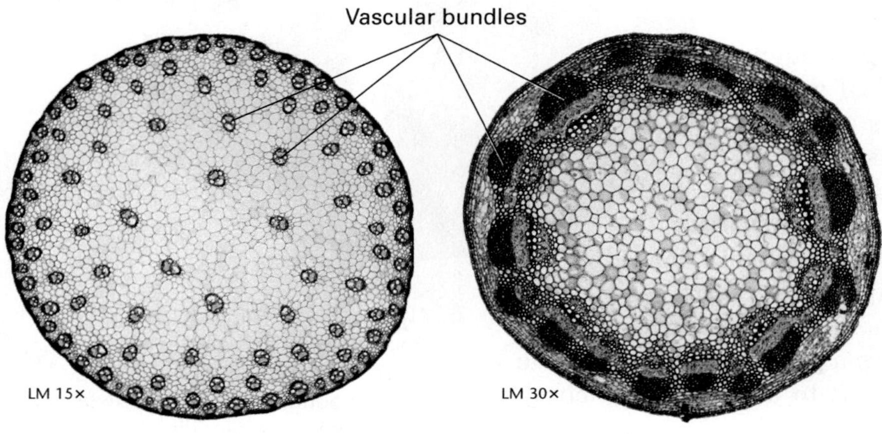

◄ **Figure 20-11** As viewed in a cross section, the vascular bundles of a monocot stem are scattered throughout the ground tissue (left). In contrast, the vascular bundles of a dicot stem are organized in a ring (right).

Ground Tissue Filling the spaces between the dermal and vascular tissues, **ground tissue** makes up most of a young, nonwoody plant and functions in photosynthesis (in the shoot), storage, and support throughout the plant. The ground tissue of the root consists primarily of a mass of cells called the **cortex.** You will read more about the root cortex in Concept 20.3.

Types of Plant Cells

The plant tissues you've been reading about are made up of three basic cell types: parenchyma, collenchyma, and sclerenchyma (Figure 20-12). The most abundant type of cell, the **parenchyma cell** (puh RENG kih muh), has thin cell walls and typically, large central vacuoles. These cells perform a variety of functions in the plant, including food storage, photosynthesis, and cellular respiration. Fruits are made up mostly of parenchyma cells. The food-conducting cells of phloem are also parenchyma cells.

Collenchyma cells (kuh LENG kih muh) have unevenly thickened cell walls. Grouped in strands or cylinders, collenchyma cells provide support in parts of the plant that are still growing. Young stems and petioles often have collenchyma just below their surface (the "strings" of a celery stalk for example). These living cells elongate with the stems and leaves they support as these regions grow.

Sclerenchyma cells (sklih RENG kih muh) are specialized for support. Sclerenchyma cells grow and then die within a mature part of a plant. But that doesn't mean they become useless to the plant after dying. Their lignin-rich cell walls are left behind, creating the "skeleton" that supports the plant. For example, the water-conducting cells of xylem are specialized sclerenchyma cells.

It is important to note that a particular type of plant tissue is not made up of just one type of plant cell. For example, ground tissue, while mostly parenchyma, may also have collenchyma (as in a celery stalk) and even sclerenchyma (as in the gritty spots of a pear's otherwise soft parenchyma).

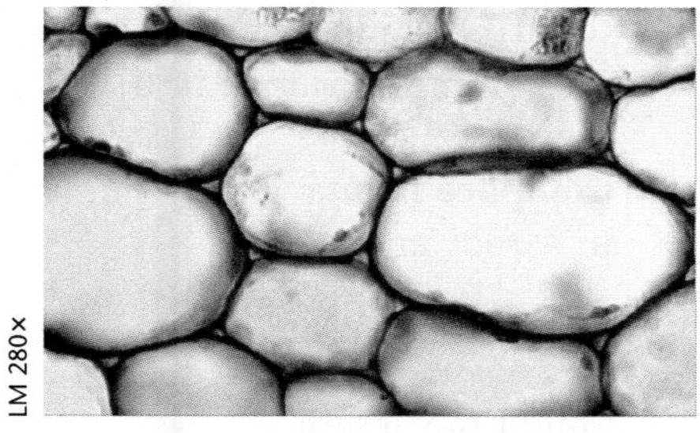

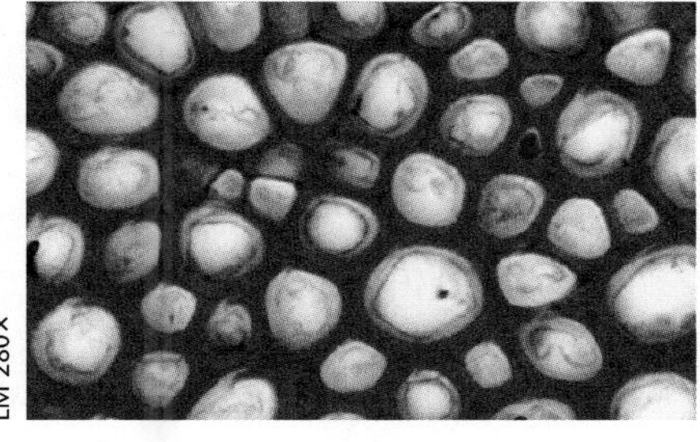

▲ **Figure 20-12** Plant tissues consist of three basic cell types. Parenchyma have thin cell walls (top). Collenchyma have unevenly thickened cell walls (middle). Sclerenchyma have lignin-rich cell walls (bottom).

Online Activity 20.2

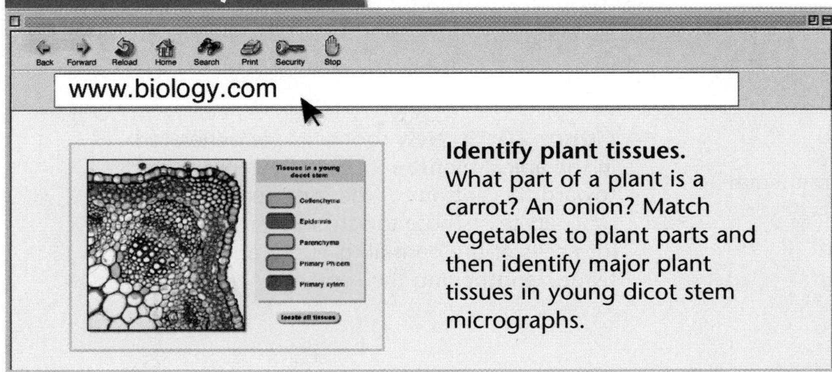

Back
Forward
Reload
Home
Search
Print
Security
Stop
www.biology.com
Identify plant tissues.
What part of a plant is a carrot? An onion? Match vegetables to plant parts and then identify major plant tissues in young dicot stem micrographs.

Concept Check 20.2

1. Compare and contrast the functions of roots and shoots.
2. List the functions of dermal, ground, and vascular tissues.
3. Describe characteristics of the three main plant cell types.

CONCEPT 20.3

Primary growth lengthens roots and shoots.

OBJECTIVES
- Identify the locations of meristematic tissue in a plant.
- Compare primary growth in a root and a shoot.

KEY TERMS
- meristem
- apical meristem
- primary growth
- root cap

What's Online

www.biology.com

Online Activity 20.3
Dissect a root.

While you will reach your maximum height sometime within the next few years, most plants grow their entire lives. This lifelong growth enables plants to continue increasing their exposure to sunlight, air, and soil.

Meristematic Tissue

Tissues called **meristems** (MEHR uh stemz) generate new dermal, vascular, and ground tissue in plants throughout their lives. A meristem consists of groups of cells that divide by mitosis, generating new cells that will later differentiate into one of the three main cell types. Meristems located in the tips of roots and buds of shoots are called **apical meristems** (AP ih kul). The apical meristems produce the new cells that enable a plant to grow in length, both above and below ground, as well as to branch. Growth in plant length is called **primary growth.**

Primary Growth of Roots

The very tip of the root is the **root cap,** a thimble-like cone of cells that protects the delicate, actively dividing cells of the apical meristem. The root's apical meristem has two roles: It replaces the cells of the root cap that are scraped away by the soil, and it produces the cells for primary growth. Cells produced during primary growth form three concentric cylinders of developing tissue (Figure 20-13). The outermost cylinder develops into the dermal tissue of the root. The middle cylinder—the bulk of the root tip—develops into the root's cortex (ground tissue). The innermost cylinder becomes the vascular tissue.

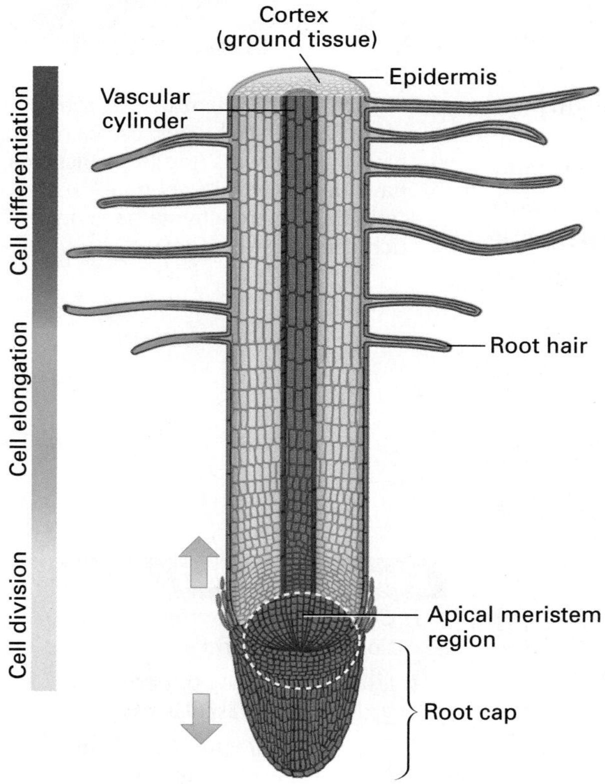

Figure 20-13 New root cells are generated in the apical meristem. Those cells produced toward the bottom of the meristem replenish root cap cells. Those toward the top differentiate into cells of the dermal, ground, and vascular tissue, lengthening the root.

Primary growth depends not only on the addition of new cells by the apical meristem, but on those new cells getting longer. The new cells become longer mainly by taking up water. This process of elongation is what actually forces the root tip through the soil.

Primary Growth of Shoots

A shoot's apical meristem is a dome-shaped mass of dividing cells at the very tip of the terminal bud (Figure 20-14). Elongation occurs just below this meristem. The elongating cells push the apical meristem upward, instead of downward as in the root. As the apical meristem advances upward, some of its cells are left behind. These pockets of meristematic cells form axillary buds at the bases of new leaves. Axillary buds give rise to branches that also show primary growth as they grow outward from the main stem. As in the root, the apical meristem forms three concentric cylinders of developing tissue. Similarly, each cylinder in the shoot develops into one of the shoot's three main tissue systems—dermal, ground, or vascular tissues.

Primary growth accounts for a plant's lengthwise growth. The stems and roots of many plants increase in thickness, too. You will explore how this happens in Concept 20.4.

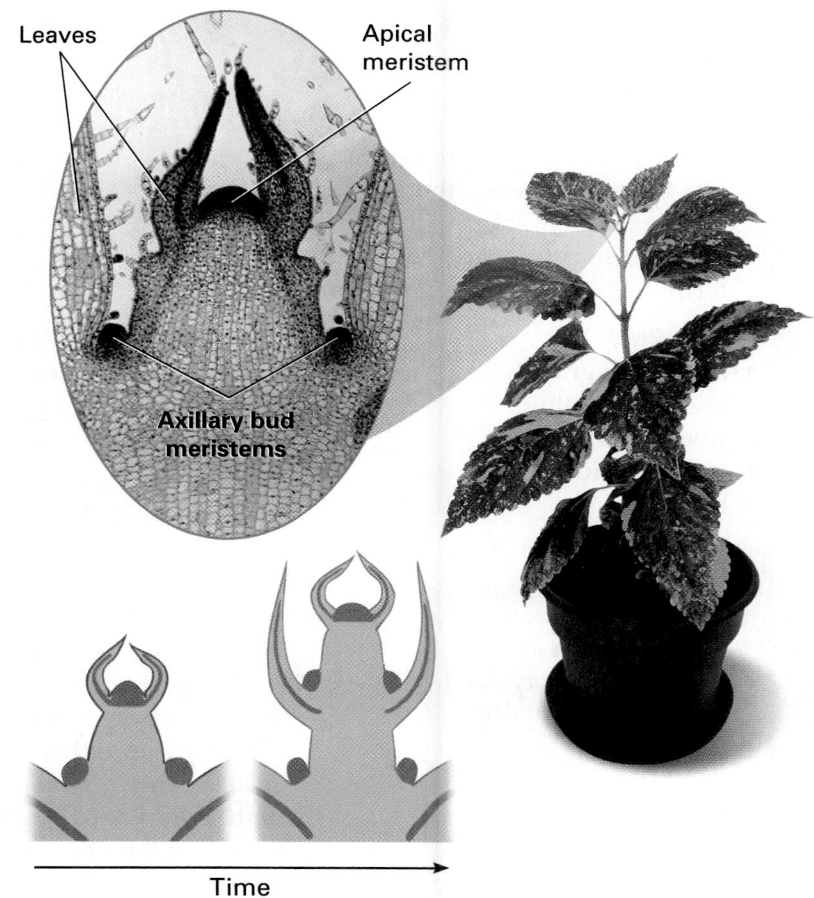

▲ **Figure 20-14** The micrograph of the tip of a *Coleus* plant shows the tightly packed cells characteristic of a meristem. The diagrams show growth of the meristem over time. Note that as the apical meristem is pushed upward, new axillary buds have formed in each new axil.

Online Activity 20.3

Dissect a root.
Go online to watch a video of root growth. Then use an online magnifier to closely examine the internal structure of a root.

Concept Check 20.3

1. Draw a simple plant and note the locations of meristems.
2. Compare and contrast primary growth in a root and a shoot.
3. Describe the function of the root cap.

CONCEPT 20.4

Secondary growth increases the thickness of woody plants.

OBJECTIVES

- Identify the two meristematic tissues that contribute to secondary growth.
- Describe how tree rings form.

KEY TERMS

- secondary growth
- vascular cambium
- wood
- cork cambium
- bark

What's Online

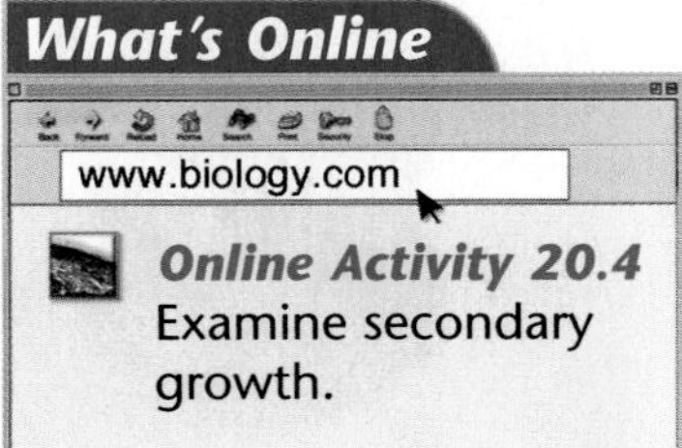

Thousands of useful products are made from wood—from construction lumber to fine furniture and musical instruments. Wood is produced by many plants as they increase in thickness.

Secondary Growth Tissues

Growth in plant width is referred to as **secondary growth.** Secondary growth occurs in the woody plants—vines, shrubs, and trees. Secondary growth involves cell division in two meristematic tissues, called vascular cambium and cork cambium.

The **vascular cambium** is a cylinder of actively dividing cells located between the xylem and phloem. The vascular cambium adds cells on either side, producing secondary xylem toward the inside of the stem and secondary phloem toward the outside of the stem (Figure 20-15). This secondary vascular tissue is added to the primary xylem and primary phloem produced by the apical meristem during primary growth. The secondary xylem that is laid down in the growing season of each year accumulates as **wood.** (In temperate climates, the vascular cambium is dormant during winter.) With each added layer of xylem, the stem or the root thickens.

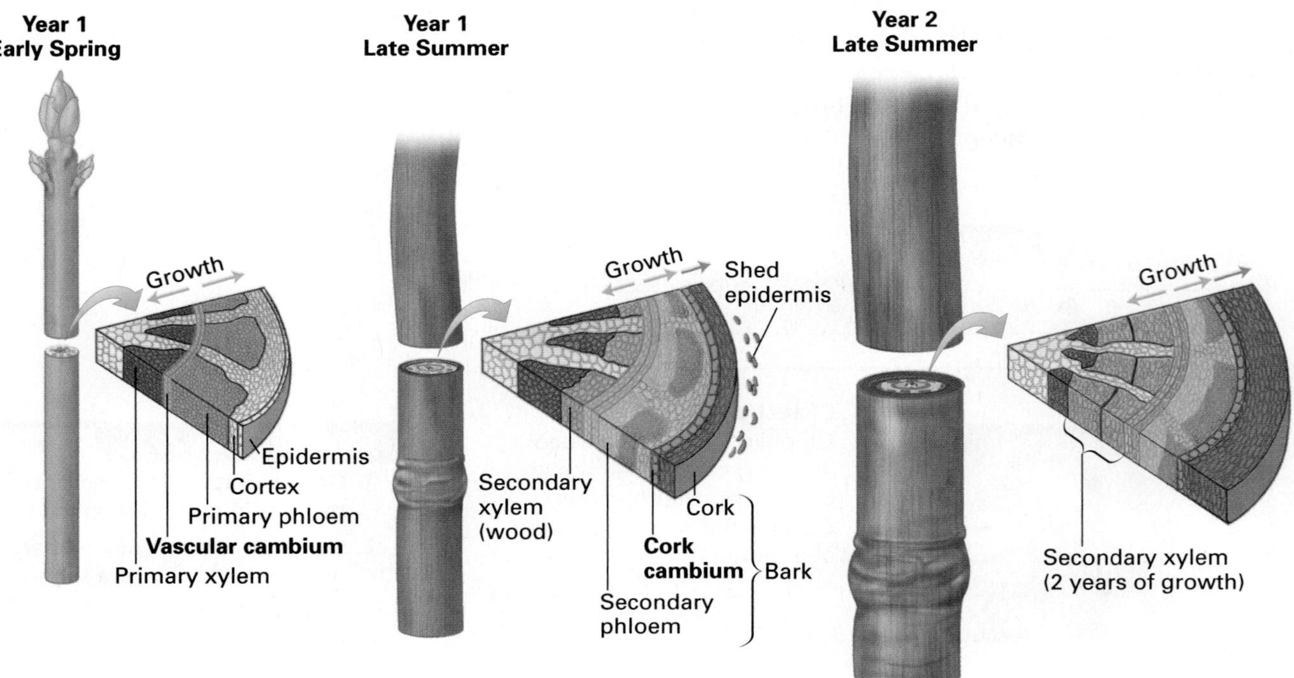

▼ **Figure 20-15** Cell division in the vascular cambium and cork cambium contributes to secondary growth.

As secondary growth begins and the stem or root thickens, the original soft dermal tissue and cortex cells of the young stem are shed. A meristem called **cork cambium** develops from parenchyma cells in the remaining cortex. It produces a tough outer layer of cork. As these cork cells die, they leave behind thick, waxy walls that help prevent water loss from the stem. Cork also functions as a barrier that helps protect the internal tissues from physical damage and pathogens.

Everything outside of the vascular cambium is called **bark:** the phloem, cork cambium, and cork. The older phloem dies as it is pushed outward. Along with the cork, this dead phloem helps protect the stem until the bark is shed.

The cork cambium produces a steady supply of new cork, keeping pace with growth from the vascular cambium. Because cork cambium is shed with the rest of the bark, new cork cambium continuously regenerates from parenchyma cells in the still-living phloem left behind.

Figure 20-16 A cross section through a tree trunk reveals different layers of tissues. (Note that in the diagram, colors are used to distinguish the different layers.) Sapwood is new xylem that is still actively transporting water. Heartwood is old xylem that no longer transports water.

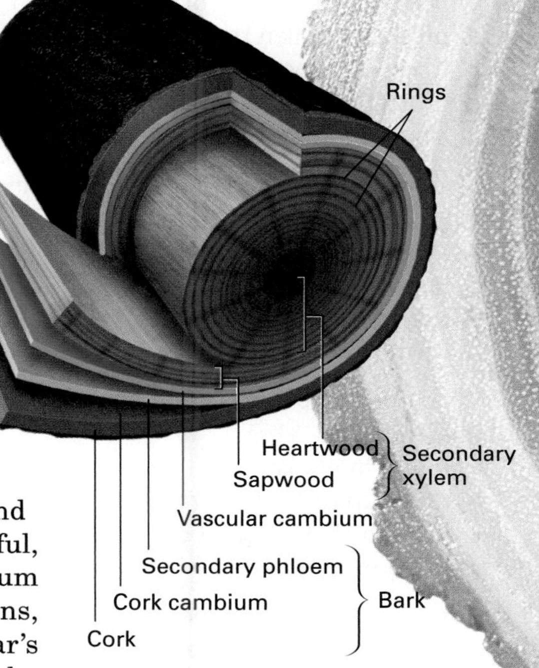

Tree Rings

Examining an old tree trunk in cross section enables you to "read" the history of the plant. You can estimate the tree's age by counting its annual growth rings. These rings result from the yearly activity of the vascular cambium (Figure 20-16).

Environmental conditions during the growing season affect xylem growth. The vascular cambium produces xylem cells that can carry a lot of water—cells that are large and thin-walled—when temperatures are cool and water is plentiful, as in the typical spring. In contrast, the vascular cambium produces narrow, thick-walled cells under hot, dry conditions, as in the typical summer. Each tree ring represents a year's growth. It consists of a cylinder of spring wood surrounded by a cylinder of denser summer wood. Differences in ring width reveal the variation in weather patterns from year to year, such as a particularly wet or dry spring.

Online Activity 20.4

Examine secondary growth. Go online to identify the secondary tissues in a young woody stem. Then explore animations of how the secondary xylem and secondary phloem develop.

Concept Check 20.4

1. What two tissues does the meristematic vascular cambium tissue produce?
2. In which tissue of a tree trunk are "tree rings" formed? Describe how they can be used to determine a tree's age.
3. Describe how the cork cambium protects a woody plant.

Multiple Choice

Choose the letter of the best answer.

1. Which choice below lists the modified leaves of a typical flower from outermost to innermost?
   a. carpels, stamens, petals, sepals
   b. sepals, stamens, carpels, petals
   c. stamens, carpels, petals, sepals
   d. sepals, petals, stamens, carpels

2. Which best states the role of the pollen tube?
   a. produces pollen grains in the stamen
   b. transports sperm to the embryo sac
   c. protects pollen during air travel
   d. all of the above

3. A stem may carry out all of the following functions *except*
   a. storing nutrients.
   b. absorbing water from the soil.
   c. transporting food to the roots.
   d. conducting photosynthesis.

4. Which of the following best characterizes sclerenchyma cells?
   a. found in meristems
   b. make up majority of root cortex
   c. have thick, hardened cell walls
   d. perform photosynthesis

5. Which is the correct order of the three cylinders of developing root tissue from innermost to outermost?
   a. vascular, ground, dermal
   b. dermal, vascular, ground
   c. ground, vascular, dermal
   d. ground, dermal, vascular

6. Apical meristem is to primary growth as
   a. cork cell is to cork cambium.
   b. tree ring is to secondary growth.
   c. secondary growth is to width.
   d. vascular cambium is to secondary growth.

7. The structures that are part of bark include cork, cork cambium, and
   a. vascular cambium.
   b. secondary xylem.
   c. heartwood.
   d. phloem.

Short Answer

8. Trace what happens to a pollen grain after it lands on another flower's stigma. What results from the two fertilizations?

9. List four ways that seeds can be dispersed and give an example of each.

10. Describe three environmental conditions that can trigger germination of certain plants.

11. Define vegetative reproduction. Explain its advantages in farming and cultivating decorative plants.

12. Compare and contrast a fibrous root system and a taproot system.

13. Compare and contrast the organization of vascular tissue in monocot and dicot stems.

14. How are new dermal, vascular, and ground tissues generated?

15. Describe how elongation occurs during the primary growth of roots and shoots.

16. Identify and describe the two types of tissue generated by the vascular cambium that contribute to secondary growth.

Visualizing Concepts

17. Copy and complete the table below that summarizes the functions of plant structures. Add as many additional rows as you can for other structures you learned about in this chapter.

Plant Structure	Function
Sepal	Covers and protects flower bud
a.	Attaches leaf blade to plant stem
Meristem	b.

Analyzing Information

18. Analyzing Diagrams Examine the diagrams below and answer the following questions.

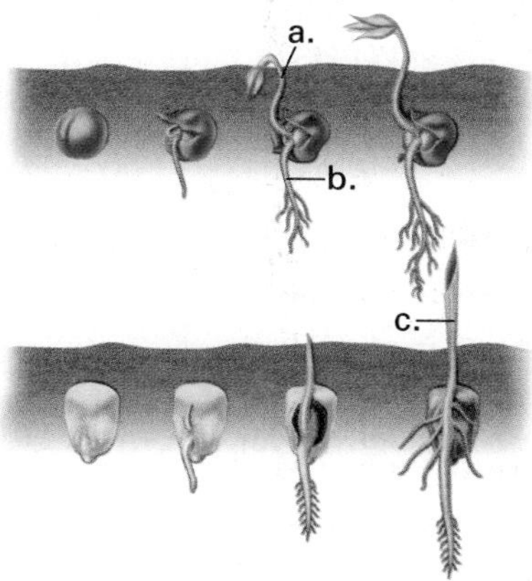

a. Which process do both diagrams show?

b. Describe an adaptation shown in each diagram. Explain its effect in aiding the process shown.

c. Name the structures indicated by the labels *a, b,* and *c.*

19. Analyzing Photographs Examine the photograph showing a cross section of a tree trunk.

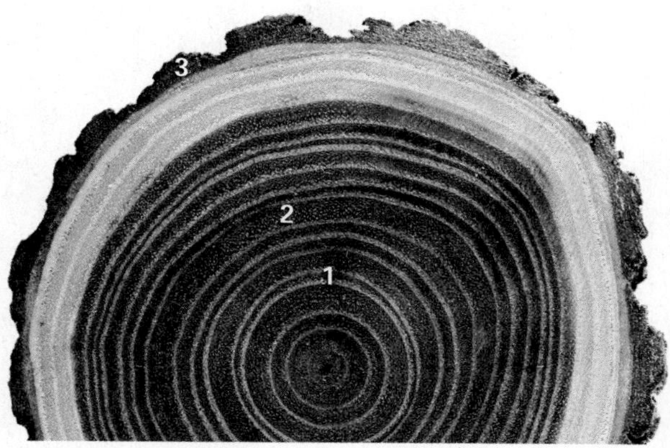

a. Approximately how old was this tree when it was cut down? 5, 10, 20, or 30 years old?

Match numbers on the photo with the descriptions below and explain your choice.

b. In this year, there was probably a drought.

c. In this year, spring was probably long and wet, and the short summer was hot.

Critical Thinking

20. Comparing and Contrasting Biologists generally define an "animal tissue" as a unit of many similar cells that together perform a specific function. How does this definition of a tissue contrast with what biologists call a "tissue system" in plants?

21. Relating Cause and Effect If a plant's terminal buds were clipped, would the plant's growth stop? Explain your answer.

22. Problem Solving Suppose two trees are damaged by two different bark-eating animals. The first animal eats a ring of bark all the way around the tree. The second animal eats the same amount as the first, but peels off a vertical strip of bark. Do they do the same amount of damage to the tree? Explain.

23. What's Wrong With These Statements? *Briefly explain why each statement is inaccurate or misleading.*

a. Within the ovaries of a flower, meiosis produces spores that develop into pollen grains.

b. Putting a seed in a warm, moist environment causes germination.

c. Tree trunks are made of dead cells.

Performance Assessment

Biology Research Project Plant scientists are searching Peru, Mexico, and the Middle East for the wild ancestors of potatoes, corn, and wheat, respectively. Research one of these crops and include details in your report about the crop's ancestry and the biology and cultivation of the crop today.

Online Assessment/Test Preparation

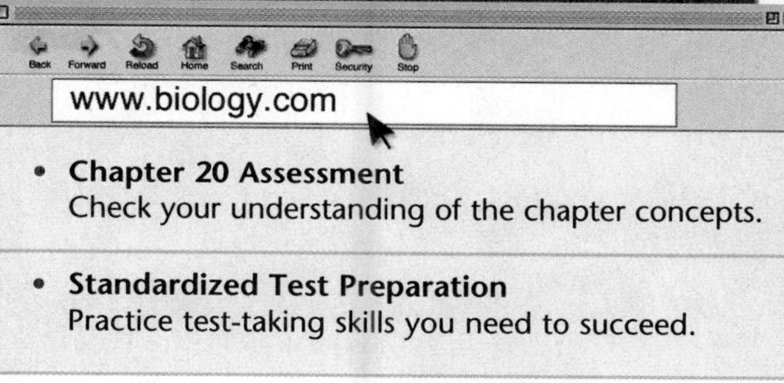

- **Chapter 20 Assessment**
  Check your understanding of the chapter concepts.
- **Standardized Test Preparation**
  Practice test-taking skills you need to succeed.

Plant Nutrition and Transport

A redwood tree can reach tens of meters in height and several meters in diameter. Where does all the mass come from to build such a huge plant? And how does the plant move the materials it needs for growth over vast distances to reach all its cells? In this chapter you'll read about the sources of a plant's nutrition as well as mechanisms for transporting these nutrients and water within the plant. Before you begin, go online to the *WebQuest* to learn about carnivorous, or meat-eating, plants.

Key Concepts

Concept 21.1

Plants acquire nutrients from the soil and air.

Concept 21.2

Vascular tissue transports sap within a plant.

Concept 21.3

Some plants have unique adaptations for nutrition.

Assessment

Chapter 21 Review

What's Online

www.biology.com

WebQuest
CarnivorousPlantQuest

Online Activity 21.1
Discover the role of nutrients in plants.

Careers
Meet a Farmer

Online Activity 21.2
Open and close leaf stomata.

Lab 21 Online Companion
Zip Up the Xylem

Online Collaborative Science 2
Exploring Patterns in Leaf Stomata

Online Activity 21.3
Trigger a Venus' flytrap.

Chapter 21 Assessment

CONCEPT 21.1

Plants acquire nutrients from the soil and air.

OBJECTIVES
- List the three sources of a plant's mass.
- List some mineral nutrients important to plants.
- Trace the path of nitrogen from the atmosphere to a plant's roots.
- List the typical contents of fertilizers.

KEY TERMS
- nitrogen fixation
- legume
- root nodule

What's Online

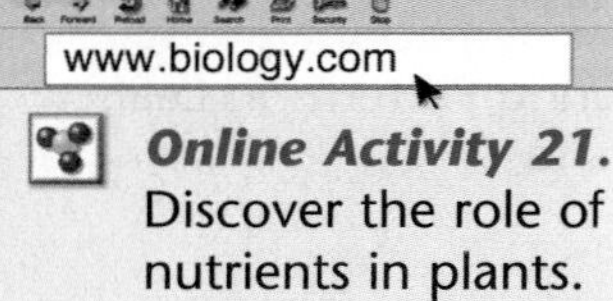

Online Activity 21.1 Discover the role of nutrients in plants.

Careers Meet a Farmer

In the 4th century B.C.E., the philosopher and scientist Aristotle proposed that soil provides all the substance (mass) necessary for plant growth. Almost 2,000 years passed before his hypothesis was tested and rejected. The process of science often advances knowledge by rejecting old hypotheses and proposing new ones in their place.

Seeking the Source of a Plant's "Substance"

Aristotle's idea was accepted as fact until the 1600s, when a Belgian physician named Jan Baptista van Helmont actually tested the hypothesis. Van Helmont grew a small willow tree in a pot containing 90 kilograms (kg) of soil. As the tree grew, he added nothing to the soil except water. Five years later, van Helmont found that the tree had gained nearly 75 kg while the soil had lost less than 0.1 kg (Figure 21-1). Since the tree gained far more mass than the soil lost, his data contradicted Aristotle's hypothesis that a plant gains its substance (mass) from soil. He proposed a new hypothesis: Growing plants gain substance from water added to the soil. A century after van Helmont's experiment, Stephen Hales, an English botanist, proposed a third hypothesis: Plants gain their substance from the air.

Van Helmont's Data

	Start	After 5 years
Soil mass (kg)	90.9	90.8
Tree mass (kg)	2.3	76.8

Figure 21-1 Van Helmont tested Aristotle's hypothesis using a young willow tree grown in a pot. The photograph shows a mature willow.

More recent research has indicated that there is some truth in *all* these early ideas about plant nutrition (Figure 21-2). Air supplies the plant with carbon dioxide. As you learned in Chapter 8, the carbon and oxygen of carbon dioxide are used in photosynthesis, generating sugar molecules. These sugars are the building blocks for the other organic molecules, such as cellulose, that make up the plant's tissues. Water (absorbed by the plant from the soil) supplies the hydrogen used in photosynthesis, serves as the solvent for the transport of other molecules through the plant, and makes up about 80–85 percent of a nonwoody plant's mass. Soil is the source of inorganic nutrients called minerals that are dissolved in water and absorbed by the plant's roots.

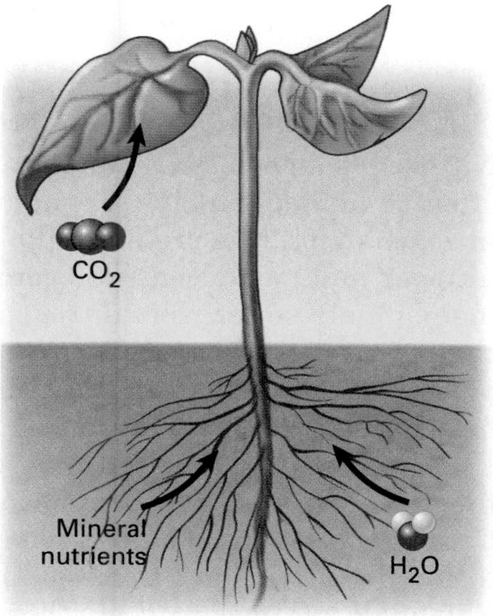

CO_2

Mineral nutrients

H_2O

▲ **Figure 21-2** A plant obtains nutrients from both the air and the soil. Carbon dioxide and water are used to make sugar in photosynthesis.

The Mineral Requirements of Plants

While many animals require a complex diet of large organic molecules, plants have simpler needs. In addition to air and water, plants require only simple ions from the soil to survive and grow. Combining these with the products of their photosynthesis, plants can make all the proteins, carbohydrates, and other molecules they need.

Most plants need 17 chemical elements to complete their life cycles—that is, to grow from a seed and produce another generation of seeds. Three of these are not obtained as minerals from the soil, as you just read: Carbon and oxygen come from CO_2 in the air and hydrogen comes mainly from water in the soil. The other elements, however, are mineral nutrients absorbed in ionic form from the soil. Figure 21-3 lists six of the mineral nutrients plants require in greatest abundance, along with their functions in the plant.

Like animals, plants can suffer from nutritional deficiencies. Without proper nutrition, plant growth may be stunted or the plant may fail to flower. Stems, roots, and leaves may also die. A plant that is magnesium-deficient, for example, is unable to synthesize chlorophyll, and shows a yellowing of its young leaves.

Some Essential Plant Mineral Nutrients

Mineral Nutrient	Functions in Plant
Nitrogen	Protein and nucleic acid synthesis
Sulfur	Protein synthesis
Phosphorus	Nucleic acid and ATP synthesis
Potassium	Protein synthesis; regulation of osmosis
Calcium	Cell wall formation; enzyme activity
Magnesium	Chlorophyll synthesis; enzyme activity

Figure 21-3 Nutrient deficiencies affect a plant's functioning. These potato plants growing in magnesium-poor soil cannot make chlorophyll, which causes their leaves to yellow.

A Closer Look at Nitrogen

Nitrogen is a particularly important plant nutrient because it is often in limited supply in a plant's environment. A plant uses nitrogen to produce proteins, nucleic acids, and hormones. With nitrogen making up nearly 80 percent of the atmosphere, why do many plants suffer from nitrogen deficiencies? The problem is that atmospheric nitrogen (N_2) is a gaseous form of nitrogen that plants can't use. Plants must absorb nitrogen from the soil in the form of mineral ions (Figure 21-4).

For plants to absorb nitrogen from the soil, the nitrogen must first be converted to ammonium ions (NH_4^+) or nitrate ions (NO_3^-). Certain species of soil bacteria convert atmospheric nitrogen (N_2) to ammonia (NH_3) in a process called **nitrogen fixation.** Each NH_3 molecule picks up another hydrogen ion from the soil, becoming NH_4^+. Other bacteria called ammonifying bacteria also contribute ammonia to the soil by breaking down organic material such as feces and dead leaves. A third group of bacteria called nitrifying bacteria convert NH_4^+ ions to NO_3^-.

Many nitrogen-fixing bacteria live freely in the soil. However, you can see that a plant adaptation that concentrates this nitrogen-fixing power close to the roots would be beneficial. In fact, some plants, including plants called **legumes,** such as peas, peanuts, alfalfa, and beans, house their own nitrogen-fixing bacteria. The bacteria are found in lumps on the legumes' roots, called **root nodules.** The relationship between the legume and the nitrogen-fixing bacteria usually benefits both organisms. The bacteria fix nitrogen, while the plant provides carbohydrates and other organic nutrients to the bacteria.

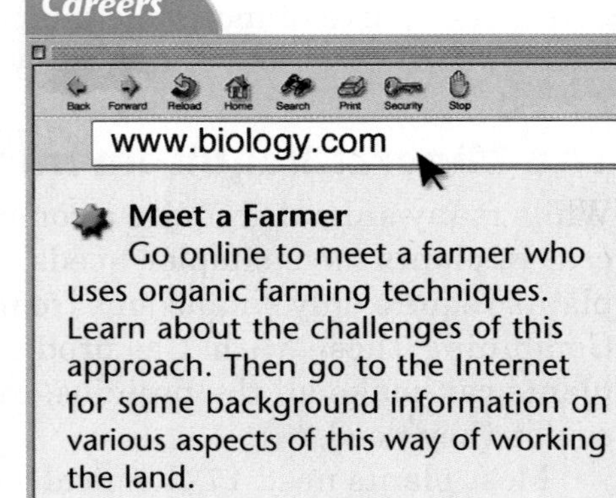

Careers
Back Forward Reload Home Search Print Security Stop
www.biology.com
Meet a Farmer
Go online to meet a farmer who uses organic farming techniques. Learn about the challenges of this approach. Then go to the Internet for some background information on various aspects of this way of working the land.

Figure 21-4 Bacteria help convert atmospheric nitrogen to ammonium and nitrate ions, forms of nitrogen that plants can use.

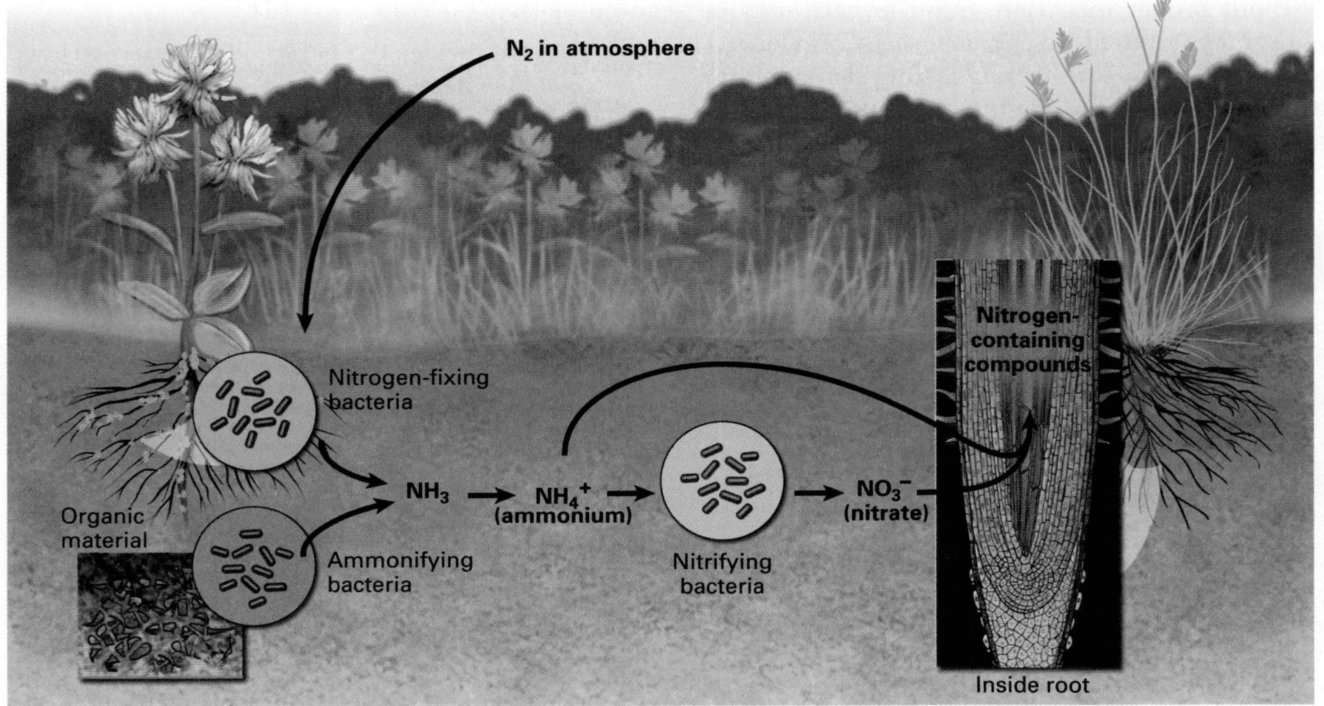

▲ **Figure 21-5** This farm is practicing crop rotation between soybeans, a legume (left), and corn (right). Next year, the placement of the crops will be switched.

Farmers use this adaptation of legumes to improve their fields in the practice of crop rotation (Figure 21-5). A field that is planted with a non-legume crop, such as corn, gets depleted of nitrogen. But if the farmer plants a legume the following year, the soil's nitrogen supply will be replenished. The farmer can rotate the crops on a yearly basis, maximizing the quality of the soil and the crops.

Fertilizers

Most farmers in the United States and other industrialized countries use commercially produced fertilizers containing minerals. These fertilizers are usually enriched in nitrogen, phosphorus, and potassium, the three mineral nutrients most commonly deficient in farm and garden soils. The next time you're in a garden shop, take a minute to examine the sacks of various fertilizers. You'll see that each one has a three-number code. A fertilizer marked "10-12-8," for instance, is 10 percent nitrogen, 12 percent phosphorus, and 8 percent potassium.

Unfortunately, any minerals from commercial fertilizers in excess of what crops need are not stored in the soil for later use. They are usually wasted because they are leached from the soil by rainwater or irrigation, and may end up polluting groundwater, streams, and lakes. Rotating crops is one way to reduce nitrogen fertilizer use. There are also some advantages in using mulch or manure instead of industrial fertilizers because they release the minerals more gradually.

Online Activity 21.1

Back Forward Reload Home Search Print Security Stop

www.biology.com

Discover the role of nutrients in plants.
Drag and drop molecules onto an interactive leaf illustration to discover how certain nutrients contribute to a plant's growth and survival. Then explore the role that bacteria play in providing nitrogen to plants.

Concept Check 21.1

1. Did van Helmont's experiment support or disprove Aristotle's hypothesis? Explain.
2. List at least three mineral nutrients required by plants, and describe their contributions to plant function.
3. Describe the role of three different kinds of bacteria in making nitrogen available to plants.
4. Describe the benefits and possible problems from fertilizer use.

CONCEPT 21.2

Vascular tissue transports sap within a plant.

OBJECTIVES

- Explain how water and minerals from the soil reach the xylem of a root.
- Describe how water moves through the xylem to leaves.
- Explain how water loss from a plant is regulated.
- Trace the path of sugar movement in phloem.

KEY TERMS

- root hair
- root pressure
- endodermis
- transpiration
- tracheid
- vessel element
- guard cell
- sieve-tube member
- companion cell
- pressure-flow mechanism

What's Online

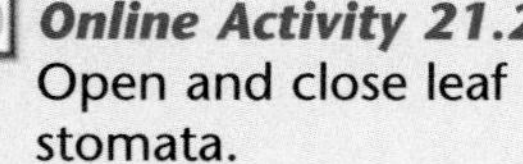

Online Activity 21.2 Open and close leaf stomata.

Lab 21 Online Companion Zip Up the Xylem

Online Collaborative Science 2 Exploring Patterns in Leaf Stomata

From the outside a tree trunk appears silent and unmoving, hardly even alive. But there is much activity inside. If you place a stethoscope on a tree trunk, especially during early spring just before leaves appear, you might hear the whoosh of sap running through the tree. In this section, you will learn how plants move water and sugars in their vascular tissues.

How Roots Absorb Water and Minerals

You have learned that a plant's roots absorb water and mineral nutrients from the soil. How does this work? **Root hairs** are tiny outgrowths of the root's epidermal cells (Figure 21-6). These root hairs grow into the spaces between soil particles. They greatly increase the surface area available for absorbing water and dissolved minerals. In addition, recall from Chapter 18 that the roots of most vascular plants form an association with fungi called mycorrhizae. This association increases the ability of the root to absorb water and inorganic ions, especially phosphate. As much as 3 m of fungal hyphae (filaments) can extend from each centimeter along a root.

Once the water gets inside the root, two main forces operate (usually at different times of day) in moving water upward from the roots and throughout the plant. The first force, called **root pressure,** helps push water up the xylem and usually operates at night. The root's epidermal cells and ground tissue cells use energy from ATP to accumulate certain minerals. The minerals can then move from cell to cell through cytoplasmic channels. Water and minerals move via this pathway into the xylem. Surrounding the vascular tissue is a layer of cells called the **endodermis,** which has waxy cell walls. The wax prevents water and minerals from leaking back out of the xylem. As minerals accumulate in the xylem, water tends to enter by osmosis, pushing xylem sap upward ahead of it.

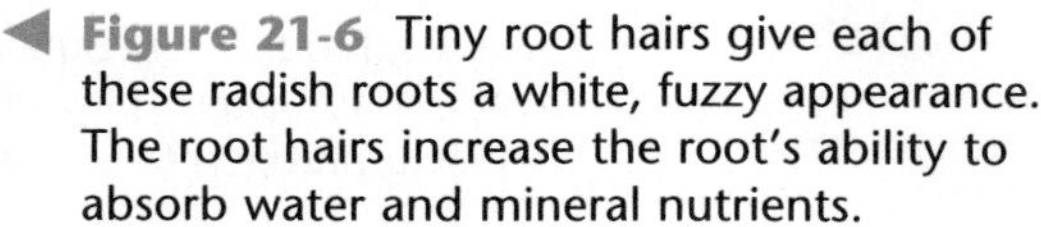

Figure 21-6 Tiny root hairs give each of these radish roots a white, fuzzy appearance. The root hairs increase the root's ability to absorb water and mineral nutrients.

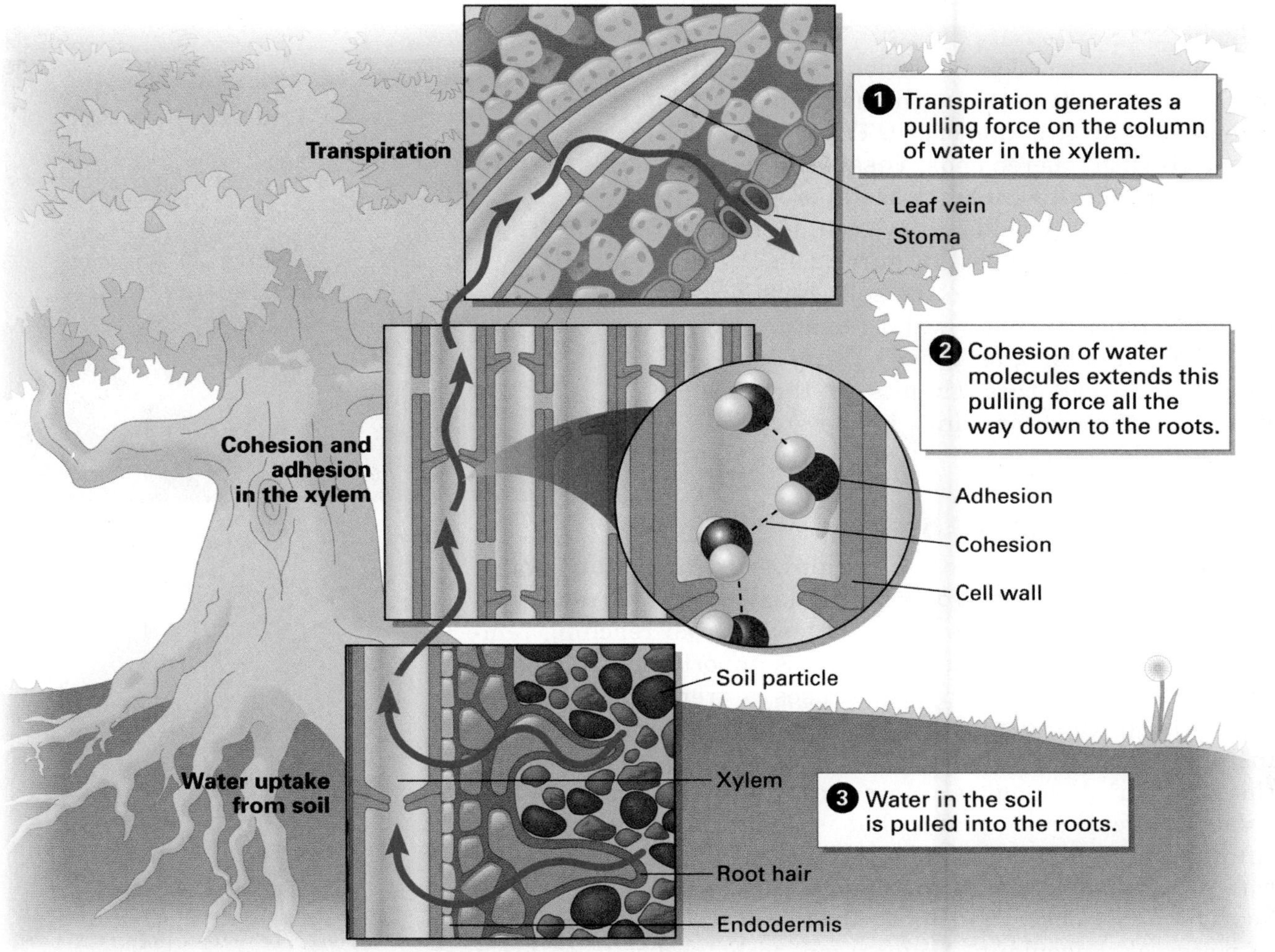

Transpiration

1 Transpiration generates a pulling force on the column of water in the xylem.

Leaf vein

Stoma

Cohesion and adhesion in the xylem

2 Cohesion of water molecules extends this pulling force all the way down to the roots.

Adhesion

Cohesion

Cell wall

Soil particle

Water uptake from soil

Xylem

3 Water in the soil is pulled into the roots.

Root hair

Endodermis

▲ **Figure 21-7** The force of transpiration is so strong that it can pull water from the soil into the roots and all the way up the tree.

The Upward Movement of Xylem Sap

Root pressure only accounts for a small part of the sap's ascent. To get water to the top of the plant, another stronger force is involved. And rather than *push* water up the plant from the bottom, this force *pulls* it from the top. Drinking water with a straw is a useful analogy—the suction you create at the top is a pulling force somewhat like the pulling force in plants. **Transpiration,** the loss of water through leaves due to evaporation, generates the pull (called *transpiration-pull*). Transpiration can pull xylem sap up a tree because of two properties of water that you learned about in Chapter 4: cohesion and adhesion.

Recall that cohesion is the tendency of molecules of the same kind to stick to one another. In water, hydrogen bonds make the water molecules stick to one another. The water molecules in the xylem tubes form continuous strings, extending all the way from the leaves down to the roots (Figure 21-7). Adhesion is the attraction between unlike molecules. Water molecules adhere, or stick to, cellulose molecules in the xylem walls. This assists the upward movement of xylem sap by counteracting the downward pull of gravity. Adhesion also prevents water from falling back down to the roots at night.

Online Collaborative Science 2

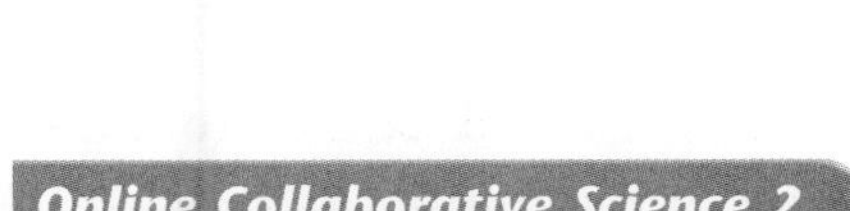

Exploring Patterns in Leaf Stomata

In this field investigation you will use a simple technique to determine the number of stomata on a leaf's surface and whether they are open or closed. After identifying stomata patterns in your local environment, share, compare, and discuss your results online with students in other classes.

There are two types of xylem "straws" in which water travels through the plant, each composed of its own kind of cell. **Tracheids** are long cells with tapered ends. **Vessel elements** are wider, shorter, much less tapered cells. The ends of tracheids or vessel elements overlap, forming tubes (Figure 21-8). The tubes are hollow because the cells have died. Only their lignified cell walls remain, creating the walls of the tubes. Water passes from cell to cell through pits in these cell walls and through openings in the end walls of vessel elements.

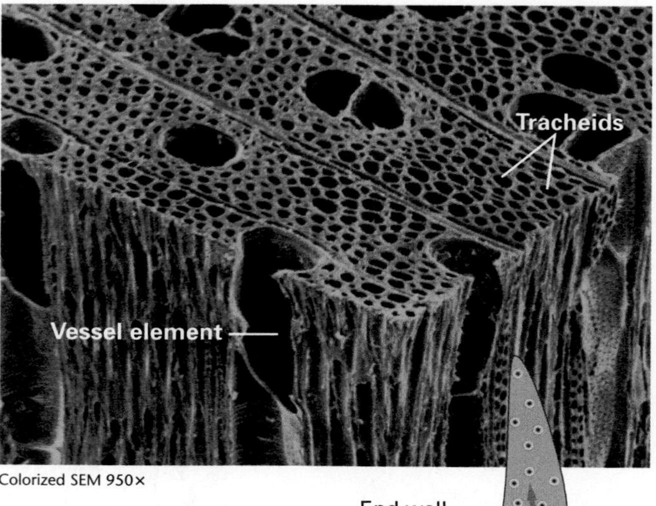

Colorized SEM 950×

Regulating Water Loss

Transpiration is required for the upward transport of water and minerals from the roots to the leaves. It also results in evaporative cooling. This prevents leaves from reaching temperatures that could denature enzymes important to photosynthesis. Yet, transpiration also causes a tremendous loss of water from the plant. An average-sized maple tree, for instance, loses more than 220 liters of water per hour during the summer. As long as water moves up from the soil fast enough to replace the water that is lost, this amount of transpiration presents no problem. But if transpiration exceeds the rate of water delivery to the leaves, the leaves will wilt. You have probably observed this result if you have ever forgotten to water a houseplant. A plant can withstand wilting for a short time, but eventually without a sufficient supply of water to the roots the plant will die.

Leaf stomata are adaptations that help plants regulate their transpiration and adjust to changing environmental conditions. Recall from Chapter 19 that stomata (singular, *stoma*) are pores located in the epidermis of leaves. The stomata can open and close, affecting the movement of gases in and out of the leaf. A pair of **guard cells** around each stoma open and close the stoma by changing shape (Figure 21-9).

During the day the stomata of most plants are open, allowing carbon dioxide required for photosynthesis to enter. Sunlight and low carbon dioxide levels within the leaf cue the guard cells to actively accumulate potassium ions (K^+) from surrounding cells. Due to osmosis, water follows the potassium ions into the guard cells, causing the guard cells to swell. The swollen guard cells buckle away from their centers in such a way that a gap (the stoma) opens between them.

Stomata typically close at night or when the plant is losing water from transpiration at a faster rate than it is gaining water from the soil. Potassium ions are lost from the guard cells, and water follows. The guard cells sag together as they lose water pressure, closing the stoma.

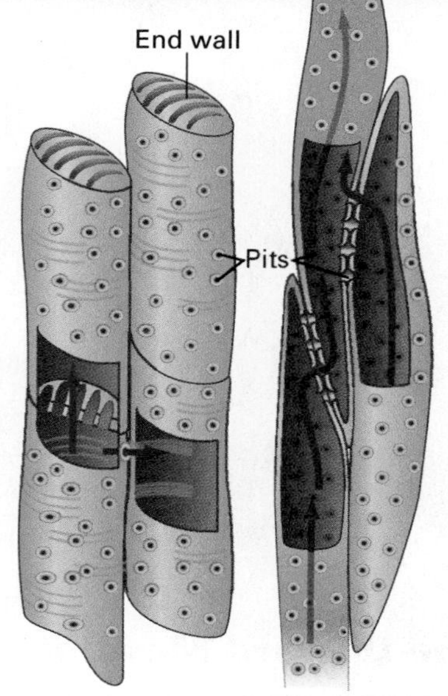

▲ **Figure 21-8** Both tracheids and vessel elements are stacked, forming hollow tubes that carry water through a plant.

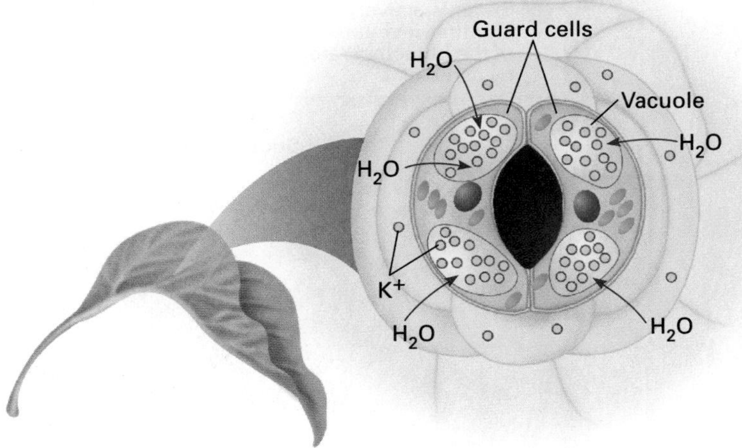

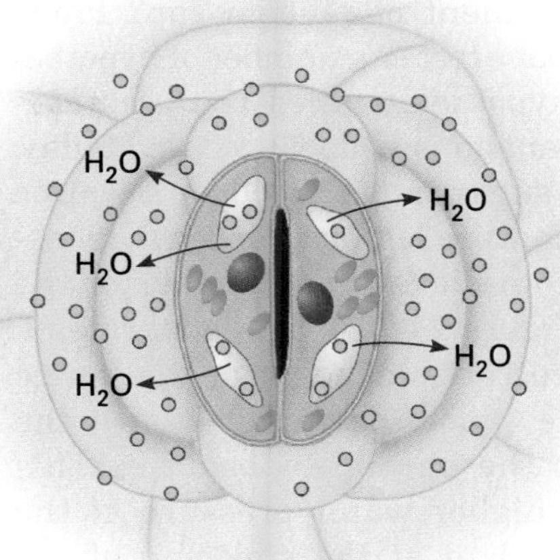

▲ **Figure 21-9** Water follows potassium ions from surrounding cells into guard cells, causing them to bulge and push apart at their centers. This forms a gap, opening the stoma. The flow of potassium ions and water out of the guard cells causes them to sag together, closing the stoma.

The Flow of Phloem Sap

The phloem of vascular tissue transports sucrose and other organic compounds along with water. This stream of phloem sap occurs through chains of cells called **sieve-tube members.** They are named this because the end walls are like sieves, allowing the flow of the fluid through pores (Figure 21-10). The chain of end-to-end cells forms a *sieve tube*. In contrast to the xylem cells, sieve-tube members remain alive. However, as they mature, sieve-tube members lose their nuclei and some other organelles. This means they lose the ability to perform some of their necessary cellular functions. **Companion cells** alongside sieve tubes may provide proteins and other resources to the sieve-tube members.

From Source to Sink What determines the direction of movement for phloem sap within a sieve tube? Phloem moves sugars from where they are made to where they are used. The mature leaves or other sites where sugar is being produced by photosynthesis or released from storage are referred to as sugar sources. Phloem moves sugar from a sugar source to a part of the plant where the sugar will be used or stored, called a sugar sink. Roots, developing shoot tips, and fruits are examples of sugar sinks.

Within a plant, the location of sugar sources and sinks can change with the seasons. For example, some storage structures such as beet taproots or potato tubers are sugar sinks during the summer. These plants stockpile sugars (stored in polysaccharides such as starch) in these structures when growing conditions are favorable. During the early spring of the following year, these same structures become sugar sources. The plant consumes its stored carbohydrates as it produces new stems and leaves.

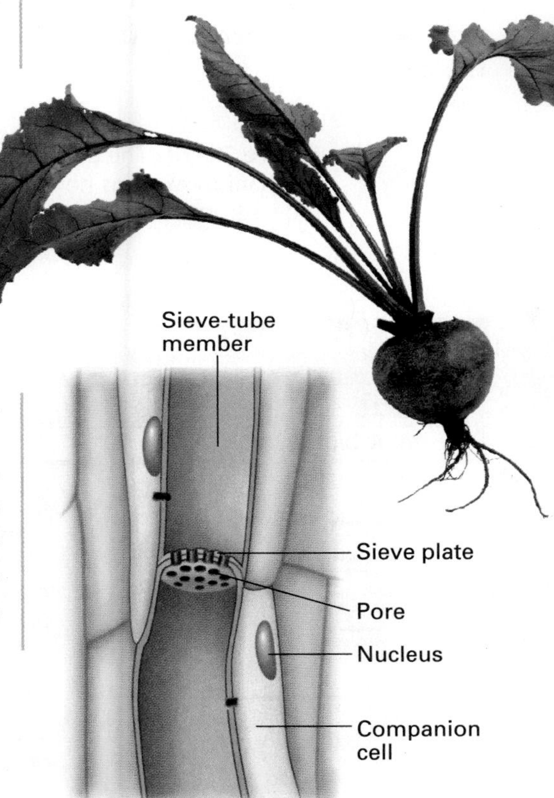

▶ **Figure 21-10** Sieve tubes carry phloem sap from sugar sources to sugar sinks. During the summer, this beet stockpiles sugars in its large taproot.

The Pressure-Flow Mechanism What drives movement of phloem sap? Plant biologists have tested a number of hypotheses. The hypothesis called the pressure-flow mechanism is widely accepted today.

When sugar is produced in a source such as a mature leaf, it is actively transported into a sieve-tube member of the phloem (Figure 21-11). This generates a high concentration of sugar at the source end of the phloem. Water follows the sugar into the phloem by osmosis. This generates higher water pressure at the source end than at the sink end of the phloem. The reverse happens at the sink end. Sugars leave the sieve-tube members, water follows, and pressure is reduced. Water, like any fluid, flows from where its pressure is higher to where it is lower. This process is called the **pressure-flow mechanism.**

In summary, the pressure-flow mechanism explains how sap flows through the phloem from areas of high sugar concentration and high water pressure to areas of low sugar concentration and low water pressure—from source to sink. (The water is returned to the source via the xylem.)

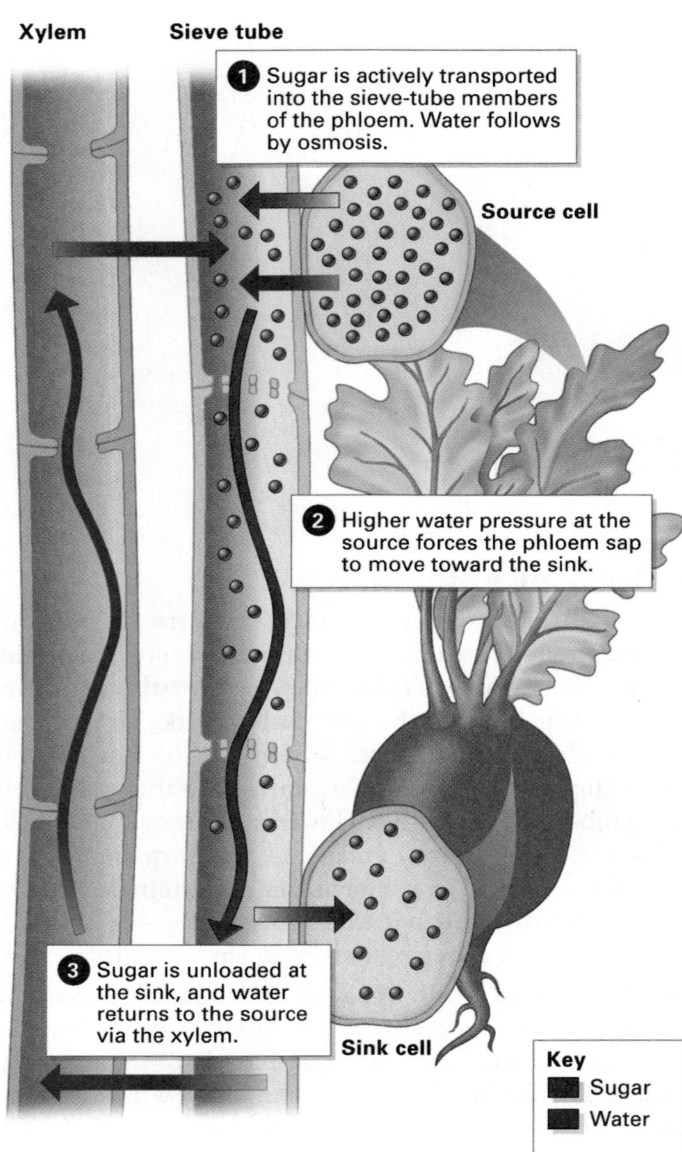
Xylem
Sieve tube
1 Sugar is actively transported into the sieve-tube members of the phloem. Water follows by osmosis.
Source cell
2 Higher water pressure at the source forces the phloem sap to move toward the sink.
3 Sugar is unloaded at the sink, and water returns to the source via the xylem.
Sink cell
Key
Sugar
Water

▶ **Figure 21-11** The pressure-flow mechanism explains how sugar moves from source to sink.

Online Activity 21.2

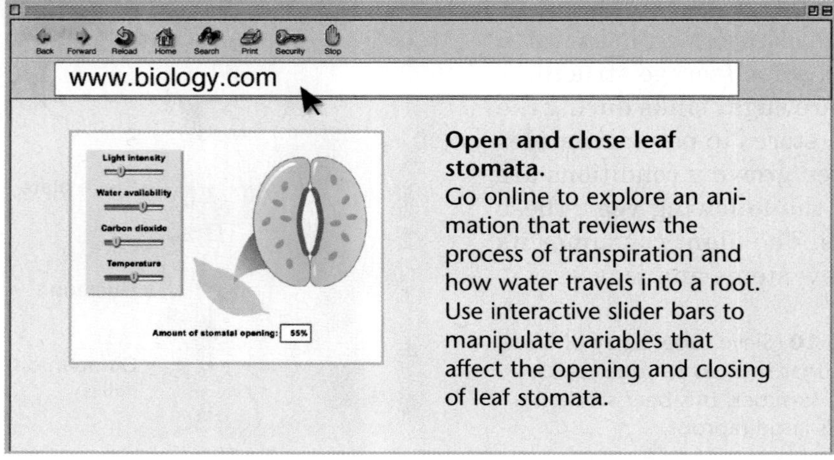
Back
Forward
Reload
Home
Search
Print
Security
Stop
www.biology.com
Light intensity
Water availability
Carbon dioxide
Temperature
Amount of stomatal opening: 55%

Open and close leaf stomata.
Go online to explore an animation that reviews the process of transpiration and how water travels into a root. Use interactive slider bars to manipulate variables that affect the opening and closing of leaf stomata.

Concept Check 21.2

1. Why is root pressure a pushing force? Explain.
2. Explain the role of transpiration in water movement.
3. Describe the mechanism that opens and closes stomata.
4. Explain how phloem sap flows from a sugar source to a sugar sink.

Zip Up the Xylem

Measuring Transpiration Rates

Question How do plants control the rate at which water is transported through the xylem?

Lab Overview In this investigation you will perform an experiment to measure and compare the transpiration rates of leaves under varying environmental conditions such as intense light, wind, or humidity. You will also make imprints of the bottom surfaces of some of the leaves to observe the stomata and guard cells.

Preparing for the Lab To help you prepare for the investigation, go to the *Lab 21 Online Companion.* ····➔ Find out more about transpiration, and develop hypotheses about environmental conditions that affect transpiration rate. Prepare for the lab procedure by previewing the steps you will take.

Completing the Lab Use your Laboratory Manual or lab page printouts from the *Lab 21 Online Companion* to do the investigation and analyze your results. **CAUTION:** *Be sure to follow your teacher's instructions and all safety guidelines in the investigation.*

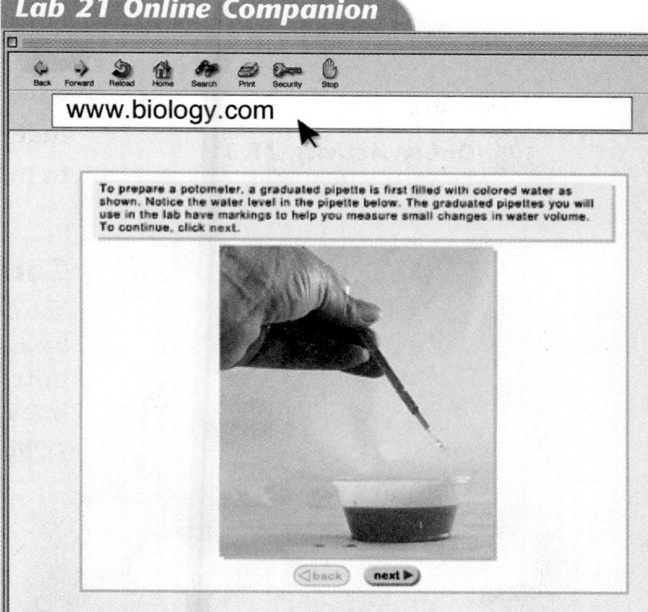
Lab 21 Online Companion
Back
Forward
Reload
Home
Search
Print
Security
Stop
www.biology.com
To prepare a potometer, a graduated pipette is first filled with colored water as shown. Notice the water level in the pipette below. The graduated pipettes you will use in the lab have markings to help you measure small changes in water volume. To continue, click next.
back
next

CONCEPT 21.3 Some plants have unique adaptations for nutrition.

OBJECTIVE

- Identify the adaptations of some plants to a carnivorous, parasitic, or epiphytic lifestyle.

KEY TERM

- epiphyte

What's Online

Online Activity 21.3
Trigger a Venus' flytrap.

Earlier you read that some plants harbor bacteria in root nodules, providing a ready supply of nitrogen. And you read that many plant roots associate with fungi, allowing access to more water and phosphorus. Now you will read about some interesting ways that plants take advantage of other plants, and even animals, to meet their nutritional needs.

Carnivorous Plants

You know that many animals, including humans, obtain nutrients by eating plants. But did you know that a few plants obtain nutrients, especially nitrogen, by eating animals? Carnivorous (meat-eating) plants, including sundews, Venus' flytraps, and pitcher plants, obtain some of their nitrogen by consuming insects. The structures that carnivorous plants use to trap and digest their prey are usually modified leaves (Figure 21-12).

Why would a plant require nitrogen from animals? The bogs where most carnivorous plants live are wetland areas containing cold, acidic water. Organic matter decays slowly in these acidic environments, and there is little inorganic nitrogen available for plant growth. Some bog plants supplement their nitrogen intake by consuming nitrogen-rich insects. Note that carnivorous plants are green and still photosynthesize in addition to eating insects. They are both producers *and* consumers.

▲ **Figure 21-12** The modified leaves of the carnivorous sundew plant have tentacle-like extensions. A sticky, sugary solution secreted from their tips attracts and traps insects. The "tentacles" then bend over the top of the prey.

Epiphytes

An **epiphyte** grows on the surface of another plant, usually on the branches or trunks of trees, but makes all its own food by photosynthesis (Figure 21-13a). Epiphytes do not absorb water and minerals from soil but rather from rain containing dissolved nutrients that falls on their leaves. For example, the threadlike leaves of the epiphyte Spanish "moss" are covered with scales adapted for absorbing moisture and nutrients.

Epiphytes often live in dense forests where light rarely penetrates to the forest floor. Growing on other plants brings epiphytes close to sunlight and puts them in the path of water dripping from foliage in the treetops. Examples of epiphytes are staghorn ferns, some mosses, Spanish "moss" (which is actually an angiosperm), and many species of bromeliads and orchids.

▲ **Figure 21-13** Although both these plants hang from trees, their adaptations for nutrition are very different. **a.** Spanish moss is an epiphyte. **b.** Mistletoe is a parasite.

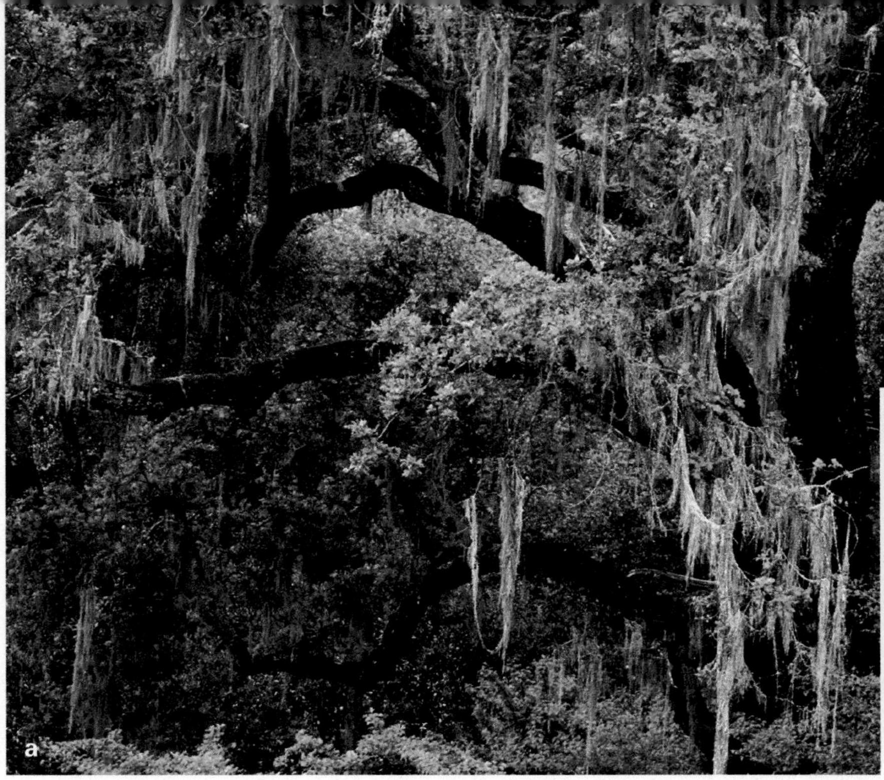

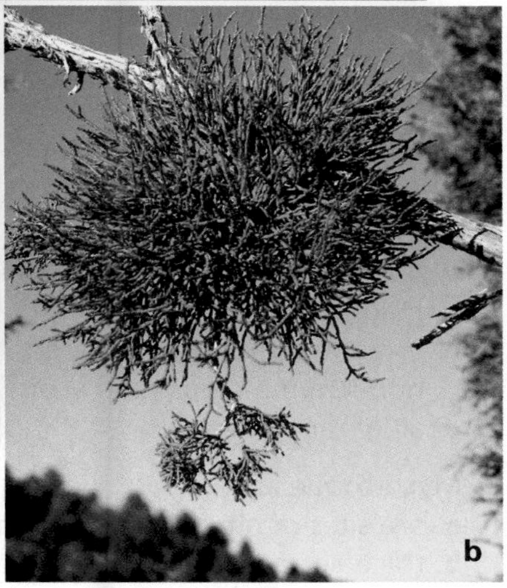

Parasitic Plants

Parasitic plants obtain some or all of their nutrients from other plants by tapping into the host plant's vascular tissue. Epiphytes such as the Spanish "moss" in Figure 21-13a are not parasites—they grow on other plants but do not steal from them. The most familiar example of a parasitic plant is mistletoe (Figure 21-13b). A mistletoe seed germinates on branches of its host tree. It then grows through the bark and into the host's xylem, from which it takes both water and minerals. Mistletoe and other parasites may kill their hosts by blocking out sunlight or robbing too many nutrients.

While mistletoe makes some of its own food through photosynthesis, there are a few plant species that lack chlorophyll entirely and are therefore completely parasitic on other plants. Fortunately for humans and other consumers, the vast majority of plants are producers.

Online Activity 21.3

Back Forward Reload Home Search Print Security Stop

www.biology.com

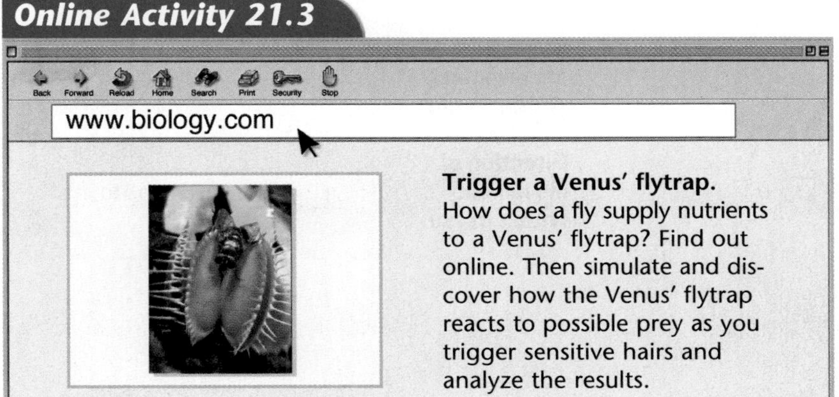

Trigger a Venus' flytrap.
How does a fly supply nutrients to a Venus' flytrap? Find out online. Then simulate and discover how the Venus' flytrap reacts to possible prey as you trigger sensitive hairs and analyze the results.

Concept Check 21.3

1. Give an example of a carnivorous plant.
2. Describe how an epiphyte makes its food.
3. List some nutritional adaptations of a parasitic plant.

Multiple Choice

Choose the letter of the best answer.

1. What is a plant's primary source of carbon?
   a. soil
   b. water
   c. air
   d. fertilizer

2. Crop rotation involves
   a. moving plants to face the sun.
   b. taking advantage of corn's ability to fix magnesium.
   c. rotating nitrogen-fixing legume crops with non-legume crops each year.
   d. all of the above.

3. Mycorrhizae are
   a. the sites of nitrogen fixation in nodules.
   b. the associations of many plants' roots with fungi.
   c. cells that control the exchange of gases by leaves.
   d. extensions of the leaves that increase water absorption.

4. Which of the following is true of transpiration?
   a. generates a pulling force within a plant
   b. causes plant to lose water through its leaves
   c. occurs via stomata
   d. all of the above

5. Companion cells
   a. surround stomata in leaves.
   b. form partnerships with xylem tissue.
   c. fix nitrogen.
   d. neighbor sieve tubes in the phloem.

6. Epiphytes are not like other plants because they
   a. can't photosynthesize.
   b. eat animals.
   c. grow in extremely dry deserts.
   d. grow without soil.

7. Mistletoe is
   a. a plant.
   b. photosynthetic.
   c. a parasite.
   d. all of the above.

Short Answer

8. Explain how the nutritional requirements of plants differ from those of animals.

9. Explain why nitrogen fixation is important.

10. What are root hairs? What is their function in a plant?

11. How are cohesion and adhesion involved in the movement of water through a plant?

12. Compare and contrast two kinds of xylem cells.

13. Describe what happens to the guard cells around an opening stoma.

14. Describe the direction of sugar movement in a plant.

15. Give two examples of plant parts that are sugar sinks.

16. Describe the typical habitat of an epiphyte.

17. Compare and contrast the nutritional adaptations of a carnivorous plant and a parasitic plant.

Visualizing Concepts

18. Complete the table below by filling in the blanks.

Type of vascular tissue	Xylem	Phloem
Function	a.	b.
Types of cells	c. , vessel element	d. , companion cell
Mechanisms of movement within tissue	root pressure, e.	f.
Direction of movement within tissue	g.	from h. to i.

Analyzing Information

19. **Analyzing Data** The table below records temperature and rates of transpiration at different hours of the day.

Transpiration Rates

Time of day	Temperature (°C)	Transpiration rate (g/m²/hr)
8 A.M.	14	57
10 A.M.	21	83
12 P.M.	27	161
2 P.M.	31	186
4 P.M.	29	137
6 P.M.	18	78

   a. Describe the apparent relationship between temperature and transpiration rate. It may help you to draw a line graph first.
   b. Hypothesize a reason why temperature affects transpiration rate in this way.

20. **Analyzing Photos** Examine the photo below and answer the questions.

   a. What kinds of sap do you expect to find in the veins of this leaf?
   b. Hypothesize the direction of travel for each kind of sap. Explain.

Critical Thinking

21. **Evaluating the Impact of Research** Describe how van Helmont's result contradicted Aristotle's hypothesis that a plant obtains its mass from the soil.

22. **Evaluating Promotional Claims** A bag of 5-10-5 fertilizer at the garden shop claims to give your house plants "everything they need." Evaluate this claim.

23. **Comparing and Contrasting** How are the effects of root pressure and the pressure-flow mechanism of phloem sap similar? How are they different?

24. **Problem Solving** Your new job as a field biologist requires you to classify new plant species with unique adaptations for nutrition. One of the first things you must determine is whether a specimen's mode of nutrition is carnivorous, epiphytic, or parasitic. Form a list of questions about each new specimen's anatomy and habitat that you would need to answer in order to classify it.

25. **What's Wrong With These Statements?** *Briefly explain why each statement is inaccurate or misleading.*
   a. Plants absorb proteins from the soil.
   b. Mycorrhizae are parasitic fungal growths on plant roots.
   c. Transpiration prevents a plant from wilting.

Performance Assessment

Design an Experiment Use glassware and/or other materials in the classroom or your kitchen to design a non-living model for how water moves up a tree.

Online Assessment/Test Preparation

Back Forward Reload Home Search Print Security Stop

www.biology.com

- **Chapter 21 Assessment**
  Check your understanding of the chapter concepts.
- **Standardized Test Preparation**
  Practice test-taking skills you need to succeed.

Control Systems in Plants

Such a spectacular display of wildflowers in the Anza-Borrego Desert of California happens only about once every 10 years. Seeds of desert annuals are quite particular in their requirements for germination. Winter must have been neither too hot nor too cold, and spring rainfall must be relatively plentiful. Rainfall affects the ratio of plant hormones in the seed, as it washes out certain hormones that inhibit germination. From the very start of a plant's life, hormones play important roles. In this chapter, you will read about hormones and other factors affecting plant functions. Before you begin, go online to the *WebQuest* to learn about some unusual plant adaptations.

Key Concepts

Concept 22.1

Hormones coordinate plant functions.

Concept 22.2

Plants respond to changes in the environment.

Concept 22.3

Plants keep track of the hours and the seasons.

Assessment

Chapter 22 Review

What's Online

WebQuest
AdaptQuest

Online Activity 22.1
Build up auxin in a plant.

Science, Technology, & Society
Genetic Control of Fruit Ripening

Lab 22 Online Companion
How Do Plants Grow Up?

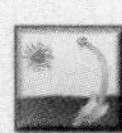

Online Activity 22.2
Activate phototropism.

Online Activity 22.3
Simulate plant reactions.

Closer Look
Phytochromes

Chapter 22 Assessment

CONCEPT 22.1 Hormones coordinate plant functions.

OBJECTIVES

- Describe the experiments that eventually led to the discovery of auxin, one of the plant hormones.
- Compare and contrast the effects of various plant hormones.

KEY TERMS

- plant hormone
- auxin
- cytokinin
- gibberellin
- dormancy
- abscisic acid
- ethylene

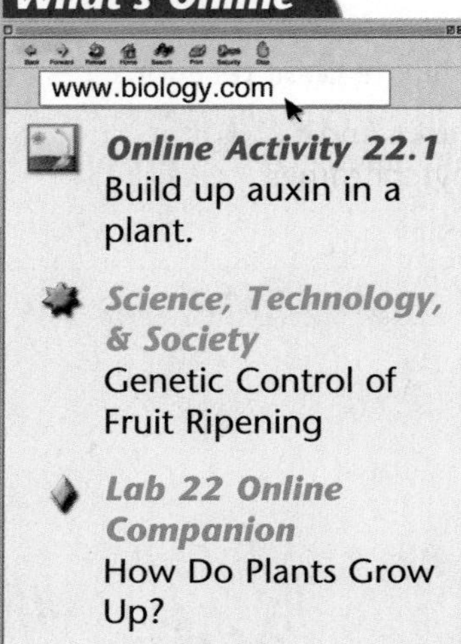

Have you ever observed how a plant on a windowsill grows toward the sunlight? Its growth may become so uneven that the plant may topple over. What causes the plant to grow in this lopsided manner?

Discovery of a Plant Hormone

Earlier in this book you read about Charles Darwin's theory of natural selection. But Darwin also studied other topics in biology. In the late 1800s, Charles Darwin and his son Francis conducted some of the first experiments to answer the question of how plants grow toward light (Figure 22-1). The Darwins observed that grass seedlings would bend toward light while they were growing. But when they cut off the tips of the seedlings, the shoots grew straight up, without bending (Figure 22-2 on the facing page). Next, the Darwins placed dark caps on the tips of the seedlings, shielding out light. Again, the seedlings grew straight up rather than bending toward the light source. However, when the Darwins placed clear caps over the tips of the seedlings or shielded only the lower part of the seedlings, they observed the normal bending response to light.

The results of these experiments suggested that something in the tip of a shoot is responsible for sensing light. However, the response, the bending of the shoot, occurs below the tip. The Darwins hypothesized that a shoot tip detects light and transmits a signal down to the growing region of the shoot.

Other scientists later confirmed that the signal is a chemical messenger produced in the shoot tip. They also discovered several other types of chemical messengers. These chemical messengers in plants are called **plant hormones.**

Plant hormones control many key functions in a plant's life. For example, hormones control a plant's germination from a seed, growth, flowering, and fruit production. Like animals, plants produce hormones in very small amounts, but even tiny amounts can have large effects. Just a few molecules of hormone can cause a cell to respond by turning genes on or off, by inhibiting enzymes, or by changing the properties of plasma membranes.

◀ **Figure 22-1** A plant's tendency to grow toward light is controlled by plant hormones.

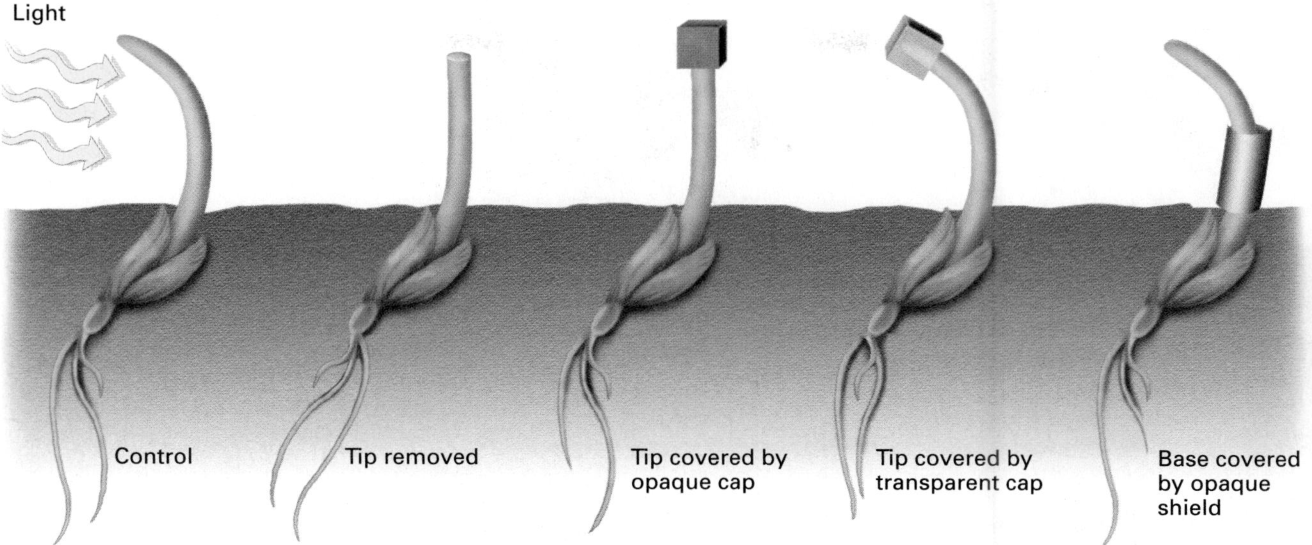

▲ **Figure 22-2** The Darwins conducted a series of controlled experiments to determine the region of a seedling responsible for detecting light.

Functions of the Five Major Hormones

Plant biologists have identified several major types of plant hormones: auxins, cytokinins, gibberellins, abscisic acid, and ethylene. No single hormone acts alone. Instead a balance of the various hormones controls the life of a plant.

Auxins The plant hormone whose effects the Darwins observed was later identified as one of a class of hormones called **auxins**. The chief function of the auxins is to promote plant growth. The name is from the Greek *auxein,* meaning "to increase."

Auxins are produced in the apical meristems at the tips of shoots. They promote cell elongation (lengthening). When a grass seedling is exposed to light from one direction, auxin builds up on the shaded side and stimulates growth beneath the tip. Because the cells on the shaded side are exposed to more auxin, they elongate (lengthen) more than the cells on the lighted side (Figure 22-3). The uneven growth rate on the two sides of the plant causes the shoot to bend toward the light.

How do auxins make cells elongate? One hypothesis is that they trigger mechanisms that loosen the bonds holding the components of the cell walls together. With its cell wall less rigid, the cell, which is hypertonic to its surroundings, is free to take up more water by osmosis. The cell elongates. Auxins also have other effects in a plant. For example, they can stimulate secondary growth of a plant stem by promoting cell division in the vascular cambium.

Seeds secrete auxins that stimulate the development of the surrounding ovary into fruit. Exposing some kinds of plants to auxins can cause fruit development without any need for pollination and seed development. Farmers use this technology to produce seedless tomatoes, cucumbers, and other fruits by spraying the flowering plants with auxins.

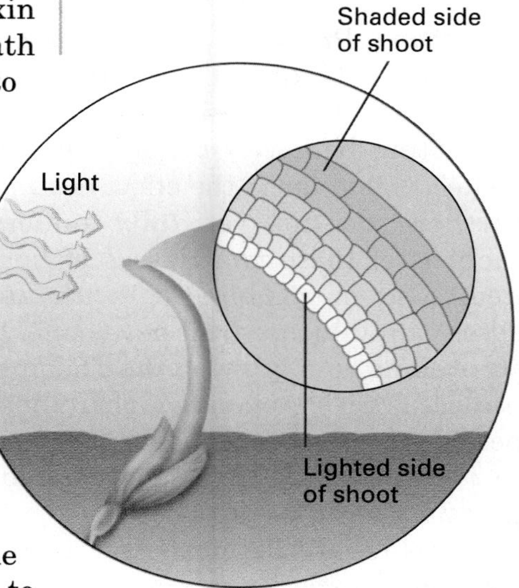

▲ **Figure 22-3** Cells on the shaded side of a plant grow faster than cells on the lighted side, causing the plant to bend toward the light.

Figure 22-4 Auxin produced and transported from the terminal bud inhibits branching (far left). In a pinched-back plant, the terminal bud has been removed, and auxin levels decrease relative to cytokinins. The plant branches more, resulting in a bushier plant.

Cytokinins Plant hormones called **cytokinins** (sy toh KY ninz) stimulate cell division. These hormones are produced in actively growing tissues, particularly in embryos, roots, and fruits. Cytokinins made in the roots reach target cells in stems by moving upward in xylem sap. One effect of cytokinins is to slow the aging of flowers and fruits.

The effects of cytokinins are often affected by the concentration of auxins present. For example, cytokinins entering the shoot system from the roots promote cell division in axillary buds. This encourages branching of the plant. But auxin traveling down the plant from the terminal bud inhibits branching. The result is fewer and shorter branches near the tip of the plant, where auxin levels are higher than cytokinin levels. To produce a bushier plant, gardeners often "pinch back" the terminal buds (Figure 22-4). This reduces auxin levels compared to cytokinin levels, causing the plant to branch more.

Gibberellins Produced at the tips of both stems and roots, **gibberellins** (jib uhr EL inz) cause a wide variety of effects. One of their main roles is to stimulate growth of stems by promoting both cell division and cell elongation. This effect is similar to the effect of auxins. However, researchers do not yet fully understand how the actions of these two classes of hormones are related. Also in combination with auxins, gibberellins can influence fruit development. One use of gibberellins is in growing the Thompson variety of seedless grapes. Applying gibberellins makes the grapes grow larger, and the clusters grow so that there is more space between the individual grapes (Figure 22-5).

Gibberellins are also important in promoting seed germination in some species. For example, with exposure to water, the embryos in some cereal grains, such as barley, release gibberellins that stimulate the breakdown of stored nutrients in the endosperm, making them available to the embryo.

Figure 22-5 Gibberellins cause some fruits to grow larger. The grapes on the left are untreated, while those on the right have been sprayed with gibberellins.

Abscisic Acid Under certain conditions, such as at the onset of winter or during a severe drought, a plant is more likely to survive if it becomes dormant. During **dormancy,** the plant stops growing. At such times, the hormone **abscisic acid** (ab SIS ik), abbreviated ABA, inhibits cell division in buds and in the vascular cambium. In other words, ABA halts primary and secondary growth. ABA also promotes dormancy in seeds—the opposite effect of gibberellins. Some seeds remain dormant until a downpour washes ABA out of the seeds. (Gibberellins do not wash out as easily.) Without the inhibitory effect of ABA, the stimulatory effect of gibberellins signals the seeds to germinate.

ABA also acts as a "stress hormone" in growing plants. For instance, when a plant is dehydrated, ABA builds up in leaves and causes stomata to close. As you learned in Chapter 21, closing stomata reduces transpiration and prevents further water loss from plants.

Ethylene In the early 1900s, oranges and grapefruits were ripened for market in sheds. Farmers would heat the sheds with kerosene stoves, believing that the heat ripened the fruit. Plant biologists later learned that the ripening was actually due to ethylene, a gas released when kerosene is burned. **Ethylene** is also a naturally occurring plant hormone that stimulates fruit ripening.

Another effect of ethylene is to promote "leaf drop," the loss of leaves from deciduous trees every autumn (Figure 22-6). Leaf drop is caused by a shift in the amounts of ethylene and auxin in leaf petioles. Ethylene concentration increases and auxin concentration decreases in response to autumn's shorter days and cooler temperatures. Leaf drop is an adaptation that helps keep trees from drying out in winter. Because their roots cannot take up water from the frozen ground during winter, trees cannot afford to lose water by evaporation from leaves.

Science, Technology, & Society

www.biology.com

Genetic Control of Fruit Ripening
Have you ever noticed that tomatoes bought at a grocery store rarely taste as good as ones grown in a home garden? What is the difference between the two? Go online to learn about a gene that controls ripening in tomatoes and how this may lead to tastier fruit on grocery store shelves.

Figure 22-6 One effect of ethylene is to promote "leaf drop" each autumn.

Online Activity 22.1

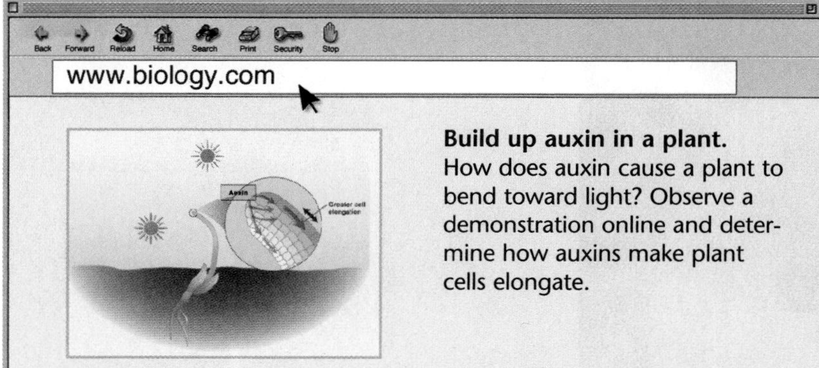

www.biology.com

Build up auxin in a plant.
How does auxin cause a plant to bend toward light? Observe a demonstration online and determine how auxins make plant cells elongate.

Concept Check 22.1

1. Explain why the Darwins did not observe any bending of the seedlings when they covered the tips of the seedlings with dark caps.
2. List five major plant hormones and state one effect of each.
3. Explain how leaf drop is an adaptive response to winter.

How Do Plants Grow Up?

Exploring Gravitropism

Inquiry Challenge How do plants respond to gravity?

Lab Overview In this inquiry investigation you will explore how plants respond to gravity, and discover how plant hormones produced in response to gravity cause a change in growth. You will develop and test your own hypotheses about the effects of gravity on young plant stems. Then you will perform an experiment of your own design using film canisters and seedlings.

Preparing for the Lab To prepare you to design your own experiment, go to the *Lab 22 Online Companion.* ······➔ Compare examples of positive and negative gravitropism.

Completing the Lab Use your Laboratory Manual or lab page printouts from the *Lab 22 Online Companion* to design and perform your own experiment and analyze your results. **CAUTION:** *Be sure to follow your teacher's instructions and all safety guidelines in the investigation.*

Lab 22 Online Companion

Back Forward Reload Home Search Print Security Stop

www.biology.com

Study the seedlings in the photograph below. Roll over the seedlings to identify their parts, Next, observe how each part of a seedling reacts to the force of gravity and enter your observations in the box below. To see a photograph taken one day later, click next.

Force of gravity

Day 1

Observations, Day 1:

Observations, Day 2:

Observations, Day 3:

back next

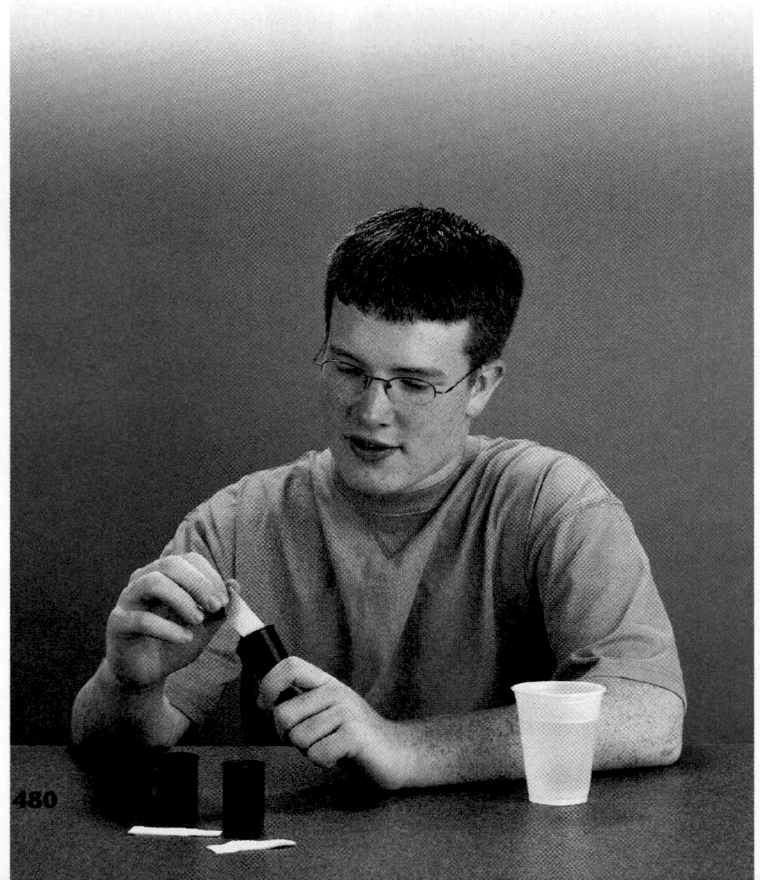

CONCEPT 22.2 Plants respond to changes in the environment.

OBJECTIVES

- Give an example of rapid plant movement.
- Define three different tropisms of plants.
- Explain some short-term and long-term adaptations of plants to stress.
- Describe plant defenses against disease.

KEY TERMS

- tropism
- thigmotropism
- phototropism
- gravitropism
- halophyte

What's Online

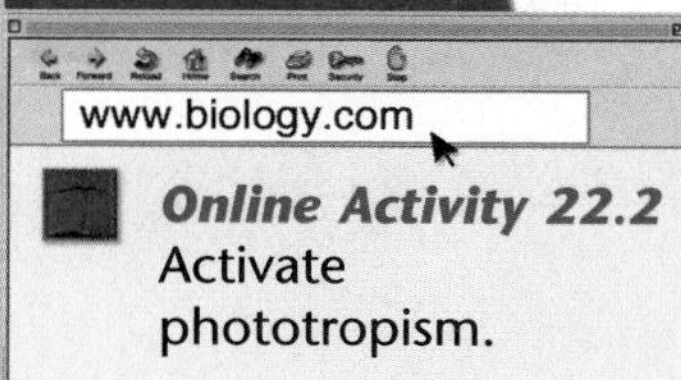

Online Activity 22.2 Activate phototropism.

A vine grows round and round the trunk of a tree. A seed in the dark ground begins to grow toward the surface. Although plants lack a nervous system, they do sense and respond to signals from their environment.

Rapid Plant Movements

All plants are sensitive to their surroundings. They respond to such stimuli as light, temperature, gravity, and touch. Most plant responses are slow—so slow that you can't see the response occurring. In a few plant species, however, the response is very rapid indeed.

The leaves of the tropical plant *Mimosa pudica* quickly fold up when touched, giving the plant a wilted appearance (Figure 22-7). After time, the leaves return to their normal position. This response is an example of a rapid plant movement. Touch triggers responses that cause cells at the base of each leaflet to lose ions. Due to osmosis, water follows the ions out of the cells. The cells shrink, causing the leaflet to droop.

What is the function of this leaf-folding behavior? Some scientists hypothesize that leaf folding in a heavy wind is an adaptation that reduces surface area and saves water. Another hypothesis states that the folding response makes the plant less attractive to animals trying to eat the plant. The rapid movement may serve to bump off (or scare off) an insect, for example.

Figure 22-7 *Mimosa,* "the sensitive plant," responds with a rapid plant movement when touched gently with a pencil.

Tropisms

Tropisms are growth responses that cause parts of a plant to grow slowly toward or away from a stimulus. Tropisms are typically regulated by plant hormones, especially auxins. Unlike rapid plant movements, tropisms are not rapidly reversible.

Responses to Touch A change in plant growth due to touch is called **thigmotropism.** For example, in the photo at right, the pea tendrils grew straight until they touched the wires (Figure 22-8). Then, the cells touching the wires slowed in growth while those on the opposite side of the tendril grew faster. These different rates of growth made the tendrils wrap around the wires. Most climbing plants have tendrils that respond by coiling and grasping when they touch rigid objects. Thigmotropism enables climbing plants to use objects for support while growing toward sunlight.

Another example of thigmotropism is a seedling's response to mechanical stress. For example, a growing seedling may press against a rock in the soil. It is advantageous for the seedling to bend, avoiding the obstacle, instead of damaging itself by growing straight into it and failing to reach the soil surface. Researchers have shown that ethylene plays a role in this response.

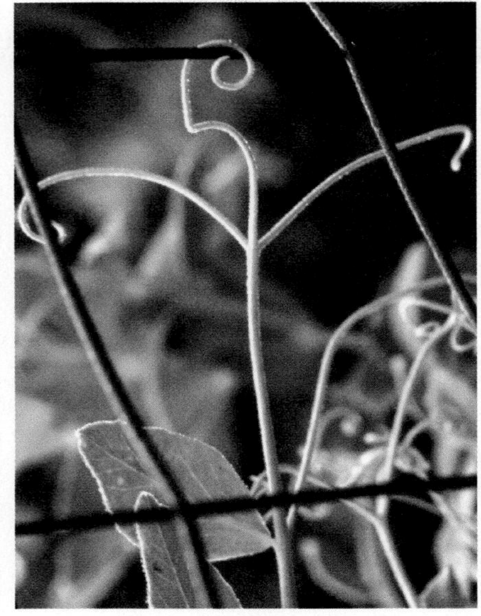

▲ **Figure 22-8** Thigmotropism enables these pea tendrils to curl around the wires.

Responses to Light The growth of a plant part toward or away from light is an example of **phototropism.** You have already learned how auxins regulate this response in grass seedlings. Shining light on one side of a shoot tip causes an uneven distribution of auxins, with more on the shaded side than on the lighted side. The shoot tips contain a protein with an attached light-absorbing molecule. When activated by light, this protein signals molecules that affect auxin transport down from the shoot tip.

Responses to Gravity A plant's growth response to gravity is called **gravitropism.** One example of gravitropism is seen in germinating seeds. A seedling's shoot grows upward and its root downward into the soil, no matter how the seed landed or was planted in the soil. Roots and shoots of mature plants respond to gravity as well (Figure 22-9).

How do plants "know" up from down? Is a plant hormone involved? Because gravitropism has opposite effects in shoots and roots, different explanations (and hormones) may be responsible. Plant biologists have yet to answer this question. One hypothesis is that gravity pulls organelles containing dense starch grains to the low points of cells. The uneven distribution of these organelles may in turn signal the cells to move auxins within the root or shoot, thus affecting the cell's direction of growth.

▼ **Figure 22-9** A plant's shoot continues to grow "up" after its pot is tipped over. This response to gravity is called gravitropism.

▲ **Figure 22-10** These Arctic plants have small leaves and shallow roots and grow close to the ground. These are adaptations to an environment that is dry, windy, and permanently frozen just a few centimeters below the soil surface.

Coping With Stressful Environments

Plants are often exposed to stressful environmental conditions. Changes in levels of water, salt, and temperature can affect a plant's growth, as well as its ability to reproduce and even to survive. Drought, flooding, or salty soil can devastate natural plant populations as well as agricultural crops. But many plants are adapted to withstand temporary stress. And some plants are especially adapted to live where conditions are always too stressful for other plants.

Drought A drought is a prolonged period of inadequate rainfall. When plants adapted to more moderate climates are exposed to drought, they can become stressed and weakened. In a drought, a plant may lose more water through transpiration than it takes up from the soil. This shortage of water inhibits the growth of young leaves, causes existing leaves to wilt, and reduces photosynthesis. Plants respond to drought by conserving water. As you learned in Chapter 21, one way plants conserve water is by closing their stomata, thereby slowing down the rate of transpiration. You read earlier in this chapter that the hormone ABA initiates this response.

Some plants have adaptations that enable them to withstand a very dry climate. Cacti and similar plants (called succulents) store water in their fleshy stems and thrive in the desert. The stems of succulents have a thick cuticle. These plants often have modified leaves (spines) instead of broad flat leaves that would lose a lot of water to evaporation. The green, fleshy stems are the main photosynthetic organs.

Plants adapted to cold, dry arctic regions tend to have very small leaves and grow very low to the ground (Figure 22-10). These adaptations help reduce transpiration during the short growing season by minimizing exposure to the harsh, dry winds that blow over the landscape.

Figure 22-11 Mangrove trees have some aboveground roots, an adaptation for growing in flooded conditions.

Flooding Did you know that an overwatered houseplant can suffocate? Waterlogged soil lacks the air spaces that provide oxygen for cellular respiration in the roots. In addition, oxygen moves more slowly through water than through air. Yet, some plants are adapted to live in very wet habitats. Mangrove trees, for example, grow in coastal marshes but have roots that are partly above ground. These aboveground roots provide oxygen for the underwater parts of roots (Figure 22-11).

How do plants that are less specialized for aquatic environments respond to unusually wet conditions, such as temporarily waterlogged soil? Plant cells that are deprived of oxygen release the hormone ethylene. The ethylene causes some of the cells in the submerged roots to die (Figure 22-12). Killing these cells creates air tubes that function as "snorkels." These air tubes carry oxygen to the submerged roots.

Salt Stress Too much salt can also threaten the health of plants. When excess salt builds up in the soil, root cells lose water to the soil through osmosis.

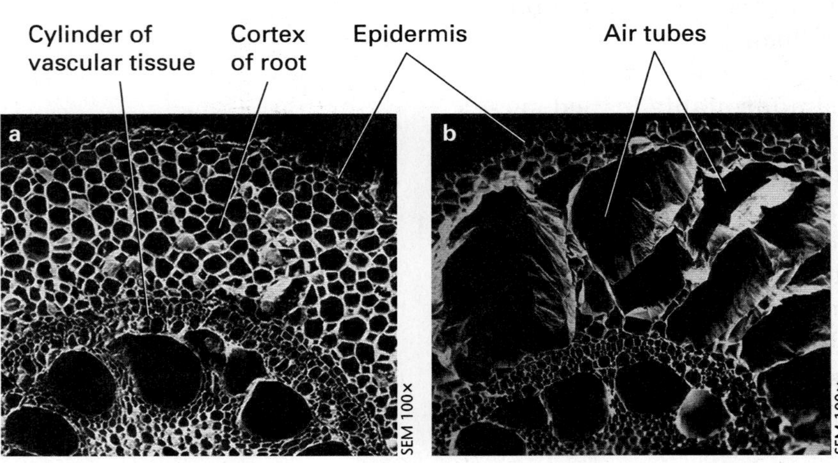

Figure 22-12 Some plants produce air tubes by destroying cells in their roots in response to temporary flooding. **a.** The corn root on the far left is growing in well-oxygenated soil. **b.** After the soil has flooded, however, the corn root releases ethylene, prompting cells in the cortex to self-destruct. These dead cells serve as snorkels for the flooded roots.

Most plants cannot survive salt stress for long. The exceptions are the **halophytes** (HAL oh fyts), salt-tolerant plants with adaptations such as salt glands. These glands pump salt out of the plant across the leaf epidermis, and rain washes the salt away. There are other adaptations, too. One salt marsh plant called pickleweed pumps excess salt to stems at the tips of the plant. Then the pickleweed sheds these stems, getting rid of the salt (Figure 22-13).

▲ **Figure 22-13** The pickleweed (*Salicornia*) is well adapted to grow in salt marshes. Pickleweed can tolerate high salt levels by pumping excess salt into its tips and then dropping the tips.

Defending Against Disease

Plants do not live in isolation in their communities. They interact with many other species. As you read in Chapter 21, some of these interactions, such as mycorrhizae and root nodules containing nitrogen-fixing bacteria, benefit both species. But many of the interactions are not beneficial to the plant. Plants are subject to infection by viruses, bacteria, and fungi. Each of these pathogens may damage tissues or even kill the plant.

Plants have adaptations that defend against infection. A plant's first line of defense against infection is the physical barrier of the plant's "skin," its epidermis. However, pathogens can cross this barrier through wounds or openings in the plant, such as the stomata. Once infected, the plant uses chemicals as a second line of defense. Some of the chemicals are antimicrobial. For example, some chemical defenses attack molecules in the cell wall of a bacterium. Other chemicals signal lignin production. This hardens the cell walls around the infected area and seals off the invading pathogen from the rest of the plant.

A plant also inherits the ability to recognize and attack certain pathogens. In fact, plant breeders often select for this ability of plants to resist specific diseases. And one goal of making transgenic plants is to introduce disease-resistance genes from different plant species into crop plants (see Chapter 13).

In addition to defending against disease, many plants defend themselves against being eaten. They may have physical defenses such as thorns or chemical defenses such as poisons.

Online Activity 22.2

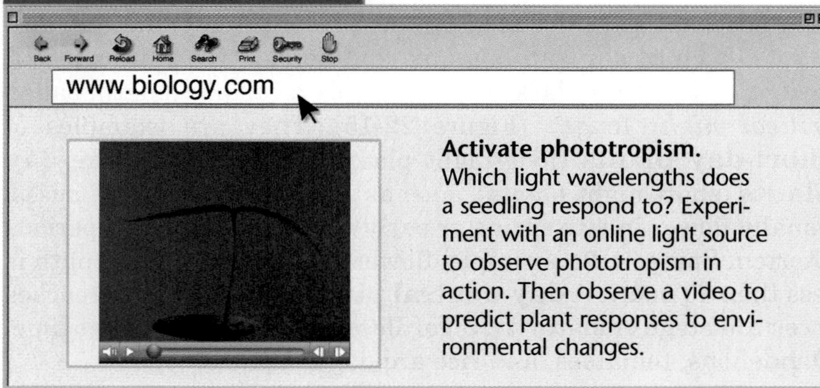

Activate phototropism. Which light wavelengths does a seedling respond to? Experiment with an online light source to observe phototropism in action. Then observe a video to predict plant responses to environmental changes.

Concept Check 22.2

1. Describe the role of osmosis in controlling the rapid plant movements of *Mimosa pudica*.
2. Distinguish among thigmotropism, phototropism, and gravitropism.
3. Contrast a desert plant's adaptations with the adaptations of a houseplant experiencing a temporary drought.
4. Describe the two main adaptations in a plant's defense against disease.

CONCEPT 22.3

Plants keep track of the hours and the seasons.

OBJECTIVES

- Define *circadian rhythm.*
- Explain how day length may affect plant flowering.

KEY TERMS

- circadian rhythm
- photoperiodism
- short-day plant
- long-day plant
- day-neutral plant
- phytochrome

What's Online

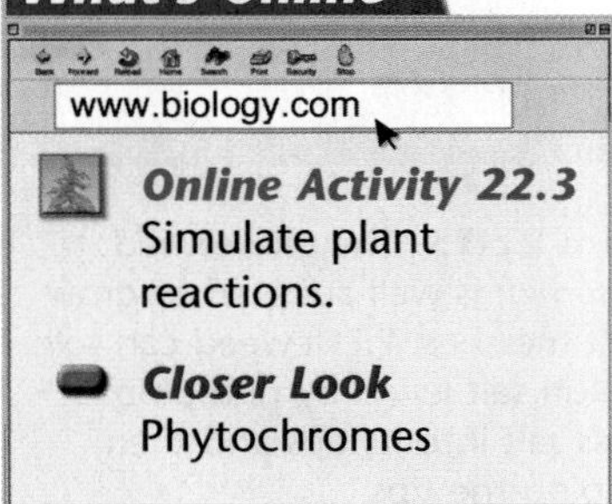

▼ **Figure 22-14** The "prayer plant" unfolds its leaves during the day (a) and folds them at night (b). This circadian rhythm continues even when the plant is kept in constant darkness, though the cycle will not be exactly 24 hours.

In addition to responding quickly to touch, every day at dusk the sensitive plant *Mimosa* folds its leaves. Every day at dawn, it unfolds its leaves. These movements, seen in many other plants as well, form a regular daily pattern.

Circadian Rhythms

Perhaps you've experienced jet lag when you've traveled rapidly to a new time zone. This is because your body is still operating on the clock from your old time zone. For example, with jet lag you feel tired when it's time for bed at home, say 10 P.M., even though it's only 7 P.M. at your destination.

Your pulse rate, blood pressure, and body temperature change with the time of day. A plant's functions change throughout a 24-hour period, too. A biological cycle that occurs about every 24 hours is called a **circadian rhythm** (sur KAY dee un). An organism's "biological clock" is set by daily signals from the environment, especially light. In experiments where organisms are kept in constant darkness, the circadian rhythms continue, but the cycle lengths become either shorter or longer than 24 hours (Figure 22-14). The changing of night and day is required to set the clock exactly to a 24-hour cycle.

Day Length and Seasons

In addition to maintaining a 24-hour cycle, plants also respond to changes in environmental cues that come with the seasons. For example, most plants produce flowers, germinate seeds, and become dormant at specific times during the year. Some plants flower in the spring, for instance, while others flower in the fall. Some species flower on exactly the same day every year!

Plants use the relative lengths of day and night to detect the time of year. The ability to use this environmental stimulus to time seasonal activities is known as **photoperiodism.** Certain plants, such as chrysanthemums and poinsettias, flower in fall or winter when the dark period exceeds a certain length, called *critical night length* (Figure 22-15). They are examples of **short-day plants** (long-night plants). In contrast, **long-day plants** (short-night plants), such as spinach, lettuce, and irises, usually flower in late spring or early summer when dark periods shorten. Spinach, for example, flowers only when night length is less than 10 hours. A **day-neutral plant** flowers when it reaches a certain stage of maturity, regardless of day length at that time. Dandelions, tomatoes, and rice are day-neutral.

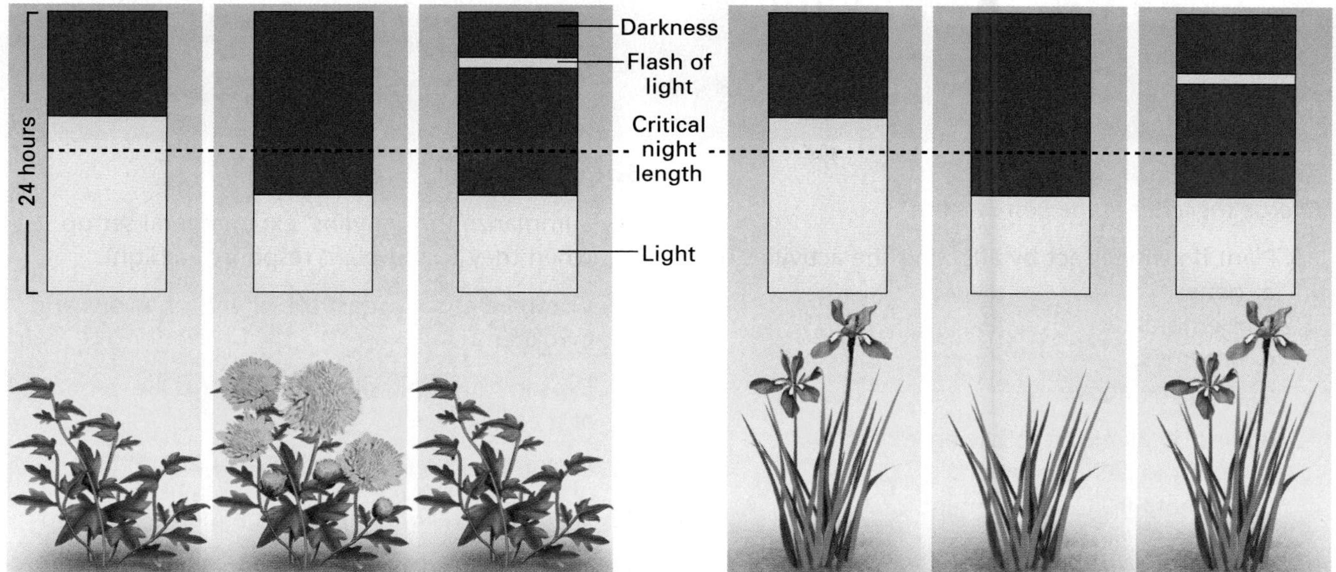

a. Short-day (long-night) plants

b. Long-day (short-night) plants

Flower growers use information about photoperiodism to produce certain flowers out of season. Chrysanthemums, for instance, are short-day plants that normally bloom in autumn. But a florist can prevent a chrysanthemum from blooming until the spring by exposing the plants to flashes of light during the long autumn and winter nights. The plant thus detects two short nights, instead of one long night, and fails to bloom.

How does a plant monitor day length as the seasons change? Sunrise and sunset are detected by pigmented proteins called **phytochromes** (FYT uh krohm). When phytochromes absorb the red light that is abundant at sunrise, they change shape to an active form that triggers a variety of plant responses. After sunset, the phytochromes gradually change back to their inactive form. These sunrise/sunset cues combine with the biological clock to indicate the proportions of day and night in a 24-hour period. This is another example of how control systems keep a plant in tune with its external world.

▲ **Figure 22-15** Night length affects blooming in many plants. **a.** Short-day (long-night) plants such as the chrysanthemum bloom when night lasts *longer* than a critical length. If that critical night length is interrupted with a flash of light, the plant fails to bloom. **b.** In contrast, long-day (short-night) plants, such as the iris, bloom when nights are *shorter* than a critical length. Interrupting a long night breaks up the night into two short nights, and the plant blooms.

Online Activity 22.3

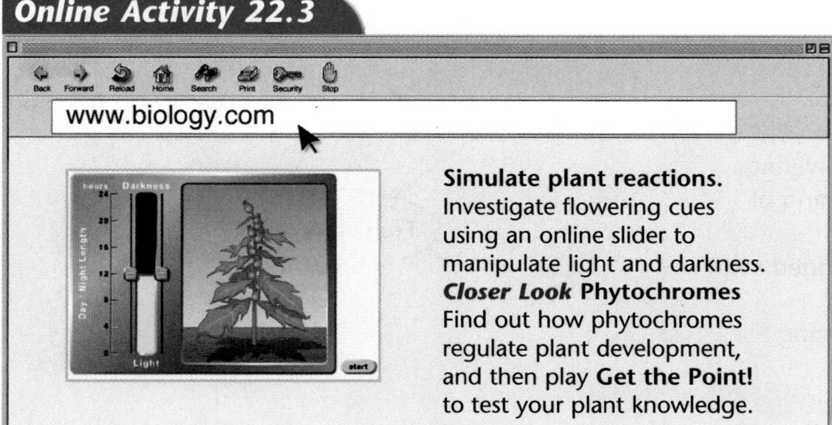

Simulate plant reactions. Investigate flowering cues using an online slider to manipulate light and darkness.
Closer Look **Phytochromes** Find out how phytochromes regulate plant development, and then play **Get the Point!** to test your plant knowledge.

Concept Check 22.3

1. Give an example of a circadian rhythm in a plant or animal.
2. Describe the difference between a short- and a long-day plant and give an example of each.
3. Explain how phytochromes are activated.

Multiple Choice

Choose the letter of the best answer.

1. Plant hormones act by affecting the activities of
   a. genes.
   b. membranes.
   c. enzymes.
   d. all of the above.

2. Auxins do all of the following *except*
   a. promote cell elongation.
   b. promote fruit development.
   c. promote "leaf drop."
   d. inhibit plant branching.

3. During winter, which plant hormone inhibits new growth?
   a. ethylene
   b. gibberellin
   c. cytokinin
   d. abscisic acid

4. Leaf drop is caused by
   a. an increase in day length.
   b. an increase in gibberellins.
   c. a change in the color of the leaves.
   d. a shift in the balance of ethylene and auxins.

5. A growth response to touch is an example of a
   a. phototropism.
   b. sleep movement.
   c. circadian rhythm.
   d. thigmotropism.

6. A species that blooms when night length exceeds a critical length is a
   a. day-neutral plant.
   b. short-day plant.
   c. long-day plant.
   d. short-night plant.

7. Phytochrome is
   a. a hormone that stimulates plant flowering.
   b. a protein that helps control the timing of flowering.
   c. a protein that responds to waterlogged soil by killing root cells.
   d. a hormone that inhibits plant flowering.

Short Answer

8. Summarize the Darwins' experimental set-up when they tested plant responses to light.

9. Compare and contrast the effects of auxins and cytokinins.

10. Explain how rapid plant movements are controlled at a cellular level.

11. Define *tropism* and give an example.

12. How can overwatering harm a plant?

13. Describe an adaptation of halophytes to salt stress.

14. How can lignin be used in plant defense?

15. Describe an example of a plant interacting with another species.

16. Explain what is meant by the term *day-neutral plant.*

17. Describe sunlight's effect on phytochrome.

Visualizing Concepts

18. Copy the graphic organizer below and add other hormones and other responses to it to show the relationships of different hormones and their effects on plants. Use green arrows to indicate stimulatory effects and red arrows to indicate inhibitory effects.

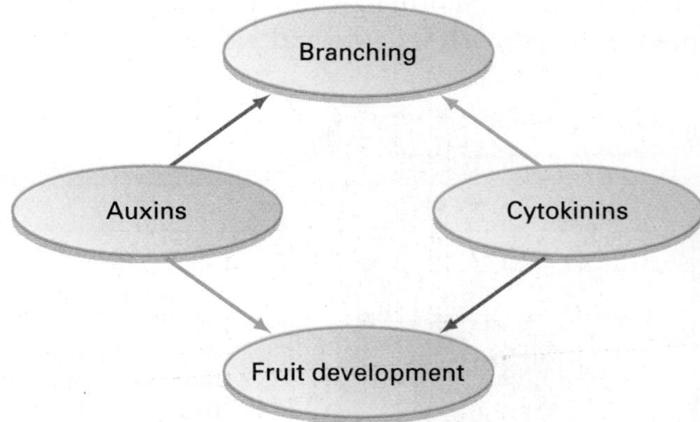

Analyzing Information

19. **Analyzing Data** The table below shows the effects of three treatments on the growth of a normal seedling and two mutant seedlings.

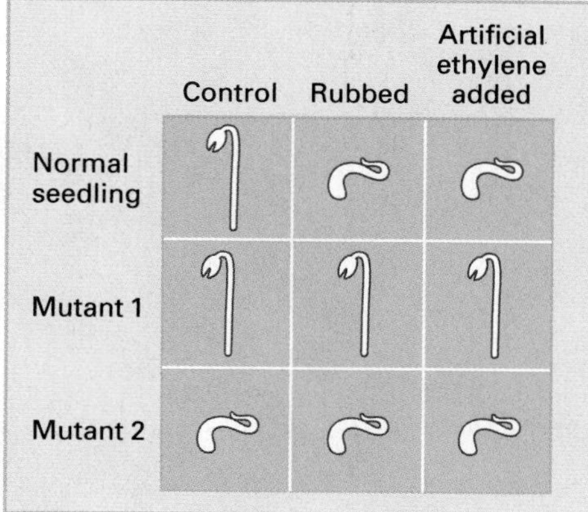

a. Hypothesize why rubbing the normal seedling had the same effect as adding artificial ethylene.
b. Which mutant is insensitive to ethylene? Explain.
c. What can you infer about the other mutant's production of ethylene?
d. How might each mutant be at a disadvantage in nature compared to the normal seedling?

20. **Analyzing Diagrams** In 1913 biologist Peter Boyce-Jensen further tested the Darwins' hypothesis that a chemical signal is responsible for phototropisms. Examine the results shown below of two treatments he applied to grass seedlings. (Note that chemicals can diffuse through gelatin, but not through mica, a rock mineral.)

Light

Tip separated by gelatin block

Tip separated by mica

a. How did the seedlings react to each treatment?
b. Why do you think the seedling with its tip separated by mica grew straight?

Critical Thinking

21. **Relating Cause and Effect** Buds and sprouts often form on tree stumps. Which group of hormones would you expect to stimulate their formation? Explain.

22. **Evaluating the Impact of Research** Give examples of at least three ways that knowledge about the control systems of plants is applied.

23. **Comparing and Contrasting** Describe how tropisms are similar to and different from rapid plant movements.

24. **Problem Solving** John just started a new job as night watchman at a plant nursery. Around midnight, he accidentally opened the door to the chrysanthemum room and turned on the lights for a moment. How could this affect the chrysanthemums (which are short-day plants)?

25. **What's Wrong With These Statements?** *Briefly explain why each statement is inaccurate or misleading.*
a. Houseplants bend toward windows because light causes them to grow more on that side.
b. The action of two different hormones together doubles the plant's response.
c. A plant loses its circadian rhythm when it is kept in the dark.

Performance Assessment

Design an Experiment Design a controlled experiment to determine the critical night length of a species of short-day plant.

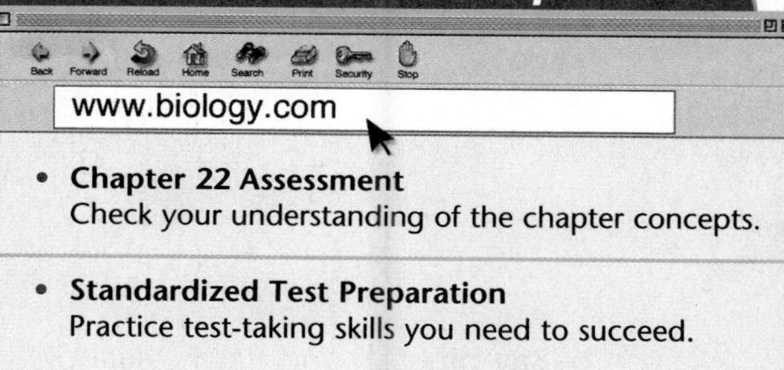

Online Assessment/Test Preparation
www.biology.com
Chapter 22 Assessment
Check your understanding of the chapter concepts.
Standardized Test Preparation
Practice test-taking skills you need to succeed.

UNIT 7

Exploring Animal Diversity

Chapters

Bay pipefish and Pacific seahorse off the coast of California

There is one quality that characterizes all of us who deal with the sciences of the earth and its life—we are never bored.

Rachel Carson

Invertebrate Diversity

Of some 1.5 million known species of organisms, more than two thirds are animals. And the vast majority of these animal species are invertebrates—animals without backbones. One place you can explore a sample of this rich diversity is in a rocky tide pool like this one off the Oregon coast. Besides its colorful sea stars and sea anemones, this habitat is home to a variety of crabs, snails, and barnacles. If you looked under a ledge, you might find brightly colored tube worms and small sponges. In fact, a typical tide pool contains examples of each of the nine phyla of invertebrates discussed in this chapter. These nine groups have the greatest number of species and are the most abundant and widespread. Before you begin the chapter, go online to the ***WebQuest*** to explore life in a rocky tide pool.

Key Concepts

Concept 23.1
Diverse animals share several key characteristics.

Concept 23.2 
Sponges are relatively simple animals with porous bodies.

Concept 23.3
Cnidarians are radial animals with stinging cells.

Concept 23.4
Flatworms are the simplest bilateral animals.

Concept 23.5
Roundworms and rotifers have complete digestive tracts.

Concept 23.6
Annelids are segmented worms.

Concept 23.7
Mollusks show diverse variations on a common body form.

Concept 23.8
Echinoderms have spiny skin and a water vascular system.

Concept 23.9
Animal diversity "exploded" during the Cambrian period.

Assessment
Chapter 23 Review

What's Online

www.biology.com

WebQuest
TidePoolQuest

Online Activity 23.1
Characterize animals.

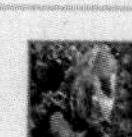
Online Activity 23.2
Explore sponges.

Online Activity 23.3
Explore cnidarians.

Online Activity 23.4
Explore flatworms.

Online Activity 23.5
Explore roundworms.

Online Activity 23.6
Explore annelids.

Online Activity 23.7
Explore mollusks.

Lab 23 Online Companion
Mapping a Mollusk

Online Activity 23.8
Explore echinoderms.

Online Activity 23.9
Activate a phylogenetic tree.

Science, Technology, & Society
Protecting Coral Reefs

Chapter 23 Assessment

CONCEPT 23.1

Diverse animals share several key characteristics.

OBJECTIVES
- List four general characteristics of animals.
- Compare and contrast vertebrates and invertebrates.

KEY TERMS
- blastula
- gastrula
- larva
- metamorphosis
- invertebrate
- vertebrate

What's Online

Online Activity 23.1
Characterize animals.

You know an animal when you see one—or do you? Can you explain why the sea anemones or sea stars in the tide pool shown on the previous pages are considered animals? This chapter begins by helping you answer this question.

What Is an Animal?

More than a million living species of animals are organized into about 35 major groups (phyla). (Different biologists have different views on the exact number of animal phyla.) But as diverse as they are, animals share four key characteristics that taken together separate them from other organisms (Figure 23-1).

1. Animals are eukaryotic.
2. Animal cells lack cell walls.
3. Animals are multicellular.
4. Animals are heterotrophs that ingest food.

The fourth characteristic refers to how animals obtain nutrition. Most animals take food into their bodies and digest it there, like you do. This mode of nutrition, called ingestion, distinguishes animals from other heterotrophs, such as fungi, that digest food outside their bodies and then absorb the nutrients. In addition, most animals have a digestive cavity, an internal sac or tube in which digestion occurs.

Comparison of Kingdoms in Domain Eukarya

	Protists	Fungi	Plants	Animals
Eukaryotic	All	All	All	All
Lack Cell Walls	Some	Few	None	All
Multicellular	Some	Most	All	All
Heterotrophic	Some	All	Few	All

Figure 23-1 Though it may look like a plant, the sea anemone above is classified as an animal because it has all four key characteristics outlined in this table.

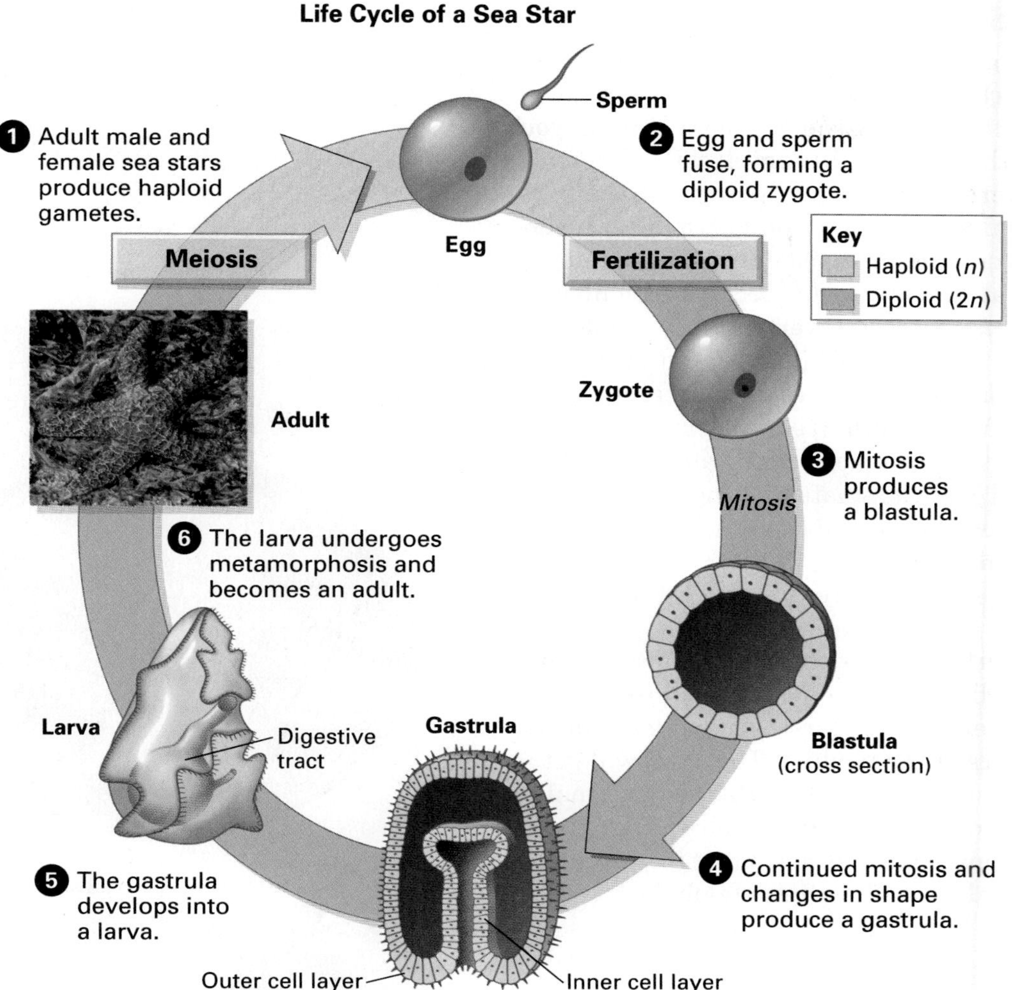
Life Cycle of a Sea Star
1 Adult male and female sea stars produce haploid gametes.
Sperm
2 Egg and sperm fuse, forming a diploid zygote.
Egg
Meiosis
Fertilization
Key
Haploid (n)
Diploid (2n)
Zygote
Adult
3 Mitosis produces a blastula.
Mitosis
6 The larva undergoes metamorphosis and becomes an adult.
Larva
Digestive tract
Gastrula
Blastula
(cross section)
4 Continued mitosis and changes in shape produce a gastrula.
5 The gastrula develops into a larva.
Outer cell layer
Inner cell layer

▲ **Figure 23-2** The life cycle of a sea star serves as an example of animal development. Most animals begin development when the zygote divides repeatedly and forms a blastula. Some animals, such as the sea star, first develop into a larva and then undergo metamorphosis. Other animals develop directly into the adult form.

The life cycles of most animals are also different from those of other organisms, especially in the early stages of development. You can note some of these characteristics of development in the life cycle of a sea star (Figure 23-2). Adult male and female animals produce haploid gametes by meiosis. During fertilization an egg and a sperm fuse and form a zygote. The zygote then undergoes mitosis. The first several cell divisions lead to an embryonic stage called a blastula that is common to all animals. Typically the **blastula** consists of a single layer of cells surrounding a hollow cavity. Later, in many animals, one side of the blastula folds inward, forming an embryonic stage called a **gastrula.** The gastrula has both an outer and an inner cell layer.

From the gastrula stage, many animals develop directly into adults. But others, including the sea star, first go through one or more larval stages. A **larva** is an immature form of an animal that looks different from the adult form and usually eats different food. The larva undergoes a change of body form, called **metamorphosis,** and becomes an adult.

Invertebrates and Vertebrates

One common way to group various animals is based on whether they have a backbone (Figure 23-3). If you examined a tide pool or the underside of rocks on a stream bottom, you would find yourself in the world of **invertebrates,** animals without backbones. Invertebrates make up approximately 95 percent of the different kinds of animals on Earth. Most invertebrate species live in aquatic or moist terrestrial habitats. And the majority of aquatic invertebrate species live in marine waters. Some familiar examples of invertebrates include sea stars, jellies ("jellyfish"), snails, clams, insects, and worms.

Vertebrates, animals with backbones, are well represented in terrestrial environments but also live in marine and freshwater habitats. Examples of common vertebrates are fishes, frogs, snakes, dogs, and the classmates sitting next to you. Since humans are land-dwelling vertebrates, it is natural that you would be most familiar with vertebrates. However, for every known vertebrate species, there are at least 19 known invertebrate species.

The diversity of invertebrates is the main subject of this chapter. In each of the following concepts, you will read about a different phylum of invertebrates. First, you will read about the general characteristics of the phylum. Then you will get a sense of the diversity of the animals within this group. Finally, at the end of this chapter, you will find a table that summarizes and compares information about how basic life processes are accomplished across all these invertebrate phyla.

Figure 23-3 At a glance, an octopus and a snake have some similarities in body structure. However, the presence of a backbone in the snake is characteristic of the animals called vertebrates. The octopus, which lacks a backbone, is an invertebrate.

Online Activity 23.1

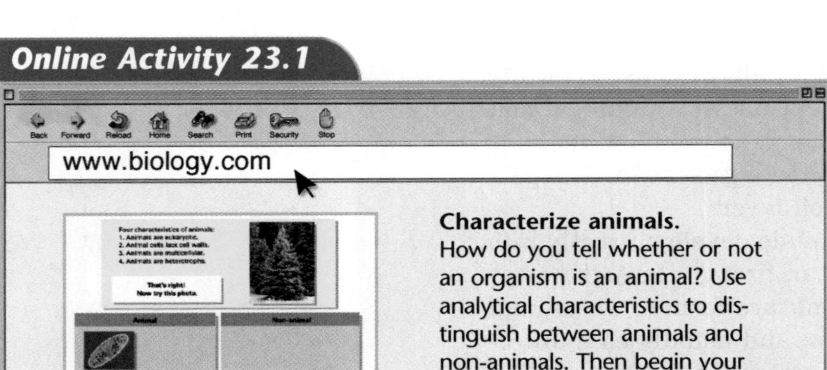

Characterize animals.
How do you tell whether or not an organism is an animal? Use analytical characteristics to distinguish between animals and non-animals. Then begin your exploration of the invertebrates by studying a cladogram.

Concept Check 23.1

1. What distinguishes an animal from animal-like protists (protozoans)?
2. Contrast invertebrates with vertebrates.
3. Explain the difference between the blastula and gastrula stages of development in most animals.

CONCEPT 23.2 Sponges are relatively simple animals with porous bodies.

OBJECTIVES

- Describe the general characteristics of sponges.
- Identify characteristics that vary among diverse sponges.

KEY TERMS

- sponge
- collar cell
- amoebocyte
- sessile

What's Online

Have you ever used a "natural sponge" to mop up a spill or wash a car? You might be surprised to learn that these large, fluffy brown sponges are actually the remains of aquatic animals.

The Body of a Sponge

Sponges (phylum Porifera) are the simplest animals. For example, *Scypha,* a small marine sponge measuring only a few centimeters, resembles a simple tube with an opening at one end (Figure 23-4). Unlike most animals, **sponges** lack true tissues and organs. Most of the different types of cells in a sponge are relatively unspecialized.

The body of most sponges consists of two layers of cells separated by a jelly-like material. The outer layer of cells protects the interior of the sponge and also has many pores (holes) through which water can enter the sponge. The inner layer of cells lines the central cavity of the sponge. These cells, called **collar cells,** have flagella. Wandering through the jelly-like material are cells called **amoebocytes** that pick up food from the collar cells, digest it, and carry the nutrients to other cells. Amoebocytes also transport oxygen, dispose of wastes, and can change into other cell types, such as support structures. In some sponges these support structures are rigid. In other types of sponges the structures are composed of a flexible protein called spongin. It is these flexible sponges that are harvested for use as bath sponges.

Sponges ingest food by the action of their collar cells. The flagella of collar cells generate water currents that move water through the sponge's pores and into the central cavity. As water flows through the sponge's body, it is filtered for food particles (mostly bacteria) in the water. Collar cells trap the food particles in mucus. Amoebocytes then engulf the particles and transport them to other cells. The water drawn in through the pores exits through the large opening at one end of the sponge.

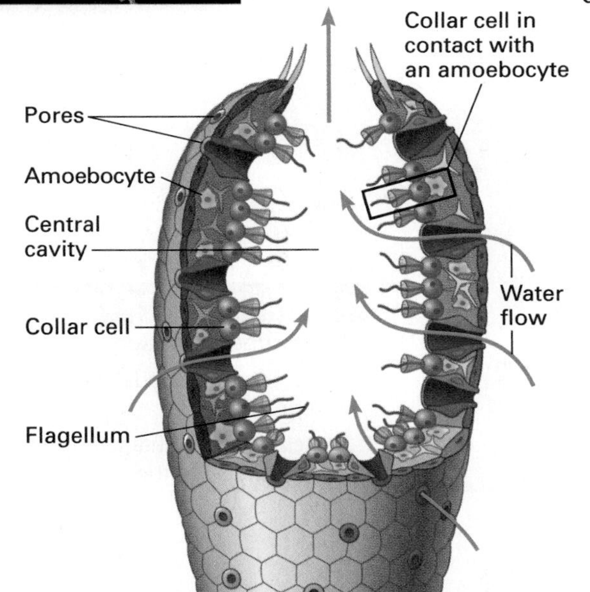

Figure 23-4 Sponges such as *Scypha* feed by filtering bacteria and other food particles from water that passes through pores in their bodies.

Sponges live singly or in clusters formed by budding. Budding is a form of asexual reproduction in which new sponges develop from an outgrowth of the parent organism. Most species of sponges have great powers of regeneration. Small fragments of a sponge body can grow into an entire new sponge. However, sponges can also reproduce sexually. Most sponges have both male and female gamete-producing structures in the same organism. The union of egg and sperm cells form zygotes that develop into flagellated larvae.

Adult sponges are **sessile,** meaning they are anchored in place. They can't run and hide. Sponges have chemical defenses that protect them from possible predators, disease organisms, and parasites. These defenses include toxins that keep predators from eating the sponges and powerful antibiotics that fight bacterial infections. Researchers are studying these unique sponge chemicals for new drugs to fight human disease.

Although sponges are animals, they have several protist-like features. Their relatively simple structure supports evidence from DNA analysis that sponges evolved very early from the protists that were ancestral to the animal kingdom. The modern protists that are most closely related to animals are colonies of protist cells that are very similar to the collar cells of sponges. Later in the chapter, you will learn about a hypothesis for how such colonial protists may have given rise to the animal kingdom.

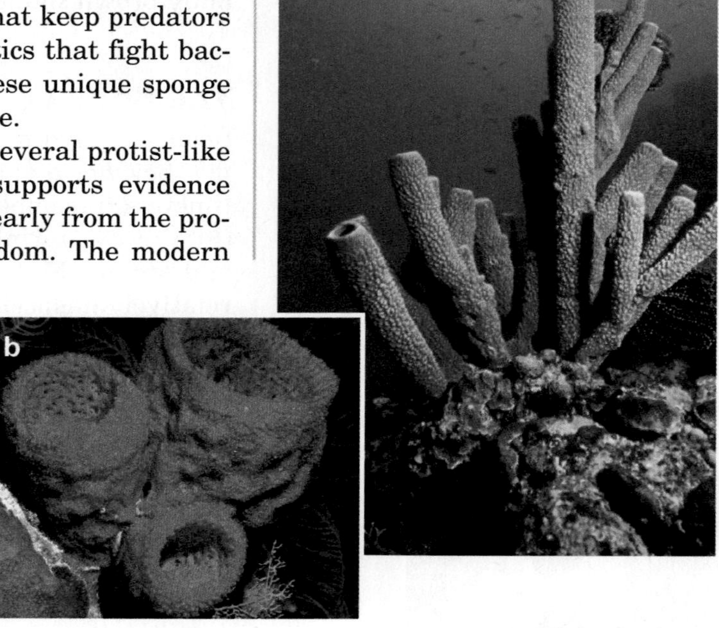

▲ **Figure 23-5** Despite being the simplest animal form, sponges show considerable diversity. **a.** The purple tube sponge can grow to be 1.5 meters tall. **b.** The tubular red sponge has an irregular body shape.

Diversity of Sponges

The 9,000 known species of sponges are diverse in shape, size, and color. Some sponges consist of a single cylinder, while other sponges branch out irregularly over the seafloor or lake bottoms (Figure 23-5). Some sponges, like *Scypha,* are quite small. Others can reach heights of 2 meters.

Online Activity 23.2

Explore sponges.
What are the key characteristics of sponges? What are their feeding habits? Learn more about sponges using an interactive chart.

Concept Check 23.2

1. Describe how a sponge feeds.
2. List three methods of sponge reproduction.
3. Describe two characteristics that vary widely in the sponge phylum.

CONCEPT 23.3

Cnidarians are radial animals with stinging cells.

OBJECTIVES

- Describe the general characteristics of cnidarians.
- Compare and contrast the body structure of a hydra with that of a marine jelly.

KEY TERMS

- cnidarian
- radial symmetry
- cnidocyte
- nematocyst
- gastrovascular cavity
- polyp
- medusa

What's Online

Online Activity 23.3
Explore cnidarians.

On a warm, sunny day in the tropics you might see thousands of harmless-looking blue bubbles floating on the surface of the ocean. Those bubbles are the top portion of a fascinating marine animal, the Portuguese man-of-war. Its tentacles extend as far as 50 meters below the surface of each bubble. Each tentacle contains stinging cells that cause a painful, temporarily paralyzing effect on fishes and other animals.

The Body of a Cnidarian

The Portuguese man-of-war is common in both tropical and temperate climates and belongs to a phylum called Cnidaria (ny DAYR ee uh). Another cnidarian, the hydra, is commonly found in ponds and lakes. The hydra has a cylindrical body, about 3 cm long, with projections called tentacles at one end (Figure 23-6). Other cnidarians include the jellies (jellyfishes), sea anemones, and coral animals. Two characteristics that all **cnidarians** share are radial symmetry and tentacles with stinging cells.

An organism with **radial symmetry** has body parts arranged like pieces of a pie around an imaginary central axis. Any imaginary slice passing longitudinally through the central axis of such an organism divides it into identical pieces. Animals with radial symmetry lack a head. Most cnidarians are slow-moving or sessile (attached to a surface). Most of the time these animals can be found on shallow ocean floors, on the bottoms of ponds, or drifting about in water currents.

Figure 23-6 The hydra in the micrograph is reproducing asexually by budding (a). *Hydra* and other cnidarians are radially symmetrical—able to be divided into identical pie-shaped segments, like a flower pot (b). Cnidarians also feature tentacles with stinging cells.

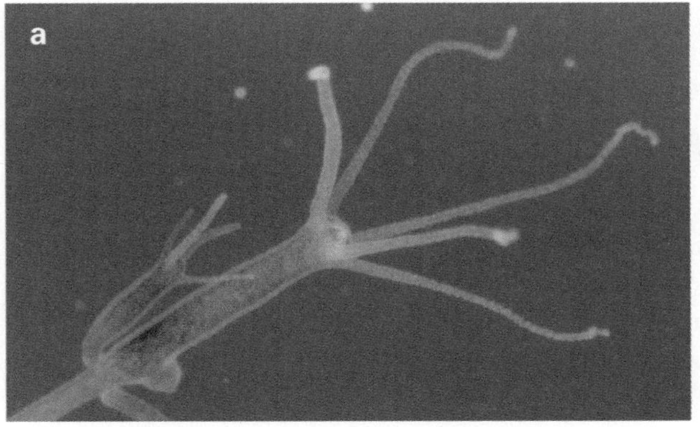

Radial Symmetry

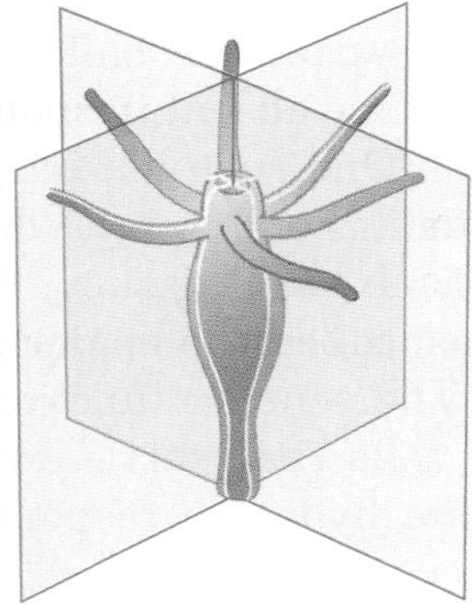

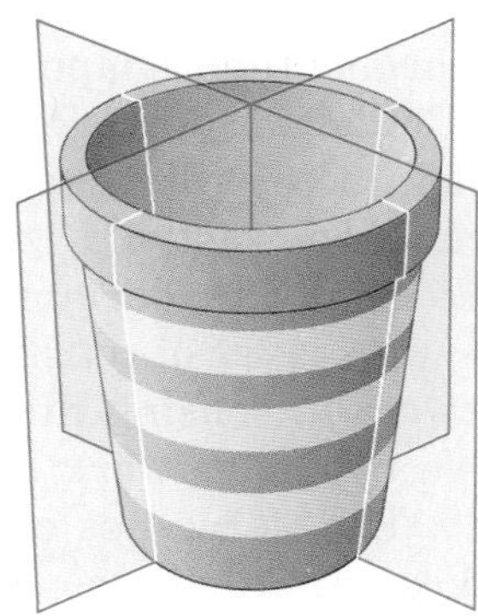

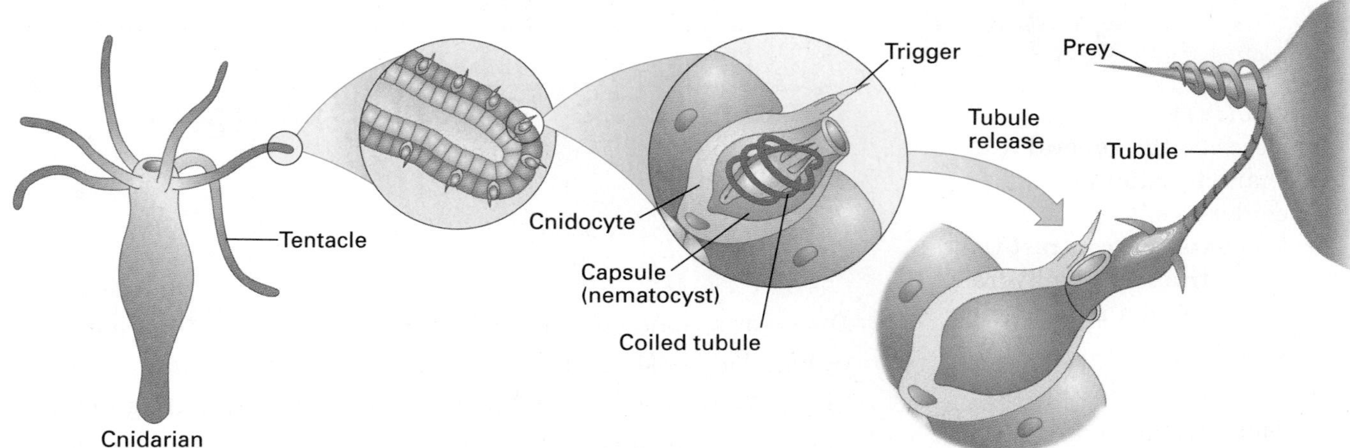

▲ **Figure 23-7** The tentacles of a hydra are armed with numerous cnidocytes. Each cnidocyte holds a stinging capsule called a nematocyst. When triggered by touch, the fine, coiled tubule within the nematocyst shoots out toward the prey.

All cnidarians have specialized stinging cells used for defense and capturing prey. The phylum is named for these stinging cells, which are called **cnidocytes** (NY duh syts). Cnidocytes are especially abundant along the tentacles. A stinging capsule is located within each cnidocyte.

One type of capsule, called a **nematocyst,** contains a fine, coiled tubule that often has a poisonous barb at the end (Figure 23-7). When released, the barb from this type of nematocyst can penetrate and release poison into the prey. Tubules of some cnidarian species have barbed ends, while tubules from other species are sticky and wrap around the prey. The speed with which a nematocyst releases its tubule is one of the quickest processes in the animal kingdom. The force that propels the tubule probably comes from a buildup of osmotic (water) pressure. Each nematocyst can only fire once.

Once a cnidarian captures its prey, its tentacles maneuver the food into its mouth, located at the center of the ring of tentacles. The mouth leads into a digestive sac called the **gastrovascular cavity.** As in other animals with a digestive sac, food enters through the mouth and is digested in the cavity. Undigested food and other wastes exit back through the mouth. Circulating fluids inside the cavity transport digested food to, and wastes from, the cells lining the cavity. This ability of the cavity to function as a circulatory (or vascular) system is the reason for "vascular" in gastrovascular (*gastro-* means "belly" or "gut"). Fluid in the cavity provides body support and helps give cnidarians their shape, much like water in a balloon.

Cnidarians have features that are absent in sponges but present in nearly all other animals. One such feature is the presence of a gastrula stage during embryonic development. Additionally, cnidarians have some basic tissues. For example, the outer layer of cells in hydras, called the epidermis, has protective and sensing functions. The sensing functions include a nerve net, a network of nerve cells that surround the hydra's body. The nerve net enables the hydra to respond to stimuli and coordinate its movements.

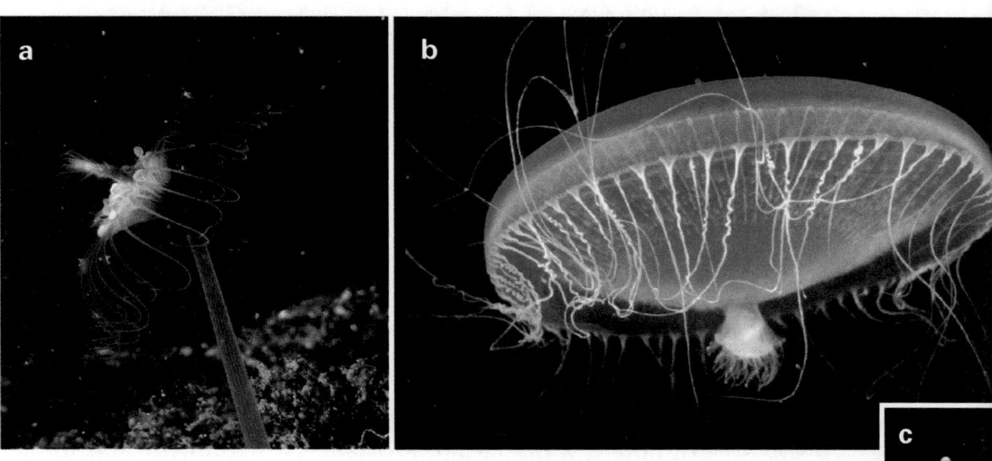

Figure 23-8 There are three classes of cnidarians. **a.** Some hydrozoans such as this nodding nosegay hydroid can be solitary. Other hydrozoans can form large colonies that serve as habitats for other animals. **b.** Scyphozoans such as this marine jelly have a medusa body shape. Some of the largest species are 2 meters in diameter and have tentacles more than 100 meters long. **c.** Anthozoans include sea anemones and closely related species, as well as most coral animals. Note the polyp body form of this species.

Diversity of Cnidarians

There are about 9,000 known species of cnidarians. These organisms have two kinds of body forms, both with radial symmetry. One body form is the **polyp,** a cylindrical body with tentacles radiating from one end. Animals with a polyp body form are mostly sessile organisms. Examples of polyp-shaped cnidarians include the hydras. The other type of cnidarian body form is the **medusa,** an umbrella-shaped form with fringes of tentacles around the lower edge. Jellies have the medusa body form. Medusas move freely about in the water, transported by wind, water currents, and rhythmic contractions of the "umbrella." Some cnidarian life cycles include both a medusa stage and a polyp stage. Others exist only as medusas. Still others such as hydras and sea anemones exist only as polyps.

Figure 23-8 shows examples of three classes of cnidarians. (Recall from Chapter 15 that *class* is a subgroup of *phylum.)* The class Hydrozoa includes the hydras, some coral animals, and the large Portuguese man-of-war (the tentacles are actually colonies of polyps). The class Scyphozoa includes the jellies. The class Anthozoa includes the sea anemones and most coral animals.

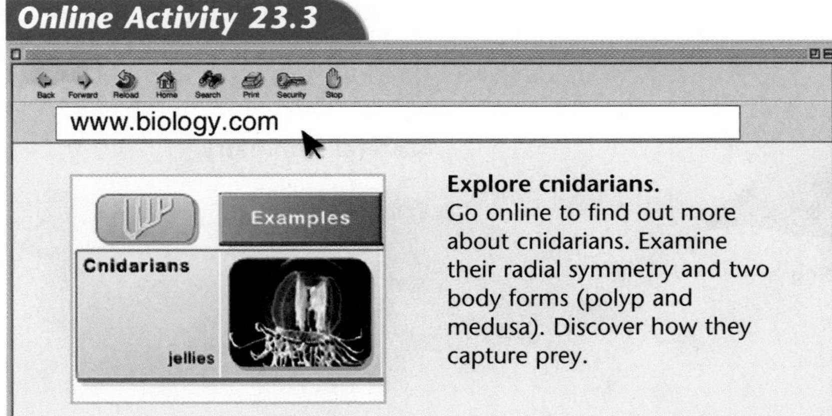

Explore cnidarians.
Go online to find out more about cnidarians. Examine their radial symmetry and two body forms (polyp and medusa). Discover how they capture prey.

Concept Check 23.3

1. What are two characteristics common to all cnidarians?
2. Describe the differences in body structure between a hydra and a marine jelly.
3. Describe the function of cnidocytes and nematocysts.

CONCEPT 23.4

Flatworms are the simplest bilateral animals.

OBJECTIVES
- Describe the general characteristics of flatworms.
- Describe three classes of flatworms.

KEY TERMS
- flatworm
- bilateral symmetry

The group of animals described here has a more complex body structure than the cnidarians. This structure enables the organism to move forward (headfirst) in response to stimuli such as prey. An example is a planarian, a small, flat organism that looks a little "cross-eyed."

The Body of a Flatworm

Planarians are examples of the mostly small, leaflike or ribbonlike **flatworms** (phylum Platyhelminthes [plat i HEL minth ez]). In contrast to radially symmetrical animals such as cnidarians, flatworms, like most other animals, are bilaterally symmetrical. An animal with **bilateral symmetry** has mirror-image right and left sides. A bilaterally symmetrical animal has a distinct head, or anterior end, and tail, or posterior end. It also has a back (dorsal) surface, a bottom (ventral) surface, and two side (lateral) surfaces. In most bilateral animals the eyes and other sense organs are located up front, on the head.

Flatworms are the simplest animals to have three tissue layers: the ectoderm, mesoderm, and endoderm (Figure 23-9). During an animal's early development, the ectoderm develops into the body covering, the mesoderm develops into an internal tissue-filled region, and the endoderm develops into the digestive sac. Like cnidarians, most flatworms have a digestive sac (gastrovascular cavity). The sac is highly branched, with a single mouth opening at one end. Food enters and wastes exit from this one opening located on the ventral surface of the planarian. When the animal is feeding, a muscular tube projects through the mouth and sucks in food.

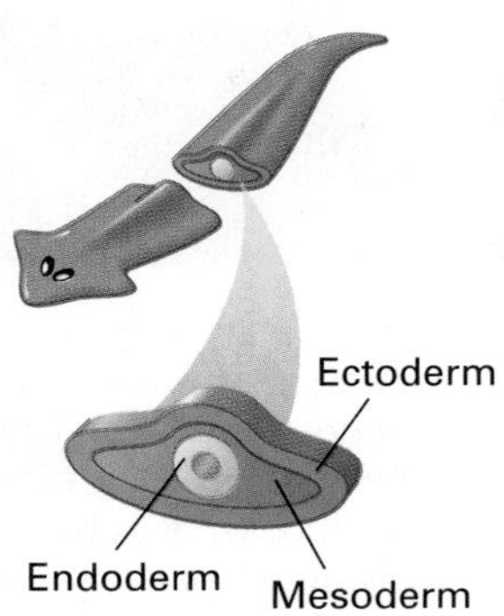

Figure 23-9 Planarians have three tissue layers (shown above) and are bilaterally symmetrical. Bilaterally symmetrical objects can be divided into identical right and left halves, like a shovel.

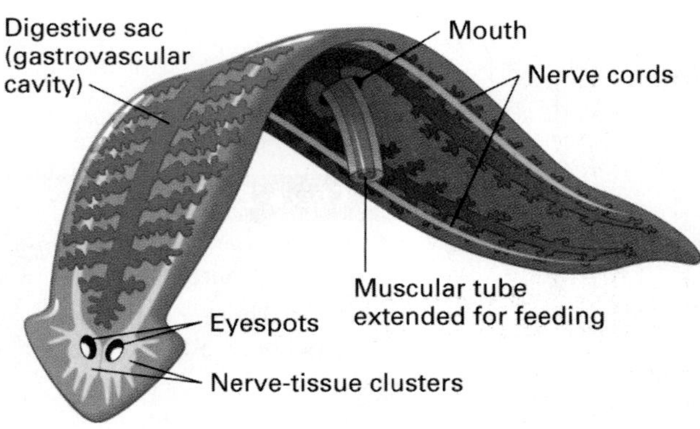

Bilateral Symmetry

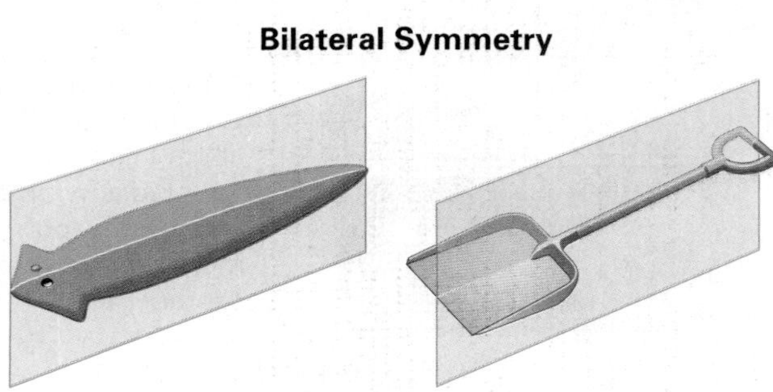

Flatworms can move in several ways. For example, using cilia on its ventral surface, the planarian slides about in search of food. It also has muscles that enable it to twist and turn. The flatworm nervous system is also more complex and centralized than that of cnidarians. A planarian's head has a pair of eyespots that detect light and side flaps that function mainly for smell.

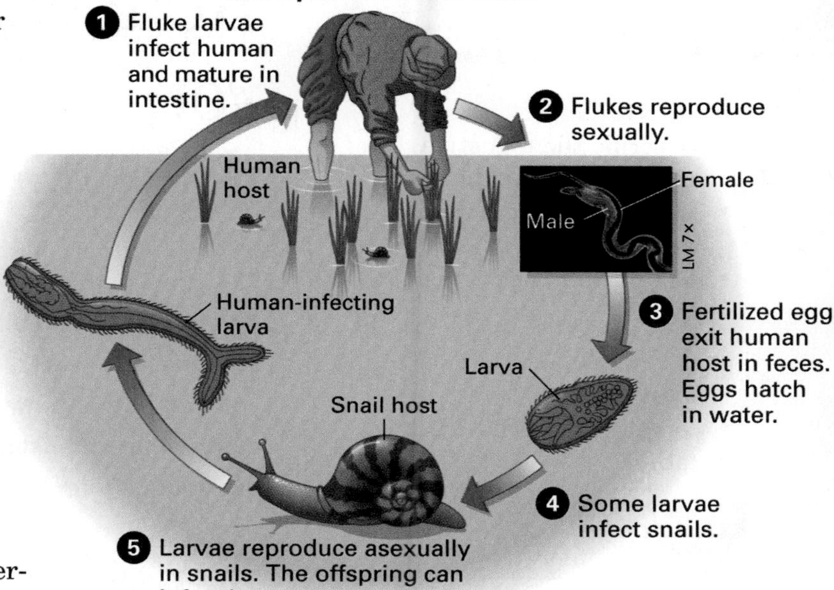

Life Cycle of a Blood Fluke
1 Fluke larvae infect human and mature in intestine.
2 Flukes reproduce sexually.
Human host
Female
Male
LM 7×
3 Fertilized eggs exit human host in feces. Eggs hatch in water.
Human-infecting larva
Larva
Snail host
4 Some larvae infect snails.
5 Larvae reproduce asexually in snails. The offspring can infect humans.

▲ **Figure 23-10** The life cycle of the parasitic blood fluke requires two hosts.

Diversity of Flatworms

The 20,000 known species of flatworms are divided into three classes. Planarians belong to the class Turbellaria. This group is mostly free-living (non-parasitic) and marine, but some planarians live in moist terrestrial environments.

Flukes (class Trematoda) are parasites—they are heterotrophs that absorb nutrients from the body fluids of a living host and in the process harm the host. For example, a blood fluke called *Schistosoma* infects humans and causes a severe, long-lasting disease called schistosomiasis (blood fluke disease). Most flukes have a complex life cycle that includes more than one host (Figure 23-10).

Tapeworms (class Cestoidea) are also parasitic (Figure 23-11). Adult tapeworms such as *Taenia solium,* the pork tapeworm, live in the digestive tracts of vertebrates. The tapeworm itself has no digestive or circulatory system. Surrounded by partially digested food in their hosts' intestines, tapeworms absorb nutrients across their body surface. Each segment of the tapeworm contains reproductive organs that produce eggs.

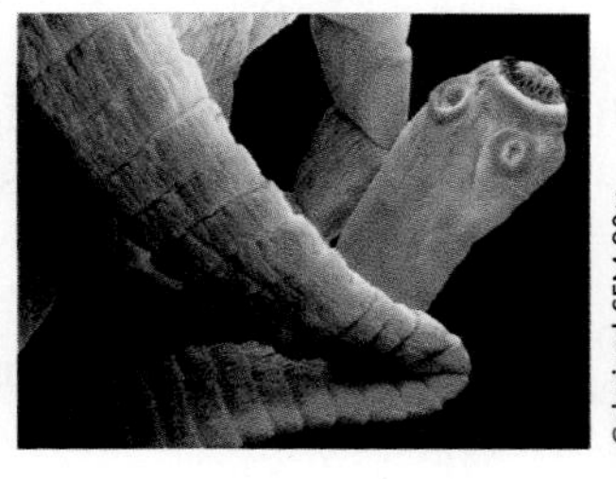

Colorized SEM 90×

◀ **Figure 23-11** The tapeworm's body consists of numerous, repeating flat units. A structure at one end of the tapeworm has hooks and suckers that anchor the worm inside the intestines of a host animal.

Online Activity 23.4

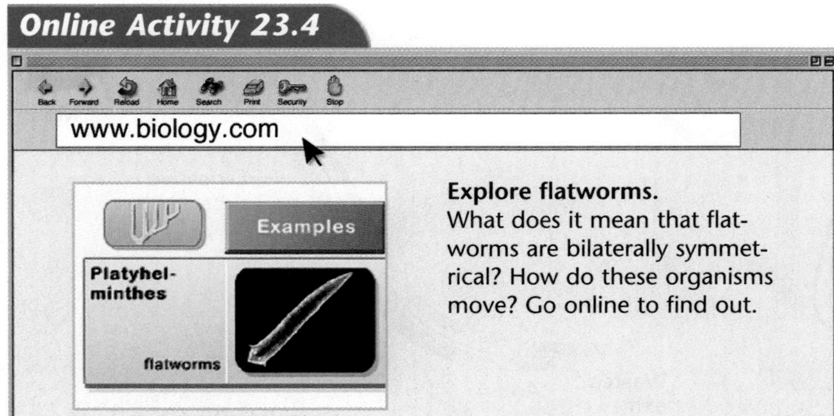

Back Forward Reload Home Search Print Security Stop
www.biology.com
Examples
Platyhel-minthes
flatworms

Explore flatworms.
What does it mean that flatworms are bilaterally symmetrical? How do these organisms move? Go online to find out.

Concept Check 23.4

1. Compare and contrast bilateral symmetry with radial symmetry.
2. List the three flatworm classes and give an example of each.

CONCEPT 23.5

Roundworms and rotifers have complete digestive tracts.

OBJECTIVES
- Describe the digestive system of a roundworm.
- List the diverse habitats of roundworms.
- Compare roundworms and rotifers.

KEY TERMS
- roundworm
- complete digestive tract
- rotifer

What's Online

www.biology.com

Online Activity 23.5
Explore roundworms.

If you take a small bit of moss or lichen from the bark of a tree, immerse it in water, and examine a sample under the microscope, you will find an unfamiliar world teeming with tiny animals. One animal that will likely catch your attention is a clear worm thrashing about—a roundworm.

The Body of a Roundworm

Roundworm

Most **roundworms,** or nematodes (phylum Nematoda), are small, cylindrical worms with somewhat pointed heads and tapered tails. Roundworms range in length from less than 1 mm to more than 7 meters. The largest roundworms are parasites found in whales. Like flatworms, roundworms have three tissue layers. One characteristic that distinguishes roundworms from cnidarians and flatworms is a complete digestive tract. In contrast to a digestive sac (gastrovascular cavity), a **complete digestive tract** has *two* openings, a mouth and an anus, at opposite ends of a continuous tube (Figure 23-12). Food travels only one way through a complete digestive tract. In animals with a digestive tract, the anterior region of the tract churns and mixes food with enzymes for digestion. The posterior region absorbs nutrients from the digested food and disposes of wastes. This step-by-step processing of food allows each part of the digestive tube to be highly specialized for its particular function.

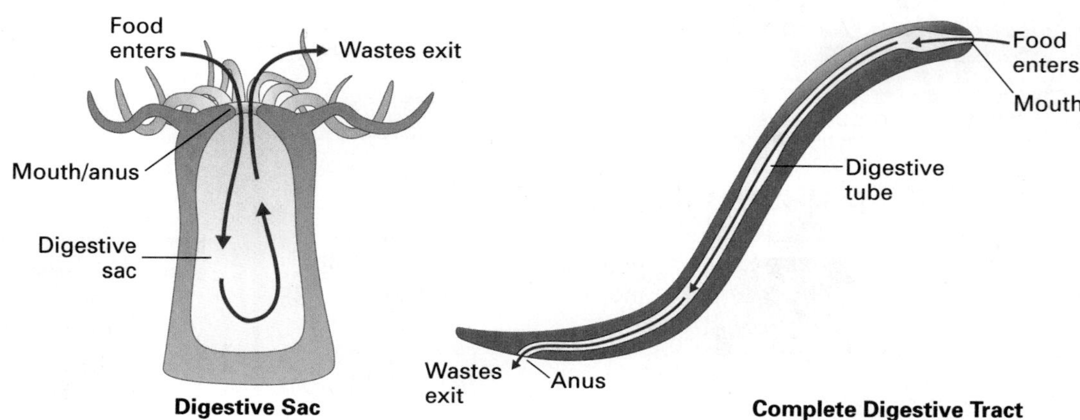

▼ **Figure 23-12** In animals with a digestive sac, such as a cnidarian, food enters and wastes exit through the same opening. In contrast, in animals with a complete digestive tract, like a nematode, food enters and wastes exit through different openings.

Abundance and Diversity of Roundworms

Roundworms are among the most numerous and diverse of all animals on Earth, totalling about 15,000 known species. (Note that "worm" is a general term for a great diversity of invertebrates with elongated bodies. Flatworms, roundworms, and segmented worms, discussed in Concept 23.6, are actually not closely related.) Roundworms live almost every place there is rotting organic matter. These worms are important decomposers in soil and on the bottom of lakes and oceans. Other roundworms thrive as parasites in the moist tissues of plants and in the body fluids and tissues of animals.

Free-living (non-parasitic) roundworms are the most abundant. However, many parasitic species of roundworms are serious agricultural pests that attack the roots of plants or the tissues of animals. Humans can be hosts to at least 50 species of roundworm parasites, including a number that can cause major health problems (Figure 23-13). One example is a disease called trichinosis. Humans acquire this disease by eating undercooked pork or other meat that is infected with worms. Roundworm parasites of animals are also known by several common names such as hookworm, pinworm, and threadworm. These names are often based on the worm's appearance or the organ it infects.

▼ **Figure 23-13** The disease called trichinosis is caused by the roundworm, *Trichinella spiralis*. This micrograph shows young *T. spiralis* within cysts in human muscle tissue.

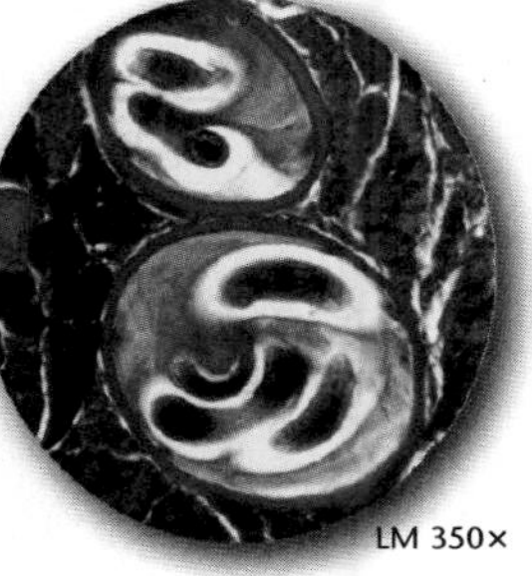

LM 350×

Rotifers

Rotifers (phylum Rotifera) are tiny animals. Most are smaller than many protists. However, the 1,800 known species of rotifers are multicellular animals with specialized organ systems. Like roundworms, rotifers have complete digestive tracts. Rotifers get their name from their unique crown of cilia. This structure directs water into the rotifer's mouth where food particles can be filtered (Figure 23-14). This crown of cilia appears to rotate like a wheel (*rotifer* means "wheel-bearer"). Rotifers are common in freshwater environments such as ponds and even puddles.

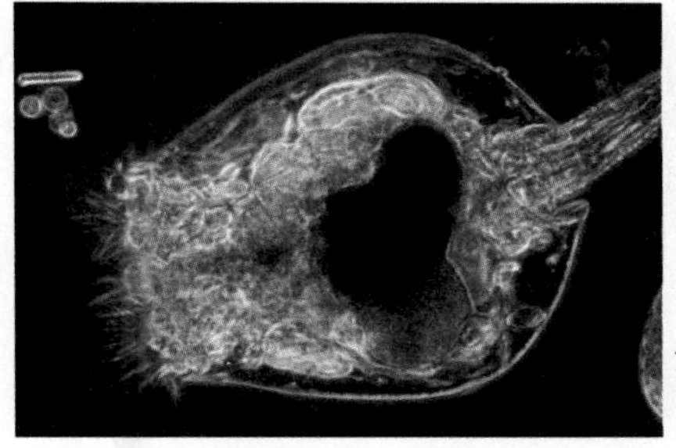

LM 100×

▲ **Figure 23-14** Rotifers are tiny animals named for whirlpool-producing cilia encircling their mouths.

Online Activity 23.5

www.biology.com

Examples

Nematodes

roundworms

Explore roundworms.
What is a hydraulic skeleton? How is a roundworm different from a flatworm? Go online to explore roundworms.

Concept Check 23.5

1. How is a roundworm's digestive system different from that of a flatworm?
2. Give an example of roundworms interacting with other organisms.
3. Describe the appearance of a rotifer.

CONCEPT 23.6

Annelids are segmented worms.

OBJECTIVES
- Describe body segmentation in annelids.
- Identify three classes of annelids.

KEY TERMS
- annelid
- closed circulatory system
- acoelomate
- pseudocoelom
- coelom

If you've ever examined an earthworm, you probably noticed that its body consists of many segments. Segmentation is the key characteristic of the phylum to which earthworms belong.

The Body of an Annelid

Earthworms and other segmented worms, called **annelids,** belong to the phylum Annelida, which means "little rings." Except for a distinct head and tail, an annelid's body segments are all very similar (Figure 23-15). For example, an earthworm's body is divided into sections by internal walls. There is a dense cluster of nerve cells and waste-excreting organs in each segment. However, the digestive tract is not segmented. It penetrates the segment walls and runs the length of the animal, as do the nerve cord and two main blood vessels. Each body segment contains smaller blood vessels connected to these two main blood vessels. Annelids have a **closed circulatory system,** where the blood remains contained within vessels. Nutrients, oxygen, and wastes diffuse in and out through the vessel walls.

Like flatworms and roundworms, annelids are bilaterally symmetrical and have three tissue layers. However, the tissue layers are organized differently in each of the three groups of worms (Figure 23-16 on the facing page). Flatworms are examples of **acoelomates**—animals that lack a body cavity. The **pseudocoelom** of roundworms is a fluid-filled body cavity in direct contact with the digestive tract. The body cavity of annelids (as well as many other animals you will read about later) is called a coelom. A **coelom** is a fluid-filled cavity that is completely lined by tissue that originated in the embryo from mesoderm tissue.

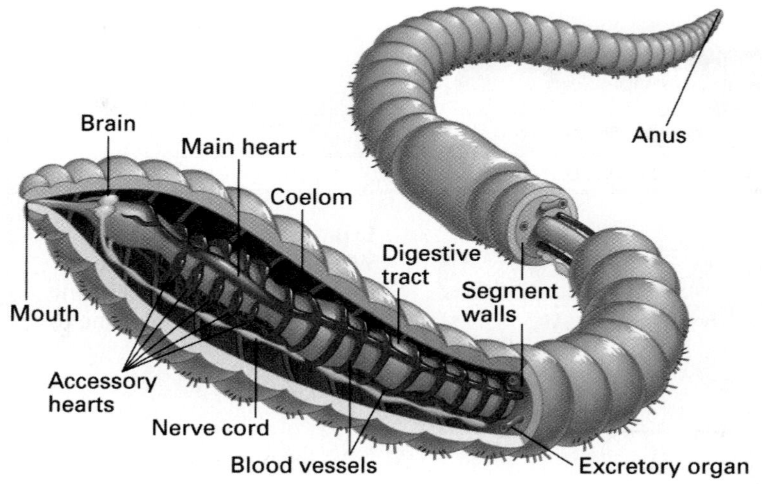

Figure 23-15 Annelid bodies, such as that of an earthworm, are segmented externally and internally.

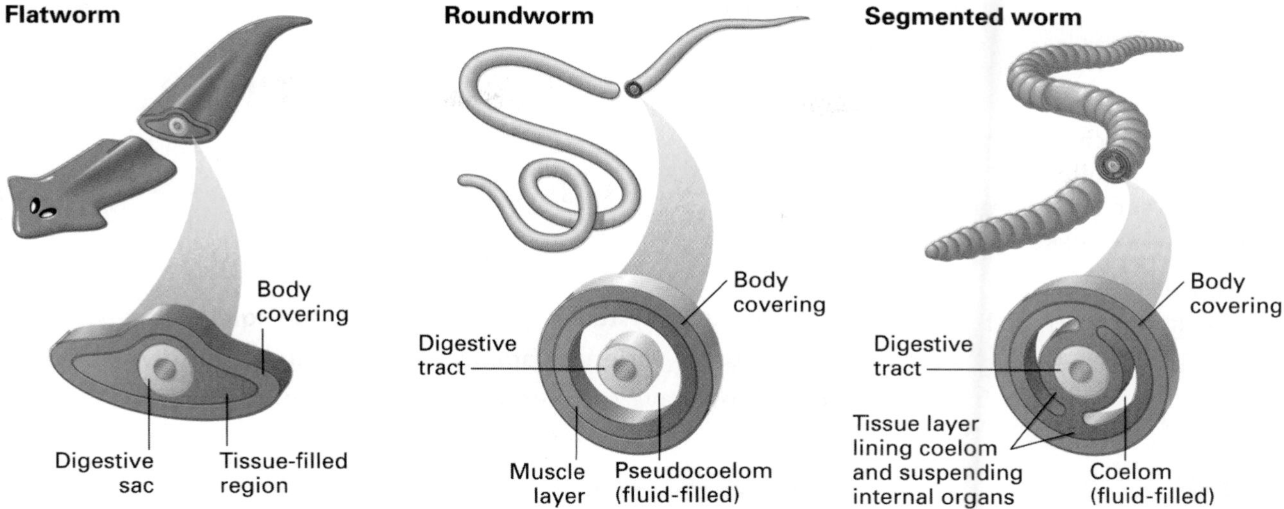

▲ **Figure 23-16** These cross sections contrast three basic body forms for animals with bilateral symmetry: acoelomate (flatworms), pseudocoelomate (roundworms), and coelomate (annelids and many other animals). The colors of the layers in the cross sections indicate body parts that develop from three tissue layers in the embryo (blue = ectoderm; red = mesoderm, and yellow = endoderm).

The Diversity of Annelids

There are about 15,000 known species of annelids, grouped into three classes (Figure 23-17). Class Polychaeta includes many species, such as sandworms, that scavenge for food on the ocean floor. Earthworms belong to class Oligochaeta. These worms are particularly important because their tunneling through soil helps air to circulate in it, which helps plants to grow. Class Hirudinea includes the parasitic leeches.

▲ **Figure 23-17** Note the body segmentation in three different annelids: a sandworm (left), an earthworm (middle), and a leech (right).

Online Activity 23.6

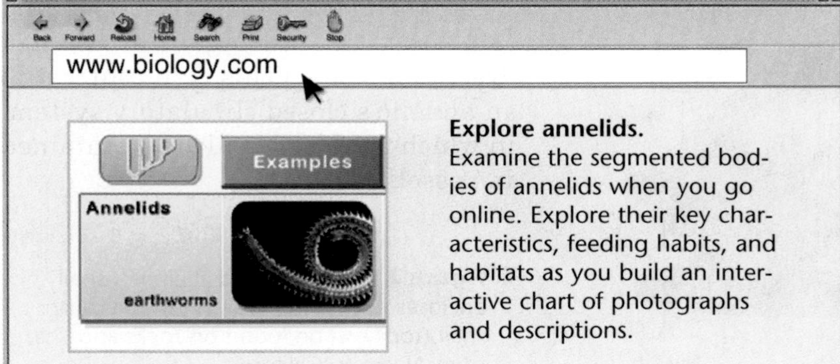

Explore annelids.
Examine the segmented bodies of annelids when you go online. Explore their key characteristics, feeding habits, and habitats as you build an interactive chart of photographs and descriptions.

Concept Check 23.6

1. Describe the body structure of an earthworm.
2. What are the three classes of annelids?

CONCEPT 23.7

Mollusks show diverse variations on a common body form.

OBJECTIVES

- Describe the characteristics common to mollusks.
- Describe the three largest classes of mollusks.

KEY TERMS

- mollusk
- mantle
- radula
- open circulatory system
- gastropod
- bivalve
- cephalopod

What's Online

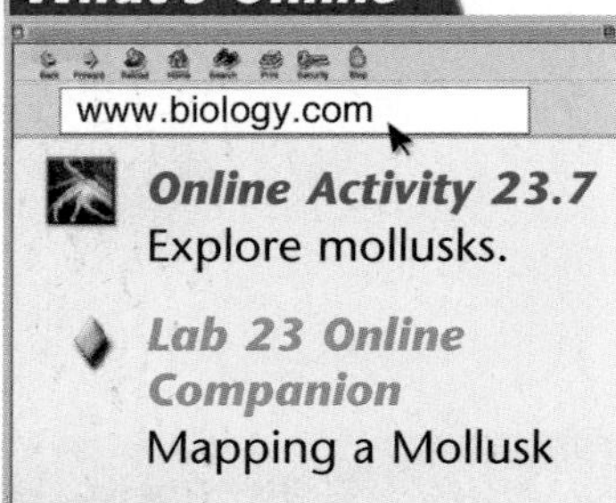

Snails, slugs, oysters, clams, octopuses, and squids are just a few of the great variety of animals that belong to this diverse phylum. Most have soft bodies protected by hard shells.

The Body of a Mollusk

Although squids, clams, and snails look different from each other, these animals have certain features in common. All **mollusks** (phylum Mollusca) have a muscular mass of tissue called a foot and a multifunctional structure called a mantle (Figure 23-18). The mollusk foot functions in locomotion, but its structure is very different from a human foot. The **mantle** is an outgrowth of the body surface that drapes over the animal. The mantle produces the shell in mollusks such as clams and snails. The mantle also functions in respiration, waste disposal, and sensory reception. In addition, the mantle is related to another distinctive feature, the mantle cavity. In aquatic snails and many other mollusks, the mantle cavity houses a gill. The gill extracts oxygen dissolved in the water and may also dispose of wastes.

Another body feature found in many mollusks is a unique rasping organ called a **radula.** An aquatic snail's radula extends from the mouth and slides back and forth like a garden rake, scraping and scooping algae off rocks. Other mollusks use their radulas to drill through shells to prey on other mollusks.

Like segmented worms, all mollusks have a coelom. A snail's coelom consists of three cavities: one around the heart, one around the reproductive organs, and another that forms part of the kidney. Most mollusks have an **open circulatory system** that includes a heart that pumps blood into vessels. The blood vessels then open into chambers where the organs are bathed directly in blood. (This is in contrast to an annelid's closed circulatory system, in which the blood is always contained in vessels.)

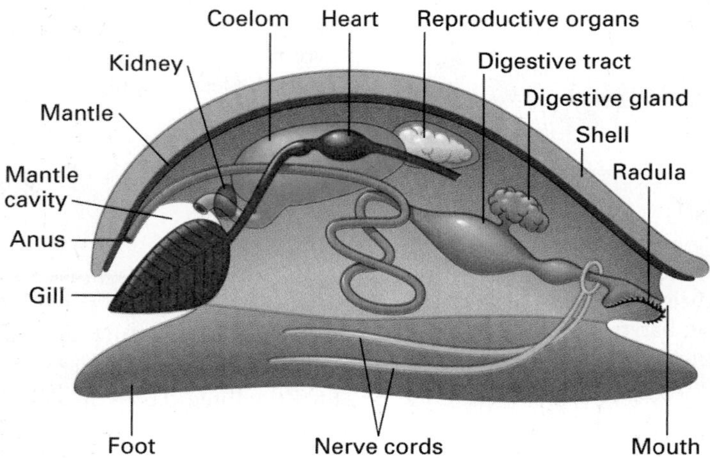

Figure 23-18 The hard shell of a snail encloses its internal organs. The ring top snail (top) can be found on rocks and kelp from Alaska to California.

a

b

c

Figure 23-19 There are three main classes of mollusks. **a.** Gastropods (meaning "stomach-foot") include snails and sea slugs. **b.** Bivalves (mollusks with shells in two halves) include scallops. **c.** Cephalopods (meaning "head-foot") include squid.

The Diversity of Mollusks

The phylum Mollusca is very diverse, with about 150,000 known species (Figure 23-19). **Gastropods** (class Gastropoda) make up the largest group of mollusks. Most organisms in this class have a single shell that is often spiral-shaped. Gastropods live in freshwater, saltwater, and terrestrial environments. Most gastropods are marine. In fact, land snails and slugs are the only mollusks that live on land.

Bivalves (class Bivalvia) include clams, oysters, mussels, and scallops. They have hinged shells divided into two halves. Most bivalves live in marine or freshwater environments. They use their muscular feet for digging and anchoring in the mud or sand. Bivalves feed by pumping water over their gills and trapping food particles that are suspended in the water.

Cephalopods (class Cephalopoda) such as squids and octopuses are faster and more agile than gastropods and bivalves. The cephalopods called chambered nautiluses have external shells, but in most cephalopods the shell is small and internal (as in squids) or missing altogether (as in octopuses). Cephalopods are marine predators, using beak-like jaws and a radula to crush or rip prey apart. Their mouth is at the center of their foot, which is surrounded by 8–10 long tentacle-like arms that catch and hold prey.

Online Activity 23.7

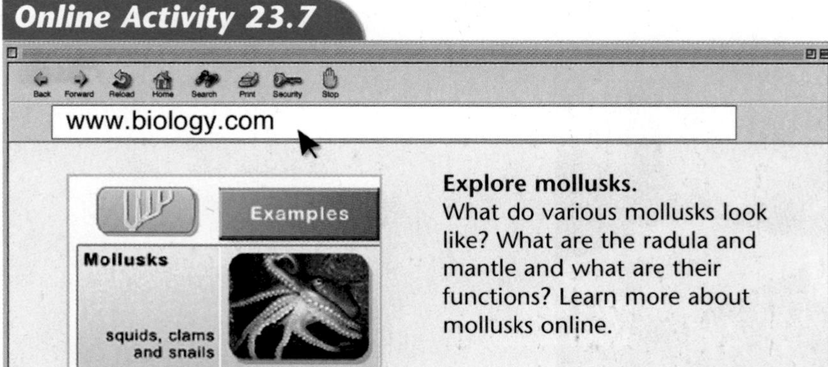

Explore mollusks.
What do various mollusks look like? What are the radula and mantle and what are their functions? Learn more about mollusks online.

Concept Check 23.7

1. What are three functions of the mantle in mollusks?
2. Compare and contrast three classes of mollusks.
3. Describe how a mollusk uses its radula for feeding.

Mapping a Mollusk

Squid Dissection

Question What are the anatomical features of a squid? How do these features allow a squid to hunt, avoid predators, and carry out basic life functions?

Lab Overview In this investigation you will explore mollusk form and function as you dissect a squid, observe features of its external and internal anatomy, and make sketches based on your observations.

Preparing for the Lab To help you prepare for the investigation, go to the *Lab 23 Online Companion*. Find out what makes a squid a mollusk, and identify the parts of a squid. Prepare for the lab procedure by previewing the steps you will take.

Completing the Lab Use your Laboratory Manual or lab page printouts from the *Lab 23 Online Companion* to do the investigation and draw conclusions from the observations you made. **CAUTION:** *Be sure to follow your teacher's instructions and all safety guidelines in the investigation.*

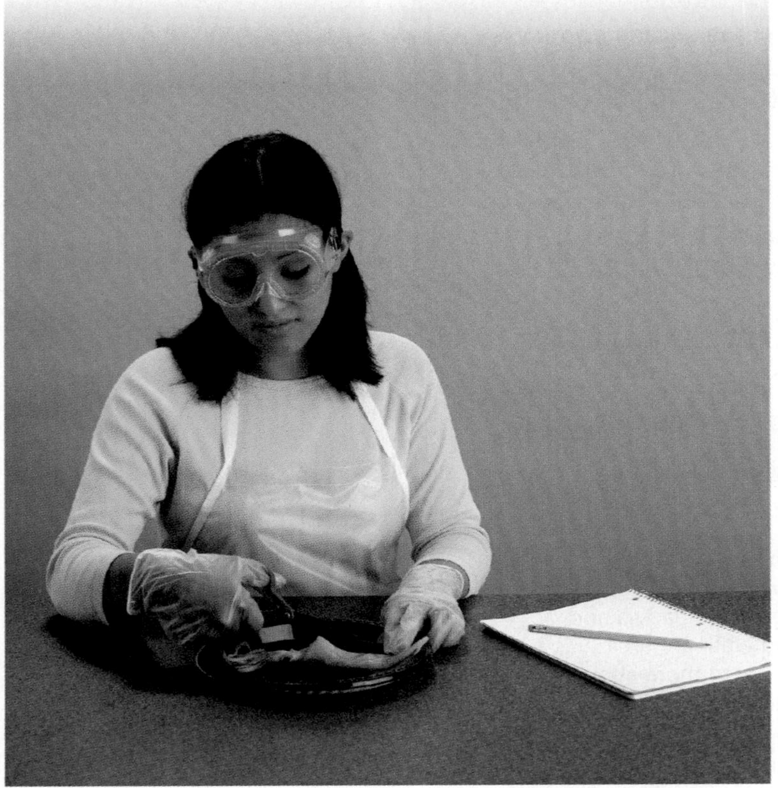

Lab 23 Online Companion

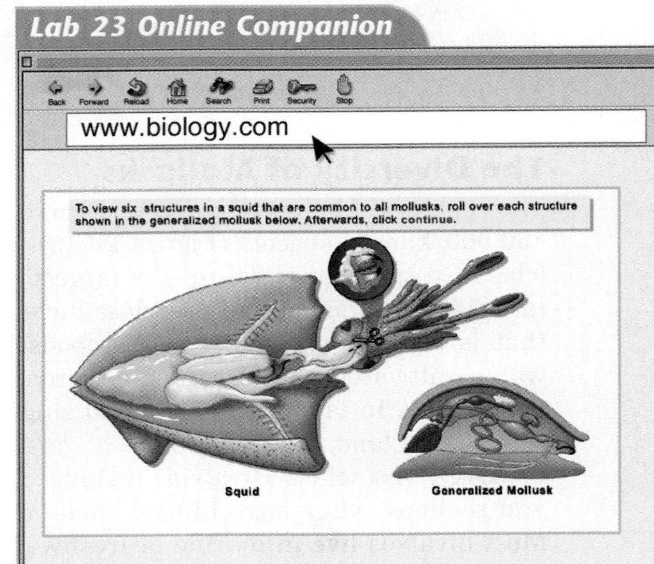
Back
Forward
Reload
Home
Search
Print
Security
Stop
www.biology.com
To view six structures in a squid that are common to all mollusks, roll over each structure shown in the generalized mollusk below. Afterwards, click continue.
Squid
Generalized Mollusk

CONCEPT 23.8

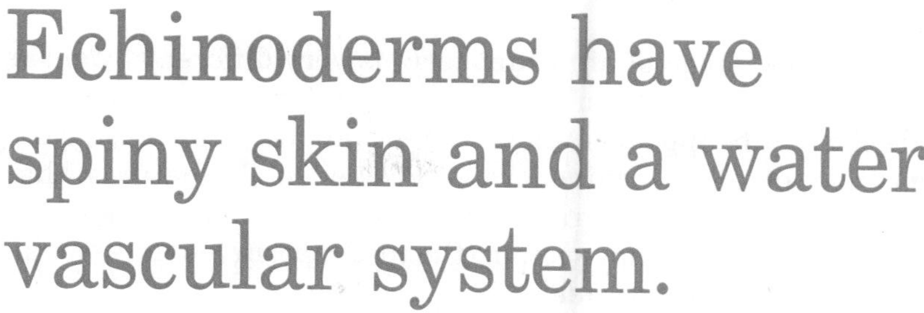

Echinoderms have spiny skin and a water vascular system.

OBJECTIVES

- Describe the characteristics of echinoderms.
- Compare and contrast three different classes of echinoderms.
- Explain the difference between protostomes and deuterostomes.

KEY TERMS

- echinoderm
- endoskeleton
- water vascular system
- tube feet
- protostome
- deuterostome

What's Online

Annelids and mollusks are part of one large evolutionary branch of the animal kingdom. Animals such as sea stars and sea urchins represent a very different evolutionary branch—the branch that also includes you.

The Body of an Echinoderm

Sea urchins, sea stars, and sea cucumbers are all slow-moving marine animals that belong to phylum Echinodermata. **Echinoderms** lack body segments, and in most adult forms the external parts of the animal radiate from the center like spokes of a wheel.

Most echinoderms have a rough and spiny surface (*echino-* means "spiny" or "prickly"; *-derm* means "skin"). The spininess of a sea star or sea urchin comes from hard spiny plates embedded under the skin. The spines and plates are actually parts of a hard internal skeleton, an **endoskeleton.**

A unique feature of echinoderms is the **water vascular system,** a network of water-filled canals (Figure 23-20). The water vascular system branches into structures called **tube feet** that function in locomotion, feeding, and respiration (gas exchange with the environment). For example, the tube feet of sea stars have suction-like structures that are used to pull the animals over the seafloor.

Sea stars and some other echinoderms have strong powers of regeneration. Tube feet and whole arms that are damaged or lost are readily regrown. One group of echinoderms, the sea cucumbers, can even regenerate some of their internal organs, such as parts of the digestive system.

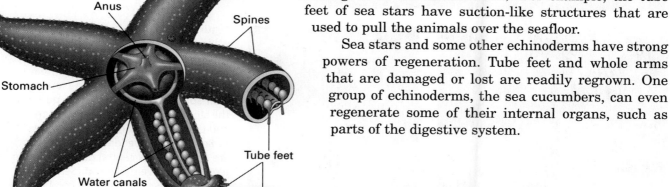

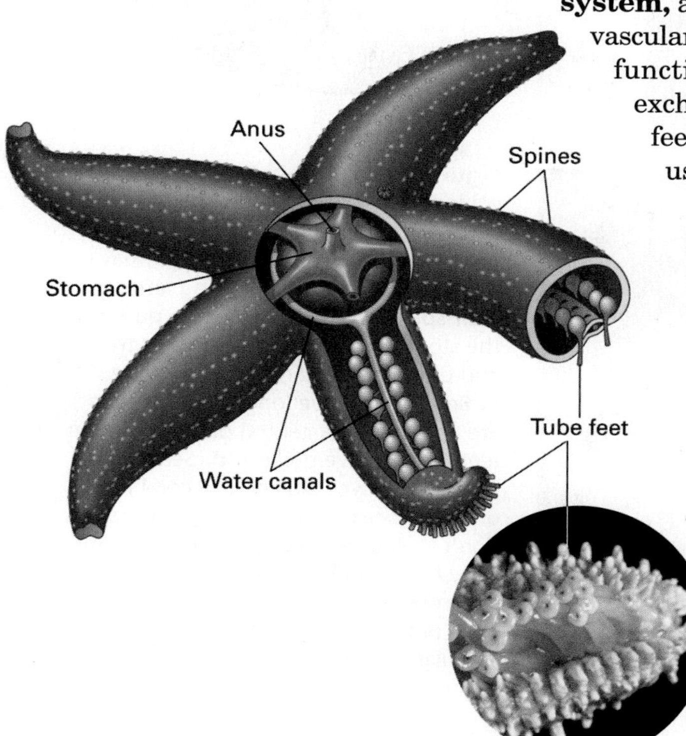

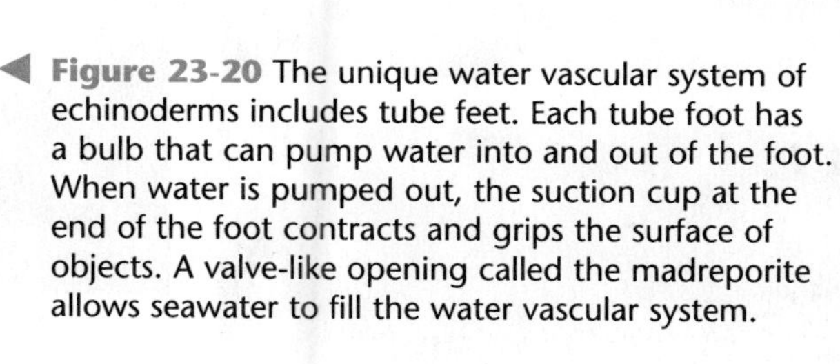

Figure 23-20 The unique water vascular system of echinoderms includes tube feet. Each tube foot has a bulb that can pump water into and out of the foot. When water is pumped out, the suction cup at the end of the foot contracts and grips the surface of objects. A valve-like opening called the madreporite allows seawater to fill the water vascular system.

The larval stage of an echinoderm is very different from the adult stage. Echinoderm larvae are bilaterally symmetrical, while the adults appear to show radial symmetry. However, close inspection of adult echinoderms reveals small features that make them bilateral, not radial. For example, the opening of the sea star's water vascular system (the madreporite) is not central, but is located off to one side.

Diversity of Echinoderms

The 7,000 or so known echinoderm species are classified into 6 classes: the sea urchins (class Echinoidea), sea stars (class Asteroidea), brittle stars (class Ophiuroidea), sea lilies (class Crinoidea), and sea cucumbers (class Holothuroidea) (Figure 23-21). The sixth group, sea daisies (class Concentricycloidea), was recently discovered. It consists of at least two species of disk-shaped animals about 1 cm in diameter. Sea daisies live on waterlogged wood deep in the sea.

Figure 23-21 Five of the six classes of echinoderms are illustrated in these photos. **a.** Sea urchins are spherical and have no arms. They do, however, have threadlike tube feet projecting among their spines. **b.** Sea stars eat by pushing the stomach out through the mouth and digesting food outside the body. **c.** Brittle stars have long, thin arms that are attached to a central disk. Their tube feet do not have suckers. **d.** Sea lilies spend their lives attached to coral reefs or to the ocean floor. **e.** Sea cucumbers don't look much like other echinoderms. They lack spines and are elongated like a cucumber. However, they do have five rows of tube feet and part of a water vascular system.

Protostomes and Deuterostomes

Echinoderms, annelids, and mollusks are coelomates, meaning they have a body cavity that is a true coelom. However, the coelom of echinoderms develops in the embryo differently than in annelids and mollusks. This difference in coelom development can be used to divide coelomates into two groups: protostomes and deuterostomes. This division is key to understanding how some animals are related to other animals. For example, annelids and mollusks are protostomes. Also included among protostomes is the very large phylum of animals called arthropods. You will read more about arthropods in Chapter 24. In **protostomes,** the coelom forms from solid masses of cells in the embryo (Figure 23-22).

In **deuterostomes,** the coelom forms from a portion of the digestive tube of the early embryo. In addition to echinoderms, chordates (the phylum that includes humans) are deuterostomes. This similarity in coelom development during the embryonic stage is important for biologists studying vertebrate origins. Evidence from embryonic development reinforces other evidence in support of the hypothesis that echinoderms are more closely related to chordates than they are to annelids and mollusks.

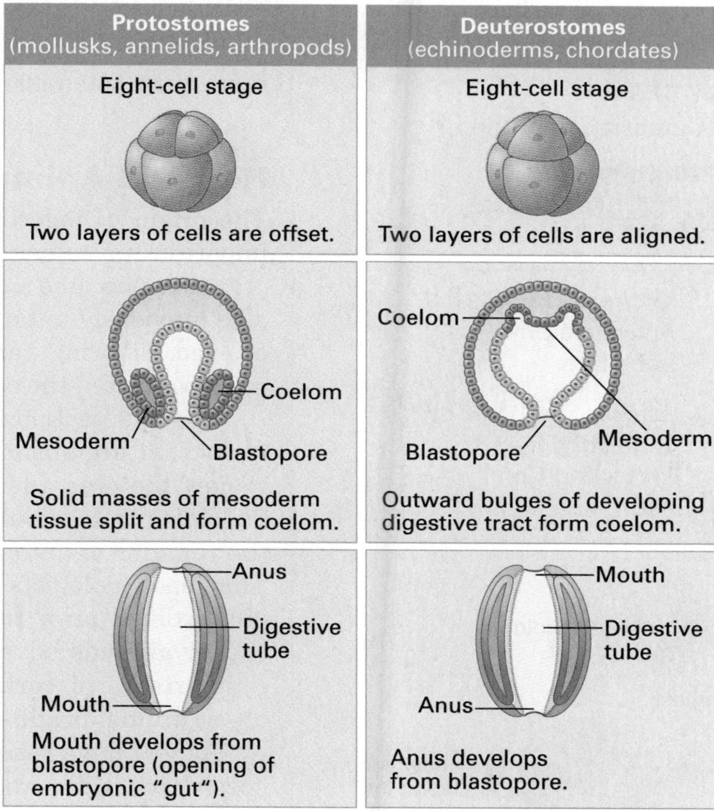

Protostomes
(mollusks, annelids, arthropods)
Deuterostomes
(echinoderms, chordates)
Eight-cell stage
Two layers of cells are offset.
Eight-cell stage
Two layers of cells are aligned.
Coelom
Mesoderm
Blastopore
Solid masses of mesoderm tissue split and form coelom.
Coelom
Blastopore
Mesoderm
Outward bulges of developing digestive tract form coelom.
Anus
Digestive tube
Mouth
Mouth develops from blastopore (opening of embryonic "gut").
Mouth
Digestive tube
Anus
Anus develops from blastopore.

Figure 23-22 This diagram depicts the differences in early embryonic development between protostomes, such as mollusks and annelids, and deuterostomes, such as echinoderms and chordates (the phylum that includes humans).

Online Activity 23.8

www.biology.com
Examples
Echinoderms
sea stars

Explore echinoderms.
To explore the echinoderms watch a video of their movement and see their unusual tube feet in action. How do echinoderms digest their food outside their bodies? Find out when you go online.

Concept Check 23.8

1. Describe the function of the water vascular system of echinoderms.
2. Compare and contrast sea cucumbers with sea stars.
3. Describe embryonic evidence that indicates echinoderms are more closely related to humans than they are to mollusks.

CONCEPT 23.9

Animal diversity "exploded" during the Cambrian period.

OBJECTIVES
- Explain the hypothesis of animals originating from colonial protists.
- Explain the meaning of the phrase "Cambrian explosion."
- Explore one hypothetical phylogenetic tree for animals.
- Compare and contrast body systems of various invertebrates.

KEY TERM
- Cambrian explosion

What's Online

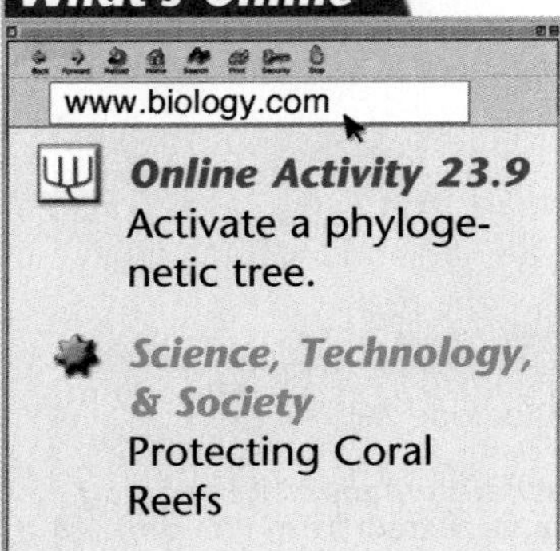

Online Activity 23.9
Activate a phylogenetic tree.

Science, Technology, & Society
Protecting Coral Reefs

Forty million years may seem like a long time. However, it is just a brief period in geologic time—less than 1 percent of the total history of Earth. Yet, fossil evidence indicates that the diversity of animals increased dramatically during a 40-million-year period more than 500 million years ago.

How Did Animal Life Begin?

The origin of ingestion (eating) as a mode of nutrition was an important milestone in the beginning of animal life. Eating other organisms became a new way of "making a living" that made available previously untapped food resources. Diverse forms of animals evolved, differing partly in their feeding adaptations. Early animals populated the oceans, then fresh water, and eventually land.

The oldest known animal fossils come from Precambrian rocks that are about 700 million years old. (See Figure 15-18 to review the eras and periods of geologic time.) These fossils tell biologists little about the *origin* of the animal kingdom. They are the remains of animals with relatively complex body structures. This leads biologists to conclude that simpler animal forms probably existed prior to these complex animals. No fossils of such earlier animals have been found so far, so biologists mainly use comparisons of certain modern organisms to test hypotheses about animal origins.

As you have read, animals are multicellular organisms with specialized cells and, in most cases, specialized tissues and organs. How did this specialization arise? One hypothesis is that animals evolved from protists that lived as colonies of cells (Figure 23-23). Some of these colonies of identical cells may have, over time, formed hollow spherical colonies. Gradually, some of these cells may have become specialized for certain functions. As a result of this specialization, each cell was no longer independent. This is a key characteristic of multicellular organisms—their cells are highly specialized and interdependent.

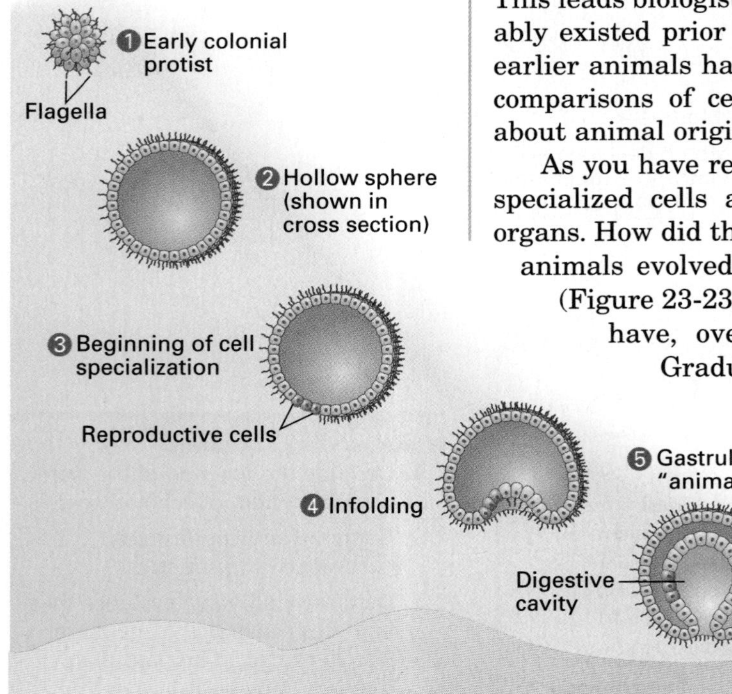

Figure 23-23 This diagram illustrates one hypothesis about the gradual evolution of animals from a colonial protist.

Another fundamental feature of animals is multiple cell layers. One hypothesis proposes that one side of the hollow sphere folded inward, much like the development of a gastrula from a blastula embryo. Originally the "pocket" may have provided a primitive digestive cavity where cells eventually became specialized for feeding and digestion.

DNA analysis points to certain colonial protists as the modern organisms most closely related to animals. This evidence supports the hypothesis that both modern animals and modern colonial protists have a common ancestor. But what the earliest animals really looked like remains a mystery. The two main stages described above—the hollow colony and the "infolded" stage—are modeled after the blastula and gastrula stages in animal development. Indeed, these embryonic stages may resemble organisms that were early ancestors of animals.

The Cambrian "Explosion"

Regardless of how they evolved, the great diversity of animals appears rather suddenly in the fossil record. There is fossil evidence of Precambrian sponges and cnidarians that lived about 550 million years ago. However, most of the major phyla of animals make their first fossil appearance during the first part of the Cambrian period. This burst of animal diversity is called the **Cambrian explosion.** It is marked by a rich collection of fossils that record the first animals with hard skeletons (Figure 23-24).

This relatively brief episode in the history of life probably lasted about 40 million years (between 565 and 525 million years ago). Fossil evidence indicates that during late Precambrian times, the seas contained various soft-bodied animals, which could have given rise to more complex forms. Still, the much greater diversity of Cambrian animals is striking compared to the relatively simple, less diverse soft-bodied animals of the late Precambrian. Biologists are currently exploring various hypotheses to explain the Cambrian explosion, including genetic changes that made a greater diversity of body forms possible.

Figure 23-24 An artist created this painting based on data from fossils found in British Columbia, Canada. The scene illustrates some of the diversity of animals that existed during the early Cambrian period.

Hypothetical Phylogeny of Animals

Due to the relatively short period of time during which animals diversified, it is difficult from the fossil record to sort out the sequence of branching in the evolutionary history of animals. So how can biologists test hypotheses about evolutionary relationships among the animal phyla? As you read in Chapter 15, biologists use data from comparative anatomy, embryology, genetics, and molecular studies of living species to search for clues about common ancestry.

▼ **Figure 23-25** This phylogenetic tree, based mainly on molecular data, summarizes one set of hypotheses about evolutionary relationships among several of the 35 animal phyla.

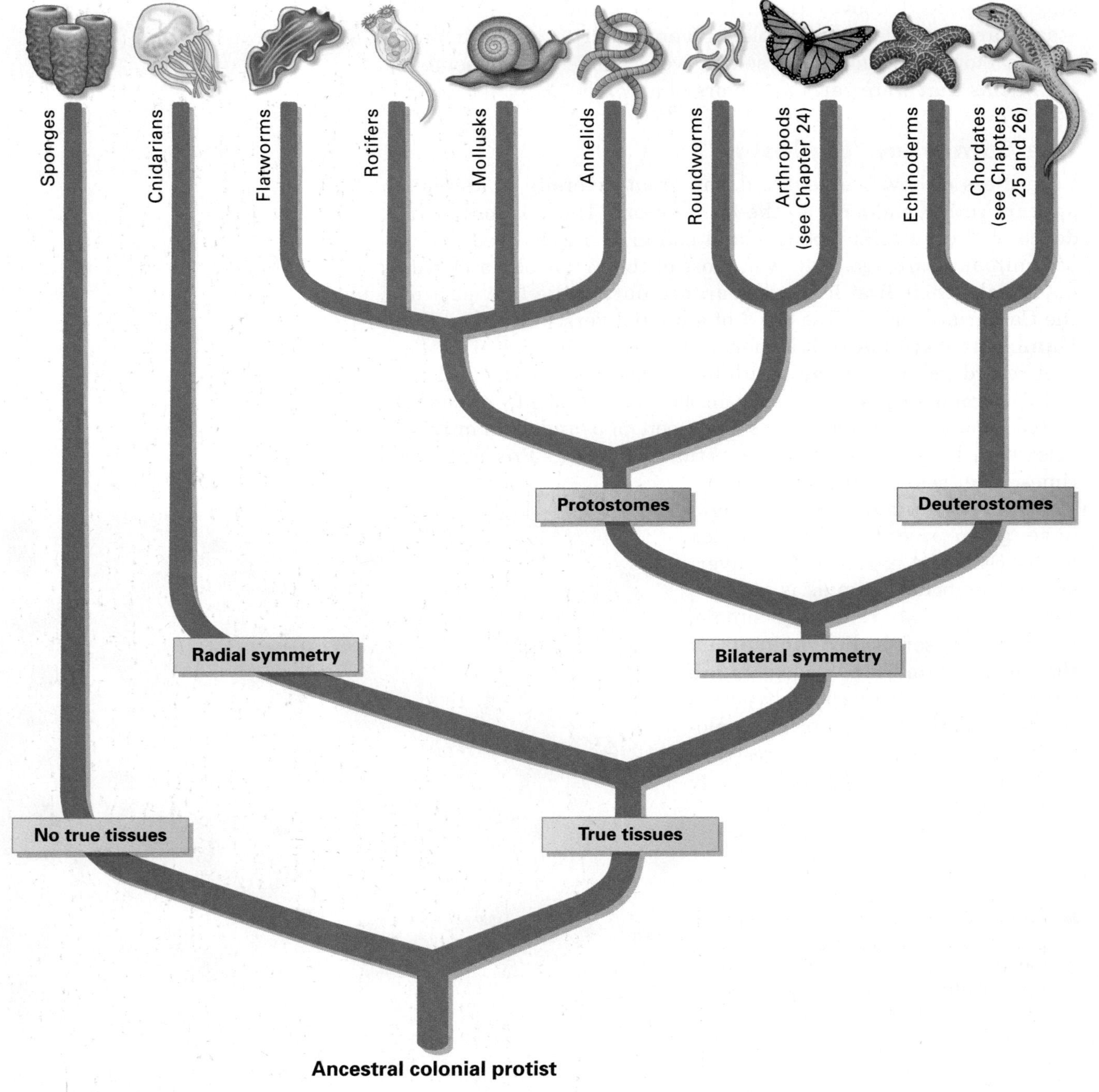

The phylogenetic tree in Figure 23-25 on the facing page represents one hypothetical view of the evolutionary history of the animal kingdom. This tree is based mainly on an analysis of nucleotide sequences in certain genes (DNA) and RNA molecules. In addition to the invertebrates mentioned in this chapter, this tree also includes two phyla that you will study in Chapters 24 and 25—the arthropods (such as insects, crabs, and spiders) and the chordates (vertebrates and closely related invertebrates).

At the bottom of the phylogenetic tree is the hypothetical colonial protist that may have given rise to the earliest animals. The tree has a series of branching points. The first branching splits the sponges, which lack true tissues, from all other animals, which do have tissues. Among the "tissue animals," the next branching divides the radial animals, such as cnidarians, from animals with bilateral symmetry. The bilateral animals are further split into protostomes and deuterostomes.

This tree tracing the evolutionary history of animals is based on the best available data from fossils, molecular analysis, comparative anatomy, and comparisons of embryonic development. Like other phylogenetic trees, this one serves as a hypothesis to stimulate further research and discussion. The hypothetical tree of animal origins will undoubtedly be revised to be compatible with new information as research continues.

Comparison of Body Systems of Invertebrates

On the following pages you will find a large table that summarizes the body systems of some major phyla of invertebrates (Figure 23-26). Phyla are listed in the first column, starting with the sponges at the top left page. Across the top of the pages are the body systems. In some cases, especially in the relatively simple animals, the descriptions span several columns because the same tissues or organs accomplish several body functions. In other cases, the descriptions span several rows because there is no major difference in that body function from one phylum to the next. One of the phyla listed is the arthropods, about which you will read in the next chapter.

Science, Technology, & Society

Back Forward Reload Home Search Print Security Stop

www.biology.com

Protecting Coral Reefs

Coral reefs are one of the richest, most diverse ecosystems in the world. But today many coral reefs are threatened with possible extinction. What are the causes, and how are scientists and others trying to protect them? Find out when you go online.

Online Activity 23.9

Back Forward Reload Home Search Print Security Stop

www.biology.com

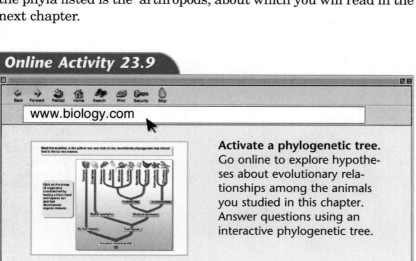

Activate a phylogenetic tree. Go online to explore hypotheses about evolutionary relationships among the animals you studied in this chapter. Answer questions using an interactive phylogenetic tree.

Concept Check 23.9

1. Describe stages of the evolution of protists that may have led to the first animals.
2. Explain the significance of the phrase "Cambrian explosion."
3. Explain why biologists consider the phylogenetic tree in Figure 23-25 to be hypothetical.
4. Which invertebrate phyla have an open circulatory system? (*Hint:* Consult Figure 23-26.)

Figure 23-26 Invertebrate Body Systems

Phylum (with examples)	Body Support/Movement	Nervous Control	Reproduction
Porifera: Sponges	Amoebocytes produce a protein called spongin or mineral-based, needle-like structures for support. Adults are sessile.	None	Asexual: budding Sexual: male and female structures are present in same individual; zygotes develop into flagellated larvae.
Cnidaria: Hydras, jellies, and anemones	Fluid in gastrovascular cavity gives body shape. Microfilaments within cells are arranged into fibers that contract.	Nerve net	Asexual: budding Sexual: male and female structures are present in same individual.
Platyhelminthes: Flatworms	True muscle tissue—muscles run along the length of the animal (longitudinally).	Primitive brainlike ganglia (nerve clusters) and ventral nerve cords	Asexual: fragmentation and regeneration Sexual: male and female structures present in same individual; cross-fertilization between individuals.
Nematoda: Roundworms	Exoskeleton—called the cuticle—has to be shed as animal grows. Muscles are all longitudinal, causing thrashing movements.	Central brainlike ganglion with nerve cords extending to the front and rear	Sexual: most species have separate males and females; internal fertilization in most species.
Annelida: Segmented worms	Fluid-filled compartments provide support; two sets of muscles—circular and longitudinal	Two ventral nerve cords connect to ganglia in each segment; pair of cerebral ganglia in the head	Sexual: male and female structures are present in same individual (except in polychaetes); internal fertilization (external in polychaetes)
Mollusca: Snails, clams, squids	Mantle produces a shell in most species; muscular foot	Nerve ring around the esophagus with attached nerve cords	
Arthropoda: Insects, crustaceans, spiders	Exoskeleton of protein and chitin; muscles attached to knobs on interior of exoskeleton	Ventral nerve cord with several ganglia. In the head region, the two cords meet and fuse into a larger ganglion (brain).	Sexual: separate males and females; internal fertilization
Echinodermata: Sea stars, sea urchins, sea cucumbers	Endoskeleton of hard plates; water vascular system	Nerve ring plus nerve cords along each arm	Sexual: separate males and females; gametes are released externally in water.

<table>
<tr><th>Digestion</th><th>Circulation</th><th>Excretion</th><th>Gas Exchange</th></tr>
<tr><td colspan="4">Digestion, circulation, excretion, and gas exchange are accomplished by multi-purpose amoebocytes. Amoebocytes ingest food particles, and digest and transport the nutrients throughout the sponge. Gas exchange also occurs at the cellular level, primarily by diffusion.</td></tr>
<tr><td colspan="2" rowspan="2">Digestion takes place in a gastrovascular cavity (digestive sac), which has a single opening that is both mouth and anus. The nutrients are distributed to cells that line the cavity. In flatworms the gastrovascular cavity is finely branched, helping the distribution of nutrients throughout the body.</td><td>Expulsion from gastrovascular cavity; simple diffusion of wastes from cells into surrounding water</td><td rowspan="2">No specialized structures. Diffusion across cell membranes helped by circulation in the gastrovascular cavity.</td></tr>
<tr><td>Most wastes diffuse from cells into the surrounding water. Ciliated cells move fluid containing wastes through branched ducts opening to the outside.</td></tr>
<tr><td rowspan="4">Complete digestive tract (tube) with openings at both ends—mouth and anus; digestive tract has specialized regions for digestion, the stomach and intestine.</td><td>No specialized circulatory system. Nutrients are transported by fluid in the body cavity, which is a pseudocoelom.</td><td>A ventral gland or a tubular system is connected to an excretory pore; mostly used for maintaining water balance</td><td>Diffusion across cell membranes</td></tr>
<tr><td>Closed circulatory system; dorsal and ventral vessels connected by two vessels per segment; blood with oxygen-carrying hemoglobin; accessory hearts</td><td>Tubular structures called metanephridia in each segment remove wastes from blood.</td><td>The moist skin serves as the organ for gas exchange; oxygen absorbed across the skin is transported by the circulatory system.</td></tr>
<tr><td>Open circulatory system in most species; dorsal heart circulates fluid to body cavities.</td><td>Specialized structures called nephridia remove wastes from blood.</td><td>Mantle cavity with gills in aquatic species; mantle cavity can serve as a lung for terrestrial species.</td></tr>
<tr><td>Open circulatory system with a dorsal heart; bloodlike fluid transports materials.</td><td>In insects and arachnids, Malpighian tubules remove wastes from the bloodlike fluid.</td><td>Feathery gills in aquatic species; tracheal tubes inside the body in terrestrial species; book lungs in spiders</td></tr>
<tr><td>Short digestive tract with mouth and anus</td><td>Fluid in the body cavity (coelom) transports nutrients throughout the body.</td><td>No specialized excretory system; wastes are removed by diffusion from the fluid in the coelom and the water vascular system.</td><td>Water vascular system</td></tr>
</table>

Multiple Choice

Choose the letter of the best answer.

1. Which of the following is *not* a characteristic of animals?
   a. They are multicellular.
   b. They have no cell walls.
   c. They are autotrophic.
   d. They are eukaryotic.

2. Animals called invertebrates all lack
   a. nerve cells.
   b. a backbone.
   c. a body cavity.
   d. a shell.

3. Which animal phylum lacks true tissues?
   a. cnidarians
   b. annelids
   c. sponges
   d. nematodes

4. Radial symmetry is a characteristic of
   a. flatworms.
   b. roundworms.
   c. mollusks.
   d. cnidarians.

5. Which of the following organisms is parasitic?
   a. jellyfish
   b. planarian
   c. tapeworm
   d. squid

6. Which two features are commonly found in mollusks?
   a. cell wall and chloroplast
   b. amoebocyte and flagellum
   c. closed circulation and accessory hearts
   d. mantle and foot

7. Which phylum of invertebrates is named for their spiny skin?
   a. echinoderms
   b. sponges
   c. annelids
   d. rotifers

Short Answer

8. Describe the function of amoebocyte cells in sponges.

9. Define nematocysts. What function do nematocysts have in cnidarians?

10. Explain the difference between a pseudocoelom and a coelom.

11. Explain the difference between a digestive sac (gastrovascular cavity) and a digestive tube (complete digestive tract).

12. Describe the circulatory system of earthworms.

13. Describe the role colonial protists might have played in the evolution of multicellular organisms.

14. Explain what is meant by the phrase "Cambrian explosion."

15. Compare and contrast the process of digestion in cnidarians and echinoderms.

Visualizing Concepts

16. On a separate sheet of paper, copy the life cycle of a sea star below.

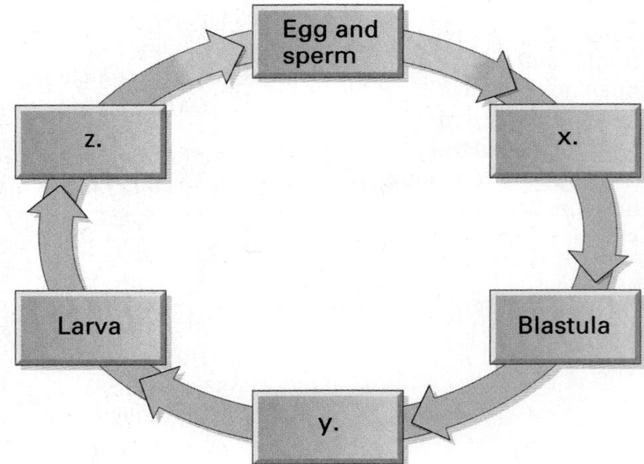

   a. Fill in the empty boxes in the cycle.
   b. Identify the haploid and diploid stages in the diagram.
   c. What process occurs between the larval stage and the stage labeled *z*?

Analyzing Information

17. **Analyzing Diagrams** Use this diagram, which shows the internal structure of an earthworm, to answer the questions below.

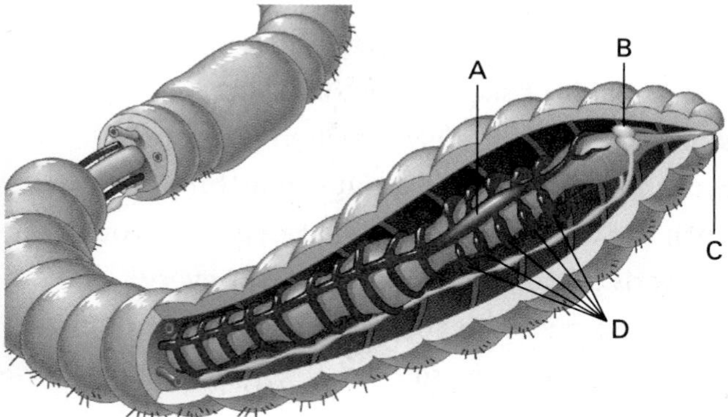

   a. What type of circulatory system is depicted above?
   b. Which structures in the diagram are responsible for pumping blood?
   c. Contrast this type of circulatory system with the circulatory system found in mollusks.
   d. To what phylum of invertebrates does this organism belong?

18. **Analyzing Photographs** Use the photo of the underside of a marine invertebrate to answer the questions below.

   a. The tube-shaped feet visible in the photograph are part of what system?
   b. What are some functions of this system?
   c. To which phylum does this animal belong?

Critical Thinking

19. **Comparing and Contrasting** Compare radial symmetry with bilateral symmetry. Give one example of an organism with each.

20. **Problem Solving** You are a zoologist working in a laboratory. An animal you are observing has the following characteristics: bilateral symmetry, a pseudocoelom, and a complete digestive tract. To which phylum does this animal belong? Explain.

21. **Comparing and Contrasting** Compare and contrast the body cavity types of flatworms, roundworms, and annelids.

22. **Making Generalizations** Describe how embryonic development can indicate the evolutionary relationships between different invertebrates.

23. **What's Wrong With These Statements?** *Briefly explain why each statement is inaccurate or misleading.*
   a. There are approximately the same numbers of invertebrate and vertebrate species.
   b. The digestive systems of cnidarians and annelids are similar.
   c. Sea stars are more closely related to sea anemones than they are to humans.

Performance Assessment

Design an Experiment Design an experiment to demonstrate water flow in a sponge, using living sponges, a confined water environment (aquarium), and non-toxic colored dye.

Online Assessment/Test Preparation

Back Forward Reload Home Search Print Security Stop

www.biology.com

- **Chapter 23 Assessment**
  Check your understanding of the chapter concepts.
- **Standardized Test Preparation**
  Practice test-taking skills you need to succeed.

CHAPTER 24

A Closer Look at Arthropods

This colorful Sally Lightfoot crab is one of many interesting species of the Galápagos Islands of Ecuador. Named for its habit of skipping across short stretches of water, this crab represents one of approximately 1 million arthropod species. In this chapter, you will read about the three major groups of arthropods: the crustaceans (including Sally Lightfoot), the arachnids, and the insects. And you will learn some of the reasons why arthropods successfully inhabit almost every nook and cranny of Earth. Before you begin, go online to the ***WebQuest*** to learn more about the arthropod that is often called a "living fossil."

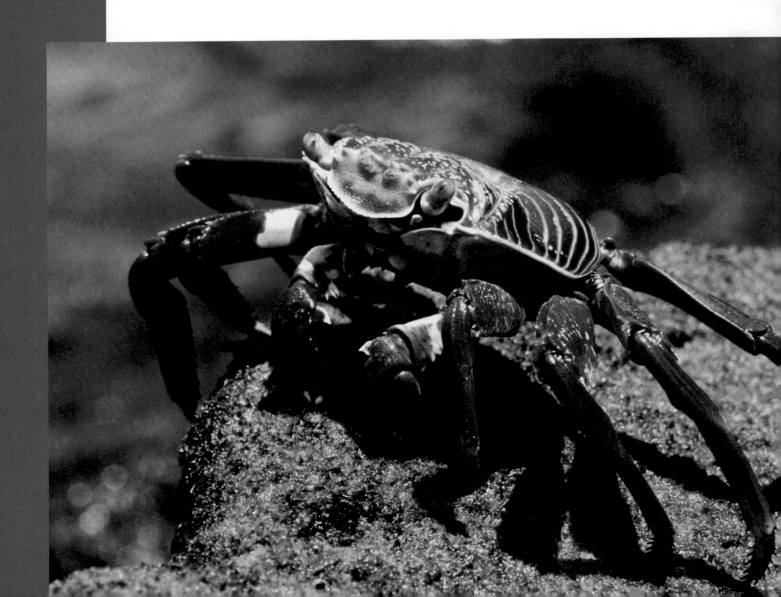

Key Concepts

Concept 24.1 Arthropods are the most numerous and diverse animals.

Concept 24.2 Arachnids include spiders and scorpions.

Concept 24.3 Crustaceans are the most common aquatic arthropods.

Concept 24.4 Insects play major roles in terrestrial environments.

Assessment Chapter 24 Review

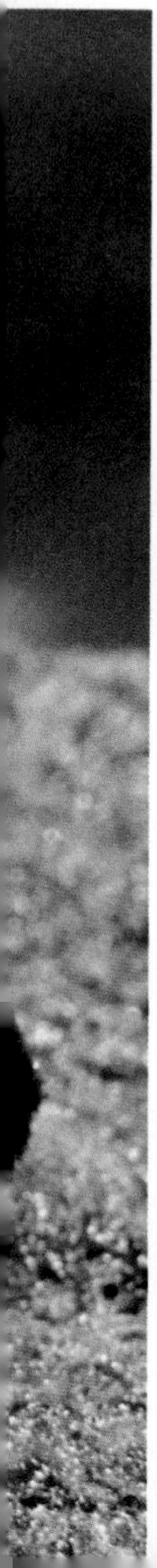

What's Online

www.biology.com

WebQuest
HorseshoeCrabQuest

Online Activity 24.1
Build an arthropod.

Online Activity 24.2
Explore arachnids.

Online Activity 24.3
Explore crustaceans.

Guided Research Lab 4
Diversity of Soil Invertebrates

Online Activity 24.4
Explore insects.

Science, Technology, & Society
Controlling Mosquitoes With Pesticides

Lab 24 Online Companion
The Life of WOWBugs

Chapter 24 Assessment

CONCEPT 24.1

Arthropods are the most numerous and diverse animals.

OBJECTIVES
- List the general characteristics of arthropods.
- Name the main groups of arthropods, both living and extinct.

KEY TERMS
- arthropod
- thorax
- jointed appendage
- exoskeleton
- chitin
- molting
- ganglia
- compound eye
- trachea
- spiracle
- crustacean
- arachnid
- insect

Biologists have identified nearly 1 million arthropod species. All the other animal species combined number less than one third as many. Arthropods thrive in almost every habitat on Earth, and their global population is estimated at 1 billion billion, or 10^{18} individuals.

General Characteristics of Arthropods

Arthropods are characterized by their segmented bodies, jointed appendages, and hard external skeletons. In contrast to annelids, which have similar segments throughout the body, arthropods have distinct groupings of segments. A dragonfly, for example, has three distinct groupings: a head, a thorax, and an abdomen (Figure 24-1). The head consists of fused segments bearing sensory antennae (an TEN ee), eyes, and mouthparts (specialized appendages near the mouth). The middle section of fused segments bears legs and wings. This midsection of an arthropod is called the **thorax.** Finally, the dragonfly's abdomen section bears reproductive appendages. An arthropod's appendages, the parts attached to its segments, are jointed. In fact, **jointed appendages** are the source of the name *arthropod* (Greek *arthron* for "joint," and *pod* for "foot").

The arthropod body, including the appendages, is covered by a hard external skeleton, or **exoskeleton.** The exoskeleton of arthropods contrast with the endoskeletons of some other animal phyla. An endoskeleton, such as your own, is *inside* the body instead of on the surface. Your endoskeleton grows continuously along with the rest of your body, whereas an exoskeleton cannot. The exoskeleton consists of layers of proteins mixed with a polysaccharide called **chitin** (KY tun). It is waterproofed by lipids. The exoskeleton protects the arthropod. Knobs on the inner surface of the exoskeleton provide points of attachment for muscles that move the appendages.

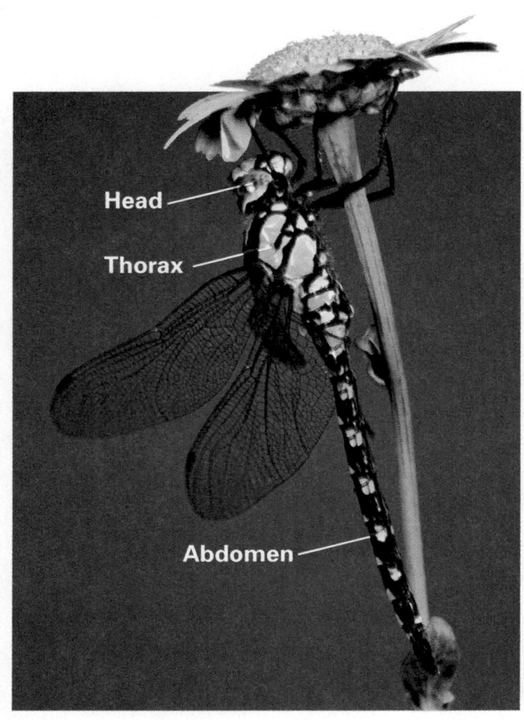

Figure 24-1 An arthropod such as this dragonfly has distinct groupings of segments, jointed appendages, and a hard exoskeleton.

As it grows, an arthropod must periodically shed its old exoskeleton and secrete a larger one, a process called **molting.** Before molting, the arthropod secretes a new layer of chitin beneath its exoskeleton, then forces fluid between the old and new exoskeletons. The outer exoskeleton splits open and the arthropod crawls out (Figure 24-2). At first, the new exoskeleton is quite soft, but it hardens over time. Just after molting, the "soft" arthropod is especially vulnerable to predators and other dangers.

▲ **Figure 24-2** This treehopper (an insect) has just molted, leaving behind its old exoskeleton. Its new exoskeleton will take several hours to harden completely.

Arthropods show a great variety of adaptations in their body systems. But there are some features that all arthropods share (Figure 24-3). Arthropods have an open circulatory system, in which blood is pumped through a tube-like heart into chambers that bathe the organs. The nervous system consists of a ventral nerve cord and brain. All along the nerve cord are clusters of nerve cell bodies called **ganglia** (GANG glee uh). Optic nerves leading from the eyes transmit visual information to the brain. Most arthropods have **compound eyes** with many facets, each with its own lens. However some arthropods, such as most spiders, have camera-like, single-lens eyes. And there are arthropods that have both single-lens and compound eyes.

Aquatic arthropods have gills that function in respiration (the exchange of oxygen and carbon dioxide with the surrounding environment). Most terrestrial arthropods have **tracheae** (TRAY kee ee), chitin-lined tubes that lead from the internal parts of the body to the outside. Tracheae (singular, *trachea*) allow the exchange of carbon dioxide and oxygen through holes in the exoskeleton called **spiracles.**

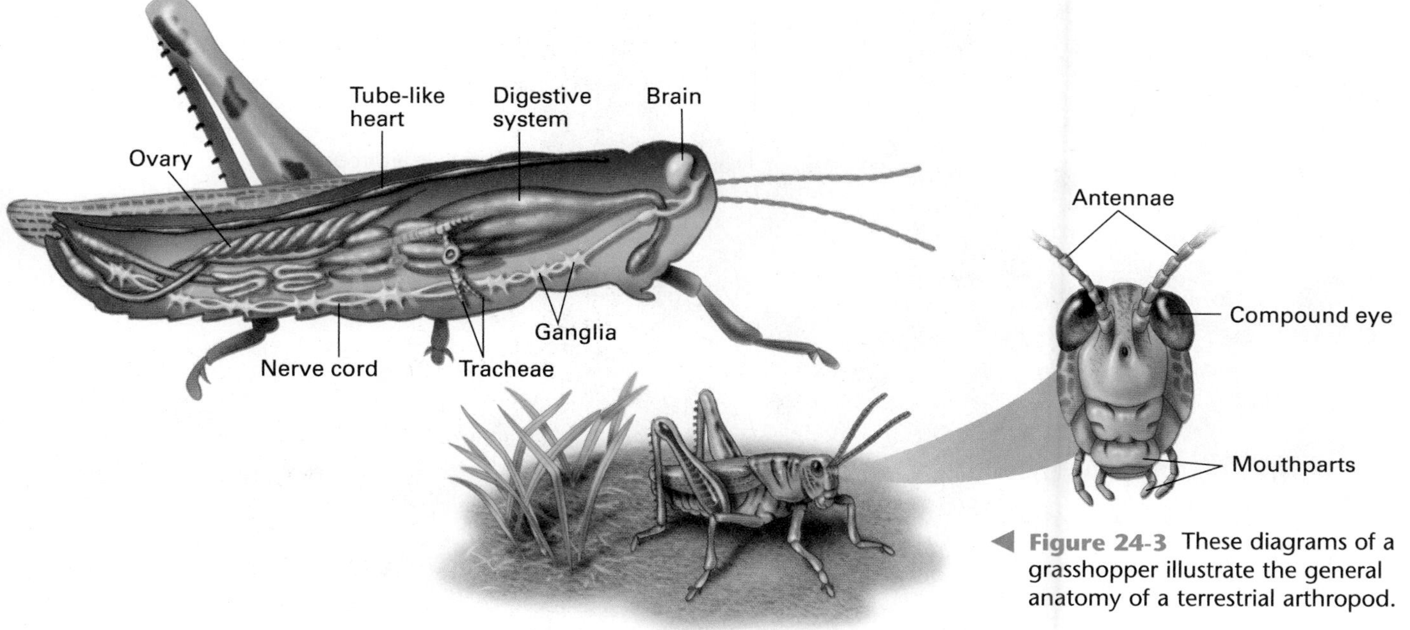

◀ **Figure 24-3** These diagrams of a grasshopper illustrate the general anatomy of a terrestrial arthropod.

An Overview of Arthropod Diversity

Fossil evidence indicates that the first arthropods evolved in the sea about 560 million years ago. These early arthropods had more body segments and less specialization of those segments than most modern arthropods. Examples of early arthropods, now extinct, are the trilobites (Figure 24-4). Paleontologists have described about 4,000 trilobite species. Because of their hard exoskeleton, trilobites and other early arthropods have left an excellent fossil record.

▲ **Figure 24-4** This fossil trilobite shows characteristics typical of the early arthropods. Its body segments are less fused and less specialized than in most modern arthropods.

A group of spiderlike arthropods was abundant in the sea about 300 million years ago. Today only four species of this ancient group still exist, the horseshoe crabs. Horseshoe crabs have changed very little during their long existence on Earth. North America has just one species, which gathers on the Atlantic and Gulf coasts of the United States in groups of thousands to spawn—to release eggs and sperm (Figure 24-5a). The females release eggs at the ocean's edge. Many of the eggs become an essential food source for other animals. For example, many migrating shorebirds "refuel" for the next leg of their long flights by feeding on these eggs.

One other group of arthropods in existence today lives mostly in aquatic environments: the **crustaceans.** This group includes lobsters, crabs, crayfish, shrimp, and barnacles, among others. The fiddler crab is one example of a modern aquatic arthropod (Figure 24-5b). Note the specialization of its appendages. For instance, male fiddler crabs have one claw that is larger than the other. By waving the large claw back and forth, the male signals to mates and rivals.

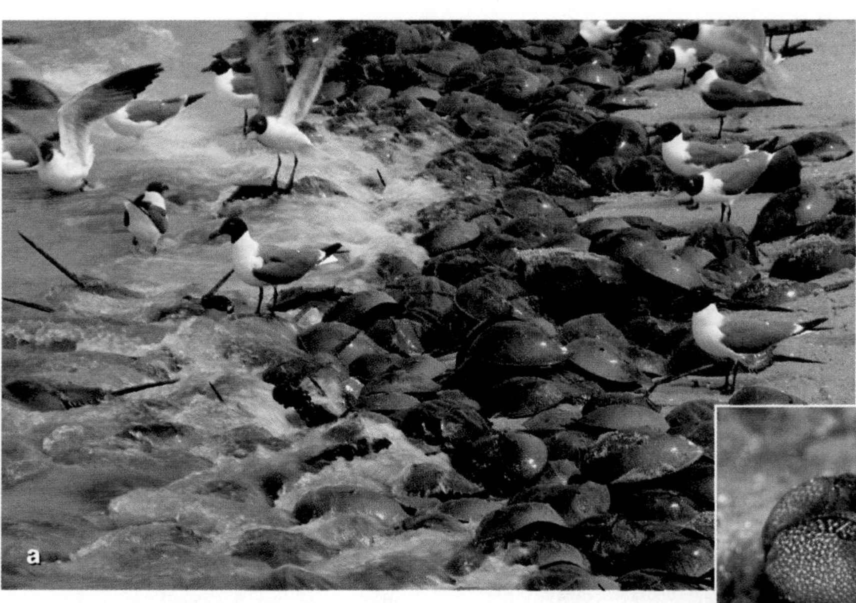

Figure 24-5 Two examples of aquatic arthropods are shown. **a.** Horseshoe crabs gather in large groups to spawn. **b.** This male fiddler crab is a crustacean that lives in burrows in salt marshes.

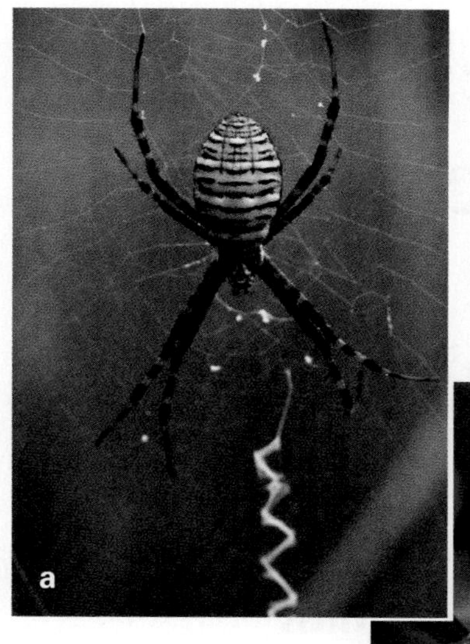

Figure 24-6 These three species are all terrestrial arthropods. **a.** The banded argiope, a common garden spider, is an example of an arachnid. **b.** The emerald fruit chafer, a beetle found in Africa, is an insect. **c.** This millipede represents the group of many-legged arthropods that includes all millipedes and centipedes.

The majority of arthropods have adapted to living on land. The move onto land was made possible in part by the exoskeleton, which prevents water loss and provides structural support. Today, the terrestrial arthropods include three groups: the arachnids, the insects, and the myriapods, or many-legged arthropods (Figure 24-6). **Arachnids** include spiders, scorpions, mites, and ticks. **Insects** include beetles, ants, grasshoppers, butterflies, dragonflies, and many others. The myriapods include the centipedes and millipedes.

Centipedes and millipedes live in humid environments, and can be found in soil, in leaf litter, or under stones and wood. Compared with insects, they have many more pairs of legs. In centipedes, each body segment behind the head bears a single pair of long legs. The head includes a pair of claws that secrete a poison used to stun or kill prey. Millipedes have two pairs of legs per segment and eat dead and decaying plant material. They defend themselves by curling up into a ball, and some species secrete a foul-smelling or toxic chemical when threatened.

In the next three concepts, you will explore in more detail the diversity, anatomy, and lifestyles of the largest groups of arthropods: the arachnids, crustaceans, and insects.

Online Activity 24.1

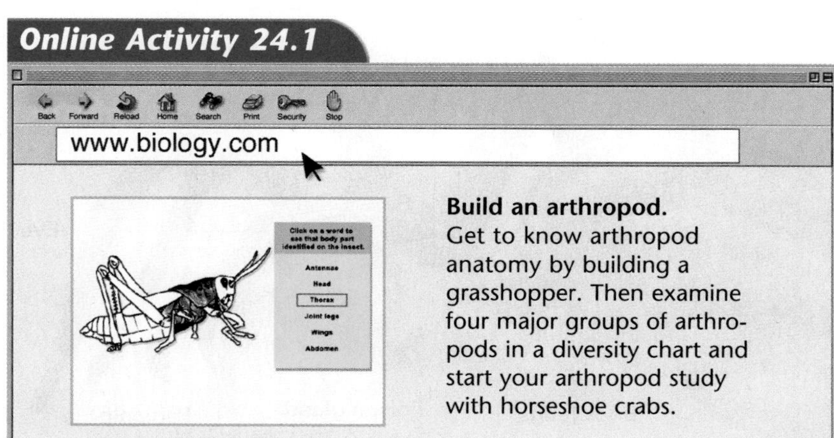

Build an arthropod.
Get to know arthropod anatomy by building a grasshopper. Then examine four major groups of arthropods in a diversity chart and start your arthropod study with horseshoe crabs.

Concept Check 24.1

1. List three characteristics of arthropods that unite them as a single large group.
2. Name one group of arthropods that is now extinct. Name at least three groups still in existence today.

CONCEPT 24.2 Arachnids include spiders and scorpions.

OBJECTIVES
- List the general characteristics of arachnids.
- Compare and contrast the three main groups of arachnids.

KEY TERMS
- cephalothorax
- chelicera
- pedipalp
- Malpighian tubule
- book lung
- spinneret

What's Online

Online Activity 24.2
Explore arachnids.

Through the night, the spider waits in the dark on its silk web. At daybreak, the web gently sways in a breeze. Finally, breakfast arrives. A fly has flown into the web. Silk webs are just one of many interesting ways arachnids obtain meals.

General Characteristics of Arachnids

Scorpions, spiders, ticks, and mites and several smaller groups are collectively called arachnids. Arachnids have two body sections and four pairs of legs (Figure 24-7). The two body sections are a fused head and thorax, called a **cephalothorax** (sef ul loh THAWR aks), and an abdomen. Arachnids have two pairs of mouthparts. **Chelicerae** (kuh LIS ur ee) are fanglike mouthparts used to paralyze prey with poison. **Pedipalps** are mouthparts typically used to manipulate prey once it has been paralyzed.

Almost all arachnids live on land and have several adaptations that help them retain water. In addition to their water-tight exoskeleton, arachnids have excretory structures called **Malpighian tubules** (mal PIG ee un) that remove wastes from the fluid in the body cavity. These tubules also work with the gut in reducing water loss by reabsorbing most water before wastes leave the body. Many arachnids also have specialized respiratory structures called **book lungs.** Book lungs contain many flaps of tissue, like the sheets of a book, that provide a large surface area for gas exchange. They exchange gases with the atmosphere through an opening in the exoskeleton. Some arachnids transport respiratory gases through tracheae in addition to or instead of book lungs.

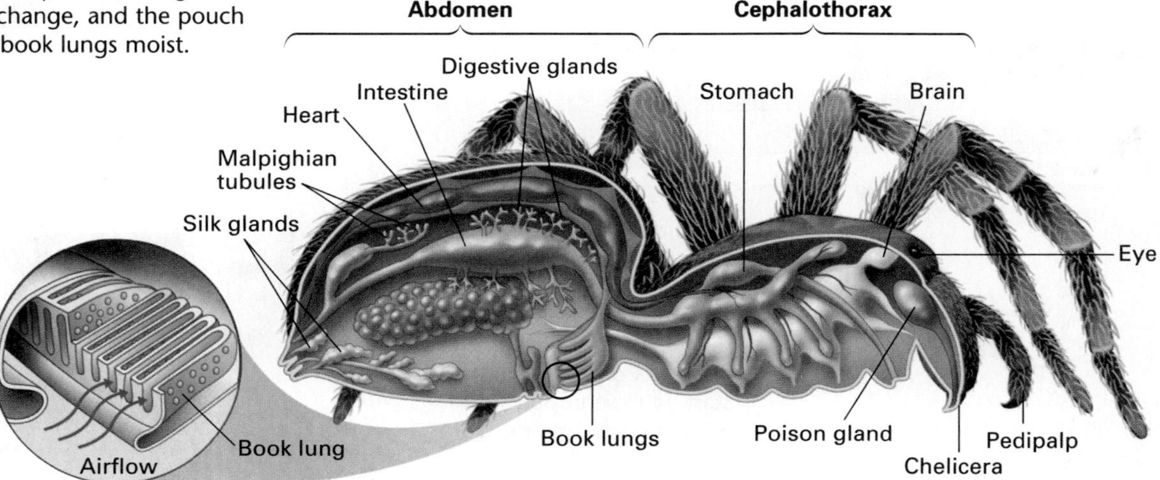

▼ **Figure 24-7** This diagram of a spider illustrates the basic anatomy of an arachnid. Book lungs, shown in the inset, are a unique adaptation of arachnids for respiration on land. The folded tissues provide a large surface for gas exchange, and the pouch keeps the book lungs moist.

Diversity of Arachnids

As you get to know the arachnids, you'll learn that they encompass a great variety of species in many habitats. Figure 24-8 shows examples of the three subgroups of arachnids.

Spiders Generally, spiders are characterized as hunters or weavers. Hunters include tarantulas and wolf spiders that roam the ground, searching for prey. The weavers, on the other hand, are "sit-and-wait" predators. They catch prey in a web that they weave, using silk proteins produced by silk glands inside the abdomen. The silk is spun into fibers by organs near the end of the abdomen called **spinnerets.**

Although not all spiders weave webs, all produce silk. Spiders may use silk to wrap prey in tight bundles for storage. Many baby spiders eject a small line of silk that catches the wind and carries them to new locations. Some hunting spiders use silk as a covering for their underground burrows. A variety of other uses for silk have been observed.

Scorpions Scorpions are nighttime hunters that mainly live in deserts. Their pedipalps are modified as pincers that function in defense and capturing prey. The tip of the tail bears a poisonous stinger. Scorpions eat mainly insects and spiders. They will attack people only when prodded or stepped on. Only a few species of scorpions are dangerous to humans.

Mites and Ticks Mites and ticks are small, often microscopic arachnids. Many are parasites that suck sap from plants or blood from mammals, but most are free-living. Mites and ticks with sucking mouthparts often have needlelike chelicerae and pedipalps equipped with claws for holding onto the host. Some ticks, notably the deer tick, can transmit serious diseases to humans, including Lyme disease.

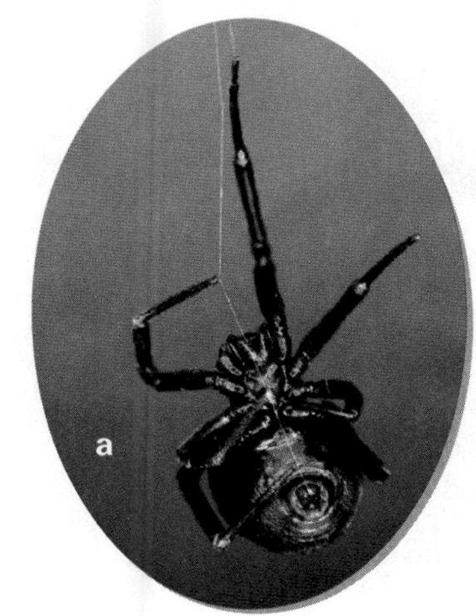

Figure 24-8 Arachnids are diverse. **a.** While most spiders are harmless, the black widow spider is one of two dangerously venomous species in North America. Note the silk being extruded from her spinnerets. **b.** Most scorpions live in very dry habitats, such as deserts. **c.** Many mites, like these shown on a flower, are plant parasites.

Online Activity 24.2

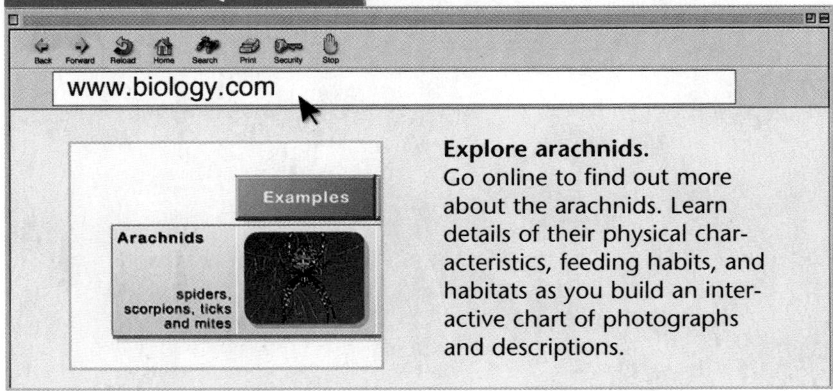

Back
Forward
Reload
Home
Search
Print
Security
Stop
www.biology.com
Examples
Arachnids
spiders, scorpions, ticks and mites
Explore arachnids.
Go online to find out more about the arachnids. Learn details of their physical characteristics, feeding habits, and habitats as you build an interactive chart of photographs and descriptions.

Concept Check 24.2

1. List at least two adaptations of arachnids for life on dry land.
2. Compare and contrast the food-gathering methods of different arachnids.

CONCEPT 24.3

Crustaceans are the most common aquatic arthropods.

OBJECTIVES
- List the characteristics of decapods.
- Contrast the habitats of barnacles, copepods, and isopods.

KEY TERMS
- carapace
- mandible

What's Online

A whale hurtles toward the ocean surface, her huge mouth gaping open. After breaking the surface, her jaws clamp down. While water pours back out through the slits in sieve-like plates lining her mouth, thousands of tiny crustaceans called krill are trapped. As prey, many crustaceans support populations of animals much larger than themselves.

Decapods

Of all the crustaceans, you are probably most familiar with the decapods (meaning "ten legs"). Their common names include lobster, crab, and shrimp. The "ten legs" refer to the pair of pincers (claws) and four pairs of walking legs that are characteristic of most decapods. While most decapods are marine, crayfish live in fresh water, and a few tropical crabs live on land.

Like arachnids, decapods have two main body regions: a cephalothorax and abdomen (Figure 24-9). A decapod's exoskeleton is harder than that of many arthropods because it is reinforced with calcium carbonate (limestone). The portion of the exoskeleton that covers the back of the cephalothorax forms a shield called the **carapace.** Decapods and other crustaceans have two pairs of sensory antennae attached to the head. The mouthparts closest to the mouth are hard **mandibles,** which bite and grind food.

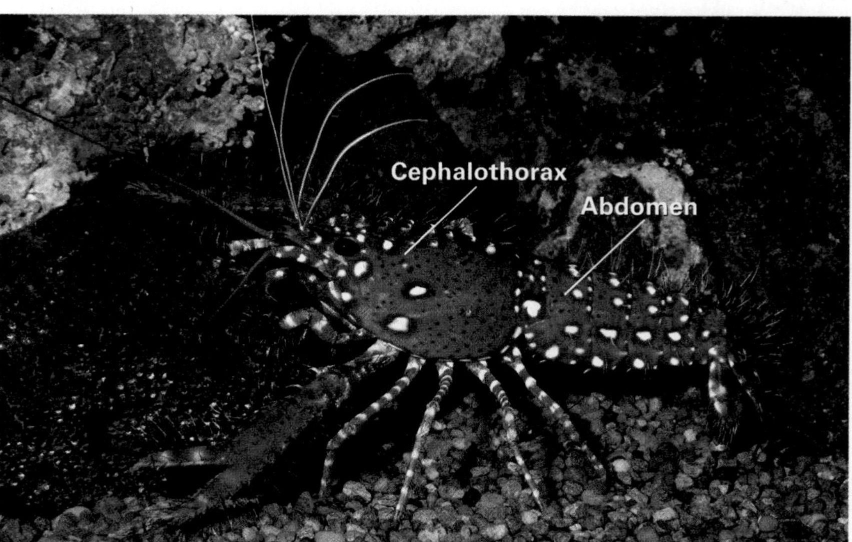

Figure 24-9 This red reef lobster lives in tropical ocean waters. Like other decapods, it has a cephalothorax protected by a hard carapace. Decapods obtain food by both scavenging on dead organic material and attacking live prey.

Barnacles, Copepods, and Isopods

Barnacles are marine crustaceans that secrete calcium carbonate shells in which they live. Perhaps you have seen them covering rocks at the seashore. They also grow on wooden piers, ships' hulls, and even on the skin of whales. During low tide a barnacle is sealed tightly in its shell, protected from drying out. During high tide, when covered with water, its jointed, feathery appendages poke out from the shell and beat back and forth (Figure 24-10a). The jointed appendages sweep small invertebrates and organic particles toward the mouthparts inside the shell. Barnacle larvae disperse on ocean currents and settle on rocks and other surfaces that are sometimes hundreds of kilometers from their parents.

Copepods are very small but like the krill you read about at the beginning of the concept, they play a big role in the food chains of marine and freshwater communities. A copepod is typically under 2 mm long (Figure 24-10b). They feed on photosynthetic bacteria and phytoplankton, and in turn are fed upon by larger animals. Copepods are one of the main food sources for younger stages of many commercially important fishes, such as cod.

Most isopods are small marine crustaceans. Some species are numerous at the bottom of deep oceans. Isopods also include the familiar land-dwelling pill bugs, sometimes called wood lice, which you may have seen underneath wet leaves or a rotting log (Figure 24-10c). Like millipedes, pill bugs curl into a ball when threatened.

▲ **Figure 24-10** Crustaceans are diverse in their appearance and habitats. **a.** Barnacles adhere to rocks or other surfaces in the ocean. **b.** Copepods are numerous in the ocean and are the food source of many larger organisms. **c.** Pill bugs are isopods that live in damp terrestrial environments.

Guided Research Lab 4

Diversity of Soil Invertebrates
In this field investigation, you will collect samples of the rich diversity of arthropods and other invertebrates that live in soil. After learning this technique, you will apply what you have learned to design and carry out your own investigation into the diversity of soil invertebrates.

Online Activity 24.3

Explore crustaceans.
What are the common characteristics of crustaceans? What do they eat? What are their habitats? Explore the world of crustaceans when you go online.

Concept Check 24.3

1. List at least three features of a decapod.
2. Describe the habitat and feeding mechanism of a barnacle.
3. Explain the importance of copepods to the fishing industry.

CONCEPT 24.4 Insects play major roles in terrestrial environments.

OBJECTIVES
- Summarize the general characteristics of insects.
- List eight major insect orders.
- Explain some positive and negative impacts of insects on human populations.

KEY TERMS
- pupa
- entomology
- biological control

What's Online

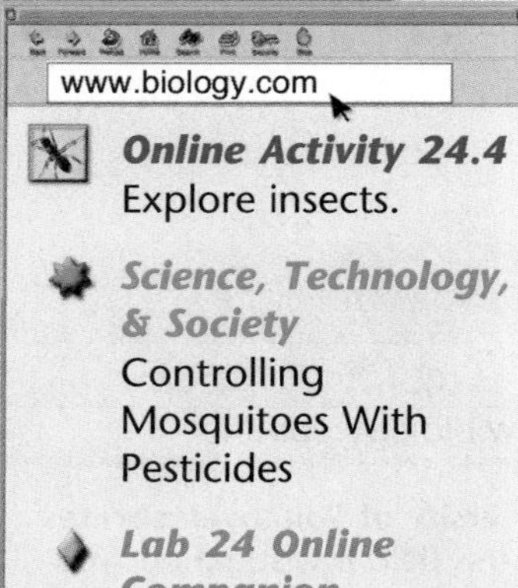

Maybe you've watched ants crawl across the sidewalk, heard crickets chirping on a summer night, or seen a butterfly land on a flower. Insects seem to be everywhere, and there are so many different kinds! What are the keys to their success?

General Characteristics of Insects

Insects have three main body parts: head, thorax, and abdomen. They have three pairs of walking legs and usually one or two pairs of wings attached to the thorax. Insect wings are extensions of the exoskeleton of the thorax.

Like spiders, insects have Malpighian tubules that serve in excretion. But instead of book lungs, they have an extensive tracheal system that transports gases throughout the body. Like most crustaceans, insects typically have compound eyes, but they have just one pair of sensory antennae (Figure 24-11). One function of antennae is to detect chemical signals released by individuals of the same and different insect species. Those signals released by the same species are called pheromones (FER uh mohnz). For example, many male moths detect female pheromones, helping guide them to mates. In social species such as honeybees, some of the activities of the hive are coordinated by pheromones.

Ability to Fly Flight is one key to the great success of insects. Most species have wings in adulthood. An animal that has the ability to fly can escape many predators, find food and mates, and disperse to new habitats faster than an animal that is limited to walking or crawling around.

Diverse Feeding Habits The ability of diverse insects to thrive in a variety of habitats is another key to their success. This is partly due to their diverse types of mouthparts. Some insects, including grasshoppers, use mandibles to handle, bite, and chew food such as leaves. Other insects have mouthparts that are fused together into a sucking tube. A mosquito uses this structure to

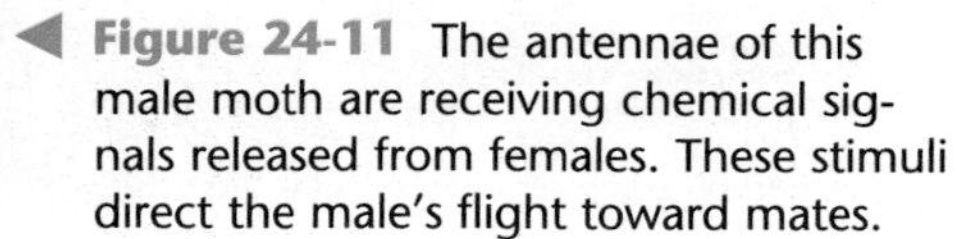

Figure 24-11 The antennae of this male moth are receiving chemical signals released from females. These stimuli direct the male's flight toward mates.

pierce skin and suck blood. Some insects, such as fruit flies, lap their food. Many insects have a combination of feeding mouthparts, giving them access to various types of food. Furthermore, some insects have specialized digestive enzymes (or have microorganisms with such enzymes in their guts) that allow them to take advantage of some unusual food sources that other animals cannot, such as beeswax, wool, and wood.

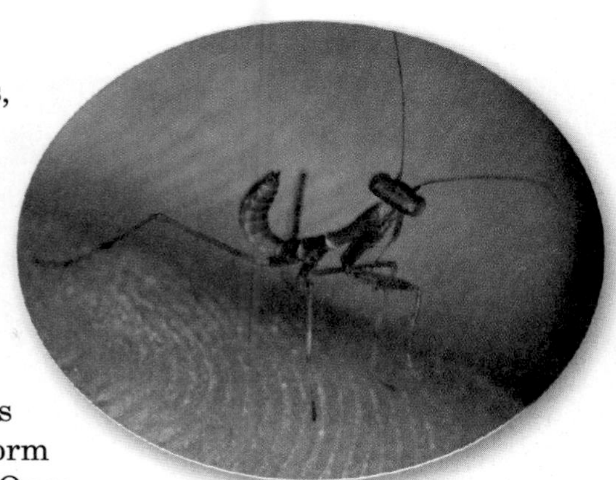

▲ **Figure 24-12** This newly hatched praying mantis (shown on a fingertip) will molt many times until its final molt to adulthood. The adult will be much bigger, sexually mature, and winged, but will otherwise look similar to this hatchling (incomplete metamorphosis).

Metamorphosis During their development many insects undergo metamorphosis, a process in which their body form changes from the sexually immature to the mature stage. Once metamorphosis is complete, the adult no longer grows. Molting and metamorphosis are controlled by insect hormones.

In some insects, the change from juvenile to adult is not very dramatic, and is called *incomplete metamorphosis*. For example, juvenile grasshoppers look like miniature adults, except that the proportions are a little different (Figure 24-12). The juveniles also lack wings and sexual organs. Changes in size occur at several molts during the juvenile stage. The final molt is the one that produces the adult stage.

But other insects, such as butterflies, flies, and beetles, have an adult stage that looks and functions very differently from the larva (Figure 24-13). These insects undergo what is called *complete metamorphosis*. Typically in these cases, the larval stage is specialized for eating and growing, and the adult is specialized for moving to a new location and reproducing. Complete metamorphosis may be part of the key to insect success in that it allows the insect to take advantage of more than one habitat and food source at different life stages.

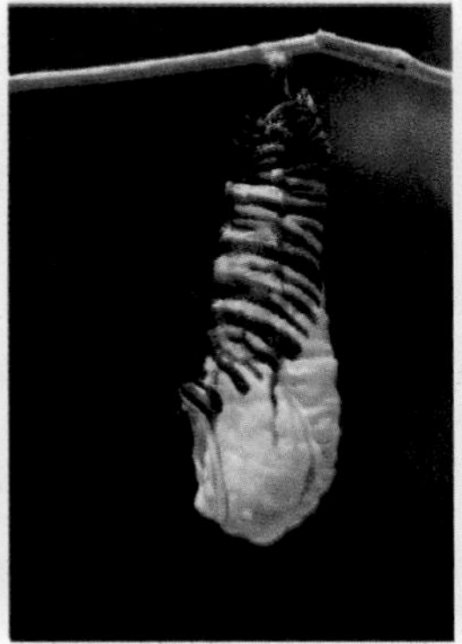
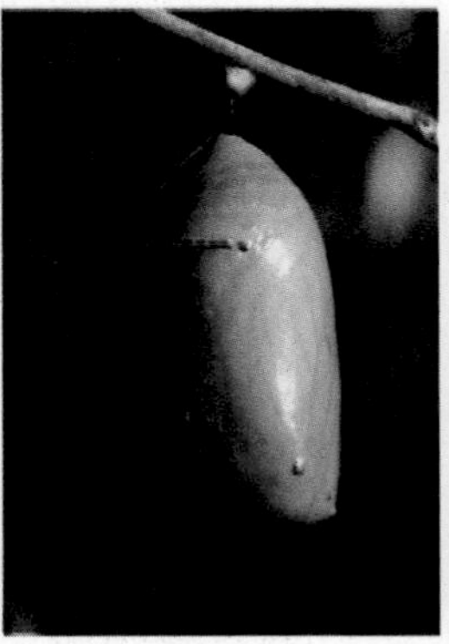

▲ **Figure 24-13** A monarch butterfly is an insect that undergoes complete metamorphosis.

The larva molts several times into larger and larger larval stages. During the transition between the larval and adult stages, an insect with complete metamorphosis becomes a **pupa** (PYOO puh). During the pupal stage, the insect larva stops feeding and becomes inactive. Major chemical and physical changes occur in the insect during this time of transformation.

Figure 24-14 Some Major Orders of Insects

Order	Familiar Name	Approximate Number of Species	Characteristics	Example
Coleoptera	Beetles	500,000	Two pairs of wings—front pair is chitinous (hardened by chitin) and shields the back pair when insect is not flying	 Japanese beetle
Lepidoptera	Moths, butterflies	140,000	Two pairs of wings covered with tiny scales	 Swallowtail butterfly
Diptera	Flies, mosquitoes	120,000	One pair of membranous (transparent) wings	 Horsefly
Hymenoptera	Ants, bees, wasps	100,000	Two pairs of membranous wings; abdomen of most females has stinging organ; many species live in social colonies	 Cicada-killer wasp
Hemiptera	The true "bugs"	55,000	Two pairs of wings—front half of front pair is chitinous	 Leaf-footed bug
Orthoptera	Crickets, grasshoppers	30,000	Two pairs of wings; back pair of legs often enlarged and function in jumping	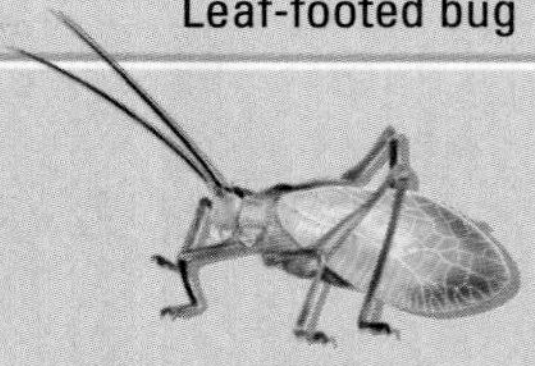 Katydid
Odonata	Dragonflies, damselflies	5,000	Two pairs of wings; large compound eyes and almost 360° vision	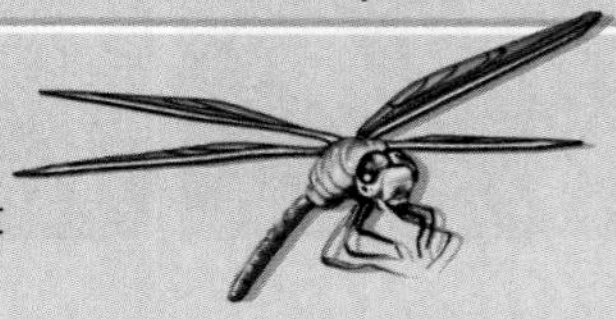 Green darner dragonfly
Isoptera	Termites	2,000	Reproductive adults of some species have two pairs of membranous wings (other species are wingless); live in social colony	 Subterranean termite

Insect Diversity

There are more insect species than all the other animal species combined. They live in almost every habitat on land and in fresh water. They are rare only in the ocean, where crustaceans are the most common arthropods. You are probably already familiar with some if not all of the major orders of insects, at least by their common names (Figure 24-14, on the facing page).

The Impact of Insects

Animals so numerous, diverse, and widespread as insects are bound to affect the lives of many other organisms, including humans. On one hand, humans and other organisms depend on insects. Bees, beetles, and many other insects pollinate the majority of flowering plants, including crops and orchard trees. This allows plants to reproduce and bear fruit. Termites and ants break down organic matter, helping produce new soil and recycling nutrients (Figure 24-15).

On the other hand, certain insects are carriers of diseases that affect humans. For example, there has been recent concern in parts of the United States about mosquito-spread viruses, in particular West Nile virus. These viruses can cause encephalitis (an inflammation of the brain) or meningitis (an inflammation of spinal cord tissues) in humans and other mammals. Insects also compete with humans for food (Figure 24-16). In parts of Africa, for instance, insects destroy about 75 percent of the crops.

There is an entire field of biology called **entomology** devoted to classifying and understanding the biology of insects. The focus of some entomologists is on developing ways to control pest insects. The use of toxins (pesticides, or insecticides) has been the standard approach in the past. But many of these toxins had unexpected effects. Some, like DDT, were found to be deadly to other animals such as beneficial insects and birds. Additionally, resistance to toxins often evolves in insects through the process of natural selection, as you read in Chapter 14. As a result, farmers and public health officials have had to apply stronger doses or new combinations of toxins.

▲ **Figure 24-15** Insects play valuable roles in the environment. For example, termites can enrich soil by decaying wood.

◄ **Figure 24-16** Insects can also be pests. Larvae of the diamondback moth chewed the holes in this crop of cabbages in Thailand.

One challenge of entomologists today is to solve problems caused by pest insects without hurting beneficial insects and the rest of the environment. One solution is **biological control,** the control of pest organisms by interfering with their natural ecological interactions. For example, introducing ladybird beetles or wasps that naturally prey on pest insects can help keep pest populations in check. Other methods involve finding ways to expose a toxin to just the targeted pest insect and not other animals. Practices like these are used in a method of pest control called integrated pest management, or IPM. IPM relies on closely monitoring the presence of insect pests and their life cycles in order to prevent the use of unnecessary chemical controls. The strategy behind IPM is to use physical barriers, planting practices, or biological controls whenever possible as alternatives to traditional chemical pesticides. Another approach, which you read about in Chapter 13, is genetic engineering of plants to resist particular insects.

Still another control strategy is to manipulate the pest insect's behavior. For example, to defend against the apple maggot fly, some farmers hang a sticky red ball from the apple trees. Flies that would normally mate and lay eggs (that hatch into apple maggots) on real apples are lured to the exaggerated shape and color of the fakes (Figure 24-17). They get trapped on the sticky surface and die.

Some methods of pest insect control, especially of disease-carrying insects, rely on education campaigns. One role of public health officials is to warn people about dangerous insects and ways to avoid contact with them. For example, perhaps you have noticed campaigns in your neighborhood or city to clean up old tires and other sources of standing water. Simple measures such as these can help reduce mosquito populations.

Learning how to live with (or despite) insects is a necessity. As one entomologist has pointed out, insects are not going to inherit the Earth. They already own it!

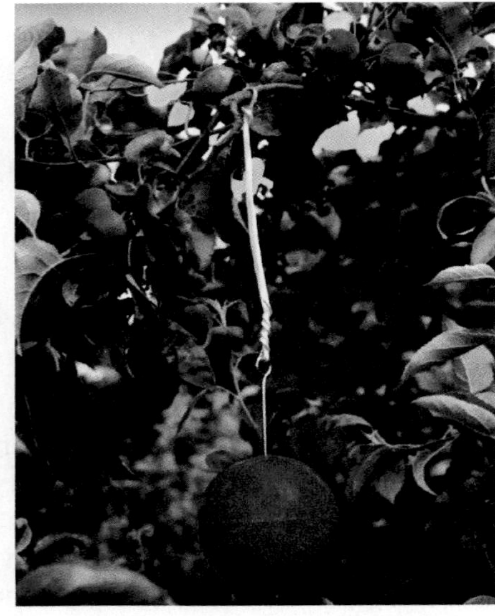

▲ **Figure 24-17** One non-toxic way to control pest insects is to lure them with something that naturally attracts them. This sticky fake apple attracts and traps the apple maggot fly.

Science, Technology, & Society

www.biology.com

Controlling Mosquitoes With Pesticides

Do you live in an area where mosquitoes are found during summer months? If so, you know what a nuisance they can be. Mosquitoes can also cause disease. In some communities mosquitoes are sprayed with poisons, but is this a good idea? Go online to explore both sides of this controversial issue and make a recommendation of your own.

Online Activity 24.4

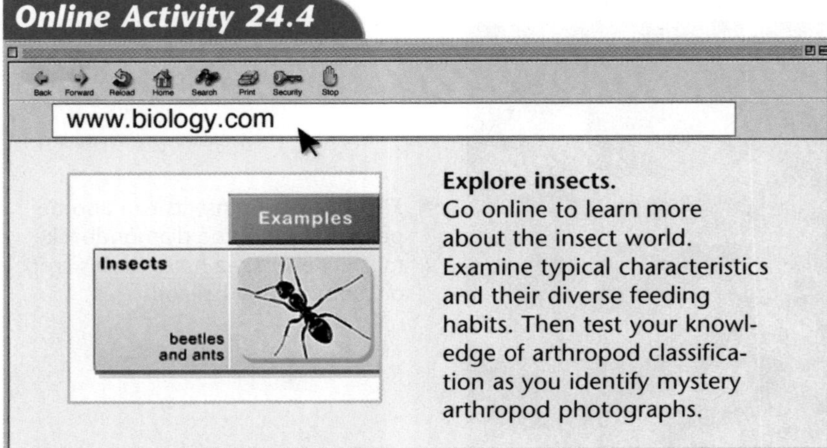

Explore insects.
Go online to learn more about the insect world. Examine typical characteristics and their diverse feeding habits. Then test your knowledge of arthropod classification as you identify mystery arthropod photographs.

Concept Check 24.4

1. List three keys to insect success.
2. List at least five major orders of insects and describe the main characteristics of each.
3. Describe at least two positive effects insects have on the world, and two negative effects some insects have on humans.

The Life of WOWBugs

Observing WOWBug™ Behavior

Question How do WOWBugs interact and communicate with each other?

Lab Overview In this investigation you will observe an active culture of WOWBugs, identify the males and females, and compare their behaviors. Then, you will perform an experiment to discover how WOWBugs communicate over a distance.

Preparing for the Lab To help you prepare for the investigation, go to the *Lab 24 Online Companion.* ····→ Learn what WOWBugs are and find out more about their life cycles. Prepare for the lab procedure by previewing the steps you will take.

Completing the Lab Use your Laboratory Manual or lab page printouts from the *Lab 24 Online Companion* to do the investigation and draw conclusions from the observations you made. **CAUTION:** *Be sure to follow your teacher's instructions and all safety guidelines in the investigation.*

Lab 24 Online Companion

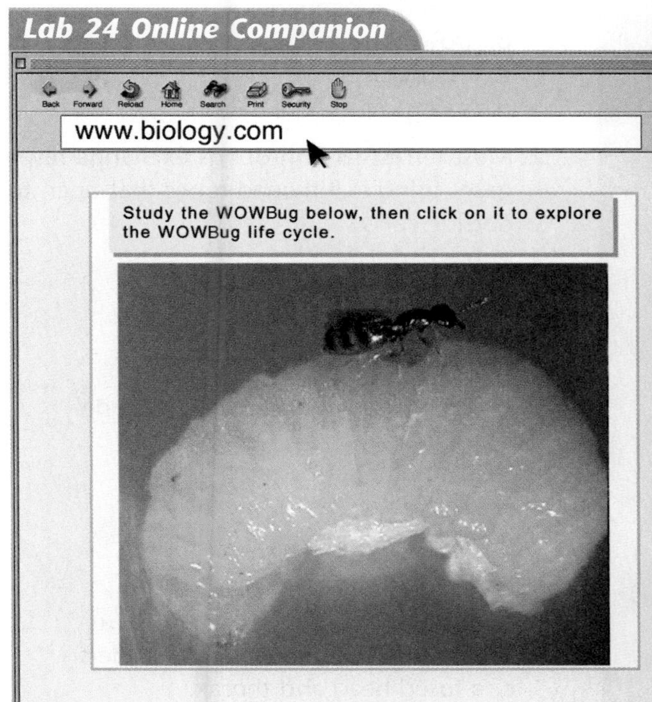
Back
Forward
Reload
Home
Search
Print
Security
Stop
www.biology.com
Study the WOWBug below, then click on it to explore the WOWBug life cycle.

Multiple Choice

Choose the letter of the best answer.

1. Which characteristic is *not* typical of an arthropod?
   - **a.** jointed appendages
   - **b.** growth in size by molting
   - **c.** internal skeleton
   - **d.** brain

2. Most terrestrial arthropods exchange respiratory gases using chitin-lined tubes that open to the outside called
   - **a.** tracheae.
   - **b.** ganglia.
   - **c.** book lungs.
   - **d.** gills.

3. The characteristics of spiders include
   - **a.** spinnerets and silk production.
   - **b.** jointed appendages.
   - **c.** Malpighian tubules.
   - **d.** all of the above

4. A cephalothorax is
   - **a.** found in all insects.
   - **b.** a specialized mouthpart of spiders.
   - **c.** a fused head and thorax.
   - **d.** a component of chitin.

5. How is a decapod different from an insect?
   - **a.** A decapod has antennae.
   - **b.** A decapod has a segmented body.
   - **c.** A decapod has a cephalothorax.
   - **d.** A decapod lives only on land.

6. An insect with incomplete metamorphosis
   - **a.** dies in a juvenile stage.
   - **b.** continues to molt as an adult.
   - **c.** changes its diet dramatically as an adult.
   - **d.** has an adult stage that looks and behaves much like the juvenile stage.

7. During the pupal stage, an insect
   - **a.** molts many times.
   - **b.** feeds and grows.
   - **c.** changes in body form.
   - **d.** flies.

Short Answer

8. Identify two functions of an arthropod's exoskeleton.
9. In which habitat did the first arthropods evolve? Describe two ways they differed from modern arthropods.
10. Describe the diet and defenses of a millipede.
11. Compare and contrast a spider and a beetle.
12. Give three examples of arachnids.
13. Compare and contrast a lobster and a barnacle.
14. Define pheromones and give two examples of their function.
15. Trace the stages of an insect with complete metamorphosis.
16. Name the field of biology devoted to the study of insects and give an example of one question this field of biology studies.
17. Give an example of a positive interaction and an example of a negative interaction between insects and humans.

Visualizing Concepts

18. Use the terms below to make lists of characteristics for each of three groups of arthropods: arachnids, crustaceans, and insects. You can use terms more than once.

Arthropod Characteristics		
Arachnid	Crustacean	Insect

tracheae, book lungs, spiracles, Malpighian tubules, ganglia, spinnerets, brain, wings, pedipalps, exoskeleton, cephalothorax, blood, carapace

Analyzing Information

19. Analyzing Graphs Use the pie chart showing the diversity of different groups of animals as percentages of the total number of animal species to answer the questions below.

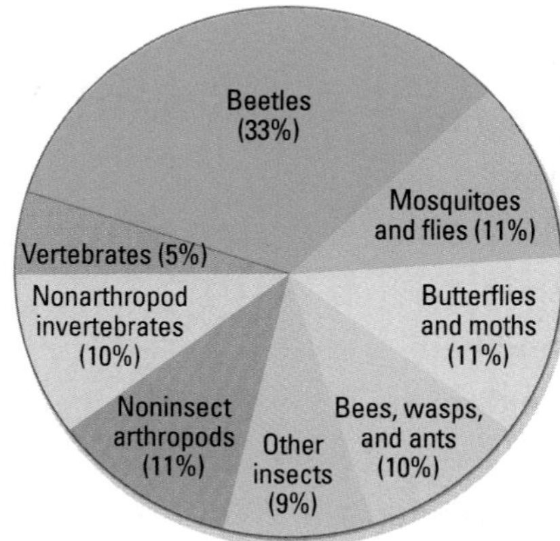

a. What general conclusion about arthropods can you draw from this pie chart?
b. Which arthropod group is most diverse?
c. Name at least three groups that fall within the "Non-insect arthropod" category.
d. Approximately what percentage of insects are butterflies and moths? Explain your calculation.

20. Analyzing Photos The photo below shows a close-up of the coiled mouthpart of an arthropod. Use the photo to answer the questions.

a. Is this arthropod most likely an arachnid, crustacean, or insect? Explain your choice.
b. Does this arthropod most likely chew, lap, or suck its food? Explain.

Critical Thinking

21. Comparing and Contrasting Describe two features of an arthopod's structure and function that are similar to your own. Describe two features that are different.

22. Comparing and Contrasting One key characteristic of arthropods is their jointed appendages. Contrast the functions of four different appendages found in four different arthropods.

23. Developing Hypotheses Insects with complete metamorphosis are more diverse and numerous than insects with incomplete metamorphosis, and evolved more recently. Hypothesize how this adaptation may have provided advantages.

24. Evaluating the Impact of Research How did the research of apple maggot fly behavior help entomologists develop a non-toxic way to manage this pest? List some advantages of this method.

25. What's Wrong With These Statements? *Briefly explain why each statement is inaccurate or misleading.*

a. A characteristic of all spiders is web-weaving.
b. Insects are flying arthropods.
c. Insects are pests.

Performance Assessment

Writing Suppose you were able to eliminate all the insects from your schoolyard, community garden, or local park. Describe the changes that would happen as a result. Before you start writing, make a survey of insects at that location.

Online Assessment/Test Preparation

Back Forward Reload Home Search Print Security Stop

www.biology.com

- **Chapter 24 Assessment**
  Check your understanding of the chapter concepts.
- **Standardized Test Preparation**
  Practice test-taking skills you need to succeed.

CHAPTER 25

Vertebrates: Fishes and Amphibians

This stained skeleton of a piranha dramatically highlights a feature common to animals classified as "vertebrates." This feature is a segmented backbone, shown here as the yellow line running from the head to the tail. Vertebrates are the most common large animals in both aquatic and land habitats. Fishes, frogs, turtles, snakes, birds, alligators, and mammals are all familiar vertebrates.

Since humans are vertebrates, many people find this group of animals particularly interesting. Learning about the biology of vertebrates may help you to learn more about your own biology. Before you begin the chapter, go online to the *WebQuest* to learn about some discoveries of unusual fishes.

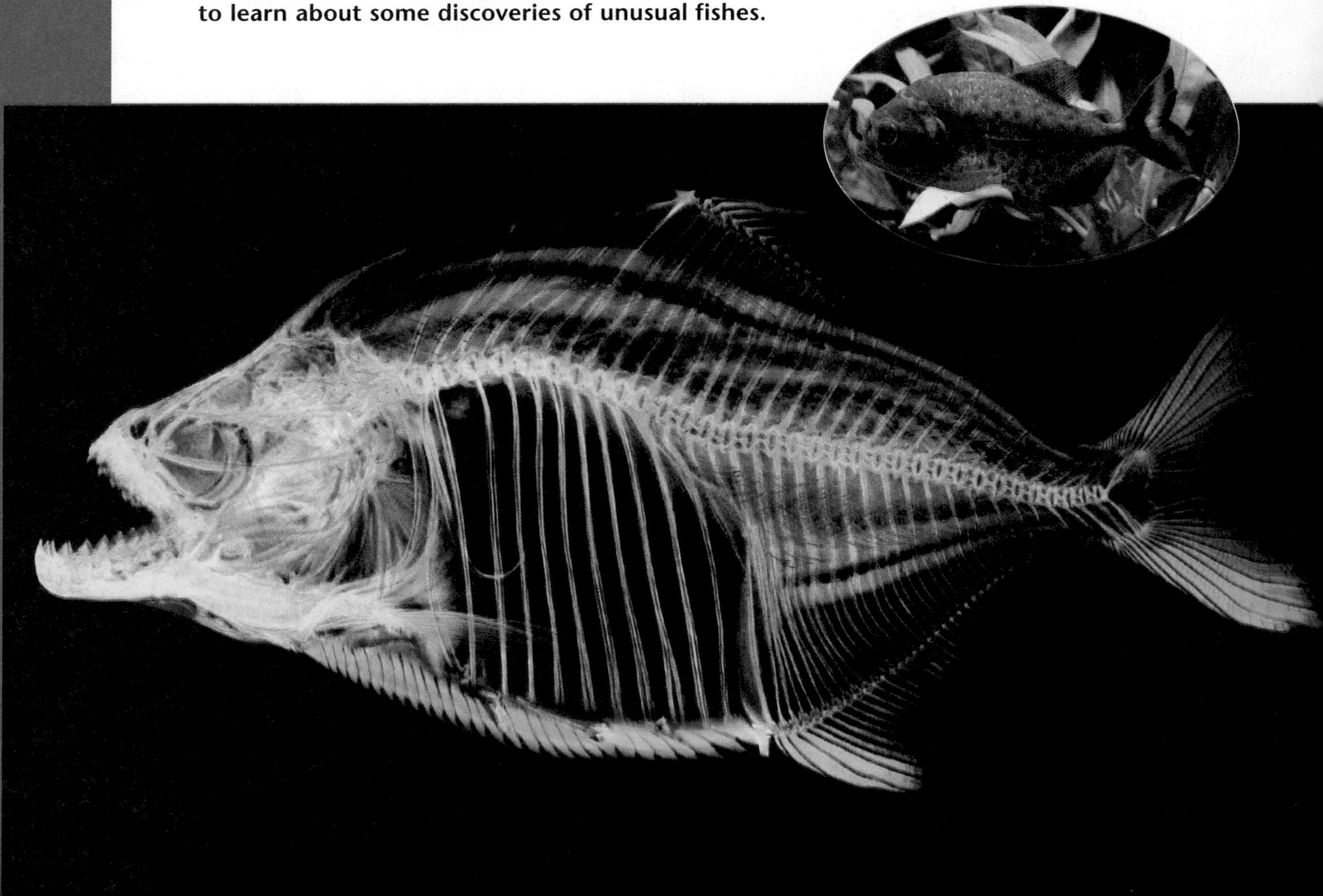

Key Concepts

Concept 25.1

Vertebrates are chordates.

Concept 25.2

Sharks and rays are fishes with skeletons made of cartilage.

Most fishes have bony skeletons.

The amphibians include frogs and salamanders.

Chapter 25 Review

What's Online

www.biology.com

WebQuest
CoelacanthQuest

Online Activity 25.1
Connect the chordates.

Online Activity 25.2
Explore sharks and rays.

Online Activity 25.3
Explore bony fishes.

Careers
Meet a Commercial Fisher

Lab 25 Online Companion
Voyagers and Acrobats

Online Activity 25.4
Explore amphibians.

Chapter 25 Assessment

CONCEPT 25.1

Vertebrates are chordates.

OBJECTIVES

- Describe four unique characteristics of chordates.
- Distinguish invertebrate chordates from other invertebrates.
- Describe the general characteristics of vertebrates.
- Identify the main groups of vertebrates.

KEY TERMS

- chordate
- notochord
- vertebra
- endoskeleton
- tetrapod

What's Online

www.biology.com

Online Activity 25.1 Connect the chordates.

What could animals as different as a blue whale and the tiny lancelet shown below possibly have in common? Both organisms belong to the phylum known as chordates. In this section, you'll explore the unique features shared by all chordates—including you.

Characteristics of Chordates

The animals known as the **chordates** (phylum Chordata) are named for a structure that is found in all chordate embryos. This structure, called the **notochord,** is a flexible rod that extends through much of the length of the body (Figure 25-1). Chordates include two groups of invertebrates as well as all of the vertebrate animals. (Recall from Chapter 23 that vertebrates are animals with segmented backbones like your own.) In some invertebrate chordates, the notochord remains as the skeleton in the adult animals. In vertebrates, however, only remnants of the notochord remain—such as the discs of cartilage in your backbone.

In addition to a notochord, all chordate embryos also share three other distinctive features. The first is a hollow nerve cord located along the dorsal (back) side of the animal. This hollow nerve cord develops into the brain and the spinal cord. In contrast, non-chordates have either no nerve cord or a solid nerve cord that usually runs along the ventral (front) side.

All chordate embryos also have slits located in the pharynx, the region of the digestive tube just behind the mouth. In vertebrates that keep these pharyngeal slits as adults, water enters the organism's mouth and exits through the slits, without traveling through the entire digestive system. In some invertebrate chordates these slits filter water for suspended food. In other groups of vertebrates, the pharyngeal slits and surrounding structures develop into different organs, including organs for gas exchange (gills), jaw support, hearing, and other functions.

The final distinguishing characteristic of chordate embryos is a tail that extends beyond the anus. In many chordates, the tail contains backbone segments and muscles. The tail provides much of the force that enables aquatic chordates to swim.

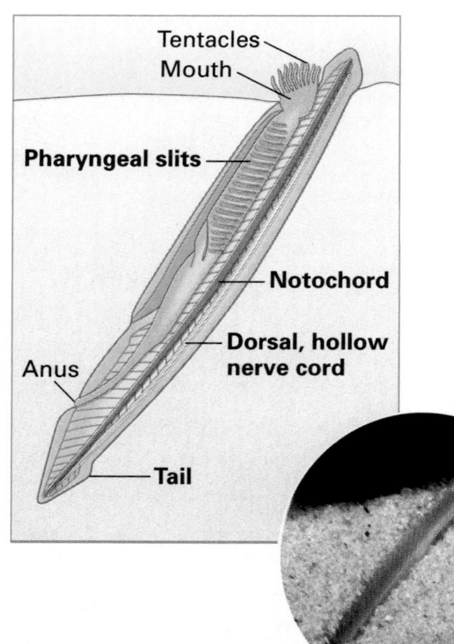

Figure 25-1 An adult lancelet displays all four chordate characteristics. Lancelets spend most of their time in sand on the seafloor, feeding on small particles in the water.

Invertebrate Chordates

Invertebrate chordates illustrate the chordate body structure in its simplest form. There are two main groups of invertebrate chordates: the tunicates and the lancelets. Tunicates are marine animals that look like small sacs (Figure 25-2). The adults are sessile and often attach to rocks, the underside of boats, or coral reefs. They filter seawater through their pharyngeal slits and feed on small organic particles suspended in the water. Adult tunicates have no trace of a notochord, nerve cord, or tail. However, the tunicate larva is a swimming, tadpole-like organism with all four chordate features.

Lancelets, such as the one in Figure 25-1 on the facing page, are small (5–15 cm), blade-like chordates that resemble tunicate larvae. They live in the sand on the ocean floor and filter tiny food particles from seawater.

▲ **Figure 25-2** These adult blue tunicates, or "sea squirts," are sessile filter-feeders.

General Characteristics of Vertebrates

Vertebrates make up most of the phylum Chordata. Figure 25-3 illustrates two unique features of vertebrates: a skull and a backbone. These skeletal features protect the main parts of the animal's nervous system. The skull forms a hard case for the brain. The backbone is composed of a series of skeletal segments called **vertebrae** (singular, *vertebra*), which enclose the nerve cord. In addition to the skull and vertebrae, most vertebrates have skeletal parts (such as shoulders and a pelvis) that support paired limbs (such as pairs of legs).

The vertebrate skeleton is inside the animal's body and is therefore called an **endoskeleton.** In some vertebrates, such as sharks, the endoskeleton is made entirely of flexible cartilage—the same material that makes up your outer ear. In other vertebrates, such as humans and other mammals, the skeleton is a combination of hard bone and cartilage. Bone and cartilage are mostly nonliving material, but they do contain living cells that secrete new bone or cartilage. These living cells enable the endoskeleton to grow with the animal. Contrast this with an arthropod's nonliving exoskeleton, which must be shed (molted) as the organism outgrows it.

Almost all vertebrates have an important feeding adaptation—a hinged jaw. Not having hinged jaws limits the size and shape of an animal's food and the ability to begin processing food by chewing. For example, think about trying to eat an apple if your mouth were 3 centimeters in diameter and you could not chew. The evolution of hinged jaws enabled vertebrates to capture and eat a wide variety of prey.

▼ **Figure 25-3** A cat's skeleton illustrates two distinguishing characteristics of vertebrates: a backbone consisting of segmented units (vertebrae) and a skull enclosing the brain. Like most vertebrates, cats also have hinged jaws.

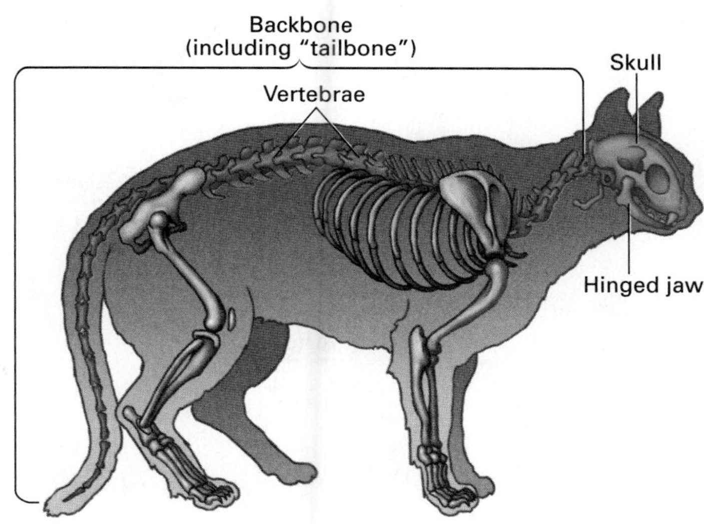

Overview of Vertebrate Diversity

The cladogram in Figure 25-4 is based on one set of hypotheses for the evolutionary history of living vertebrates. To construct this diagram, biologists relied on a combination of anatomical, molecular, and fossil evidence. The branching points represent important developments in vertebrate evolution.

The first two branches near the bottom of the diagram lead to two animal groups thought to be most closely related to the ancestors of vertebrates: hagfishes and lampreys. Both of these classes

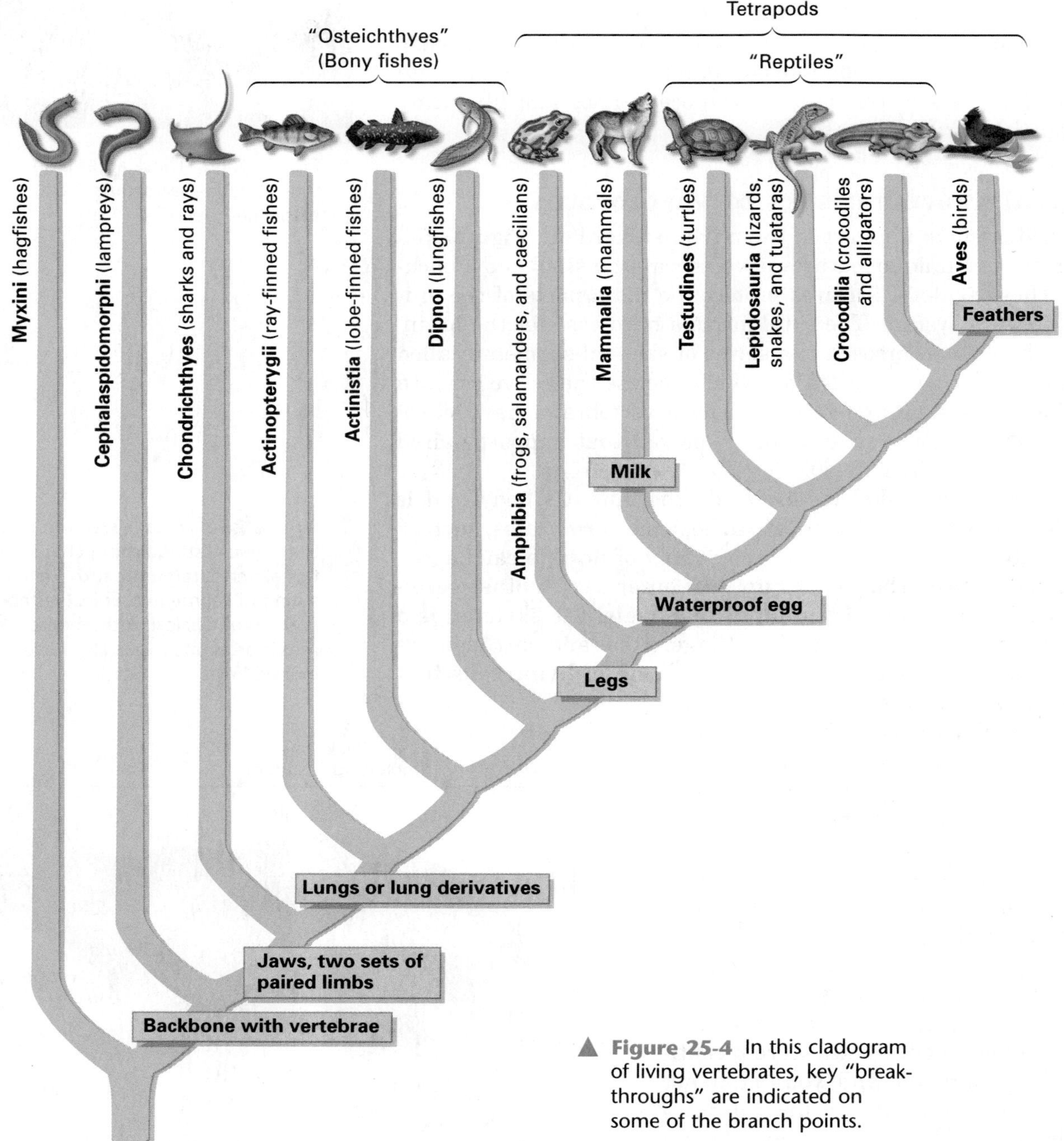

Figure 25-4 In this cladogram of living vertebrates, key "breakthroughs" are indicated on some of the branch points.

of vertebrates are aquatic animals that at first glance look something like eels. They are not closely related to eels, however. Both lampreys and hagfishes lack the hinged jaws and paired limbs found in all other vertebrates (Figure 25-5a). Lampreys have a cartilage skeleton that is more complex than a hagfish's cartilage skeleton. Although hagfishes have skulls, they do not have vertebrae: Their main body support is an adult version of the embryo's notochord. This primitive skeleton is one reason many biologists consider hagfishes to be the closest living relatives of the invertebrate chordates that were the ancestors of vertebrates.

As you have read, all vertebrates other than lampreys and hagfishes have hinged jaws (Figure 25-5b). Evidence from fossils and the study of embryos indicates that hinged jaws evolved from some of the skeletal supports of pharyngeal slits. Included among jawed vertebrates are the various classes of aquatic, finned animals generally called fishes. (Note that the term *fish* is the plural when referring to several of one species of fish, such as several sharks of the same species. However, the plural *fishes* is used when referring to more than one species, such as tuna and sharks.)

All other jawed vertebrates are *tetrapods,* a term that means "four-footed." The tetrapods include the amphibians (frogs and salamanders), the animals traditionally called reptiles (turtles, lizards, snakes, and crocodiles), birds, and mammals. A **tetrapod** has two sets of paired limbs that are modified as legs that can support the animal. This adaptation made it possible for vertebrates to inhabit the land, another key development in the evolution of vertebrates. Some tetrapods, however, adapted to their environments by becoming legless. For example, snakes are considered tetrapods because they most likely evolved from a four-legged ancestor. The rest of this chapter focuses on fishes and amphibians.

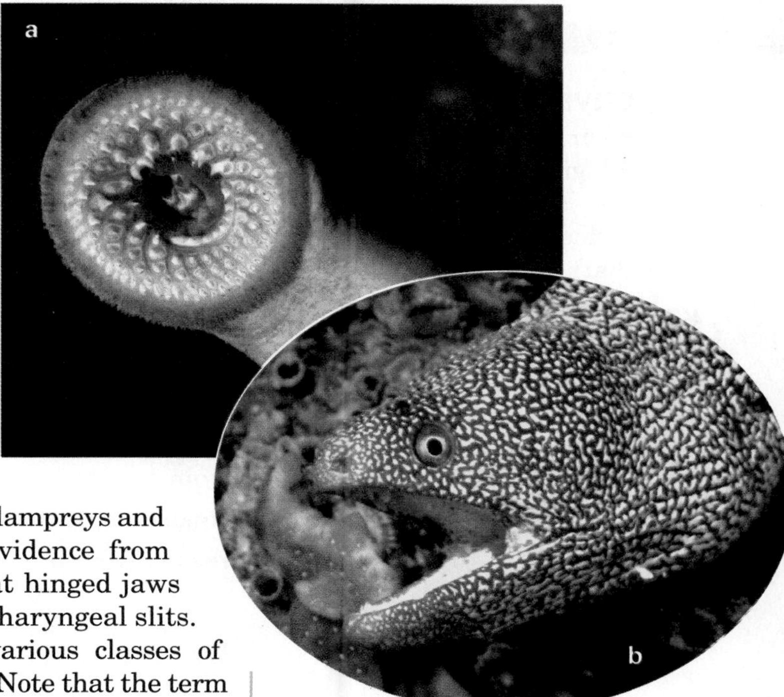

▲ **Figure 25-5** Though these two vertebrates have similar shapes, you can see an important difference in their mouths. **a.** Lacking a hinged jaw, the sea lamprey attaches its round mouth to the side of a fish, bores a hole through the skin, and absorbs the fish's blood and tissues. **b.** The goldentail moray eel uses its hinged jaw to capture and ingest small fish, shrimp, and a variety of other prey.

Online Activity 25.1

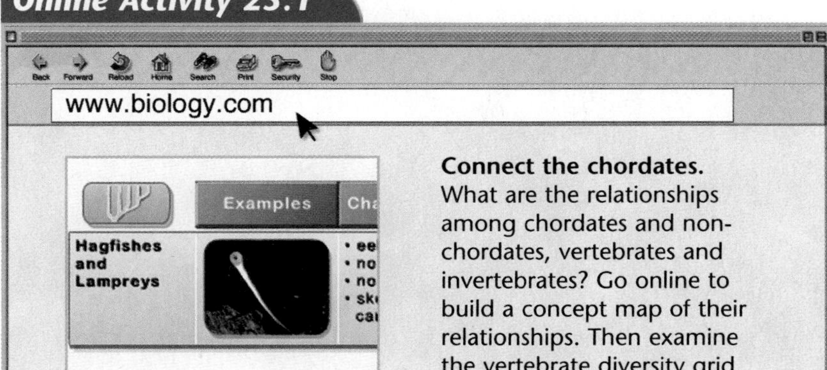

Connect the chordates. What are the relationships among chordates and non-chordates, vertebrates and invertebrates? Go online to build a concept map of their relationships. Then examine the vertebrate diversity grid.

Concept Check 25.1

1. List the four distinguishing characteristics of chordates.
2. Explain how invertebrate chordates are different from vertebrate chordates.
3. List the general characteristics of vertebrates.
4. List the four sub-groups of the group of vertebrates called tetrapods.

CONCEPT 25.2 Sharks and rays are fishes with skeletons made of cartilage.

OBJECTIVES
- Compare and contrast cartilaginous and bony fishes.
- Describe some adaptations of sharks and rays.

KEY TERMS
- cartilaginous fish
- bony fish
- lateral line system

What's Online

Online Activity 25.2
Explore sharks and rays.

Sharks have been hunting in the oceans for hundreds of millions of years. In addition to highly developed senses of touch, smell, hearing, vision, and taste, the shark has one sense you do not have. This "sixth" sense is the ability to detect small electric fields from a meter or more away. Since living organisms produce these small electric fields, this sense helps the shark find prey . . . one reason why some people call sharks "The Perfect Predator."

Diversity of Fishes

Fishes, the first jawed vertebrates, make up about 30,000 of the more than 55,000 species of vertebrates on Earth today. There are two main groups of fishes (Figure 25-6). One group is the **cartilaginous fishes,** class Chondrichthyes (kahn DRIK theez), so named because they have a flexible skeleton made entirely of cartilage. Cartilaginous fishes include the sharks and rays. All other fishes are called **bony fishes** (formerly, class Osteichthyes (ohs tee IK theez) now divided into three classes) because their skeletons contain bone hardened by calcium compounds.

Figure 25-6 This reef scene includes both a cartilaginous fish—the great white shark *(Carcharodon carcharias)*—and smaller bony fishes, swimming in the school.

Sharks

Nearly all sharks live in marine habitats. Sharks have streamlined bodies and are swift swimmers (Figure 25-7). Powerful muscles in their tail propel them forward. The dorsal (back or top) fins function mainly as stabilizers. And the lateral (side) fins provide lift in the water. However, these fins are not very movable, and as a result sharks do not maneuver very well. A shark must swim constantly to avoid sinking, since its body is actually denser than water. Continual swimming also ensures that water flows into the shark's mouth and through its gills, enabling the exchange of oxygen and carbon dioxide. Some sharks spend time resting on the seafloor. When not swimming, they must use muscles in their jaws and pharynx to pump water over their gills.

Most sharks are predators—fast and powerful with acute senses. Sharks have sharp eyesight, a powerful sense of smell, and highly developed electrosensor organs on their heads. These electrosensors can detect very small changes in electrical fields produced by muscle contractions in nearby animals. Sharks, as well as most other aquatic vertebrates, also have a **lateral line system,** a row of sensory organs running along each side of the body. The lateral line system is sensitive to very small changes in water pressure. This enables a shark to "feel" minor vibrations caused by swimming animals.

▲ **Figure 25-7** This scalloped hammerhead shark gets its name from its wide head. The function of the flattened head is unknown. It may increase the shark's ability to maneuver.

Rays

Although rays are closely related to sharks, they have adapted to a very different lifestyle. Most rays are bottom-dwellers that feed by using their jaws to crush mollusks and crustaceans. Other rays cruise in open water, scooping food into their gaping mouths. A ray's front fins are greatly enlarged. These fins propel the animal through water much like a bird flaps its wings to move through air. The tail of many rays is whip-like and, in some species, has poisonous spines that function in defense. The largest of the rays is the manta ray, with a "wingspan" of more than 7 meters (Figure 25-8).

▲ **Figure 25-8** This manta ray gets its name from the Spanish word *manta,* meaning "blanket."

Online Activity 25.2

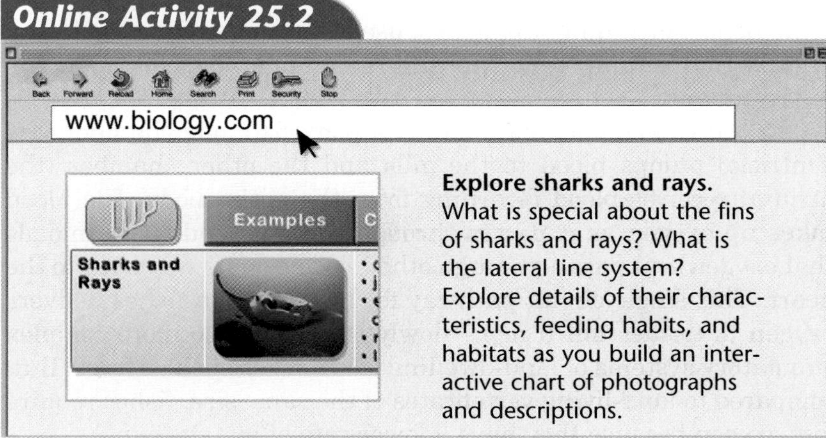

Explore sharks and rays. What is special about the fins of sharks and rays? What is the lateral line system? Explore details of their characteristics, feeding habits, and habitats as you build an interactive chart of photographs and descriptions.

Concept Check 25.2

1. What is the major difference between cartilaginous and bony fishes?
2. Describe the function of the lateral line system.

CONCEPT 25.3

Most fishes have bony skeletons.

OBJECTIVES

- Describe the general characteristics of bony fishes.
- Compare and contrast three groups of bony fishes.

KEY TERMS

- operculum
- swim bladder

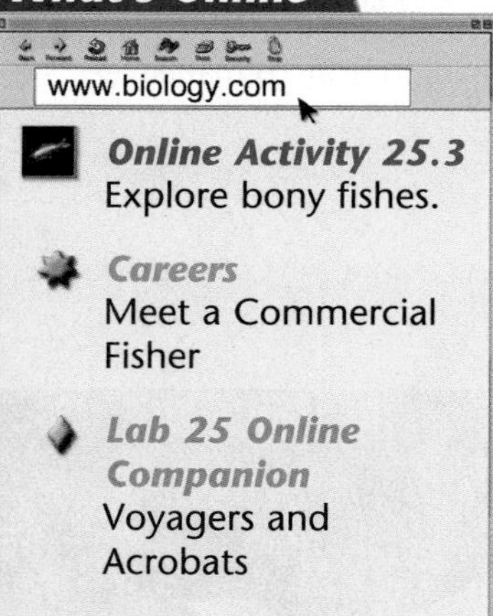

There are more species of bony fishes than of any other single group of vertebrates. Ranging in size from about 1 centimeter to more than 6 meters long, bony fishes are common in nearly all marine and freshwater habitats.

General Characteristics of Bony Fishes

Bony fishes have a relatively stiff skeleton reinforced by hard calcium compounds. Like sharks and rays, bony fishes have gills that extract oxygen from the surrounding water. On each side of the head of bony fishes, a protective flap called the **operculum** (plural, *operculi*) covers a chamber housing the gills (Figure 25-9). Movement of the operculum pumps water through the gills and allows the fish to obtain oxygen from the water even when it is not swimming. The sharks you read about in Concept 25.2 lack operculi, which is why they must swim or use jaw and pharyngeal muscles to continuously pump water over their gills for gas exchange.

Like sharks, bony fishes have a lateral line system, a keen sense of smell, and good eyesight. Flattened, stiff scales made of bone often cover the skin. Glands in the skin secrete a slimy mucus that helps fishes glide more easily through the water. The "limbs" of fishes include paired front fins and hind fins, which help maneuver their bodies when swimming. Like sharks and rays, most bony fishes are carnivores. Many species, however, feed on plankton or algae, such as seaweed.

Two key internal features of bony fishes are an air sac and a two-chambered heart (Figure 25-10 on the facing page). In most fishes, the air sac functions as a "swim bladder," which makes the animal more buoyant. The air sac also aids "hearing" in many fishes by transmitting vibrations to sensory organs. And some fishes, including lungfishes, use their air sacs as respiratory organs that supplement the gills' exchange of gases with the environment.

In the two-chambered heart of a bony fish, one chamber (the ventricle) pumps blood to the gills and the other chamber (the atrium) receives blood returning from the entire body. The blood takes up oxygen as it passes through the gills and then unloads that oxygen as it passes through other organs on its way back to the heart. This single-circuit pathway for blood flow in fishes delivers oxygen to tissues much more slowly than does the more complex circulatory systems of land-dwelling vertebrates such as frogs. But, compared to land-living vertebrates of the same size, fishes require less oxygen because they have a lower rate of metabolism.

▼ **Figure 25-9** Bony fishes breathe by opening and closing a flap over their gills, the operculum (shown close-up in the inset). The movement of the operculum forces water through the fish's gills (the feathery pink structures).

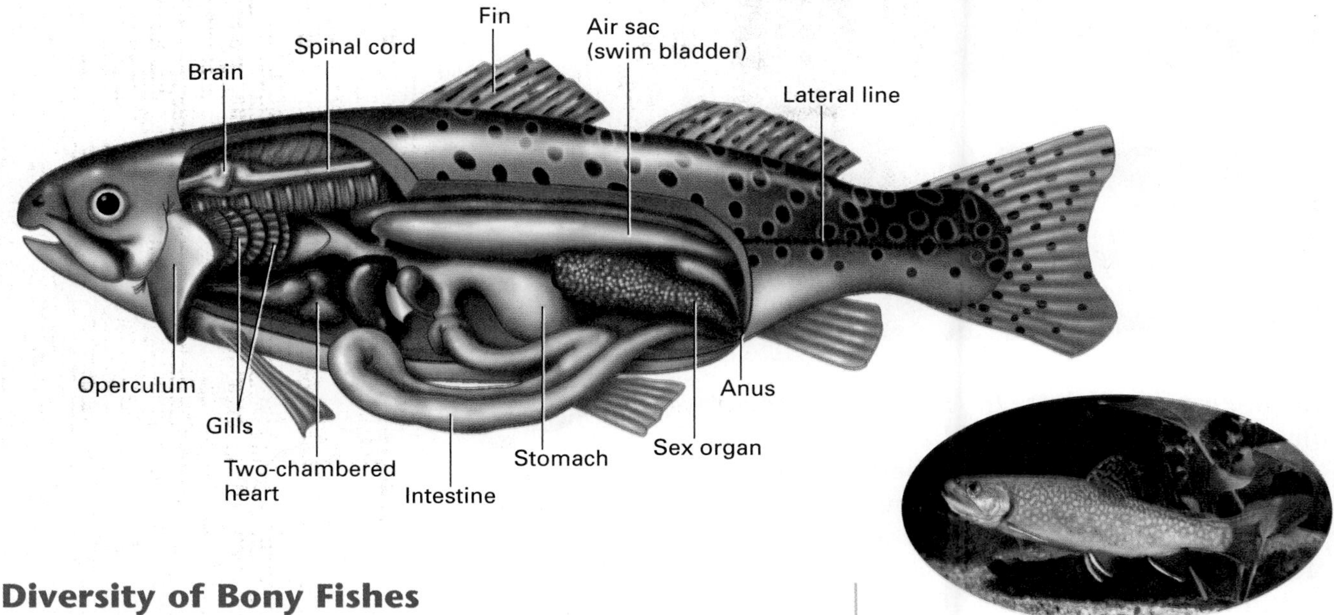

Diversity of Bony Fishes

Until recently, all bony fishes were grouped together in class Osteichthyes. Most biologists now recognize three separate classes of bony fishes: ray-finned fishes (class Actinopterygii), lobe-finned fishes (class Actinistia), and lungfishes (class Dipnoi).

Ray-Finned Fishes There are more than 20,000 species of Actinopterygii. Most bony fishes, including trout, bass, perch, and tuna, are ray-finned fishes. Ray-finned fishes are named for their fins, which consist of webs of skin supported by bony rays or spines (Figure 25-11). The thin, flexible fins help fishes maneuver while swimming. They are also used by some fishes for defense from predators.

In most ray-finned fishes, the air sac is adapted as a **swim bladder,** which is an organ that regulates buoyancy. This swim bladder is a gas-filled sac that enables a fish to control its density and thereby its depth in the water. Because of the swim bladder, bony fishes can remain motionless in water without sinking, unlike most sharks.

▲ **Figure 25-10** Trout are ray-finned fishes. A trout's internal anatomy is shown above left. The diagram below illustrates the two-chambered heart and single circulatory system typical of bony fishes.

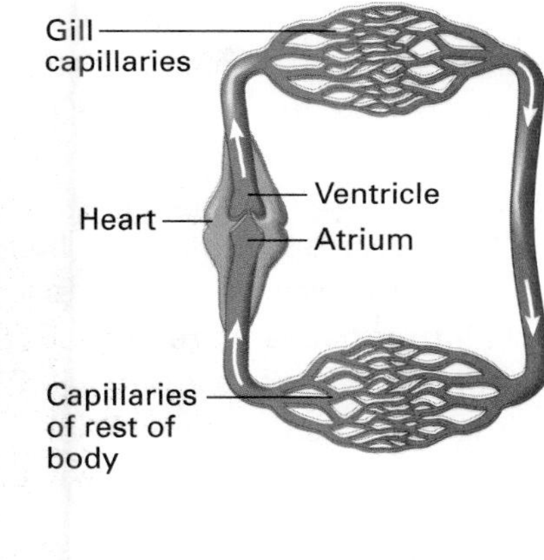

◀ **Figure 25-11** This anthias (a type of sea bass) is another ray-finned fish. Note the bony spines in the dorsal fin and the web of skin stretched between the spines.

◀ **Figure 25-12** Besides ray-finned fishes, there are two other classes of bony fishes. **a.** Lobe-finned fishes such as this coelacanth have muscular fins with stout bones. **b.** Lungfishes have the unique ability to either breathe through gills or gulp air into lungs as an oxygen source.

Lobe-Finned Fishes In contrast to the ray-finned fishes, lobe-finned fishes have muscular fins supported by stout bones. Lobe-finned fishes are not common today and are known mainly from the fossil record. Many fossil lobe-finned fishes from the Devonian period (about 400–350 million years ago) were large and apparently lived and fed on the bottom of shallow, freshwater habitats. They may have used their muscular fins to "walk" along the bottom of bodies of water. The only lobe-finned fishes to survive today are the coelacanths (SEE luh kanths) (Figure 25-12a). Coelacanths are found in the deep waters off the coast of Madagascar and Indonesia.

Lungfishes The third class of bony fishes are lungfishes (Figure 25-12b). Today, lungfishes can be found on continents in the Southern Hemisphere. They generally inhabit still ponds and swamps. The air sac of a lungfish branches into two lobes that function as lungs. A network of tiny blood vessels around the lungs take oxygen from the air that the fish gulps in when it comes to the surface of the water. Lungfishes also have gills that enable the animals to obtain oxygen from water.

The precise relationship between lungfishes and lobe-finned fishes is an area of continuing research. During the Devonian period, lungfishes were abundant predators in shallow, freshwater habitats. Recent analysis of molecular and fossil data point to lungfishes as the living fishes most closely related to tetrapods (land-dwelling vertebrates with legs).

Careers

www.biology.com

Meet a Commercial Fisher Go online to meet a successful fisher who leads an experienced crew. Read her description of her job's challenges and rewards, and find out how a knowledge of fish biology is critical to her work. Then link to Web sites to learn more about how fish develop and grow.

Online Activity 25.3

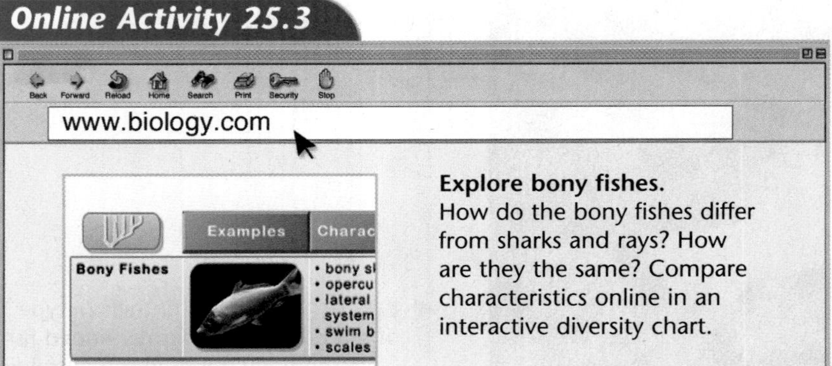

www.biology.com
Examples
Bony Fishes
scales
Explore bony fishes.
How do the bony fishes differ from sharks and rays? How are they the same? Compare characteristics online in an interactive diversity chart.

Concept Check 25.3

1. List the general characteristics of bony fishes.
2. List and contrast the three classes of bony fishes.

Voyagers and Acrobats

Comparing Fish Body Shapes

Questions What body shapes can be observed in cartilaginous and bony fishes? How does body shape affect the way a fish moves?

Lab Overview In this investigation you will study examples of fishes with different body shapes and learn how each body shape is an adaptation for survival in a specific environment. You will make a model of one of the fish body shapes and test how fast the model can move across an aquarium.

Preparing for the Lab To help you prepare for the investigation, go to the *Lab 25 Online Companion.* ····➔ Learn the basic fish body plan and see examples of different body shapes. Prepare for the lab procedure by previewing the steps you will take.

Completing the Lab Use your Laboratory Manual or lab page printouts from the *Lab 25 Online Companion* to do the investigation and draw conclusions from the observations you made. **CAUTION:** *Be sure to follow your teacher's instructions and all safety guidelines in the investigation.*

Lab 25 Online Companion

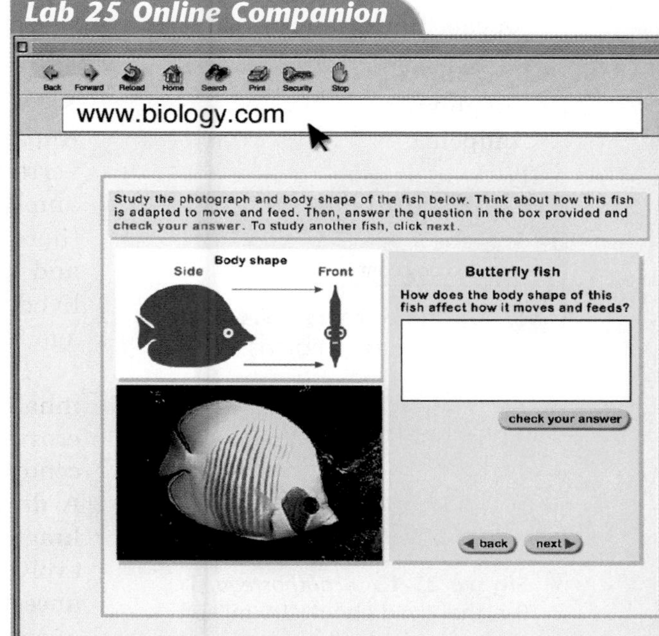

Back
Forward
Reload
Home
Search
Print
Security
Stop
www.biology.com
Study the photograph and body shape of the fish below. Think about how this fish is adapted to move and feed. Then, answer the question in the box provided and check your answer. To study another fish, click next.
Body shape
Side
Front
Butterfly fish
How does the body shape of this fish affect how it moves and feeds?
check your answer
back
next

CONCEPT 25.4 The amphibians include frogs and salamanders.

OBJECTIVES
- Discuss tetrapod evolution from fishes.
- Describe the "double life" of frogs.
- Describe the diet and habitat of salamanders.
- Identify the adaptations of caecilians.

KEY TERMS
- amphibian
- tadpole

What's Online
www.biology.com
Online Activity 25.4
Explore amphibians.

In Greek, the word *amphibios* means "living a double life." Most amphibians exhibit a mixture of aquatic and terrestrial adaptations. While spending much of their adult life on land, most amphibians return to water to reproduce.

The Origin of Tetrapods

Amphibians (class Amphibia) are tetrapods. They were the first vertebrates with adaptations for living on land. But before amphibians resembling the frogs and salamanders of today, there were other four-limbed ancestors that were fully aquatic and more like fish with sturdy legs. These earliest tetrapods lived in shallow aquatic habitats about 400 to 350 million years ago, during the Devonian period.

During this period, a diversity of plants and arthropods already inhabited the land. Some organic material from these terrestrial ecosystems dropped into aquatic habitats. This created new living conditions and food supplies for fishes living near the water's edge. A diversity of fishes resembling modern lobe-finned fishes and lungfishes had already evolved. In addition, limbs and lungs evolved in certain fishes that scientists hypothesize included the ancestors of terrestrial vertebrates. Leg-like limbs may have allowed these animals to paddle and crawl through the dense vegetation in shallow water, and could also support their weight as they moved onto land. Lungs might have supplemented gills for more efficient gas exchange at the water's edge.

Fossils record this transition to life on land over a 50-million-year period. For example, the fossils of the early tetrapod *Acanthostega* have the bony supports of gills, like a fish, but also have four legs (Figure 25-13). The skeletal parts of *Acanthostega's* legs are similar to the skeletal parts of the limbs of amphibians, reptiles, and mammals, including humans.

The lush swamps and forests of the Carboniferous period (350 to 280 million years ago) provided an ideal habitat for early amphibians. In fact, they became so widespread that the Carboniferous period is sometimes called the Age of Amphibians. As the Carboniferous swamps and forests declined, about 300 million years ago, so did those early amphibians. Many evolutionary branches became extinct. Some gave rise to modern amphibians, and another gave rise to the reptiles.

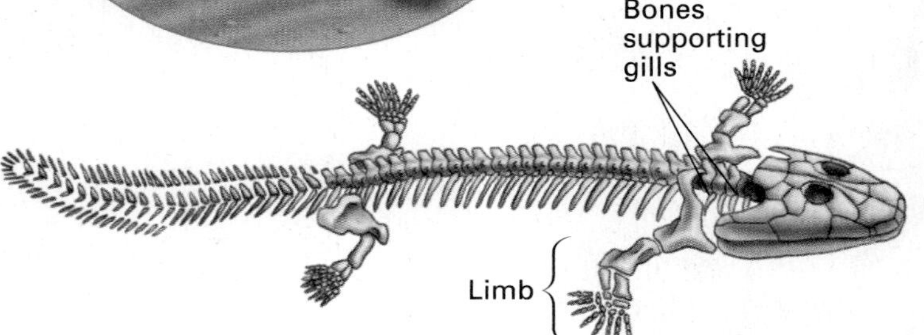

Figure 25-13 *Acanthostega,* a fish that lived about 400 million years ago, had gills and appendages for walking through underwater vegetation. The fossil record shows that early amphibians had similar skeletons to *Acanthostega.*

Figure 25-14 Most tadpoles are aquatic planteaters with fishlike tails and gills. During metamorphosis, the tissues of the gills and tail break down, and walking legs develop. Most adult frogs are air-breathing meateaters.

General Characteristics of Amphibians

Many **amphibians** live part of their life cycle in water and part on land. In general, the larval stage lives in water, while the adult stage lives on land. Amphibian adults generally utilize lungs to breathe air; have a smooth, moist skin; and lack scales.

The eggs of amphibians do not have shells and dry out quickly in the air. For this reason, most amphibians are tied to water because that is where they lay their eggs. The eggs hatch and develop into larvae called tadpoles (Figure 25-14). **Tadpoles** are generally legless aquatic planteaters with gills; a lateral line system resembling that of fishes; and a long, finned tail. In developing into adults, tadpoles undergo a dramatic metamorphosis, or change in body form. When young adults crawl onto shore, most species have four legs, air-breathing lungs instead of gills, a pair of external eardrums, and no lateral line system. Because of metamorphosis, many amphibians truly live a double life, first in water and then on land. However, there is great diversity among amphibians. Some species do not have a terrestrial stage, while other species do not have an aquatic stage.

The smooth skin of adult amphibians is generally moist and often serves to supplement their lungs for gas exchange. Amphibian skin usually has mucous glands as well as poison glands that often play a role in defense against predators.

In contrast to the two-chambered heart of fishes, the amphibian heart has three chambers (Figure 25-15). One chamber (the ventricle) pumps blood away from the heart, and the blood then divides into two pathways of vessels. One pathway delivers blood to the lungs and skin for gas exchange through tiny blood vessels called capillaries. The other pathway transports blood to the rest of the body. The remaining two chambers (the atria) collect blood that is returning to the heart—one atrium for each circulatory path. This two-circuit circulation makes it possible for oxygen-rich blood to be more efficiently transported to the brain, muscles, and other organs.

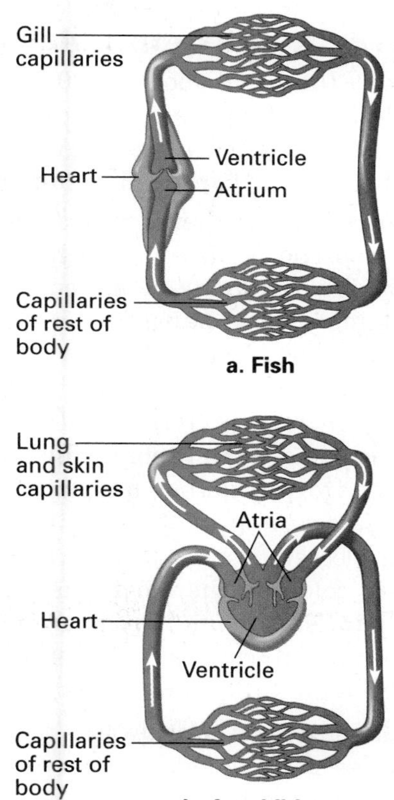

▲ **Figure 25-15** The circulatory system of fishes (a) includes a two-chambered heart and one circuit of blood flow. Amphibians (b) have a three-chambered heart and two circuits of blood flow. The two-circuit system supports the higher metabolic rate of amphibians compared to fishes.

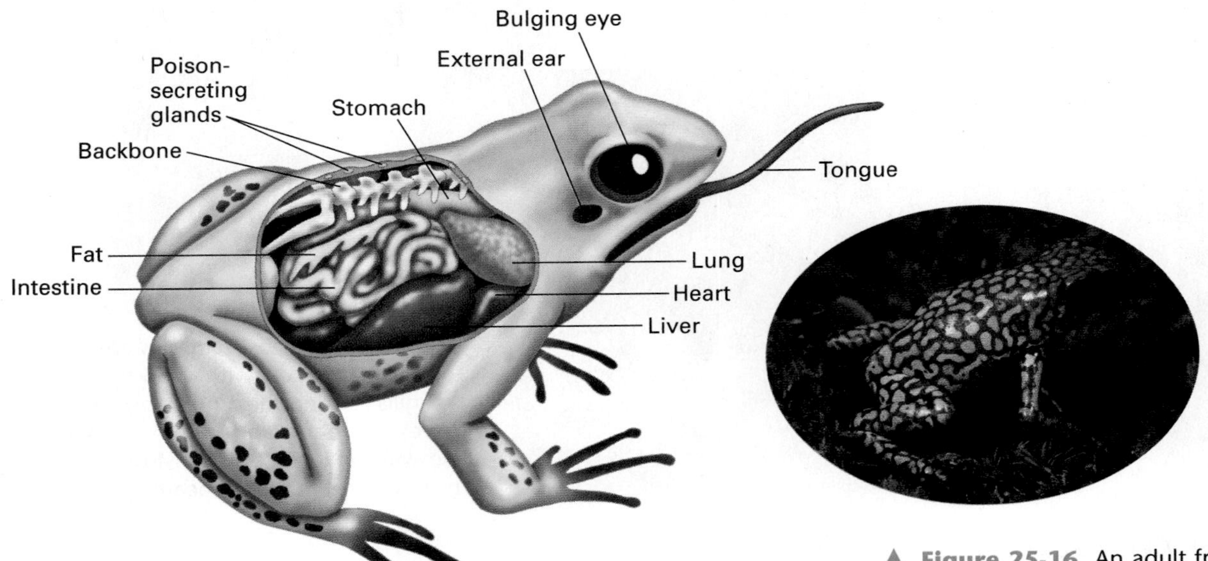

▲ **Figure 25-16** An adult frog has strong rear legs that function in jumping. All frogs have poison glands in their skin, but poison arrow frogs have particularly deadly poisons. The vivid coloration of these poisonous frogs may be an adaptation that warns away potential predators.

Diversity of Amphibians

Today there are about 4,800 species of amphibians. The world's oldest surviving class of tetrapods accounts for only about 8 percent of today's vertebrates. Amphibians can be divided into three orders: frogs, salamanders, and caecilians (see SIL ee unz).

Frogs Due to their great diversity (4,200 known species) and widespread occurrence, frogs (order Anura, "tailless ones") are probably the amphibians most familiar to you. Most frogs have bulging eyes, a pair of external eardrums, no tail, strong hind legs, webbed feet, and smooth, moist skin (Figure 25-16). *Toad* is a term generally used to refer to frogs that have rough skin and live entirely in terrestrial environments. Frogs mainly eat insects and catch them by flicking out their long, sticky tongues. Some frogs eat other frogs and small rodents. For defense from predators, frogs rely on camouflage and glands on the skin that secrete toxins. In contrast to camouflaged frogs, the vivid colors of the most poisonous species warn predators to "stay away." Frogs are usually quiet creatures. However, during breeding season, many species will fill the air with their mating calls.

Salamanders Worldwide, there are only about 500 species of salamanders (order Urodela, "tailed ones"). Most salamanders and the closely related newts do not lose their tail as they develop into adults (Figure 25-17). Usually, salamander bodies are long and slender. Instead of jumping like frogs, salamanders scurry

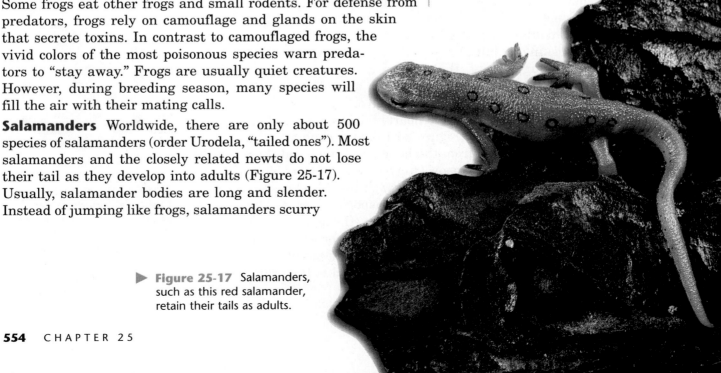

▶ **Figure 25-17** Salamanders, such as this red salamander, retain their tails as adults.

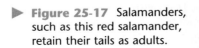

about on all four equal-sized legs. The side-to-side style of walking exhibited by some salamanders is thought to be similar to the way early terrestrial tetrapods walked.

Some species of salamanders live in aquatic environments, while other species live entirely in terrestrial habitats. Some terrestrial species do not have lungs. Instead they exchange oxygen and carbon dioxide with the environment through their thin, moist skin and mouth lining.

Salamanders are mainly meateaters that eat insects and other small invertebrates. In the forest soils of eastern North America, salamanders have a big impact on the ecosystem. The salamanders that inhabit even relatively small sections of forest habitat can consume tons of insects each year.

▲ **Figure 25-18** Caecilians, including the Costa Rican species shown here, are legless and nearly blind.

Caecilians There are about 150 species of caecilians (order Apoda, "legless ones"), amphibians that are legless and nearly blind (Figure 25-18). Caecilians evolved from an ancestor that had legs. The legless adaptation is a clue to their habitat. Like earthworms, most caecilians inhabit burrows in moist soil. The reduced limbs of caecilians are adaptations to a burrowing lifestyle. A few South American caecilians have adapted to freshwater ponds and streams.

Compared to fishes, amphibians exhibit evolutionary changes that enabled them to inhabit the land for at least part of their life cycles. Further evolutionary adaptations in vertebrates are evident in "reptiles," birds, and mammals—vertebrates that filled diverse land habitats. These vertebrate groups quickly became the dominant large animals on land and continue their success today. Their story is the subject of the next chapter.

Online Activity 25.4

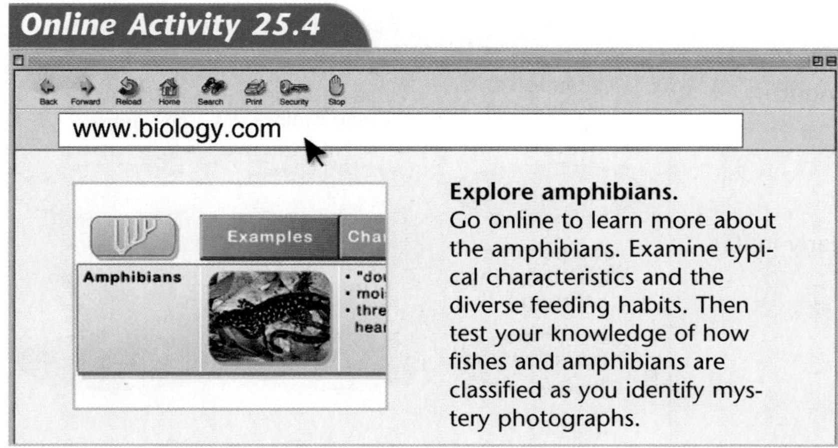

Explore amphibians.
Go online to learn more about the amphibians. Examine typical characteristics and the diverse feeding habits. Then test your knowledge of how fishes and amphibians are classified as you identify mystery photographs.

Concept Check 25.4

1. Describe how tetrapods may have evolved from fish-like ancestors.
2. Explain why frogs are described as having a double lifestyle.
3. Describe the salamander's habitat.
4. Describe how caecilians are adapted to their environment.

Multiple Choice

Choose the letter of the best answer.

1. In addition to a notochord, which of the following is also a characteristic of all chordate embryos?
   a. vertebrae
   b. exoskeleton
   c. pharyngeal slits
   d. hinged jaw

2. All of the following are tetrapods *except*
   a. mammals. b. fishes.
   c. reptiles. d. amphibians.

3. Which of the following is an example of an invertebrate chordate?
   a. lancelet b. shark
   c. salamander d. toad

4. The function of the operculum in fishes is
   a. to pump water through gills.
   b. to maneuver while swimming.
   c. to control buoyancy.
   d. to sense vibrations in the water.

5. The type of fishes thought to be most closely related to the ancestors of amphibians are
   a. lampreys.
   b. ray-finned fishes.
   c. lungfishes.
   d. rays.

6. Based on fossil evidence, the first vertebrates that lived on land were
   a. lobe-finned fishes.
   b. amphibians.
   c. cartilaginous fishes.
   d. ray-finned fishes.

7. A vertebrate with a three-chambered heart, external eardrums, strong hind legs, and smooth, moist skin is most likely a
   a. shark. b. lungfish.
   c. caecilian. d. frog.

8. Which animal breathes through gills early in its life and through lungs as an adult?
   a. ray-finned fish
   b. shark
   c. frog
   d. lamprey

Short Answer

9. Describe the four distinguishing features of all chordate embryos.

10. Give one example of a vertebrate without a hinged jaw, and one example of a vertebrate with a hinged jaw.

11. Identify general characteristics of most vertebrates.

12. Explain the differences between a bony and a cartilaginous skeleton.

13. Describe the function of a swim bladder.

14. Describe the distinguishing physical characteristics of ray-finned fishes.

15. Describe the body structure and habitat of the earliest tetrapods.

16. Explain why amphibians must lay their eggs in a moist environment.

17. Summarize the life cycle of a typical frog.

Visualizing Concepts

18. On a separate sheet of paper, copy and complete the concept map below summarizing information about amphibians.

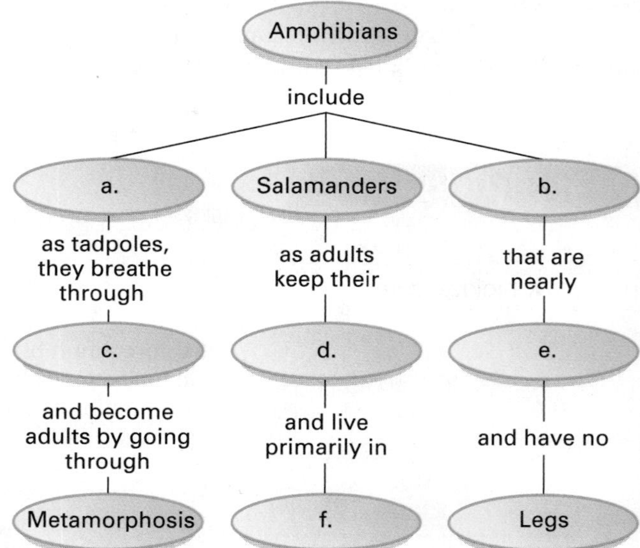

Analyzing Information

19. Analyzing Diagrams The diagram below illustrates the circulatory system of fishes.

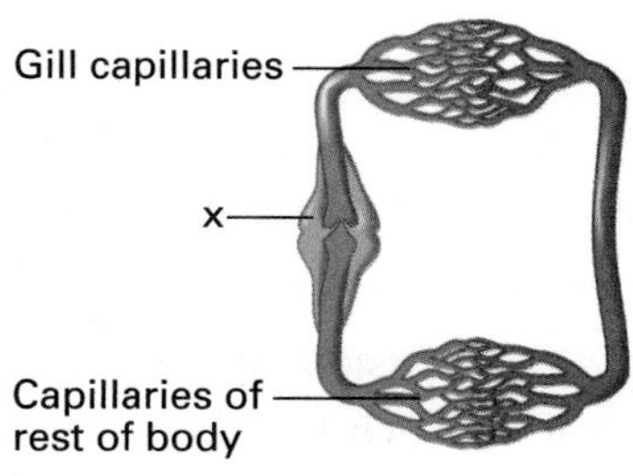

a. Describe the direction of blood flow starting at the gill capillaries.
b. What is the structure labeled *x*? What is this structure's function?
c. Is this an example of an open or closed circulatory system? Explain.

20. Analyzing Diagrams The diagram below illustrates the anatomy of a bony fish.

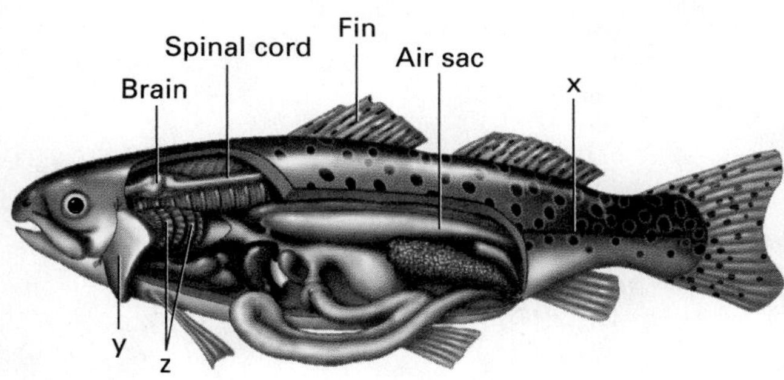

a. What does structure *x* enable the fish to do? Explain.
b. How does the air sac function in fishes?
c. Identify two structures that enable the fish to move in water.
d. How does structure *y* function with the structures labeled *z*?

Critical Thinking

21. Relating Cause and Effect A certain pond is found to contain bacteria that cause gill disease. Explain how over time these bacteria might affect the population of frogs that live near the pond.

22. Comparing and Contrasting Compare the single-circuit circulatory system of fishes with the double-circuit system of amphibians.

23. Making Generalizations In what ways are most amphibians adapted to a terrestrial life? In what ways are they adapted to an aquatic life?

24. Comparing and Contrasting In what ways are humans similar to lancelets? What are some common characteristics they share?

25. What's Wrong With These Statements? *Briefly explain why each statement is inaccurate or misleading.*
a. All chordates have a backbone.
b. A hinged jaw is characteristic of all vertebrates.
c. All amphibians spend part of their life cycle in water.
d. Most vertebrates are tetrapods.
e. Fishes do not need oxygen.

Performance Assessment

Biology Research Project Some people are very concerned about shark attacks on humans. Based on what you have learned about sharks, write a statement about whether you think sharks pose a significant danger to people. Then use your library or the Internet to research the facts about shark attacks on humans over a 20-year period. Based on your research, revise your conclusion.

Online Assessment/Test Preparation

- **Chapter 25 Assessment**
  Check your understanding of the chapter concepts.
- **Standardized Test Preparation**
  Practice test-taking skills you need to succeed.

Vertebrates: Reptiles, Birds, and Mammals

Adaptation to life on land that began with amphibians continued with the evolution of reptiles, birds, and mammals. The feathered birds and the hairy mammals such as this lionness and her cubs are the most visible and diverse land-dwelling vertebrates today. But the scaly reptiles had a much longer reign. A hundred million years ago, reptiles, including giant dinosaurs, were the most diverse and widespread tetrapods on land. In fact, ancient reptiles included the ancestors of birds and mammals, which still show signs of their reptilian roots. Before you begin tracing this history, go online to the *WebQuest* to explore the ancient vertebrates trapped in the La Brea tar pits in California.

Key Concepts

Concept 26.1 Reptiles were the first amniotes.

Concept 26.2 Birds began as feathered reptiles.

Concept 26.3 Mammals diversified during the Cenozoic Era.

Concept 26.4 Humans have a relatively short history.

Assessment Chapter 26 Review

What's Online

www.biology.com

WebQuest
TarPitQuest

Online Activity 26.1
Explore reptiles.

History of Science
Bird Evolution

Lab 26 Online Companion
Suitcases for Life on Land

Online Activity 26.2
Explore birds.

Online Activity 26.3
Explore mammals.

Closer Look
Mammal Diversity

Online Activity 26.4
Explore a human time line.

Chapter 26 Assessment

CONCEPT 26.1 Reptiles were the first amniotes.

OBJECTIVES

- Identify three main characteristics of amniotes.
- Describe the general characteristics of reptiles.
- Describe the reptiles that dominated the Mesozoic Era.
- Name and describe three groups of modern reptiles.

KEY TERMS

- amniote
- amniotic egg
- scale
- ectotherm
- endotherm

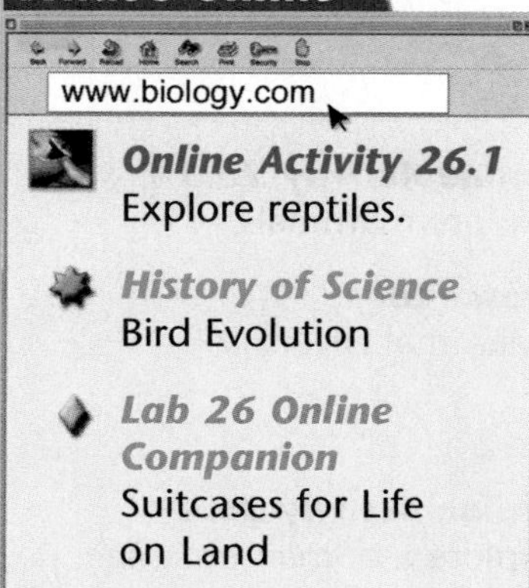

As you have read, most amphibians spend part of their life cycles in aquatic habitats, at least to lay their eggs. In contrast, the tetrapods known as amniotes—reptiles, birds, and mammals—are more completely adapted to living on land. Able to complete their life cycles without returning to water, amniotes diversified throughout land ecosystems, including the driest deserts.

General Characteristics of Amniotes

Reptiles, birds, and mammals together make up a vertebrate clade (evolutionary branch) called the **amniotes.** Three key adaptations for life on land distinguish amniotes from most amphibians and fishes: the amniotic egg, internal fertilization, and water-tight skin.

Amniotic Egg The adaptation for which the clade is named is the **amniotic egg,** a waterproof egg with a shell. The amniotic egg is named for one particular membrane—the amnion—formed by the developing embryo. The amnion protects the embryo from drying out and surrounds a fluid-filled cavity that cushions it (Figure 26-1). The other membranes formed during development of the embryo function in gas exchange, waste removal, and supplying nutrients. (Note that eggs also contain other membranes, such as the "skins" you'll observe in a chicken egg in Investigative Lab 26, that form before the egg is fertilized.)

The amniotic egg contrasts with the amphibian egg, which lacks a shell and amnion and is not waterproof. Amphibians such as frogs must deposit their eggs in a pond or other wet place. The amniotic egg, with its self-contained "pond," makes it possible for the embryo to develop within an egg laid on land.

Internal Fertilization In internal fertilization, the male deposits sperm within the female's body. The sperm then swim inside the reproductive tube toward the egg. This contrasts with external fertilization, which occurs in most fishes and amphibians. In external fertilization a large quantity of eggs is deposited in a watery environment. The sperm are then deposited nearby into the water, and they swim to the eggs. External fertilization would not work on land.

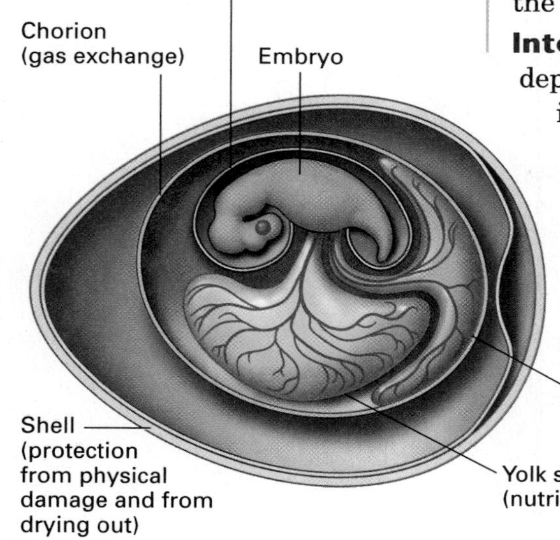

Figure 26-1 This diagram shows a cross section of a generalized amniotic egg. The shell encloses the embryo and four specialized membranes that form during the embryo's development.

Water-tight Skin Amniotes have water-tight skin enriched with a waterproofing protein called keratin. The "keratinized" skin prevents dehydration. Keratin is found in different structures in various amniotes. Reptile skin has **scales,** hard overlapping structures made of keratin. Birds have feathers made of keratin. In mammals, hair, nails, and horns are made of keratin. With water-tight skin, amniotes can maintain an internal environment that is mostly water even if the external environment is dry.

General Characteristics of Reptiles

Among amniotes, reptiles (traditionally called class Reptilia) are most easily recognized by their scaly skin (Figure 26-2). Turtles, lizards, snakes, crocodiles, and alligators are reptiles.

Most reptiles lay eggs, although a few species give birth to live young. The eggshells of lizards and most snakes are leathery and flexible. The eggshells of other reptiles, such as turtles and crocodiles, are hard and thin.

As you have read, reptiles have water-tight skin covered in scales. Consequently, reptiles cannot exchange gases across their skin, as amphibians do. Instead, most reptiles rely entirely on lungs for breathing. Also, since a scaly skin cannot expand as an animal grows, many reptiles molt. Molting is the process in which an animal sheds its skin as it grows. The shed skin is replaced by a new, larger skin.

Have you ever heard reptiles described as "cold blooded"? This common saying is somewhat inaccurate. Most reptiles do not actually have cold blood most of the time. However, reptiles do regulate their body temperatures differently than mammals do. The main source of body heat for most reptiles is their environment. Animals whose main source of body heat is the external environment are called **ectotherms.** Ectotherms do generate some metabolic heat, but they rely mainly on environmental heat. In contrast, most body heat for **endotherms,** such as birds and mammals, is generated from cell metabolism. However, most endotherms also use the environment to help regulate body temperature. For example, on a cool day a cat might nap in the sun instead of in the shade. As ectotherms, reptiles are even more dependent on such behavior to regulate their temperature. A desert lizard, for example, may move back and forth between sun and shade, maintaining a relatively stable, warm body temperature.

Figure 26-2 Most reptiles lay eggs and have water-tight skin covered with scales. **a.** This turtle is hatching from its hard, thin shell. **b.** The scales of the eyelash viper are rough and sharp.

Reptiles of the Mesozoic Era

▲ **Figure 26-3** An artist drew this duck-billed dinosaur based on fossil evidence from 80 million years ago. Fossilized nests that contain eggs and baby dinosaurs provide evidence that these dinosaurs cared for their young. In fact, the scientific name of this dinosaur, *Maiasaura,* means "good mother lizard."

The oldest reptile fossils have been found in rocks from the Carboniferous period (about 300 million years ago). Reptiles diversified greatly 55 million years later, in the Mesozoic Era. During that time, dinosaurs occupied many terrestrial habitats and ecological roles. Aquatic reptiles, such as plesiosaurs and ichthyosaurs, cruised the seas. Flying pterosaurs roamed the skies. In fact, reptiles were so widespread, numerous, and diverse that the Mesozoic Era is sometimes called the "Age of Reptiles."

For 150 million years, dinosaurs were the most diverse group of reptiles (Figure 26-3). Dinosaurs were mostly land-dwellers that walked upright on their hind legs. They ranged in size from as small as a hamster to larger than a whale. Some dinosaurs were the largest animals ever to inhabit land. Most dinosaurs ate plants. However, there were also many carnivores, including species that chased prey by running on their hind legs. There is evidence that some predators hunted in packs and attacked prey larger than themselves.

New discoveries are constantly changing how biologists think of dinosaurs. For example, dinosaurs used to be thought of as slow, sluggish creatures. However, there is increasing evidence that many dinosaurs were quick and agile. Most highly active animals living today, such as birds and mammals, are endotherms. If some dinosaurs were quick and active, were they also endothermic? Dinosaurs were very diverse with many different body forms. They may have had a number of different body temperature adaptations—perhaps including some that are no longer present among reptiles today. It is possible that at least one group of dinosaurs was endothermic. That group could have included the ancestor of birds.

The dominance of dinosaurs came to a relatively sudden end 65 million years ago. In Chapter 15, you read that scientists have found evidence of a collision between a large asteroid and Earth that may have contributed to the extinction of dinosaurs and many other forms of life. The fossil record also indicates that Earth's climate became cooler at the end of the Mesozoic Era. If most dinosaurs were ectothermic, the environment may have become too cold too quickly. This, as well as other possible changes, may have contributed to the mass extinction of dinosaurs.

History of Science

Back Forward Reload Home Search Print Security Stop

www.biology.com

Bird Evolution

Scientists often collaborate on a common goal during their research, but they may not always agree. Discussion and debate is essential to the process, and scientific debate can open doors to new interpretations and hypotheses. Go online to investigate the role such debates have played in developing current ideas about the origin of birds.

Diversity of Living Reptiles

There are about 6,500 known species of vertebrates traditionally referred to as reptiles. Three of the major orders of reptiles are turtles; lizards and snakes; and crocodiles and alligators (the crocodilians). In some classification schemes these orders are elevated to classes.

Turtles Modern turtles (order Testudines) seem to be very much like fossil turtles, indicating that turtles have changed little since their origin in the Mesozoic Era. The most familiar physical characteristic of turtles is a large shell of bony plates covered by scales (Figure 26-4). The shell provides protection from predators. Not all turtle shells are hard, however. The shells of some aquatic turtles are soft and leathery. Another unusual feature of turtles is a jaw with horny ridges instead of teeth.

Turtles range in size from over 3 meters long and over 600 kilograms to under 12 centimeters and less than 1 kilogram. Many turtles are terrestrial (these are also called *tortoises*), while other turtles live in freshwater or marine environments. Some turtles, like the terrestrial Galápagos tortoises, eat mainly plants. Other turtles, such as the aquatic soft-shelled turtles, are mostly carnivores that eat fishes and invertebrates.

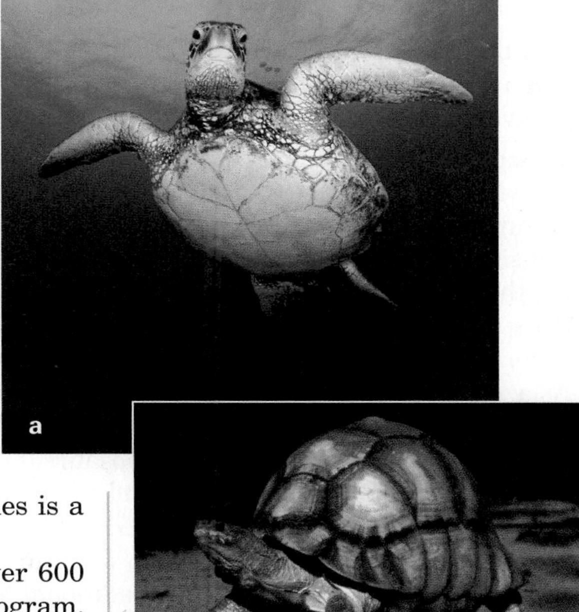

▲ **Figure 26-4** Turtles are shelled reptiles. **a.** Aquatic turtles, such as this green sea turtle, generally have reduced claws and webbed feet that function in swimming. **b.** This eastern box turtle is terrestrial, although it prefers moist habitats.

Lizards and Snakes Lizards and snakes (order Squamata) are closely related. Many lizards, like the thorny devil in Figure 26-5, may look fierce and resemble your mental image of a dinosaur in miniature. However, fossil and DNA evidence indicate that lizards and snakes are not as closely related to the dinosaurs as are crocodilians.

The physical characteristics of most lizards include four legs, a tail, and scaly skin. The legs project outward from the body, and each foot has five toes. Lizards are ectotherms, and most species live in warm habitats. Insects make up the largest part of smaller lizards' diet, but a larger lizard such as a Komodo dragon can devour mammals the size of young deer. The large lizards called iguanas, including the green iguana that peers from this book's cover, are mostly plant eaters.

Snakes are legless reptiles with long, narrow bodies. As ectotherms, they mostly live in warm habitats. All snakes are carnivores—they eat other animals. As predators, snakes have a

◀ **Figure 26-5** The spiny skin of an Australian thorny devil lizard can make it look fierce, an adaptation that probably discourages predators. This lizard uses its quick, sticky tongue to capture and eat ants. A thorny devil can eat 45 ants per minute and up to 2000 ants in one meal.

number of adaptations that aid them in hunting and eating prey (Figure 26-6). Some snake species are poisonous. They have grooved or hollow fangs that deliver poison to their prey.

Crocodiles and Alligators Together called the "crocodilians," crocodiles and alligators (order Crocodilia) are among the largest living reptiles (Figure 26-7). Some crocodiles grow longer than a full-sized car. Crocodilians spend most of their time in water breathing through turned-up nostrils. They can lie mostly hidden beneath the surface waiting to ambush prey that may approach the water's edge. Crocodiles and alligators are located in warm areas of Africa, Asia, Australia, and North and South America.

Extensive fossil evidence points to crocodiles as the living reptiles most closely related to dinosaurs. Though traditionally grouped with the lizards, snakes, and turtles as "reptiles," crocodilians are actually more closely related to birds. In fact, crocodilians have a four-chambered heart—also a feature of birds as you will read in the next section. Of all the traditional "reptiles," crocodilians have the most highly developed brain. This more complex brain probably contributes to some of the complex social behavior observed in crocodilians. They conduct courting rituals, build nests, and care for their young. These behaviors are also common in birds, the closest living relatives of crocodilians.

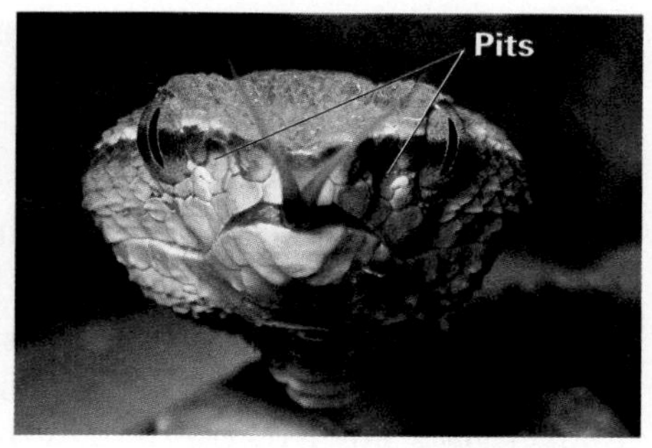

▲ **Figure 26-6** Some reptiles have unique sense organs. This Wagler's viper has heat-sensing "pits" on its head. Snakes flick their tongues as a method of sampling the air for odors. Both of these senses help the viper locate prey.

▲ **Figure 26-7** Alligators (left) have rounded snouts and generally live in fresh water. In the United States, they are found in swamps and waterways from North Carolina to the Florida Keys. Crocodiles (right) have pointed snouts and salt-secreting glands on their tongues. These glands are adaptations to living in salt water areas. In the United States, crocodiles only live in southernmost Florida.

Online Activity 26.1

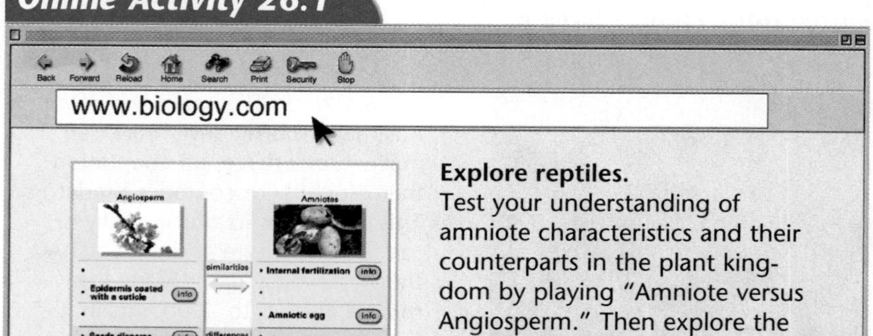

Explore reptiles.
Test your understanding of amniote characteristics and their counterparts in the plant kingdom by playing "Amniote versus Angiosperm." Then explore the diversity of reptiles as you delve into an interactive diversity chart.

Concept Check 26.1

1. Explain the evolutionary significance of the amniotic egg, water-tight skin, and internal fertilization.
2. How does the mechanism of temperature regulation distinguish reptiles from other amniotes?
3. Which terrestrial vertebrates dominated the Mesozoic Era?
4. List the three main groups of living reptiles.

Suitcases for Life on Land

Discovering the Adaptations of a Bird Egg

Question What are the structures in a bird egg that support the growth and development of an embryo?

Lab Overview In this investigation you will take apart an unfertilized chicken egg. You will locate and observe the many structures that support the growth and development of the chick, and examine certain structures with a microscope.

Preparing for the Lab To help you prepare for the investigation, go to the *Lab 26 Online Companion.* ····➔ See how a chicken egg develops and learn the functions of the egg yolk, albumen (egg white), shell, and other structures. Prepare for the lab procedure by previewing the steps you will take.

Completing the Lab Use your Laboratory Manual or lab page printouts from the *Lab 26 Online Companion* to do the investigation and draw conclusions from the observations you made.
CAUTION: *Be sure to follow your teacher's instructions and all safety guidelines in the investigation.*

Lab 26 Online Companion

Back
Forward
Reload
Home
Search
Print
Security
Stop
www.biology.com
To find out how the structures of a chicken egg develop, click on the hen below.

CONCEPT 26.2

Birds began as feathered reptiles.

OBJECTIVES

- List some general characteristics of birds.
- Describe the most widely accepted hypothesis of the origin of birds.
- Describe various bird adaptations.

KEY TERMS

- feather
- gizzard
- crop

What's Online

Molecular and fossil evidence has convinced many biologists that birds are reptiles. This evidence indicates that dinosaurs, crocodilians, and birds are more closely related to each other than any one of them is to turtles and lizards. Other biologists, however, prefer the traditional taxonomy that places birds in a separate class (class Aves).

General Characteristics of Birds

Birds are endothermic amniotes with specialized adaptations for flight. These adaptations include a specialized wing shape that produces lift for flight; feathers, which function in both flight and endothermy; and numerous weight-reducing features.

Bird wings are shaped like airfoils (like airplane wings). The top surface of the wing is curved in a way that creates lift as air moves past the wing (Figure 26-8). The shape and arrangement of the feathers form the wing into an airfoil. **Feathers** are modified scales that are made of keratin. Feathers may have first evolved as an adaptation that insulated the animal and helped conserve heat. In modern birds, feathers still provide insulation and contribute to birds being endotherms.

Birds have a system of branching air sacs that function with their lungs in respiration. The air-sac system helps supply the high levels of oxygen that support a high rate of metabolism. This provides the energy necessary for the hard-working flight muscles. This high metabolic activity also provides heat that contributes to endothermy. Another advantage of the air-sac system is a reduction of the overall density of the bird—a weight-reducing adaptation for flight.

Many other parts of a bird's anatomy are also modified in some way that reduces weight. The bones have a honeycombed structure that makes them strong but light (see Figure 1-11b on page 13). For example, the frigate bird found along coastlines in warm climates has a wingspan of about 2 meters, but its whole skeleton weighs only about 100 grams. Another adaptation that reduces weight in birds is the absence of some internal organs found in other vertebrates. Female birds, for instance, have only one ovary instead of a pair. Also, birds are toothless, an adaptation that reduces the weight of the head. Instead, birds have a

▼ **Figure 26-8** Like most birds, the frigate bird has airfoil-shaped wings. This male's red throat pouch becomes inflated when he is courting a female.

Airfoil

Lift

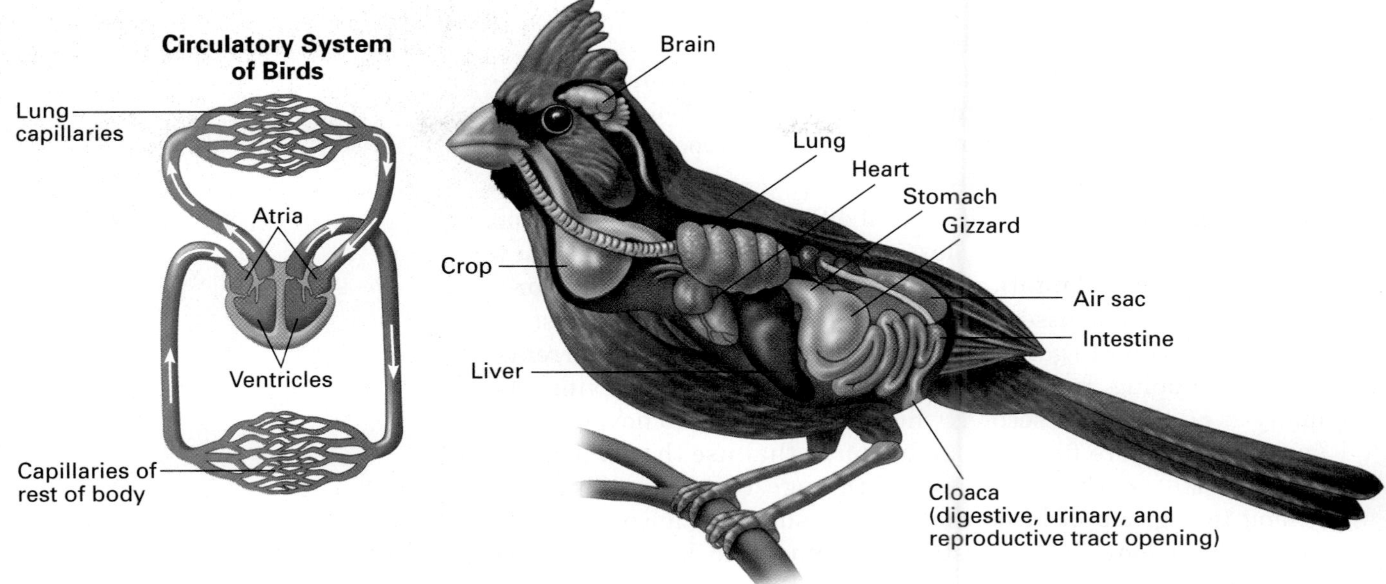

▲ **Figure 26-9** The internal structures of birds include the crop, gizzard, air sacs, and four-chambered heart with two completely separate circuits of blood flow.

hard beak and a **gizzard**—a muscular organ, often containing small stones, that grinds seeds and other food. The gizzard is a feature that birds share with crocodiles and alligators. Some dinosaurs also had gizzards. Most birds also have a **crop,** a sac-like organ used for temporarily storing food (Figure 26-9).

Birds have circulatory systems that are very efficient in delivering oxygen to cells. Like amphibians and reptiles, birds have two pathways of blood flow: one from the heart to the lungs and back, and the other from the heart to the rest of the body and back. But amphibians and most reptiles have three-chambered hearts. In these animals, oxygen-rich and oxygen-depleted blood mix in a heart chamber called a ventricle. In contrast, birds have a four-chambered heart with two separate ventricles. This keeps oxygen-rich blood from the lungs separate from the oxygen-depleted blood that passes through the heart. By improving the efficiency of delivering oxygen-rich blood to cells, the four-chambered heart is an adaptation for an active, endothermic lifestyle.

The Origin of Birds

Based on fossils, most paleontologists agree that the ancestor of birds was a type of small, feathered dinosaur. Recent fossil discoveries in China support this hypothesis of a close relationship between dinosaurs and birds. They show dinosaurs from more than 100 million years ago that are covered from tail to beak with structures that appear to be feathers.

The most famous bird fossil, *Archaeopteryx,* represents an animal that lived about 150 million years ago during the Mesozoic Era (Figure 26-10). Unlike modern birds, *Archaeopteryx* had clawed forelimbs, teeth, and a long tail with vertebrae—all reptilian characteristics. In fact, if the feathers had not been preserved in the fossil, *Archaeopteryx* probably would have been identified as a small dinosaur.

▲ **Figure 26-10** The ancestor of the feathered animal *Archaeopteryx* may also have given rise to the lineage that includes modern birds.

Diversity of Birds

There are about 9,000 species of birds living today, far outnumbering mammal species. Among those species of birds there is tremendous diversity of flying styles, beak and foot adaptations, and behavioral characteristics.

Flying Styles Birds exhibit several different styles of flying. For example, cardinals and finches rapidly change altitude as they fly. This is an adaptation that helps them avoid predators. Falcons and albatrosses are raptors (hunting birds) that soar, using their wings to gain altitude and then gliding on air currents without flapping. In contrast, hummingbirds flap their wings as many as 80 times per second, which enables them to hover in one spot. Penguins are flightless diving birds that use the same basic flight stroke as other birds to "fly" through the water. Chickens belong to a group of birds that can fly short distances, but are incapable of long flights. Ostriches, emus, and kiwis are birds that cannot fly at all.

Beak Adaptations Birds exhibit a great variety of beak shapes that reflect their various functions (Figure 26-11). Also called "bills," bird beaks are made of keratin and are tough but fairly lightweight. Bird nostrils, which function in breathing, are located in the beak. Birds do not use their beaks, which are toothless, for chewing. However, some species use their beaks to break apart fruit, seeds, nuts, and other food.

Figure 26-11 Bird beaks provide a clue to the food eaten by each species. **a.** The bald eagle and other raptors have hooked beaks ideal for tearing flesh. **b.** The toucan beak is long, but lightweight. It enables the toucan to pluck difficult-to-reach fruit off trees. **c.** The cardinal's cone-shaped beak is typical of seed-eating birds. The short, stout beak is well-suited to breaking seeds open.

Foot Structures Various birds use their feet for walking, perching on branches, wading, and paddling through water. Feet also function in grasping food, in defense, and in some courtship rituals. Most bird legs and feet are covered in scales. Each foot of most birds has four toes, although some birds, such as the ostrich, have only two toes. The arrangement of toes also varies from species to species (Figure 26-12 on the facing page). Aquatic birds have webbed feet with skin connecting the toes, an adaptation to their paddling lifestyle.

Figure 26-12 Form fits function in bird feet. Perching birds hold onto branches. Grasping birds cling to tree trunks. Raptors use their feet to seize prey. The webbed feet of aquatic birds help them swim.

Behavioral Adaptations Bird brains are relatively highly developed. Among vertebrates, the size of a bird brain compared to body size is second only to mammals. As a result, birds are capable of complex behavior, especially in elaborate courtship rituals, caring for their young, and communication.

Generally, male birds attract female mates through a combination of colorful plumage (feathers) and elaborate displays that include "dances." However, one group of birds in Australia and nearby islands builds a hut or platform of twigs called a bower (Figure 26-13a). These bowers are often decorated with colorful items. The male of one species of bower bird even uses a twig as a paintbrush and chewed berries as paint to paint the interior walls of its bower. The bower functions to attract females.

Another example of complex behavior is caring for offspring. This includes incubating the eggs, often by sitting on them for several weeks. In many species, both the male and female birds take turns incubating the eggs, keeping them warm enough for the embryo to develop inside (Figure 26-13b). In many species, when baby chicks are born, the male and female birds take turns foraging for food and bringing it back to the nest.

One of the most interesting behavioral characteristics is bird song. "Songs" are the main method by which birds communicate. The great diversity of songs have a variety of functions—to attract mates, defend territory, and send alarms about danger. Many humans, of course, enjoy hearing the variety of bird songs. More generally, "birdwatching," usually with the help of binoculars, is one of the most popular hobbies in the United States.

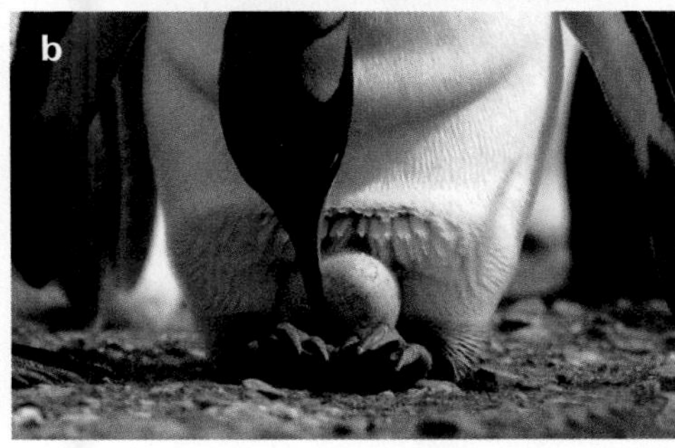

Figure 26-13 The complex social behaviors of many birds include courtship rituals and caring for young. **a.** Male bower birds build a courtship structure (a bower) and decorate it with colorful objects. **b.** Male and female king penguins take turns incubating their egg, balancing it on their feet.

Online Activity 26.2

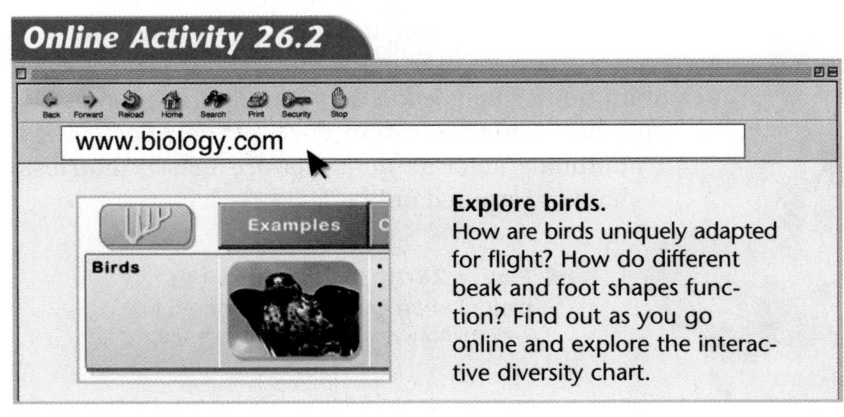

Explore birds.
How are birds uniquely adapted for flight? How do different beak and foot shapes function? Find out as you go online and explore the interactive diversity chart.

Concept Check 26.2

1. Identify some flight adaptations of birds.
2. What does fossil evidence indicate about the origin of birds?
3. Describe two behavioral adaptations of birds.

CONCEPT 26.3

Mammals diversified during the Cenozoic Era.

OBJECTIVES

- Describe the general characteristics of mammals.
- Explain the most widely accepted hypothesis for the origin of mammals.
- Describe the key characteristics of the three main groups of mammals.

KEY TERMS

- mammal
- monotreme
- marsupial
- placental mammal

What's Online

Online Activity 26.3
Explore mammals.

Closer Look
Mammal Diversity

Think of a wild animal or an animal in a zoo. Name a circus animal or the first animal that comes to mind when you think of a pet. In each of these cases, chances are your first thoughts are mammals. Many of the most familiar animals—deer, wolves, elephants, giraffes, tigers, dogs, and cats—are all mammals, and so are you.

Origin and General Characteristics of Mammals

The oldest fossils of mammals (class Mammalia) date back about 220 million years to the early Mesozoic Era. The fossil evidence supports the hypothesis that mammals evolved from mammal-like reptiles called therapsids. The early mammals co-existed with dinosaurs throughout the Age of Reptiles. During that time, there was a variety of mouse-sized, insect-eating mammals (Figure 26-14). The large eye sockets of the fossilized skulls suggest that these tiny mammals were nocturnal (active at night). This characteristic probably helped protect early mammals from carnivorous dinosaurs, which were mostly active during the day. About 65 million years ago, mammals diversified as they adapted to habitats and ecosystem roles that were vacated due to the extinction of dinosaurs.

Mammals are endothermic vertebrates that possess mammary glands and hair. Mammary glands are present in both male and female mammals. However, they do not fully develop in males. Adult female mammals produce milk in mammary glands, and offspring feed on this nutritious milk. Mammal hair, like bird feathers, is made of the protein keratin. Hair may have evolved initially as a sensory adaptation. Evidence of root-like structures in the fossils of some therapsids could indicate the presence of whiskers that functioned in the sense of touch. The main function of hair in modern mammals is to insulate the body and help maintain a warm, constant internal temperature. Some mammals have fur, a dense combination of long and short hairs. Other mammals only have hair on certain parts of their body. A few mammals such as dolphins are mostly hairless, having retained only a few bristles.

Figure 26-14 An artist drew this picture of an early mammal based on 145 million-year-old fossil evidence.

Internally, all mammals have lungs, even aquatic mammals such as whales and dolphins. All mammals also have a muscular diaphragm that separates the lungs and heart from the rest of the body cavity. The diaphragm aids in breathing. Like birds, mammals are endothermic and have a four-chambered heart with two separate circuits of blood flow. And like birds and reptiles, mammals reproduce sexually by internal fertilization. Most mammals give birth to young, but one group, about which you will read below, lays eggs.

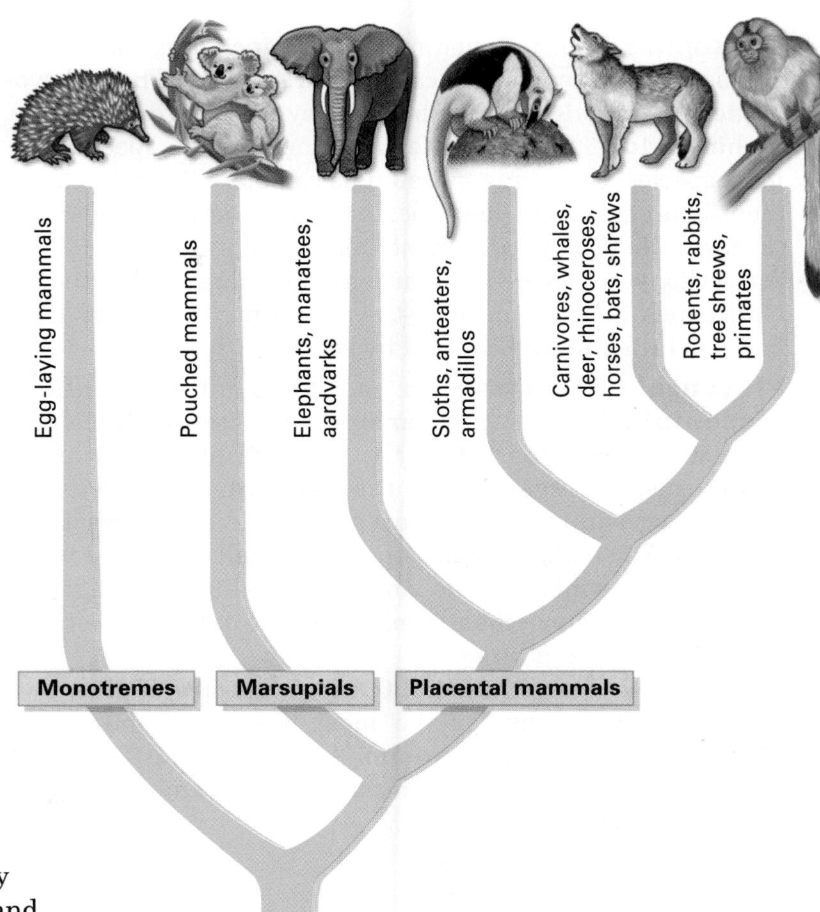

▲ **Figure 26-15** This hypothetical phylogenetic tree of modern mammals is based mainly on analysis of nucleic acid sequences in various species.

Diversity of Mammals

There are about 4,500 known species of mammals on Earth today. They are divided into three main groups: the monotremes, the marsupials, and placental mammals (Figure 26-15).

Monotremes Mammals that lay eggs are called **monotremes**. Today the only living monotremes are the platypuses and echidnas of Australia and nearby islands (Figure 26-16). These mammals are unique in their mixture of ancestral reptilian traits and mammalian characteristics. For example, the shoulders and forelimbs of monotremes are angled from the body in a way that is very similar to some reptiles. The eggs of monotremes have relatively soft shells, like those of many reptiles. Monotremes have an exit passage called the cloaca where the digestive, reproductive, and urinary systems all empty. You might recall that reptiles and birds also have cloacas. However, monotremes are classified as mammals because they have hair and the females produce milk.

The hypothesis that monotremes descended from an early branch in the evolution of mammals is supported by molecular evidence. Nucleic acid comparisons suggest that monotremes are the mammals most closely related to reptiles.

▶ **Figure 26-16** The duckbill platypus is a monotreme that inhabits freshwater streams in Australia. Electrosensors in its bill enable the platypus to locate electrical fields given off by its small prey.

Marsupials The "pouched mammals," including kangaroos, koalas, and opossums, are called **marsupials.** The embryos of these mammals are born before they are fully developed—within 12 to 16 days after fertilization in some species. In most species, the young marsupials complete their development in an external pouch, located on the mother's abdomen (Figure 26-17). While most marsupials are found in Australia, you may be familiar with one marsupial native to North and South America—the opossum. Opossums have hairless tails that are covered by scales.

Figure 26-17 Perhaps the best known marsupial is the Australian kangaroo. This female is carrying her baby (called a joey) in her pouch.

Placental Mammals In most mammals, called **placental mammals,** the embryo completes its development while protected within the mother's uterus. Inside the uterus, an organ called the placenta provides the embryo with nutrients and oxygen and removes waste products. The embryo is also bathed in fluid contained by a protective membrane, the amnion. The amnion encloses a fluid-filled compartment similar to that in the amniotic eggs of reptiles and birds.

There are more than 4,200 known species of placental mammals, by far the most diverse of the three main groups of mammals. Figure 26-18 highlights the variety of form and habitat among the placental mammals.

Figure 26-18 The photo gallery on these two pages shows representatives of a few of the many diverse orders of placental mammals.

▼ **Order Cetacea** Whales, dolphins, and porpoises are fish-shaped aquatic mammals with paddle-like forelimbs and no hind limbs. Cetaceans have little hair but have a thick layer of insulating blubber (fat). Bottlenose dolphins such as those shown below inhabit all coastal waters of the world except in polar regions. Dolphins feed on a variety of fishes and mollusks. Groups of dolphins, called pods, have been observed working together to surround schools of fish and herd them into a small circle for easier feeding.

▲ **Order Sirenia** The sea cows, or manatees, are aquatic herbivores with finlike forelimbs and no hind limbs. *Trichechus manatus* is an endangered species of manatee found in coastal waters from the Gulf of Mexico to the Carolinas.

▶ **Order Edentata** Sloths (such as the three-toed sloth shown here), anteaters, and armadillos belong to this group of mammals. Mostly insectivores (insect eaters) and herbivores, members of this order inhabit Central and South America and range northward to the south-central United States.

▲ **Order Rodentia** There are about 2,000 species of rodents, including squirrels, beavers, rats, porcupines, and mice. Most have chisel-like front teeth that continually grow and are ideally suited for gnawing. The capybara, shown above, is the largest species of rodent in the world, weighing as much as an adult human.

▶ **Order Carnivora** Dogs, wolves, cats, weasels, otters, seals, walruses, and bears are among the mammals in this order. Members of this group have sharp, pointed teeth for tearing and flattened teeth for chewing. The red panda is an endangered species that lives in the mountains of East Asia.

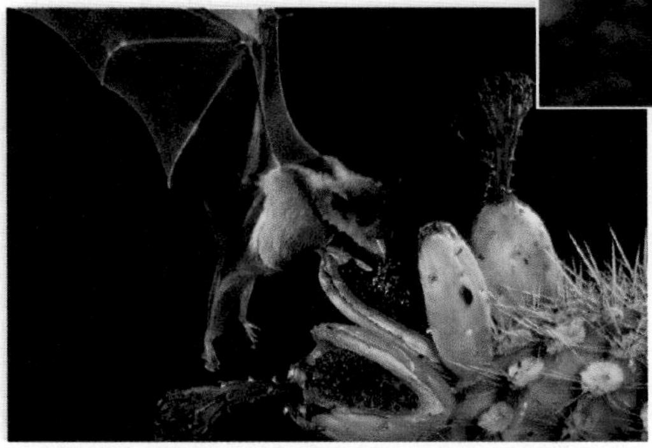

◀ **Order Chiroptera** Bats are the only mammals capable of true flight. Bats account for nearly 25 percent of all species of placental mammals and have diverse lifestyles. Some bats, such as the lesser long-nosed bat, shown here, feed on fruit and nectar. Other bats use sonar to locate insect prey. There are only three species of vampire bats, bats that eat blood. Their range extends from Mexico to South America, and they feed mostly on the blood of cattle and other livestock.

Online Activity 26.3

Explore mammals.
Why are marsupials classified as mammals? How is the placenta involved in reproduction? Go online to find out.

Closer Look **Mammal Diversity**
Learn more about the different orders of mammals.

Concept Check 26.3

1. List two unique characteristics of mammals.
2. How did the extinction of dinosaurs affect the evolution of mammals?
3. How are monotremes different from other mammals?

CONCEPT 26.4

Humans have a relatively short history.

OBJECTIVES
- Describe some general characteristics of primates.
- Describe two key evolutionary adaptations in the origin of humans.
- Explain two hypotheses for the origin of modern humans from *Homo erectus*.

KEY TERMS
- primate
- prehensile tail
- hominid
- bipedalism

What's Online

www.biology.com

Online Activity 26.4 Explore a human time line.

Fossils of humans and human ancestors provide a connection to the past. The fossil record indicates that modern humans have a relatively recent history that began in Africa. In only a short time, humans have become the most numerous and widespread large animal on Earth.

A Closer Look at Primates

The mammals called **primates** (order Primates) include lemurs, monkeys, apes, and humans. There are approximately 300 primate species living today. Fossil evidence supports the hypothesis that primates evolved from a small tree-dwelling, insect-eating ancestor about 65 million years ago. Recent analysis of molecular data suggests an even earlier origin 85 million years ago.

Primates, even those that now live on the ground, retain adaptations for living in the trees. For example, primates have flexible shoulder joints, which make it possible to swing from one branch to another. The hands of primates can hang onto branches and manipulate food. Many primate species have sensitive fingers with nails instead of claws. Primates have binocular vision, meaning that the two eyes are close together on the front of the face. The fields of vision of the two eyes overlap—like a pair of binoculars—enhancing depth perception, which is the ability to estimate how far away an object is. This is a valuable adaptation for animals that maneuver in trees. The excellent eye-hand coordination of primates is also important for maneuvering in the treetops.

Mammals devote more energy to caring for their young than do most other vertebrates. And primates are among the most attentive parents of all mammals. Most primates have single births and nurture their offspring for a long time.

Biologists divide living primates into two groups. One group includes lorises, galagos, and lemurs (Figure 26-19). Today lemurs are found on Madagascar and the Comoro Islands, off the east coast of Africa. Lorises live in Africa and southern Asia. With the exception of some lemurs, most primates of this group are nocturnal tree-dwellers. Many have claws rather than nails.

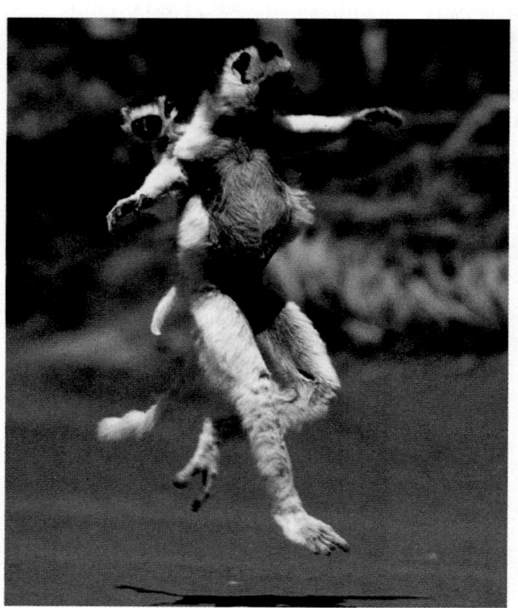

Figure 26-19 Lemurs are primarily arboreal (tree-living). However, this sifaka (a type of lemur) shows that this group of primates is capable of short periods of bipedal locomotion (walking-upright on two feet).

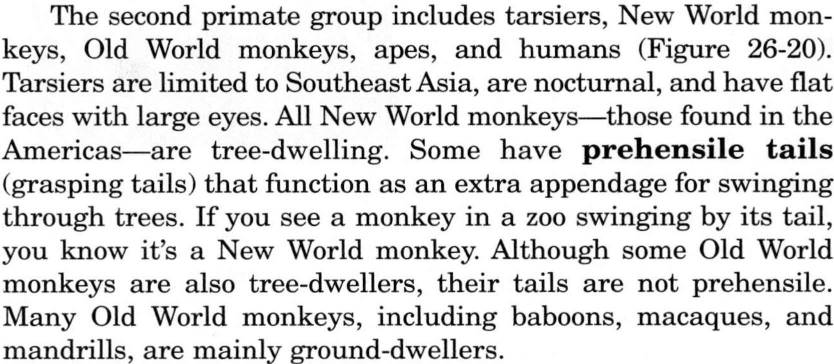

Figure 26-20 The second group of primates includes tarsiers, New World monkeys, Old World monkeys, and apes. **a.** Tarsiers are small nocturnal tree-dwellers that eat insects, birds, and small mammals. **b.** This woolly spider monkey is a New World monkey and lives in the forests of coastal Brazil. Notice its prehensile tail, used for grasping tree branches. **c.** This mandrill, an Old World monkey, lives mostly on the ground, but seeks the shelter of trees at night. **d.** Orangutans are apes that live in trees.

The second primate group includes tarsiers, New World monkeys, Old World monkeys, apes, and humans (Figure 26-20). Tarsiers are limited to Southeast Asia, are nocturnal, and have flat faces with large eyes. All New World monkeys—those found in the Americas—are tree-dwelling. Some have **prehensile tails** (grasping tails) that function as an extra appendage for swinging through trees. If you see a monkey in a zoo swinging by its tail, you know it's a New World monkey. Although some Old World monkeys are also tree-dwellers, their tails are not prehensile. Many Old World monkeys, including baboons, macaques, and mandrills, are mainly ground-dwellers.

The apes include gibbons, orangutans, gorillas, and chimpanzees. Modern apes live only in tropical regions of the Old World. Except for some gibbons, apes are generally larger than other primates. They have relatively long arms, short legs, and no tail. While all apes can move by swinging through trees, only gibbons and orangutans are mainly tree-dwellers. Gorillas and chimpanzees are highly social. Of all primates, chimpanzees are biologically the closest relatives of humans, differing in about 5 percent of their DNA sequences.

Early Hominids

Mammals that are more closely related to humans than to any other species are called **hominids** (family Hominidae). Only one species of hominid exists today—*Homo sapiens,* modern humans. However, a diversity of hominids lived in the past, including the probable ancestors of *H. sapiens.*

The earliest hominid may have lived as long as 6 or 7 million years ago. In the summer of 2001, researchers discovered fragments of a skull that old in the desert of northern Chad (a country in Africa). The fossil has certain facial features and teeth that are more hominid-like than ape-like. An important question about this species is whether it was the ancestor of the diverse hominids that appear about a million years later in the fossil record.

Two important developments in the evolution of hominids were upright posture (leading to two-legged walking) and enlargement of the brain.

Walking Upright Fossilized bones of a hominid species named *Australopithecus afarensis* provide the oldest evidence of upright posture and walking on two feet, called **bipedalism.** *A. afarensis* was walking upright at least 4 million years ago. One of the most complete fossil skeletons of *A. afarensis* dates to about 3.2 million years ago and was found in East Africa. Nicknamed "Lucy" by her discoverers, the individual was a female, only about 3 and a half feet tall, and had a head about the size of a softball (Figure 26-21).

All *Australopithecus* species were extinct by about 1.2 million years ago. Some of the later species overlapped in time with early species of the genus *Homo*. What is the evolutionary relationship of *Australopithecus* to *Homo*? Were the different *Australopithecus* species all evolutionary side branches? Or were some of them ancestors to later humans? Either way, these early hominids indicate that walking upright evolved millions of years before a greatly enlarged brain.

Enlarged Brain An enlarged brain relative to body size in hominids first appears in fossils from East Africa that are about 2.5 million years old. Scientists have found many skulls with braincase sizes that are between those of the most recent *Australopithecus* species and those of *H. sapiens*. Simple handmade stone tools are sometimes found with the larger-brained fossils of this species, which has been named *Homo habilis* ("handy man"). About 2 million years after first walking upright, the ancestors of modern humans were using their skilled hands and big brains to invent tools (Figure 26-22). These tools probably enhanced the ability to hunt, gather, and scavenge for food.

The first hominid species to appear as fossils on continents other than Africa was *Homo erectus*. *H. erectus* was taller than *H. habilis* and had a larger brain (Figure 26-23 on the facing page). During the 1.5 million years the species existed, the *H. erectus* brain increased to as large as 1,200 cubic centimeters, within the normal range for modern humans. Increased intelligence enabled humans to continue their success in Africa and also to survive in the colder climates of the north. One hypothesis about the spread of humans from Africa about 1.8 million years ago centers on the

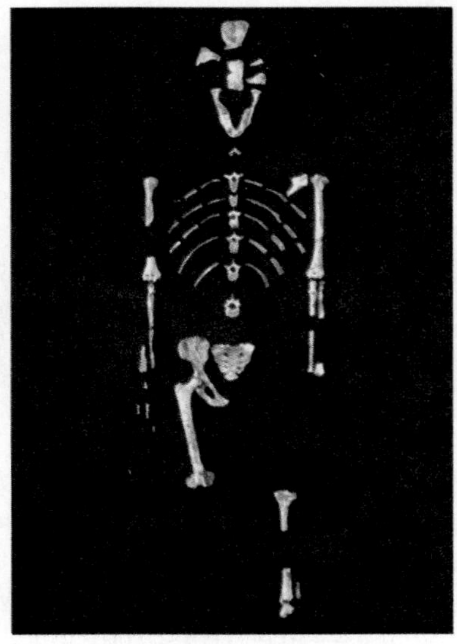

▲ **Figure 26-21** Researchers discovered these bones of "Lucy," a representative of the hominid species *A. afarensis*.

▼ **Figure 26-22** This time line is based on hominid fossils. Longer than previous hominid time lines, it includes a skull recently discovered in Chad (called *Sahelanthropus tchadensis*) as a hominid. Note that there were times in the past when two or more different hominid species lived at the same time.

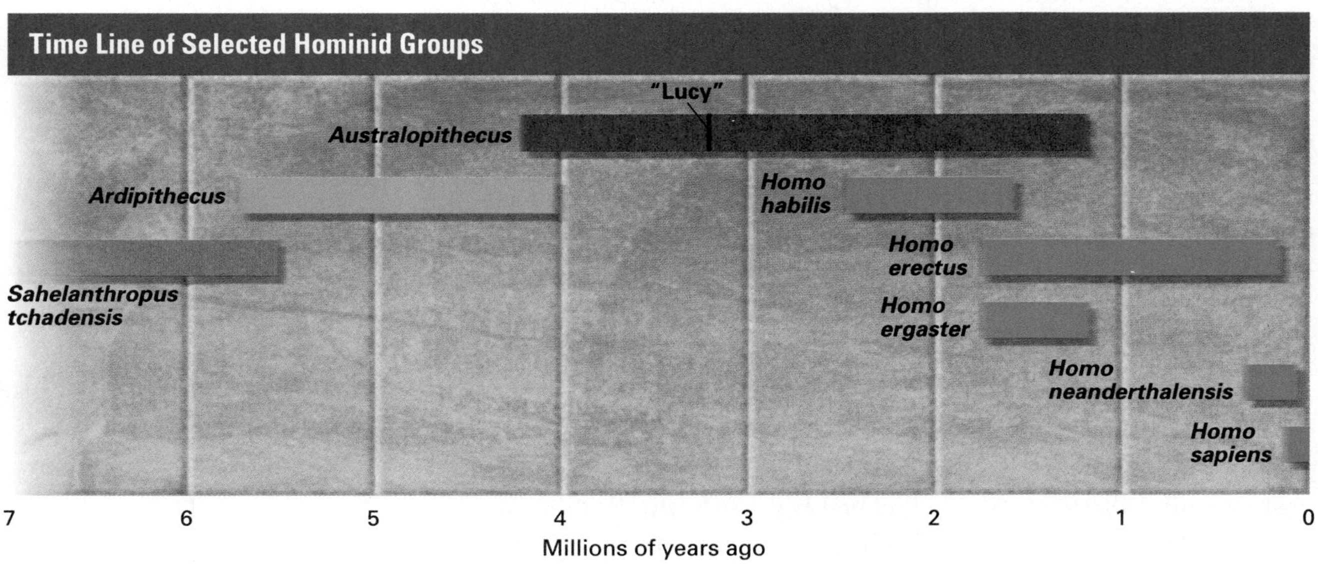

gradual change in diet to include a larger proportion of meat. In general, hunting for food requires living in a larger territory than does feeding on plants. However, in 2001 researchers found skulls that may challenge the view that *H. erectus* was the first hominid to leave Africa. In the country of Georgia, near Russia, hominid skulls have been found with relatively small brain cases. Some scientists have inferred from these finds that a *H. habilis*-like ancestor may have been the first hominid to leave Africa.

Figure 26-23 By comparing skulls like these, scientists can trace the evolution of the enlarged brain through hominid history.

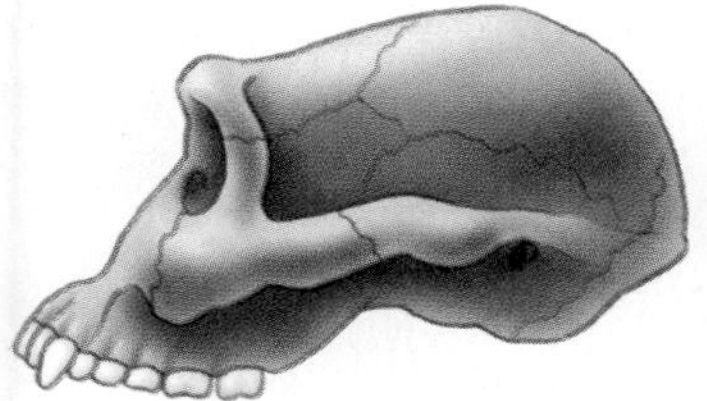

Australopithecus afarensis
(approx. 4.2 – 3.2 million years ago)

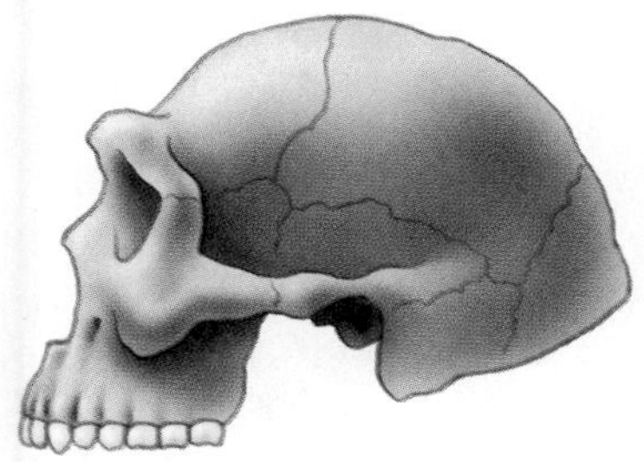

Homo erectus
(approx. 1.75 – 0.25 million years ago)

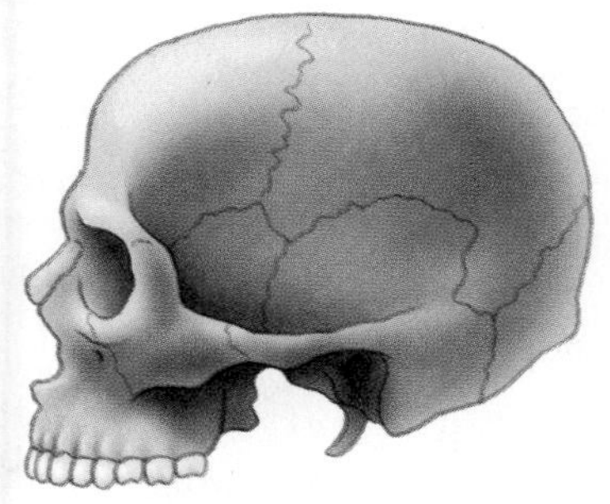

Homo sapiens
(approx. 100,000 years ago – today)

The Origin of Modern Humans

The fossil record suggests that *H. erectus* gave rise to diverse hominids in different regions. For example, the Neanderthals were *H. erectus* descendants who lived in what are now Europe, the Middle East, and Asia. The oldest fully-modern fossils of *H. sapiens*—skulls and other bones that look like those of today's humans—are about 100,000 years old and were discovered in Africa. Similar fossils almost as old have been discovered in Israel.

There are two hypotheses for the origin of fully-modern humans from earlier hominids. According to the "multiregional hypothesis," fully-modern humans evolved in several parts of the world from *Homo erectus* descendants that spread from Africa over 1.5 million years ago. Occasional inbreeding among regional populations could explain how *H. sapiens* evolved as a single species. But according to the second hypothesis, all regional descendants of *H. erectus,* outside of Africa, including the Neanderthals, became extinct. According to this view, fully-modern humans evolved from a population of *H. erectus* descendants that remained in Africa. These fully-modern humans spread out of Africa less than 100,000 years ago, "replacing" the then-extinct descendants of the much earlier *H. erectus* migration. Comparisons of DNA samples from human populations around the world today support a very recent split from a common ancestor. This molecular evidence favors the "replacement hypothesis."

When you review these two chapters on vertebrates, you can trace human ancestry back to the earliest animals with backbones. To help with your review, Figure 26-24 on the next two pages summarizes the body systems of the major vertebrate groups.

Online Activity 26.4

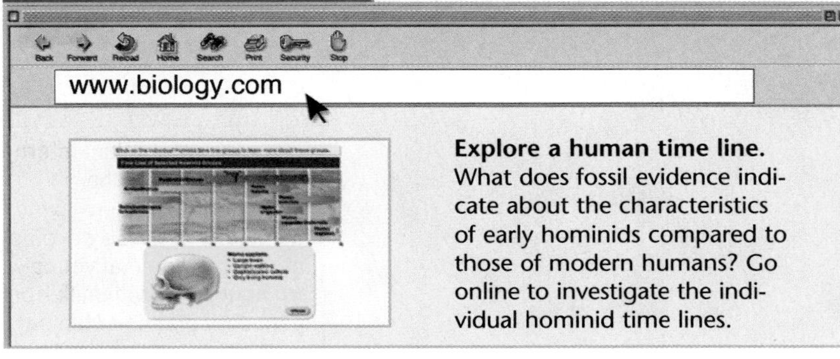

Explore a human time line. What does fossil evidence indicate about the characteristics of early hominids compared to those of modern humans? Go online to investigate the individual hominid time lines.

Concept Check 26.4

1. Identify examples of the two primate groups.
2. Who is "Lucy" and why is she important?
3. Explain the differences between the multiregional and replacement hypotheses.

Figure 26-24 Vertebrate Body Systems

Vertebrate Group	Skeleton/Movement	Nervous System	Reproduction
Fishes 	Skeleton includes a skull and a backbone composed of a series of segmented units called vertebrae. The skull forms a case for the brain, and the vertebrae enclose the nerve cord. Most vertebrates have a hinged jaw. Most vertebrates have paired limbs (legs, wings, or fins). Muscles attached by tendons to the bones move the jointed skeleton, enabling the animal to walk, fly, and/or swim.	The brain and spinal cord make up the central nervous system. Nerves transmitting impulses to and from the central nervous system make up the peripheral nervous system.	Sexual reproduction; mostly external fertilization. Embryo develops within non-waterproof egg in an aquatic environment. Usually thousands of offspring are produced. Parental care is not common.
Amphibians 			
Turtles 			Sexual reproduction; internal fertilization. Generally eggs develop externally and are protected within a leathery, waterproof shell. Some snakes retain eggs internally. There is little parental care.
Snakes and lizards 			
Crocodiles and alligators 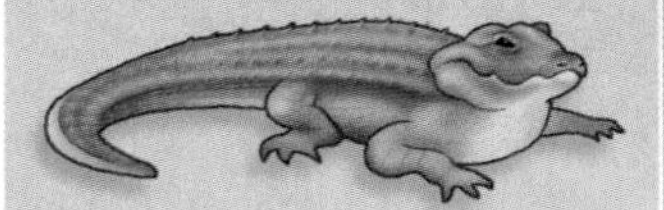			Sexual reproduction; internal fertilization. Eggs develop externally and are protected with a hard, waterproof shell. Parental care exists in most species.
Birds 			
Mammals 			Sexual reproduction; internal fertilization. With the exception of the egg-laying mammals, embryos develop internally. Mammal young are nourished with milk from mammary glands of female.

Digestion	Circulation	Water Balance and Waste Disposal	Gas Exchange
Complete digestive tract; organs include mouth, pharynx, esophagus, stomach, intestines, liver, pancreas, and anus.	Two-chambered heart with a single circuit of blood flow. Blood is pumped from heart ventricle to gill capillaries where the blood is oxygenated.	Kidneys maintain water balance and excrete nitrogen wastes. In freshwater fishes nitrogen wastes are excreted as ammonia; in marine fishes, as urea. Gills also aid in excretion and salt/water balance.	Gills; one group (lungfishes) also has lungs.
	Three-chambered heart, with two circuits of blood flow. Some mixing of oxygen-rich and oxygen-poor blood in the ventricle, but a ridge in ventricle maintains some separation.	Kidneys maintain water balance and excrete nitrogen-containing wastes. Adult amphibians and turtles excrete waste in the form of urea.	Gills as larva (some groups have external gills). Lungs and moist skin in most adults. In most amphibians the skin is important for gas exchange.
	Three-chambered heart with two circuits of blood flow. The ventricle is partially divided and less mixing of oxygen-rich and oxygen-depleted blood occurs than in amphibians.		Lungs and the cloacal lining (back end of the digestive tract).
		Kidneys maintain water balance and excrete nitrogen-containing wastes. Most reptiles and birds excrete waste in the form of uric acid.	Lungs
Complete digestive tract; organs include mouth, pharynx, esophagus, stomach, intestines, liver, pancreas, and anus; plus birds have crop for storage and gizzard for grinding food.	Four-chambered heart with two circuits of blood flow. A small opening between the ventricles allows some mixing of oxygen-rich and oxygen-depleted blood.		
	Four-chambered heart with two completely separated circuits of blood flow—one to the lungs and one to the rest of the body.		Lungs and air sacs
Complete digestive tract; organs include mouth, pharynx, esophagus, stomach, intestines, liver, pancreas, and anus.		Kidneys maintain water balance and excrete nitrogen-containing wastes in the form of urea.	Lungs

Multiple Choice

Choose the letter of the best answer.

1. Which structure is correctly paired with the group of animals in which it is found?
   a. diaphragm—reptiles
   b. air sacs—mammals
   c. four-chambered heart—amphibians
   d. eggs—monotremes

2. The dominant land vertebrates of the Mesozoic Era were
   a. birds.
   b. amphibians.
   c. reptiles.
   d. mammals.

3. Which of the following groups of animals has a four-chambered heart and two separate circuits of blood flow?
   a. fishes   b. birds
   c. amphibians   d. lizards

4. Which of the following groups of animals is ectothermic?
   a. reptiles
   b. mammals
   c. birds
   d. all of the above

5. Two characteristics of all mammals are
   a. hair and teeth.
   b. mammary glands and external fertilization.
   c. bipedalism and prehensile tails.
   d. mammary glands and hair.

6. Which of the following correctly lists probable ancestors of modern humans, from the oldest to the most recent?
   a. *Homo erectus, Australopithecus, Homo habilis*
   b. *Homo erectus, Homo habilis, Australopithecus*
   c. *Australopithecus, Homo erectus, Homo habilis*
   d. *Australopithecus, Homo habilis, Homo erectus*

7. Which hominid was probably the first to spread out of Africa?
   a. *Australopithecus*
   b. *Homo neanderthalensis*
   c. *Homo erectus*
   d. *Homo sapiens*

Short Answer

8. What is an amniotic egg? Describe an evolutionary advantage of an amniotic egg.
9. Describe the general characteristics of reptiles.
10. What characteristics do crocodiles and alligators share with other reptiles? What characteristics do they share with birds?
11. Describe one hypothesis that explains the sudden decline in diversity of dinosaurs.
12. Identify three flight adaptations in birds.
13. Use examples to explain how beak shape and the structure of a bird's feet provide clues to the bird's feeding habits and lifestyle.
14. Give two examples of complex behavior in birds.
15. Explain why mammals are considered amniotes even though most mammals do not produce an amniotic egg.
16. How did the extinction of dinosaurs influence the diversity of mammals?
17. Describe one key difference between New World and Old World monkeys.
18. Describe three adaptations of primates for living in the trees.
19. Describe two key characteristics of hominids.

Visualizing Concepts

20. On a separate sheet of paper copy and complete the table below that summarizes methods of reproduction in three groups of mammals.

Group	Example	Offspring complete embryonic development in
u.	v.	Egg
Marsupials	w.	x.
y.	Dolphin	z.

Analyzing Information

21. Analyzing Data Review the information about vertebrate body systems summaraized in Figure 26-24 on pages 578-579. Use the data in the table to answer the questions that follow.

a. Identify at least five similarities in body systems among all the groups listed in the table.

b. How do the egg shells of birds differ from those of most reptiles?

c. Describe how gas exchange in amphibians differs from gas exchange in the other groups.

d. List the groups that have circulatory systems in which oxygen-rich blood and oxygen-depleted blood do not mix. Explain how the structure of the heart in these animals relates to this characteristic.

e. Which group of organisms has organs in their digestive system that are not found in the other groups? What are these organs and what is the function of each?

22. Analyzing Diagrams Examine the diagram below of a typical amniotic egg.

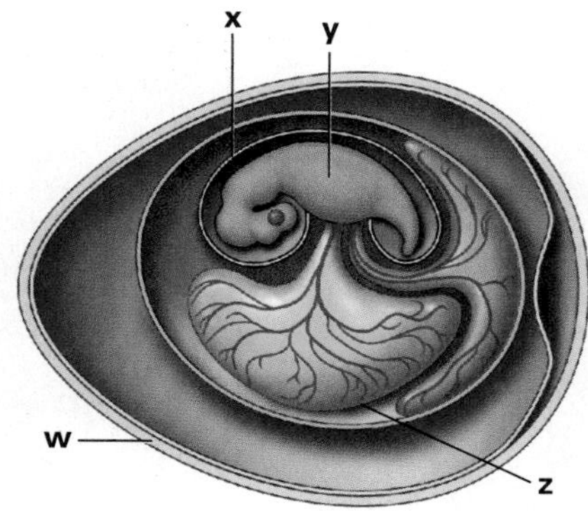

a. Which letter represents the embryo?

b. Which letters represent structures that help prevent the embryo from drying out? What are the names of these structures?

c. Which letter represents a structure that functions in supplying nutrients to the embryo? What is the name of this structure?

Critical Thinking

23. Comparing and Contrasting In what ways are the circulatory systems of lizards and birds similar? How are they different?

24. Making Generalizations An amphibian might produce hundreds or thousands of eggs that are fertilized externally. Some mammal species produce only one offspring at a time. How might the number of offspring produced be related to care the parents provide their offspring? Explain your answer.

25. Relating Cause and Effect Like all endotherms, humans sometimes take actions similar to those of ectotherms that help regulate their internal temperature. List two such actions that humans might take and explain how those actions would influence internal temperature.

26. What's Wrong With These Statements? *Briefly explain why each statement is inaccurate or misleading.*

a. Snakes and other reptiles are cold-blooded.

b. Mammals and birds are the only animals that provide care for their young.

c. Humans originated on Earth during the Age of Reptiles.

Performance Assessment

Writing Use an encyclopedia, your school library, or online resources to research *Homo habilis.* Then, write a one-page summary of what daily life might have been like for *H. habilis.* Include an estimate of when and where *H. habilis* might have lived.

Online Assessment/Test Preparation

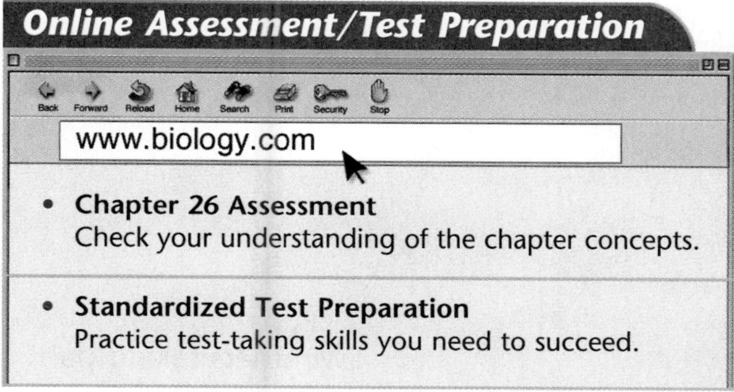

- **Chapter 26 Assessment**
  Check your understanding of the chapter concepts.
- **Standardized Test Preparation**
  Practice test-taking skills you need to succeed.

UNIT 8

Exploring Human Structure and Function

Chapters

27 The Human Organism: An Overview

28 The Nervous System

29 Nutrition and Digestion

30 The Circulatory and Respiratory Systems

31 The Body's Defense System

32 Regulation of the Internal Environment

33 Reproduction and Development

▶ Swimmers taking part in a triathlon

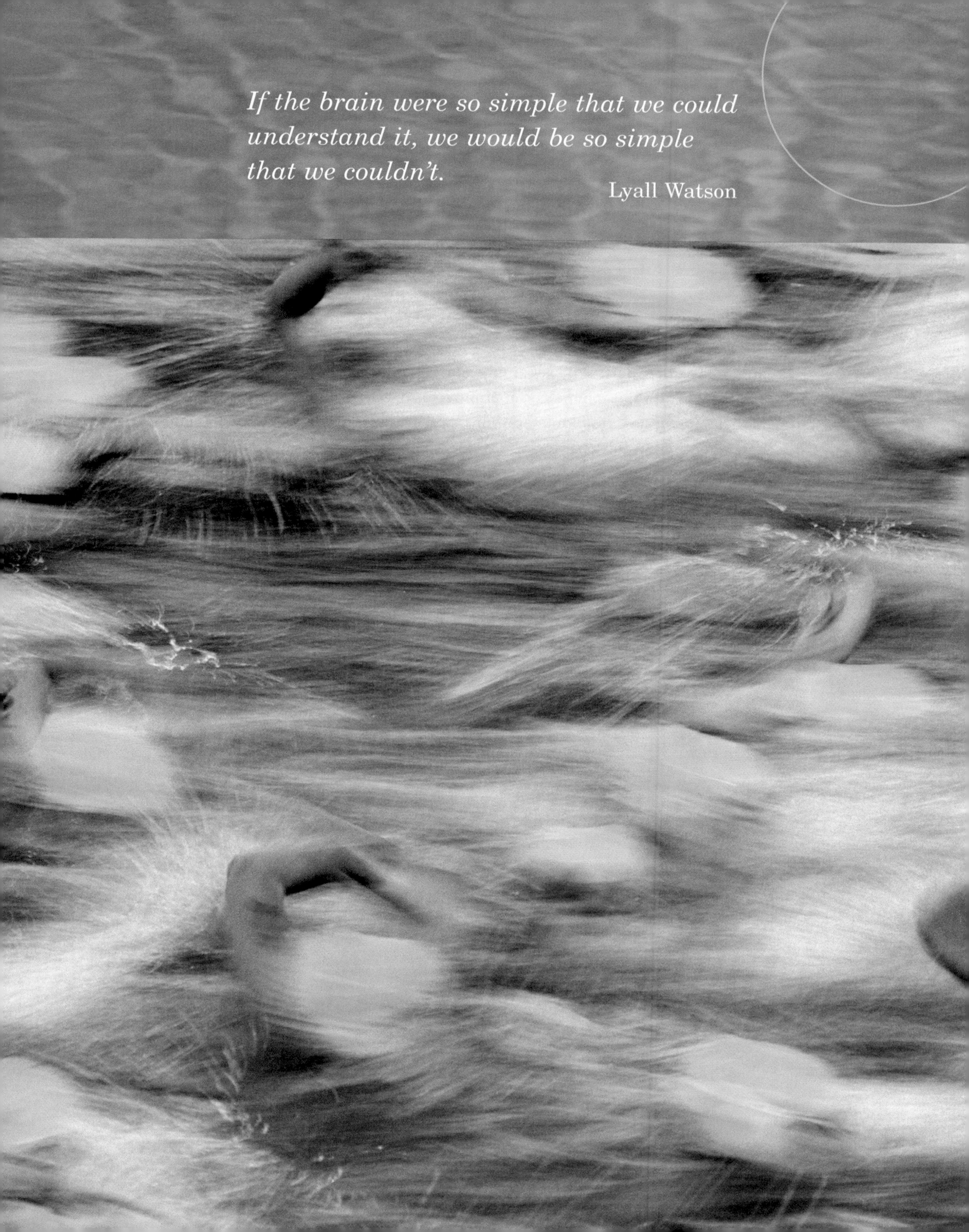

If the brain were so simple that we could understand it, we would be so simple that we couldn't.

Lyall Watson

The Human Organism: An Overview

The human body is a coordinated assembly of blood, nerves, skin, bones, muscles, and many other parts. This assembly allows humans to walk and run, talk and sing, read and think. Humans can also perform extraordinary feats: scaling the highest mountains, running marathons, and creating masterpieces of art, music, and invention. In this chapter, you will learn about how your body is constructed and how it works. But first, go online to the *WebQuest* to explore how one artist depicted human body systems many centuries ago.

Key Concepts

Concept 27.1 Structure fits function in the human body.

Concept 27.2 A tissue is a group of cells with the same structure and function.

Concept 27.3 The body regulates its internal environment.

Concept 27.4 The skeleton functions in support and movement.

Concept 27.5 Muscles move the skeleton by contracting.

Assessment Chapter 27 Review

What's Online

www.biology.com

WebQuest
DaVinciQuest

Online Activity 27.1
Match structure and function.

Online Activity 27.2
Locate and examine tissues.

Online Activity 27.3
Investigate a feedback loop.

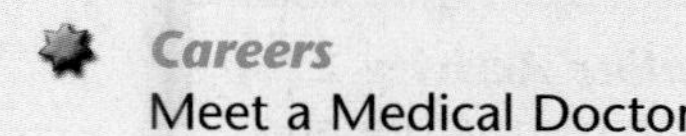

Careers
Meet a Medical Doctor

Online Activity 27.4
Build the skeleton.

Online Activity 27.5
Flex a muscle.

Lab 27 Online Companion
Every Flex Is Quite Complex

Chapter 27 Assessment

CONCEPT 27.1

Structure fits function in the human body.

OBJECTIVES
- Relate anatomy and physiology.
- Identify the levels of structure in the human body.

KEY TERMS
- anatomy
- physiology
- tissue
- organ
- organ system

What's Online

Online Activity 27.1 Match structure and function.

How does your favorite band make good music? The drummer keeps rhythm, the singer provides the melody, and the guitarist holds it all together. Likewise, each organ system in your body has a unique role to play. All systems work together, allowing your body to function smoothly.

Anatomy and Physiology

A close look at a biological structure often provides clues about its function. Structures that look alike often have similar functions. For example, if you look at your teeth in a mirror, you'll see thin-edged, sharp teeth in front called incisors (Figure 27-1). Their shape may remind you of the sharp blade of a cutting tool, such as a knife. Indeed, the function of incisors is to cut through pieces of food. The teeth in the back of your mouth, molars, have many sharp bumps that resemble a meat tenderizer's hard, bumpy surface. Just as a chef pounds a tenderizer against a tough piece of meat to soften it before cooking, molars grind and mash food before it is swallowed.

The study of the structure of an organism and its parts is called **anatomy.** For example, the anatomy of your mouth reveals how many teeth you have, their shapes, and their position in your jaw. **Physiology** (fiz ee AWL uh jee) is the study of what structures do, and how they do it—in other words, their function. Studying how your jaw moves your teeth when you chew and how your teeth cut and mash your food is physiology. Knowing anatomy is important to understanding physiology. Keep this relationship between structure and function in mind as you begin your study of the human body systems.

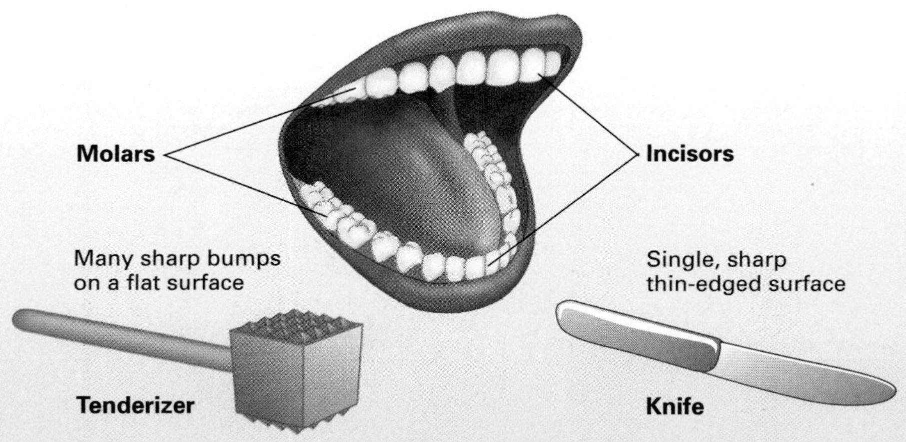

Figure 27-1 Incisors and molars have different structures that fit their different functions. Molars have a bumpy surface that mashes food. Incisors have a sharp, thin edge that cuts food.

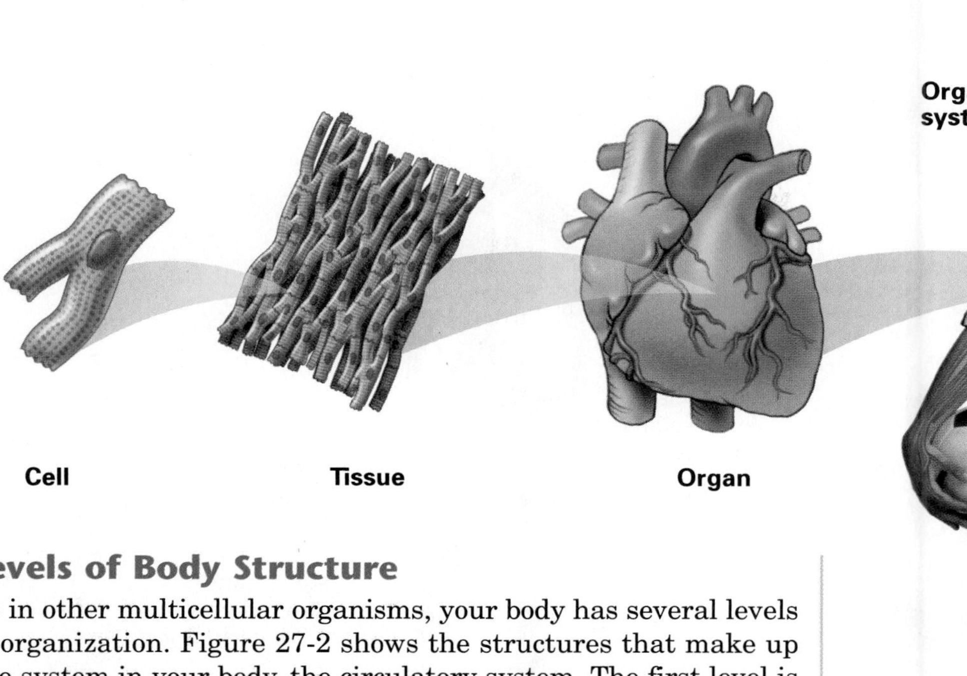

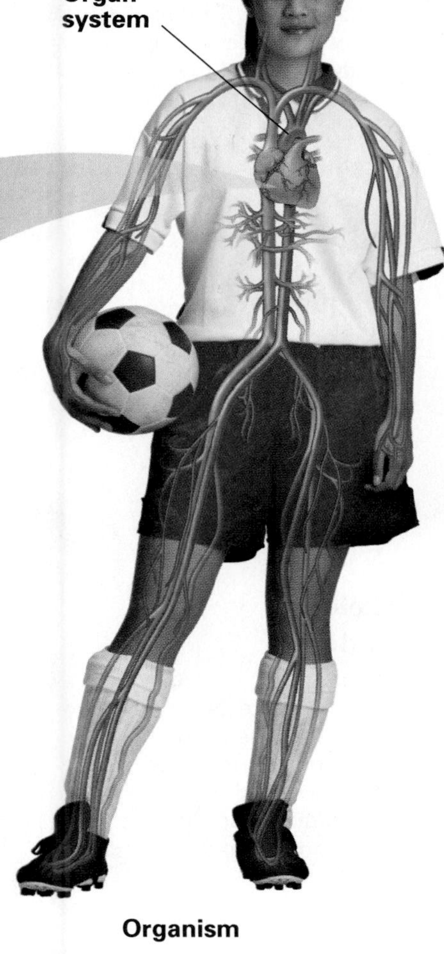

▲ **Figure 27-2** The smallest level of organization shown in this diagram is the cell. Cells working together make up a tissue, which in turn is part of an organ. Organs working together form the different organ systems that make up a whole organism.

Levels of Body Structure

As in other multicellular organisms, your body has several levels of organization. Figure 27-2 shows the structures that make up one system in your body, the circulatory system. The first level is the cell, such as a muscle cell in your heart. Each heart muscle cell is branched, allowing it to interlock with other surrounding heart muscle cells, much as jigsaw puzzle pieces fit together. This interlocking helps coordinate the actions of neighboring cells. Together, these cells form a muscle tissue. A **tissue** is a cooperating unit of many similar cells that perform a specific function. In this case, the tight organization of the muscle cells allows the muscle tissue to produce heartbeats that pump blood. In addition to muscle tissue, the other major types of tissue are epithelial, connective, and nervous tissue. You will learn about all four tissue types in the next section.

An **organ** consists of several tissues that together perform a specific task. For example, your heart is an organ composed of muscle and other tissues, such as nervous tissue, that together produce a pumping action. An **organ system** consists of multiple organs that together perform a vital body function. The organs of the circulatory system are the heart and blood vessels. Together, they constantly transport blood throughout the body.

The highest level of structure is the whole organism, in this case a human. Different organ systems work together, contributing to the successful function of the whole organism. For example, without oxygen supplied by the respiratory system and nutrients provided by the digestive system, the heart cannot pump blood and the circulatory system cannot function. Another example is the coordination of the nervous, muscular, and skeletal systems in moving parts of the body. Nerves stimulate muscles to contract, and the muscles in turn move the bones of the skeleton to which they are attached.

Figure 27-3 on the next two pages introduces the major functions and organs of 12 organ systems in the human body. The remainder of this unit will provide more details on these functions and the structures that make them possible.

▼ **Figure 27-3** These pages show 12 organ systems in the human body. Note the major organs that make up each system.

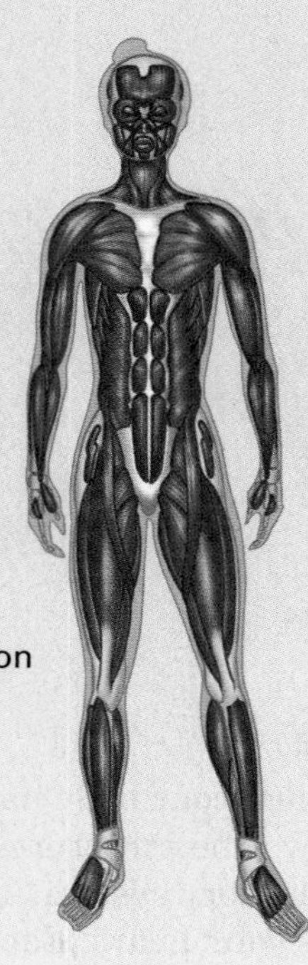

Muscular System

Enables body movement and facial expressions essential to human communication

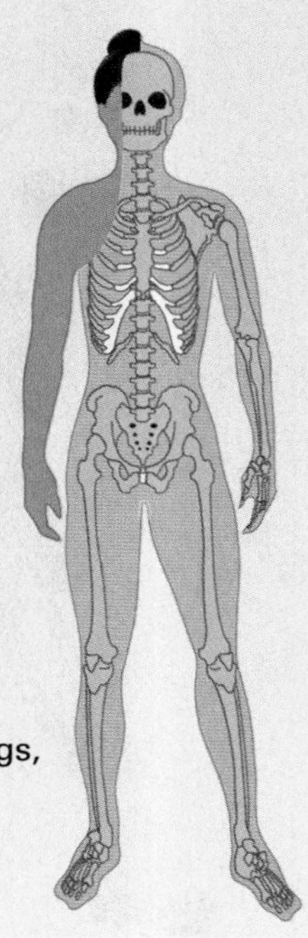

Integumentary System

Covers the body and protects it from injury, infection, excessive heat or cold, and drying out

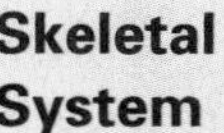

Skeletal System

Provides body support, protects certain organs such as the brain and lungs, and works with the muscular system in body movements

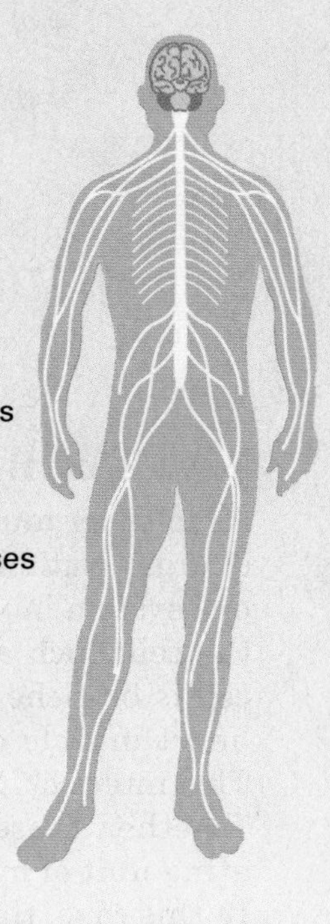

Nervous System

Coordinates body's activities by detecting stimuli and directing the body's responses

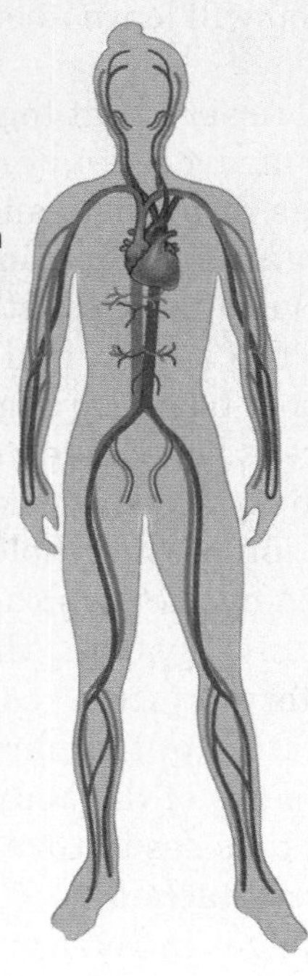

Circulatory System

Delivers oxygen and nutrients to body cells and transports waste products to excretory organs

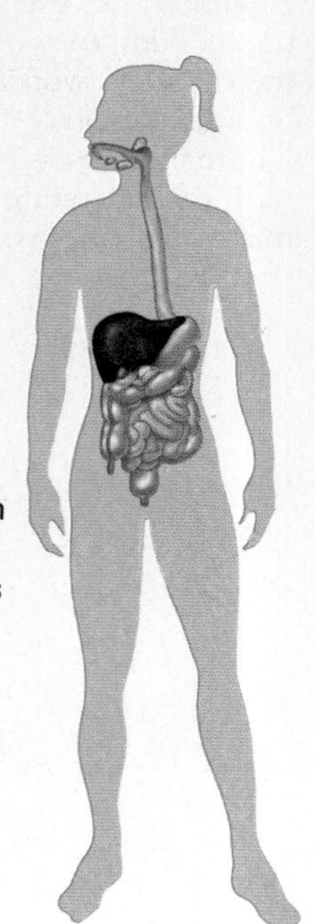

Digestive System

Ingests food, breaks it down into smaller chemical units for use by the body, and eliminates undigested material

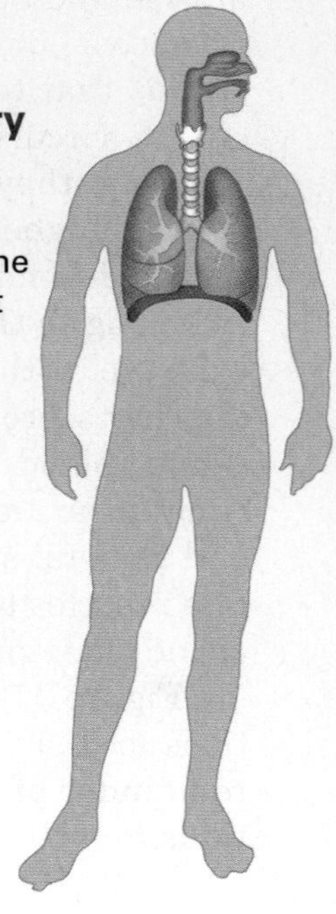

Respiratory System

Exchanges gases with the environment

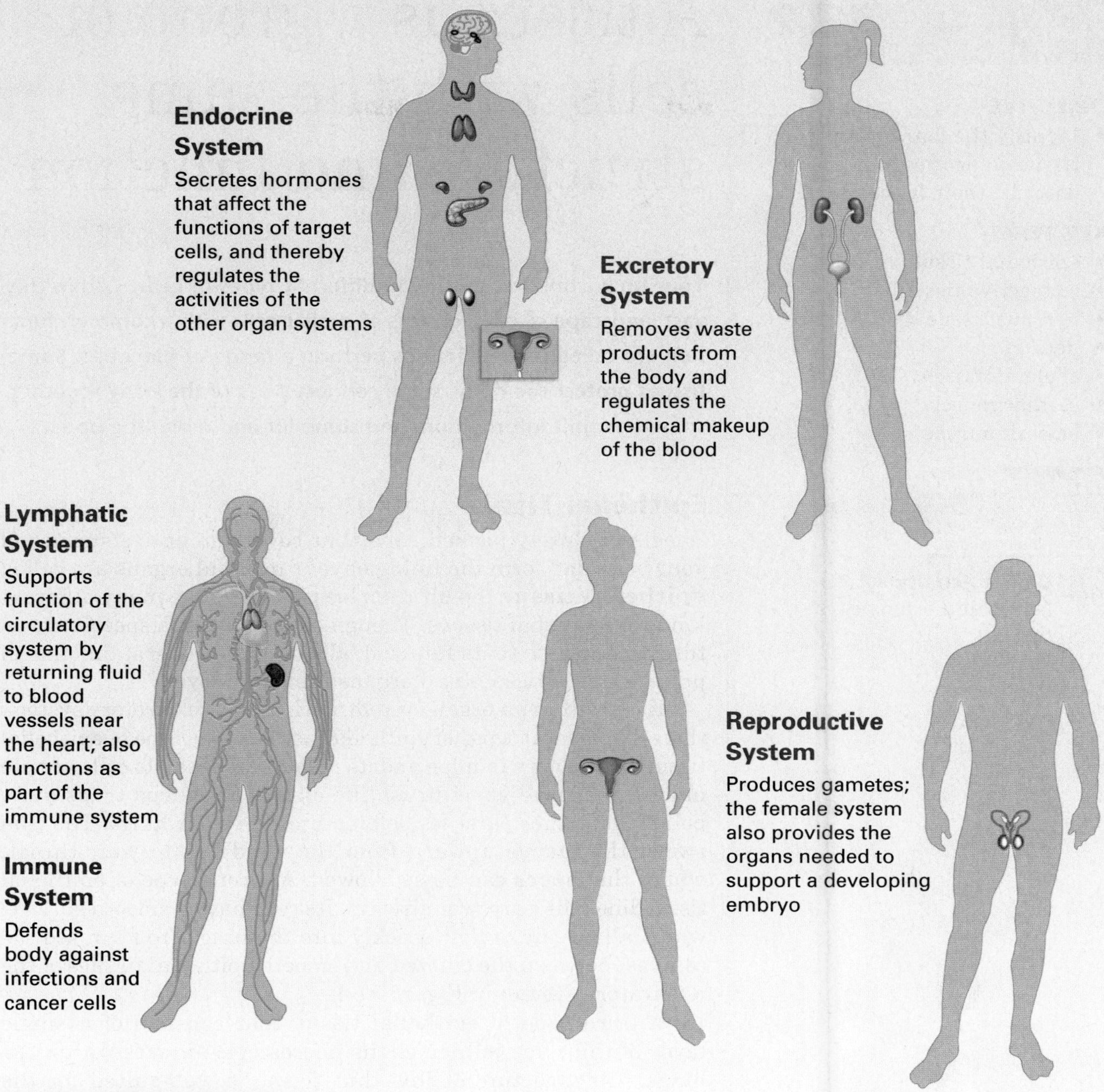

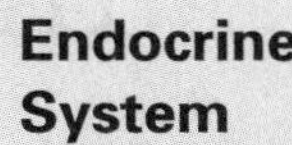

Endocrine System

Secretes hormones that affect the functions of target cells, and thereby regulates the activities of the other organ systems

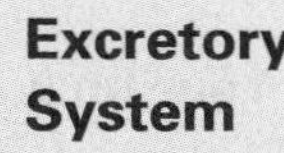

Excretory System

Removes waste products from the body and regulates the chemical makeup of the blood

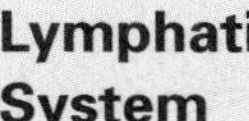

Lymphatic System

Supports function of the circulatory system by returning fluid to blood vessels near the heart; also functions as part of the immune system

Immune System

Defends body against infections and cancer cells

Reproductive System

Produces gametes; the female system also provides the organs needed to support a developing embryo

Online Activity 27.1

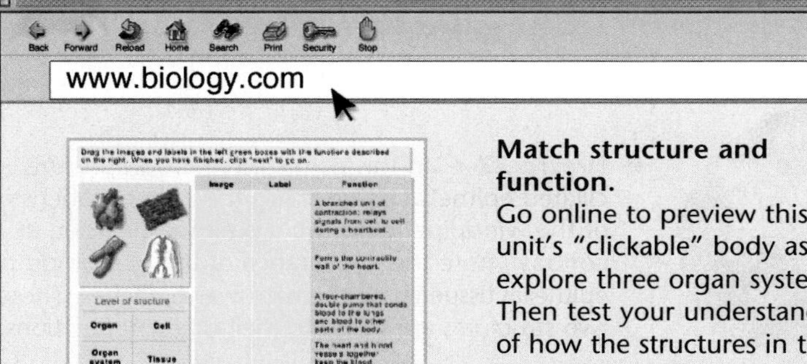

Match structure and function.
Go online to preview this unit's "clickable" body as you explore three organ systems. Then test your understanding of how the structures in the circulatory system relate to their function.

Concept Check 27.1

1. Explain how anatomy and physiology are related.
2. List in order from smallest to largest the five levels of structure in the human body.
3. List 12 different organ systems in one column of a table. In the second column, state the major functions of each system.

CONCEPT 27.2

A tissue is a group of cells with the same structure and function.

OBJECTIVE

- Identify the four major tissue categories and describe their functions.

KEY TERMS

- epithelial tissue
- connective tissue
- nervous tissue
- neuron
- skeletal muscle
- cardiac muscle
- smooth muscle

What's Online

Online Activity 27.2
Locate and examine tissues.

Your body contains about 250 different types of cells. Within this vast landscape of cells, groups of similar cells with a common function are called tissues. Tissues perform a range of functions. Some tissues protect the body, some connect parts of the body together, some transmit information, and some lift and move the body.

Epithelial Tissue

Sheets of closely packed cells that cover the entire surface of your body and form the lining of your internal organs are called **epithelial tissue** (ep uh THEE lee ul). There are many different kinds of epithelial tissues. Though each type has a specific structure appropriate to its function, all serve the general function of protecting the tissues and organs that they cover.

Even within an organ system, such as the respiratory system, there are several types of epithelial tissues. One type of epithelial tissue lines your windpipe and its major branches. Its cells secrete mucus and have short brushlike cilia. The mucus traps dust, pollen, and other particles before air enters your lungs. The cilia sweep the mucus upward from the windpipe to your throat, where the mucus can be swallowed. A second type of epithelial tissue lines the narrower airways. Its cells have a smooth surface, which allows air to flow quickly into the lungs. You can see the contrast between the ciliated and smooth epithelial tissues of the respiratory system in Figure 27-4.

A third type of epithelial tissue that consists of a single layer of thin, flat cells lines the microscopic air sacs within the lungs. The structure of this thin tissue is well-suited for the transfer of carbon dioxide and oxygen between your blood and the air you breathe. The fact that this tissue is only one cell thick minimizes the distance these gases have to travel.

Colorized SEM 2,900×

Figure 27-4 In this colorized micrograph, the ciliated epithelial tissue lining the major branches of the windpipe looks like a pink shag carpet. In contrast, note the appearance of the blue smooth epithelial tissue lining the narrower branches. These two structures are suited to their different functions.

LM 1,900×

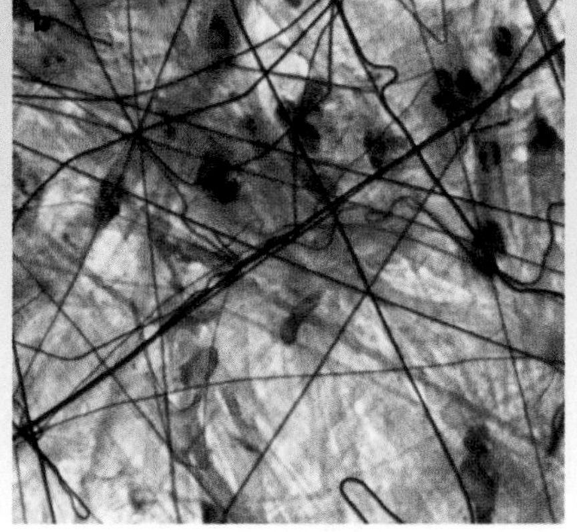
LM 550×

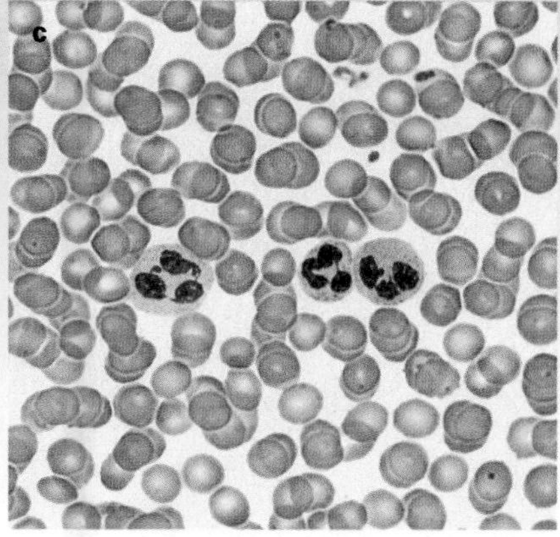

LM 1,900×

▲ **Figure 27-5** Shown above are three of the many types of connective tissue in your body. **a.** The cells of bone tissue are embedded in a dense matrix of mineral deposits and proteins. **b.** In loose connective tissue, the main cell bodies (containing dark nuclei) are embedded in a net-like matrix of fibers (pink and blue threads). **c.** Blood tissue is made of different types of blood cells suspended in a fluid matrix.

Connective Tissue

The main functions of **connective tissue** are to hold together and support other tissues, and to cushion, insulate, and connect organs. The cells that make up connective tissues are scattered in a matrix of fibers. Loose connective tissue is the most common type, so-called because its matrix is a loose weave of fibers. Like a "living glue," loose connective tissue holds other tissues and organs in place and connects the skin to underlying muscle tissue. Other types of connective tissue include bone, cartilage, blood, and fat (adipose tissue). Connective tissues vary widely in appearance (Figure 27-5).

Nervous Tissue

Your survival depends upon your ability to respond appropriately to sudden changes in the environment. For instance, if you touch a hot pan on the stove, your arm pulls away very quickly—even before you know what you've done. Your rapid response minimizes the damage to your body. **Nervous tissue** forms the communication system that makes this behavior possible. The basic unit of nervous tissue is the **neuron,** or nerve cell (Figure 27-6). Neurons can transmit signals very rapidly over long distances. For example, the neurons in your arm reach all the way from the muscles in the tips of your fingers to your spinal cord. The signal to move your arm is communicated through this connection. In Chapter 28 you'll explore the structure and function of nervous tissue in more detail.

LM 290×

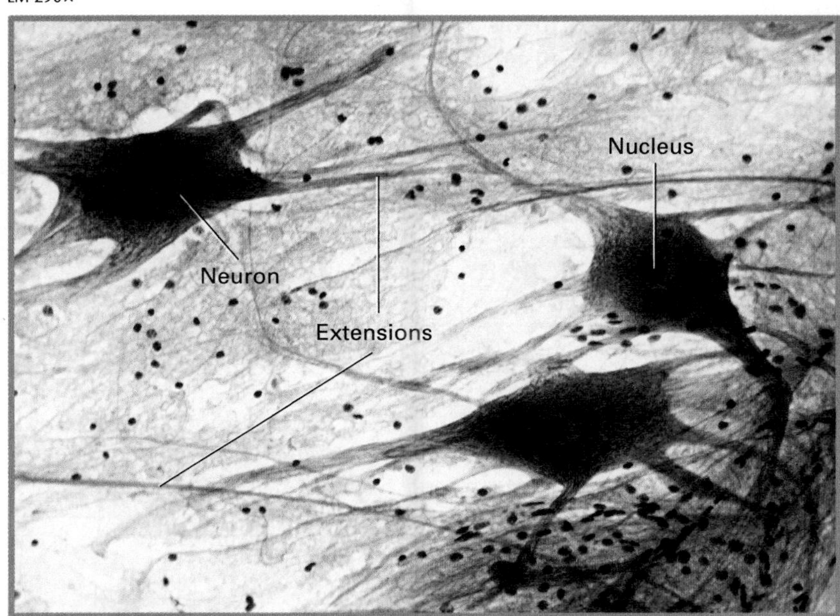

▶ **Figure 27-6** Nerve cells (neurons) are the basic unit of the communication network of the body, the nervous tissue. Neurons have long extensions that transmit signals.

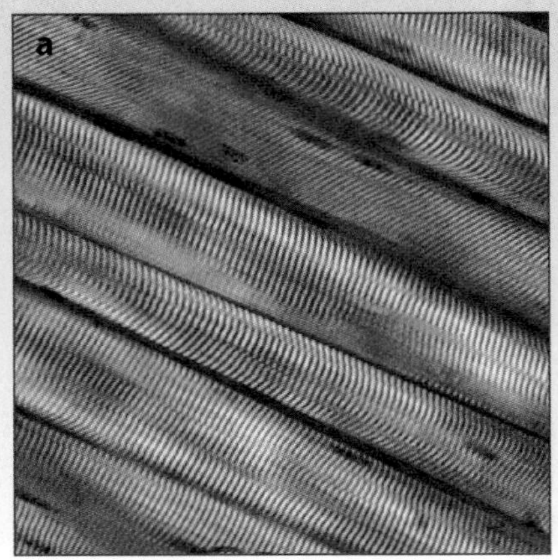

LM 260×

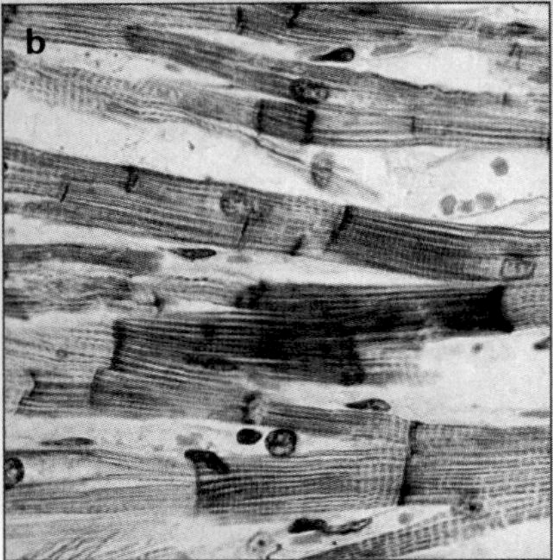

LM 160×

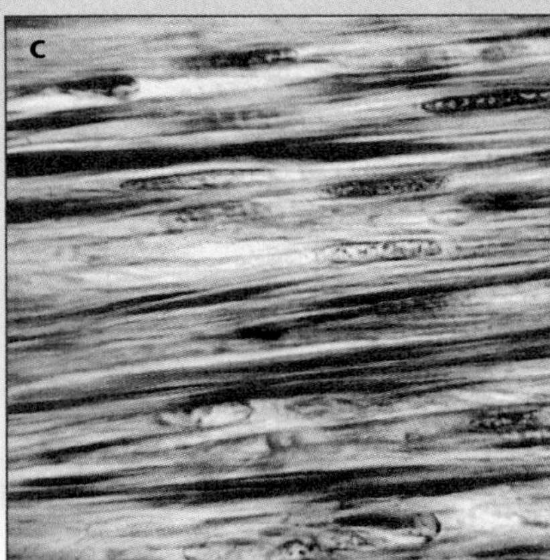

LM 260×

▲ **Figure 27-7** The three main types of muscle tissue have different structures. **a.** Skeletal muscle cells are long and cylinder-shaped—the cells stretch far beyond the edges of this micrograph. **b.** Cardiac muscle cells make branching connections with each other. **c.** Smooth muscle cells are spindle-shaped, meaning tapered at the ends.

Muscle Tissue

Muscles are organs that enable humans to move, to run, to dance, and to swim. They aid in moving your blood and digesting your food. Muscles are composed of several different types of tissue, including connective tissue, nervous tissue, and muscle tissue.

There are three types of muscles. A muscle that you can control under your own will, such as a muscle in your arm or leg, is called a *voluntary muscle.* A voluntary muscle is also called a **skeletal muscle** because it is attached to the bones of your skeleton. Skeletal muscles are composed of skeletal muscle tissue and allow you to move the various parts of your body.

A muscle that works without you consciously controlling it is called an *involuntary muscle.* The involuntary muscles that cause your heart to pump blood and contain cardiac muscle tissue are called **cardiac muscles.** Involuntary muscles that contain smooth muscle tissue and are found in most of your other organs are called **smooth muscles.** They perform many necessary functions without you having to think about them. For example, smooth muscles in your intestine move food through your digestive system. You'll read more about how muscles work in Concept 27.5.

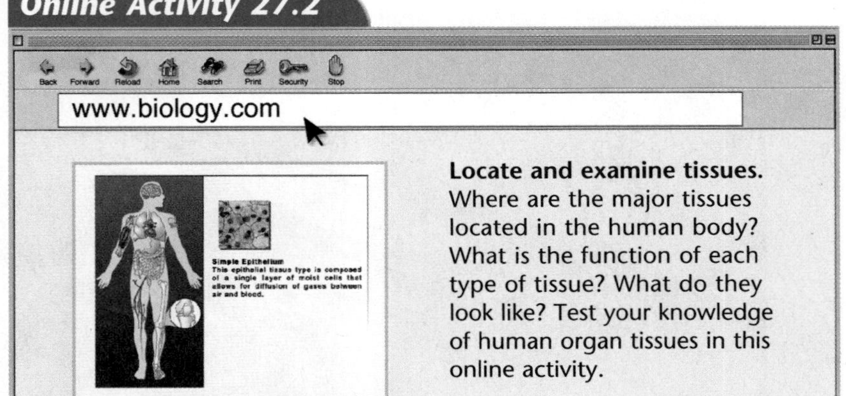

Locate and examine tissues. Where are the major tissues located in the human body? What is the function of each type of tissue? What do they look like? Test your knowledge of human organ tissues in this online activity.

Concept Check 27.2

1. Make a table listing the four major types of tissue in your body and stating their functions.
2. Give an example of how structure and function are related in a type of tissue.
3. Describe the differences between skeletal, cardiac, and smooth muscles.

CONCEPT 27.3 The body regulates its internal environment.

OBJECTIVES

- Define homeostasis and explain its importance.
- Explain how homeostasis involves chemical exchange.
- Describe how the integumentary system contributes to homeostasis.

KEY TERMS

- homeostasis
- hormone
- interstitial fluid
- integumentary system
- epidermis
- melanin
- dermis
- hypodermis

What's Online

Online Activity 27.3
Investigate a feedback loop.

Careers
Meet a Medical Doctor

On a brisk winter day, you shiver in response to the cold temperature. On a hot and sticky summer day, you may sweat profusely. These two very different physiological responses to temperature extremes are your body's ways of achieving the same thing: stability.

Homeostasis

In both cold and hot weather, your body maintains a steady temperature of about 37°C (98.6°F). This is just one example of how your body buffers itself from changes in the *external* environment, providing a relatively stable *internal* environment. This stability is important because your tissues can only survive within a narrow range of conditions. The internal stability or "steady state" maintained by your body is called **homeostasis** (hoh mee oh STAY sis).

The narrow range of operating conditions is defined by *set points*. You can think of set points as "normal" levels. To better understand this idea, think about the thermostat in your home. You set your thermostat at a comfortable temperature—this is its set point. The thermostat turns on the furnace when the indoor temperature drops below the set point and turns it off when the temperature rises above the set point. This keeps the home temperature close to the set point.

Your body's "thermostat," located in your brain, switches on and off many mechanisms that maintain a nearly constant temperature. Two of these mechanisms are shivering and sweating. Shivering is caused by the rapid contraction of skeletal muscles. The muscles release heat that helps maintain your body temperature on a cold day. And on a hot day or during exercise, sweating causes evaporative cooling (see Chapter 4). Sweating thus helps keep the body from overheating.

Many chemical signals help regulate the body systems that contribute to homeostasis. For example, your neurons release signal molecules that stimulate the muscles that make you shiver. Other signal molecules called **hormones** are released by glands into the bloodstream. The hormones are carried to other parts of the body where they trigger particular responses. You can investigate one type of hormonal regulation in Online Activity 27.3, and you can learn more about your body's ability to maintain homeostasis in Chapter 32.

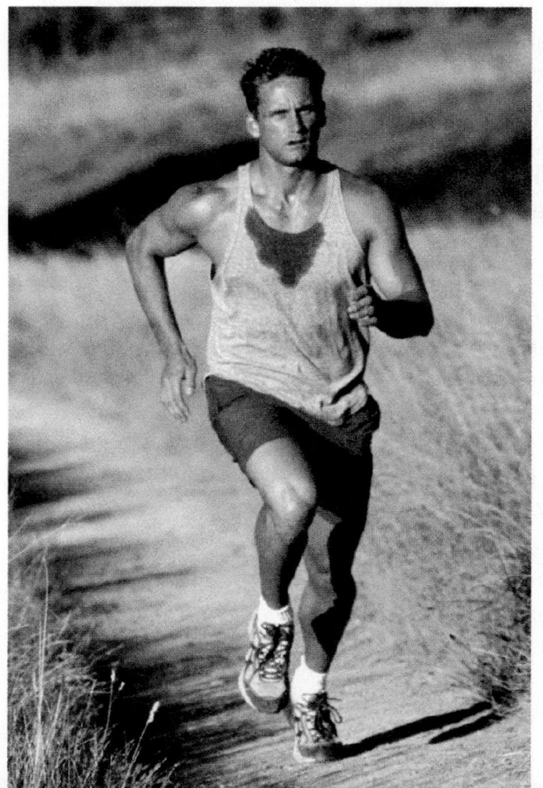

Figure 27-8 Sweating causes evaporative cooling, helping the body maintain a stable temperature.

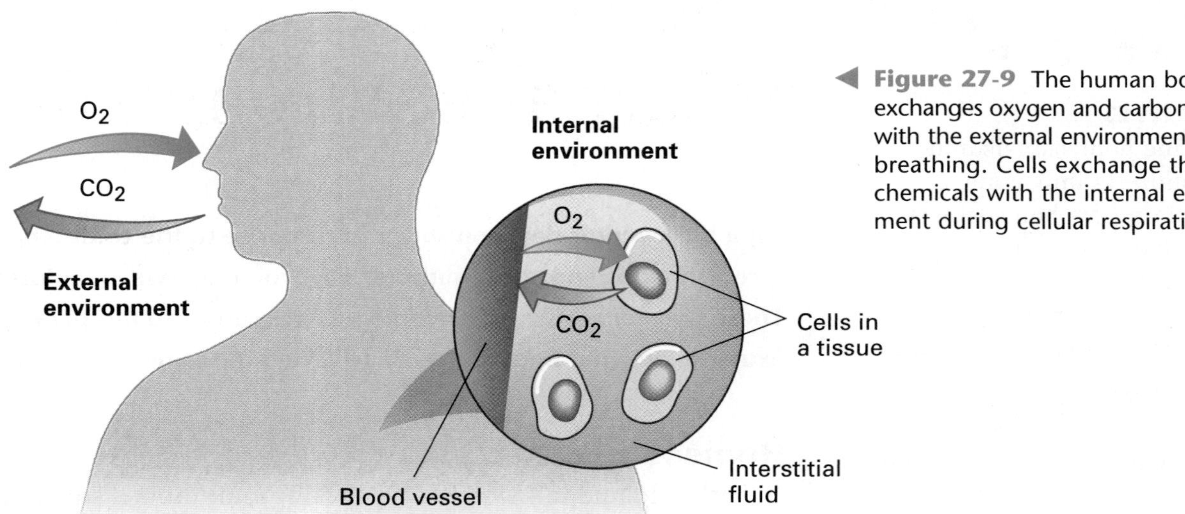

Figure 27-9 The human body exchanges oxygen and carbon dioxide with the external environment during breathing. Cells exchange these chemicals with the internal environment during cellular respiration.

Chemical Exchange With the Surroundings

In maintaining homeostasis, two environments are important: the external environment surrounding your body and the internal environment surrounding your individual cells. Your body exchanges chemicals with the external environment, and then your cells exchange materials with the internal environment (Figure 27-9). The internal exchange takes place through an aqueous solution called **interstitial fluid** (in tur STISH ul) that fills the gaps between cells in a tissue. Chemicals traveling between the blood and tissue cells pass through the interstitial fluid. For example, oxygen enters your body from the external environment when you inhale. In your lungs, oxygen diffuses through interstitial fluid into the blood. From the blood, oxygen moves to your cells by passing through the interstitial fluid and the plasma membranes of individual cells. Cells use oxygen for cellular respiration and produce carbon dioxide. This carbon dioxide passes from a cell to the interstitial fluid and then to the blood. The carbon dioxide is then carried to your lungs where it can be exhaled.

Your circulatory, respiratory, digestive, and excretory systems in particular perform a great deal of chemical exchange with the rest of the body. For all the cells of these systems to receive and deliver chemicals, they must be bathed in interstitial fluid. In another example of structure fitting function, the epithelial tissues of these systems have textured or branched surfaces that enhance chemical exchange. For example, your lungs have millions of microscopic air sacs with a total gas-exchanging surface about the size of a tennis court. Oxygen and carbon dioxide move across the surface between these air sacs and the bloodstream. Figure 27-10 illustrates another example, the finger-like bumps on the lining of the small intestine. In contrast to a flat surface, this bumpy surface greatly expands the total area across which nutrients can pass from your intestine to your bloodstream after you eat.

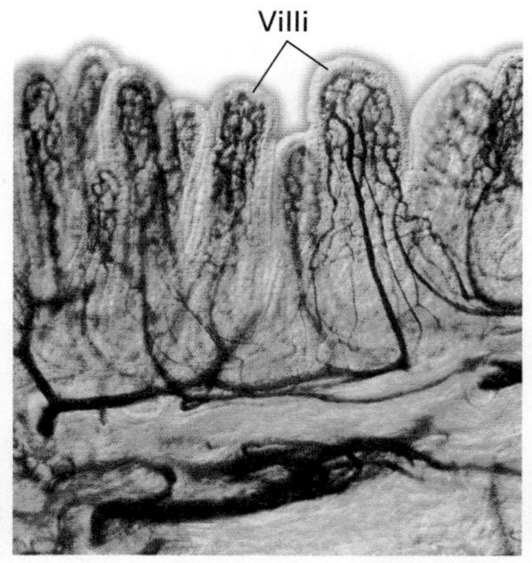

Figure 27-10 The epithelium lining the small intestine has many tiny bumps, called villi. These villi increase the surface area across which chemicals can be exchanged.

The Integumentary System

While maintaining homeostasis is a function of all your organ systems, the **integumentary system** (in teg yoo MEN tuh ree)—the body's outer covering—has the important task of physically separating the body from the external environment. This barrier is important for maintaining homeostasis.

The Skin The largest and most familiar organ of the integumentary system is the skin. Though it is only about 2 millimeters thick (the thickness of two compact discs), the skin consists of two main layers: the epidermis and the dermis (Figure 27-11). The **epidermis,** the outermost layer of skin, is made mostly of dead epithelial cells that continually flake and fall off. New cells pushing up from lower layers are constantly replacing the cells that are lost. This ongoing renewal of your outer covering is necessary because your skin is often scratched or otherwise damaged. Not all the cells of the epidermis are dead, however. For example, the bottom region of the epidermis contains living cells that produce **melanin,** a pigmented protein that gives your skin its color.

The **dermis** is the skin layer that lies beneath and supports the epidermis. The dermis is made mostly of fibrous connective tissue, giving the skin its strength and elasticity. The dermis also contains hair follicles, oil and sweat glands, muscles, nerves, and blood vessels. Below the dermis is a tissue layer called the **hypodermis.** The hypodermis contains a kind of connective tissue called adipose tissue, which includes fat-storing cells and blood vessels.

Careers

www.biology.com

Meet a Medical Doctor
Meet a doctor of internal medicine who relies on her education and experiences to treat patients with a variety of ailments. Listen as she describes one interesting way that she treats patients, physically and mentally. Then go to the Internet to examine some of the tools she uses in her practice.

Figure 27-11 Note the layers in this cross section of an area of skin. Each layer contains different tissue types.

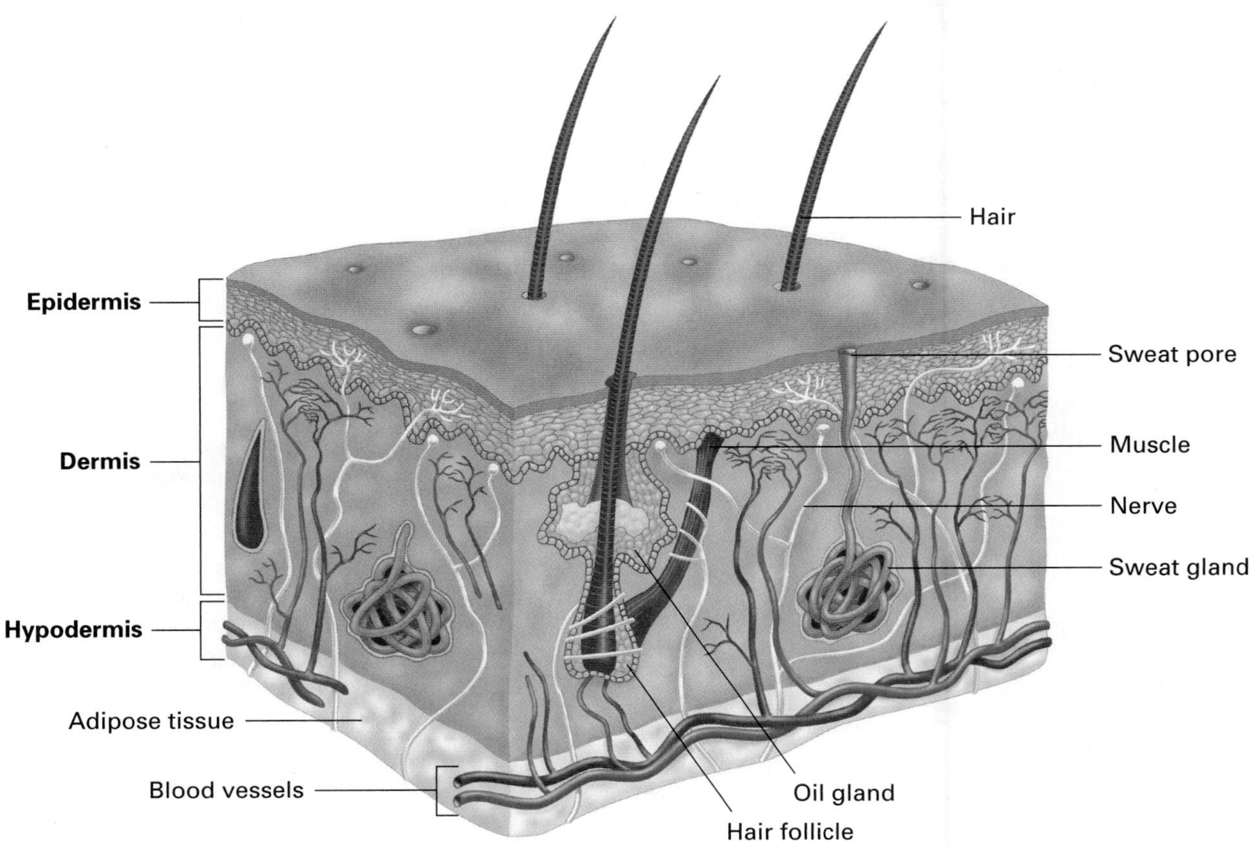

Hair and Nails Hair and nails are also part of your integumentary system. Hair covers almost all of your body. Over much of the body surface, hair is so short and sparse that you hardly notice it. Hair is composed of a protein called keratin. It is formed in pockets called hair follicles deep in the dermis layer. The follicle cells produce and deposit keratin at the base of each hair shaft, causing the hair to grow (Figure 27-12). Your fingernails and toenails are also made of keratin, and they too grow as they are pushed outward by living cells beneath.

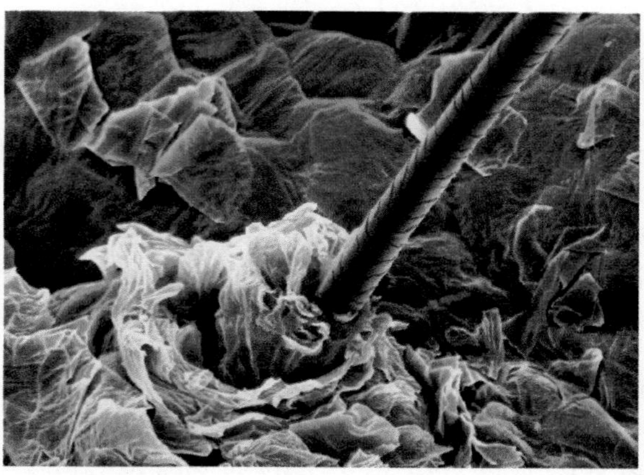
Colorized SEM 90×

▲ **Figure 27-12** A hair emerges from the skin. In this micrograph, you can see the layers of keratin making up the hair (green) and some dead cells shedding from the surface of the epidermis (orange).

Role in Homeostasis Your integumentary system helps your body maintain homeostasis in several ways. The skin provides a physical barrier against dirt and microorganisms entering your body. Its layered construction also helps to insulate the body on cold days and to cushion internal organs against physical injury. Your skin further helps maintain homeostasis by responding to such stimuli as slight changes in body temperature and water content. For example, you read at the beginning of this section that if your body temperature begins to rise above normal, you respond in part by sweating through pores in your skin.

Hair also helps maintain homeostasis. Hair on the top of your head protects your scalp from the harming effects of ultraviolet radiation from the sun. It also provides a layer of insulation from the changing outside temperatures. Your eyebrows and eyelashes prevent dirt and other small particles from entering your eyes.

Despite all the protection it provides, your integumentary system is not failproof. For example, cuts and other injuries break the barrier of the integumentary system and may allow microorganisms to enter the body. Excessive exposure to the sun may cause damage to connective tissues in the dermis, leading to wrinkles. Excessive sun exposure over time may also cause skin cancer.

Online Activity 27.3

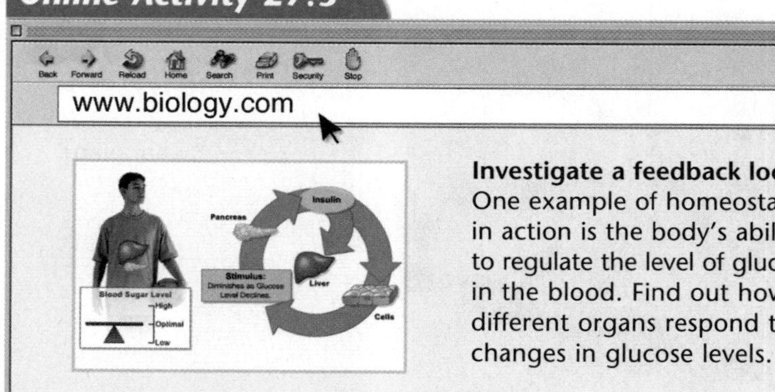

Investigate a feedback loop. One example of homeostasis in action is the body's ability to regulate the level of glucose in the blood. Find out how different organs respond to changes in glucose levels.

Concept Check 27.3

1. Explain why homeostasis is important to your body's functioning.
2. Give an example of an organ that exchanges chemicals, and explain how its structure allows this.
3. Give three examples of ways your skin helps maintain homeostasis in your body.
4. Explain one way that your body maintains a constant temperature while outside on a cold day.

CONCEPT 27.4

The skeleton functions in support and movement.

OBJECTIVES

- List the main functions and parts of the skeleton.
- Describe the structure of a typical bone.
- Compare and contrast three types of joints in your body.
- Identify three disorders of the skeletal system.

KEY TERMS

- vertebra
- cartilage
- marrow
- joint
- ligament
- arthritis
- osteoporosis

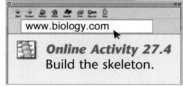

What's Online

Online Activity 27.4
Build the skeleton.

Without your skeleton supporting your body from within, you would sag from your own weight into a formless heap. You would also be unable to move—without bones to anchor them, your muscles would be useless.

Anatomy of the Skeleton

The skeleton provides a strong framework that holds your body up and maintains its shape (Figure 27-13). The skeleton also protects soft organs and provides attachment sites for your muscles. Starting from the top of the skeleton, the skull houses and protects the brain. The backbone, which protects the spinal cord, consists of a column of small bones, each of which is called a **vertebra** (plural, *vertebrae*). Between the vertebrae are disks made of **cartilage** (KARH tuh lij), a type of connective tissue that is softer than bone. The cartilage disks act as cushions for the vertebrae and permit the spinal cord to twist and bend. Stretching out from some of the vertebrae is a set of ribs that form a protective cage around the heart and lungs. Your skeleton also includes the bones of your arms, hands, legs, and feet. The bones of your shoulder girdle (the scapula and clavicle) connect your arms to your "core" skeleton. The bones of your pelvic girdle, or hip, join your legs to the core.

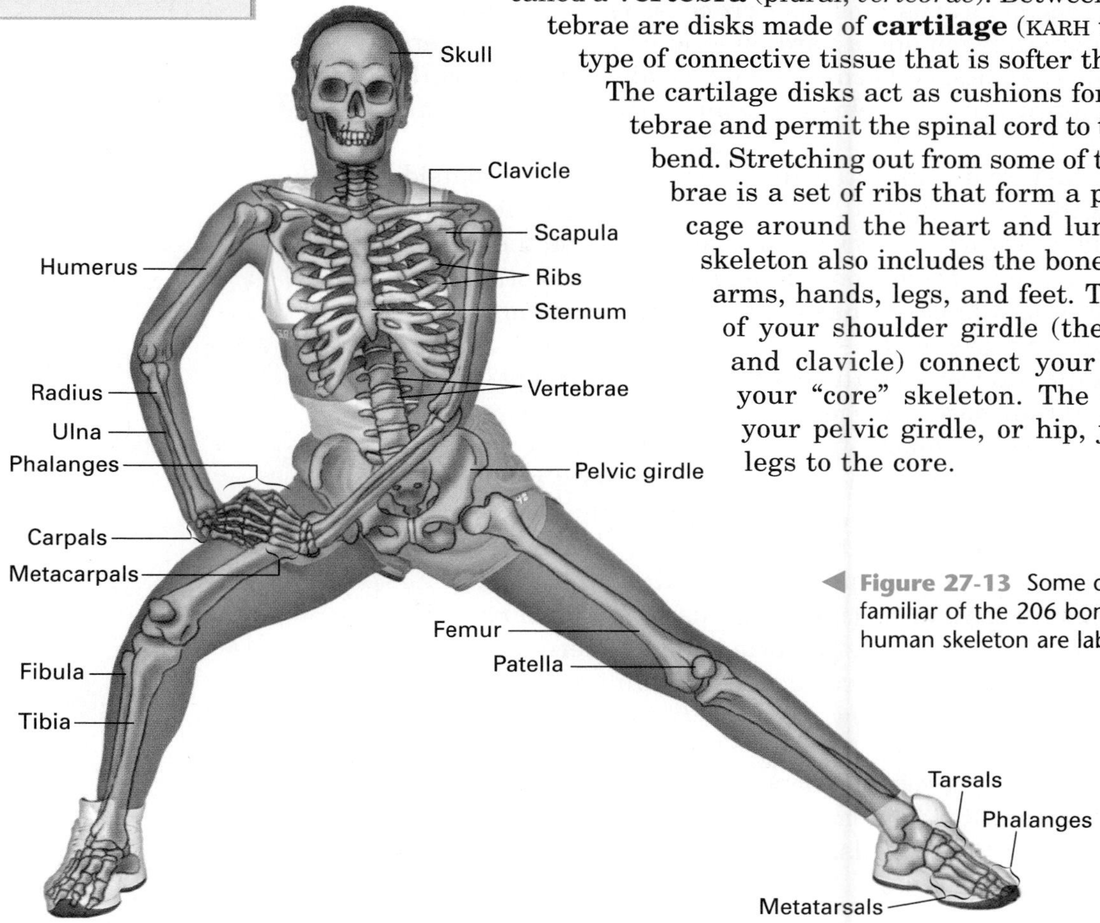

Figure 27-13 Some of the most familiar of the 206 bones in the human skeleton are labeled here.

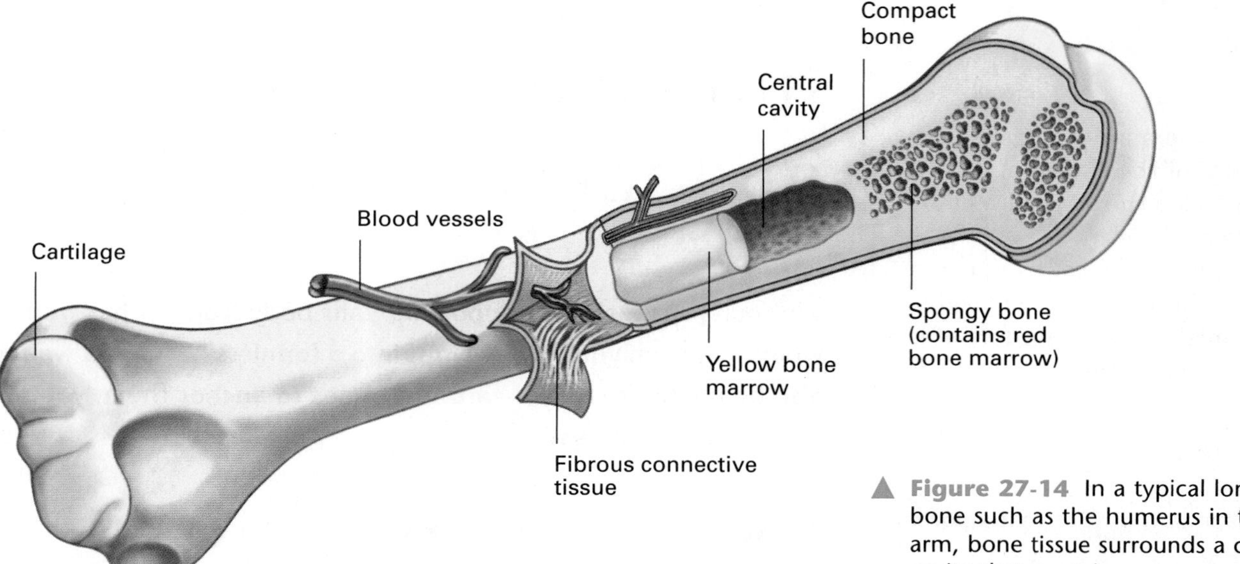

▲ **Figure 27-14** In a typical long bone such as the humerus in the arm, bone tissue surrounds a central cavity that contains marrow. Cartilage cushions the ends.

Bones as Living Organs

Although you might think of bones as dry and lifeless, your bones are organs made up of living connective tissue. Within this very dense connective tissue, a material known as *bone matrix* surrounds the bone cells. Bone matrix consists of flexible fibers of the protein collagen and a hard mineral made of calcium and phosphate. The collagen keeps the bone flexible and non-brittle, while the hard mineral helps the bone withstand forces that push on it.

A sheet of fibrous connective tissue covers most of the outside surface of the bone (Figure 27-14). This tissue helps form new bone in the event of a fracture. Cartilage cushions the ends of bones and prevents them from rubbing against each other. Your elbows, hips, and knees in particular depend upon cartilage to ensure smooth movement.

In addition to covering the ends of bones, cartilage is found in the tip of your nose and the outer portion of your ears. When you were a newborn, much of your skeleton was made up of cartilage. As you grew, this cartilage was gradually replaced by bone as minerals circulating in the blood accumulated in the developing bone. Bones continue to grow in length in women until about age 18, and in men until about age 21.

Many bones contain specialized tissues called **marrow.** The shafts of long bones, such as the arm bone (humerus) shown in Figure 27-14, have a central cavity containing yellow bone marrow. Yellow bone marrow consists of stored fat and serves as an energy reserve for the body. Cavities in certain bones, such as the humerus, your hip bones, and your sternum, contain red bone marrow. Red bone marrow produces cells that develop into your body's blood cells, replenishing your blood supply when old blood cells die.

How Joints Work

An area where one bone meets another bone is called a **joint.** Some joints connect bones in a way that allows little or no movement. Such joints are called immovable joints. For example, the bones in your skull are fused together with immovable joints. Similarly, your ribs are attached to the vertebrae with immovable joints. By being unable to move, these bones better protect the soft organs that lie beneath them. Yet, if all your bones were fused together in one continuous skeleton, you would not be able to move. Movable joints allow you to bend, twist, and rotate your limbs, neck, and torso. The bones in a movable joint are held together by a strong, fibrous connective tissue called a **ligament.**

Movable joints can be classified by the way in which the bones come together. The different structures of the joints allow your body to move in a variety of ways. Think about some of the motions a pitcher makes when throwing a softball (Figure 27-15). The pitcher checks the runner at first by turning her head to the side. The top of her neck and base of her skull form a *pivot joint,* which enables one bone to rotate around another bone. When she winds up for the pitch, she rotates her arm from the shoulder. The shoulder is an example of a *ball-and-socket joint,* which enables a bone to rotate and move back-and-forth and side-to-side. The "ball" at the end of the humerus fits into the cup-like socket of the scapula. Of all the joints, a ball-and-socket joint allows the greatest range of motion. Next, a *gliding joint* in the pitcher's wrist (not shown) enables her to bend and flex her wrist to put extra spin on the ball. Gliding joints allow small bones to slide gently over one another. Finally, as the pitcher releases the ball, she leans forward by bending her knee. The knee is an example of a *hinge joint,* which permits movement only in a single plane—a back-and-forth type of movement.

Many daily activities cause wear and tear on your joints and ligaments. Stretching regularly, especially before exercising, may keep your ligaments flexible and reduce joint injuries.

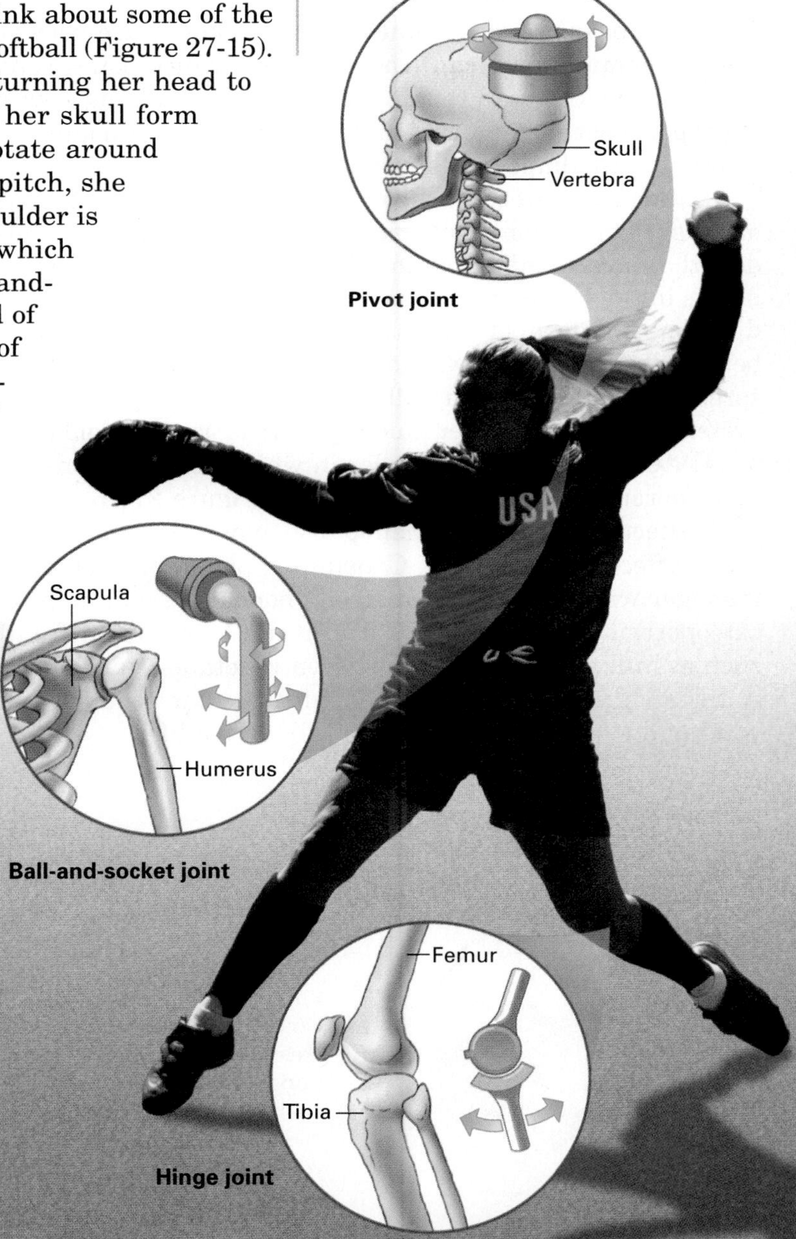

Figure 27-15 The many motions required to pitch a softball are provided by different types of joints.

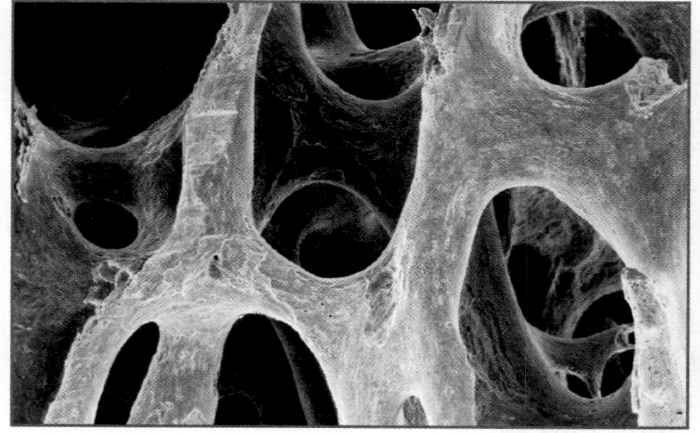

Colorized SEM 50×

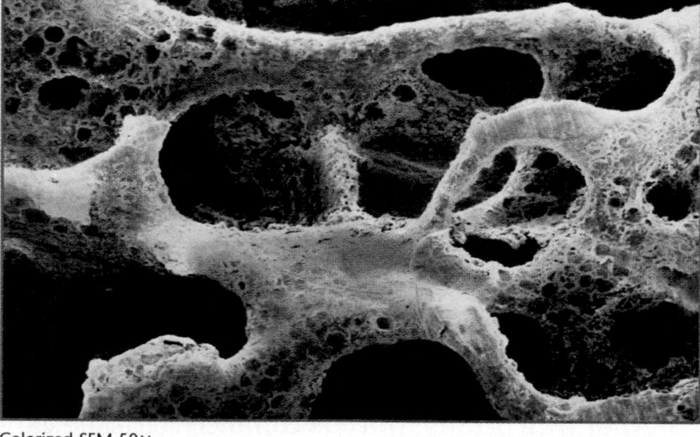

Colorized SEM 50×

▲ **Figure 27-16** Healthy spongy bone tissue (above left) contrasts with bone diseased by osteoporosis (above right).

Skeletal Disorders

Have you ever broken a bone? Although bones are very strong, a great enough force can fracture them. Since bones consist of living tissue, they can repair themselves by building new tissue. If properly set using a cast or splint, a bone will usually return to its normal shape and strength.

Besides fractures, bones and joints can be affected by disorders of the skeletal system. **Arthritis** refers to a group of skeletal disorders that involve inflammation of the joints. One out of every three adults in the United States suffers from arthritis or a related joint disorder. One form of arthritis occurs as part of aging—cartilage between bones wears down, and the joints become swollen, stiff, and sore. In Chapter 31, you will learn how the body's own immune system can cause another kind of arthritis (rheumatoid arthritis).

Osteoporosis is a disorder in which bones become thinner, more porous, and more easily broken (Figure 27-16). It particularly affects women after menopause, when changes in hormone levels affect bone strength. Consuming plenty of calcium while a teenager will help you build strong bones and will help prevent osteoporosis in the future. Calcium can be obtained from foods such as milk, cheese, and dark green vegetables such as broccoli. A diet rich in calcium combined with regular exercise will help you build a strong skeleton for a full, active life.

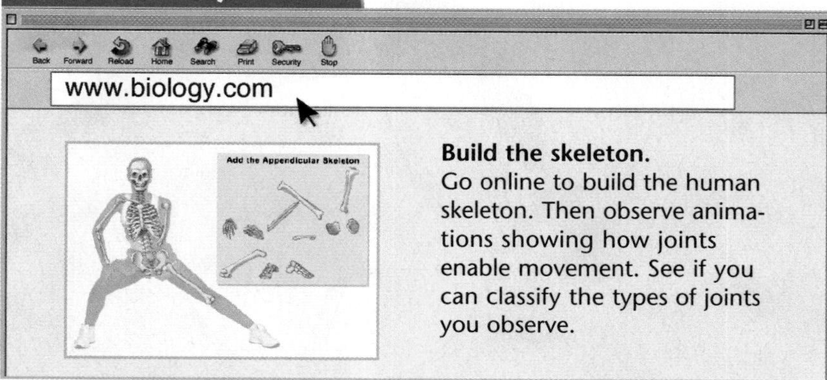

Build the skeleton.
Go online to build the human skeleton. Then observe animations showing how joints enable movement. See if you can classify the types of joints you observe.

Concept Check 27.4

1. List three structures within the skeletal system and describe the function of each.
2. Describe the structures that make up an arm bone.
3. Describe the differences between a hinge joint and a ball-and-socket joint.
4. Describe one way to prevent osteoporosis.

CONCEPT 27.5

Muscles move the skeleton by contracting.

OBJECTIVES

- Explain how muscles and bones move the body.
- Describe the structure of a skeletal muscle.
- Relate the anatomy and physiology involved in a simple task.

KEY TERMS

- tendon
- muscle fiber
- myofibril
- sarcomere
- actin
- myosin

What do you and the fastest runner on Earth have in common? Star athletes depend on the same type of interaction between skeletal muscles and the skeleton that you depend on when you run to catch the bus in the morning. More than 600 skeletal muscles help drive your body's movement.

How Muscles and Bones Work Together

Skeletal muscles interact with parts of your skeleton in moving your body. A muscle is attached to a bone by a type of dense connective tissue called a **tendon.**

As a muscle contracts, it pulls on the attached bone. Since muscles cannot push, only pull, an opposing motion is needed to return the bone to its original position. Therefore muscles must work in pairs. For each skeletal muscle that is contracting, there is an opposing muscle—one that is relaxed but that can contract to pull the bone back in the opposite direction. For instance, when the bass drummer in a marching band beats the drum, his biceps contracts and his triceps relaxes (Figure 27-17). The opposite occurs when he pulls his arm away from the drum. His biceps relaxes, and his triceps contracts. If you had only one muscle in your arm, you would only be able to move your arm in one direction—and you would not be able to move it back again.

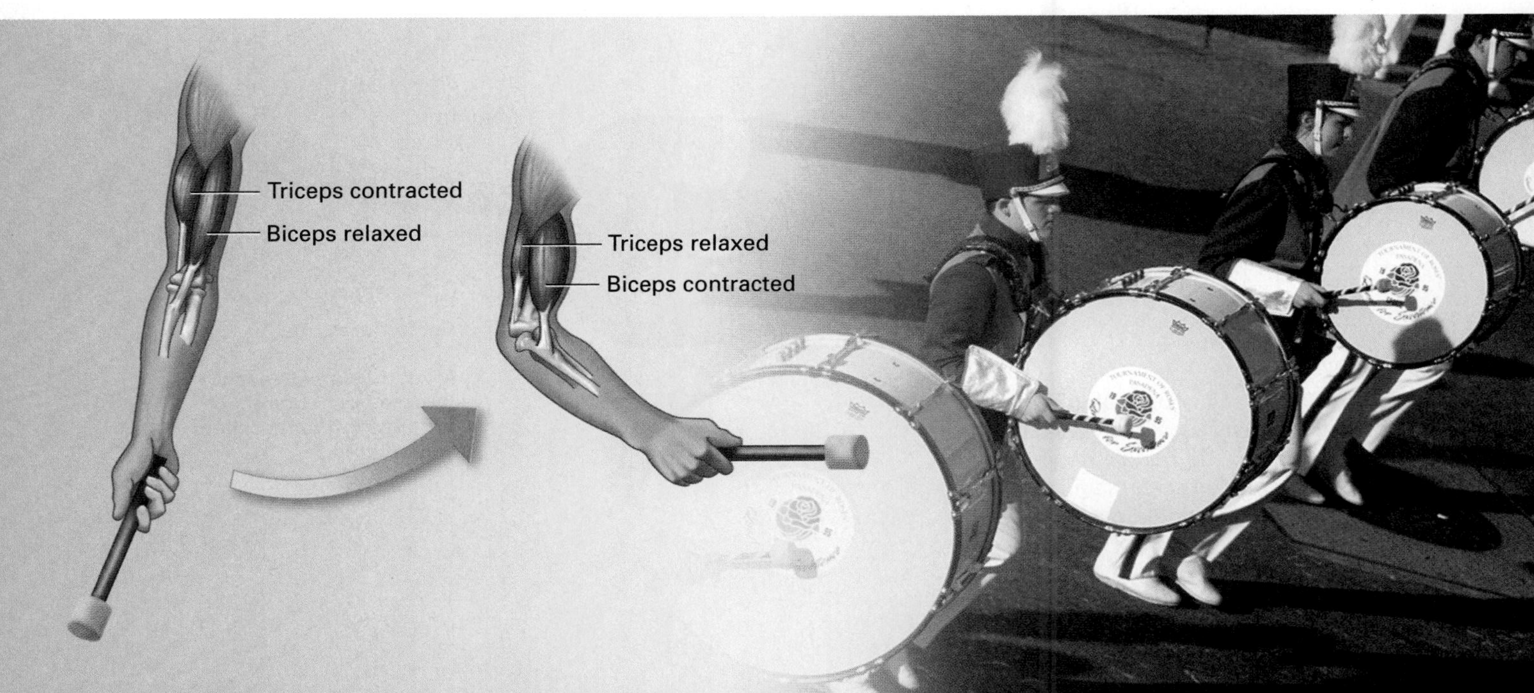

▼ **Figure 27-17** Skeletal muscles work in pairs. When the bass drummer's biceps contracts, his triceps relaxes. When his triceps contracts, his biceps relaxes.

The Structure of a Muscle

Remember from Concept 27.2 that skeletal muscles are voluntary muscles. Picking up a book, walking down the street, or performing any one of thousands of other conscious motions all require using skeletal muscles. For example, you use the muscles in your arm frequently throughout the day for activities as varied as writing notes during class and scratching an itch on your nose.

Taking a closer look, a skeletal muscle such as your calf muscle consists of bundles of parallel muscle fibers along with a supply of nerves and blood vessels (Figure 27-18). A **muscle fiber** is a single long cylindrical muscle cell that contains many nuclei. A large skeletal muscle contains hundreds of thousands of these cells.

Inside a muscle fiber are bundles of smaller units called **myofibrils.** If you observe a myofibril under a microscope, you will see that it has alternating light and dark bands (shown as red and white stripes in Figure 27-18). For this reason, skeletal muscle is also known as *striated* muscle, which means "striped."

A single myofibril consists of repeating units called sarcomeres. The **sarcomere** (SAHR koh mir) is the muscle fiber's basic unit of action—it is the unit that contracts. Each sarcomere is composed of two kinds of filaments, thin and thick. The thin filaments

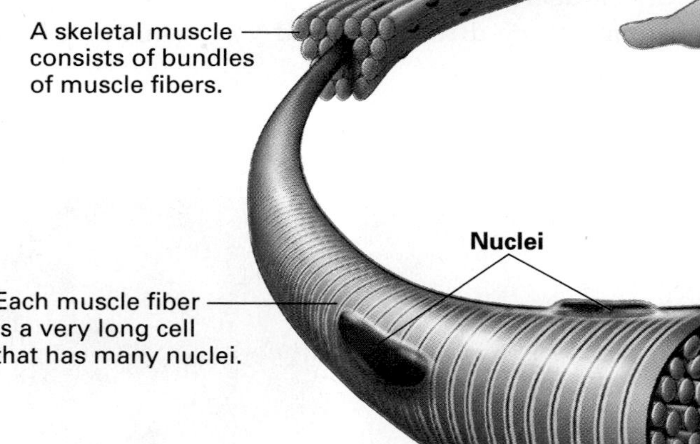
A skeletal muscle consists of bundles of muscle fibers.
Nuclei
Each muscle fiber is a very long cell that has many nuclei.
Myofibril
Sarcomeres
Myofibrils inside each muscle fiber consist of repeating units called sarcomeres.

▲ **Figure 27-18** This "dissection" shows the organization of a skeletal muscle from muscle bundle down to the sarcomere. The sarcomere is the basic unit of contraction in a muscle.

are composed of the protein **actin** and have a twisted, ropelike structure. The thick filaments are composed of the protein **myosin** and have bumplike projections called myosin heads.

The interaction of myosin heads with the thin filaments is the key to muscle contraction. As with many other cell processes that you have read about, the energy-storage molecule ATP plays an important role in this process. In each mini-contraction (shown below in Figure 27-18), myosin heads first bind to thin filaments. Next, the myosin heads bend, pulling the thin filaments toward the center of the sarcomere. ATP then binds to each myosin head, releasing it from the thin filament. The myosin head is now free to attach at a new spot and further pull the thin filament along. Note that the filaments themselves don't get shorter, but as they slide across one another, their overlap increases. The sarcomere shortens. The process can continue until the sarcomere is fully contracted. As the sarcomeres of many muscle fibers shorten together, the entire muscle contracts.

Though only a few myosin heads are shown in the figure below, a typical thick filament has about 350 myosin heads. Each head can bind and unbind to a thin filament about 5 times per second. The myosin heads do not all release from the thin filament at the same time—if that were the case, the thin filament could slide back to its former position. Instead, some of the heads hold the thin filaments in position, while others release and connect to new binding sites. You can observe an animation of a contracting muscle as part of Online Activity 27.5.

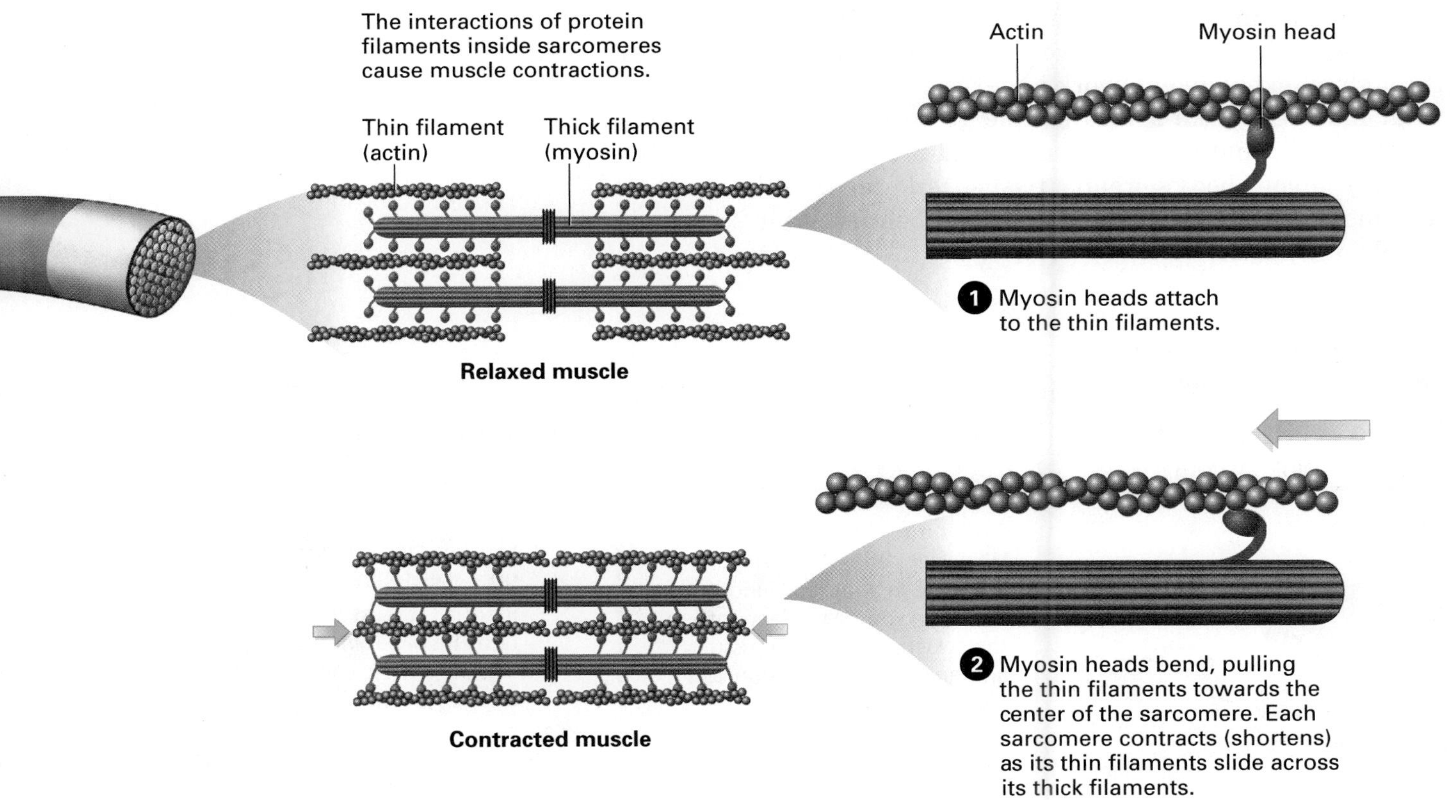
The interactions of protein filaments inside sarcomeres cause muscle contractions.
Thin filament (actin)
Thick filament (myosin)
Relaxed muscle
Actin
Myosin head
1 Myosin heads attach to the thin filaments.
Contracted muscle
2 Myosin heads bend, pulling the thin filaments towards the center of the sarcomere. Each sarcomere contracts (shortens) as its thin filaments slide across its thick filaments.

The Anatomy and Physiology of a Handshake

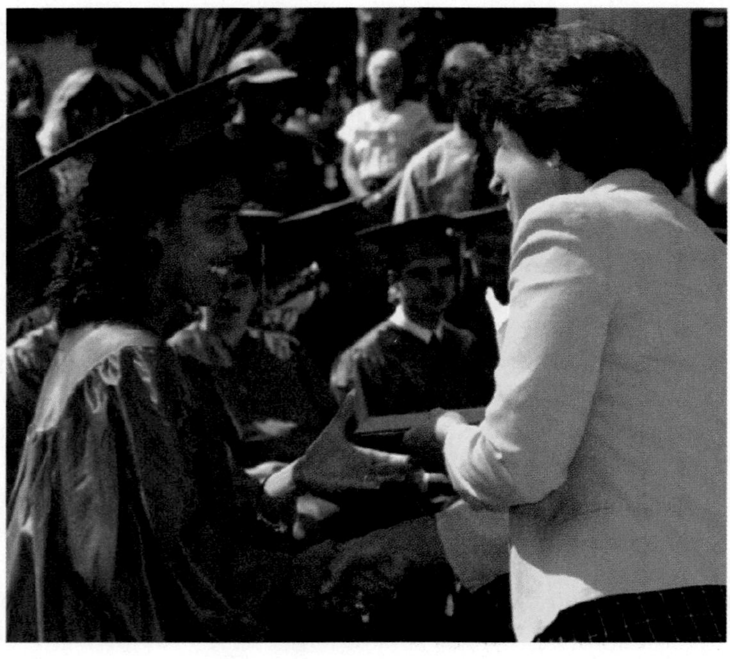

▲ **Figure 27-19** A simple handshake requires the coordination of many body systems.

A handshake may at first seem like a simple task: You grab someone's hand and give it a squeeze. But physiologically, shaking someone's hand is a complicated procedure requiring many muscles, bones, and nerves working simultaneously and in coordination. You must extend your hand at precisely the right moment, in just the right position, and with the polite amount of grip.

All this coordination occurs in your brain, the main control center of your body. First, your eyes sense the presence of the other person and relay that information to your brain. The thinking part of your brain decides to initiate the handshake. Then other brain regions send out messages along your nerves to an array of muscles. The response consists of coordinated contractions and relaxations in the muscles of your back, shoulder, upper arm, forearm, and wrist. These muscles lift and extend the right bones in the right sequence to extend your hand. Finally, many muscles manipulate the 27 bones in your hand into place.

Throughout this process, blood cells travel through your blood vessels, providing a constant supply of nutrients and oxygen to hand muscles. The brain acts as the control center, directing each and every movement involved in the handshake through an extensive network of nerves. As this example shows, what may seem like a very simple gesture is in fact a complicated process that requires energy and involves the cooperation of many of your body's organs, tissues, and cells. In the chapters to come, you will learn the physiology behind other seemingly simple daily tasks.

Online Activity 27.5

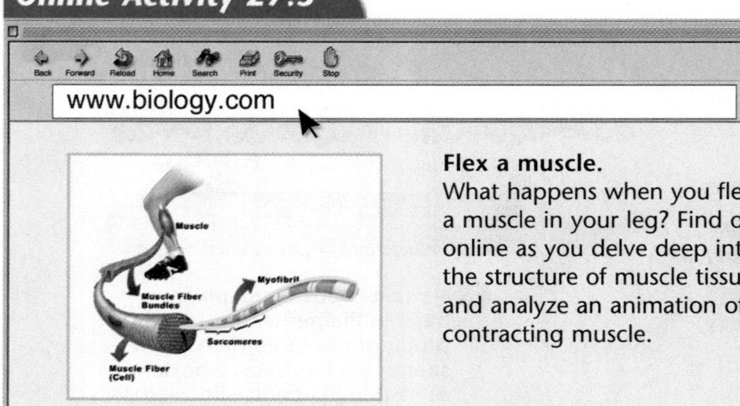

Flex a muscle.
What happens when you flex a muscle in your leg? Find out online as you delve deep into the structure of muscle tissue and analyze an animation of a contracting muscle.

Concept Check 27.5

1. Explain how muscles work in pairs in moving limbs.
2. Identify the structures that make up a skeletal muscle.
3. Identify at least three organ systems involved in a handshake. Describe what each system contributes to the handshake.
4. Explain how actin and myosin interact as a muscle cell contracts.

Every Flex Is Quite Complex

Structure and Function in a Chicken Wing

Question How do the tissues of a chicken wing work together during movement?

Lab Overview In this investigation you will carefully examine and dissect the tissues of a chicken wing to learn about its structure and to discover how bones, muscles, tendons, ligaments, and skin work together and function in movement.

Preparing for the Lab To help you prepare for the lab, go to the *Lab 27 Online Companion.* Explore structure and function in the human arm and make predictions about the structures that make a chicken wing move. Prepare for the lab procedure by previewing the steps you will take.

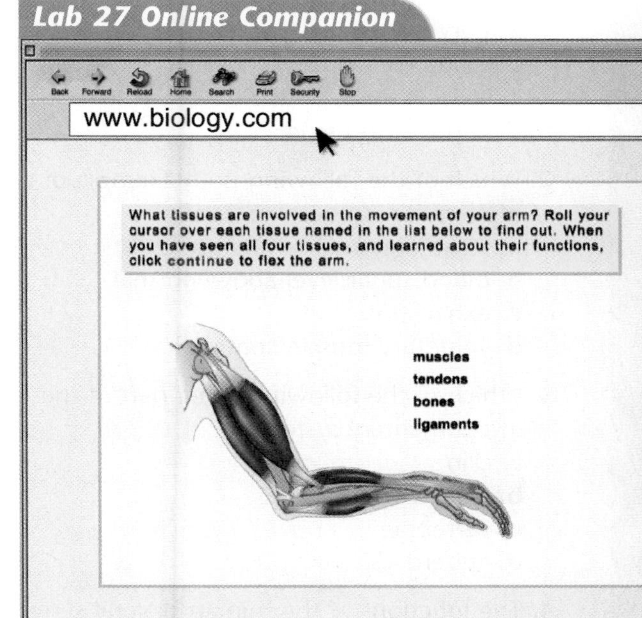
Lab 27 Online Companion
Back
Forward
Reload
Home
Search
Print
Security
Stop
www.biology.com
What tissues are involved in the movement of your arm? Roll your cursor over each tissue named in the list below to find out. When you have seen all four tissues, and learned about their functions, click continue to flex the arm.
muscles
tendons
bones
ligaments

Completing the Lab Use your Laboratory Manual or lab page printouts from the *Lab 27 Online Companion* to do the investigation and draw conclusions from the observations you made. **CAUTION:** *Be sure to follow your teacher's instructions and all safety guidelines given in the investigation.*

Multiple Choice

Choose the letter of the best answer.

1. Which type of tissue covers your body and lines your internal organs?
   a. nervous tissue
   b. epithelial tissue
   c. muscle tissue
   d. connective tissue

2. Which of the following is an example of a result of maintaining homeostasis?
   a. steady internal temperature
   b. blood sugar level above normal
   c. exhaustion
   d. voluntary muscle contraction

3. Which of the following is *not* part of the integumentary system?
   a. skin
   b. hair
   c. vertebrae
   d. fingernails

4. The functions of the human skeletal system include
   a. building muscle cells.
   b. exchanging chemicals with muscles.
   c. providing attachment sites for muscles.
   d. preventing fluid loss.

5. Pick the answer that accurately pairs a structure with its function:
   a. sharp front teeth: grinding food
   b. hinge joint: rotating one bone around another bone
   c. highly folded lining of intestine: exchanging nutrients
   d. all of the above

6. Which is *not* true of skeletal muscles?
   a. They work in pairs.
   b. Their cells each have many nuclei.
   c. Myosin and actin interact, which causes contractions.
   d. Their contractions produce heartbeats.

Short Answer

7. Explain the relationship between anatomy and physiology.
8. Give an example of how one of your body structures matches its function(s).
9. Name two general functions of connective tissue.
10. Describe one function of smooth muscles.
11. Describe the cause and effect of shivering.
12. Describe the structure and function of the epidermis, dermis, and hypodermis.
13. What function does the cartilage between your vertebrae have?
14. Name two ways people can reduce their risk of osteoporosis.
15. Describe the difference between ligaments and tendons.
16. Describe the structure of a skeletal muscle.
17. Describe the role myosin heads play during muscle contraction.

Visualizing Concepts

18. Arrange the steps below into a flowchart showing the process of a skeletal muscle contraction.

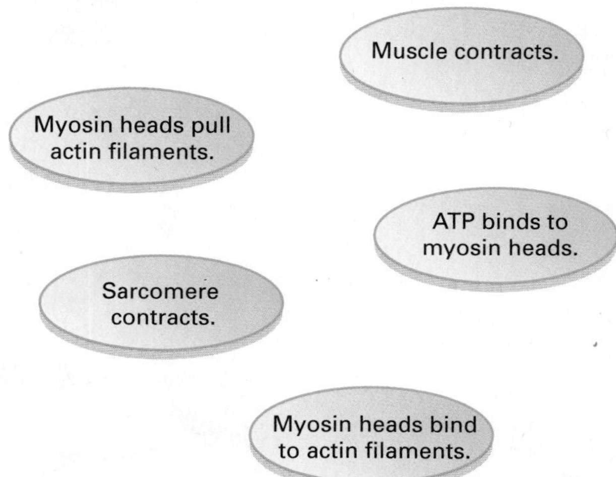

Muscle contracts.
Myosin heads pull actin filaments.
ATP binds to myosin heads.
Sarcomere contracts.
Myosin heads bind to actin filaments.

Analyzing Information

19. Analyzing Photographs Examine the photo to answer the questions below.

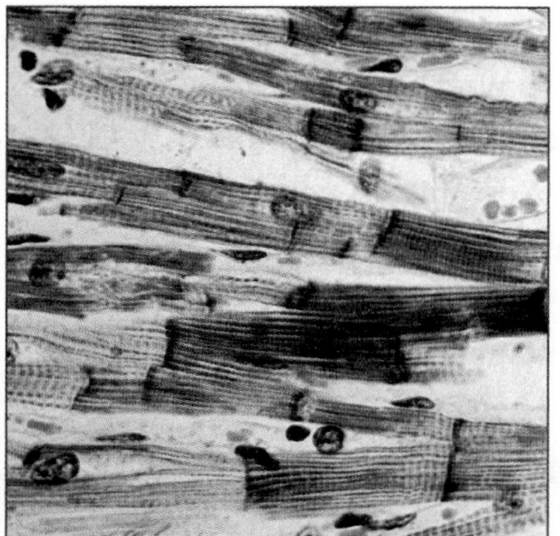
LM 160×

a. Which kind of muscle tissue is shown in the photo?
b. Where in the body is this tissue found?
c. How does the shape of the cells of this tissue contribute to the tissue's function?
d. Is the contraction of the muscles containing this tissue voluntary or involuntary?

20. Analyzing Data Use the data table below to answer the questions.

Temperature Readings

	6 A.M.	8 A.M.	10 A.M.	Noon
Temp. Outdoors	14°C	15°C	17°C	19°C
Temp. Indoors	23°C	23°C	23°C	24°C
Temp. Inside Human	37°C	37°C	37°C	37°C

a. Which location has the greatest change in temperature?
b. Which of these three locations do you think has some kind of homeostatic mechanism? Why?
c. Do the data allow you to conclude whether the human is indoors or outdoors between 8:00 A.M. and noon? Why or why not?

Critical Thinking

21. Comparing and Contrasting Give examples of organs in your body with skeletal muscle tissue and with smooth muscle tissue. Describe the similarities and differences between the two types of muscles.

22. Relating Cause and Effect How might a burn injury to the skin affect your body's ability to maintain homeostasis? Explain.

23. What's Wrong With These Statements? *Briefly explain why each statement is inaccurate or misleading.*
a. Homeostasis prevents your body from changing.
b. Your bones are hard and brittle.
c. While beating a drum, your arm muscles are contracted.
d. Nonliving cells have no function in the human body.

24. Making Generalizations Name an object in your home or classroom that is similar in structure to a hinge joint found in your body. Describe how their functions are similar.

Performance Assessment

Writing You learned that shaking someone's hand requires tight coordination of your body's systems. Write your own description of your body's coordination during an action you perform while playing your favorite sport.

Online Assessment/Test Preparation

Back Forward Reload Home Search Print Security Stop

www.biology.com

- **Chapter 27 Assessment**
  Check your understanding of the chapter concepts.
- **Standardized Test Preparation**
  Practice test-taking skills you need to succeed.

The Nervous System

Inside the dark movie theater, the smell of popcorn wafts up your nose, and soda fizz settles on your tongue. On the screen a car chase unfolds, complete with screeching tires and blaring horns. You shift in your seat, cramped and restless from sitting for so long. The friend sitting next to you bumps your arm.

All these incoming bits of information—the scents, sounds, and other sensations—trigger messages that travel along a network of nerves to your brain. Within milliseconds, your brain initiates responses to the different sensations. The buttery odor of popcorn might result in your salivary glands secreting saliva. Maybe the sights and sounds from the screen will scare you, causing adrenaline to course through your body.

In this chapter you will investigate how your complex circuitry of nerve cells and the control center known as your brain enable you to perceive and respond to your environment. Before you begin, go online to the *WebQuest* to explore some of the brain's functions.

Key Concepts

What's Online

www.biology.com

WebQuest
BrainQuest

Concept 28.1

The nervous system links sensation to response.

Online Activity 28.1
Analyze a reflex arc.

Concept 28.2

Neurons conduct nerve impulses.

Online Activity 28.2
Examine how neurons function.

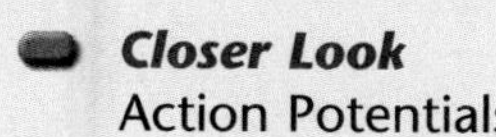

Closer Look
Action Potentials

Concept 28.3

The PNS carries information to and from the CNS.

Online Activity 28.3
Compare PNS divisions.

Concept 28.4

The CNS integrates nervous information.

Online Activity 28.4
Build a brain.

Concept 28.5

Sensory receptors link the environment to the nervous system.

Online Activity 28.5
Get an inside view of vision.

Science, Technology, & Society
Smell and Behavior

Lab 28 Online Companion
What Gives Your Vision Precision?

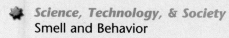

Concept 28.6

Certain drugs alter brain function.

Online Activity 28.6
Analyze the effects of drugs.

Assessment

Chapter 28 Review

Chapter 28 Assessment

CONCEPT 28.1 The nervous system links sensation to response.

OBJECTIVES
- Describe the basic structure and functions of the nervous system.
- Explain the pathway of a reflex arc.

KEY TERMS
- central nervous system (CNS)
- peripheral nervous system (PNS)
- nerve
- stimulus
- sensory neuron
- sensory receptor
- interneuron
- motor neuron
- reflex

What's Online

Online Activity 28.1
Analyze a reflex arc.

Each second your brain processes thousands of messages. As you read this sentence, for instance, your brain receives information from your eyes, assesses it, and forms a response—perhaps directing your hand to write notes. Simultaneously, your brain monitors your heart rate and temperature. Your nervous system's intricate organization makes all this activity possible.

Structure and Functions of the Nervous System

Just as muscle cells are the basic units of the muscular system, nerve cells (neurons) are the basic units of the nervous sytem. While there are many types of neurons, they all have specialized structures that enable them to convey electrical signals.

The organs of the nervous system form two subsystems. The brain and the spinal cord make up the **central nervous system (CNS),** the body's main information processing center. All the nervous tissue outside the CNS makes up the **peripheral nervous system (PNS).** The PNS delivers information to the CNS and carries messages from the CNS to other organs through communication lines called nerves. A **nerve** consists of one or more bundles of neuron fibers surrounded by connective tissue. The PNS and CNS together carry out three main functions (Figure 28-1). Different types of neurons are involved in each function.

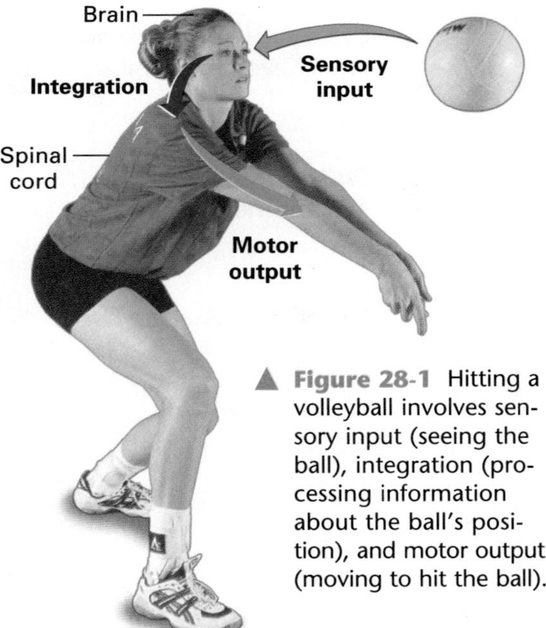

▲ Figure 28-1 Hitting a volleyball involves sensory input (seeing the ball), integration (processing information about the ball's position), and motor output (moving to hit the ball).

Sensory Input First, the PNS receives information about an environmental change, or **stimulus** (plural, *stimuli*). Examples of stimuli include the colors of a sunset, a change in temperature, or a tap on the shoulder. Neurons that carry information about stimuli to the CNS are called **sensory neurons.** Some sensory neurons detect stimuli directly, such as the neurons that sense pain. But most stimuli are received by highly specialized cells called **sensory receptors.**

Integration Next, the CNS interprets the information. This step, called integration, involves neurons located entirely within the CNS, which are called **interneurons.** For example, when you sit down, your CNS integrates sensory input about the positions of the chair and your body and plans your response.

Motor Output Next, the CNS orders a response—perhaps instructing a muscle to contract or a gland to secrete a hormone. Neurons that carry such signals away from the CNS are called **motor neurons.**

The Knee-Jerk Reflex: An Example

Here's a familiar example that shows the roles of the three kinds of neurons in responding to a stimulus. During a physical your doctor has probably performed a test by striking your knee with a rubber hammer. Without your thinking about it, your lower leg quickly jerks forward—a rapid, automatic response known as a **reflex.** The nervous system pathway that regulates a reflex is called a reflex arc (Figure 28-2). Next, you'll explore how the structure of neurons enables them to perform their functions in a reflex arc or other response.

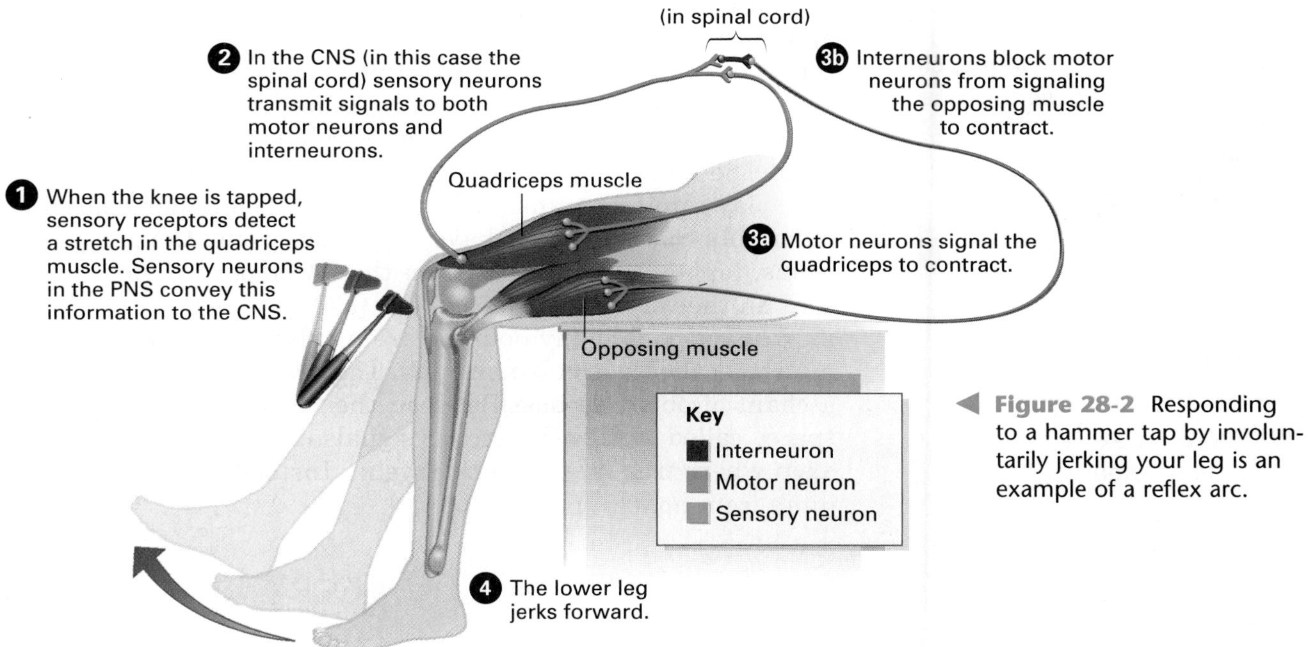
(in spinal cord)
2 In the CNS (in this case the spinal cord) sensory neurons transmit signals to both motor neurons and interneurons.
3b Interneurons block motor neurons from signaling the opposing muscle to contract.
Quadriceps muscle
1 When the knee is tapped, sensory receptors detect a stretch in the quadriceps muscle. Sensory neurons in the PNS convey this information to the CNS.
3a Motor neurons signal the quadriceps to contract.
Opposing muscle
Key
Interneuron
Motor neuron
Sensory neuron
4 The lower leg jerks forward.

Figure 28-2 Responding to a hammer tap by involuntarily jerking your leg is an example of a reflex arc.

Online Activity 28.1

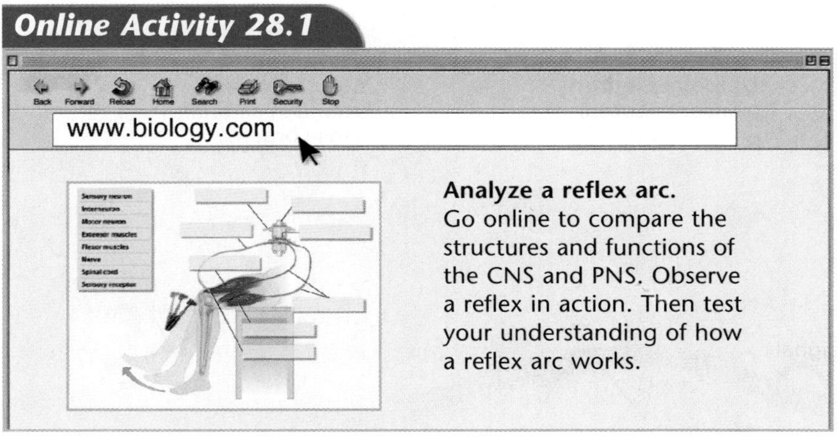
Back
Forward
Reload
Home
Search
Print
Security
Stop
www.biology.com

Analyze a reflex arc.
Go online to compare the structures and functions of the CNS and PNS. Observe a reflex in action. Then test your understanding of how a reflex arc works.

Concept Check 28.1

1. Define the two subdivisions of the nervous system, and list the nervous system's three main functions.
2. Explain how the three types of neurons are involved in a simple reflex arc.
3. Give two examples of environmental stimuli other than those discussed in the text.

CONCEPT 28.2

Neurons conduct nerve impulses.

OBJECTIVES

- Describe the basic structure of a neuron.
- Explain how a neuron at rest stores potential energy.
- Relate how a nerve signal begins, travels, and crosses synapses.
- Identify effects of neurotransmitters.

KEY TERMS

- dendrite
- axon
- myelin sheath
- node
- resting potential
- depolarization
- threshold
- action potential
- synapse
- synaptic cleft
- neurotransmitter

What's Online

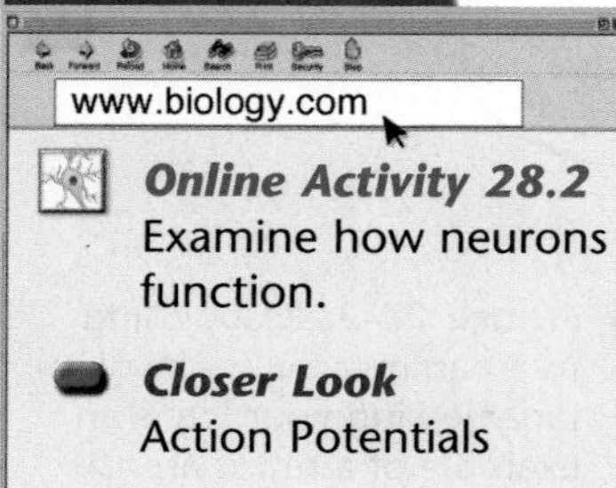

Throughout this book you have explored how biological structures are related to their functions. Neurons, the specialized cells that make up your nervous system, have structures that fit their function of communicating signals throughout your body.

Structure of a Neuron

Though there are many different types of neurons in your body, most neurons share several common features (Figure 28-3). A typical neuron has a cell body that houses the neuron's nucleus and most of the organelles. Two types of fibers project from the cell body. Fibers called **dendrites** receive signals and carry them toward the neuron's cell body. A fiber called the **axon** carries electrical impulses away from the cell body and toward other cells. The end of the axon forms a clump of knobbed branches that play a role in transmitting messages to another neuron or other cell. Some neurons have very long axons. Certain motor axons, for instance, stretch from the lower part of your spinal cord all the way to muscles in your toes.

The axons of many neurons are insulated by a thick coat of material called a **myelin sheath.** The myelin sheath resembles a chain of oblong beads. Between the "beads" are uninsulated spaces called **nodes.** Electrical signals cannot travel along the axon where it is insulated by myelin. Instead, the signal must jump from node to node.

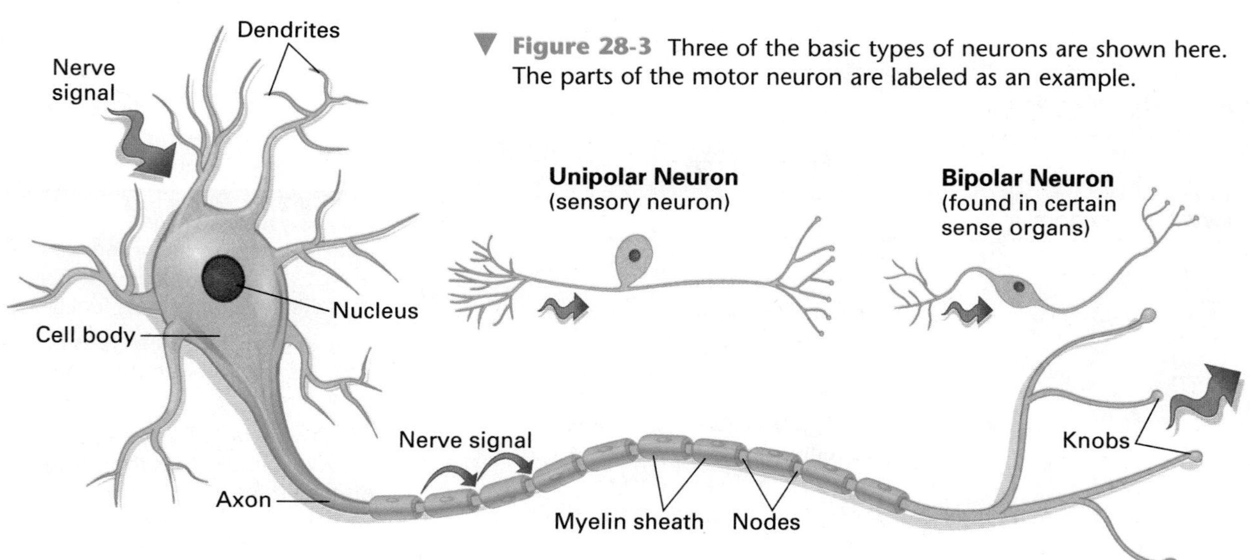

▼ **Figure 28-3** Three of the basic types of neurons are shown here. The parts of the motor neuron are labeled as an example.

A Neuron at Rest

To understand nerve signals, you first need to examine a resting neuron—a neuron that is not yet transmitting a signal.

Resting Potential Much like a battery, a resting neuron stores electrical energy. The key is the neuron's plasma membrane, which separates ions located inside and outside the cell. (Recall that ions are electrically charged atoms and molecules.) Because opposite charges attract, separating them is a form of potential energy—the electrical version of water stored behind a dam. Just as the water produces pressure on the dam, holding opposite charges apart produces an electrical "pressure" called voltage. Voltage is measured in units called volts. For example, the voltage of a new flashlight battery is 1.5 volts (V), or 1500 millivolts (mV). A resting neuron is a smaller "battery," with a voltage of –70 mV (about 5 percent of a flashlight battery's voltage). The minus sign in front of the 70 indicates that the inside of the nerve cell is negative in charge compared to the outside. This voltage across the plasma membrane of a resting neuron is called the **resting potential.** The word *potential* refers to potential energy.

Ion Channels The resting potential is based on the concentrations of various ions on opposite sides of the plasma membrane. As Figure 28-4 illustrates, sodium ions (Na^+) are more concentrated outside the neuron than inside. In contrast, potassium ions (K^+) are more concentrated inside the cell than outside.

Specific proteins built into the membrane act as channels for each kind of ion. These channels allow the ions to diffuse across the membrane from where they are more concentrated to where they are less concentrated. So, Na^+ ions diffuse into the cell and K^+ ions diffuse out. However, the membrane has many more K^+ channels than Na^+ channels. Positive charge exits the cell as K^+ ions faster than it enters as Na^+ ions. This unbalanced diffusion of positive charge is the main cause of the outside of the cell being positive compared to the inside.

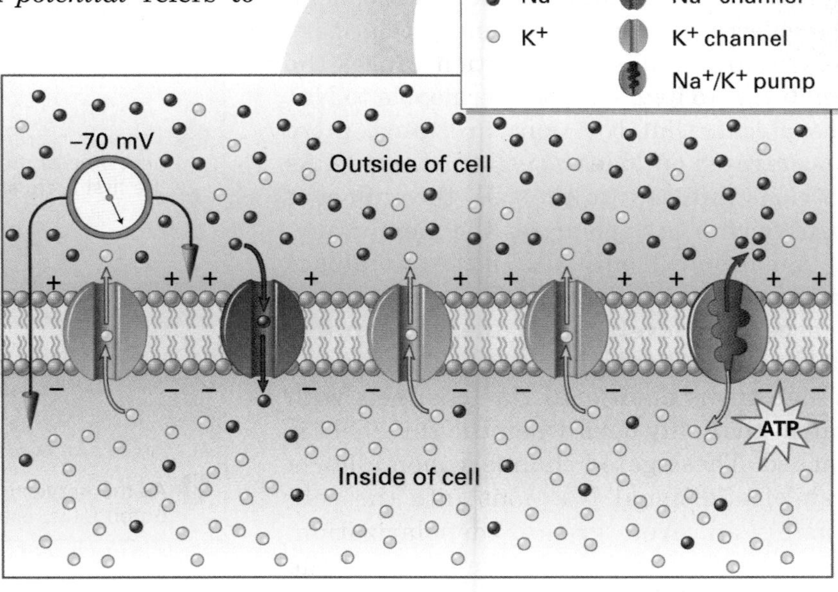

▲ **Figure 28-4** The concentration differences of ions across the plasma membrane result in a voltage of approximately –70 mV in a resting neuron.

Ion Pumps What causes the ion concentration differences? In addition to the ion channels that allow diffusion, the membrane contains a protein, called the sodium-potassium (Na^+/K^+) pump, that pumps these ions back across the membrane (Figure 28-4). Pumping chemicals in a direction opposite to diffusion requires energy, like pumping water uphill against gravity. ATP is the energy source that powers the ion pumps.

The neuron's resting potential (voltage) and steep concentration differences of Na^+ ions and K^+ ions make it sensitive to stimulation. Like a flashlight with its switch in the "off" position, the resting neuron is ready to "fire"—to transmit a nerve signal.

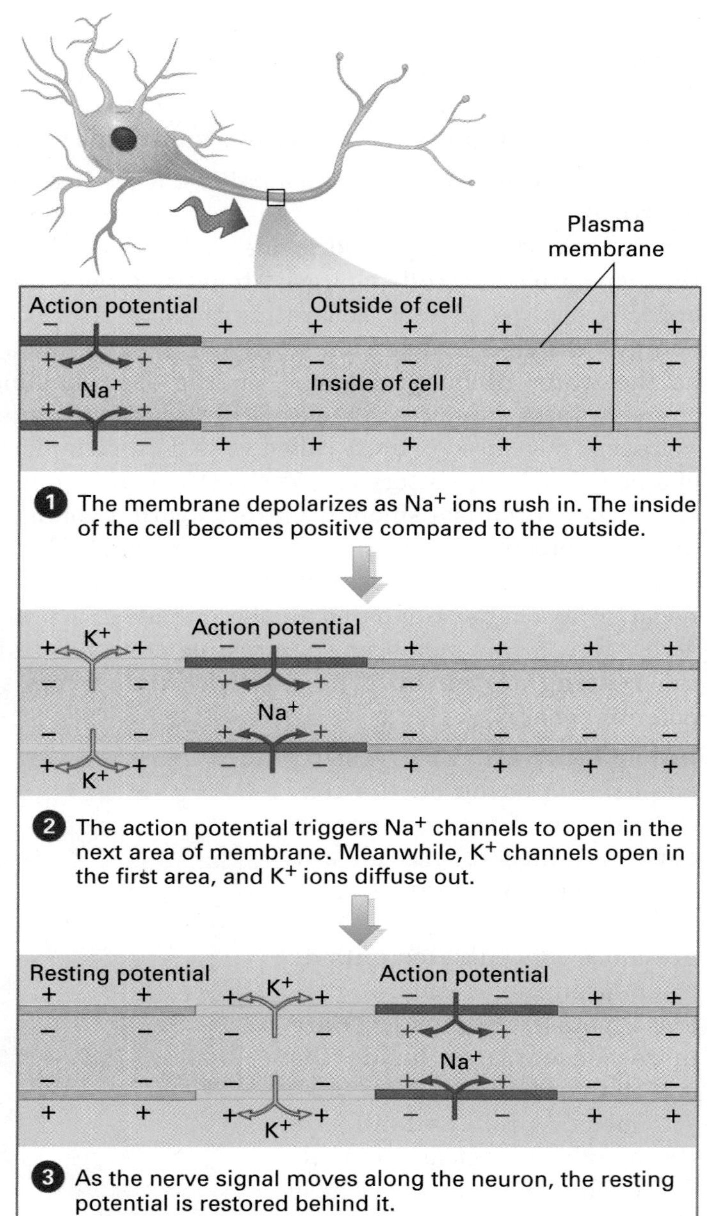

Plasma membrane
Action potential
Outside of cell
Na+
Inside of cell
1 The membrane depolarizes as Na+ ions rush in. The inside of the cell becomes positive compared to the outside.
K+
Action potential
Na+
K+
2 The action potential triggers Na+ channels to open in the next area of membrane. Meanwhile, K+ channels open in the first area, and K+ ions diffuse out.
Resting potential
K+
Action potential
Na+
K+
3 As the nerve signal moves along the neuron, the resting potential is restored behind it.

▲ **Figure 28-5** Once the neuron's membrane is depolarized to the threshold level, an action potential occurs. This triggers an action potential in a neighboring section of the membrane, transmitting the nerve signal along the axon.

How a Nerve Signal Travels

All cells—not just neurons—have voltages across their plasma membranes. But only certain specialized cells, including neurons and muscle cells, can use this stored energy to transmit signals.

Triggering the Nerve Signal If a neuron is stimulated—by a tap on the knee, for example—the voltage across the membrane changes at the point of stimulation. This voltage change is called a **depolarization,** because the charge difference across the membrane decreases (the membrane depolarizes). This occurs because stimulation causes the membrane to become more permeable to Na^+ ions. Recall that Na^+ ions are much more concentrated outside the cell than inside. As Na^+ ions diffuse into the cell, the inflow of positive charge depolarizes the membrane.

A neuron will only "fire" if the stimulus is strong enough to depolarize the membrane to a certain level, called the **threshold,** which is usually about –50 mV. This voltage change opens additional Na^+ channels with "gates" that only open when the threshold is reached. These gated channels then allow a rush of additional Na^+ ions into the cell, causing an even greater depolarization. This stronger depolarization, called the **action potential,** is the start of the nerve signal. In Figure 28-5 Step 1, notice that the inside of the neuron becomes positive compared to the outside as the Na^+ ions rush in. This change indicates the action potential.

Transmitting the Nerve Signal The initial action potential occurs at the point of stimulation. But the voltage change of the action potential then opens Na^+ gates nearby, causing an action potential there. This in turn triggers an action potential a little farther along the neuron, and so on. You can compare this to tipping over the first domino in a long row. The first domino does not itself travel the length of the row, but its fall is relayed all along the row, domino by domino. In the case of a neuron, "news" of the stimulus is transmitted over the length of the neuron as a series of action potentials.

Notice in Step 2 of Figure 28-5 on page 614 that after the nerve signal passes a region of the neuron, the resting potential is restored. This is indicated by the outside of the cell returning to positive compared to the inside. The return to resting potential is caused by the opening of K^+ gates. The K^+ ions, more concentrated inside the cell than outside, diffuse out.

With each action potential, there is actually little change in the concentration differences of Na^+ ions and K^+ ions. This is because the gated channels close again very quickly. It is like rapidly opening and closing the water gates in a dam. With each release of water, the lake level doesn't change much. However, this will eventually drain a lake that is not refilled. The neuron "refills its reservoir"—restores its concentration differences of Na^+ and K^+ ions—by using the Na^+/K^+ pumps you read about earlier.

The Speed of Transmission The nerve signal can travel along a neuron's membrane at a rate of about 5 meters per second. But most of your neurons can transmit signals even faster because of the myelin sheath. The sheath surrounds the axon as a chain of cells separated by nodes. As shown in Figure 28-6, the action potential "jumps" from node to node. This transmits the nerve signal much faster than if the message had to travel the entire length of the membrane.

Neurons with myelin sheaths transmit nerve signals at a rate of about 150 meters per second—30 times faster than if the signal had to take the longer route along the entire axon. A nerve signal can travel along a nerve from your spinal cord to your toes in less than 7 milliseconds!

Measuring Stimulus Strength If the stimulus is too weak to push the neuron's voltage to the threshold level, then the stimulus is "ignored"—there is no action potential. If the stimulus is strong enough to reach the threshold, then the neuron fires an action potential. But a very strong stimulus produces an action potential identical to one caused by a weaker stimulus that barely reaches the threshold. In other words, action potentials—and thus nerve signals—are all-or-none events.

If all action potentials are identical, how can the nervous system distinguish a strong stimulus such as a crashing cymbal from a weaker stimulus such as a chiming xylophone? As a stimulus becomes more intense, the frequency and number of action potentials increase, though the strength of each action potential remains the same. The brain hears the cymbals as loud because their crash stimulates many ear neurons, each firing many action potentials per millisecond.

▼ **Figure 28-6** In a neuron with a myelin sheath, a nerve signal jumps from node to node.

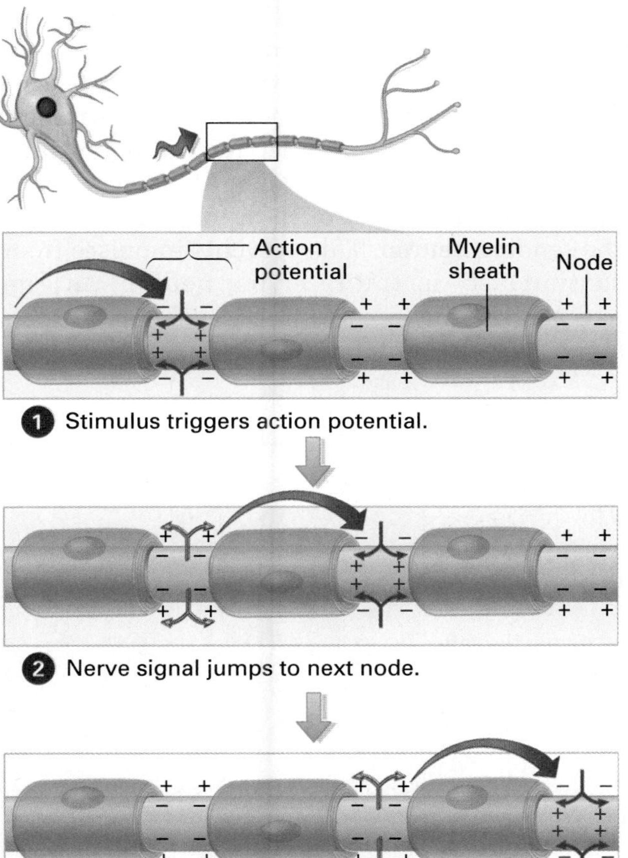
Action potential
Myelin sheath
Node
1 Stimulus triggers action potential.
2 Nerve signal jumps to next node.
3 Resting potential is restored at the nodes behind the nerve signal.

Crossing Synapses

The nervous system works by transmitting information from sensory neurons to interneurons for processing, and then to motor neurons for carrying out the response. Now that you have studied how a nerve signal travels along a neuron, the next step is to see how signals pass from one neuron to another.

As you read earlier, the end of a neuron's axon has many fine branches with knoblike tips. The junction between these knobs and another cell is called a **synapse** (SIN aps). Synapses may be electrical or chemical. In an electrical synapse, the action potential at the end of the axon directly causes an electrical change in the receiving cell. Such synapses are common in your heart and digestive organs, where nerve signals maintain steady, rhythmic muscle contractions.

In a chemical synapse, the nerve signal must be transmitted across a tiny space called the **synaptic cleft** (Figure 28-7). For this to occur, the action potential (an electrical signal) is converted to a chemical signal. The chemical signal mostly consists of small, nitrogen-containing organic compounds called **neurotransmitters.**

Neurotransmitters are contained in tiny vesicles, or sacs, in the axon's knobs. When the action potential reaches the knob, it causes the vesicles to release the neurotransmitter into the synaptic cleft. The neurotransmitter diffuses across the gap and reaches the receiving neuron. Receptor molecules on the receiving neuron's membrane accept the neurotransmitter. Sometimes the result is a new impulse (action potential) in the receiving neuron. After the neurotransmitter triggers the new signal, the neurotransmitter is broken down by enzymes or reabsorbed into the sending neuron. This prevents impulses from being generated continuously in the receiving neuron. As Figure 28-7 shows, one neuron may receive hundreds or even thousands of signals simultaneously from different synapses.

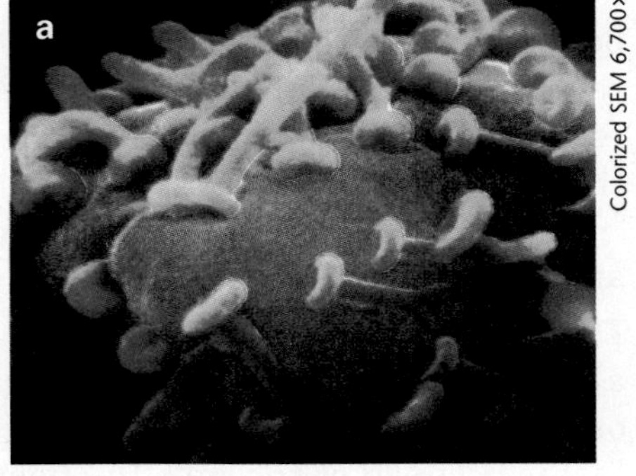

Figure 28-7 The area where one neuron meets another is the synapse. **a.** The cell body (orange) of this neuron receives input from the axon knobs (blue) of many other neurons. **b.** At each chemical synapse an action potential stimulates the release of neurotransmitters into the synaptic cleft. The neurotransmitter relays the signal from one neuron to the next.

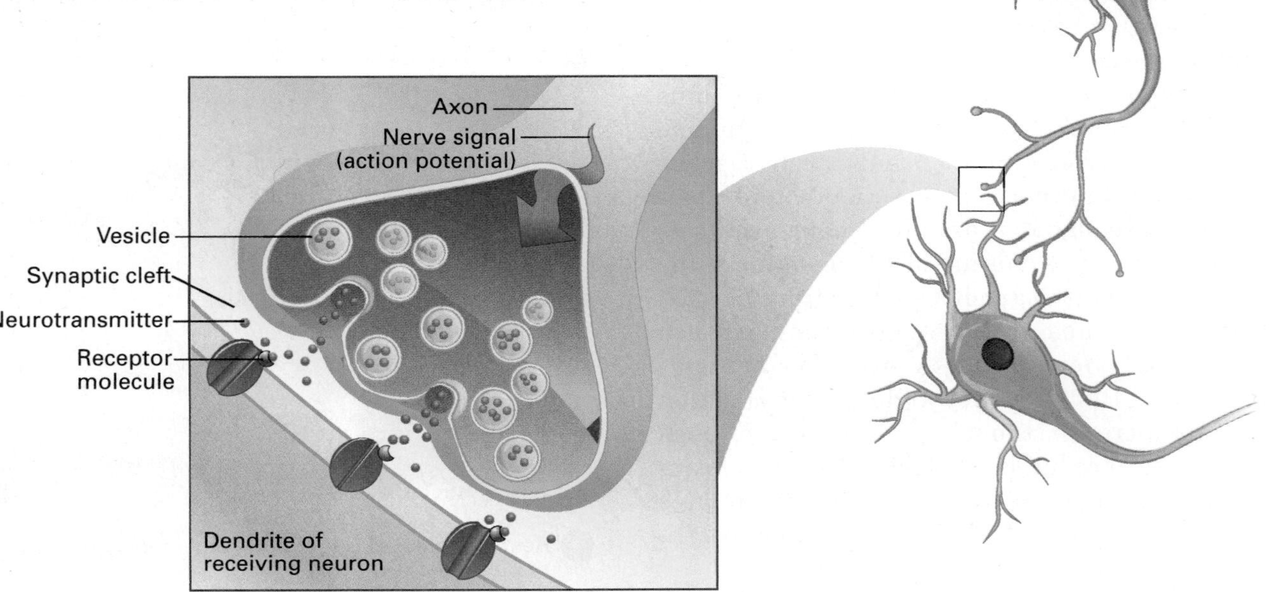

Effects of Neurotransmitters

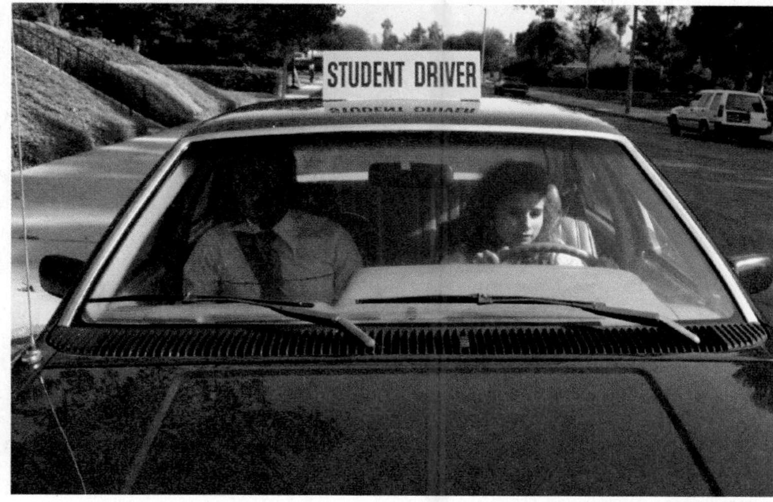

▲ **Figure 28-8** In stressful situations, such as learning to drive, epinephrine and norepinephrine trigger stress reactions in your body.

A receiving neuron may not generate a new action potential for every incoming signal. How a neuron responds depends on its receptors and on the specific chemical effects of each neurotransmitter. Some neurotransmitters help trigger action potentials in receiving neurons. Other neurotransmitters inhibit (block) the formation of action potentials in receiving neurons. A single neuron may receive a multitude of these opposing messages at the same time. The response of the neuron depends on which type of neurotransmitter is more abundant in the synapse.

Researchers have identified dozens of neurotransmitters, each with specific roles in the body. For example, the neurotransmitter acetylcholine is released by motor neurons at synapses with skeletal muscle cells. Acetylcholine triggers a change in the muscle cell membrane that results in the muscle cell contracting.

Epinephrine, norepinephrine, serotonin, and dopamine are other important neurotransmitters in the nervous system. Epinephrine and norepinephrine also function as hormones. In stressful situations, epinephrine and norepinephrine trigger physiological changes that result in increasing heart rate (Figure 28-8). In the brain, serotonin and dopamine trigger changes that affect sleep, mood, attention, and learning.

Researchers are finding that imbalances of certain neurotransmitters in the brain are associated with various kinds of mental illness. For example, low levels of norepinephrine and serotonin appear to be linked with depression. Understanding the roles of these neurotransmitters may help lead to treatments. For instance, the antidepressant drug Fluoxetine (Prozac™) blocks the removal of serotonin from the synaptic cleft. This increases the amount of serotonin available to receiving neurons.

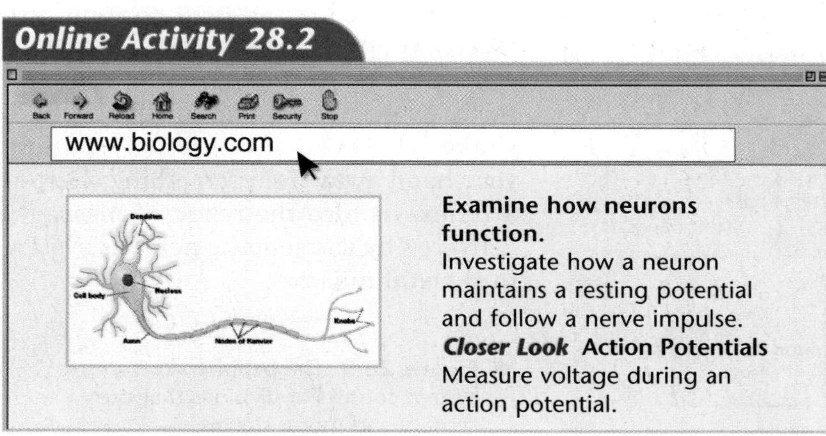

Online Activity 28.2
www.biology.com
Examine how neurons function.
Investigate how a neuron maintains a resting potential and follow a nerve impulse.
Closer Look **Action Potentials**
Measure voltage during an action potential.

Concept Check 28.2

1. Identify the two types of fibers that project from a neuron's cell body and state their functions.
2. Relate ion concentration differences across a neuron's membrane to the resting potential.
3. Explain the statement, "Action potentials are 'all-or-none' events."
4. Compare how nerve signals cross electrical and chemical synapses.
5. What are the two effects that a neurotransmitter can have on a receiving neuron?

CONCEPT 28.3

The PNS carries information to and from the CNS.

OBJECTIVES

- Summarize the roles of the sensory division.
- Describe different functions of neurons within the motor division.

KEY TERMS

- somatic nervous system
- autonomic nervous system
- sympathetic division
- parasympathetic division

What's Online

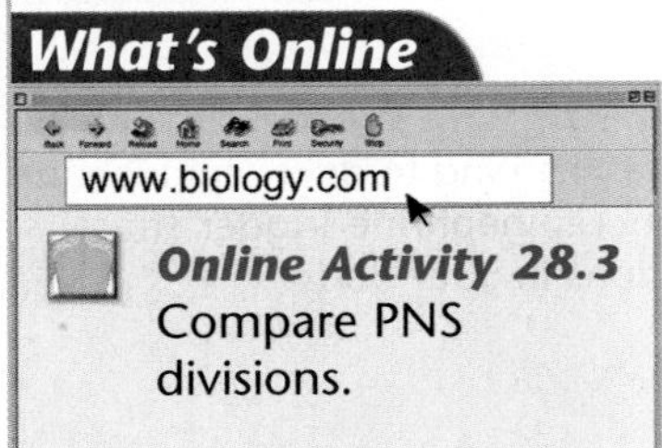

Online Activity 28.3
Compare PNS divisions.

As you have read, the peripheral nervous system (PNS) transmits signals to the central nervous system (CNS) for processing and transmits responses from the CNS to the rest of the body. Based on these two functions, the PNS can be divided into a sensory division and a motor division.

Sensory Division

The sensory division of the PNS includes two sets of sensory neurons (Figure 28-9). One set brings in information about the outside environment from the eyes, ears, skin, and other external sense organs. The other set provides the brain with internal information about the body such as temperature, heart rate, and acidity level of the blood. Both sets of sensory neurons can also provide the brain with sensations of pain, which is the body's warning that it may be suffering tissue damage.

Motor Division

Motor neurons make up the second major division of the PNS. They carry the CNS's response messages to muscle cells and gland cells. The motor division can be further divided into the somatic nervous system and the autonomic nervous system.

The Somatic Nervous System The motor neurons of the **somatic nervous system** carry signals from the CNS to skeletal muscles. The actions controlled by the somatic nervous system are mostly voluntary (under your conscious control). For example, you can voluntarily extend your hand to offer a handshake. However, involuntarily pulling your hand away from something sharp—a reflex—is also the result of messages delivered by the somatic nervous system to skeletal muscles.

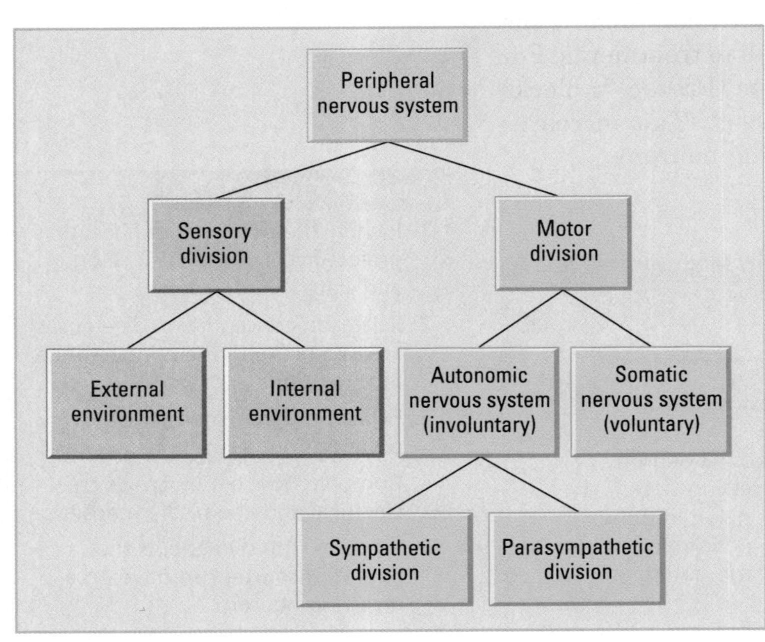

Figure 28-9 The peripheral nervous system consists of divisions that carry sensory and motor signals.

The Autonomic Nervous System The motor neurons of the **autonomic nervous system** carry signals to organs such as the intestines, the heart, and glands. These neurons cause responses that are mostly involuntary. The neurons of this system are separated into two divisions, the sympathetic and the parasympathetic. The two divisions have opposing effects on most organs (Figure 28-10).

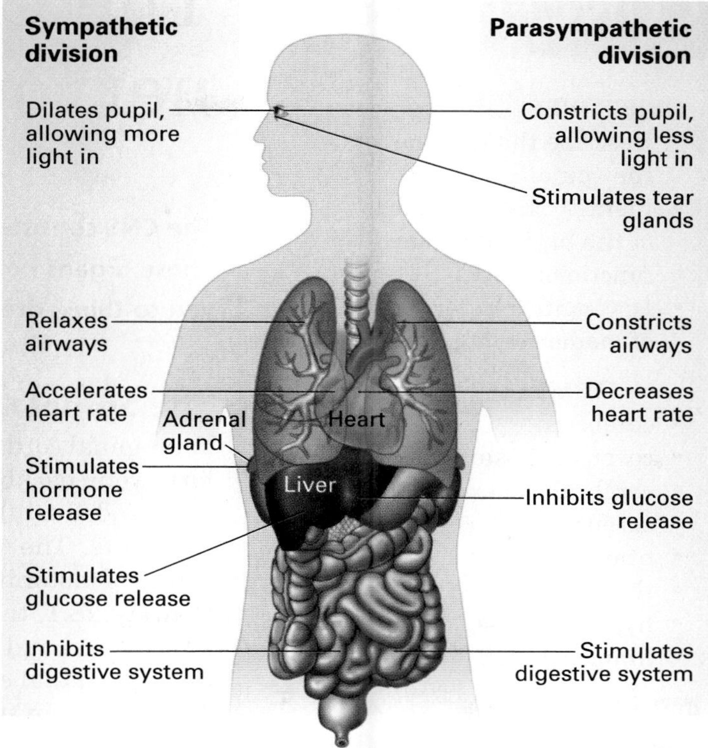

▲ **Figure 28-10** In many cases, the two divisions of the autonomic nervous system have opposing effects on the same organ.

The **sympathetic division** increases the general level of activity in the body and makes more energy available. This division prepares the body for intense activities that consume energy, such as running or taking a difficult exam. Under extreme levels of physical or emotional stress, your body undergoes what is called the "fight-or-flight response." Certain sympathetic division neurons stimulate organs directly, while others work indirectly by signaling certain glands to secrete hormones. Such hormones might increase your heart rate, cause your liver to release glucose, or relax the airways in your lungs, enabling more air to enter. The sympathetic division response also slows down your digestive system, making more blood available to carry oxygen to your brain, heart, and muscles.

In contrast, the **parasympathetic division** has a much different effect, calming the body and returning it to regular maintenance functions. This division decreases your heart rate and glucose release. It also stimulates your digestive system to continue breaking down food.

The fight-or-flight response and total relaxation are opposite extremes. Most organs receive both sympathetic and parasympathetic signals that continually adjust the organs' activity to a suitable level.

Online Activity 28.3

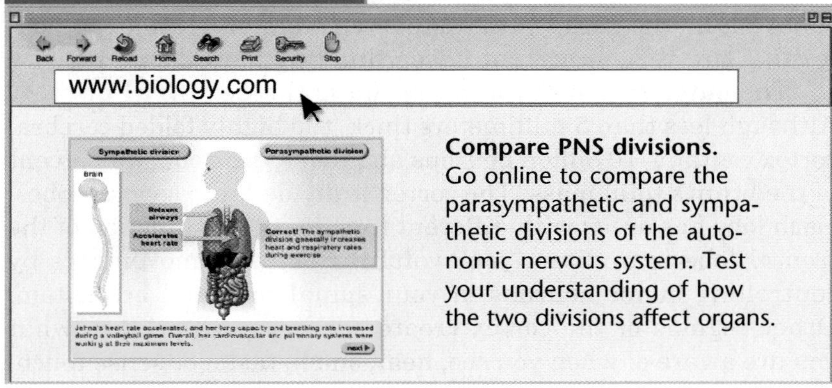

Compare PNS divisions. Go online to compare the parasympathetic and sympathetic divisions of the autonomic nervous system. Test your understanding of how the two divisions affect organs.

Concept Check 28.3

1. What are the two functions of sensory neurons in the sensory division?
2. Distinguish the functions of the somatic and autonomic nervous systems.
3. Compare and contrast the two divisions of the autonomic nervous system.

CONCEPT 28.4

The CNS integrates nervous information.

OBJECTIVES
- Describe the function of the spinal cord.
- Identify the main parts of the brain and their functions.
- Distinguish different types of memories.

KEY TERMS
- cerebrum
- corpus callosum
- cerebral cortex
- cerebellum
- brainstem
- thalamus
- hypothalamus
- limbic system

The CNS consists of two structures: the spinal cord and the brain. These organs not only enable you to survive, but they also allow you to think, dream, and plan as a creative and intelligent being.

The Spinal Cord

Your spinal cord is contained within the column of vertebrae that form your backbone, or spine (Figure 28-11). The spinal cord is surrounded by fluid that cushions the cord and provides it with nutrients. The spinal cord contains interneurons and the cell bodies of motor neurons. As described in the knee-jerk example in Concept 28.1, the spinal cord processes certain types of sensory information and sends out responses via motor neurons. In addition, the spinal cord contains neurons that convey signals to and from the brain.

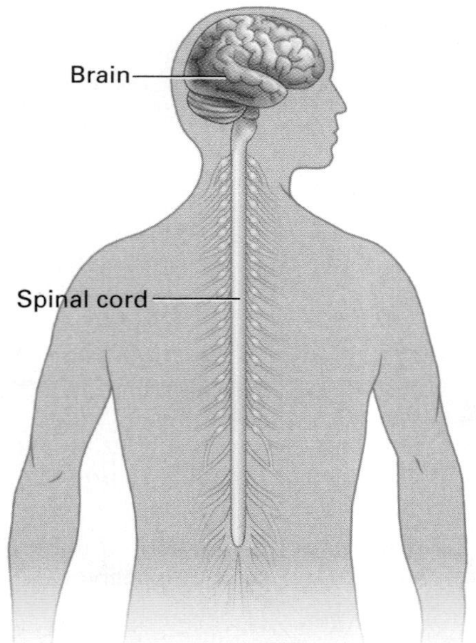

▲ **Figure 28-11** The brain and spinal cord make up the CNS.

The Brain

Composed of about 100 billion neurons, the human brain is more complex than a computer. It receives, sorts, and delivers vast quantities of information. This section discusses the brain's major structures and functions (Figure 28-12 on page 621).

Cerebrum The **cerebrum** (suh REE brum) is the largest and most complex part of the brain. It is divided into two halves called hemispheres. The left hemisphere controls movement of the right side of your body, and the right hemisphere controls movement of the left side of your body. In most people, the left hemisphere specializes in logical thinking, problem solving, and language, while the right hemisphere is more responsible for creative thoughts and imagination. The hemispheres are connected by a thick band of more than 100 million nerve fibers called the **corpus callosum.** The corpus callosum supports communication between the hemispheres. Beneath the corpus callosum lie the *basal nuclei,* small clusters of neuron cell bodies that are very important in coordinating movement.

The outer region of the cerebrum is the **cerebral cortex.** Although less than 5 millimeters thick, the highly folded cerebral cortex contains 10 billion neurons and makes up about 40 percent of the brain's total mass. The cortex is divided into several lobes. Each lobe has areas with different functions. One function of the frontal lobe is to direct your voluntary muscle movements by controlling motor neurons in your spinal cord and brainstem. Other regions of the cortex create sensory perceptions—what you are aware of when you see, hear, smell, taste, or sense touch.

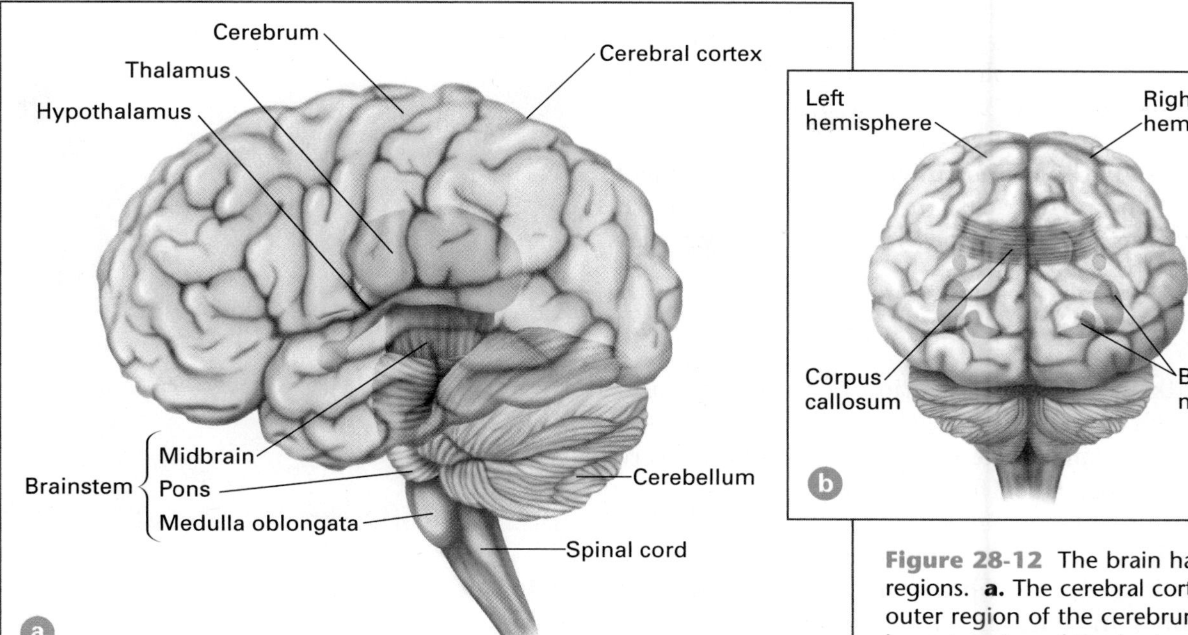

Figure 28-12 The brain has many regions. **a.** The cerebral cortex is the outer region of the cerebrum, the largest region of the brain. Other regions are located within or beneath the cerebrum. **b.** The cerebrum's right and left hemispheres are connected by a thick mass of nerve fibers called the corpus callosum. **c.** The cerebral cortex has four lobes that control different functions.

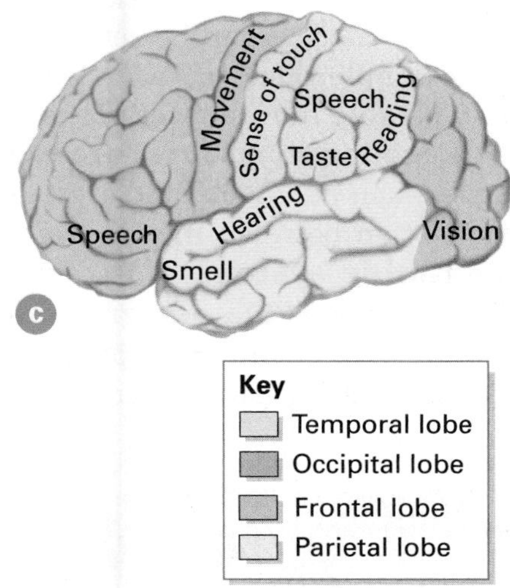

In addition, the cerebral cortex is responsible for many distinctive human mental characteristics—reasoning and mathematical abilities, language skills, imagination, artistic talent, and personality traits.

Cerebellum Located below the cerebrum near the top of the spinal cord, the **cerebellum** (sehr uh BEHL um) is the coordination center for body movements. The cerebellum receives signals from the cerebrum indicating a need to move. The cerebellum also receives information from sensory receptors regarding the positions of different body parts. The cerebellum evaluates this information and, within a few milliseconds, sends a plan for coordinated movements back to the cerebrum. For instance, as you step onto an escalator, your cerebellum evaluates your body position and relays the plan for smoothly getting the rest of your body to follow. The cerebrum then fine-tunes the plan and sends appropriate commands to the muscles.

Brainstem The lower section of your brain, called the **brainstem,** includes several structures: the medulla oblongata, the pons, and the midbrain. The brainstem filters all the information from the sensory and motor neurons going to and from the brain. The brainstem also regulates sleep, controls breathing, and helps coordinate body movements.

Thalamus Located in the middle of the brain, the **thalamus** sorts information going to and coming from the cerebral cortex. The thalamus exerts some control over what information goes from sensory receptors to the cerebrum by blocking some signals and enhancing others. An example of the thalamus in action is a parent who easily sleeps through noisy street traffic, but immediately awakens upon hearing his or her baby crying.

Hypothalamus The **hypothalamus** helps to regulate body temperature, blood pressure, hunger, thirst, and emotions. It is also the master control center of the endocrine system, as you will read in Chapter 32. Part of the hypothalamus functions as a "biological clock," your body's natural timing mechanism. With input from your eyes, the clock maintains daily cycles such as sleepiness and hunger.

Memory

As you walk to class, the location of your room and your teacher's name come quickly to mind. This is a result of your memory. Memory is the ability to store and retrieve information from past experiences.

Your brain forms different types of memories. For example, when you meet someone, his or her name typically is stored as a *short-term memory.* It may last for just a few minutes. In contrast, a *long-term memory* can be retrieved later. Long-term memory can be enhanced by associating new memories with old ones. For instance, it's easier to learn a new card game when you are familiar with other card games.

As you know, it's possible to memorize simple facts rapidly. These memories are formed by strengthening already existing nerve pathways. In contrast, learning and remembering a skill, such as tennis or skateboarding, requires nerve cells to make new connections and can be a slow process. However, once a skill memory is formed, it can be retained for a lifetime (Figure 28-13a). For example, once you have learned to ride a bike, you will probably be able to ride after years without practice.

Long-term memories are enhanced when linked with emotions, such as joy or fear, or senses, such as sight or taste. The connection between memory, emotions, and senses is related to the **limbic system.** This region of the brain involves several different areas that integrate and relay information, including the amygdala, hippocampus, and parts of the cerebral cortex, hypothalamus, and thalamus (Figure 28-13b).

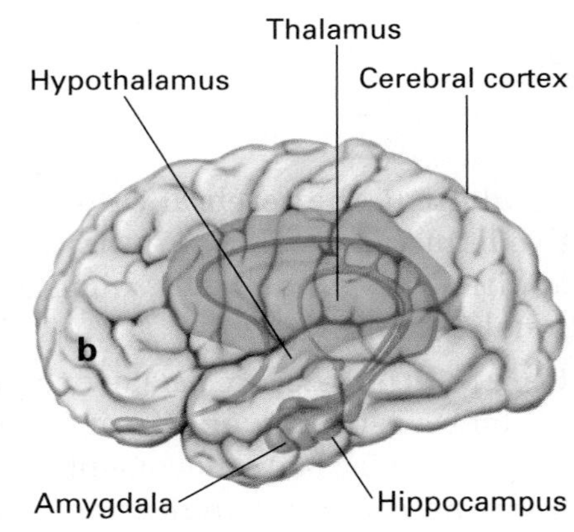

▲ **Figure 28-13** The brain creates memories from past experiences. **a.** Perfecting some skills, such as this tae kwon do maneuver, can take many years. Once learned, however, the skill is usually retained. **b.** The structures of the limbic system are involved in memories linked to emotions or the senses.

Online Activity 28.4

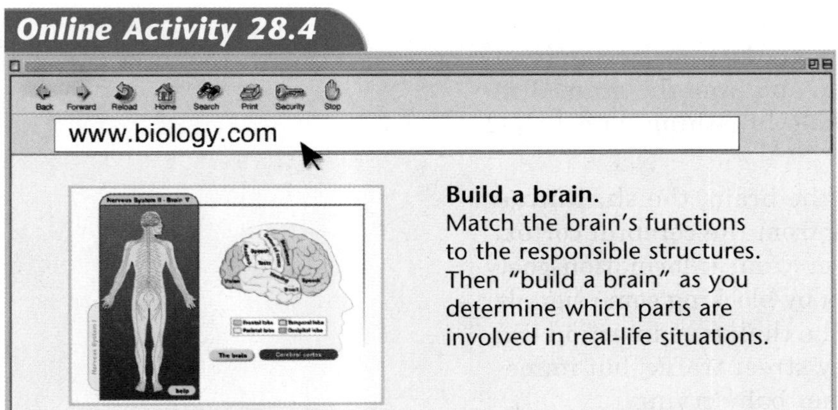

Build a brain.
Match the brain's functions to the responsible structures. Then "build a brain" as you determine which parts are involved in real-life situations.

Concept Check 28.4

1. Describe the role of the spinal cord in the CNS.
2. Describe how your cerebellum and cerebrum work together in body movements.
3. Explain why a skill is harder to learn than a simple fact.
4. How does your hypothalamus act as your "biological clock"?

CONCEPT 28.5

Sensory receptors link the environment to the nervous system.

OBJECTIVES

- Distinguish between a sensation and a perception.
- Identify five types of sensory receptors.
- Describe the processes involved in vision, hearing, balance, smell, and taste.

KEY TERMS

- sensation
- perception
- cornea
- iris
- pupil
- retina
- cone
- rod
- auditory canal
- eardrum
- auditory tube
- cochlea

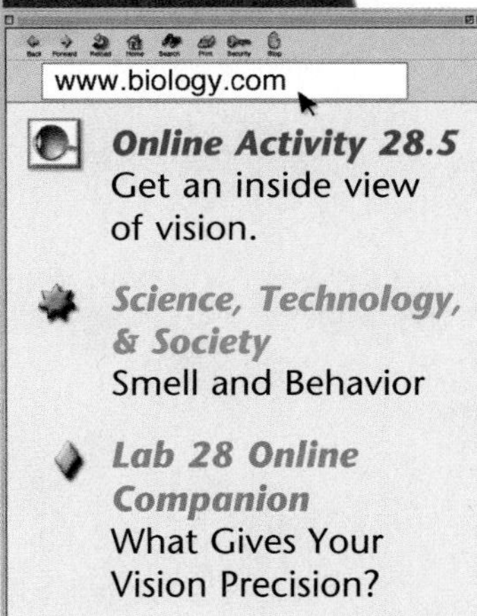

Thanks to specialized sensory receptors, humans can detect a range of stimuli. Messages transmitted from these sensory receptors enable people to see, hear, smell, taste, and sense touch.

Sensation and Perception

Sensory receptors detect stimuli, such as light, sounds, and skin temperature, and send the information to the CNS. These receptors are found in high concentrations in your sense organs—your nose, eyes, ears, mouth, and skin. When you sniff a flower, for example, the sensory receptors in your nose detect chemicals in the air near the flower. The receptors send reports about the chemicals to your brain in the form of nerve impulses. When sensory information reaches your brain, you may experience a **sensation,** an awareness of these sensory stimuli. As your brain integrates the sensory signals from your nose, you become aware of the flower's scent.

Besides receiving sensations, the brain also integrates new information and forms a **perception.** Perceptions are meaningful interpretations of sensory data. Figure 28-14 illustrates the difference between a perception and a sensation. What do you see when you look at this figure? If you only see some black splotches and green space, your brain has simply developed a sensation. If you see a person riding a horse, your brain has formed a perception—it has converted the sensation to a meaningful image.

Types of Sensory Receptors

The human body has five categories of sensory receptors that collect information from the external and internal environments.

Pain Receptors All parts of your body except the brain have *pain receptors*. Pain is sensed by free nerve endings—that is, the dendrites of sensory neurons—rather than by separate receptor cells. Pain is important because it often indicates that your tissues are in danger. Because it is difficult to ignore, pain usually protects you by making you stop the behavior causing the pain or seek medical attention.

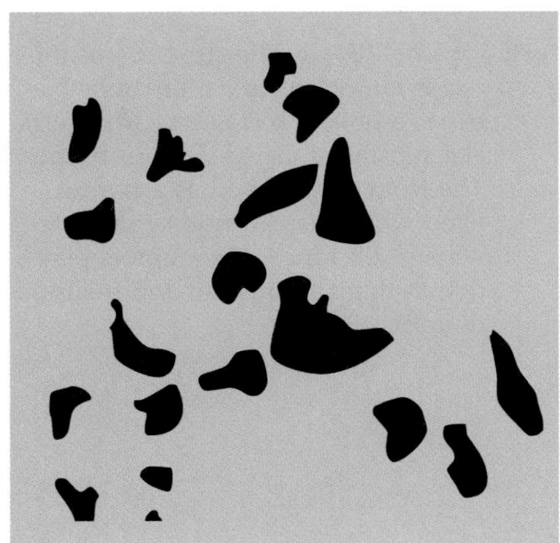

Figure 28-14 What do you see when you look at this image? If you see a person riding a horse, then your brain has formed a perception.

Thermoreceptors Found in the skin and certain internal organs, *thermoreceptors* detect heat and cold. Like pain receptors, thermoreceptors are free nerve endings rather than separate cells. These receptors report information to the hypothalamus, which acts as the body's thermostat. Receiving nerve signals from different thermoreceptors, the hypothalamus regulates the body's internal temperature within a narrow range.

Mechanoreceptors Your skin contains several types of *mechanoreceptors* that are stimulated by different forms of mechanical energy, including touch and pressure, stretch, and motion. In each mechanoreceptor, a change to the shape of its membrane alters its permeability to ions. This change can generate an action potential. One category of mechanoreceptors in the ears is the hair cells. The "hairs" are actually specialized cilia that detect movement. As you will read, hair cells play an important role in hearing and balance.

Chemoreceptors Sensory receptors such as those in your nose and taste buds that are sensitive to certain chemicals are called *chemoreceptors.* Internal chemoreceptors include sensors in arteries that detect dissolved gases in your blood.

Photoreceptors Found in your eyes, *photoreceptors* are receptive to various wavelengths of light. They relay this information to the brain, resulting in vision, as you will read below.

Science, Technology, & Society

Back Forward Reload Home Search Print Security Stop

www.biology.com

Smell and Behavior

The sense of smell frequently recalls memories from the past. But scientists are now beginning to uncover not only how this sense works, but also the extent to which it affects behavior, both consciously and subconsciously. Go online to explore the sense of smell and the role it plays in certain human behaviors.

Vision

For most humans, more than half of the sensory input to the brain is visual. The human eye is a remarkable sense organ. Millions of sensory cells in the eyes receive light and send nerve signals to the brain. The brain analyzes the information and perceives images.

As you might expect, the eye's structure is the key to its function (Figure 28-15). The outer white surface of the eye is a

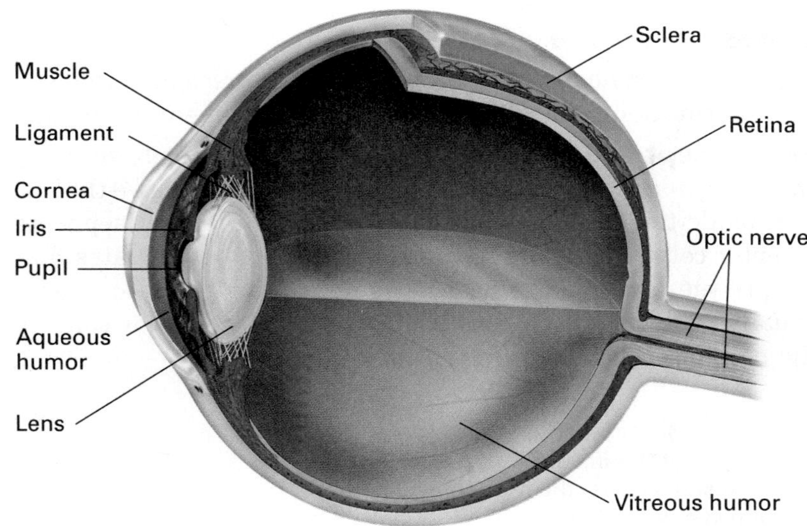

Figure 28-15 The structure of the eye is important to its function. The eye is a hollow ball filled with a jelly-like substance called vitreous humor. The front of the eye has a pocket filled with aqueous humor, a more watery substance. The humors play a role in the transmission and focusing of light.

tough layer of connective tissue called the sclera. Light enters the eyes through a transparent area of the sclera called the **cornea.** The cornea helps to focus the light as it travels to the back of the eyeball. A thin membrane that secretes mucus keeps the cornea and the rest of the sclera moist and free of debris.

Just beneath the sclera lies a pigmented layer containing blood vessels that nourish the eye. At the front of the eye, this layer forms the **iris,** which gives your eyes their color. The dark opening in the center of the iris is the **pupil.** Muscles in the iris regulate the size of the pupil and control how much light reaches the interior of the eye.

After light passes through the pupil, it passes through the disk-shaped lens. Muscles attached to ligaments pull on the lens, changing its shape as you look at near or distant objects. The lens focuses these images on the **retina,** the inner surface of the eye.

The three most common types of visual problems are nearsightedness, farsightedness, and astigmatism. These problems are related to the shape of the eyeball or a part of the eyeball (Figure 28-16). These conditions affect how well the lens can focus images on the retina.

The retina of each eye is lined with 130 million photoreceptor cells (Figure 28-17). These cells detect light as it moves into the eye and send signals along the optic nerve to the occipital lobe of the brain, where the signals are processed into images. **Cones** are one type of photoreceptor. The three types of cones respond to three colors of light: blue, red, and green. Colorblindness results from a deficiency or malfunction in one or more types of cones. **Rods,** another type of photoreceptor, do not distinguish colors, but are extremely sensitive to light. They allow people to see objects in dim light, but only in shades of gray.

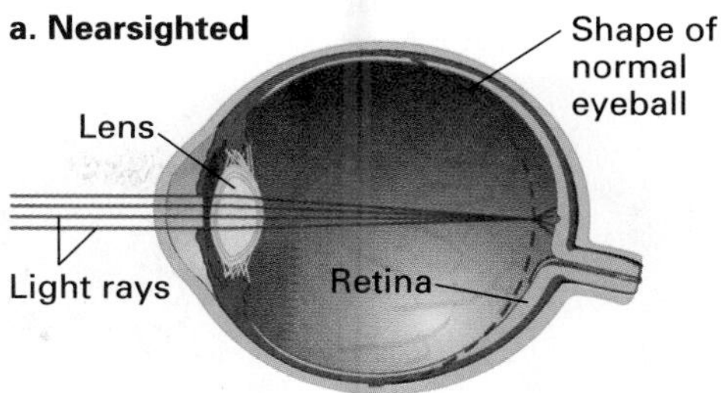

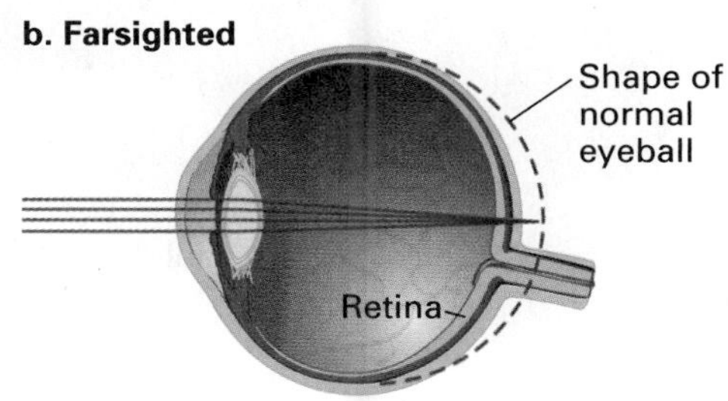

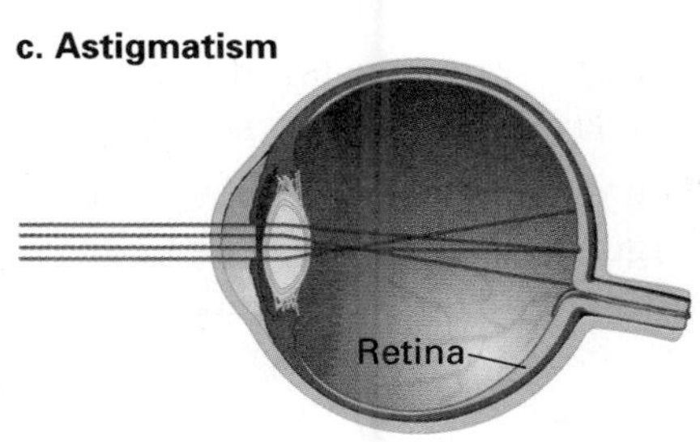

Figure 28-16 The shape of the eye or its structures can lead to vision problems. **a.** A nearsighted eye is oblong, making it difficult to see objects that are far away. **b.** A farsighted eye is too short, making it difficult to see objects up close. **c.** An eye with astigmatism has a misshapen lens or cornea that distorts how light strikes the retina.

Colorized SEM 6,700×

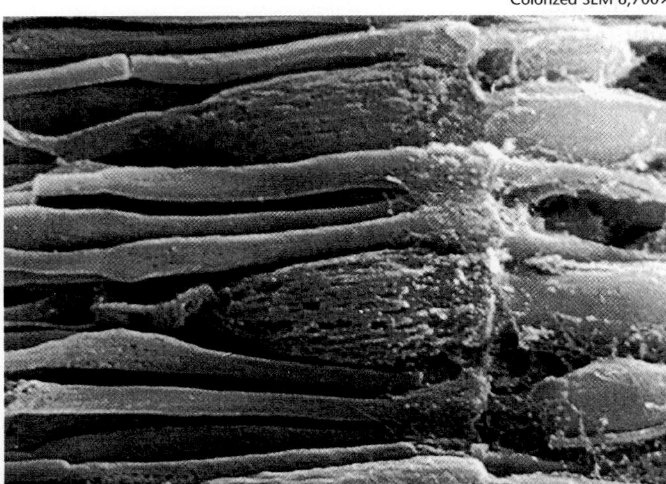

Figure 28-17 Your eyes are lined with millions of photoreceptors called cones and rods that detect light.

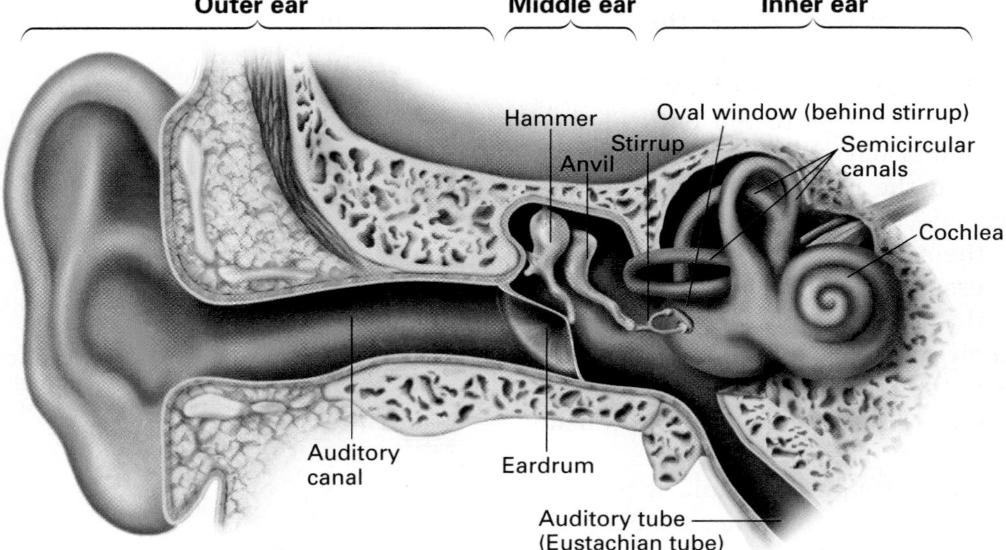

▲ **Figure 28-18** The many chambers and structures of the ear play key roles in hearing and balance.

Hearing and Balance

How is listening to music related to balancing on one foot? Both hearing and balance depend on sense organs in the ear.

Hearing The ear is composed of the outer ear, middle ear, and inner ear (Figure 28-18). The outer ear consists of the flaplike structure known as the "ear" and a tunnel-like opening called the **auditory canal.** The outer ear collects sound waves, such as those produced by strumming on a guitar, and channels them to the eardrum. The **eardrum** is a sheet of tissue that separates the outer ear from the middle ear. When sound waves strike the eardrum, it vibrates. The eardrum passes the vibrations on to three small bones: the hammer, anvil, and stirrup. Then the vibrations pass into the inner ear through a membrane-covered hole called the oval window.

The **auditory tube** (also called the Eustachian tube) conducts air between the middle ear and the back of the throat, keeping the air pressure equal on either side of the eardrum. The tube is what enables your ear to move air in or out to equalize pressure ("popping" your ears) when you change altitude in an airplane or during a drive up a mountain. Without this correction, your eardrum would bulge inward or outward, distorting your hearing.

The inner ear consists of fluid-filled channels in the skull. Sound waves set this fluid in motion. One of these channels is the **cochlea** (KAHK lee uh), a long, coiled tube shaped like a snail shell. Sound waves transferred by the eardrum and bones of the middle ear cause the oval window to vibrate. Then the pulsating oval window produces pressure waves in the fluid within the cochlea. These waves cause movements in hairlike projections along the membrane of the cochlea. The movements of these "hairs" initiate action potentials that are sent to the brain. The louder a sound, the stronger the vibrations of fluid in the cochlea and the more action potentials are created. Very loud sounds can damage the hair cells, causing hearing loss.

Balance In addition to the cochlea, the inner ear has five fluid-filled structures that help you maintain your balance. The three semicircular canals, lined by hair cells, detect changes in the head's movement in any direction. Two other chambers lined with hair cells detect the position of your head in relation to gravity. In all of these structures, fluid movement stimulates hair cells to send action potentials to the brain. The brain then provides feedback to your muscle cells so that you can keep your balance.

Smell and Taste

Smells of dinner cooking or a favorite flower can evoke pleasant feelings. Other smells such as smoke or sour milk can cause fear or distaste. All odors originate from molecules that enter your nose. Chemoreceptors in your nose have specialized cilia coated with mucus (Figure 28-19). Chemicals dissolve in the mucus and bind to receptor molecules on the cilia, triggering action potentials. The brain integrates the signals, resulting in the perception of an odor.

Taste also depends on chemoreceptors. When you take a bite of chocolate cake, the sweet and somewhat bitter taste of the chocolate begins with chemoreceptors in some of the 3,000 taste buds that line your tongue. Each taste bud contains specialized taste cells. Your sense of taste is stimulated when dissolved chemicals bind to receptor molecules on your taste cells. Besides the four basic human taste sensations—sweet, bitter, salty, and sour—researchers have recently identified receptors that sense *umami*, a meatlike taste associated with certain amino acids.

When you eat, the flavors you perceive are usually a combination of these various tastes, plus other sensory data such as texture and smell. The same chemicals that stimulate your taste buds also stimulate sensory receptors in your nose. This explains why food may seem bland and tasteless when your nose is stuffed up.

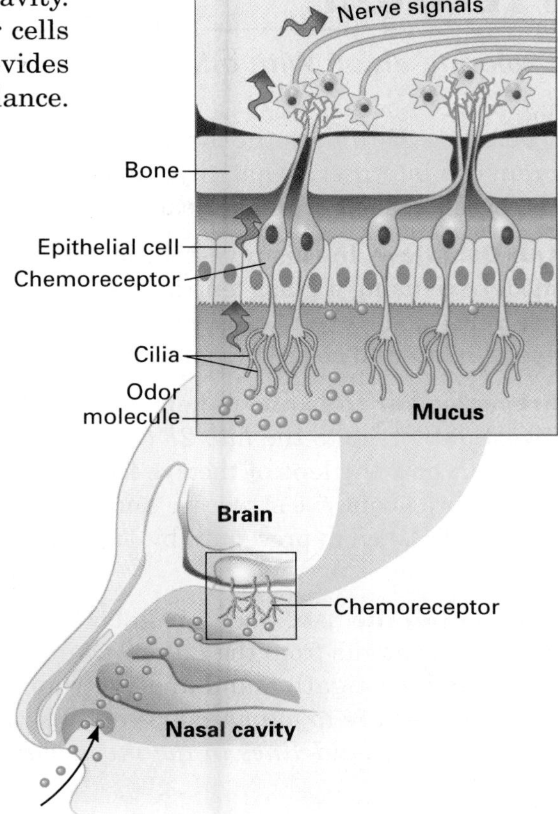

▲ **Figure 28-19** Chemicals in the air enter your nose and stimulate chemoreceptors that send signals to your brain. From these signals, your brain creates a sensation and a perception of the odor.

Online Activity 28.5

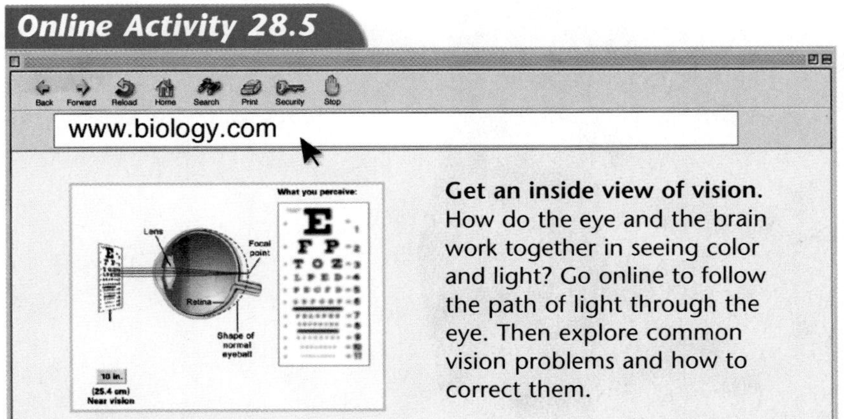

Get an inside view of vision. How do the eye and the brain work together in seeing color and light? Go online to follow the path of light through the eye. Then explore common vision problems and how to correct them.

Concept Check 28.5

1. Explain the difference between a sensation and a perception. Give an example of each that is not in the text.
2. List and describe the function of the five types of sensory receptors.
3. How is your sense of hearing related to your sense of balance?
4. In what way are your senses of smell and taste similar?

What Gives Your Vision Precision?

Exploring Vision With a Model Eye

Questions How does the eye produce an image the brain can interpret? What physical differences exist in the eyes of people who are nearsighted or farsighted?

Lab Overview In this investigation you will create a model eye using a glass lens and a shoebox. You will use your model eye to discover how the shape of the eye is related to common vision problems.

Preparing for the Lab To help you prepare for the investigation, go to the *Lab 28 Online Companion.* ······➔ Find out how the lens of the eye focuses images, and learn more about eye structure and visual perception. Prepare for the lab procedure by previewing the steps you will take.

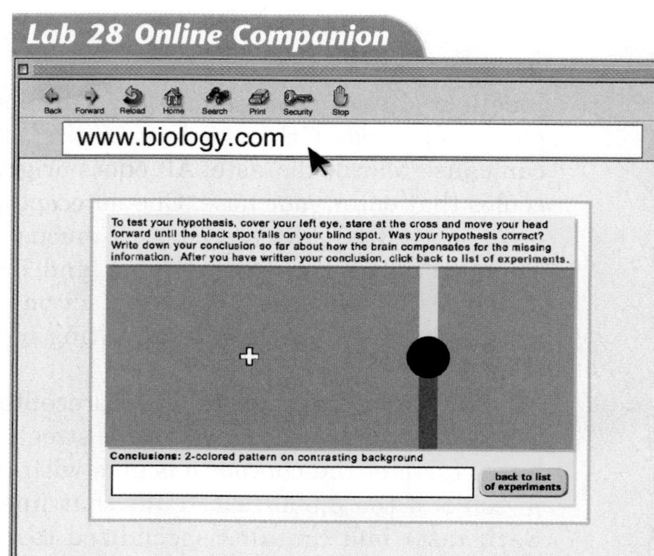

Completing the Lab Use your Laboratory Manual or lab page printouts from the *Lab 28 Online Companion* to do the investigation and analyze your results. **CAUTION:** *Be sure to follow your teacher's instructions and all safety guidelines in the investigation.*

Lab 28 Online Companion
To test your hypothesis, cover your left eye, stare at the cross and move your head forward until the black spot falls on your blind spot. Was your hypothesis correct? Write down your conclusion so far about how the brain compensates for the missing information. After you have written your conclusion, click back to list of experiments.
Conclusions: 2-colored pattern on contrasting background
back to list of experiments

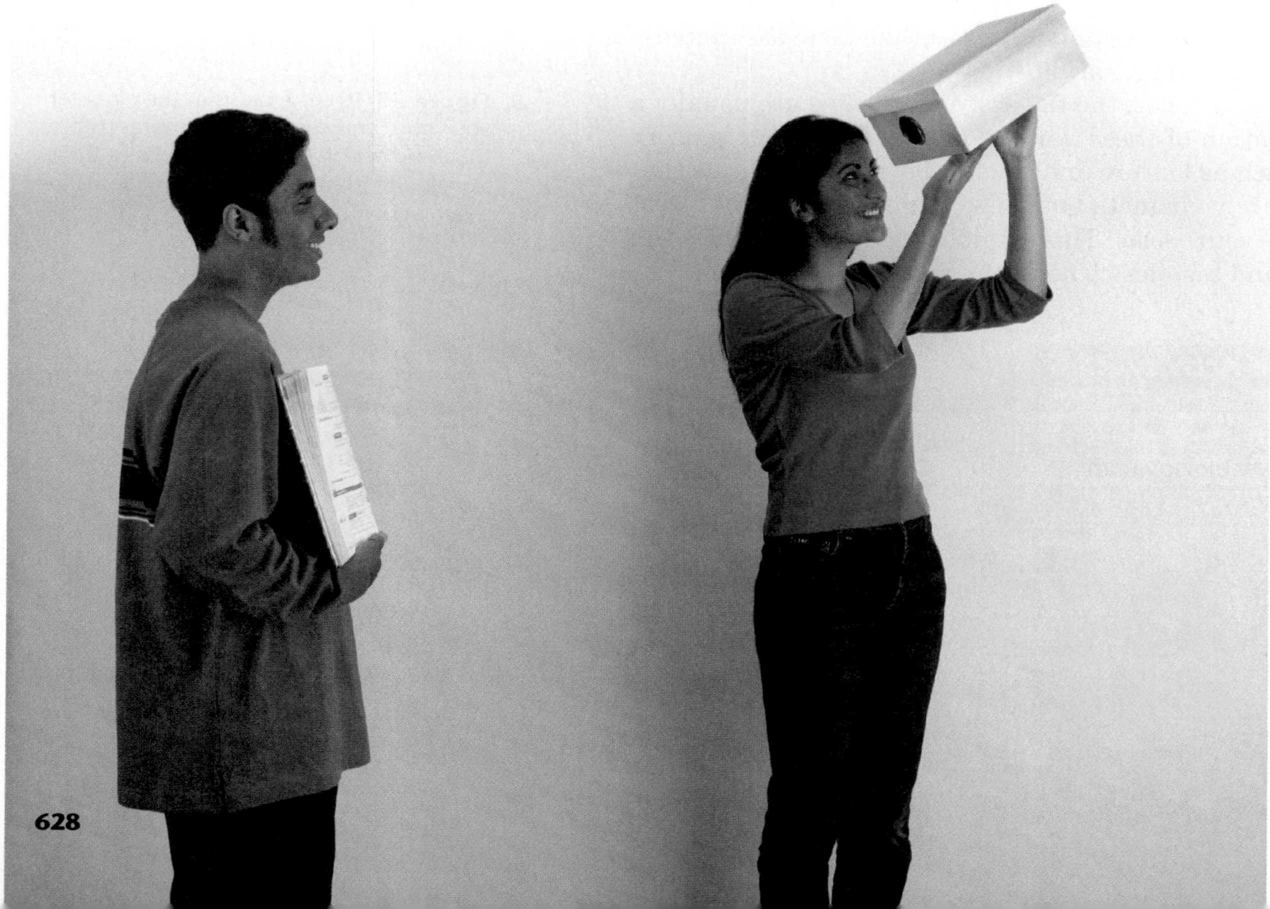

CONCEPT 28.6

Certain drugs alter brain function.

OBJECTIVES

- Explain how drugs can affect the nervous system.
- Explain how drug use can lead to addiction.
- Describe classifications of drugs.

KEY TERMS

- tolerance
- addiction
- withdrawal
- stimulant
- depressant
- marijuana
- opiate
- hallucinogen
- Ecstasy
- inhalant

What's Online

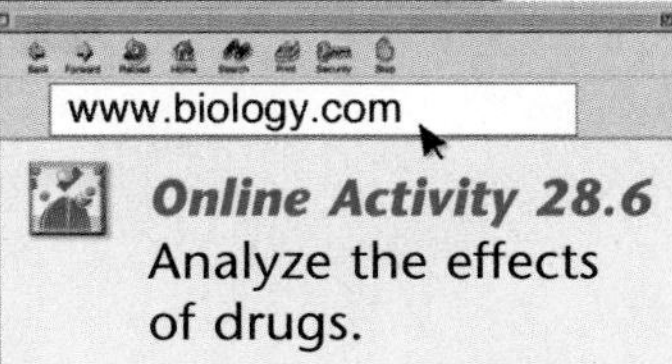

A drug is a substance that is used to produce an effect on the body. Drugs include chemicals used for medicinal purposes such as aspirin, as well as alcohol, tobacco, and illegal drugs such as marijuana and cocaine. Certain drugs affect the brain by altering the way neurons communicate.

Effects on the Nervous System

Drugs can affect the nervous system in different ways (Figure 28-20). Some drugs increase the rate at which neurons release neurotransmitters. Other drugs slow the rate at which neurotransmitters are removed from the synaptic cleft. Rather than being broken down after prompting an action potential, the neurotransmitters remain and continue to stimulate receiving neurons. Still other drugs mimic a neurotransmitter by binding to its receptor sites, creating abnormal patterns of action potentials. You will read later in this section about how some particular groups of drugs affect the nervous system.

Tolerance and Addiction

Any drug, even legal drugs, can be abused if instructions are not followed, the drug is taken in a manner in which it was not intended, or the drug is overused. With most drugs, abuse may lead to **tolerance** of the drug. This means that more and more of the drug is needed in order to produce the same effect in the person. Use of some drugs may result in **addiction,** an uncontrollable dependence on a drug. A person who is addicted will experience **withdrawal** when the drug is not taken. Withdrawal symptoms can be physical or psychological and may include shaking, sweating, nausea, rapid heart rate, hallucinations, and depression.

▼ **Figure 28-20** Different types of drugs affect the brain in various ways. This diagram shows three different mechanisms of drug action.

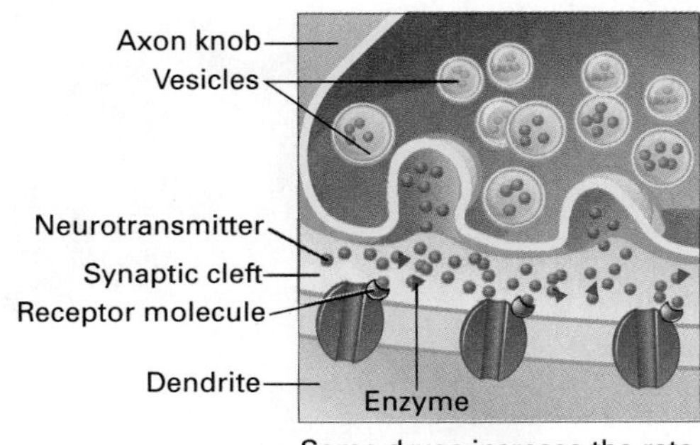

Some drugs increase the rate of neurotransmitter secretion, flooding the synaptic cleft.

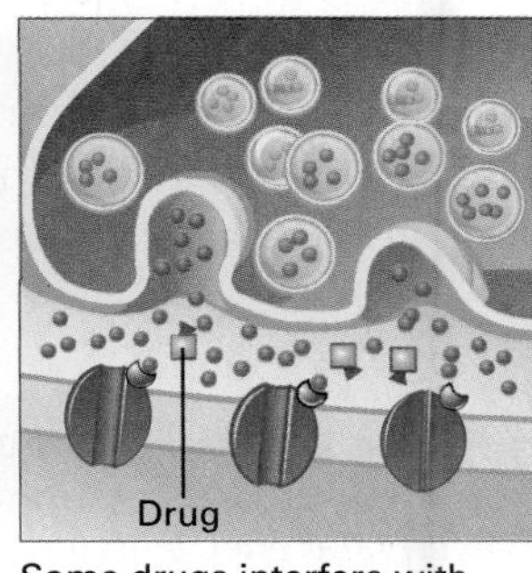

Some drugs interfere with enzymes that normally break down neurotransmitters.

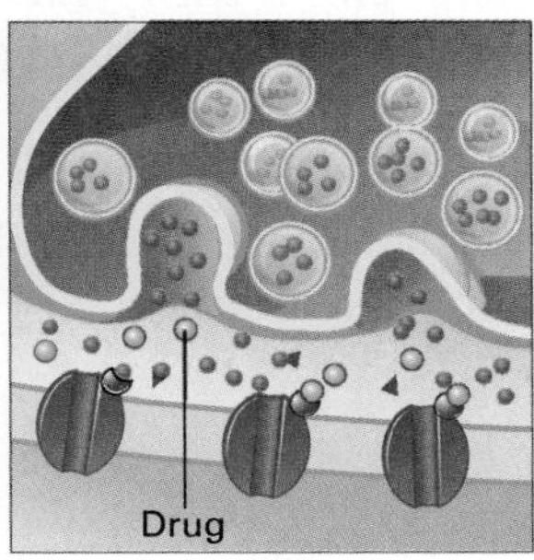

Some drugs mimic neurotransmitters and bind to their receptors.

▲ **Figure 28-21** The stimulant caffeine is found in all of these common food products.

Drug Classifications

Different types of drugs have different effects on the body.

Stimulants Drugs called **stimulants** generally increase activity in the CNS. They often do this by affecting the release or removal of neurotransmitters. For example, caffeine, which is found in colas, coffee, tea, and chocolate, raises heart rate and alertness (Figure 28-21). Nicotine, the highly addictive drug in tobacco products, is another stimulant. Nicotine can increase heart rate, blood pressure, and secretion of stomach acids.

Cocaine is another highly addictive stimulant. Cocaine blocks the normal removal of pleasure-inducing neurotransmitters. The excess neurotransmitters cause a temporary "high" that is soon followed by depression as the neurotransmitter levels fall to normal or below normal levels. Addiction to cocaine may cause permanent chemical changes in the brain.

Methamphetamine (also called speed, ice, or crank) is a stimulant that causes increased activity levels, decreased appetite, and a general sense of well-being. Chronic use can lead to violent behavior, confusion, and sleeplessness. The drug causes neurons in the brain to release large amounts of the neurotransmitter dopamine. Over time, using the drug can permanently damage the nervous system.

Depressants Drugs that are classified as **depressants** often slow CNS activity. Alcohol is an example of a strong depressant that not only interferes with coordination and judgment, but also can cause other serious health problems. Heavy drinking can lead to severe liver and brain damage and may be associated with cardiovascular disease and several forms of cancer.

Other types of depressants include tranquilizers and barbiturates (sedatives). These drugs cause reduced anxiety and a state of drowsiness. Combining depressants can be fatal if the CNS is slowed until its life-sustaining functions stop.

Marijuana Made from a mixture of dried pieces of the hemp plant, **marijuana** contains over 400 chemicals. The main mind-altering ingredient is THC (tetrahydrocannabinol). Marijuana causes many changes in the brain. Some effects include problems with memory and learning, distorted perceptions, loss of coordination, and anxiety.

► **Figure 28-22** Illegal drugs such as these can have harmful and even fatal effects on your body.

Narcotics Morphine, codeine, and heroin, called **opiates,** are narcotics derived from the opium poppy (Figure 28-23). Opiates mimic natural chemicals in the CNS and bind to their receptors. They produce feelings of euphoria, slow the brainstem's normal functioning, and block pain signals. When prescribed by a doctor, morphine and codeine can help relieve the pain of serious health problems. Heroin is too potent and addictive, however, to be used for medical purposes. Tolerance and addiction to opiates, especially heroin, can occur quickly, and withdrawal symptoms can be extremely painful.

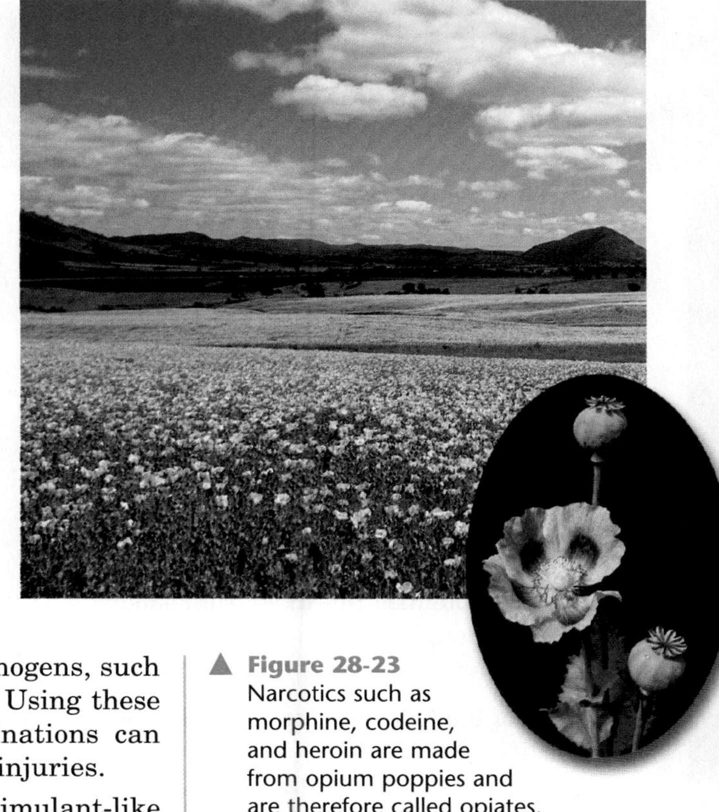

▲ **Figure 28-23** Narcotics such as morphine, codeine, and heroin are made from opium poppies and are therefore called opiates.

Hallucinogens Drugs called **hallucinogens** cause the user to see, hear, and perceive things that do not exist. Some hallucinogens are natural substances, such as certain chemicals from psilocybin mushrooms and peyote cactus. Other hallucinogens, such as LSD (lysergic acid diethylamide), are synthetic. Using these drugs is illegal and very dangerous. The hallucinations can cause confusion and panic that can lead to severe injuries.

Ecstasy A synthetic drug called **Ecstasy** causes stimulant-like effects such as increased energy level as well as hallucinogen-like effects such as an exaggerated emotional attachment to other people. As with many other drugs, effects that users of Ecstasy perceive as positive can also be accompanied by negative effects, such as blurred vision, memory loss, and lingering paranoia. Long-term use causes changes to the brain that may interfere with its functions.

Inhalants The vapors of certain substances can produce mind-altering effects. These substances, called **inhalants,** include volatile solvents, aerosols, certain gases, and nitrites. Short-term effects of inhalant use include slurred speech, clumsiness, and increased heart rate. Long-term effects can include damage to major organs, including the lungs and liver. Many healthy, first-time users of inhalants have died suddenly from heart failure or suffocation.

Online Activity 28.6

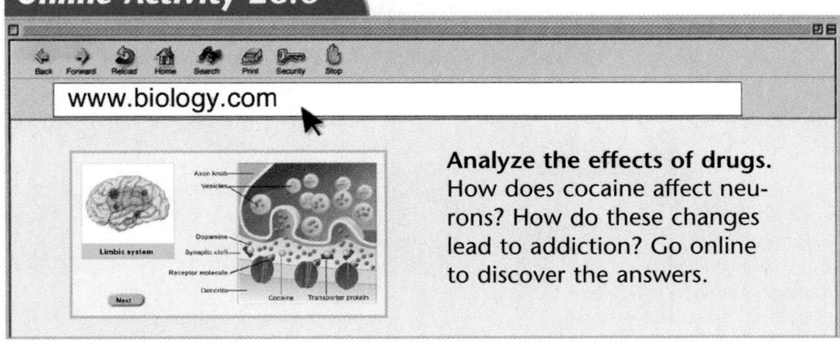

Analyze the effects of drugs. How does cocaine affect neurons? How do these changes lead to addiction? Go online to discover the answers.

Concept Check 28.6

1. Describe two ways that drugs affect the action of neurotransmitters.
2. Explain how addiction to a drug may occur.
3. Distinguish between the effects of stimulants and depressants on the body.

Multiple Choice

Choose the letter of the best answer.

1. Which sentence best describes integration in the nervous system?
   a. Sensory receptors convey signals to sensory neurons.
   b. Motor neurons convey signals to muscle cells.
   c. Sensory neurons convey signals to the CNS.
   d. Interneurons in the CNS formulate a response.
2. A nerve signal travels in what order?
   a. stimulation, resting potential, action potential
   b. action potential, threshold, stimulation
   c. stimulation, depolarization, action potential
   d. threshold, stimulation, depolarization
3. Which of the following are controlled by the somatic nervous system?
   a. blood pressure, body temperature, heart rate
   b. emotions, sensations of pain, sense of touch
   c. salivation, glucose release, relaxed airways
   d. walking, standing up, throwing a ball
4. Which region of the brain creates sensory perceptions?
   a. thalamus
   b. cerebral cortex
   c. cerebellum
   d. corpus callosum
5. Which of the following is a perception?
   a. feeling cold
   b. deciding that a new food is tasty
   c. pulling your finger away from a sharp object
   d. all of the above
6. Which part of the eye controls how much light enters through the pupil?
   a. cornea
   b. sclera
   c. retina
   d. iris
7. A substance that stimulates your CNS is
   a. marijuana.
   b. heroin.
   c. cocaine.
   d. LSD.

Short Answer

8. Describe the three types of neurons and their functions.
9. Summarize the knee-jerk reflex arc.
10. After an action potential has passed through a section of an axon, how is the resting potential restored?
11. Describe the concepts of *threshold* and "all-or-none" events in relation to action potentials.
12. Choose three organs of the human body. Describe the effects of the parasympathetic and sympathetic nervous systems on each of the organs.
13. Describe the difference between how your brain creates a skill memory, such as using a yo-yo, and how it creates the memory of a fact, such as an address.
14. Identify three types of sensory receptors found in the skin. What is the function of each type of receptor?
15. Explain why your night vision is mostly in black-and-white rather than color.
16. What are three ways that drugs interfere with neuron or neurotransmitter activities at synapses?

Visualizing Concepts

17. A signal has been initiated in this axon, which has a myelin sheath. Draw the steps that will occur as this nerve signal travels along the axon. Provide a short explanation of each step.

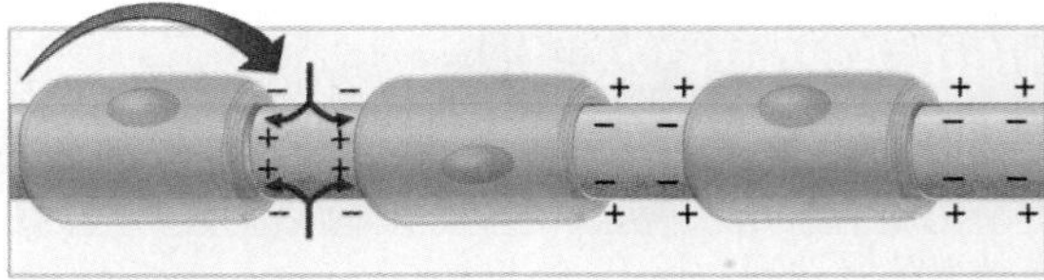

Analyzing Information

18. **Analyzing Diagrams** Review the diagram below and answer the following questions.

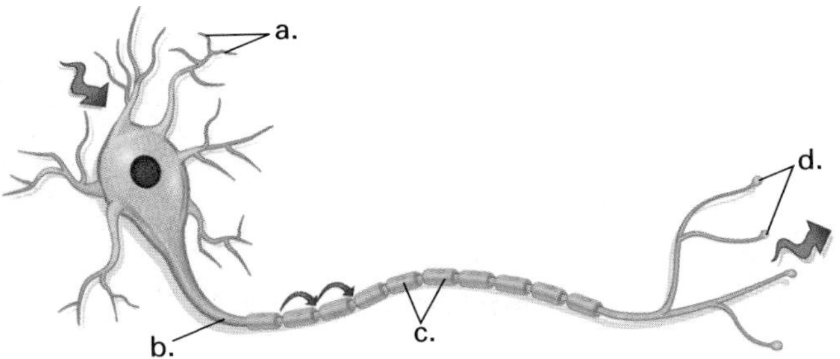

a. Identify the parts labeled *a* and *b* and describe their functions.
b. What is *c*? How would a signal travel through this neuron differently if *c* were not present?
c. What is *d*? Explain what happens when an action potential reaches *d*.

19. **Analyzing Data** Sound level is measured in decibels (dB). Many experts agree that exposure to sounds of more than 85 dB for 8 hours or more can damage hearing. Sounds of 110 dB can damage hearing in less than 15 minutes. Sounds of 140 dB can cause immediate damage.

Decibel Levels (dB) of Various Sounds

dB	Sound
10	Normal breathing
60	Normal conversation
90	Noisy restaurant
112	Headphones (high volume)
120	Nearby ambulance siren
150	Jet engine at takeoff
162	Fireworks at about 1 meter

a. Create a bar graph that depicts the data in the table above. In your graph, indicate the different ranges of sound danger.
b. Explain why prolonged exposure to loud sounds can lead to hearing loss.
c. Write a short public service announcement to explain threats to hearing loss and how to prevent hearing loss.

Critical Thinking

20. **Comparing and Contrasting** Compare and contrast your nervous system to a computer.

21. **Relating Cause and Effect** How would a drug that inhibits the parasympathetic nervous system affect a person's pulse?

22. **Making Generalizations** Walking home from a friend's house, Raoul is confronted by a large puddle. He decides to leap across it. Which regions of his brain will be involved in this action? How will they work together?

23. **Developing Hypotheses** Drawing on what you have learned about the different senses, develop a hypothesis that explains why some people experience motion sickness. What two senses are probably involved with this unpleasant reaction to movement?

24. **What's Wrong With These Statements?** *Briefly explain why each statement is incorrect or misleading.*
    a. The parasympathetic division of the autonomic nervous system slows digestion.
    b. Nerve signals travel quickly through a neuron's myelin sheath.
    c. The auditory tube passes on vibrations.

Performance Assessment

Design an Experiment Most sensory organs come in pairs. You have two eyes and two ears. Similarly, a rattlesnake has two infrared receptors, and a butterfly has two antennae. Propose a hypothesis that could explain the advantage of having pairs of sense organs. Devise an experiment to test your hypothesis.

Online Assessment/Test Preparation

Back Forward Reload Home Search Print Security Stop

www.biology.com

- **Chapter 28 Assessment**
  Check your understanding of the chapter concepts.
- **Standardized Test Preparation**
  Practice test-taking skills you need to succeed.

Nutrition and Digestion

Have you ever heard the expression, "You are what you eat"? That doesn't mean that you would turn into a salad or a fruit cup after sampling the colorful array of food below. But your body is made from compounds built from the raw materials in the food you eat. In addition to these building materials, food provides a supply of energy for all the work done by your cells.

In this chapter you'll read about how your body acquires the raw materials it needs from the food you eat. Before you begin, go online to the ***WebQuest*** to explore a familiar organ of the digestive system.

Key Concepts

Concept 29.1 Nutrition depends on digestion and absorption.

Concept 29.2 Each region of the digestive tube is specialized.

Concept 29.3 A healthful diet provides both fuel and building materials.

Concept 29.4 Nutritional disorders damage health.

Assessment Chapter 29 Review

What's Online

www.biology.com

WebQuest
StomachQuest

Online Activity 29.1
Break down a pizza.

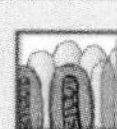

Online Activity 29.2
Tour the digestive system.

Lab 29 Online Companion
Breaking Down Fat Digestion

Online Activity 29.3
Calculate Calories and interpret a food label.

Online Activity 29.4
Investigate case studies in nutrition.

Careers
Meet a Registered Dietitian

Chapter 29 Assessment

CONCEPT 29.1

Nutrition depends on digestion and absorption.

OBJECTIVES

- List the six types of nutrients found in food.
- Summarize the four stages of food processing.

KEY TERMS

- nutrition
- ingestion
- digestion
- absorption
- elimination

Think about sliding a warm, tasty slice of cheese pizza into your mouth. You take a bite, chew, and swallow. You probably aren't saying to yourself, "There, I'm providing my cells with nutrients." However, that's exactly what you're doing. But first, your digestive system must disassemble the pizza into basic building blocks that your cells can use.

Food As a Source of Nutrients

Like all heterotrophs, humans obtain nutrients from food. These nutrients are the source of raw materials that your body uses to build tissue and fuel cellular work. There are six types of nutrients in food: carbohydrates, fats, proteins, vitamins, minerals, and water (Figure 29-1).

However, the food you eat is usually "packaged" in bulk form—like the slice of pizza—and contains large, complex molecules. These large molecules, such as starch and other polymers, are too big to pass through membranes into the cells where they are needed. In addition, the polymers are not the same polymers that make up your body. For example, the cheese on a slice of pizza is partly made up of proteins. These cheese proteins are polymers that can't be used as is by your cells. Instead, the

Figure 29-1 A slice of pizza contains the six types of nutrients in various forms. Digestion breaks down the nutrients in the pizza, enabling your body to use them.

Types of Nutrients in Foods

Nutrient Type	Structure	Some Functions in Body
Carbohydrates	Polymers constructed from monosaccharide monomers	Provide carbon skeletons for building other organic molecules; used as primary fuel source
Fats	Large molecules consisting of glycerol and fatty acids	Provide raw materials for building cellular membranes; used as fuel
Proteins	Polymers constructed from amino acid monomers	Provide raw materials to make enzymes and other proteins; may be used as fuel
Vitamins	Small organic molecules	Diverse functions; aid enzymes
Minerals	Inorganic ions	Diverse functions; some bond with organic molecules
Water	Inorganic molecule (H_2O)	Serves as the solvent in cells and body fluids

cheese proteins must be broken down into their basic building blocks (monomers)—amino acids. As you read in Chapter 5, all organisms use the same monomers to build larger polymers. So, the amino acids that make up cheese proteins are the same ones your cells can use to build your body's "brand" of proteins.

Four Stages of Food Processing

The process of how your body obtains raw materials from food is called **nutrition.** This process involves the four stages shown in Figure 29-2. The first is very familiar to you—eating. The act of eating or drinking is called **ingestion.**

After food enters the body through ingestion, the next stage of food processing, digestion, begins. **Digestion** is the process of breaking food down into molecules small enough for the body to absorb. For example, polysaccharides such as the starch in the pizza crust are broken down into monosaccharides (simple sugars).

Digestion occurs in two steps. Mechanical digestion (such as chewing) chops and grinds food into smaller pieces, increasing its surface area. This improves the effectiveness of the second step, chemical digestion. Chemical digestion breaks the chemical bonds within the large molecules that make up food, producing smaller building-block molecules. An example of chemical digestion is the action of acids and enzymes in your stomach.

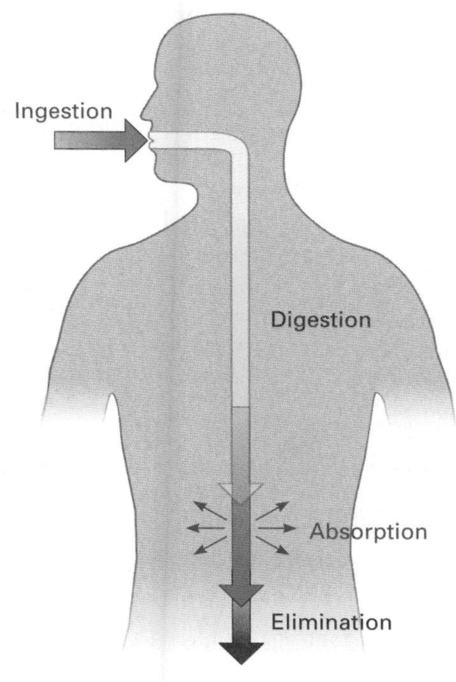

▲ **Figure 29-2** Through a four-stage process (ingestion, digestion, absorption, and elimination), your body takes what it needs from the foods you consume.

The last two stages of food processing occur after food is digested. In the third stage, **absorption,** certain cells take up (absorb) the small molecules. The circulatory system then transports the nutrients throughout the body. Finally, undigested material passes out of the body in the stage called **elimination.** In Concept 29.2, you'll read how the organs of the digestive system participate in these four stages.

Online Activity 29.1
www.biology.com
Break down a pizza.
Click on slices of a pizza to determine how carbohydrates, proteins, and fats are broken down in chemical digestion. What happens during hydrolysis? Find out online.

Concept Check 29.1

1. What are the six types of nutrients found in food?
2. Draw a flowchart showing the four stages of food processing.
3. Identify and describe two types of digestion.

CONCEPT 29.2 Each region of the digestive tube is specialized.

OBJECTIVES
- Describe the tube in which digestion occurs.
- Trace the path of food through the organs of the digestive system.

KEY TERMS
- alimentary canal
- saliva
- bolus
- pharynx
- esophagus
- peristalsis
- stomach
- chyme
- small intestine
- liver
- gallbladder
- pancreas
- villus
- large intestine
- feces

What's Online

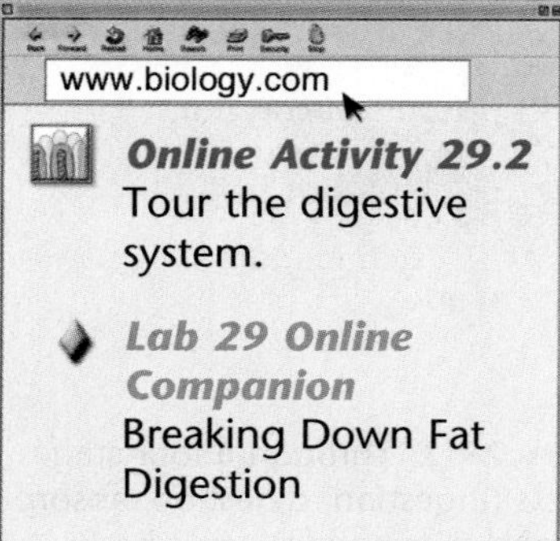

Online Activity 29.2
Tour the digestive system.

Lab 29 Online Companion
Breaking Down Fat Digestion

How is your digestive system like an automobile factory that is running in reverse? If an automobile assembly line operated in reverse, the workers would start with a complete car and disassemble it into individual parts, or building blocks. Your body processes food in a similar manner. As food travels through your digestive system, it is broken into its basic building blocks.

Digestion Occurs in a Tube

Digestion occurs in a tube called the **alimentary canal.** Food moves in one direction through the alimentary canal, which is organized into specialized regions that carry out digestion and absorption in a step-by-step process. Food enters the canal through the mouth and wastes leave through the anus. However, the alimentary canal is much longer than the distance between these two openings. For instance, a person 1.8 meters tall can have a 9-meter alimentary canal. The tube fits inside the body because portions wind and loop back and forth.

As you read in Chapter 27, epithelial tissue lines the alimentary canal. One function of the epithelial cells is to secrete mucus that lubricates the canal and helps prevent the body from digesting itself. This is important because the digestive juices in your stomach, for example, have a pH of 2—acidic enough to dissolve iron nails. Despite the mucous layer, the epithelial cells in the stomach are constantly eroded. Enough new cells are generated through mitosis to completely replace your stomach lining every three days.

Organs of the Digestive System

Six main organs make up the alimentary canal: the mouth, pharynx, esophagus, stomach, small intestine, and large intestine (Figure 29-3). Accessory glands and organs include the salivary glands, pancreas, liver, and gallbladder, which secrete digestive juices into the alimentary canal.

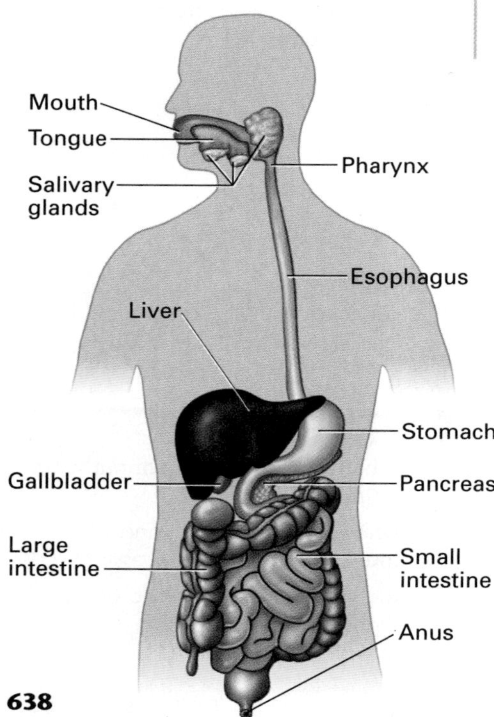

Figure 29-3 Digestion occurs in a tube called the alimentary canal that begins at the mouth and ends at the anus.

Mouth Your mouth functions both in ingestion and in the beginning of digestion. Your teeth and tongue are responsible for mechanical digestion (Figure 29-4). The various shapes of different types of teeth cut, smash, and grind food into smaller pieces. This makes the food easier to swallow and exposes more surface area to digestive enzymes.

Chemical digestion also begins in your mouth. In a typical day, salivary glands in your mouth region secrete more than one liter of liquid. This liquid, called **saliva,** contains digestive enzymes, mucus, and other chemicals. The salivary enzyme called amylase begins the chemical digestion of the polysaccharide starch in foods like pizza crust, pasta, and bread. The main products of amylase's action are smaller polysaccharides and the disaccharide maltose. Other chemicals in saliva kill bacteria and neutralize certain acids in foods, protecting your teeth from decay.

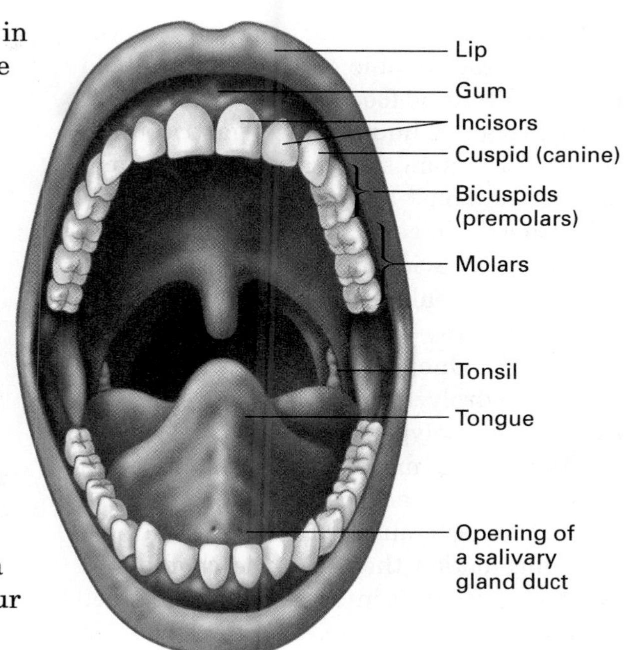

Cuspid (canine)
Bicuspids (premolars)

▲ **Figure 29-4** The mouth functions in both ingestion and digestion. The different shapes of your teeth are specialized for cutting and grinding food.

Pharynx The tongue pushes each chewed clump of food, called a **bolus,** down the throat. The upper portion of the throat, called the **pharynx** (FAR ingks), is the junction of the alimentary canal and the passageway by which air enters the lungs. When you swallow, a cartilage flap called the epiglottis temporarily seals off the airway and prevents food from entering.

Esophagus Next, the bolus enters a long, muscle-encased tube called the **esophagus** (ih SAHF uh gus), which connects the pharynx to the stomach. Although the esophagus is oriented vertically in your body, gravity is not the reason that food moves toward your stomach. (If that were the case, astronauts would not be able to eat or drink in space where there is zero gravity.) Rather, food is pushed through the esophagus by a series of muscle contractions called **peristalsis** (Figure 29-5). The muscles at the very top of the esophagus are striated (voluntary), which means that swallowing may begin voluntarily. But the muscle layers around the rest of the esophagus are smooth (involuntary). Once a bolus of food reaches the pharynx, these smooth muscles trigger the swallowing reflex. The smooth muscles contract in a wave-like motion that forces the bolus of food toward the stomach. Food continues to move along the alimentary canal by peristalsis.

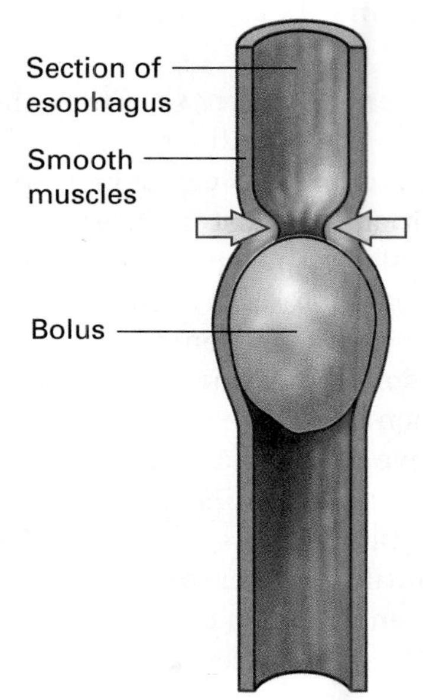

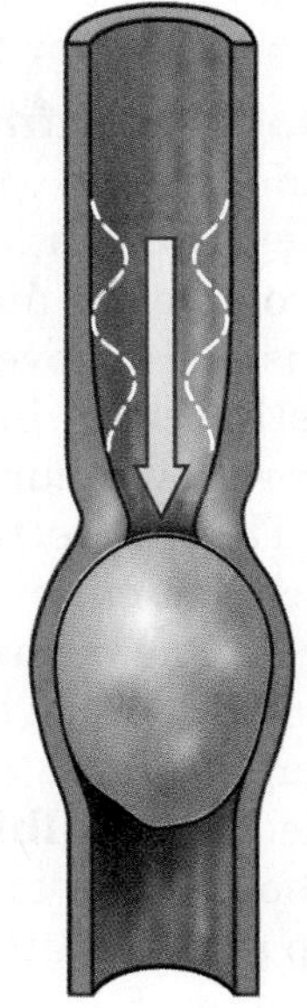

Contraction of smooth muscles behind bolus forces it forward.

Waves of muscle contractions move bolus toward stomach.

▶ **Figure 29-5** A wave of muscular contractions called peristalsis pushes food through your esophagus.

Stomach The **stomach** is an elastic, muscular sac capable of stretching to hold up to 2 liters of food (an entire medium-sized pizza). A liquid called gastric juice, secreted by glands in the stomach lining, bathes the bolus after it enters the stomach. Gastric juice is a mixture of mucus, hydrochloric acid, and enzymes. Hydrochloric acid breaks apart the cells in food. It also kills many of the bacteria swallowed with food. One of the gastric enzymes, pepsin, hydrolyzes large protein molecules into smaller polypeptides.

Meanwhile, mechanical digestion turns the bolus into an acidic liquid called **chyme** (kym). Stomach muscles contract, creating a churning motion that stirs the chyme and eventually forces it into the small intestine.

Most of the time, the stomach is pinched closed at both ends (Figure 29-6). The passageway between the esophagus and the stomach opens when peristalsis delivers a bolus. But in some people, the passageway may open at inappropriate times, allowing acidic chyme to flow backward into the esophagus. This creates a burning sensation called heartburn.

At the opposite end of the stomach, a muscular valve called the pyloric sphincter regulates the flow of chyme into the small intestine. It typically takes 2 to 6 hours after a meal for the stomach to empty.

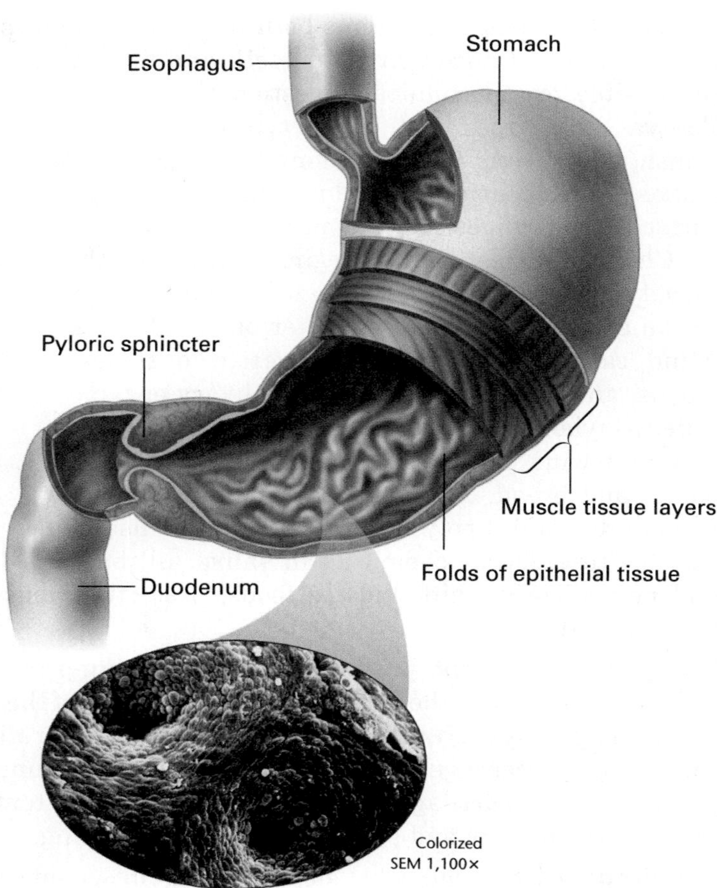

▲ **Figure 29-6** A thick layer of muscle tissue enables the stomach to break up and stir a bolus of food. The micrograph shows the surface of the stomach lining, which secretes gastric enzymes.

Small Intestine, Liver, and Pancreas From the stomach, liquid chyme passes into the small intestine. The **small intestine** is a long (6 m), narrow (2.5 cm) tube where digestion is completed and absorption of most nutrients takes place. Peristalsis moves chyme along the small intestine. Digestion mostly occurs in the first portion of the small intestine, while absorption occurs along the rest of its length.

The first section of the small intestine is called the duodenum. As chyme enters the duodenum, it mixes with several digestive juices. One of these digestive juices is a liquid called bile. Bile is produced outside of the small intestine by the body's largest internal organ, the **liver.** Bile is stored in a sac-like structure called the **gallbladder** until it is secreted into the duodenum. Although bile contains no enzymes, it contains substances that help prepare fats such as those in butter, ice cream, and nuts for digestion. Fats tend to clump together into globs, making it difficult for enzymes to reach the molecules. Bile separates small fat droplets, preventing them from clumping into globs. This enables digestive enzymes to break the fats down more efficiently.

The **pancreas** produces and secretes pancreatic juice into the duodenum. Pancreatic juice neutralizes the acid chyme and also contains enzymes that hydrolyze carbohydrates, proteins, and lipids. Other pancreatic enzymes, along with enzymes secreted by the lining of the small intestine, complete the chemical digestion of food.

As an end result of digestion, carbohydrates are hydrolyzed to monosaccharides. Monosaccharides provide your cells with a source of energy. They are also a source of carbon skeletons (chains of carbon atoms) for constructing other organic molecules. The complete digestion of proteins results in individual amino acids. As you have already read, your cells use these amino acids to build their own "brand" of proteins. Lastly, the hydrolysis of fats by the enzyme lipase (which is secreted by the pancreas) results in fatty acids and glycerol. Your cells use these raw materials to build their own lipids.

The small intestine is highly specialized for absorbing nutrients into the circulatory and lymphatic systems for transport (Figure 29-7). The wall of the small intestine is folded into many small, finger-like projections called **villi** (singular, *villus*). The epithelial cells lining each villus have microscopic projections called microvilli. The total surface area of all the villi in the small intestine is about equal to that of a tennis court!

At its core, each villus has a small lymph vessel and a network of capillaries (microscopic blood vessels). After fatty acids and glycerol are absorbed by an epithelial cell, these building blocks are recombined into fats that are then transported into the lymph vessel. Sugars and amino acids are absorbed into the bloodstream through the capillaries in each villus.

▼ **Figure 29-7** Nutrient absorption occurs in the epithelial cells of the small intestine.

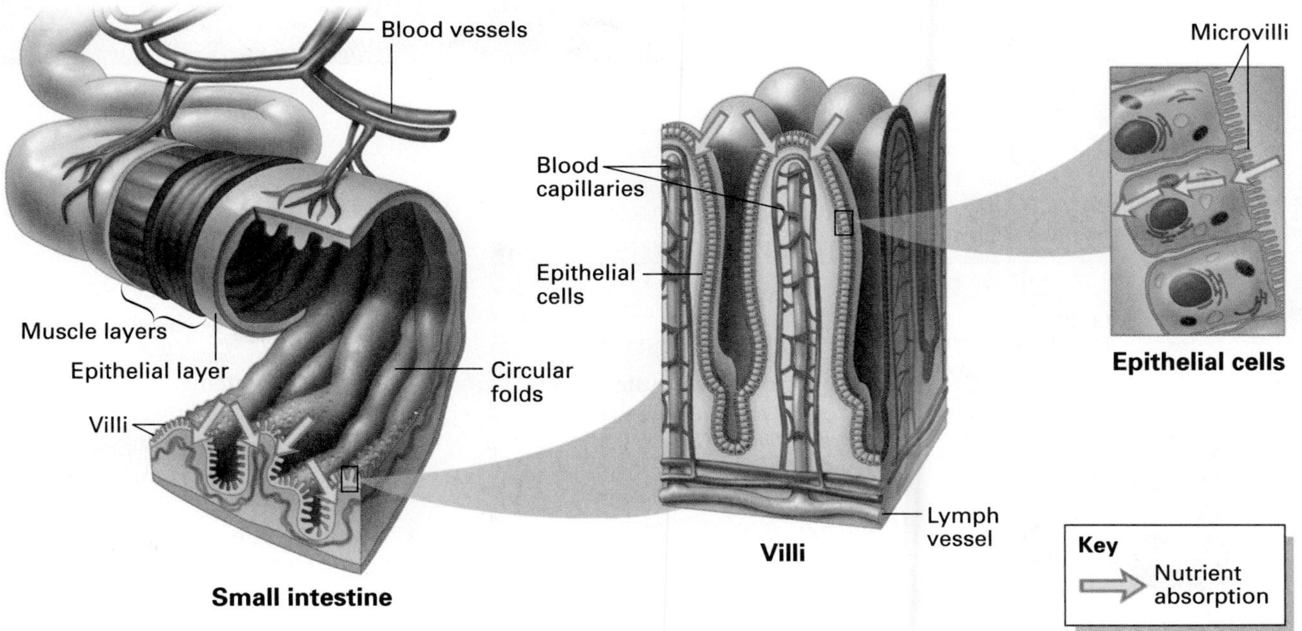

Large Intestine By the time food reaches the end of the small intestine, the nutrients have all been broken down and absorbed. Undigested material passes through another sphincter from the small intestine into the large intestine. Also called the colon, the **large intestine** is a wide (5 cm), short (1.5 m) tube from which water is absorbed into the body (Figure 29-8). The large intestine also contains certain bacteria that produce vitamin K and several B vitamins.

As you have read, a major function of the large intestine is to reabsorb water. Saliva, gastric juice, and other digestive juices all contain large amounts of water. Altogether about 7 liters of fluid are secreted into the alimentary canal each day. Much of that water is reabsorbed along with nutrients in the small intestine. The large intestine finishes the job by absorbing most of the remaining water. Together the small intestine and large intestine reclaim 90 percent of the water that enters the alimentary canal.

Undigested food material and other waste products are called **feces.** Reabsorption of water causes the feces to become more solid as it moves through the large intestine. Once again, peristalsis is the mechanism that moves this material through the large intestine. It generally takes 12 to 24 hours for waste material to travel through the colon.

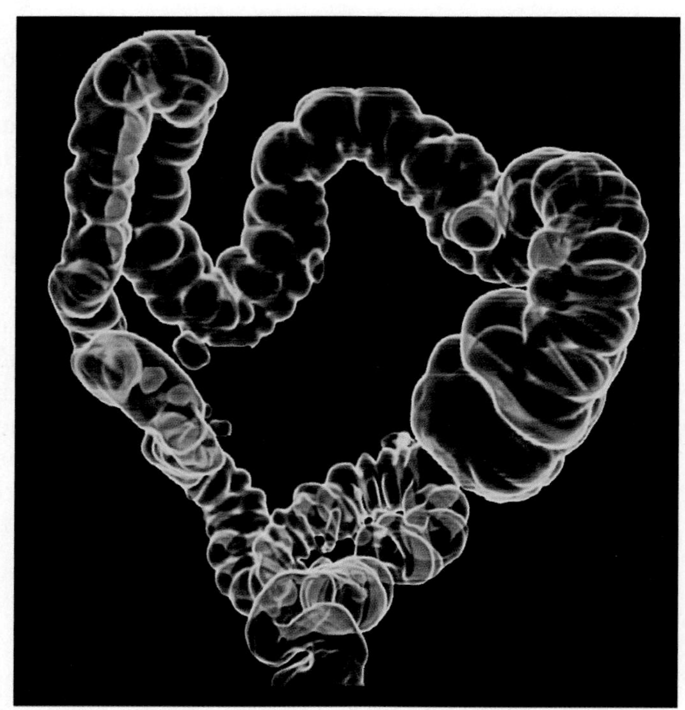

Figure 29-8 This 3-dimensional digital image of a large intestine was generated by combining images of 2-dimensional cross sections. The structure of the large intestine is suited to its function of absorbing water from undigested materials leaving the small intestine.

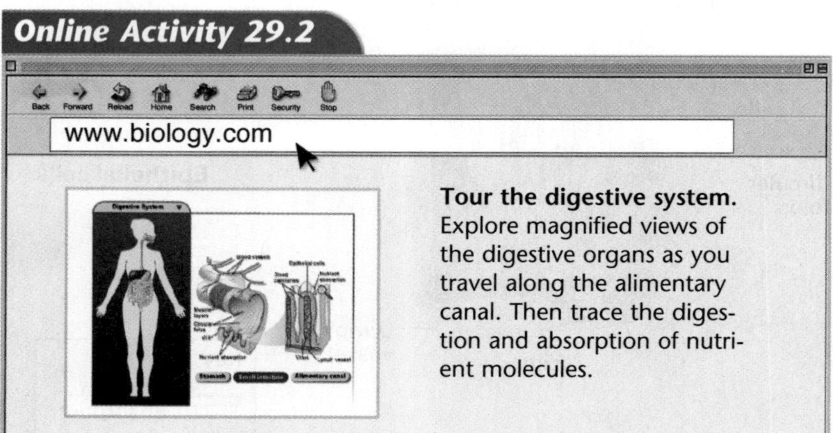

Online Activity 29.2
Back Forward Reload Home Search Print Security Stop
www.biology.com
Tour the digestive system. Explore magnified views of the digestive organs as you travel along the alimentary canal. Then trace the digestion and absorption of nutrient molecules.

Concept Check 29.2

1. Explain the statement, "Digestion occurs in a tube."
2. List the organs of the alimentary canal in the order of their interactions with food.
3. Which organ is most responsible for absorption? Explain your answer.

Breaking Down Fat Digestion

How Bile and Pancreatic Juice Affect Fat Digestion

Question What are the roles of bile and pancreatic juice in fat digestion?

Lab Overview In this investigation you will determine the roles of bile and pancreatic juice in fat digestion. You will use whole milk as a source of fat, samples of bile and pancreatic juice, and the pH indicator phenol red.

Preparing for the Lab To help you prepare for the investigation, go to the *Lab 29 Online Companion.* ·····➔ Find out more about the production of bile and pancreatic juice in the digestive system and learn how fat molecules are broken down. Prepare for the lab procedure by previewing the steps you will take.

Completing the Lab Use your Laboratory Manual or lab page printouts from the *Lab 29 Online Companion* to do the investigation and analyze your results. **CAUTION:** *Be sure to follow your teacher's instructions and all safety guidelines in the investigation.*

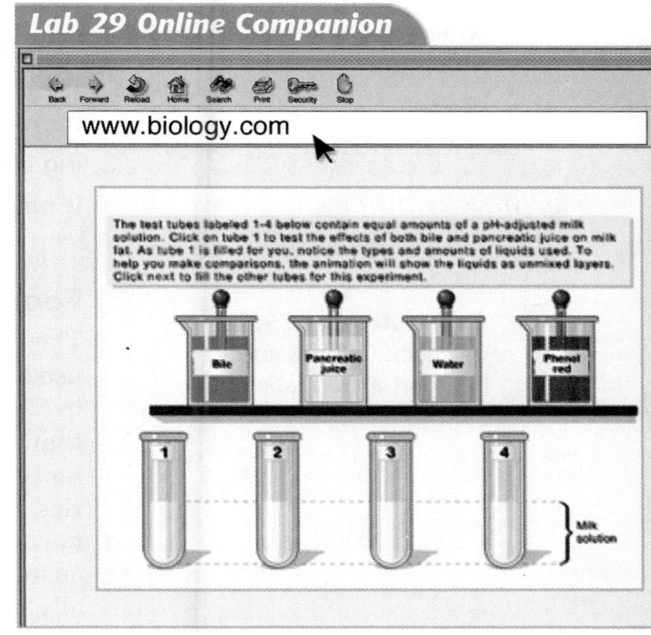

Lab 29 Online Companion
www.biology.com
The test tubes labeled 1-4 below contain equal amounts of a pH-adjusted milk solution. Click on tube 1 to test the effects of both bile and pancreatic juice on milk fat. As tube 1 is filled for you, notice the types and amounts of liquids used. To help you make comparisons, the animation will show the liquids as unmixed layers. Click next to fill the other tubes for this experiment.
Bile
Pancreatic juice
Water
Phenol red
1
2
3
4

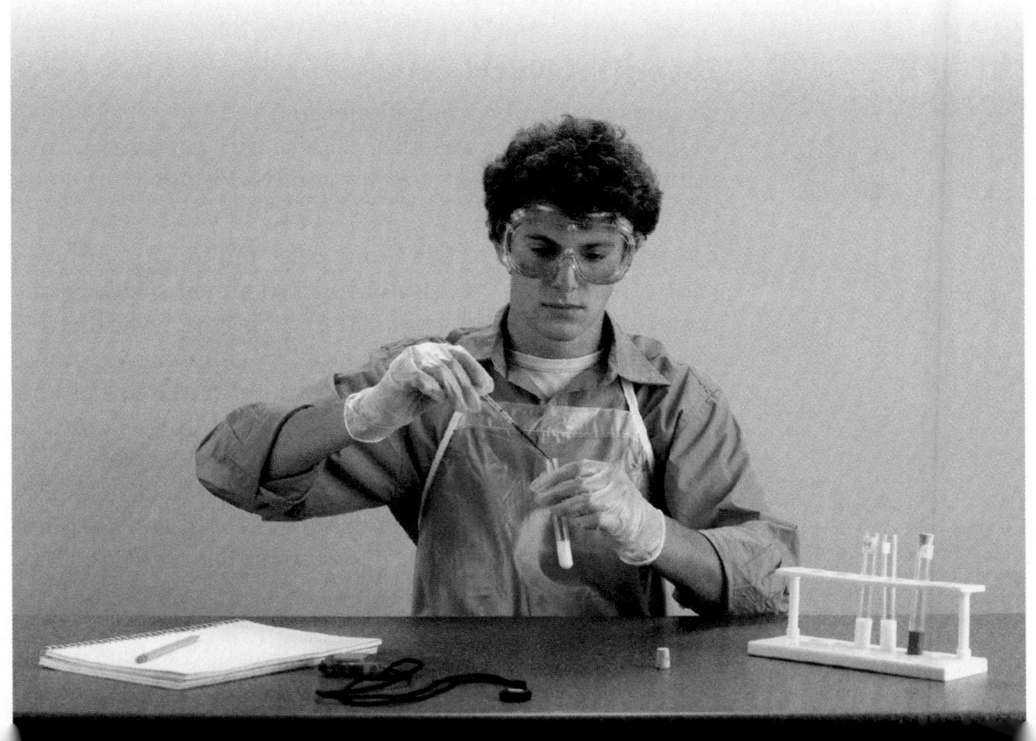

CONCEPT 29.3 A healthful diet provides both fuel and building materials.

OBJECTIVES

- Describe how the body uses food as fuel.
- Explain the significance of essential nutrients.
- Describe the information provided by the Food Guide Pyramid and food labels.

KEY TERM

- essential nutrient

What's Online

www.biology.com

Online Activity 29.3
Calculate Calories and interpret a food label.

Why do you need to eat? Your body is constantly working, even while you are sleeping. To do that work, your body needs food to burn as fuel for energy. Food is also a source of molecular building blocks that your body can use to manufacture other molecules it needs.

Food As Fuel

The building blocks of carbohydrates, proteins, and fats can all be used by cells to generate ATP by cellular respiration (as you read in Chapter 7). Fats are especially rich in energy, containing more than twice the energy of carbohydrates per gram. The energy content of food is measured in kilocalories (1 kilocalorie = 1000 calories). (Remember that one calorie is the amount of energy required to raise one gram of water one degree Celsius.) The calories listed on food labels or referred to elsewhere regarding nutrition are actually kilocalories and are written as "Calories" (with a capital "C").

Each person must consume a minimum amount of Calories every day just to maintain the metabolic processes that sustain life. For this basic maintenance plus energy needed for an active lifestyle, teenagers require about 2,200 Calories for females and 2,500 Calories for males. Figure 29-9 lists the specific Calorie requirements for several different activities.

▼ **Figure 29-9** It only takes a few minutes to eat a slice of pizza. However, burning those Calories can take much longer!

Calories Used During Different Activities

	Jogging 10.8 km/h	Swimming 3.2 km/h	Walking 3.0 km/h
Calories burned per min	11.7	8.9	2.6
Time to burn Calories in one slice cheese pizza (300 Calories)*	26 min	34 min	1 h 55 min

*Based on a 68-kg person

Essential Nutrients

Besides fuel and carbon skeletons, your diet must also supply essential nutrients. **Essential nutrients** are materials that must be ingested because your cells cannot construct them from other molecules.

Essential Fatty Acids Your cells make fats and certain other lipids by combining fatty acids with other molecules, such as glycerol. Your cells can manufacture most of the required fatty acids from simpler molecules. The fatty acids that your body can *not* make are essential fatty acids, which means that they must be obtained from your diet. An example is linoleic acid, which is required to make the phospholipids that make up your cells' plasma membranes. Most people's diets in the United States provide enough essential fatty acids, so deficiencies are rare.

Essential Amino Acids Of the 20 amino acids required to manufacture all the proteins your body needs, eight cannot be made by your cells from other organic molecules. Those eight are called essential amino acids. A deficiency in even one impairs protein synthesis. (Infants require a ninth essential amino acid, histidine, that their cells start to make as they grow older.) The body cannot store excess amino acids, making it important for your daily diet to contain the essential ones. Animal products such as meat, eggs, and cheese provide all eight. People who do not eat animal products must eat the right combinations of plant foods to obtain all the essential amino acids (Figure 29-10).

Vitamins Vitamins are organic molecules that are required in relatively small amounts and partner with enzymes (Figure 29-11). Vitamin deficiencies can cause health problems. For example, a lack of vitamin A can cause vision problems.

There are two main classes of vitamins. Water-soluble vitamins cannot be stored by your body, while fat-soluble vitamins can. If you ingest more water-soluble vitamins than you need each day, the excess will be eliminated in your urine. However, if you ingest more fat-soluble vitamins than you need, the excess will be stored. Over time, these stored vitamins can build up and cause health problems. For example, an extreme excess of vitamin A can cause hair loss, blurred vision, and liver damage.

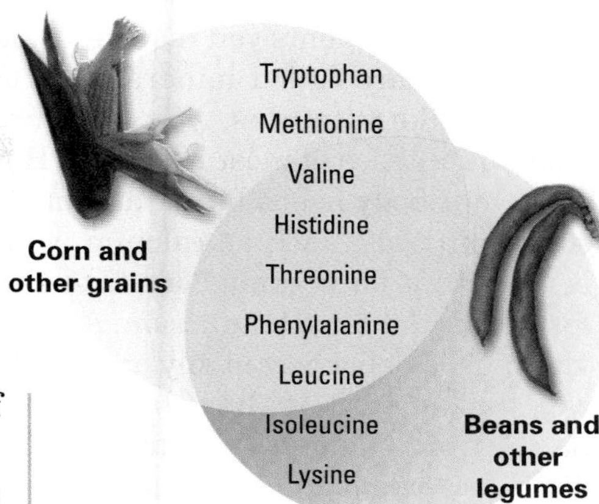

▲ **Figure 29-10** Combining corn and beans provides all of the essential amino acids.

▼ **Figure 29-11** Vitamins are vital for maintenance and proper functioning of your body.

Selected Vitamins

	Vitamin	Major Sources in Diet	Some Functions
Water-Soluble	Vitamin B_1	Pork, legumes, peanuts, whole grains	Carbohydrate use and nervous system function
	Vitamin B_2	Dairy, meats, whole grains, vegetables	Carbohydrate, protein, and fat metabolism
	Niacin	Nuts, meats, grains, legumes	Energy metabolism
	Vitamin B_6	Meats, vegetables, whole grains	Protein, fat, and carbohydrate metabolism
	Pantothenic acid	Meats, dairy, whole grains	Energy metabolism; steroid production
	Folic acid	Green vegetables, oranges, nuts, legumes	Red blood cell and protein formation
	Vitamin B_{12}	Meats, eggs, dairy products	Nervous system function; red blood cell production
	Biotin	Legumes, other vegetables, meats	Energy metabolism
	Vitamin C	Citrus, broccoli, green peppers	Bones, teeth, and skin growth and maintenance
Fat-Soluble	Vitamin A	Green and orange vegetables, fruits, dairy	Skin, bones, teeth, and hair; vision
	Vitamin D	Fortified milk, egg yolks	Bones and teeth; calcium, phosphorus use
	Vitamin E	Vegetable oils, nuts, seeds	Protection against certain toxins
	Vitamin K	Green vegetables	Blood clotting

Minerals Elements you require in inorganic form are called minerals (Figure 29-12). Like vitamins, you only need small quantities of most minerals. However, your body needs larger amounts of some minerals, such as calcium, which is important for making bone tissue and for nerve and muscle function. Also like vitamins, a deficiency in any one mineral can cause serious health problems. Recall from Chapter 27 that a calcium deficiency can lead to osteoporosis.

Minerals can also be harmful if they are consumed in high quantities. For example, excessive sodium intake is associated with high blood pressure in some individuals. Sodium is found in high levels in most prepared foods. As a result, the average American consumes 20 times the required amount of sodium.

Partial List of Minerals

Mineral	Sources in Diet	Some Functions
Calcium	Dairy, dark green vegetables, legumes	Bones and teeth; blood clotting; nerve and muscle function
Phosphorus	Dairy, meats, grains	Bones and teeth; ATP production
Potassium	Meats, dairy, fruits, vegetables, grains	Water balance; nerve and muscle function
Iodine	Seafood, dairy, iodized salt	In certain hormones
Iron	Meats, eggs, legumes, grains, leafy vegetables	In hemoglobin
Zinc	Meats, seafood, grains	In certain digestive enzymes
Sulfur	Proteins from various foods	Protein and cartilage production

▲ **Figure 29-12** Minerals play important roles in a range of body functions.

The Food Guide Pyramid

One way to learn how much of each type of food to eat is to study the Food Guide Pyramid (Figure 29-13). The pyramid shape indicates the recommended proportions of different types of food in a healthy diet. For example, notice that foods such as bread, rice, and pasta make up the pyramid's wide base. This indicates that these foods should make up the largest proportion of a person's daily diet. The foods in the tip of the pyramid (fats, oils, and sweets) should only make up a very small part of the diet. The number of small triangle and circle symbols in each block of the pyramid signifies the amount of fats and sugars in that type of food.

To fully understand and use the Food Guide Pyramid, it is important to know what is meant by a "serving" of each type of food. In some cases, a serving is less than you might expect. For example, one serving of bread is a single piece. One serving of meat, poultry, or fish equals 2 or 3 ounces. That's about the size of one medium chicken thigh. So, eating two or three chicken thighs would satisfy your daily requirement in this food group.

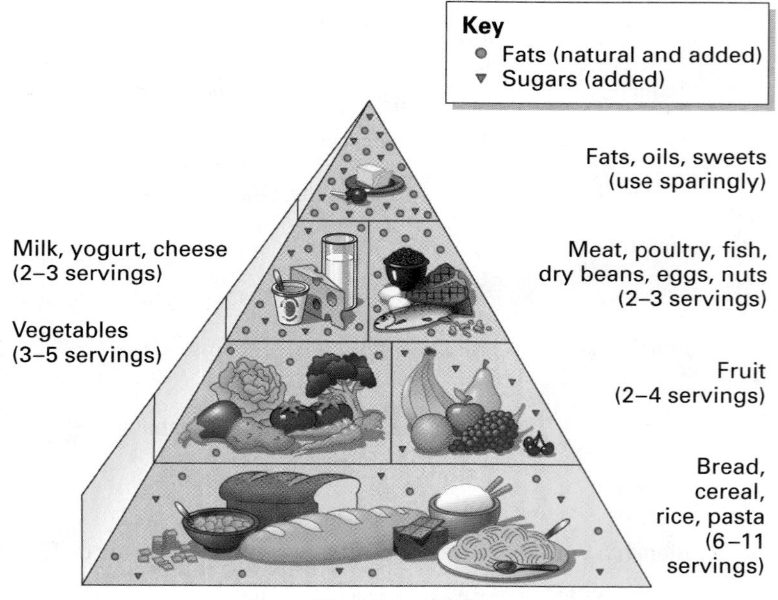

▲ **Figure 29-13** Following the recommendations of this Food Guide Pyramid will help you maintain a healthy and balanced diet.

Food Labels

Perhaps you've noticed information labels like the one in Figure 29-14 printed on food containers. The Food and Drug Administration (FDA) requires that all packaged food be labeled with detailed nutritional information. This information is presented in blocks of data.

Section A of the label indicates the size of a single serving and also how many servings are in the package. Section B indicates the total Calories in one serving of the food, as well as how many Calories are from fat. Section C provides more detail, including how many grams (g) or milligrams (mg) of fat, carbohydrate, and protein are contained in one serving. It also indicates what percentage of the Daily Value is provided in one serving. For example, one serving of this vegetable pizza contains 7 g of fat. Experts recommend that a person eating a 2,000 Calorie per day diet ingest no more than 30 percent from fat, or no more than 600 Calories from fat. Seven grams of fat provides approximately 63 Calories. (Section F lists how many Calories are contained in one gram of fat, carbohydrate, and protein). So, one serving provides approximately 11 percent of that person's Daily Value of fat.

Section D provides percentage of Daily Value information for key vitamins and minerals. For example, one serving of this pizza provides 20 percent of the Daily Value of vitamin C and 15 percent of the Daily Value of calcium (for a person consuming 2,000 Calories per day). Section E provides general information on recommended daily nutrient intake for people who require 2,000 or 2,500 Calories per day. Finally, Section G lists all the ingredients in the food, from the most abundant to the least. For instance, wheat flour is the most abundant ingredient in this vegetable pizza.

Eating a balanced diet is key to providing your body with the energy and building blocks it needs. In Concept 29.4, you will learn about the negative health effects of not eating the right amounts of healthy foods.

Nutrition Facts

Serving Size 1 Slice (142g)
Servings Per Container 3 } A

Amount Per Serving
Calories 270 Calories from Fat 63 } B

	% Daily Value*
Total Fat 7g	**11%**
Saturated Fat 3g	**15%**
Cholesterol 10mg	**4%**
Sodium 450mg	**19%**
Total Carbohydrate 41g	**14%**
Dietary Fiber 3g	**14%**
Sugars 4g	**14%**
Protein 12g	

} C

Vitamin A 10% • Vitamin C 20%
Calcium 15% • Iron 8% } D

*Percent Daily Values are based on a 2,000 calorie diet. Your daily values may be higher or lower depending on your calorie needs:

	Calories	2,000	2,500
Total Fat	Less than	65g	80g
Sat Fat	Less than	20g	25g
Cholesterol	Less than	300mg	300mg
Sodium	Less than	2,400mg	2,400mg
Total Carbohydrate		300g	375g
Dietary Fiber		25g	30

} E

Calories per gram:
Fat 9 • Carbohydrate 4 • Protein 4 } F

INGREDIENTS: CRUST: WHEAT FLOUR AND WHOLE-WHEAT FLOUR, WATER, OAT BRAN, OLIVE OIL, HONEY, YEAST, SALT. **SAUCE:** TOMATOES, WATER, BASIL, TOMATO PASTE, ONIONS, CRUSHED GARLIC, SALT, SUGAR, CRUSHED RED PEPPER. **CHEESE:** LOW MOISTURE PART-SKIM MOZZARELLA (PASTEURIZED PART-SKIM MILK, CULTURES, SALT, ENZYMES), GOAT CHEESE (PASTEURIZED GOAT'S MILK, SALT, RENNET, CULTURES). **TOPPINGS:** ROASTED CORN, EGGPLANT, ZUCCHINI, RED PEPPER. } G

▲ **Figure 29-14** The standard Nutrition Facts food label was developed to help consumers make healthy and educated choices.

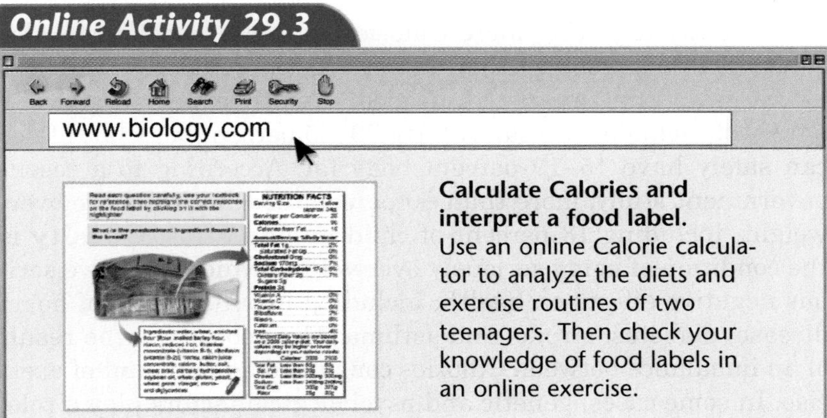

Online Activity 29.3
Back Forward Reload Home Search Print Security Stop
www.biology.com
Calculate Calories and interpret a food label.
Use an online Calorie calculator to analyze the diets and exercise routines of two teenagers. Then check your knowledge of food labels in an online exercise.

Concept Check 29.3

1. Explain why a person requires at least a minimum number of Calories each day.
2. Why are some nutrients considered essential nutrients?
3. What does the shape of the Food Guide Pyramid signify?
4. List three types of information that can be found on a food label.

CONCEPT 29.4 Nutritional disorders damage health.

OBJECTIVES

- Contrast malnutrition and undernutrition.
- Summarize the causes and consequences of obesity.
- Explain the term *eating disorder*.

KEY TERMS

- malnutrition
- undernutrition
- obesity
- anorexia
- bulimia

What's Online

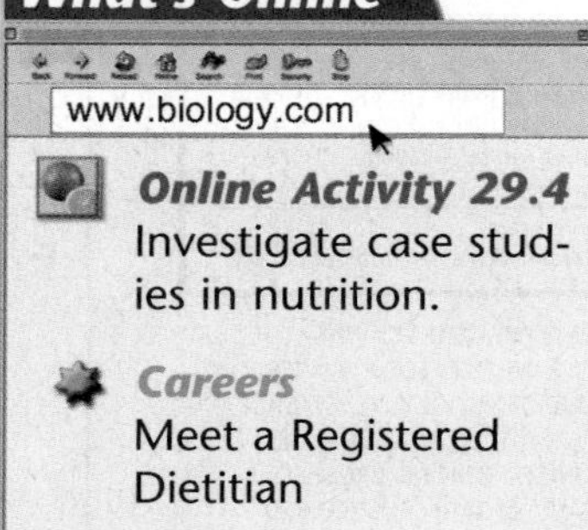

Online Activity 29.4 Investigate case studies in nutrition.

Careers Meet a Registered Dietitian

Diets lacking in essential nutrients result in health problems. In addition, the body has a basic Calorie requirement to function. What happens when the body receives too few—or too many—Calories?

Malnutrition

A diet lacking one or more essential nutrients can result in **malnutrition.** For example, a deficiency in vitamin C can result in scurvy, a disease that causes swollen gums, loose teeth, and small black and blue spots on the skin. Sailors prior to the 1800s often suffered from scurvy because on their long journeys they had no source of fresh fruit and vegetables that provide vitamin C. Today, malnutrition due to protein deficiency is a serious problem in certain parts of the world. For example, higher death rates among children are common in countries where nutrient-rich food is scarce.

Undernutrition

A person whose diet is deficient in Calories is suffering from **undernutrition.** Eventually the body begins breaking down its own protein molecules for fuel. Muscles shrink and the body may even break down its own tissues to supply energy. Undernutrition usually occurs in parts of the world where drought, war, or some other crisis has disrupted the food supply.

Even simple diets consisting only of rice or corn can provide an adequate number of Calories. However, such diets may be deficient in various nutrients (Figure 29-15).

Figure 29-15 North Korean residents line up to receive food rations. Providing staple foods such as rice can help prevent undernutrition.

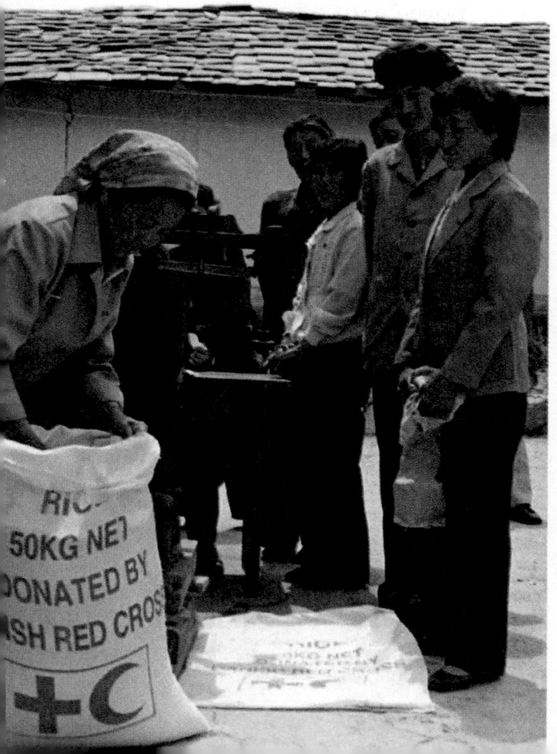

Obesity

Consistently ingesting more Calories than are needed can also cause health problems. The human body stores excess Calories as fat until that energy is needed. Health experts generally agree that females can safely have 20–25 percent body fat. Males can safely have 15–19 percent body fat. According to a recent government study, more than 60 percent of Americans are overweight, including 13 percent of children and teens. **Obesity** is the condition of being seriously overweight, which can have serious negative effects on health, including increased risk of heart disease, diabetes, stroke, and asthma. Most obesity is the result of an imbalance between Calories consumed and amount of exercise. In some cases, genetic and psychological factors play a role.

Eating Disorders

Eating disorders are psychological conditions that affect a person's eating habits and ability to obtain nutrients. Anorexia and bulimia are the two most common disorders. While they do affect males, these conditions affect a higher percentage of the females in the United States (as many as 4 percent, or more than 7 million women and girls).

Anorexia is an extreme pursuit of thinness characterized by self-starvation and excessive weight loss. A person suffering from anorexia does not consume enough Calories to maintain normal body weight. This condition can lead to disintegration of body organs, menstrual irregularities in women, irregular heartbeat, and even heart failure.

Bulimia is an eating disorder characterized by purging after bingeing (eating excessively). Purging by vomiting or using laxatives results in the premature elimination of food before the body is able to absorb its nutrients. While bulimics do not always appear extremely thin, a bulimic person will often suffer the same health disorders as an anorexic.

A third type of eating disorder is bingeing without purging. As a binge eater consumes excessive Calories, this condition can lead to obesity.

Careers

Back Forward Reload Home Search Print Security Stop

www.biology.com

Meet a Registered Dietitian

Meet a registered dietitian who specializes in eating disorders and helps patients overcome anorexia and bulimia. She works as a member of a team to identify the cause of the problem and then provides nutrition guidance and psychological assistance. Take a closer look at some tools she uses in her work when you go online.

Healthy Eating for Life

Throughout your reading in this chapter you have probably noticed some themes that can help you make healthy decisions about food. One theme is the need for balance between Calories consumed in food and Calories spent in daily activities and exercise. Another theme is the need for a variety of foods in your diet and attention to the amounts of different kinds of foods. One way to get the information you need to make healthy choices is to use the Food Guide Pyramid and to read food labels.

▲ **Figure 29-16** Developing healthy eating habits now can pay big rewards all throughout your life.

Online Activity 29.4

Back Forward Reload Home Search Print Security Stop

www.biology.com

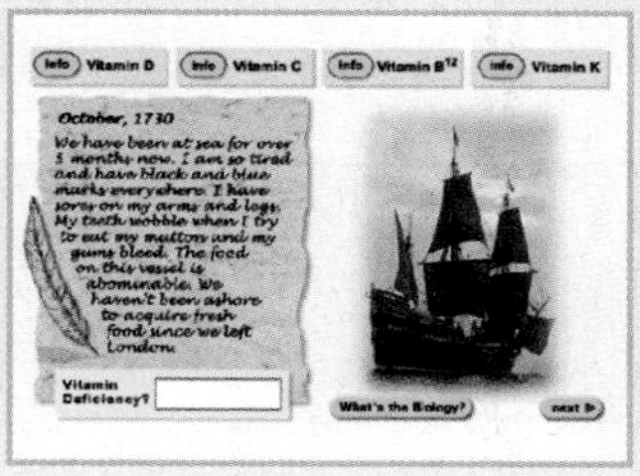

Investigate case studies in nutrition.

What's wrong with the health of a sailor in the 1700s? Read his journal to determine which vitamin deficiency is responsible for his symptoms. Analyze other medical cases when you go online.

Concept Check 29.4

1. What is the difference between malnutrition and undernutrition?
2. What are some health problems related to obesity?
3. Distinguish anorexia, bulimia, and bingeing.

Multiple Choice

Choose the letter of the best answer.

1. Proteins in food such as cheese provide the body with which monomers?
   a. monosaccharides
   b. amino acids
   c. fatty acids
   d. water molecules

2. Which list of the stages of food processing follows in the same order in which they happen in the body?
   a. ingestion, absorption, digestion
   b. absorption, elimination, ingestion
   c. digestion, absorption, elimination
   d. ingestion, elimination, digestion

3. Chemical digestion of starches begins in the
   a. mouth.
   b. liver.
   c. large intestine.
   d. pancreas.

4. The epithelial layer of the stomach is protected from self-digestion by a layer of
   a. acid.
   b. mucus.
   c. skin.
   d. cilia.

5. The role of the liver in digestion is to
   a. store bile.
   b. manufacture pepsin.
   c. manufacture bile.
   d. reabsorb water.

6. Which of the following are essential nutrients?
   a. essential amino acids
   b. essential fatty acids
   c. sodium, calcium, and iron
   d. all of the above

7. How are ingredients listed on Nutrition Facts labels?
   a. by fat content
   b. alphabetically
   c. by abundance in the food
   d. in the order that they are mixed

Short Answer

8. Describe the results of digesting carbohydrates, proteins, and fats.

9. Describe the function of the epiglottis.

10. Explain how persistalsis moves food along the alimentary canal.

11. Explain what roles the stomach plays in mechanical and chemical digestion.

12. How does heartburn occur?

13. How does the structure of the small intestine match its function?

14. Explain the relationship between Calories ingested, Calories burned, and changes in weight.

15. Why are certain amino acids considered essential amino acids?

16. What is an eating disorder? Give at least one example.

Visualizing Concepts

17. Follow the example in the completed protein flowchart to finish the similar flowchart for carbohydrates. Next, construct your own flowchart describing the digestion and absorption of fats.

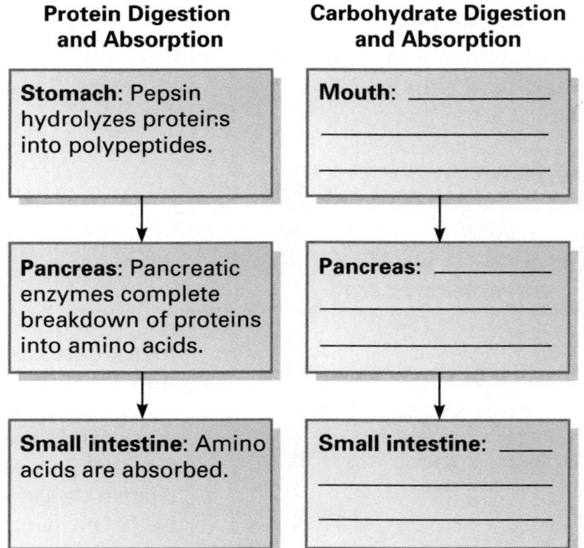

Protein Digestion and Absorption
Carbohydrate Digestion and Absorption
Stomach: Pepsin hydrolyzes proteins into polypeptides.
Mouth:
Pancreas: Pancreatic enzymes complete breakdown of proteins into amino acids.
Pancreas:
Small intestine: Amino acids are absorbed.
Small intestine:

Analyzing Information

18. Analyzing Data Use this Nutrition Facts label to answer the questions below.

Nutrition Facts
Serving Size 1/2 Cup (83g)
Servings Per Container 8

Amount Per Serving	
Calories 190 Calories from Fat 110	
	% Daily Value*
Total Fat 12g	**18%**
Saturated Fat 8g	**40%**
Cholesterol 45mg	**15%**
Sodium 75mg	**3%**
Total Carbohydrate 18g	**6%**
Dietary Fiber 0g	**0%**
Sugars 17g	
Protein 3g	
Vitamin A 10% •	Vitamin C 8%
Calcium 10% •	Iron 0%

a. What percentage of the total Calories in this product is from fat?

b. Based on the grams of saturated fat and its % Daily Value, calculate the upper limit of saturated fat that a person should consume daily.

c. Is this product an overall good source of vitamin A and calcium? Explain your answer.

19. Analyzing Diagrams Use the diagram of a villus to answer the questions.

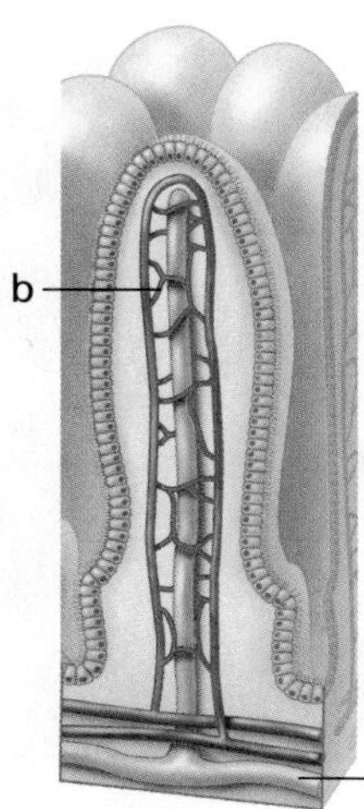

a. Which digestive system organ contains villi?

b. What is the structure labeled *a?* What is its function?

c. What is the structure labeled *b?* What is its function?

Critical Thinking

20. Evaluating Promotional Claims A snack food's packaging advertises that it is now fortified with calcium and iron. How can you decide if this product is a healthy food choice?

21. Relating Cause and Effect Describe at least one possible effect of a diet lacking in one of the nine essential amino acids.

22. Developing Hypotheses Suppose a person's body does not absorb enough nutrients even though she eats a healthy, balanced diet. What might be a possible cause of such a condition? Explain.

23. What's Wrong With These Statements? *Briefly explain why each statement is inaccurate or misleading.*

a. Digestion is completed in the large intestine.

b. You cannot drink water while standing on your head.

c. Polysaccharide digestion occurs in the liver.

d. Your cells can manufacture vitamin K.

e. Malnourished people are always underweight.

Performance Assessment

Biology Research Project Research the condition caused by childhood vitamin D deficiency called rickets. What are the signs and symptoms of rickets? What researchers were involved in determining the cause of rickets? How did these researchers build off the discoveries of each other to determine the cause of rickets and how to prevent it?

Online Assessment/Test Preparation

Back Forward Reload Home Search Print Security Stop

www.biology.com

- **Chapter 29 Assessment**
  Check your understanding of the chapter concepts.
- **Standardized Test Preparation**
  Practice test-taking skills you need to succeed.

CHAPTER 30

The Circulatory and Respiratory Systems

Blood vessels carry blood from your heart to the tips of your fingers and toes, and then back again. The image below provides a glimpse inside a human blood vessel. The vessel's walls consist of muscle tissue (pink) and connective tissue (yellow) that enable it to expand and contract as blood flows through it. Red blood cells inside the vessel carry oxygen to all parts of your body. In this chapter, you will learn how your circulatory system serves as an internal transport system, distributing nutrients to cells and removing wastes. You will also learn how your circulatory and respiratory systems work together, exchanging oxygen and carbon dioxide between your cells and the environment. Before you begin the chapter, go online to the ***WebQuest*** to explore how climbing at high altitudes affects the respiratory system.

Colorized SEM 460×

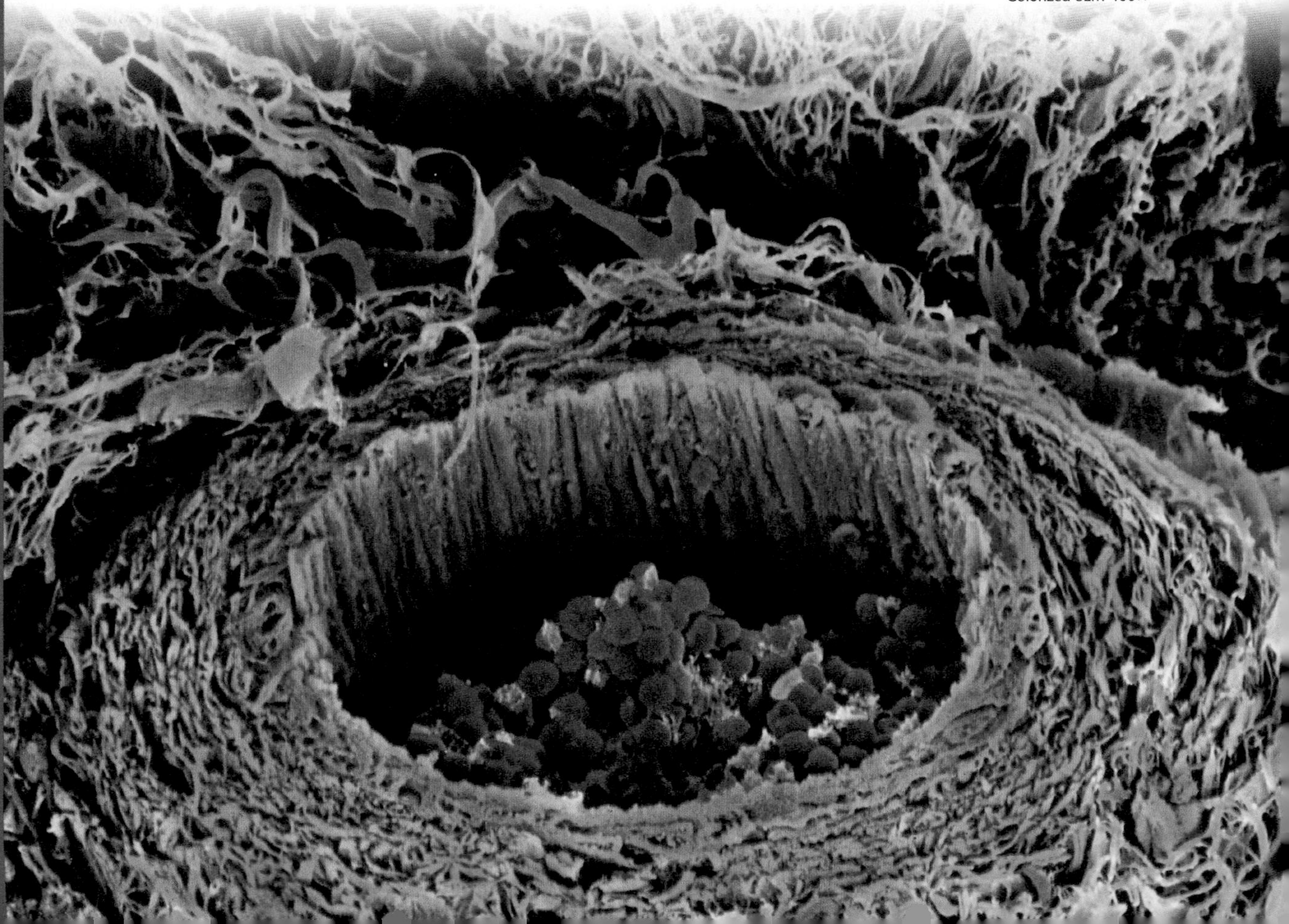

Key Concepts

Concept 30.1 The circulatory system transports materials throughout the body.

Concept 30.2 The heart pumps blood throughout the circulatory system.

Concept 30.3 Blood consists of cells suspended in plasma.

Concept 30.4 Cardiovascular disease is the leading cause of death in the United States.

Concept 30.5 The respiratory system exchanges gases between blood and air.

Concept 30.6 Smoking damages the body and shortens life.

Assessment Chapter 30 Review

What's Online

www.biology.com

WebQuest
EverestQuest

Online Activity 30.1
Go inside a capillary.

History of Science
Discovery of Blood and Circulation

Online Activity 30.2
Detect electrical activity in the heart.

Lab 30 Online Companion
Sensing Circulation

Online Activity 30.3
Break down a blood sample.

Online Activity 30.4
Track the clogging of an artery.

Online Activity 30.5
Tour the respiratory system.

Online Collaborative Science 3
Exploring Cardiorespiratory Fitness

Online Activity 30.6
Analyze the effects of tar.

Chapter 30 Assessment

CONCEPT 30.1

The circulatory system transports materials throughout the body.

OBJECTIVES

- Identify the organs and key functions of the circulatory system.
- Explain how chemicals are exchanged between the blood and other tissues.
- Describe the function of the lymphatic system.

KEY TERMS

- blood
- heart
- capillary
- artery
- vein
- lymph

What's Online

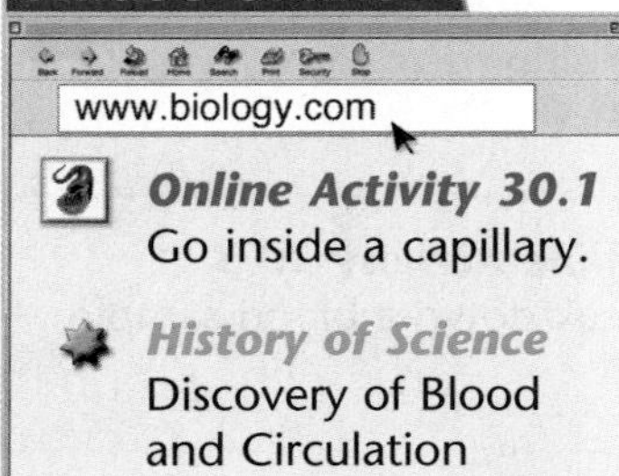

Online Activity 30.1
Go inside a capillary.

History of Science
Discovery of Blood and Circulation

Your circulatory system includes a network of about 100,000 kilometers of blood vessels. Laid end to end, they would encircle Earth two and a half times! This network of vessels supplies the trillion cells in your body with nutrients and oxygen, and removes carbon dioxide and other waste products.

Organs of the Circulatory System

As you read in Chapter 7, your cells require a constant supply of nutrients and oxygen. If diffusion were the only method of transportation, it could take as long as two years for these chemicals to travel from your small intestine to the cells in your brain. Fortunately, your body has a more efficient distribution system—the circulatory system.

In addition to delivering nutrients and oxygen to cells, the circulatory system transports hormones throughout your body and carries wastes away from cells. The circulatory system also plays important roles in repairing tissue and protecting the body from infection, as you will read in Chapter 31.

The three primary components of the circulatory system are the blood, the heart, and the blood vessels (Figure 30-1). **Blood** is a type of connective tissue made up of cells and liquid. Blood is pumped through the body by the **heart,** a multi-chambered, muscular organ. The overall flow of blood is from the heart to tissues throughout the body and back to the heart.

Blood flows throughout your body via blood vessels, tubes that form a closed pipeline within the body. Your body contains about 5 liters of blood. Under normal activity, it takes about one minute for all that blood to make a complete circuit through the body. Increased activity, such as running or dancing, causes your blood to circulate

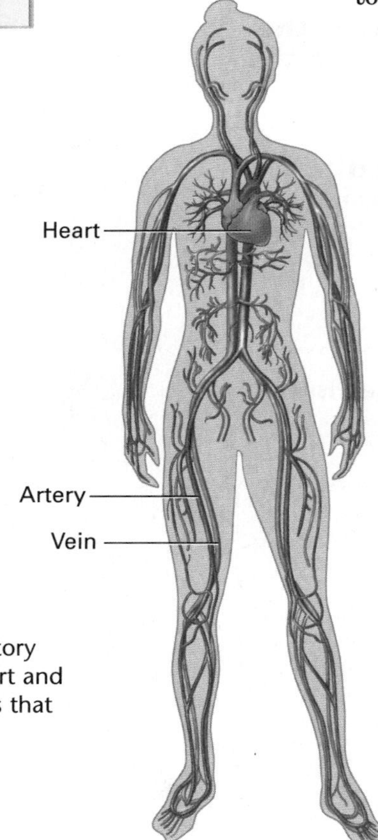

Figure 30-1 The circulatory system consists of the heart and a network of blood vessels that carry the blood.

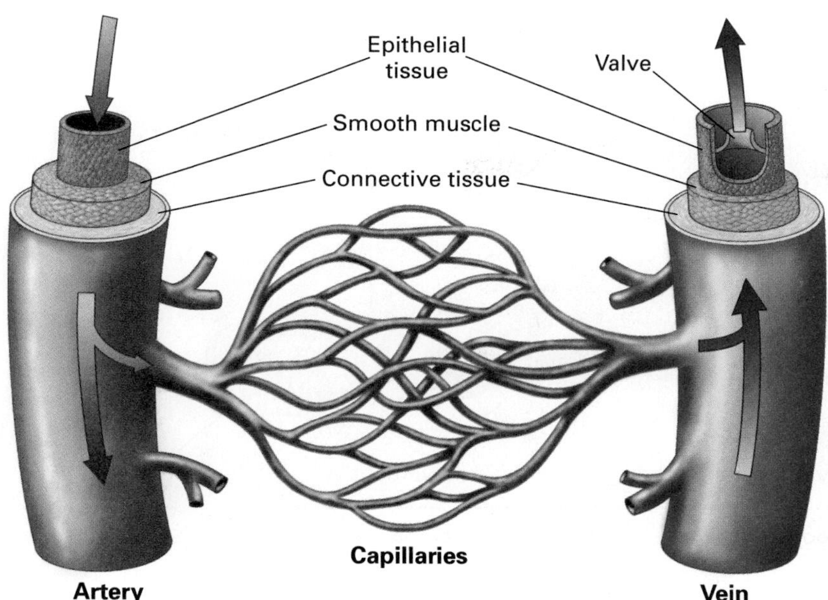

Figure 30-2 From the heart, blood flows through arteries to capillaries, then back through veins. As shown in the micrograph below, most capillary walls are only one cell thick. These thin walls allow for quick diffusion of needed materials.

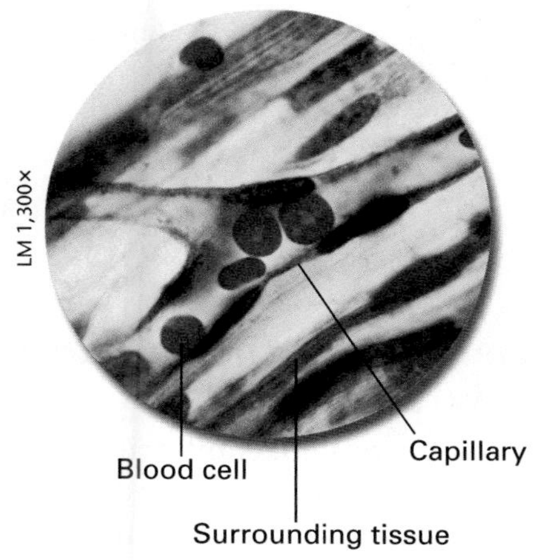

more quickly, keeping your cells supplied with oxygen and nutrients. There are three types of blood vessels that make up this pathway: capillaries, arteries, and veins.

Capillaries To distribute nutrients and oxygen effectively, the circulatory system must have close contact with all the cells of the body. This close contact is accomplished by millions of microscopic blood vessels called **capillaries.** Some capillaries are so narrow that blood cells must travel through them one at a time (Figure 30-2). The walls of capillaries consist of a very thin layer of epithelial tissue encased in a moist membrane. This structure enables the diffusion of nutrients and oxygen out of the blood and the diffusion of waste products into the blood.

Arteries Blood flows from the heart to the capillaries through a system of thick-walled blood vessels called **arteries.** The walls of arteries consist of epithelial tissue wrapped in layers of smooth muscle and connective tissue. The muscle tissue enables the artery to constrict (become more narrow) and to dilate (relax). The blood in arteries is under pressure due to the heart's pumping action. This pressure helps to ensure that blood flows only in one direction—toward the capillaries. Further from the heart, the arteries branch into smaller and smaller vessels. Eventually the narrowest arteries flow into capillaries.

Veins Blood returns from the capillaries to the heart through vessels called **veins.** The walls of veins also consist of epithelial tissue surrounded by smooth muscle and connective tissue. But the muscle layer in veins is thinner than that in arteries. The blood in veins is under very little pressure. The main force that pushes blood through the veins comes from the skeletal muscle tissue in which many veins are located. Contracting these muscles squeezes the veins and forces blood through them. Most veins contain valves that allow blood to flow only toward the heart. Small veins merge together into larger veins.

History of Science

Back Forward Reload Home Search Print Security Stop

www.biology.com

Discovery of Blood and Circulation

Blood transfusions can mean the difference between life and death for people who have been in accidents, who need surgery, or who have certain blood-related diseases. How did people gain the knowledge necessary to perform this critical treatment? Go online to learn more about the first scientists who studied blood and the circulatory system and to investigate some of the ongoing research in the field.

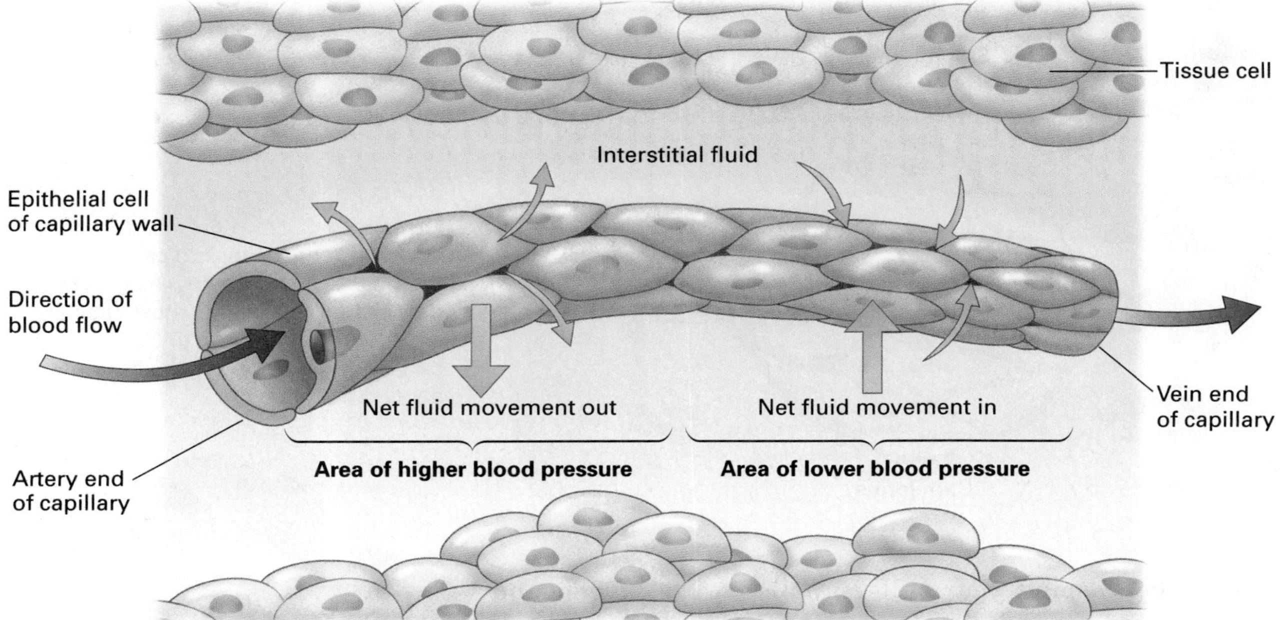

▲ **Figure 30-3** At the artery end of a capillary, the higher blood pressure forces fluid out. The lower blood pressure at the vein end allows fluid to reenter the capillary.

Chemical Exchange Between Blood and Body Tissues

As you have read, capillaries are in close contact with the cells of your body. In fact, most cells in your body are no farther than 10 micrometers (μm) from a capillary and the blood inside it. This capillary network and the structure of the individual capillaries are critical to accomplishing the main functions of the circulatory system—the distribution of oxygen and nutrients, and the removal of waste products.

As you read in Chapter 27, cells in body tissues are surrounded by interstitial fluid. Thus the substances in capillaries do not enter tissue cells directly. First these substances must enter the interstitial fluid, then enter the cells. The exchange of substances between blood and the interstitial fluid occurs in several ways. Some small molecules, such as oxygen and carbon dioxide, diffuse across membranes or pass through gaps between the epithelial cells of the capillary wall. Oxygen and nutrients move from the blood into the interstitial fluid, while carbon dioxide and other small waste products move from the interstitial fluid into the blood. Larger molecules move across the membranes by exocytosis and endocytosis. (See Chapter 6 to review these transport processes.)

Blood pressure also forces fluid through the capillary wall. At the artery end of a capillary, blood pressure forces water, small solutes, and some dissolved proteins through the gaps between cells (Figure 30-3). However, blood cells and larger proteins are too large to pass easily through these openings, so they remain in the capillary. As a result, the vein end of the capillary is hypertonic compared to the surrounding interstitial fluid.

(Recall that a hypertonic solution has a higher solute concentration than another solution.) Thus water tends to reenter the vein end of the capillary via osmosis. Blood pressure is very low at the vein end of the capillary, so it does not oppose the flow of fluid back into the capillary. In fact, 85 percent of the fluid that leaves the artery end of the capillary reenters at the vein end.

The Lymphatic System

Your blood loses about 4 liters of fluid into the interstitial fluid daily. The lymphatic system collects and returns most of this fluid to the circulatory system. Like the circulatory system, the lymphatic system consists of capillaries and larger vessels (Figure 30-4). Once inside the lymphatic vessels, this collected fluid is called **lymph.** Like veins, lymphatic vessels are embedded in muscle tissue, and they have valves that prevent lymph from flowing back toward the capillaries. The combination of muscle contractions squeezing the vessels and the one-way valves helps fluid move through the lymphatic system. Eventually, lymph drains into the circulatory system near the heart, allowing the fluid to be reused.

Located at juncture points throughout the lymphatic system are enlargements in the lymph tissue called lymph nodes. Lymph nodes help defend the body against infection. The nodes contain cells that destroy some bacteria and viruses that may enter the body. Have you ever had "swollen lymph glands" in your neck when you've had a cold or the flu? These "glands" are actually groupings of lymph nodes, swollen with infection-fighting cells. In Chapter 31 you will read more about the lymphatic system's role in fighting disease.

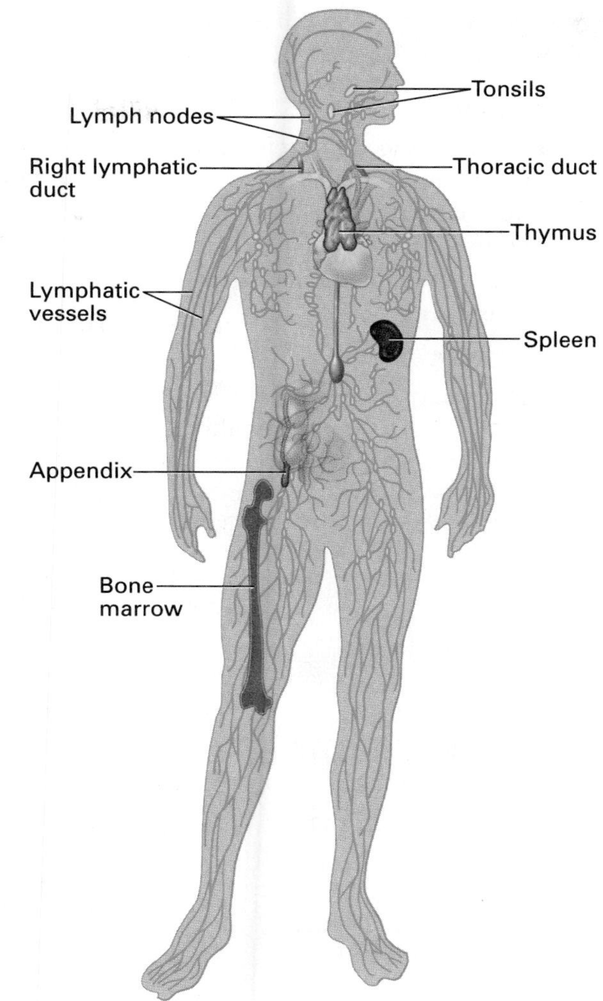

▲ **Figure 30-4** The lymphatic system includes specialized organs in addition to vessels and nodes. White blood cells develop in the bone marrow and thymus and collect in other organs of the lymphatic system where they fight infection.

Online Activity 30.1

Go inside a capillary.
Review the circulatory system as you study magnified views of arteries and veins, and the heart's structure by using the clickable body. Then test your understanding of how materials flow into and out of a capillary.

Concept Check 30.1

1. List the components of the circulatory system and describe the functions of each.
2. Describe how materials such as oxygen move from the blood into a tissue cell.
3. How does the lymphatic system return fluid to the circulatory system?

CONCEPT 30.2

The heart pumps blood throughout the circulatory system.

OBJECTIVES

- Relate the blood flow circuits to heart anatomy.
- Explain heartbeat regulation.
- Explain how blood pressure is measured.

KEY TERMS

- pulmonary circuit
- systemic circuit
- aorta
- atrium
- ventricle
- valve
- pacemaker
- AV node
- systolic pressure
- diastolic pressure

What's Online

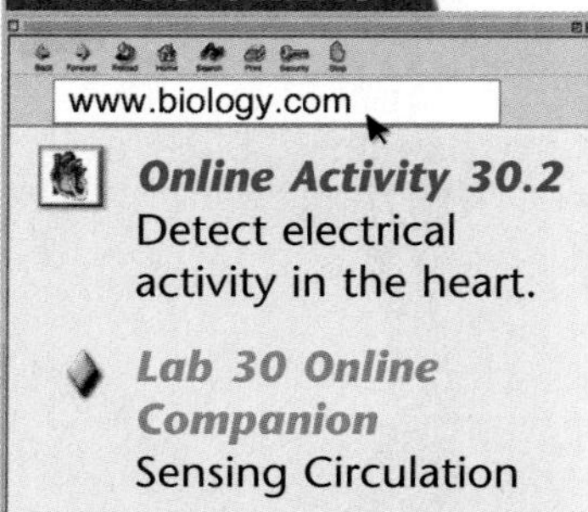

Online Activity 30.2
Detect electrical activity in the heart.

Lab 30 Online Companion
Sensing Circulation

The size of a clenched fist, your heart beats an average of 70 times per minute—over 100,000 times per day. This section explores the structure and function of this hard-working organ.

Two Circuits of Blood Flow

Blood flows along two pathways, or circuits, in the body (Figure 30-5). The **pulmonary circuit** carries oxygen-depleted blood from the heart to the lungs and oxygen-rich blood back to the heart. The **systemic circuit** carries oxygen-rich blood from the heart to the rest of the body and oxygen-depleted blood back to the heart. Blood flows through both circuits at the same time. While some blood is flowing in the pulmonary circuit, the rest is flowing through the systemic circuit. This double circuit ensures that oxygen-rich blood is constantly delivered to cells.

In the pulmonary circuit, blood travels from the right side of the heart through the pulmonary arteries to the lungs. In the lungs, blood picks up oxygen and releases carbon dioxide, which is exhaled. Pulmonary veins then return the oxygen-rich blood to the left side of the heart.

In the systemic circuit, oxygen-rich blood leaves the left side of the heart through the **aorta,** the artery that supplies oxygen-rich blood to all of the body. From the aorta, oxygen-rich blood flows through the branching arteries to the capillaries. In the capillaries, oxygen diffuses out of the blood and carbon dioxide diffuses in. The blood is now said to be oxygen-depleted. The oxygen-depleted blood returns to the right side of the heart through the veins.

Most arteries in the body carry oxygen-rich blood, while most veins carry oxygen-depleted blood. However, the vessels in the pulmonary circuit do the exact opposite. Pulmonary arteries carry oxygen-depleted blood to the lungs. Pulmonary veins carry oxygen-rich blood from the lungs to the heart.

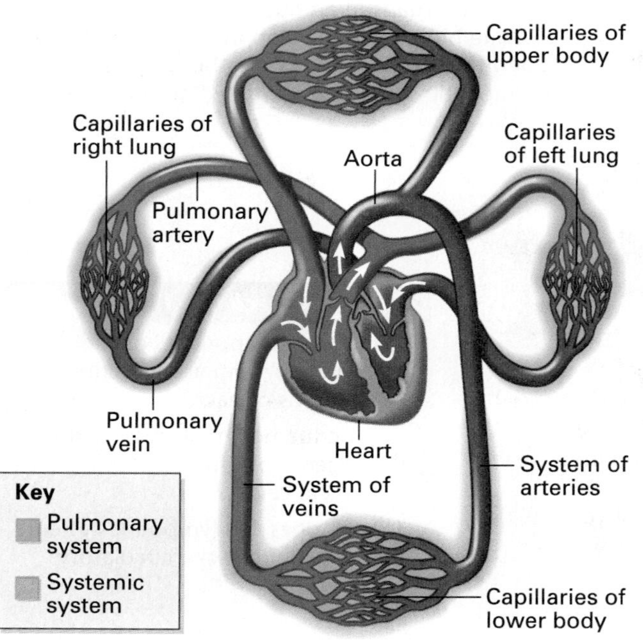

Figure 30-5 Blood flows to the pulmonary and systemic systems of the body through circuits composed of the heart and blood vessels.

Anatomy of the Heart

The heart is a muscular pump located between your lungs. A sac called the pericardium encloses the heart. As in other mammals, the human heart has four chambers (Figure 30-6). The two upper chambers, which receive blood returning to the heart, are called **atria** (singular, *atrium*). The two lower chambers are called **ventricles**, which pump blood out of the heart. The atria, which pump blood a short distance into the ventricles, have fairly thin walls. Ventricles have thicker muscular walls that enable them to pump blood throughout the body.

Oxygen-rich blood from the lungs gathers in the left atrium and is then pumped to the left ventricle. From there, blood is pumped through the aorta to the rest of the body where it delivers oxygen and nutrients to the cells. Oxygen-depleted blood returns to the right atrium via veins. Blood is then pumped into the right ventricle, which pumps it to the lungs through pulmonary arteries. After being replenished with oxygen in the lungs, blood once again returns to the heart through pulmonary veins and gathers in the left atrium.

Flaps of tissue in the heart called **valves** prevent blood from flowing backward. Valves are located between the atria and ventricles (called atrioventricular valves), and also between the ventricles and the arteries leading from the heart (called the pulmonary valve and the aortic valve). With each heartbeat, the valves open, allowing blood to flow through. Then the valves close, preventing blood from flowing back. The familiar heart sound of "lub dupp" is caused by the valves snapping shut. The "lub" sound is the atrioventricular valves closing, while the "dupp" sound happens when the pulmonary and aortic valves close.

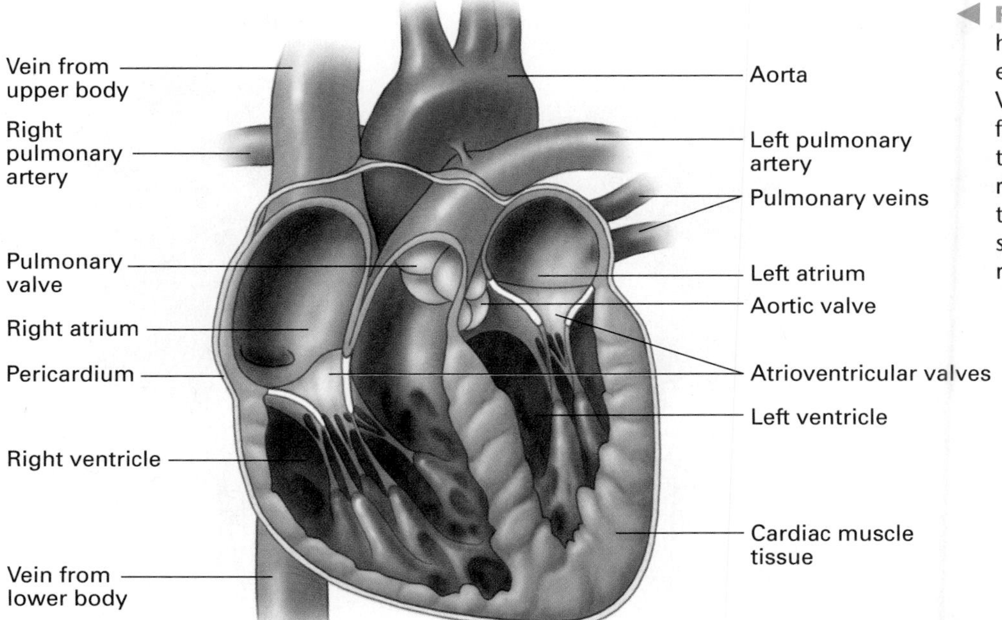

Figure 30-6 Blood enters the heart through the atria and exits through the ventricles. Valves keep the blood from flowing in the wrong direction. (Note that the left and right sides of the heart refer to the person's left and right sides, causing them to appear reversed in this face-on view.)

Regulation of the Heartbeat

When you run up a flight of stairs or are startled by a sudden noise, your heart is likely to beat faster than it does when you are at rest. A specific region of your heart muscle, known as the **pacemaker,** sets the rate at which your heart contracts (Figure 30-7). The pacemaker is located in the wall of the right atrium. It generates electrical impulses that spread rapidly over the walls of both atria, making them contract. The impulses then spread to a region of the heart called the **AV node** (atrioventricular node). From there, the electrical impulses spread to the ventricles, causing them to contract. The contracting ventricles propel blood to the rest of the body.

The pacemaker ensures that the heart beats in a rhythmic cycle. During the relaxation phase, called diastole, the atria and ventricles are relaxed, allowing blood from veins to enter the heart. The contraction phase is called systole. First the atria contract, and blood is forced into the ventricles, which are relaxed. Then the ventricles contract, pumping blood into arteries, while the atria are relaxed. This cycle repeats about every second when you are resting.

The pacemaker is controlled by both the nervous system and the endocrine system. Two sets of opposing nerves control the pacemaker by speeding it up and by slowing it down. Hormones secreted into the blood also control the pacemaker. For example, the hormone epinephrine, also called adrenaline, increases heart rate when the body is under stress.

Some diseases can disrupt the normal functioning of the pacemaker. One life-saving device is the cardiac defibrillator. When a patient's heart stops beating, paddle-like appliances are applied to the patient's chest, producing a strong electrical current that can cause the person's heart to resume beating.

▼ **Figure 30-7** The pacemaker sets the rate at which the heart contracts. Its signals generate electrical changes in the skin that can be measured as an electrocardiogram (ECG). The yellow color in the sample ECG below indicates the different stages of the heartbeat.

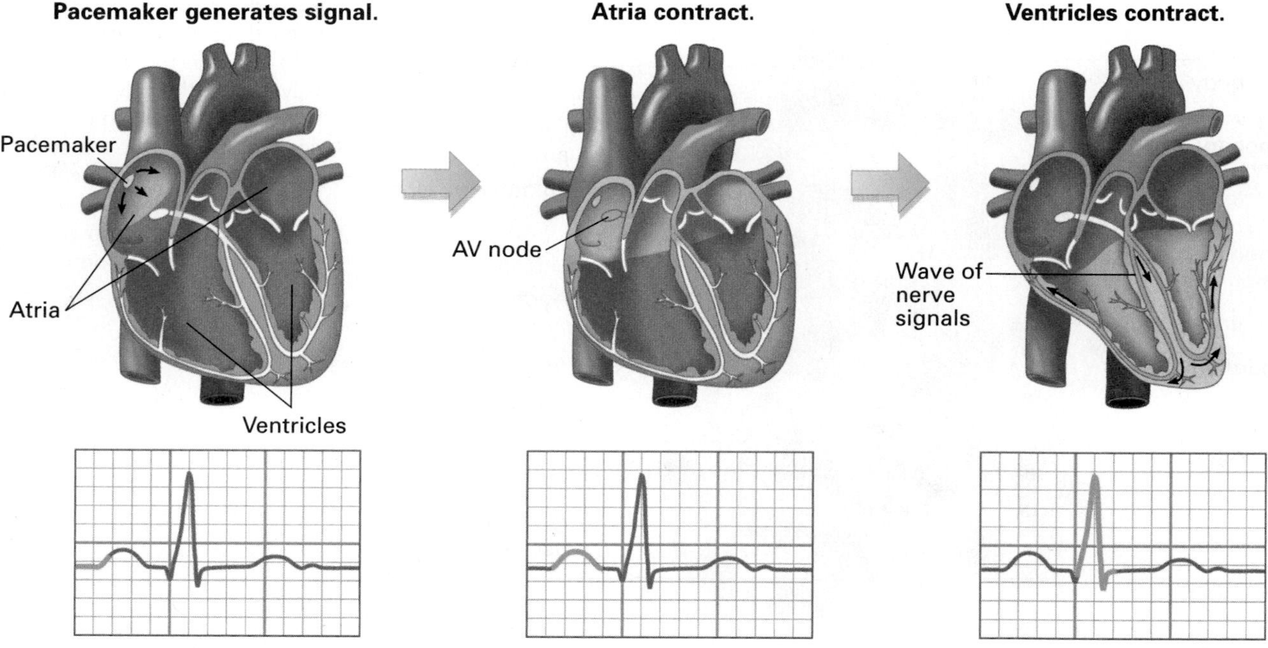

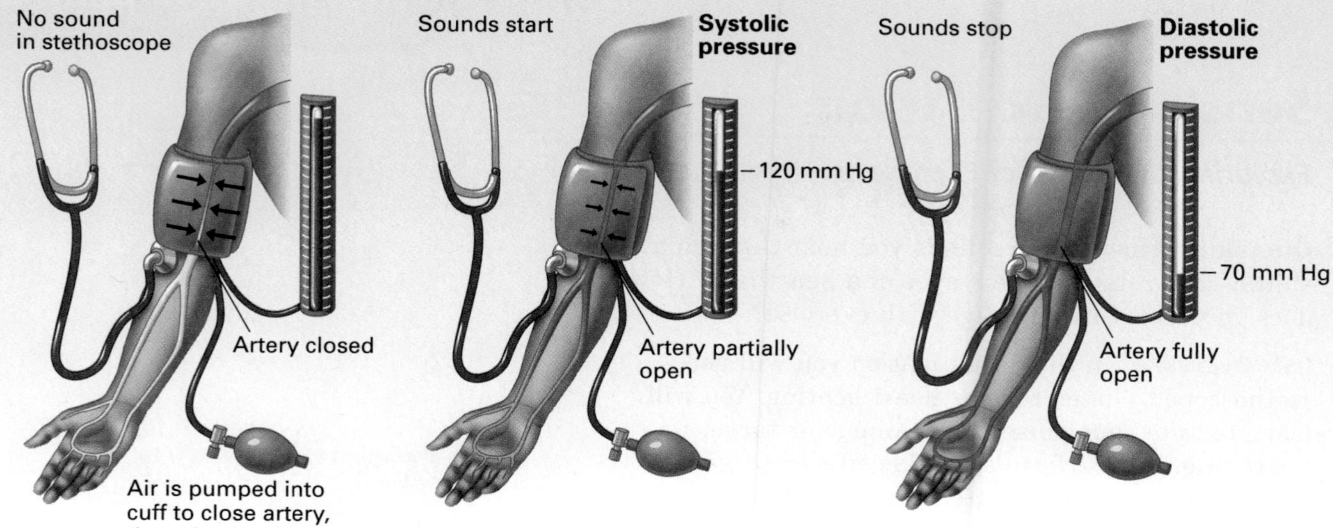

▲ **Figure 30-8** To measure blood pressure, an inflatable cuff is wrapped around a person's arm. As air is pumped in, the cuff squeezes the arm and closes a large artery. As air is slowly released from the cuff, the caregiver listens for the sounds of blood flowing through the artery.

Measuring Blood Pressure

When the ventricles contract, they increase pressure on the blood. The resulting force that blood exerts against the artery walls is called blood pressure. This force drives blood through the arteries and into the capillaries. Artery walls are elastic, which enables them to stretch in response to this force.

Blood pressure is represented by two numbers separated by a slash, such as 120/70 (Figure 30-8). It is measured in millimeters of mercury (mm Hg), a standard unit of liquid pressure. The first number is referred to as **systolic pressure,** the highest recorded pressure in an artery when the ventricles contract (systole). **Diastolic pressure,** the second number, is the lowest recorded pressure in an artery during the relaxation phase of the heartbeat (diastole).

A blood pressure of about 120/70 is the average for a healthy young adult. As a person ages, blood pressure may increase. Smoking or a fatty diet can contribute to this increase by causing arteries to become less elastic. A blood pressure above 140/90 is considered high and may lead to other cardiovascular diseases.

Online Activity 30.2

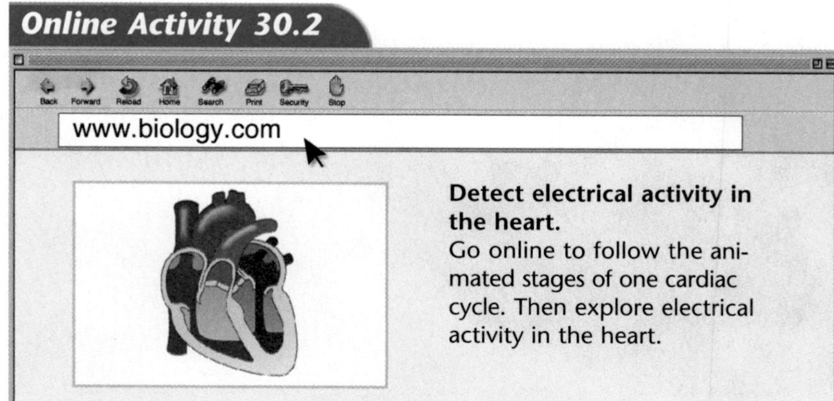

Detect electrical activity in the heart.
Go online to follow the animated stages of one cardiac cycle. Then explore electrical activity in the heart.

Concept Check 30.2

1. Starting with the right ventricle, describe the path of blood flow in the body.
2. List the four chambers of the heart and describe their functions.
3. What is the pacemaker? Describe its function in the heart.
4. Explain the difference between systolic and diastolic pressure.

Sensing Circulation

Exploring the Effects of Exercise on Heart Rate

Questions How do the sounds you hear through a stethoscope relate to the stages of a heartbeat? How does your heart rate change with exercise?

Lab Overview In this investigation you will use a stethoscope to listen to your heart beating. You will learn to take your pulse, determine your target heart rate, and perform a cardiac efficiency test to explore how your heart rate changes during and after exercise.

Preparing for the Lab To help you prepare for the investigation, go to the *Lab 30 Online Companion.* Find out more about how heart valves work and about the sounds they make. Learn how to take your pulse. Prepare for the lab procedure by previewing the steps you will take.

Completing the Lab Use your Laboratory Manual or lab page printouts from the *Lab 30 Online Companion* to do the investigation and analyze your results. **CAUTION:** *Be sure to follow your teacher's instructions and all safety guidelines in the investigation.*

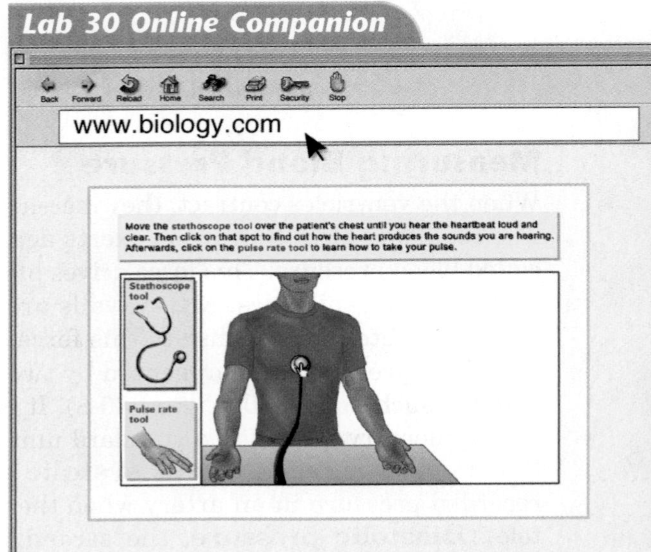
Lab 30 Online Companion
Back
Forward
Reload
Home
Search
Print
Security
Stop
www.biology.com
Move the stethoscope tool over the patient's chest until you hear the heartbeat loud and clear. Then click on that spot to find out how the heart produces the sounds you are hearing. Afterwards, click on the pulse rate tool to learn how to take your pulse.
Stethoscope tool
Pulse rate tool

CONCEPT 30.3

Blood consists of cells suspended in plasma.

OBJECTIVE
- Identify the main components that make up blood.
- Describe the process of blood clotting.

KEY TERMS
- plasma
- red blood cell
- hemoglobin
- white blood cell
- platelet

What's Online

Online Activity 30.3 Break down a blood sample.

Part liquid, part cellular material, your blood is a highly specialized tissue. It is also the only tissue you can donate to others as often as every other month, once you reach 17 years of age (according to the American Red Cross).

The Make-up of Blood

Your blood has several functions that are essential to your good health. As you have been reading, blood is responsible for transporting oxygen, water, and nutrients to cells. It also distributes hormones throughout the body. Blood removes waste products from the tissues and delivers them to the organs of the excretory system. In addition to its transport functions, blood also helps to fight infection and heal wounds.

Plasma Blood is the only liquid connective tissue in your body (Figure 30-9). Fifty-five percent of the volume of blood is a solution called **plasma.** Plasma is 90 percent water. The other 10 percent of plasma consists of dissolved salts, proteins, and other transported substances. The remaining 45 percent of blood volume consists mostly of red blood cells.

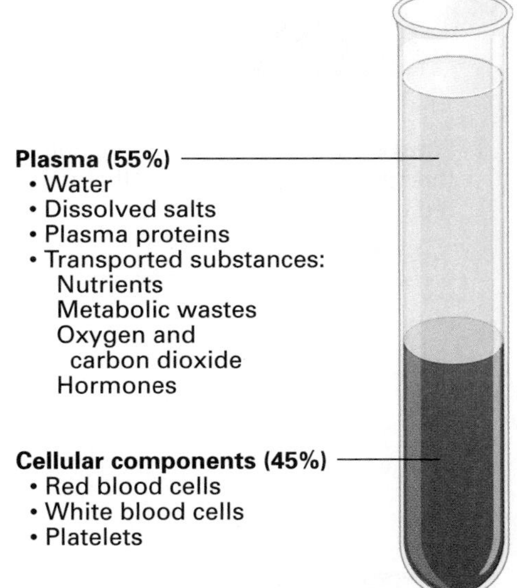

▲ **Figure 30-9** Blood consists of plasma, red blood cells, white blood cells, and platelets.

Red Blood Cells By far the most numerous cells in your blood are red blood cells, or erythrocytes. **Red blood cells** carry oxygen from the lungs to all the tissues of the body. One drop of blood (1 cubic millimeter) contains about 5 million red blood cells, and the average person has about 25 trillion in all. Each red blood cell contains about 250 million molecules of **hemoglobin,** a protein that temporarily stores oxygen for delivery to the cells. Hemoglobin is a good transporter of oxygen because it contains iron. Oxygen molecules bind to the iron portion (also called the heme group) of the hemoglobin molecule.

▲ **Red blood cells**

Red blood cells are produced in bone marrow at the rate of 2 million per second in a healthy adult. As red blood cells mature, they lose their nuclei and mitochondria. The loss of these structures helps give red blood cells their distinctive shape, like a flat disk that curves inward in the middle on both the top and bottom. This structure provides increased surface area for oxygen transfer compared to a spherical shape with the same volume.

Since a mature red blood cell has no nucleus, it cannot replace proteins, grow, or divide. The typical lifespan of a red blood cell is between 100 and 120 days. As red blood cells age, they become fragile and are eventually broken down.

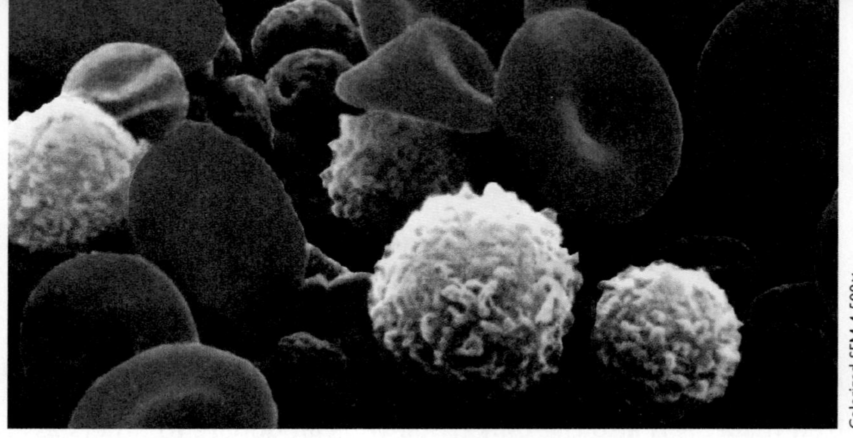

◀ **Figure 30-10** Three types of blood cells are visible in this SEM: red blood cells (red disks), white blood cells (yellowish spheres), and platelets (irregular, smaller red fragments).

White Blood Cells Also called leukocytes, **white blood cells** have nuclei and mitochondria and are responsible for fighting infection and preventing the growth of cancer (Figure 30-10). Normally, there are between 4,000 and 11,000 white blood cells in a drop (one cubic millimeter) of blood. However, when infection invades your body, the number of white blood cells increases. Most of the action of white blood cells takes place outside the blood vessels in the interstitial fluid. You will read more about white blood cells in Chapter 31.

Blood Clotting

When you get a small cut or scrape, your blood usually clots, stopping the bleeding and sealing the wound. The clotting process depends on small fragments of blood cells called **platelets** that originate in the bone marrow. Each drop of blood contains between 250,000 and 500,000 platelets.

The blood clotting process begins when platelets adhere to the site where the blood vessel is damaged. The platelets break apart and release substances called clotting factors. The clotting factors make other nearby platelets sticky and activate a series of reactions among other clotting factors in the plasma. These reactions result in the formation of a protein called fibrin. Fibrin threads trap red blood cells and additional platelets (Figure 30-11). This network of threads and cells builds up, eventually forming a patch that stretches over the torn tissue. This patch dries into a scab.

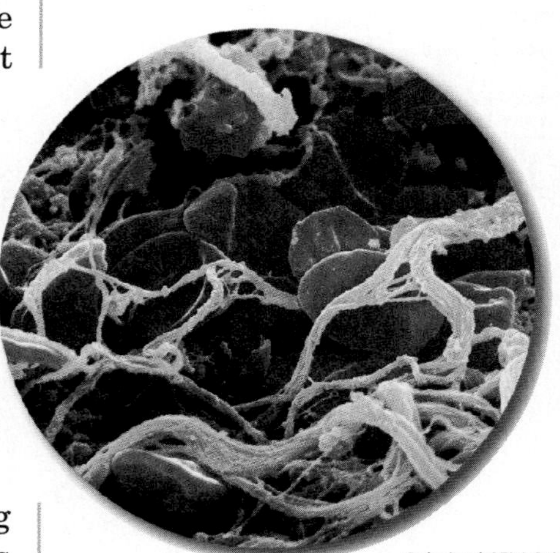

▲ **Figure 30-11** During clotting, fibrin threads (yellow) form a web that traps red blood cells and platelets.

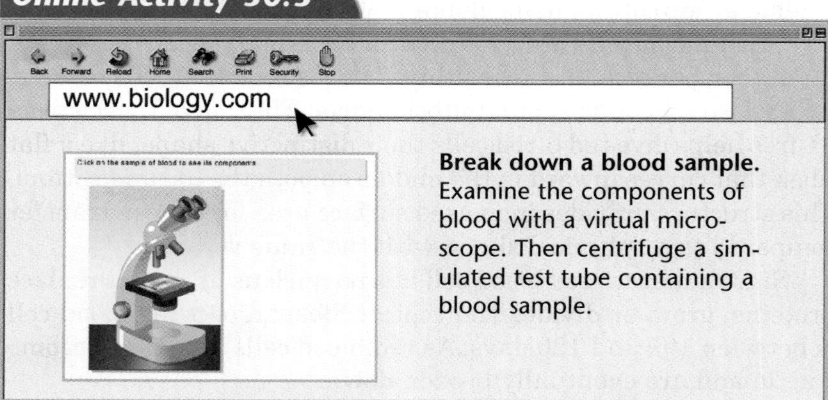

Back
Forward
Reload
Home
Search
Print
Security
Stop
www.biology.com
Break down a blood sample. Examine the components of blood with a virtual microscope. Then centrifuge a simulated test tube containing a blood sample.

Concept Check 30.3

1. List the four main components of blood.
2. What is the role of fibrin in blood clotting?
3. Describe how the structure of a red blood cell enables it to carry out its function.

CONCEPT 30.4 Cardiovascular disease is the leading cause of death in the United States.

OBJECTIVES
- Identify cardiovascular diseases and their causes.
- Describe measures you can take to prevent cardiovascular disease.

KEY TERMS
- plaque
- cardiovascular disease
- atherosclerosis
- heart attack
- arteriosclerosis
- hypertension
- stroke

What's Online

www.biology.com

Online Activity 30.4
Track the clogging of an artery.

Each year, hundreds of thousands of people, young and old, die from heart attacks and strokes. Some of these people were unaware of their disease before the fatal attack. Fortunately you can reduce the risk of heart disease by proper diet and exercise throughout your life.

Types of Cardiovascular Disease

If you could peer into the arteries of a newborn baby, you would probably see fairly smooth blood vessels. If you could inspect the arteries of an older person, however, you might find a patchwork of cholesterol, calcium, and fat deposits, called **plaque** (plak), adhering to the interior walls (Figure 30-12). Plaque builds up throughout a person's life. While a teenager may not feel any symptoms of the disease, significant buildup of plaque can ultimately lead to **cardiovascular disease,** illness of the heart and/or blood vessels.

Atherosclerosis Narrowing of the arteries, a condition called **atherosclerosis** (ath ur oh skluh ROH sis), results from plaque building up inside the artery wall. As the pathway narrows, blood pressure increases. Sometimes the narrowing completely blocks the flow of blood. If such a blockage occurs in one of the coronary arteries, the main arteries that supply the heart, the heart becomes deprived of oxygen and other nutrients. In mild cases with partial blockage, the person may feel occasional chest pains, called angina pectoris. In cases of severe blockage, a blood clot could close up the artery, leading to a **heart attack.**

▼ Figure 30-12 Compare the cross section of a clear artery (left) with a larger artery partly obstructed by plaque buildup (right).

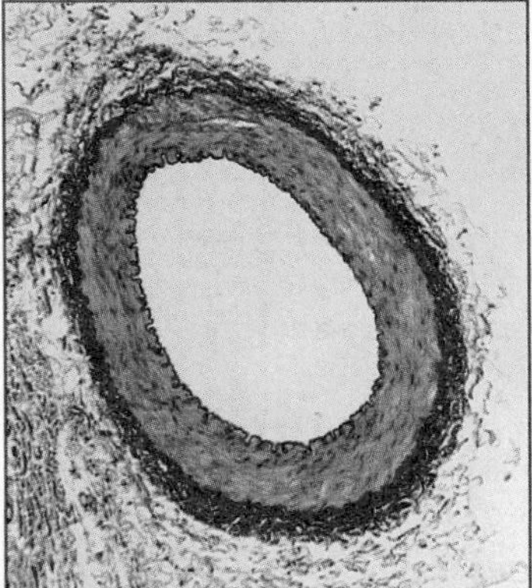

LM 130×

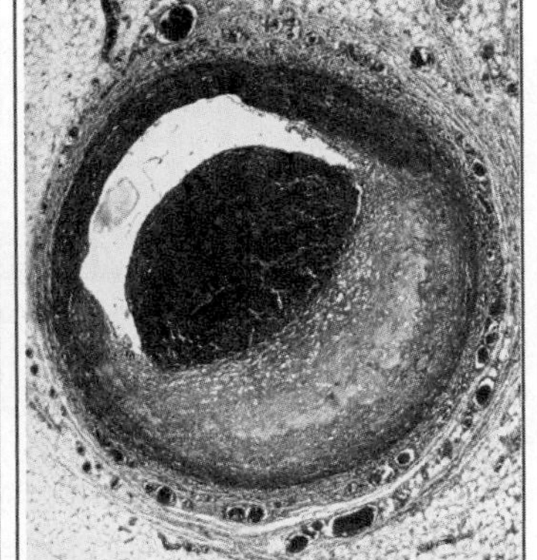

LM 25×

Arteriosclerosis A more advanced stage of plaque buildup, called **arteriosclerosis** (ar tir ee oh skluh ROH sis), occurs when the deposits on the artery wall harden. As you read in Concept 30.1, arteries are flexible and can expand and contract, which helps to control blood pressure. With arteriosclerosis, the arteries lose their ability to stretch. This disease increases blood pressure and the chance for blood clots to form within the blood vessels.

Hypertension Anger or fear can temporarily raise a person's blood pressure. However, if a person has a blood pressure of 140/90 or higher for an extended period of time, that person is said to have **hypertension,** or high blood pressure. Prolonged hypertension damages the heart and blood vessels. The heart must work harder to pump blood throughout the body, and over time the heart muscles enlarge. If these muscles expand too much, they actually become weakened and incapable of pushing blood throughout the body. Hypertension also exerts greater than normal pressure on the walls of the arteries, which can cause small tears. These tears can speed up atherosclerosis, which further increases blood pressure.

Stroke You have already read that a blood clot that forms in a coronary artery can cause a heart attack. If a blood clot forms in an artery going to the brain, it can cause a **stroke,** damage to brain tissue resulting from blocked blood flow. Tissue downstream from the blockage dies from lack of oxygen. Some consequences of stroke are partial paralysis, loss of speech, memory loss, and sometimes death. These effects depend in part on where in the brain the blockage occurred.

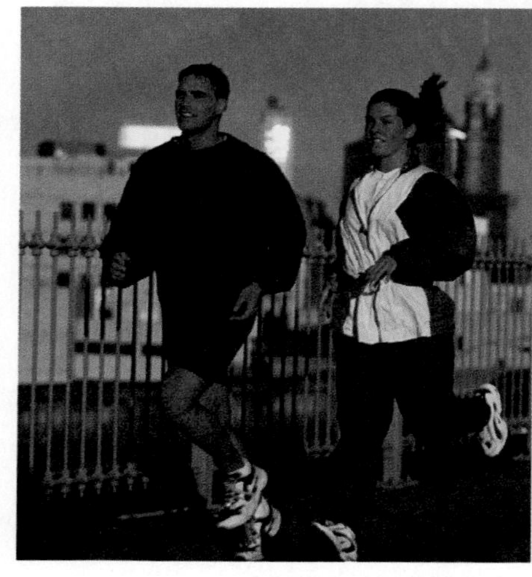

▲ **Figure 30-13** The choices you make about exercise all through your life affect your chances for a healthy adulthood and old age. The American Heart Association recommends that most people get 30 to 60 minutes of aerobic exercise 3 or 4 times a week.

Preventive Actions You Can Take Now

Although some risk for cardiovascular disease is genetic, there are also many controllable factors that play a role. For example, smoking, lack of exercise, and high-fat diets all increase risk. You can lessen your risk of future cardiovascular disease by making certain choices throughout your life (Figure 30-13). For example, you can limit your intake of cholesterol. Cholesterol is one ingredient in the plaque that coats artery walls. Cholesterol is found in foods containing saturated animal fats, such as butter and meat. High cholesterol levels increase the risk for cardiovascular disease.

Other preventive measures you can take include limiting your intake of salt (high salt levels can increase blood pressure) and eating lots of fresh fruits, vegetables, and whole-grain foods. Some researchers think that the fiber in these types of food helps to lower cholesterol levels. The proper diet, combined with regular exercise to maintain cardiovascular fitness, will help keep your circulatory system healthy.

Online Activity 30.4
www.biology.com
DANGER!
Heart attack imminent.
Track the clogging of an artery.
Monitor an artery as it becomes clogged over time. Use the images in the animation to analyze how clogged arteries can lead to heart attacks.

Concept Check 30.4

1. Describe two types of cardiovascular disease and their causes.
2. List five measures you can take to limit your risk of developing cardiovascular disease.
3. What is hypertension? How can it be avoided?

CONCEPT 30.5

The respiratory system exchanges gases between blood and air.

OBJECTIVES

- List the organs of the respiratory system.
- Explain breathing and how it is regulated.

KEY TERMS

- pharynx
- epiglottis
- larynx
- trachea
- bronchus
- lung
- bronchiole
- alveolus
- diaphragm

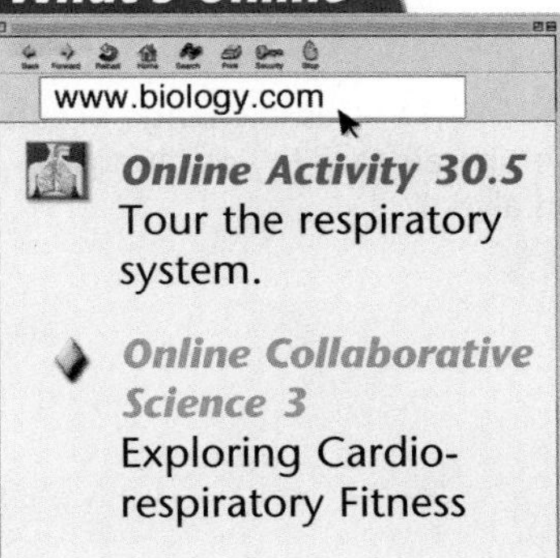

If you were stranded on a desert island or left adrift in a lifeboat, you would be able to survive for days without fresh water and for weeks without food. But if you were stranded on the moon, where there is no oxygen, you would perish within minutes. In this section, you will read about the importance of respiration to your everyday survival.

Anatomy of the Respiratory System

You read earlier in this chapter that all organisms must exchange materials with their environment. All your cells require oxygen to obtain energy efficiently from organic molecules during cellular respiration. However, most of your cells can't obtain oxygen directly from the environment. The function of the respiratory system is to provide oxygen for distribution to cells throughout your body. The respiratory system also removes the waste product carbon dioxide from the body.

The structures of the respiratory system include the mouth, nose, pharynx, larynx, trachea, and lungs (Figure 30-14). As you inhale, air enters the respiratory system through the nose or mouth. Many of the impurities in air, such as dirt and bacteria, are filtered by hair and mucus in the nose. As air enters the body through the nose or mouth, it is warmed and moisture is added. Next, air passes into the **pharynx** (the throat), where the passageways for air and food cross. The air pathway in the pharynx is always open, except when you swallow. Then a flap of tissue called the **epiglottis** momentarily covers the air pathway and prevents water or food from entering.

From the pharynx, air passes through the voice box or **larynx.** (Vocal cords in the larynx vibrate as you exhale, producing sounds.) Air next passes into the **trachea** (TRAY kee uh), or windpipe. The tubular shape of the trachea is maintained by c-shaped rings of cartilage. The trachea forks into two **bronchi** (BRAHNG ki; singular, *bronchus*), air tubes that connect the trachea to the lungs. You have two **lungs** consisting of sponge-like tissue, each about the size of a football, that function in the exchange of oxygen and carbon dioxide with the blood.

Figure 30-14 The respiratory system provides you with oxygen and removes carbon dioxide.

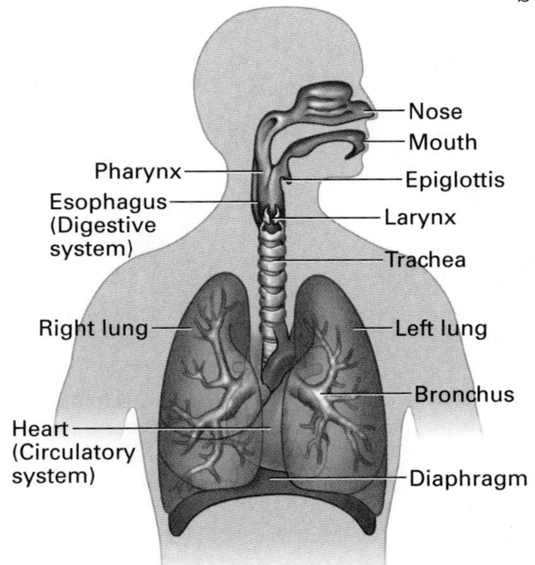

Within each lung, the bronchus branches repeatedly into finer and finer tubes called **bronchioles.** This branching pattern looks somewhat like an upside-down tree, and in fact the system of tubes is sometimes called "the respiratory tree." Each bronchiole ends in grapelike clusters of tiny air sacs called **alveoli** (singular, *alveolus*) (Figure 30-15). The lungs contain millions of these tiny air sacs. The inner surface of each alveolus is lined with a layer of moist epithelial cells. Oxygen in the air you inhale dissolves in the film of moisture on these epithelial cells. Oxygen then diffuses into a web of capillaries surrounding each alveolus and enters red blood cells, binding to hemoglobin. Carbon dioxide diffuses the opposite way, from the capillaries across the epithelial cells and into the alveoli. Then the carbon dioxide is expelled back up the trachea, through the nose or mouth, and into the air.

The respiratory system, from the nose and mouth all the way to the lungs, is lined with moist epithelial tissue. In the trachea and bronchi, the epithelial cells are covered with cilia and a fine layer of mucus, which act like cleaning elements. The mucus traps foreign particles. The cilia then sweep the mucus-trapped particles up toward the pharynx where they can be swallowed.

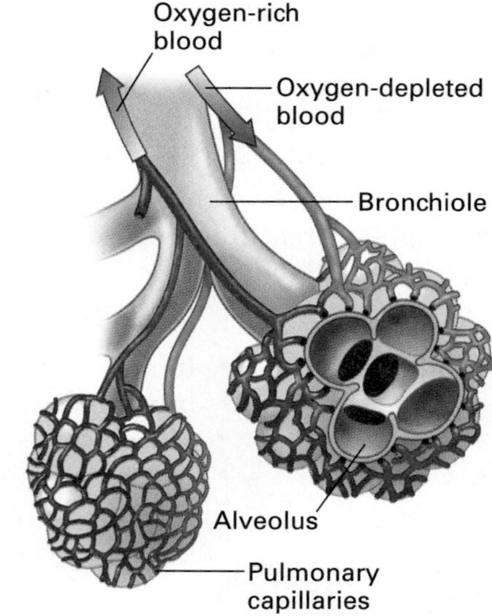

▲ **Figure 30-15** Gas exchange occurs in the tiny air sacs in your lungs called alveoli.

Breathing

The process of moving air into and out of your lungs is called breathing. Although you were most likely unaware of it, you probably took a breath of air and released it while you were reading this sentence. On average, you breathe about 15 times per minute, or more than 21,000 breaths each day.

A sheet of muscle called the **diaphragm,** which forms the bottom wall of the chest cavity, plays a key role in breathing (Figure 30-16). You inhale when your diaphragm and rib muscles contract, which expands your chest cavity. This action increases the volume of your lungs, resulting in reduced air pressure within the alveoli. Since air tends to move from an area of higher pressure to an area of lower pressure, air rushes in through the nose or mouth and fills the alveoli.

You exhale when your diaphragm and rib muscles relax. This decreases your lung volume, causing higher air pressure in the alveoli. Air rushes from your lungs out through your nose or mouth.

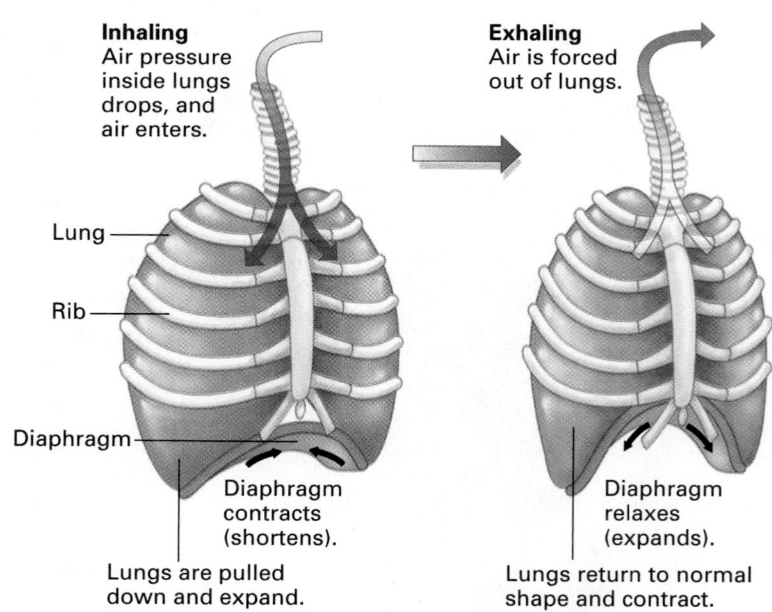

▲ **Figure 30-16** The diaphragm and rib muscles control lung volume and enable breathing.

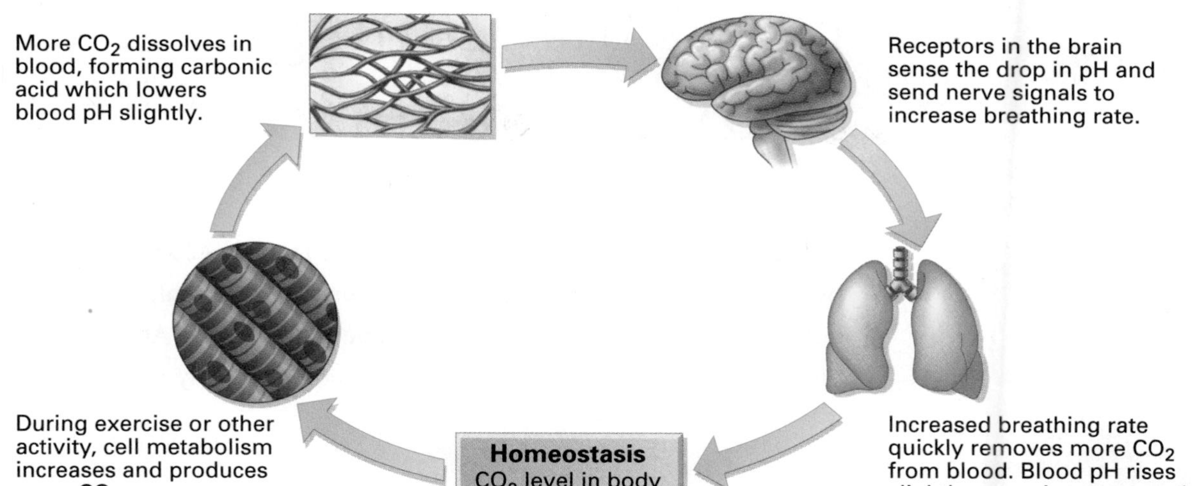
More CO_2 dissolves in blood, forming carbonic acid which lowers blood pH slightly.
Receptors in the brain sense the drop in pH and send nerve signals to increase breathing rate.
Increased breathing rate quickly removes more CO_2 from blood. Blood pH rises slightly, returning to normal.
Homeostasis
CO_2 level in body
During exercise or other activity, cell metabolism increases and produces more CO_2.

▲ **Figure 30-17** When your brain senses a lowered pH level in your blood, it initiates a faster breathing rate.

Regulation of Breathing

You might think that the rate of breathing is controlled by the level of oxygen in the body. But, surprisingly, it is usually the level of carbon dioxide that controls breathing rate (Figure 30-17). As carbon dioxide diffuses through a capillary wall, most of it dissolves in the plasma, the liquid portion of blood. When carbon dioxide dissolves in a solution containing water, it forms carbonic acid (H_2CO_3). If, for example, you exercise heavily, cell metabolism increases carbon dioxide output. This causes more carbon dioxide to dissolve in the blood. The increased carbon dioxide dissolved in the blood slightly lowers its pH. A drop in pH level causes the brain to send nerve impulses that increase breathing rate. As a result, more carbon dioxide is exhaled, and the pH returns to normal.

Breathing is usually an involuntary process that you seldom realize is occurring. Most of the time, breathing is controlled by the medulla oblongata, a part of the brain located near the top of the spinal cord. The medulla oblongata sends nerve signals to the diaphragm and rib muscles, causing them to contract and relax. However, you can temporarily exert conscious control over breathing, such as when you hold your breath under water.

Online Collaborative Science 3

www.biology.com

Exploring Cardiorespiratory Fitness

In this investigation, you will explore the effect of exercise on various measurements of cardiorespiratory fitness. Then share, compare, and discuss your results with other classrooms around the country to explore patterns and ask your own questions.

Online Activity 30.5

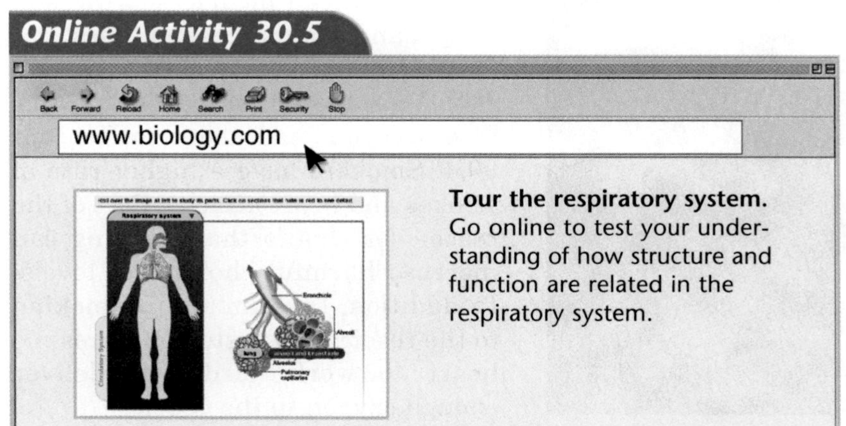
Back
Forward
Reload
Home
Search
Print
Security
Stop
www.biology.com

Tour the respiratory system. Go online to test your understanding of how structure and function are related in the respiratory system.

Concept Check 30.5

1. Describe the pathway of air beginning with the intake of air and ending at the alveoli.
2. Describe the processes of inhalation and exhalation.
3. How is breathing controlled?

CONCEPT 30.6

Smoking damages the body and shortens life.

OBJECTIVES

- Describe the effects of smoking on the respiratory system.
- Explain why tobacco is addictive.

KEY TERM

- emphysema

What's Online

www.biology.com

Online Activity 30.6
Analyze the effects of tar.

In the United States, smoking contributes to over 400,000 deaths per year—more than all the deaths caused by alcohol, cocaine, heroin, homicide, suicide, traffic accidents, fire, and AIDS combined. Why is smoking unhealthy? And why do many people find it hard to quit smoking?

Smoking-Related Diseases

Smoking a cigarette exposes the smoker to more than 4,000 different chemicals, including carbon monoxide, ammonia, and hydrogen cyanide. The toxic substances in tobacco smoke irritate the cells lining the bronchi and destroy the cilia. Without cilia, these cells lose the ability to move particles out of the respiratory system. Without the ability to remove these harmful particles from the lungs, smokers are at greater risk for diseases caused by these particles. In addition to the toxins from cigarette smoke, damage to the respiratory system also increases the risk of damage from air pollution, dust, and airborne bacteria.

Compared with non-smokers, smokers also have an increased risk for developing cancers of the lung, bladder, pancreas, mouth, throat, and several other organs. For example, people who smoke tobacco products account for 90 percent of all lung cancer cases (Figure 30-18).

Figure 30-18 Toxic substances in tobacco products cause severe damage to the respiratory system. Compare the healthy lung (above) with the cancerous lung (right).

Another disease, **emphysema** (em fuh SEE muh), can develop when tobacco smoke causes the walls of the alveoli to lose their elasticity. This results in air becoming trapped inside the alveoli during exhalation. Breathing becomes more difficult, and the smoker becomes more easily tired. Other symptoms of emphysema can include shortness of breath and dramatic weight loss.

Smoking also increases a person's risk for some of the cardiovascular diseases you read about in Concept 30.4. Smokers have a higher rate of strokes and heart attacks. Part of the reason for this is that smoking can increase harmful cholesterol levels. In addition, the damage of smoking to the respiratory system requires the heart to work harder to deliver enough oxygen to the cells.

According to life insurance companies, someone who smokes a pack or more of cigarettes each day lives an average of seven years less than someone who has never smoked. Fortunately for smokers, after 10 years of not smoking, the chances of getting lung cancer and heart disease return to normal levels. But with all that is known about the negative consequences of smoking, why do so many people still do it? Part of the answer is related to the addictive nature of tobacco products.

▲ **Figure 30-19** Many teens who understand the health risks of smoking get involved in spreading the word to others.

Why Is Tobacco Addictive?

Among the many dangerous chemicals in tobacco smoke, nicotine is the substance that makes tobacco addictive. Nicotine is easily absorbed through the skin and mucous membranes. Inhaling cigarette smoke into the lungs increases the speed of absorption. High levels of nicotine can reach the brain within 10 seconds of inhaling. Once it reaches the brain, nicotine increases the level of dopamine, a neurotransmitter in the part of the brain that controls pleasurable feelings. Dopamine causes the nerves to transmit signals more frequently, causing the person to experience pleasure.

However, the effects of nicotine disappear quickly. In order to maintain the high dopamine levels, the body craves more nicotine. A typical smoker takes 10 puffs on a single cigarette. A person who smokes a pack and a half (30 cigarettes) a day consumes 300 doses of nicotine each day.

Since all tobacco products contain nicotine, even users of smokeless tobacco, as well as pipe and cigar smokers, are absorbing nicotine and risking exposure to its addictive nature. Nearly 35 million people try to stop smoking every year. Unfortunately, less than 7 percent successfully stop smoking for more than one year. People who start smoking may not realize how hard it is to quit. The majority of adult smokers say they wish they had never started smoking (Figure 30-19).

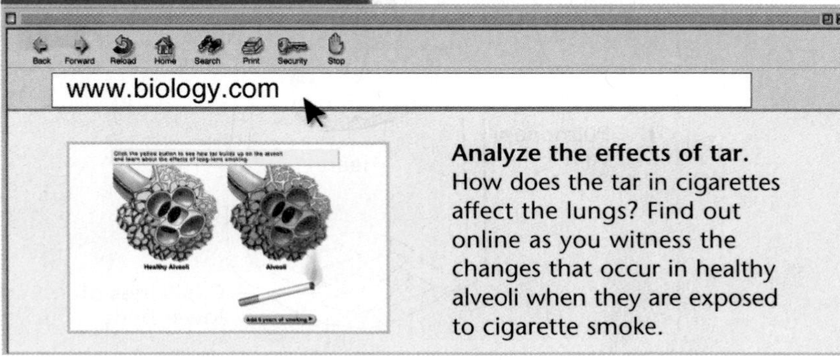

Analyze the effects of tar. How does the tar in cigarettes affect the lungs? Find out online as you witness the changes that occur in healthy alveoli when they are exposed to cigarette smoke.

Concept Check 30.6

1. How does smoking affect the respiratory system?
2. Explain the role of nicotine in tobacco addiction.
3. Describe what happens in the lungs of a person with emphysema.

Multiple Choice

Choose the letter of the best answer.

1. Which structure is *not* a component of the circulatory system?
   a. heart
   b. lung
   c. blood
   d. artery

2. What is the main function of the lymphatic system?
   a. to bind oxygen to hemoglobin
   b. to remove wastes from the body
   c. to return fluids to the circulatory system
   d. to release substances for blood clotting

3. Where is blood pressure greatest?
   a. lymphatic system
   b. veins
   c. vein end of capillary
   d. artery end of capillary

4. In the systemic circuit, blood returns to the heart via
   a. lymph vessels.
   b. arteries.
   c. capillaries.
   d. veins.

5. What is the function of the pulmonary circuit?
   a. to deliver blood to body cells
   b. to oxygenate blood
   c. to absorb nutrients
   d. to deliver blood to the brain

6. What is the main function of the diaphragm?
   a. to vibrate, producing sound
   b. to exchange O_2 and CO_2
   c. to expand the chest cavity
   d. to control the rate of breathing

7. Which substance is known to make tobacco addictive?
   a. ammonia
   b. carbon monoxide
   c. hydrogen cyanide
   d. nicotine

Short Answer

8. Describe the differences between capillaries, arteries, and veins.

9. How do larger molecules move across epithelial membranes in the capillaries?

10. Explain how heart contractions are regulated.

11. Explain the major differences between red and white blood cells.

12. What is the main function of blood platelets?

13. Why is hypertension dangerous to the circulatory system?

14. Describe the pathway of air from the mouth (or nose) to the lungs.

15. What characteristic of blood is monitored by the brain in controlling the rate of breathing?

16. Discuss the effects of smoking on the circulatory and respiratory systems.

Visualizing Concepts

17. Copy the diagram below and use red and blue colored pencils to follow the path of blood. Use blue when the blood is oxygen-depleted and red when the blood is oxygen-rich.

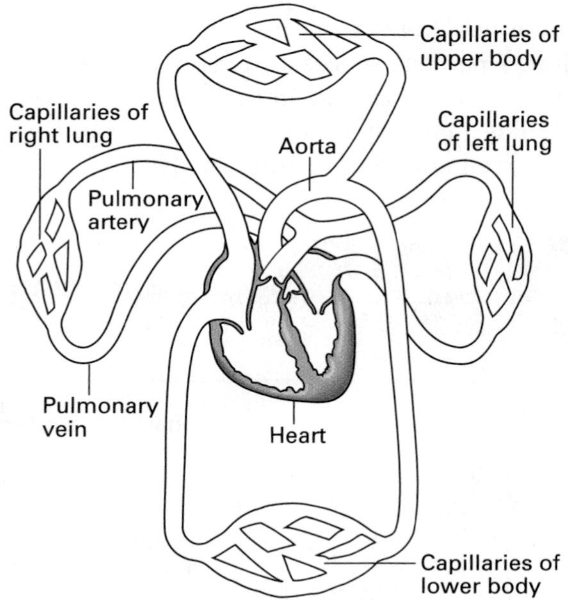

Analyzing Information

18. Analyzing Diagrams Below is a diagram of blood that has been separated into its components.

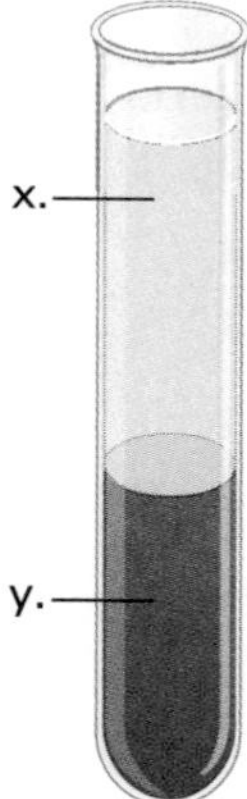

a. In which part of the test tube would you expect to find the greatest concentration of hemoglobin?

b. What are four substances you might find dissolved in the part labeled *x*?

c. Considering what you have read about the materials that make up blood, why do you think the materials in part *x* rise to the top?

19. Analyzing Graphs The graph below shows blood pressures in different parts of the cardiovascular system. Use it to answer the questions that follow.

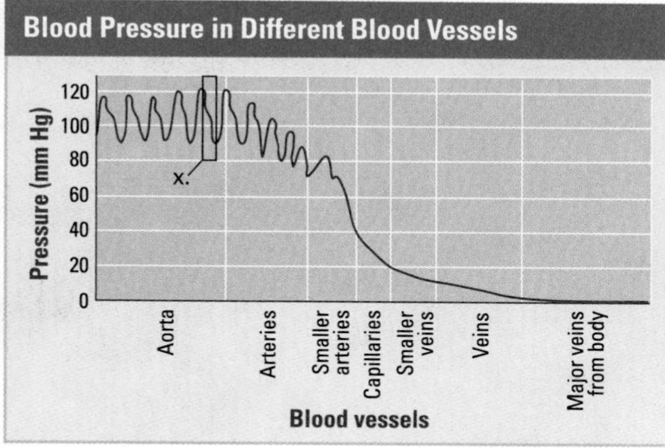

a. In the area of the graph labeled *x*, what is the systolic and diastolic pressure of this person?

b. In which blood vessels is blood pressure the highest? Lowest?

c. What mechanism allows blood to return to the heart?

Critical Thinking

20. Evaluating Promotional Claims Certain tobacco products claim to have less nicotine than other products. Do you think the lower nicotine product would be less harmful? Explain the reason for your conclusion.

21. Relating Cause and Effect A certain person used to have normal blood pressure. But now this person's blood pressure has risen to 140/90 for an extended period of time. What are some possible reasons for the increased blood pressure? What are some actions this person could take to try to decrease blood pressure?

22. Making Generalizations Some people say the heart is the most important organ in the body. Do you agree or disagree with this statement? Explain your answer.

23. What's Wrong With These Statements? *Briefly explain why each statement is inaccurate or misleading.*

a. All blood flowing in veins is oxygen-depleted.

b. Platelets are the only factors involved in blood clotting.

c. The main factor that controls breathing rate is the level of O_2 in the blood.

Performance Assessment

Design an Experiment Develop a hypothesis about the relationship between heart rate and breathing rate. Design an experiment that would allow you to test your hypothesis. Be sure to check with your teacher before carrying out any experiments.

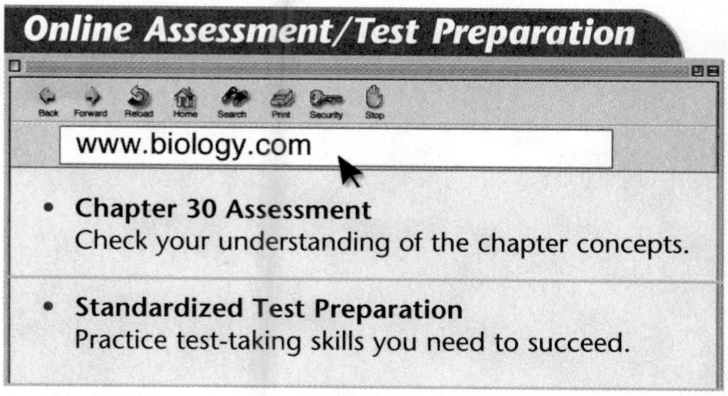

Online Assessment/Test Preparation

Back Forward Reload Home Search Print Security Stop

www.biology.com

- **Chapter 30 Assessment**
  Check your understanding of the chapter concepts.
- **Standardized Test Preparation**
  Practice test-taking skills you need to succeed.

The Body's Defense System

It might surprise you to learn that the human body contains far more bacteria than it has body cells. Some of these bacteria are helpful. Most are merely harmless. But some have the potential to make you sick and even kill you. Your body wages a constant battle against harmful microscopic organisms. This micrograph shows a specialized white blood cell (blue) attacking bacteria (yellow) and foreign debris (green) that have entered the body. A single red blood cell is also visible. In this chapter, you will read about the full array of defenses your body uses in fighting infections. Before you begin the chapter, go online to the ***WebQuest*** to explore some early medical pioneers' research on infections and disease prevention.

Colorized SEM 5,400×

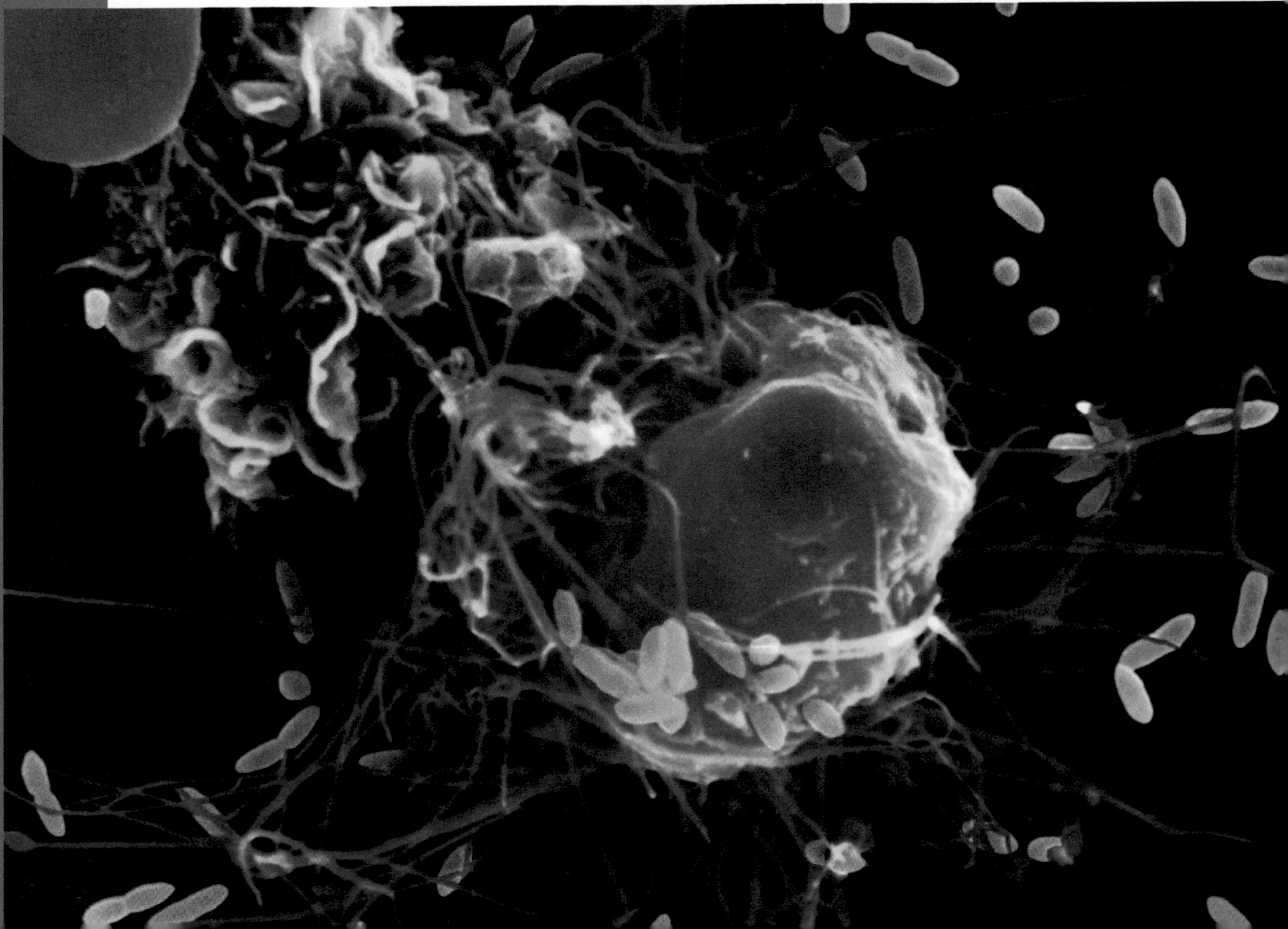

Key Concepts

Concept 31.1

Infectious diseases are caused by pathogens.

Concept 31.2

The human body has three lines of defense against infections.

Concept 31.3

The immune system recognizes specific invaders.

Concept 31.4

Vaccines stimulate the immune response.

Concept 31.5

Disorders of the immune system are major health problems.

Assessment

Chapter 31 Review

What's Online

www.biology.com

WebQuest
ImmuneQuest

Online Activity 31.1
Investigate how diseases spread.

Online Activity 31.2
Trigger an inflammatory response.

Online Activity 31.3
Track an immune response.

Lab 31 Online Companion
Detecting Disease

Online Activity 31.4
Vaccinate a patient.

Online Activity 31.5
Generate an allergic reaction.

Science, Technology, & Society
Living Organ Donors

Chapter 31 Assessment

CONCEPT 31.1

Infectious diseases are caused by pathogens.

OBJECTIVES

- Describe the germ theory of disease.
- List four ways by which infectious diseases can be transmitted.

KEY TERMS

- pathogen
- infectious disease

What's Online

www.biology.com

Online Activity 31.1 Investigate how diseases spread.

Between 1345 and 1350 C.E. approximately 25 million people (one out of four) in Europe died from a disease called the plague. Many people at the time believed the disease was caused by breathing foul-smelling air. Some treatments therefore included burning pleasant-smelling incense. Not surprisingly, this method did little to ward off the disease, which is actually caused by a bacterium carried by rats. Knowing the real cause of a disease helps scientists develop useful methods of prevention and cures.

The Germ Theory of Disease

Today, scientists know more about **pathogens,** or disease-causing organisms or viruses. Pathogens include certain bacteria, protozoans, fungi, worms, and viruses. Diseases that are caused by pathogens are known as **infectious diseases** (Figure 31-1).

Most of the current understanding about infectious disease has developed in the last 150 years. In the mid-1800s, the French biochemist Louis Pasteur conducted a series of experiments involving the microorganisms (yeasts) responsible for alcoholic fermentation. Pasteur demonstrated that other microorganisms could contaminate fermenting wine or beer. These contaminations interfered with the normal fermentation process.

Around the same time in England, surgeon Joseph Lister read about Pasteur's work. Lister was dismayed that as many as 50 percent of patients who had surgery died from infections afterward. Pasteur's work led Lister to hypothesize that microorganisms caused these infections. Lister's experiments involved using carbolic acid to wash instruments and the surgeons' hands before operations. As a result, deaths from infections after surgery in his hospital dropped to 15 percent.

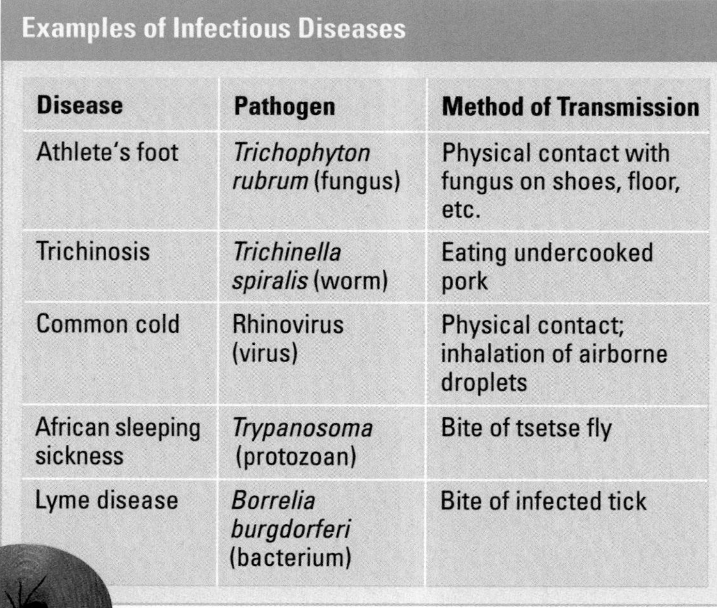

Examples of Infectious Diseases

Disease	Pathogen	Method of Transmission
Athlete's foot	*Trichophyton rubrum* (fungus)	Physical contact with fungus on shoes, floor, etc.
Trichinosis	*Trichinella spiralis* (worm)	Eating undercooked pork
Common cold	Rhinovirus (virus)	Physical contact; inhalation of airborne droplets
African sleeping sickness	*Trypanosoma* (protozoan)	Bite of tsetse fly
Lyme disease	*Borrelia burgdorferi* (bacterium)	Bite of infected tick

◀ **Figure 31-1** Infectious diseases can be transmitted in a variety of ways, including through insects such as this deer tick, which can spread Lyme disease.

Pasteur, Lister, and other researchers contributed to the development of the *germ theory of disease.* This theory states that infectious disease is caused by pathogens that can spread the disease from one organism to another organism.

A few years later Robert Koch, a German physician, built upon the previous work of Pasteur and Lister. Koch developed a process to identify numerous specific pathogens, such as the different bacteria that cause anthrax and tuberculosis. Koch's method is still used to establish whether or not a specific pathogen causes a certain illness (Figure 31-2).

Transmission of Infectious Disease

Once the cause of an infectious disease is determined, the next step in controlling the disease is to understand how it is transmitted. Some diseases are transmitted when airborne pathogens are inhaled. Some are transmitted by physical contact such as a handshake. For example, a virus can be transferred from an infected person's hand to your hand. If you then touch your nose, mouth, or eyes, you can transfer the virus to your mucous membranes—ideal locations for the virus to invade cells and multiply.

Other diseases are transmitted through contaminated water or food. And some are passed along by sexual contact. In other cases, an animal acts as an agent to transmit the disease. For example, deer ticks (black-legged ticks) can transmit the bacterium that causes Lyme disease to humans (Lyme disease causes fatigue, joint and muscle pain, and nerve tissue damage). Ticks feed by penetrating the skin of a host and slowly taking in blood. When a tick infected with the bacterium *Borrelia burgdorferi* bites a human, the bacterium can be transferred. Lyme disease can be treated with antibiotics if caught early.

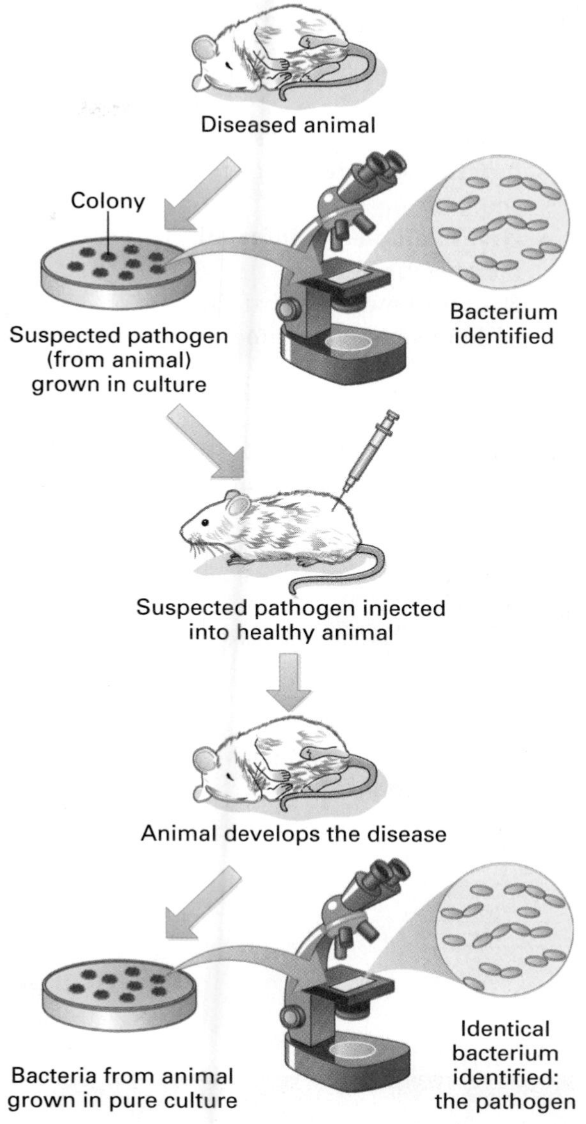

▲ **Figure 31-2** Koch's method is used to identify the pathogens that cause specific diseases.

Online Activity 31.1

Investigate how diseases spread.
An employee at a factory has contracted the flu virus. Will others be infected? Investigate the spread of an historic flu epidemic.

Concept Check 31.1

1. Describe how Pasteur and Lister contributed to the development of the germ theory of disease.
2. Give two examples of pathogen-caused diseases and explain how they can be transmitted.

CONCEPT 31.2

The human body has three lines of defense against infections.

OBJECTIVES
- Explain how barriers function in defending the body.
- Give examples of internal nonspecific defenses.
- Explain how the third line of defense is a targeted defense.

KEY TERMS
- nonspecific defense
- inflammatory response
- histamine
- interferon

What's Online

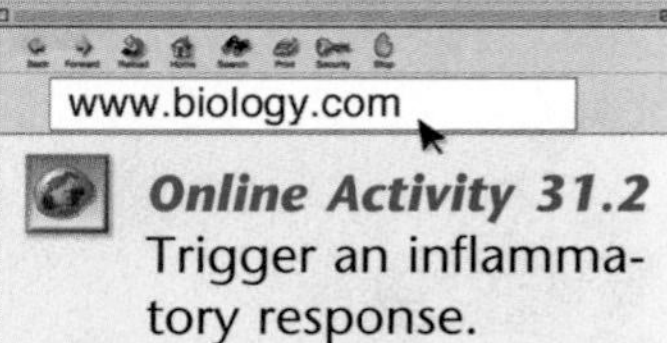

Online Activity 31.2
Trigger an inflammatory response.

The first line of defense consists of barriers against invasion, somewhat like a wall around a castle. The second line includes chemicals and cells that attack pathogens that get past the "wall." And the third line of defense targets specific pathogens and is responsible for identifying and quickly attacking the same pathogens in the future.

The First Line: Barriers

Your body's first line of defense against pathogens consists of physical and chemical barriers that prevent pathogens from entering the body. These barriers are **nonspecific defenses,** meaning they do not distinguish one invader from another. Your skin is one example of such a barrier (Figure 31-3). The outer layer of the skin is comprised of tough, dead cells that most bacteria and other organisms cannot penetrate. Also this layer of skin is constantly shedding, which makes it difficult for bacteria to embed in it and grow.

As you read in Chapter 27, your skin also contains sweat and oil glands. These glands secrete acids and oils that prevent the growth of many microorganisms, acting as a chemical barrier. Furthermore, sweat contains lysozyme, an enzyme that breaks down the cell walls of many bacteria.

While skin covers most of your body, the mouth, eyes, and nostrils are all areas through which pathogens could enter. Saliva and tears contain lysozyme, which helps protect the mouth and eyes from bacterial invasion. In addition, your digestive and respiratory passageways are lined with mucous membranes, another barrier. Mucus in the trachea, for example, creates a sticky barrier that traps microorganisms. Cilia move these trapped particles up to the pharynx where they are swallowed. Then, stomach acids and enzymes help to destroy the pathogens, as well as many other microorganisms in your food and drink.

Figure 31-3 A researcher examines a piece of "artificial skin" grown in the laboratory. Since skin is such an important physical barrier against infections, biologists are studying ways to repair human skin damaged by such traumas as burns.

The Second Line: Internal Nonspecific Defenses

Pathogens are always present in the environment (Figure 31-4). Sometimes pathogens gain access to your body despite the barriers of your first line of defense. For example, when you are bitten by an insect or prick your finger with a pin, your skin is broken, and pathogens can enter your body tissues. When this happens, the invaders are met by your body's second line of defense. The second line of defense includes certain pathogen-destroying white blood cells, the inflammatory response, and certain specialized proteins. Since they do not single out specific pathogens, these defenses are also said to be nonspecific, like the first line of defense.

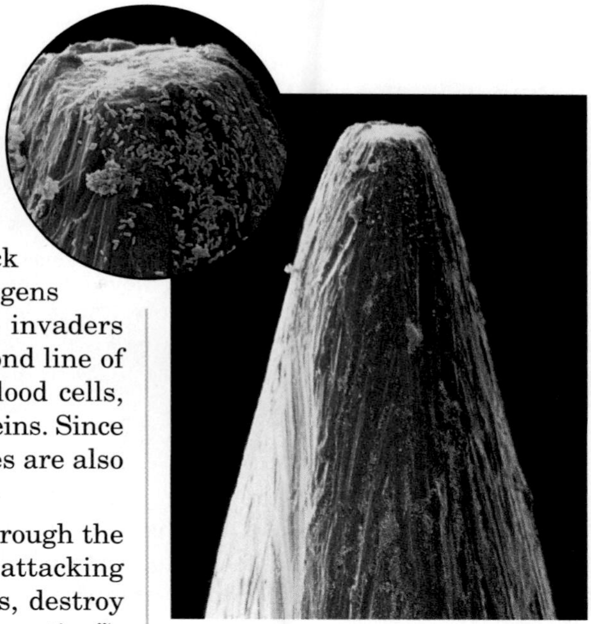

Colorized SEM 130×. Inset: colorized SEM 430×

▲ **Figure 31-4** Bacteria live just about everywhere. This enlarged view of a pin shows hundreds of bacteria (yellow) on its tip.

White Blood Cells Certain white blood cells roam through the bloodstream, interstitial fluid, and lymphatic system attacking invaders. Some, such as macrophages and neutrophils, destroy microorganisms through phagocytosis (meaning "cellular eating"). Macrophages (meaning "big eaters") are found mainly in interstitial fluid. When a macrophage encounters an invading pathogen, the macrophage engulfs the organism much as an amoeba ingests food. The pathogen is drawn into the macrophage, where enzymes such as lysozyme kill the pathogen.

Neutrophils are smaller and more numerous in the body than macrophages. Neutrophils also kill by phagocytosis. Once the pathogen is inside the neutrophil, the neutrophil releases chemicals (similar to bleach) that kill the invading pathogen. However, these chemicals also kill the neutrophil.

Key to these responses is the white blood cells' ability to identify which structures to attack, and which to leave alone. White blood cells can identify certain proteins and carbohydrates on the surface of an invading pathogen. Recognizing these "foreign" molecules triggers the cells' responses.

Another type of white blood cell called a natural killer (NK) cell is found in the bloodstream. Unlike macrophages and neutrophils, NK cells do not attack pathogens directly or kill by phagocytosis. Instead, they recognize body cells that have become infected by a virus and kill them by releasing chemicals that poke holes in the infected cell's membrane (Figure 31-5). NK cells also recognize and attack abnormal body cells such as cancer cells. They play a key role in defending against cancer by killing abnormal cells before they can form a tumor.

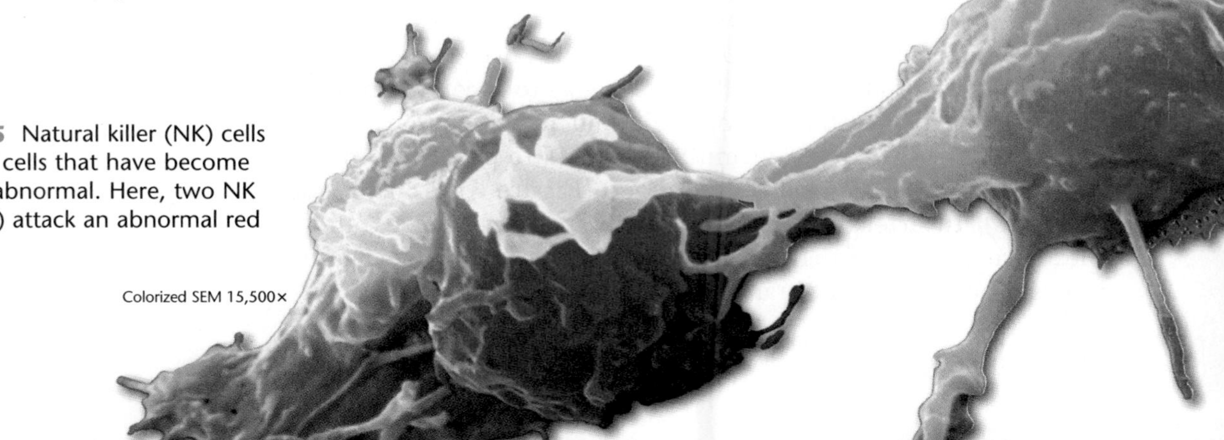

▶ **Figure 31-5** Natural killer (NK) cells attack body cells that have become infected or abnormal. Here, two NK cells (yellow) attack an abnormal red blood cell.

Colorized SEM 15,500×

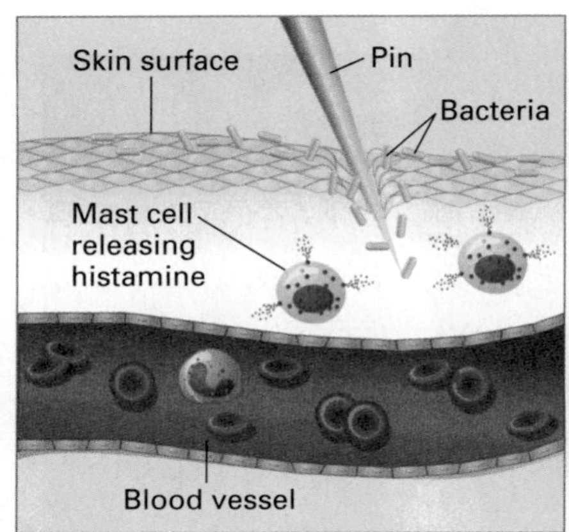

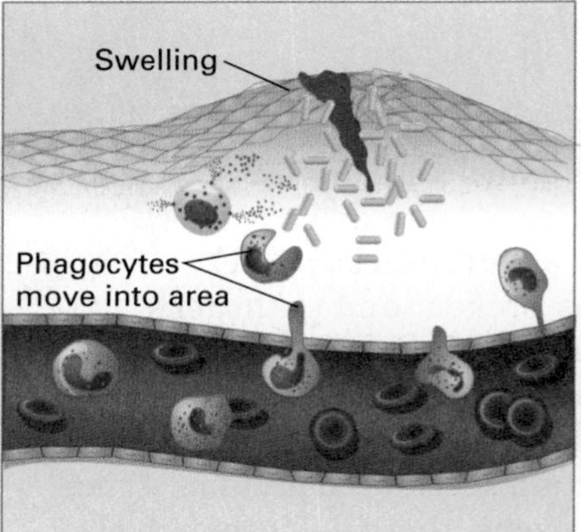

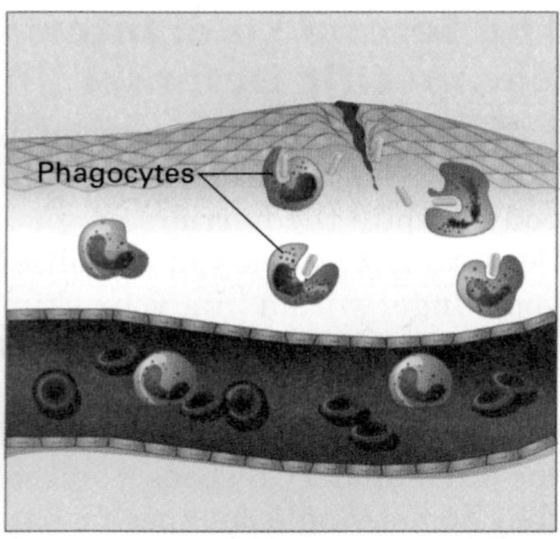

▲ **Figure 31-6** During an inflammatory response, chemical signals trigger changes in blood vessels and attract white blood cells that help destroy the invaders.

Inflammatory Response At the site of pathogen invasion, such as a pinprick or an insect bite, certain cells release a variety of chemical "alarms." These chemical alarms trigger an **inflammatory response,** a nonspecific defense characterized by redness, heat, swelling, and pain. For example, cells called mast cells release a type of chemical alarm called **histamine,** which causes nearby blood vessels to dilate (expand). The expanded blood vessels increase the volume of blood flowing to the injured tissue. In addition, the vessels become more porous, allowing more blood plasma to leak into the interstitial fluid. Other chemicals attract additional phagocytes and other white blood cells to the area, where they pass through the leaky blood vessel walls into the interstitial fluid (Figure 31-6). This local increase of blood flow, fluid, and white blood cells produces the redness, heat, swelling, and pain you may experience around the injured area.

The major function of the inflammatory response includes removing pathogens and cleaning injured tissues. Inflammation may occur in a tiny area, such as the site of a mosquito bite (Figure 31-7). Or, if pathogens get into the blood or release toxins that are carried throughout the body by the circulatory system, the whole body may react with an inflammatory response. In such a response white blood cells increase and a fever (an abnormally high body temperature) may occur. A very high fever may be dangerous, because it can destroy proteins and cause other damage. But a moderate fever may contribute to defense by stimulating phagocytosis and stopping the growth of many kinds of microorganisms.

▲ **Figure 31-7** A mosquito bite can become a site for pathogens to get past the physical barrier of the skin. The inflammatory response is triggered, resulting in the familiar swollen red bump and itching.

Specialized Proteins Other internal nonspecific defenses include specialized proteins that either attack invaders directly or block their reproduction. One example is **interferon,** a family of proteins produced by cells in response to becoming infected by a virus. The infected cell may die, but its interferon reaches healthy cells in the area, stimulating them to produce proteins that interfere with virus reproduction (Figure 31-8 on the facing page). Interferon is effective against many viruses and is therefore nonspecific. Interferon seems to be effective against viruses that cause the flu and the common cold.

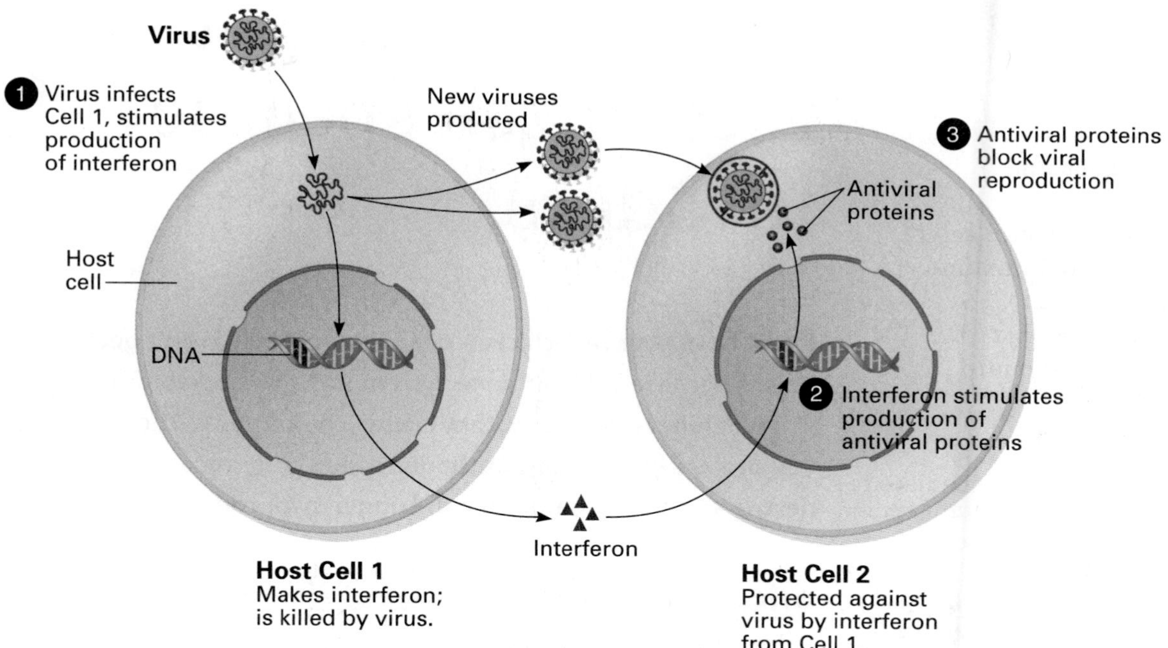

New viruses produced
3 Antiviral proteins block viral reproduction
Antiviral proteins

2 Interferon stimulates production of antiviral proteins

Host Cell 1

Host Cell 2
Protected against virus by interferon from Cell 1.

▲ **Figure 31-8** Infected cells produce interferon, which stimulates noninfected cells to manufacture substances that block virus reproduction.

The body can only produce interferon in small amounts. However, the recombinant DNA technology described in Chapter 13 has enabled the drug industry to manufacture interferon in large quantities to be used to treat certain viral infections.

The Third Line: Targeted Defense

Supporting the nonspecific defenses is your body's third line of defense, the immune system. This system recognizes and defends against *specific* pathogens, cancer cells, and certain chemicals. The third line is therefore a specific, or targeted, defense. To accomplish this, the immune system must be able to distinguish between its own body cells ("self") and intruders ("non-self"). When non-self cells or other intruders are identified, the immune system launches a customized response, as you will read in Concept 31.3. Such a response may take longer, but it is longer-lasting and often more effective than nonspecific defenses.

Online Activity 31.2

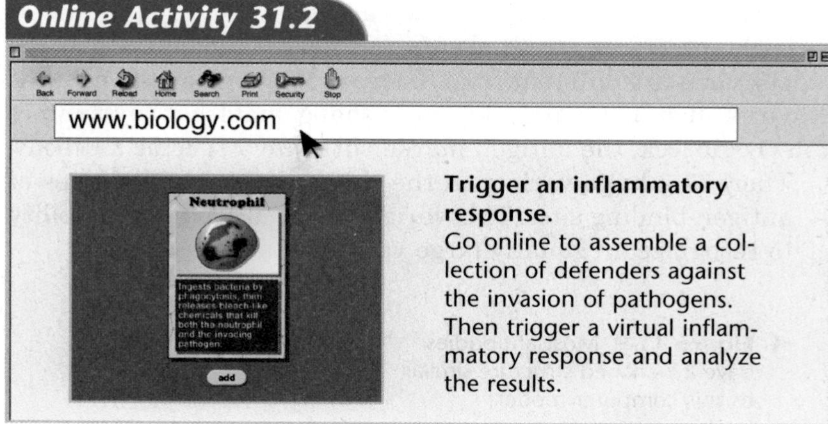

www.biology.com
Neutrophil
Ingests bacteria by phagocytosis, then releases bleach-like chemicals that kill both the neutrophil and the invading pathogen.
add

Trigger an inflammatory response.
Go online to assemble a collection of defenders against the invasion of pathogens. Then trigger a virtual inflammatory response and analyze the results.

Concept Check 31.2

1. List two barriers to pathogen invasion and explain how each stops invaders.
2. Describe the body's inflammatory response at a small site, such as a mosquito bite.
3. What is the body's third line of defense?
4. Explain the role of interferon in the second line of defense.

CONCEPT 31.3

The immune system recognizes specific invaders.

OBJECTIVES

- Relate antigens and antibodies.
- Explain the roles of B cells and T cells in the immune system.
- Describe the primary and secondary immune responses.

KEY TERMS

- immunity
- antigen
- antibody
- B cell
- T cell
- plasma cell
- humoral immunity
- cell-mediated immunity
- cytotoxic T cell
- helper T cell
- memory cell

What's Online

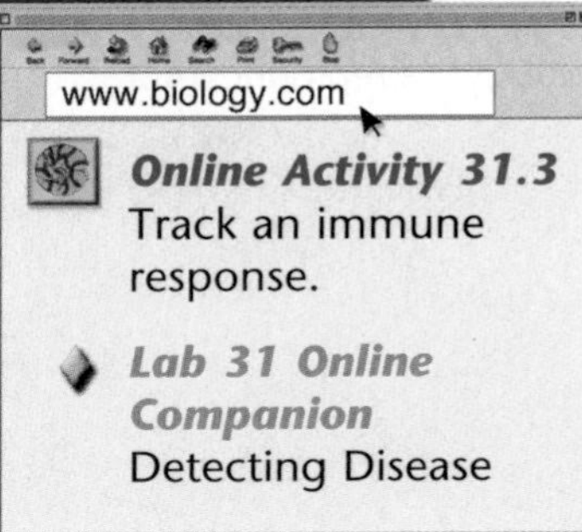

Online Activity 31.3
Track an immune response.

Lab 31 Online Companion
Detecting Disease

If you have ever had chicken pox, you probably won't get it again. This is because your immune system has a remarkable "memory." It "remembers" the virus that causes chicken pox. The next time you are exposed to this pathogen, your body recognizes and destroys the virus before it can trigger symptoms of the illness.

Antigens and Antibodies

After you have had the chicken pox, mumps, or measles, you become immune to those diseases. **Immunity** means that your body is resistant to the pathogen that causes a specific disease. In general, you acquire immunity by becoming infected by the pathogen. But how does your body recognize and remember each pathogen it encounters?

The surfaces of viruses, bacteria, fungi, cancer cells, pollen, and other cells contain certain molecules called antigens. An **antigen** is a large molecule, usually a protein, that provokes an immune response. The word *antigen* is a contraction meaning "*anti*body-*gen*erating." **Antibodies** are proteins found on the surface of certain white blood cells, or in blood plasma, that attach to particular antigens.

The most common antibodies are Y-shaped molecules that look a bit like "rabbit-ear" antennae (Figure 31-9). At the tip of each arm of the Y is an antigen-binding site, or antigen receptor. The shape of this binding site makes it possible for the antibody to recognize a specific antigen with a complementary shape. Each antigen sits on the surface of the invading particle and has a particular shape with knobs that protrude from the surface. The knobs, also known as "markers," are unique for each antigen. For example, the markers found on the chicken pox virus are different from the markers found on the measles virus. Just as a particular key's shape enables it to fit into a specific lock, the antigen marker fits into a specific antibody. There is a huge variety in the three-dimensional shapes of antigen-binding sites. This variety gives antibodies the ability to recognize an equally large variety of antigens.

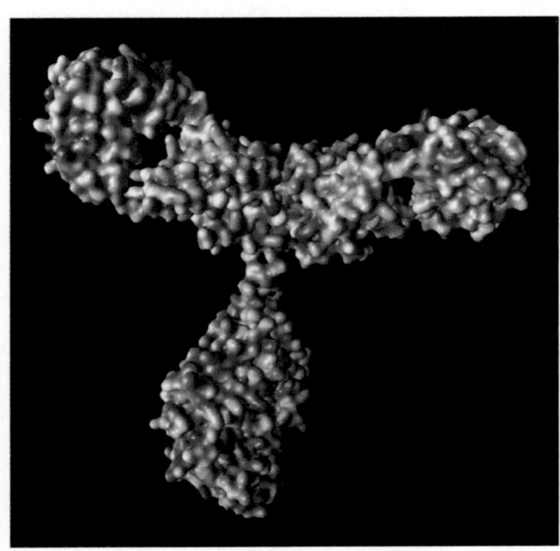

Figure 31-9 Most antibodies have a Y-shaped structure similar to this computer model.

Rather than directly engulfing pathogens, antibodies work indirectly in destroying them. An antibody "tags" the invader by binding to the antigen molecule (Figure 31-10). This triggers mechanisms that neutralize or destroy the invader.

In one such mechanism, the binding of antibodies stops viruses from attaching to a host cell. This disables the virus and halts further infection. In another example, an antibody might bind to the toxin-producing molecules on the surface of a bacterial cell. This makes the pathogen harmless and tags it for destruction by phagocytes. In still another mechanism, antibodies cause pathogens to clump together. This clumping makes the cells easy targets for phagocytes to capture and destroy.

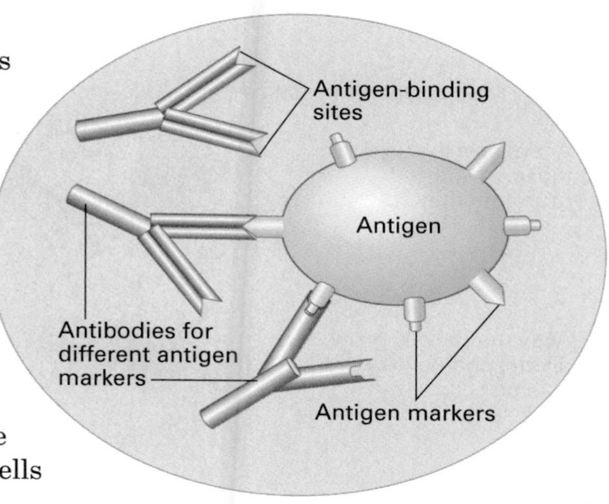

▲ **Figure 31-10** Antigens bind to antibodies that have a complementary or matching shape.

Antibodies may also activate immune system chemicals called complement proteins that can attach to viral surfaces or bacterial membranes. These proteins help to clump viruses for phagocytosis by white blood cells or puncture holes in a bacterial outer membrane, causing the pathogen to break open. All of these antibody mechanisms involve a specific recognition and attack phase, followed by a nonspecific destruction phase.

Lymphocytes

The white blood cells that recognize specific invaders are called lymphocytes. Lymphocytes originate in bone marrow from stem cells, which also give rise to various other kinds of cells (Figure 31-11). Some lymphocytes, called **B cells** or B lymphocytes, continue their development in bone marrow. Others, called **T cells** or T lymphocytes, are transported to the thymus gland where they mature. Eventually both B and T cells travel in the blood to the lymph nodes and other parts of the lymphatic system.

Not all B cells or T cells are alike. The body has an enormous diversity of these cells, each specialized to recognize and react to a particular antigen marker. This ability to target a particular antigen is due to the specific shapes of the antigen receptors on the lymphocyte surface.

During the development of lymphocytes, many different antigen receptors are generated. However, the body destroys those lymphocytes with antigen receptors that could react against the body's own molecules and cells. Thus, the immune system can distinguish self (the body's own cells) from non-self (foreign substances).

The types of lymphocytes have different functions. B cells play a key role in humoral immunity, while T cells play the major role in cell-mediated immunity.

▼ **Figure 31-11** All lymphocytes begin development in the bone marrow. B cells complete their development there (think "B for bone"). T cells are transported to the thymus gland where they mature (think "T for thymus").

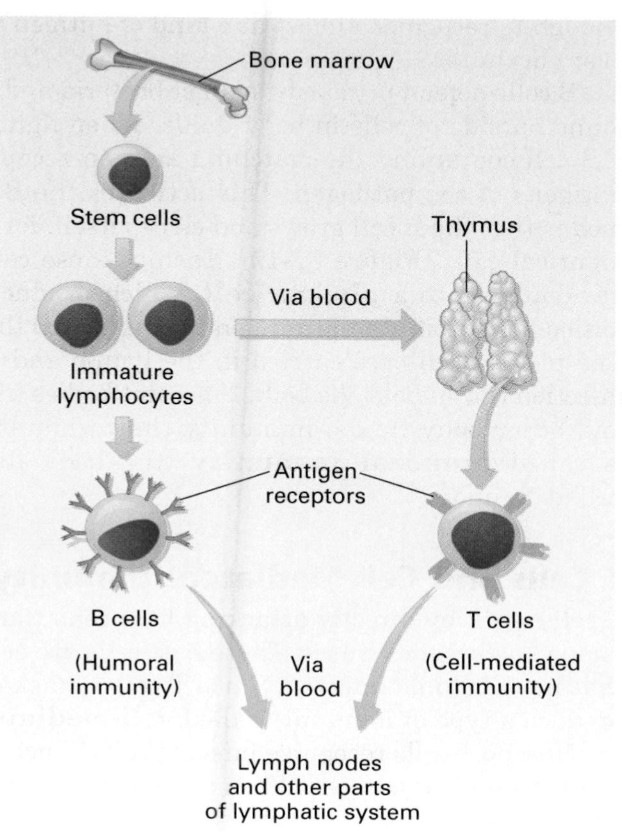

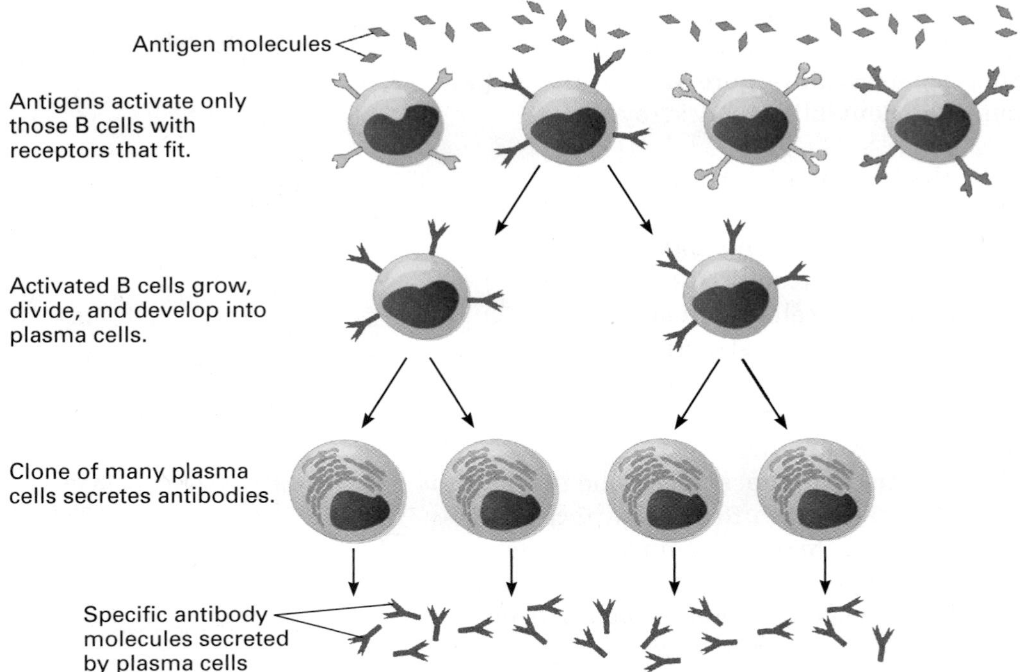
Antigen molecules
Antigens activate only those B cells with receptors that fit.
Activated B cells grow, divide, and develop into plasma cells.
Clone of many plasma cells secretes antibodies.
Specific antibody molecules secreted by plasma cells

▲ **Figure 31-12** A particular type of antigen activates a specific B cell. The activated B cell produces a clone of millions of plasma cells that produce antibodies to the specific antigen.

B Cells and Humoral Immunity

Antibody proteins are embedded on the surface of B cells as specific receptors for antigens. In total, researchers estimate there are approximately 100 million different B cell surfaces. That's enough to recognize almost any kind of antigen you are likely to ever encounter.

B cells defend primarily against bacteria and viruses that are found outside of cells in body fluids. When fighting a pathogen, a B cell containing the matching antigen receptor binds to the antigens of the pathogen. This activates the B cell. Activation means that the B cell grows and clones itself, forming millions of identical cells (Figure 31-12). Each of those cells is capable of developing into a **plasma cell,** which produces and secretes antibodies specific to the antigen that activated the original B cell. The plasma cells are carried in the lymph and blood to sites of infection throughout the body. Since antibodies travel in the blood and other body fluids, immunity that originates from B cells is called **humoral immunity** (the body fluids were once called "humors").

T Cells and Cell-Mediated Immunity

T cells work by directly attacking host cells that contain multiplying bacteria or viruses. These host cells are actually body cells that have become infected. Since T cells attack other cells, they produce a type of immunity called **cell-mediated immunity.**

How do T cells recognize infected cells? Each T cell has receptors for a specific antigen. When a pathogen infects a body cell, the pathogen's antigens are displayed on the surface of the body cell.

Those antigens bind to the receptors of the "matching" T cell, which activates the T cell. The activated T cell then divides and produces millions of identical clones. These clones develop into **cytotoxic T cells,** which then attack cells infected with the pathogen that triggered the response. Cytotoxic T cells bind to an infected cell's membrane and poke holes in it by secreting a protein called perforin (think "perforate"). The infected cell leaks fluid, breaks open, and dies.

T Cells and Cancer Research indicates that individuals with weakened immune systems are more likely to get cancer. This suggests that the immune system is important in fighting some cancers. Certain B cells play a role in this battle. Researchers are studying how T cells may also be involved. They have learned that some changes that lead to cancer occur on the outer membrane of body cells. Scientists have hypothesized that the altered membrane may alert T cells to an intruder in the body. Cytotoxic T cells then proceed to destroy the cancer cells (Figure 31-13). Why this system sometimes fails is a key question in cancer research.

Central Role of Helper T Cells So far you have read that the immune system has two different responses to pathogens: humoral and cell-mediated immunity. During the humoral response, B cells produce antibodies after being activated by free antigens present in body fluids. During the cell-mediated response, cytotoxic T cells attack infected cells that display the antigens of pathogens on their surface.

Both humoral and cell-mediated immunity get a boost from a particular type of lymphocyte called **helper T cells**. Like all lymphocytes, helper T cells are present in many versions, each with surface receptors that recognize a specific antigen (Figure 31-14). Like cytotoxic T cells, the helper T cells are activated by binding to cells that display antigens of a pathogen. But the antigen-displaying cells that helper T cells recognize are macrophages, the white blood cells that eat pathogens by phagocytosis. The marked macrophages serve as an "announcement" that a pathogen is present. Helper T cells respond to this announcement by secreting chemicals that activate both cytotoxic T cells and B cells.

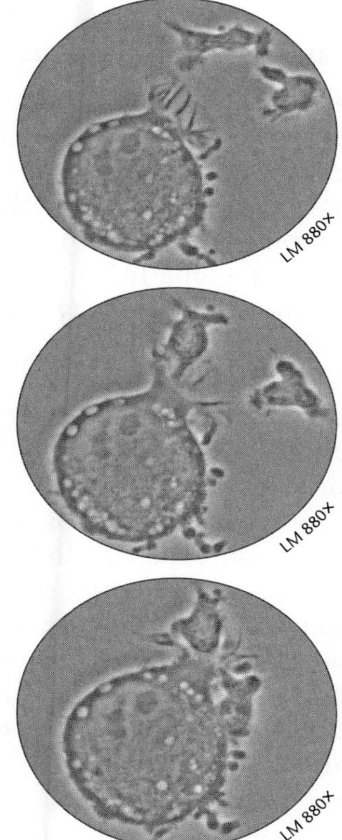

▲ **Figure 31-13** These images show two cytotoxic T cells attacking a larger cancer cell, causing its membrane to break open.

▼ **Figure 31-14** Macrophages display the antigens of pathogens they have "eaten." This display activates a specific version of helper T cells. The activated helper T cells in turn stimulate cytotoxic T cells and B cells.

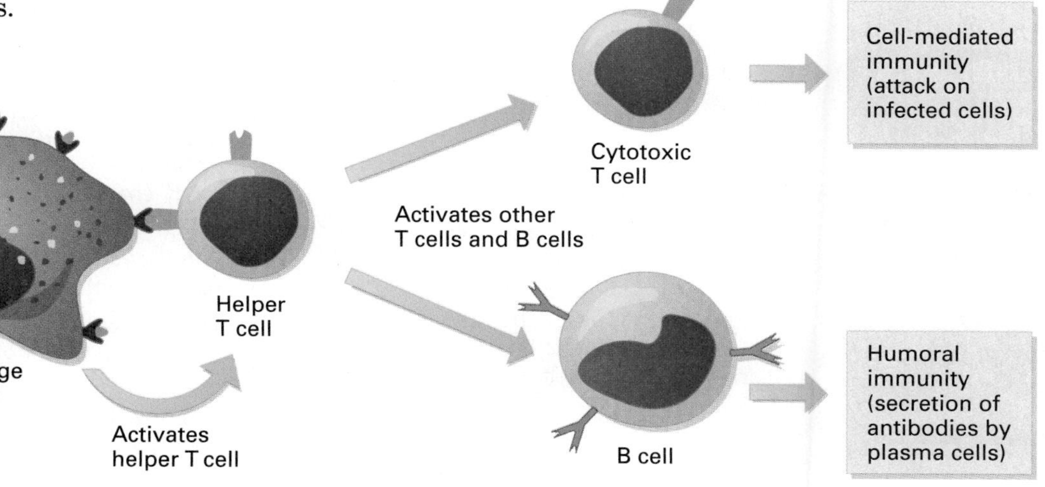

Primary and Secondary Immune Responses

When you are first exposed to a pathogen, specific B and T cells multiply and defend against that particular pathogen. Some of that "brand" of B and T cells remain in your body. These long-lasting lymphocytes are called **memory cells** (Figure 31-15). The first formation of B and T cells to battle a new invading pathogen is called the primary immune response. This first response is relatively slow and weak because time is needed for enough specific lymphocytes to form to defeat the pathogen.

A second exposure to the same pathogen triggers a much quicker and stronger response called the secondary immune response. The B and T memory cells for that pathogen recognize and quickly respond to this repeat visit. The second exposure stimulates the memory B cells to rapidly produce plasma cells that will secrete antibodies specific to that antigen. Meanwhile memory T cells rapidly produce large numbers of cytotoxic T cells that attack cells infected with the pathogen. The process is so quick that you don't develop symptoms of the disease. Your body destroys the invader before you feel sick.

How the Immune System "Remembers" Pathogens

B or T cell

First exposure to antigen

Primary immune response
(First clone)

Pathogen-fighting cells

Memory cells

Second exposure to same antigen

Secondary immune response
(Second clone)

New pathogen-fighting cells

More memory cells

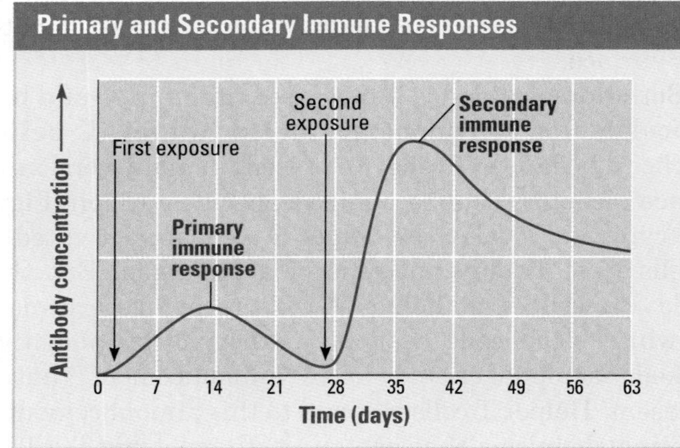

▶ **Figure 31-15** The first exposure to a pathogen produces B and T memory cells specific to that pathogen. A second exposure activates those memory cells.

Online Activity 31.3

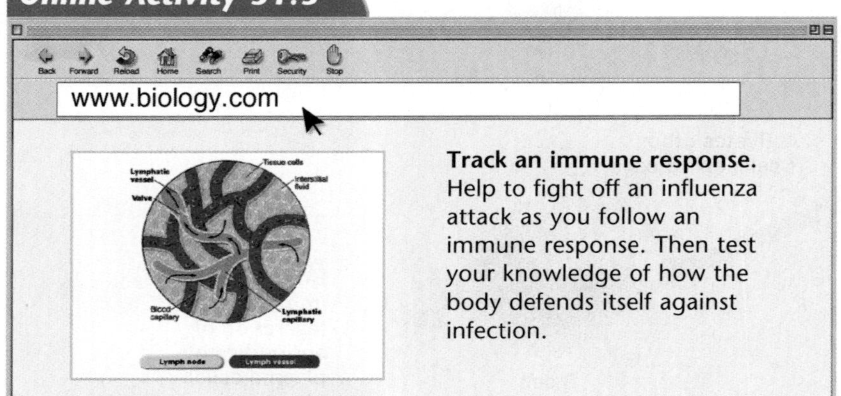

Track an immune response. Help to fight off an influenza attack as you follow an immune response. Then test your knowledge of how the body defends itself against infection.

Concept Check 31.3

1. Describe how the shape of an antibody enables it to recognize a specific antigen.
2. Explain the role of B cells and T cells in the immune response.
3. Explain why a second exposure to chicken pox does not usually result in illness.
4. Explain how T cells might protect against cancer.

Detecting Disease

Performing a Lyme Disease Assay

Question How can you tell if a person is infected with the bacteria that cause Lyme disease?

Lab Overview You will take on the role of a medical laboratory technician in a diagnostic lab and test simulated blood serum samples using a test called an Enzyme-Linked Immunosorbent Assay (ELISA).

Preparing for the Lab To prepare for the investigation go to the *Lab 31 Online Companion.* ····➔ Find out how antibodies can be used to detect the bacteria that cause Lyme disease and see how the test for Lyme disease could be performed in a medical diagnostic lab. Prepare for the lab procedure by previewing the steps you will take.

Completing the Lab Use your Laboratory Manual or lab page printouts from the *Lab 31 Online Companion* to do the investigation and analyze your results. **CAUTION:** *Be sure to follow your teacher's instructions and all safety guidelines in the investigation.*

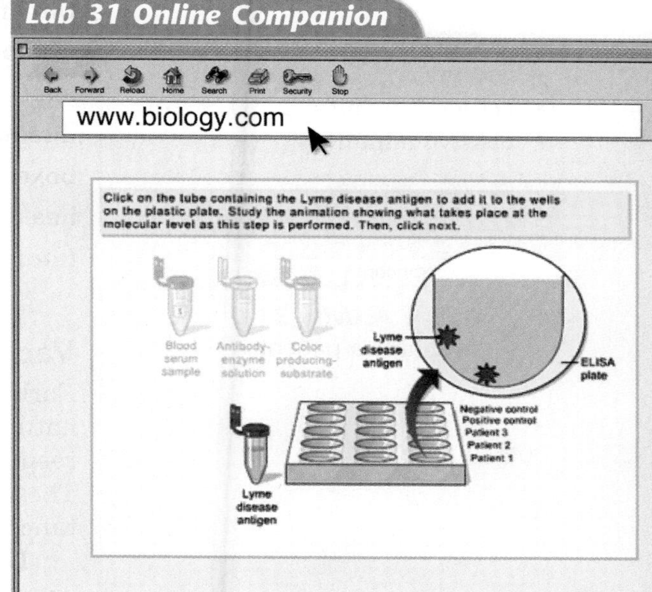

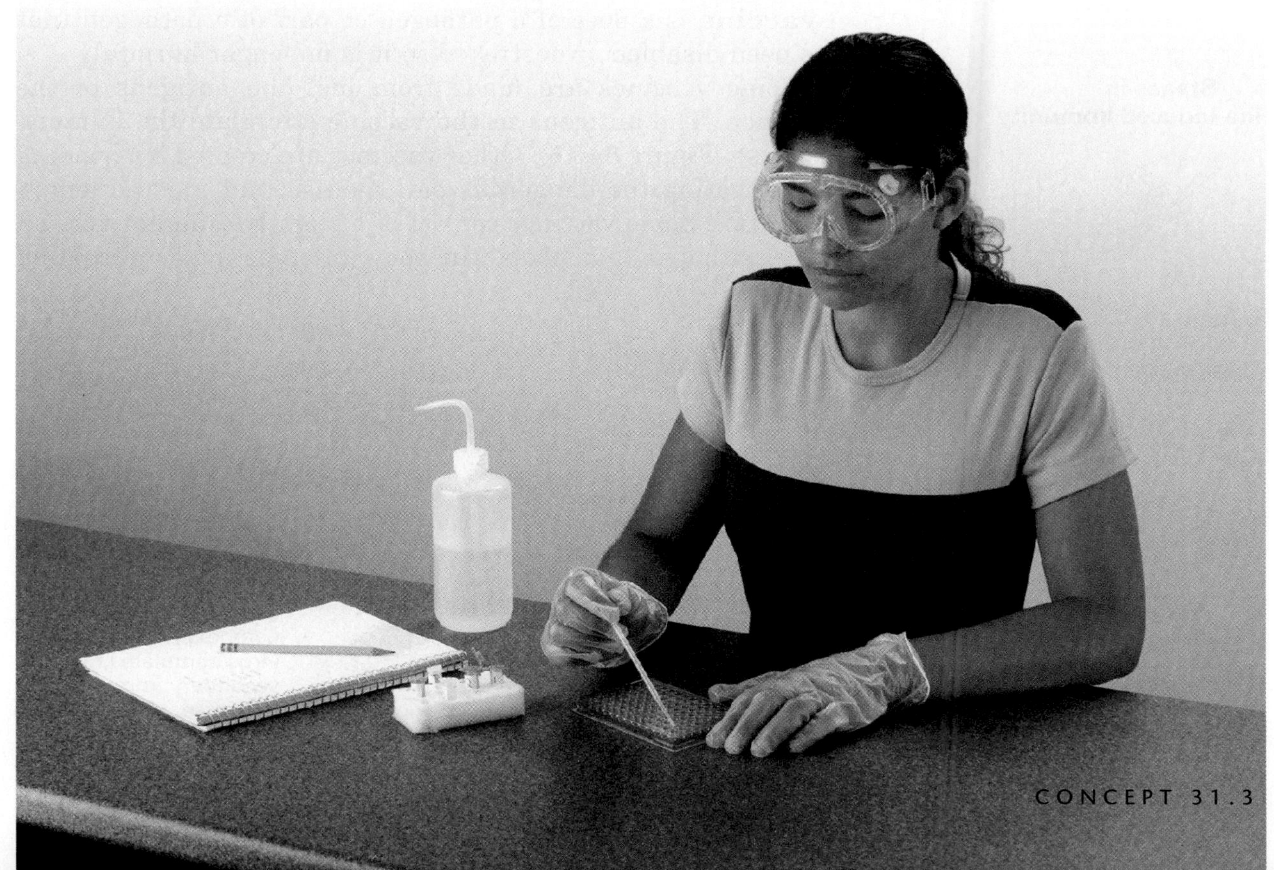

CONCEPT 31.4

Vaccines stimulate the immune response.

OBJECTIVES
- Describe how vaccines work.
- Compare and contrast active and passive immunity.

KEY TERMS
- vaccine
- active immunity
- passive immunity

What's Online

Until the 1950s, a disease called polio crippled and killed hundreds of thousands of people. Dr. Jonas Salk developed a procedure to inject healthy children with poliovirus that had been chemically disabled. Much like a sparring partner functions to prepare a boxer for a future boxing match, the disabled virus stimulates healthy immune systems to produce antibodies that can fight future invasions by the functional poliovirus.

Vaccines

Earlier you read that being infected with a pathogen can result in natural immunity. Antigens of the pathogen stimulate an immune response and, among other results, memory cells are formed. These memory cells reside in the body and provide lasting resistance to that specific pathogen.

However, some pathogens can cause serious illness or death as a result of the first exposure, as in the case of polio. For those pathogens, or when a person's immune system is in a weakened state, natural immunity isn't much help. For some of these diseases, a vaccine can stimulate the immune response and formation of memory cells before exposure to the real pathogen. A **vaccine** is a dose of a pathogen or part of a pathogen that has been disabled or destroyed so it is no longer harmful.

Some vaccines are made from just the antigens of the pathogen. The antigens in the vaccine stimulate the immune response (Figure 31-16). Other vaccines are created by grinding up or heating the dangerous pathogen so that it is no longer functional. Some vaccines consist of a slightly different version of the pathogen that "fools" the body into reacting as if exposed

▼ **Figure 31-16** A vaccine stimulates the production of antibodies and memory cells that protect against future exposure to the pathogen.

Stages in Vaccine-Induced Immunity

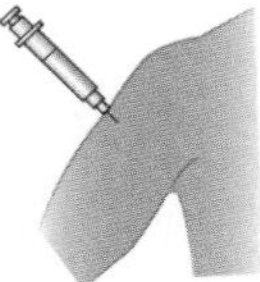

Stage 1
Deactivated virus (vaccine) is injected into body.

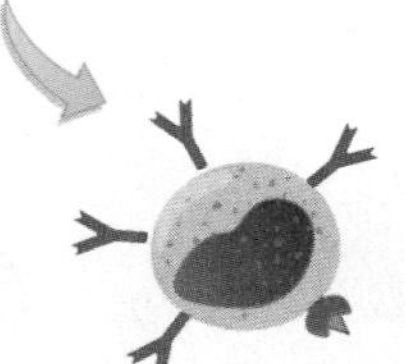

Stage 2
Antigens in vaccine stimulate primary immune response.

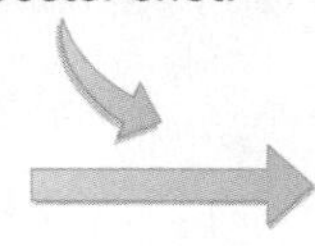

Booster Stage
Some vaccines require a booster shot.

Stage 3
Memory cells are formed that match the antigens in the vaccine.

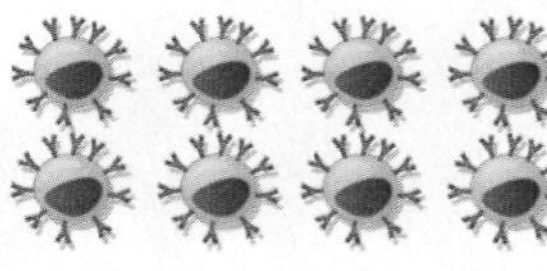

Stage 4
Later exposure to same virus stimulates rapid secondary immune response.

to the real antigen. For example, the vaccine for the virus that causes smallpox (a deadly disease) is actually made from a closely related virus that causes cowpox (a mild disease). The two antigens are so similar that your immune system launches a full fight in the presence of either antigen. Vaccines have proven to be effective in reducing the occurrence of many diseases (Figure 31-17).

You may remember receiving a "booster" shot of a vaccine, such as the one for tetanus, at a doctor's visit. This shot is an additional dose of an antigen that "boosts" antibody production and extends the memory for that antigen. The booster is necessary because some of the initial memory cells that were produced after the first shot have died.

Reported Cases of Measles in the United States

Reported cases of measles (in thousands): 1000, 900, 800, 700, 600, 500, 400, 300, 200, 100

Year: 1950, 1956, 1962, 1968, 1974, 1980, 1986

Measles vaccine licensed (1963)

▲ **Figure 31-17** The introduction of the measles vaccine in the early 1960s helped to greatly reduce the number of reported cases of measles.

Active and Passive Immunity

Whenever your body produces antibodies against infection, the result is called **active immunity.** Active immunity can develop from catching a disease such as chicken pox or from receiving a vaccine, such as that for polio. In contrast, when your body receives antibodies for a particular disease from another source, the result is called **passive immunity.** For example, a fetus receives antibodies by transfer from the mother's bloodstream to its own. In another example, travelers to some foreign countries receive various shots containing antibodies rather than antigens. These antibodies temporarily protect the travelers in the event of exposure to particular diseases, such as various forms of hepatitis, in the country they will be visiting. Passive immunity only lasts a few weeks or months because the antibodies in the shots disintegrate over time, and the recipient does not make his or her own antibodies against that pathogen.

Online Activity 31.4

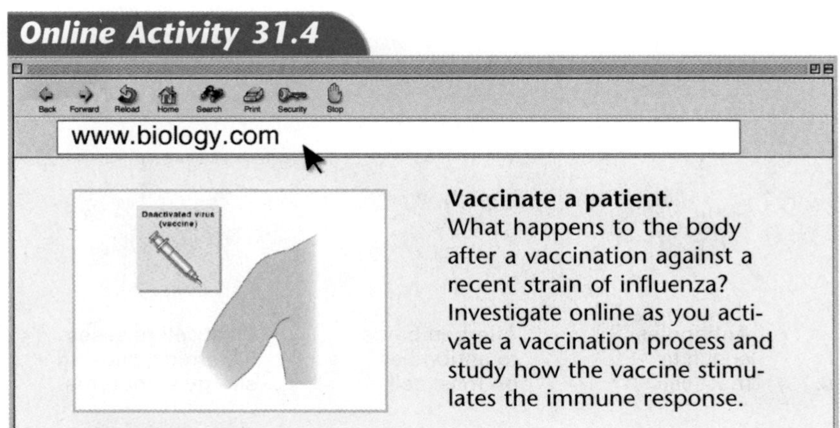

Back Forward Reload Home Search Print Security Stop
www.biology.com
Deactivated virus (vaccine)
Vaccinate a patient.
What happens to the body after a vaccination against a recent strain of influenza? Investigate online as you activate a vaccination process and study how the vaccine stimulates the immune response.

Concept Check 31.4

1. Explain how vaccines can protect against deadly pathogens.
2. Distinguish between active and passive immunity.
3. What is the function of a booster shot?

CONCEPT 31.5

Disorders of the immune system are major health problems.

OBJECTIVES

- Describe an allergic reaction.
- Explain how autoimmune diseases affect the body.
- Explain how HIV causes AIDS.
- Describe how the body reacts to organ transplants.
- List ways to keep your immune system healthy.

KEY TERMS

- allergy
- autoimmune disease
- AIDS
- HIV

What's Online
www.biology.com
Online Activity 31.5
Generate an allergic reaction.
Science, Technology, & Society
Living Organ Donors

The immune system is the body's protector against disease. But occasionally the immune system malfunctions or attacks the body's own tissues with harmful effects. And sometimes a pathogen, such as the virus that causes AIDS, actually attacks the immune system itself and destroys it.

Allergies

You may be one of several million people who sneeze and cough around pollen, dust, cats, or dogs. The runny, itchy nose, watery eyes, and frequent sneezing that accompany exposure to these substances are allergic reactions. An **allergy** is an abnormal over-sensitivity to an otherwise non-harmful antigen, called an allergen. If you are allergic to dust, for instance, your immune system is overly sensitive to allergens in the feces of tiny mites that live in household dust. Many people who are allergic to cats or dogs are actually responding to allergens in the animal's saliva.

Another example, hay fever, is an allergic response to pollen released from grasses or plants such as ragweed (Figure 31-18). The pollen grains have allergens on their surface that trigger B cells to produce a class of antibodies different from those that protect against pathogens. These "allergic antibodies" attach to receptor proteins on the surface of cells called mast cells that produce histamine. As you read in Concept 31.2, histamine triggers the inflammatory response, which, in the case of allergies, includes watery eyes and a runny nose. These "watery" symptoms

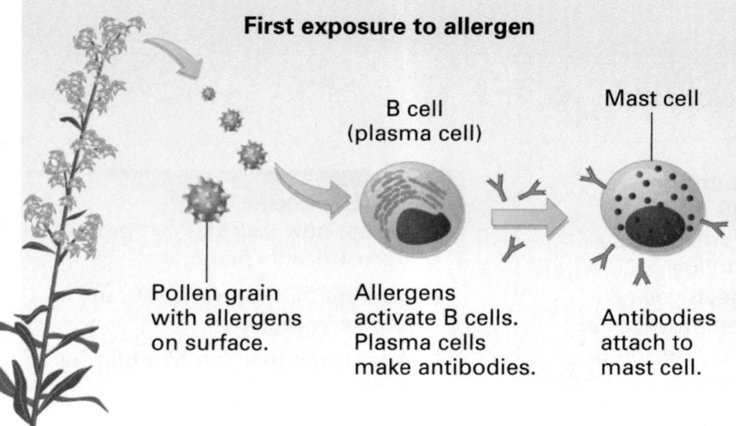
First exposure to allergen
B cell
(plasma cell)
Mast cell
Pollen grain with allergens on surface.
Allergens activate B cells. Plasma cells make antibodies.
Antibodies attach to mast cell.

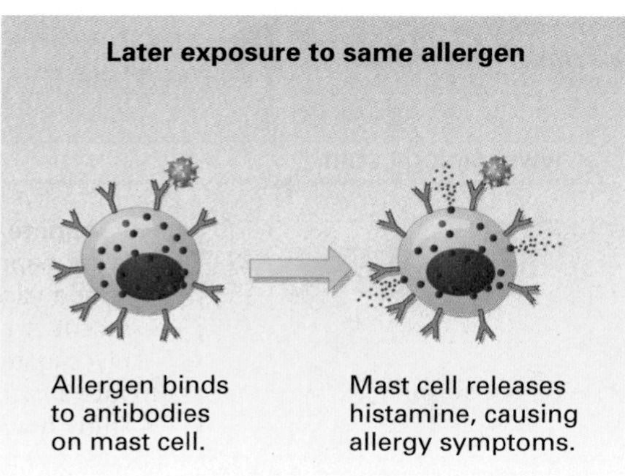
Later exposure to same allergen
Allergen binds to antibodies on mast cell.
Mast cell releases histamine, causing allergy symptoms.

Figure 31-18 An allergic reaction releases histamine, which causes the characteristic allergy symptoms. These symptoms may include a runny nose and watery eyes.

are caused by histamine dilating local blood vessels, which results in more liquid filling the interstitial area of the eyes and nose. One treatment for allergies is a class of medications called "antihistamines." These drugs block the action of histamine, minimizing the symptoms of an allergic reaction.

Most allergies are a nuisance. But some allergies are life-threatening. For example, when some people eat peanuts or are stung by a bee, they suffer a sudden, dramatic drop in blood pressure and have difficulty breathing. This dangerous type of allergic reaction, called anaphylactic shock, can be a potentially fatal condition. People who are severely allergic to bees often carry a self-injection kit containing epinephrine (adrenaline), a hormone that counteracts the allergy's symptoms.

Autoimmune Diseases

The human immune system is highly effective. It protects the body against a vast diversity of harmful invaders. But, in some individuals, the immune system cannot always distiguish between self and non-self. In such cases, the immune system turns against some of the body's own molecules, resulting in an **autoimmune disease.** Examples of autoimmune diseases include lupus, rheumatoid arthritis, and multiple sclerosis.

Lupus occurs when the body makes antibodies that react with some of the body's own tissues as if they were foreign. Since any tissue or organ of the body can be attacked, symptoms of the disease are varied (Figure 31-19a). They can include fever, weakness, weight loss, anemia, and a butterfly-shaped rash on the face.

Rheumatoid arthritis is another autoimmune disease characterized by the formation of antibodies that attack the body's own tissues. The immune system attacks cartilage and bone joints, causing damage and painful inflammation (Figure 31-19b). When rheumatoid arthritis strikes people under the age of 16, the disease is referred to as juvenile rheumatoid arthritis.

Multiple sclerosis (MS) is an autoimmune disease that strikes the central nervous system. T cells attack the myelin sheaths that cover the axons of some neurons. As you read in Chapter 28, the myelin sheath plays a key role in the transmission of nerve signals. Disrupting the signals can cause mild symptoms, such as fatigue, tingling, and numbness. More advanced cases may interfere with walking, talking, memory, and concentration.

Scientists have not determined the exact causes of autoimmune diseases. Evidence points to a combination of contributing factors including genetics, exposure to toxic chemicals, and certain viruses. Medicines for autoimmune diseases generally replace the destroyed "self" molecules, suppress the immune response, or treat specific symptoms.

▼ **Figure 31-19** Autoimmune diseases are caused by the immune system attacking "self" cells. **a.** Lupus can result in the body attacking and destroying its own red blood cells. **b.** Rheumatoid arthritis causes painfully swollen and deformed joints.

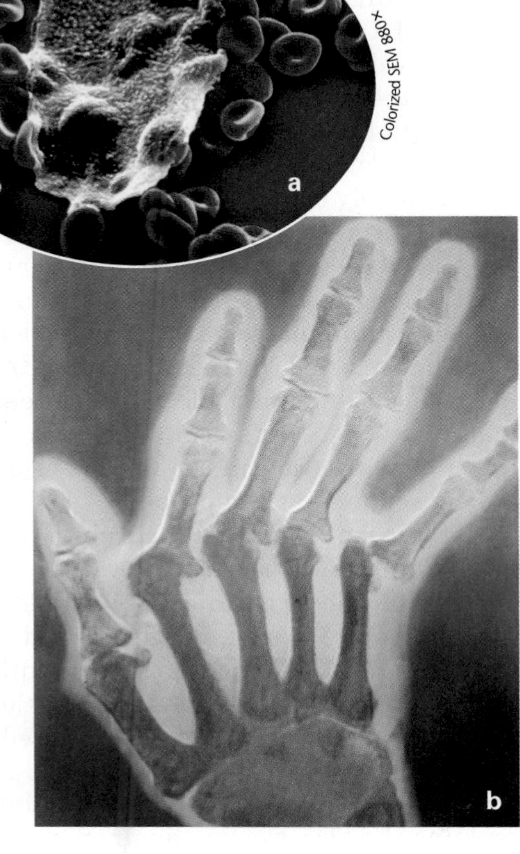

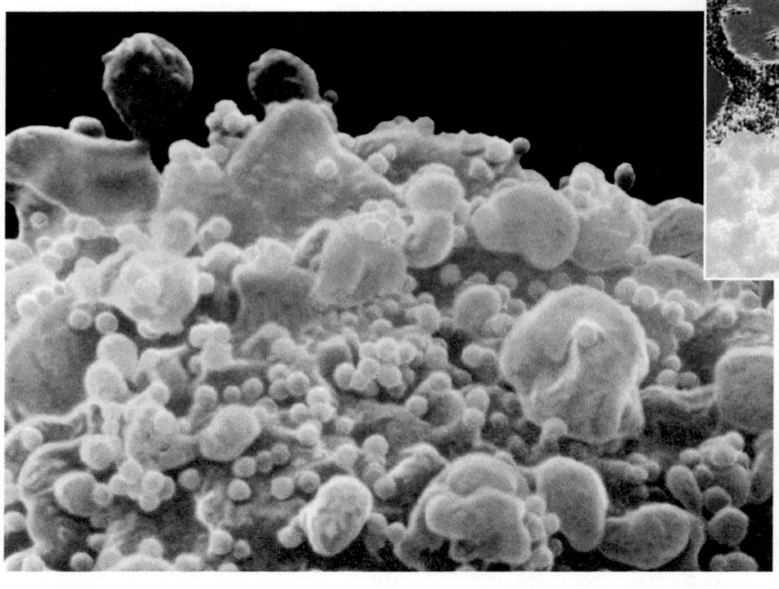

Figure 31-20 The micrograph at left shows HIV viruses (green) attacking a T cell (pink). Once inside a T cell, the virus can multiply. The above image shows viruses emerging from the surface of a T cell.

AIDS—A Disease of the Immune System

In the past two decades, AIDS has killed more than 11 million people worldwide. **AIDS** stands for acquired immune deficiency syndrome. A virus called **HIV,** or human immunodeficiency virus, causes AIDS. More than 40 million people are now infected with the AIDS virus, HIV.

HIV is deadly because it destroys the immune system, leaving the body unable to defend itself against pathogens and certain cancers. HIV infects a variety of immune system cells, especially helper T cells (Figure 31-20). When HIV destroys the body's helper T cells, the immune system cannot activate other T cells or B cells. Both the humoral and cell-mediated immune responses are impaired, and the body cannot fight pathogens (Figure 31-21). Death usually occurs from another infection, such as pneumonia, or from certain types of cancer.

The AIDS virus is transmitted mainly in semen and blood. Most often it enters a person's body during sexual contact or via needles contaminated with infected blood. Screening of donated blood has reduced the risk from blood transfusions, but the sharing of needles to inject illegal drugs remains a major source of infection. The rate of new infections also continues to rise worldwide among sexually active people.

At present AIDS is incurable, although newly developed drugs have slowed the progress of AIDS in infected individuals and decreased the number of deaths in the United States. Unfortunately, HIV mutates frequently and evolves rapidly. This makes the development of a vaccine difficult, since the mutated forms of the virus have different antigens. At present, education about preventing infection remains the best weapon against AIDS.

▼ **Figure 31-21** Over time, the total number of T cells declines as a result of HIV infection.

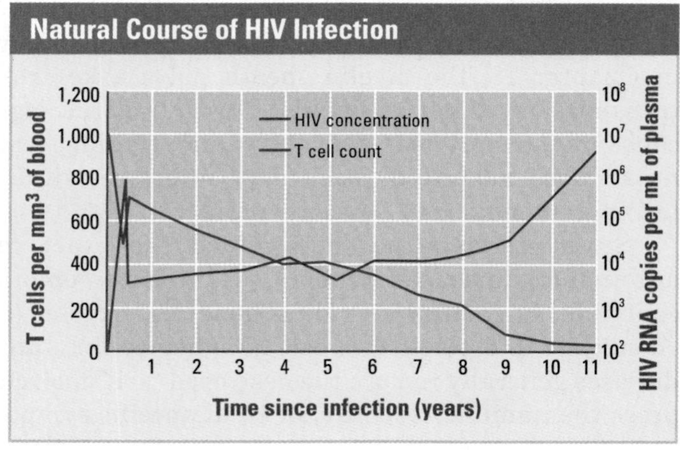

The Body's Reaction to Organ Transplants

▲ **Figure 31-22** Chris Klug, a liver transplant recipient, went on to medal in the Olympic Games.

An organ transplant replaces a damaged organ or part of an organ with a healthy organ or tissue. Some common organ transplants involve the kidney, cornea, skin, and liver. Just about every time a transplant occurs, the recipient's immune system wages a battle against the transplanted organ. This reaction is the normal process of self/non-self recognition. The transplanted organ is identified as non-self tissue and triggers an immune response.

Transplants that raise the fewest complications are those between identical twins or if the transplant is within the same individual, as in a skin graft. The immune system will more likely recognize genetically similar tissue as self tissue. In all transplants, medications are necessary to suppress the immune response to foreign organs. Cyclosporine is a drug commonly used to suppress the immune system and decrease the possibility of rejection. However, suppressing the immune system increases the patient's risk of infection. Despite the complications, transplant recipients can often lead full and active lives (Figure 31-22).

Keeping Your Immune System Healthy

Although you cannot always avoid illnesses, you can take steps to help your immune system in fighting many infectious diseases. Washing your hands before eating and after using the bathroom reduces the number of pathogens that enter your body. Eating a balanced diet will provide your body with adequate nutrients to maintain your immune system. Getting enough sleep will give your body time to restore itself.

The immune system is especially affected by the body's response to stress. As you will read in Chapter 32, the body releases certain chemicals when experiencing stress. These chemicals can suppress the immune system, making you more vulnerable to disease. Stress may be unavoidable, but learning to manage your stress will help your immune system function.

Science, Technology, & Society

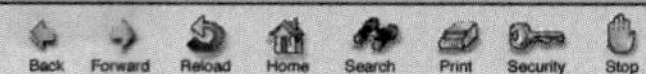

www.biology.com

Living Organ Donors

Liver transplants have saved thousands of lives. While most livers come from deceased donors, surgeons can now transplant partial livers from living donors as well. Go online to learn how these live donations are improving the chances of successful transplants.

Online Activity 31.5

www.biology.com

Generate an allergic reaction. Go online to identify some common allergens and find out how they affect the immune system. Then investigate the mechanics of an allergic reaction at the cellular level.

Concept Check 31.5

1. Explain what causes the allergic reaction called *anaphylactic shock.*
2. Describe two autoimmune diseases and their effects.
3. Explain how infection by HIV weakens the immune system and causes AIDS.
4. Explain why an immune response is triggered by organ transplants.
5. List three ways you can help your body fight infections.

Multiple Choice

Choose the letter of the best answer.

1. An organism that causes an infectious disease is called a(n)
a. antibody.
b. vaccine.
c. pathogen.
d. histamine.

2. Infectious disease can be spread from one person to another by
a. shaking hands.
b. touching a doorknob.
c. inhaling.
d. all of the above.

3. An example of a nonspecific defense to infection is
a. the inflammatory response.
b. plasma cells.
c. cytotoxic T cells.
d. all of the above.

4. One role of T cells in the immune response is to
a. secrete antibodies.
b. secrete histamine.
c. produce antigens.
d. directly attack infected cells.

5. To what type of cells do helper T cells bind?
a. macrophages
b. cancer cells
c. red blood cells
d. stem cells

6. Which of the following is *not* a method of making a vaccine?
a. grinding up bacteria
b. using the antigens of a pathogen
c. using a pathogen with a similar antigen
d. using cytotoxic T cells

7. Which treatment would be used to reduce the symptoms of allergies?
a. vaccine
b. allergens
c. antihistamine
d. interferon

Short Answer

8. Identify the body's physical barriers to pathogen invasion.

9. How does phagocytosis help protect your body from infection?

10. Explain the importance of the shape of an antibody's antigen-binding site.

11. How do T cells help protect the body against cancer?

12. Why is a booster shot sometimes necessary?

13. Give one example of how passive immunity is acquired.

14. Explain the role of self/non-self distinction in autoimmune disease.

15. Explain why destruction of helper T cells by HIV is so harmful to the immune system.

16. Explain why organ rejection is not a disorder of the immune system.

Visualizing Concepts

17. Complete the table below with the role of the given cell or chemical, or with the term that matches the given role.

Cell or Chemical	Role in Immune System
a.	Chemical "alarm" signal that causes nearby blood vessels to dilate during an inflammatory response
Helper T cell	b.
Interferon	c.
B cell	d.
Plasma cell	e.
f.	Cells that attack infected cells as part of the body's nonspecific defense

Analyzing Information

18. Analyzing Drawings Examine the drawings below to answer the following questions.

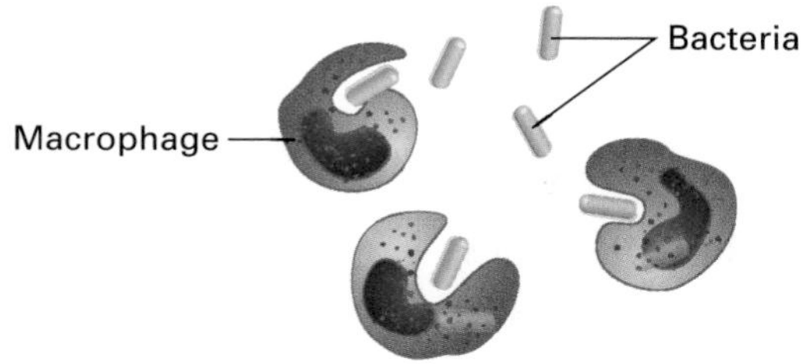

a. Is the above an example of nonspecific or specific immune system response? Explain.
b. How does the action of macrophages differ from the action of natural killer cells?

19. Analyzing Data Use the data in the table to answer the questions that follow.

Leading Causes of Death in the United States

1900		1999	
1. Pneumonia/Flu (ID)*	12%	1. Heart disease	30%
2. Tuberculosis (ID)	11%	2. Cancer	23%
3. Diarrhea (ID)	8%	3. Stroke	7%
4. Heart disease	8%	4. Lung disease	5%
5. Stroke	6%	5. Accidents	4%
6. Kidney disease	5%	6. Diabetes	3%
7. Accidents	4%	7. Pneumonia/Flu (ID)	3%
8. Cancer	4%	8. Alzheimer's disease	2%
Other	42%	Other	23%

*(ID) indicates an infectious disease

a. Create two circle graphs of the leading causes of death in 1900 and 1999. Shade in the infectious disease sections in both graphs. (See the Skills Appendix to review circle graphs.)
b. Summarize the similarities and differences between the two graphs and suggest reasons for the differences.
c. Pose a new question about the data. For example, you might ask if the leading causes of death are different for males and females.

Critical Thinking

20. Comparing and Contrasting What are the major similarities and differences between nonspecific and specific defensive responses?

21. Relating Cause and Effect A biologist is trying to determine whether a pathogen is causing a disease in mice. Describe how the scientist might use Koch's method to find out.

22. Relating Cause and Effect Flu viruses undergo frequent genetic mutations that produce viruses with a new combination of antigens. How would this affect the immune system's ability to defend against the flu?

23. What's Wrong With These Statements? *Briefly explain why each statement is inaccurate or misleading.*
a. Plasma cells attack pathogens by phagocytosis.
b. Interferon can prevent bacteria from growing.
c. Lyme disease can be transmitted by touching an infected object.
d. Once you have had an infectious disease, the same pathogen cannot attack you again.

Performance Assessment

Biology Research Project Go to the Web site for the Centers for Disease Control and Prevention (CDC). Choose ten diseases from the Health Topics list. Try to choose diseases that were not covered in this chapter. With a partner, write and illustrate a children's story that explains how the diseases are caused and transmitted, and how they can be prevented.

Online Assessment/Test Preparation

Back Forward Reload Home Search Print Security Stop

www.biology.com

- **Chapter 31 Assessment**
  Check your understanding of the chapter concepts.
- **Standardized Test Preparation**
  Practice test-taking skills you need to succeed.

Regulation of the Internal Environment

The hot desert sun beats down on this bicyclist in California's Death Valley National Park. Despite the extreme conditions in the external environment, the bicyclist's internal environment remains within a certain range of conditions. The body's relatively constant internal environment compared to the outside is called homeostasis. In this chapter you will investigate the roles of the excretory system, the liver, and the endocrine system in maintaining homeostasis. Before you begin, go online to the *WebQuest* to explore how and why you sleep.

Key Concepts

Concept 32.1

Homeostasis depends on mechanisms of regulation.

Concept 32.2

The kidneys function in excretion and water balance.

Concept 32.3

The liver helps maintain homeostasis.

Concept 32.4

Hormones function in growth, development, reproduction, and homeostasis.

Assessment

Chapter 32 Review

What's Online

www.biology.com

WebQuest
SleepQuest

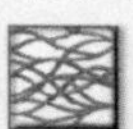

Online Activity 32.1
Regulate body temperature.

Online Activity 32.2
Activate a kidney.

Lab 32 Online Companion
You Are a Medical Technologist

Online Activity 32.3
Analyze the liver's role.

Online Activity 32.4
Trigger hormone responses.

Science, Technology, & Society
Thermoregulation

Chapter 32 Assessment

CONCEPT 32.1

Homeostasis depends on mechanisms of regulation.

OBJECTIVES

- Describe how body temperature is regulated by negative feedback.
- Explain the role your kidneys play in waste disposal and water regulation.
- Explain how hormones affect homeostasis.

KEY TERMS

- negative feedback
- urea
- excretion
- hormone
- endocrine gland
- target cell

What's Online

Online Activity 32.1 Regulate body temperature.

Have you ever noticed that when you are very thirsty, it's hard to think about anything else? This is related to the fact that maintaining the proper level of water inside your body is critical to your survival. As you read in Chapter 27, the stable internal environment in your body is called homeostasis. Maintaining water balance, regulating temperature, and removing metabolic wastes are examples of homeostasis.

Temperature Regulation

Your body has internal processes that respond to changing external conditions (Figure 32-1). For example, when you are cold, you shiver. When you are hot, you sweat. These responses help keep your internal body temperature within a narrow range close to 37°C (98.6°F). But what triggers these responses?

Your body has a temperature regulation (thermoregulation) system that works in much the same way as a home thermostat. This type of regulation is called **negative feedback,** because a change in conditions triggers responses in your body that counteract (negate) that change. Figure 32-2 on the facing page shows how negative feedback regulates your body's internal temperature. If your body temperature rises above the set point, the thermoregulation portion of your brain senses the change. The brain then stimulates activity that counteracts the temperature increase. For example, you may sweat, which cools your body through evaporation. Also the blood vessels in your skin may dilate. This allows more blood to flow near the surface of your body, releasing heat. These responses return your internal temperature to its normal range.

Your body also responds if your temperature falls below the set point. Blood vessels in your skin constrict, which reduces blood flow near the surface, conserving heat. Your brain may also send signals that result in the rapid contraction of your skeletal muscles—shivering—which generates more heat.

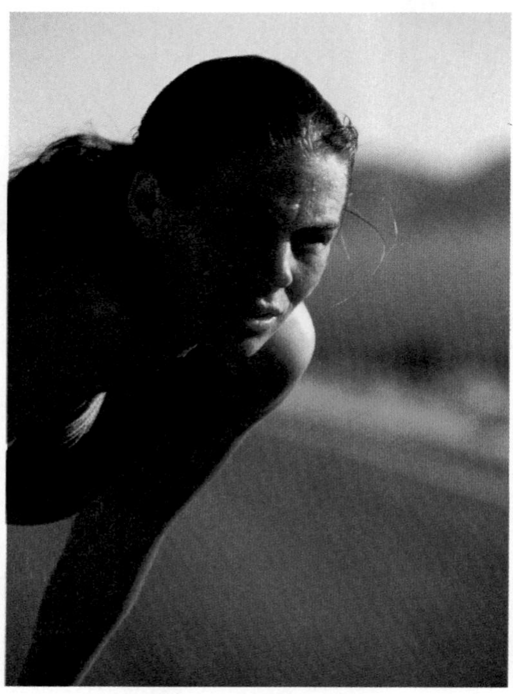

Figure 32-1 Exercising raises body temperature, especially on a hot day. Two responses that counteract the change are sweating and dilation of blood vessels in the skin.

Waste Disposal and Water Regulation

In addition to temperature regulation, homeostasis depends on regulating the chemical makeup of body fluids such as blood and interstitial fluid. This is accomplished by removing waste products and balancing the intake and loss of water.

Your cells produce wastes as a result of their normal metabolism. For example, when a cell breaks down amino acids, a toxic substance called ammonia (NH_3) is produced. In the liver, ammonia combines with carbon dioxide, forming **urea.** While urea is less toxic than ammonia, it must still be eliminated from the body. The removal of nitrogen-containing wastes from the body is called **excretion.** The primary organs of the excretory system, including the kidneys, remove urea.

In addition to excreting metabolic wastes, your kidneys play a role in regulating the balance of water and salts in your body. For example, when you sweat heavily, your body loses large amounts of water. Unless the water lost by sweating is replaced, the internal environment becomes unbalanced. Too little water in body fluids results in too high a concentration of dissolved substances, which negatively affects many body functions. In response, you feel thirsty. Drinking replaces the water lost through sweating. In addition, the kidneys are stimulated to allow more water to reenter your bloodstream. In Concept 32.2 you will read more about how your body maintains water balance.

Sweat glands secrete sweat that evaporates, cooling the body.
Thermoregulation center in brain is activated.
Blood vessels in skin dilate and heat escapes.
Temperature rises above normal.
Homeostasis: Internal body temperature of approximately 36–38°C
Temperature falls below normal.
Blood vessels in skin constrict, minimizing heat loss.
Skeletal muscles rapidly contract, causing shivering which generates heat.
Thermoregulation center in brain is activated.

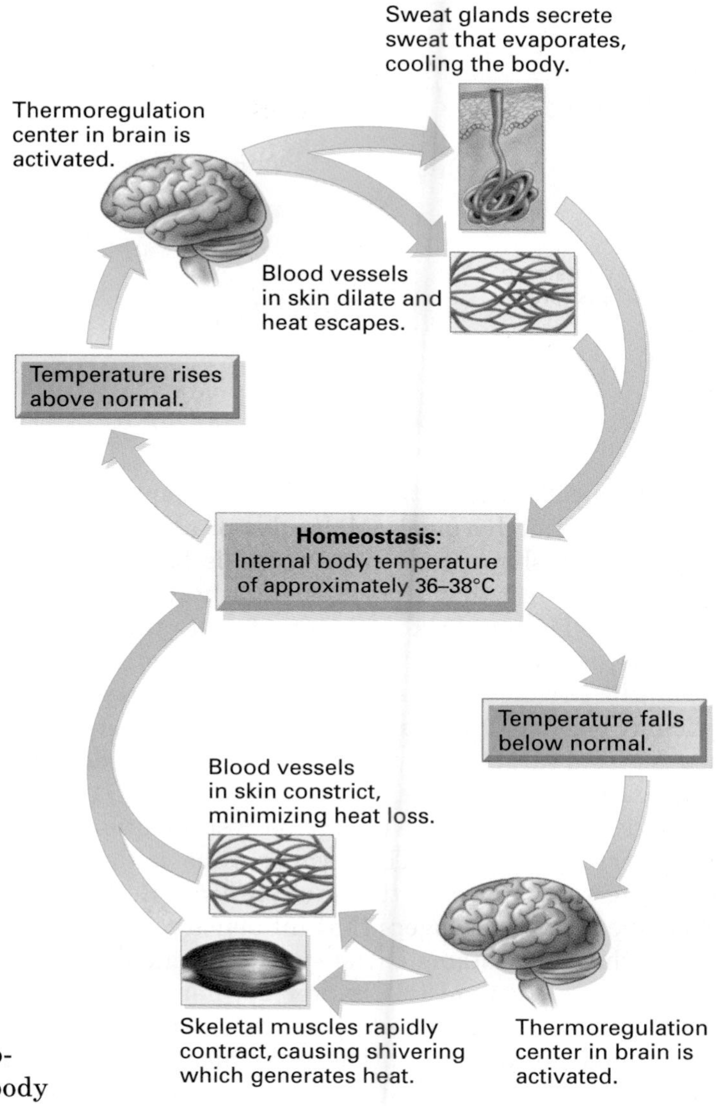

▲ **Figure 32-2** Your body's temperature regulation system can be compared to a home thermostat. When the brain senses a change in internal temperature it activates mechanisms that result in regaining homeostasis.

Hormones and Homeostasis

As you read in Chapter 27, chemical messengers called **hormones** trigger many of the responses that maintain homeostasis. Hormones are secreted by organs of the endocrine system called **endocrine glands.** These glands secrete more than 40 different hormones. Various hormones regulate blood pressure, heart rate, muscle tone, digestion, cellular metabolism, calcium and glucose levels in the blood, and salt and water balance.

Hormones are secreted into body fluids, usually directly into the bloodstream. A hormone may reach all parts of the body, but

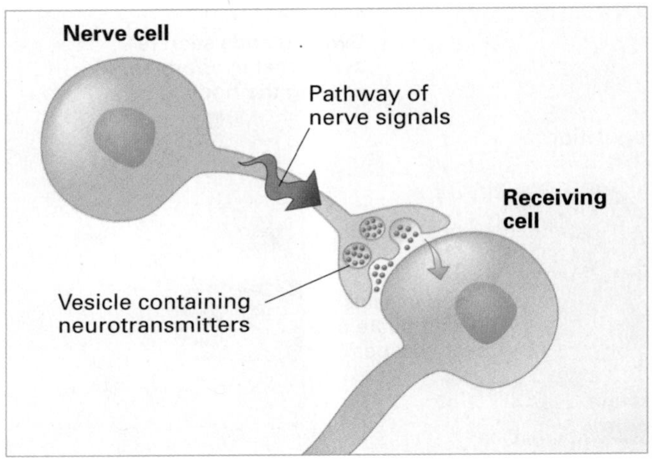

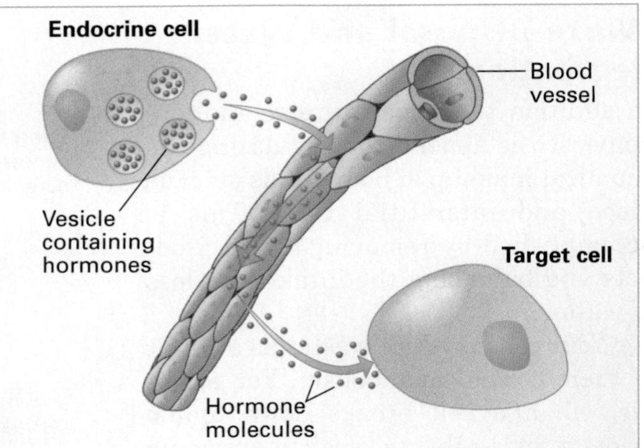

▲ **Figure 32-3** Nerve cells and endocrine cells both play important roles in regulating body systems and maintaining homeostasis.

only certain cells, called **target cells,** are equipped to respond to that particular hormone. Molecules of a particular hormone have a specific shape, and its target cells have chemical receptors that recognize that shape. When a hormone comes in contact with cells that lack receptors for it, those cells do not respond. However, when a hormone reaches an appropriate target cell, the hormone triggers an action within that cell. Thus, a particular hormone can travel through the body and stimulate a response from target cells, while non-target cells do not respond to that particular hormone.

How is the action of the endocrine system different from that of the nervous system? The two systems both play roles in responding to changes in the environment. Both systems also rely on chemical messengers that influence cells. One difference between the two systems is the speed at which their messages can travel. As you read in Chapter 28, nerve signals traveling through nerve cells as action potentials trigger the release of chemical neurotransmitters. These chemical signals can directly affect other cells and result in split-second responses. In contrast, the chemical messengers of the endocrine system, hormones, travel through the blood. As a result, their effects may take minutes or even days to occur.

Online Activity 32.1

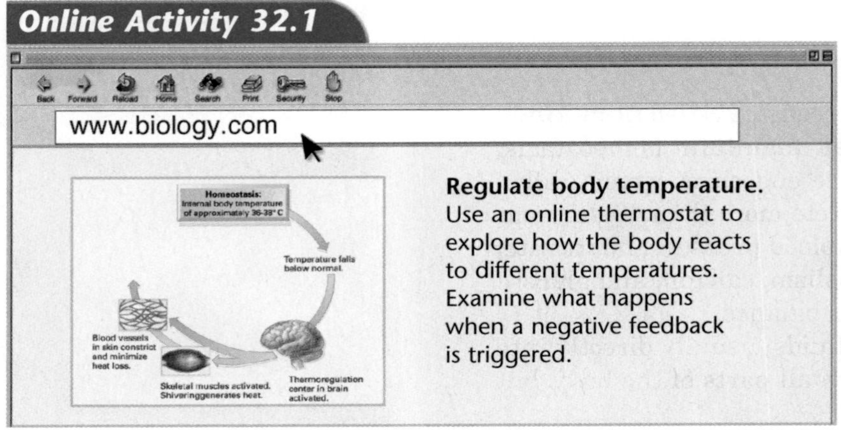

Regulate body temperature. Use an online thermostat to explore how the body reacts to different temperatures. Examine what happens when a negative feedback is triggered.

Concept Check 32.1

1. How does negative feedback help regulate your internal body temperature?
2. Describe how your body removes nitrogen-containing wastes.
3. Explain how a hormone might stimulate some cells, but not others.

CONCEPT 32.2

The kidneys function in excretion and water balance.

OBJECTIVES

- Identify the organs of the excretory system.
- Describe how the structure of the kidney fits its functions.
- Describe how the body regulates water balance.
- Explain two ways in which kidney failure is treated.

KEY TERMS

- kidney
- urine
- ureter
- urinary bladder
- urethra
- nephron
- glomerulus
- dialysis

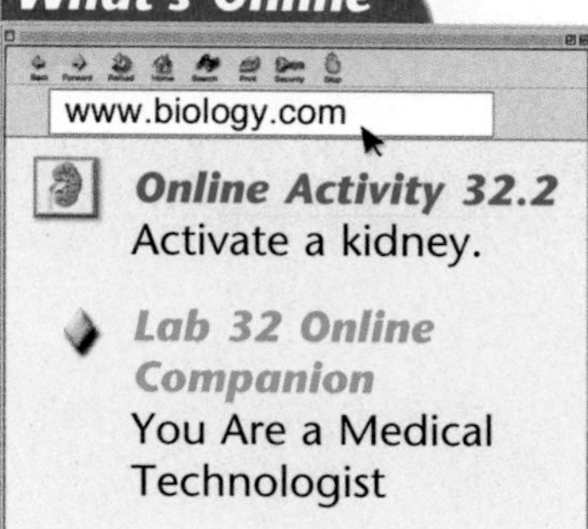

Nutritionists recommend that adults drink nearly 2 liters of water each day. On a day when you are exercising or otherwise very active, you require even more water to replace the water lost in sweat. The water you drink is transported by your circulatory system to your cells. But for homeostasis to be maintained, the water level of blood must stay within a certain range. How does your body regulate the amount of water in blood? In this chapter, you'll learn how the kidneys regulate water balance and also how they help excrete metabolic wastes.

Organs of the Excretory System

The primary organs of the excretory system are the **kidneys,** two bean-shaped structures that excrete waste products and regulate water and salt balance. Each kidney is about the size of a clenched fist. Your kidneys are tucked up under your ribcage on either side of your spinal cord (Figure 32-4). The kidneys filter blood and produce **urine,** a liquid composed of water, urea, and other waste products. Extending from each kidney is a tube, the **ureter** (yoo REET ur), which carries urine to the urinary bladder. The **urinary bladder** is a collapsible sac that temporarily stores urine until it is eliminated from the body. Urine leaves the bladder through another tube called the **urethra** (yoo REE thruh). The urethra extends through an opening near the vagina in females and through the penis in males.

While the kidneys are the primary organs involved in the removal of nitrogen-containing wastes, the skin also functions as an excretory organ. Glands in the skin secrete sweat, which contains small amounts of urea. In addition, the lungs are sometimes considered excretory organs, since they remove another metabolic waste product, carbon dioxide, from the body when you exhale.

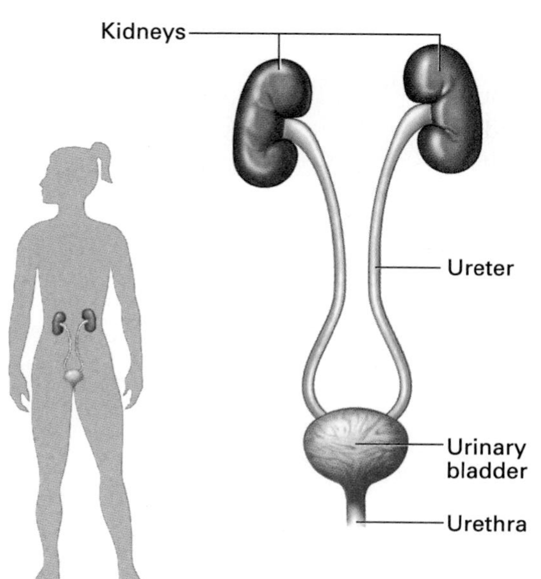

Figure 32-4 The kidneys filter blood and produce urine, which exits the body through the ureters, urinary bladder, and urethra.

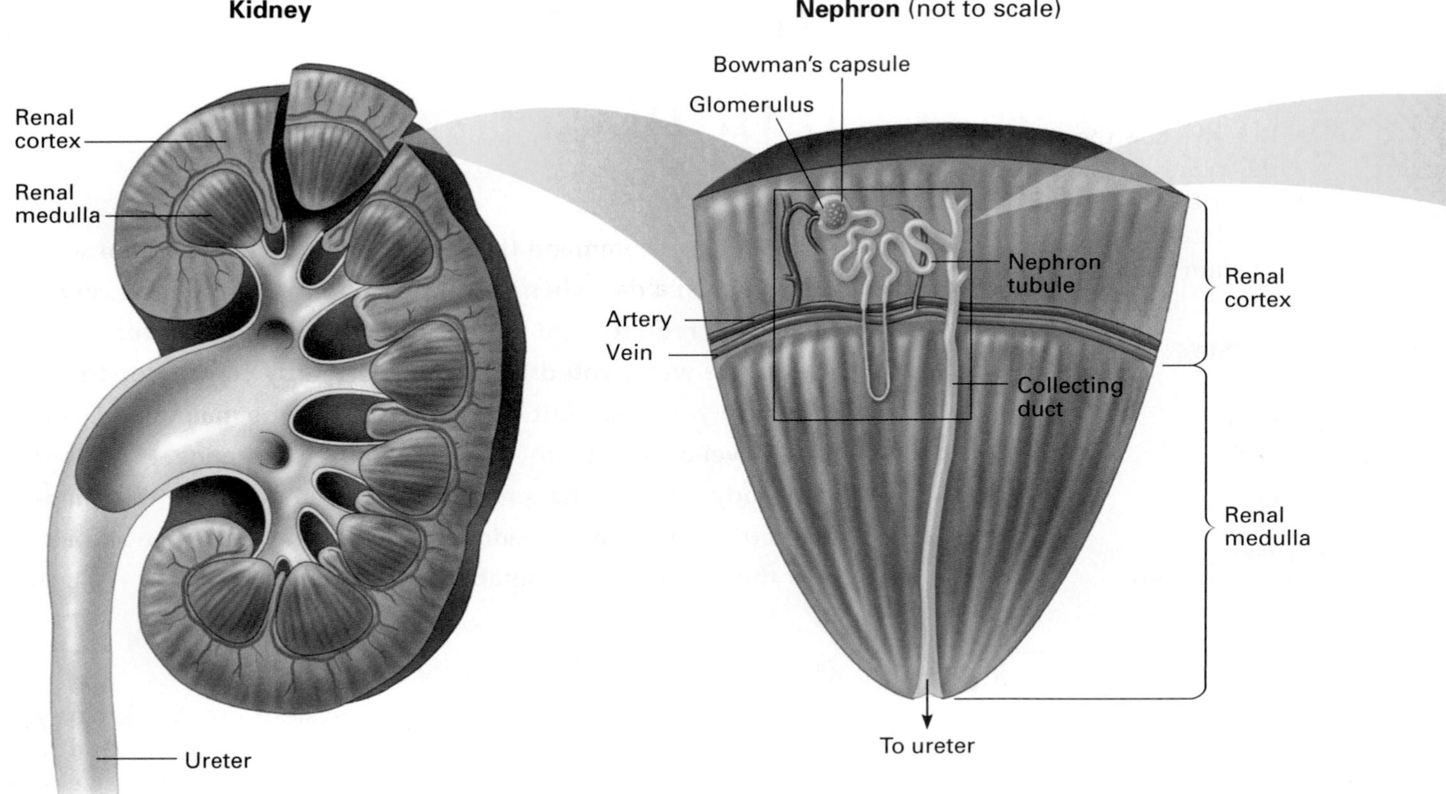

Kidney Structure and Function

As with the other organs you have studied in this unit, the kidney's structure fits its function. Each kidney consists of an outer region, called the renal cortex, and an inner region, called the renal medulla (Figure 32-5). (*Renal* means "related to the kidney.") Each kidney contains approximately one million microscopic filtering tubules called **nephrons.** A nephron consists of one tubule and its associated blood vessels.

When blood enters the kidneys, it is distributed through a network of branching arteries to the nephrons. Blood is processed and urine is excreted in four steps. The first step, filtration, occurs at a tiny ball of capillaries called the **glomerulus,** located at the beginning of each nephron tubule. In the glomerulus, blood pressure forces fluid through the capillary walls. This fluid, called filtrate, includes water, urea, glucose, salts, and amino acids. The filtrate is collected in a cup-shaped portion of the nephron called Bowman's capsule. From Bowman's capsule, the filtrate flows through the nephron tubule, which has two winding portions connected by a long, U-shaped region.

The next two steps refine the filtrate. The second step, reabsorption, takes place as the filtrate flows through the tubule. Water and dissolved nutrients, such as glucose, salts, and amino acids, are reabsorbed from the filtrate into the

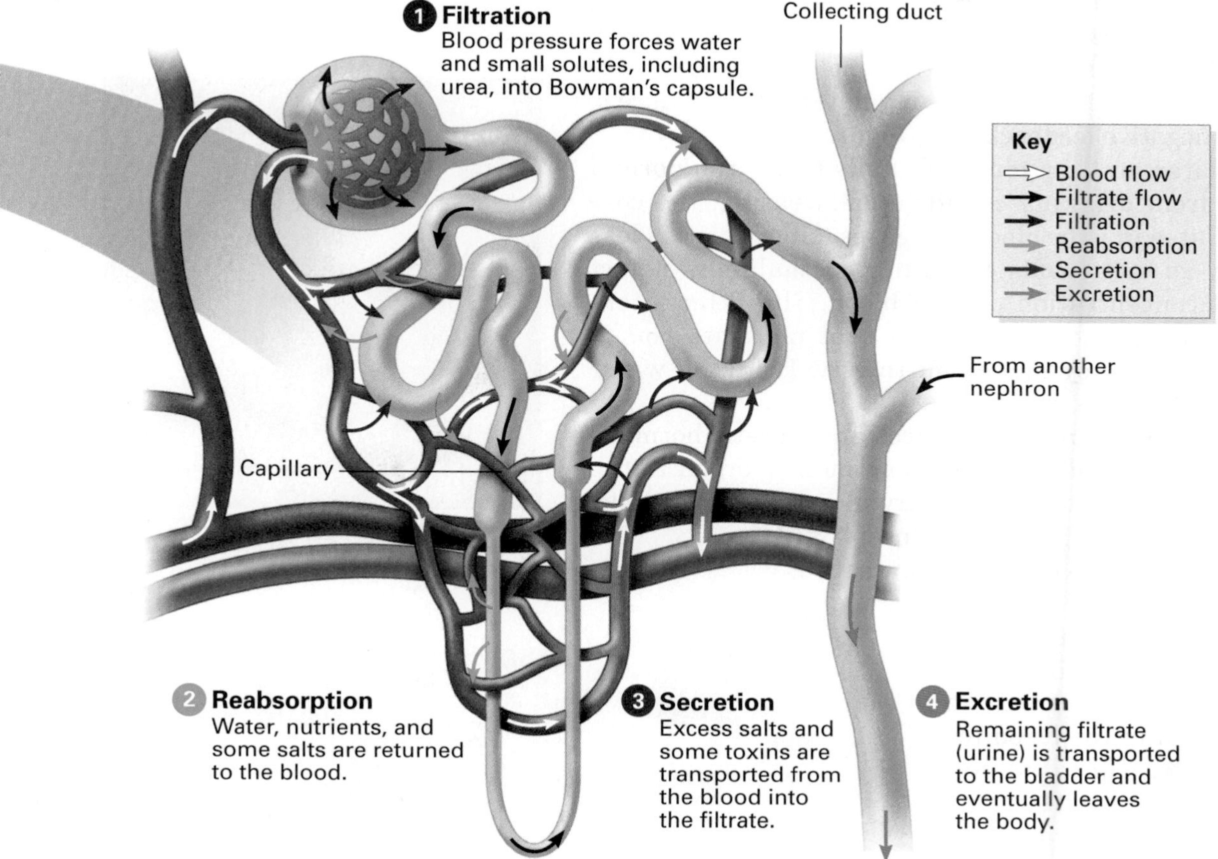

Nephron and Surrounding Capillaries
1 Filtration
Blood pressure forces water and small solutes, including urea, into Bowman's capsule.
Collecting duct
Key
Blood flow
Filtrate flow
Filtration
Reabsorption
Secretion
Excretion
From another nephron
Capillary
2 Reabsorption
Water, nutrients, and some salts are returned to the blood.
3 Secretion
Excess salts and some toxins are transported from the blood into the filtrate.
4 Excretion
Remaining filtrate (urine) is transported to the bladder and eventually leaves the body.

▲ **Figure 32-5** The working units of the kidney, called nephrons, filter blood, process the filtrate, and excrete urine in four steps.

blood. Active transport returns most sodium and most of the other dissolved salts and nutrients to the blood. Since the filtrate within the nephron is hypotonic compared with the surrounding blood and interstitial fluid, about 99 percent of the water in the filtrate is returned to the blood by osmosis.

In the third step, secretion, the kidneys remove certain substances from the blood and add them to the filtrate. For example, excess potassium ions or hydrogen ions in the blood are transported into the nephron. Secretion can also eliminate certain drugs and toxic substances from the blood. After the first three steps, filtrate contained within the nephron is called urine. In the final step, excretion, urine exits the body via the ureters, urinary bladder, and urethra.

The kidneys perform their function continuously. They filter your entire blood supply, approximately 5 liters, as many as 400 times each day. From this enormous traffic of blood, the kidneys process about 180 liters of filtrate per day—nearly the volume of three automobile gas tanks. Most of this fluid is returned to the blood. In a typical day, a person excretes only about 1.5 liters of urine.

Regulating Water Balance

Every cell in the body is composed mostly of water. Cells also exist in a watery environment—interstitial fluid. Survival depends on regulating the level of water in the body to within a certain range, which is one of the most important functions of the kidneys. Mechanisms of homeostasis regulate the amount of water reabsorbed at the kidneys. The process that regulates water balance is an example of a negative feedback loop (Figure 32-6).

When the water level in your body falls below the normal range, such as from drinking too little or sweating, the concentration of solutes in your blood increases (since there is less water). Certain receptor cells in your hypothalamus detect this high solute concentration in your blood. This "thirst center" in your brain produces sensations that motivate you to drink water—that is, they make you thirsty. Drinking water replaces the lost fluid.

This region of the brain also produces antidiuretic hormone (ADH), which is stored and released from another organ in the endocrine system, the posterior pituitary gland. (You will read more about the pituitary gland in Concept 32.4.) ADH travels in the blood to the kidneys, where it stimulates nephrons to reabsorb more water. This increased reabsorption moves water from kidney filtrate into the blood. The result is a decrease in solute concentration in the blood to the normal range. Since more water is reabsorbed, the water content of the urine decreases, causing it to be more concentrated and deeper in color.

When you drink too much water, your blood solute concentration can drop below the normal range. The hypothalamus and pituitary respond by releasing less ADH. The lower level of ADH decreases the amount of water reabsorbed in nephrons. As a result, the urine contains relatively more water and is lighter in color.

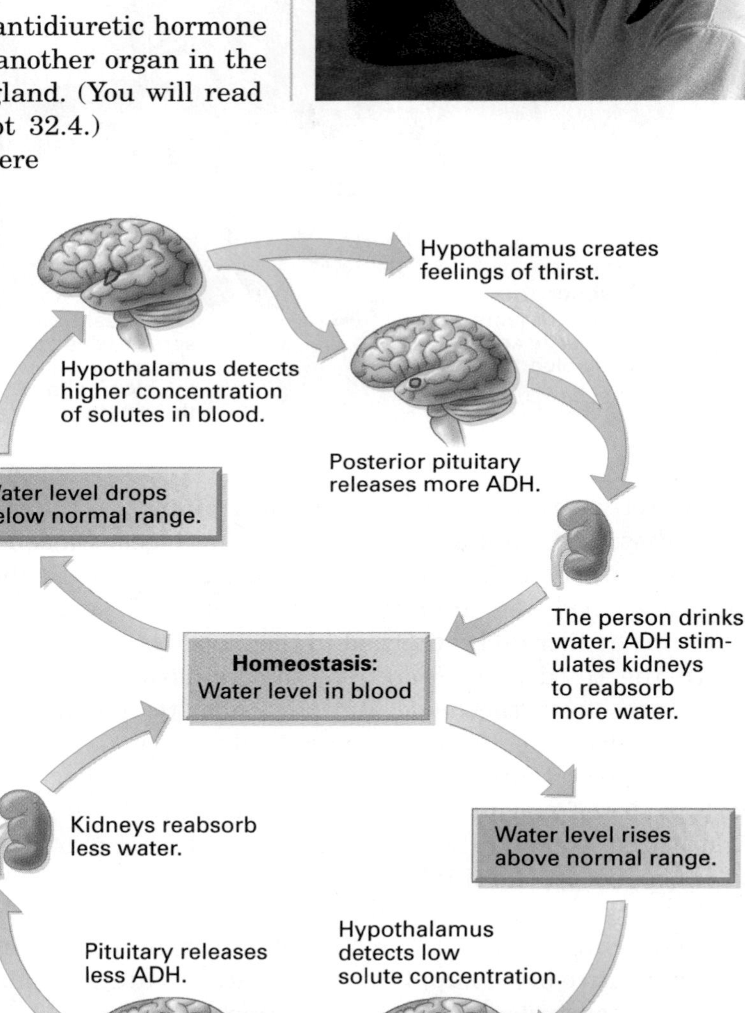
Hypothalamus creates feelings of thirst.
Hypothalamus detects higher concentration of solutes in blood.
Posterior pituitary releases more ADH.
Water level drops below normal range.
The person drinks water. ADH stimulates kidneys to reabsorb more water.
Homeostasis: Water level in blood
Kidneys reabsorb less water.
Water level rises above normal range.
Pituitary releases less ADH.
Hypothalamus detects low solute concentration.

▶ **Figure 32-6** Water balance in your body is regulated by a negative feedback loop. The only way to replace water lost from the body is to drink water.

Treating Kidney Disease

Some people inherit a tendency for kidney disease. Illness, injury, or poisoning can also damage the kidneys. For example, the microscopic nephron tubules can become clogged, or diseases such as arteriosclerosis can block blood flow to the kidneys. A person can survive with only one working kidney. However, if both kidneys stop functioning, toxic wastes build up in the body, resulting in life-threatening conditions.

One treatment for kidney failure is to process the blood outside the body, a process called **dialysis** (Figure 32-7). During dialysis the patient's blood is pumped through tubes that function like nephrons. Urea and excess salts diffuse out of the blood across a membrane. Glucose and other required substances that diffuse out of the blood may also be restored. The blood is then returned to the person's body. Dialysis treatments take about four hours, and most dialysis patients require three treatments a week.

Another treatment for failing kidneys is to transplant a healthy kidney into the patient. But there is a risk that the recipient's body will reject the transplanted organ. Medicines that counteract organ rejection have increased the number of successful transplants. Many kidney recipients live long, healthy lives.

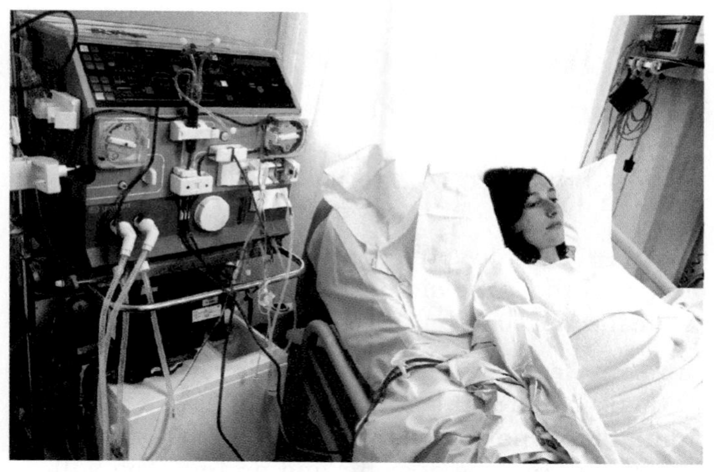

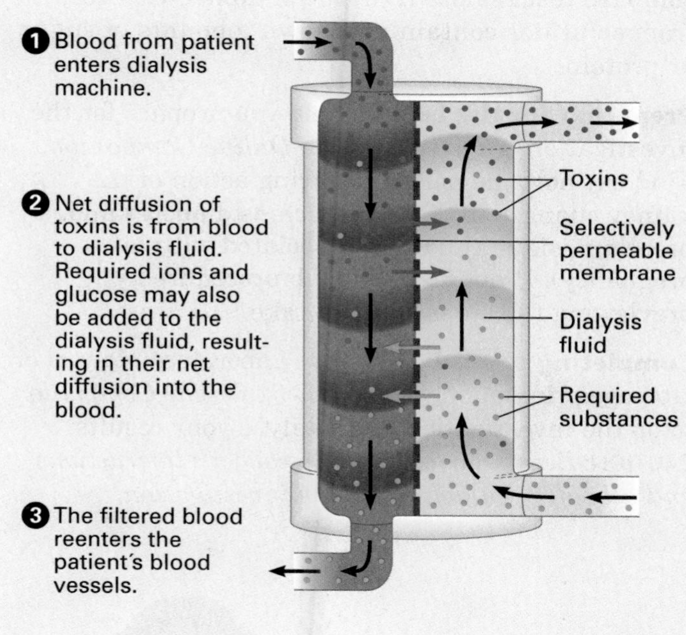

1 Blood from patient enters dialysis machine.
2 Net diffusion of toxins is from blood to dialysis fluid. Required ions and glucose may also be added to the dialysis fluid, resulting in their net diffusion into the blood.
3 The filtered blood reenters the patient's blood vessels.
Toxins
Selectively permeable membrane
Dialysis fluid
Required substances

▶ **Figure 32-7** Dialysis simulates the functioning of the kidneys and removes toxic substances from the body.

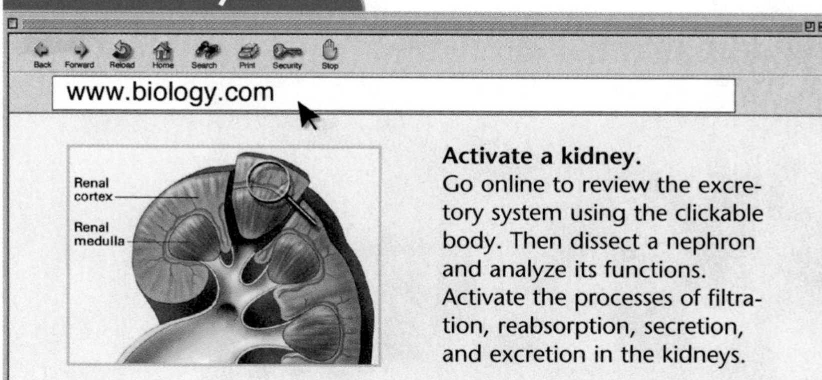

Activate a kidney.
Go online to review the excretory system using the clickable body. Then dissect a nephron and analyze its functions. Activate the processes of filtration, reabsorption, secretion, and excretion in the kidneys.

Concept Check 32.2

1. List four primary organs of the excretory system and explain the function of each.
2. Describe how kidney structure is suited to its function of removing wastes from blood.
3. Explain how ADH helps regulate water balance.
4. Explain how dialysis is used to treat certain kidney diseases.

You Are a Medical Technologist

Testing Simulated Urine for Protein and Sugar

Question How does the detection of sugar or protein in the urine aid in the diagnosis of certain medical conditions?

Lab Overview In this investigation you will take on the role of a medical technologist as you test simulated urine samples from three "patients" to detect the presence of sugar and protein. You will compare test results from the samples with results from solutions containing known amounts of sugar or protein.

Preparing for the Lab To help you prepare for the investigation, go to the *Lab 32 Online Companion.* ······➔ Find out how the normal filtering action of the kidney changes in diseases such as diabetes and preeclampsia (a condition associated with late pregnancy). Prepare for the lab procedure by previewing the steps you will take.

Completing the Lab Use your Laboratory Manual or lab page printouts from the *Lab 32 Online Companion* to do the investigation and analyze your results.
CAUTION: *Be sure to follow your teacher's instructions and all safety guidelines in the investigation.*

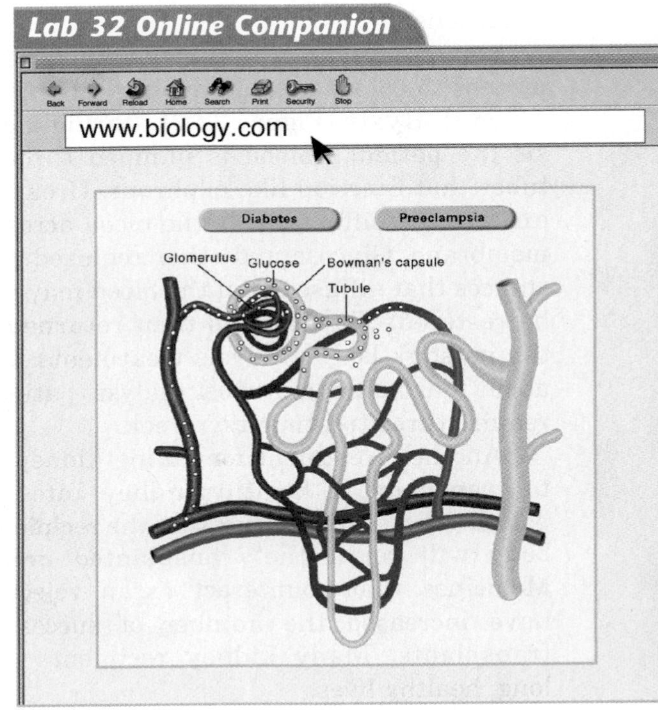

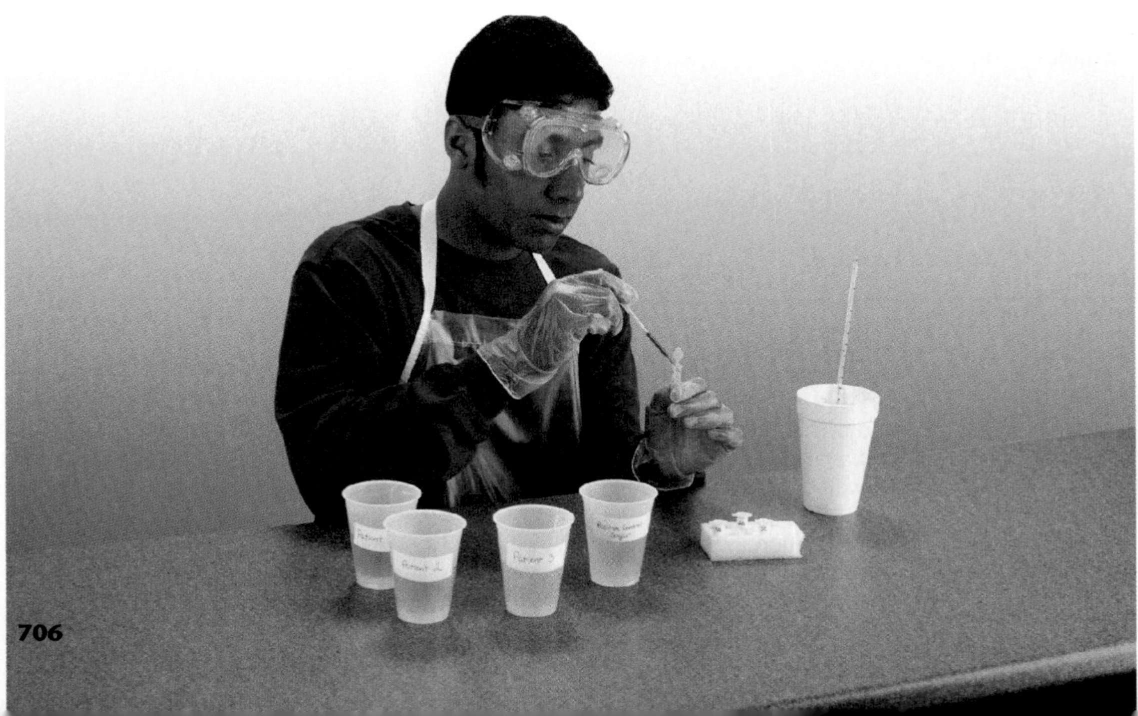

CONCEPT 32.3

The liver helps maintain homeostasis.

OBJECTIVES

- Describe how the liver helps maintain homeostasis.
- Describe liver diseases and their causes.

KEY TERMS

- hepatitis
- cirrhosis

What's Online

www.biology.com

Online Activity 32.3 Analyze the liver's role.

Your liver is like a chemical processing plant within your body. It secretes bile, processes many different organic molecules, destroys old red blood cells, stores nutrients, produces blood-clotting factors, converts ammonia to urea, and changes many toxic substances to less harmful compounds. The liver also interacts with several organ systems to help maintain homeostasis.

The Liver and Homeostasis

As you have been reading, maintaining homeostasis requires coordinated activity between several organ systems—circulatory, endocrine, digestive, nervous, excretory, and others. Your liver interacts with many of these systems. For example, the liver modifies nutrients and detoxifies substances that are absorbed by the blood in the digestive tract. The liver's key location in the pathway of blood—between the intestines and the heart—enables it to perform this job before the blood is distributed to the rest of the body (Figure 32-8). This maintains nutrient levels in the blood and helps ensure that toxins reach as few cells as possible.

Liver cells have enzymes that chemically alter many substances. For example, as you read in Concept 32.1, the liver converts ammonia into urea. The liver also carries out chemical reactions that detoxify certain poisons, such as alcohol. Additionally, the liver helps regulate the amount of glucose in the blood. One of the liver's most important functions is to convert excess glucose into glycogen (a storage polysaccharide similar to starch). The liver then stores glycogen, which can be broken down to glucose at a later time. Maintaining a constant level of glucose in the blood supports cellular metabolism and helps to maintain homeostasis in the body. The liver also manufactures most of the proteins found in blood plasma. Plasma proteins have a variety of functions. For example, the plasma protein fibrinogen can be converted to fibrin, which plays an important role in blood clotting, as described in Chapter 30.

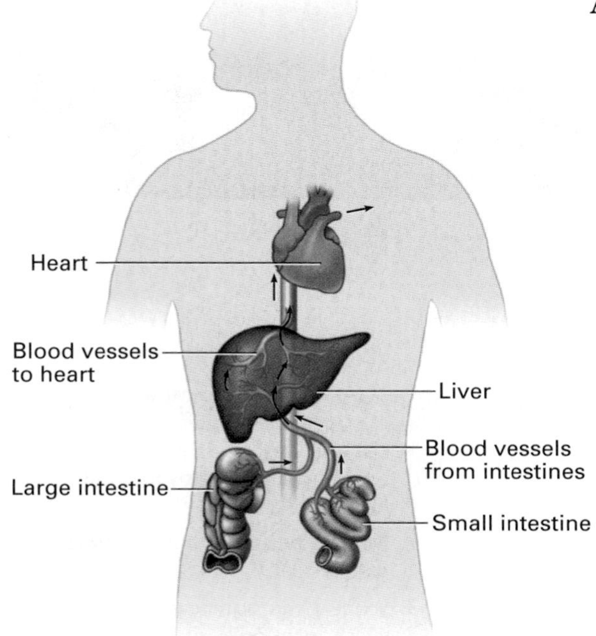

Figure 32-8 The liver is located between the intestines and the heart. This means that nutrients are processed and most poisons are removed from the blood before it is distributed to the rest of the body.

Hepatitis and Other Liver Diseases

The liver plays a central role in homeostasis. When the liver is not working properly, the body's internal environment becomes unstable. Damage to the liver may be caused by a viral or bacterial infection, an injury, abuse of alcohol or another chemical, or other factors.

One liver disease is **hepatitis,** a name that means "inflammation of the liver." Although hepatitis can be caused by several factors, many cases of hepatitis are traced to viral infections. Scientists have identified six types of viruses that cause hepatitis. The virus called hepatitis B is the most infectious (Figure 32-9). Approximately 10 to 30 million people worldwide are infected each year. The hepatitis B virus is found in the saliva, semen, and blood of infected persons. The disease can be transmitted through sexual contact, kissing, the sharing of needles to inject illegal drugs, and, rarely, blood transfusions (blood banks in the United States test donated blood for hepatitis). It also can be transmitted from mother to baby during birth. Hepatitis B or alcohol abuse may lead to cirrhosis (suh ROH sis) of the liver (Figure 32-10). **Cirrhosis** occurs when the liver is so scarred that it can no longer function effectively.

Colorized TEM 310,000×

▲ **Figure 32-9** This micrograph shows the virus that causes hepatitis B (small circles), the most infectious form of hepatitis.

When the liver is not functioning properly, several symptoms can occur. For example, the scarring of the liver tissue blocks blood vessels. The increased blood pressure can rupture small vessels, causing internal bleeding. The liver is also responsible for manufacturing proteins that are critical for blood clotting. Liver disease can interfere with the production of these substances, making internal bleeding even more cause for concern. Also, if a diseased liver fails to make bile, the patient's ability to digest fats decreases.

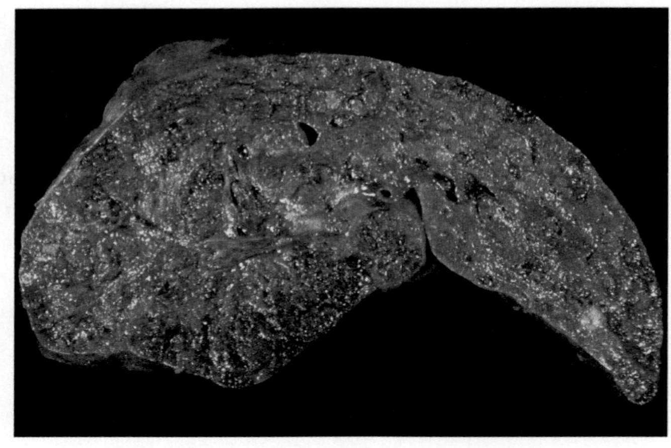

▶ **Figure 32-10** This cross section of a liver from a person who had cirrhosis reveals large amounts of scar tissue (dark areas).

Online Activity 32.3

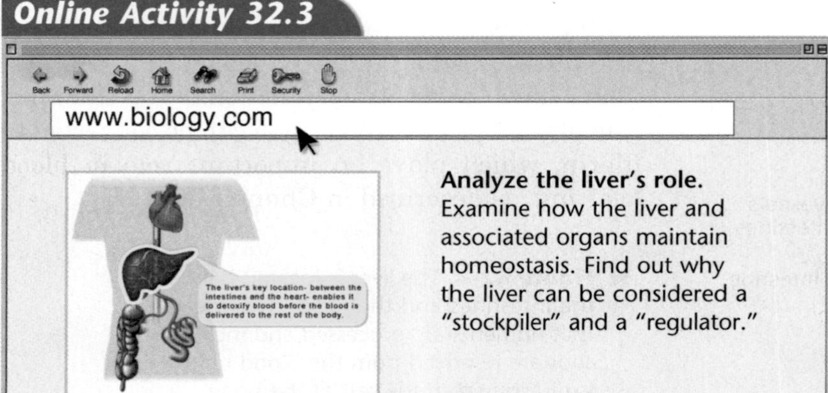
Back
Forward
Reload
Home
Search
Print
Security
Stop
www.biology.com
The liver's key location- between the intestines and the heart- enables it to detoxify blood before the blood is delivered to the rest of the body.

Analyze the liver's role. Examine how the liver and associated organs maintain homeostasis. Find out why the liver can be considered a "stockpiler" and a "regulator."

Concept Check 32.3

1. List and describe three ways in which the liver helps maintain homeostasis.
2. What is hepatitis B and how is it spread?
3. What is the significance of the liver's location?

CONCEPT 32.4

Hormones function in growth, development, reproduction, and homeostasis.

OBJECTIVES

- Explain the role of the endocrine system in the body.
- Contrast how steroid and nonsteroid hormones affect target cells.
- Identify the major endocrine glands and their functions.

KEY TERMS

- hypothalamus
- pituitary gland
- releasing hormone
- thyroid
- pancreas
- diabetes
- adrenal gland

What's Online

www.biology.com

Online Activity 32.4
Trigger hormone responses.

Science, Technology, & Society
Thermoregulation

Have you ever had trouble staying awake while reading a book late at night? Your eyelids are heavy, and you are finding it difficult to concentrate on your reading. Your head nods and you jerk upright, shaking your head to clear your thoughts. The sleepiness you feel could be the result of a hormone called melatonin, secreted by a tiny gland of your endocrine system.

Introduction to the Endocrine System

The feeling of drowsiness is one example of how the endocrine system helps regulate your body (Figure 32-11). The pineal gland, a pea-sized endocrine gland in the brain, manufactures and secretes the hormone melatonin, which helps regulate the body's daily and seasonal rhythms. Research indicates that light stimulates nerve signals to the brain that inhibit melatonin secretion. At night, when light is generally absent or dim, the inhibiting signals stop, allowing the pineal gland to secrete melatonin. Melatonin affects receptor areas in the brain and contributes to the feeling of drowsiness. Part of the evidence for this conclusion is that peak levels of melatonin in the body are found at night, while lowest levels are found during daylight hours.

Many hormones such as melatonin help regulate human body functions. The pineal gland and several other endocrine glands make up the endocrine system. A few of these glands, such as the thyroid and pituitary, have the sole function of secreting hormones. Other glands, however, have both endocrine and non-endocrine functions. The pancreas, for example, contains endocrine cells that secrete hormones that influence the level of glucose in the blood. But as you read in Chapter 29, the pancreas also has non-endocrine cells that secrete digestive enzymes into the small intestine.

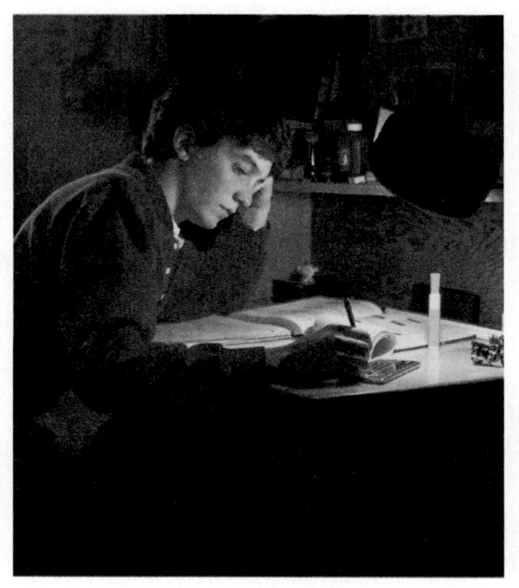

Figure 32-11 One reason you naturally feel drowsy late at night is the secretion of melatonin by your pineal gland.

a. Steroid Hormone Response

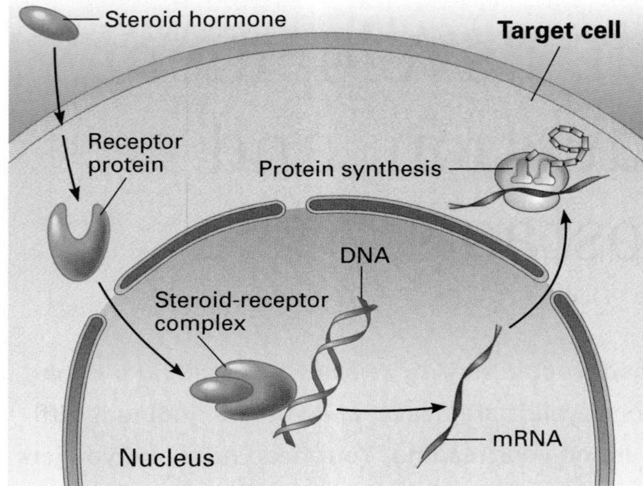

b. Nonsteroid Hormone Response

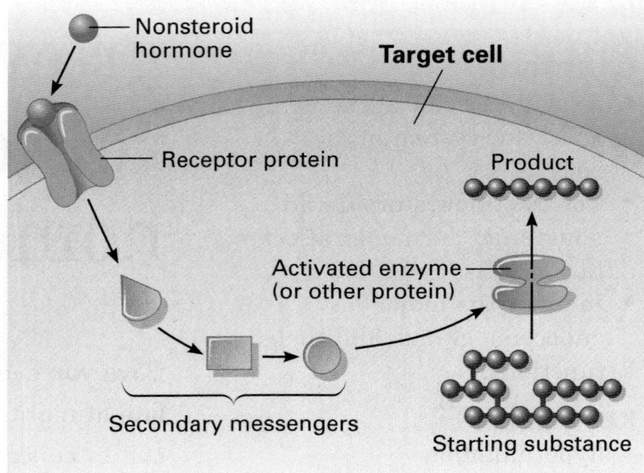

▲ **Figure 32-12** Steroid and nonsteroid hormones affect target cells through different mechanisms.

How Hormones Affect Target Cells

Hormones can be classified as steroid or nonsteroid. Steroid hormones include the sex hormones, such as estrogen, progesterone, and testosterone, as well as certain hormones secreted by the adrenal gland. Steroid hormones are lipid-soluble and can move across the plasma membrane and into a cell (Figure 32-12a). Once in the cell, each type of steroid hormone binds to a specific receptor protein, forming a steroid-receptor complex. Inside the nucleus, the steroid-receptor complex binds to DNA. This process can turn on specific genes that program the production of proteins, thus completing the response to the hormone.

Many of the nonsteroid hormones are modified amino acids or small polypeptides. Because they are not lipid-soluble, most nonsteroid hormones do not cross the plasma membrane. Instead, these hormones bind to specific receptor proteins located in the plasma membrane of target cells (Figure 32-12b). This action stimulates secondary messengers in the cell to activate proteins that carry out the cell's response. Figure 32-13 on the facing page lists the major steroid and nonsteroid hormones secreted by the endocrine system.

Once a hormone reaches a target cell, it causes that cell to respond in a specific manner. Some target cells respond with a change in the permeability of their membranes. This change affects the transport of substances into and out of cells. Other cells respond by making proteins and activating (or deactivating) enzymes. Some cells respond by secreting another hormone or other product, such as a digestive enzyme.

The Hypothalamus and the Pituitary

The human endocrine system includes many organs, some of which also belong to other organ systems (Figure 32-13). The **hypothalamus** is often referred to as the master control center of the endocrine system. First, it manufactures hormones that direct the activities of many endocrine glands, particularly

Major Endocrine Glands and Hormones

Pituitary gland

Posterior lobe (stores and releases hormones made in the hypothalamus)

- **Antidiuretic hormone (ADH)**
  Stimulates kidneys to reabsorb water
- **Oxytocin**
  Stimulates uterine contractions and mammary gland cells

Anterior lobe

- **Growth hormone (GH)**
  Stimulates growth and metabolism
- **Prolactin (PRL)**
  Stimulates milk production
- **Follicle-stimulating hormone (FSH)**
  Stimulates egg and sperm production
- **Luteinizing hormone (LH)**
  Stimulates ovaries and testes
- **Thyroid-stimulating hormone**
  Stimulates thyroid gland
- **Adenocorticotropic hormone (ACTH)**
  Stimulates adrenal cortex

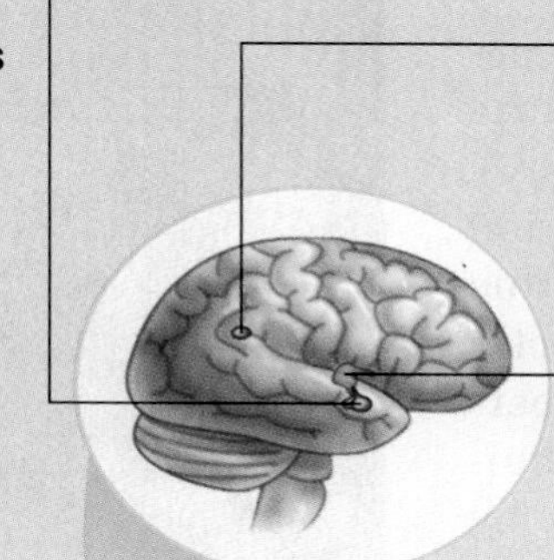

Pineal gland

- **Melatonin**
  Involved in day/night cycles

Hypothalamus

- **Releasing hormones**
  Trigger the anterior pituitary to secrete hormones

Thyroid gland

- **Thyroxine**
  Stimulates and maintains metabolic processes
- **Calcitonin**
  Lowers blood calcium level

Parathyroid glands (4)

- **Parathyroid hormone (PTH)**
  Raises blood calcium level

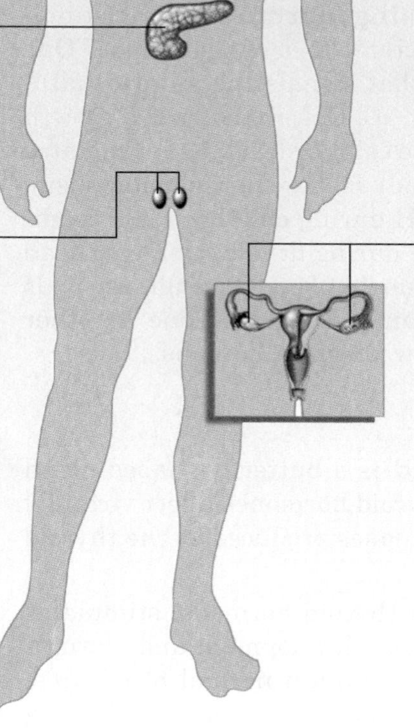

Thymus

- **Thymosin**
  Stimulates T cell development (immune system)

Adrenal glands

Adrenal medulla

- **Epinephrine and norepinephrine**
  Increase blood glucose; increase metabolic activities; constrict certain blood vessels

Adrenal cortex

- **Corticosteroids**
  Promote glucose synthesis, reduce inflammation, increase blood glucose

Pancreas

- **Insulin**
  Decreases blood glucose level
- **Glucagon**
  Increases blood glucose level

Testes

- **Testosterone**
  Supports sperm formation and male secondary sex characteristics

Ovaries

- **Estrogen**
  Stimulates uterine lining growth and development of female secondary sex characteristics
- **Progesterone**
  Promotes uterine lining growth

▲ **Figure 32-13** This table lists the major glands and hormones of the endocrine system and describes their functions.

the pituitary gland, as you will read in a moment. In addition, the hypothalamus receives and sends nerve signals, making the link between the nervous and endocrine systems.

As you read in Chapter 28, the hypothalamus receives information from the nerves about the status of the body's internal systems and about the condition of the external environment. With this information, the hypothalamus indirectly regulates body functions such as temperature, hunger, and thirst. The hypothalamus acts on the endocrine system by controlling the neighboring pituitary gland. The hypothalamus stimulates the **pituitary gland** to secrete hormones that influence other glands and body functions.

▲ **Figure 32-14** Much like a conductor directs the individual members of an orchestra to work together as a group, the hypothalamus directs the rest of the endocrine system.

The pituitary gland consists of two parts: the posterior (meaning "in the back") lobe and the anterior (meaning "in the front") lobe. The posterior pituitary stores and releases hormones made in the hypothalamus. For instance, the hypothalamus synthesizes antidiuretic hormone (ADH), the kidney-regulating hormone described in Concept 32.2. ADH is then channeled into the posterior pituitary for storage. When the hypothalamus detects a change indicating a low water level, it sends nerve signals that stimulate the posterior pituitary to release the stored ADH into the blood.

Together, the hypothalamus and pituitary gland regulate most of the endocrine system. The hypothalamus controls the anterior pituitary through **releasing hormones** that stimulate the anterior pituitary to secrete its own hormones. One example is a releasing hormone that signals the anterior pituitary to secrete growth hormone (GH). GH promotes the growth and development of the body. At the cellular level, GH stimulates protein synthesis and the use of body fat for energy metabolism. One result of overproduction of GH during childhood is a condition called giantism. Too little GH during development can lead to dwarfism. One dramatic achievement of genetic engineering is the ability to manufacture human growth hormone in other organisms for treating pituitary dwarfism in humans.

The Thyroid

Located in your neck, the **thyroid** is a butterfly-shaped gland wrapped around your trachea. Thyroid hormones affect virtually every tissue in your body. Two hormones produced by the thyroid are thyroxine and calcitonin.

Thyroxine Thyroxine, the major thyroid hormone, stimulates cellular respiration. It also influences development and maturation of the body. Thyroxine helps maintain normal blood pressure, heart rate, digestion, and reproductive functions. Having

Science, Technology, & Society

Back Forward Reload Home Search Print Security Stop

www.biology.com

Thermoregulation

How can people survive exposure in extreme environments? The rare stories of survival in icy waters or searing heat provide interesting lessons on the body's ability to regulate its internal environment. Go online to learn more about the role of homeostasis in some amazing cases.

too much thyroxine in the blood can result in a disease called hyperthyroidism. This disorder can cause high blood pressure, weight loss, irritability, and overheating. Having too little thyroxine, a condition called hypothyroidism, can cause weight gain, tiredness, and intolerance to cold.

Precise regulation of the thyroid hormones is important for homeostasis. The thyroid is regulated by a releasing hormone secreted by the hypothalamus. This hormone causes the anterior pituitary to secrete thyroid-stimulating hormone (TSH). Under the influence of TSH, the thyroid secretes its hormones.

You have already read that the hypothalamus receives cues about the environment via signals from the nervous system. For instance, cold temperatures cause the hypothalamus to signal increased TSH secretion from the pituitary. In response to TSH, the thyroid makes and secretes thyroxine. This increases cellular respiration, which helps warm the body.

A negative-feedback mechanism controls the secretion of TSH. An increase in thyroxine levels in the blood inhibits the secretion of releasing hormone from the hypothalamus. This negative-feedback loop is an important mechanism in controlling thyroxine levels in the blood.

Calcitonin The thyroid also secretes calcitonin (kal sih TOH nin), a hormone involved in the regulation of calcium levels (Figure 32-15). Calcium contributes to nerve signal transmission, muscle contraction, blood clotting, the movement of materials across membranes, and bone production. Ninety-nine percent of the calcium in your body is stored in your bones. The movement of calcium between the bones and the blood ensures the smooth functioning of the body processes described above.

Eating calcium-rich foods increases blood calcium levels. The thyroid responds to high calcium levels by secreting calcitonin, which causes more calcium to be deposited in the bones. This action lowers the level of calcium in the blood. When the blood levels drop too low, another gland called the parathyroid releases parathyroid hormone. This reverses calcitonin's effects, releasing calcium ions from the bones.

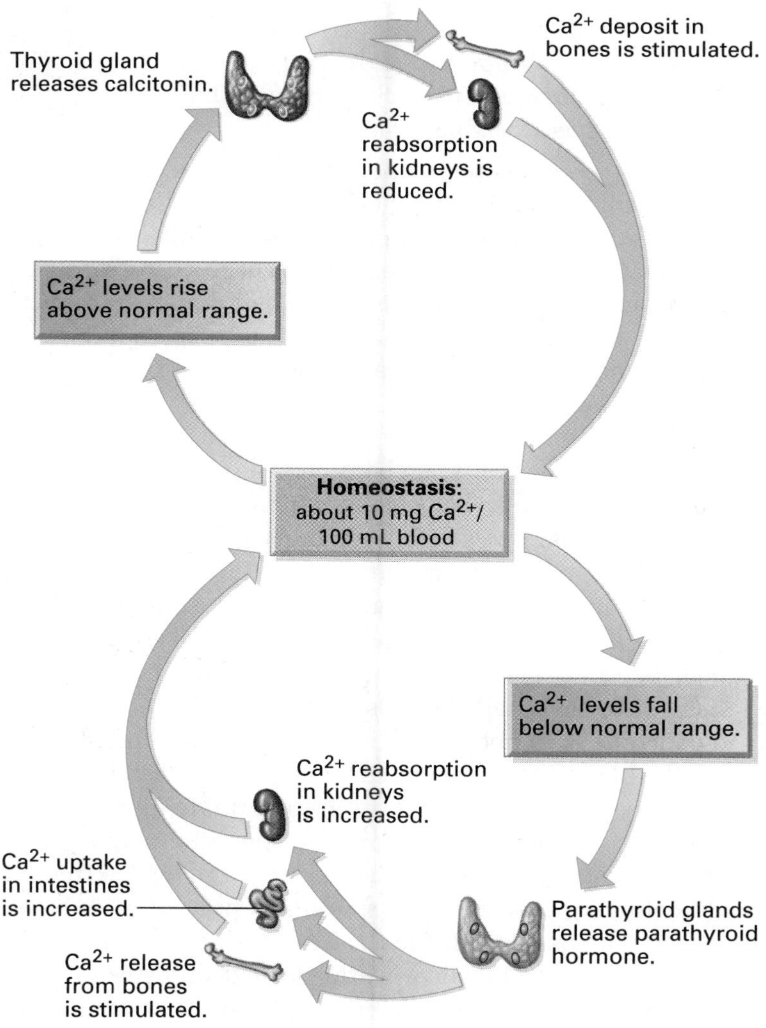
Ca^{2+} deposit in bones is stimulated.
Thyroid gland releases calcitonin.
Ca^{2+} reabsorption in kidneys is reduced.
Ca^{2+} levels rise above normal range.
Homeostasis: about 10 mg Ca^{2+}/ 100 mL blood
Ca^{2+} levels fall below normal range.
Ca^{2+} reabsorption in kidneys is increased.
Ca^{2+} uptake in intestines is increased.
Parathyroid glands release parathyroid hormone.
Ca^{2+} release from bones is stimulated.

▶ **Figure 32-15** When you eat foods such as milk, cheese, and dark leafy greens, your blood calcium level rises, stimulating an endocrine response.

The Pancreas

The **pancreas** produces insulin and glucagon, two hormones that manage the body's energy supply by regulating the amount of glucose in the blood. Glucose is used in cellular respiration to provide energy. Insulin and glucagon are opposing hormones and work in a negative-feedback circuit (Figure 32-16).

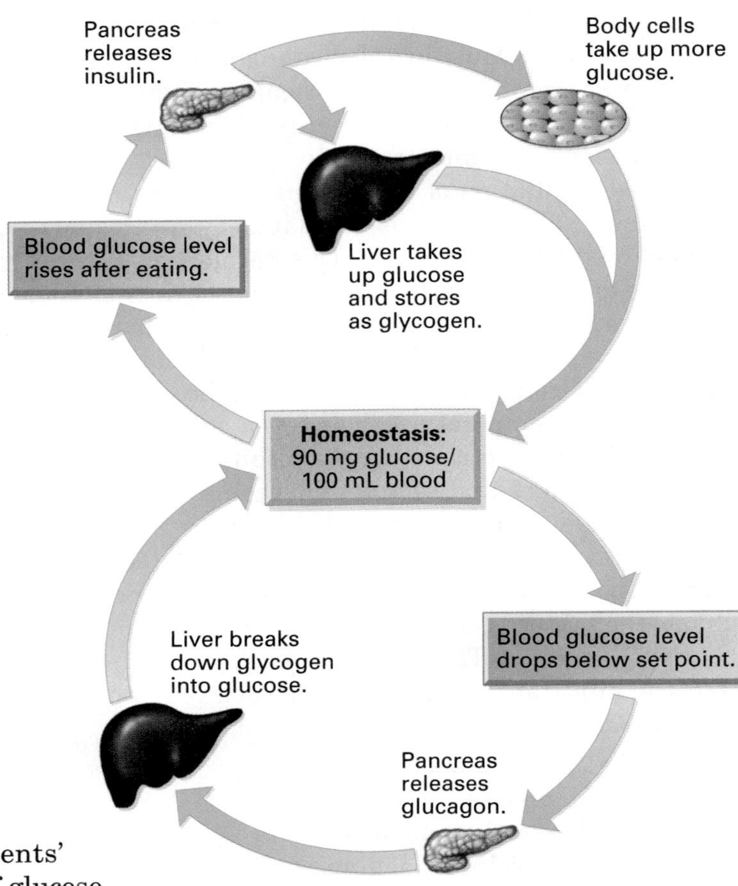

Pancreas releases insulin.
Body cells take up more glucose.
Blood glucose level rises after eating.
Liver takes up glucose and stores as glycogen.
Homeostasis: 90 mg glucose/ 100 mL blood
Liver breaks down glycogen into glucose.
Blood glucose level drops below set point.
Pancreas releases glucagon.

▲ **Figure 32-16** Insulin and glucagon are two hormones that work in opposition to each other in a feedback loop that maintains homeostasis for blood glucose level.

Insulin and Glucagon After a person eats a meal, the rising level of glucose in the blood stimulates the pancreas to secrete insulin. Insulin increases the amount of glucose that enters body cells, thereby increasing cell metabolism and decreasing the blood glucose level. The liver stores excess glucose as glycogen. When the blood glucose level falls, as it may between meals or during exercise, the pancreas responds by secreting glucagon. Glucagon is a hormone that stimulates liver cells to break down glycogen into glucose. The glucose is then released into the blood, becoming available for body cells.

Diabetes During physical exams, patients' urine samples are tested for the presence of glucose. Sugar in urine is a symptom of the disease **diabetes,** in which body cells are unable to absorb glucose from the blood. (Note that there are two diseases called diabetes: diabetes mellitus and diabetes insipidus. Here the term diabetes refers to diabetes mellitus.) More than 5 percent of the United States population suffers from this disease.

The symptoms of diabetes occur when there is not enough insulin in the blood or when body cells do not respond normally to insulin. As a result, body cells cannot obtain enough glucose. Starved for fuel, body cells will burn fat and protein supplies. Meanwhile, glucose accumulates in the blood. This excess glucose is excreted in urine and can be detected in a simple test.

There are two types of diabetes mellitus. Type I diabetes (also called insulin-dependent diabetes) is an autoimmune disease in which white blood cells (T cells) attack pancreas cells. As a result, the pancreas does not produce enough insulin, and glucose builds up in the blood. Type I diabetes often develops before the age of 15 and requires daily doses of insulin to regulate glucose levels.

In type II diabetes, cells fail to respond to insulin. A tendency for this disease seems to be inherited through a gene that codes for malfunctioning insulin receptors. Ninety percent of diabetes in the United States is type II. Most cases appear after age 40 in overweight individuals. People with this form of diabetes can help manage their disease by exercising and by controlling sugar intake.

The Adrenal Glands

The two **adrenal glands** are located on top of the kidneys (*adrenal* means "on, or near, the kidneys"). These glands produce hormones in response to stress. Each adrenal gland consists of a central portion called the adrenal medulla and an outer portion called the adrenal cortex (Figure 32-17).

Imagine that you are walking down a quiet street at night. Suddenly a large dog jumps out at you, growling and barking. Luckily, the dog is on a leash and can't reach you. Nevertheless, even several minutes later, you can probably feel your heart pounding faster than normal within your chest. In response to the apparent threat of danger, your hypothalamus sent nerve signals directly to your adrenal glands, causing them to release a hormone called epinephrine (also called adrenaline). This hormone prepares your body for urgent action by stimulating faster breathing and heart rate. The adrenal medulla also secretes norepinephrine, which works with epinephrine to stimulate liver cells to release glucose, making more fuel available for cellular respiration. These hormones are fast-acting and have a short-term effect.

Hormones secreted by the adrenal cortex provide a slower, longer-acting response to stress. In stressful situations, the hypothalamus secretes a releasing hormone, which causes the anterior pituitary to secrete an adrenal-stimulating hormone called ACTH. ACTH signals cells in the adrenal cortex to make and secrete other hormones called corticosteroids. Some corticosteroids help regulate water and ion reabsorption in the kidneys. Others promote fat and protein breakdown and glucose synthesis.

Other hormones of the endocrine system play a major role in the reproductive system, which you will read about in the next chapter.

▼ **Figure 32-17** The adrenal cortex and adrenal medulla secrete hormones that help your body manage stressful situations.

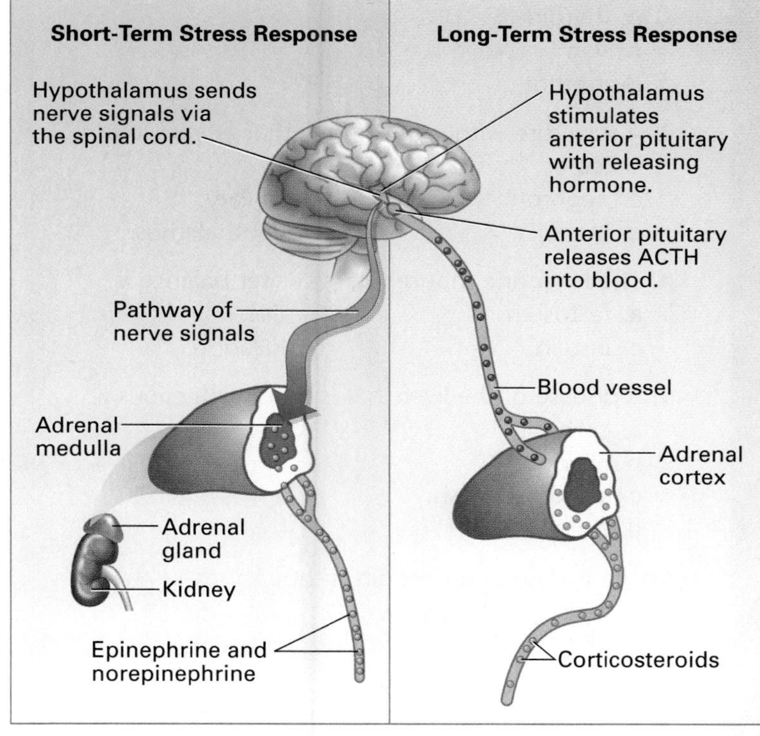

Online Activity 32.4

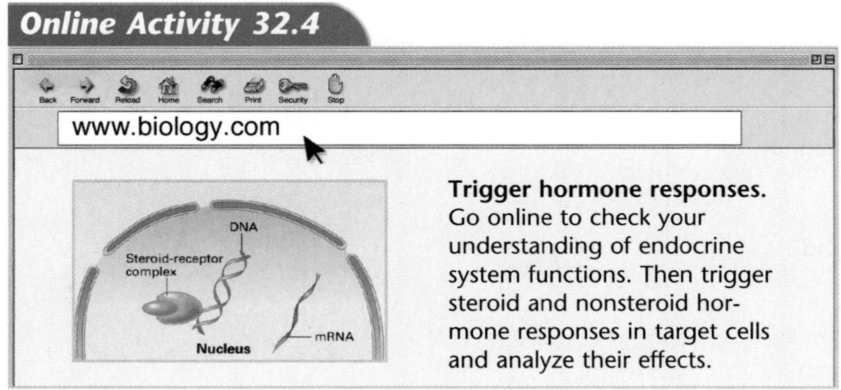

Trigger hormone responses. Go online to check your understanding of endocrine system functions. Then trigger steroid and nonsteroid hormone responses in target cells and analyze their effects.

Concept Check 32.4

1. Give an example of how the endocrine system regulates certain body functions.
2. Explain how steroid and nonsteroid hormones affect target cells.
3. Describe how the hypothalamus and pituitary glands control the endocrine system.
4. How do insulin and glucagon affect the level of blood glucose?

Multiple Choice

Choose the letter of the best answer.

1. The liver converts the toxic substance ammonia to
   a. urine.
   b. urea.
   c. glycogen.
   d. glucose.

2. Which of the following is *not* considered part of the excretory system?
   a. kidney
   b. thyroid
   c. skin
   d. urethra

3. A structure within the kidney that filters blood is called a
   a. nephron.
   b. capillary.
   c. medulla.
   d. hypothalamus.

4. The hormone that regulates water balance is
   a. testosterone.
   b. ADH.
   c. insulin.
   d. glucagon.

5. A disease of the liver that is highly infectious is
   a. cirrhosis.
   b. hepatitis B.
   c. artherosclerosis.
   d. diabetes.

6. The hormone melatonin is thought to
   a. make you feel drowsy.
   b. prepare your body for urgent action.
   c. regulate calcium levels.
   d. increase water absorption in the kidneys.

7. The pancreas
   a. secretes insulin.
   b. secretes glucagon.
   c. helps regulate blood glucose levels.
   d. all of the above.

8. When the hypothalamus sends nerve signals to the adrenal medulla, it is initiating
   a. a stress response.
   b. the uptake of calcium from the blood.
   c. shivering.
   d. the release of ADH into the blood.

Short Answer

9. Explain the result of excretion.

10. Name four structures of the excretory system and explain the function of each.

11. Name and describe each of the four steps of fluid processing by nephrons.

12. Describe two functions of the liver.

13. Explain why being lipid-soluble is an important characteristic of steroid hormones.

14. What is the relationship between the hypothalamus and the two lobes of the pituitary gland?

15. Explain the relationship between TSH and thyroxine.

16. Explain how calcium level in the blood is regulated.

17. What is diabetes mellitus? Contrast the two types of diabetes mellitus.

18. Describe how the body responds to epinephrine.

Visualizing Concepts

19. Copy the terms below and arrange them into a flowchart of the events leading to a long-term stress response. Then write a sentence for each term, explaining its position in the flowchart.

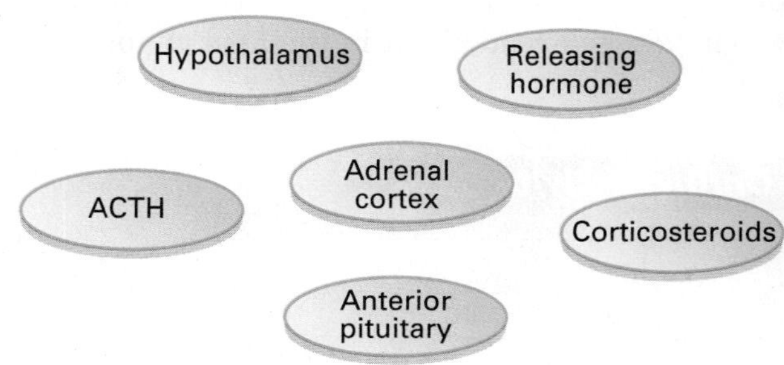

Analyzing Information

20. Analyzing Diagrams Use the diagram of a nephron to answer the questions below.

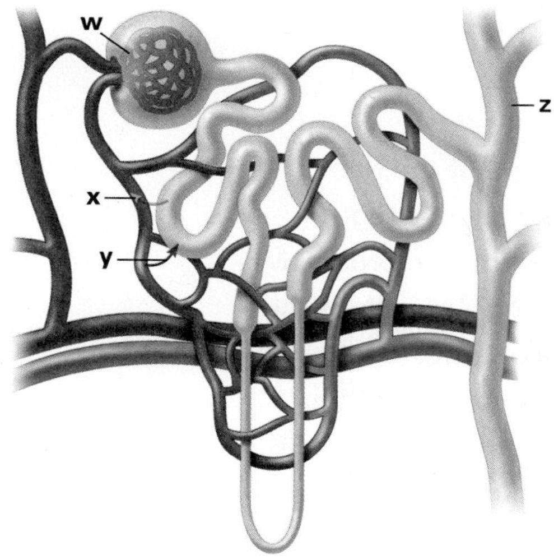

a. Name the capillary structure labeled *w*. What stage of fluid processing occurs here?
b. Describe what the arrows labeled *x* and *y* represent.
c. What is the function of the structure labeled *z*?

21. Analyzing Graphs This graph depicts changes in blood glucose level in two people over time.

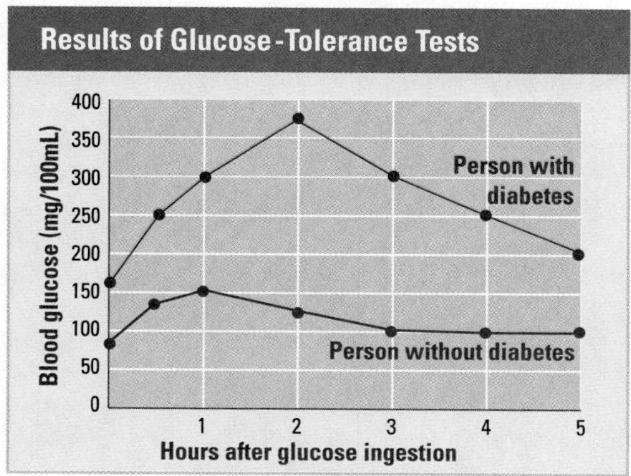

a. Describe the change for each individual.
b. Suggest a reason for the difference in the two graphs.

Critical Thinking

22. Relating Cause and Effect Describe two health problems that might result if a person's liver stopped functioning.

23. Making Generalizations Describe how endocrine glands contribute to homeostasis.

24. Comparing and Contrasting Explain the difference between steroid and nonsteroid hormones, including how both types of hormones influence target cells.

25. What's Wrong With These Statements? *Briefly explain why each statement is inaccurate or misleading.*

a. Secretion eliminates drugs and toxic substances from the filtrate.
b. ACTH stimulates the liver to manufacture glycogen.
c. All cells respond to each type of hormone that circulates in the body.
d. Calcitonin stimulates the release of calcium from bones.

Performance Assessment

Biology Research Project Select an endocrine gland and one of its hormones from Figure 32-13 on page 711. Research and write a report on the role that hormone plays in homeostasis, including a description of how it is regulated—for instance, by a negative feedback loop. What health effects may result if the endocrine gland that secretes your chosen hormone stops functioning?

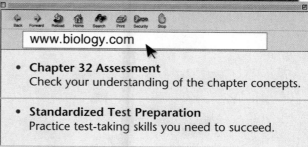

Online Assessment/Test Preparation

Back Forward Reload Home Search Print Security Stop

www.biology.com

- **Chapter 32 Assessment**
  Check your understanding of the chapter concepts.
- **Standardized Test Preparation**
  Practice test-taking skills you need to succeed.

Reproduction and Development

The SEM image below provides a glimpse of one of the first events in human reproduction. A single female gamete (egg) is shown within a narrow tube that is part of the female reproductive system. Cilia, the hair-like structures you see lining the walls of the tube, beat rhythmically, moving the egg cell along the length of the tube. Attached to the surface of the egg are dozens of much smaller male gametes, or sperm cells. If one of these sperm cells penetrates the egg cell, the nuclei of the gametes fuse and development begins. In this chapter, you will learn about the human reproductive systems and about the development that follows the events described above. But first, go online to the ***WebQuest*** to explore the worlds of identical and fraternal twins.

Colorized SEM 3,300×

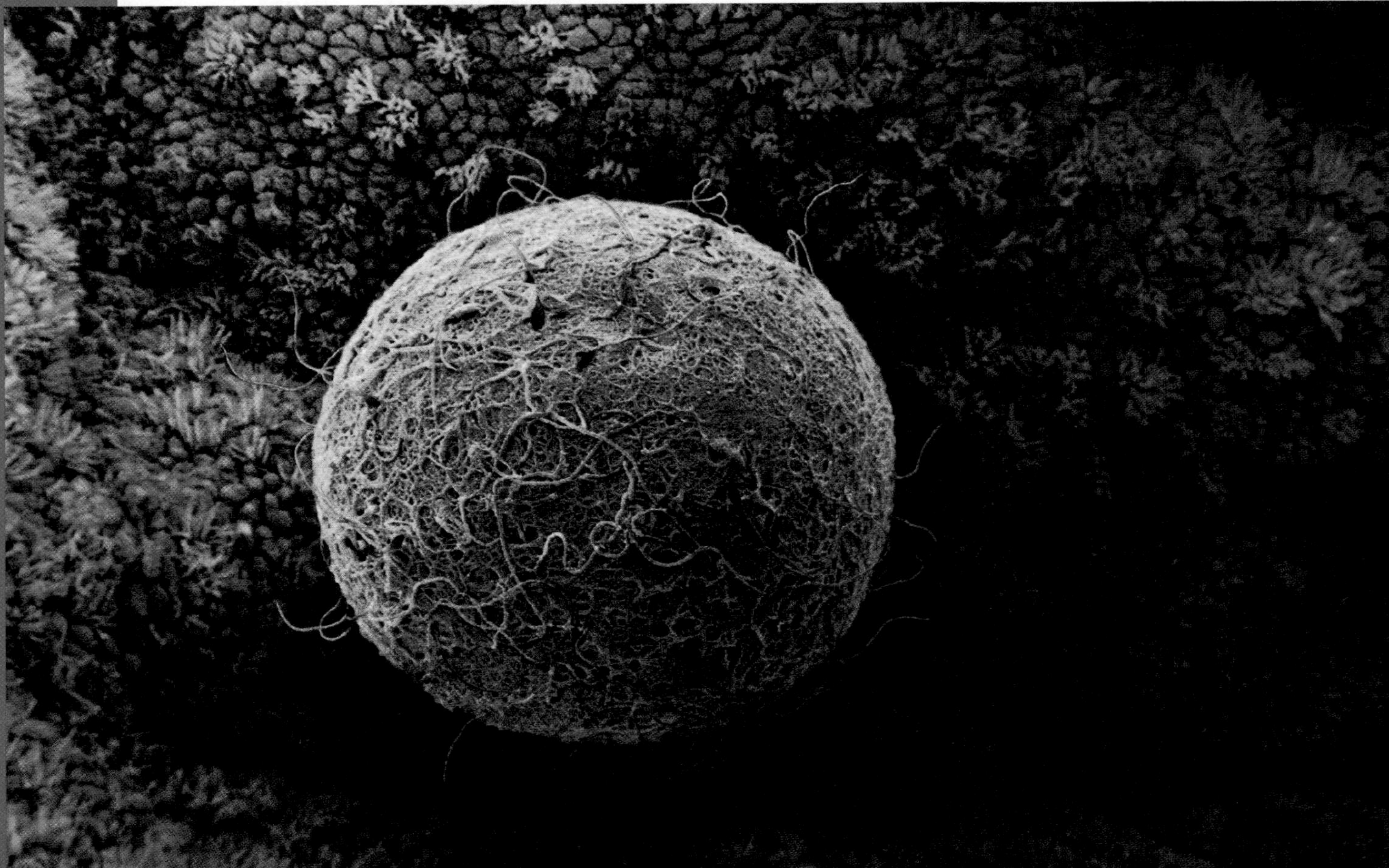

Key Concepts

Concept 33.1 — Reproductive organs produce and transport gametes.

Concept 33.2 — Hormones regulate the reproductive systems.

Concept 33.3 — Fertilization occurs in the oviduct.

Concept 33.4 — Embryonic and fetal development occurs in the uterus.

Concept 33.5 — Development is a lifelong process.

Concept 33.6 — Maintaining a healthy reproductive system requires knowledge.

Assessment — Chapter 33 Review

What's Online

www.biology.com

WebQuest
TwinQuest

Online Activity 33.1
Play a reproductive system matching game.

Lab 33 Online Companion
Name That Tube

Online Activity 33.2
Analyze the female reproductive cycles.

Online Activity 33.3
Follow an oocyte.

Online Activity 33.4
Trace an embryo's development.

Science, Technology, & Society
Fetal Surgery

Online Activity 33.5
Take the life stages challenge.

Online Activity 33.6
Investigate STD causes and symptoms.

Chapter 33 Assessment

CONCEPT 33.1

Reproductive organs produce and transport gametes.

OBJECTIVES

- Identify key female and male reproductive structures and their functions.
- Compare and contrast egg cell and sperm cell development.

KEY TERMS

- ovary
- follicle
- oviduct
- uterus
- cervix
- vagina
- testis
- scrotum
- epididymis
- semen
- vas deferens
- penis
- ovulation
- ovum

What's Online

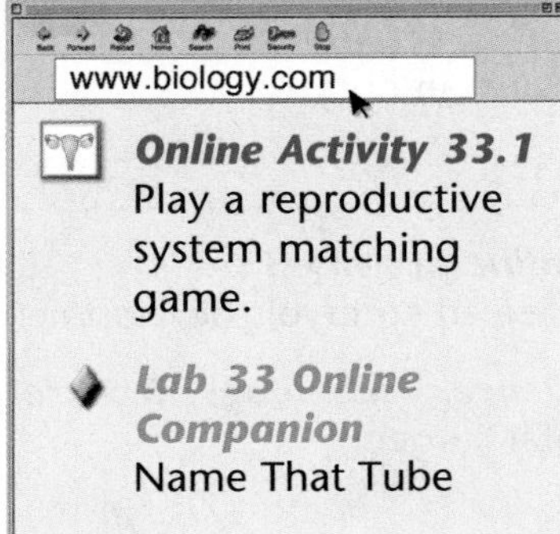

In mammalian reproduction, the female produces eggs and gives birth to offspring. Humans are no exception. The female reproductive system produces the egg cell and nurtures the developing baby. The male reproductive system generates sperm cells. In this section you will read about the specialized organs that carry out these functions. You will also read more about the processes involved in producing egg and sperm cells.

The Female Reproductive System

The female reproductive structures include the ovaries, oviducts, uterus, and vagina (Figure 33-1). Each of the two **ovaries** are shaped like, and are about twice the size of, an almond. They are the organs in which egg cells are produced. Within the ovaries, each developing egg cell is contained inside a **follicle,** a cluster of cells that surround, protect, and nourish a developing egg cell. Just above each ovary is the open end of an **oviduct** (also called a fallopian or uterine tube). The oviduct is a narrow tube about 10 cm long, which serves as a passageway to the uterus. The oviduct is normally the site of fertilization. The **uterus** is a hollow, muscular organ with thick walls, roughly the size and shape of a pear. If an egg is fertilized by a sperm cell, the uterus functions to contain and protect the developing baby. The neck of the uterus, called the **cervix,** connects the uterus to the vagina. The **vagina** is a flexible, thin-walled organ about 9 cm long. The vagina has several functions: it receives the penis and sperm during intercourse; it is the birth canal through which the baby exits during birth; and it is a passageway for menstrual flow.

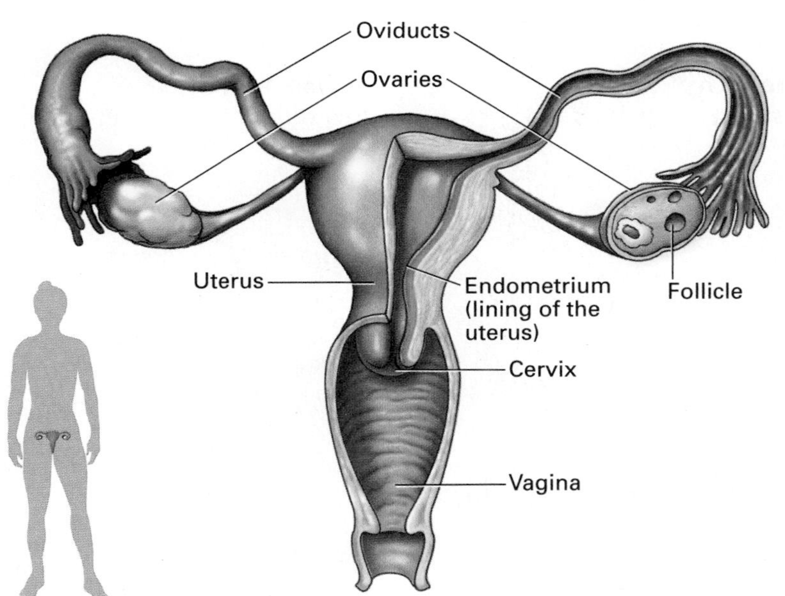

Figure 33-1 The female reproductive system produces female gametes (eggs), provides a receptacle for male gametes (sperm), and provides structures for nourishing and protecting a baby.

The Male Reproductive System

The main male reproductive structures are the testes, scrotum, epididymis, vas deferens, and penis (Figure 33-2). Sperm cells begin their development in a pair of organs called **testes** (singular, *testis*). The testes are contained in a sac-like structure called the **scrotum.** Since sperm cells cannot develop at normal body temperature, one function of the scrotum is to house the testes outside the main body cavity, a location that is 1° to 3°C cooler than normal body temperature. Sperm complete their development and are stored in the **epididymis,** a long, thin, coiled tube attached to each testis.

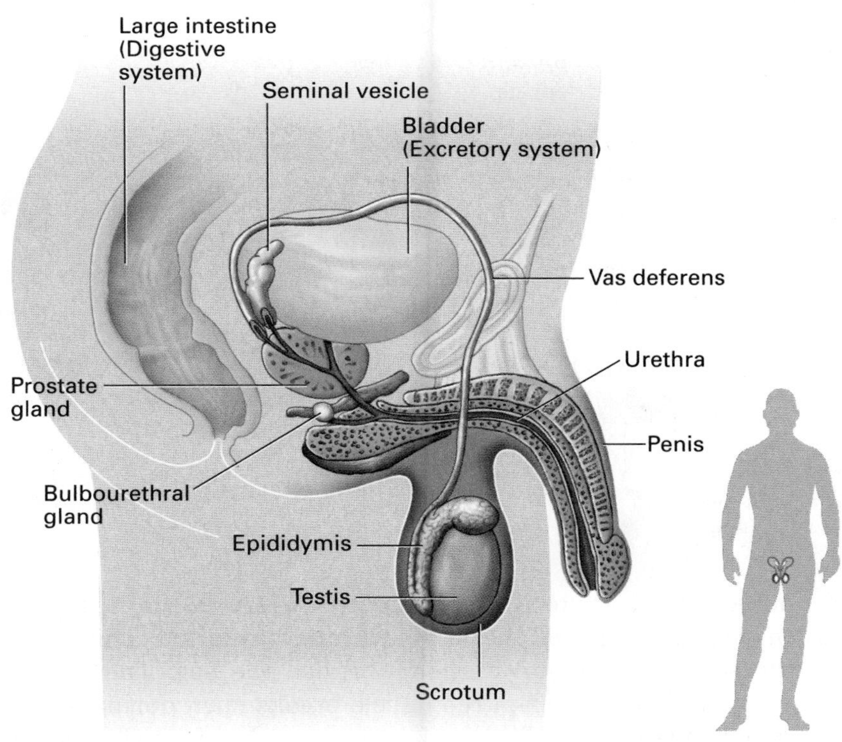

▲ **Figure 33-2** The male reproductive system produces sperm cells and provides a mechanism for delivering them to the female's body.

The male reproductive system also includes the seminal vesicles, the prostate gland, and the bulbourethral glands. These glands secrete fluids that function in the transport and survival of sperm. The fluids, along with sperm cells, make up **semen,** the substance that is emitted during the process called ejaculation. During ejaculation, muscular contractions propel sperm from the epididymis through connecting ducts called the **vas deferens** and finally through the urethra. The urethra is also the tube through which urine flows. When ejaculation takes place, muscles at the base of the urethra contract and close off the outlet from the bladder. This enables the urethra to perform its dual functions. The urethra passes through the **penis,** an organ consisting mainly of specialized tissue called erectile tissue. Filling of this tissue with blood causes an erection.

Development of Eggs and Sperm

As you read in Chapter 9, animals that reproduce sexually produce sex cells (gametes) through the process of meiosis. Most of the cells in the human body are diploid and contain 46 chromosomes (23 pairs). However, sex cells (eggs and sperm) are haploid and contain 23 single chromosomes. You can follow the process through which these cells are produced in Figure 33-3 on the next page.

Egg Cells Development of egg cells actually begins before a female is born, when a diploid cell in each follicle begins meiosis. The result is a primary oocyte (OH oh syt), a diploid cell that is in the prophase stage of meiosis I. At this stage the process pauses. Some of the oocytes disintegrate, and by the time a human female reaches puberty her ovaries contain about 400,000 follicles. Each follicle contains a resting primary oocyte that could develop into a mature egg cell. Beginning at

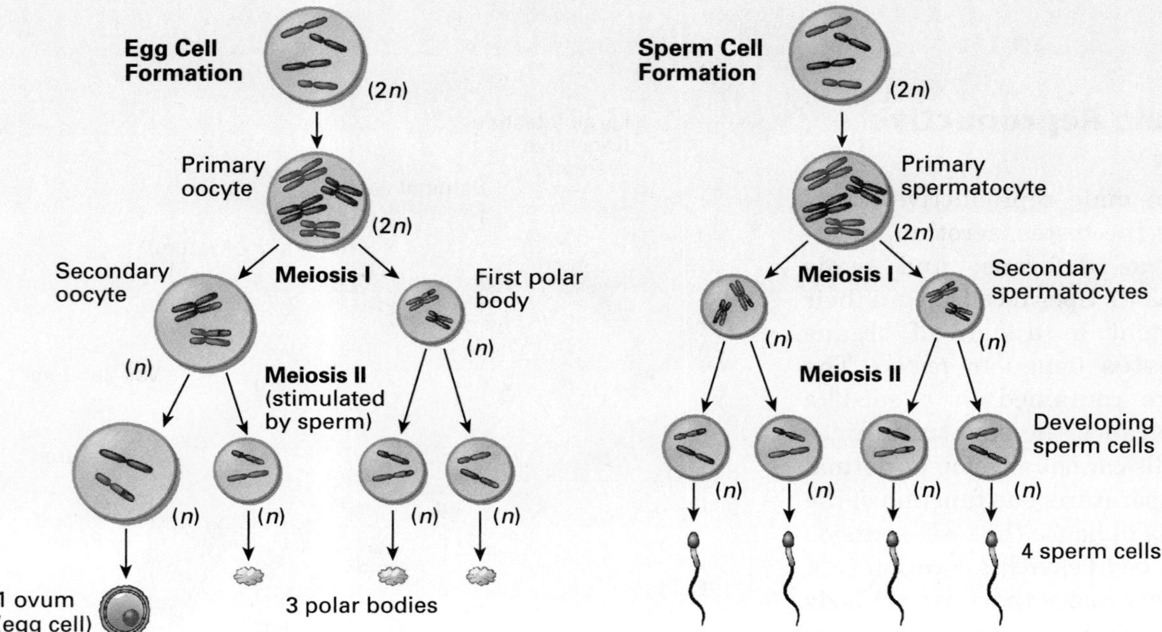

puberty, and occuring approximately every 28 days, hormones cause one follicle and the oocyte within it to mature. This produces the secondary oocyte, commonly called the egg. The secondary oocyte is released when the follicle breaks open during a process called **ovulation.** Meiosis II is not completed unless the egg is penetrated by a sperm cell. As soon as this occurs, the secondary oocyte undergoes its final meiotic division. This forms the **ovum,** the mature egg cell with a haploid nucleus that is capable of fusing with the sperm nucleus.

Sperm Cells The development of sperm cells begins when males reach puberty and lasts well into old age. The process begins with the primary spermatocyte within the testis. In contrast to meiosis of the primary oocyte, which produces just one egg cell, meiosis of the primary spermatocyte produces four haploid sperm cells. Sperm cells move from the testes to the epididymis where they complete their development. A mature sperm has a tail (flagellum) that enables it to swim within the female reproductive tract. A male has the potential to produce up to 400,000,000 sperm cells each day.

▲ **Figure 33-3** This figure simplifies the processes of egg and sperm cell development by beginning with only four chromosomes. Note that for each primary oocyte that undergoes meiosis, only one of the four cells produced survives as the ovum (egg). The other three cells, called polar bodies, break down. In contrast, for each primary spermatocyte that undergoes meiosis, all four cells produced normally develop into sperm cells.

Online Activity 33.1

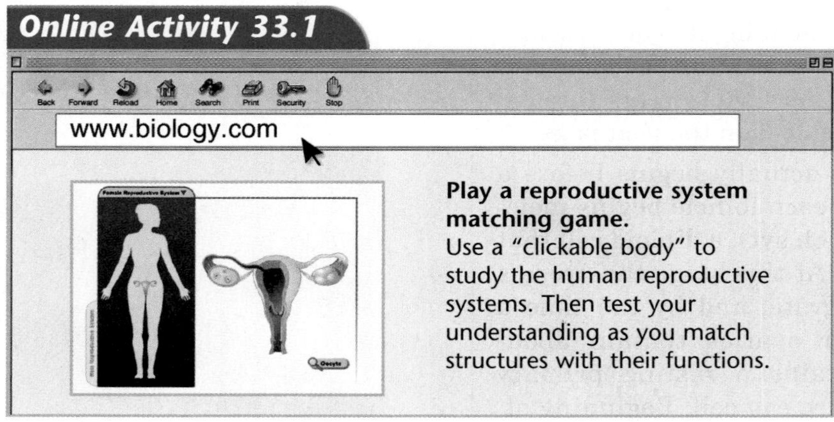

Play a reproductive system matching game.
Use a "clickable body" to study the human reproductive systems. Then test your understanding as you match structures with their functions.

Concept Check 33.1

1. List the major structures of the female reproductive system and describe the function of each.
2. List and describe the structures involved in the production and transport of sperm.
3. Describe one way in which the development of sperm cells differs from the development of egg cells.

Name That Tube

Form and Function in Tubules of the Reproductive System

Questions How are the structural features of tubules (very thin tubes) involved in sperm and egg transport related to their functions? How can structural features help you identify these tubules under a microscope?

Lab Overview In this investigation you will use a microscope to view slides with cross sections of unidentified mammalian reproductive tubules. Then use your observations of structural features to identify male and female tubules.

Preparing for the Lab To help you prepare for the investigation, go to the *Lab 33 Online Companion.* ···➔ Find out more about tubules in the reproductive system and discover how form follows function. Prepare for the lab procedure by previewing the steps you will take.

Completing the Lab Use your Laboratory Manual or lab page printouts from the *Lab 33 Online Companion* to do the investigation and draw conclusions from the observations you made. **CAUTION:** *Be sure to follow your teacher's instructions and all safety guidelines in the investigation.*

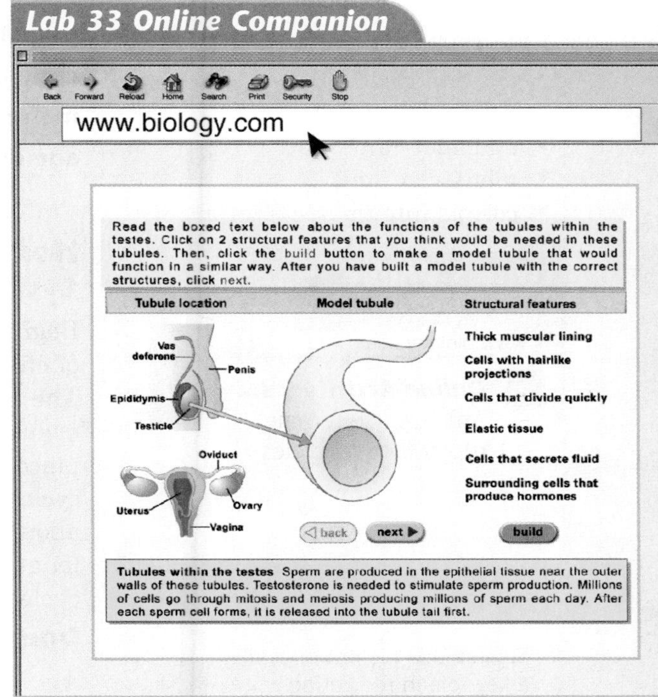

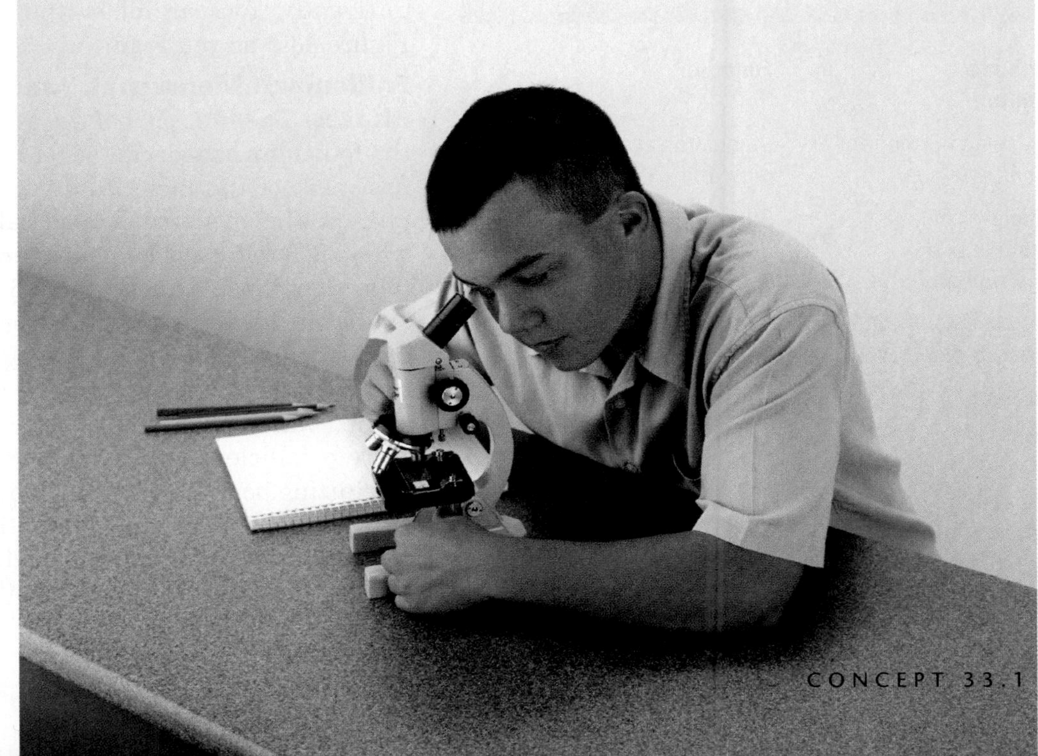

CONCEPT 33.2

Hormones regulate the reproductive systems.

OBJECTIVES
- Describe the role of hormones in the ovarian and menstrual cycles.
- Describe how hormones regulate the testes.

KEY TERMS
- ovarian cycle
- menstrual cycle
- endometrium
- menstruation
- corpus luteum

What's Online

www.biology.com

Online Activity 33.2 Analyze the female reproductive cycles.

Each month the mature female body prepares for the possibility of pregnancy. If pregnancy does not occur, the body sheds the prepared tissues and the process starts all over again. This monthly cycle is controlled by hormones. Meanwhile, hormones in the mature male body continuously regulate the production and storage of hundreds of millions of sperm cells each day.

Hormonal Control of the Female Reproductive System

Beginning at puberty, female reproductive organs undergo a cycle of changes that prepare the body for the possibility of pregnancy. The **ovarian cycle** refers to cyclic changes that occur in the ovaries. The **menstrual cycle** refers to cyclic changes that take place in the uterus. The secretion of hormones coordinates the two cycles (Figure 33-4). The ovarian and menstrual cycles average about 28 days in length. However, it is not unusual for cycle lengths to vary between 24 to 35 days. The length of a woman's cycles may also change from one cycle to the next.

One Cycle, Two Organs The ovarian and menstrual cycles are really two processes of one coordinated cycle. They occur during the same period of time and are regulated by hormones. These hormones, however, affect the two organs—the ovaries and uterus—differently. You can follow the cycles together in Figure 33-5 as you read.

Follicular, Menstrual, and Proliferation Phases The first part of the ovarian cycle, called the follicular phase, can be 9 to 20 days long. The first part of the menstrual cycle consists of two phases: the menstrual (also called flow) phase, which is 3 to 5 days long on average; and the proliferation phase, which can be 6 to 14 days long.

At the beginning of the cycles, estrogen levels in the body are low. Low estrogen levels trigger the hypothalamus to secrete a releasing hormone, which causes the anterior pituitary to secrete follicle-stimulating hormone (FSH) and luteinizing hormone (LH). In one of the ovaries, the rising levels of FSH cause one of the follicles and its oocyte to start to mature. Meanwhile, in the uterus, the low levels of estrogen cause the uterine lining,

▼ **Figure 33-4** Hormones play a key role in regulating female reproductive cycles.

Effects of Reproductive Hormones in Females

Hormone *(Source)*	Function
Releasing hormone *(Hypothalamus)*	Stimulates anterior pituitary
Follicle-stimulating hormone (FSH) *(Anterior pituitary)*	Stimulates follicle and oocyte development in ovary
Luteinizing hormone (LH) *(Anterior pituitary)*	Causes follicle to mature and break open
Estrogen *(Follicle and corpus luteum)*	Causes endometrium thickening; development of secondary sex characteristics
Progesterone *(Corpus luteum)*	Causes and maintains endometrium thickening

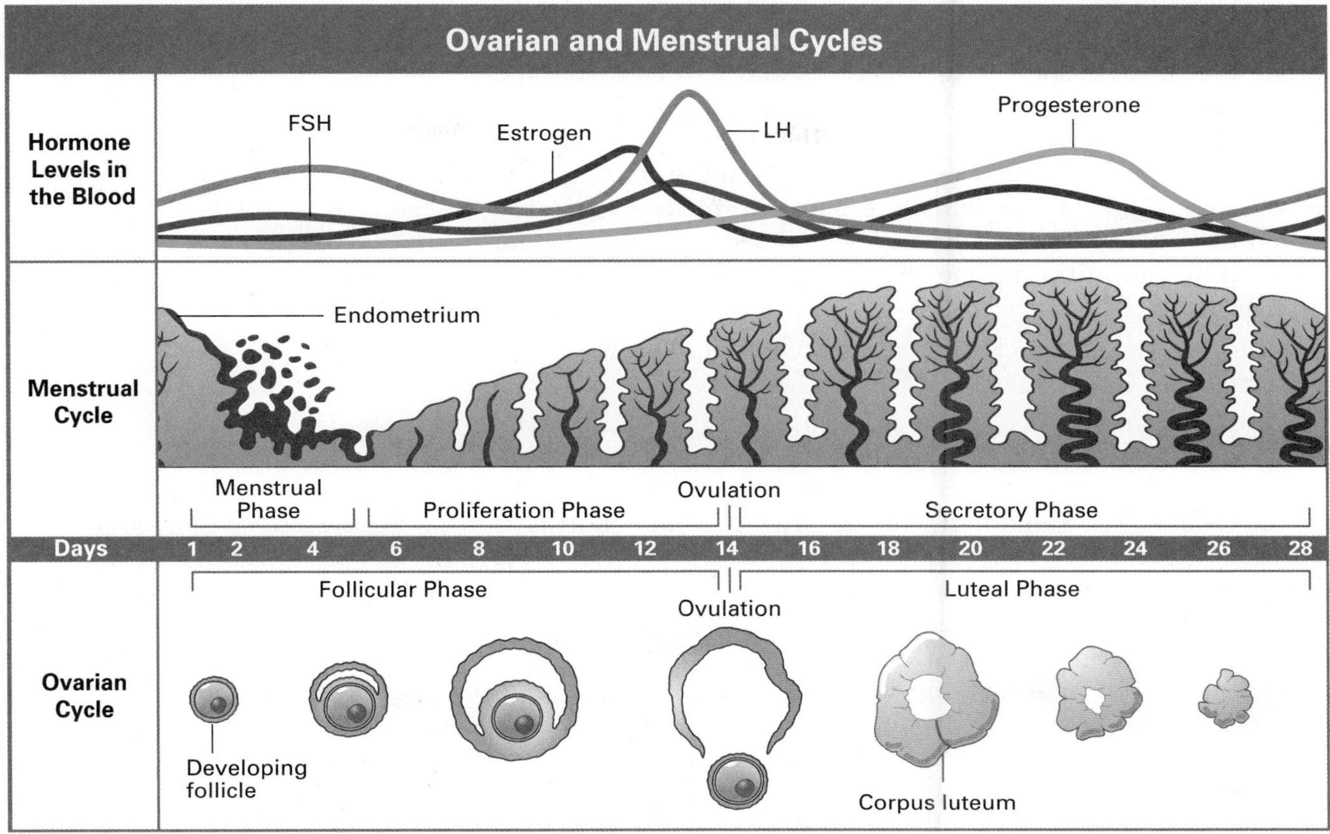

▲ **Figure 33-5** Changes occur in the ovaries and uterus as a result of different hormone levels over a 28-day period. Notice how these hormones have different effects on the ovaries and the uterus.

the **endometrium,** to break down. Epithelial cells, mucus, and about 40 mL of blood are discharged through the vagina in a process called **menstruation** (the flow phase of the menstrual cycle).

As the follicle matures, it secretes estrogen. The larger it becomes, the more estrogen it secretes. The slow rise of estrogen signals the hypothalamus to slow the secretion of releasing hormone. In turn, the anterior pituitary secretes less FSH and LH. In the ovaries, the lower FSH and LH levels prevent additional follicles from developing. In the uterus, the rising estrogen levels cause the endometrium to thicken, which is the proliferation phase. The thickened lining is a necessary preparation in case of pregnancy.

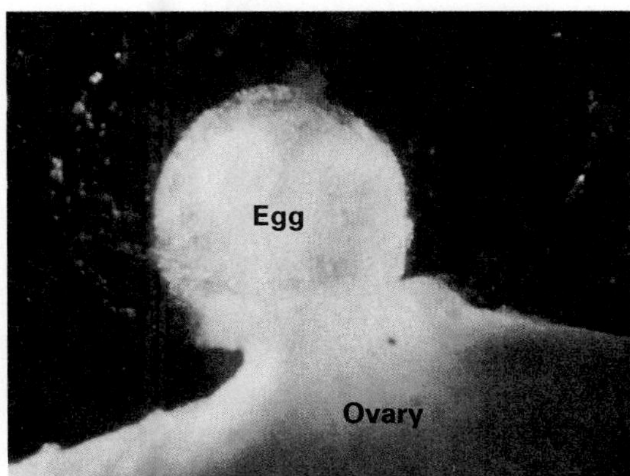

▲ **Figure 33-6** After ovulation, shown in this image, the cells remaining from the ruptured follicle form the corpus luteum.

Ovulation Phase (1 day) Around day 12 of an average-length cycle, the follicle reaches maturity, causing a rapid rise in levels of estrogen. This rapid rise in estrogen signals the hypothalamus to secrete high levels of releasing hormone. The anterior pituitary responds by secreting FSH and LH. In the ovaries, the high levels of LH cause the follicle to break open and release the egg into the oviduct in the process of ovulation (Figure 33-6).

Luteal and Secretory Phases (14 days) After the follicle breaks open, the remaining follicle cells form a structure called the corpus luteum (meaning "yellow body"). The **corpus luteum** secretes estrogen and progesterone, which stimulate the endometrium to thicken further in preparation for pregnancy.

If pregnancy does not occur, the corpus luteum begins to break down. As it does, it secretes less and less estrogen and progesterone. The lower levels of estrogen and progesterone signal the hypothalamus to secrete releasing hormone. This makes the anterior pituitary secrete FSH and LH. In the ovaries, high FSH levels signal a new follicle to mature. In the uterus, the falling estrogen and progesterone levels cause the endometrium to break down, initiating menstruation and starting the cycle all over again.

Hormonal Regulation of the Testes

The hypothalamus and anterior pituitary gland also control the male reproductive system (Figure 33-7). Note that the hypothalamic and pituitary hormones are named for their function in the female. The same hormones exist in the male, but have different effects. Beginning at puberty, the hypothalamus starts secreting a releasing hormone. As in females, this causes the anterior pituitary to secrete FSH and LH. In males, rising levels of LH signal the testes to produce and secrete testosterone. The combination of FSH and testosterone stimulates sperm production within the testes. Increases in testosterone levels signal the hypothalamus to decrease secretion of releasing hormone. Likewise, decreases in testosterone levels signal the hypothalamus to increase secretion of releasing hormone. In this way, the body regulates hormone levels and sperm production by a negative feedback loop. (To review negative feedback loops, see Concept 32.1.)

Figure 33-7 Hormone secretions regulate sperm production in males.

Effects of Reproductive Hormones in Males

Hormone ***(Source)***	**Function**
Releasing hormone *(Hypothalamus)*	Stimulates anterior pituitary
Follicle-stimulating hormone (FSH) *(Anterior pituitary)*	Stimulates sperm production
Luteinizing hormone (LH) *(Anterior pituitary)*	Stimulates testes to produce testosterone
Testosterone *(Testes)*	Stimulates sperm production; development of secondary sex characteristics

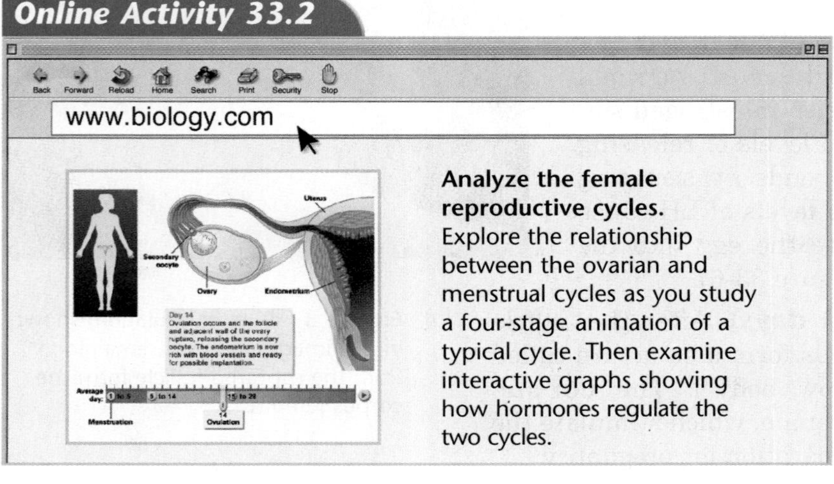

Concept Check 33.2

1. How does estrogen help prepare the female body for pregnancy?
2. What hormones in males stimulate sperm production in the testes?
3. Compare and contrast the role of FSH and LH in the female and male reproductive systems.

CONCEPT 33.3 Fertilization occurs in the oviduct.

OBJECTIVES
- Describe the process of fertilization.
- Follow the human developmental process from a zygote to an embryo.
- Explain how fertilization can result in twins.

KEY TERMS
- fertilization
- zygote
- cleavage
- blastocyst
- trophoblast
- embryo
- implantation

What's Online

Human development begins when the nuclei of a sperm and egg cell fuse. After fertilization, the zygote (fertilized egg) begins dividing. At first all the cells look identical, but they eventually differentiate, forming a complex organism. In this section, you will read about the developmental events from fertilization through the time the embryo enters the uterus.

Fertilization

Fertilization occurs when the egg and sperm cells fuse. When a sperm cell penetrates the egg, meiosis II is completed and the ovum is formed. Within the ovum, the nuclei of the sperm and ovum fuse, forming a diploid nucleus. This fertilized egg cell is called a **zygote.** Successful fertilization requires living sperm in the oviduct on the day of, or shortly after, ovulation. On average, hundreds of millions of sperm are deposited in the female's vagina during intercourse. Yet, only one sperm is necessary to fertilize the egg. Why so many sperm? Once deposited in the vagina, each sperm must travel approximately 18 cm to reach an oviduct. Only a few hundred sperm survive the trip due to a variety of factors including the 50/50 chance of entering the wrong oviduct (the one that doesn't contain the egg).

If an oocyte is present when sperm are in the oviduct, many sperm will attach to the oocyte's surface. Each sperm cell has a capsule at the forward end, called an acrosome, which contains enzymes that help the sperm cell penetrate the protective coats of the oocyte (Figure 33-8). Once one sperm successfully contacts the plasma membrane of the oocyte, a barrier forms on the oocyte's surface that prevents other sperm from entering. This ensures that just one sperm nucleus will be present to fuse with the ovum nucleus.

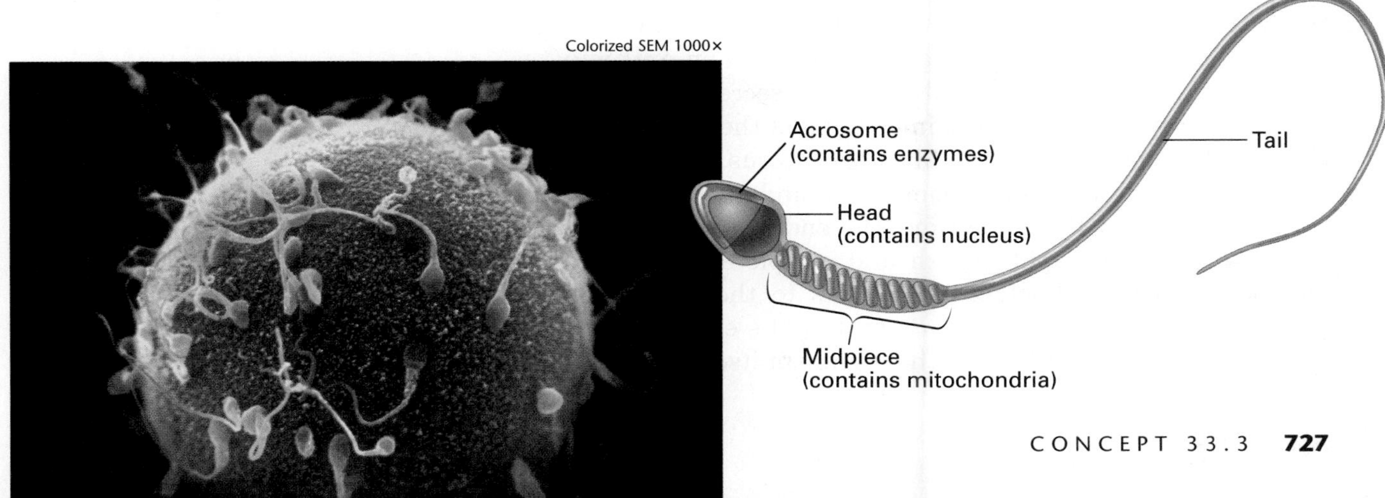

▼ **Figure 33-8** This colorized micrograph shows numerous sperm cells on the surface of a much larger secondary oocyte. Numerous mitochondria provide energy to move the tail, enabling the sperm cell to "swim" through the female reproductive system. Enzymes in the acrosome enable the sperm to penetrate the protective coats of the oocyte.

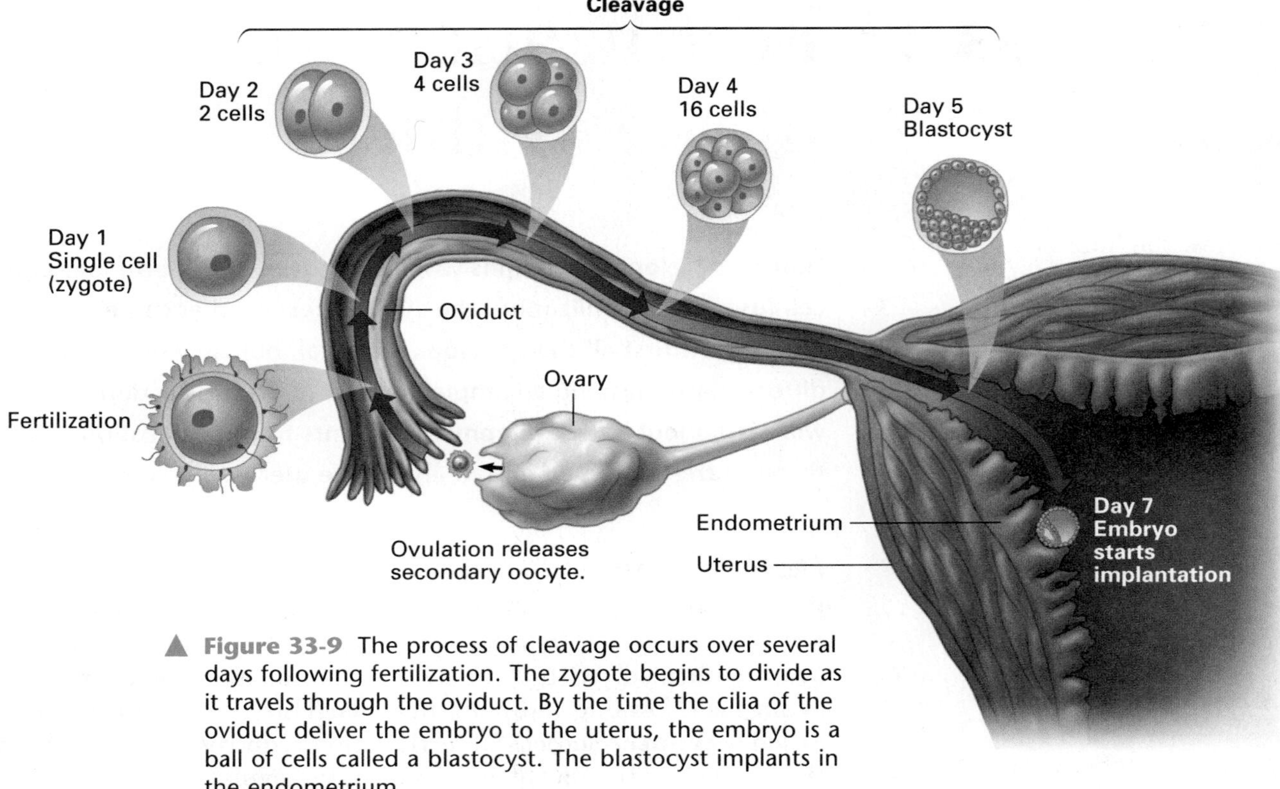

▲ **Figure 33-9** The process of cleavage occurs over several days following fertilization. The zygote begins to divide as it travels through the oviduct. By the time the cilia of the oviduct deliver the embryo to the uterus, the embryo is a ball of cells called a blastocyst. The blastocyst implants in the endometrium.

Human Development: The First Week

Fertilization usually occurs in the region of the oviduct nearest the ovary. By about 36 hours after fertilization, a process called **cleavage** has begun, during which the zygote undergoes a series of rapid mitotic divisions (Figure 33-9). The process of cleavage produces a large number of daughter cells that serve as building blocks for the developing organism.

By about the fifth day, cleavage has produced a ball of about 100 cells that has reached the uterus with the help of cilia in the oviduct. This ball of cells is called a **blastocyst,** a fluid-filled sphere consisting of an outer layer of cells and a group of cells inside the sphere (Figure 33-10). The outer layer of cells is called the **trophoblast,** and the cluster of cells within the sphere is called the inner cell mass. From the beginning of cleavage until the first body structures begin to appear (about nine weeks after fertilization), the developing organism is called an **embryo.**

Within the uterus, trophoblast cells secrete enzymes that stimulate **implantation,** the imbedding of the blastocyst in the thickened endometrium that lines the uterus. The trophoblast grows, extending into the endometrium and anchoring the blastocyst in place. At the same time, the endometrium responds to implantation with rapid growth and completely surrounds the blastocyst. The trophoblast contributes to the development of membranes that will nourish and protect the embryo. The inner cell mass will eventually form the organism itself.

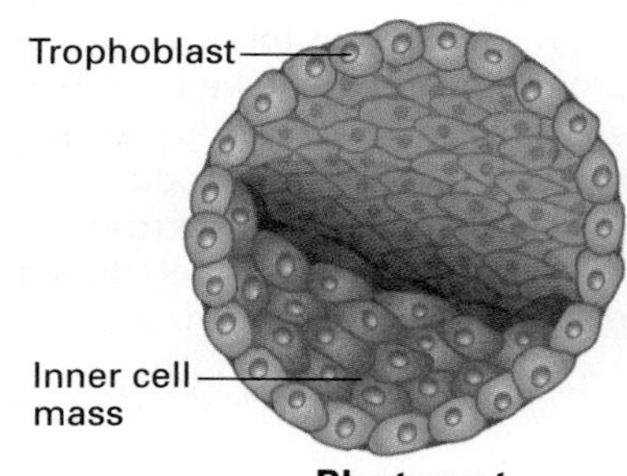

▲ **Figure 33-10** A blastocyst forms nearly a week after fertilization.

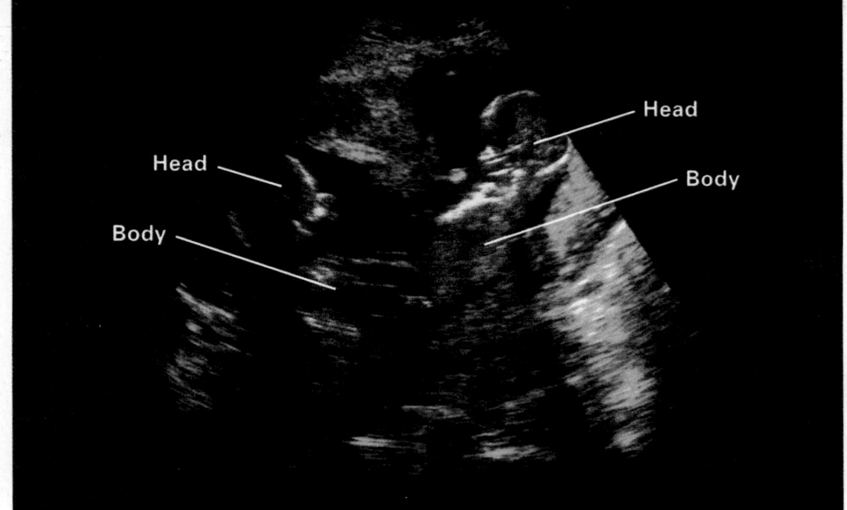

◀ **Figure 33-11** This image is the result of an ultrasound, a procedure that can show if twins are present.

▲ **Figure 33-12** Because identical twins both come from a single zygote, they carry the same genetic information.

Twins and "Supertwins"

Although fertilization usually results in one embryo, occasionally multiple embryos are produced (Figure 33-11). Two embryos are called twins, and more than two are called "supertwins" (triplets, quadruplets, quintuplets, etc.). Twins and supertwins may be either fraternal or identical (Figure 33-12). Fraternal twins are the result of more than one egg being fertilized during an ovarian cycle. For this to happen, both ovaries must release an egg, or one ovary must release two eggs. Occasionally, one or both ovaries will release multiple eggs. If three or more of these eggs become fertilized, fraternal supertwins can result. Each zygote of fraternal twins and supertwins is formed from a different egg and sperm. As a result, the genetic information for fraternal twins is different for each individual, in the same way that brothers and sisters born at different times have different genetic material.

Identical twins are the result of one early-stage embryo splitting into two. For example, after the zygote divides for the first time, the two cells may separate and give rise to two embryos. This is an example of natural "cloning," or creating a genetic duplicate. Identical twins carry the same set of chromosomes from the original sperm and egg that formed the initial zygote. That is why identical siblings look so much alike and are the same gender. Although less likely, the embryo can split multiple times producing identical supertwins.

Online Activity 33.3

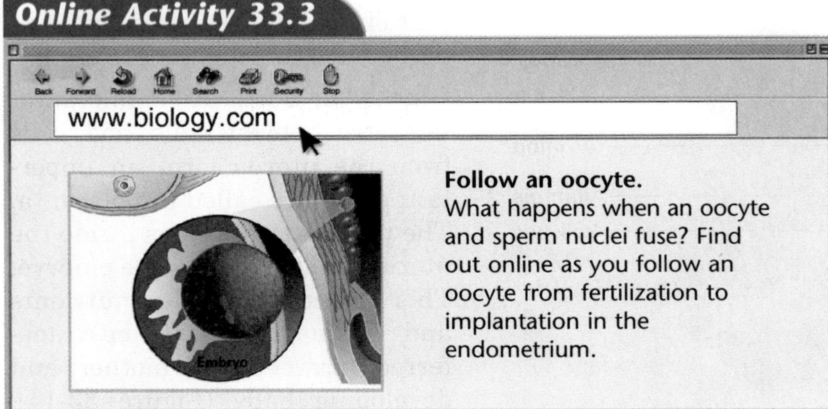

Follow an oocyte.
What happens when an oocyte and sperm nuclei fuse? Find out online as you follow an oocyte from fertilization to implantation in the endometrium.

Concept Check 33.3

1. What role does a sperm cell's acrosome play in fertilization?
2. Describe the first week of human development.
3. Compare and contrast identical and fraternal twins.

CONCEPT 33.4

Embryonic and fetal development occurs in the uterus.

OBJECTIVES
- Identify changes that take place during the first, second, and third trimesters of pregnancy.
- Explain the importance of good nutrition during pregnancy.
- Describe how hormones regulate childbirth.

KEY TERMS
- gastrulation
- placenta
- fetus
- labor
- oxytocin

What's Online

www.biology.com

Online Activity 33.4
Trace an embryo's development.

Science, Technology, & Society
Fetal Surgery

A human female carries a developing baby for about nine months before giving birth. During the nine months leading up to a human's birth, a vast number of changes occur. Development that takes place in the uterus is divided into three trimesters, which are each about three months long. As the moment of birth nears, it is once again hormonal secretions that regulate the process.

The First Trimester

At implantation the embryo consists of the trophoblast and an inner mass of cells. The inner cell mass gradually gives rise to the organs and tissues of the embryo. The cells of this inner mass are also called stem cells.

Gastrulation Approximately three weeks after fertilization, a process called gastrulation takes place. **Gastrulation** forms three cell layers: ectoderm, endoderm, and mesoderm. The ectoderm (outer layer) forms the outer part of the embryo's skin and the central nervous system. The endoderm (inner layer) forms the digestive tract and lungs. The mesoderm (middle layer) forms most of the other organs (Figure 33-13).

Membranes During the first few weeks, membranes form that protect and nourish the embryo. One membrane, the amnion, forms a fluid-filled sac. The amniotic membrane protects the embryo from physical impact. The yolk sac membrane produces the first blood cells and is the source of cells that eventually form gametes. The chorion is a third membrane that becomes the embryo's portion of the placenta. Lastly, the allantois forms part of the umbilical cord that connects the embryo to the placenta.

Placenta Soon after implantation, trophoblast cells and cells from the uterus form an important structure called the placenta. The **placenta** develops inside the uterus and surrounds the embryo. This structure enables nutrients and waste products to be transferred between the mother and developing baby (Figure 33-14).

Figure 33-13 Four membranes protect and nourish the embryo, which consists of three tissue layers.

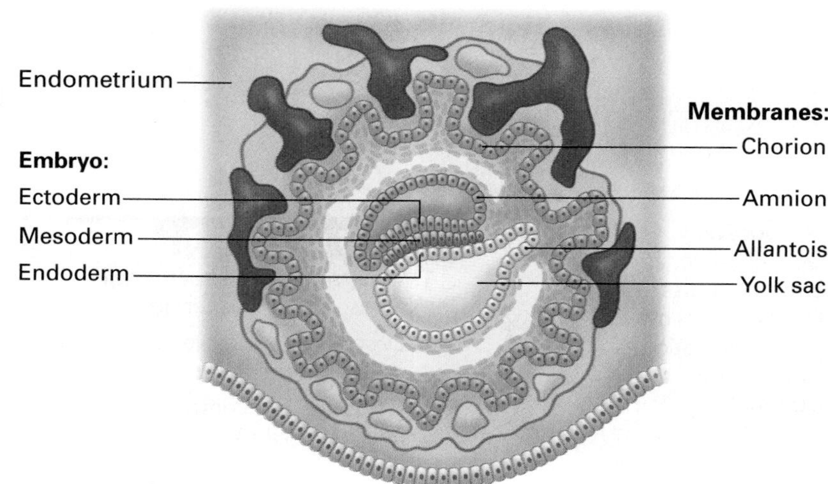

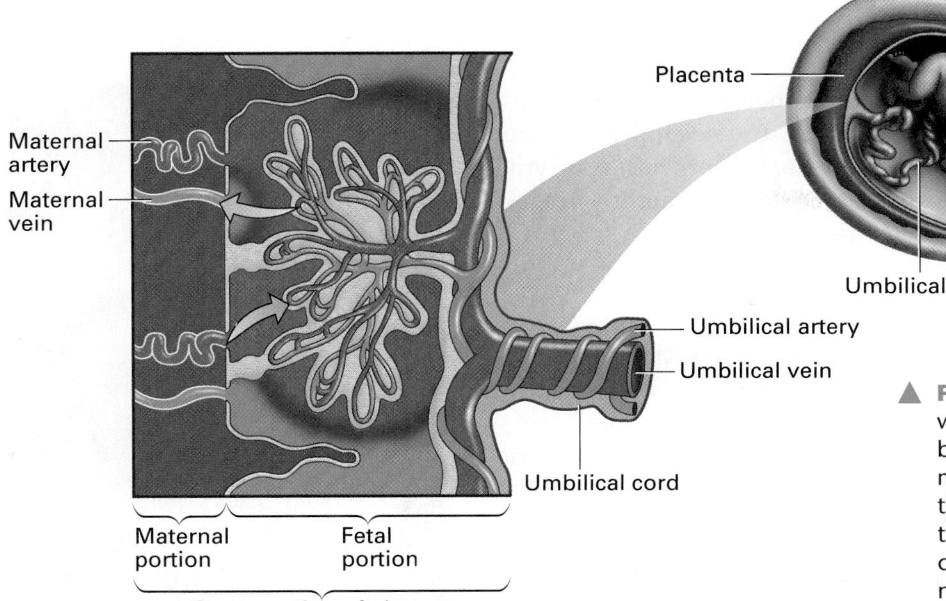

▲ **Figure 33-14** Nutrients and waste products are exchanged between the fetus and the mother within the placenta. Note that the umbilical vein is red in this diagram, indicating that it is carrying oxygen-rich blood and nutrients to the fetus. The umbilical arteries are blue, indicating that they carry oxygen-depleted blood and waste products away from the fetus.

By the end of the third month, the placenta is fully formed and functional. In the wall of the placenta, the mother's blood and baby's blood remain isolated in separate circulatory systems. However, the mother's blood vessels release pools of blood very close to the baby's blood vessels. Nutrients and waste products are able to diffuse back and forth through interstitial fluid from one blood system to the other.

From week 9 until birth, the developing human is called a **fetus.** At nine weeks, the fetus is approximately 3 cm long, about the length of a paper clip. It has all of its organs and major body parts, including a head that is large in proportion to its body (Figure 33-15a). By the end of the first trimester, the fetus can move its arms and legs, turn its head, frown, and make sucking motions.

The Second Trimester

During weeks 12 through 23, the period of the second trimester, the fetus increases in length to about 25 cm. By the end of this period, the fetus weighs about 0.5 kg and has the face of an infant, complete with eyebrows and eyelashes (Figure 33-15b). At this point, the fetal heartbeat is easily detected and the fetus can be quite active. The mother can usually feel this activity, which ranges from flutters to kicks and pokes. Because the fetus is now filling up much of the space in the uterus, it curls forward into what is referred to as the "fetal position."

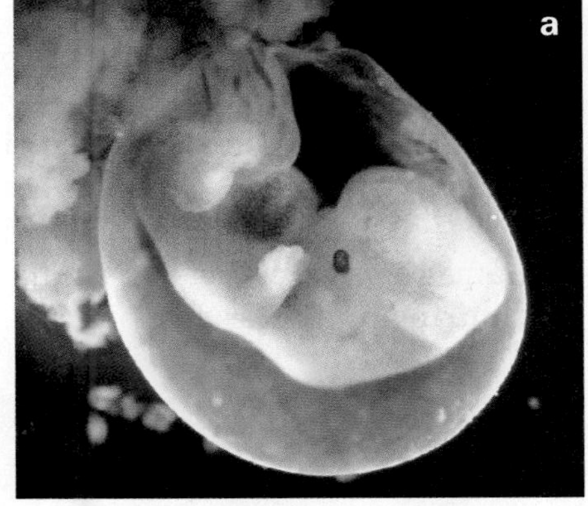

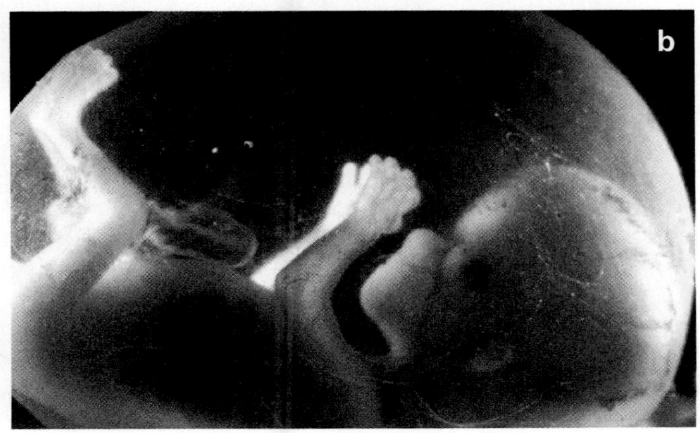

▶ **Figure 33-15** Embryo and fetal development occurs over about 38 weeks. **a.** The arms and legs of this 6-week-old embryo have started to develop. **b.** This 16-week-old fetus shows further development of body structures.

During this period there is also an important change in hormone secretion by the placenta. Early in the second trimester, the placenta starts secreting progesterone, rather than receiving it from the corpus luteum. No longer needed to secrete progesterone, the corpus luteum disintegrates.

The Third Trimester

From week 24 until birth, the period of the third trimester, the fetus experiences rapid growth, becoming larger and gaining stronger bones and muscles (Figure 33-16). The respiratory and circulatory systems undergo changes that will enable the baby to start breathing air and perform other vital functions outside the mother's uterus when it is born. As it fills more and more of the available space in the uterus, the fetus becomes less active.

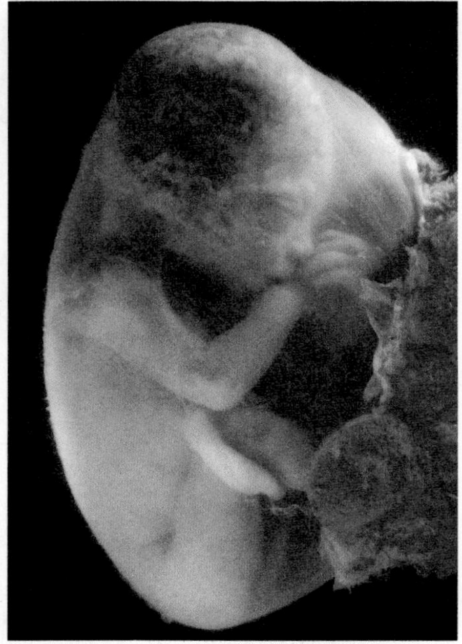

▲ **Figure 33-16** This fetus is nearing the end of the third trimester. At this stage, the further development of the head, arms, and legs is visible.

Importance of Nutrition During Pregnancy

During pregnancy, substances in the mother's bloodstream are transferred to the fetus's bloodstream. This is how the fetus is nourished for nine months. But this transfer process can pose a serious risk for the fetus if the mother doesn't have a healthy lifestyle. Alcohol, tobacco compounds, other drugs, and certain poisons can be transferred to the fetus and can impair normal development. It is important for the mother to eat a balanced diet and avoid alcohol and other damaging substances during her pregnancy.

As an example, excessive alcohol use during pregnancy is linked to a condition in the baby known as fetal alcohol syndrome. Symptoms of this condition include delayed physical development, decreased mental functioning, and abnormal facial features. Maintaining a healthy lifestyle, including a balanced diet and regular exercise, is important to the mother's health both during and after pregnancy.

Science, Technology, & Society

Back Forward Reload Home Search Print Security Stop

www.biology.com

Fetal Surgery

Advances in medicine are enabling doctors to surgically repair some medical problems in babies even before they are born. Examples include blocked airways, tumors, and problems associated with a condition called spina bifida. Though some risks to the mother and baby are involved, the benefits can be profound. Find out more about fetal surgery when you go online.

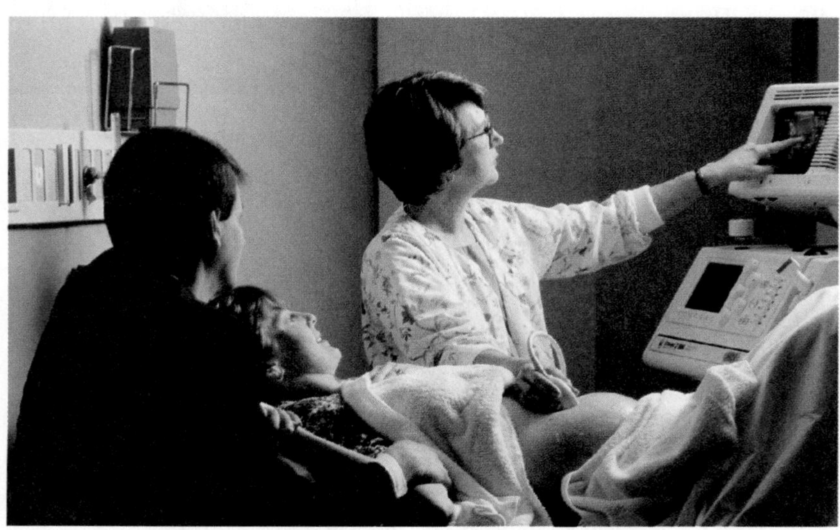

◀ **Figure 33-17** Ultrasound technology allows health-care providers and parents to get a glimpse of a fetus in the uterus.

Childbirth

At birth, the average baby is 40–50 cm long and weighs 2.7–4.5 kg (7–12 lbs), or about the size of a small watermelon. The baby is born as a result of a series of strong, rhythmic contractions of the muscles of the mother's uterus—a condition called **labor.** Once again, hormones of the endocrine system regulate the process. During the final weeks of pregnancy, estrogen levels peak. This causes cells to form in muscles of the uterus that serve as receptors for a hormone called **oxytocin.** As it reaches the final stages of development, the fetus and the mother's pituitary gland start to secrete oxytocin. This secretion causes the muscles of the uterus to begin contracting. These muscle contractions stimulate the secretion of more oxytocin, which causes more contractions, in an increasingly intense cycle that results in the baby being forced out of the uterus (Figure 33-18).

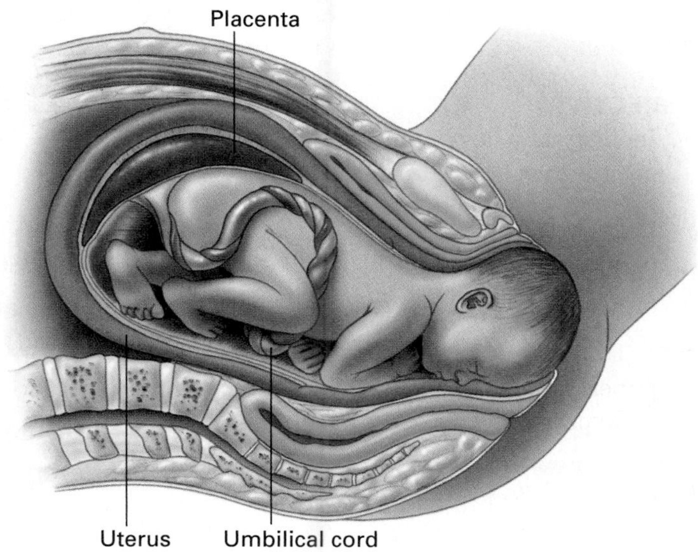

▲ **Figure 33-18** During labor, hormones stimulate the uterus to contract. The contractions push the baby out of the mother's body.

Within moments of entering its new world, the baby gasps its first breaths of air. Television and movies have not painted a very accurate picture of what a newborn really looks like. Immediately after birth, most infants are bluish in color and are covered with blood and mucus. Often the facial features are distorted from having been forced through the narrow opening of the cervix and vagina. Usually, these distortions disappear within a few hours, and of course each baby looks beautiful to its parents.

Shortly after birth, additional contractions force the placenta out of the uterus. This is sometimes called the afterbirth. The umbilical cord is tied off and cut. The remnant of the cord will eventually dry up and fall off on its own, leaving a familiar scar known as the navel, or belly button.

Online Activity 33.4

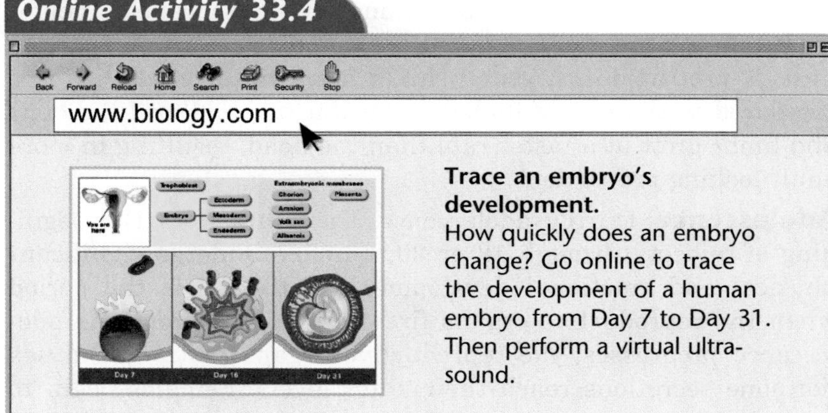

Trace an embryo's development.
How quickly does an embryo change? Go online to trace the development of a human embryo from Day 7 to Day 31. Then perform a virtual ultrasound.

Concept Check 33.4

1. What is the function of the placenta during pregnancy?
2. How can poor nutrition affect a developing fetus?
3. Explain what role hormones play in childbirth.
4. Describe the fetus during the second trimester.

CONCEPT 33.5

Development is a lifelong process.

OBJECTIVES

- Identify key developmental events that occur during infancy, childhood, and adolescence.
- Describe changes that occur during the aging process.

KEY TERMS

- puberty
- menopause

What's Online

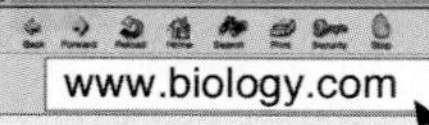

www.biology.com

Online Activity 33.5
Take the life stages challenge.

Infants are born with several basic reflexes. For example, an infant will suck on anything put into its mouth, and will tightly close its fingers around an object placed into its palm. Beyond these basic reflexes, all other growth and behavior from infancy through adulthood are the result of ongoing developmental events. Each stage of life—childhood, adolescence, adulthood, and old age—has its own biological milestones.

Infancy Through Adolescence

Though it may seem never-ending at the time, the infant, childhood, and adolescent years are only a small part of the average human's life. During that time, however, tremendous changes are taking place.

Infancy The first year of a baby's life is filled with rapid physical growth and major developmental gains. A newborn's muscular and nervous systems are poorly developed. However, a baby is born with vital basic reflexes. The sucking reflex enables a baby to respond to the touch of a nipple and receive nourishment. Another basic reflex that babies have is the ability to cry, signaling that they are hungry, tired, wet, or in pain.

Although a baby comes into the world still dependent on an adult's care, within a year or so the baby will be well on the way to eating solid foods, communicating, and walking (Figure 33-19).

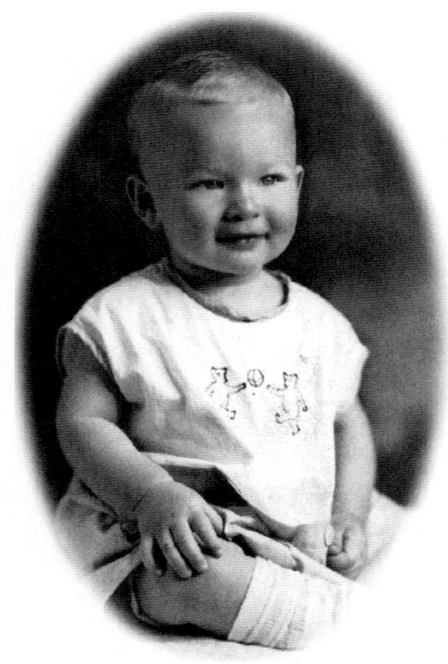

▲ **Figure 33-19** The photos on these two pages show the physical changes that occurred in the same person at ages 1, 18, 41, and 72.

Childhood From 12 months until around 12 or 13 years is the period called childhood. Most children absorb new information and skills quickly and learn to communicate effectively through speaking and writing. Children learn how to interact socially and emotionally with people inside and outside of their families.

Most physical changes during childhood are more gradual than those that occur during infancy. With each year, height increases and muscles are toned. There is also a gradual change in body proportions. A young child's head, for example, is large compared to the rest of its body. But during childhood the body and limbs grow at a faster rate than the head, resulting in more adult-looking proportions.

Adolescence During adolescence, the years from the beginning of puberty through 18 or 20, humans undergo significant physical and emotional development. **Puberty** is the period when the reproductive organs first become functional. As adolescence progresses, the reproductive organs mature, and sex hormone secretions reach their adult levels. Females begin to

▲ Age 18

ovulate and menstruate. Males start to produce sperm.

In response to sex hormones, female secondary sex characteristics develop, such as breasts and pubic hair. Males develop secondary sex characteristics such as broader shoulders, larger muscles, deeper voice, and pubic and facial hair. Emotionally, adolescence is a period when both females and males become more aware of themselves as independent humans and learn how they fit into the world.

Adulthood and Aging

After adolescence, the human body stops growing in height, and organ systems have matured. During the next couple of decades, many people focus on careers and family lives, seeking out mates and having children. However, the body changes with age. Women cannot become pregnant after they stop ovulating, usually in their 50s. **Menopause** is the time in life when a woman stops ovulating. Hormonal changes at menopause can cause physical symptoms. For example, low estrogen levels can cause decreased bone density. As men age, they produce decreasing levels of testosterone, but they continue to produce sperm well into old age.

As people age, they often experience more health problems. For example, decreased flexibility and memory loss can be sources of frustration for the elderly. A lifelong commitment to a healthy lifestyle can help minimize some of the negative aspects of aging.

▼ Age 41

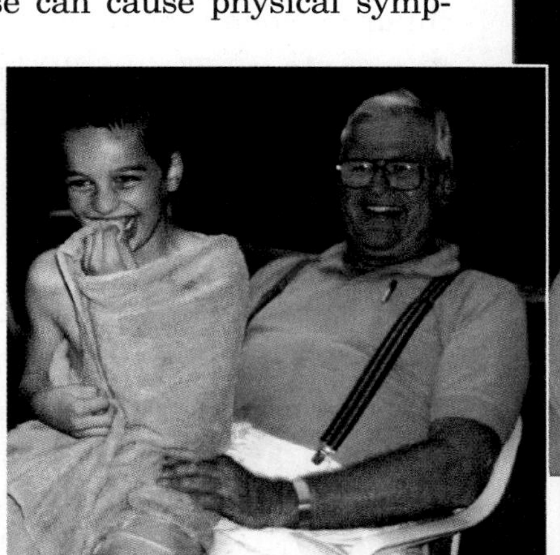

▲ Age 72

Online Activity 33.5

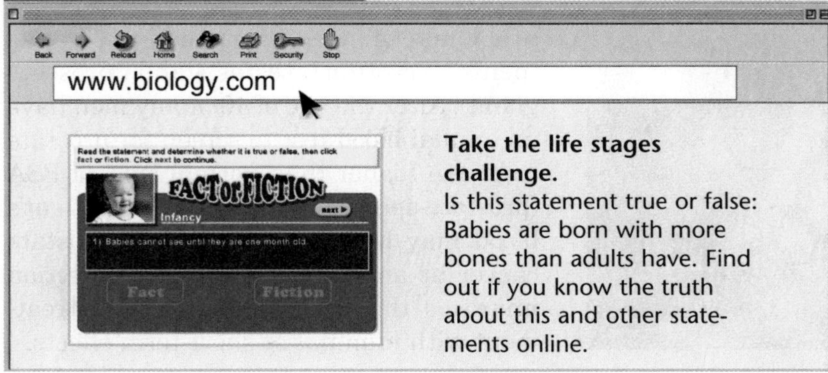

Take the life stages challenge.
Is this statement true or false: Babies are born with more bones than adults have. Find out if you know the truth about this and other statements online.

Concept Check 33.5

1. Describe an important developmental event for infancy, childhood, adolescence, adulthood, and old age.
2. Give one example of how adulthood is different from the three previous life stages.
3. Describe menopause and explain when it normally occurs.

CONCEPT 33.6

Maintaining a healthy reproductive system requires knowledge.

OBJECTIVES

- Identify medical specialties that focus on reproductive health.
- Describe different STDs and how they are treated.

KEY TERMS

- gynecology
- urology
- sexually transmitted disease (STD)

What's Online

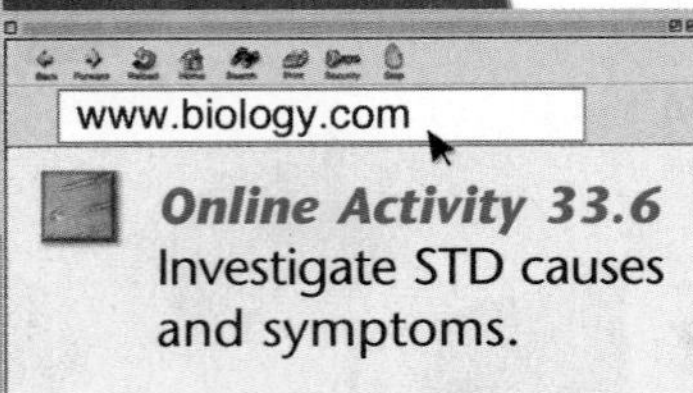

Online Activity 33.6 Investigate STD causes and symptoms.

As with other organ systems, there are steps you can take throughout life to maintain the good health of your reproductive system. It is especially important to be aware of and prevent diseases that can affect your ability to have children in the future, or diseases that can even be fatal.

A Wellness Approach to Reproductive Health

Discussing personal health issues related to reproductive systems can seem awkward and embarrassing, especially for adolescents. However, maintaining a healthy reproductive system is important to a person's overall health and critical to one's ability to have children when that time comes.

Gynecology The medical specialty that focuses on the wellness of female reproductive organs is called **gynecology.** Many females, as early as adolescence, have annual gynecological exams to monitor the health of reproductive organs. These exams usually include examination of the breasts for abnormalities. A typical exam would also include Papanicolaou (Pap) testing to screen for cervical cancer. The test consists of gently scraping the cervix with a plastic spatula to collect a sample of tissue, which is then tested in a laboratory (Figure 33-20).

Many gynecologists are also obstetricians, resulting in the abbreviation for both specialties, OB/GYN. The obstetrician focuses on maternal and fetal health during pregnancy and childbirth.

▼ **Figure 33-20** Tests, such as a Pap test, detect early signs of diseases such as cervical cancer.

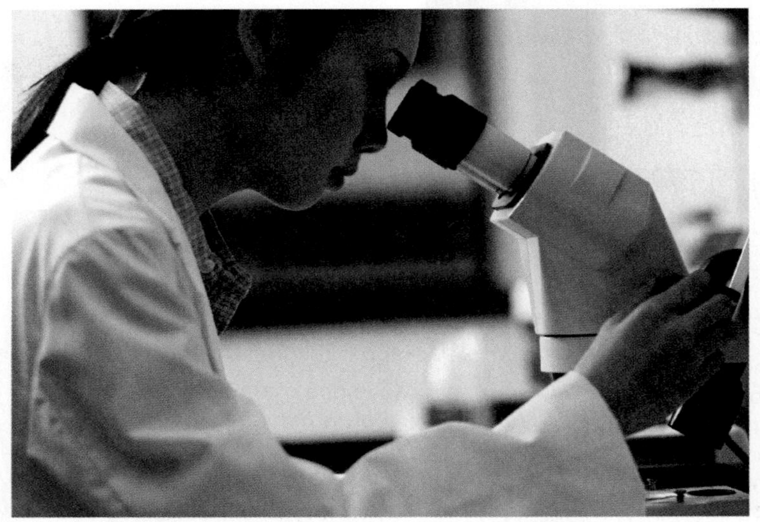

Urology The medical specialty that focuses on the wellness of the urinary tract and bladder for females and males is called **urology.** Males also see urologists for problems of the reproductive organs (penis, scrotum, testes, and prostate gland). After the age of 40, many men have an annual blood test to screen for prostate cancer. A higher than normal level of PSA (prostate-specific antigen) in a patient's blood may help doctors discover prostate cancer at an early stage. Early detection improves the chance of successful treatment with minimal or short-term effects.

Common Sexually Transmitted Diseases (STDs)			
	Disease	**Symptoms**	**Treatment**
Bacterial	Chlamydia	Women: no symptoms until chlamydia advances to pelvic inflammatory disease, which can cause infertility. Men: genital discharge, itching, painful urination.	Antibiotics
Bacterial	Gonorrhea	Women: sometimes no symptoms. Men: genital discharge, painful urination.	Antibiotics
Bacterial	Syphilis	Initial symptoms: open sore on the genitals, swollen lymph nodes. Secondary symptoms: rash on the hands and feet. If untreated, spreads throughout the body and can be fatal.	Antibiotics can cure in early stages.
Viral	Genital warts	Small, hard, painless fleshy growths on genitals; highly contagious; easily spread through sexual contact. Linked to some forms of cancer.	Can be removed by freezing. No cure.
Viral	Genital herpes	Recurring symptoms: painful blisters, intense itching, painful urination. Linked to cervical cancer, miscarriage, birth defects.	Medicines can shorten duration of symptoms. No cure.
Viral	Human immuno-deficiency virus (HIV)	No initial symptoms for some people. Others have flu-like symptoms within a month of exposure, such as fever, headache, and enlarged lymph nodes. HIV leads to acquired immune deficiency syndrome (AIDS) which destroys the immune system.	Combination of drugs can minimize symptoms. No cure.

▲ **Figure 33-21** Sexually transmitted diseases are caused by a variety of pathogens and sometimes have no obvious symptoms.

Sexually Transmitted Diseases (STDs)

Sexual contact introduces the possibility of spreading infectious diseases, called **sexually transmitted diseases (STDs).** There are two main groups of STDs: bacterial and viral. Figure 33-21 lists some common STDs and their symptoms. Bacterial STDs can usually be cured with antibiotics, especially if treated early. For most viral STDs there is no cure. Some, like HIV, have fatal consequences.

Maintaining the health of your reproductive system is required in order to have children. But it is also essential for a healthy adulthood and even, in the case of some diseases, your survival. It is important to bring unusual symptoms to the attention of your doctor as early as possible for a better chance of treating any disease.

Online Activity 33.6

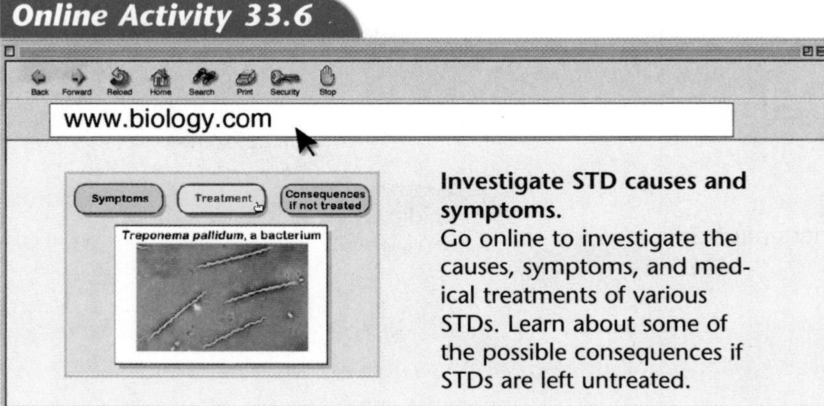

Investigate STD causes and symptoms.
Go online to investigate the causes, symptoms, and medical treatments of various STDs. Learn about some of the possible consequences if STDs are left untreated.

Concept Check 33.6

1. Describe the roles of gynecologists and urologists.
2. List one viral and one bacterial STD and describe their cures or treatments.
3. Give one reason why it is important to understand how your reproductive system functions.

Multiple Choice

Choose the letter of the best answer.

1. Which organ of the female reproductive system produces eggs?
   a. oviduct
   b. ovary
   c. uterus
   d. vagina

2. Which list best describes the path of sperm from the testis to the site of fertilization?
   a. penis, vas deferens, ovary, oviduct
   b. ovary, oviduct, penis, epididymis
   c. vas deferens, penis, vagina, oviduct
   d. scrotum, oviduct, penis, ovary

3. What process stimulates the secondary oocyte to complete meiosis II?
   a. ovulation
   b. sperm penetrating egg
   c. ejaculation
   d. menstruation

4. The breakdown of the endometrium each month is caused by
   a. high levels of estrogen.
   b. high levels of progesterone.
   c. low levels of estrogen.
   d. low levels of FSH and LH.

5. Which list shows stages of development in the order in which they occur?
   a. zygote, embryo, fertilization
   b. blastocyst, zygote, embryo
   c. trophoblast, embryo, blastocyst
   d. zygote, embryo, fetus

6. During which developmental period do secondary sex characteristics usually appear?
   a. adulthood
   b. adolescence
   c. childhood
   d. infancy

7. Which statement correctly describes menopause?
   a. It occurs during adolescence.
   b. The endometrium breaks down.
   c. Ovulation stops.
   d. Men stop manufacturing sperm.

Short Answer

8. Describe the differences and similarities between egg and sperm production.

9. What role does FSH have in the ovarian and menstrual cycles?

10. Compare and contrast the effects of releasing hormone from the hypothalamus on the female and male reproductive systems.

11. What is ovulation? What organs are involved in ovulation?

12. If it only takes one sperm to fertilize an egg, explain an advantage of hundreds of millions of sperm being deposited during intercourse.

13. Describe the process of cleavage.

14. Explain the two ways twins are formed.

15. Describe the structure and function of the placenta.

16. Describe the role of oxytocin in childbirth.

17. At what point in the human development process do reproductive organs become functional?

18. What is an STD? Give an example of a bacterial STD and a viral STD.

Visualizing Concepts

19. Use the ovals below to complete a flowchart showing the pathway of sperm in the male reproductive system. Explain what occurs at each step.

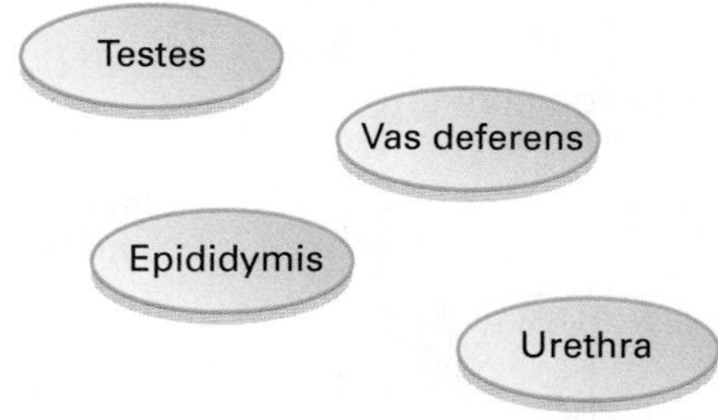

Analyzing Information

20. Analyzing Graphs This graph indicates hormone levels during a portion of an average ovarian/menstrual cycle. Use the graph to answer the questions below.

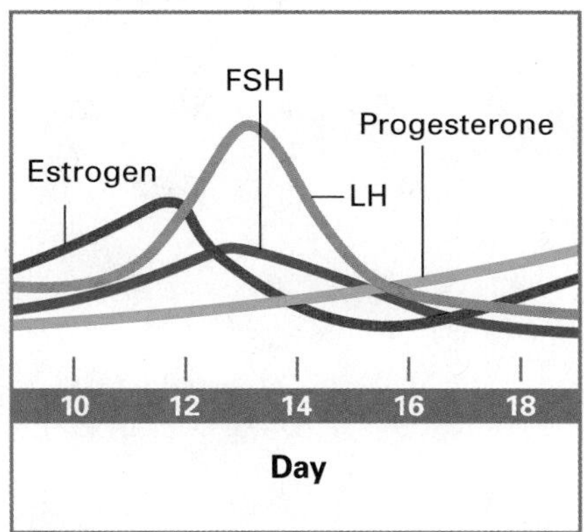

a. On which day is the estrogen level highest? What effect does this peak in estrogen have on the levels of FSH and LH? Explain.

b. Around day 13, which hormone is at the highest level? Why?

c. What ovarian structure contributes to the rising level of progesterone during the last half of the time frame shown? What effect does increased progesterone levels have on the uterus?

21. Analyzing Diagrams Use the diagram below to answer the following questions.

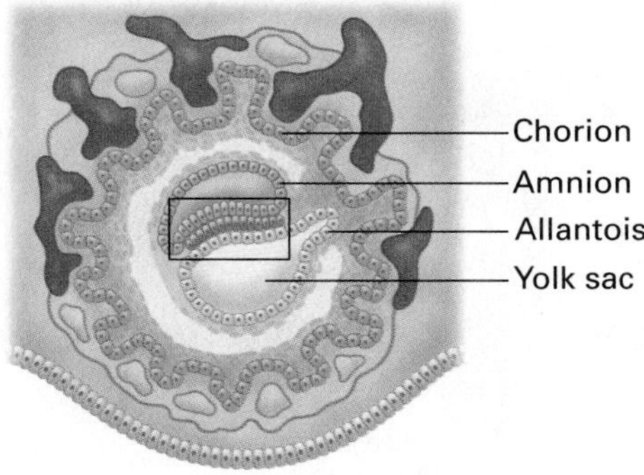

a. What is the significance of the area within the box?

b. Which labeled structure produces the first blood cells in the embryo?

c. Describe the events from fertilization to the stage of development shown in the diagram.

Critical Thinking

22. Relating Cause and Effect From what you have read in this chapter about how nutrients are passed from mother to baby, explain the dangers to the baby if the mother drinks alcohol, smokes tobacco, or takes drugs during pregnancy.

23. Relating Cause and Effect Other than regulating ovarian and menstrual cycles in females and sperm production in males, name other effects estrogen and testosterone have on adolescents.

24. Making Generalizations Suppose a friend tells you that only people who are ready to have children need to worry about their reproductive health. How would you respond to this statement?

25. What's Wrong with These Statements? *Briefly explain why each statement is inaccurate or misleading.*

a. Fertilization of an egg by a sperm can only take place on the day of ovulation.

b. The hormone estrogen regulates the menstrual and ovarian cycles.

c. Mothers share blood with the fetus.

d. Twins always develop from a single fertilized egg.

Performance Assessment

Writing In this chapter you read about the many stages of life. Choose which stage you think is the best time of life. Describe the reasons for your choice. Then, interview a grandparent or an older family friend. Ask him or her which stage has been the most enjoyable. Were your choices the same?

Online Assessment/Test Preparation

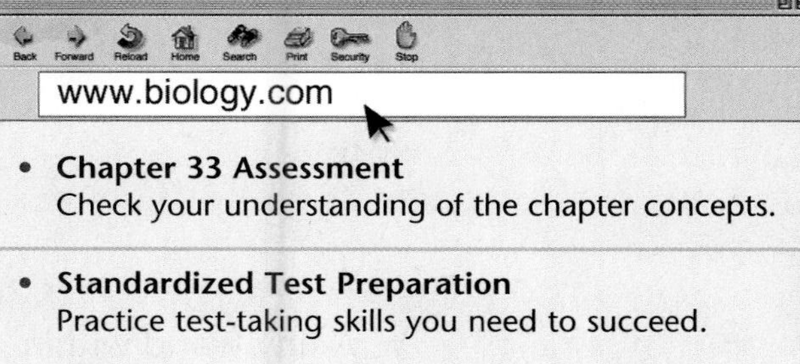

- **Chapter 33 Assessment**
  Check your understanding of the chapter concepts.
- **Standardized Test Preparation**
  Practice test-taking skills you need to succeed.

UNIT 9 Exploring Ecology

Chapters

▶ A tiny world within a tropical bromeliad

The first law of ecology is that everything is related to everything else.

Barry Commoner

The Biosphere

Gazing at a view like that below, *Apollo* astronaut Rusty Schweickart once remarked, "On that small blue-and-white planet is everything that means anything to you. National boundaries and human artifacts no longer seem real. Only the biosphere, whole and home of life."

In the vastness of space, Earth is a tiny, fragile home to trillions of living things. All these organisms, from single-celled bacteria to gigantic blue whales to you and your friends, continuously interact with planet Earth. Organisms exchange gases with the atmosphere; obtain energy and raw materials; and release wastes to their surroundings. In this chapter you'll explore the diverse environments that support Earth's living things. But first, go online to the ***WebQuest*** to explore the ecosystems of the Chesapeake Bay on the mid-Atlantic coast.

Key Concepts

Concept 34.1

The biosphere is the global ecosystem.

Concept 34.2

Climate determines global patterns in the biosphere.

Concept 34.3

Biomes are the major types of terrestrial ecosystems.

Concept 34.4

Aquatic ecosystems make up most of the biosphere.

Assessment

Chapter 34 Review

What's Online

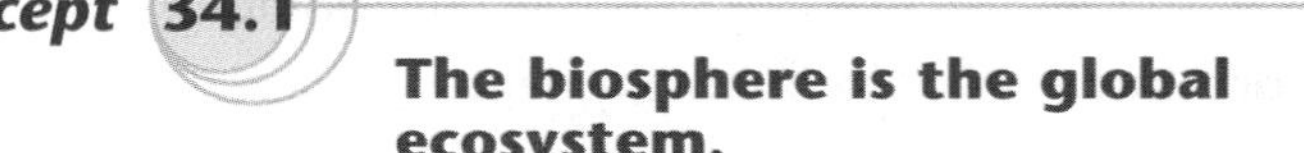

WebQuest
ChesapeakeBayQuest

Online Activity 34.1
Predict the role of abiotic factors in an ecosystem.

Lab 34 Online Companion
Life As a Pond Organism

Online Activity 34.2
Discover the effects of climate on Earth.

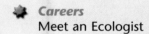

Closer Look
Circulation Cells

Careers
Meet an Ecologist

Online Activity 34.3
Build a climatograph.

Online Activity 34.4
Match ocean organisms with their zones.

Chapter 34 Assessment

CONCEPT 34.1

The biosphere is the global ecosystem.

OBJECTIVES
- Describe the five levels of ecological study.
- Explain how the patchiness of the biosphere creates different habitats.
- Identify key abiotic factors.

KEY TERMS
- ecology
- biotic factor
- abiotic factor
- population
- community
- ecosystem
- biosphere
- habitat

What's Online

www.biology.com

Online Activity 34.1
Predict the role of abiotic factors in an ecosystem.

Lab 34 Online Companion
Life As a Pond Organism

Millions of species live in Earth's diverse environments, which range from scorching deserts to bubbling deep-sea vents, from lush rain forests to your school's grounds. This section introduces the study of how living things interact with these varied environments.

The Study of Ecology

The scientific study of the interactions among organisms and between organisms and their environments is called **ecology.** Ecologists, scientists who conduct research in ecology, test their hypotheses outdoors in the field as well as in the laboratory. Ecologists also use computer models to understand these complex interactions. Understanding ecology helps people make decisions about environmental issues, such as how best to manage forests, rivers, and other natural resources.

An organism's environment consists of other organisms as well as nonliving factors. The prokaryotes, protists, animals, fungi, and plants in the environment are called **biotic factors.** The nonliving physical and chemical conditions are called **abiotic factors.** Ecologists study the relationships among biotic and abiotic factors at five increasingly broad levels: organisms, populations, communities, ecosystems, and the biosphere.

Individual Organisms The smallest unit of ecological study is the individual organism. This blue sweetlip fish is one example of an organism in the coral reef environment shown in Figure 34-1 on the facing page. Other examples of organisms in this environment include the orange fish, the sponges, and the small coral animals that make up the reef. Ecologists ask questions about the adaptations that enable organisms to meet the challenges posed by their environments. For example, how are the reef organisms affected by the changing sunlight levels to which they are exposed?

▼ Organism

Populations A **population** is a group of individual organisms of the same species living in a particular area. The group of sweetlip fish in the reef scene is an example of a population. In contrast, all the fish living around this reef do not form a single population because they represent more than one species. Ecologists often ask questions about factors that affect the size and growth of a population. For instance, what factors limit the number of sweetlip fish living around this reef?

▼ Population

Communities The coral reef is home to a collection of living things including fish, coral animals, microscopic algae, and all other organisms living in and around the reef. All of the organisms inhabiting a particular area make up a **community.** Ecologists investigate interactions among the organisms in a community. For example, how do different species of algae-eating fish compete for food? How might a disease that strikes coral animals affect the other species in the community?

▲ Community

Ecosystems An **ecosystem** includes the abiotic factors and the biotic factors in an area. A coral reef ecosystem includes the reef's many species and its nonliving conditions, such as the water temperature and amount of sunlight (Figure 34-1). Questions at the ecosystem level may relate to the flow of energy and chemicals. For example, how does nitrogen move within the reef ecosystem?

Biosphere The broadest level of ecological study is the biosphere. The **biosphere** is the sum of all Earth's ecosystems. You can picture the biosphere as the "envelope" of air, land, and water that supports and includes all life on Earth: the atmosphere to an altitude of several kilometers; the land to a depth of about 2 kilometers; lakes and streams; and the oceans to a depth of several kilometers. Questions at the biosphere level involve global issues, such as investigating the effects of climate change on living things.

Aside from energy, which enters the biosphere as sunlight and exits as heat, the biosphere is essentially a closed system. This means that the chemicals in the biosphere's living and nonliving things mostly come from within the system—they are not supplied from the outside. (One exception is the occasional meteorite that adds material to Earth.) You'll read more about how the biosphere's raw materials are recycled in Chapter 36.

▼ **Figure 34-1** This coral reef ecosystem includes both biotic and abiotic factors. It is one small part of the global ecosystem, or biosphere.

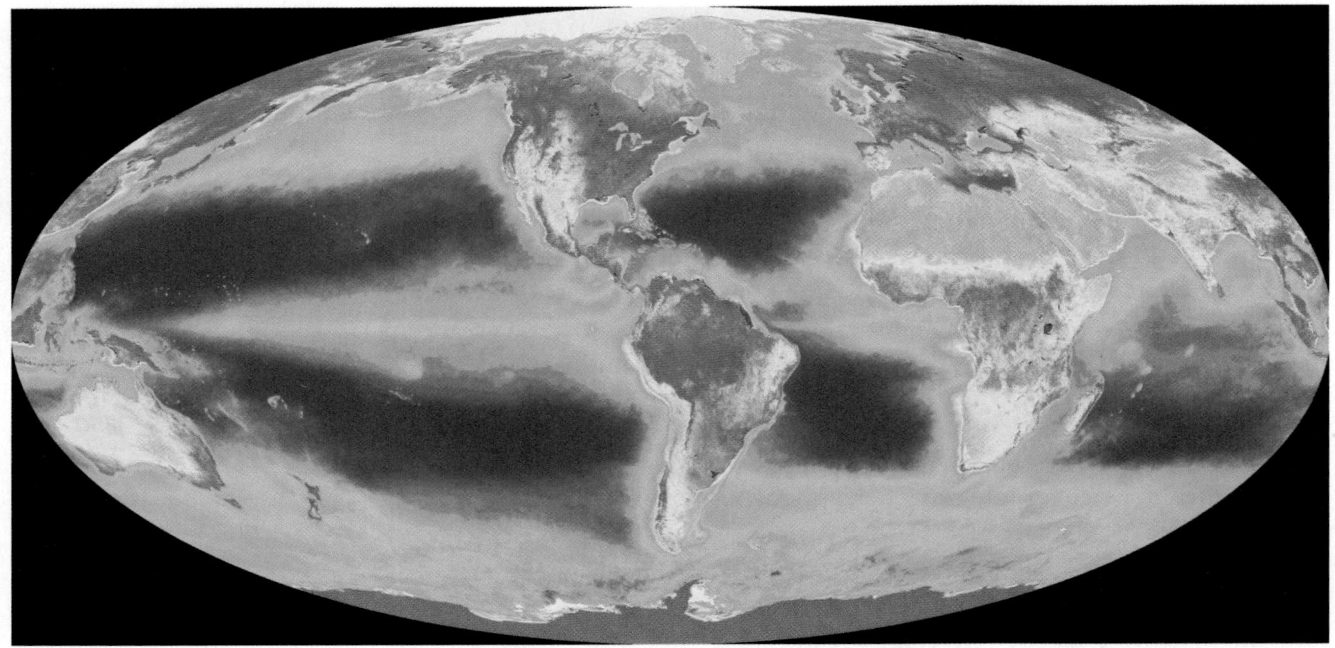

▲ **Figure 34-2** This image shows the amount of chlorophyll (which indicates the abundance of living things) in different parts of the globe. The dark green and red areas are ecosystems that are especially rich in life, including forests and certain aquatic environments. The tan and gold areas are deserts and other ecosystems where living things are less concentrated.

Patchiness of the Biosphere

The biosphere is not spread out uniformly around the planet. Looking at Earth from a space shuttle, you would see that the biosphere is "patchy"—like a quilt of different environments, including land and oceans, lakes and ice (Figure 34-2). Zoom in closer to observe just one continent, and you would see an uneven distribution of ecosystems such as deserts, grasslands, forests, and rivers. A still smaller area, such as the wilderness in Figure 34-3, may contain patches of woods, fresh water, and marshes. All these environmental variations are due mainly to differences in abiotic factors such as temperature, soil type, and the availability of water and light.

This patchiness creates a number of different **habitats,** or specific environments in which organisms live. Each habitat has characteristic abiotic and biotic factors. For example, the wilderness in Figure 34-3 includes several habitats: patches of forest, marshy areas, and the river. The forest patches are home to trees and certain species of birds and animals. The marshy land areas provide a habitat for many species of prokaryotes, fungi, and insects that live in and on top of the wet soil. And within the river habitat is a surface "microhabitat" that supports floating plankton and swimming animals, while the deeper water is a separate microhabitat, with different light and temperature conditions and a different community of organisms.

▼ **Figure 34-3** This wilderness area in Finland contains many habitats.

Key Abiotic Factors

The organisms that inhabit the forest in Figure 34-4 are adapted to the characteristic physical conditions of forest habitats. These abiotic factors include sunlight, water, temperature, soil, and wind.

Sunlight The sun provides light and warmth and is the energy source for almost all ecosystems on Earth. Sunlight powers photosynthesis by plants, the main producers in most terrestrial (land) ecosystems. Within the forest, much less sunlight reaches the forest floor than reaches the tops of the tall trees. This varying amount of sunlight creates different microhabitats. In aquatic (water) environments, sunlight provides energy for photosynthetic producers such as algae. The fact that sunlight only penetrates a short distance into a body of water affects where algae live within a lake or ocean.

Water Water is essential to all life on Earth. All organisms contain water—in fact, you consist of nearly 70 percent water! Among its many important properties, water can dissolve gases such as oxygen and solutes such as salt, as you read in Chapter 4. Terrestrial organisms have adaptations that keep them from losing too much water and drying out. For example, some plants such as pine trees have needle-shaped leaves with a waxy coating. These leaves minimize the amount of water that evaporates into the air. Aquatic organisms also must balance their water uptake and water loss. Otherwise, their cells may burst or shrivel due to osmosis (Chapter 6 describes this process).

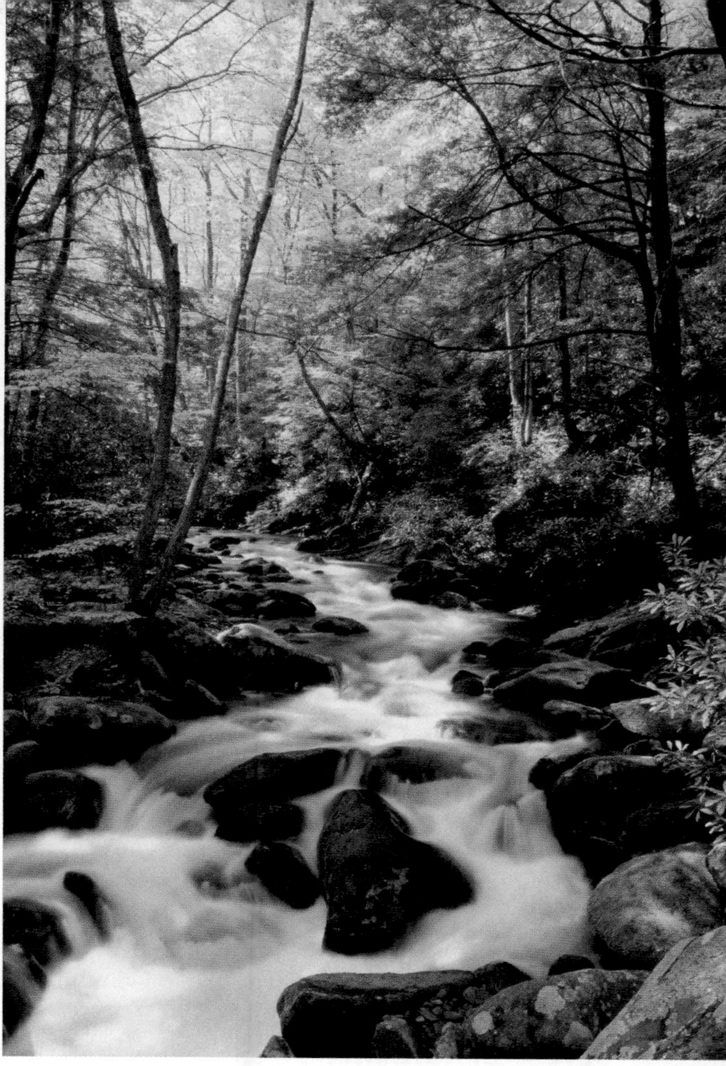

▲ **Figure 34-4** Abiotic factors in this ecosystem include the intensity of sunlight, the availability of water, the types of rock and soil, and the temperature range.

Temperature Most life exists within a fairly narrow range of temperatures, from about 0°C to about 50°C. Few organisms can maintain an active metabolism below 0°C for long, and most organisms' enzymes are denatured (they lose their shape and stop working) above 50°C. However, extraordinary adaptations enable certain species to live at extreme temperatures. Some species of prokaryotes, for example, can thrive in hot springs as hot as 80°C and around deep-sea vents, which are even hotter.

Soil Soil is the product of abiotic forces (such as ice, rain, and wind) and the actions of living things (such as microorganisms, plants, and earthworms) on the rocks and minerals of Earth's crust. The structure and chemical makeup of soil and rock in an area affect the types of plants that grow there. For example, areas with a certain type of dry, nutrient-poor soil are often dominated by little bluestem grasses. These grasses have extensive roots that obtain scarce moisture in the soil. Their long, narrow leaves roll up in hot, dry weather, reducing water loss. In aquatic environments as well, the characteristics of the underlying sand or rock affect the types of plants and algae that can grow. This in turn influences the other organisms found there.

▲ **Figure 34-5** Strong winds gradually caused the "flagging" of this Jeffrey pine tree in Yosemite National Park, California. The wind keeps branches from growing on the upwind side (the left in this picture) of the tree, while branches on the downwind side (the right in this picture) grow normally.

Wind Wind can affect the distribution and the activities of organisms in several ways. Wind moves clouds and rain over Earth's surface. Wind also stirs up water in ponds, lakes, and streams, creating currents that in turn bring up nutrients from the bottom. Many land plants depend on wind to help disperse their pollen and seeds. Figure 34-5 shows another possible effect of wind on organisms.

Severe Disturbances Major natural disturbances that affect ecosystems include fires, hurricanes, tornadoes, droughts, floods, and volcanic eruptions. Some disturbances, such as volcanic eruptions, are so infrequent that organisms have not acquired evolutionary adaptations to them. Other disturbances, such as fires, occur frequently in some communities. Many organisms in such communities have adapted to these disturbances. For example, in dry scrublands where fires are common, many plants can regrow from their roots after a brush fire destroys their aboveground parts.

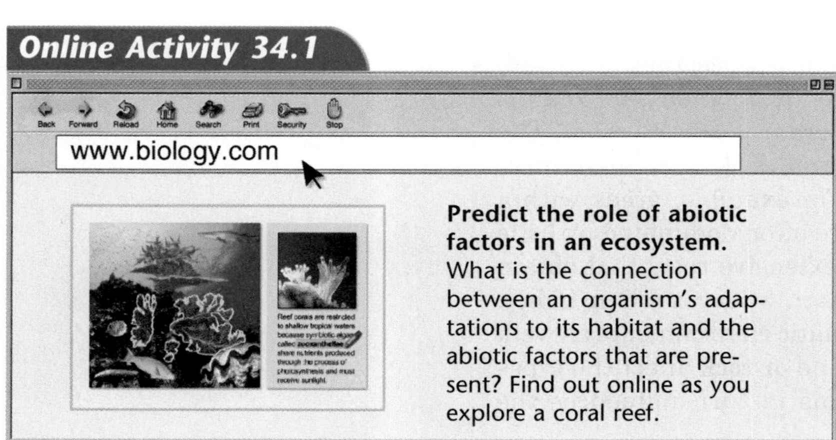

Online Activity 34.1
Back
Forward
Reload
Home
Search
Print
Security
Stop
www.biology.com
Predict the role of abiotic factors in an ecosystem.
What is the connection between an organism's adaptations to its habitat and the abiotic factors that are present? Find out online as you explore a coral reef.

Concept Check 34.1

1. Draw a diagram showing the relationship among the five levels of ecological study.
2. Describe what is meant by the "patchiness" of the environment.
3. Explain the importance of sunlight as an abiotic factor in terrestrial ecosystems.
4. Define biotic and abiotic factors and give an example of each for a particular ecosystem.
5. Explain why it is more accurate to define the biosphere as the global ecosystem than as the global community.

Life As a Pond Organism

Changes and Interactions in a Pond Environment

Question How do changes in abiotic factors affect organisms living in a pond ecosystem?

Lab Overview In this investigation you will use a microscope to observe various organisms living in a pond water sample and choose one type of pond organism to observe more closely. Then you will change the water temperature or light conditions. You will make observations over time to discover how the life of "your" pond organism changes in response to different environmental conditions.

Preparing for the Lab To help you prepare for the lab, go to the *Lab 34 Online Companion.* Learn to find and identify typical pond organisms and get an idea of their relative sizes. Then make predictions about how pond organisms might be affected by changing environmental conditions. Prepare for the lab procedure by previewing the steps you will take.

Completing the Lab Use your Laboratory Manual or lab page printouts from the *Lab 34 Online Companion* to do the investigation and draw conclusions from the observations you made. **CAUTION:** *Be sure to follow your teacher's instructions and all safety guidelines in the investigation.*

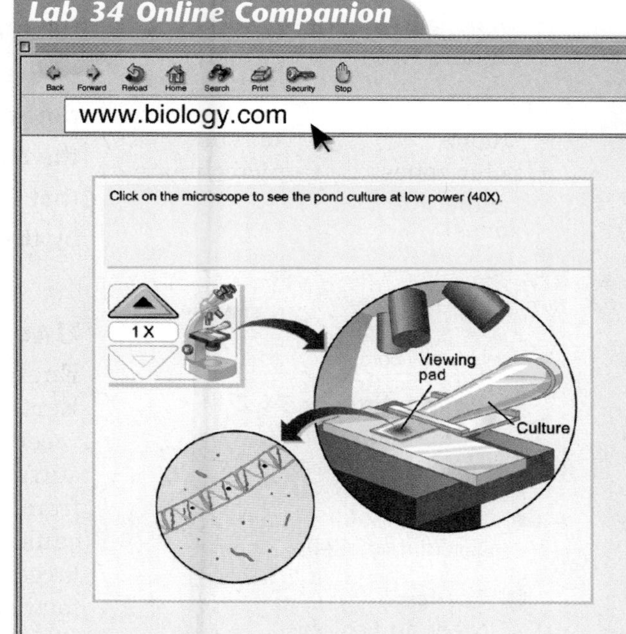

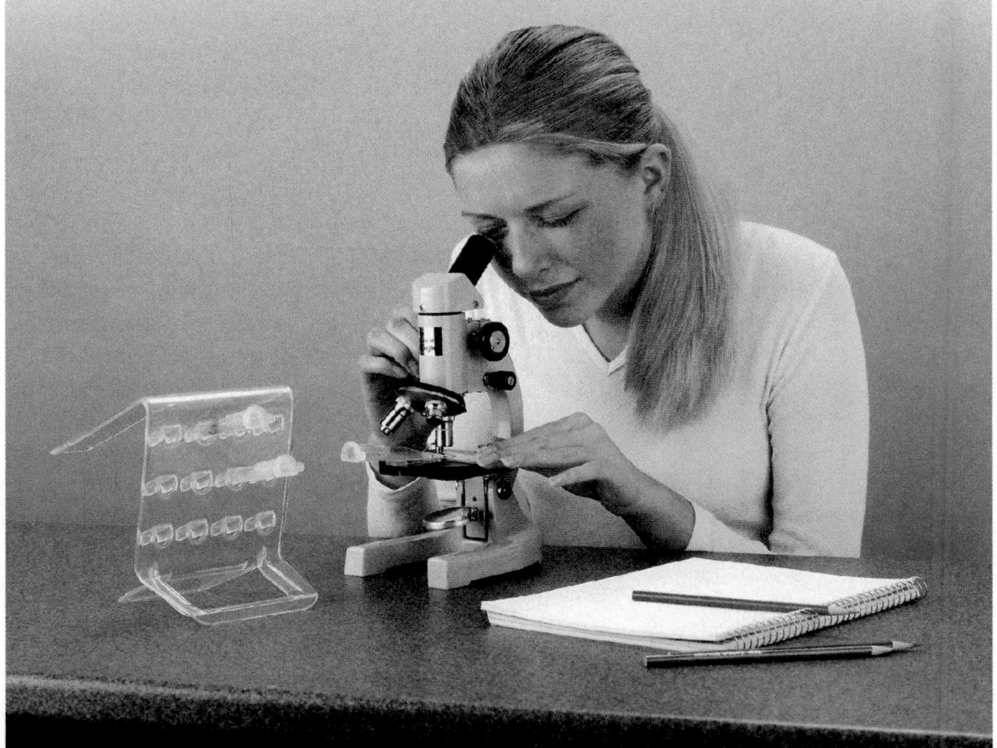

CONCEPT 34.2

Climate determines global patterns in the biosphere.

OBJECTIVES

- Explain how the sun heats Earth's surface unevenly.
- Describe global patterns of wind, precipitation, and ocean currents.
- Distinguish between local climates and microclimates.

KEY TERMS

- tropics
- polar zones
- temperate zones
- current
- microclimate

What's Online

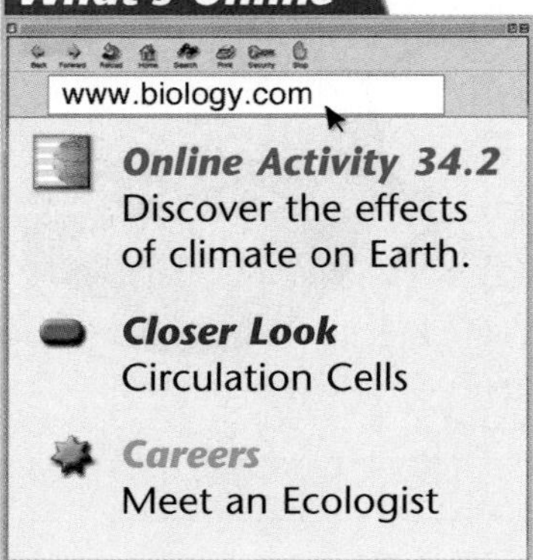

Online Activity 34.2 Discover the effects of climate on Earth.

Closer Look Circulation Cells

Careers Meet an Ecologist

What determines the types of ecosystems found in a certain part of the world? Usually the climate of the region—particularly the range of temperature and amount of rainfall—is a major part of the answer. These abiotic factors influence the types of organisms that live in the region. Earth's climate patterns are largely produced by the uneven heating of the planet by the sun.

Uneven Heating of Earth's Surface

Energy from the sun warms Earth's surface. But because of Earth's spherical shape, different locations on Earth's surface receive different amounts of solar energy. Near the equator, the sun's rays strike the surface most directly. At latitudes farther from the equator the rays strike Earth's surface at lower angles, causing the same amount of solar energy to be spread over a larger area (Figure 34-6). As a result, regions on Earth's surface farther from the equator absorb less heat and generally experience cooler temperatures than regions closer to the equator. These temperature differences also drive global air and water movements.

Earth's surface can be divided into different temperature zones based on lines of latitude. The region that lies between 23.5° N latitude (the Tropic of Cancer) and 23.5° S latitude (the Tropic of Capricorn), called the **tropics,** is the warmest temperature zone. The region north of the Arctic Circle (66.5° N) and the region south of the Antarctic Circle (66.5° S), called the **polar zones,** receive the least amount of direct sunlight year-round. The polar zones are the coldest temperature zones. The latitudes in between the tropics and the polar zones in each hemisphere are called the **temperate zones.** Most of the United States is located within the northern temperate zone. Seasonal temperature changes can be very large in some temperate zones. But in general, the temperate zones experience less extreme heat than the tropics and less extreme cold than the polar zones.

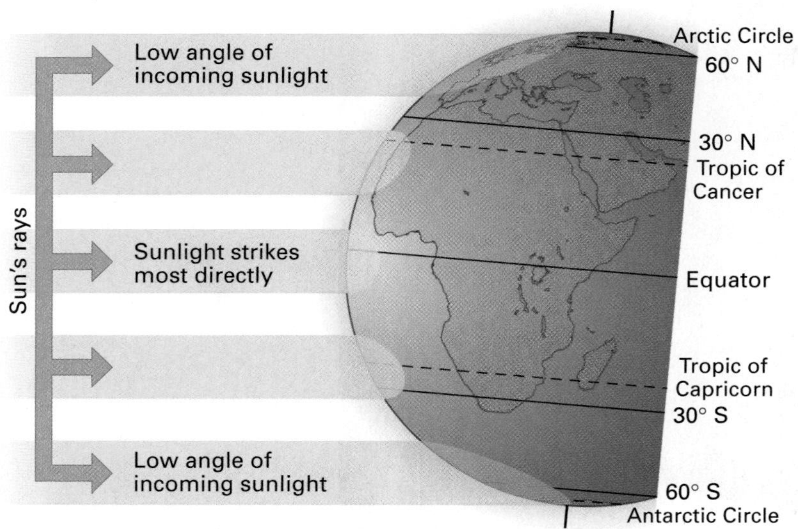

▼ **Figure 34-6** The sun's rays strike Earth most directly near the equator. Near the poles, the same amount of solar energy is spread over a much greater area.

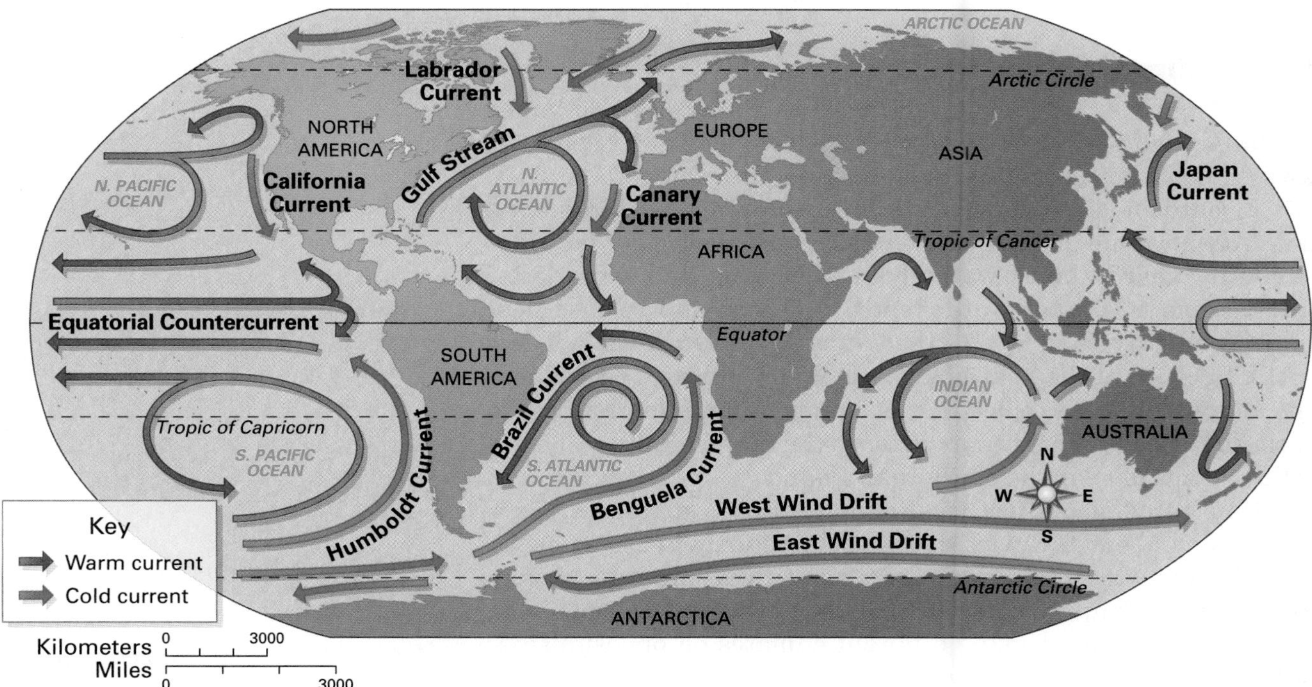

Wind, Precipitation, and Ocean Currents

The uneven heating of Earth's surface by the sun is also a driving force behind global patterns of winds and precipitation (rain, snow, and sleet). When air is warmed it can absorb more moisture, and it also tends to rise. Thus air near the equator, heated by the direct rays of the sun, absorbs moisture and rises. Higher in the atmosphere the air cools again, forming clouds that produce rainfall. This pattern means that many areas of Earth close to the equator tend to have warm temperatures and heavy rainfall year-round. Most rain forests are found in this part of the world, as you will read in Concept 34.3.

After losing moisture over the equator, air masses spread away from the tropics. The dry air descends again and warms at latitudes of about 30° N and 30° S. Some of the world's largest deserts are found in these regions. At higher latitudes, the moving air absorbs more moisture and produces precipitation again.

The rising and falling of air masses, combined with Earth's rotation, produce predictable wind patterns. These wind patterns combine with the uneven heating of Earth's surface, the rotation of the Earth, and the shapes of the continents, producing surface currents. A **current** is a river-like flow pattern within a body of water. Notice in Figure 34-7 that some surface currents move warm water from the tropics toward the polar zones, while others move cold water from the polar zones back toward the tropics. Surface currents can greatly affect regional climates. For instance, the Gulf Stream carries warm water northward from the tropics. This makes the climate in western Europe warmer than other areas at similar latitudes.

▲ **Figure 34-7** Global wind patterns and Earth's rotation create warm and cold surface currents in the oceans. These surface currents affect the climate on the continents.

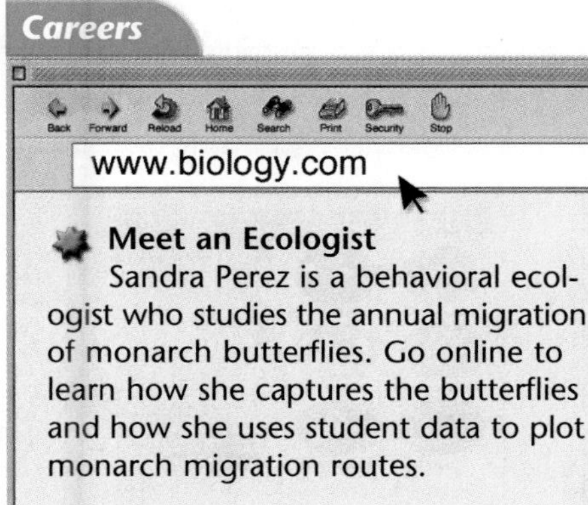

Meet an Ecologist
Sandra Perez is a behavioral ecologist who studies the annual migration of monarch butterflies. Go online to learn how she captures the butterflies and how she uses student data to plot monarch migration routes.

Local Climate

On an August day, people in Los Angeles' San Fernando Valley might face temperatures of 38°C (100°F), while just 30 kilometers away, people at the beach are enjoying the comfortable 24°C (75°F) outdoor air. What causes this difference within such a small geographic area? Local climate variations may be influenced by nearby large water bodies. Oceans and large lakes affect climate because water tends to absorb and release heat more gradually than most other substances (such as soil and rock). Because of the heat-absorbing ability of water, areas near the shore tend to be cooler in the summer than inland areas. In turn, the release of heat from water to the air generally results in milder winters near the shore than inland.

Mountains also affect local climate. First, air temperature declines by about 6°C with every 1000-meter increase in elevation. This is why it becomes cooler as you hike up a mountain. Second, mountains near a coast can block the flow of cool, moist air from the ocean, causing different climates on opposite sides of the mountain range. For example, in California, Oregon, and Washington, precipitation falls on the western, coastal side of the mountain ranges. The eastern side of the mountains can be dry and even desert-like.

Microclimate

Organisms living in the same climate region may be exposed to different conditions created by shade, snow cover, or windbreaks. For example, the kangaroo rat in Figure 34-8 avoids the hot, dry daytime conditions on the desert surface by living underground in a dark, moist burrow. Turn over a fallen log, and it is teeming with life that thrives under conditions quite different from those on top of the log. Such small-scale differences in climate result in a **microclimate,** the climate in a specific area that varies from the surrounding climate region. In the next concept, you'll return to the global scale to explore how climate patterns determine the distribution of Earth's major ecosystems.

▼ **Figure 34-8** This kangaroo rat spends most of the hot summer days in a microclimate within the New Mexico desert. The kangaroo rat's burrow is cooler, darker, and moister than the desert surface just above it.

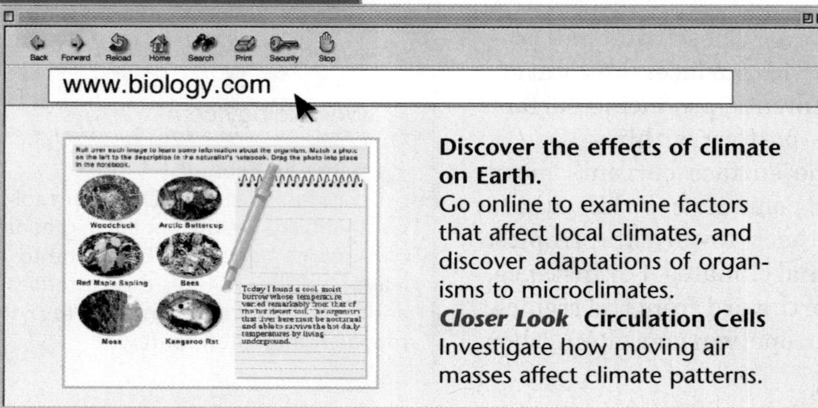

Discover the effects of climate on Earth.
Go online to examine factors that affect local climates, and discover adaptations of organisms to microclimates.
Closer Look **Circulation Cells**
Investigate how moving air masses affect climate patterns.

Concept Check 34.2

1. Explain how the uneven heating of Earth's surface creates different temperature zones.
2. How do surface currents affect climate patterns?
3. Why might a town located on a large lake be cooler in the summer than a town 100 kilometers away from the lake?
4. Give an example of a microclimate.

CONCEPT 34.3

Biomes are the major types of terrestrial ecosystems.

OBJECTIVES

- Describe what defines a biome.
- List and describe eight major terrestrial biomes.

KEY TERMS

- biome
- tropical rain forest
- savanna
- desert
- chaparral
- temperate grassland
- temperate deciduous forest
- coniferous forest
- tundra
- permafrost

What's Online

www.biology.com

Online Activity 34.3
Build a climatograph.

Ecologists studying the distribution of Earth's organisms observe that areas with similar climates tend to have similar ecosystems.

What Is a Biome?

The major types of terrestrial ecosystems that cover large regions of Earth are called **biomes.** Each biome is characterized by communities of plants and other organisms that are adapted to its climate and other abiotic factors. But while the landscapes may appear similar across a biome, the specific organisms vary in different parts of the world. For example, bison and pronghorns graze in North American grasslands, while the grazing mammals in Asian grasslands include saiga (also called "antelope goats") and yaks. The species in both places have similar feeding behavior and other characteristics because they are adapted to similar conditions. Figure 34-9 shows the natural distribution of eight major biomes, plus large areas of ice found near both poles. Notice that there are some latitudinal patterns—certain biomes appear at similar latitudes on several different continents.

▼ **Figure 34-9** Miniature versions of this map will keep you oriented as you read about each biome.

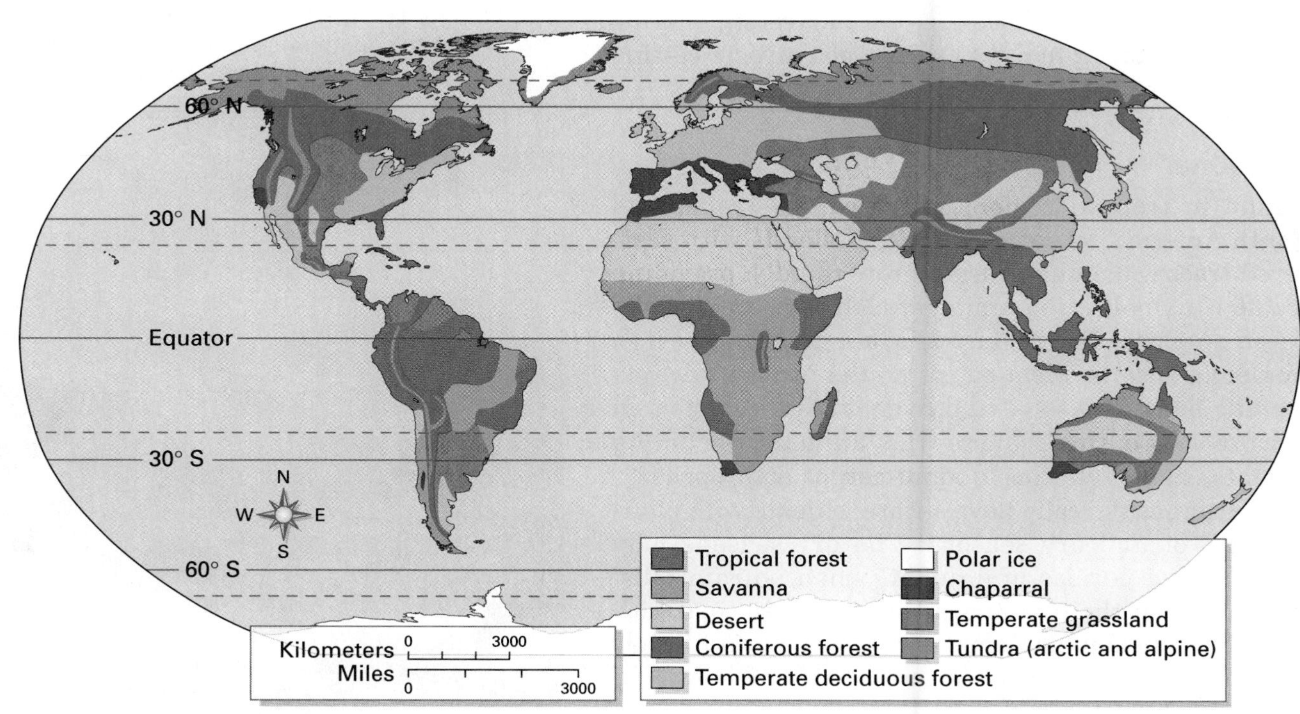

Tropical Forest

Tropical forests occur near the equator where temperatures are warm year-round. One major type of tropical forest, the **tropical rain forest,** can receive as much as 350 centimeters of rainfall yearly. These ideal growing conditions result in a lush diversity of plants growing in vertical layers. Tall broad-leaved trees form vast overhead canopies more than 30 meters in height (17 times the height of an average adult man). Although light is plentiful at the canopy level, little light reaches the forest floor. The short plants that live there are adapted to the shaded, moist conditions. Many trees are covered with mosses, vines, and other plants such as orchids and bromeliads. These plants grow on other plants rather than on the ground. Many rainforest animals are tree-dwellers too, including monkeys, birds, snakes, and bats.

Of all biomes, tropical rain forests have the greatest diversity of life, with an estimated 50 percent of all known species on Earth. Rain forests on the island of Madagascar, off the coast of Africa, are home to some 8,000 species of flowering plants, 80 percent of which occur only there. Many of the unique species provide food, medicine, and other valuable products. However, rain forests in Madagascar and many other parts of the world are shrinking. Clearing forests for mining, lumber, and farmland has affected many rainforest species. Losing large areas of forest may also affect global weather patterns, as you'll read in Chapter 36. Governments and researchers are investigating ways to preserve remaining rain forests. Solutions may include different farming methods and the harvesting of nuts, fruits, and other products that do not involve cutting down trees.

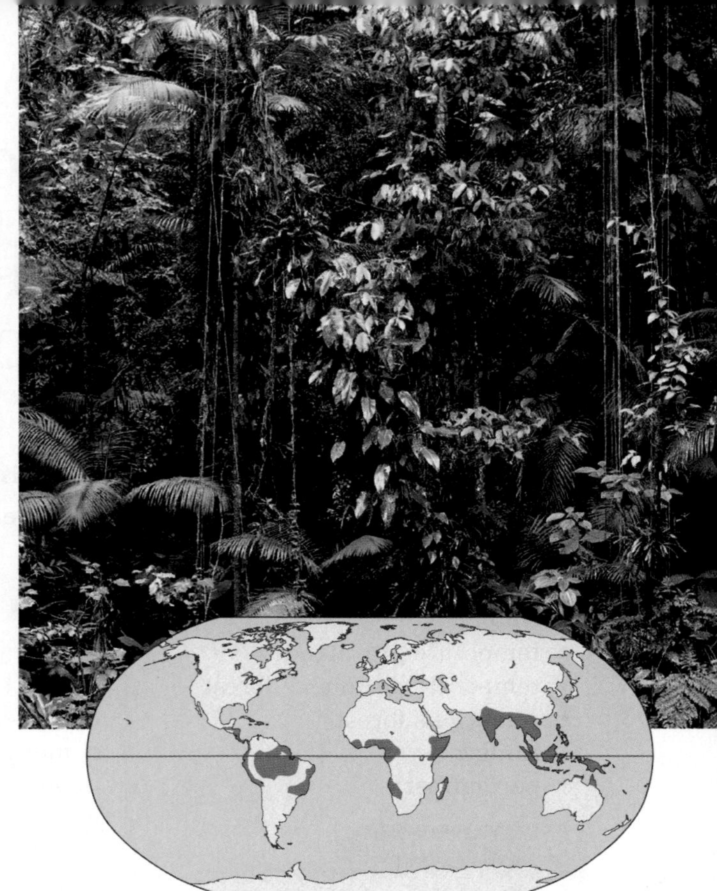

▲ **Figure 34-10** Notice the variety of plant life in this lush tropical rain forest in Brazil.

▼ **Figure 34-11** The herd of springbok on this South African savanna are examples of the grazing animals found in this biome.

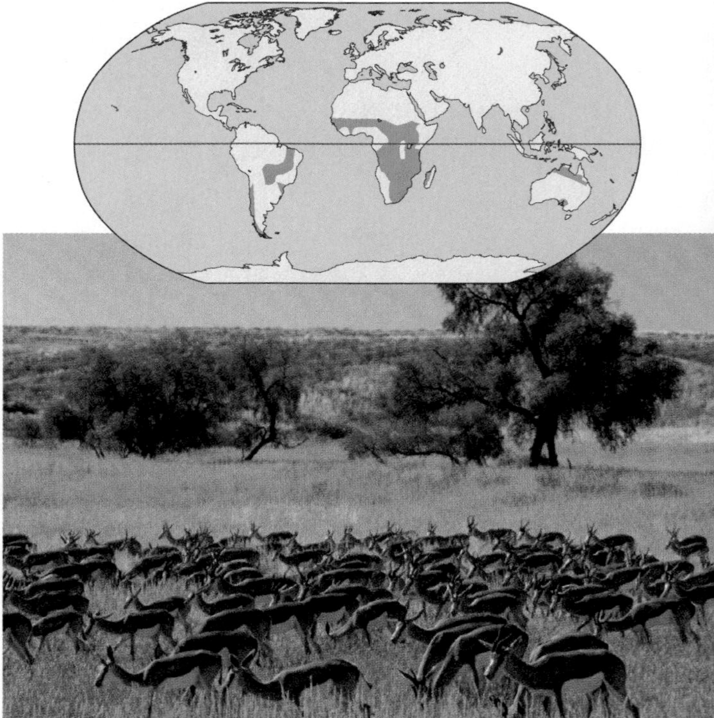

Savanna

Found in tropical regions of Africa, Australia, and South America, **savannas** are grasslands with scattered trees. Savanna grasses grow rapidly, providing food for many grazing animals, such as zebras, wildebeest, antelope, and, in Australia, kangaroos, as well as numerous insects. Meat eaters on the African savanna include lions, cheetahs, and hyenas. Also common on savannas are small burrowing animals, including rodents, snakes, worms, and numerous arthropods.

Savannas typically have a warm climate with alternating wet and dry seasons. The dry seasons may include long periods of drought, when no rain falls. Organisms in the savanna must be able to cope with drought. For example, some animals wander until they find greener pastures or scattered watering holes.

Desert

Land areas receiving less than 30 centimeters of rain per year are typically classified as **deserts.** Though you may think of all deserts as very hot places, temperatures vary widely. Some deserts have surface soil temperatures above 60°C during the day and then cool off at night. Other deserts, such as those in central Asia, are relatively cold, especially during winter nights. The driest deserts, such as those in central Australia and Africa, have little or no plant life. Others are populated by scattered shrubs and cacti (Figure 34-12).

A remarkable array of ways to conserve water have evolved in desert organisms. The saguaro cacti in Figure 34-12 have "pleats" that enable the plants to expand and to store water during wet periods. Many desert animals, such as the kangaroo rat in Figure 34-8, are small burrowers that are active in the cool evenings. This unusual mammal does not need to drink—it derives water mainly from the seeds it eats.

▲ **Figure 34-12** The saguaro cacti in Arizona's Sonoran Desert store water after rains, enabling the plants to survive dry periods.

▼ **Figure 34-13** This dry California scrubland is a typical chaparral ecosystem.

Chaparral

The **chaparral** (shap uh RAL) is a temperate coastal biome dominated by dense evergreen shrubs. The climate consists of mild, rainy winters and hot, dry summers. While the largest area of chaparral occurs around the Mediterranean Sea, similar ecosystems are found elsewhere in the world, including California (Figure 34-13).

The chaparral's dry, woody shrubs are frequently ignited by lightning and are adapted to survive periodic brushfires. In fact, some of the plant species produce seeds that will germinate only after a hot fire. Animals of the chaparral include deer, birds, and rodents that feed on the shrubs and their seeds, as well as lizards and snakes.

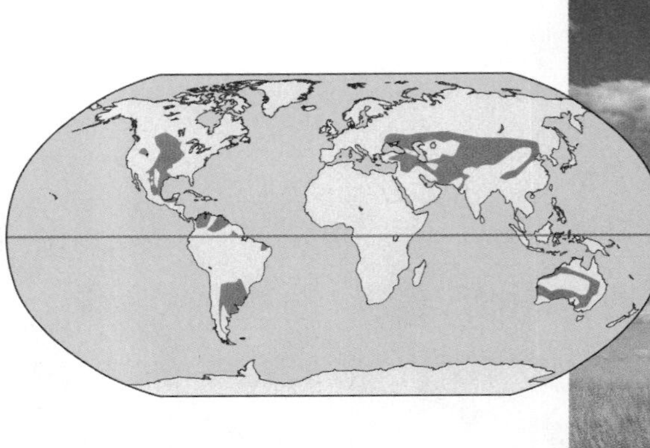

▲ **Figure 34-14** A bison grazes in a short-grass prairie in South Dakota.

Temperate Grassland

The **temperate grassland** biome is characterized by deep, nutrient-rich soil that supports a variety of grass species and other plants. The winters are colder than in the tropical savannas. Seasonal drought, occasional fires, and grazing by large mammals all prevent the growth of woody shrubs and trees. The height of the vegetation in a grassland depends mainly on the amount of yearly rainfall. Drier areas, such as the South Dakota grassland in Figure 34-14, tend to have shorter grass species, whereas wetter areas, such as eastern Kansas, support grasses and other plants that grow to over 2 meters in height.

Grassland soils contain a great diversity of microorganisms and animals, including worms, arthropods, and burrowing rodents. Above ground, the North American grasslands (also known as prairies) include grazing mammals such as bison and pronghorns, as well as coyotes, snakes, lizards, and insects.

Temperate Deciduous Forest

Dense stands of deciduous trees—trees that drop their leaves each year—characterize **temperate deciduous forests.** These forests occur throughout the temperate zone where there is enough precipitation to support the growth of large trees. In this region winters tend to be very cold, while summers can be quite hot. Common deciduous trees such as maples, oaks, beeches, and hickory shed their leaves in autumn, which helps reduce evaporation during the winter when water is not easily replaced from frozen soil.

Though not as rich in species diversity as tropical rain forests, temperate deciduous forests provide habitats for a wide variety of species. Many microorganisms, fungi, and arthropods live in the soil and leaf litter on the forest floor. Mammals found in the temperate deciduous forests of eastern North America include deer, squirrels, chipmunks, foxes, and bears. During the cold winter, many of these animals conserve energy by greatly reducing their activity levels. Some bird species migrate to warmer climates.

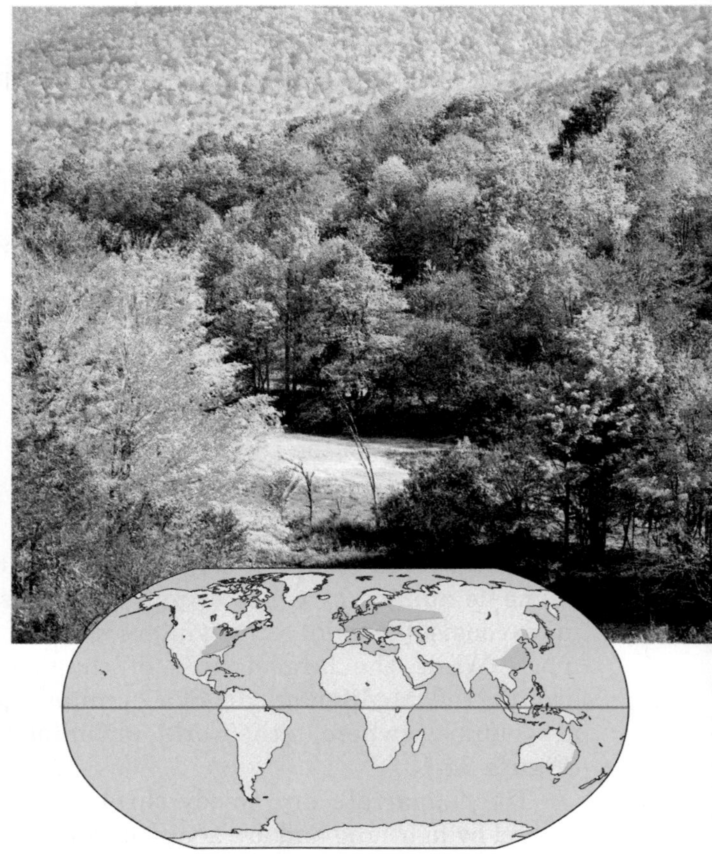

▲ **Figure 34-15** These vibrant deciduous trees in New York's Catskill Mountains will shed their leaves before the cold winter arrives.

Coniferous Forest

Towering cone-bearing evergreen trees such as pine, spruce, fir, and hemlock characterize the **coniferous forest.** The northern regions of the biome, also called the *taiga,* have long, cold winters with heavy snowfall. The conical shape of the trees prevents too much snow from collecting and breaking branches. The needle-like leaf is low in surface area, which limits water loss from evaporation during dry periods. Typical taiga animals include hares, moose, elk, wolves, and bears.

In coastal Oregon, Washington, and British Columbia, Canada, conditions are warmer and wetter than in most other coniferous forest areas. These forests are actually considered temperate rain forests because of the amount of precipitation they receive.

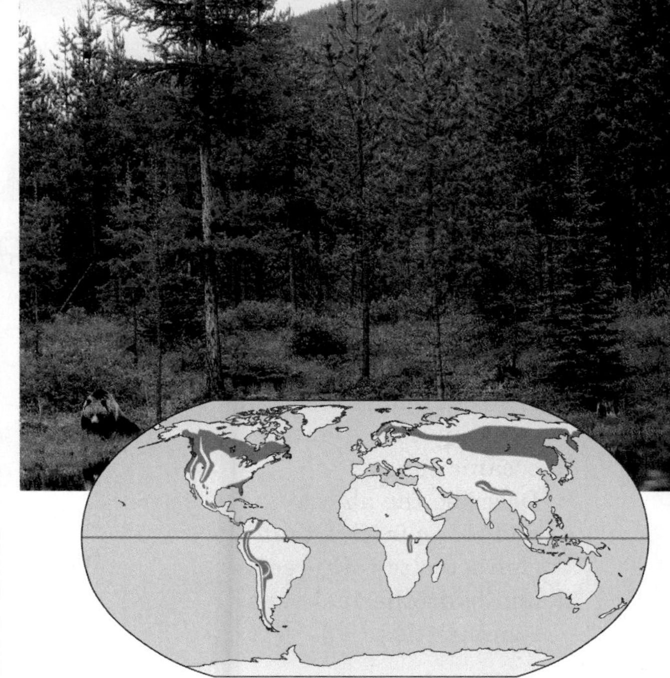

▲ **Figure 34-16** This coniferous forest in Montana is dominated by a few species of cone-bearing evergreen trees.

Tundra

Bitterly cold temperatures and high winds characterize the **tundra.** Tundra communities are found within the Arctic Circle and on high mountaintops at all latitudes due to the similar conditions there. The permanently frozen subsoil, called **permafrost,** ranges in depth from a few meters to 1,500 meters. During the short summer season, only the top few centimeters of the permafrost melt. Puddles accumulate in the shallow topsoil. Mosses, lichens, and grasses thrive, but large plants are rare since their roots cannot penetrate the permafrost or absorb water and nutrients from it.

During the brief Arctic growing season, clouds of mosquitoes fill the air. Lemmings, caribou, and reindeer eat the tundra ground cover. Some tundra animals, including the arctic hare and snowy owl, turn white in the winter, allowing them to blend in with the snow. During the summer they turn brown, better enabling them to hide in their rock-strewn environment.

▲ **Figure 34-17** Colorful lichens and mosses thrive in the soggy surface soil of the Norwegian tundra.

Online Activity 34.3

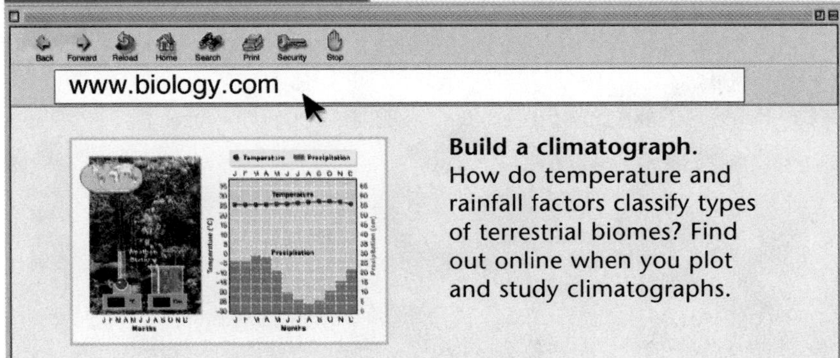

Build a climatograph. How do temperature and rainfall factors classify types of terrestrial biomes? Find out online when you plot and study climatographs.

Concept Check 34.3

1. What factors determine the type of biome in an area?
2. Compare and contrast tropical rain forests, temperate deciduous forests, and coniferous forests.
3. Give an example of how a desert organism has adapted to the abiotic conditions there.

CONCEPT 34.4

Aquatic ecosystems make up most of the biosphere.

OBJECTIVES

- Compare and contrast ponds, streams, and estuaries.
- Compare conditions and typical organisms in the intertidal, neritic, and oceanic zones.
- Describe the abiotic and biotic factors that characterize coral reefs and hydrothermal vent communities.

KEY TERMS

- photic zone
- phytoplankton
- aphotic zone
- benthic zone
- estuary
- pelagic zone
- intertidal zone
- neritic zone
- oceanic zone
- zooplankton
- hydrothermal vent

What's Online

Online Activity 34.4 Match ocean organisms with their zones.

Nearly three quarters of Earth's surface is covered with water, most of it in the world's oceans. Aquatic (water) ecosystems provide homes to many of Earth's organisms. Major abiotic factors affecting aquatic ecosystems include the amount of dissolved salt, the water temperature, and the availability of sunlight.

Ponds and Lakes

Freshwater ecosystems include water bodies with very little dissolved salt, such as most ponds, lakes, streams, and rivers. Ponds and lakes are standing (not flowing) bodies of water. They range from ponds of a few square meters to large lakes such as the Great Lakes, which are thousands of square kilometers in area.

Lakes and large ponds are divided into zones based on water depth and distance from shore. The shallow water close to shore and the upper zone of water away from shore make up the **photic zone,** so named because light is available for photosynthesis. **Phytoplankton,** microscopic algae and cyanobacteria that carry out photosynthesis, live in the photic zone, along with water plants. The deep, murky areas of a lake, where light levels are too low to support photosynthesis, are called the **aphotic zone.**

The bottom of any aquatic ecosystem is called the **benthic zone.** The benthic zone consists of rock, sand, and sediment. The organisms of deep (aphotic) benthic areas feed on wastes that sink down from the photic zone. When you wade in a pond, the soft material you feel between your toes is part of the benthic zone.

Figure 34-18 This serene Colorado pond is an example of a standing freshwater body. The water plants growing throughout much of the pond indicate that the water is relatively shallow.

Streams and Rivers

A body of flowing fresh water is known as a stream or a river. (Streams are smaller bodies of flowing water, and rivers are larger.) Streams and rivers generally support different communities of organisms from those found in ponds and lakes.

A river changes greatly between its source and the point at which it empties into a lake or the ocean. Near the source, the water is usually cold, low in nutrients, and clear. The river channel tends to be shallow and narrow. Few phytoplankton inhabit this part of a river. Instead, the major producers near a river's source are algae attached to rocks on the river bed. Many species of arthropods live in the benthic zone, feeding on algae, fallen leaves, and one another. The most common fish are often trout, which eat insects in the river.

Downstream from its source, a river generally becomes wider and deeper. Marshes and other wetlands are common in these downstream areas. The water is usually warmer and murkier than it is upstream. More phytoplankton live in this part of a river, as do waterfowl, frogs, catfish, and other fishes that find food more by scent and taste than by sight. Worms and insect larvae that burrow into the mud are abundant in the benthic zone.

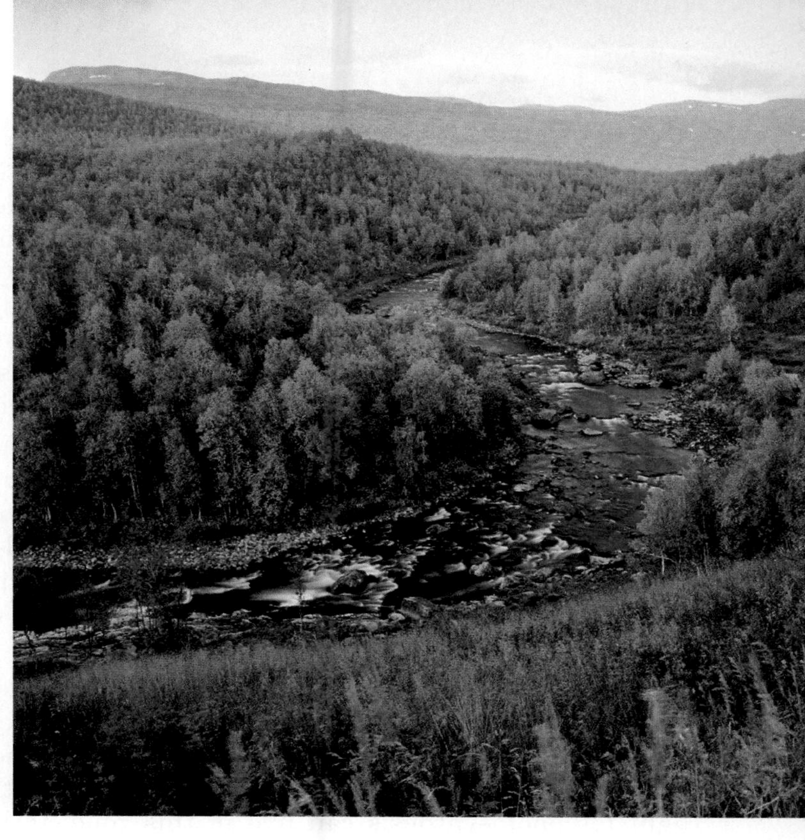

▲ **Figure 34-19** Organisms in this river in Sweden are adapted to the swiftly moving water.

Estuaries

Streams and rivers merge with ocean water in areas known as **estuaries.** Estuary organisms experience changes in salt concentration and temperature as the fresh water and salt water mix. Nutrient-rich soil carried into estuaries by rivers supports a rich diversity of life both in the water and on the surrounding land. The result is one of Earth's most productive ecosystems. Estuaries serve as breeding grounds for many invertebrate and fish species, and as nesting and feeding areas for a great diversity of birds.

Along most of the east coast of the United States, the major ecosystems found in estuaries are salt marshes (Figure 34-20). Grasses that can grow in salty water and algae are the major photosynthetic organisms in salt marshes. These producers support a variety of animals, including crabs, oysters, clams, and small fish. In this chapter's WebQuest, you can explore the ecosystems of the Chesapeake Bay estuary on the mid-Atlantic coast.

In tropical areas, the typical estuary ecosystems are mangrove swamps. These swamps are dominated by mangrove trees, which are anchored by tangled networks of arching roots.

▼ **Figure 34-20** Salt marshes like this one are typical estuary ecosystems. The blue crab is one inhabitant of the Chesapeake Bay estuary.

Ocean Zones

More than 250,000 known species live in ocean habitats. Like lakes, the ocean can be divided into different zones based on depth and on distance from shore (Figure 34-21). Zones of depth include the benthic zone, or ocean floor, and the **pelagic zone** (pi LAJ ik), or open water above the ocean floor. Also as in freshwater ecosystems, the ocean has a photic zone, which receives enough sunlight to support photosynthesis, and a dark aphotic zone. Zones of distance from shore include the intertidal zone, neritic zone, and oceanic zone.

Intertidal Zone The area of shore between the high-tide and low-tide lines is called the **intertidal zone.** Pounded by waves during high tide and exposed to the sun and drying winds during low tide, benthic organisms in this zone must be well-adapted to survive these harsh conditions. Barnacles, for example, cement themselves to rocks and have trap door-like plates in their shells that hold in moisture during low tide.

Neritic Zone The area of the ocean from the low-tide line out to the edge of the continental shelf is the **neritic zone.** Since the ocean here is fairly shallow, some sunlight reaches the bottom in most of the neritic zone. As a result, many organisms that require light for photosynthesis can live in this zone, including seaweeds and phytoplankton. Most coral reefs are also found in the neritic zone. The benthic community may include mollusks, sponges, crustaceans, and worms that feed on sinking wastes and remains. Swimming animals include sea turtles, fish, and marine mammals such as seals.

Oceanic Zone The vast open ocean from the edge of the continental shelf outward is called the **oceanic zone.** Phytoplankton drifting in the photic layer are the major producers in this zone. Microscopic animals called **zooplankton** also inhabit the photic zone and in turn are a source of food for other animals. Swimming organisms in the pelagic zone include dolphins, whales, squid, and numerous species of fish adapted to life at different depths.

Figure 34-21 The ocean can be divided into zones based on depth and distance from shore.

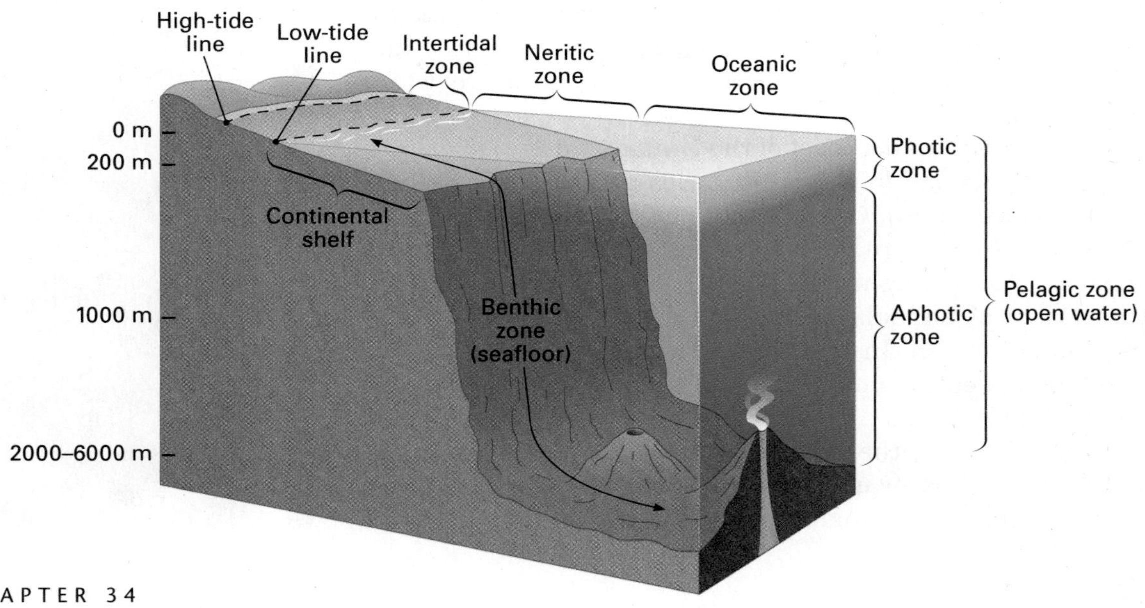

Coral Reefs

▲ **Figure 34-22** A coral reef in Micronesia is among Earth's most diverse ecosystems.

Coral reefs are a visually spectacular and biologically diverse ecosystem—the marine equivalent of tropical rain forests. More than one of every four marine species inhabits a coral reef. All the invertebrate phyla are found on coral reefs, including sponges, sea anemones, worms, sea stars, and mollusks. Vertebrates such as sea turtles and fishes also roam the reefs.

Most reefs are formed by colonies of coral polyps, animals in the phylum Cnidaria that secrete hard external skeletons. These skeletons form the stonelike bases that serve as home to more coral polyps, sponges, and algae. During the day, coral polyps obtain food mainly from photosynthetic algae that live within their tissues. The coral polyps can also use their stinging tentacles to capture zooplankton.

Deep-sea Vents

Imagine the surprise of biologists when they first glimpsed giant tube worms like those in Figure 34-23 living at depths of 2,500 meters. These unfamiliar organisms live around deep-sea **hydrothermal vents,** spots on the ocean floor where hot gases and minerals escape from Earth's interior into the water.

No sunlight reaches this deep, dark zone. The vent communities use the chemical energy from Earth's interior as their energy source. The producers in these ecosystems are prokaryotes that, instead of carrying out photosynthesis, can extract energy from sulfur compounds spewing from the vents and use this energy to make carbohydrates. The tube worms and clams consume these prokaryotes and their energy-rich compounds. In turn, these animals are eaten by other organisms in the community, such as crabs.

▲ **Figure 34-23** Giant tube worms, which can grow as long as 3 meters, are among the unusual organisms in hydrothermal vent communities.

Online Activity 34.4

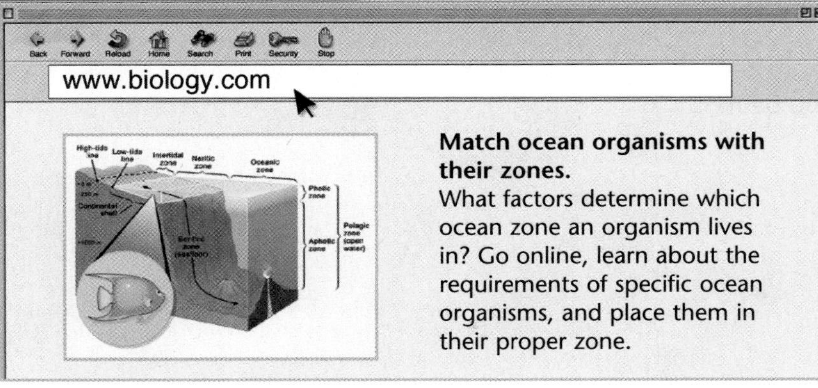

Back
Forward
Reload
Home
Search
Print
Security
Stop
www.biology.com
Match ocean organisms with their zones.
What factors determine which ocean zone an organism lives in? Go online, learn about the requirements of specific ocean organisms, and place them in their proper zone.

Concept Check 34.4

1. Describe the abiotic factors that affect organisms in ponds, streams, and estuaries.
2. Compare and contrast the intertidal zone, neritic zone, and oceanic zone.
3. Discuss sunlight as an abiotic factor in coral reefs and vent communities.

Multiple Choice

Choose the letter of the best answer.

1. An ecologist counting the whooping cranes in a wildlife refuge over a five-year period is studying ecology at the level of a(n)
   a. organism.
   b. population.
   c. community.
   d. ecosystem.

2. Which of the following experiments is studying the effect of an abiotic factor?
   a. investigating how the amount of precipitation affects the growth of a species of grass
   b. identifying the sources of food for an elephant population
   c. observing the interactions between different fish inhabiting a coral reef
   d. investigating how goats on a mountain compete for food

3. The sun's rays strike Earth's surface most directly near
   a. 60° N and S latitude.
   b. 30° N and S latitude.
   c. the equator.
   d. the poles.

4. Warm grasslands with a few trees characterize the
   a. tundra.
   b. desert.
   c. mangrove swamp.
   d. savanna.

5. In which biome would you most expect to find maple and birch trees?
   a. temperate deciduous forest
   b. chaparral
   c. tropical rain forest
   d. coniferous forest

6. In a lake or the ocean, where would you be most likely to find phytoplankton?
   a. in the photic zone
   b. in the aphotic zone
   c. in the benthic zone
   d. in a hydrothermal vent

Short Answer

7. List the five levels of ecological organization from smallest to largest. Which levels include abiotic as well as biotic factors?

8. Define the term *habitat.* Give an example of an organism and its habitat.

9. Explain how wind might affect living things in an ecosystem.

10. List Earth's three main temperature zones. In which zone do you live?

11. How are surface currents in the ocean linked to climate patterns?

12. Define the term *microclimate.* How might a microclimate create a microhabitat?

13. What is permafrost? How does permafrost affect biotic factors in the tundra?

14. Describe the different ecological zones in a large lake. What types of organisms live in each zone?

Visualizing Concepts

15. Make and complete a table like the one shown below to compare and contrast the eight major terrestrial biomes.

Terrestrial Biome	Climate Conditions	Typical Organisms
Desert	Less than 30 cm of rain per year. Temperatures may be hot or cold.	Cacti, small burrowing mammals
Savanna		
Chaparral		

Analyzing Information

16. Analyzing Diagrams Use the diagram to answer the questions.

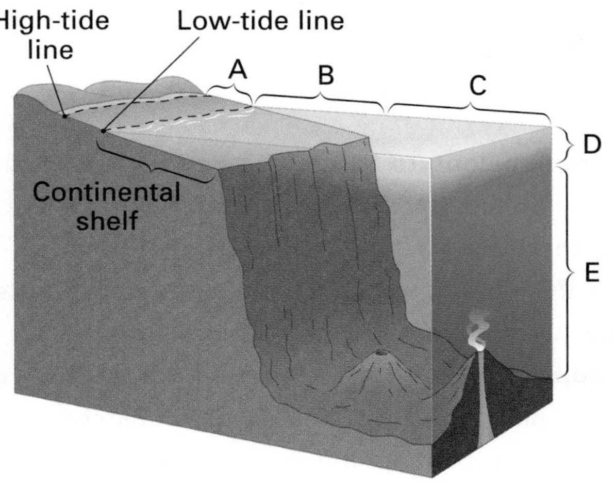

a. Name the ocean zone labeled *A* in the diagram. Describe conditions in this zone.

b. In which depth zone *(D* or *E)* do phytoplankton live? Explain why this is true.

c. In which ocean zone *(A, B,* or *C)* would a hydrothermal vent ecosystem most likely be found? Describe conditions and a typical organism found in this ecosystem.

17. Analyzing Data An ecologist has been collecting climate data from three locations: a desert, a tundra, and a temperate deciduous forest. After several years, the ecologist averaged the measurements to find a mean annual temperature and mean annual precipitation for each location. Based on the data below, suggest which set of data came from which location. Explain your reasoning.

Climate Data

	Data Set A	Data Set B	Data Set C
Mean annual temperature (°C)	2	15	20
Mean annual precipitation (cm)	55	15	130

Critical Thinking

18. Giving an Example Identify three biotic factors and three abiotic factors in your classroom environment.

19. Relating Cause and Effect Many of the world's largest deserts are located around 30° N and 30° S latitudes. Describe how global patterns of temperature, wind, and precipitation help explain this fact.

20. Relating Cause and Effect What accounts for the great diversity of organisms in tropical rain forests?

21. Comparing and Contrasting Describe at least two similarities and two differences between lake and ocean ecosystems.

22. Making Generalizations Explain how abiotic factors help to shape biotic communities.

23. What's Wrong With These Statements? *Briefly explain why each statement is inaccurate or misleading.*

a. Ecologists study Earth's living things.

b. Deserts are hot, dry places.

c. Nothing can grow in the harsh tundra climate.

Performance Assessment

Biology Research Project Use an almanac or the Internet to find temperature and precipitation data for your city or state. What biome describes your area? Identify three other locations along the same longitude line, but at different latitudes. Predict how the climate in these areas compares to yours. Research their climate and make a visual aid of your findings. How do your results compare with your predictions? Suggest a reason for any differences.

Online Assessment/Test Preparation

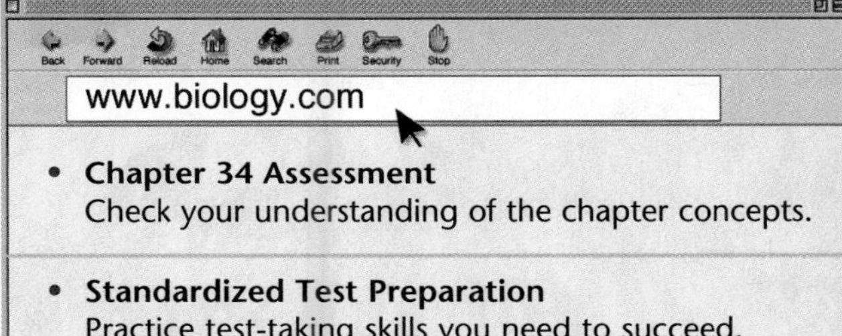

- **Chapter 34 Assessment**
  Check your understanding of the chapter concepts.
- **Standardized Test Preparation**
  Practice test-taking skills you need to succeed.

Population and Community Ecology

The monarch butterflies in this photograph belong to a population of hundreds of millions that migrate each winter from the United States to particular forests in Mexico. As large as this monarch population is, there are limits to its growth. Each female monarch lays hundreds of eggs, and yet the world is not overrun with monarch butterflies. What factors influence the number of monarchs in a population? Does harsh weather kill many of these insects? Is population size related to food supply? How do other species of organisms affect monarch numbers? How, in turn, do monarchs affect populations of the other species in their community? Asking questions such as these is part of studying the ecology of populations and communities, the topics of this chapter. Before you begin, go online to the ***WebQuest*** to explore what happens when a population is introduced into a new location.

Key Concepts

Concept 35.1 — **A population is a local group of organisms of one species.**

Concept 35.2 — **There are limits to population growth.**

Concept 35.3 — **Biologists are trying to predict the impact of human population growth.**

Concept 35.4 — **Species interact in biological communities.**

Concept 35.5 — **Disturbances are common in communities.**

Assessment — **Chapter 35 Review**

What's Online

www.biology.com

WebQuest
KillerBeeQuest

Online Activity 35.1
Study population dynamics.

Online Collaborative Science 4
Exploring Lawn Biodiversity

Lab 35 Online Companion
Dynamic Populations

Online Activity 35.2
Analyze population growth data.

Online Activity 35.3
Plot human population growth over time.

Online Activity 35.4
Classify interactions of populations.

Online Activity 35.5
Build a temperate rainforest community.

Science, Technology, & Society
The Alaskan Wilderness

Chapter 35 Assessment

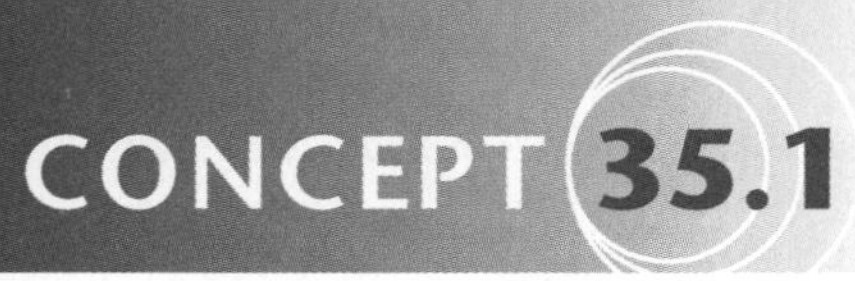

A population is a local group of organisms of one species.

OBJECTIVES
- Explain how ecologists define a population for study.
- Explain how population density is calculated.
- Describe several methods scientists use to measure population density.

KEY TERM
- population density

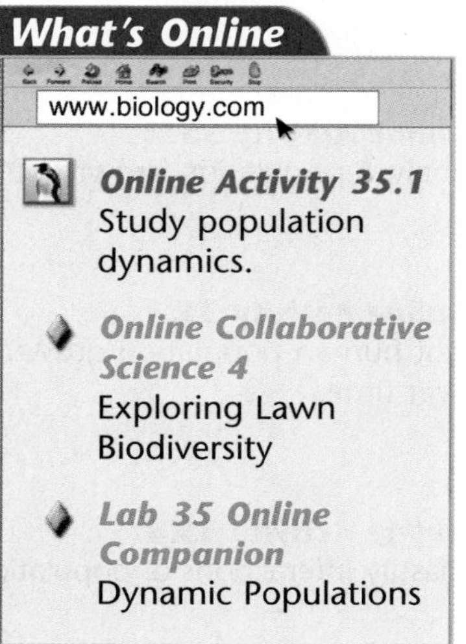

The alligators in the swamp shown below make up a population—members of the same species living in a specific geographic area. Other populations in the swamp include diverse species of trees, egrets and other birds, and the various species of fishes, algae, and microorganisms in the swamp water. This section explains how ecologists identify, measure, and study such populations.

Defining Populations

Some populations change in size dramatically over time, increasing rapidly and then decreasing again. Other populations are more stable, with only small increases or decreases in the number of members over time. Several factors influence a population's size and how much it changes over time. They include the availability of food and space, weather conditions, and breeding patterns.

In studying how these factors affect a population, ecologists need to define the population's geographic boundaries. These boundaries might be natural, such as the edges of a lake where a particular species of catfish lives. The boundaries might be chosen to make the population easy to study, such as the walls of an aquarium in which algae are growing. A researcher exploring the effects of hunting on a deer species might define the study population as all the deer within a particular state. Another researcher studying the AIDS epidemic's effect on the human population might focus on the HIV infection rate in one nation or throughout the world.

▼ **Figure 35-1** Alligators in a Florida swamp sun themselves on the shore. Together, the alligators in the swamp make up a population.

Population Density

Ecologists often describe a population in terms of its density. **Population density** is the number of individuals of a particular species per unit area or volume. The number of alligators per square kilometer of swamp, the number of bacteria per square centimeter of an agar plate, and the number of earthworms per cubic meter of soil are all examples of population density measurements.

On rare occasions you can count all the individuals in a population, such as the number of beech trees in a forest measuring 50 square kilometers (km^2). If there were 1000 beech trees in this forest, the population density would be 1000 trees per 50 km^2. Reducing this fraction allows you to express the density of trees in a single square kilometer (20 trees per km^2).

$$\text{Population density} = \frac{\text{Individuals}}{\text{Unit area}} = \frac{\text{1000 trees}}{50\ km^2} = \frac{\text{20 trees}}{km^2}$$

Population density is a helpful measurement for comparing populations in different locations. For example, beech trees are more dense in the above forest (20 trees/km^2) than in a 100 km^2 forest with 500 beech trees (5 trees/km^2).

Sampling Techniques

It usually isn't practical to count every member of a population. There may be too many individuals, or they may move around too quickly to be counted accurately, as with many species of insects, birds, and fish. In such cases, ecologists use a variety of sampling techniques to estimate the size of the population.

Quadrats The researchers in Figure 35-2 have marked off an area of tundra. They are counting the number of a particular species of plant within this boundary, called a quadrat. After repeating this procedure in several locations within the ecosystem, the ecologists will average their results to estimate the population density of this plant in the ecosystem. The more quadrats they study, the more accurate the estimate.

Indirect Counting A sampling technique for organisms that move around a lot or are difficult to see is indirect counting. This method involves counting nests, burrows, or tracks rather than the organisms themselves (Figure 35-3).

Online Collaborative Science 4

www.biology.com

Exploring Lawn Biodiversity
The community of organisms in a lawn is more diverse than you might expect. In this field investigation, you and your classmates will investigate the biodiversity of a lawn or park area. Then share, compare, and discuss your results with other classrooms from around the country to explore patterns and ask your own questions.

▲ **Figure 35-2** These scientists are using a quadrat to sample a plant population in the Canadian Arctic tundra.

◀ **Figure 35-3** The individuals of an African termite population are too numerous to count. Instead, the size and number of termite mounds can be used to estimate the population size.

Mark-Recapture Another technique commonly used to estimate animal populations is the mark-recapture method. The biologist traps animals in the study area and marks them, such as with a drop of colored dye. The researcher then releases the marked individuals. After a period of time, the researcher again captures animals from the population and counts the marked and unmarked individuals in the second sample. The following formula then gives an estimate of the total population size:

$$\text{Total population} = \frac{\text{number in first capture} \times \text{number in second capture}}{\text{number of marked animals recaptured}}$$

You can learn how to use this technique in Online Activity 35.1.

Limits to Accuracy Most sampling techniques involve making some assumptions about the population being studied. If these assumptions are not valid, then the estimate will not be accurate. For example, the quadrat method assumes that organisms are distributed fairly evenly throughout the study area. But some populations may be arranged in "clumps," such as cottonwood trees clustered near sources of water in a dry ecosystem (Figure 35-4). If the quadrat includes a clump, the estimate for the total population may be too high. If the quadrat does not include a clump, the estimate may be too low. To minimize this problem, biologists must consider how a study population is distributed when choosing an appropriate quadrat size.

The mark-recapture technique assumes that both marked and unmarked animals have the same chance of surviving and of being caught in the second capture. In reality, animals that have been captured once may be wary of traps and avoid being recaptured. This behavior change in previously captured animals could lead to overestimating the population size. To lessen this problem, researchers try to minimize the effects of trapping on the captured animals.

▼ **Figure 35-4** Rather than being distributed randomly in this desert ecosystem in Utah, cottonwood trees line the creekbeds. Quadrats may not be the best method for sampling this clumped population.

Online Activity 35.1

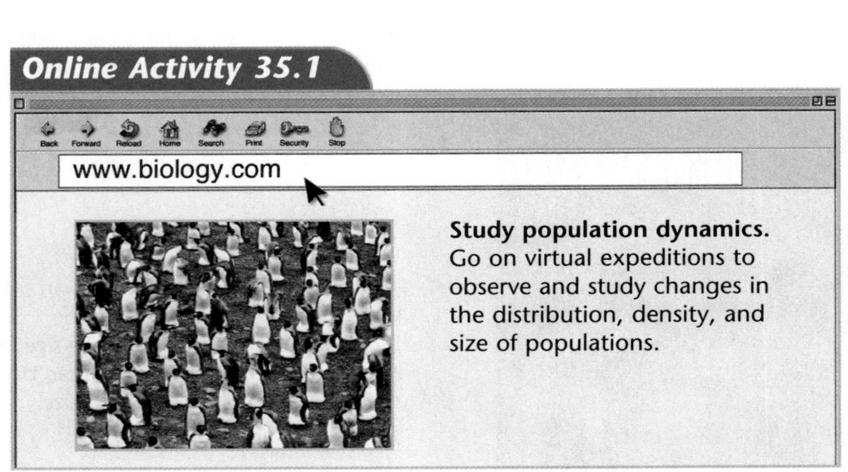

Back
Forward
Reload
Home
Search
Print
Security
Stop
www.biology.com
Study population dynamics.
Go on virtual expeditions to observe and study changes in the distribution, density, and size of populations.

Concept Check 35.1

1. Give an example of boundaries that ecologists use to study populations.
2. Contrast population *size* with population *density.*
3. Give an example of a population of organisms located near your school. Describe a method you could use to measure the density of this population.
4. What is the relationship between the terms *species* and *population?*

Dynamic Populations

Determining the Size of a Moving Population

Question How can you determine the size of a population of organisms when the organisms move around or are hard to locate?

Lab Overview In this field investigation you will discover how to use the mark-recapture method to estimate the size of a population of moving organisms. You will then use the mark-recapture method to do your own population study of local garden invertebrates.

Preparing for the Lab To help you prepare for the investigation, go to the *Lab 35 Online Companion* ·····➔ where you'll take on the role of a fisheries biologist. Explore the use of the mark-recapture method as you estimate the trout population of a flood-affected stream two years after the flood. Prepare for the lab procedure by previewing the steps you will take.

Completing the Lab Use your Laboratory Manual or lab page printouts from the *Lab 35 Online Companion* to do the investigation and analyze your results. **CAUTION:** *Be sure to follow your teacher's instructions and all safety guidelines in the investigation.*

CONCEPT 35.2 There are limits to population growth.

OBJECTIVES

- Describe the pattern of exponential growth.
- Relate limiting factors and carrying capacity.
- Compare and contrast density-dependent and density-independent factors.
- Identify hypotheses for the causes of population growth cycles.

KEY TERMS

- exponential growth
- limiting factor
- carrying capacity
- density-dependent factor
- density-independent factor

What's Online

Online Activity 35.2
Analyze population growth data.

The population of crows in your neighborhood can grow, decline, or stay constant over time. If conditions were ideal for crows, the population would grow until your neighborhood was completely overrun with crows. Fortunately, this does not occur. The crow population's ability to grow is limited by predators, disease, food supply, and other factors in the crows' environment.

Exponential Growth of Populations

A population's ability to grow depends partly on the rate at which its organisms can reproduce. Bacteria are among the fastest-reproducing organisms. A single bacterium can reproduce every 20 minutes under laboratory conditions of unlimited food, space, and water. After just 36 hours, this rate of reproduction would result in enough bacteria to form a layer almost half a meter deep covering the entire planet.

In general, larger mammals reproduce at slower rates than smaller mammals. For example, elephants produce fewer offspring than mice and have longer time intervals between offspring. But even so, in theory, the descendants of a single pair of mating elephants would number 19 million elephants within 750 years.

In these theoretical examples, the bacteria and elephant populations are undergoing **exponential growth,** in which the population multiplies by a constant factor at constant time intervals. Consider the bacteria example. The constant factor for this population is 2, because each parent cell splits, forming two offspring cells. The constant time interval is 20 minutes. So every 20 minutes, the population is multiplied by 2. Graphing these data forms the J-shaped curve in Figure 35-5. Notice that the larger the population of bacteria, the faster the population grows—the curve gets steeper with time.

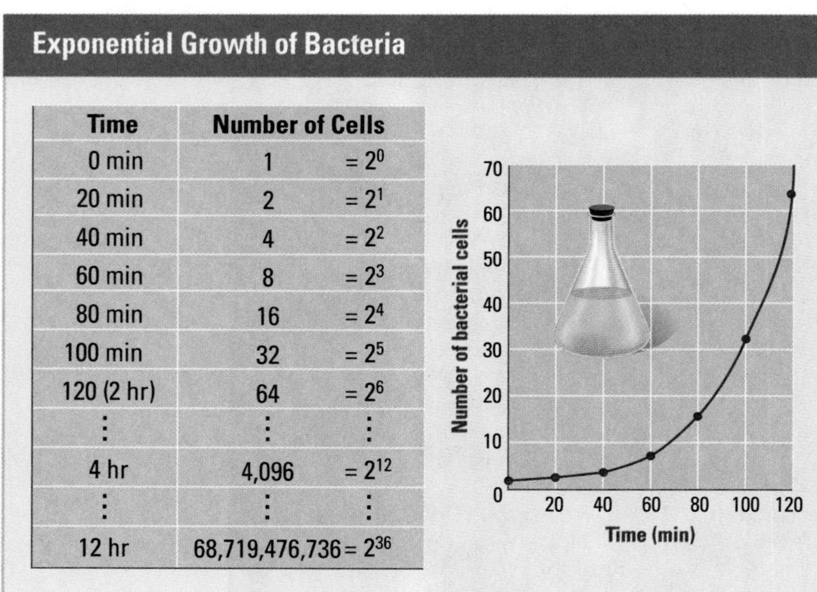

Exponential Growth of Bacteria

Time	Number of Cells	
0 min	1	$= 2^0$
20 min	2	$= 2^1$
40 min	4	$= 2^2$
60 min	8	$= 2^3$
80 min	16	$= 2^4$
100 min	32	$= 2^5$
120 (2 hr)	64	$= 2^6$
⋮	⋮	⋮
4 hr	4,096	$= 2^{12}$
⋮	⋮	⋮
12 hr	68,719,476,736	$= 2^{36}$

Figure 35-5 This table shows how many bacteria are in a population that doubles every 20 minutes. The graph is another way to show the same data.

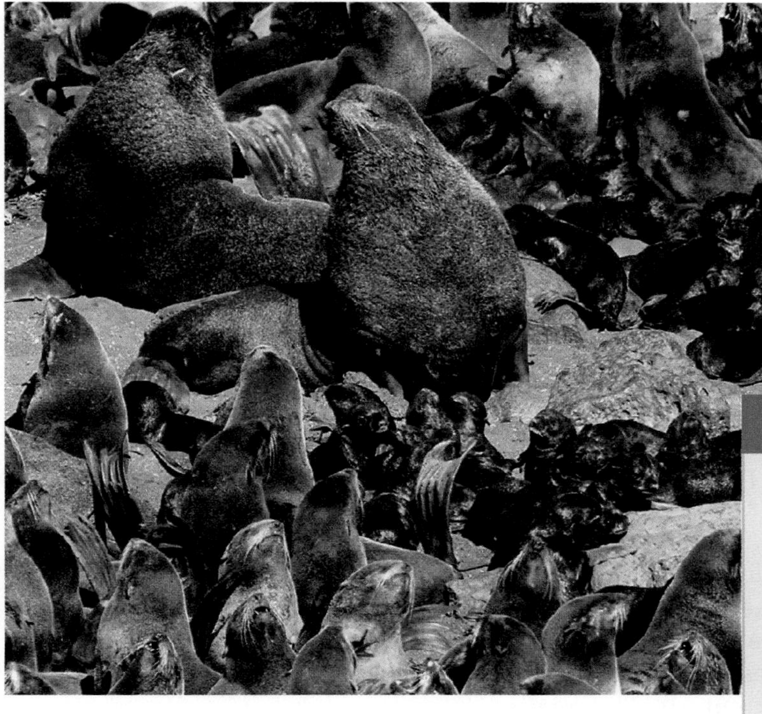

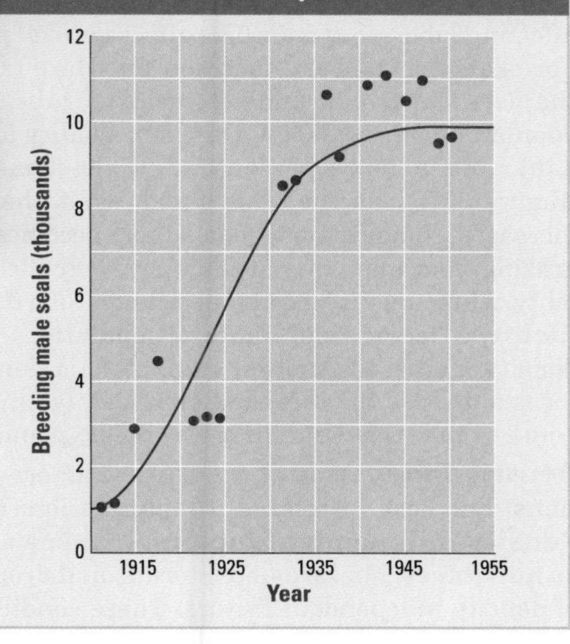

▲ **Figure 35-6** Before the early 1900s, hunting kept this population of fur seals below the carrying capacity of the environment. Then, after hunting was reduced, the population grew almost exponentially for two decades. The population began to level off as it reached the carrying capacity.

Carrying Capacity

In nature, a population may start growing exponentially, but eventually one or more environmental factors will limit its growth. The population then stops growing or may even begin to decrease. For example, consider lily pads growing and spreading across the surface of a pond. Once the pond is covered in lily pads, no more can grow. Space is one example of a **limiting factor,** a condition that can restrict a population's growth. Other limiting factors include disease and availability of food.

Figure 35-6 shows the growth of a population of fur seals on Saint Paul Island off the coast of Alaska. Until the early 1900s, hunting kept the seal population small and fairly stable. Then hunting on the island was reduced, and the seal population began to increase almost exponentially. By about 1935, the population leveled off again. Ecologists hypothesized that the population became limited by a variety of factors, including disease and competition for food.

When such environmental factors limit a population's growth rate, the population is said to have reached its carrying capacity. The **carrying capacity** is the number of organisms in a population that the environment can maintain, or "carry," with no net increase or decrease. As a growing population approaches carrying capacity, the birth rate may decrease or the death rate may increase (or both), until they are about equal. Over time the balance in births and deaths keeps the change in the population size close to zero. Notice the S-shaped curve of the seal population graph in Figure 35-6. The seal population increased rapidly for a time, but then stabilized when it reached the carrying capacity of the environment.

Factors Affecting Population Growth

In the laboratory, you can observe the effects of environmental factors such as food availability or temperature on population growth. For example, if you put fruit flies in a container and add the same amount of food each day, the population rapidly increases until the daily food supply cannot support more flies. If you place another container of fruit flies on a sunny window ledge, the heat may cause that population to decrease despite a sufficient food supply.

Density-Dependent Factors Factors similar to those affecting laboratory fruit flies affect natural populations. For example, the best nutrition for white-tailed deer is the new leaves and buds of woody shrubs. When deer population density is low, this high-quality food is abundant, and a large percentage of the females bear offspring (Figure 35-7). On the other hand, when the population density increases, the nutritious food supply becomes scarce due to overgrazing, and many females do not reproduce at all. The availability of high-quality food is one example of a **density-dependent factor,** a factor that limits a population more as population density increases. Another example of a density-dependent factor is a disease that spreads more easily among organisms in a dense population than in a less dense population.

▲ **Figure 35-7** In deer populations, twin fawns are much more common when population densities are low than when densities are high.

Density-Independent Factors Factors that limit populations but are unrelated to population density are called **density-independent factors.** Extreme weather events, such as hurricanes, blizzards, ice storms, and droughts, are examples of density-independent factors. These conditions have the same effect on a population regardless of its size.

Many insect populations are particularly vulnerable to density-independent factors. For example, aphids produce large numbers of offspring in warm, damp conditions (Figure 35-8). But if the weather suddenly turns hot and dry, the aphids will die off in large numbers. (This was the same effect observed in the fruit fly population that was placed on a sunny shelf.) Other examples of density-independent factors include fires, floods, and major changes in a habitat, such as the trees in a forest being cut down.

▼ **Figure 35-8** A population of aphids typically grows exponentially in the wet spring months. The population nearly dies off in the hot, dry summer. Weather is a density-independent factor that limits the aphid population.

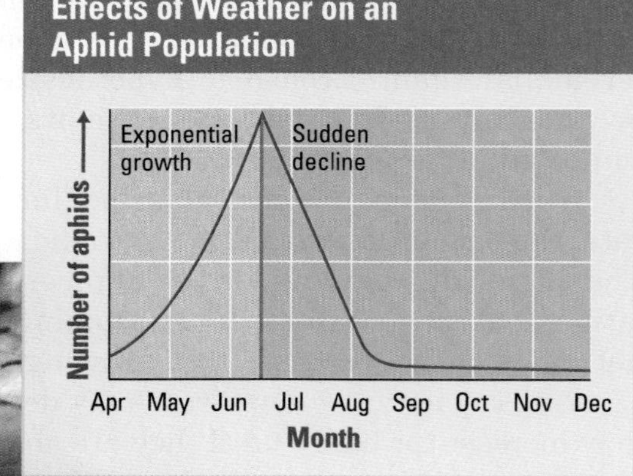

Population Growth Cycles

Some populations have “boom-and-bust” growth cycles: They increase rapidly for a period of time (the “boom”), but then rapidly decline in numbers (the “bust”). Populations of various rodents exhibit boom-and-bust cycles. A striking example is lemming populations, which can cycle dramatically every three to five years. Some researchers hypothesize that natural changes in the lemmings’ food supply may be the underlying cause. Another hypothesis is that stress from crowding during the “boom” may affect the lemmings’ hormonal balance and reduce the number of offspring produced, causing a “bust.”

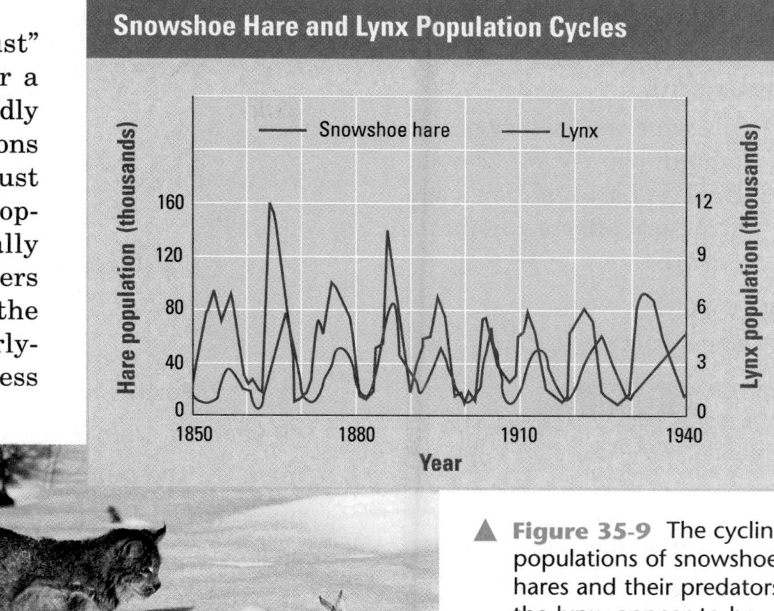

▲ **Figure 35-9** The cycling populations of snowshoe hares and their predators, the lynx, appear to be related. Increases in the hare population are followed closely by increases in the lynx population.

Some populations’ growth cycles appear to be influenced by those of other populations in their environments. For example, in the forests of northern Canada, both the lynx and the snowshoe hare follow boom-and-bust cycles (Figure 35-9). About every 10 years, the hare population reaches a high point, followed by a sharp decrease. The lynx, which feeds on the hare, has a population cycle that seems to follow that of the hares. When the hare population increases, the lynx population follows closely. You might hypothesize that the greater availability of food enables the lynx population to grow. Then, as more and more lynx feed on the hares, the hare population decreases again, which in turn becomes a limiting factor for the lynx. This complicated relationship is still not fully understood. Are the two species directly influencing each other’s population growth? Or is there another underlying cause for the changes, such as a cycle in the hares’ food supply? The causes of boom-and-bust cycles vary among species.

Online Activity 35.2

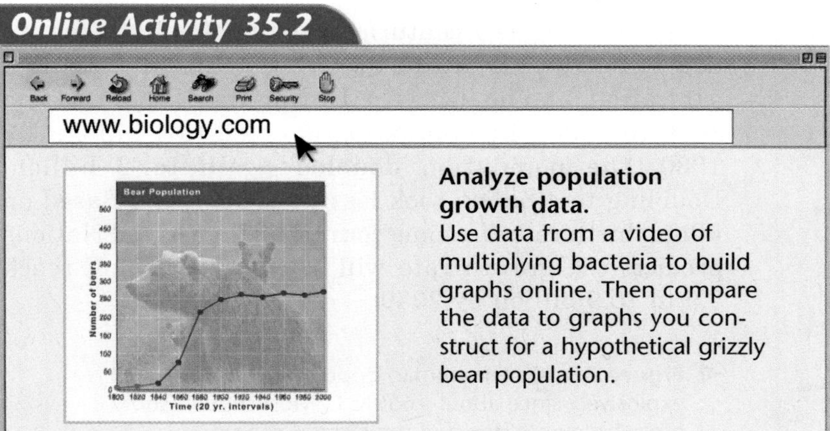

Analyze population growth data.
Use data from a video of multiplying bacteria to build graphs online. Then compare the data to graphs you construct for a hypothetical grizzly bear population.

Concept Check 35.2

1. Describe how a population grows with unlimited food, space, and water.
2. Describe what happens when a population reaches its carrying capacity in a particular environment.
3. Compare density-dependent and density-independent factors, and give an example of each.
4. What is a “boom-and-bust” population growth cycle? What might cause such a cycle?

CONCEPT 35.3

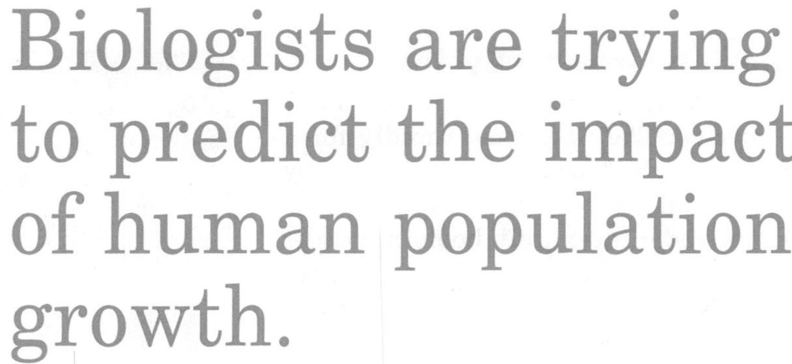

Biologists are trying to predict the impact of human population growth.

OBJECTIVES

- Describe the history of human population growth.
- Explain how a nation's age structure affects population growth.

KEY TERM

- age structure

What's Online

www.biology.com

Online Activity 35.3
Plot human population growth over time.

In 1959, Earth's human population numbered three billion. Just 40 years later, in 1999, the population had passed the six billion mark. As the population continues to expand in the 21st century, humans will require more and more resources, including space to live, land to raise food, and places to dump wastes. As with any species, there is a limit to the population of humans that the environment can support.

History of Global Population Growth

For most of human history, the population has grown extremely slowly or not at all (Figure 35-10). But for the last few centuries, the human population has grown so rapidly that it resembles the exponential growth curve you read about in Concept 35.2. What circumstances accompanied this dramatic change?

As with other species, human population growth depends on birth rates and death rates. When birth rates go up and death rates go down, the population increases. About 10,000 years ago, in 8000 B.C.E. (before the common era), some changes in human culture started causing such an increase. Wide-scale farming began to replace hunting and gathering, providing a more plentiful food supply. More food meant people reproduced more and lived longer, and the population began to climb. Scientists estimate that by 1650 C.E. (common era), the population was 500 million.

In the past few centuries, death rates have continued to decline because of improvements in nutrition, sanitation, and health care. During the 150 years from 1650 to 1800, the population doubled to 1 billion. By 1930, the population doubled again to 2 billion. Doubling to 4 billion took less than 50 years. Based on falling birth rates in some countries, the United Nations predicts the growth rate will slow, but will still reach 7.9 to 10.9 billion by 2050.

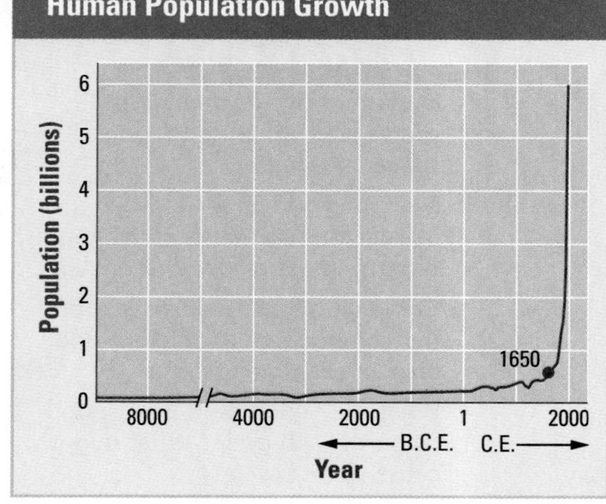

Figure 35-10 The human population has increased explosively since about 1650 C.E. Most models show growth slowing down in the current century.

Predicting Future Population Growth

The future of human population growth is difficult to predict. Scientists use a variety of data and assumptions to develop hypotheses about future growth. Many predictions of growth in specific countries are partly based on a characteristic called age structure. The **age structure** of a population is the proportion of people in different age groups. Figure 35-11 shows the age structures of the United States and Kenya. Each bar represents an age group, such as 15- to 19-year-olds. The length of the bar indicates what portion of the total population falls within that age group. (Note that the scale on the x-axis is different in the two graphs because their population sizes are so different.)

Kenya's population includes many more individuals who are under 30 than who are over 45. Because young people are likely to have children in the future, the population of Kenya is likely to continue to increase rapidly. In the United States, there is more of a balance in different age groups. However, there is still a bulge in the age groups that are likely to have children, and so the population is predicted to grow. In addition, high rates of immigration (people moving into the country) contribute more people to the U.S. population. Some nations currently have declining growth rates. For example, Sweden has a low birth rate and a top-heavy age structure.

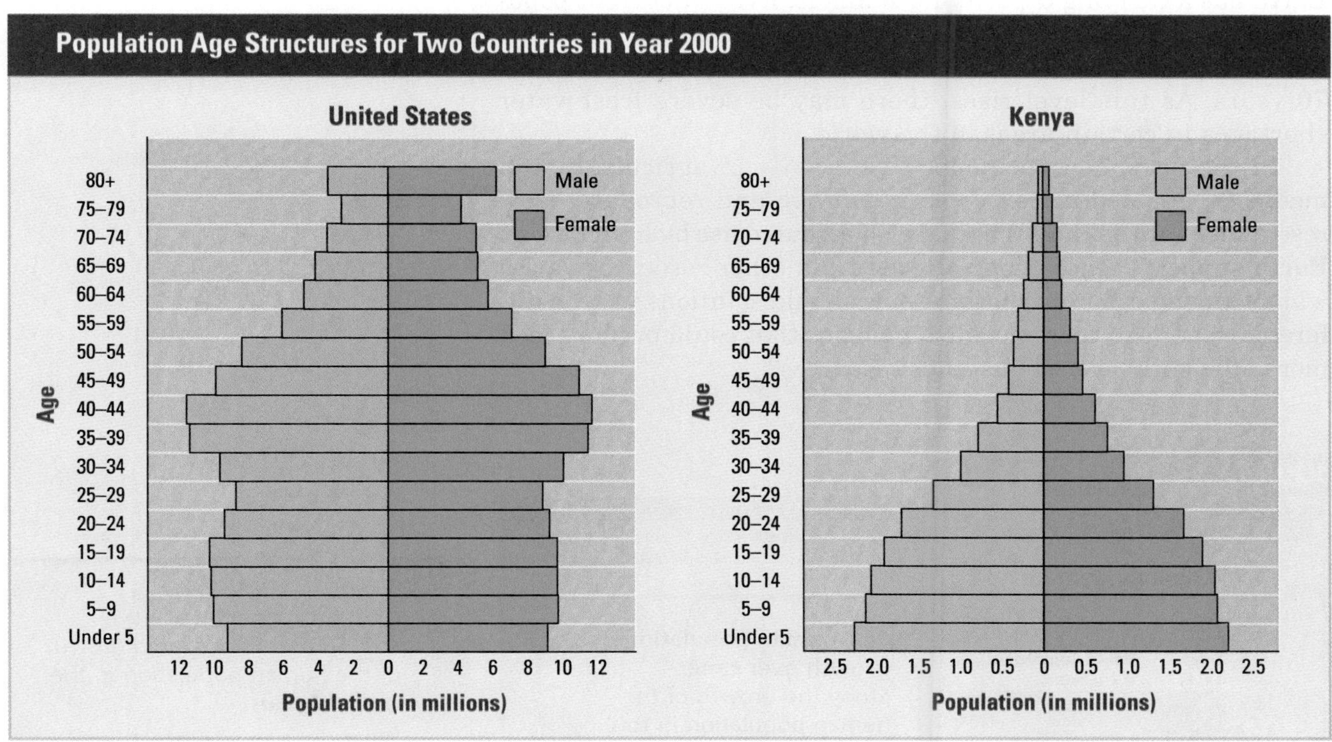

▲ **Figure 35-11** Age-structure graphs for the United States and Kenya show striking differences in the ages of people making up the two populations. Analyzing age structures can help scientists predict future growth in a particular country.

Predictions of future trends in worldwide human population growth vary. One reason for the variation is that the projections depend on assumptions about how birth and death rates will change in various nations in the future. In many developed nations, populations are experiencing very little growth or are even declining, due to low birth rates. Most of the current population growth is occurring in less developed countries. Historically, as nations have become more developed, the birth rate has tended to decline. Will this trend continue? There is a great deal of debate and uncertainty about these assumptions and projections.

The different predictions also raise the question of whether Earth has a carrying capacity for humans. Even at current population levels, humans are straining the planet's natural resources. For example, water use has increased 600 percent over the past 70 years. As this level rises, there may be severe freshwater shortages in certain areas of the world.

In the past, new technology, especially in agriculture and medicine, enabled more people to survive and reproduce. Now researchers are asking: What level of resource use by humans can Earth support? Since usage of water and other resources varies widely among different nations, how should solutions vary in different areas? Are there new technologies that could produce food more efficiently or provide other resources?

▲ **Figure 35-12** A city population's demands for food, water, energy, and other supplies can strain resources far from the city.

Online Activity 35.3

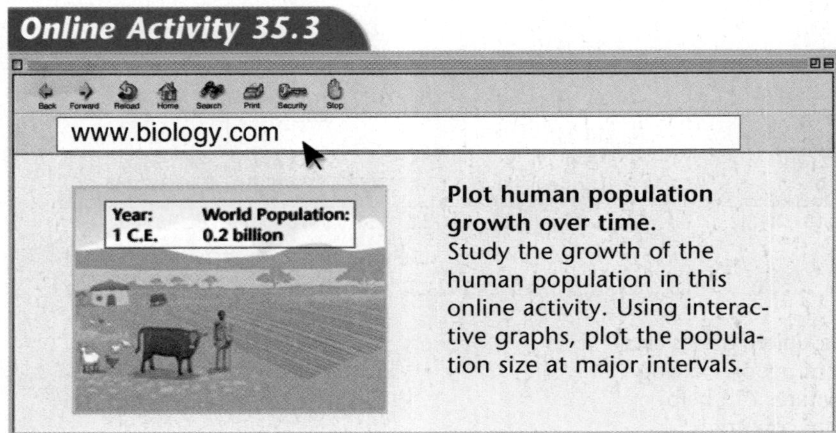

Plot human population growth over time.
Study the growth of the human population in this online activity. Using interactive graphs, plot the population size at major intervals.

Concept Check 35.3

1. List some factors that have contributed to the rapid growth of the human population in the last 500 years.
2. What does an age-structure graph show? How might a scientist use this information to make predictions about future population growth?

CONCEPT 35.4 Species interact in biological communities.

OBJECTIVES

- Identify causes and possible results of interspecific competition.
- Identify some adaptations of predators and prey.
- Compare and contrast symbiotic relationships.

KEY TERMS

- interspecific competition
- competitive exclusion
- niche
- predation
- symbiotic relationship
- parasitism
- mutualism
- commensalism

What's Online

www.biology.com
Online Activity 35.4
Classify interactions of populations.

On your next walk through a patch of woods or park, or even down a city street, look for examples of different species interacting with each other. You might observe birds nesting in trees, bees collecting pollen from flowers, or ferns growing in the shade of larger plants. Populations do not live in isolation—instead, they interact with other populations living in the same area. In some cases, populations compete for resources such as food, water, or shelter.

Competition Between Species

The massive elephant in Figure 35-13 cannot survive without other organisms. The elephant is part of a herd of elephants that form a population. The herd is part of a larger community of organisms. Recall from Chapter 34 that a community is a group of species living in the same geographic area. The elephants' community includes gazelles, giraffes, and birds; ants, beetles, fungi, and bacteria in the soil; and grasses and trees.

In Concept 35.2 you read that members of a population may compete for limited resources in the environment. This competition within a single species limits the growth of the population. Within a community, **interspecific competition** (competition between species) takes place when two or more species rely on the same limited resource. For example, in the African savanna community, many species feed on grasses. In times of drought, the grasses may be in short supply, and competition may become especially intense.

▼ **Figure 35-13** Elephants, gazelles, and various kinds of trees and shrubs are just a few of the many species in this African savanna community.

Competitive Exclusion If two species are so similar in their requirements that the same resource limits both species' growth, one species may succeed over the other. This process is referred to as **competitive exclusion.** A Russian biologist named G.F. Gause demonstrated this principle in the laboratory. He cultured two different species of *Paramecium, P. aurelia* and *P. caudatum,* feeding them a constant amount of food every day. When he grew them in separate containers, both thrived. But when he grew them together, the two species competed for the limited food available. Because *P. aurelia* could gather food more quickly, *P. aurelia* survived and reproduced, while *P. caudatum* starved. Eventually only *P. aurelia* remained in the culture.

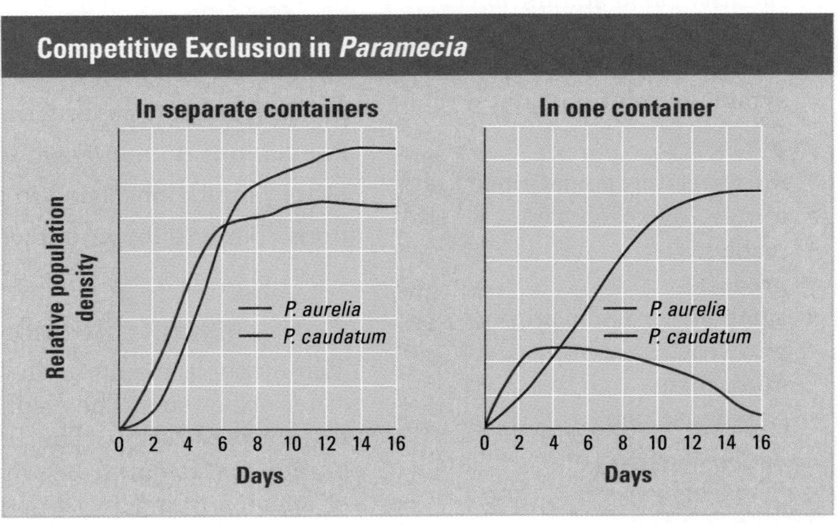

▲ **Figure 35-14** Two similar species may each thrive in separate locations, but one may exclude the other when they are placed together. The results of an experiment with two *Paramecium* species demonstrate this principle of competitive exclusion.

In nature, the degree to which two species can require the same resources and still coexist depends on other factors in the ecosystem. For example, predators may keep competing populations below the levels at which resources such as food would become limiting factors. Gause's laboratory experiment demonstrated the process of competitive exclusion because he was able to isolate the two species and their common limiting resource (food) in the laboratory.

Niches Within a community, each species has a unique living arrangement called its niche. A **niche** includes an organism's living place (habitat), its food sources, the time of day it is most active, and many other factors specific to that organism's way of life. The local loss of a species due to competitive exclusion is most likely to occur if two species have niches that are very similar. But even when species compete for some of the same resources, their niches are rarely identical. For example, one lizard species in a tropical forest may feed on insects in low shrubs, while a similar lizard species may eat insects high in the trees.

Predation

Within the same savanna community where grazing animals may compete for grass, other interactions between species are taking place. For instance, a lion chases down an injured zebra, while nearby an egret targets a fish for its meal. These two interactions are examples of **predation,** an interaction in which one organism eats another. The lion and the egret are examples of predators, the organisms doing the eating. The food species being eaten are the prey. Because eating and avoiding being eaten are so important to survival, it is not surprising that many effective adaptations have evolved in both predators and prey.

Predator Adaptations Predators that pursue their prey are generally fast and agile. Many predators have coloring that hides, or camouflages, them in their surroundings (Figure 35-15). Some predators, such as wolves and killer whales, may team up in packs to capture their prey. Most predators have acute senses that enable them to find prey. Rattlesnakes, for example, locate their prey with heat-sensing organs located between each eye and nostril. Adaptations such as claws, teeth, fangs, and stingers help many predators catch prey.

Prey Adaptations Several adaptations help prey avoid being eaten. Some organisms retreat to safe locations; others flee from predators. And, while predators use camouflage to ambush prey, prey may use camouflage to hide from predators. Another type of defensive coloring has the opposite effect—it makes the organism stand out. Such "warning coloration" serves as a caution to predators (Figure 35-16).

Some organisms aren't poisonous or dangerous themselves, but they look like organisms that are. This type of defense is called mimicry. For instance, the hawk moth larva puffs up its head and thorax when disturbed, looking like the head of a small poisonous snake (Figure 35-17). It even weaves its head back and forth and hisses like a snake.

Animals aren't the only prey organisms that have elaborate defense adaptations. Plants cannot run away from predators, but they have other defenses that include poisonous chemicals and structures such as spines and thorns (Figure 35-18).

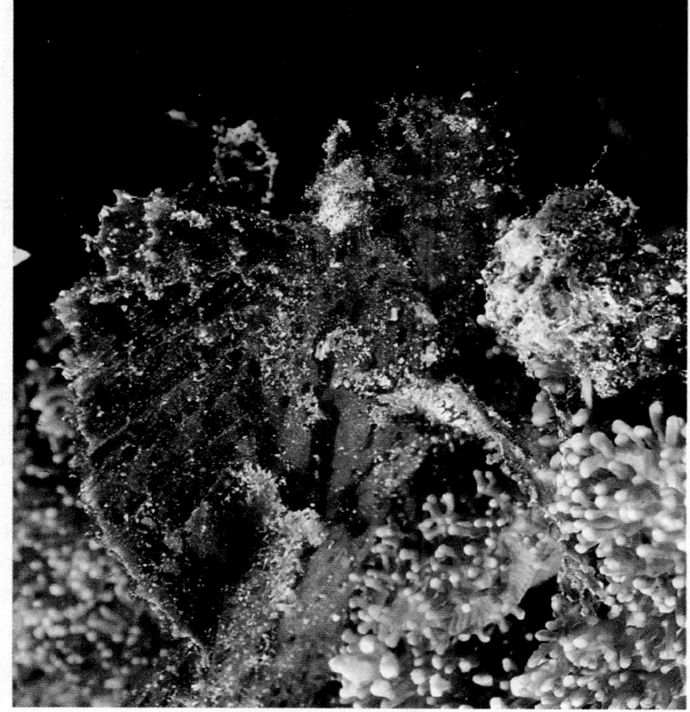

▲ **Figure 35-15** A leaf scorpionfish is a predator that blends into its environment.

◀ **Figure 35-16** Most predators learn to avoid black and yellow coloration, a common characteristic of poisonous prey such as this poison arrow frog.

▼ **Figure 35-17** Which is the caterpillar and which is the snake? Although the caterpillar on the left is harmless, it mimics the poisonous snake on the right, scaring away its potential predators.

◀ **Figure 35-18** Thorns on this rose plant provide defense against predators.

Symbiotic Relationships

A **symbiotic relationship** (sim bee AHT ik) is a close interaction between species in which one of the species lives in or on the other. There are three main types of symbiotic relationships: parasitism, mutualism, and commensalism.

Parasitism is a relationship in which one organism, the parasite, obtains its food at the expense of another organism, the host. Usually the parasite is smaller than the host. Both blood-sucking mosquitoes and tapeworms that live and feed in the intestines of larger animals are examples of parasites. Figure 35-19 shows a tiny parasitic crustacean that burrows into the skin of fish.

The process of natural selection, described in Chapter 14, works on both the parasite and the host. Parasites that can locate and feed on their hosts efficiently are most successful. For example, some aquatic leeches locate their hosts first by detecting movement in the water. Then they confirm their selection by using temperature and chemical cues on the host's skin. Usually the effect of the parasite does not kill the host quickly, which would result in the death of the parasite as well. Natural selection has also produced defensive adaptations that help hosts resist parasites. The immune system of humans and other vertebrates is an example.

In **mutualism,** both organisms benefit from the symbiotic relationship. One example of mutualism occurs inside your own body. Your large intestine is inhabited by millions of bacteria. The bacteria benefit by having a warm, moist home with a constant stream of nourishment, your food. In turn, some intestinal bacteria produce vitamin K. As discussed in Chapter 29, vitamin K is essential for blood clotting. Both you and the bacteria benefit from this relationship.

Commensalism is a relationship in which one organism benefits, while the other organism is neither harmed nor helped significantly. For example, a spider crab may place seaweed on its back. The crab benefits by being camouflaged from its predators. The seaweed does not seem to be significantly affected. True commensalism in nature is rare, since most interactions harm one species (parasitism) or help both species (mutualism) to some degree.

▲ **Figure 35-19** This fish, called a lingcod, is covered with tiny crustaceans that burrow into its skin. Because the crustacean benefits while harming the fish, this symbiotic relationship is an example of parasitism.

Online Activity 35.4

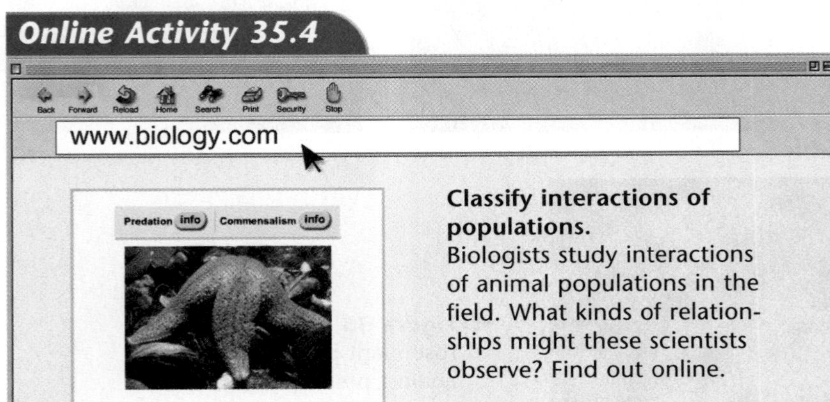

Classify interactions of populations.
Biologists study interactions of animal populations in the field. What kinds of relationships might these scientists observe? Find out online.

Concept Check 35.4

1. How did Gause's experiment with *Paramecium* demonstrate competitive exclusion?
2. Describe two methods predators use to help them capture their prey and two methods prey use to help them avoid being eaten.
3. Define and give an example of each of the three types of symbiotic relationships.

CONCEPT 35.5 Disturbances are common in communities.

OBJECTIVES
- Describe how disturbances can have positive and negative effects.
- Compare primary and secondary succession.
- Explain how human activities can affect species diversity.

KEY TERMS
- ecological succession
- primary succession
- secondary succession
- introduced species

What's Online

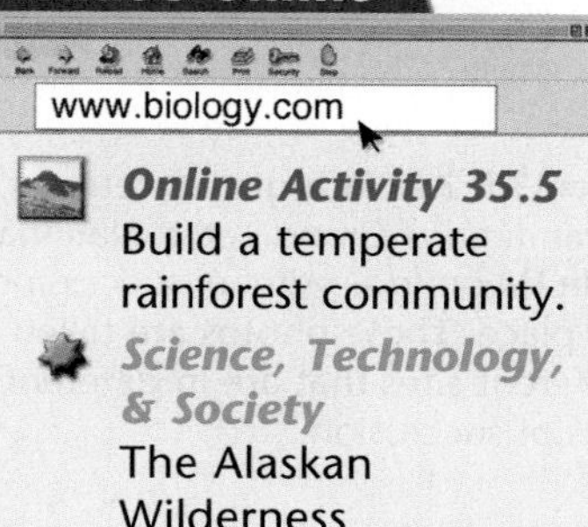

Online Activity 35.5
Build a temperate rainforest community.

Science, Technology, & Society
The Alaskan Wilderness

Raging fires transformed thousands of acres of wilderness in Yellowstone National Park in 1988. Mt. St. Helen's violent volcanic eruption in 1980 leveled thousands of hectares of forest and killed millions of animals. Hurricanes that bear down on the Caribbean topple trees and disturb coral reef communities. These are all examples of disturbances that happen naturally to communities. But human activities can also disturb communities. In this section you will read about the long-term effects of disturbances on communities.

Disturbances to Communities

Communities tend to be in a continual state of change. Natural disturbances such as fires, volcanic eruptions, floods, storms, and droughts affect communities by destroying organisms and changing the availability of resources such as shelter and water (Figure 35-20a). The effects of the disturbance are not necessarily negative. Despite the deaths caused by the disturbance, some organisms thrive in the wake of the destruction. For example, seeds of some plant species require exposure to the extremely high temperature of a forest fire before they can sprout. Disturbances can also be caused by human activities, such as clearing a forest to grow crops or build homes. Like natural disturbances, certain disturbances caused by human activities can have some positive effects. For example, when a ship sinks in the ocean, it disturbs the ocean floor. However, the wreckage also provides new nooks and crannies in which fish can hide. Barnacles, mussels, seaweed, and other marine species can attach to its surfaces (Figure 35-20b).

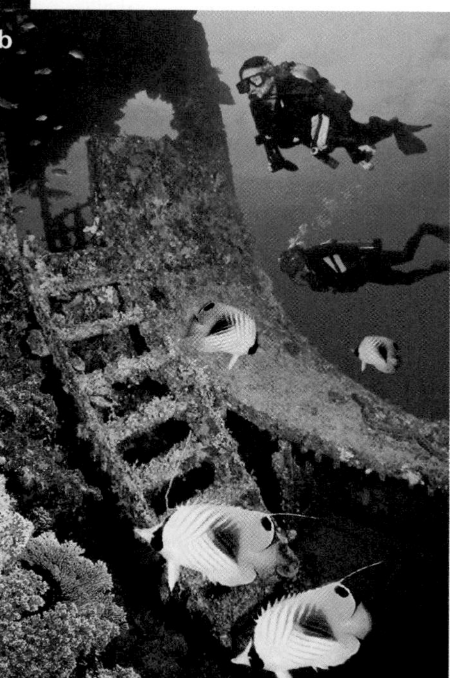

Figure 35-20 Disturbances to communities can be large or small. **a.** Fire is a typically large-scale natural disturbance affecting forested ecosystems. **b.** A sunken ship creates a local, small-scale disturbance to the ocean floor community.

▲ **Figure 35-21** As a glacier retreats from an area of Grand Teton National Park in Wyoming, primary succession takes place. These photos are taken at different sites that are in different stages of succession.

Ecological Succession

Communities may change drastically as a result of a disturbance. A variety of species may colonize the disturbed area. These species may be replaced as yet other species move into the area later. This process of community change is called **ecological succession.**

Primary Succession When a community arises in a lifeless area that has no soil, the change is called **primary succession.** Examples of such areas are new islands created by erupting volcanoes, or the bare rock left behind a retreating glacier. Autotrophic microorganisms are generally the first organisms to appear. Then lichens and mosses, which grow from windblown spores, colonize the barren ground. Soil develops gradually from the action of these early colonizers and from their decomposed remains. Once soil is present, the lichens and mosses may be overgrown by grasses, shrubs, and trees. These plants' seeds may have blown in from other areas or been carried in by animals. Primary succession from barren ground to a community such as a deciduous forest can take hundreds or even thousands of years (Figure 35-21).

Secondary Succession When a disturbance damages an existing community but leaves the soil intact, the change that follows is called **secondary succession.** An example is a forested area that has been cleared for farming and then abandoned. Grasses that grow from seeds carried by animals or the wind may be the first plants to grow in abandoned fields. They may be replaced by shrubs, and eventually by trees similar to those in the original forest.

Science, Technology, & Society

Back Forward Reload Home Search Print Security Stop

www.biology.com

The Alaskan Wilderness

The state of Alaska contains vast stretches of wilderness that are home to many species of plants and animals. It is also a place that contains valuable natural resources, such as oil. Is it possible to tap into some of these resources and also protect the wildlife communities? Go online to investigate this topic and write about it.

Human Activities and Species Diversity

Of all species, humans have had the greatest impact on communities worldwide. Currently 60 percent of Earth's land is used by humans, mostly as cropland or rangeland. Unfortunately, human disturbances usually have a negative effect on species diversity in those communities.

Clearing the Land Many areas of forest have been cut down for lumber or to provide land for farming and building (Figure 35-22). Similarly, much of the natural North American prairie has been converted to farmland. In some cases the diverse forest or grassland community is replaced with crops of a single plant species, such as corn. Other areas may be paved over or eventually recolonized by weeds and shrubs, as in abandoned city lots. Usually the species diversity of these environments is reduced by the disturbances.

▲ **Figure 35-22** A clearcut hillside is an example of human disturbance to a community. Here, secondary succession can be seen in its early stages.

Introduced Species Sometimes called exotic species, **introduced species** are organisms that humans move from the species' native locations to new geographic areas, either intentionally or accidentally. One intentional introduction is kudzu, a Japanese plant that was planted widely in the American South in the 1930s to help control erosion, especially along irrigation canals. But kudzu soon grew out of control, taking over vast expanses of landscape (Figure 35-23).

Many introduced species are ill-suited to their new environment and don't survive to reproduce. However, some introduced species gain a foothold and may disrupt their new community. Some introduced species prey on native species. Introduced species may also outcompete native species that have similar niches.

▲ **Figure 35-23** Introduced species can dramatically change the appearance of a landscape. Kudzu is a vine that covers everything in its path, including abandoned vehicles.

Online Activity 35.5

Build a temperate rainforest community.
What happens to a community during succession? How can you predict the sequence of events that occur in succession? Find out online when you study succession in a temperate rain forest.

Concept Check 35.5

1. Provide an example of an ecological disturbance and describe its effects on a community.
2. What is the main difference between primary and secondary succession?
3. Give an example of an introduced species and describe its effect on species diversity.

Multiple Choice

Choose the letter of the best answer.

1. If there are 50 alligators in a swamp that measures 10 square kilometers (km^2), what is the alligators' population density?
   a. 10 alligators/km^2
   b. 5 alligators
   c. 50 alligators/km^2
   d. 5 alligators/km^2
2. A species of bacteria in a laboratory undergoes exponential growth, reproducing every 30 minutes. Starting with one bacterial cell, how many bacterial cells will there be after 3 hours?
   a. 6
   b. 64
   c. 90
   d. 270
3. Which of the following is an example of a density-dependent factor that limits population growth?
   a. hurricane
   b. flood
   c. food availability
   d. drought
4. The current human population of Earth is closest to
   a. 600,000
   b. 60,000,000
   c. 600,000,000
   d. 6,000,000,000
5. Poison ivy vines often climb tree trunks toward light. They do not harm the trees. What form of symbiotic relationship is this?
   a. mutualism
   b. commensalism
   c. predation
   d. parasitism
6. Which of the following is an example of primary succession?
   a. Trees start growing in a meadow.
   b. Wildflowers colonize abandoned farmland.
   c. Lichens grow on lava rock after a volcanic eruption.
   d. Weeds grow in the soil of an empty city lot.

Short Answer

7. Give two examples of geographic boundaries of populations.
8. Explain the concept of carrying capacity.
9. Give an example of a density-dependent factor, and describe how it might affect a population's growth.
10. Give an example of a density-independent factor, and describe how it might affect a population's growth.
11. Describe the pattern of human population growth over the last 500 years. What are some factors that have contributed to this pattern?
12. Explain how researchers use age-structure graphs to help predict future population growth.
13. Describe the experimental design that Gause used in his study of *Paramecium* species, and summarize his results and conclusions.
14. Describe what factors are included in an organism's niche.
15. Describe three adaptations of prey that help them avoid being eaten.
16. Explain the difference between mutualism and parasitism.
17. Explain how a disturbance might affect one population negatively, while affecting another population in the same community positively.
18. Explain two ways that introduced species may disrupt their new communities.

Visualizing Concepts

19. Construct a concept map showing the main types of interactions among species and the characteristics of those interactions.

Analyzing Information

20. Analyzing Graphs Examine the graph below to answer the questions.

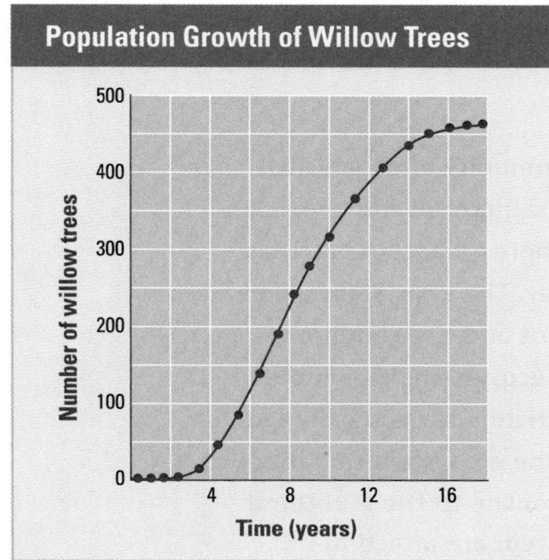

a. During which years is this population of willow trees growing almost exponentially?
b. What is the carrying capacity of the population?
c. Explain why a population in nature cannot grow exponentially forever.

21. Analyzing Data Use the data table below to answer the following questions.

Populations (in millions) of Two Countries

Age Category	Country A		Country B	
	Male	*Female*	*Male*	*Female*
Under 20	4.4	4.2	32.6	32.4
20 – 39	6.5	6.3	15.9	15.5
40 – 59	4.8	4.9	7.9	7.4
60 +	3.7	4.8	2.8	2.8

a. Construct an age-structure graph for each country.
b. Based on the data, which country is more likely to have an increase in population size over the next 10 years? Explain your reasoning.

Critical Thinking

22. Making Generalizations Describe camouflage in animals. How is it an effective adaptation for both predators and prey?

23. Problem Solving As a field biologist, you are studying the wildlife in a local forest. You want to know the population size of three forest species: maple trees, raccoons, and bees. Choose the sampling method you think will best estimate each population. Explain your choices.

24. Developing Hypotheses A scientist staked out two plots of land with the same five wildflower species in roughly equal numbers. Around one plot, she installed a fence to keep out kangaroo rats, which feed on wildflower seeds. After two years, four of the wildflower species were gone from the fenced-in plot, but one species had increased drastically. In the unfenced plot, all five types of flowers flourished. Suggest a hypothesis to explain these results.

25. What's Wrong With These Statements? *Briefly explain why each statement is inaccurate or misleading.*

a. A population always grows until it reaches its carrying capacity.
b. Symbiotic relationships benefit both species.

Performance Assessment

Biology Research Project Choose two similar species that are often found together (like pigeons and sparrows). Find three locations where both species live. Hypothesize how the features of each location affect the population of each species. Is there evidence of competitive exclusion or niche differences? Explain.

Online Assessment/Test Preparation

Back Forward Reload Home Search Print Security Stop

www.biology.com

- **Chapter 35 Assessment**
  Check your understanding of the chapter concepts.
- **Standardized Test Preparation**
  Practice test-taking skills you need to succeed.

Ecosystems and Conservation Biology

This desert ecosystem supports a rich community of organisms, such as the curved-bill thrasher and the saguaro cactus seen below. Even the desert soil is alive with fungi and bacteria actively at work breaking down dead organic matter. This ecosystem seems hardy in its ability to persist in the very hot and dry conditions of the American Southwest. But as in any ecosystem, its complex network of relationships is vulnerable to change. As you will read in this chapter, changes in one aspect of the ecosystem can affect the entire network. Before you begin, go online to the ***WebQuest*** to investigate how changes in one ecosystem are affecting its community of organisms.

Key Concepts

Concept 36.1

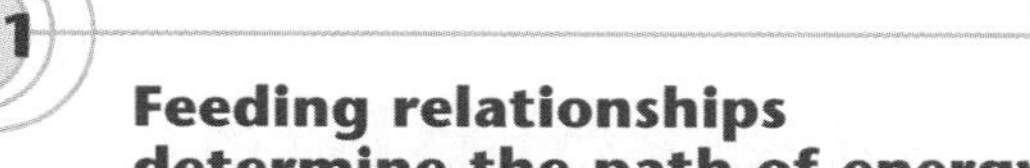

Feeding relationships determine the path of energy and chemicals in ecosystems.

Concept 36.2

Energy flows through ecosystems.

Concept 36.3

Chemicals cycle in ecosystems.

Concept 36.4

Human activities can alter ecosystems.

Concept 36.5

Conservation biology can slow the loss of biodiversity.

Assessment

Chapter 36 Review

What's Online

WebQuest
FrogQuest

Online Activity 36.1
Build an aquatic food chain.

Online Activity 36.2
Graph primary productivity in ecosystems.

Online Activity 36.3
Examine the nitrogen cycle.

Online Activity 36.4
Analyze effects of deforestation.

Lab 36 Online Companion
Can Lake Life Remain Despite Acid Rain?

Online Activity 36.5
Investigate threats to biodiversity.

Science, Technology, & Society
Releasing Genetically Modified Salmon

Chapter 36 Assessment

CONCEPT 36.1

Feeding relationships determine the path of energy and chemicals in ecosystems.

OBJECTIVES

- Contrast the flow of energy and chemicals in ecosystems.
- Explain how trophic levels relate to food chains and food webs.

KEY TERMS

- producer
- consumer
- decomposer
- trophic level
- food chain
- herbivore
- carnivore
- omnivore
- primary consumer
- secondary consumer
- tertiary consumer
- detritus
- food web

What's Online

Online Activity 36.1
Build an aquatic food chain.

As small as it is, a terrarium like the one pictured below is an ecosystem. A terrarium includes a community of organisms such as plants, snails, and bacteria as well as their nonliving environment—the soil, minerals, water, and air. Just as in larger ecosystems such as forests and streams, the terrarium illustrates two key processes of all ecosystems: energy flow and chemical cycling.

Energy Flow and Chemical Cycling

Every organism requires energy to carry out life processes such as growing, moving, and reproducing. Photosynthetic **producers** such as plants convert the light energy from sunlight to the chemical energy of organic compounds (Figure 36-1). Organisms called **consumers** obtain chemical energy by feeding on the producers or on other consumers. Finally, organisms called **decomposers** break down wastes and dead organisms. As living things use chemical energy, they release thermal energy in the form of heat to their surroundings. To summarize, energy enters an ecosystem as light, is converted to chemical energy by producers, and exits the ecosystem as heat. Energy is not recycled within an ecosystem, but flows through it and out. Producers must continue to receive energy as an input for the ecosystem to survive.

In contrast to energy, chemicals such as carbon, oxygen, and nitrogen can be recycled between the living and nonliving parts of ecosystems and the biosphere. In Concept 36.3 you will read about the different chemical cycles in more detail.

Although energy flows through an ecosystem, while chemicals can be used again and again, the movements of both energy and chemicals are related to patterns of feeding within the ecosystem.

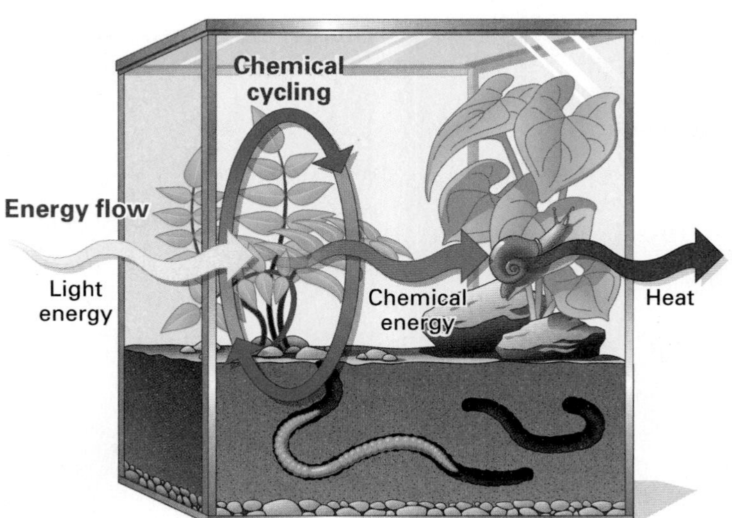

◀ **Figure 36-1** As in larger ecosystems, energy flows through the terrarium ecosystem, while chemicals cycle within it.

Food Chains

In the desert, a grasshopper munches on a brittlebrush's bright yellow flowers. Suddenly, a mouse seizes the grasshopper for its own meal. These feeding relationships, from flower to grasshopper to mouse, relate to how energy and chemicals move through the desert ecosystem. Each of these organisms represents a feeding level, or **trophic level,** in the ecosystem. The pathway of food transfer from one trophic level to another is called a **food chain.**

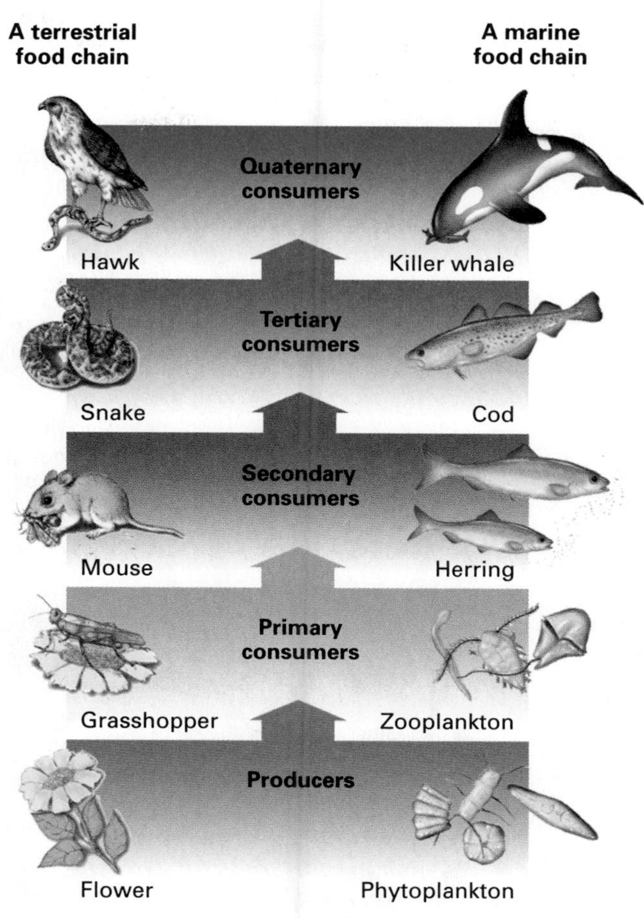

▲ **Figure 36-2** Each of these food chains includes five trophic levels. The arrows indicate the direction of food transfer between trophic levels.

Producers Figure 36-2 compares a terrestrial food chain and an aquatic food chain. In both food chains, the producers make up the trophic level that supports all other trophic levels. In terrestrial ecosystems, plants are the main producers. In aquatic ecosystems, phytoplankton—photosynthetic protists and bacteria—multicellular algae, and aquatic plants are the main producers.

Consumers Organisms in the trophic levels above the producers are consumers. They may be categorized according to what they eat. A consumer (such as a horse) that eats only producers is an **herbivore.** A consumer (such as a lion) that eats only other consumers is a **carnivore.** And a consumer (such as a bear) that eats both producers and consumers is an **omnivore.**

Consumers may also be categorized by their position in a particular food chain. For instance, when a consumer feeds directly on producers it is referred to as a **primary consumer,** or first-level consumer. In terrestrial ecosystems, primary consumers often include insects and birds that eat seeds and fruit, as well as grazing mammals such as antelope and deer. In aquatic ecosystems, primary consumers include a variety of zooplankton (mainly protists and microscopic animals such as small shrimps) that feed on phytoplankton. **Secondary consumers** (second-level consumers) eat primary consumers. On land, secondary consumers include many small mammals and reptiles that eat insects, as well as large carnivores that eat rodents and grazing mammals. In aquatic ecosystems, secondary consumers are mainly small fish that eat zooplankton. **Tertiary consumers** (TUR shee ehr ee)—third-level consumers—eat secondary consumers. On land, a tertiary consumer may be a snake eating a mouse. Some ecosystems, such as those in Figure 36-2, can even support quaternary (fourth-level) consumers. As you will read in Concept 36.2 the number of fourth-level consumers in an ecosystem is usually low.

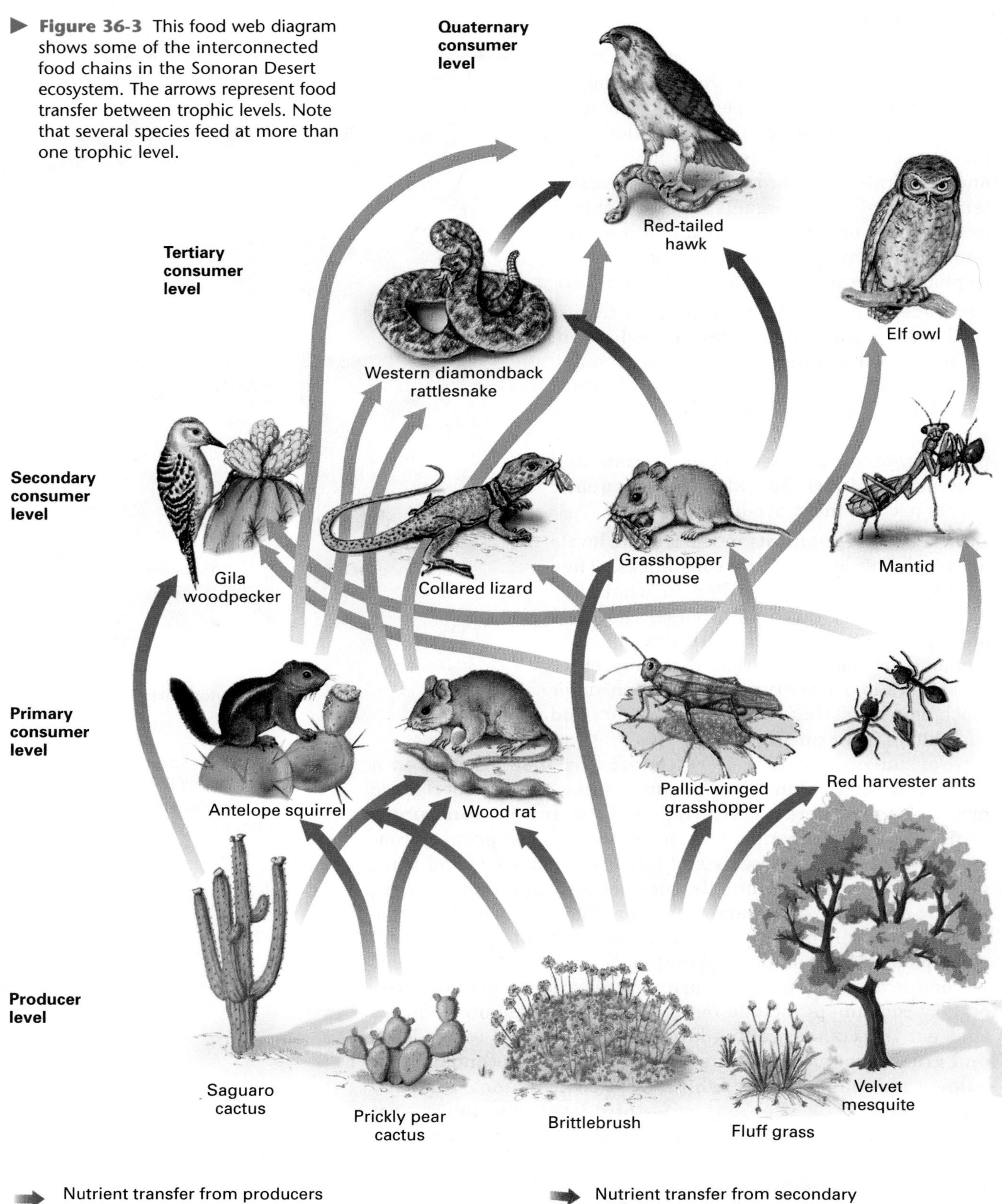

Figure 36-3 This food web diagram shows some of the interconnected food chains in the Sonoran Desert ecosystem. The arrows represent food transfer between trophic levels. Note that several species feed at more than one trophic level.

Decomposers At each trophic level, organisms produce waste and eventually die. These wastes and remains of dead organisms are called **detritus.** Decomposers are consumers that obtain energy by feeding on and breaking down detritus. Animals that eat detritus, often called scavengers, include earthworms, some rodents and insects, crayfish, catfish, and vultures. But an ecosystem's main decomposers are bacteria and fungi. These organisms, found in enormous numbers in the soil and in the sediments at the bottom of lakes and oceans, recycle chemicals within the ecosystem.

Diagrams of food chains, such as those in Figure 36-2, generally do not depict the decomposers that break down the remains of the organisms at each trophic level in the food chain. But all ecosystems do include decomposers—their role is vital to the ongoing recycling of chemicals in the ecosystems.

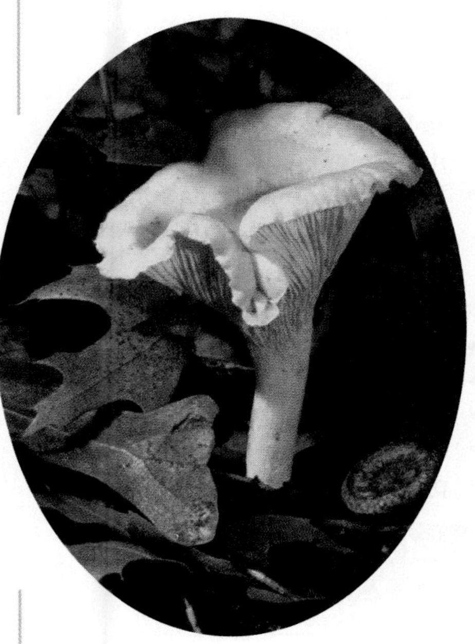

▲ **Figure 36-4** This mushroom, called a smooth chanterelle, recycles chemicals as it decomposes fallen leaves and other plant remains.

Food Webs

The feeding relationships in an ecosystem are usually more complicated than the simple food chains you have just read about. Since ecosystems contain many different species of animals, plants, and other organisms, consumers have a variety of food sources. The pattern of feeding represented by these interconnected and branching food chains is called a **food web.**

Figure 36-3 on the facing page shows how food chains within a food web are interconnected. For example, the rattlesnake eats several animal species that may also be eaten by other consumers, such as the hawk. In addition, some consumers can feed at several different trophic levels. The woodpecker, for instance, is a primary consumer when it eats cactus seeds, and a secondary consumer when it eats ants or grasshoppers. The hawk can be a secondary, tertiary, or even quaternary consumer depending on its prey. Note that like food chains, food web diagrams typically do not show decomposers. In the next section you'll read more about how trophic levels in food webs relate to energy flow in an ecosystem.

Online Activity 36.1

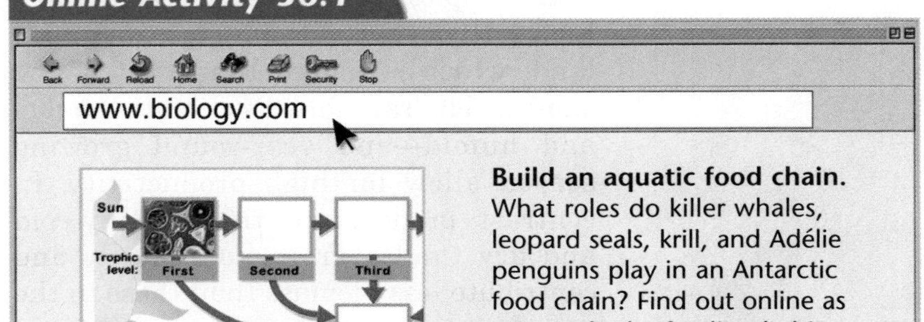

Build an aquatic food chain. What roles do killer whales, leopard seals, krill, and Adélie penguins play in an Antarctic food chain? Find out online as you study the feeding habits of these organisms and build a food chain.

Concept Check 36.1

1. How are the movement of energy and the movement of chemicals in ecosystems different?
2. In the following food chain, identify the trophic levels: An owl eats a mouse that ate berries.
3. Using Figure 36-3, identify a food chain with at least three trophic levels in the Sonoran Desert ecosystem (other than that featured in Figure 36-2).

CONCEPT 36.2 Energy flows through ecosystems.

OBJECTIVES
- Relate ecosystem productivity to biomass.
- Describe the information provided by the three types of ecological pyramids.

KEY TERMS
- biomass
- primary productivity
- energy pyramid
- biomass pyramid
- pyramid of numbers

What's Online

www.biology.com

Online Activity 36.2
Graph primary productivity in ecosystems.

All organisms require energy for growth, reproduction, and, in some species, movement. But there is a limited amount of energy available in an ecosystem—an "energy budget" that is divided among the different trophic levels. This energy budget influences the types and numbers of organisms in the ecosystem.

Productivity of Ecosystems

What determines an ecosystem's energy budget? For most ecosystems, the answer begins with the amount of sunlight that enters the ecosystem. Much of the sunlight that bombards Earth every day bounces back into space or is absorbed by the atmosphere. Of the light energy that reaches plants and other producers, only a tiny fraction—about 1 percent—is captured by photosynthesis. The producers convert this light energy to the chemical energy stored in organic compounds. Even such a small percentage of the sun's total energy output is enough to enable Earth's producers to manufacture billions of kilograms of organic material, or **biomass,** each year.

The rate at which producers in an ecosystem build biomass is called **primary productivity.** The level of primary productivity in an ecosystem sets the energy budget. In other words, primary productivity determines the maximum amount of energy available to all the higher trophic levels in an ecosystem.

Figure 36-5 An ecosystem's primary productivity is the rate at which the producers build biomass. Factors such as rainfall and temperature influence productivity.

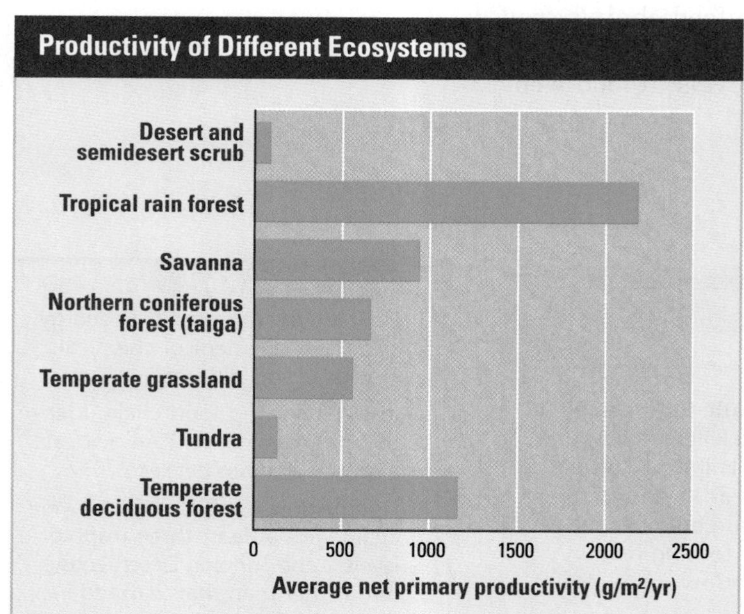

Figure 36-5 contrasts the net primary productivity of several different terrestrial ecosystems. (Net productivity refers to the total amount of organic material produced minus the amount used by the producers themselves to fuel their own life processes.) Notice that the productivity of the tropical rain forest is considerably higher than that of the temperate grassland, which is higher than that of the tundra. The rain forest's climate—warm and humid—and year-round growing season allow for high productivity. In contrast, producers in the typically cold and dry tundra grow more slowly and contribute less biomass than those in the rain forest. Conditions for producers in the grasslands fall in between, and so does their productivity.

Ecological Pyramids

While the producers set an ecosystem's total energy budget, energy is "spent" at each step of the food web. As each consumer feeds, some energy is transferred from the lower trophic level to the higher trophic level. But most of the available energy stored in the prey organism's biomass is lost. For example, when a caterpillar eats a leaf, about 50 percent of the energy stored in the leaf passes out of the caterpillar's body in its wastes (feces). The caterpillar uses 35 percent of the leaf's stored energy to support its life processes, such as moving and reproducing. The caterpillar transforms only about 15 percent of the leaf's stored energy into new caterpillar biomass (Figure 36-6).

To depict information about energy, biomass, and numbers of organisms at different trophic levels, ecologists use three types of diagrams: energy pyramids, biomass pyramids, and pyramids of numbers. In each case, the foundation of the pyramid is the producer level. The primary consumers form the next block, and so on.

Energy Pyramids An **energy pyramid,** sometimes called a food pyramid, emphasizes the energy loss from one trophic level to the next (Figure 36-7). In general, an average of only 10 percent of the available energy at a trophic level is converted to biomass in the next higher trophic level. The rest of the energy—about 90 percent—is lost from the ecosystem as heat.

Notice in Figure 36-7 that the amount of energy available to the top-level consumer is tiny compared to that available to primary consumers. For this reason, it takes a lot of vegetation to support higher trophic levels. This explains why most food chains are limited to three or four levels; there is simply not enough energy at the top of an energy pyramid to support another trophic level. For instance, lions and killer whales have no natural predators; the energy stored in populations of these top-level consumers is not enough to feed yet another trophic level.

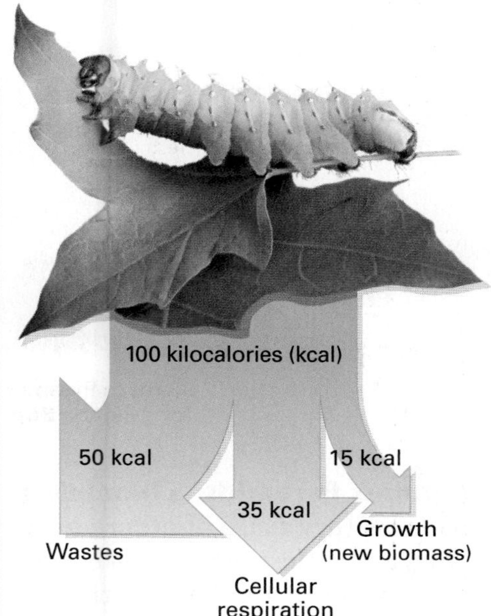

▲ **Figure 36-6** Only 15 percent of the energy stored in this leaf will be converted to new caterpillar biomass through growth of new tissue. (The caterpillar converts slightly more energy to biomass than the average 10 percent.)

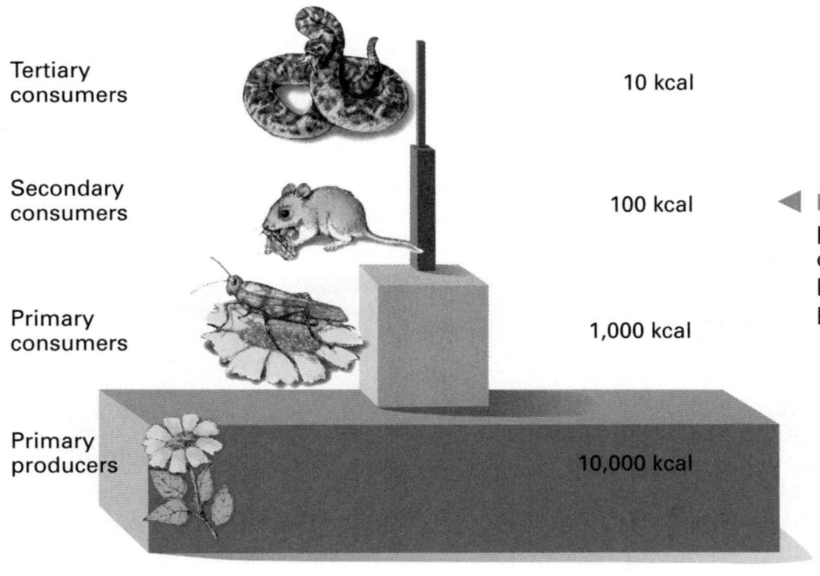

◀ **Figure 36-7** This generalized energy pyramid indicates that only 10 percent of the energy available at a trophic level is typically converted to new biomass in the next trophic level.

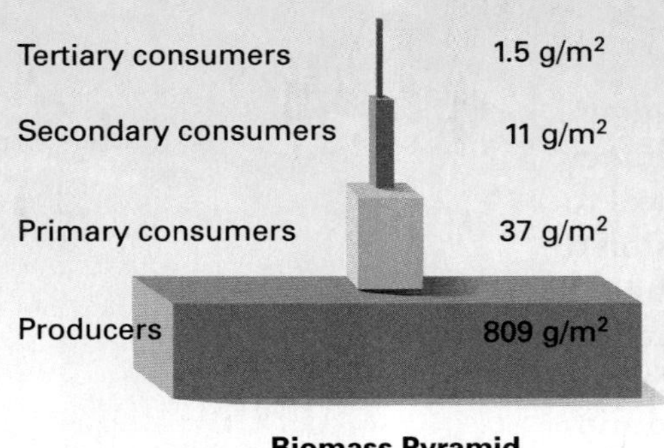

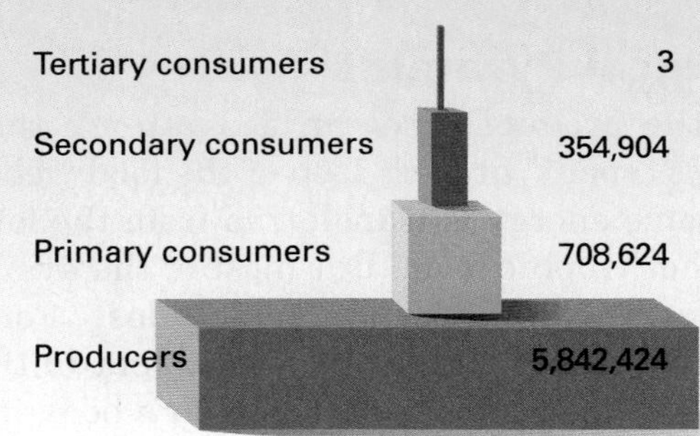

▲ **Figure 36-8** Biomass pyramids and pyramids of numbers are two other ways of modeling information about an ecosystem. A biomass pyramid (left) represents the dry mass of all organisms at each trophic level in an ecosystem. A pyramid of numbers (right) depicts the number of organisms at each trophic level.

Biomass Pyramids A **biomass pyramid** represents the actual biomass (dry mass of all organisms) in each trophic level in an ecosystem. Most biomass pyramids narrow sharply from the producer level at the base to the top-level consumers at the peak (Figure 36-8). There are some exceptions, however. In certain aquatic ecosystems, the zooplankton (primary consumers) consume the phytoplankton (producers) extremely rapidly. As a result, the zooplankton have a greater mass at any given time than the phytoplankton. The phytoplankton grow and reproduce at such a rapid rate that they can support a consumer population that has a greater biomass. A biomass pyramid for this ecosystem would appear top-heavy.

Pyramids of Numbers A **pyramid of numbers** depicts the number of individual organisms in each trophic level of an ecosystem. These pyramids are also organized like energy pyramids, with producers found at the foundation and higher trophic levels on each step above them. In most cases, the foundation is again the widest section, indicating that there are more individual producers than there are primary consumers, and so on (Figure 36-8). This pyramid emphasizes how few top-level consumers an ecosystem can support. Exceptions to the usual shape of a number pyramid occur when small organisms eat larger ones. For example, a single tree (producer) may be the sole food source for hundreds of insects (primary consumers).

Online Activity 36.2

Graph primary productivity in ecosystems.
Go online to analyze the primary productivity of eight different ecosystems and graph the results. Then build an energy pyramid by calculating available food energy at different trophic levels.

Concept Check 36.2

1. What does primary productivity measure? What does it tell you about an ecosystem?
2. What point does each type of ecological pyramid emphasize?
3. What does the shape of the energy pyramid indicate?

CONCEPT 36.3

Chemicals cycle in ecosystems.

OBJECTIVES

- Summarize the basic pattern of chemical cycling.
- Describe how carbon and oxygen are cycled through an ecosystem.
- Describe the movement of nitrogen through an ecosystem.
- Describe the processes that make up the water cycle.

KEY TERMS

- nitrogen fixation
- nitrification
- transpiration

What's Online

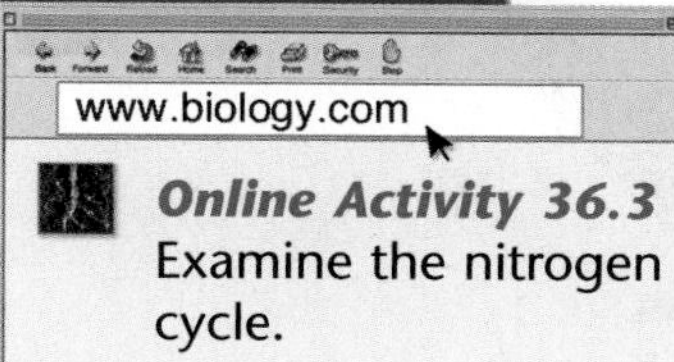

Online Activity 36.3
Examine the nitrogen cycle.

Did you know that some of the carbon atoms in an apple in your lunch might once have been in a panda's lungs? Carbon dioxide molecules exhaled by a panda in China could have been carried to North America by global air currents. During photosynthesis, some of the carbon atoms could have been incorporated into sugar by an apple tree, and then finally reached your lunch tray. It's possible for some of life's important chemicals to travel the globe as they cycle through and between ecosystems.

The Basic Pattern of Chemical Cycling

Many chemicals cycle within an ecosystem. This section explores some of the most important cycles: the carbon and oxygen cycle, the nitrogen cycle, and the water cycle. Chemical cycles typically involve three general steps:

1. Producers incorporate chemicals from the nonliving environment into organic compounds.
2. Consumers feed on the producers, incorporating some of the chemicals into their own bodies and releasing some back to the environment in waste products.
3. As organisms die, decomposers break them down, further supplying the soil, water, and air with chemicals in inorganic form. The producers gain a renewed supply of raw materials for building organic matter, and the cycles continue.

In addition, at least part of each chemical's cycle involves nonliving processes such as rain and fires. As you read about the cycles, look for the three basic steps, as well as for nonliving processes that move chemicals around and between ecosystems.

Figure 36-9 Due to chemical cycling, it's possible that a carbon atom exhaled by this panda in the Wolong Reserve in China could now be in your lunch.

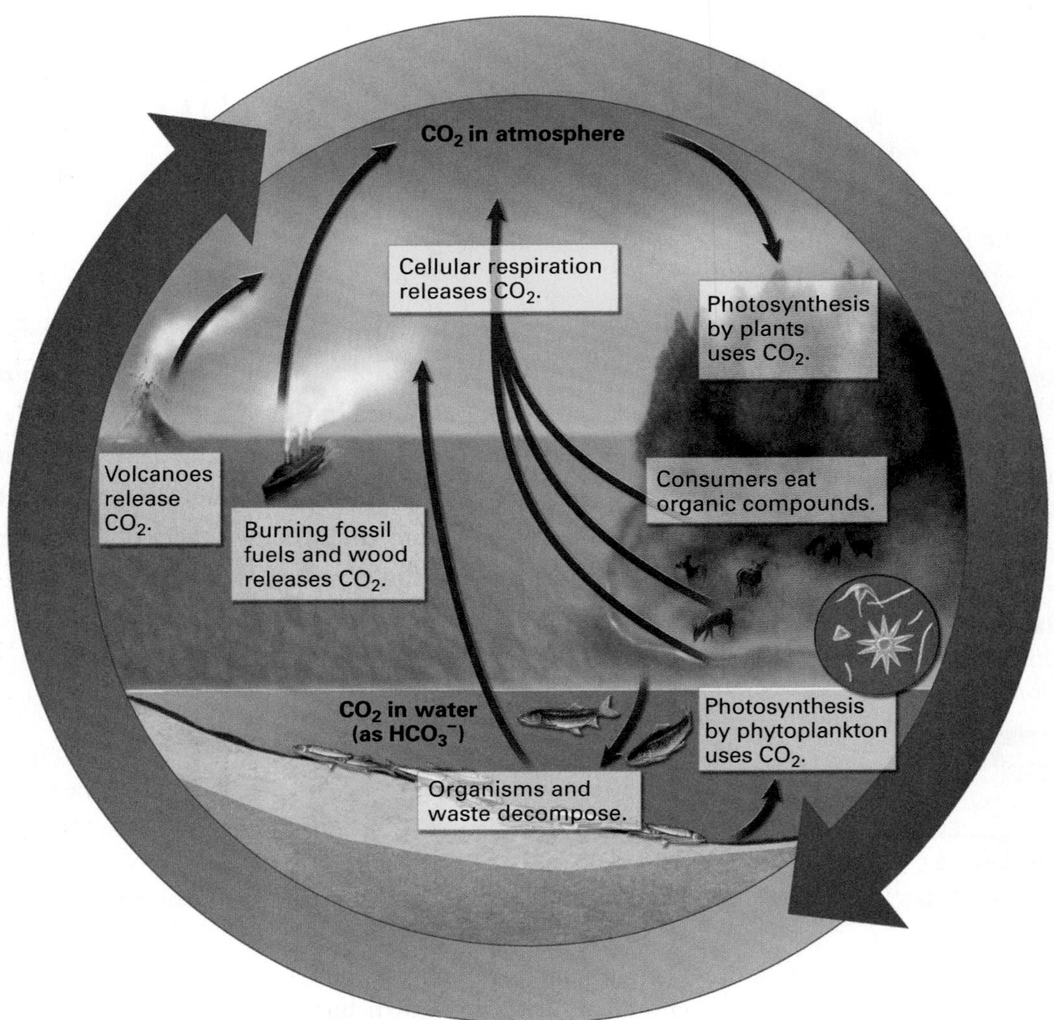
CO2 in atmosphere
Cellular respiration releases CO2.
Photosynthesis by plants uses CO2.
Volcanoes release CO2.
Burning fossil fuels and wood releases CO2.
Consumers eat organic compounds.
CO2 in water (as HCO3−)
Photosynthesis by phytoplankton uses CO2.
Organisms and waste decompose.

▲ **Figure 36-10** Many life processes and human activities contribute to the cycling of carbon in the biosphere.

The Carbon and Oxygen Cycle

Since many of the movements of carbon in an ecosystem are closely linked to those of oxygen, their paths are sometimes described together as the carbon and oxygen cycle. In the atmosphere, carbon is found in inorganic form as carbon dioxide gas (CO_2). Significant amounts of inorganic carbon are also found in water in dissolved form as HCO_3^-. Producers use the carbon and oxygen atoms of these inorganic compounds to form organic compounds during photosynthesis (Figure 36-10). Some of this organic carbon cycles to consumers as food.

During cellular respiration, both producers and consumers break down organic compounds such as sugars and release carbon dioxide gas as a waste product. Carbon dioxide also is released to the atmosphere as decomposers break down detritus.

Nonliving processes also play a role in the carbon cycle. Burning fossil fuels—oil, coal, and natural gas—releases carbon dioxide to the atmosphere. (Fossil fuels form over hundreds of millions of years from the remains of living things.) Burning wood, both from natural forest fires and from human activities, also releases carbon dioxide gas. Geologic events such as volcanic eruptions add more carbon dioxide gas to the atmosphere.

The Nitrogen Cycle

Nitrogen is found in all living organisms as an element in amino acids and other essential molecules. But although almost 80 percent of Earth's atmosphere is nitrogen gas (N_2), most producers can only use nitrogen in the form of compounds such as ammonium (NH_4^+) and nitrate (NO_3^-). Certain types of bacteria convert the nitrogen gas to ammonia (NH_3) through a process called **nitrogen fixation** (Figure 36-11). These nitrogen-fixing bacteria live in the soil and in nodules on the roots of plants such as peas, beans, alfalfa, and clover. In the soil the ammonia picks up another hydrogen ion from water, forming ammonium. Other bacteria in the soil can convert ammonium to nitrates in a process called **nitrification.** Producers absorb the ammonium and nitrates from the soil and use them to build amino acids, proteins, and nucleic acids. Consumers that eat the producers thereby obtain their nitrogen in the form of organic molecules. Eventually, decomposers release the nitrogen (as ammonium) from the wastes and decaying bodies of organisms, and the cycle continues. Denitrifying bacteria in the soil convert some nitrates back to nitrogen gas and release it into the atmosphere.

Free N_2 in atmosphere
Consumer eats plants.
Denitrifying bacteria convert NO_3^- to N_2.
Plants use NO_3^- and NH_4^+.
Nitrogen-fixing bacteria convert N_2 to NH_3.
Decomposers return NH_4^+ to the soil.
NH_3 becomes NH_4^+ in soil.
Nitrifying bacteria convert NH_4^+ to NO_3^-.

▼ **Figure 36-11** From the atmosphere, nitrogen is converted by bacteria to forms that plants and animals can use to build amino acids, proteins, and nucleic acids.

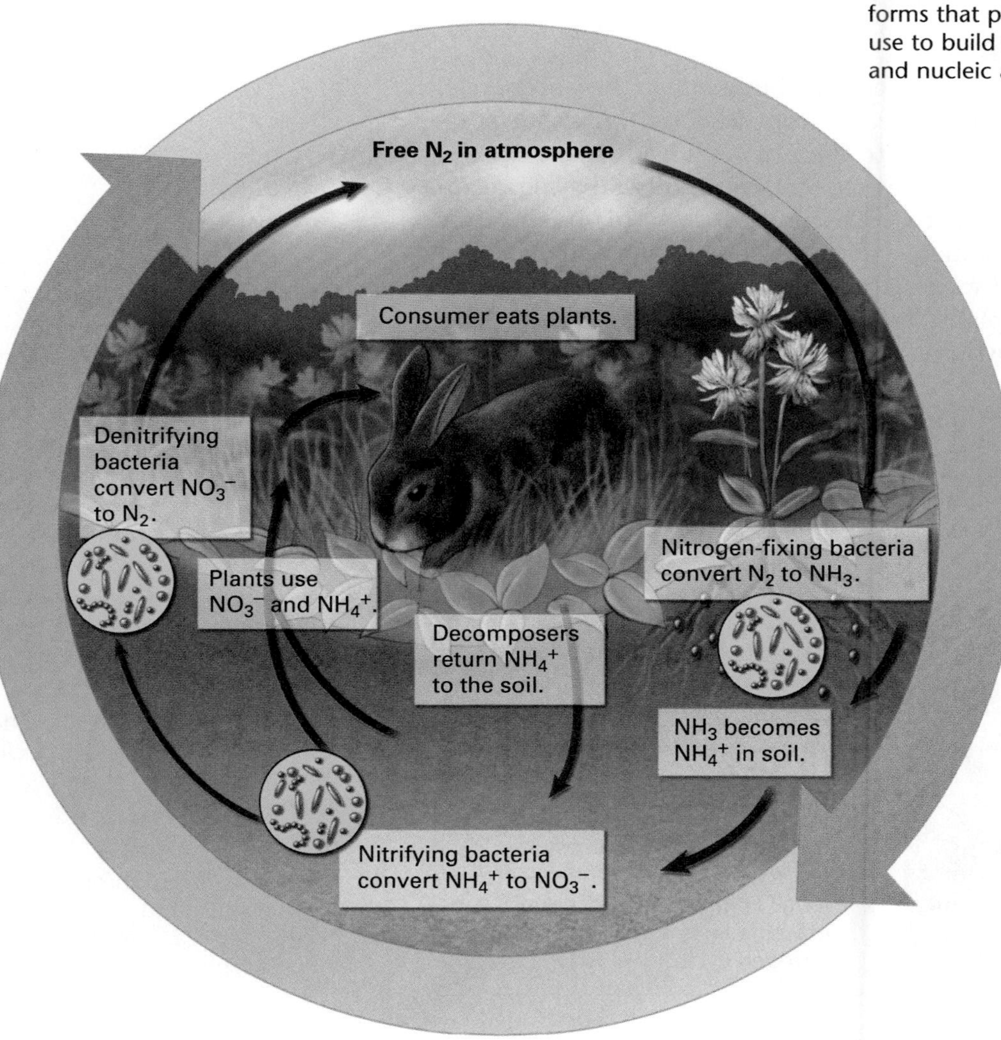

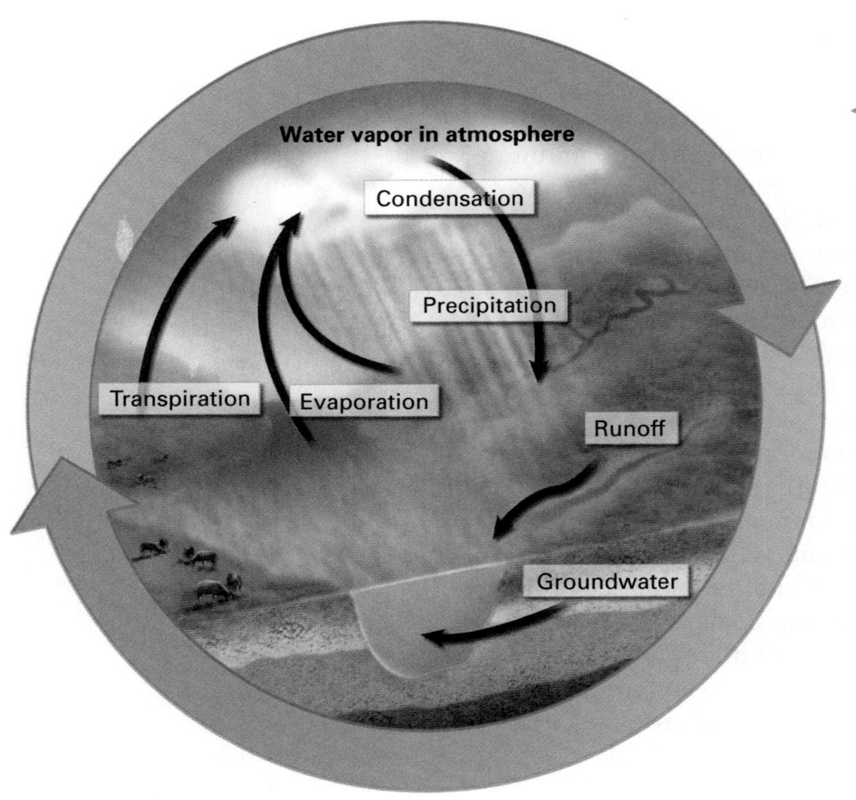

Figure 36-12 The three major processes of evaporation (including transpiration), condensation, and precipitation continuously move water between the land, bodies of water, and the atmosphere.

The Water Cycle

Nonliving processes play an especially large role in the water cycle. The sun's energy evaporates water from land and water surfaces, adding gaseous water vapor to the atmosphere (Figure 36-12). As it cools, water vapor condenses and eventually falls as precipitation (rain, snow, hail, or sleet). Plants absorb this fresh water from the soil, and consumers obtain water by eating and drinking.

A large amount of water exits plants during **transpiration,** evaporation from the plant's leaves. On a hot summer day 200 liters of water could reenter the atmosphere from just one average-sized maple tree.

Water that is not retained by plants or bound to soil particles either runs off into rivers and streams or restores groundwater. Eventually, this water may reenter the atmosphere through evaporation, and the cycle continues.

Online Activity 36.3

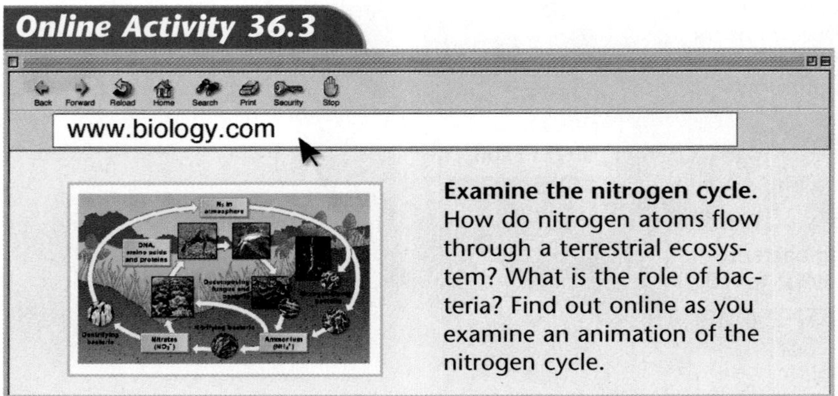

Examine the nitrogen cycle. How do nitrogen atoms flow through a terrestrial ecosystem? What is the role of bacteria? Find out online as you examine an animation of the nitrogen cycle.

Concept Check 36.3

1. Identify three basic steps of chemical cycling.
2. Explain how photosynthesis and respiration are involved in cycling carbon and oxygen.
3. Describe three roles that bacteria play in the nitrogen cycle.
4. Follow a raindrop through one possible path through the water cycle, ending as water vapor in the atmosphere.

CONCEPT 36.4 Human activities can alter ecosystems.

OBJECTIVES
- Explain how human activities can impact chemical cycles.
- Explain how pollution can affect food chains.

KEY TERMS
- deforestation
- greenhouse effect
- global warming
- eutrophication
- acid rain
- pollution
- biological magnification
- ozone

What's Online

www.biology.com

Online Activity 36.4 Analyze effects of deforestation.

Lab 36 Online Companion Can Lake Life Remain Despite Acid Rain?

Throughout this unit you have explored the complexity and interconnectedness of ecosystems. Over the past few centuries, many ecosystems have been affected by the rapidly growing human population's need for resources. The effects of human activities are sometimes felt in only a small area. Sometimes, though, the ecological impact is more widespread or even global.

Impact on Chemical Cycles

Human activities can affect chemical cycling by literally moving nutrients from one place to another. In contrast to a deer, which might eat plants in a forest and return the raw materials to the same forest in its waste, a human might eat a salad containing vegetables from many different parts of the country. And the human's waste might be carried out into the ocean in sewage, far from the sources of the raw nutrients. On an even larger scale, some human activities can disrupt the processes within global chemical cycles.

Carbon Cycle Impacts As you have read, the burning of wood and fossil fuels is one source of carbon dioxide in the atmosphere. As nations have become more industrialized, atmospheric carbon dioxide levels have risen steadily (Figure 36-13). **Deforestation,** the clearing of forests for agriculture, lumber, and other uses, also affects the carbon cycle by eliminating plants that absorb carbon dioxide during photosynthesis. Sometimes after being cut down, the trees are then burned, releasing more carbon dioxide. Burning after deforestation in the tropics accounts for about 20 percent of the carbon dioxide added to the atmosphere by human activities. Worldwide burning of fossil fuels accounts for most of the other 80 percent.

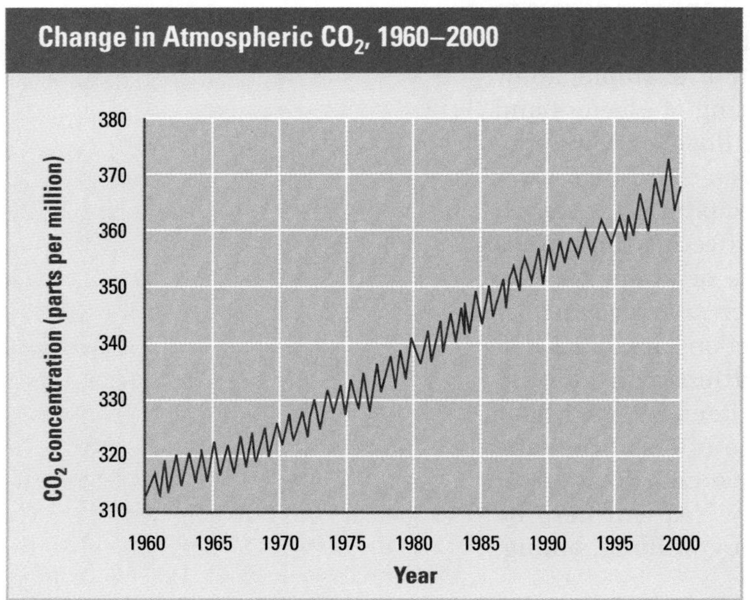

Figure 36-13 The zig-zag shape of this graph is due to seasonal changes in atmospheric levels of carbon dioxide. Levels decrease each year during the summer growing season and increase during the winter. The overall level of carbon dioxide has climbed during the last four decades.

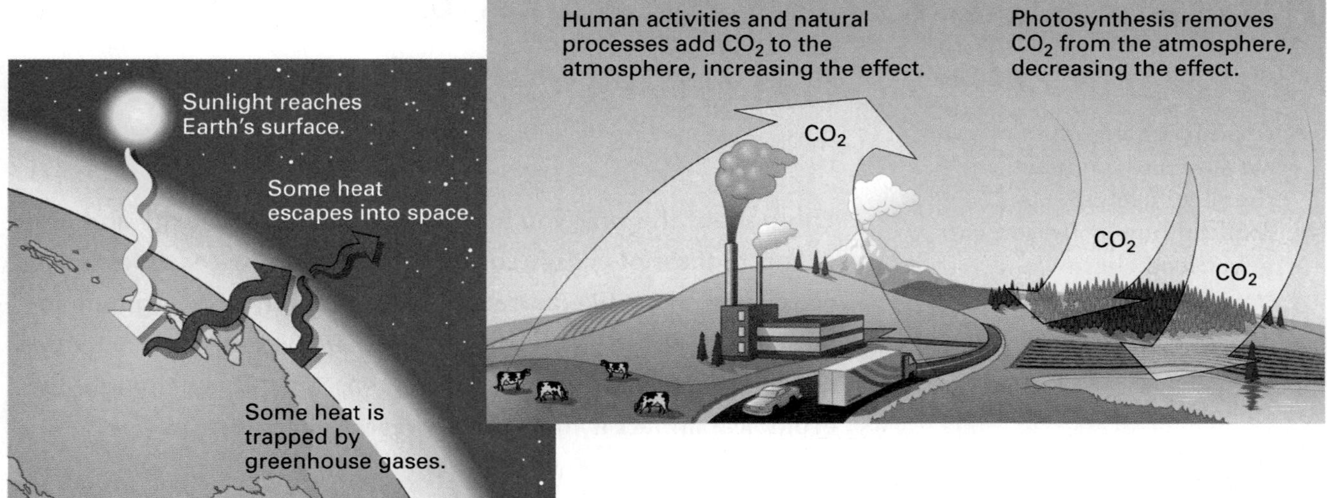
Sunlight reaches Earth's surface.
Some heat escapes into space.
Some heat is trapped by greenhouse gases.
Human activities and natural processes add CO_2 to the atmosphere, increasing the effect.
Photosynthesis removes CO_2 from the atmosphere, decreasing the effect.
CO_2
CO_2
CO_2

▲ **Figure 36-14** The greenhouse effect is a natural process that stops all of the sun's heat from escaping rapidly back to space. This process can be altered by human activities that affect the levels of greenhouse gases in the atmosphere.

How are increased carbon dioxide levels in the atmosphere significant? Carbon dioxide is one of a few gases in the atmosphere that allow sunlight to pass through to Earth, but trap some heat as it is reflected and radiated from Earth's surface (Figure 36-14). As a result, the temperature of Earth's surface is higher than it would be if all heat escaped into space. These gases act somewhat like the glass windows of a greenhouse that allow light in, but prevent heat from escaping. Because of this analogy, the process by which atmospheric gases trap heat is called the **greenhouse effect.** As the levels of carbon dioxide and other "greenhouse gases" rise, the greenhouse effect becomes stronger, trapping more heat in the atmosphere and raising Earth's average temperature. Such an overall rise in Earth's average temperature is called **global warming.**

Using a variety of computer models, scientists make predictions about the long-term effects of increasing carbon dioxide levels. Global warming predictions range from just tenths of a degree to a few degrees Celsius. Scientists also have different hypotheses about the possible effects of global warming. For example, a few degrees of warming could cause enough melting of glaciers and polar ice caps to cause a rise in sea levels, flooding low-lying coastal areas. Small changes in temperatures could also have large effects on weather, such as changing precipitation patterns. The boundaries between biomes might shift, affecting the species that live in them. Which species could move or adapt quickly enough to survive these changes? The answer is unknown.

International cooperation and individual actions are all needed to lessen the chance of these outcomes. Nations can identify ways that people in the tropics can support themselves without burning forests. Nations can also reduce use of fossil fuels by conserving energy and developing alternative energy sources, such as wind, solar, and geothermal energy. You can help by making your home more energy-efficient and by walking, biking, or riding public transportation.

Nitrogen Cycle Impacts Human activities impact the nitrogen cycle primarily by moving large amounts of nitrogen compounds into the water or the air. For example, some sewage treatment plants release dissolved nitrogen compounds into streams and rivers. Fertilizers applied to crops are another source of nitrogen compounds—excess fertilizer may run off into nearby streams and ponds. The high levels of nitrogen, often along with phosphates, feed the rapid growth of algae in these bodies of water, a condition called **eutrophication** (Figure 36-15). As the algae die, the bacteria decomposing them can use up so much of the oxygen in the water that there is no longer enough to support other organisms.

Smokestacks and automobile exhaust pipes release certain nitrogen and sulfur compounds into the atmosphere. There these compounds combine with water, forming nitric and sulfuric acids. Precipitation that carries this acid back to Earth's surface is called **acid rain.** The Clean Air Act has helped lessen the acid rain problem in the United States by reducing levels of sulfuric acids. However, precipitation in some areas is still acidic enough to cause damage.

Water Cycle Impacts One human activity that can impact the water cycle is deforestation. A primary way that fresh water returns to the atmosphere is transpiration from dense tropical forests. As a result, tropical deforestation greatly reduces the amount of water vapor added to the atmosphere. This changes precipitation patterns and affects ecosystems. Drawing water from rivers or underground aquifers for household use or crop irrigation also affects the water cycle. If the rate of water use is faster than the rate at which the water cycle can replace it, the river or aquifer may eventually run dry.

Case Study: Hubbard Brook Experimental Forest About 40 years ago, scientists started a long-term study on the effects of deforestation on chemical cycling in a New Hampshire forest. The study measured chemical cycling in an area of the forest where all the trees were cut down (the altered area) compared to an untouched area (the reference area). Scientists recorded nutrient levels in streams flowing out of each area. For several years following the cut, the water volume flowing from the altered area increased by 30 to 40 percent. Without trees to absorb excess water, the water ran off from the soil. Most remarkable was the loss of nitrate along with the water, which increased 60-fold (or 6000 percent) in concentration in the stream flowing from the altered area (Figure 36-16). However, as new plants grew in the treatment area, transpiration increased and runoff decreased. The Hubbard Brook research shows that plants play a large role in chemical cycling in a forest ecosystem. In Online Activity 36.4, you can use a virtual laboratory to collect and analyze water and soil samples in the Hubbard Brook Forest.

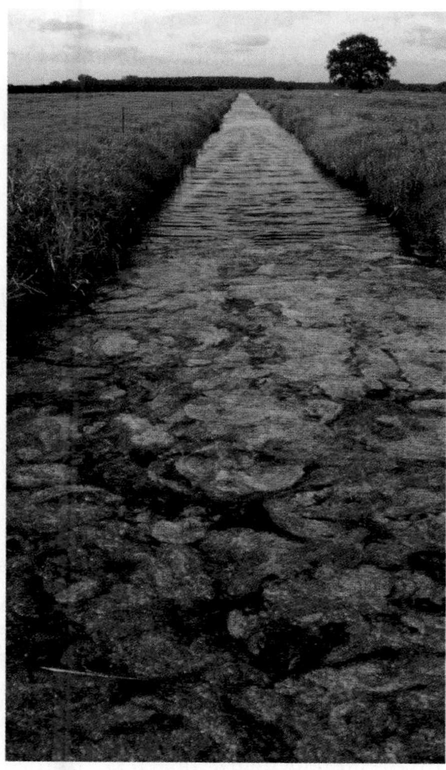

▲ **Figure 36-15** The algal bloom developing in this agricultural canal is due to fertilizer runoff from the crop fields.

▼ **Figure 36-16** Deforestation in the altered area of Hubbard Brook Forest increased the concentration of nitrates in runoff for several years.

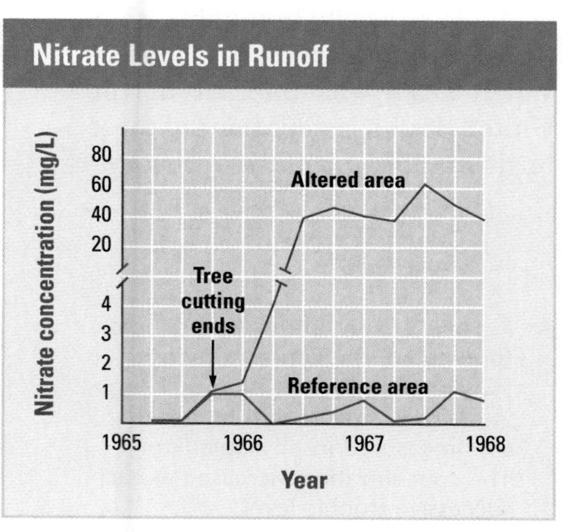

Other Effects of Pollution

The addition of substances to the environment that result in a negative effect is called **pollution.** You have just read how pollution can affect chemical cycles. Two more examples show how pollution can affect food chains and Earth's atmosphere.

Biological Magnification As organisms take in nutrients and water from the environment, they may also take in pollutants. Though some pollutants may be excreted, others accumulate in an organism's tissues. For example, a group of chemicals called PCBs are soluble in lipids and collect in the fatty tissues of animals. PCBs that are disposed in industrial wastes can remain in the environment for a long time. In the Great Lakes, studies detected PCBs in the tissues of organisms throughout the food web. As higher trophic levels fed on each other, the PCBs accumulated in each predator's fatty tissues at even higher concentrations. As you can see in Figure 36-17, the concentration of PCBs increased from 0.025 parts per million (ppm) in phytoplankton to 124 ppm in herring gull eggs. The process by which pollutants become more concentrated in successive trophic levels of a food web is called **biological magnification.**

One of the first studied examples of biological magnification involved the pesticide DDT. Before 1971, DDT was used in the United States to control mosquitoes and agricultural pests. As with PCBs, DDT concentrates in fats and becomes magnified at each step of the food chain. When ecologists studying a decline in the populations of top-level consumers such as pelicans, ospreys, and eagles found high levels of DDT in the birds' eggs, they realized that DDT was a serious environmental problem. DDT caused the birds' egg shells to be easily breakable, thus fewer young survived to hatch. When DDT was banned in the United States, populations of these birds made a dramatic recovery.

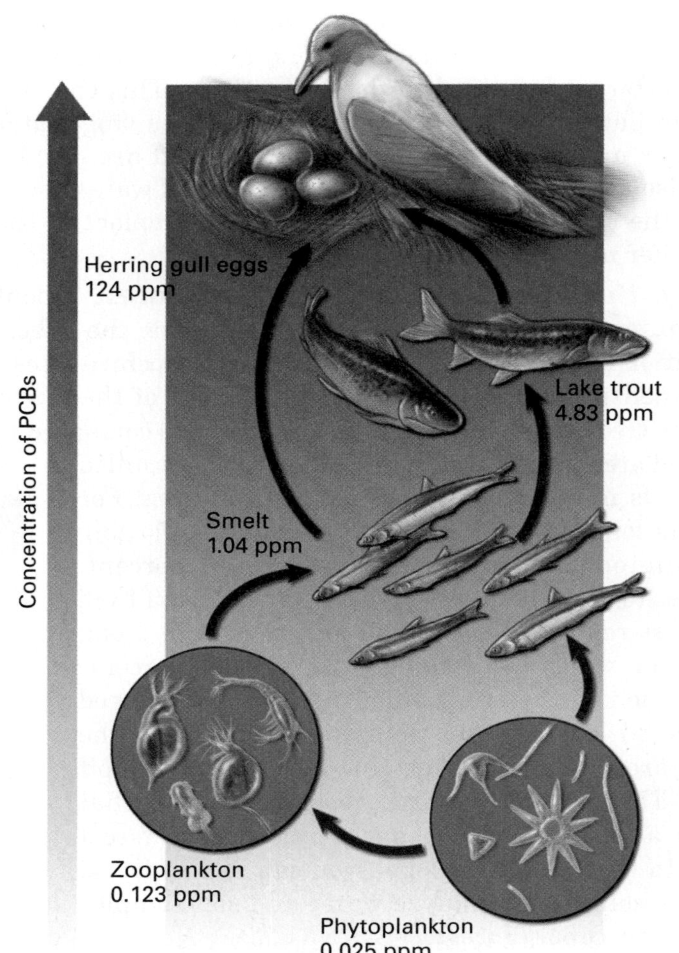

Figure 36-17 In this Great Lakes food chain, the concentration of PCBs measured in herring gull eggs was almost 5000 times higher than that measured in phytoplankton. The concentration increased at each successive trophic level.

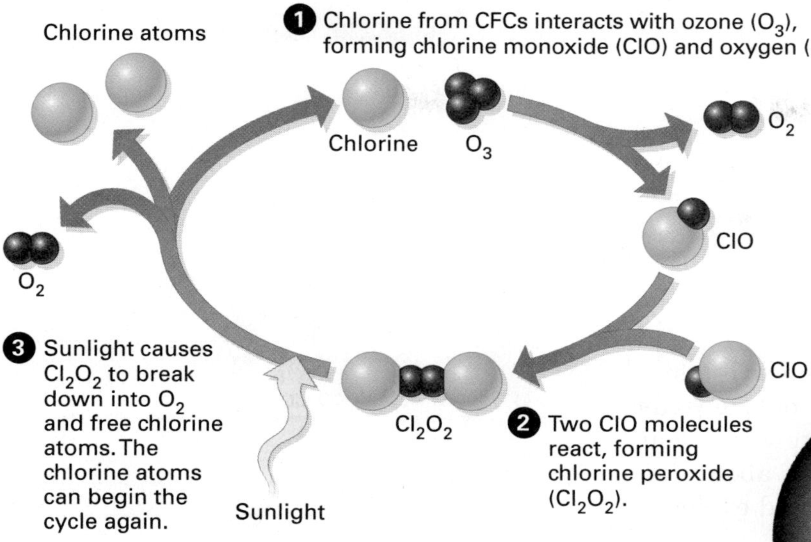
Chlorine atoms
1 Chlorine from CFCs interacts with ozone (O_3), forming chlorine monoxide (ClO) and oxygen (O_2).
Chlorine
O_3
O_2
ClO
ClO
O_2
3 Sunlight causes Cl_2O_2 to break down into O_2 and free chlorine atoms. The chlorine atoms can begin the cycle again.
Sunlight
Cl_2O_2
2 Two ClO molecules react, forming chlorine peroxide (Cl_2O_2).

Figure 36-18 Free chlorine atoms in the atmosphere react with and destroy ozone molecules. Over time, the loss of ozone has resulted in an ozone "hole"—an area of very low ozone concentrations, shown as blue in the image below—located over Antarctica.

Damage to the Ozone Shield Some pollution in the atmosphere affects a gas called **ozone** (O_3) that has particular importance to living things. The ozone layer, a region of the atmosphere between 17 and 25 kilometers above Earth's surface, contains concentrations of ozone that absorb ultraviolet radiation, shielding organisms from its damaging effects.

Scientists have recorded the thinning of the ozone layer since the 1970s. A major contributor to the destruction of the layer are chlorofluorocarbons (CFCs) released from aerosol cans, refrigeration units, and certain manufacturing processes. These compounds destroy ozone molecules (Figure 36-18).

The consequences of ozone depletion for humans may include an increase in health problems such as skin cancer and cataracts, caused by more intense ultraviolet radiation reaching Earth's surface. The radiation may also harm crops and other producers.

International efforts may help to minimize ozone loss and to aid in its recovery. Nearly 200 nations, including the United States, are working to eliminate the use of ozone-destroying chemicals. For example, CFCs have been banned in many countries.

Online Activity 36.4

Back
Forward
Reload
Home
Search
Print
Security
Stop
www.biology.com

Analyze effects of deforestation.
Go online to a virtual laboratory at the Hubbard Brook Forest. Analyze water and soil samples from a watershed; measure their nitrate content; and then plot your data in a graph.

Concept Check 36.4

1. Describe how increased quantities of carbon dioxide in the atmosphere may contribute to global warming.
2. Give an example showing how pollution relates to biological magnification.
3. How can deforestation impact the carbon and water cycles?
4. What is the relationship between chlorofluorocarbons and ozone?

Can Lake Life Remain Despite Acid Rain?

Acid Rain and the Chemistry of Lake Water

Question Why does acid rain harm some lakes more than others?

Lab Overview In this investigation you will test how simulated acid rain changes the pH of lake water samples, including a sample of local lake water. You will use your results to make predictions about the effects of acid rain on lake ecosystems and explore how these effects may vary.

Preparing for the Lab To help you prepare for the lab, go to the *Lab 36 Online Companion.* Compare and contrast three Adirondack lakes that receive significant amounts of acid rain, and develop possible hypotheses explaining why acid rain affects each lake differently. Prepare for the lab procedure by previewing the steps you will take.

Completing the Lab Use your Laboratory Manual or lab page printouts from the *Lab 36 Online Companion* to do the investigation and analyze your results. **CAUTION:** *Be sure to follow your teacher's instructions and all safety guidelines in the investigation.*

Lab 36 Online Companion

Back Forward Reload Home Search Print Security Stop

www.biology.com

Roll your cursor over the word food web in the picture below to see the relationships between the organisms in the lake. When you are ready, change the pH of the lake by moving the slider along the pH scale between pH 7.0 and pH 3.5. As you decrease the pH, note the species that are present at each 0.5 pH unit.

Phytoplankton
(5x)
(20x)
Bass
Baby trout
(20x)
(200x)
Zooplankton
Crayfish
Detritus
Food Web

7.0 6.5 6.0 5.5 5.0 4.5 4.0 3.5
Neutral → More acidic

CONCEPT 36.5

Conservation biology can slow the loss of biodiversity.

OBJECTIVES
- Explain the importance of biodiversity.
- List four main threats to biodiversity.
- Identify four approaches to conserving biodiversity.

KEY TERMS
- biodiversity
- overexploitation
- conservation biology
- zoned reserve
- buffer zone
- sustainable development

What's Online

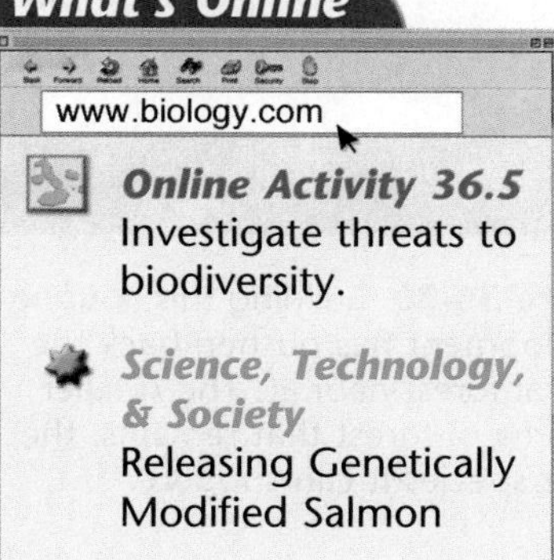

Do you take part in a community recycling program or strive to save energy by turning off the lights when you leave a room? If so, you probably know that your efforts are helping to conserve natural resources and energy. The idea of conservation—protecting and sustaining resources for the future—can also be applied to biology. In this section you will read about what individuals and nations can do to protect habitats and conserve the diversity of life on Earth.

Why Diversity Matters

The rain forest shown in Figure 36-19 is one of Earth's most diverse ecosystems. The number of species in an ecosystem is one aspect of **biodiversity,** a term that encompasses the variety of life on Earth. The other aspects of biodiversity are the variety of ecosystems in the biosphere and the genetic variety among individuals within a species.

Why does biodiversity matter? One basic reason is that many of the species in an ecosystem are interconnected. Species depend on community interactions for food, shelter, and other needs. If a key species disappears, other species—and the health of the whole ecosystem—may be affected.

People value biodiversity for many other reasons as well. For instance, organisms and ecosystems are a source of beauty and inspiration to many people. People also rely on a great variety of organisms as sources of oxygen, food, clothing, and shelter. Beyond providing these basics, biodiversity has aided the development of many medicines. In the United States, 25 percent of all medicines contain substances originally derived from plants.

For many people, the possibility of identifying new products that could help humans is a strong argument for conserving biodiversity. For example, the rosy periwinkle, which grows in the rain forests of Madagascar, yields a medicine used to treat two types of cancer: childhood leukemia and Hodgkin's disease. Deforestation in Madagascar and other rain forests threatens many rainforest species.

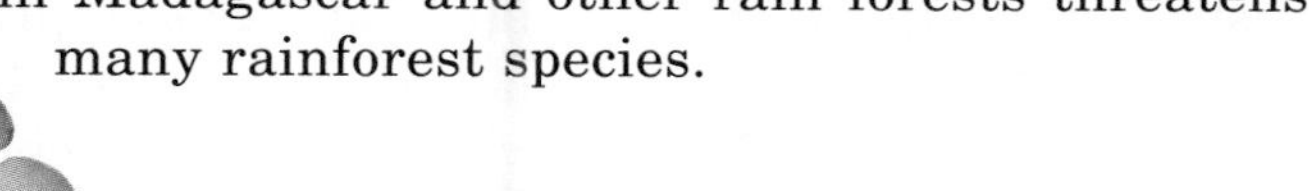
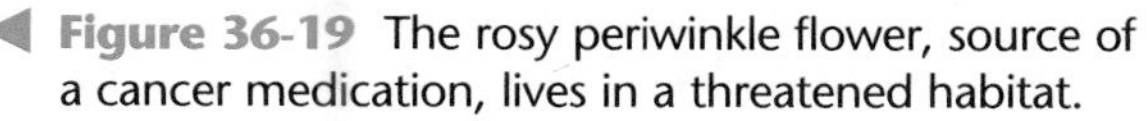
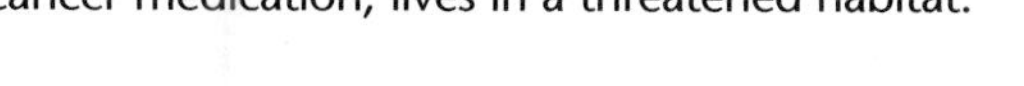

Figure 36-19 The rosy periwinkle flower, source of a cancer medication, lives in a threatened habitat.

Threats to Biodiversity

Throughout Earth's history, species have become extinct—the last members of the population died—and the species no longer exists on the planet. Periods of mass extinction occurred as a result of drastic climate change caused by volcanic eruptions or asteroid collisions. You are probably familiar with the story of one such event during the Cretaceous period, which scientists hypothesize resulted in the extinction of Earth's many dinosaur species.

There is currently another period of mass extinction taking place on Earth. Its exact scale is uncertain since the 1.5 million living species known to biologists are probably only a fraction of the total number of species on Earth. But there are signs that species are disappearing at a dramatic rate:

- About 11 percent of the 9,040 known bird species in the world are endangered.
- Of the approximately 20,000 known plant species in the United States, at least 680 species are endangered.
- Conservation biologists estimate that about 20 percent of the known freshwater fishes in the world have either become extinct during historical times or are threatened.

What is causing these threats to biodiversity? The main factors are pollution, which you read about in Concept 36.4, habitat destruction, introduced species, and overexploitation.

▲ **Figure 36-20** Building this housing development has pushed back the natural forest habitat. The smaller the area of forest that remains, the fewer species it can support.

Habitat Destruction As the human population grows, more land is needed for agriculture, roads, and communities (Figure 36-20). Clearing land for these uses and for obtaining natural resources such as lumber, coal, and minerals may harm or even destroy natural communities. If the organisms that require that habitat do not adapt or move to a new area, they will not survive.

Some changes cause a habitat to become fragmented. For example, building a road through a forest creates a barrier that may prevent species from using resources in all parts of the forest. The smaller the habitat fragments become, the fewer species each fragment can support.

Introduced Species As you read in Chapter 35, introduced (non-native) species often prey on native species or compete with them for resources. If you live in a city, there's a good chance that many of the birds you see are introduced species—starlings, house sparrows, and rock doves (often called pigeons). Since starlings and house sparrows were brought to the United States from Europe, these birds have competed with bluebirds for nesting spots (Figure 36-21). Losing nesting sites affected the bluebird's ability to reproduce, thereby reducing its population. As a result of recent efforts to build artificial "bluebird only" nest boxes, bluebirds are again increasing in number. (Reducing the use of pesticides on farmland has also helped bluebird populations.)

▲ **Figure 36-21** The native bluebird (left) has lost nesting sites to the similarly-sized, aggressive house sparrow (right), an introduced species.

Overexploitation The right whale and the Galápagos tortoise are two examples of populations that have experienced **overexploitation**—the practice of harvesting or hunting to such a degree that the small number of remaining individuals may not be able to sustain the population. For example, many fish populations and mollusks, such as scallops, have been overfished. Governments have placed strict limits on fishing certain species that have been threatened in this way, such as the Atlantic cod, but the ability of these species to rebound remains uncertain.

Another category of overexploitation includes animals that are poached, or hunted illegally, for economic reasons. Often poachers sell animal products such as elephant tusks and rhinoceros horns for large amounts of money. Other species are sold as exotic pets or decorative plants.

▲ **Figure 36-22** The Sumatran rhino is a victim of overexploitation. Poachers kill rhinos for their horns, which are used in many traditional Far East medicines.

Conservation Biology Approaches

What measures can be taken to protect ecosystems and species? Finding solutions and carrying them out are two goals of **conservation biology,** the application of biology to counter the loss of biodiversity.

Focusing on Hot Spots Many conservation biologists have focused their attention on biodiversity "hot spots." These hot spots are small geographic areas with high concentrations of species. The total area of the hottest of these spots covers less than 1.5 percent of Earth's land surface. But this tiny area is home to one third of all species of plants and vertebrates.

Biodiversity hot spots also tend to be hot spots of extinction. Eleven of the hot spots shown in Figure 36-23 have lost at least 90 percent of their original habitats. They are a top priority demanding strong global conservation efforts. Conservation biologists, lawmakers, and local communities are working to preserve areas of some hot spots as nature reserves. They are exploring ways to manage these areas with the goal of meeting human needs, while still supporting the many other species living there.

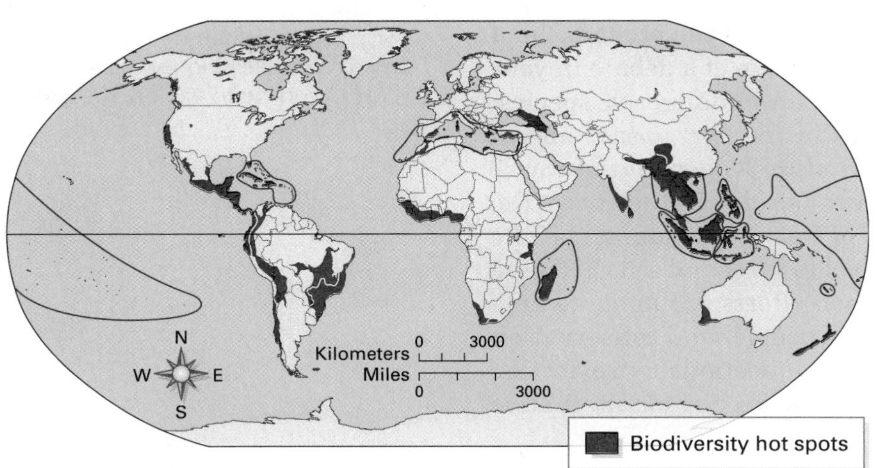

◀ **Figure 36-23** Earth's biodiversity "hot spots" are home to an enormous variety of species, many of which are endangered.

Figure 36-24 The red-cockaded woodpecker's preferred habitat is longleaf pine trees surrounded by low-growing vegetation. Careful observation gave conservation biologists the understanding needed to create protected habitat areas for the endangered bird.

Understanding an Organism's Habitat Understanding the habitat requirements of a species can help biologists manage its existing habitat or create new habitat areas. Consider the example of the red-cockaded woodpecker *(Picoides borealis),* an endangered species found in very specific locations in the southeastern United States. The species prefers to nest in longleaf pines (Figure 36-24). Fungi soften the wood of these trees, making it easy for the woodpecker to drill its nest. Another critical habitat factor for this woodpecker is low-growing vegetation surrounding the pines. The birds benefit by having a clear flight path between their home trees and neighboring feeding grounds. Periodic fires that sweep through the pine forests keep the undergrowth low.

Although the red-cockaded woodpecker nearly became extinct due to habitat destruction caused by housing developments, it is now making a comeback. By recognizing and protecting the key habitat factors, conservation biologists are giving the woodpecker a second chance. They have set aside some protected areas of longleaf pine forests and set controlled fires to help control plant undergrowth and promote growth of the pine. As a result, the woodpeckers have survived and continue to reproduce.

Balancing Demands for Resources In many cases, a tug of war exists between efforts to save species and the economic and social needs of people. Perhaps you are aware of a debate in your town or state regarding protection of an endangered species. Should a wooded habitat be conserved in an effort to save an owl population if it means putting hundreds of loggers out of work? Should work proceed on a new highway bridge if it destroys the only remaining habitat of a species of freshwater mussel? If the bridge isn't built, how will people travel to work and school? These are the types of questions raised when efforts are made to help protect biodiversity. Politicians, townspeople, and conservation biologists can reach resolution to these questions by reviewing scientific data, weighing costs and benefits, looking for alternative solutions, and casting their votes.

Science, Technology, & Society

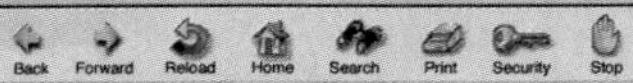

www.biology.com

Releasing Genetically Modified Salmon

In recent years, scientists discovered how to alter the genetic makeup of certain salmon so that they can grow twice as fast. What are the benefits and risks of releasing these fish in the wild? Go online to explore the issue.

Planning for a Sustainable Future One way for nations to help protect ecosystems is to establish **zoned reserves.** A zoned reserve includes areas of land that are relatively undisturbed by humans, surrounded by areas that are minimally impacted by humans called **buffer zones.** The small Central American nation of Costa Rica has become a world leader in establishing zoned reserves. The Costa Rican government set aside eight zoned reserves with the goal of maintaining at least 80 percent of its natural species (Figure 36-25). Although humans live in the buffer zones, destructive environmental practices such as massive logging, large-scale single-crop agriculture, and extensive mining are discouraged. The zoned reserves encourage long-term ecosystem conservation through a balance of human needs and habitat preservation.

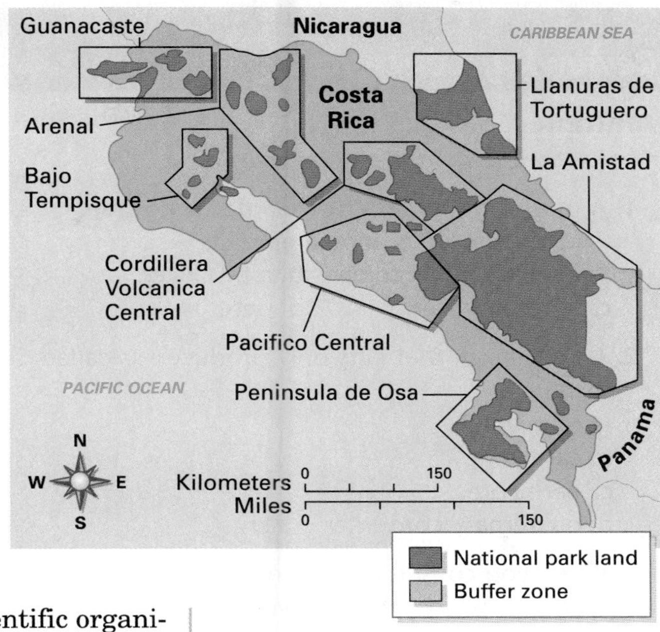

▲ **Figure 36-25** Costa Rica has established eight zoned reserves in an effort to conserve biodiversity while meeting the needs of humans. People live and work in the buffer zones surrounding the park preserves.

With such efforts as a model, many nations, scientific organizations, and private foundations are working toward a goal of **sustainable development**—developing natural resources so that they can renew themselves and be available for the future. People practicing sustainable development can continue to farm food and harvest timber while still protecting biodiversity. For example, a forest corridor through farmland may be left to connect two parts of an ecosystem, preventing habitat fragmentation. Timber may be harvested selectively, with only mature trees taken, instead of cutting down all the vegetation in an area.

Sustainable development depends on the continued research and applications of basic ecology and conservation biology. The challenge for individuals and nations is to find a way to meet the needs of Earth's human population, while conserving ecosystems and resources for the planet's other populations as well. By exploring life in your biology class this year, you and your classmates have taken an important step toward an understanding of nature that is essential to the future of the biosphere.

Online Activity 36.5

Investigate threats to biodiversity.
Meet "Lonesome George," the last tortoise on the Island of Santa Cruz. Find out why tortoises and other organisms are endangered here, and devise a plan to help.

Concept Check 36.5

1. Describe two arguments for preserving biodiversity.
2. What are four main threats to biodiversity?
3. Describe how zoned reserves may help conservation efforts.

Multiple Choice

Choose the letter of the best answer.

1. A mushroom breaks down a decaying tree. The mushroom is an example of
   a. a secondary consumer. b. a producer.
   c. a decomposer. d. detritus.

2. An organism that eats only producers is called a(n)
   a. omnivore.
   b. carnivore.
   c. herbivore.
   d. quaternary consumer.

3. When you consume a serving of broccoli, you represent which trophic level?
   a. producer
   b. primary consumer
   c. secondary consumer
   d. tertiary consumer

4. Which of the following lists only includes ways that carbon is released into the atmosphere?
   a. photosynthesis, nitrogen fixation, cellular respiration
   b. forest fires, transpiration, decomposers breaking down detritus
   c. greenhouse effect, nitrification, burning of fossil fuels
   d. cellular respiration, forest fires, volcanic eruptions

5. The process through which certain bacteria convert nitrogen gas (N_2) to ammonia (NH_3) is
   a. nitrogen fixation. b. evaporation.
   c. nitrification. d. decomposition.

6. Which of the following events might be a sign of biomagnification of a pollutant?
   a. an increase in global temperatures
   b. a decline in the phytoplankton population
   c. rising pH levels in aquatic ecosystems
   d. a decline in the population of top-level consumers

7. Building a highway through a forest is an example of
   a. habitat fragmentation. b. poaching.
   c. eutrophication. d. biomagnification.

Short Answer

8. Describe a meal in which a person would be feeding at two or more trophic levels and identify the levels.

9. Predict whether a temperate deciduous forest or a desert ecosystem would have a higher level of annual primary productivity per square meter. Explain your answer.

10. Explain why food chains generally are limited to three or four levels.

11. Discuss the information represented in an energy pyramid, a biomass pyramid, and a pyramid of numbers.

12. Summarize the basic pattern of a chemical cycle in an ecosystem.

13. List three roles that bacteria play in the nitrogen cycle.

14. What is the greenhouse effect? Explain how it is significant to Earth's ecosystems.

15. Describe the concept of sustainable development.

Visualizing Concepts

16. Copy the cycle diagram below and complete it to show one possible path of carbon through the carbon cycle.

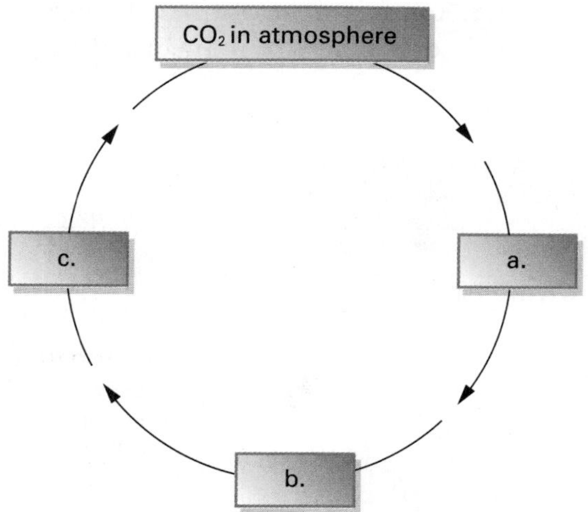

Analyzing Information

17. Analyzing Diagrams Use the food web diagram to answer the questions below.

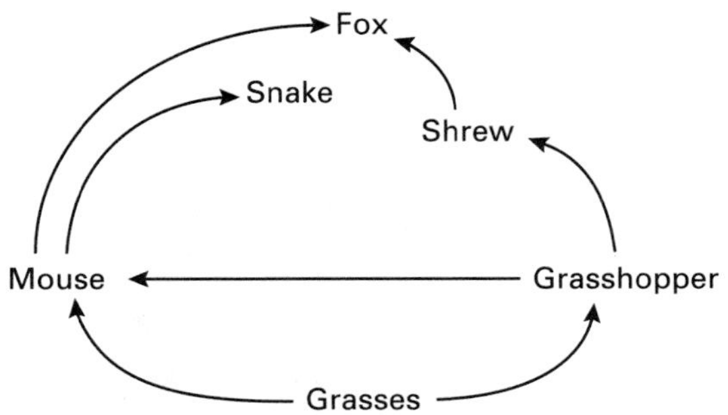

a. Which organism(s) are tertiary consumers?
b. Which organisms consume the grasshopper? What trophic level do they represent?
c. Use the diagram to create one simple food chain with at least three trophic levels.

18. Analyzing Graphs Use the graph to answer the following questions.

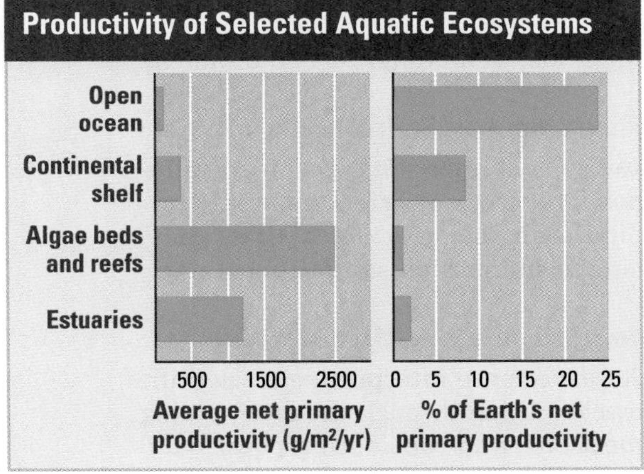

a. Which ecosystem shown has the lowest primary productivity per square meter? Which has the highest?
b. Which ecosystem shown represents the greatest percentage of Earth's total primary productivity? Which represents the least?
c. Does an ecosystem's average net primary productivity match its percent of Earth's primary productivity? Explain why or why not.

Critical Thinking

19. Relating Cause and Effect Explain two ways that deforestation can affect levels of carbon dioxide in the atmosphere.

20. Relating Cause and Effect Explain how eutrophication can lead to the death of fish in a lake.

21. Developing Hypotheses Suggest one reason why, although CFCs are no longer used in many countries, the ozone layer continues to shrink.

22. Making Generalizations Use an example to explain one reason that people value biodiversity.

23. Evaluating Promotional Claims A cleaning product claims that it is "good for the environment" because it uses a natural plant chemical to dissolve grease. Is this product necessarily "good for the environment"? Explain.

24. What's Wrong With These Statements? *Briefly explain why each statement is inaccurate or misleading.*
a. In the water cycle, all water returns to the atmosphere by transpiration.
b. Poaching threatens biodiversity because it releases large amounts of pollution.
c. When a spider eats a fly, the spider will use most of the energy stored as biomass in the fly to build new biomass of its own.

Performance Assessment

Writing You are one of six people chosen to live on a self-contained space station. What organisms would you bring with you? Describe the functions you'd need each organism to perform.

Online Assessment/Test Preparation

www.biology.com

- **Chapter 36 Assessment**
  Check your understanding of the chapter concepts.
- **Standardized Test Preparation**
  Practice test-taking skills you need to succeed.

Skills in *Biology: Exploring Life*

There's more to science than "just the facts." Throughout your exploration of biology this year, you are developing a set of skills to interpret information and to design and carry out scientific investigations. In this appendix, you'll find explanations and examples of some key skills, including

- **Making Measurements**
- **Organizing Information**
- **Graphing**
- **Critical Thinking**

Plus, go online to the *Biology: Exploring Life* Web site for more skills instruction and practice in the following areas:

Making Measurements

Learn the "language of data" and develop good measuring skills with conversion tables, practice problems, and common equivalents.

Conducting a Scientific Investigation

Through virtual experiments, practice making observations and inferences, developing hypotheses, designing experiments, collecting and interpreting data, drawing conclusions, and communicating your results.

Using a Microscope

Learn the parts of a microscope and important techniques for using one effectively in the lab.

Lab Safety Primer

Learn about the safety precautions in your *Biology: Exploring Life* Laboratory Manual. Then check your safety IQ.

Math Review

Sharpen your math skills with tutorials and practice problems on fractions, percents, decimals, exponents, probability, and significant figures.

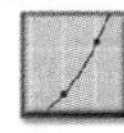

Graphing

Practice reading, interpreting, and making line, bar, and circle graphs.

Organizing Information

Learn how to create graphic organizers such as concept maps, flowcharts, cycle diagrams, Venn diagrams, and tables.

Studying for Standardized Tests

Review test question types and strategies for selecting correct answers and eliminating incorrect ones. Practice your techniques on sample questions.

Reading a Scientific Article

Get experience interpreting a scientific article. Sifting through the facts, posing questions, and considering potential bias will help you understand and critically evaluate information.

Critical Thinking for Web Research

Find out how to select research topics and locate appropriate Web sites for information. Asking the right questions, using search engines, and evaluating the results will help you to harness the research power of the Web.

Making Measurements

Measurement plays a critical role in science. Quantitative observations yield precise data that can be mathematically analyzed and easily communicated to others. Scientists around the world use the International System of Measurements, abbreviated as SI (from the French name, Système International d'Unités). SI is derived from the metric system. The table below lists the SI and metric units you will use most frequently in your study of biology. For more practice, go online to the *Making Measurements Skills Activity.*

Metric-English Equivalents

1 kilogram (kg) = 2.2 pounds (lb)

1 gram (g) = 0.04 ounce (oz)

1 kilometer (km) = 0.67 mile (mi)

1 meter (m) = 39.36 inches (in.)

1 centimeter (cm) = 0.39 inch (in.)

1 liter (L) = 1.06 quarts (qt)

$°C = \frac{5}{9} \times (°F–32)$

Common SI and Metric Units of Measurement

Quantity	Unit	Symbol	Useful Equivalents
Mass (the amount of matter in an object) Balance	kilogram gram	kg g	1 kg = 1000 g 1 g = 0.001 kg
Length (the distance from one point to another) Ruler	kilometer meter centimeter millimeter micrometer nanometer	km m cm mm μm nm	1 km = 1000 m 1 m = 100 cm 1 cm = 10 mm 1 mm = 0.001 m 1 μm = 0.001 mm 1 nm = 0.001 μm
Volume (the space occupied by an object) Graduated cylinder	liter milliliter cubic centimeter	L mL cm^3	1 L = 1000 mL 1 mL = 1 cm^3
Temperature (the average energy of random motion of particles in an object) Thermometer	degrees Celsius	°C	0°C = freezing point of water 100°C = boiling point of water

Organizing Information

Your study of biology involves understanding concepts, making connections between ideas, and communicating your ideas to others. These tasks often become easier when you organize information in concept maps, flowcharts, tables, and other methods of visualizing concepts. This summary explains how to use some common graphic organizers. As you become familiar with using graphic organizers, you will find them helpful not only in your study of biology but in other courses, too. For more practice, go online to the *Organizing Information Skills Activity.*

Concept Maps

A concept map is a word diagram that shows how ideas (concepts) are connected. The organization of a concept map reveals relationships between the ideas, making them easier to understand and remember.

A concept map consists of concepts (usually nouns, noun phrases, or adjectives) written in ovals and connected with linking words. To build a concept map, start with the most general concept at the top. Increasingly specific concepts and examples follow in a branching pattern down the map. Related concepts are connected by straight lines and linking words that describe how the concepts are connected. Any two concepts and their linking words should form a sentence or phrase that makes sense. You can also link concepts on different branches using arrows.

Matter
may be
Elements
Compounds
Mixtures
consist of
may be
include
Atoms
Ionic
Molecular
Solutions
such as
such as
Table salt
Water
are often made with

Flowcharts

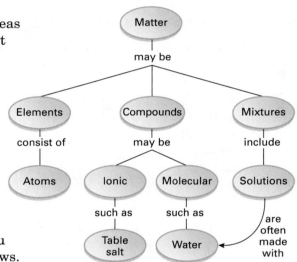

Flowcharts diagram the sequence of steps in a process or a procedure. For example, this simplified flowchart shows the steps in the process of blood clotting after an injury. Flowcharts are good study tools because they help you review and reinforce what you know about a process.

To construct a flowchart, first make a list of the steps in the process. Working vertically or horizontally, write the steps in the correct order and draw a box around each one. Use arrows between the boxes to show the direction of the process from beginning to end.

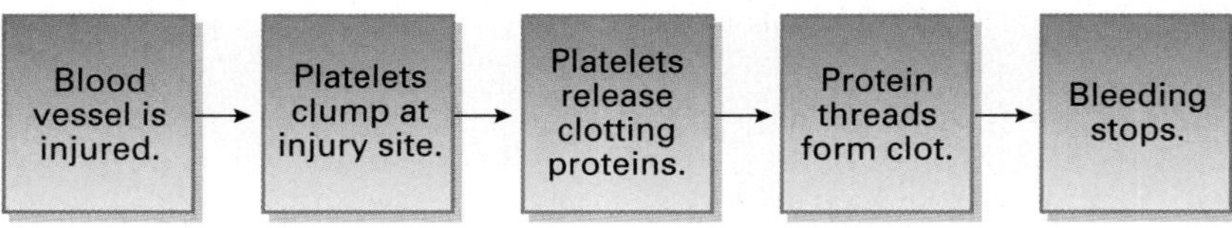

Cycle Diagrams

Many processes in nature occur as cycles, such as the nitrogen cycle or the life cycle of an organism. Cycles have no specific beginning or end. Instead they occur as a series of steps that lead to the same events over and over. For example, the cycle diagram at the right shows a series of recurring events in the water cycle. Each step always follows in the same order, and the cycle has no end. Like flowcharts, cycle diagrams can help you remember the sequence of events in a continuing process.

Construct a cycle diagram similarly to how you would construct a flowchart, but draw the steps in a circle rather than in a straight line. Connect the steps with arrows. Include a title with your diagram.

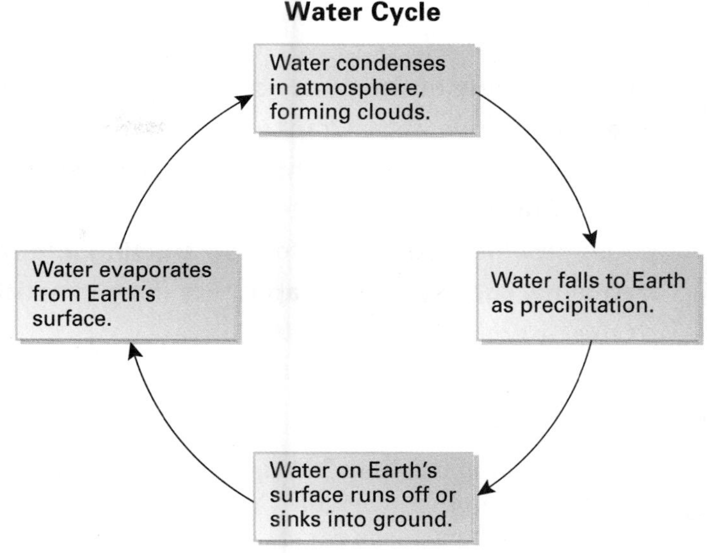
Water Cycle
Water condenses in atmosphere, forming clouds.
Water falls to Earth as precipitation.
Water on Earth's surface runs off or sinks into ground.
Water evaporates from Earth's surface.

Venn Diagrams

A Venn diagram is a way to summarize the similarities and differences between processes or objects. The simplest Venn diagram compares two items, such as this example comparing and contrasting sharks and dolphins. To construct this type of diagram, draw two circles (or ovals) that partially overlap. Above each circle, write the name of the process or object represented. In the area of overlap, list characteristics shared by both items. In the non-overlapping areas, list characteristics that make each item different.

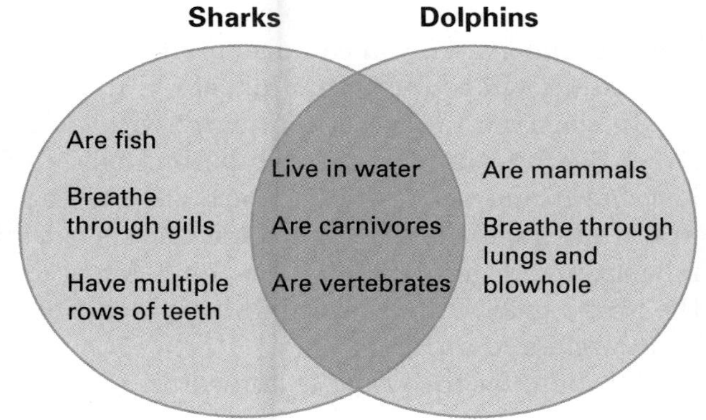
Sharks
Dolphins
Are fish
Breathe through gills
Have multiple rows of teeth
Live in water
Are carnivores
Are vertebrates
Are mammals
Breathe through lungs and blowhole

Tables

A table provides a way to record data, organize information visually, or compare the characteristics of two or more subjects. Tables help you summarize information in an easy-to-read format.

To construct a table, first identify how many items, groups, or categories of information you want to include. Draw a table with that number of columns, and write a heading at the top of each column. If your table lists quantitative data, include the proper units of measurement. If you are creating a data table or a compare-contrast table (in which you list differences and similarities among groups), list the groups to be compared in a column at the left. Then list the characteristics to be compared at the top of the other columns, as in the nutritional classification table at the right. Complete the table by filling in the appropriate information.

Nutritional Classification of Organisms

Nutritional Type	Energy Source	Carbon Source
Photoautotroph (photosynthesizers)	Sunlight	CO_2
Chemoautotroph	Inorganic chemicals	CO_2
Photoheterotroph	Sunlight	Organic compounds
Chemoheterotroph	Organic compounds	Organic compounds

Graphing

Graphs are one of the most useful ways to organize and analyze quantitative data. Graphs reveal patterns, communicate information, and allow scientists to make predictions. Different types of graphs are suited to different purposes. These two pages provide instructions for constructing and reading three frequently used types of graphs. For more practice, go online to the *Graphing Skills Activity.*

Line Graphs

A line graph shows how changes in one variable are linked to changes in another variable. You may be able to make predictions based on patterns revealed by the graph. For example, the graph below on the left indicates how the size of a bacterial population is related to time. The graph shows that the number of bacteria approximately doubles every 20 minutes. Based on the shape of the graph, you can also predict that at 240 minutes the population will be more than 6,000.

To construct a line graph, start with a grid (graph paper). Draw two lines at the left and bottom edges of the grid as the horizontal and vertical axes. Next, divide each axis into equal units and label it with the name of the variable, the unit of measurement, and a range of values. Mark each data point on the graph grid. Draw a straight or curved line through the data points and add a title.

The data for the graph at the left fit neatly on a smooth curve. But if you were to connect each data point on the graph at the right, you would have a mess that yielded little useful information. For data like these, scientists draw a line or curve that reflects the general trend. Such a line runs as closely as possible to all the points and allows you to make generalizations or predictions based on the data.

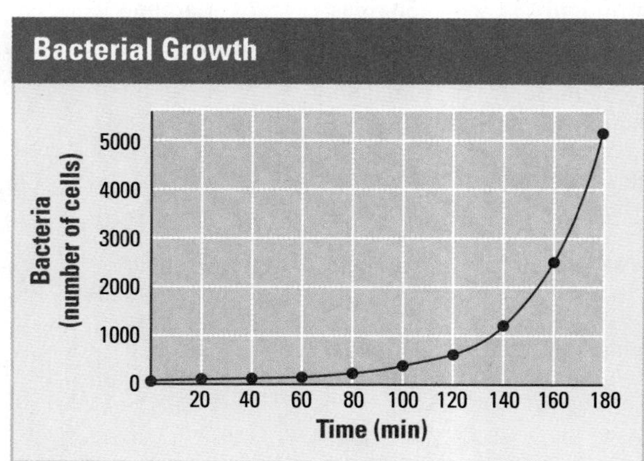

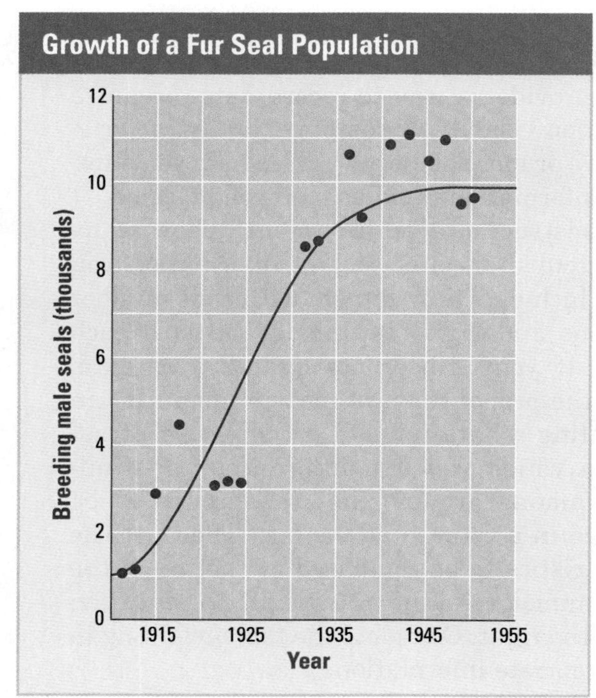

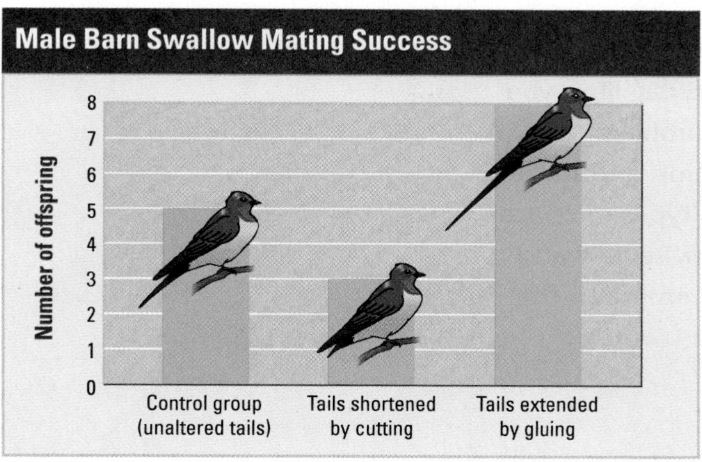

Bar Graphs

A bar graph is useful for comparing data from two or more distinct categories. For example, the sample bar graph above compares the length of bird tail feathers with the number of offspring produced by the birds. Each group of birds has tail feathers of a distinct length.

As with a line graph, construct a bar graph by first drawing the axes. On one axis (usually the horizontal), write the name of each category to be represented. Then label the vertical axis, and mark off a range of values. For each group, draw a short bar at the appropriate value. Then fill in the space from the bar to the horizontal axis. Include a title for your graph.

Circle Graphs

Like a bar graph, a circle graph also compares data from several different categories. Circle graphs, sometimes called pie charts, display data as parts of a whole. To use a circle graph, you must have data that add up to 100 percent. The example compares the abundance of different groups of insects to one another and to other animals. Each sector of the graph represents one group, such as beetles. The entire graph accounts for all the known animal species.

To construct a circle graph using percentages, first draw a circle and mark the center. Then draw a radius line from the center to the circle's edge. Next, determine the size of each sector by calculating the number of degrees that correspond to the percentage you wish to represent. For example, in the graph shown, bees, wasps, and ants make up 10 percent of all animals. Therefore,

$$360° \times 0.10 = 36°$$

With a protractor fixed at the center of the circle, measure an angle—in this case 36°—from the first radius, and draw a second radius at that point. Label the sector. Repeat for each of the other categories. For easier reading, color or shade each sector differently. Remember to include a title for the graph.

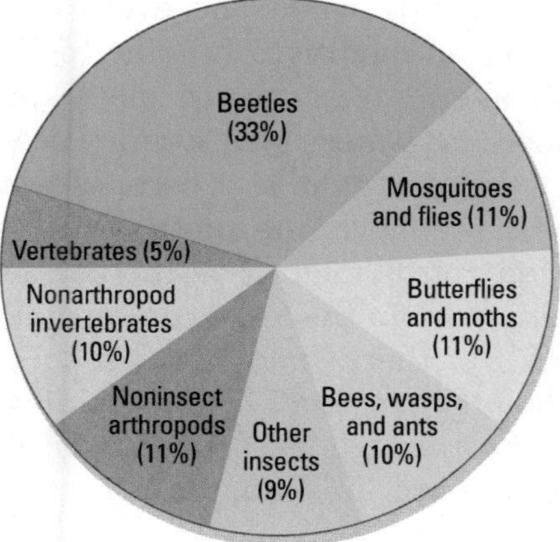

Critical Thinking

When you think critically—in science or in everyday life—you use logic and reasoning to find an answer to a problem. Critical thinking skills also help you evaluate information and make decisions. Below are summaries of a few of the types of critical thinking questions you will find in the Chapter Review and elsewhere in this book. For more practice, go online to the *Critical Thinking for Web Research* and *Conducting a Scientific Investigation Skills Activities.*

Comparing and Contrasting

When you identify similarities and differences between two objects, groups, or processes, you are comparing and contrasting. In comparing, you seek to identify shared characteristics. In contrasting, you search for differences. These details help you better understand the topic under examination.

For example, plants and animals represent two kingdoms of organisms. Comparing them reveals that both are made of cells, both are eukaryotic, and both carry out cellular respiration. Contrasting the two groups reveals that only plants are made of cells that have cell walls. You also find out that most plants are autotrophic (can make their own food), while animals are heterotrophic (must get their food by eating other organisms).

Relating Cause and Effect

Does pollen make you sneeze? If so, you have first-hand experience with cause and effect. Relating cause and effect involves recognizing when one event or condition leads to another event or condition. Inhaling pollen, for example, triggers an allergic response in many people that may include sneezing, watery eyes, a runny nose, and other symptoms.

Keep in mind that because two events occur together or in sequence, one may not necessarily cause the other. Many birds migrate in the fall, for example. That's also a time when the leaves on certain trees turn color and drop off. But there is no evidence that either of these events causes the other to occur. Scientists identify cause-and-effect relationships through experiments or by using prior knowledge and experience. You can, too.

Developing Hypotheses

A hypothesis is a suggested, testable answer to a scientific question. Hypotheses form the basis of inquiry by leading to predictions that can be tested in experiments. Refer to Chapter 2 for more information about hypotheses and their role in science.

A hypothesis is a statement that describes the cause of what you have observed. An example is: "The direction in which a plant grows is affected by the position of a light source." From your hypothesis, you should be able to make a prediction that can be tested in an experiment. For example, "If the light source that shines on a plant is moved, the direction of the plant's growth will change."

Problem Solving

Problem solving can mean working out a calculation or solving a word problem. Or, it can mean finding the shortest route to your next class. Problem solving involves reasoning and other critical thinking skills. When solving a problem, try breaking the problem into parts. Identify exactly what you are asked to find and what information you are given. Then take stock of what you know from other sources and apply your knowledge to the problem. In some cases, the trial-and-error approach can lead you to test different solutions until you find the right one. In other cases, you may need to work through a series of steps, construct a diagram, or brainstorm with a classmate (if appropriate) until you can find an answer.

Evaluating Models

Models are thinking tools frequently used by scientists to help them better understand a process or an idea. Chapter 2 describes different kinds of models and their uses. An example of a scientific model is Darwin's theory of natural selection.

Mental models often are a complex collection of ideas. Physical models do not always look like the objects they represent. And mathematical models can be abstract. How do you know when a model is useful? Examine the model and ask yourself, "What strengths and weaknesses does the model have?" A model should

1) explain all the observations related to it;
2) allow you to make predictions that can be tested; and
3) work with other, related models.

a. A beetle population includes individuals of different colors.

b. Birds capture more light beetles than dark beetles.

c. Survivors (mostly dark beetles) reproduce.

d. Dark beetles become more frequent in the population over time.

Glossary

A

abiotic factor nonliving physical or chemical condition in an environment (p. 744)
abscisic acid plant hormone that inhibits cell division in buds and vascular cambium (p. 479)
absorption uptake of small nutrient molecules; the third stage of food processing (p. 637)
absorptive nutrition method by which fungi absorb small organic molecules from their surroundings (p. 403)
acid compound that donates H^+ ions to an aqueous solution and measures less than 7 on the pH scale (p. 85)
acid rain precipitation that contains nitric and/or sulfuric acids (p. 801)
acoelomate animal lacking a body cavity (p. 506)
actin twisted, thin filament in a muscle fiber (p. 603)
action potential change in voltage across the plasma membrane of a neuron resulting in a nerve signal (p. 614)
activation energy minimum amount of energy required to trigger a chemical reaction (p. 103)
active immunity immunity provided by the body producing its own antibodies against an antigen; results from exposure to the antigen via infection or vaccine (p. 689)
active site region of an enzyme into which a particular substrate fits (p. 104)
active transport movement of molecules across a membrane requiring energy to be expended by the cell (p. 121)
adaptation inherited characteristic that improves an organism's ability to survive and reproduce in a particular environment (pp. 17, 292)
adaptive radiation evolution from a common ancestor of many species adapted to diverse environments (p. 328)
addiction uncontrollable dependence on a drug (p. 629)
adhesion attraction between unlike molecules (p. 82)
adrenal gland one of a pair of endocrine glands located on top of the kidneys (p. 715)
aerobic requiring oxygen (p. 145)
age structure proportion of people in different age groups in a population (p. 775)
aggressive behavior symbolic threat display or a physical struggle between individuals of the same species (p. 62)
AIDS acquired immune deficiency syndrome; the late stages of HIV infection (p. 692)
alga (plural, *algae*) plant-like protist; makes its own food by photosynthesis (p. 381)
alimentary canal digestive tube that extends from the mouth to the anus (p. 638)
allele alternative form of a gene (p. 209)
allergy abnormal immune system sensitivity to an otherwise harmless antigen (p. 690)
alternation of generations alternation between gametophyte and sporophyte in a plant life cycle (p. 424)
alveolus one of millions of tiny sacs within the lungs where gas exchange occurs (p. 668)
amino acid monomer that makes up proteins; contains carboxyl and amino functional groups (p. 101)
amniote vertebrate having an amnion surrounding the embryo; reptile, bird, or mammal (p. 560)
amniotic egg waterproof egg with a shell (p. 560)
amoebocyte cell found in sponges and other animals that may digest and distribute food, dispose of wastes, and change into other cell types (p. 497)
amphibian member of a group of vertebrates that includes frogs, toads, and salamanders, most of which spend part of their life cycles in an aquatic environment and part in a terrestrial environment (p. 553)
anaerobic without oxygen (p. 154)
analogous structures similarities among unrelated species that result from convergent evolution (p. 343)
anaphase third phase of mitosis and of meiosis I and II, in which the sister chromatids separate and move toward the poles of the spindle (p. 187)
anatomy study of an organism's structure (p. 586)
angiosperm flowering plant (p. 434)
animal behavior what an animal does when interacting with its environment (p. 48)
annelid segmented worm (p. 506)
anorexia eating disorder brought about by an extreme pursuit of thinness characterized by self-starvation and excessive weight loss (p. 649)
anther long stalk at the top of a flower's stamen where meiosis produces spores that develop into pollen (p. 442)
antibiotic medicine that kills or slows the growth of bacteria (p. 318)
antibody protein in blood plasma that attaches to a particular antigen (p. 682)
anticodon in tRNA, a triplet of nitrogenous bases that is complementary to a specific codon in mRNA (p. 239)
antigen foreign molecule that provokes an immune response (p. 682)
aorta artery that carries blood directly from the heart to the rest of the body (p. 658)
aphotic zone deep areas of a body of water where light levels are too low to support photosynthesis (p. 758)
apical meristem meristem located in the tip of a root or the bud of a plant shoot (p. 452)
aqueous solution solution in which water is the solvent (p. 84)
arachnid member of a group of arthropods that includes spiders, scorpions, mites, and ticks (p. 527)
archaea domain of prokaryotic organisms that are biochemically and genetically distinct from bacteria (p. 361)
arteriosclerosis condition that occurs when plaque hardens on artery walls (p. 665)
artery vessel that carries blood away from the heart to other parts of the body (p. 655)
arthritis group of skeletal disorders characterized by inflamed joints (p. 600)
arthropod member of a group of invertebrates characterized by segmented bodies, jointed appendages, and exoskeletons (p. 524)
artificial selection selective breeding of domesticated plants and animals to produce offspring with desired genetic traits (p. 307)
asexual reproduction process in which a single cell or set of cells produces offspring that inherit all their genetic material from one parent (p. 181)
atherosclerosis narrowing of the arteries that results from a buildup of plaque (p. 665)
atom smallest particle of an element (p. 74)
atomic number number of protons in an atom's nucleus; is unique for each element (p. 75)
ATP (adenosine triphosphate) main energy source that cells use for most of their work (pp. 129, 143)

ATP synthase protein structure in cell mitochondria that uses energy from H^+ ions to convert ADP to ATP (p. 151)
atrium heart chamber that receives blood returning to the heart from other parts of the body (p. 659)
auditory canal part of the outer ear that channels sounds from the outside to the eardrum (p. 626)
auditory tube air passage between the middle ear and throat that equalizes air pressure on either side of the eardrum; also called the Eustachian tube (p. 626)
autoimmune disease disorder in which the immune system attacks the body's own molecules (p. 691)
autonomic nervous system subdivision of the motor division of the peripheral nervous system that regulates the internal environment (p. 619)
autotroph organism that makes its own food (p. 136)
auxin plant hormone that promotes plant growth (p. 477)
AV node (atrioventricular node) region of the heart between the right atrium and right ventricle from which electrical impulses spread to the ventricles during a heartbeat (p. 660)
axon neuron fiber that carries electric impulses away from the cell body and toward other cells (p. 612)

B

B cell lymphocyte that matures in bone marrow and produces antibodies; responsible for humoral immunity (p. 683)
bacillus a rod-shaped bacterium (p. 362)
bacteria domain of prokaryotic organisms that are biochemically and genetically distinct from archaea (p. 361)
bacteriophage virus that infects bacteria; also called a "phage" (p. 227)
bark all plant tissues outside the vascular cambium; includes phloem, cork cambium, and cork (p. 455)
base compound that removes H^+ ions from an aqueous solution and that measures more than 7 on the pH scale (p. 85)
benign tumor mass of cells that remain at their original site (p. 190)
benthic zone bottom of an aquatic ecosystem; consists of sand and sediment and supports its own community of organisms (p. 758)
bilateral symmetry body plan in which an animal can be divided into two equal sides (p. 502)
binary fission mode of prokaryote asexual reproduction in which each daughter cell receives an identical copy of the parent cell's chromosome (p. 363)
binomial two-part Latin name of a species (p. 342)
biodiversity variety of life on Earth (p. 805)
biological control control of pest organisms by interfering with their natural ecological interactions, as in introducing predators (p. 536)
biological magnification process by which pollutants become more concentrated in successive trophic levels of a food web (p. 802)
biological species concept definition of a species as a population or group of populations whose members can breed with one another in nature and produce fertile offspring (p. 324)
biomass organic material manufactured by producers (p. 792)
biomass pyramid diagram representing the biomass in each trophic level of an ecosystem (p. 794)
biome major type of terrestrial ecosystem that covers a large region of Earth (p. 753)
bioremediation use of organisms to remove pollutants from water, air, and soil (p. 368)
biosphere all the parts of the planet that are inhabited by living things; sum of all Earth's ecosystems (pp. 4, 745)
biotechnology use of organisms to perform practical tasks (p. 266)
biotic factor any living part of an environment (p. 744)
bipedalism ability to walk upright on two feet (p. 575)
bivalve member of a group of mollusks with hinged shells, such as clams, mussels, scallops, and oysters (p. 509)
blade main part of a leaf (p. 449)
blastocyst stage in human embryonic development; fluid-filled ball of cells that implants in the endometrium (p. 728)
blastula embryonic stage in most animals consisting of a single layer of cells surrounding a hollow cavity (p. 495)
blood fluid connective tissue of the circulatory system; consists of blood cells and plasma (p. 654)
bolus chewed clump of food that leaves the mouth and travels through the alimentary canal (p. 639)
bony fish member of a group of fishes with skeletons made mainly of bone (p. 546)
book lung respiratory structure in many arachnids (p. 528)
brainstem lower section of the brain including the medulla oblongata, pons, and midbrain that filters information going to and from the brain (p. 621)
bronchiole thin tube that branches from a bronchus within a lung (p. 668)
bronchus one of two tubes connecting the trachea to each lung (p. 667)
bryophyte plant, such as a moss, lacking lignin-hardened vascular tissue (p.425)
bud undeveloped shoot of a plant (p. 449)
buffer substance that maintains a fairly constant pH in a solution by accepting H^+ ions when their levels rise and donating H^+ ions when their levels fall (p. 86)
buffer zone area of a reserve that is minimally impacted by humans (p. 809)
bulimia eating disorder characterized by bingeing and purging (p. 649)

C

calorie amount of energy required to raise the temperature of 1 g of water 1°C (p. 141)
Calvin cycle cycle in plants that makes sugar from carbon dioxide, H^+ ions, and high-energy electrons carried by NADPH (p. 162)
Cambrian explosion burst of diverse animal species originating during the Cambrian period (p. 515)
cancer disease caused by severe disruption of the mechanisms that normally control the cell cycle (p. 190)
capillary microscopic blood vessel that carries blood between an artery and a vein, allowing the exchange of substances between the blood and interstitial fluid (p. 655)
carapace hard shield reinforced with calcium carbonate that covers the back of a decapod's cephalothorax (p. 530)
carbohydrate organic compound made of sugar molecules (p. 95)
carbon cycle process by which carbon moves from inorganic to organic compounds and back (p. 172)

cardiac muscle involuntary muscle that causes the heart to pump blood (p. 592)
cardiovascular disease illness of the heart and/or blood vessels (p. 665)
carnivore consumer that eats only other consumers (p. 789)
carpel female reproductive organ of a flower (p. 434)
carrier individual who has one copy of the allele for a recessive disorder and does not exhibit symptoms (p. 256)
carrying capacity number of organisms in a population that an environment can maintain (p. 771)
cartilage type of connective tissue softer than bone (p. 597)
cartilaginous fish member of a group of fishes with flexible skeletons made entirely of cartilage (p. 546)
catalyst agent that speeds up chemical reactions (p. 103)
cell basic unit of living matter; separated from its environment by a plasma membrane (p. 6)
cell cycle sequence of events from the production of a eukaryotic cell to the time the cell itself reproduces (p. 183)
cell plate disk containing cell wall material that develops in plant cells during cytokinesis, eventually dividing the cell into two daughter cells (p. 188)
cell theory generalization that all living things are composed of cells, and that cells are the basic unit of structure and function in living things (p. 110)
cell wall strong wall outside a plant cell's plasma membrane that protects the cell and maintains its shape (p. 113)
cell-mediated immunity type of immunity produced by T cells that attack infected or abnormal body cells (p. 684)
cellular differentiation increasing specialization in structure and function of cells during development of a multicellular organism (p. 283)
cellular respiration chemical process that uses oxygen to convert chemical energy stored in organic molecules into ATP (adenosine triphosphate) (p. 137)
cellular slime mold protist with both unicellular and multicellular stages in its life cycle; is a decomposer (p. 388)
cellulose polysaccharide consisting of glucose monomers that reinforces plant-cell walls (p. 97)
central nervous system (CNS) the body's primary information processing system; includes the brain and spinal cord (p. 610)
centromere region where two sister chromatids are joined tightly together (p. 182)
centrosome region of cytoplasmic material that in animal cells contains structures called centrioles (p. 185)
cephalopod member of a group of mollusks that includes squids and octopuses (p. 509)
cephalothorax fused head and thorax characteristic of arachnids and some crustaceans (p. 528)
cerebellum part of the brain located below the cerebrum and above the spinal cord; planning center that coordinates body movement (p. 621)
cerebral cortex the outer region of the cerebrum containing integration centers for higher brain functions (p. 620)
cerebrum largest and most complex part of the brain, made up of the left and right hemispheres (p. 620)
cervix neck of the uterus, opening into the vagina (p. 720)
chaparral temperate coastal biome dominated by dense evergreen shrubs (p. 755)
chelicera fanglike mouthpart characteristic of arachnids (p. 528)
chemical energy potential to perform work due to the arrangement of atoms within molecules (p. 139)
chemical reaction breaking of old and formation of new chemical bonds that result in new substances (p. 80)
chitin polysaccharide in arthropod exoskeletons (p. 524)
chlorophyll pigment that gives a chloroplast its green color; uses light energy to split water molecules during photosynthesis (p. 160)
chloroplast organelle found in some plant cells and certain unicellular organisms where photosynthesis takes place (pp. 128, 160)
cholesterol steroid molecule present in the plasma membranes of animal cells (p. 99)
chordate member of a group of animals that have a notochord in their embryonic form (p. 542)
chromatin combination of DNA and protein molecules, in the form of long, thin fibers, making up the genetic material in the nucleus of a eukaryotic cell (p. 182)
chromosome condensed threads of genetic material formed from chromatin as a cell prepares to divide (p. 182)
chromosome theory of inheritance generalization that genes are located on chromosomes and that the behavior of chromosomes during meiosis and fertilization accounts for inheritance patterns (p. 218)
chyme liquid mixture of food and stomach fluids released from the stomach into the small intestine (p. 640)
cilia short structures projecting from a cell and containing bundles of microtubules that move a cell through its surroundings or move fluid over the cell's surface (p. 130)
ciliate member of a group of protozoans that move and feed by means of hairlike projections (cilia) (p. 384)
circadian rhythm rhythmic pattern of behavior (in an animal) or biological cycle (in a plant) that follows an approximately 24-hour natural cycle (pp. 55, 486)
cirrhosis condition in which the liver is so scarred that it can no longer function (p. 708)
cladogram phylogenetic tree constructed from a series of two-way branch points, suggesting ancestral relationships among species (p. 346)
cleavage series of rapid mitotic divisions of a zygote (p. 728)
closed circulatory system blood transport system in which blood remains enclosed in vessels; and nutrients, oxygen, and wastes diffuse through vessel walls (p. 506)
cnidarian member of a group of invertebrates with radial symmetry and tentacles with stinging cells (p. 499)
cnidocyte specialized cell in cnidarians that functions in defense and capturing prey (p. 500)
coccus a spherical bacterium (p. 362)
cochlea coiled tube in the inner ear containing hairlike projections that function in hearing (p. 626)
codominance inheritance pattern in which a heterozygote expresses the distinct traits of both alleles (p. 216)
codon in RNA, a three-base "word" that codes for one amino acid (p. 236)
coelom fluid-filled body cavity completely lined by a layer of mesoderm cells (p. 506)
cohesion tendency of molecules of the same kind to stick to one another (p. 82)
collar cell flagellated cell in a sponge's inner layer (p. 497)
collenchyma cell type of plant cell with unevenly thickened cell walls that is grouped in strands or cylinders; provides support in the growing parts of a plant (p. 451)

commensalism symbiotic relationship in which one organism benefits, while the other organism is neither harmed nor helped (p. 780)

communication signals among animals that include sounds, odors, visual displays, and touches (p. 64)

community all the organisms living in an area (p. 745)

companion cell cell found alongside a sieve tube in a plant that may provide resources to the sieve-tube members (p. 467)

competitive exclusion one species succeeding over another when the growth of both species is limited by the same resource (p. 778)

complete digestive tract continuous digestive tube with a separate mouth and anus (p. 504)

compound substance containing two or more elements chemically combined in a fixed ratio (p. 73)

compound eye eye with many facets, each with its own lens (p. 525)

conditioning type of learning in which a particular stimulus or response is linked to a reward or punishment (p. 59)

cone photoreceptor cell in the retina that is stimulated in bright light, enabling color vision (p. 625)

coniferous forest forest populated by cone-bearing evergreen trees; mostly found in northern latitudes (p. 757)

connective tissue groups of cells that hold together and support other tissues and cushion, insulate, and connect organs (p. 591)

conservation biology application of biology to counter the loss of biodiversity (p. 807)

consumer organism that obtains food by eating producers (autotrophs) or other consumers (pp. 15, 136, 788)

continental drift motion of continents about Earth's surface on plates of crust floating on the hot mantle (p. 339)

controlled experiment experiment that tests the effect of a single variable (p. 33)

convergent evolution process in which unrelated species from similar environments have adaptations that seem very similar (p. 343)

cooperation group of behaviors in which individuals work together in a way that benefits the group (p. 65)

cork cambium meristem that develops from parenchyma cells in the cortex and produces a tough outer layer of cork in the stem and root of a woody plant (p. 455)

cornea transparent area at the front of the eye through which light enters (p. 625)

corpus callosum band of nerve fibers that support communication between the two cerebral hemispheres (p. 620)

corpus luteum ovarian structure that forms from a follicle after ovulation; secretes progesterone and estrogen (p. 725)

cortex mass of cells forming the ground tissue of a plant's root; also found in ground tissue of stems (p. 451)

cotyledon structure in a seed that functions in the storage and transfer of nutrients to the embryo (p. 444)

courtship ritual elaborate behavior of individuals of the same species before mating (p. 63)

covalent bond chemical bond that forms when two atoms share electrons (p. 79)

crop saclike food storage organ found in most birds (p. 567)

cross-fertilization process by which sperm from one flower's pollen fertilizes the eggs in a flower of a different plant (p. 207)

crossing over exchange of genetic material between homologous chromosomes during prophase I of meiosis (p. 199)

crustacean member of a group of arthropods that includes lobsters, crabs, crayfish, shrimp, and barnacles (p. 526)

current riverlike flow pattern within a body of water (p. 751)

cuticle waxy coating on the leaves and other aboveground parts of plants that helps the plant retain water (p. 421)

cyanobacteria group of prokaryotes that generate oxygen as a waste product of their photosynthesis (p. 366)

cytokinesis process by which the cytoplasm of a cell is divided in two; usually follows mitosis and meiosis (p. 184)

cytokinin plant hormone that stimulates cell division (p. 478)

cytoplasm region of a cell between the nucleus and the plasma membrane (p. 113)

cytotoxic T cell lymphocyte that attacks body cells infected with pathogens (p. 685)

data recorded observations or items of information (p. 25)

day-neutral plant plant that blooms when it reaches a certain stage of maturity, regardless of day length (p. 486)

decomposer organism that breaks down wastes and dead organisms (p. 788)

deforestation clearing of forests for agriculture, lumber, or other uses (p. 799)

deletion change to a chromosome in which a fragment of the chromosome is removed (p. 252)

denaturation loss of normal shape of a protein due to heat or other factor (p. 102)

dendrite neuron fiber that receives signals and carries them toward the cell body (p. 612)

density-dependent factor factor that limits a population more as population density increases (p. 772)

density-independent factor factor unrelated to population density that limits a population (p. 772)

deoxyribonucleic acid (DNA) molecule responsible for inheritance; nucleic acid that contains the sugar deoxyribose (pp. 6, 229)

depolarization voltage change that occurs when the difference in charge across a membrane decreases (p. 614)

depressant drug such as alcohol or tranquilizers that, in general, slows central nervous system activity (p. 630)

derived character homologous characteristic that unites organisms as a group (p. 346)

dermal tissue outer covering or "skin" of a plant (p. 450)

dermis layer of skin beneath and supporting the epidermis, made up mostly of fibrous connective tissue that gives the skin its strength and elasticity (p. 595)

descent with modification process by which descendants of ancestral organisms spread into various habitats and accumulate adaptations to diverse ways of life (p. 297)

desert land area that receives less than 30 centimeters of rain per year (p. 755)
detritus wastes and remains of dead organisms (p. 791)
deuterostome member of a group of organisms that includes echinoderms and chordates in which the coelom forms from part of the early embryo's digestive tube (p. 513)
diabetes disease in which body cells cannot absorb enough glucose from the blood (p. 714)
dialysis treatment that processes blood outside the body (p. 705)
diaphragm sheet of muscle that forms the bottom wall of the chest cavity; contracts during inhaling and relaxes during exhaling (p. 668)
diastolic pressure second number of a blood pressure reading; measurement of the pressure on artery walls when the heart is relaxed (p. 661)
diatom member of a group of unicellular algae with glasslike cell walls (p. 392)
diffusion net movement of the particles of a substance from where they are more concentrated to where they are less concentrated (p. 118)
digestion mechanical and chemical breakdown of food into molecules small enough for absorption; the second stage of food processing (p. 637)
dihybrid cross mating of two organisms that differ in two characters (p. 212)
dikaryotic having two haploid nuclei per cell, one from each parent, in a fungal mycelium (p. 406)
dinoflagellate member of a group of unicellular, photosynthetic algae with cell walls made of cellulose and having two flagella (p. 391)
diploid having two homologous sets of chromosomes (p. 194)
disaccharide sugar with two monosaccharides (p. 96)
DNA fingerprint an individual's unique banding pattern on an electrophoresis gel, determined by restriction fragments of the person's DNA (p. 280)
DNA polymerase enzyme that makes the covalent bonds between the nucleotides of new DNA strands (p. 234)
DNA replication process of copying DNA molecules (p. 233)
domain broadest category used to classify life forms (p. 9)
dominance hierarchy ranking of individuals in a group based on aggressive behavior (p. 62)
dominant descriptive of an allele in a heterozygous individual that appears to be the only one affecting a trait (p. 209)
dormancy period when a plant stops growing (p. 479)
double helix two strands of nucleotides wound about each other; structure of DNA (p. 231)
Down syndrome general set of symptoms in people with trisomy 21 (p. 250)
duplication change to a chromosome in which part of the chromosome is repeated (p. 252)

E

eardrum tissue separating the outer ear from the middle ear that vibrates when stimulated by sound waves (p. 626)
echinoderm member of a group of marine invertebrates that includes sea urchins and sea stars (p. 511)
ecological succession series of changes in the species in a community, often following a disturbance (p. 782)
ecology scientific study of the interactions among organisms and between organisms and their environment (p. 744)
ecosystem community of living things plus the nonliving features of the environment that support them (pp. 5, 745)
Ecstasy synthetic drug that causes stimulant-like and hallucinogenic-like effects in the user (p. 631)
ectotherm animal whose main source of body heat is the external environment (p. 561)
electromagnetic spectrum range of types of electromagnetic energy from gamma waves to radio waves (p. 163)
electron subatomic particle with a single unit of negative electric charge (–) (p. 74)
electron transport chain sequence of electron carrier molecules that transfer electrons and release energy during cellular respiration (p. 147)
element pure substance that cannot be broken down into other substances by chemical or physical means (p. 72)
elimination passage of undigested material from the digestive tract; the fourth stage of food processing (p. 637)
embryo stage in human development from the first division of the zygote until about nine weeks after fertilization (p. 728)
embryo sac female gametophyte in a flower containing seven haploid cells, one of which is an egg cell (p. 443)
embryology study of multicellular organisms as they develop from fertilized eggs to fully formed organisms (p. 333)
emphysema respiratory disease in which alveoli lose their elasticity, leading to difficulty breathing (p. 670)
endocrine gland organ of the endocrine system that secretes hormones (p. 699)
endocytosis process of taking material into a cell within vesicles that bud inward from the plasma membrane (p. 122)
endodermis layer of cells surrounding a plant's vascular tissue (p. 464)
endometrium inner lining of the uterus; site of implantation of the embryo (p. 725)
endoplasmic reticulum network of membranes within a cell's cytoplasm that produce a variety of molecules (p. 125)
endoskeleton skeleton located inside the body; characteristic of all vertebrates and some invertebrates (pp. 511, 543)
endosperm nutrient-storing tissue that nourishes the developing embryo of a plant (p. 435)
endospore dormant cell formed by certain bacteria that can survive very harsh conditions (p. 365)
endosymbiosis process by which eukaryotic cells may have evolved from small symbiotic prokaryotes that lived within other, larger host cells (p. 396)
endotherm animal whose main source of body heat is generated from cell metabolism (p. 561)
energy pyramid diagram representing energy loss from one trophic level to the next (p. 793)
entomology the study of insects (p. 535)
enzyme specialized protein that catalyzes the chemical reactions of a cell (p. 103)
epidermis outermost layer of skin (p. 595)
epididymis long, thin coiled tube where sperm mature and are stored (p. 721)
epiglottis flap of tissue that covers the trachea during swallowing, preventing food from entering the lungs (p. 667)

epiphyte plant that grows on another plant and absorbs nutrients through rain that falls on its leaves (p. 470)

epithelial tissue sheets of closely packed cells that cover the surface of the body and line the internal organs (p. 590)

equilibrium point at which the number of diffusing molecules moving in one direction is equal to the number moving in the opposite direction (p. 118)

esophagus muscle-encased tube of the alimentary canal between the pharynx and the stomach (p. 639)

essential nutrient raw material that must be ingested because cells cannot make it from other molecules (p. 644)

estuary area where fresh water from rivers merges with salty ocean water; productive ecosystem (p. 759)

ethylene plant hormone that stimulates fruit ripening and leaf drop (p. 479)

euglenoid member of a group of unicellular photosynthetic protists with one or two flagella and no cell wall (p. 390)

eukaryotic cell cell with a nucleus (surrounded by its own membrane) and other internal organelles (pp. 9, 114)

eutrophication rapid growth of algae in bodies of water, due to high levels of nitrogen and often phosphate (p. 801)

evidence collected body of data from observations and experiments (p. 37)

evolution generation-to-generation change in the proportion of different inherited genes in a population that accounts for all of the changes that have transformed life over an immense time (pp. 18, 292)

excretion removal of nitrogen-containing wastes from the body (p. 699)

exocytosis process of exporting proteins from a cell by a vesicle fusing with the plasma membrane (p. 122)

exon coding region in RNA transcript (p. 239)

exoskeleton hard external skeleton; characteristic of some invertebrates (p. 524)

exponential growth growth of a population that multiplies by a constant factor at constant time intervals (p. 770)

extinct no longer existing as a living species on Earth (p. 300)

F

facilitated diffusion pathway provided by transport proteins that helps certain molecules pass through a membrane (p. 119)

fat organic compound consisting of a three-carbon backbone (glycerol) attached to three fatty acids (p. 98)

feather type of modified scale made of keratin; characteristic of birds (p. 566)

feces undigested food material and other waste products that exit the body through the anus (p. 642)

fermentation cellular process of making ATP without oxygen (p. 153)

fertilization the fusion of the nuclei and cytoplasm of a haploid sperm cell and a haploid egg cell, forming a diploid zygote (pp. 194, 727)

fetus stage of human development from nine weeks after fertilization until birth (p. 731)

fibrous root type of thin root that makes up a highly branched root system (p. 448)

fitness contribution that an individual makes to the gene pool of the next generation compared to the contributions of other individuals (p. 315)

fixed action pattern (FAP) innate behavior that occurs as an unchangeable sequence of actions (p. 54)

flagella long, thin, whip-like structures, with a core of microtubules, that enable some cells to move (p. 130)

flatworm member of a group of small, leaflike or ribbon-like invertebrates that includes planarians (p. 502)

flower specialized plant shoot that functions in reproduction; unique to angiosperms (p. 434)

follicle cluster of cells that surround, protect, and nourish a developing egg cell in an ovary (p. 720)

food chain pathway of food transfer from one trophic level to another (p. 789)

food web pattern of feeding in an ecosystem consisting of interconnected and branching food chains (p. 791)

foram member of a group of marine protozoans with porous shells made of organic material and calcium carbonate (p. 383)

fossil preserved remains or marking left by an organism that lived in the past (p. 299)

fossil record chronological collection of life's remains in sedimentary rock layers (p. 299)

fruit ripened ovary of a flower (p. 435)

fruiting body aboveground reproductive structure of a fungus (p. 406)

functional group group of atoms within a molecule that interacts in predictable ways with other molecules (p. 93)

G

gallbladder organ that stores bile from the liver and releases it into the small intestine (p. 640)

gamete egg or sperm sex cell that contains a single set of chromosomes, one from each homologous pair (p. 194)

gametophyte haploid generation of a plant; produces gametes (p. 424)

ganglia clusters of nerve cell bodies found along the nerve cords of some animals (p. 525)

gastropod member of a group of mollusks that includes snails and slugs (p. 509)

gastrovascular cavity digestive sac (p. 500)

gastrula emybronic stage following the blastula that has an inner and outer cell layer (p. 495)

gastrulation developmental process in which three distinct cell layers form in an embryo: the endoderm, mesoderm, and ectoderm (p. 730)

gel electrophoresis technique for sorting molecules or fragments of molecules by length (p. 279)

gene unit of inherited information in DNA (p. 6)

gene expression transcription and translation of genes into proteins (p. 283)

gene flow exchange of genes between populations (p. 313)

gene locus specific location of a gene on a chromosome (p. 218)

gene pool all of the alleles in all the individuals that make up a population (p. 310)

generalization general conclusion (p. 28)

genetic counselor person trained to collect, analyze, and explain data about human inheritance patterns (p. 259)

genetic drift change in the gene pool of a population due to chance (p. 312)

genetic linkage tendency for alleles of genes on the same chromosome to be inherited together (p. 219)
genetic marker specific portion of DNA that varies among individuals (p. 280)
genetic recombination new combination of genetic information in a gamete as a result of crossing over during prophase I of meiosis (p. 199)
genetically modified organism (GMO) organism that has acquired genetic material by artificial means (p. 274)
genetics study of heredity (p. 206)
genome complete set of an organism's genetic material (p. 248)
genomic library complete collection of cloned DNA fragments from an organism (p. 271)
genotype genetic makeup of an organism; an organism's combination of alleles (p. 211)
geographic isolation separation of populations as a result of geographic change or migration to geographically isolated places (p. 327)
geologic time scale Earth's history organized into four eras: Precambrian, Paleozoic, Mesozoic, and Cenozoic (p. 336)
germination process by which a plant embryo begins to grow (p. 445)
gibberellin plant hormone that stimulates growth of stems (p. 478)
gizzard muscular organ, often containing small stones, that grinds seeds and other foods (p. 567)
global warming rise in Earth's average temperature (p. 800)
glomerulus ball of capillaries in each nephron of a kidney that is the site of filtration (p. 702)
glycogen polysaccharide in animal cells that consists of many glucose monomers (p. 97)
glycolysis the splitting in half of a glucose molecule; the first stage of cellular respiration and fermentation (p. 149)
Golgi apparatus cellular organelle that modifies, stores, and routes cell products (p. 126)
gravitropism growth of a plant in response to gravity (p. 482)
greenhouse effect process by which atmospheric gases trap heat close to Earth's surface and prevent it from escaping into space (pp. 173, 800)
ground tissue tissue between the dermal tissue and vascular tissue of a non-woody plant that functions in photosynthesis, storage, and support (p. 451)
growth factor protein that initiates cell division (p. 260)
guard cell one of a pair of cells that open and close the stoma of a plant by changing shape, allowing gas exchange with the surrounding air (p. 466)
gymnosperm plant that bears seeds that are not enclosed in an ovary (p. 431)
gynecology medical specialty that focuses on wellness of the female reproductive system (p. 736)

H

habitat an organism's specific environment, with characteristic abiotic and biotic factors (p. 746)
habituation type of learning in which an animal stops responding to a repeated stimulus that conveys little or no important information (p. 57)
half-life time it takes for 50 percent of a radioactive isotope sample to decay (p. 338)
hallucinogen drug that causes a person to see, hear, and perceive things that do not exist (p. 631)
halophyte salt-tolerant plant (p. 485)
haploid having a single set of chromosomes (p. 194)
Hardy-Weinberg equilibrium condition that occurs when the frequency of alleles in a particular gene pool remain constant over time (p. 311)
heart multi-chambered, muscular organ that pumps blood throughout the body (p. 654)
heart attack condition that occurs when an artery becomes blocked, disrupting blood flow to the heart (p. 665)
helper T cell lymphocyte that activates cytotoxic T cells and stimulates B cells to produce antibodies (p. 685)
hemoglobin iron-containing protein in red blood cells that carries oxygen for delivery to cells (p. 663)
hepatitis disease, usually viral, characterized by inflammation of the liver (p. 708)
herbivore consumer that eats only producers (p. 789)
heterotroph organism that obtains food by eating other organisms (p. 136)
heterozygous having different alleles for a gene (p. 209)
histamine chemical alarm signal released by mast cells that causes blood vessels to dilate during an inflammatory response (p. 680)
histone small protein that DNA wraps around (p. 248)
HIV (human immunodeficiency virus) virus that destroys helper T cells and causes AIDS (p. 692)
homeostasis internal stability or "steady state" maintained by the body (pp. 16, 593)
homeotic gene master control gene in many organisms that directs development of body parts (p. 284)
hominid member of the family of species that includes *Homo sapiens* (modern humans) (p. 575)
homologous chromosome one of a matching pair of chromosomes, one inherited from each parent (p. 192)
homologous structure similar structure found in more than one species that share a common ancestor (p. 301)
homozygous having identical alleles for a gene (p. 209)
hormone signal molecule released into the bloodstream that triggers particular responses (pp. 593, 699)
humoral immunity specific immunity produced by B cells that produce antibodies that circulate in body fluids (p. 684)
hybrid offspring of two different true-breeding varieties (p. 208)
hydrocarbon organic molecule composed of only carbon and hydrogen atoms (p. 92)
hydrogen bond bond created by the weak attraction of a slightly positive hydrogen atom to a slightly negative portion of another molecule (p. 81)
hydrophilic attracts water molecules (p. 93)
hydrophobic avoids water molecules (p. 98)
hydrothermal vent opening in the ocean floor where hot gases and minerals escape from Earth's interior (p. 761)
hypertension condition of having a blood pressure of 140/90 or higher for an extended period; also called high blood pressure (p. 666)
hypertonic having a higher concentration of solute than another solution (p. 120)

hypha (plural, *hyphae*) a thread of cytoplasm; many hyphae together make up the body of a fungus (p. 402)
hypodermis tissue layer beneath the dermis; contains adipose tissue, a connective tissue that includes fat-storing cells and blood vessels (p. 595)
hypothalamus region of the brain that is the "master control center" of the endocrine system; functions in maintaining homeostasis by regulating temperature, blood pressure, and other conditions (pp. 622, 710)
hypothesis suggested, testable answer to a well-defined scientific question (p. 31)
hypotonic having a lower concentration of solute than another solution (p. 120)

I

immediate cause explanation of an organism's behavior based on its immediate interactions with the environment (p. 51)
immunity resistance to a specific pathogen (p. 682)
imperfect fungi informal category of fungi with no known sexual stage of reproduction (p. 408)
implantation imbedding of a blastocyst into the endometrium (p. 728)
imprinting a usually irreversible type of learning limited to a specific time period in an animal's life (p. 58)
infectious disease disease caused by a pathogen (p. 676)
inference logical conclusion based on observations (p. 27)
inflammatory response nonspecific defense against infection, characterized by redness, heat, swelling, and pain (p. 680)
ingestion the act of eating food or drinking; the first stage of food processing (p. 637)
inhalant substance, such as certain aerosols, whose vapors produce mind-altering effects (p. 631)
innate behavior behavior performed correctly and in the same way by all individuals of a species, without previous experience (p. 53)
inorganic molecule non-carbon-based molecule (p. 92)
insect member of a group of arthropods that includes beetles, ants, butterflies, bees, and many others (p. 527)
insight performing a behavior correctly or appropriately in a new situation, without previous experience (p. 60)
integumentary system outer covering that physically separates the body from the external environment (p. 595)
interferon protein produced by cells in response to being infected by a virus; helps other cells resist the virus (p. 680)
intermediate inheritance inheritance in which heterozygotes have a phenotype intermediate between the phenotypes of the two homozygotes (p. 215)
interneuron nerve cell located entirely in the central nervous system that integrates sensory information and sends motor commands (p. 610)
interphase stage of the cell cycle during which a cell carries out its metabolic processes and performs its functions in the body (p. 183)
interspecific competition competition between species that depend on the same limited resource (p. 777)
interstitial fluid aqueous solution that fills the gaps between cells in a tissue (p. 594)
intertidal zone area of shore between the high-tide and low-tide lines (p. 760)
introduced species species moved by humans to new geographic areas, either intentionally or accidentally (p. 783)
intron internal noncoding region in RNA transcript (p. 239)
inversion change to a chromosome in which a fragment of the original chromosome is reversed (p. 252)
invertebrate member of a group of animals without a backbone (p. 496)
ion atom that has become electrically charged as a result of gaining or losing an electron (p. 78)
ionic bond chemical bond that occurs when an atom transfers an electron to another atom (p. 78)
iris colored part of the eye; controls the amount of light that enters the eye by regulating the size of the pupil (p. 625)
isotonic having a solute concentration equal to that of another solution (p. 120)
isotope one of several forms of an element, each containing the same number of protons in their atoms but a different number of neutrons (p. 76)

J

joint area where one bone meets another (p. 599)
jointed appendage appendage with joints, or points where it can bend (p. 524)

karyotype display of a person's 46 chromosomes (p. 192)
kidney main organ of the excretory system; excretes waste products and regulates water and salt balance (p. 701)
kinetic energy energy of motion (p. 138)
Krebs cycle stage of cellular respiration that finishes the breakdown of pyruvic acid molecules to carbon dioxide, releasing energy (p. 150)

L

labor series of rhythmic contractions of the uterus that expel the baby from the uterus, resulting in birth (p. 733)
large intestine portion of the alimentary canal from which water is reabsorbed into the body (p. 642)
larva immature form of an animal that looks different from the adult form (p. 495)
larynx voicebox; contains the vocal cords (p. 667)
lateral line system row of sensory organs running along each side of the body in fishes (p. 547)
learning a change in behavior resulting from experience (p. 57)
legume member of a group of plants that house their own nitrogen-fixing bacteria (p. 462)
lichen mutualistic pairing of a fungus and an alga (p. 410)
ligament strong fibrous connective tissue that holds together the bones in movable joints (p. 599)
light reactions chemical reactions that convert the sun's energy to chemical energy; take place in the membranes of thylakoids in the chloroplast (p. 162)
lignin chemical that hardens certain plant cell walls (p. 421)

limbic system system of regions of the brain that interact with the cerebral cortex in emotion and memory (p. 622)
limiting factor condition that restricts a population's growth, such as space, disease, and food availability (p. 771)
lipid one of a class of water-avoiding compounds (p. 98)
liver largest organ in the body; performs many functions such as producing bile, storing glucose as glycogen, and transforming ammonia to urea (p. 640)
long-day plant plant that blooms when the dark period is shorter than a critical length (p. 486)
lung organ consisting of sponge-like tissue that exchanges oxygen and carbon dioxide with the blood (p. 667)
lymph fluid similar to interstitial fluid that circulates in the lymphatic system (p. 657)
lysogenic cycle a viral reproductive cycle in which the viral DNA is added to the host cell's DNA and is copied along with the host cell's DNA (p. 372)
lysosome membrane-bound sac containing digestive enzymes that can break down proteins, nucleic acids, and polysaccharides (p. 127)
lytic cycle a viral reproductive cycle in which copies of a virus are made within a host cell, which then bursts open, releasing new viruses (p. 372)

M

macroevolution major biological changes evident in the fossil record (p. 325)
malignant tumor mass of abnormal cells resulting from uncontrolled cancer cell division (p. 190)
malnutrition condition caused by a diet lacking one or more essential nutrients (p. 648)
Malpighian tubule excretory structure that works with the gut in reducing water loss in land arthropods (p. 528)
mammal member of a group of endothermic vertebrates with mammary glands and hair (p. 570)
mandible hard mouthpart used to bite and grind food, characteristic of decapods and some insects (p. 530)
mantle body surface outgrowth that drapes over a mollusk (p. 508)
marijuana drug made from dried pieces of the hemp plant (p. 630)
marrow specialized tissue found in bone; yellow bone marrow consists of stored fat that serves as an energy reserve; red bone marrow makes cells that develop into blood cells (p. 598)
marsupial member of a group of pouched mammals whose embryos are born before development is complete (p. 572)
mass extinction episode of great species loss (p. 340)
matter anything that occupies space and has mass (p. 72)
medusa cnidarian body form that is umbrella-shaped with fringes of tentacles (p. 501)
meiosis type of cell division that produces four cells, each with half as many chromosomes as the parent cell (p. 192)
melanin pigmented protein that gives skin its color (p. 595)
memory cell long-lasting lymphocyte formed during the primary immune response that is reactivated on exposure to the same pathogen, quickly producing many clones (p. 686)
menopause point in life when a woman stops ovulating, usually in her 50s (p. 735)
menstrual cycle cyclic changes that occur in the uterus (p. 724)
menstruation discharge resulting from shedding of the endometrium during the menstrual cycle (p. 725)
meristem structure that generates new dermal, vascular, and ground tissue in a plant (p. 452)
messenger RNA (mRNA) RNA molecule transcribed from a DNA template (p. 238)
metabolism all of a cell's chemical processes (p. 148)
metamorphosis complete change of body form in some animals from a larva to an adult (p. 495)
metaphase second stage of mitosis and of meiosis I and II when the spindle is fully formed and all of the chromosomes are held in place (p. 186)
metastasis spread of cancer cells beyond their original site in the body (p. 190)
microclimate climate in a specific area that varies from the surrounding climate region (p. 752)
microevolution evolution on the smallest scale—a generation-to-generation change in the frequencies of alleles within a population (p. 311)
microfilament solid rod of protein, thinner than a microtubule, that enables a cell to move or change shape (p. 130)
micrograph photograph of the view through a microscope (p. 111)
microtubule straight, hollow tube of proteins that gives rigidity, shape, and organization to a cell (p. 130)
mitochondria cellular organelles where cellular respiration occurs (p. 129)
mitosis process by which the nucleus and duplicated chromosomes of a cell divide and are evenly distributed, forming two daughter nuclei (p. 184)
mitotic phase stage of the cell cycle when a cell is actively dividing (p. 184)
model physical, mental, or mathematical representation of how people understand a process or an idea (p. 39)
mold fungus that grows very rapidly on a surface (p. 408)
molecule two or more atoms held together by covalent bonds (p. 79)
mollusk member of a group of invertebrates characterized by a muscular foot and a mantle (p. 508)
molting process of shedding an old exoskeleton (in arthropods) or skin (in reptiles) and producing a new one (p. 525)
monohybrid cross mating of two organisms that differ in only one character (p. 208)
monomer small molecular unit that is the building block of a larger molecule (p. 93)
monosaccharide sugar containing one sugar unit (p. 95)
monotreme member of a group of mammals that lays eggs (p. 571)
motor neuron nerve cell that carries signals from the central nervous system to muscle or gland cells (p. 611)
multicellular consisting of many cells (p. 9)
muscle fiber single, long cylindrical muscle cell containing many nuclei (p. 602)
mutagen physical or chemical agent that causes mutations (p. 243)
mutation any change in the nucleotide sequence of DNA (p. 242)
mutualism type of symbiotic relationship in which both organisms involved benefit (p. 780)

mycelium interwoven mat of hyphae that functions as the feeding structure of a fungus (p. 402)
mycorrhizae symbiotic relationships between fungal hyphae and plant roots (p. 411)
myelin sheath thick coat of material that surrounds and insulates the axon of some neurons (p. 612)
myofibril unit of muscle fiber made up of smaller units that contract (sarcomeres) (p. 602)
myosin thick filament in a muscle fiber; has bump-like projections (p. 603)

N

natural selection process by which individuals with inherited characteristics well-suited to the environment leave more offspring than do other individuals (pp. 17, 298)
negative feedback type of regulation that responds to a change in conditions by initiating responses that will counteract the change (p. 698)
nematocyst stinging capsule found in a cnidocyte (p. 500)
nephron one of millions of tubes and its associated blood vessels in a kidney that extracts filtrate from the blood and refines it into urine (p. 702)
neritic zone area of ocean that extends from the low-tide line out to the edge of the continental shelf (p. 760)
nerve bundle or bundles of neuron fibers surrounded by connective tissue (p. 610)
nervous tissue tissue that transmits signals in the body in response to changes in the environment (p. 591)
neuron nerve cell; basic unit of nervous tissue (p. 591)
neurotransmitter chemical messenger that carries information from one neuron to another or to another cell (p. 616)
neutron subatomic particle that has no charge (is electrically neutral) (p. 74)
niche unique living arrangement of an organism defined by its habitat, food sources, time of day it is most active, and other factors (p. 778)
nitrification process by which certain bacteria convert ammonium to nitrates (p. 797)
nitrogen fixation process by which certain bacteria convert nitrogen gas to ammonia (pp. 462, 797)
nitrogenous base single or double ring of carbon and nitrogen atoms with attached functional groups, found in nucleic acids (p. 229)
node uninsulated spaces between the "beads" of a myelin sheath where an action potential can be transmitted (p. 612)
nondisjunction event during meiosis in which homologous chromosomes or sister chromatids fail to separate (p. 251)
nonspecific defense physical or chemical barrier that prevents pathogens from entering the body (p. 678)
notochord flexible rod that extends through much of the length of a chordate embryo (p. 542)
nuclear envelope double membrane that surrounds a cell nucleus (p. 124)
nucleic acid probe radioactively labeled nucleic acid molecule used to tag a particular DNA sequence (p. 271)
nucleolus ball-like mass of fibers and granules in a cell nucleus (p. 124)
nucleotide building block (monomer) of nucleic acid polymers (p. 229)
nucleus in an atom, the central core that contains protons and neutrons (p. 75); in a cell, the part that houses the cell's genetic material in the form of DNA (p. 112)
nutrition the process of obtaining raw materials from food (p. 637)

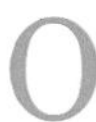

obesity condition of being significantly overweight (p. 648)
observation use of the senses to gather and record information about structures or processes in nature (p. 25)
oceanic zone vast open ocean from the edge of the continental shelf outward (p. 760)
omnivore consumer that eats both producers and consumers (p. 789)
oncogene cancer-causing gene (p. 260)
open circulatory system blood transport system in which blood is pumped into chambers where it comes in direct contact with tissues and organs (p. 508)
operator control sequence on an operon that acts as a switch, determining whether or not RNA polymerase can attach to the promoter (p. 281)
operculum protective flap covering the gills of bony fishes (p. 548)
operon cluster of genes and their control sequences (p. 281)
opiate narcotic, such as morphine or heroin, that is derived from opium poppies (p. 631)
organ unit consisting of several tissues that together perform a specific task (p. 587)
organ system unit of multiple organs that together perform a vital body function (p. 587)
organelle part of a cell with a specific function (p. 112)
organic molecule carbon-based molecule (p. 92)
organism living thing (p. 5)
osmosis passive transport of water across a selectively permeable membrane (p. 120)
osteoporosis disorder in which bones become thinner, more porous, and more easily broken (p. 600)
ovarian cycle cyclic changes that occur in the ovaries (p. 724)
ovary in flowering plants, protective organ inside a flower that bears seeds (p. 423); in animals, female reproductive organ that produces egg cells and hormones (p. 720)
overexploitation practice of harvesting or hunting to such a degree that remaining individuals may not be able to replenish the population (p. 807)
oviduct tube that conveys egg cells away from the ovary toward the uterus; the usual site of fertilization (p. 720)
ovulation release of a secondary oocyte from an ovarian follicle (p. 722)
ovule structure in seed plants in which the female gametophyte develops (p. 432)
ovum mature egg cell with a haploid nucleus (p. 722)
oxytocin hormone secreted by pituitary gland that stimulates contractions of the uterus (p. 733)
ozone atmospheric gas (O_3) that absorbs ultraviolet radiation, shielding organisms from its damaging effects (p. 803)

pacemaker specific region of the heart that sets the rate at which the heart contracts (p. 660)

pancreas gland that makes digestive enzymes and secretes them into the small intestine; makes the hormones insulin and glucagon and secretes them into the blood (pp. 641, 714)
paper chromatography laboratory technique used to observe the different pigments in a material (p. 164)
parasitism relationship in which a parasitic organism obtains its food at the expense of a host organism (p. 780)
parasympathetic division division of the autonomic nervous system that conserves energy (p. 619)
parenchyma cell type of plant cell that has thin walls and typically a large central vacuole; functions in food storage, photosynthesis, and cellular respiration (p. 451)
passive immunity resistance to a particular pathogen that results when the body acquires antibodies for it, as when a baby receives antibodies from its mother (p. 689)
passive transport diffusion across a membrane requiring only the random motion of molecules with no energy expended by the cell (p. 119)
pathogen a disease-causing organism or virus (pp. 369, 676)
pedigree family tree that records and traces the occurrence of a trait in a family (p. 255)
pedipalp mouthpart characteristic of arachnids that is used to manipulate prey (p. 528)
pelagic zone open water above the ocean floor (p. 760)
penis male reproductive organ; also contains the urethra and functions in eliminating urine from the body (p. 721)
perception meaningful interpretation of sensory data by the central nervous system (p. 623)
peripheral nervous system (PNS) network of nerves carrying signals into and out of the central nervous system (p. 610)
peristalsis series of smooth muscle contractions that push food through the alimentary canal (p. 639)
permafrost permanently frozen subsoil (p. 757)
petal one of the modified leaves of the second ring of a flower (inside the sepals) (p. 442)
petiole stalk that connects a leaf to a plant stem (p. 449)
pH scale a range of numbers used to describe how acidic or basic a solution is; ranges from 0 (most acidic) to 14 (most basic) (p. 85)
pharynx the junction in the throat of the alimentary canal and the trachea (pp. 639, 667)
phenotype observable traits of an organism (p. 211)
phloem vascular tissue that transports food from a plant's leaves to its roots and other parts (p. 450)
phospholipid bilayer two-layer "sandwich" of molecules that surrounds a cell (p. 116)
photic zone regions of a body of water where light penetrates, enabling photosynthesis (p. 758)
photoperiodism plant response to cycles of light and darkness (p. 486)
photosynthesis process by which plants use the sun's energy to convert water and carbon dioxide into sugars (pp. 14, 136)
photosystem cluster of chlorophyll and other molecules in a thylakoid (p. 165)
phototropism growth of a plant part toward or away from light (p. 482)
phylogenetic tree branching diagram, suggesting evolutionary relationships, that classifies species into groups within groups (p. 343)
physiology study of functions or processes in an organism (p. 586)
phytochrome pigmented plant protein that detects light (p. 487)
phytoplankton microscopic algae and cyanobacteria that carry out photosynthesis (pp. 391, 758)
pigment chemical compound that determines a substance's color (p. 164)
pituitary gland gland consisting of the anterior pituitary and posterior pituitary, which is controlled by the hypothalamus and influences many body functions (p. 712)
placenta organ that develops inside the uterus and enables the transfer of nutrients, gases, and waste products between the mother and developing baby (p. 730)
placental mammal member of a group of mammals whose embryos complete their development within the mother's uterus (p. 572)
plankton mostly microscopic organisms that drift or swim near the surface of ponds, lakes, and oceans (p. 391)
plant multicellular autotroph in which the embryo develops within the female gametophyte (p. 420)
plant hormone chemical messenger in a plant (p. 476)
plaque deposits of cholesterol, calcium, and fat that build up on artery walls and can lead to cardiovascular disease (p. 665)
plasma liquid portion of blood made up of water, dissolved salts, proteins, and other substances (p. 663)
plasma cell antibody-secreting B cell (p. 684)
plasma membrane thin outer boundary of a cell that regulates the traffic of chemicals between the cell and its surroundings (p. 112)
plasmid small, circular DNA molecule found in bacteria that is separate from the bacterial chromosome (p. 268)
plasmodial slime mold member of a group of funguslike protists that grows in a branching pattern (p. 387)
plasmodium mass of cytoplasm, undivided by membranes or cell walls and containing many nuclei; characteristic of certain protists (p. 387)
platelet fragment of a blood cell originating in the bone marrow that is involved in blood clotting (p. 664)
polar molecule molecule in which opposite ends have opposite electric charges (p. 81)
polar zones the regions north of the Arctic Circle (66.5° N) and south of the Antarctic Circle (66.5° S), that receive the smallest amount of direct sunlight year-round (p. 750)
pollen much-reduced male gametophyte of seed plants that contains cells that develop into sperm (p. 431)
pollen tube structure that extends from a pollen grain and carries sperm to the female gametophyte (p. 443)
pollination process in which pollen grains released from anthers land on the stigma of a flower (p. 443)
pollution addition of substances to the environment that result in a negative effect (p. 802)
polygenic inheritance combined effect of two or more genes on a single character (p. 216)
polymer long chain of small molecular units (monomers) (p. 93)
polymerase chain reaction (PCR) technique that makes many copies of a certain segment of DNA without using living cells (p. 278)
polyp cnidarian body form consisting of a cylindrical body with tentacles radiating from one end (p. 501)

polypeptide chain of linked amino acids (p. 101)
polysaccharide long polymer chain made up of simple sugar monomers (p. 96)
population group of individuals of the same species living in a particular area at the same time (pp. 17, 305, 744)
population density number of individuals of a particular species per unit area or volume (p. 767)
potential energy energy stored due to an object's position or arrangement (p. 138)
predation interaction in which one organism consumes another (p. 778)
prehensile tail grasping tail that functions as an extra appendage, such as for swinging through trees (p. 575)
pressure-flow mechanism process by which phloem sap moves through a plant (p. 468)
primary consumer consumer that feeds directly on producers (p. 789)
primary growth growth in plant length (p. 452)
primary productivity rate at which producers in an ecosystem build biomass (p. 792)
primary succession process by which a community arises in a virtually lifeless area with no soil (p. 782)
primate member of a group of mammals that includes lemurs, monkeys, apes, and humans (p. 574)
producer organism that makes its own food (autotroph) and produces organic molecules that serve as food for other organisms in its ecosystem (pp. 15, 136, 788)
product material created as a result of a chemical reaction (p. 80)
prokaryotic cell cell lacking a nucleus and most other organelles (pp. 9, 114)
promoter control sequence on an operon where RNA polymerase attaches to the DNA (p. 281)
prophase first stage of mitosis and of meiosis I and II, when the already replicated chromosomes condense (p. 186)
protein polymer constructed from a set of 20 amino acid monomers (p. 100)
protist eukaryotic organism that is not an animal, a plant, or a fungus (p. 380)
proton subatomic particle with a single unit of positive electric charge (+) (p. 74)
protostome member of a group of organisms with a coelom that develops from a solid cell mass in the embryo, such as mollusks, annelids, and arthropods (p. 513)
protozoan animal-like protist; is a heterotroph (p. 381)
pseudocoelom fluid-filled internal space that is in direct contact with the wall of the digestive tract (p. 506)
pseudopodium temporary extension of a cell's cytoplasm and plasma membrane; used by certain protozoans in movement and feeding (p. 383)
pteridophyte member of a group of seedless vascular plants with lignin-hardened support tissues that includes ferns (p. 427)
puberty stage of human development when reproductive organs become functional and secondary sex characteristics develop (p. 734)
pulmonary circuit circuit of blood flow that carries blood between the heart and lungs (p. 658)
punctuated equilibrium evolutionary model suggesting species often diverge in spurts of relatively rapid change, followed by long periods of little change (p. 329)
Punnett square diagram showing the probabilities of the possible outcomes of a genetic cross (p. 210)
pupa transition stage between larva and adult in insects with complete metamorphosis (p. 533)
pupil opening in the iris that admits light into the eye (p. 625)
purine double-ring nitrogenous base (p. 230)
pyramid of numbers representation of the number of individual organisms in each trophic level of an ecosystem (p. 794)
pyrimidine single-ring nitrogenous base (p. 230)

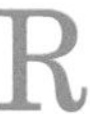

R

radial symmetry body plan in which an organism can be divided into equal parts around a central axis (p. 499)
radioactive isotope isotope in which the nucleus decays (breaks down) over time, giving off radiation in the form of matter and energy (p. 76)
radiometric dating determination of absolute ages of rocks and fossils through calculations based on a radioactive isotope's fixed rate of decay (p. 338)
radula scraping organ characteristic of mollusks (p. 508)
reactant starting material for a chemical reaction (p. 80)
recessive descriptive of an allele in a heterozygous individual that does not appear to affect a trait (p. 209)
recombinant DNA technology technology that combines genes from different sources into a single DNA molecule (p. 267)
red blood cell blood cell containing hemoglobin, which transports oxygen; also called an erythrocyte (p. 663)
reflex rapid, automatic response to a stimulus (p. 611)
releasing hormone hormone secreted by the hypothalamus that regulates the release of other hormones from the anterior pituitary (p. 712)
repressor protein that binds to the operator and blocks attachment of RNA polymerase to the promoter (p. 282)
reproductive isolation condition in which a reproductive barrier keeps two species from interbreeding (p. 325)
resting potential voltage across the plasma membrane of a resting neuron (p. 613)
restriction enzyme enzyme that cuts sugar-phosphate bonds in the DNA backbone at specific points within particular nucleotide sequences in DNA (p. 269)
retina inner surface of the eye that is lined with millions of photoreceptor cells (p. 625)
retrovirus member of a group of viruses such as HIV that carry reverse transcriptase, which catalyzes the synthesis of DNA from an RNA template (p. 374)
ribonucleic acid (RNA) nucleic acid containing the sugar ribose (p. 236)
ribosomal RNA (rRNA) RNA component of ribosomes (p. 240)
ribosome cluster of proteins and nucleic acids that constructs proteins in a cell (p. 125)
RNA polymerase transcription enzyme that links RNA nucleotides together (p. 238)
RNA splicing process by which the introns are removed from RNA transcripts and the remaining exons are joined together (p. 239)
rod photoreceptor in the retina that enables vision in dim light (p. 625)
root cap thimble-like cone of cells at the tip of a plant root that protects the actively dividing cells of the apical meristem (p. 452)

root hair outgrowth of a root's epidermal cell that increases the surface area available for absorption (p. 464)
root nodule lump on a plant root that contains nitrogen-fixing bacteria (p. 462)
root pressure force that helps push water up the xylem in a plant (p. 464)
rotifer member of a group of invertebrates with a complete digestive tract and a crown of rotating cilia (p. 505)
roundworm member of a group of cylindrical invertebrates with pointed heads and tapered tails (p. 504)

S

saliva liquid secreted into the mouth that contains mucus and digestive enzymes that start chemical digestion (p. 639)
sarcomere unit of contraction in a muscle fiber (p. 602)
saturated fat fat in which all three fatty acid chains contain the maximum possible number of hydrogen atoms (p. 98)
savanna grassland with scattered trees; found in tropical regions of Africa, Australia, and South America (p. 754)
scale hard structure made of keratin that is part of the skin of reptiles, fishes, and some other animals (p. 561)
sclerenchyma cell cell with lignin-rich cell walls that is specialized for support in the mature part of a plant (p. 451)
scrotum sac that houses the testes outside the abdomen (p. 721)
seaweed a large, multicellular marine alga (p. 392)
secondary consumer consumer that eats primary consumers (p. 789)
secondary growth growth in plant width (p. 454)
secondary succession change following a disturbance that damages an existing community but leaves the soil intact (p. 782)
seed plant embryo packaged along with a food supply within a protective coat (p. 431)
selectively permeable membrane membrane that allows some substances to pass more easily than others and blocks the passage of some substances altogether (p. 119)
semen sperm-containing fluid that is released from the penis during ejaculation (p. 721)
sensation awareness of sensory stimuli (p. 623)
sensory neuron nerve cell that carries information from the environment to the central nervous system (p. 610)
sensory receptor specialized cell that transmits signals to sensory neurons (p. 610)
sepal modified leaf of the outermost ring of a flower; covers and protects the flower bud before it opens (p. 442)
sessile anchored in place (p. 498)
sex chromosome one of two chromosomes of the 23rd pair of human chromosomes, which determine an individual's gender (p. 193)
sex-linked gene gene located on a sex chromosome (p. 220)
sexual reproduction process in which genetic material from two parents combines and produces offspring that differ genetically from either parent (p. 181)
sexually transmitted disease (STD) infectious disease spread by sexual contact (p. 737)
short-day plant plant that blooms when the dark period exceeds a critical length (p. 486)
sieve-tube member one of a chain of cells that forms a sieve tube, through which phloem sap flows in a plant (p. 467)
sister chromatid one of a pair of identical chromosomes created before a cell divides (p. 182)
skeletal muscle voluntary muscle attached to the skeleton that allows movement of the body (p. 592)
small intestine long, narrow tube where digestion is completed and most absorption occurs (p. 640)
smooth muscle involuntary muscle found in most organs of the body (p. 592)
solute substance in a solution that is dissolved and is present in a lesser amount (p. 84)
solution uniform mixture of two or more substances (p. 84)
solvent substance in a solution that dissolves the other substance and is present in the greater amount (p. 84)
somatic nervous system subdivision of the motor division of the peripheral nervous system that controls the voluntary movement of skeletal muscles (p. 618)
speciation formation of new species (p. 325)
species distinct form of life (p. 7)
spindle framework of microtubules that guide the movement of chromosomes during mitosis and meiosis (p. 185)
spinneret organ in a spider's abdomen that spins silk into fibers (p. 529)
spiracle hole in an arthropod's exoskeleton that allows the exchange of carbon dioxide and oxygen (p. 525)
spirochete member of a group of large spiral-shaped bacteria (p. 362)
sponge member of a group of animals that lack true tissues and organs (p. 497)
sporangia reproductive structures on a plasmodial slime mold; also called fruiting bodies (p. 387); spore-forming structures at the tips of fungal hyphae (p. 405)
spore haploid single cell with a thick wall that functions in the dispersal stage in fungal reproduction (p. 404)
sporophyte diploid generation of a plant; produces spores (p. 424)
stamen male reproductive organ of a flower (p. 434)
starch polysaccharide in plant cells that consists entirely of glucose monomers (p. 96)
stem structure of a plant that supports leaves and flowers (p. 448)
stem cell cell with the potential to develop into one of several types of differentiated cells (p. 284)
steroid lipid molecule with four fused carbon rings (p. 99)
stigma sticky tip of the style in a flower carpel (p. 443)
stimulant drug, such as caffeine, nicotine, and cocaine, that generally increases activity in the central nervous system (p. 630)
stimulus environmental change that triggers a response (p. 610)
stomata (singular, *stoma*) microscopic pores in a leaf's surface (p. 421)
stomach elastic, muscular sac where some chemical and some mechanical digestion take place (p. 640)
stroke damage to brain tissue resulting from a clot blocking blood flow to the brain (p. 666)
stroma thick fluid contained in the inner membrane of a chloroplast (p. 160)

stromatolite dome-shaped rock composed of thin layers of sediment pressed tightly together (p. 356)
style narrow structure in a flower; has a sticky tip (the stigma) and leads to the ovary (p. 443)
substrate specific reactant acted on by an enzyme (p. 104)
sustainable development use of natural resources in a way that allows them to renew themselves and be available for the future (p. 809)
swim bladder gas-filled sac that controls buoyancy in fishes (p. 549)
symbiotic relationship close interaction between species in which one species lives in or on the other (p. 780)
sympathetic division division of the autonomic nervous system that generally prepares the body for energy-consuming activities (p. 619)
synapse junction between two neurons or a neuron and another cell where electrical or chemical signals are relayed (p. 616)
synaptic cleft tiny space separating a knob of a transmitting neuron from a receiving neuron or other cell (p. 616)
system complex organization formed from a simpler combination of parts (p. 11)
systemic circuit circuit of blood flow that carries blood between the heart and the rest of the body (p. 658)
systolic pressure first number of a blood pressure reading; measures the pressure on artery walls when heart ventricles contract (p. 661)

T

T cell lymphocyte that matures in the thymus; is responsible for cell-mediated immunity and also plays a role in humoral immunity (p. 683)
tadpole legless aquatic larva of an amphibian (p. 553)
taproot large vertical plant root with many smaller branches (p. 448)
target cell cell with chemical receptors that cause it to respond to a particular hormone (p. 700)
taxonomy identification, naming, and classification of species (p. 341)
technology application of scientific understanding for a specific purpose (p. 41)
telophase final stage of mitosis and of meiosis I and II, in which the chromosomes reach the spindle poles, nuclear envelopes form around each set of daughter chromosomes, and the nucleoli reappear (p. 187)
temperate deciduous forest forest in a temperate region, characterized by trees that drop their leaves annually (p. 756)
temperate grassland biome characterized by deep, nutrient-rich soil that supports many grass species (p. 756)
temperate zones latitudes between the tropics and polar regions in each hemisphere (p. 750)
temperature measure of the average energy of random motion of particles in a substance (p. 83)
tendon dense connective tissue that attaches a muscle to a bone (p. 601)
territory area defended by an individual, usually excluding other members of the same species (p. 63)
tertiary consumer consumer that eats secondary consumers (p. 789)
testcross mating of an individual of unknown genotype but dominant phenotype with a homozygous recessive individual (p. 211)
testis male reproductive organ that produces sperm and hormones (p. 721)
tetrad group of four chromatids formed during prophase I of meiosis by the two sister chromatids in each of the two homologous chromosomes (p. 196)
tetrapod member of a group of animals with two sets of paired limbs modified as legs (p. 545)
thalamus brain region that sorts and exerts some control over information going to and from the cerebral cortex (p. 621)
theory well-tested explanation that makes sense of a great variety of scientific observations (p. 39)
thermal energy total amount of energy associated with the random movement of atoms and molecules in a sample of matter (pp. 83, 138)
thigmotropism plant growth in response to touch (p. 482)
thorax midsection of an arthropod (p. 524)
threshold minimum change in a membrane's voltage that must occur to generate an action potential (p. 614)
thylakoid disk-shaped sac in the stroma of a chloroplast; site of the light reactions of photosynthesis (p. 161)
thyroid endocrine gland that secretes hormones including thyroxin and calcitonin (p. 712)
tissue cooperating unit of many similar cells that perform a specific function (p. 587)
tolerance resistance to a drug's effects such that more of the drug is needed to produce the same effect (p. 629)
trace element element critical to health that makes up less than 0.01 percent of body mass (p. 72)
trachea in some arthropods, chitin-lined air tube that forms part of the respiratory system (p. 525); in humans, tube between the larynx and bronchi through which air travels to the lungs; also called the windpipe (p. 667)
tracheid long cell with tapered ends that transports water in the xylem (p. 466)
trait variation of a particular inherited character (p. 206)
transcription process by which a DNA template is used to produce a single-stranded RNA molecule (p. 236)
transcription factor protein that regulates transcription by binding to promoters or to RNA polymerases (p. 283)
transfer RNA (tRNA) RNA that translates the three-letter codons of mRNA to amino acids (p. 239)
transgenic genetically modified organism whose source of new genetic material is a different species (p. 274)
translation process by which a sequence of nucleic acids in RNA is used to direct the production of a chain of specific amino acids (p. 236)
translocation change to a chromosome in which a fragment of one chromosome attaches to a nonhomologous chromosome (p. 252)
transpiration evaporation of water from a plant's leaves (pp. 465, 798)
transposon genetic element that moves from one location to another in a genome (p. 253)
trisomy 21 condition in which an individual has three number 21 chromosomes, resulting in Down syndrome (p. 250)
trophic level feeding level in an ecosystem (p. 789)

trophoblast outer cells of the blastocyst that secrete enzymes that allow implantation (p. 728)

tropical rain forest type of forest near the equator that receives as much as 250 cm of rainfall yearly (p. 754)

tropics regions between 23.5° N latitude and 23.5° S latitude; warmest temperature zones on Earth (p. 750)

tropism growth response that causes parts of a plant to grow toward or away from a stimulus (p. 482)

tube feet in echinoderms, structures that are part of the water vascular system and function in locomotion, feeding, and gas exchange (p. 511)

tumor-suppressor gene gene that codes for a protein that stops cell division in particular situations (p. 260)

tundra biome in the Arctic Circle or on high mountaintops, characterized by bitterly cold temperatures and high winds (p. 757)

U

ultimate cause explanation of an organism's behavior based on its evolutionary adaptations (p. 51)

undernutrition condition caused by a diet deficient in Calories (p. 648)

unicellular consisting of a single cell (p. 9)

unsaturated fat fat with less than the maximum number of hydrogens in one or more of its fatty acid chains (p. 99)

urea compound formed in the liver from ammonia and carbon dioxide and excreted primarily by the kidneys (p. 699)

ureter tube extending from each kidney that carries urine to the urinary bladder (p. 701)

urethra tube leading from the urinary bladder through which urine exits the body (p. 701)

urinary bladder sac that stores urine until it is eliminated from the body (p. 701)

urine liquid composed of water, urea, and other waste products; produced by the kidneys (p. 701)

urology medical specialty that focuses on the wellness of the urinary tract in males and females, and also the male reproductive system (p. 736)

uterus in female mammals, the organ where the young develop before birth (p. 720)

V

vaccine dose of a disabled or destroyed pathogen (or part of a pathogen) used to stimulate a long-term immune defense against the pathogen (pp. 375, 688)

vacuole membrane-bound sac that buds from the endoplasmic reticulum or the Golgi apparatus (p. 126)

vagina part of the female reproductive system that leads from the uterus to the outside of the body; functions as the birth canal and the passageway for menstrual flow (p. 720)

valve flap of tissue in the heart that prevents blood from flowing in the wrong direction (p. 659)

variable any factor in an experiment that is not constant (any factor that can change) (p. 33)

variation difference among members of a species (p. 306)

vas deferens tube that conveys sperm between the epididymis and the urethra (p. 721)

vascular cambium cylinder of actively dividing cells located between the xylem and phloem of a plant (p. 454)

vascular tissue system of tube-shaped cells that branches throughout a plant and transports water, mineral nutrients, and organic molecules (pp. 420, 450)

vegetative reproduction method of asexual reproduction in plants (p. 446)

vein vessel that returns blood to the heart (p. 655)

ventricle heart chamber that pumps blood out of the heart (p. 659)

vertebra segment of the backbone; encloses and protects the nerve cord (pp. 543, 597)

vertebrate animal with a backbone (p. 496)

vesicle small membrane-bound sac that functions in moving products into, out of, and within a cell (p. 122)

vessel element short, wide cell that transports water in the xylem of a plant (p. 466)

vestigial structure remnant of a structure that may have had an important function in a species' ancestors, but has no clear function in the modern species (p. 302)

villus fingerlike projection of the inner surface of the small intestine that functions in absorbing nutrients (p. 641)

virus package of nucleic acid wrapped in a protein coat that must use a host cell's machinery to reproduce itself (p. 227)

W

water vascular system in echinoderms, a network of water-filled canals that function in movement, food gathering, and as a basic circulatory system (p. 511)

wavelength distance between adjacent waves (p. 163)

white blood cell blood cell that functions in defending the body against infections and cancer cells; also called a leukocyte (p. 664)

withdrawal psychological and/or physical symptoms experienced when a person stops taking a drug to which he or she is addicted (p. 629)

wood secondary xylem that accumulates during the annual growing season of a plant (p. 454)

xylem vascular tissue that transports water and dissolved minerals from the roots of a plant to the shoots (p. 450)

yeast unicellular fungus that inhabits liquid or moist habitats, including plant sap and animal tissues (p. 408)

Z

zoned reserve area of land that is relatively undisturbed by humans and is surrounded by buffer zones that are minimally impacted by humans (p. 809)

zooflagellate member of a group of protozoans that move by means of one or more flagella (p. 382)

zooplankton microscopic animals that swim or drift near the surface of aquatic environments (pp. 391, 760)

zygosporangium thick-walled reproductive structure formed from the fusion of the cytoplasm of the mycelia of two neighboring fungi (p. 405)

zygote diploid cell formed when the nucleus of a haploid sperm cell fuses with the nucleus of a haploid egg cell (pp. 194, 727)

Index

Credits

Staff Credits

The people who made up the *Biology: Exploring Life* team—representing design services, editorial, editorial services, market research, marketing services, online services & multimedia development, production services, project office, and publishing processes—are listed below.

Jennifer Angel, Amy C. Austin, Joyce Barisano, Neil Benjamin, Barbara A. Bertell, Peggy Bliss, Jim Brady, Brienn A. Buchanan, Roger Calado, Sarah J. Garrett, Julia Gecha, Sandy Graff, Maria B. Green, Sarah C. Greene, Iris Martinez Kane, Toby Klang, Melissa Levine, Marcia Lord, Dorothy Marshall, Anne C. McConnell, Carolyn B. McGuire, Joan Paley, Judith Pinkham, Robert Runck, Shelley Ryan, Robin Samper, Robin Santel, Hope E. Schuessler, Laurel Smith, Amanda Watters, Beth N. Winickoff

Additional Acknowledgments

The team credits the significant contributions to *Biology: Exploring Life* of Dan Breslin, Todd Christy, Patrick Finbarr Connolly, Bob Craton, Donald Gagnon, Jon R. Hansen, Daniel R. Hartjes, Ellen Levinger, Meredith Mascola, Brent McKenzie, Ken Pratt, Peter Reid, Crystal Streck, Kira Thaler Marbit, Jeff Weidenaar, Amy Winchester, Michelle York

Design Credits

Cover Design Judith Pinkham
Cover Production David Julian
Front Cover Photo David Maitland/Getty Images, Inc.
Back Cover Photo JC Carton/Bruce Coleman, Inc.
Interior Prototype Design Kokopelli Design Studio, Inc.

t=top, b=bottom, l=left, r=right, m=middle

Art Credits
Argosy **770, 771, 772, 773, 774, 775, 778, 785;** Articulate Graphics **25, 28, 35, 40, 44, 45, 92b, 93, 94, 95, 96, 96, 98, 99, 101, 104, 107, 115, 117, 119, 120, 121, 122, 132, 133bl, 287;** Carlyn Iverson **789, 790, 793t, 794;** Jen Paley **174b, 320, 321;** Jennifer Fairman **112, 113, 114, 116, 124, 125, 126, 127, 128, 129, 133tl, 384, 385, 388, 390, 395, 397, 402, 411, 415, 421, 461, 462, 796, 797, 798, 802;** Mark Foerster **188, 324, 328, 332, 338, 339, 351, 357, 363, 372, 375, 525, 528, 552, 553, 557t, 567, 576, 577, 587, 597, 599, 640, 641, 651, 658, 659, 660, 661, 669, 672, 702–3, 704, 705, 710, 717t, 727, 728, 733,** Karen Minot **293, 294, 304, 306, 311, 312, 316, 318, 337, 342, 516, 518–519, 544, 571, 578–579;** Kathryn Smith **623;** Laurie O'Keefe **298, 300, 301, 308;** Matt Mayerchak **55, 66, 67, 67, 251b, 256t, 258, 286, 321, 350, 351, 376, 377, 398, 399, 414, 460, 461, 472, 473, 488, 494, 539, 556, 557b, 636, 644, 645, 646t, 686, 689, 692, 695, 698, 792, 799, 801, 810, 811, 814, 815, 816, 817;** Nadine Sokol **72, 75, 76, 77, 78, 79, 80, 81, 82, 84, 85, 89, 92tr, 226, 228, 229, 230, 231, 233, 234, 236, 237, 238, 239, 240, 241, 242, 245;** Phillip Guzy **325, 330, 343, 345, 346, 347, 348, 374, 534, 543, 549, 560, 581, 588–89; 590, 601, 602–603, 619, 620, 637, 638, 654, 657, 667, 701, 707, 711, 713, 715, 720, 721, 731;** Quade and Emi Paul, Fivth Media **8, 12, 14, 15, 17, 20, 21, 268, 269, 270, 271, 275, 278, 279, 281, 282, 283, 284, 285, 287, 334, 358, 423, 425, 427, 431, 434, 439, 445, 449, 450, 452, 453, 454, 455, 457, 466, 467, 468, 477, 487, 489, 611, 612, 613, 614, 615, 616, 621, 622, 624, 625, 626, 627, 629, 632, 633, 676, 677, 680, 681, 683, 684, 685, 688, 690, 716, 717b, 819;** Steve McEntee **30, 31, 34, 48, 50, 54, 56, 59, 64, 65, 103, 137, 139, 140, 143, 144, 145, 146, 147, 148, 149, 150, 151, 152, 153, 154, 157, 161, 162, 163, 164, 165, 166, 167, 168, 169, 170, 173, 174t, 175, 183, 184, 186–187, 193, 195, 196–197, 198, 199, 200, 202, 207, 208, 209, 210, 211, 212, 213, 215, 216, 218, 219, 221, 222, 223, 248, 251t, 252, 253, 256b, 261, 262, 263b, 296, 299, 405, 406, 407, 415, 422, 424, 425, 428, 432, 435, 438, 442, 443, 465, 495, 497, 502l, 503, 506, 507, 508, 511, 520, 521, 646b, 750, 751, 754, 755, 756, 757, 760, 763, 788, 793, 800, 803, 807, 809, 813, 817;** Stephen McMath **180, 191, 358, 363, 364, 365, 373, 502, 542, 554, 586, 594, 595, 598, 655, 656, 663, 668, 722, 724, 725, 726, 730, 815b**

Photo Credits
Cover Photos; Front Cover, David Maitland/Getty Images, Inc.; **Back Cover,** JC Carton/Bruce Coleman, Inc.

Unit Opener Photos
Unit 1, pages xxiv–001, Joe McDonald/Corbis**; Unit 2, pages 68–69,** K.G. Murti/Visuals Unlimited; **Unit 3, pages 176–177,** Gary Vestal/Getty Images, Inc.; **Unit 4, pages 288–289,** Jonathan Blair/Corbis; **Unit 5, pages 352–353,** Peter Parks/IQ3d/V&W/Bruce Coleman, Inc.; **Unit 6, pages 416–147,** David Julian/Sweetlight Creative Partners; **Unit 7, pages 490–491,** G. Ochocki/Photo Researchers, Inc.; **Unit 8, 582–583,** Jake Martin/Getty Images, Inc.; **Unit 9, 740–741,** Paul A. Zahl/Getty Images, Inc.

Front Matter: ii, David Maitland/Getty Images, Inc.; **iv,** Stone/Bryan Mullennix; **v,** Macduff Everton/Corbis; **vi,** JC Carton/Bruce Coleman, Inc.; **viii–ix,** Marc Epstein/DRK Photo; **x t,** WorldSat International/Photo Researchers, Inc.; **x b,** Dr. Gopal Murti/Phototake ; **xi t,** ELSCINT/ SPL / Photo Researchers, Inc.; **xi m,** Dr. David Patterson/SPL/Photo Researchers, Inc.; **xi bl,** Alfred Pasieka/Science Photo Library/Photo Researchers, Inc.; **xi bml,** J. Olson/National Marine Mammal Lab; **xi bm,** Gerry Ellis/Minden Pictures; **xi bmr,** Will & Deni McIntyre/Getty Images, Inc.; **xi br,** Dennis Kunkel/Phototake; **xii t,** Lester Lefkowitz/Getty Images Inc.; **xii m,** Adrian T Sumner/Getty Images, Inc.; **xii b,** Dwight R. Kuhn; **xii inset,** Bettmann/Corbis; **xiii t,** Lee D. Simon/Science Source/Photo Researchers, Inc.; **xiii b,** Peter Essick/Aurora Photos; **xiv t,** Ken Lucas/Visuals Unlimited; **xiv b,** Dennis Kunkel/Phototake; **xv tl,** Runk/Schoenberger/Grant Heilman Photography; **xv tml,** Alan & Linda Detrick/Photo Researchers, Inc.; **xv tm,** Douglas Peebles/Corbis; **xv tmr,** R.G. Kessel/C.Y. Shih/Visuals Unlimited; **xv tr,** Courtesy of Fred Jensen; **xv m,** Oliver Meckes/Photo Researchers, Inc.; **xv b,** Dan Cheatham/DRK Photo; **xvi t,** Okapia-Frankfurt/Photo Researchers, Inc.; **xvi m,** Frans Lanting/Minden Pictures; **xvi bl,** Dave Fleetham/Getty Images, Inc.; **xvi bml,** Gerry Ellis/Minden Pictures; **xvi bm,** Fred Bavendam/Minden Pictures; **xvi bmr,** Barry Runk/Grant Heilman Photography; **xvi br,** Mitsuaki Iwago/Minden Pictures; **xvii t,** Planet Earth/Peter Gasson /Getty Images, Inc.; **xvii b,** PhotoDisc/Getty Images, Inc.; **xviii t,** Andrew Syred /Getty Images, Inc; **xviii bl,** NCI /Photo Researchers, Inc. **xviii bml,** Collection CNRI /Phototake; **xviii bm,** Oliver Meckes/Ottawa/Photo Researchers, Inc.; **xviii bmr,** Myrleen Ferguson Cate/PhotoEdit; **xviii br,** David Phillips/The Population Council/Photo Researchers, Inc.; **xix t,** UHB Trust /Getty Images, Inc.; **xix b,** CNRI/Science Photo Library/Photo Researchers, Inc.; **xx t,** Fred Bavendam/Minden Pictures; **xx m,** Matt Meadows/Peter Arnold, Inc.; **xx b,** John D. Cunningham/Visuals Unlimited; **xxi,** Stuart Westmorland/Corbis; **xxii t,** David Maitland/Getty Images, Inc.; **xxii b,** Kevin Collins/Visuals Unlimited; **xxiii,** Richard Haynes

Chapter 1: 2-3, Norbert Wu/DRK Photo; **4 l,** WorldSat International/Photo Researchers, Inc.; **4 r,** Spot Image/CNES/Photo Researchers, Inc.; **5 l,** Joseph Pobereskin/Getty Images, Inc.; **5 r,** Lightwave Photography Inc./Animals Animals/Earth Scenes; **6 t,** BioDisc/Visuals Unlimited; **6 b,** Alfred Pasieka/Science Photo Library/Photo Researchers, Inc.; **7 t,** Tom McHugh/Photo Researchers, Inc.; **7 inset,** CC Lockwood/DRK Photo; **7 b,** Color-Pic/Animals Animals/Earth Scenes; **8 t,** Michael Fogden/DRK Photo; **8 m,** John Shaw/NHPA; **8 b,** Luiz C. Marigo/Peter Arnold, Inc.; **9 tl,** Ralph Robinson/Visuals Unlimited; **9 tr,** Dennis Kunkel/Phototake; **9 ml,** Eric Soder/NHPA; **9 mr,** Carolina Biological Supply Company/Phototake; **9 bl,** Andrea Pistolesi/Getty Images, Inc.; **9 br,** Guido Alberto Rossi/Getty Images, Inc.; **10,** Richard Haynes; **11 l,** David Young-Wolff/PhotoEdit; **11 r,** Mehau Kulyk/Science Photo Library/Photo Researchers, Inc.; **12,** Bill Beatty/Ag Pix.com; **13 tl,** Janice Sheldon; **13 tm,** M.P. Kahl/DRK Photo; **13 tr,** Don Fawcett/Science Source/Photo Researchers, Inc.; **13 b,** Steve Kaufman/DRK Photo; **14,** C Squared Studios/Getty Images, Inc.; **15,** Wild & Natural/Animals Animals/Earth Scenes; **16 t,** Richard Hamilton Smith/Corbis; **16 b,** Jim Zipp/Photo Researchers, Inc.; **17 t,** Michael Fogden/DRK Photo; **17 m,** G I Bernard/NHPA; **17 b,** Art Wolfe/Photo Researchers, Inc.; **18 l,** USDA/Science Source/Photo Researchers, Inc.; **18 m,** Bill Banaszewski/Visuals Unlimited; **18 r,** Barry Slaven/Visuals Unlimited; **19,** Lynda Richardson/Peter Arnold, Inc.; **21,** Gerry Ellis/Minden Pictures

Chapter 2: 22 both, Mark Moffett/Minden Pictures; **24,** M.T. Frazier/Photo Researchers, Inc.; **25 t,** Tony Freeman/PhotoEdit; **25 m,** Tim Ridley/Dorling Kindersley; **25 b,** Karl Ammann/Corbis; **26 t,** Rob & Ann Simpson/Visuals Unlimited; **26 b,** Christine Case/Visuals Unlimited; **27,** Duncan Smith/Corbis; **28 tl,** Ed Reschke/Peter Arnold, Inc.; **28 tr,** J. C. Revy/ISM/Phototake; **28 ml,** J. C. Revy/ISM/Phototake; **28 m,** BioDisc/Visuals Unlimited; **28 mr,** J. C. Revy/ISM/Phototake; **28 b,** Eric Grave/Photo Researchers, Inc.; **29,** Dannielle Hayes/Omni Photo Communications Inc.; **32 l,** Hans Pfetschinger/Peter Arnold, Inc.; **32 r,** John Alcock/Visuals Unlimited; **33 l,** Breck P. Kent; **33 r,** E.R. Degginger/Photo Researchers, Inc.; **34 both,** David Pfennig; **36,** Richard Haynes; **37,** Carolyn A. Mckeone/Photo Researchers, Inc.; **38,** Steve Austin/Corbis; **39,** EyeWire, Inc./Getty Images, Inc.; **41,** George Riley/Courtesy of Biogen Corp.; **45,** Matthias Breiter/Minden Pictures

Chapter 3: 46, Francois Gohier/Photo Researchers, Inc.; **48 t,** J. Olson/National Marine Mammal Lab; **48 b,** Cheryl A. Ertelt/Visuals Unlimited; **49,** Michael K. Nichols/National Geographic Image Collection **51,** Fred Bruemmer/Peter Arnold, Inc.; **52,** Richard Haynes; **53,** Jeff Foott/Bruce Coleman, Inc.; **55 t,** Gerry Ellis/Minden Pictures; **55 b,** Richard Alan Wood/Animals Animals/Earth Scenes; **57,** Hal H. Harrison/Grant Heilman Photography; **58 l,** Thomas D. McAvoy/TimePix; **58 r,** Mitsuaki Iwago/Minden Pictures; **59,** Harry Engels/Animals Animals/Earth Scenes; **60 all,** John G. Shedd Aquarium/Edward G. Linus Jr.; **61,** Michio Hoshino/Minden Pictures; **62,** Charles Melton/Visuals Unlimited; **63 t,** Mitsuaki Iwago/Minden Pictures; **63 b,** Frans Lanting/Minden Pictures; **64 t,** S.J. Krasemann/Peter Arnold, Inc.; **64 b,** J.P.Varin/Jacana/Photo Researchers, Inc.; **65,** Kenneth Lorenzen, UC Davis

Chapter 4: 70, David Young-Wolff/Getty Images, Inc.; **73 l,** Richard Menga/Fundamental Photographs; **73 m,** Stephen Frisch/Stock Boston; **73 r, 73 inset,** Barry Runk/Grant Heilman Photography; **74 l,** Runk/Schoenberger/Grant Heilman Photography; **74 r,** Barry Runk/Grant Heilman Photography; **75,** Joseph Sohm; ChromoSohm Inc./Corbis; **76,** ELSCINT/SPL/Photo Researchers, Inc.; **82,** Antony Edwards/Getty Images, Inc.; **83,** Bill Sumner/Corbis Stock Market; **84 t,** Dave Spier/Visuals Unlimited; **84 b,** Martyn F. Chillmaid/Science Photo Library/Photo Researchers, Inc.; **86,** PhotoDisc/Getty Images, Inc.; **87** Richard Haynes

Chapter 5: 90, Will & Deni McIntyre/Getty Images, Inc.; **93,** Jan Tove Johansson/Getty Images Inc.; **96,** Bob Daemmrich/Stock Boston; **98,** Terry Brandt/Grant Heilman Photography; **99,** Len Rue Jr./Photo Researchers, Inc.; **100 t,** Foto Sorrel/Peter Arnold, Inc.; **100 m,** Ron Kimball/Ron Kimball Stock; **100 b,** Gary W. Carter/Corbis; **102,** Ken Eward/Science Source/Photo Researchers, Inc.; **105,** Richard Haynes

Chapter 6: 108, David Becker/Getty Images, Inc.; **110 l,** Science Museum/Science & Society Picture Library; **110 r,** Leonard Lessin/Peter Arnold, Inc.; **111 l,** Kevin Collins/Visuals Unlimited; **111 tr,** Mike Abbey/Visuals Unlimited; **111 mr,** Dennis Kunkel/Phototake; **111 br,** Nina Lampen/Phototake; **114 l,** Dr. Gopal Murti/Phototake; **114 r,** Kwangshin Kim/Photo Researchers, Inc.; **118 both,** Robin Samper; **120 l,** Stan Fiegler/Visuals Unlimited; **120 m, 120 r,** David M. Phillips/Visuals Unlimited; **121 both,** Runk/Schoenberger/Grant Heilman Photography; **122,** Michael Abbey/SS/Photo Researchers, Inc.; **123,** Richard Haynes; **124,** W.B. Saunders Company; **125,** Dennis Kunkel/Phototake; **126 t,** Professors P. Motta & T. Naguro/Science Photo Library/Photo Researchers, Inc.; **126 m,** Dr. David Patterson/SPL/Photo Researchers, Inc.; **126 b,** BioPhoto Associates/Photo Researchers, Inc.; **128,** Dr. Jeremy Burgess/Photo Researchers, Inc.; **129,** Professors P. Motta & T. Naguro/Science Photo Library/Photo Researchers, Inc.; **130 t,** Dr. Gopal Murti/Science Photo Library/Photo Researchers, Inc.; **130 b,** Dr. John Heuser; **131 t,** Professor P. Motta/Science Photo Library/Photo Researchers, Inc.; **131 b,** Lennart Nilsson/Boehringer Ingelheim International

Chapter 7: 134, Joe McDonald/DRK Photo; **136 l,** Lewis Trusty/Animals Animals/Earth Scenes; **136 m,** Larry Lefever/Grant Heilman Photography; **136 r,** M.I.

Walker/Photo Researchers, Inc.; **137,** Lynn Stone/Animals Animals/Earth Scenes; **138,** Kelly-Monney Photography/Corbis; **142,** Richard Haynes; **145,** Carl Schneider/Getty Images, Inc.; **147,** Robert W. Ginn/PhotoEdit; **151,** R.J. Erwin/Photo Researchers, Inc.; **154 t,** Bob Daemmrich/The Image Works; **154 b,** EyeWire Collection/Getty Images, Inc.; **155,** Premium Stock/Corbis

Chapter 8: 158-159, Andy Sacks/Getty Images Inc.; **160 t,** Stephen Downer/Animals Animals/Earth Scenes; **160 b,** Lester Lefkowitz/Getty Images Inc.; **161 l,** Dr. Kenneth R. Miller/Photo Researchers, Inc.; **161 r,** Newcomb & Wergin/BPS/Getty Images Inc.; **165,** Lester Lefkowitz/Corbis Stock Market; **168,** Michael Fogden/Animals Animals/Earth Scenes; **171,** Richard Haynes; **172,** A. & M. Shah/Animals Animals/Earth Scenes

Chapter 9: 178, Dr. Conly L. Rieder, Division of Molecular Medicine, Wadsworth Center, N.Y. State Dept. of Health, Albany, New York **180,** Richard Haynes; **181 tl,** Carolina Biological Supply Company/Phototake; **181 tr,** Jerome Wexler/Visuals Unlimited; **181 b,** Ron Austing/Photo Researchers, Inc.; **182 t,** Ed Reschke; **182 b,** Adrian T. Sumner/Getty Images, Inc.; **185,** Peter Essick/Aurora Photos; **186 both,** Ed Reschke; **187 all,** Ed Reschke; **188 l,** R. Calentine/Visuals Unlimited; **188 r,** Russ Lappa; **189,** Richard Haynes; **190,** Simon Fraser/Science Photo Library/Photo Researchers, Inc.; **192,** American Images, Inc./Taxi/Getty Images, Inc.; **193 t,** L. Willatt, East Anglian Regional Genetics Services/Science Photo Library/Photo Researchers, Inc.; **193 b,** BioPhoto Associates/Photo Researchers, Inc.; **194 t,** John D. Cunningham/Custom Medical Stock Photo; **194 ml,** CNRI/SPL/Photo Researchers, Inc.; **194 mr,** D.W. Fawcett/Photo Researchers, Inc.; **194 bl,** Pascal Goetgheluck/Science Photo Library/Photo Researchers, Inc.; **194 br,** CC Studio/Science Photo Library/Photo Researchers, Inc.; **203,** Runk/Schoenberger/Grant Heilman Photography, Inc.

Chapter 10: 204, Macduff Everton/Corbis; **206,** Bettmann/Corbis; **207,** Dwight R. Kuhn; **212,** A. D. Darleishire, "Breeding and the Mendelian Discovery," 1911/Mary Evans Picture Library; **214,** Russ Lappa; **216,** David Young-Wolff/PhotoEdit; **217,** PhotoDisc/Getty Images, Inc.; **220 both,** George Bernard/Animals Animals/Earth Scenes

Chapter 11: 224, Will & Deni McIntyre/Photo Researchers, Inc.; **227 t,** Science Photo Library/Photo Researchers, Inc.; **227 b,** Lee D. Simon/Science Source/Photo Researchers, Inc.; **231,** Science Source/Photo Researchers, Inc.; **232,** Richard Haynes; **234,** Dr. Gopal Murti/SPL/Photo Researchers, Inc.; **235 t,** Gary R. Robinson/Visuals Unlimited; **235 b,** John Burwell/Getty Images, Inc.; **243 t,** Jo Prater/Visuals Unlimited; **243 b,** John Serrao/Photo Researchers, Inc.

Chapter 12: 246, Andy Sacks/Getty Images Inc.; **248 l,** Pamela McTurk/Science Photo Library/Photo Researchers, Inc.; **248 r,** BioPhoto Associates/Science Source/Photo Researchers, Inc.; **249,** H. Raguet/Eurelios/Phototake; **250 l,** Richard Hutchings/PhotoEdit; **250 r,** L. Willatt, East Anglian Regional Genetics Service/Science Photo Library/Photo Researchers, Inc.; **253 t,** Bettmann/Corbis; **253 b,** Virginia Walbot/Stanford University; **254,** Richard Haynes; **255 l,** Alain Dex/Publiphoto/Photo Researchers, Inc.; **255 r,** Martin Dohrn/Science Photo Library/Photo Researchers, Inc.; **257 t,** Suzanne Alford/AP/Wide World Photo; **257 b,** Steve Uzzell; **258 l,** Corel Corp.; **258 r,** Digital imaging by Michael Douma/webexhibits.org/Corel Corp.; **259,** Will & Deni McIntyre/Photo Researchers, Inc.; **260,** Nancy Kedersha/Photo Researchers, Inc.

Chapter 13: 264, Jean Claude Revy/ISM/Phototake; **266,** Dennis Kunkel/ Phototake; **267,** Hank Morgan/Photo Researchers, Inc.; **268,** Science Photo Library/Photo Researchers, Inc.; **272,** George Riley; **273,** Richard Haynes; **274,** P. Dumas/Phototake; **274 inset,** P. Dumas/Phototake; **275,** Aqua Bounty Farms/AP/Wide World Photos; **276 l,** PPL Therapeutics /AP/Wide World Photos; **276 r,** Derek Bromhall/Oxford Scientific Films Ltd.; **277,** Gary Wagner/Stock Boston; **279,** Bob Anderson/Masterfile Corporation; **280,** AP/Wide World Photos; **281,** Manfred Kage/Peter Arnold, Inc.; **283 t, inset,** Hans Pfletschinger/Peter Arnold, Inc.; **283 b,** Volker Steger/Science Photo Library/Photo Researchers, Inc.; **284,** Professor Walter Gehring/Science Photo Library/Photo Researchers, Inc.;

Chapter 14: 290, Biophoto Associates/Photo Researchers, Inc.; **292,** Mitsuaki Iwago/Minden Pictures; **293 t,** Michael S. Yamashita/Corbis; **293 bl,** ARCHIV/Photo Researchers, Inc.; **293 br,** The Granger Collection; **294,** Tue De Roy/Minden Pictures; **295 t,** Tim Fitzharris/Minden Pictures; **295 bl,** Walter Bibkow/Getty Images Inc.; **295 br,** Rod Feldman; **297 t,** Jack Novak/Corbis; **297 b,** Joe McDonald/Corbis; **300 t,** Victor R. Boswell Jr./National Geographic Image Collection; **300 m,** Gerry Ellis/Minden Pictures; **300 b,** Tom Van Sant/Photo Researchers, Inc.; **302 t,** Darrell Gulin/Corbis; **302 b,** Custom Medical Stock Photography; **303 l,** Dwight Kuhn; **303 r,** Lennart Nilsson/Albert Bonniers Forlag AB; **305 t,** Tui De Roy/Minden Pictures; **305 m,** Frans Lanting/Minden Pictures; **305 b,** Tui De Roy/Minden Pictures; **306 l,** Richard Parker/Photo Researchers, Inc.; **306 r,** Patti Murray/Animals Animals/Earth Scenes; **307,** Ron Kimball/Ron Kimball Studios; **309,** Richard Haynes; **310,** Earth Imaging/Getty Images, Inc.; **311,** Eastcott Momatiuk /Getty Images, Inc.; **313,** Ron Kimball/Ron Kimball Studios; **314,** Yann Arthus-Bertrand/Corbis; **315 t,** Glenn M. Oliver/Visuals Unlimited; **315 m, 315 b,** B.R. Grant/Princeton University Department of Ecology; **317,** Eye of Science/Photo Researchers, Inc.; **318** Russ Lappa; **319 l,** Simon Fraser/Photo Researchers, Inc.; **319 r,** S. Lowry/University of Ulster/Getty Images, Inc.

Chapter 15: 322-323, Frans Lanting/Minden Pictures; **324 l, 324 r,** Konrad Wothe/Minden Pictures; **325 l,** California Academy of Sciences, Special Collections; **325 r,** W.J. Weber/Visuals Unlimited; **326 l,** Kit Houghton Photo/Corbis; **326 m,** Grant Heilman/Grant Heilman Photography; **326 r,** Bjorn Bolstad/Photo Researchers, Inc.; **327 l,** John Shaw/Bruce Coleman, Inc.; **327 m,** Richard Sisk/Panoramic Images, Chicago; **327 r,** Michael Fogden/Bruce Coleman, Inc.; **329,** Frans Lanting/Minden Pictures; **331,** Joe McDonald/Visuals Unlimited; **332 t,** A. Kerstitch/Visuals Unlimited; **332 b,** Pascal AEF.Goetgheluck/Getty Images, Inc.; **333 tl,** Gerad Lacz/Peter Arnold, Inc.; **333 tr,** Sea World of California/Corbis; **333 b,** David Scharf/Peter Arnold, Inc.; **334 l,** Steinhart Aquarium/Photo Researchers, Inc.; **334 r,** Gary Meszoros/Visuals Unlimited; **335 l,** Ken Lucas/Visuals Unlimited; **335 r,** Maurice Nimmo/Frank Lane Picture Agency/Corbis; **336,** Jeff J. Daly/Visuals Unlimited; **340,** Benjamin Cummings; **341,** Gilbert S. Grant/Photo Researchers, Inc.; **343 l, both,** Tom McHugh/Photo Researchers, Inc.; **344 l,** Francois Gohier/Photo Researchers, Inc.; **344 m,** Staffan Widstrand/Corbis; **344 r,** John Klausmeyer/Science Magazine; **349,** Richard Haynes

Chapter 16: 354-355, Jack Dykinga/Getty Images, Inc.; **356 t,** S.M. Awramik/University of California/Biological Photo Service; **356 m,** Kevin & Betty Collins/Visuals Unlimited; **356 b,** François Gohier/Photo Researchers, Inc.; **359,** B. Murton/Southampton Oceanography Centre/SPL/Photo Researchers, Inc.; **360,** Meckes/Ottawa/Photo Researchers, Inc.; **361,** Martin G. Miller/Visuals Unlimited; **362 t,** Dennis Kunkel/Phototake; **362 m,** David Scharf/Peter Arnold, Inc.; **362 b,** Tina Carvalho/Visuals Unlimited; **363 l,** Peres/Custom Medical Stock Photo; **363 r,** Peres/Custom Medical Stock Photo; **365,** H.S. Pankratz & TC Beaman/Biological Photo Service; **366,** T.E. Adams/Visuals Unlimited; **367 l,** Wally Eberhart/Visuals Unlimited; **367 r,** E.R. Degginger/Animals Animals/Earth Scenes; **368 l,** Michael Abbey/Photo Researchers, Inc.; **368 r,** Still Pictures/Peter Arnold, Inc.; **369 t,** Gary Gaugler/Visuals Unlimited; **369 b,** Tony Freeman/PhotoEdit; **370,** Raymond B Otero/Visuals Unlimited; **371,** Richard Haynes; **372,** Biozentrum, University of Basel/SPL/Photo Researchers, Inc.; **373,** CNRI/SPL/Photo Researchers, Inc.; **374,** Chris Bjornberg/Photo Researchers, Inc.; **375,** Bettmann/Corbis; **377,** Jack M Bostrack/Visuals Unlimited

Chapter 17: 378, A. Smith/Photo Researchers, Inc.; **380,** Science Vu/Visuals Unlimited; **381 t,** Roland Birke/Peter Arnold, Inc.; **381 b,** Alfred Pasieka/Peter Arnold, Inc.; **382 l,** Jerome Paulin/Visuals Unlimited; **382 r,** Oliver Meckes/Photo Researchers, Inc.; **383 series of four,** Mike Abbey/Visuals Unlimited; **383 b,** Manfred Kage/Peter Arnold, Inc.; **384 tl,** Dr. David J. Patterson/Science Photo Library/Photo Researchers, Inc.; **384 tr,** Bruce Coleman, Inc.; **384 b,** M. Abbey/Visuals Unlimited; **385,** Moredun Scientific Ltd/Photo Researchers, Inc.; **386,** Richard Haynes; **387 l,** Robert Calentine/Visuals Unlimited; **387 r,** Ray Simons/Photo Researchers, Inc.; **388,** Carolina Biological/Visuals Unlimited; **389 t,** James W. Richardson/Visuals Unlimited; **389 bl,** Astrid & Hanns-Frieder Michler/Science Photo Library/Photo Researchers, Inc.; **389 br,** R. Calentine/Visuals Unlimited; **390,** BioPhoto Associates/Photo Researchers, Inc.; **391,** Sanford Berry/Visuals Unlimited; **391 inset,** David M. Phillips/Visuals Unlimited; **392 t,** Kent Wood/Photo Researchers, Inc.; **392 b,** Chuck Davis/Getty Images, Inc.; **393,** David Wrobel/Visuals Unlimited; **394 t,** David L. Kirk; **394 m,** Manfred Kage/Peter Arnold, Inc.; **394 b,** Andrew J. Martinez/Photo Researchers, Inc.; **396,** Carolina Biological Supply Company/Phototake; **399,** Mike Abbey/Visuals Unlimited

Chapter 18: 400, Biotic/Photonica; **403 tl,** Richard Walters/Visuals Unlimited; **403 tr,** Dick Poe/Visuals Unlimited; **403 bl,** Cabisco/Visuals Unlimited; **403 br,** Michael P. Gadomski/Photo Researchers, Inc.; **404 l,** OSF/R. Packwood/Animals Animals/Earth Scenes; **404 r,** Biophoto Associates/Photo Researchers, Inc.; **405 l,** BioPhoto Associates/Photo Researchers, Inc.; **405 r,** M.F. Brown/Visuals Unlimited; **406 t,** David M. Dennis/Animals Animals/Earth Scenes; **406 bl,** Michael Fogden/Oxford Scientific Films/Animals Animals/Earth Scenes; **406 br,** James W. Richardson/Visuals Unlimited; **407 tl,** Corbis Digital Stock; **407 tr,** M.F. Brown/Visuals Unlimited; **407 b,** Rob Simpson/Visuals Unlimited; **408 t,** David M. Phillips/Visuals Unlimited; **408 b,** David Cavagnaro/Visuals Unlimited; **409,** Russ Lappa; **410 t,** Philippe Colombi/PhotoDisc/Getty Images, Inc.; **410 b,** Ned Therrien/Visuals Unlimited; **411 t,** V. Ahmadjian/Visuals Unlimited; **411 bl,** Stanley L. Flegler/Visuals Unlimited; **411 br,** Rod Planck/Photo Researchers, Inc.; **412 t,** Rene Dulhoste/Photo Researchers, Inc.; **412 bl,** Owen Franken/Corbis; **412 br,** Rob & Ann Simpson/Visuals Unlimited; **413 t,** Sian Irvine/StockFood; **413 b,** Michael P. Gadomski/Photo Researchers, Inc.

Chapter 19: 418, Adam Jones/Photo Researchers, Inc.; **420,** Runk/Schoenberger/Grant Heilman Photography; **421,** Ed Reschke/Peter Arnold, Inc.; **422 t,** Graham Kent; **422 bl,** Oliver Meckes/Photo Researchers, Inc.; **422 br,** Dennis Kunkel/Phototake; **425,** Dwight Kuhn; **426 l,** Robert & Linda Mitchell Photography; **426 m, 426 r,** Runk/Schoenberger/Grant Heilman Photography; **427,** Ludeck Pesek/Science Photo Library/Photo Researchers, Inc.; **428,** David M. Dennis/Animals Animals/Earth Scenes; **429 t,** Jim Steinberg/Photo Researchers, Inc.; **429 m, 429 b,** Runk/Schoenberger/Grant Heilman Photography; **430,** Richard Haynes; **431 l,** Glenn Oliver/Visuals Unlimited; **431 tr, 431 br,** Runk/Schoenberger/Grant Heilman Photography; **433 l,** Runk/Schoenberger/Grant Heilman Photography; **433 tm, 433 bm,** Grant Heilman/Grant Heilman Photography; **433 r,** Adam Jones/Photo Researchers, Inc.; **434 l,** Alan & Linda Detrick/Photo Researchers, Inc.; **434 r,** David Dennis/Animals Animals/Earth Scenes; **435 t,** Corel Corp.; **435 bl,** C Squared Studios/Getty Images, Inc; **435 br,** Eisenhut & Mayer/Getty Images, Inc.; **436 l,** Stephen McCabe; **436 r,** Runk/Schenberger/Grant Heilman Photography; **437 l,** Bob & Ann Simpson/Visuals Unlimited; **437 m,** Michael P. Gadomski/Photo Researchers, Inc.; **437 r,** M.H. Sharp/Photo Researchers, Inc.; **439,** R.J. Erwin/Photo Researchers, Inc.

Chapter 20: 440, Marc Epstein/DRK Photo; **444 t,** Dwight Kuhn; **444 bl,** D. Cavagnaro/Visuals Unlimited; **444 bm,** Gregory K. Scott/Photo Researchers, Inc; **444 br,** Stephen Dalton/NHPA; **446 t,** Norbert Wu/Peter Arnold, Inc.; **446 b,** Geoff Kidd/Oxford Scientific Films; **447,** Richard Haynes; **448 both,** Dwight Kuhn; **449 t,** George Bernard/Animals Animals/Earth Scenes; **449 b,** Douglas Peebles/Corbis; **450 both,** Ed Reschke/Peter Arnold, Inc.; **451 all,** BioPhoto Associates/Science Source/Photo Researchers, Inc.; **453 l,** Ed Reschke; **453 r,** Russ Lappa; **455,** Runk/Schoenberger/Grant Heilman Photography; **457,** Runk/Schoenberger/Grant Heilman Photography

Chapter 21: 458, Jim Zuckerman/Corbis; **460,** Sylvester Allred/Visuals Unlimited; **461,** Nigel Cattlin/Holt Studios International/Photo Researchers, Inc.; **463,** Sylvan Wittwer/Visuals Unlimited; **464,** R.J. Erwin/DRK Photo; **466,** R.G. Kessel/C.Y. Shih/Visuals Unlimited; **467,** Okapia-Frankfurt/Photo Researchers, Inc.; **469,** Richard Haynes; **470,** Runk/Schoenberger/ Grant Heilman Photography; **471 t,** Enlightened Images/Animals Animals/Earth Scenes; **471 b,** D. Cavagnaro/Visuals Unlimited; **473,** Anthony Saint James/Getty Images, Inc.

Chapter 22: 474, Carr Clifton/Minden Pictures; **476,** Runk/Schoenberger/Grant Heilman Photography; **478 tl, 478 tr,** Walter Chandoha Photography; **478 b,** Courtesy of Fred Jensen; **479,** Michael Melford/Getty Images, Inc.; **480,** Richard Haynes; **481 both,** David Sieren/Visuals Unlimited; **482 t,** Doug Wechsler/ Animals Animals/Earth Scenes; **482 b,** Runk/ Schoenberger/Grant Heilman Photography; **483,** John Warden/Index Stock Imagery, Inc.; **484 t,** Theo Allofs/Corbis; **484 b,** M.C. Drew and M. B. Jackson; **485,** Robert Clay/Visuals Unlimited; **485 inset,** John D. Cunningham/Visuals Unlimited; **486 both,** Jerome Wexler/Visuals Unlimited

Chapter 23: 492, Stuart Westmorland/Corbis; **494,** George Grall/Getty Images, Inc.; **495,** Dave Schiefelbein/Getty Images, Inc.; **496 t,** Dave Fleetham/Getty Images, Inc.; **496 b,** J.H. Pete Carmichael/Getty Images, Inc.; **497,** Charles R. Wyttenbach/Biological Photo Service; **498 l,** Carl Roessler/Animals Animals/Earth Scenes; **498 r,** Marty Snyderman/Corbis Digital Stock/Corbis; **499,** C. Milkins/OSF/Animals Animals/Earth Scenes; **501 l,** Fred Bavendam/Minden Pictures; **501 m,** Herb Segars/Animals Animals/Earth Scenes; **501 r,** David Hall/Photo Researchers, Inc.; **503 t,** Oliver Meckes/Eye of Science/Photo Researchers, Inc.; **503 b,** Andrew Syred/Science Photo Library/Photo Researchers, Inc.; **504,** Juergen Berger, Max-Planck Institute/SPL/Photo Researchers, Inc.; **505 t,** Andrew Syred/Science Photo Library/Photo Researchers, Inc.; **505 b,** W. I. Walker/Photo Researchers, Inc.; **507 t,** OSF/Michael Birkhead/Animals Animals/Earth Scenes; **507 m,** David M. Dennis/Animals Animals/Earth Scenes; **507 b,** Breck Kent/Animals Animals/Earth Scenes; **508,** F. Stuart Westmorland/Photo Researchers, Inc.; **509 l,** David Wrobel/Visuals Unlimited; **509 m,** Ken Lucas/Visuals Unlimited; **509 r,** W. Gregory Brown/Animals Animals/Earth Scenes; **510,** Richard Haynes; **511,** John D. Cunningham/Visuals Unlimited; **512 tl,** Richard Hermann/Visuals Unlimited; **512 tr,** Marc C. Chamberlain; **512 ml,** Lawrence Migdale/Photo Researchers, Inc.; **512 mr,** Marty Snyderman/Visuals Unlimited; **512 b,** Gerald & Buff Corsi/Visuals Unlimited; **515,** Benjamin Cummings; **521,** Anthony Bannister; Gallo Images/Corbis

Chapter 24: 522, Frans Lanting/Minden Pictures; **524,** Geoff du Feu/Getty Images, Inc.; **525,** Patricia Fogden/Corbis; **526 t,** Francois Gohier/Photo Researchers, Inc; **526 bl,** Jeff Lepore/Photo Researchers, Inc.; **526 br,** Rod Planck/Photo Researchers, Inc.; **527 l,** Jakub Jasinski/Visuals Unlimited; **527 m,** Gerry Ellis/Minden Pictures; **527 r,** Planet Earth/Peter Gasson/Getty Images, Inc.; **529 t,** Bill Beatty/Visuals Unlimited; **529 m,** Tim Flach/Getty Images, Inc.; **529 b,** D. Cavagnaro/Visuals Unlimited; **530,** Mark Smith/Photo Researchers, Inc.; **531 l,** Carolina Biological Supply Co./Phototake; **531 m,** Tom Branch/Photo Researchers, Inc.; **531 r,** James Robinson/Animals Animals/Earth Scenes; **532,** Stephen Dalton/Photo Researchers, Inc.; **533 t,** Steve Hoffmann; **533 br,** D. Cavagnaro/Visuals Unlimited; **533 the rest,** Frans Lanting/Minden Pictures; **535 t,** Kenneth H. Thomas/Photo Researchers, Inc.; **535 b,** Nigel Cattlin/Holt Studios Int'l/Photo Researchers, Inc.; **536,** Courtesy of The Tanglefoot Company; **537,** Richard Haynes; **539,** James Robinson/Animals Animals/Earth Scenes

Chapter 25: 540, Dave Roberts/Science Photo Library/Photo Researchers, Inc.; **542 inset,** Zig Leszczynski/Animals Animals/Earth Scenes; **542,** Runk/Schoenenberger/Grant Heilman Photography; **543,** Corbis Digital Stock; **545 t,** Breck P. Kent; **545 b,** W. Gregory Brown/Animals Animals/Earth Scenes; **546,** Mike Parry/Minden Pictures; **547 t,** Fred Bavendam/ Minden Pictures; **547 b,** Flip Nicklin/Minden Pictures; **548,** Norbert Wu/Peter Arnold, Inc.; **548 inset,** Breck Kent/Animals Animals/Earth Scenes; **549 t,** Gerard Lacz/Animals Animals/Earth Scenes; **549 b,** Peter Pinnock/Getty Images, Inc.; **550 l,** Dr. Hans Fricke; **550 r,** J.D. Cunningham/Visuals Unlimited; **551,** Richard Haynes; **553 l,** Breck Kent/Animals Animals/Earth Scenes; **553 m,** Runk/Schoenenberger/Grant Heilman Photography; **553 r,** L.L. Rue III/Animals Animals/Earth Scenes; **554 t,** Breck P. Kent/Animals Animals/Earth Scenes; **554 b,** Barry Runk/Grant Heilman Photography; **555,** Michael Fogden/Animals Animals/Earth Scenes

Chapter 26: 558, Mitsuaki Iwago/Minden Pictures; **561 t,** Joe McDonald/Visuals Unlimited; **561 b,** Zig Leszczynski/Animals Animals/Earth Scenes; **562,** Benjamin Cummings; **563 t,** Dave Fleetham/Tom Stack & Associates, Inc.; **563 m,** Patti Murray/Animals Animals/Earth Scenes; **563 b,** Fred Bavendam/Minden Pictures; **564 t,** Jim Meril/Visuals Unlimited; **564 bl, 564 br,** Author C. Smith III/Grant Heilman Photography; **565,** Richard Haynes; **566,** John Gerlach/Visuals Unlimited; **567,** James L. Amos/Photo Researchers, Inc.; **568 l, 568 m,** Frans Lanting/Minden Pictures; **568 r,** John Cancalosi/Peter Arnold, Inc.; **569 t,** Patti Murray/Animals Animals/Earth Scenes; **569 b,** Mitsuaki Iwago/Minden Pictures; **570,** Mark A. Klingler /Carnegie Museum of Natural History; **571,** Shin Yoshino/Minden Pictures; **572 t,** Erik Svenson/Getty Images, Inc.; **572 bl,** Flip Nicklin/Minden Pictures; **572 br,** Fred Bavendam/Peter Arnold, Inc.; **573 tl,** Michael & Patricia Fogden/Minden Pictures; **573 tr,** Frans Lanting/Minden Pictures; **573 m,** Michael Dick/Animals Animals/Earth Scenes; **573 b,** Merlin D. Tuttle/Bat Conservation International/Photo Researchers, Inc.; **574,** Martin Harvey/DRK Photo; **575 tl,** Frans Lanting/Minden Pictures; **575 tm,** Manoj Shah/Animals Animals/Earth Scenes; **575 tr,** Frans Lanting/Minden Pictures; **575 b,** Martin Harvey/Peter Arnold, Inc.; **576,** The Natural History Museum, London

Chapter 27: 584, Don Mason/Corbis Stock Market; **586,** Richard Haynes; **587,** PhotoDisc/Getty Images, Inc.; **590,** Meckes/Ottawa/Photo Researchers, Inc.; **591 tl, 591 tm,** Biophoto Associates/Photo Researchers, Inc.; **591 tr,** Dr. Gopal Murti/Science Photo Library/Photo Researchers, Inc.; **591 b,** Ed Reschke/Peter Arnold, Inc.; **592 l,** Michael Abbey/Science Source/Photo Researchers, Inc.; **592 m,** Manfred Kage/Peter Arnold, Inc.; **592 r,** Biology Media/Photo Researchers, Inc.; **593,** Tim McGuire Images, Inc./Getty Images, Inc.; **594,** Biophoto Associates/Photo Researchers, Inc.; **596,** Quest/Science Photo Library/Photo Researchers, Inc.; **597,** John Garrett/Dorling Kindersley; **599,** Doug Pensinger/Allsport; **600 both,** Professor P. Motta/Dept. of Anatomy, University "La Sapienza" Rome/Science Photo Library/Photo Researchers, Inc.; **601,** David Young-Wolff/PhotoEdit; **604,** Tony Freeman/PhotoEdit; **605,** Richard Haynes; **607,** Manfred Kage/Peter Arnold, Inc.

Chapter 28: 608, Dandy Zipper/Getty Images, Inc.; **610,** Rod Kaye Photography; **616,** Omikron/Science Source/Photo Researchers, Inc.; **617,** Jose Carillo/PhotoEdit; **622,** Todd Powell/Index Stock Imagery, Inc.; **625,** Ralph C. Eagle Jr. MD/Photo Researchers, Inc.; **628,** Richard Haynes; **630 t,** Russ Lappa; **630 b,** Tom Croke/Getty Images, Inc.; **631,** Joyce Photo graphics/Photo Researchers, Inc.; **631 inset,** Scott Camazine/Photo Researchers, Inc.

Chapter 29; 634, John E. Kelly/Getty Images, Inc.; **636,** Hunter-StockFood Munich/StockFood; **640,** Fred Hossler/Visuals Unlimited; **642,** Kelly Wise/Vital Imaging; **643,** Richard Haynes; **645 l,** Burke/Triolo/ Brand X Pictures/PictureQuest; **645 r,** Burke/Triolo/ Brand X Pictures/PictureQuest; **648,** Lasse Norgaard-Red Cross/AP/Wide World Photo; **649,** David Young-Wolff /PhotoEdit

Chapter 30: 652, Quest/Science Photo Library/Photo Researchers, Inc.; **655,** Lennart Nilsson/Albert Bonniers Forlag AB; **662,** Richard Haynes; **663,** Andrew Syred /Getty Images, Inc.; **664 t,** NCI /Photo Researchers, Inc.**664 b,** Eye of Science/Science Photo Library/Photo Researchers, Inc.; **665 l,** Chuck Brown/Photo Researchers, Inc.; **665 r,** BioPhoto Associates/Photo Researchers, Inc.; **666,** Al Bello/Getty Images Inc.; **670 t,** A. Glauberman/Photo Researchers, Inc.; **670 b,** James Stevenson/Science Photo Library/Photo Researchers, Inc.; **671,** Douglas C. Pizac/AP/Wide World Photos; **671 inset,** David Young-Wolff/PhotoEdit

Chapter 31: 674, Dennis Kunkel/Phototake; **676,** Scott Camazine/Photo Researchers, Inc.; **678,** Collection CNRI /Phototake; **679 tl,** and **679 tr,** Dr. Tony Brain & David Parker/Science Photo Library/Photo Researchers, Inc.; **679 b,** Meckes/Ottawa/Photo Researchers, Inc.; **680,** Hans Pfletschinger/Peter Arnold, Inc.; **682,** Alfred Pasieka/Science Photo Library/Photo Researchers, Inc.; **685 all,** James A. Sullivan/Cells Alive; **687,** Richard Haynes; **691 t,** Manfred Kage/Peter Arnold, Inc.; **691 b,** CNRI/Science Photo Library/Photo Researchers, Inc.; **692 l,** NIBSC/Science Photo Library/Photo Researchers, Inc.; **692 r,** NIBSC/Science Photo Library/Photo Researchers, Inc.; **693,** REUTERS/Jeff J. Mitchell/TimePix

Chapter 32: 696-697, Simeone Huber/Getty Images, Inc.; **698,** Peter Griffith/Masterfile Corporation; **704,** Myrleen Ferguson Cate/PhotoEdit; **705,** Laurent/Mangado/BSIP/Phototake; **706,** Richard Haynes; **708 t,** Oliver Meckes/Ottawa/Photo Researchers, Inc.; **708 b,** Martin M. Rotker/Photo Researchers, Inc.; **709,** Kevin Morris/Getty Images, Inc.; **712,** Robert Brenner/PhotoEdit; **713,** Mitch Hrdlicka/Getty Images, Inc.

Chapter 33: 718, Yorgos Nikas/Getty Images, Inc.; **723,** Richard Haynes; **725,** Claude Edelmann/Photo Researchers, Inc.; **727,** David Phillips/The Population Council/Photo Researchers, Inc.; **729 l,** UHB Trust /Getty Images, Inc.; **729 r,** Mary Kate Denny/PhotoEdit; **731 t,** Lennart Nilsson/Albert Bonniers Forlag; **731 b,** Claude Edelmann/Photo Researchers, Inc.; **732 t,** Lennart Nilsson/Albert Bonniers Forlag; **732 b,** Will & Deni McIntyre/Photo Researchers, Inc.; **734,** Courtesy of Don Manning; **735 all,** Courtesy of Don Manning; **736,** Ryan McVay/Getty Images, Inc.

Chapter 34: 742, Stone/Getty Images, Inc.; **744 both,** Fred Bavendam/Minden Pictures; **745 both,** Fred Bavendam/Minden Pictures; **746 t,** Provided by the SeaWiFS Project, NASA/Goddard Space Flight Center and Orbimage; **746 b,** BIOS (P. Bertrand)/Peter Arnold, Inc.; **747,** Russ Gutshall/SuperStock, Inc.; **748,** John D. Cunningham/Visuals Unlimited; **749,** Richard Haynes; **752,** Bob & Clara Calhoun/Bruce Coleman Inc.; **754 t,** Fabio Colombini/Animals Animals/Earth Scenes; **754 b,** Michael & Patricia Fogden/Corbis; **755 t,** Ed Reschke/Peter Arnold, Inc.; **755 b,** Ken Lucas/Visuals Unlimited; **756 t,** Jake Rajs/Getty Images, Inc.; **756 b,** Larry Lefever/Grant Heilman Photography; **757 t,** Stephen J. Krasemann/Photo Researchers, Inc.; **757 b,** B. & C. Alexander/Photo Researchers, Inc.; **758,** Willard Clay/Getty Images, Inc.; **759 t,** Roine Magnusson/Getty Images, Inc.; **759 bl,** Andy Martinez/Photo Researchers, Inc.; **759 br,** Maresa Pryor/Animals Animals/Earth Scenes; **761 t,** Jeff Hunter/Getty Images, Inc.; **761 b,** J. Frederick Grassle

Chapter 35: 764, Frans Lanting/Minden Pictures; **766,** David Hosking/Photo Researchers, Inc.; **767 t,** Brian Milne/Animals Animals/Earth Scenes; **767 b,** Gunter Ziesler/Peter Arnold, Inc.; **768,** Rod Planck/Photo Researchers, Inc.; **769,** Diane Sweeney; **771,** John Eastcott & Yva Momatiuk/Animals Animals/Earth Scenes; **772 t,** Wolfgang Kaehle/Corbis; **772 b,** David Spears; Science Pictures Limited/Corbis; **773,** Tom & Pat Leeson/Photo Researchers, Inc.; **776,** Alan Cary/The Image Works; **777,** BIOS (M. Laboureur)/Peter Arnold, Inc.; **779 t,** David Hall/Photo Researchers, Inc.; **779 inset,** Zig Leszczynski/Animals Animals/Earth Scenes; **779 ml,** S.J. Krasemann/Peter Arnold, Inc.; **779 mr,** Gary McVicker/Index Stock Imagery, Inc.; **779 b,** Geoff Bryant/Photo Researchers, Inc.; **780,** Norbert Wu/Peter Arnold, Inc.; **781 l,** AP/Wide World Photos; **781 r,** Jeff Hunter /Getty Images, Inc.; **782 l,** John Elk III/Stock Boston; **782 ml,** Don Pitcher/Stock Boston; **782 mr,** McCutheon/Visuals Unlimited; **782 r,** David Newman/Visuals Unlimited; **783 t,** Jim Steinberg/Photo Researchers, Inc.; **783 b,** Robert Ginn/PhotoEdit

Chapter 36: 786, Jen and Des Bartlett/Bruce Coleman, Inc.; **791,** Ray Coleman/Photo Researchers, Inc.; **793,** Matt Meadows/Peter Arnold, Inc.; **795,** Joseph Van Os/Getty Images Inc.; **801,** Chinch Gryniewicz; Ecoscene/Corbis; **803,** NASA; **804,** Richard Haynes; **805,** Frans Lanting/Minden Pictures; **805 inset,** Richard Parker/Photo Researchers, Inc.; **806 t,** Steve Dunwell Photography/Getty Images Inc.; **806 bl,** Larry West/Getty Images Inc.; **806 br,** M. C. Rainey; **807,** Terry Whittaker/Photo Researchers, Inc.; **808 l,** Raymond K Gehman/National Geographic Image Collection; **808 r,** John Snyder/Bruce Coleman, Inc.

Skills Appendix: 818 t, Lynn Stone/Animals Animals/Earth Scenes; **818 b,** Oliver Meckes/Photo Researchers, Inc.; **819,** Runk/Schoenberger/Grant Heilman Photography